176-194

Modern Labor Law
in the Private and
Public Sectors

Modern Labor Law in the Private and Public Sectors

Cases and Materials

THIRD EDITION

Seth D. Harris
DISTINGUISHED SCHOLAR
SCHOOL OF INDUSTRIAL & LABOR RELATIONS
CORNELL UNIVERSITY

Joseph E. Slater
EUGENE N. BALK PROFESSOR OF LAW AND VALUES
UNIVERSITY OF TOLEDO COLLEGE OF LAW

Anne Marie Lofaso
ARTHUR B. HODGES PROFESSOR OF LAW
WEST VIRGINIA UNIVERSITY COLLEGE OF LAW

Charlotte Garden
PROFESSOR OF LAW &
LITIGATION DIRECTOR, KOREMATSU CENTER FOR LAW & EQUALITY
SEATTLE UNIVERSITY SCHOOL OF LAW

Richard F. Griffin, Jr.
OF COUNSEL BREDHOFF & KAISER, P.L.L.C.

CAROLINA ACADEMIC PRESS
Durham, North Carolina

ISBN   978-1-5310-1852-8
e-ISBN   978-1-5310-1853-5
LCCN   2020943175

Carolina Academic Press
700 Kent Street
Durham, North Carolina 27701
Telephone (919) 489-7486
Fax (919) 493-5668
www.cap-press.com

Printed in the United States of America
2023 Printing

Contents

Table of Agency Decisions

[References are to pages.]

Table of Cases

[References are to pages.]

Preface

About fourteen years ago, Seth Harris, at that time a professor and Director of Labor and Employment Law Programs at New York Law School, approached University of Toledo College of Law Professor Joseph Slater, about co-authoring a casebook that would address both private-sector and public-sector labor law and also discuss modern organizing procedures outside the NLRA process. They agreed that Harris would write the book's private-sector labor law sections, including those aspects of private-sector labor relations that fell outside the gambit of traditional organizing, while Slater would draft the historical and the public-sector labor law sections. About one year after commencing this ambitious project, President Barack Obama appointed Harris to the position of Deputy U.S. Secretary of Labor, which effectively removed him from this casebook project. That meant recruiting two additional co-authors to finish the project. In spring 2009, Harris and Slater recruited two of the best in the business: West Virginia University Law Professor Anne Marie Lofaso and St. John's University Law Professor David Gregory.

No one could have anticipated what happened next. After the mid-term elections of 2010, attacks on the collective-bargaining rights of public-sector unions and their members by some governors and state legislatures significantly restricted such rights in several states. The changes in public-sector labor laws and the new debates over policy in the public sector meant significant updates and re-writing just to keep up. While this was challenging (and at times aggravating), the project is all the better for our efforts. The events in the public-sector, plus some important controversies and shifts in private-sector labor law, have challenged decades of thinking about labor law in general, in both the private and public sectors. The first edition was finally published in 2013. We now have a casebook that is truly modern in its approach to labor law in the United States.

Our vision for the second edition, published in January 2016, was to incorporate the Obama Board's more progressive view of labor law and to compare that vision with take backs in the public sector and push backs from the judicial branch. Harris returned to his co-author responsibilities in 2014 after leaving the Obama Administration. Soon thereafter, rising star labor law scholar and teacher Charlotte Garden agreed to join as a fourth co-author to take the place of David Gregory who retired from his role with this casebook.

The past four-plus years were once again exciting for labor scholars and practitioners, resulting in a third edition with a uniquely modern approach to labor law instruction. The dawn of this period coincides with Colin Kaepernick's protests during the playing of "The Star-Spangled Banner" at the opening of football games. In the great tradition of U.S. labor history, Kaepernick's protests mixed political with workplace grievances. Our third edition also covers the transition from the Obama Board to the Trump Board. During this period, we welcomed Dick Griffin, former NLRB General Counsel (2013–2017), who has helped us meticulously and accurately navigate these changes. While the Trump Board has used rulemaking and adjudication to cut back on workers' rights, public-sector employees fought against the political tide, which included a devastating blow to public-sector unions imposed by the Supreme Court in *Janus v. AFSCME* (June 2018) (declaring unconstitutional agency fee payments without prior employee consent). The years 2018–2019 witnessed a wave of teachers' strikes that began in West Virginia. The success of that statewide, two-week strike — a strike that included all 55 counties, enjoyed public support, and ended with a pay raise — inspired similar education workers' strikes in Oklahoma, Arizona, Kentucky, Georgia, Virginia, North Carolina, Chicago, Los Angeles, and Denver. This national strike wave has sparked the Red for Ed movement — a fight that links the educators' cause with students' educational rights. The period ends, as it began, with a growth in private-sector collective action which connects workplace with political goals. These concerted activities have been bolstered by a surging interest in labor law reform within the Democratic Party, as evidenced by the Protecting the Right to Organize Act, a bill that, if enacted, would greatly strengthen workers' rights to engage in concerted activity.

Acknowledgments

The preparation of *Modern Labor Law in the Private and Public Sectors: Cases and Materials* was supported by funds from the University of Toledo College of Law, the West Virginia University College of Law, Cornell University's School of Industrial & Labor Relations, New York Law School, and Seattle University School of Law. The authors wish to express their gratitude to these law schools, especially the Eugene N. Balk Professorship (Toledo) and the Hodges Foundation (West Virginia), for their generous financial support.

The authors also wish to thank the following individuals. Without their work, this book would not be possible.

Seth Harris: Thank you to my co-authors Joe Slater and Anne Marie Lofaso for their excellent and disproportionately sizeable contributions to this project. I owe particular thanks to Joe Slater. Joe shepherded this project brilliantly and with his characteristic wit, energy, and insight after I returned to the public sector. We began this project as partners, but life took over and so did Joe. I am glad to be working with him again, and with Anne and Charlotte. Thank you, also, to Dean Harry Katz, who welcomed me back to my alma mater as a scholar and teacher and provided valuable support to my research. Dean Kevin Hallock has generously continued that support. I am grateful to my Cornell research assistants, Benjamin Hawkins and Carolyn Wald, and my New York Law School research assistants on this project Marcelo Martinez and Damien Maree. New York Law School and its former Dean Richard Matasar also supported this project and many others in ways that extended well beyond financial assistance. Thank you to the countless scholars, teachers, and practitioners of labor and employment law and policy, collective bargaining, organizing, dispute resolution, labor economics, and related subjects who educated me over three and one-half decades and made my contributions to this book possible. Finally, thank you to Karen, Jonathan and Daniel—sine qua non.

Joe Slater: Thanks to the teaching assistants who helped me with this project over the years, especially Kelly Walsh, Sarah Corney, and Elijah Welenc. Thanks to the Eugene N. Balk Professorship for financial resources, and to my very patient and supportive Deans, Dan Steinbock and Ben Barros. Thanks to my co-authors who taught me so much. Thanks to the members of the ABA Section on Labor and Employment Law, Committee on State and Local Government Bargaining and Employment Law, for putting together extremely useful reports on public-sector labor law; this book features many cases I discovered in these reports that I probably wouldn't have found otherwise. Finally, profound thanks to my inimitable wife Krista Schneider and my awesome son Isaac Slater for all that they do.

Anne Lofaso: I wish to express my sincerest gratitude to my co-authors, Seth Harris, Joe Slater, Charlotte Garden, and Dick Griffin for their intellectual companionship and inspiration throughout the book drafting and publication process. Thank you to the Hodges summer research fund and the Arthur B. Hodges Professorship for supporting this project. I also wish to acknowledge the loving support of my husband Jim and daughter Giorgi, especially these past several months as we finalized publication during the COVID-19 pandemic. Working from home to finalize our third edition allowed me to spend additional time with my now sixteen-year-old child who took daily breaks with me—I from writing this book, and she from her AP studies. These moments I will forever cherish.

Charlotte Garden: I remain grateful to Joe, Anne, and Seth for having invited me to join them in the second edition of this casebook, and for making the project such an enjoyable one. I have learned a tremendous amount from each of them—and also from Dick Griffin, whose willingness to join the book for its third edition has made the final product even stronger. I am also grateful to Dean Annette Clark of the Seattle University School of Law for research support, and Henry Brudney for excellent, careful research assistance. Finally, thank you to Owen Davies, without whose indefatigable love and support I would not be where I am today.

Dick Griffin: Thank you to my co-authors who so generously welcomed me to their exciting project; thank you to Claire C. Pettengill for more than 38 years of wedded bliss; thank you to our children, Charlie and Emma, who I love more than words can express; and thank you to my parents, Richard F. Griffin, Sr. and Jane Flanigen Griffin, for their example and their support.

We wish to dedicate this edition to the memory of a member of our original team, David L. Gregory, whose passing in December 2019 leaves a hole in the hearts of all who knew him.

SETH D. HARRIS
Distinguished Scholar
School of Industrial & Labor Relations
Cornell University

JOSEPH E. SLATER
Eugene N. Balk Professor of Law and Values
University of Toledo College of Law
Toledo, OH

ANNE MARIE LOFASO
Arthur B. Hodges Professor of Law
West Virginia University College of Law
Morgantown, WV

CHARLOTTE GARDEN
Professor of Law and
Litigation Director, Korematsu Center for Law & Equality
Seattle University School of Law

RICHARD GRIFFIN
Of Counsel
Bredhoff & Kaiser, P.L.L.C.

October, 2020

Introduction

The practice of labor law has changed considerably in recent years. First, a significant portion of it is now in the public sector. While union density rates in the private sector have dropped to around seven percent, union rates in the public sector have climbed to nearly 40 percent. Thus, beginning in 2009, around half of all union members in the U.S. have been public employees. Public-sector labor laws are typically modeled in part on the main private-sector labor statute, the National Labor Relations Act (NLRA), but with some significant differences. For example, most public employees cannot legally strike; many are significantly limited in the subjects over which they can bargain; and a significant number have no legal right to bargain collectively at all. Beyond differences in legal rules, the policy debates and political context of public-sector labor law and labor relations are often different from those in the private sector. For example, the first half of 2011 witnessed a wave of state laws restricting the rights of public employees and their unions in ways still unimaginable in the private sector.

Second, unions in the private sector are increasingly abandoning traditional NLRA practices and procedures and adopting new strategies that do not depend on traditional labor law mechanisms. Whether this is because, as union advocates claim, evolving labor law doctrines and the National Labor Relations Board (NLRB) have become too biased against labor to offer unions a fair opportunity, or due simply to frustration with declining density numbers, private-sector unions and worker advocacy organizations are increasingly looking to alternate strategies and even alternate forms of organization, from card-check and neutrality agreements in lieu of NLRB elections, to Workers' Centers in lieu of traditional union representation.

This book incorporates both these modern trends, so that students entering the practice of labor law—on the side of unions, employers, or government agencies—will understand what they are likely to encounter. One of the authors of this book started a labor law job fresh out of law school and, having taken a traditional labor law class, expected to encounter at least mostly the issues his class covered: contract negotiations that could lead to strikes or lockouts, secondary boycotts, and perhaps even some of the more colorfully named NLRA doctrines, such as *Boys Market* injunctions and hot cargo clauses. Instead, he worked on cases involving a union of school employees in Virginia, a state in which public-sector unions could neither strike nor bargain collectively. In that same era, the "Justice for Janitors" campaign of the Service Employees International Union (SEIU), which explicitly made a practice of avoiding NLRB proceedings, was achieving high-profile successes around the country. Students today should be prepared to deal with these sorts of situations and developments, which have been a significant part of the practice for decades.

Other factors have shifted the turf in labor relations. In the past two decades, some important unions experimented by splitting from the AFL-CIO, an umbrella organization that has, since the 1950s, included nearly all the significant unions in the U.S., to form the Change-to-Win coalition. While a number of those unions have returned to the AFL-CIO, the nature of union leadership is evolving and debates over the best uses of union resources continue. The NLRB under the George W. Bush administration issued a series of decisions interpreting the NLRA in new ways, in a number of cases overturning decades of precedent and giving a more restrictive reading to worker and union rights. The NLRB under the Obama Administration reversed some of those cases and issued new rules broadening the scope of worker and union rights. The NLRB under Trump has swung the pendulum aggressively the other way.

While the NLRA seems almost immune to formal amendment, in the public sector, labor statutes are amended with some regularity. The attacks on public-sector collective bargaining rights in 2011 and 2012 (summarized near the end of Chapter 1) were the most radical in decades, but since the 1960s and through the present, political battles have led to public employees winning and losing important legal rights in many different jurisdictions.

Amidst the swirl of legal and political battles, students of labor law must always be mindful of the tremendous importance of the working relationship to the parties involved. For employees, jobs provide not only income necessary to live, but also, at least often, a sense of identity and pride. Unions, at their best, provide not only increased bargaining power for individual employees *vis-a-vis* their employers, but also a measure of democratic control over, or at least input into, the workplace. For employers, labor is not only a cost of production but also, at least often, the backbone of the enterprise. Unlike all other factors of production, labor power is produced by human beings who have legal and human rights. Still, employers often feel that decisions regarding the enterprise should be made by the owners and managers, not the workers. Both sides appeal to visions of liberty and freedom that resonate in the American tradition. Labor relies on the freedom to associate and act collectively to gain a democratic voice in workplace decisions that affect the lives of employees. Employers appeal to the freedom to own and control their private property and to run their businesses as they please. How the law mediates these competing ideas is fraught with moral, philosophical, political, and economic concerns.

In the public sector, there is an added concern about the role of private bodies, such as unions, influencing democratically accountable public institutions. This relates to the broader question of whether public-sector unions should have at least mostly the same types of rights as private-sector unions. One could argue that workplace issues that unions address—wages, hours, and working conditions— are basically the same for, say, a janitor in a public school and a janitor in a private school, and thus that the labor law rules governing both should be fairly similar.

That is the approach of most western democracies. In the U.S., however, public-sector labor laws developed much later and on a much different track than private-sector labor law. Modern concerns about public-sector laws center on the question of whether collective bargaining interferes too much with public budgets and the decisions of elected officials. For example, even if collective bargaining is allowed, should public-sector laws exclude certain subjects from bargaining—subjects that private-sector workers are allowed to negotiate—because in government employment, such subjects rightly should be in the sole discretion of elected officials? Should all types of public workers be allowed to bargain, or just some types? Should strikes in the public sector be banned—and if so, for all government employees or just some? If we ban strikes but allow collective bargaining—as a plurality of states now do—how should bargaining impasses be resolved?

Because public-sector labor laws developed after private-sector law, much of the debate in designing public-sector rules has centered on whether and how private-sector rules should be imported: when to essentially copy them in state public-sector statutes, and when they should be modified or avoided entirely because of concerns specific to the public sector. Students are encouraged to track these debates and develop their own opinions. Moreover, though, the relative success of unions in the public sector in the past several decades as compared to private-sector unions raises the question of whether certain aspects of public sector labor law might profitably be adopted in the private sector. While states are largely preempted from innovating in private-sector labor law, it is fair to ask what decision-makers at the Board, in the federal courts, and the federal legislature can learn from experiences in the public sector.

Acknowledging that public-sector labor law is now a significant part of labor law also challenges some conventional wisdom about unions in the U.S. The "rise and fall" periodization of the history of American labor that focuses essentially exclusively on the private sector changes considerably if we include what is now many decades of experience in the public sector. The story that American workers are too "individualistic" or otherwise culturally disinclined to join unions becomes problematic if we count those who, for example, clean public schools or otherwise labor on behalf of a government entity as authentic "workers." On the other hand, should declining union rates in the private sector be blamed primarily on an unfavorable legal climate (as some critics claim), given that public sector unions have achieved impressive successes under labor laws which generally give unions similar but fewer rights than the rights the NLRA grants in the private sector?

This book is structured around the life cycles of the organizing and collective bargaining processes. The first phase consists of workers' organizing efforts or protests and (typically, albeit not always) employers' efforts to persuade workers not to organize or their responses to protests. Workers may choose to organize themselves into a traditional union or some other type of organization, or simply to protest perceived injustices without creating an organization. Protests and union organizing in the private sector are protected by the NLRA. In the public sector, most states have labor laws that protect these activities, and the Constitution also protects the right to organize.

Workers who decide to organize a union move to a second phase. They either pursue a union representation election administered by the appropriate labor relations agency or choose some alternative means of acquiring union representation, such as a voluntary recognition agreement with an employer. If the workers succeed in organizing a union, the union and the employer enter a third phase. In the private sector, unions use collective bargaining and both sides deploy economic weapons to influence bargaining outcomes. In the public sector, a majority of jurisdictions allow union collective bargaining, but most limit the subjects of bargaining more strictly than does the NLRA, and most prohibit economic weapons such as strikes and lockouts. Instead, public-sector laws often provide for some combination of mediation, fact-finding, and arbitration to resolve bargaining impasses, and unions and employers use political tactics to influence outcomes. When bargaining produces a collective bargaining agreement, then the fourth phase is reached: the parties administer their agreement and use dispute resolution mechanisms as part of that administration process.

The first part of this casebook provides a history of labor relations in the United States, and the coverage of labor statutes in the private and public sectors. It then moves to organizing and collective worker protests, with one chapter mostly dedicated to modern alternatives to traditional union organizing, and other chapters explaining the traditional labor law protections for worker protests. This part also explores why and how the law of public-sector labor relations developed so much later and, in many ways, so differently, than private-sector law. The bulk of the rest of the book studies the life cycle of unions: collective bargaining; strikes, economic weapons, and impasse resolution in the public sector; contract administration; and secondary activity and related actions. It concludes with three chapters that examine the rights of individual workers within their unions, bargaining relationships in transition (successorship), and preemption.

Two themes are repeated throughout the casebook. The first theme is how policymakers wrestle with the appropriateness of applying private-sector doctrine to government employees and their unions. In some areas of labor law, the rules in both sectors are quite similar because policymakers did not believe the public sector context required a different approach. In other areas, the rules are quite different because policymakers felt that private-sector rules were not appropriate for the public sector. This theme arises in legislative decisions over rights explicitly granted or denied in statutes (e.g., whether a public-sector law should cover certain types of public employees at all, and whether certain public employees should have the right to strike). It also arises when agencies and courts try to decide which of the myriad rules devised by the NLRB and courts in the private sector should be used in the public sector. Even if broad statutory language in a public-sector labor law is the same as the language in the NLRA, do different policy concerns dictate that courts should adopt different rules, at least sometimes, in the public sector? Should the default assumption be that if the statutory language is the same, all the rules flowing from that language should be the same, because that is more efficient or because the public sector should benefit from the much longer and wider experience in the private sector? If so, what if the law in the private sector changes (as it inevitably does) because a new political alignment on the NLRB interprets the NLRA in a new and different way? Should public sector rules—based on interpreting the same statutory language in a state public sector statute—change along with it automatically? Or might the discontents of private-sector labor law give those making policy for the public sector reason to reconsider private-sector rules? This could permit more experimentation and allow states to act even more as "laboratories of democracy" in this area.

The second theme is that, while the law of private-sector labor relations has stagnated, workers and their organizations, including unions, have responded by finding new ways to organize, both inside and outside traditional forms. Thus, while a comprehensive understanding of modern American labor law requires studying the governing statutes and the doctrines that have emerged from them, it also requires considering how actors in the field have worked around existing doctrine to create new systems, new structures, and new legal issues. Students will be challenged to predict the outcomes of these new strategies—including, but not limited to, analyzing the legal issues they raise.

Each of the book's chapters addresses particular issues that arise in that phase of the relationship between organizing or organized workers and their employers. Each chapter begins with cases and materials relating to private-sector workers and also includes materials relating to the same issue in the context of public-sector employment. In some instances, the public-sector materials are in substantial additional sections, in some cases in quite short additional sections, and in a few sections, the public sector materials are interwoven with the private-sector materials. Notes follow most of the cases, and problems are often provided as well. Key cases that are discussed at length but do not appear as excerpts appear in bold [*e.g., NLRB v. Hearst Publications*, 322 U.S. 111 (1944)]. Throughout, the goal is to provide students with the knowledge and background that will prepare them for the labor law and labor relations of the 21st century.

Modern Labor Law
in the Private and
Public Sectors

Chapter 1

The History of Public- and Private-Sector Labor Law: Unions Before Collective Bargaining Statutes and Beyond

I. The History of Labor Law and Labor Relations in the Private and Public Sectors

The history of labor relations and labor law is crucial to understanding modern labor law doctrines. First, labor law statutes often contain broad or vague language, and often the language contains significant gaps. Interpreting vague language or filling in gaps often involves policy judgments. These judgments, not infrequently, rely in part on opinions about efficiency, freedom, equality, economics, and/or democracy. In many instances, judges and agency decision-makers seem to bring in values and assumptions from an earlier time. In a surprising number of cases, court decisions in labor law cases seem to be at least arguably contrary to the actual text of the National Labor Relations Act (NLRA). Large swaths of labor law are almost inexplicable without understanding certain notions about unions and the economy that predates the NLRA. *See generally* James Atleson, Values and Assumptions in American Labor Law (1983).

Related, labor law has always been and remains a fascinating forum for tensions in our values as a society, as union supporters and opponents appeal to different parts of our cultural and political heritage. Unions cite traditions of democracy, rights of association, and self-government, and they try to apply those traditions to the work arena. Private employers call on traditions of property rights, individualism, and free market capitalism. Public employers cite the importance of public, democratic control over government functions. Generally, the two sides, historically and currently, have used terms such as "freedom" and "democracy" to mean quite different things.

Second, the historical materials help in understanding three issues that are central to labor law: what ends unions may lawfully pursue; what means unions may lawfully use to pursue lawful ends; and what tactics employers may lawfully use in response. Courts and legislators have struggled with these issues since unions first emerged in the U.S. more than 200 years ago, and these issues will occupy much of the material in this casebook. As to lawful ends, what goals should unions be allowed to pursue, legally? Higher wages? Control over subcontracting? Control over the types of products produced and where and when plants should be opened or closed? As to lawful means to pursue a lawful end, for example, what limits should there be on strikes, boycotts, and pickets? As to employer responses, what tools—from propaganda and persuasion to economic weapons (*e.g.*, "permanently replacing" strikers)—should employers be allowed to use when unions are acting lawfully? Labor statutes often do not answer these basic questions with any specificity. The rules that courts and boards have created are often deeply rooted in historical understandings.

Third, in both the public and private sectors, labor statutes were passed both to address long-standing problems and to accommodate unions that were active well before the statutes were passed. But you may find, especially with the NLRA, that statutes have not kept up with the times. History is also important as we look to what labor law should be in the 21st century. Unions look at new trends in the economy—shifting types of work and a workforce that is quite demographically different from the 1930s workforce—and argue that labor law should expand to new types of workers in new types of jobs (*e.g.*, Uber drivers) and in new contexts (*e.g.*, Facebook posts). Unions also argue that the current legal protections for workers have proven inadequate in modern times. Employers, in contrast, tend to think the modern economy requires alternatives to traditional unions and the "adversarial model" they represent. Some of the alternatives employers have advocated would violate current law (*e.g.*, worker participation committees that run afoul of the ban on employer-dominated labor organizations).

As a result of globalization and other trends, the economy now features much more foreign competition, outsourcing, temporary workers, workers who may or may not be properly classified as independent contractors, and service work, and less traditional manufacturing work, than in the past. In the public sector, recent years have seen severe budget problems and angry debates over whether and to what extent collective bargaining rights for public workers have helped cause such problems. In both cases, understanding why current laws were created is vital to an informed opinion about where the law should go.

Further, to what extent should the answers to these questions be different for public workers than for private workers? Should public-sector unions be able to negotiate all the topics private-sector unions can negotiate, or are some of those issues best left to the unilateral control of public officials because the issues involve matters of public policy? Should any public employees be allowed to strike as private-sector workers are? Should public employees have the right to bargain collectively at all? History is vital to answering these questions as well.

In the private sector up through the mid-1930s, and in the public sector for much longer, courts had largely exclusive power to answer these questions, because there was no relevant labor law statute. Today, the NLRA covers much of the private sector, and a large majority of states permit at least a significant number of public employees to bargain collectively. Labor law matters are generally first brought before an agency: the National Labor Relations Board (NLRB or Board) in the private sector, or for public-sector unions, an analogous state agency. But even though the boards and courts are interpreting statutes, they often seem quite influenced by older ideas of rights and liberties.

Even in the age of statutes, history looms large. Private-sector labor law has proven quite resistant to change in statutory language. The last major amendment to the NLRA came in 1959, and that law mostly regulated the internal conduct of unions. Most of the NLRA's language regarding the relations of unions and employers was enacted in the 1930s and 1940s. Thus, changes in private-sector law in recent decades have been made by courts and agencies. Many of these changes have been dramatic, and again, history plays a role. In contrast, public-sector labor statutes are altered much more frequently. The statutory amendments that several states passed in 2011 limiting the rights of public-sector unions were much more radical than previous changes, but changes in statutes were relatively common in the public sector before then. Also, some states have not adopted laws granting public-sector unions the right to bargain collectively at all. In such jurisdictions, public-sector labor law today is in many ways quite similar to the way it was a century ago.

This casebook, unlike others, looks in depth at both private and public-sector labor law. In some important ways, the history of public-sector unions and public-sector labor law is separate from the history of private-sector unions and private-sector labor law. Private-sector unions arose as a truly significant force, economically and politically, decades before public-sector unions did. While both private- and public-sector unions existed in the 19th century and early 20th century, private-sector unions were at their strongest in the middle decades of the 20th century. Public-sector unions have been at their strongest beginning in the latter decades of that century through today, a period when private-sector unions have been declining.

Laws giving rights to unions in the different sectors followed different tracks. The main private-sector labor statute, the NLRA, explicitly excludes government employees, and public-sector labor statutes do not cover employees of private employers. The NLRA was enacted in 1935, while public-sector labor laws were passed mainly in the 1960s–80s. The NLRA is a federal statute that applies to private-sector workers in all states, counties, and cities. Public-sector labor laws are typically state and local laws that apply at most to the public workers in the given state, often only to some public workers in a state, and sometimes only to public workers in a given county or even city (federal public-sector labor laws apply only to employees of the federal government). Most broadly, throughout history and through today, a significant set of policymakers in the U.S. have insisted that union rights in the private sector were quite a different matter than union rights in the public sector.

On the other hand, the two histories, while in many ways asynchronous, have important similarities. Unions in both the private and public sectors were active long before they won formal rights to bargain collectively. Indeed, both public and private-sector labor statutes were passed in part to deal with that reality. In both cases, a significant body of court-made labor law preceded and in various ways influenced the later statutes. While private-sector labor relations featured considerably more bloodshed than public-sector relations, both types of unions faced determined opposition, often from many of the same constituencies (private-sector businesses have long actively opposed public- as well as private-sector unions). Also, while public-sector labor law raises some different policy issues than private-sector law, throughout the 20th century to the present day, unions and their advocates have stressed the common concerns public and private workers share: a desire for better wages, hours, and working conditions, and the desire for unions to provide workers with a voice in the workplace.

Two quotes from the 1940s sum up the different approaches. In *Perez v. Bd. of Police Commissioners of the City of Los Angeles*, 78 Cal. App. 2d 638, 647 (1947), the court stated, "[n]othing can be gained by comparing public employment with private employment; there can be no analogy in such a comparison." In contrast, in 1942, the Transport Workers Union urged that, "[g]overnment workers who are unorganized can be and are exploited as cruelly as unorganized workers in private industry. Whatever progress government workers have made in recent years they have made only through labor organization." JOSEPH SLATER, PUBLIC WORKERS: GOVERNMENT EMPLOYEE UNIONS, THE LAW, AND THE STATE, 1900–1962 192 (2004). As you go through these materials, consider these opposing perspectives and how they should affect legal rules.

II. Private-Sector Unions and Labor Law[*]

A. Work and Unions Before the Civil War

From the later 18th century through the Civil War, work relations in the U.S. were quite different than they were in the 20th century and beyond. First, much

---

[*] There is a rich literature on the history of private-sector labor and labor law. This section has drawn information from the following works which are recommended for students interested in this history. JAMES ATLESON, VALUES AND ASSUMPTIONS IN AMERICAN LABOR LAW (1983); IRVING BERNSTEIN, THE TURBULENT YEARS: A HISTORY OF THE AMERICAN WORKER, 1933–1941 (1969); IRVING BERNSTEIN, THE LEAN YEARS: A HISTORY OF THE AMERICAN WORKER, 1920–1933 (1960); EILEEN BORIS & NELSON LICHTENSTEIN, MAJOR PROBLEMS IN THE HISTORY OF AMERICAN WORKERS (1991); DAVID BRODY, WORKERS IN INDUSTRIAL AMERICA: ESSAYS ON THE TWENTIETH CENTURY STRUGGLE (1980); MELVYN DUBOFSKY, LABOR IN AMERICA: A HISTORY (7th ed. 2003); MELVYN DUBOFSKY, THE STATE AND LABOR IN MODERN AMERICA (1994); DANIEL ERNST, LAWYERS AGAINST LABOR: FROM INDIVIDUAL RIGHTS TO CORPORATE LIBERALISM (1995); LEON FINK, WORKINGMEN'S DEMOCRACY: THE KNIGHTS OF LABOR AND AMERICAN POLITICS (1983); WILLIAM FORBATH, LAW AND THE SHAPING OF THE AMERICAN LABOR MOVEMENT (1989); NELSON LICHTENSTEIN, STATE OF THE UNION, A CENTURY OF AMERICAN LABOR (2001); DAVID MONTGOMERY, CITIZEN WORKER: THE EXPERIENCE OF WORKERS IN THE UNITED STATES WITH DEMOCRACY AND THE FREE MARKET

labor was quite dramatically "unfree": slaves were a major part of the economy, as, to some extent were indentured servants. Even beyond those categories, work was far from what it is today: apprentices, servants, farm labor, and independent artisans dominated the scene. The law in this time was in significant ways based on old English "master-servant" law. As Blackstone had observed, "master-servant" law equated employment law with the laws regulating parents and children. Among other things, this law included the presumption that employment contracts were for one year, and it penalized workers under such default arrangements for leaving work before a year's end. 1 WILLIAM BLACKSTONE, COMMENTARIES 413 (1765). In earlier days in the U.S., workers could be jailed for quitting before the end of the year; as the 19th century wore on, the penalty was to deprive workers of any claim to wages, including claims for work actually performed.

Some workers' associations existed in the 18th century. The first reported labor case in the U.S. was *Commonwealth v. Pullis*, 3 Commons & Gilmore 59 (Mayor's Ct. 1806) (often called the "Philadelphia Cordewainers' Case"). In this case, some cordewainers (shoemakers) were indicted for striking for higher wages. Judge Levy charged the jury as follows: "a combination of workmen to raise their wages may be considered from a twofold point of view; one is to benefit themselves . . . the other is to injure those who do not join their society. The rule of law condemns both." Individual workers could legally have quit or threatened to quit unless they received the higher rates, but the issue in the case was whether workers could legally act in concert for this purpose. The case held they could not: "an act innocent in an individual is rendered criminal by a confederacy to effect it." Further, collective action of this type was an "unnatural" means that would injure the public. *See* Walter Nelles, *The First American Labor Case*, 41 YALE L.J. 165 (1931).

Thus began decades of using the law of criminal conspiracy against a wide variety of union actions, especially strikes. Early cases held that unions constituted criminal conspiracies merely for forming associations that bound members to union rules, *e.g.*, forbidding members to work with non-union workers, and requiring them to

---

DURING THE NINETEENTH CENTURY (1993); DAVID MONTGOMERY, THE FALL OF THE HOUSE OF LABOR: THE WORKPLACE, THE STATE, AND AMERICAN LABOR ACTIVISM, 1865–1925 (1987); DAVID MONTGOMERY, WORKERS CONTROL IN AMERICA: STUDIES IN THE HISTORY OF WORK, TECHNOLOGY, AND LABOR STRUGGLES (1979); PATRICIA SEXTON, THE WAR ON LABOR AND THE LEFT: UNDERSTANDING AMERICA'S UNIQUE CONSERVATIVISM (1991); KATHERINE V.L. STONE, FROM WIDGETS TO DIGITS: EMPLOYMENT REGULATION FOR THE CHANGING WORKPLACE (2004); ROBERT STEINFELD, COERCION, CONTRACT, AND FREE LABOR IN THE NINETEENTH CENTURY (2001); ROBERT STEINFELD, THE INVENTION OF FREE LABOR: THE EMPLOYMENT RELATION IN ENGLISH AND AMERICAN LAW AND CULTURE, 1350–1870 (1991); CHRISTOPHER TOMLINS, LAW, LABOR AND IDEOLOGY IN THE EARLY AMERICAN REPUBLIC (1993); CHRISTOPHER TOMLINS & ANDREW KING, EDS., LABOR LAW IN AMERICA (1992); CHRISTOPHER TOMLINS, THE STATE AND THE UNIONS: LABOR RELATIONS LAW AND THE ORGANIZED LABOR MOVEMENT IN AMERICA (1985); Dianne Avery, *Images of Violence in Labor Jurisprudence: The Regulation of Picketing and Boycotts, 1894–1921*, 37 BUFF. L. REV. 1 (1989); John Nockleby, *Two Theories of Competition in the Early 19th Century Labor Cases*, 38 AM. J. OF LEGAL HIST. 452, 452–81 (1994).

work only for union wage rates. Notably, at the same time, it was not a conspiracy for masters (employers) to combine to lower wages. John Nockleby, *Two Theories of Competition in the Early 19th Century Labor Cases*, 37 Am. J. Of Legal History 452 (1994). *See, e.g., People v. Melvin*, 2 Wheeler Crim. Cas. 262 (1810) (finding a union attempting to raise wages to be an illegal conspiracy while rejecting the union's defense that their employers had combined to depress wages).

In 1842, the Massachusetts Supreme Judicial Court held that merely organizing into a union and refusing to work for employers who employed non-union workers was not a criminal conspiracy in and of itself. The court analogized internal union rules to an organization of workers who agreed not to work in any shop in which "ardent spirit" was furnished, which was not illegal. *Commonwealth v. Hunt*, 45 Mass. (4 Metc.) 111, 130 (1842). Still, under *Hunt* and similar cases, it was not clear what unions could actually do, beyond organizing and setting internal rules for members, to avoid falling afoul of criminal conspiracy law. The court explained that union activity would constitute an illegal conspiracy if it either used unlawful means or pursued an unlawful end. "Unlawful," the court noted, did not simply refer to criminal acts. "We use the terms criminal or unlawful, because it is manifest that many acts are unlawful, which are not punishable by indictment or other public prosecution; and yet there is no doubt, we think, that a combination by numbers to do them would be an unlawful conspiracy, and punishable by indictment." 45 Mass. 111, 123.

Later in the 19th century, criminal conspiracy prosecutions were increasingly replaced with civil conspiracy prosecutions. These cases used the same basic analysis: did the union use lawful means to pursue lawful ends? It remained unclear what unions could legally do, beyond setting internal rules for their members.

Meanwhile, as the 19th century progressed, new types of work and workers began to emerge, and union activity increased. Even before the "industrial revolution" of the later 19th century, more business enterprises were organizing their workers in less traditional, often less secure ways. In the mid- and later 19th century, a new managerial class began to form, and workers chafed under their often impersonal and harsh direction. Fewer journeymen became masters. In the north, more immigrants arrived, as did some former slaves who had fled the south. Many of these types of employees flocked to workers' associations. Craft unions date back to the 1830s, and in 1853, a national craft union, the National Typographers, was born. The Cigar Makers International Union was formed in 1864. *See* Katherine V.W. Stone, From Widgets to Digits 13–22 (2004).

B. The Context of the Late 19th–Early 20th Century

Unions had existed since the American Revolution, but they picked up steam after the Civil War and began to create national organizations. The National Labor Union, founded in 1866, lasted about six years. In 1886, the American Federation of Labor (AFL) formed as an umbrella group for national unions in various trades.

Samuel Gompers, an early head of the AFL, led it through 1924. By the end of the century, there were sixty-two national craft unions. Other national umbrella groups rose as well, but they did not have the staying power of the AFL. The Knights of Labor was born in 1869, peaked in the mid-1880s (with some large and successful railroad strikes), but was in serious decline by the beginning of the 20th century. In the early 20th century, the more radical Industrial Workers of the World (IWW) would experience a similar rise and fall. The AFL, in contrast to the Knights and the IWW, focused mostly on the skilled trades and the idea of craft unionism, and it had the most staying power.

Despite a very hostile legal environment, the AFL experienced significant growth in the later 19th and early 20th century. Why this interest in the AFL and other unions? Increasing industrialization led to much more factory work. Such work was dangerous, and often involved very long hours. Arguably as important, factory employees lacked the control over their working lives—determining how jobs were done and hours of work—that artisans at least sometimes enjoyed.

In this period, it is important to understand how dramatic and violent labor relations were in the U.S., and how important law has always been to labor relations. The U.S. has the bloodiest, most violent labor history of any industrial nation. From 1890–97, more than 90 people were killed during major strikes; and then from 1902–04 alone, about 200 were killed and almost 2,000 injured. The dead and injured were almost all strikers and their supporters. These numbers are much higher than they were in Western European countries. *See* Patricia Sexton, The War on Labor and the Left: Understanding America's Unique Conservativism 55–56 (1991). For example, in the infamous "Ludlow Massacre" of 1913, during a strike against the Colorado Fuel and Iron company, national guard and company agents attacked a miner's camp while the working men were away, shooting and burning to death a number of the workers' wives and children. Kim Phillips Fein, *Corporate Strike Strategy, in* The Encyclopedia of Strikes in American History 66 (Aaron Brenner, Benjamin Day & Immanuel Ness eds., 2009). Employers routinely used spies, vigilantes, and other means to attack—often physically—union supporters.

Consider also the Homestead steel strike of 1892, in Pittsburgh. Historians have called it "one of the greatest conflicts of American labor history," Bernstein, The Turbulent Years, *supra*, 433, and "a battle which for bloodthirstiness and boldness was not excelled in actual warfare." Melvyn Dubofsky & Foster Rhea Dulles, Labor In America: A History 160 (4th ed. 1984). Ten people were killed, including seven workers, many more injured, and it took 8,000 state militia men to break the strike. Law was central in labor relations here and elsewhere, and it could be quite harsh. During the Homestead strike, the Carnegie Steel company filed rioting and murder charges against the strikers. The judge sustained those charges and the judge himself added charges of traitorously intending to levy war, and insurrection and rebellion against Pennsylvania. Robin Archer, Why is There No Labor Party in the United States? 117–18 (2010).

Other famous strikes include the Pullman railroad strike of 1894. Courts issued ten separate injunctions against strikers in the Pullman strike, and Eugene Debs was jailed for violating one. The legal rule at the time allowed employers to get an injunction merely by showing that a strike could threaten future goodwill and expectations of the company's customers. Thus, even a threatened strike was a conspiracy in restraint of trade.

Society perceived labor issues to be extremely important. After the 1877 railroad strikes, a southern newspaper remarked that, "the Southern question is dead," superseded by "the question of labor and capital." DUBOFSKY, THE STATE AND LABOR IN MODERN AMERICA, *supra*, xvii. Further, unions and strikes sharply divided opinion throughout the country. William Howard Taft wrote the following to his wife about the Pullman Railroad Strike of 1894: "It will be necessary for the military to kill some of the mob. . . . They have only killed six . . . as yet. This is hardly enough to make an impression." KERMIT HALL, ED., THE OXFORD COMPANION TO THE SUPREME COURT OF THE UNITED STATES 855 (1992).

Still, unions grew. By the end of 1904, union membership surpassed the two million mark. Bad working conditions spurred this growth and labor militancy. To pick just one example, in the early 20th century, there were a number of strikes by mineworkers. Why did they strike? In one typical instance, miners worked ten hours a day and had to dig thousands of pounds of coal per day. The work was hard, dangerous, and unhealthy. Four hundred forty-one miners died in work accidents in 1901. In 1905–06, the fatality rate for miners was 7.5 per thousand employees a year (and this did not include those seriously injured or maimed). Notably, there was no compensation for injured employees. For this work, miners earned an average of less than $300 a year, and were often paid in company scrip, redeemable only in the company stores. *See* DUBOFSKY & DULLES, *supra*, 180–81; Gerald Ronning, *Mesabi Iron Miners' Strikes*, *in* BRENNER, DAY, AND NESS, *supra*, 463.

Contemporaries used different, often opposing, theoretical lenses to view these facts. The concept of "freedom" was always important in labor law, but advocates and opponents of unions have applied the term "freedom" in very different ways. Employers and their allies stressed the concept of "free labor" and the "freedom of contract." These theories influenced courts in such famous, or perhaps infamous, cases as *Lochner v. New York*, 198 U.S. 45 (1905). *Lochner* struck down a state law capping the number of hours bakers could work. In this era, state and federal courts, using a variety of theories, struck down or vitiated more than 150 laws that provided various rights (relating to unions, wages, hours, and etc.) for workers. *See* WILLIAM FORBATH, LAW AND THE SHAPING OF THE AMERICAN LABOR MOVEMENT 178–92 (1991) (citing such cases in the period 1885–1930).

While these cases turned on a number of different legal theories, employers consistently argued that various types of worker-protective legislation, including laws giving rights to unions, impinged on the rights of individual workers to form their own contracts. Employers stressed that freedom was at the core of "employment at will," the default legal status, adopted in the U.S. in the latter part of the

19th century. Under employment at will, an employer can fire an employee at any time, for any reason, and an employee can quit any time, for any reason.

In contrast, unions and their supporters defined "freedom" differently. For them, freedom included a legally protected right for workers to join a union, and have their union take certain actions on their behalf: negotiate, boycott, strike, and picket. They linked these rights with notions of democracy at the workplace and the right of association. They frequently noted that employers had organized into groups, as had professional employees such as doctors and lawyers. Instead of individual bargaining and the "employment at will" version of freedom, unions and their allies emphasized the unequal bargaining and power relationships in employment. This included the belief that workers should have some control over how they performed their work and that workers have certain rights in continued employment if they do good work (*i.e*, the right not to be fired absent good cause). Most basically, it included the idea that workers should have the freedom to organize and bargain with management collectively without fear of being fired or disciplined. For an explanation of this paradigm, see Anne Marie Lofaso, *Toward a Foundational Theory of Workers' Rights: The Autonomous Dignified Worker*, 76 U.M.K.C. L. Rev. 1 (2007).

In the later 19th and early 20th century, however, laws governing employers and employees gave employers almost total power. By the later 19th century, in reaction to both master-servant law and slavery, some courts and some commentators started pushing the idea of what they called "free labor." Essentially, the idea was that if the relationship was not like slavery—the employee was legally allowed to quit at any time, for any reason—the employment relationship was "free." And, the contemporary reasoning continued, if the employee could quit for any reason, surely the employer should have the ostensibly analogous right to fire employees at any time for any reason. Thus, "at will" employment rules were born.

Was this "free"? Such rules gave employers essentially complete power in discipline, discharge, and rule-setting. Consider *Payne v. Western & Atl. R.R. Co.*, 81 Tenn. 507 (1884). In *Payne*, a railroad manager barred his workers from shopping at a certain store. (Why might the manager have imposed this rule?) The Supreme Court of Tennessee upheld the rule, stating that an employer could give the same orders to an employee that the master of a house could give to a house servant. "May I not dismiss my domestic servant for dealing, or even visiting, where I forbid? And if my domestic, why not my . . . mechanic or teamster? And, if one of them, then why not all four? And if all four, why not a hundred or a thousand of them?" 81 Tenn. 507, 518. Of course, employees were free, legally, to quit. But how realistic was this vision of freedom? The dissent in *Payne* worried that the majority opinion would allow employers "to require employees to trade where they may demand, to vote as they may require, or do anything not strictly criminal that employer may dictate" on pain of discharge. "Employment is the means of sustaining life to himself and family to the employee, and so he is morally though not legally compelled to submit." Employers could thus "control the employment of others to an extent that in time may sap the foundations of our free institutions." 81 Tenn. 507, 543–44.

Indeed, workers in the factories during the industrial revolution often did not perceive themselves as having much freedom. In the north, the phrase "wage slavery" became popular. And workers increasingly turned to union organizing.

C. Central Questions of Labor Law

This forced the question of what legal rights unions should have. What actions should they be free to take? This turned on what workers and their unions wanted to do. What were their goals?

First, unions wanted the power to set wages. In modern times, we think of the power to set wages above the legal minimum as a function of negotiation between the employer and the individual worker or union. It was not always so. Before the Revolutionary War, wages and even prices were often set by the government. This practice was in decline by the late 18th century, and partly in reaction, some workers organized and tried to set wages themselves by using private economic action. In early years, courts held this was a criminal conspiracy in cases such as the *Philadelphia Cordewainers* case discussed above.

In the late 19th and early 20th century, unions and progressives tried to set minimum wages by supporting minimum wage statutes. Courts often rejected such laws; even some attempts to limit such laws to women (ostensibly because they needed more protection) failed. *See, e.g., Adkins v. Children's Hospital*, 261 U.S. 525 (1923) (D.C. minimum wage for women is unconstitutional); *Morehead v. New York ex rel. Tipaldo*, 298 U.S. 587 (1936) (state minimum wage law for women is unconstitutional under freedom of contract theory). So, unions in the early 20th century began to focus more on private economic bargaining power to win higher pay.

Unions and their allies also wanted to limit the hours of work. In the late 19th and early 20th century, workers routinely worked 60–80 hours a week. Here again, unions tried to pass laws to limit hours. But again, these were frequently declared unconstitutional through the late 1930s, for example in *Lochner v. New York, supra*, and also in *Carter v. Carter Coal Co.*, 298 U.S. 238 (1936) (holding that Federal Coal Board rules, including maximum hours for miners, were unconstitutional). So, again, unions increasingly tried using private economic muscle to improve hours.

Third, unions wanted some power to control the means and methods of work. One of the most important transformations of work in the 19th century was the decline of the independent artisan and the rise of the factory worker, discussed above. Skilled workers often found it galling that they no longer controlled how their work was done. Instead, a new class of managers and supervisors felt that it was their job to design and run the work process. In the late 19th and early 20th century, there were many significant strikes over who would control how work was done. *See* DAVID MONTGOMERY, THE FALL OF THE HOUSE OF LABOR: THE WORKPLACE,

THE STATE, AND AMERICAN LABOR ACTIVISM, 1865–1925 (1987). While the law has always given management broad discretion to direct how work is performed, there has long been an opposing current in the culture that believes that workers should have significant input into how they do their work.

Fourth, unions often sought to impose rules that required employees in a given shop to become union members. This included what was called the "closed shop"— an agreement that the employer would only hire workers who were already union members—and the "union shop"—an agreement that employees had to join the union shortly after being hired.

These issues remain central in labor law, in both the private and public sectors, under the rubric of "scope of bargaining." What topics should unions have a right to negotiate and strike (or engage in other processes to resolve a bargaining impasse) about? Wages? Control of at least some parts of the work process? Whether a union and an employer could agree that employees must join the union or at least pay union dues as a condition of employment? Should employers be required to bargain with unions about these things? Are there some things that the employer should be allowed, but not required, to bargain over? Are there some issues that unions and employers should not be allowed to agree to in contracts, even if both sides would be willing to agree? And should the answers be the same for the public and private sectors? *See* Chapter 10.

The next issue was what means unions could use to pursue their goals. Strikes? Boycotts? Pickets? Before the 1930s, unions had very few formal legal rights to use these weapons. Many pickets, boycotts, and strikes were held to be illegal. As noted above, from the early to late 19th century, employers used criminal and then later civil conspiracy claims. Later, as discussed below, anti-trust and other actions were effectively deployed. Still, this did not stop workers from organizing, and it did not stop unions from trying to use economic muscle.

D. The Rise of Labor Organizations and Early Legal Responses

The following case sets out opposing views on the legality of the means and ends of a common union activity. As an introduction, Vegelahn owned a furniture-making company, and Guntner was the business agent for the Upholsterer's Union. At this time, the basic law of picketing was evolving such that there was a two-part test. To be legal, picketing had to be done by lawful means and also for a lawful end.

The union picketed the employer in *Vegelahn*, and the employer sought a temporary injunction. The lower court granted the injunction, which restrained union members from interfering with plaintiff's business by patrolling the walk or street in the vicinity of the premises for the purpose of preventing anyone who was currently or might thereafter be employed by plaintiff from entering or leaving the premises, by intimidation, threats, or otherwise. It also barred any obstruction or interference with any such persons "by any scheme or conspiracy . . . organized for the purpose of annoying, hindering, interfering, or preventing" any person in plaintiff's employ or desiring to be in such employ from entering or maintaining employment with plaintiff.

The initial appeal was heard only by Justice Holmes of the Massachusetts Supreme Judicial Court. Among other things, Holmes found that no actual violence was used, but threats (albeit "a good deal disguised") of personal harm were. Holmes continued the injunction to the extent it barred physically obstructing entrance and egress from plaintiff's business intimidating threats against those who worked for plaintiff or were considering working for plaintiff. He did not continue the injunction in full, however: *e.g.*, it no longer barred "annoying" employees or applicants. Acts involving physical force, threats of physical force, and attempts to cause current employees to break employment contracts remained enjoined.

After that, the entire state Supreme Court ruled on the matter, with Justice Allen giving the majority opinion and Holmes one of the dissents.

Vegelahn v. Guntner

Supreme Judicial Court of Massachusetts
167 Mass. 92, 44 N.E. 1077 (1896)

ALLEN, J.

The principal question in this case is whether the defendants should be enjoined against maintaining the patrol. The report shows that, following upon a strike of the plaintiff's workmen, the defendants conspired to prevent him from getting workmen, and thereby to prevent him from carrying on his business, unless and until he should adopt a certain schedule of prices. The means adopted were persuasion and social pressure, threats of personal injury or unlawful harm conveyed to persons employed or seeking employment, and a patrol of two men in front of the plaintiff's factory, maintained from half past 6 in the morning till half past 5 in the afternoon, on one of the busiest streets of Boston. The number of men was greater at times, and at times showed some little disposition to stop the plaintiff's door. The patrol proper at times went further than simple advice, not obtruded beyond the point where the other person was willing to listen; and it was found that the patrol would probably be continued if not enjoined. There was also some evidence of persuasion to break existing contracts. The patrol was maintained as one of the means of carrying out the defendants' plan, and it was used in combination with social pressure, threats of personal injury or unlawful harm, and persuasion to break existing contracts. It was thus one means of intimidation, indirectly to the plaintiff, and directly to persons actually employed, or seeking to be employed, by the plaintiff, and of rendering such employment unpleasant or intolerable to such persons.

Such an act is an unlawful interference with the rights both of employer and of employed. An employer has a right to engage all persons who are willing to work for him, at such prices as may be mutually agreed upon, and persons employed or seeking employment have a corresponding right to enter into or remain in the employment of any person or corporation willing to employ them. These rights are secured by the constitution itself. No one can lawfully interfere by force or intimidation to prevent employers or persons employed or wishing to be employed from the exercise of these rights. It is in Massachusetts, as in some other states, even made a criminal offense for one, by intimidation or force, to prevent, or seek to prevent, a person from entering into or continuing in the employment of a person or corporation. . . . Intimidation is not limited to threats of violence or of physical injury to person or property. It has a broader signification, and there also may be a moral intimidation which is illegal. Patrolling or picketing, under the circumstances stated in the report, has elements of intimidation like those which were found to exist in *Sherry v. Perkins*, 147 Mass. 212. . . . The patrol was an unlawful interference both with the plaintiff and with the workmen, within the principle of many cases; and, when instituted for the purpose of interfering with his business, it became a private nuisance. . . .

The defendants contend that these acts were justifiable, because they were only seeking to secure better wages for themselves, by compelling the plaintiff to accept their schedule of wages. This motive or purpose does not justify maintaining a patrol in front of the plaintiff's premises, as a means of carrying out their conspiracy. A combination among persons merely to regulate their own conduct is within allowable competition, and is lawful, although others may be indirectly affected thereby. But a combination to do injurious acts expressly directed to another, by way of intimidation or constraint, either of himself or of persons employed or seeking to be employed by him, is outside of allowable competition, and is unlawful. . . .

A question is also presented whether the court should enjoin such interference with persons in the employment of the plaintiff who are not bound by contract to remain with him, or with persons who are not under any existing contract, but who are seeking or intending to enter into his employment. A conspiracy to interfere with the plaintiff's business by means of threats and intimidation, and by maintaining a patrol in front of his premises, in order to prevent persons from entering his employment, or in order to prevent persons who are in his employment from continuing therein, is unlawful, even though such persons are not bound by contract to enter into or to continue in his employment; and the injunction should not be so limited as to relate only to persons who are bound by existing contracts. . . . We therefore think that the injunction should be in the form as originally issued. So ordered.

FIELD, C.J., dissenting.

The practice of issuing injunctions in cases of this kind is of very recent origin. . . .

[I]n the absence of any power given by statute, the jurisdiction of a court of equity, . . . does not, I think, extend to enjoining acts like those complained of in the case at bar, unless they amount to a destruction or threatened destruction of property, or an irreparable injury to it. . . .

As a means of prevention, the remedy given by Pub.St. c. 74, § 2, would seem to be adequate where the section is applicable, unless the destruction of, or an irreparable injury to, property is threatened; and there is the additional remedy of an indictment for a criminal conspiracy at common law, if the acts of the defendant amount to that. If the acts complained of do not amount to intimidation or force, it is not in all respects clear what are lawful and what are not lawful at common law.

It seems to be established in this commonwealth that, intentionally and without justifiable cause, to entice, by persuasion, a workman to break an existing contract with his employer, and to leave his employment, is actionable, whether done with actual malice or not. . . . What constitutes justifiable cause remains in some respects undetermined. Whether to persuade a person who is free to choose his employment not to enter into the employment of another person gives a cause of action to such other person, by some courts has been said to depend upon the question of actual malice; . . . . For myself, I have been unable to see how malice is necessarily decisive. To persuade one man not to enter into the employment of another, by telling the truth to him about such other person and his business, I am not convinced is actionable at common law, whatever the motive may be. . . .

In the present case, if the establishment of a patrol is using intimidation or force, within the meaning of our statute, it is illegal and criminal. If it does not amount to intimidation or force, but is carried to such a degree as to interfere with the use by the plaintiff of his property, it may be illegal and actionable. But something more is necessary to justify issuing an injunction. If it is in violation of any ordinance of the city regulating the use of streets, there may be a prosecution for that, and the police can enforce the ordinance; but if it is merely a peaceful mode of finding out the persons who intend to enter the plaintiff's premises to apply for work, and of informing them of the actual facts of the case, in order to induce them not to enter the plaintiff's employment, in the absence of any statute relating to the subject, I doubt if it is illegal, and I see no ground for issuing an injunction against it. . . .

HOLMES, J., dissenting.

. . . There was no proof of any threat or danger of a patrol exceeding two men. . . . Again, the defendants are enjoined by the final decree from intimidating by threats, express or implied, of physical harm to body or property, any person who may be desirous of entering into the employment of the plaintiff, so far as to prevent him from entering the same. . . . The important difference between the preliminary and the final injunction is that the former goes further, and forbids the defendants to interfere with the plaintiff's business "by any scheme . . . organized for the purpose of . . . preventing any person or persons who now are or may hereafter be . . . desirous of entering the [plaintiff's employment] from entering it." I quote only a part, and the part which seems to me most objectionable. This includes refusal of social intercourse, and even organized persuasion or argument, although free from any threat of violence, either express or implied. And this is with reference to persons who have a legal right to contract or not to contract with the plaintiff, as they may see fit. Interference with existing contracts is forbidden by the final decree. . . . It appears to me that the opinion of the majority turns in part on the assumption that the patrol necessarily carries with it a threat of bodily harm. That assumption I think unwarranted, for the reasons which I have given. Furthermore, it cannot be said, I think, that two men, walking together up and down a sidewalk, and speaking to those who enter a certain shop, do necessarily and always thereby convey a threat of force. I do not think it possible to discriminate, and to say that two workmen, or even two representatives of an organization of workmen, do; especially when they are, and are known to be, under the injunction of this court not to do so. . . . With this I pass to the real difference between the interlocutory and the final decree.

I agree, whatever may be the law in the case of a single defendant . . . that when a plaintiff proves that several persons have combined and conspired to injure his business, and have done acts producing that effect, he shows temporal damage and a cause of action, unless the facts disclose or the defendants prove some ground of excuse or justification. . . .

Nevertheless, in numberless instances the law warrants the intentional infliction of temporal damage, because it regards it as justified. It is on the question of what shall amount to a justification, and more especially on the nature of the considerations which really determine or ought to determine the answer to that question, that judicial reasoning seems to me often to be inadequate. The true grounds of decision are considerations of policy and of social advantage, and it is vain to suppose that solutions can be attained merely by logic and general propositions of law which nobody disputes. Propositions as to public policy rarely are unanimously accepted, and still more rarely, if ever, are capable of unanswerable proof. They require a special training to enable any one even to form an intelligent opinion about them. . . .

To illustrate what I have said in the last paragraph: It has been the law for centuries that a man may set up a business in a small country town, too small to support more than one, although thereby he expects and intends to ruin some one already there, and succeeds in his intent. In such a case he is not held to act "unlawfully and without justifiable cause." . . . The reason, of course, is that the doctrine generally has been accepted that free competition is worth more to society than it costs, and that on this ground the infliction of the damage is privileged. *Com. v. Hunt*, 4 Metc. (Mass.) 111, 134. . . .

. . . [T]his illustration . . . shows without the need of further authority that the policy of allowing free competition justifies the intentional inflicting of temporal damage, including the damage of interference with a man's business by some means, when the damage is done, not for its own sake, but as an instrumentality in reaching the end of victory in the battle of trade. In such a case it cannot matter whether the plaintiff is the only rival of the defendant, and so is aimed at specially, or is one of a class all of whom are hit. The only debatable ground is the nature of the means by which such damage may be inflicted. We all agree that it cannot be done by force or threats of force. We all agree, I presume, that it may be done by persuasion to leave a rival's shop, and come to the defendant's. It may be done by the refusal or withdrawal of various pecuniary advantages, which, apart from this consequence, are within the defendant's lawful control. It may be done by the withdrawal of, or threat to withdraw, such advantages from third persons who have a right to deal or not to deal with the plaintiff, as a means of inducing them not to deal with him either as customers or servants. *Com. v. Hunt*, 4 Metc. (Mass.) 111, 112, 133; *Bowen v. Matheson*, 14 Allen 499; *Heywood v. Tillson*, 75 Me. 225; *Steamship Co. v. McGregor* [1892] App.Cas. 25. I have seen the suggestion made that the conflict between employers and employed was not competition. But I venture to assume that none of my brethren would rely on that suggestion. If the policy on which our law is founded is too narrowly expressed in the term "free competition," we may substitute "free struggle for life." Certainly, the policy is not limited to struggles between persons of the same class, competing for the same end. It applies to all conflicts of temporal interests.

I pause here to remark that the word "threats" often is used as if, when it appeared that threats had been made, it appeared that unlawful conduct had begun. But it depends on what you threaten. As a general rule, even if subject to some exceptions, what you may do in a certain event you may threaten to do—that is, give warning of your intention to do—in that event, and thus allow the other person the chance of avoiding the consequence. So, as to "compulsion," it depends on how you "compel." *Com. v. Hunt*, 4 Metc. (Mass.) 111, 133. So as to "annoyance" or "intimidation." . . . In *Sherry v. Perkins*, 147 Mass. 212, it was found as a fact that the display of banners which was enjoined was part of a scheme to prevent workmen from entering or remaining in the plaintiff's employment, "by threats and intimidation." The context showed that the words as there used meant threats of personal violence and intimidation by causing fear of it.

So far, I suppose, we are agreed. But there is a notion, which latterly has been insisted on a good deal, that a combination of persons to do what any one of them lawfully might do by himself will make the otherwise lawful conduct unlawful. It would be rash to say that some as yet unformulated truth may not be hidden under this proposition. But, in the general form in which it has been presented and accepted by many courts. I think it plainly untrue, both on authority and principle. *Com. v. Hunt*, 4 Metc. (Mass.) 111. . . . There was combination of the most flagrant and dominant kind in *Bowen v. Matheson*, and in the *Steamship Co. Case*, and combination was essential to the success achieved. But it is not necessary to cite cases. It is plain from the slightest consideration of practical affairs, or the most superficial reading of industrial history, that free competition means combination, and that the organization of the world, now going on so fast, means an ever-increasing might and scope of combination. It seems to me futile to set our faces against this tendency. Whether beneficial on the whole, as I think it, or detrimental, it is inevitable, unless the fundamental axioms of society, and even the fundamental conditions of life, are to be changed.

One of the eternal conflicts out of which life is made up is that between the effort of every man to get the most he can for his services, and that of society, disguised under the name of capital, to get his services for the least possible return.

Combination on the one side is patent and powerful. Combination on the other is the necessary and desirable counterpart, if the battle is to be carried on in a fair and equal way. . . .

If it be true that workingmen may combine with a view, among other things, to getting as much as they can for their labor, just as capital may combine with a view to getting the greatest possible return, it must be true that, when combined, they have the same liberty that combined capital has, to support their interests by argument, persuasion, and the bestowal or refusal of those advantages which they otherwise lawfully control. I can remember when many people thought that, apart from violence or breach of contract, strikes were wicked, as organized refusals to work. I suppose that intelligent economists and legislators have given up that notion today. I feel pretty confident that they equally will abandon the idea that an organized refusal by workmen of social intercourse with a man who shall enter their antagonist's employ is unlawful, if it is dissociated from any threat of violence, and is made for the sole object of prevailing, if possible, in a contest with their employer about the rate of wages. The fact that the immediate object of the act by which the benefit to themselves is to be gained is to injure their antagonist does not necessarily make it unlawful, any more than when a great house lowers the price of goods for the purpose and with the effect of driving a smaller antagonist from the business. Indeed, the question seems to me to have been decided as long ago as 1842, by the good sense of Chief Justice Shaw, in *Com. v. Hunt.* . . .

Notes

1. Would Allen's opinion allow any picketing under any circumstances? Consider this part of the opinion: "Intimidation is not limited to threats of violence or of physical injury to person or property . . . there also may be a moral intimidation which is illegal." Could there be picketing that did not involve "moral intimidation"? On what grounds should "moral intimidation" be illegal?

2. Under Allen's opinion, what if a mother and father ask an adult son not to work in a shop the parents think is dangerous? Would *Vegelahn* allow the employer to sue the parents successfully? What if the parents attempt to dissuade the son from working at a shop because, in the parents' view, the shop was unfair to unions? What if it were several friends?

3. Would Allen's opinion allow any "economic competition" by a group of workers against their employer? Any type of strike, picket, boycott, or other act intended to pressure the employer to agree to improve wages, hours, or working conditions?

4. Holmes admits that the workers were attempting to accomplish their goal by inflicting some economic harm on the employer, but Holmes makes an analogy to a new competing business doing economic harm to an existing business (which is legal). Is this a good analogy? Are employees who engage in economic competition through union organizing and picketing so different from employers competing with other employers that even peaceful persuasion by a union trying to

convince potential workers not to work for an employer should be considered an illegal conspiracy?

5. Would Holmes's opinion have been a good guide for determining the types of union activities that were legal and illegal? He says that some economic competition by a combination of workers against their employer should be allowed. Can you tell what type of picketing he would have allowed, and what types of appeals to current or potential workers?

6. Justice Field's opinion focuses on whether the remedy of an injunction is appropriate. In general, injunctions are considered extraordinary remedies, not available in most civil cases. Why would employers be especially eager to get an injunction in cases involving labor picketing?

Plant v. Woods

Supreme Judicial Court of Massachusetts
176 Mass. 492, 57 N.E. 1011 (1900)

HAMMOND, J.

This case arises out of a contest for supremacy between two labor unions of the same craft, having substantially the same constitution and by-laws. The chief difference between them is that the plaintiff union is affiliated with a national organization having its headquarters in Lafayette, in the state of Indiana, while the defendant union is affiliated with a similar organization having its headquarters in Baltimore, in the state of Maryland. The plaintiff union was composed of workmen who, in 1897, withdrew from the defendant union. There does not appear to be anything illegal in the object of either union, as expressed in its constitution and by-laws. . . .

The contest became active early in the fall of 1898. In September of that year the members of the defendant union declared 'all painters not affiliated with the Baltimore headquarters to be nonunion men,' and voted 'to notify bosses' of that declaration. The manifest object of the defendants was to have all the members of the craft subjected to the rules and discipline of their particular union, in order that they might have better control over the whole business, and to that end they combined and conspired to get the plaintiffs, and each of them, to join the defendant association, peaceably, if possible, but by threat and intimidation if necessary. Accordingly, on October 7th, they voted that, 'If our demands are not complied with, all men working in shops where Lafayette people are employed refuse to go to work.' The plaintiffs resisting whatever persuasive measures, if any, were used by the defendants, the latter proceeded to carry out their plan. . . .

[T]he general method of operations was substantially as follows: A duly authorized agent of the defendants would visit a shop where one or more of the plaintiffs were at work, and inform the employer of the action of the defendant union with reference to the plaintiffs, and ask him to induce such of the plaintiffs as were in his employ to sign applications for reinstatement in the defendant union. As to the general nature of these interviews the master finds that the defendants have been courteous in manner, have made no threats of personal violence, have referred to the plaintiffs as nonunion men, but have not otherwise represented them as men lacking good standing in their craft; that they have not asked that the Lafayette men be discharged, and in some cases have expressly stated that they did not wish to have them discharged, but only that they sign the blanks for reinstatement in the defendant union. The master, however, further finds, from all the circumstances under which those requests were made, that the defendants intended that employers of Lafayette men should fear trouble in their business if they continued to employ such men, and that employers to whom these requests were made were justified in believing that a failure on the part of their employés who were Lafayette men to sign such reinstatement blanks, and a failure on the part of the employers to discharge them for not doing so, would lead to trouble in the business of the employers in the nature of strikes or a boycott . . . and the defendants did not deny that such results might occur; that the strikes which did occur appear to have been steps taken by the defendants to obtain the discharge of such employés as were Lafayette men who declined to sign application blanks for reinstatement; that these defendants did not in all cases threaten a boycott of the employers' business, but did threaten that the place of business of at least one such employer would be left off from a so-called 'fair list' to be published by the Baltimore union. . . .

We have, therefore, a case where the defendants have conspired to compel the members of the plaintiff union to join the defendant union, and, to carry out their purpose, have resolved upon such coercion and intimidation as naturally may be caused by threats of loss of property by strikes and boycotts, to induce the employers either to get the plaintiffs to ask for reinstatement in the defendant union, or, that failing, then to discharge them. It matters not that this request to discharge has not been expressly made. . . . It is well to see what is the meaning of this threat to strike, when taken in connection with the intimation that the employer may 'expect trouble in his business.' It means more than that the strikers will cease to work. That is only the preliminary skirmish. It means that those who have ceased to work will by strong, persistent, and organized persuasion and social pressure of every description do all they can to prevent the employer from procuring workmen to take their places. It means much more. It means that, if these peaceful measures fail, the employer may reasonably expect that unlawful physical injury may be done to his property; that attempts in all the ways practiced by organized labor will be made to injure him in his business, even to his ruin, if possible; and that by the use of vile and opprobrious epithets and other annoying conduct, and actual and threatened personal violence, attempts will be made to intimidate those who enter or desire to enter his employ; and that whether or not all this be done by the strikers or only by their sympathizers, or with the open sanction and approval of the former, he will have no help from them in his efforts to protect himself. . . .

If the defendants can lawfully perform the acts complained of in the city of Springfield, they can pursue the plaintiffs all over the state in the same manner, and compel them to abandon their trade, or bow to the behests of their pursuers. It is to be observed that this is not a case between the employer and employed, or, to use a hackneyed expression, between capital and labor, but between laborers all of the same craft, and each having the same right as any one of the others to pursue his calling. . . . The same rule is stated with care and discrimination by Wells, J., in *Walker v. Cronin*, 107 Mass. 555: 'Every one has a right to enjoy the fruits and advantages of his own enterprise, industry, skill, and credit. He has no right to be protected against competition, but he has a right to be free from malicious and wanton interference, disturbance, or annoyance. . . .' In this case the acts complained of were calculated to cause damage to the plaintiffs, and did actually cause such damage; and they were intentionally done for that purpose. Unless, therefore, there was justifiable cause, the acts were malicious and unlawful. . . .

The defendants contend . . . that a person may work for whom he pleases, and, in the absence of any contract to the contrary, may cease to work when he pleases, and for any reason whatever, whether the same be good or bad, that he may give notice of his intention in advance, with or without stating the reason; that what one man do several men acting in concert may do, and may agree beforehand that they will do, and may give notice of the agreement; and that all this may be lawfully done, notwithstanding such concerted action may, by reason of the consequent interruption of the work, result in great loss to the employer and his other employés, and that such a result was intended. In a general sense, and without reference to exceptions arising out of conflicting public and private interests, all this may be true. . . . [B]ut in many cases the lawfulness of an act which causes damage to another may depend upon whether the act is for justifiable cause. . . .

In cases somewhat akin to the one at bar this court has had occasion to consider the question how far acts manifestly coercive and intimidating in their nature, which cause damage and injury to the business or property of another, and are done with intent to cause such injury, and partly in reliance upon such coercion, are justifiable. In *Bowen v. Matheson*, 14 Allen 499, it was held to be lawful for persons engaged in the business of shipping seamen to combine together into a society for the purpose of competing with other persons engaged in the same business, and it was held lawful for them, in pursuance of that purpose, to take men out of a ship if men shipped by a nonmember were in that ship, to refuse to furnish seamen through a nonmember, to notify the public that they had combined against nonmembers and had 'laid the plaintiff on the shelf,' to notify the plaintiff's customers and friends that the plaintiff could not ship seamen for them, and to interfere in all these ways with the business of the plaintiff as a shipping agent, and compel him to abandon the same. The justification for these acts so injurious to the business of the plaintiff, and so intimidating in their nature, is to be found in the law of competition. No legal right of the plaintiff was infringed upon, and, as stated by Chapman, J., . . . 'if the effect of these acts was to destroy the business of shipping masters who are not members of the association, it is such a result as, in the competition of business, often follows from a course of proceeding that the law permits.'

The primary object of the defendants was to build up their own business, and this they might lawfully do to the extent disclosed in that case, even to the injury of their rivals. Similar decisions have been made in other courts where acts somewhat coercive in their nature and effect have been held justifiable under the law of competition. *Steamship Co. v. McGregor* (1892) App. Cas. 25. . . .

On the other hand, it was held in *Carew v. Rutherford*, 106 Mass. 1, that a conspiracy against a mechanic — who is under the necessity of employing workmen in order to carry on his business — to obtain a sum of money from him, which he is under no legal obligation to pay, by inducing his workmen to leave him, or by deterring others from entering into his employ, or by threatening to do this, so that he is induced to pay the money demanded under a reasonable apprehension that he cannot carry on his business without yielding to the demands, is illegal, if not criminal, conspiracy; that the acts done under it are illegal, and that the money thus obtained may be recovered back. . . . That case bears a close analogy to the one at bar. The acts there threatened were like those in this case, and the purpose was, in substance, to force the plaintiff to give his work to the defendants, and to extort from him a fine because he had given some of his work to other persons.

Without now indicating to what extent workmen may combine, and in pursuance of an agreement may act by means of strikes and boycotts to get the hours of labor reduced, or their wages increased, or to procure from their employers any other concession directly and immediately affecting their own interests, or to help themselves in competition with their fellow workmen, we think this case must be governed by the principles laid down in *Carew v. Rutherford, ubi supra.* The purpose of these defendants was to force the plaintiffs to join the defendant association, and to that end they injured the plaintiffs in their business, and molested and disturbed them in their efforts to work at their trade. It is true they committed no acts of personal violence, or of physical injury to property, although they threatened to do something which might reasonably be expected to lead to such results. In their threat, however, there was plainly that which was coercive in its effect upon the will. . . . The necessity that the plaintiffs should join this association is not so great, nor is its relation to the rights of the defendants, as compared with the right of the plaintiffs to be free from molestation, such as to bring the acts of the defendant under the shelter of the principles of trade competition. Such acts are without justification, and therefore are malicious and unlawful, and the conspiracy thus to force the plaintiffs was unlawful. Such conduct is intolerable, and inconsistent with the spirit of our laws. . . . See, in addition to the authorities above cited, *Com. v. Hunt*, 4 Metc. (Mass.) 111; . . . *Vegelahn v. Guntner*, 167 Mass. 97. . . . As the plaintiffs have been injured by these acts, and there is reason to believe that the defendants contemplate further proceedings of the same kind, which will be likely still more to injure the plaintiffs, equity lies to enjoin the defendants. Vegelahn v. Guntner, ubi supra. . . .

HOLMES, C. J., dissenting.

. . . If the decision in the present case simply had relied upon *Vegelahn v. Guntner*, I should have hesitated to say anything. . . . But, much to my satisfaction, if I may say so, the court has seen fit to adopt the mode of approaching the question which I believe to be the correct one, and to open an issue which otherwise I might have thought closed. The difference between my Brethren and me now seems to be a difference of degree, and the line of reasoning followed makes it proper for me to explain where the difference lies.

I agree that the conduct of the defendants is actionable unless justified. . . . I agree that the presence or absence of justification may depend upon the object of their conduct; that is, upon the motive with which they acted. *Vegelahn v. Guntner.* . . . On the other hand, I infer that a majority of my Brethren would admit that a boycott or strike intended to raise wages directly might be lawful, if it did not embrace in its scheme or intent violence, breach of contract, or other conduct unlawful on grounds independent of the mere fact that the action of the defendants was combined. . . . To come directly to the point, the issue is narrowed to the question whether, assuming that some purposes would be a justification, the purpose in this case of the threatened boycotts and strikes was such as to justify the threats. That purpose was not directly concerned with wages. It was one degree more remote. The immediate object and motive was to strengthen the defendants' society as a preliminary and means to enable it to make a better fight on questions of wages or other matters of clashing interests.

I differ from my Brethren in thinking that the threats were as lawful for this preliminary purpose as for the final one to which strengthening the union was a means. I think that unity of organization is necessary to make the contest of labor effectual, and that societies of laborers lawfully may employ in their preparation the means which they might use in the final contest.

Although this is not the place for extended economic discussion, and although the law may not always reach ultimate economic conceptions, I think it well to add that I cherish no illusions as to the meaning and effect of strikes. While I think the strike a lawful instrument in the universal struggle of life, I think it pure phantasy to suppose that there is a body of capital of which labor, as a whole, secures a larger share by that means.

. . . Organization and strikes may get a larger share for the members of an organization, but, if they do, they get it at the expense of the less organized and less powerful portion of the laboring mass. They do not create something out of nothing. . . .

But, subject to the qualifications which I have expressed, I think it lawful for a body of workmen to try by combination to get more than they now are getting, although they do it at the expense of their fellows, and to that end to strengthen their union by the boycott and the strike.

Notes

1. The majority found both the means and the ends of labor action illegal. The means were illegal because, even though there was no violence yet, the union was essentially making a threat of a strike, which would (in the majority's view)

inevitably be violent or at least intimidating and threatening. Also, the end of requiring workers to join a union was illegal.

Holmes, dissenting, would have found both the means and ends legal. The union's actions had been peaceful, and strikes for a legal end are (or at least should be) legal. Further, the real "end" the union sought here was the legal goal of trying to raise wages. Workers joining the union was not the end in itself; rather, it was a necessary part of the true end of raising wages, as organizing into a union would be a more effective way of achieving higher wages.

Who is more convincing? Labor law is predicated on the notion that workers generally have more power when bargaining collectively than when bargaining individually, and statistics bear this out. Unionized workers usually have significantly greater compensation than comparable, non-union workers. Still, what sorts of pressure should unions be able to use to encourage workers to join a specific union, or to get employers to agree to use workers from a specific union?

2. In modern law, we refer to agreements between employers and employees that obligate employees to pay at least a large portion of union dues as "union security agreements." As Chapter 14 explains, some jurisdictions permit union security agreements, and some (the so-called "right to work" jurisdictions) do not. The closed shop and the union shop are illegal in all jurisdictions. What types of union security agreements should be legal ends for unions? Are there any specifics about such agreements, or other labor law rules, you might want to know, before deciding?

3. At the time of the case, under "at will" employment rules, it was entirely legal for employers to bar employees from joining a union or other organization, on pain of discharge, and it was entirely legal for employers to require employees to join pretty much any sort of organization the employer wished them to join, on pain of discharge, including an employer's preferred employee organization (notably including "company unions," discussed further *infra*). Should that be relevant in deciding whether the union in *Plant* was pursuing a legal end?

4. As to the means, under the majority opinion in *Plant*, what types of strikes, if any, might be legal? Holmes says he "infers that a majority of my Brethren" would agree that a strike for wages could be legal. Is that a fair inference? Note that while the *Plant* majority does seem to imply that some kinds of economic harm would be allowed, it does not cite any cases allowing strikes.

5. The majority in *Plant* cited both *Bowen v. Matheson*, 96 Mass. 499 (1867) and *Mogul Steamship Co. v. McGregor, Gow & Co.*, 23 Q.B.D. 598 (Eng. 1889). Both cases involved competition between businesses, which the courts found permissible.

In *Bowen*, plaintiff company and defendant companies all were in the business of supplying workers to ships. The defendant companies joined together to control the business. This included agreeing together to set terms such as the minimum wages of the workers that they supplied. Also, defendant companies agreed not to furnish any workers to any ship which used workers from the plaintiff company. Plaintiff company sued, and the court held for defendants. The decision reasoned that business competition is allowed, even if it involves setting wages of workers of other businesses, and even if the effect is to destroy the business of those not in the association.

Thus, it was legal in that era for businesses to compete against each other and cause economic harm specifically by affecting the wages of the workers of another business. Also, in much of the 19th century, employers could form combinations to lower wages of employees. But, Holmes's dissents to the contrary notwithstanding, courts did not see competition by unions against business in the same way. Unions were not allowed to compete against companies by trying to set wages. Does this represent a double standard, or is there a distinction that should make a difference?

6. Judges in that era and beyond were quite hostile to the goal of a union shop. For example, *State v. Glidden*, 8 A. 890 (Conn. 1887), involved a peaceful boycott by printers to try to win a union shop. The judge enjoined the boycott, and he characterized the union position as follows. The union was telling the employer that: "You shall discharge the men you have in your employ, and you shall hereafter employ only such men as we shall name. It is true we have no interest in your business, we have no capital invested therein, we are in no wise responsible for its losses or failures, we are not directly benefitted by its success, and we do not participate in its profits; yet we have a right to control its management and compel you to submit to our dictation." 8 A. 890, 894.

––––––––––

So, in the late 19th and early 20th centuries, what could unions do, legally? In *Hopkins v. Oxley Stave Co.*, 83 F. 912 (8th Cir. 1897), the union tried a public boycott to protest use of new machines at a barrel manufacturer. The court enjoined the boycott. Note that this case did not involve a strike, but merely requests to the public not to patronize the store. *United Shoe Machinery Corp. v. Fitzgerald*, 237 Mass. 537 (1921), held that a strike with the purpose of getting the employer to agree to bargain collectively with the union was an illegal end, because the employer had individual employment contracts in place.

Still, in the early 20th century, despite such cases, unions continued to grow. Beyond the courtroom, employers attacked unions both physically and via other means. Employers began using "scientific management" and speedup systems which often made work both less fulfilling and more difficult, because workers did fewer and more minute tasks with less discretion and were pressured to do such tasks much more rapidly. *See generally* DAVID NOBLE, AMERICA BY DESIGN: SCIENCE, TECHNOLOGY AND THE RISE OF CORPORATE CAPITALISM (1977). In the early 20th century, the National Association of Manufacturers (NAM) was born. In 1903, NAM started its "open shop" campaign, a drive to either destroy unions or replace them with "company unions," groups that were really run by the employer. Voicing one conception of American values, NAM President David Parry said in 1903: "The principles and demands of organized labor are absolutely untenable to those believing in the individualistic social order." BRUCE KAUFMAN, MANAGING THE HUMAN

FACTOR: THE EARLY YEARS OF HUMAN RESOURCE MANAGEMENT IN AMERICAN INDUSTRY 102 (2008). The open shop campaign continued into the 1920s.

Meanwhile, labor argued for a fundamental right of freedom to associate in a union. The AFL and other independent labor unions hated company unions. But the law at this time allowed employers to treat employees in a company union better than employees in a real union. Indeed, the law allowed employers simply to fire employees for joining an independent union.

Along these lines, employers often compelled workers to sign "yellow dog contracts": a promise that the employee was not a union member and would not become a union member as a condition of employment. Yellow dog contracts were enforceable until the early 1930s, and they were widely used. By 1929, 1,250,000 workers had signed such contracts, including almost all the miners in West Virginia. BERNSTEIN, THE LEAN YEARS *supra*, 200 (1960).

Given that under at-will employment rules, it was still legal to fire an employee for joining or even sympathizing with a union, why did employers use yellow dog contracts? In large part, it was to get injunctions against union organizers. If employees had signed yellow dog contracts, then employers could claim organizers were interfering with the contracts and seek an injunctive remedy. *See, e.g., Hitchman Coal & Coke Co. v. Mitchell*, 245 U.S. 229 (1917) (upholding an injunction against union organizers because what would otherwise have been lawful persuasion was unlawful interference with the yellow dog contracts); *United Mine Workers v. Red Jacket Consol. Coal & Coake Co.*, 18 F.2d 839 (4th Cir. 1927) (broadly enjoining union organizers from organizing in West Virginia, because of yellow dog contracts).

Unions helped to pass state laws which outlawed the use of yellow dog contracts. But the Supreme Court held—twice—that such laws violated the Constitution. *Adair v. U.S.*, 208 U.S. 161 (1908) (striking down a federal law barring such contracts); *Coppage v. Kansas*, 236 U.S. 1 (1915) (same for a state law).

Injunctions were a central part of the arsenal of employers at time. Indeed, this period was later labeled the era of "government by injunction." Courts issued thousands of injunctions against labor unions in the early 20th century, with the numbers increasing each decade, including more than 2,000 in the 1920s. Many were issued *ex parte*, meaning unions had no opportunity to contest the injunction before it was issued. *See* FELIX FRANKFURTER & NATHAN GREENE, THE LABOR INJUNCTION (1930); Forbath, *supra*, 59 (25 percent of all strikes in the 1920s were enjoined).

Still, unions grew. Membership in the AFL increased from two million to five million members from 1914–20. Thus, there was an increasing disconnect between the reality on the ground of union organization and court decisions that were extremely hostile to unions.

The legal theories employers used against unions changed a bit in the early 20th century. The employer's cause of action moved from conspiracy to the tort of intentionally inflicted economic loss. But it was the same basic analysis. The courts looked at the means and the ends, and asked if the infliction of economic loss was justified. Often the answer was "no." It remained unclear what exactly unions could do to further their goals. Some courts adopted Holmes's view that a peaceful strike for wages by the employees at the shop of their employer was legal. But beyond that, there were many means and ends that the courts found illegal. ERNST, *supra*, 81–89, 104–05.

E. Early Rules on Secondary Activity

1. Controversies over Secondary Activity

Among the most significant limits courts placed on the means unions could use to pursue their goals were the limits on what is now called "secondary" activity. Secondary activity, most broadly, refers to activities in which the union tries to pressure or persuade parties beyond the primary parties (the union and employer it has a direct dispute with). So, if Employer A employs members of Union Local 1, and Local 1 goes on strike against Employer A, the primary parties to the labor dispute are Employer A and Local 1. Everyone else in the world — other employers, employees at other employers, customers, and the general public — are secondary parties. Thus, Local 1 engages in secondary activity if it pickets or calls for a boycott of employers other than Employer A (typically businesses who are suppliers or customers of Employer A), or if Local 1 calls for workers of other employers to strike their own employer (again, typically employers which are customers or suppliers of Employer A). Local 1 also engages in secondary activity if it appeals to the public, for example, by calling for consumer boycotts of Employer A or for consumer boycotts of other employers that do business with Employer A.

Chapter 12 covers modern rules on secondary activity, but such tactics have always been controversial: unions have long wanted to use them because they can be powerful tools for influencing employers by putting pressure on them. Employers have long opposed them, partly for that very reason and partly because they can enmesh employers who are "innocent," or at least those who have no direct way to resolve the labor dispute themselves.

Before the NLRA, courts generally found secondary activities to be illegal. This included unions calling for consumer boycotts of the primary employer. Employers often sought injunctions against such boycotts, and frequently got them. Some judges held that a secondary boycott was an unlawful means because it was inherently coercive. Other judges reached the same ultimate result by finding that the ends of union actions were unlawful. Even if a union claimed it was only trying to raise wages, judges would hold that the real end was to interfere with the right of employers to choose, *e.g.*, their own employees, suppliers, work rules, etc. ERNST, *supra*, 71–76.

Some boycott cases drew national attention and notoriety. *Buck's Stove & Range Co. v. A.F.L.*, 36 Wash. L. Rptr. 822 (D.C. 1908), was particularly infamous. In this case, a union of metal workers went on strike against Buck's Stove Company. The lower court issued an injunction barring AFL officials from placing Buck's Stove on the AFL newspaper's "We Don't Patronize" list. The injunction even barred AFL members from calling attention to the fact that workers were on strike against the company. The AFL ignored this injunction. So, the court sentenced Samuel Gompers, the AFL's president, to a year in jail, and sentenced other union officials to nine months. Finally, in 1911, the Supreme Court overturned the sentences on a procedural technicality: the strike was over, and a settlement had made the issues moot, in part because the contempt was civil, not criminal. But the Supreme Court seemed to accept the principle that simply publicizing a boycott was an illegal conspiracy in restraint of trade. ***Gompers v. Bucks Stove & Range Co.***, 221 U.S. 418 (1911). The court explained that the law:

> recognizes the right of workingmen to unite and to invite others to join their ranks, thereby making available the strength, influence, and power that come from such association. By virtue of this right, powerful labor unions have been organized.
>
> But the very fact that it is lawful to form these bodies, with multitudes of members, means that they have thereby acquired a vast power, in the presence of which the individual may be helpless. This power, when unlawfully used against one, cannot be met, except by his purchasing peace at the cost of submitting to terms which involve the sacrifice of rights protected by the Constitution; or by standing on such rights, and appealing to the preventive powers of a court of equity. . . .
>
> In the case of an unlawful conspiracy, the agreement to act in concert when the signal is published gives the words 'Unfair,' 'We Don't Patronize,' or similar expressions, a force not inhering in the words themselves, and therefore exceeding any possible right of speech which a single individual might have. Under such circumstances they become what have been called 'verbal acts,' and as much subject to injunction as the use of any other force whereby property is unlawfully damaged. 221 U.S. 418, 439.

Were this case to be decided today, entirely apart from labor law doctrines, would it be decided the same way?

Courts repeatedly found secondary boycotts illegal. Still, unions continued to use this tactic, attempting to convince other workers, the public, and other businesses not to deal with the struck employer. Consider ***Matthews v. Shankland***, 25 Misc. 604, 56 N.Y.S. 123 (Sup. Ct. 1898). In *Matthews*, a typographical union wanted higher wages and a union shop from its employer, a newspaper called the Express. All the unions in Buffalo called for a boycott of firms that continued to advertise in the Express. This was a secondary boycott because it involved parties beyond the typographical union and the primary employer, the Express. *Matthews* held that this boycott was a criminal conspiracy to hurt business relations. The decision explained that a primary boycott would have been legal; the newspaper workers themselves could have decided to not patronize the newspaper or its advertisers. But it was illegal to appeal to other workers and the public. The court stressed that property rights must be protected. Further, were this type of labor boycott to be allowed, "industry will become precarious and anarchy will prevail." The newspaper should not have to "place the management of their property under the control of" the union. 25 Misc. 604, 610.

Samuel Gompers denounced this decision. He argued that the paper and its advertisers had no vested right to patronage; if the primary employees at the paper could legally withdraw their patronage, then a group of unions should be able to withdraw their patronage as well. The distinction between primary and secondary boycotts made no sense. "The principle is the same . . . whether you are alone in threatening the withdrawal of your custom or a member of a vast combination." He called the law on this issue, "vague, obscure, and . . . tyrannical." Samuel Gompers, Labor and the Employer 208 (1920).

Again, the distinction between primary and secondary activity is a major issue in labor law today. Who was right? The *Matthews* court or Gompers? Does the primary/secondary distinction make sense, in the context of a boycott or otherwise? What concerns should guide policymakers in deciding the rules on these sorts of actions?

2. Anti-Trust Laws and Secondary Activity

Employers also used anti-trust laws against unions that employed boycotts or related tactics. In 1890, Congress passed the Sherman Act. The Sherman Act made illegal, among other things, "combinations in the form of trust or otherwise, or conspiracy in restraint of trade." This law was passed with business monopolies in mind, but employers soon began arguing that unions restrained trade as well.

Perhaps the most famous case involving anti-trust law and unions was the following case, often referred to as the "*Danbury Hatters* case." The union's ends in this case were straightforward. It wanted to organize Dietrich Loewe's hat making business and win an agreement for a union shop. This was part of a larger campaign by the AFL to organize hat finishers. By 1902, only 12 of 120 hat manufacturers in the country were nonunion. Loewe refused to be organized, insisting that he could not do so and afford to stay in business.

Loewe v. Lawlor

Supreme Court of the United States
208 U.S. 274, 28 S. Ct. 301, 52 L. Ed. 488 (1908)

[The complaint alleged that the United Hatters of North America, an AFL affiliate, intended to unionize plaintiff hat manufacturers, located in Danbury, Connecticut, and all hat maker workers, by "restraining and destroying" their interstate trade, by "intimidation and threats" made to manufacturers and customers, and by boycotting them and their customers by appeals to union members throughout the U.S. This included inducing strikes at plaintiffs' facilities and calls for boycotts of the hats, of wholesalers selling them, and of dealers who purchased from the wholesalers being boycotted. The boycott of the wholesalers and dealers was done through distributing circulars and publicizing the boycott in various newspapers and union publications, including the journals of the Hatters' union and the AFL.

For example, the complaint alleged that, "the boycott was used against the products of the firm of F. Berg & Company, of Orange, New Jersey, and H.H. Roelofs & Company, of Philadelphia, Pennsylvania, hat manufacturers, to their very great injury, and until the said firms successively yielded to [union] demands." The AFL and the Hatters Union "have frequently declared boycotts . . . against the business and product of various hat manufacturers, and have vigorously prosecuted the same . . . to the great damage and loss of business of said manufacturers and particularly during the years of 1901 and 1902."

The complaint also alleged that plaintiffs conducted businesses "upon the broad and patriotic principle of not discriminating against any person seeking employment because of his being or not being connected with any labor or other organization, and have refused to enter into agreement with any person or organization whereby the rights and privileges, either of themselves or any employee, would be jeopardized, surrendered to, or controlled by, said person or organization." The complaint further alleged that defendants did "falsely represent to said wholesale dealers and their customers, that the plaintiffs . . . had driven their employees to extreme measures 'by their persistent, unfair, and un-American policy of antagonizing union labor, forcing wages to a starvation scale, and given boys and cheap, unskilled foreign labor preference over experienced and capable union workmen.'"

Plaintiffs claimed this violated the Sherman Anti-Trust Act, alleged actual damages of $80,000, and requested treble damages, as provided by the Act. The District Court sustained a demurrer for defendants, and the Second Circuit certified the legal question to the Supreme Court.]

FULLER, C.J.:

The question is whether, upon the facts therein averred and admitted by the demurrer, this action can be maintained under the anti-trust act. . . .

In our opinion, the combination described in the declaration is a combination 'in restraint of trade or commerce among the several states,' in the sense in which those words are used in the act, and the action can be maintained accordingly.

And that conclusion rests on many judgments of this court, to the effect that the act prohibits any combination whatever to secure action which essentially obstructs the free flow of commerce between the states, or restricts, in that regard, the liberty of a trader to engage in business.

The combination charged falls within the class of restraints of trade aimed at compelling third parties and strangers involuntarily not to engage in the course of trade except on conditions that the combination imposes; and there is no doubt that (to quote from the well-known work of Chief Justice Erle on Trade Unions) 'at common law every person has individually, and the public also has collectively, a right to require that the course of trade should be kept free from unreasonable obstruction.'

But the objection here is to the jurisdiction, because, even conceding that the declaration states a case good at common law, it is contended that it does not state one within the statute. Thus, it is said that the restraint alleged would operate to entirely destroy plaintiffs' business and thereby include intrastate trade as well; that physical obstruction is not alleged as contemplated; and that defendants are not themselves engaged in interstate trade.

We think none of these objections are tenable, and that they are disposed of by previous decisions of this court. . . .

In *W.W. Montague & Co. v. Lowry*, 193 U. S. 38, which was an action brought by a private citizen under § 7 against a combination engaged in the manufacture of tiles, defendants were wholesale dealers in tiles in California, and combined with manufacturers in other states to restrain the interstate traffic in tiles by refusing to sell any tiles to any wholesale dealer in California who was not a member of the association, except at a prohibitive rate. The case was a commercial boycott against such dealers in California as would not or could not obtain membership in the association. The restraint did not consist in a physical obstruction of interstate commerce, but in the fact that the plaintiff and other independent dealers could not purchase their tiles from manufacturers in other states because such manufacturers had combined to boycott them. This court held that this obstruction to the purchase of tiles, a fact antecedent to physical transportation, was within the prohibition of the act. Mr. Justice Peckham, speaking for the court, said, concerning the agreement, that it 'restrained trade, for it narrowed the market for the sale of tiles in California from the manufacturers and dealers therein in other states, so that they could only be sold to the members of the association, and it enhanced prices to the nonmember.'

The averments here are that there was an existing interstate traffic between plaintiffs and citizens of other states, and that, for the direct purpose of destroying such interstate traffic, defendants combined not merely to prevent plaintiffs from manufacturing articles then and there intended for transportation beyond the state, but also to prevent the vendees from reselling that hats which they had imported from Connecticut, or from further negotiating with plaintiffs for the purchase and intertransportation of such hats from Connecticut to the various places of destination. So that, although some of the means whereby the interstate traffic was to be destroyed were acts within a state, and some of them were, in themselves, as a part of their obvious purpose and effect, beyond the scope of Federal authority, still, as we have seen, the acts must be considered as a whole, and the plan is open to condemnation, notwithstanding a negligible amount of intrastate business might be affected in carrying it out. If the purposes of the combination were, as alleged, to prevent any interstate transportation at all, the fact that the means operated at one end before physical transportation commenced, and, at the other end, after the physical transportation ended, was immaterial.

Nor can the act in question be held inapplicable because defendants were not themselves engaged in interstate commerce. The act made no distinction between classes. It provided that 'every' contract, combination, or conspiracy in restraint of trade was illegal. The records of Congress show that several efforts were made to exempt, by legislation, organizations of farmers and laborers from the operation of the act, and that all these efforts failed, so that the act remained as we have it before us.

In an early case (*United States v. Workingmen's Amalgamated Council*, 54 Fed. 994) the United States filed a bill under the Sherman act in the circuit court for the eastern district of Louisiana, averring the existence of 'a gigantic and wide-spread combination of the members of a multitude of separate organizations for the purpose of restraining the commerce among the several states and with foreign countries,' and it was contended that the statute did not refer to combinations of laborers. But the court, granting the injunction, said:

> 'I think the congressional debates show that the statute had its origin in the evils of massed capital; but, when the Congress came to formulating the prohibition, which is the yardstick for measuring the complainant's right to the injunction, it expressed it in these words: 'Every contract or combination in the form of trust, or otherwise in restraint of trade or commerce among the several states or with foreign nations, is hereby declared to be illegal.' The subject had so broadened in the minds of the legislators that the source of the evil was not regarded as material, and the evil in its entirety is dealt with. They made the interdiction include combinations of labor as well as of capital; in fact, all combinations in restraint of commerce, without reference to the character of the persons who entered into them.... [I]ts meaning, as far as relates to the sort of combinations to which it is to apply, is manifest, and that it includes combinations which are composed of laborers acting in the interest of laborers.
>
> 'It is the successful effort of the combination of the defendants to intimidate and overawe others who were at work in conducting or carrying on the commerce of the country, in which the court finds their ... violation of the statute....'

Subsequently came the litigation over the Pullman strike and the decisions *In re Debs*, 64 Fed. 724, 745, 755 (C.C.N.D. Ill. 1894), 158 U. S. 564 (1895). The bill in that case was filed by the United States against the officers of the American Railway Union, which alleged that a labor dispute existed between the Pullman Palace Car Company and its employees; that thereafter the four officers of the railway union combined together and with others to compel an adjustment of such dispute by creating a boycott against the cars of the car company; that, to make such boycott effective, they had already prevented certain of the railroads running out of Chicago from operating their trains; that they asserted that they could and would tie up, paralyze, and break down any and every railroad which did not accede to their demands, and that the purpose and intention of the combination was 'to secure unto themselves the entire control of the interstate, industrial, and commercial business in which the population of the city of Chicago and of the other communities along the lines of road of said railways are engaged with each other, and to restrain any and all other persons from any independent control or management of such interstate, industrial, or commercial enterprises, save according to the will and with the consent of the defendants.'

The circuit court proceeded principally upon the Sherman anti-trust law, and granted an injunction. . . .

[T]he complaint averred that plaintiffs were manufacturers of hats in Danbury, Connecticut, having a factory there, and were then and there engaged in an interstate trade in some twenty states other than the state of Connecticut; that they were practically dependent upon such interstate trade to consume the product of their factory, only a small percentage of their entire output being consumed in the state of Connecticut; that, at the time the alleged combination was formed, they were in the process of manufacturing a large number of hats for the purpose of fulfilling engagements then actually made with consignees and wholesale dealers in states other than Connecticut, and that, if prevented from carrying on the work of manufacturing these hats, they would be unable to complete their engagements.

That defendants were members of a vast combination called The United Hatters of North America, comprising about 9,000 members, and including a large number of subordinate unions, and that they were combined with some 1,400,000 others into another association known as The American Federation of Labor, of which they were members, whose members resided in all the places in the several states where the wholesale dealers in hats and their customers resided and did business; that defendants were 'engaged in a combined scheme and effort to force all manufacturers of fur hats in the United States, including the plaintiffs, against their will and their previous policy of carrying on their business, to organize their workmen in the departments of making and finishing, in each of their factories, into an organization, to be part and parcel of the said combination known as the United Hatters of North America, or, as the defendants and their confederates term it, to unionize their shops, with the intent thereby to control the employment of labor in and the operation of said factories, and to subject the same to the direction and control of persons other than the owners of the same, in a manner extremely onerous and distasteful to such owners, and to carry out such scheme, effort, and purpose by restraining and destroying the interstate trade and commerce of such manufacturers, by means of intimidation of and threats made to such manufacturers and their customers in the several states, of boycotting them, their product, and their customers, using therefor all the powerful means at their command as aforesaid, until such time as, from the damage and loss of business resulting therefrom, the said manufacturers should yield to the said demand to unionize their factories.'

That the conspiracy or combination was so far progressed that out of eighty-two manufacturers of this country engaged in the production of fur hats, seventy had accepted the terms and acceded to the demand that the shop should be conducted in accordance, so far as conditions of employment were concerned, with the will of the American Federation of Labor; that the local union demanded of plaintiffs that they should unionize their shop under peril of being boycotted by this combination, which demand plaintiffs declined to comply with; that thereupon the American Federation of Labor, acting through its official organ and through its organizers, declared a boycott. . . .

We think a case within the statute was set up and that the demurrer should have been overruled. Judgment reversed and cause remanded with a direction to proceed accordingly.

Notes

1. Review the *Montague* case as described in *Loewe.* Is there a relevant distinction in the fact patterns of the two cases? Did *Montague* involve a boycott, or something else? Do the factual differences in the cases justify a different result?

2. As a result of this decision, the hatters' local union was fined $252,000, and workers in the local union were held individually liable for these damages. The only reason they were not all driven into poverty was that the national AFL agreed to pay the fines.

3. Were this case to come up today, do you see any potential legal problems in interpreting a statute to bar peaceful persuasion, via literature, of customers of a business not to patronize that business?

4. The workers at the Danbury plant had also tried to strike to further their goals. That tactic was not at issue in the decision above, but if the strike had been successful in preventing production entirely, would that have been a Sherman Act violation under the logic of this decision? Note that the Court says, regarding the union's acts, "some of them were, in themselves, as a part of their obvious purpose and effect, beyond the scope of Federal authority." On the other hand, is there a plausible argument under this decision that a union action that shuts down a business doing interstate commerce is a "combination . . . in restraint of trade or commerce among the several states"?

5. Note the competing visions of freedom, liberty, and what it means to be an American in this case. The union referred to the employers' "persistent, unfair, and un-American policy of antagonizing union labor [and] forcing wages to a starvation scale." Unions also argued that they should have the liberty to try to persuade people not to patronize employers that labor thought were unfair, for the goal of improved wages. Loewe countered that he conducted business, "upon the broad and patriotic principle of not discriminating against any person seeking employment because of his being or not being connected with any labor or other organization."

6. Defendants in *Loewe* unsuccessfully argued that at least some of their actions lacked sufficient connection to interstate commerce to be covered by the Sherman Act. **Coronado Coal v. United Mine Workers**, 268 U.S. 295 (1925), focused even more on that issue. In *Coronado Coal*, the union had used dynamite to destroy mine property, and two people were killed. (Labor relations in the mining industry often featured considerable violence on both sides).

The legal issue in *Coronado Coal* was not whether these acts were illegal under state laws, but rather whether the Sherman Act covered such activity. At the time, but not today, the Court generally took the position that activities like mining, agriculture, and manufacturing were beyond the scope of Congress's legislative authority under the Commerce Clause. In the first round of litigation, plaintiff mine owners won a verdict of $600,000 ($200,000 actual damages trebled). On appeal, the Supreme Court remanded the action: there was only a "local motive" for a "local strike." Although the acts were "reprehensible," they were not covered by the Sherman Act, which required interstate commerce.

On remand, however, the lower court found that the union's objective was not merely local. It was also designed to prevent plaintiffs' non-union mines from being able to compete with unionized mines in adjacent states. This was found to be sufficient connection to interstate commerce, even in 1925, when that concept was significantly more limited than it would be later.

————————

Unions were not happy about how courts were interpreting the Sherman Act. So, labor and its supporters successfully lobbied for certain language to be added to the Clayton Antitrust Act of 1914. Unions relied on two parts of the Clayton Act. First, §6, which said that "the labor of a human being is not a commodity or article of commerce." Section 6 also provided that unions did not *per se* violate anti-trust laws, and it added that anti-trust laws shall not bar labor organizations "from lawfully carrying out the legitimate objects thereof." Second, §20 provided that no injunction would be issued "in any case between an employer and employees, or between employers and employees . . . growing out of a dispute concerning terms or conditions of employment, unless necessary to prevent irreparable injury to property."

Samuel Gompers called this "labor's charter of freedom." And there were other encouraging signs for labor in the second decade of the 20th century. AFL membership grew dramatically, up to nearly five million by 1920. The public increasingly accepted unions. Also, during World War I, President Woodrow Wilson set up the National Labor Board (NLB). Designed to resolve labor disputes short of strikes which would interfere with wartime production, the NLB adopted the following as a principle: "The right of workers to organize in trade unions and to bargain collectively, through chosen representatives, is recognized and affirmed. This right shall not be denied, abridged, or interfered with by the employers in any manner whatsoever." Russell Smith, *The Evolution of the "Duty to Bargain" Concept in American Law*, 39 Mich. L. Rev. 1065, 1068 & n. 6 (1941).

But the 1920s proved to be "lean years" for labor. First, labor suffered setbacks in a few radical general strikes in 1919, including the Boston police strike discussed in Section III-B. Second, employer resistance stiffened, both through "open shop" campaigns and through company unions and "welfare capitalism" (which sometimes did bring better benefits and less arbitrary management). Third, the AFL's strategy of focusing almost exclusively on skilled workers left out the increasing number of unskilled manufacturing workers. The AFL lost hundreds of thousands of members in the 1920s. The legal environment remained quite hostile, and the Clayton Act did not provide the protection Gompers had hoped.

The key case in that regard was **Duplex Printing Press Co. v. Deering**, 254 U.S. 443 (1921). In *Duplex*, the union was pursuing the ends of a closed shop, an eight-hour day, and union wage levels. The means were mostly secondary. The union tried a strike, which had little effect. It then led a boycott against products of Duplex's factory. Among other things, the union told Duplex's business customers (typically newspapers) that it would be better for them not to purchase or install Duplex presses. The union threatened these business customers with strikes; it told a trucking company not to haul presses; it told repair shops not to work on Duplex presses; and it told union workers that they would lose their union cards if they installed Duplex presses.

The Court majority found an anti-trust violation by the union. The union argued that §§ 6 and 20 of the Clayton Act protected them. However, Justice Pitney, writing for the Court, said that § 6 only allowed "normal and legitimate objects of unions," not restraint of trade. Responding to the suggestion that a closed shop was, in fact, a normal object of unions, Pitney reasoned that even if so, the closed shop was not a legitimate object in the eyes of the law (it was not entirely clear what Pitney thought the normal and legitimate objects § 6 protected were). The majority then said that § 20 "is but declaratory of the law as it stood before." 254 U.S. 443, 469–70. The majority added that since these parts of the Clayton Act imposed an exceptional restriction on equity powers of courts (their power to issue injunctions), that restriction should be read narrowly. Thus, courts could still enjoin secondary activity, and the Clayton Act restrictions should only apply "to those who are proximately and substantially concerned as parties to an actual dispute." Proper union activity must be in "proximate relation to a controversy" between an employer and an employee. In this case, the dispute between Duplex and its employees did not allow other members of the Machinists' union who worked for other employers to "make that dispute their own." The others were "standing in no relation of employment" to Duplex. *Id.* at 470–72. This secondary boycott "cannot be deemed 'peaceful and lawful' persuasion." Rather, "it is a threat to inflict damage on the immediate employer, between whom and his employees no dispute exists, in order to bring him against his will into a concerted plan to inflict damage upon another employer who is in dispute with his employees." *Id.* at 474.

The majority also expressed fear of what could happen were secondary boycotts allowed.

> An ordinary controversy in a manufacturing establishment, said to concern the terms or conditions of employment there, has been held a sufficient occasion for imposing a general embargo upon the products of the establishment and a nation-wide blockade of the channels of interstate commerce against them, carried out by inciting sympathetic strikes and a

secondary boycott against complainant's customers, to the great and incalculable damage of many innocent people far remote from any connection with or control over the original and actual dispute—people constituting, indeed, the general public upon whom the cost must ultimately fall. *Id.* at 477–78.

The majority's holding that the only people who could be involved in a boycott were "those who are proximately and substantially concerned as parties to an actual dispute" made the sharp distinction between primary and secondary activity that is still present in modern U.S. labor law.

Justice Brandeis dissented, joined by Justices Holmes and Clarke. The dissent argued that other machinists in the other shops were substantially concerned with the primary dispute, and all the union defendants had a common-law justification: they were injuring Duplex in self-defense. The dissent noted that the town had four press manufacturers, three of which were already organized. Two of those employers had stated that they could not abide by union rules unless Duplex did also. Under these circumstances, the dissent reasoned, the fate of all machinists in the press industry was obviously affected by what happened at Duplex. *Id.* at 480–81.

More generally, Brandeis and the dissenters did not make a point of distinguishing between secondary and primary activities. Rather, the dissent focused on what it called "unity of interest" of the workers. Thus, the dissent distinguished *Loewe v. Lawlor* in part by stressing that *Loewe* involved people "not united by common interest but only by sympathy." *Id.* at 483.

Using this logic, the dissent reasoned that a boycott becomes illegal when, as in *Loewe*, unions appealed to the public to engage in secondary boycotts. Is that a convincing distinction? Should it be legal for workers to appeal to some secondary workers but illegal to appeal to the public? Modern labor law does draw distinctions between appeals to secondary workers and appeals to the public but, as Chapter 12 explains, modern law allows more appeals to the public than appeals to secondary workers.

The dissent also read the anti-trust laws differently. Notably, it observed that the Clayton Act was trying to address the following problem: "the social and economic ideas of judges ... were prejudicial to a position of equality between workingman and employer." *Id.* at 485. Also, as to § 20, "Congress did not restrict the provision to employers and workingmen in their employ." Section 20 refers to "'employers and employees' and 'persons employed and persons seeking employment'"; this "showed that it was not aiming merely at ... a specific employer and his employees." *Id.* at 487–88.

The case raised questions that still figure significantly in modern labor law. What sort of economic weapons should be legal for labor to use? Much secondary activity is illegal under modern NLRA law (*see* § 8(b)(4) and Chapter 12). As a matter of good labor policy, what sorts of secondary activities should be legal? Appeals to the public to boycott secondary employers who do business with the primary employer?

Picketing secondary employers? Appeals to workers at the secondary employer to strike, or not to handle struck goods?

In any case, despite labor's hopes, through the 1920s, the Clayton Act did unions little or no good. Unions would get no further statutory protections until the 1930s. At most, some courts acknowledged that peaceful, nonthreatening primary strikes and pickets for wages and hours were legal (meaning not barred by common law or anti-trust laws). But through the 1920s, courts continued to issue thousands of injunctions against labor activities, enforce yellow dog contracts, and allow employers to fire employees for organizing or joining a union, or taking part in any union activities.

Still, there was a growing disconnect between this harsh legal climate and the continued existence of unions and increased public acceptance of the idea that unions had a proper role.

F. The Beginning of Modern Private-Sector Labor Law

1. The Railway Labor Act and the Norris-LaGuardia Act

The first federal statute giving rights to unions was the Railway Labor Act of 1926 (RLA). While this casebook does not focus on RLA rules in detail, students should be aware of its existence. It applies to at least most employees and employers in the railway and airline industries. Many RLA rules are at least similar to those in the NLRA, but some (especially those regarding strikes and other methods of resolving bargaining impasses) are different.

The broader break in the hostile legal climate was the Norris-LaGuardia Act of 1932 (29 U.S.C. §§ 101–115). It was passed largely due to the increasing unpopularity of yellow dog contracts, the widespread use of injunctions against unions, and increased public sympathy toward labor. *See* Frankfurter & Greene, *supra.* This Act did two important things. First, § 3 made yellow dog contracts unenforceable. This was a significant victory for labor (although workers still did not have an affirmative legal right to unionize). Second, the Act barred courts from using injunctions in most nonviolent labor disputes. Section 1 of the Act states "No court of the United States, shall have jurisdiction to issue any restraining order or temporary or permanent injunction in a case involving or growing out of a labor dispute, except in conformity with the provisions of this Act." Section 4 then lists exceptions to this rule, essentially conduct involving violence or fraud. And even then, §§ 7, 9, and 10 provide that injunctions can only be issued after notice and hearings, that any injunction must be narrowly tailored, and that appeals may be expedited under specified rules. The Act also specifically overturned a key part of *Duplex Printing.* Section 13, paragraph C, states that its ban on most injunctions was applicable "whether or not the disputants stand in the proximate relation of employer and employee." For the moment, it appeared that secondary activities could not be enjoined, at least not under federal law.

Also demonstrating a turning of the tide in labor law, the Norris LaGuardia Act contained some strong, pro-union language. Section 2 of the Act explained:

> Whereas under prevailing economic conditions, developed with the aid of governmental authority for owners of property to organize in the corporate and other forms of ownership association, the individual unorganized worker is commonly helpless to exercise actual liberty of contract and to protect his freedom of labor, and thereby to obtain acceptable terms and conditions of employment, wherefore, though he should be free to decline to associate with his fellows, it is necessary that he have full freedom of association, self-organization, and designation of representatives of his own choosing, to negotiate the terms and conditions of his employment, and that he shall be free from the interference, restraint, or coercion of employers of labor, or their agents, in the designation of such representatives or in self-organization or in other concerted activities for the purpose of collective bargaining or other mutual aid or protection.

2. Resolving the Anti-Trust Issue

The anti-trust issue was finally resolved in 1940 and 1941, by two Supreme Court cases. First, *Apex Hosiery Co. v. Leader*, 310 U.S. 469 (1940), involved a violent strike for the end of a closed shop. The Supreme Court held that primary activities, for the end of improving wages, hours, health or safety, or union recognition, did not violate anti-trust laws. The purpose of the union's actions was not to suppress competition or fix prices. Rather, it was an attempt to compel a particular employer to comply with the union's demands. Union activity in itself was not a restraint of trade at common law, and the Clayton Act affirmed that normal union activities did not violate anti-trust statutes. Still, *Apex* distinguished both *Loewe v. Lawlor* and *Duplex Printing*; in those two cases, the *Apex* decision insisted, "the activities affecting interstate commerce were directed at control of the market and were so widespread as substantially to affect it. There was thus a suppression of competition in the market." 310 U.S. at 506.

This decision still left a considerable range of union actions subject to anti-trust prosecutions, but this range was greatly narrowed soon thereafter by *United States v. Hutcheson*, 312 U.S. 219 (1941). *Hutcheson* involved a criminal anti-trust prosecution against a union engaged in a jurisdictional dispute (two unions disagreeing about whose members had the right to do certain work for the primary employer, Anheuser-Busch). Defendant (the Carpenters' union), had used various tactics, including strikes and pickets at the primary employer and at secondary employers (*e.g.*, a separate construction company doing work for the primary employer), pickets at another employer, and a campaign urging that union members not buy Anheuser-Busch beer.

Hutcheson created what is often called the "labor exemption from the Sherman Act." The Supreme Court held that reading the Sherman Act, Clayton Act, and Norris-LaGuardia Act together revealed a congressional intent to overrule *Duplex*

Printing. The Court stressed that, "[s]o long as a union acts in its self-interest and does not combine with non-labor groups, the licit and the illicit under § 20 are not to be distinguished by any judgment regarding the wisdom or unwisdom . . . the selfishness or unselfishness of the end of which the particular union activities are the means." 312 U.S. at 232. This decision apparently exempted secondary activity from federal prosecution. But the secondary activity issue would reemerge with a vengeance later.

3. The Creation of the National Labor Relations Act

The next and most important step was the creation of the NLRA. The revolutions in law, politics, and the economy that occurred during the New Deal years could be the subject of an entire course. Many of these changes were driven by labor relations and labor and employment laws, which will be the focus here.

Before the NLRA, there was the National Industrial Recovery Act of 1933 (NIRA). The NIRA was one of President Franklin Roosevelt's early New Deal Programs. NIRA § 7(a)(1) gave employees the right to organize and bargain collectively free of interference by employers. It even set up an agency to decide labor cases — first called the National Labor Board, then later renamed the National Labor Relations Board (not to be confused with the agency of the same name under the NLRA). The NIRA's main drawback, at least from labor's perspective, was that it had no enforcement mechanism. So, major employers often ignored it. This issue became moot, because two years later, the Supreme Court held the NIRA unconstitutional (for reasons unrelated to the specific rules regarding unions) in *Schechter Poultry Corp. v. U.S.*, 295 U.S. 495 (1935).

Meanwhile, problems on the ground continued as the Depression worsened. In 1932, there were 840 strikes; in 1933, 1,700; in 1936, 2,200; and in 1937, 4,700. Boris & Lichtenstein, eds., *supra*, 308. Strikes were big and often violent. In 1934 alone, about 1.5 million workers went on strike, which was about seven percent of the total labor force (this is perhaps especially remarkable given how high unemployment was during the Great Depression). In 1934, 40 strikers were killed. Some strikes featured genuine radicalism. For example, in 1934, Trotskyists helped lead a strike at the Electric Auto-Lite plant in Toledo. Citizens and unemployed workers fought the Ohio National Guard. Although two people were killed, the union ultimately won the strike. *Id.* at 305; Bernstein, The Turbulent Years, *supra*, 221–29.

At this point, the system of labor relations was in crisis. Law and reality were increasingly out of synch. This all led to the National Labor Relations Act of 1935, the original version of which is often called as "the Wagner Act," after its author, Senator Robert Wagner. This Act, as amended, is the main, current private-sector labor law statute.

In debates over the original NLRA, Wagner urged a conception of freedom that was consistent with what union leaders and supporters had long urged. Wagner argued: "What does it profit a man to have so-called 'political freedom' if he is made an economic slave?" Dubofsky, The State and Labor, *supra*, 119.

Section 1 set out the "Findings and Policies" of the Wagner Act. This included the following:

> the denial by employers of the right of employees to organize and the refusal by employers to accept the procedure of collective bargaining lead to strikes and other forms of industrial strife or unrest, which have the intent of the necessary effect of burdening or obstructing commerce. . . .
>
> The inequality of bargaining power between employees who do not possess full freedom of association or actual liberty of contract, and employers who are organized in the corporate or other forms of ownership association substantially burdens and affects the flow of commerce, and tends to aggravate recurrent business depressions, by depressing wage rates and the purchasing power of wages earners. . . .
>
> It is hereby declared to be the policy of the United States to eliminate the causes of certain substantial obstructions to the free flow of commerce . . . by encouraging the practice and procedure of collective bargaining. . . .

There were four main goals behind the Act, and in modern labor law cases and debates about labor law, advocates and judges stress different aspects. Notably, some of the goals can be, in some contexts, in tension with others. First was the goal of stability and labor peace. Congress wanted less violence in labor relations, and arguably that included fewer strikes. While the Act allowed strikes (indeed, it was essentially the only tool which labor had to resolve bargaining impasses), the idea was that a framework for collective bargaining would limit strikes and worker protests. Second, as seen in the last quoted paragraph above, Congress wanted to encourage unionization, collective bargaining, and even industrial democracy. The idea here was in part that the economy would be strengthened by unions, as they would insist on a more equitable division of profits, and thus raise purchasing power. Atleson, *supra*, 112. Third, the Act was designed to provide a fair but neutral playing field, allowing unions and employers to settle their own disputes, without the government setting terms. Finally, Congress likely wanted to bring the law into conformity with the reality of union organization.

Section 7 of the Wagner Act sets out some of the most important, basic rights in labor law. It provides, in part, that: "Employees shall have the right to self-organization, to form, join, or assist labor organizations, to bargain collectively through representatives of their own choosing, and to engage in other concerted activities for the purposes of collective bargaining or other mutual aid or protection." As we will see, these rights are not absolute, but they are the basic building blocks of labor law.

Section 8 of the Wagner Act (now §8(a) of the NLRA) provided for certain "unfair labor practices" (ULPs) by employers. Under what was §8(1) and now is §8(a)(1), it is a ULP for employers to interfere with, restrain, or coerce employees in their exercise of their § 7 rights (most basically, *e.g.*, by firing employees because they supported a union). In addition, unions were happy about the ban on company unions in § 8(2), now § 8(a)(2). Section 8(3), now § 8(a)(3), barred discrimination against workers based on their position on unions. Section 8(4), now § 8(a)(4), barred discrimination in the context of NLRB complaints and proceedings. Section 8(5), now § 8(a)(5), imposed a duty on employers to bargain in good faith with unions.

Why do these sections now all have "(a)" added to them? The Wagner Act (the original version of the NLRA) contained employer ULPs, but no union ULPs. That would change in 1947 with the Taft-Hartley Act, described further below. Since Taft-Hartley, employer ULPs have been in § 8(a) and union ULPs in § 8(b).

Section 9 of the Act discussed representation elections, including the concepts of exclusive representation, majority rule, and appropriate bargaining units.

Also important to unions, the Wagner Act contained an enforcement mechanism for the rights it granted workers and unions. Sections 3 and 4 created the National Labor Relations Board (the NLRB or Board). Section 10 gave the Board enforcement power to investigate and prosecute employer violations of the Act. It also empowered the Board to hear cases and issue orders, including remedies, and authorized courts to enforce orders of the Board.

The Wagner Act was considered a huge victory for labor. On the other hand, the Wagner Act did not, and the NLRA still does not: mandate or require unions be formed in any particular employer or industry; allow the state to set the terms of contracts between the parties; or require an employer to enter into a contract with a union or agree to any particular terms in a contract.

Still, business reacted furiously against the NLRA, claiming it was unconstitutional and refusing to comply with it. The war on the ground continued between labor and management for three years. A Senate investigation reported that from 1934 to 1937, 2,500 corporations spent almost $9.5 million on hiring agents to spy on unions, sow discontent, and generally discourage organizing. In preparation for the Steel Strikes of 1937 (called the "Little Steel" strikes), the Youngstown Sheet and Tube Company acquired 369 rifles, eight machine guns, 190 shotguns, 450 revolvers, and 109 gas guns. Republic Steel had even more weapons: 7,855 tear and sickening gas grenades and shells, 105 gas guns, 247 revolvers, 142 shotguns, 75,650 rounds of ammunition, and 400 magazines for rifles. It was the largest buyer of arms and ammunition in the US outside the US armed forces. United States Congress, *National Labor Relations Act and Proposed Amendments, Hearings, Feb. 6–7 (1940)* 4643–4644; Robert Bruno, "Steel on Strike: From 1936 to the Present," in BRENNER, DAY AND NESS, EDS. *supra*, 262.

But in 1937, the Supreme Court upheld the constitutionality of the NLRA in **NLRB v. Jones & Laughlin Steel Corp.**, 301 U.S. 1 (1937). This case also helped mark the beginning of a new, more expansive interpretation of the Commerce Clause which began during the New Deal. The Court explained, "[a]lthough activities may be intrastate in character when separately considered, if they have such a close and substantial relation to interstate commerce that their control is essential or appropriate to protect that commerce from burdens and obstructions, Congress cannot be denied the power to exercise that control." 301 U.S. 1 at 37. The Court also added some language indicating at least some shift in judicial attitudes toward unions.

> Long ago we stated the reason for labor organizations. We said that they were organized out of the necessities of the situation; that a single employee was helpless in dealing with an employer; that he was dependent ordinarily on his daily wage for the maintenance of himself and family; that, if the employer refused to pay him the wages that he thought fair, he was nevertheless unable to leave the employ and resist arbitrary and unfair treatment; that union was essential to give laborers opportunity to deal on an equality with their employer. *Id.* at 33.

This, the end of the Depression, and moves during World War II to prevent labor strife (including another War Labor Relations Board) helped spur significant increases in union membership. In 1933, fewer than 2,700,000 workers were in unions. In 1937 alone, unions recruited 3,000,000 workers, bringing the total to more than 7,000,000. By 1945, total union membership was more than 14,300,000. Michael Goldfield, The Decline of Organized Labor in the United States (1987), 10; Dubofksy, The State and Labor, *supra*, 137.

Contributing greatly to this was a new wing of the labor movement, the Congress of Industrial Organizations (CIO). The CIO was composed mostly of assembly line and other "unskilled" workers in industries such as auto, steel, rubber, glass and clothing—unlike the AFL which mostly organized skilled craft workers. Some of the main unions in the CIO had split off from the AFL in 1938 over issues such as whether to organize union bargaining units by craft (*e.g.*, all the electricians working for an employer in the electricians' union, all the carpenters in the carpenters union, etc.) or on a "wall to wall" model (with all the union-eligible employees of an employer in one bargaining unit). The CIO also organized more minorities and women, was more politically radical than the AFL, and was often more militant in its tactics (*e.g.*, using "sit down strikes" in the auto industry). Perhaps competition between the AFL and CIO pushed both organizations to be better at organizing. By the end of 1937, the CIO had 3.5 million members and the AFL had more than 4.5 million. In the 1950s, the AFL and CIO merged, creating the AFL-CIO, which still exists today as the main umbrella organization for most major unions in the United States (although as we will see later, a few important public-sector unions, including one of the largest unions in the country, the National Education Association, and the Fraternal Order of Police, remain outside the AFL-CIO, for reasons discussed in Section III, *infra*).

From the late 1930s to the mid-50s, union membership rose dramatically. By 1939, more than 8,750,000 people were in unions, which was nearly 29 percent of the nonagricultural workforce. By 1954, more than 17,000,000 million people were in unions, which was nearly 35 percent of the non-agricultural workforce.

Private-sector labor density began declining soon thereafter, although the absolute number of union members continued to increase for some time. In 1980, while union density had fallen to 24.7 percent, more than 22,300,000 people in the U.S. were union members. GOLDFIELD, *supra*, 10–11.

4. The Labor Management Relations Act of 1947 (Taft-Hartley)

Immediately after World War II, the size and power of unions was a concern to some. This helped lead, in 1947, to the Labor Management Relations Act (the Taft-Hartley Act or LMRA). The factors that led to Taft-Hartley included the increased power of unions, and a major strike wave in 1946, which featured a number of secondary actions that caused a significant amount of economic damage to employers: in the twelve months after Japan surrendered in August 1945, there were 4,630 strikes involving around five million workers and more than 120 million workdays. DUBOFSKY, THE STATE AND LABOR, *supra*, 193. Also, the Republicans won majorities in Congress (President Truman vetoed the bill, but Congress overrode his veto).

As an overview, the most significant changes Taft-Hartley made were as follows. First, again, Taft-Hartley added union ULPs, contained in the new § 8(b). For example, union ULPs included a ban on almost all secondary activities in § 8(b)(4), and a ban on various forms of union intimidation and discrimination against employees in §§ 8(b)(1) and 8(b)(2). Second, Taft-Hartley made the closed shop illegal in amendments to § 8(a)(3). Third, Taft-Hartley also added the "right to work" provision in § 14(b). This provision—the only provision in the NLRA that permits states to choose among options for NLRA rules—allows states to make any form of union security agreement illegal. Currently, about half the states are "right to work" states, mostly, but not entirely, in the south and southwest. For more on this, *see* Chapter 14. Fourth, Taft-Hartley excluded "supervisors" from the NLRA's coverage § 2(3). Fifth, in a move with symbolic as well as substantive import, § 7 was amended to make it explicit that workers had a right to "refrain from" certain § 7 activities. Sixth, Taft-Hartley added § 301, which provided federal court jurisdiction over suits alleging a violation of a collective bargaining agreement. As Chapter 13 shows, quite a bit of labor law has emerged under § 301.

5. The Labor Management Reporting and Disclosure Act (Landrum-Griffin)

The final major amendment to the NLRA came in 1959: the Labor Management Reporting and Disclosure Act (the Landrum-Griffin Act or LMRDA). The LMRDA tightened even further the restrictions on secondary boycotts (*e.g.*, by barring so-called "hot cargo" clauses, in which union members asserted rights not to work on products from "unfair" secondary employers in § 8(e)). It limited the right to picket employers for recognition in § 8(b)(7). *See* Chapter 12. It also added significant provisions regulating the internal conduct of unions and rights of individual union members *vis-a-vis* their unions. Landrum-Griffin was passed in an era when union corruption was much in the news and popular culture (consider the movie "On the Waterfront," for example). Although union opponents exaggerated it, real mob influence and corruption existed in certain unions, most famously in the International Brotherhood of Teamsters.

6. Labor Law and Unions Through to the Present

The LMRDA was the last major amendment to the NLRA. In 1974, language was added extending jurisdiction to, and creating some special rules for, hospitals. In later decades, attempts to amend the NLRA have failed. Advocates of these amendments have mostly argued that the NLRA, and interpretations of it by the NLRB and courts, have not sufficiently protected the rights of unions and pro-union workers. The most recent bill promoted for these reasons was the Employee Free Choice Act, which foundered and ultimately never passed in Congress during the first years of the Obama administration.

Union density in the private sector has been declining since the mid-1950s. In 1953, union density (the percentage of non-agricultural workers who were union members) was 35 percent. In 1983, union density was 20.1 percent with 17.7 million members. In 2019, those figures were 10.3 percent and 14.6 million. Bureau of Labor Statistics, U.S. Dept. of Labor, *Union Member Summary* (Jan. 22, 2020), USDL-20-1018. The decline in the private sector has been even more precipitous; overall union density numbers have been somewhat bolstered by much higher union density rates in the public sector. In 2019, union density in the private sector was 6.2 percent, while in the public sector it was 33.6 percent. *Id.* Note that these numbers measure only actual union members. Figures for those covered by union contracts are somewhat higher, as not everyone covered by a union contract is required to be a union member (*see* Chapter 14). So, for example, in 2019, unions represented 16.4 million employees, for an overall density of 11.6%, including 7.2 percent of eligible private workers and 37.2 percent of public workers. Local government employment had the highest figures: 40.3 percent of such employees were union members and unions represented 43.4% of these employees. Also, local government employees (as opposed to state and federal government employees) made up over half the public-sector workforce. *Id.*, Table 3.

The decline of union rates in the private sector has been accompanied by, and arguably has helped cause, increased inequality in wages in the economy as a whole. First, as one study explains:

> At least since the 1980s, real compensation received by American workers has remained fairly flat, even though productivity has steadily risen. From 1979–2009, the index of average real hourly compensation for American nonfarm business workers rose . . . just 36.6%, while the index of hourly productivity for those workers rose . . . 82.9%.

> The gap is even more striking if one examines only the wages of nonsupervisory workers whose average real hourly wages increased merely 2%, between 1979 and 2009. The wealth . . . became ever more concentrated

in the highest income earners . . . From 1979 to 2007, the percent of total income going to the top 5% of income earners increased from 15.5% to 20.1% and the ratio of their average income to the average income of families in the bottom 20% of the income distribution rose from 11.4 to 19.7. Similarly, between 1978 and 2006, average CEO pay increased from thirty-five times the average worker's pay to 275 times the average worker's pay — over $12 million per year. As a result, the decline in the rewards to labor is even more pronounced if one examines just non-supervisory salaries. Kenneth Dau-Schmidt, *Promoting Employee Voice in the American Economy: A Call for Comprehensive Reform*, 94 MARQ. L. REV. 765, 793–94 (2011).*

Second, another recent study explicitly linked increased wage inequality with the decline of unions. It noted that from 1973 to 2007, wage inequality in U.S. private-sector employment increased by more than 40 percent among men and by about 50 percent among women. The study then found that declines in unionization rates explained about 33 percent of the rise in inequality among men, and 20 percent of the rise in inequality among women. Bruce Western and Jake Rosenfeld, *Unions, Norms, and the Rise in American Wage Inequality*, 76 AMERICAN SOCIOLOGICAL REV. 513 (2011).

There are a variety of explanations for the decline of private-sector unions in the U.S. Have they outlived their usefulness, in an age of more enlightened employers and more employment law statutes giving rights to all workers? Did unions become more corrupt and/or bureaucratic, thus limiting their appeal and effectiveness? Does U.S. culture have such a strong strain of "individualism" that unions are less attractive here than elsewhere? Did changes in the economy — a shift from manufacturing to service sector work, and more international competition, for example — hurt unions? On the other hand, some have stressed the aggressive anti-union stance employers have taken, especially since the 1970s, featuring among other things, increased use of anti-union consultants and anti-union campaigns, and permanently replacing strikers. One study shows that the number of times the NLRB ordered reinstatement for employees discharged for pro-union activities during union organizing campaigns went from an average of around 1,500 per year in the period of 1971–75 to almost 3,000 a year in 1981–85. COMMISSION ON THE FUTURE OF WORKER-MANAGEMENT RELATIONS, U.S. DEPARTMENT OF LABOR, FACT FINDING REPORT, 84, Exhibit III-4 (1994). Another study found that from 1992–95, more than a third of employers fired workers for union activity during NLRB elections. Another study in the late 1990s concluded that employers illegally fired or otherwise retaliated against one of every 18 private-sector workers who support a union during an organizing campaign. One poll found that 79 percent of workers thought it was either "somewhat" or "very" likely that employees "will get fired if they try to organize a union." *See* Joseph Slater, *The 'American Rule' That Swallows*

---

the Exceptions, 11 Employee Rights and Employment Policy Journal 53, 79–80 (collecting sources).

When answering this question, and throughout the materials in this book, consider the contrast in the public sector, where union density is over five times the rate in the private sector. What explains this difference? It is hard to believe that public workers are so much different than private-sector workers as a group. Further, as we will see, public-sector labor laws tend to give unions fewer rights than private-sector law does. Why is the public sector so much more highly unionized than the private sector?

Consider also, what difference does it make if private-sector unions exist or not?

Charles Craver, *Why Labor Unions Must (and Can) Survive*
1 U. Pa. J. Lab. & Emp. L. 15 (1998)*

Many people believe that labor organizations are outmoded institutions providing representational services no longer needed by individuals employed by enlightened business enterprises. The unconscionable sweatshop conditions that were pervasive in the early twentieth century have been mainly eliminated, and the labor movement has directly or indirectly caused significantly enhanced employment conditions for most workers. . . .

The introduction of new technologies in the workplace has substantially modified the structure of the American economy. The substitution of capital for labor in the manufacturing sector has caused the displacement of many organized blue-collar personnel and has generated a concomitant increase in nonunion white-collar positions. The service sector has experienced similar growth, and labor unions have discovered that organizing campaigns that used to appeal to traditional blue-collar workers are not well received by white-collar and service personnel.

The technological developments that have altered the structure of the American economy have also contributed to the internationalization of the global economic system. By the twenty-first century, several hundred multinational corporations will dominate world trade. The developed nations provide the capital-intensive technologies, the consumer markets, and the distribution system, while the developing countries provide low-cost labor. The proliferation of low-cost "export platforms" has caused the exporting of many blue-collar jobs. If labor organizations hope to meaningfully influence the employment policies of international business enterprises, they must coordinate their efforts with trade unions located in the other countries in which those firms operate. . . .

Empirical evidence demonstrates that workers who have selected bargaining agents have enhanced their individual economic benefits. Their wage rates have

---

improved, and they have obtained health care coverage, pension programs, supplemental unemployment benefits, day-care centers, and other important fringe benefits. Similar studies indicate that unorganized personnel have received indirect financial gain from the labor movement, as their employers have provided them with wage and benefit packages competitive with those enjoyed by unionized employees. . . .

Labor organizations do not merely advance the economic interests of their members. Through the "collective voice" exerted by united groups, workers have also advanced important noneconomic interests. Collective bargaining agreements generally preclude worker discipline except for "just cause." This protection contrasts with the traditional "employment-at-will" doctrine, under which employers are authorized to discharge employees for good cause, bad cause, or no cause at all. Other contractual provisions typically establish orderly layoff and recall procedures, and require the application of relatively objective criteria to promotional opportunities.

When employees are not satisfied with the way in which contractual terms are applied, they may invoke grievance-arbitration procedures. During grievance-adjustment sessions, labor and management representatives are usually able to negotiate mutually acceptable solutions for their outstanding contractual disputes. When no mutual accords are achieved, the dissatisfied parties may ask neutral arbitrators to determine the controverted issues. Grievance-arbitration procedures prevent arbitrary employer action and provide workers with access to impartial determinations of controversies concerning the interpretation and application of contractual terms. Without the rights and protections contained in bargaining agreements, individual employees could rarely challenge questionable employer decisions. . . .

Business firms depend on the input of three fundamental groups for their success: investors, managers, and workers. Shareholders provide the necessary capital; managers provide the requisite managerial skills; and employees create the commercial goods or provide the business services. As each of these groups competes for a greater share of company profits and a more significant degree of control over corporate decision making, individual employees are at a distinct disadvantage. . . . Shareholders have the right to vote on significant corporate issues, and they can limit their exposure to particular firm financial difficulties through diversified investment strategies. When investors become disenchanted with the performance of specific corporations, they can sell their shares in that firm and invest the proceeds elsewhere.

Professional managers may similarly protect their own interests. Those with relatively unique personal skills can negotiate long-term employment contracts that may provide them with "golden parachutes" in the event the business relationship is terminated prematurely. High-level executives have access to confidential financial information, apprising them of their firm's economic well-being. They are usually well-connected at the upper levels of other business entities, and can use those contacts to locate other employment when they decide to leave their current positions.

Rank-and-file employees do not enjoy any of these privileges. They are fortunate to have one or two job opportunities at any one time. Employers feel no need to give job applicants detailed information regarding firm affairs. Once they accept employment with a specific company, workers enjoy minimal mobility. They possess limited information about other job openings, and the transaction costs associated with relocation may be substantial. To change jobs, they may lose some or all of their pension rights. They may also be forced to forfeit accrued seniority and to start at the bottom of the ladder in their new work environment, greatly jeopardizing their future employment security.

. . . Unorganized workers are generally powerless to negotiate with their corporate employers over their wages, hours, and working conditions. They must accept the terms unilaterally offered or else look for alternative employment. If they are directed to submit to drug testing or to engage in particularly arduous tasks, they have no real choice but to comply. This loss of personal freedom results directly from the considerable inequality of bargaining power that exists between individual employees and corporate managers.

The labor movement was initiated to provide individual workers with a collective voice that could effectively counter the aggregate power possessed by corporate enterprises. Without organizational strength, there is no broad-based institution to represent the interests of rank-and-file employees. A lack of such power would render workers one of the few groups in America without a collective voice. Business firms have organizations like the National Chamber of Commerce and the National Association of Manufacturers to represent their interests. More specific groups speak for pharmaceutical companies, chemical manufacturers, retail establishments, media groups, and other similar businesses. Lawyers have the American Bar Association; doctors have the American Medical Association. . . . In large corporations, however, individual employees often lack the assistance of representative organizations. Workers who think it would be "unprofessional" or "lower class" to join labor organizations should remember that their employers are all affiliated with business "unions" that effectively advance their economic interests. It is hypocritical for these business enterprises to tell their employees that they do not need a collective voice to further their employment interests. . . .

Over the past ten to fifteen years, union membership has steadily declined. While corporate profits have doubled, enhancing stock prices and firm dividends, and the compensation levels of corporate managers have increased dramatically, employee wage rates have stagnated and even declined. It is easy to understand why employees have been left behind economically: they lack the economic power to demand and obtain their fair share of increased corporate profits. . . .

The United States prides itself on being one of the world's great democracies. . . . The importance of democratic employment environments was recognized by Senator Robert Wagner, the principal author of the NLRA:

> [W]e must have democracy in industry as well as in government . . . democracy in industry means fair participation by those who work in the decisions vitally affecting their lives and livelihood; and . . . the workers in our great mass production industries can enjoy this participation only if allowed to organize and bargain collectively through representatives of their own choosing.

The increasingly unorganized employment setting remains the most significant arena in which democratic participation is denied to employees. Representative labor organizations remain a sine qua non to meaningful industrial democracy.

Notes

1. Since the time this article was written in the late 1990s, the trends the author decries have continued and, if anything, intensified. This chart shows the changes from 1970–2008 within various economic subgroups.

INCOME LEVEL	NUMBER OF PEOPLE	AVERAGE INCOME	OVERALL CHANGE 1970–2008	
Top 0.1%	152,000	$5.6 million	+385%	
Top 0.1-0.5%	610,000	$878,139	+141%	
Top 0.5-1%	762,000	$443,102	+90%	
Top 1-5%	6.0 million	$211,476	+59%	
Top 5-10%	7.6 million	$127,184	+38%	
Bottom 90%	137.2 million	$31,244	-1%	

This study noted that executive pay began to grow around the same time as income inequality in the U.S., and that executive pay has increased about 400 percent since 1970, while average wages for all workers have remained relatively flat. Further, while the gap between the top earners and everyone else has risen in some other countries, the disparity is greater in the U.S. *Not Spreading the Wealth: The Income Gap Between the Wealthy and the Rest of the Country has Grown Along with Dramatic Increases in CEO Pay*, Washington Post, June 18, 2011, *available at* http://www.washingtonpost.com/wp-srv/special/business/income-inequality/.

2. At the same time, union density overall and in the private sector has continued to decline. How, specifically, could this decline and the increase in income inequality be in some ways related? *See* Western and Rosenfeld, *supra*. If they are

correct that the two are linked, and if you share Prof. Craver's view that high rates of income inequality are injurious to a free and democratic society, what can or should be done to reverse these trends?

It is at least intuitive that lower unionization rates affect the wages of lower- and middle-income earners. Intriguingly, though, a 2015 study by the International Monetary Fund found "strong evidence that lower unionization is associated with an increase in top income shares in advanced economies during the period 1980–2010." The study concluded that on average, "the decline in unionization explains about half of the 5 percentage point rise in the top 10 percent income share." Florence Jaumotte and Carolina Osorio Burton, "Power from The People," International Monetary Fund Finance & Development, March 2015, Vol. 53, No. 1, *available at* http://www.imf.org/external/pubs/ft/fandd/2015/03/jaumotte.htm

3. As noted above, unlike public-sector labor law, private-sector labor law has been almost impervious to any statutory amendment since 1959. After the election of 2008, labor advocates hoped that the Employee Free Choice Act (EFCA) would be enacted. In short, EFCA would have done three things. First, it would have required that employers recognize a union if the union presented the employer with cards signed by a majority of members of an appropriate union bargaining unit (unless the cards were produced by fraud or coercion). Under pre-existing (and current) NLRA law, employers presented with such cards have the option of voluntarily recognizing the union but are not required to do so. They may insist on an election instead. Notable here, seven states have authorized such "mandatory card check recognition" in their public-sector labor laws. *See* Chapter 8 for more details. Second, EFCA would have increased the penalties for employer ULPs during union organizing campaigns. *See* Chapter 6 for more details. Finally, when a union and employer could not reach agreement on a first contract within a specified or mutually agreed-upon time frame, EFCA would have required a process similar to the interest arbitration procedures used in the public sector to resolve the bargaining impasse. *See* Chapter 12 for more details.

As you go through the materials on both the public and private sectors in this book, consider whether any or all of these provisions of EFCA would be good policy.

4. In June 2014, the Supreme Court decided in *NLRB v. Noel Canning, et al.*, 134 S. Ct. 2550 (2014), that three appointments President Obama had made to the NLRB were not valid exercises of the President's power to make "recess appointments." The U.S. Constitution's Article II, Section 2 grants the president the authority to "fill up all Vacancies that may happen during the Recess of the Senate" without the typically required advice and consent of the Senate. The issue in *Noel Canning* was whether the Senate was in "recess" for the purpose of this clause when it met only in very brief, *pro forma* sessions during which no business was conducted. The D.C. Circuit had held that it was not, and thus the recess appointments to the NLRB were invalid. *Noel Canning v. NLRB*, 705 F.3d 490 (D.C. Cir.

2013). That decision was in some tension with decisions of other circuit courts. *See, e.g., Evans v. Stephens*, 387 F.3d 1220 (11th Cir. 2004), *cert. den.*, 544 U.S. 942 (2005) (upholding presidential authority to make the recess appointment of federal judge William Pryor).

Specifically, this meant that the appointments President Obama made on January 4, 2012, of Board members Sharon Block, Richard Griffin, and Terence Flynn were invalid. Had President Obama not made these appointments on that day, the Board would have had only two members. Previously, the Supreme Court had held that the Board cannot exercise its powers without a quorum of three members. *New Process Steel, LP v. NLRB*, 560 U.S. 674 (2010). The range of dates of decisions at issue was roughly bounded by the invalidated appointments on January 4, 2012, and the dates on which new Senate-confirmed Board members Nancy Schiffer, Kent Hirozawa, Phillip Miscimarra, and Harry Johnson were sworn in during the period of August 2 to August 12, 2013.

The NLRB then began reconsidering, *de novo*, decisions made in this period. The NLRB decisions *Noel Canning* invalidated contain, as a group, more controversial cases than the decisions *New Process Steel* voided. The latter group included decisions made by a two-member Board consisting of one Democrat and one Republican, and thus were mainly noncontroversial decisions.

III. Unions and Labor Law in the Public Sector*

A. Early History and the Boston Police Strike

In the past half-century, public-sector unions have been a major success story of the American labor movement. One result of the increased union density in the

---

* Far fewer academic works discuss the history of public-sector unions and public-sector labor law than discuss the private sector. *See* Joseph McCartin, *Bringing the State's Workers In: Time to Rectify an Imbalanced U.S. Labor Historiography*, 47 LABOR HISTORY 73 (2006) and Robert Shaffer, *Where are the Organized Public Employees? The Absence of Public Employee Unionism from U.S. History Textbooks, and Why it Matters*, 43 LABOR HISTORY 315 (2002). Two main overviews are JOSEPH SLATER, PUBLIC WORKERS: GOVERNMENT EMPLOYEE UNIONS, THE LAW, AND THE STATE, 1900–1962 (2004) and the much older but still useful STERLING SPERO, GOVERNMENT AS EMPLOYER (1948). Some works focus on specific unions (*e.g.*, AFSCME) or a specific type of employee (*e.g.*, teachers' or police unions). For interested students, the following are recommended. JOHN BURPO, THE POLICE LABOR MOVEMENT: PROBLEMS AND PERSPECTIVES (1971); STEPHEN COLE, THE UNIONIZATION OF TEACHERS: A CASE STUDY OF THE UFT (1969); WINSTON CROUCH, ORGANIZED CIVIL SERVANTS (1978); WILLIAM EATON, THE AMERICAN FEDERATION OF TEACHERS, 1916–1961 (1975); JOSHUA FREEMAN, IN TRANSIT: THE TRANSPORT WORKERS UNION IN NEW YORK CITY, 1933–1966 (1989); RICHARD FREEMAN AND CASEY ICHNIOWSKI, WHEN PUBLIC SECTOR WORKERS UNIONIZE (1988); JOSEPH GOULDEN, JERRY WURF: LABOR'S LAST ANGRY MAN (1982); JOYCE NAJITA & JAMES STERN, EDS., COLLECTIVE BARGAINING IN THE PUBLIC SECTOR: THE EXPERIENCE OF EIGHT STATES (2001); RICHARD KEARNEY & PATRICE MARESCHAL LABOR RELATIONS IN THE PUBLIC SECTOR (5th ed. 2014); LARRY KRAMER, LABOR'S PARADOX: THE AMERICAN FEDERATION OF STATE,

public sector and decreased density in the private sector is that, for several years now, nearly half of all union members in the U.S. were public workers. In 2019, about 7.2 million public workers belonged to a union and about 7.9 million were represented by a union, while in the private sector those numbers were around 7.6 million and 8.5 million, respectively. *Union Members Summary, supra.*

Public workers did not begin to get the formal legal right to bargain collectively or, in most cases, even the right to form unions until the 1960s. Not surprisingly, union density in the public sector was significantly lower before then. Yet, just as private-sector workers organized unions and took collective action before the NLRA, so did public workers in the decades before any law gave them institutional rights. This history is important in part because, despite their successes, public-sector unions have still not won collective bargaining rights on a national scale. A minority of states still do not grant any public employees the right to bargain, and a number of states only provide such rights to a few discrete categories of employees (*e.g.*, police, fire, and/or teachers). Thus, for many public employees, the present legal regime is similar to that of the early 20th century.

Some public workers organized unions as early as the 1830s. In the 19th century, unionized public workers were usually members of mostly private-sector craft unions, for example, carpenters working in naval yards. Like private-sector workers, public workers tried to pass worker-protective legislation. In 1840, President Martin Van Buren signed an executive order establishing a ten-hour day on federal works projects. In 1861, Congress passed laws providing that the compensation and hours for Navy employees would be comparable to those for similar jobs in private

---

County, and Municipal Employees, AFL-CIO (1962); David Lewin, Peter Feuille, et al., eds., Public Sector Labor Relations: Analysis and Readings (1988); John Lyons, Teachers and Reform: Chicago Public Education, 1929–1970 (2008); Joseph McCartin, Collision Course: Ronald Reagan, The Air Traffic Controllers, and the Strike that Changed America (2011); M. Brady McKusko, Carriers In A Common Cause: A History of Letter Carriers and the NALC (1986); Marjorie Murphy, Blackboard Unions: The AFT and The NEA, 1900–1980 (1990); Murray Nesbitt, Labor Relations In The Federal Government Service (1976); Wayne Urban, Why Teachers Organized (1982); John Walsh, Labor Struggle In The Post Office: From Selective Lobbying to Collective Bargaining (1992); Julia Wrigley, Class Politics and Public Schools: Chicago, 1900–1950 (1982); Miller Berkeley and William Canak, *There Should Be No Blanket Guarantee: Employer Opposition to Public Employee Unions*, 24 J. Of Collective Negotiations In The Public Sector 17 (1995); Marick Masters, *AFSCME as a Political Union*, 19 Journal of Labor Research 313 (1998); Gregory Saltzman, *Bargaining Laws as a Cause and a Consequence of the Growth of Teacher Unionism*, 38 Industrial and Labor Relations Rev. 335 (1985); Joseph McCartin, *Unexpected Convergence: Values, Assumptions and the Right to Strike in Public and Private Sectors, 1945–2005*, 57 Buff. L. Rev. 727 (2009); Joseph McCartin, *A Wagner Act for Public Workers: Labor's Deferred Dream and the Rise of Conservatism, 1970–1976*, 95 J. Am. Hist. 123 (2008); Joseph Slater, *Public Workers: Labor and the Boston Police Strike of 1919*, 38 Lab. Hist. 7 (1997); Joseph Slater, *The Court Does Not Know 'What a Labor Union Is': How State Structures and Judicial (Mis)Constructions Deformed Public Sector Labor Law*, 79 Or. L. Rev. 981 (2000).

industry. Public-sector unions also promoted civil service statutes in an attempt to eliminate political patronage "machines" that the merit system was designed to undercut. Slater, Public Workers, *supra*, 16–17.

The second decade of the 20th century saw an increase in public-sector unionism that was cut short by the Boston police strike of 1919.

Joseph Slater, *Labor and the Boston Police Strike of 1919*

in Brenner, Day, and Ness, eds., The Encyclopedia of Strikes in American History (2009)[*]

When almost all of Boston's police officers went on strike in September 1919, they did so for reasons similar to those that motivated other workers before and since to do the same, but with unique consequences for the history of American labor. Although the strikers were concerned with wages, hours, and working conditions, it was immediately and ominously clear that this event would be like no other job action. As the policemen walked off the job, they were attacked by a crowd of more than 1,000 volunteer substitute policemen, and for the following three days many denizens of the city engaged in a variety of criminal acts, including assaults, public gambling (with attendant thefts and violence), robbery, and destruction of property. Parts of the city were frighteningly lawless. . . . State guards finally intervened, firing point-blank into the crowds, killing nine and wounding twenty-three others. Hundreds more were injured during the strike. Property damage was estimated in the hundreds of thousands of dollars. . . . With peace finally restored, all 1,147 strikers were fired.

Unfortunately for public-sector unions, the most searing and enduring image of their history in the first half of the twentieth century was the Boston police strike. The strike was routinely cited by courts and officials through the end of the 1940s. Even in later decades, opponents of public-sector unions would invoke the strike as a cautionary tale of the evils of such unions. It provided evidence that strikes by government workers were dangerous and destructive and made it more difficult for officials to see public employees as "workers"—the type of people who should have the right to form unions. Although the Boston police strike was as atypical as it was dramatic, it contributed far more than any other single event to the peculiarly American view that public-sector labor relations were something entirely distinct from private-sector labor relations.

The Boston police strike can only be understood as part of the larger narrative of the period's labor history. From 1916 to 1922 historian David Montgomery explains . . . , "workers' demands became too heady for the AFL . . . to contain . . . and too menacing for business and the state to tolerate." During and directly after

---

World War I, the union movement was growing in both the public and private sectors. In 1919, police unions were affiliating with the AFL at an impressive rate. . . .

Opposition to police affiliation with the labor movement caused the Boston strike. . . . [T]he cause of the walkout was [Boston Police Commissioner Edwin] Curtis's ban on police affiliating with the AFL, and the broader trend on which contemporaries focused was the nationwide increase in public workers, including police, joining the AFL. In fact, government officials, businessmen, union leaders, and socialists all predicted that public-sector unions would shift the balance of power in all labor relations. The AFL maintained that government employees were members of the working class. Opponents insisted that they had nothing in common with labor and that AFL organizing in the public sector would lead to union interests dominating the state.

. . . After fitful starts in the first decade of the century, the movement took off around World War I. In 1906, the AFL created its first national union of government workers, the National Federation of Post Office Clerks. In 1902, the Chicago Teachers Federation had affiliated with the Chicago AFL, and the national AFL directly chartered a teachers' local in San Antonio. After a few abortive attempts to create a national teachers' union, in 1916 the AFL formed the American Federation of Teachers (AFT). In the year before the Boston strike, the AFT grew from 2,000 to 11,000 members. In 1917, the AFL established the National Federation of Federal Employees (NFFE). That same year, the National Association of Letter Carriers (NALC), founded in 1889, affiliated with the AFL, as did the Railway Mail Carriers. The AFL chartered its first firefighters local in 1903 and created the International Association of Fire Fighters (IAFF) in 1918. The IAFF soon grew from about 5,000 to over 20,000 members. . . .

The overall rate of unionization in the public sector reflected this activity. From 1900 to 1905, union density in the public sector was less than 2 percent, increasing to only around 3.5 percent in 1910. Then from 1915 to 1921, density increased from 4.8 to 7.2 percent, an especially impressive increase given that the total number of government employees in these years grew by more than one-quarter, from 1,861,000 to 2,397,000. . . . Thus, from 1915 to 1921, the total number of public workers in unions nearly doubled. . . .

[In 1919, the AFL reversed its previous policy against chartering police unions]. The response was immediate. By September 1919, the AFL had received sixty-five requests from police organizations and had chartered thirty-seven locals. Samuel Gompers remarked . . . that in his thirty-six years as AFL president, in no other trade had he ever seen as many applications in as short a time. . . .

In addition to fears of police themselves striking, union opponents were also extremely concerned about how police officers in the AFL might act during strikes by other unions. . . . They spoke of "divided loyalty" and "charges of favoritism" if police officers were called on to handle strikes by members of other AFL unions. . . . Ironically, this concern seemed to assume a greater set of common interests among public and private-sector workers than that side of the debate would normally admit. Gompers parried that the AFL merely wanted the police to be neutral and "not throw their full weight" against workers. . . .

In contrast to labor's approach, leaders of the Boston Police Department sharply differentiated their employees from other workers. The conflict began in 1918 when Police Commissioner Steven O'Meara learned that Boston police officers were considering AFL affiliation. O'Meara issued an order stating that even rumors of unionization were "likely to injure the discipline, efficiency and even the good name of the Force." If officers had obligations to an outside organization, he stated, they would be "justly suspected of abandoning their impartial attitude." He claimed that he did not dispute the "wisdom or even necessity" of unions in the private sector. Public-sector unions, however, were "of doubtful propriety," and police in particular should not be allowed to organize because they were responsible for impartial law enforcement. On July 29, 1919, in response to more talk of affiliation, the new police commissioner, Edwin Curtis, promulgated Rule 102, which stated that he was "firmly of the opinion that a police officer cannot consistently belong to a union and perform his sworn duty," and that a police officer "should realize that his work is sharply differentiated from that of the worker in private employ."

Undeterred, police in Boston affiliated with the AFL on August 9, 1919. Their complaints were typical of all workers: low wages, long hours, unhealthy conditions, and despotic supervisors. . . .

Police Commissioner Curtis would not allow a union affiliated with the AFL, and this position, coupled with the refusal of the police officers to leave the AFL, caused the strike. . . .

The striking police were vilified by the press, public officials, and employers. In one of the more temperate responses, the *New York Times* editorialized on September 10 that a "policeman has no more right to belong to a union than a soldier or sailor."

More broadly, the debate over the Boston Police Union turned on a central issue in American labor history: the extent to which government employees could be part of organized labor. The [Boston] *Labor World* consistently supported police and other public-sector unions throughout the country, affirming that they were part of a public-sector movement and a larger struggle for workers' rights . . . police had "grievances just the same as men in other walks of life." All workers should have the right to bargain collectively. . . .

Similarly, opponents of the Police Union made objections that applied to all public-sector unions. The heads of many private businesses wrote to Curtis recommending that no government employee of any kind be allowed to join the AFL. Using logic that could be extended to any public worker, Governor Coolidge declared that police were not "employees" or even "holders of a job," because no private concern made a profit from their efforts. Police "are not in any sense labor bodies," the Buffalo *Courier* on September 14 protested, and "their duties do not constitute a trade." . . . . Taking a page from private-sector employers, O'Meara and Curtis claimed that "agents of an outside organization" could not help police. . . .

In 1919, the year of the "Red Scare" and unprecedented militancy by workers [including general strikes in Seattle and Winnipeg earlier in the year], . . . radical visions of union power stiffened opposition to the Police Union and placed organized labor in a difficult position. . . .

The aftermath of the Boston strike significantly restrained the movement for public-sector unions. All police locals affiliated with the AFL were soon destroyed . . . Congress quickly prohibited police and firefighters in the District of Columbia from striking or affiliating with the AFL, and a number of local governments and police departments followed suit. There would be no AFL-affiliated police locals until the 1930s and 1940s, and these too would meet strong opposition. A national AFL-CIO police union would be proposed only in 1969 and not created until 1979.

While other public-sector unions tried to avoid association with the Boston disaster by emphasizing or adopting no-strike policies, many were still devastated. . . . The IAFF lost fifty locals, including its Boston affiliate. The strike also led to losses in membership of the AFT and other public-sector unions.

Thus, the strike stopped the first dawn of public-sector organizing in its tracks. After years of increases, the number of unionized government employees fell . . . and the rate of unionization in the public sector, which had bolted up rapidly in the preceding years, now stagnated, hovering just below the 1921 rate of 7.2 percent for nearly all the 1920s. . . . Beyond the numbers, memories of the Boston strike inhibited the growth of public-sector unions for decades; it was easy to equate any form of public-sector unionism with the calamitous confrontation. The strike also helped separate government employees from the labor movement. Rules against affiliation with the AFL forced public workers into "associations" that often resembled company unions. The national AFL also took less of an interest. . . .

At a minimum, police in Boston showed that many public "officers"—even police—were also workers, both in their own minds and in the minds of the labor movement.

Notes

1. The Boston strike left a lasting legacy in the history of public-sector labor relations. President Ronald Reagan cited the Boston strike as precedent for firing illegally striking members of the Professional Air Traffic Controllers Union in 1981.

2. While police are one of the most heavily unionized occupations in the country, the largest police union (the Fraternal Order of Police) is not affiliated with the AFL-CIO. This is in large part due to the practice—common until the 1960s—of

local governments banning certain types of public employees from affiliating with the broader labor movement. Another example is the National Education Association, one of the largest unions in the country, which is not affiliated with the AFL-CIO.

3. Had you been alive in Boston in 1919, which arguments would you have found most and least convincing? Which arguments do you think are most and least convincing today, given our experiences with public-sector unions and police unions?

4. The claim that private-sector unions are usually appropriate but public-sector unions are quite different and inappropriate has been made for a long time. In 1920, Senator Charles Thomas (D-Col.) stated that the "fundamental idea lying at the foundation of organized labor . . . has been the assumption . . . of an antagonism of interest and of purpose between employer and employee. . . . That situation cannot be applied to public employment." In contrast, union supporters stressed the similarity of public and private-sector employees. Government workers had "grievances just the same as men in other walks of life," insisted Boston's labor newspaper in 1919. Slater, Public Workers, *supra*, 1, 27.

5. These debates continue today, and they intensified in 2011 with the wave of laws limiting the rights of public-sector unions (see below). One editorial in 2011 challenged the idea that public-sector workers should not get union rights because they "work for us." The author insisted that performing public service did not "cancel[] their rights as organized workers." He argued that it was a false distinction to claim, "We're not anti-union, we're just against certain kinds of unions." It was "delusional" to think that exploitation was unique to private sector employers. Further, the public sector "is a profit-making entity; it profits me." Garret Keizer, *Public or Private, It's Work*, New York Times, A19, June 24, 2011.

6. More recently, in the context of calls for reforming and "defunding" police departments, some have blamed police unions for protecting "bad cops." *See generally* Robert Iafolla, *Defunding Is One Place Police Unions See Vaunted Powers Limited*, Bloomberg (June 12, 2020) https://news.bloomberglaw.com/daily-labor-report /defunding-is-one-place-police-unions-see-vaunted-powers-limited. Unlike the private sector, public-sector labor law often has special rules for certain occupations. As you study the public-sector materials in this book, consider how, if at all, labor law rules could be used to address underlying issues in policing. Consider also in this regard the role of police management, and the role of political power independent of collective bargaining rights.

B. The Lengthy "Pre-Collective Bargaining Era"

In the "pre-collective bargaining era" (before the 1960s, when states began passing public-sector labor laws), public-sector unions faced unsympathetic courts.

Perhaps not surprisingly, in the era before the New Deal, courts were unsympathetic to public, as well as private-sector unions, and gave public employers wide latitude to simply forbid union membership or enforce "yellow dog" contracts. For example, in 1917, more than half of the 7,000 teachers in the Chicago Public Schools were members of the Chicago Teachers' Union. The local school board then barred membership in that union, and Illinois Supreme Court upheld that rule. *People ex. rel. Fursman v. City of Chicago*, 278 Ill. 318 (1917).

Even during and after the New Deal, courts and legislatures treated public-sector unions quite differently than private-sector unions. For example, in 1943, a New York state court explained, "we all recognize the value and the necessity of collective bargaining in industrial and social life," but "bargaining is impossible between the government and its employees, by the reason of the very nature of government itself." *Railway Mail Ass'n v. Murphy*, 44 N.Y.S.2d 601, 607–08 (1943), *rev'd on other grounds sub nom. Railway Mail Ass'n v. Corsi*, 267 App. Div. 470 (1944). Before 1959, no statute in the U.S. authorized collective bargaining for any public employees. So, before the 1960s, courts effectively made public-sector labor law, and those courts uniformly approved whatever bars on unions public employers imposed. Federal workers had the Lloyd-LaFollette Act of 1912, which gave them the right to form unions without being disciplined for so doing, but this law did not authorize union bargaining.

This "pre-collective bargaining era" for government employees lasted decades longer in the U.S. than in many comparable nations. For example, public workers in Britain and France won bargaining rights in the first part of the 20th century largely similar to those of private-sector workers in those countries. *See* SLATER, PUBLIC WORKERS, *supra*, 92–93.

Why did public-sector labor law develop relatively late and unevenly in the U.S.? As discussed above, the Boston strike was a major factor. Second, the highly divided nature of the state in the U.S. was crucial. Serious concerns over federalism and states' rights helped prevent any federal law giving rights to unions of state or local government. Also, the highly subdivided state governments played a major role. Through the early 1960s, judges endorsed rules which led to considerable judicial deference to local public government bodies. Case after case held that public employers had the discretion to decide whether unions were appropriate in public employment, and judges should defer to this discretion. This meant, in effect, that local government employers often had the effective power to set the rules of public-sector labor relations. Further, some cases held that collective bargaining and arbitration violated the constitutional "non-delegation" doctrine: the rule that certain public powers cannot be "delegated" to private bodies such as unions (in collective bargaining) or arbitrators. *See* SLATER, PUBLIC WORKERS, *supra*, Ch. 3. While most jurisdictions eventually rejected non-delegation objections to public-sector labor law, the doctrine was crucial in early decades, and it still makes occasional and sometimes significant appearances today.

Finally, judges often simply could not believe that public-sector unions would behave any differently than private-sector unions, and such behavior could not be allowed in government.

Joseph Slater, *The Court Does Not Know "What a Labor Union Is": How State Structures and Judicial (Mis)Constructions Deformed Public-Sector Labor Law*

79 Or. L. Rev. 981 (2000)[*]

[J]udges falsely constructed the term "union." . . . [E]ven though public-sector unions had all formally renounced strikes and most were willing to forego traditional collective bargaining, at least over wages, courts insisted on seeing unions as institutions that inevitably bargained and struck. Especially in the aftermath of the infamous Boston police strike of 1919, judges could not imagine giving public workers such rights. . . .

In forming their construction of unions, judges seemed, at best, blind to relevant events outside their courtrooms. First, public-sector unions in this era, while not as large or prominent as in recent decades, did exist in significant numbers. . . . In 1934, public-sector unions represented 9% of the nearly 3,300,000 government workers in the United States, who in turn constituted 12.7% of all non-agricultural workers in the country. Second, these unions took actions on behalf of their members, from representing employees in civil service proceedings, to lobbying government officials . . . to providing information to their members and the public. Third, these unions almost never struck. After the Boston police strike of 1919, AFL and later CIO public-sector unions renounced the strike weapon, and in fact strikes by public-sector unions from 1919 to 1945 were rare, small in scale, and short. But in the courtroom, unionists lacked the power to make this image of unionism real.

Instead, judges clung exclusively to the private-sector image of unions, ignoring the ongoing presence of active public-sector unions that did not formally bargain or strike and rejecting the sworn statements and binding documents that unions proffered as evidence of their different nature. In 1947, *King v. Priest* [357 Mo. 68], upheld a rule banning an AFSCME local that more than eight hundred police officers had joined. The union's charter barred striking and bargaining and stated that the oath that police officers took regarding their duties came before any obligation to the union. Instead of tactics used in the private sector, the charter continued, the local would, "by publicity, direct public attention to conditions that need correcting, . . . seek legislative action, . . . represent individuals in administrative procedure, and prevent discriminatory and arbitrary practices."

The Missouri Supreme Court would have none of it: "[T]he court, of course, knows what a labor union is. . . ." Defining the institution, the court took judicial notice of the "common knowledge" that "some of the most common methods used by labor unions . . . are strikes, threats to strike, [and] collective bargaining agreements. . . ." Refusing to accept an alternate model of "union," but without claiming that any AFSCME local had ever attempted to strike or bargain, the court asserted that "all of the rights and powers ordinarily inherent in a labor union would exist actually or potentially" in the local, "regardless of the form of its charter and the present admissions of appellants."

Similarly, *CIO v. City of Dallas* [198 S.W.2d 143 (Tex.App. 1946)] discounted the fact that the union had renounced formal collective bargaining and that its constitution and bylaws barred strikes "or other concerted economic weapons or procedures." The court ruled that the "declaration of the local to abandon the usual procedure pursued by labor unions to accomplish their purposes, is in irreconcilable conflict with the declared purposes and objects of the unions." The decision cited documents from the national CIO, not the public-sector local involved. . . .

One lone dissent credited the claims of public-sector unions that they would behave differently than private-sector unions. In *City of Jackson v. McLeod*, [199 Miss. 676] Justice McGehee of the Mississippi Supreme Court would have held that membership in AFSCME was not sufficient cause to discharge police officers under a civil service law. Among other things, the "jury was entitled to find . . . that there is a fundamental difference between [AFSCME] and the labor unions in general." McGehee noted that the union's charter denied policemen the right to strike and that no AFSCME local had ever struck a police department. Further, the union did not advocate negotiating contracts by collective bargaining or the closed shop. McGehee even quoted a statement from former AFL president Samuel Gompers, issued in 1919 in response to the Boston turmoil, that it was the position of the AFL that police would neither strike nor assume any obligation that conflicted with their duty. Yet beyond this single voice, which itself did not come until 1946, judges uniformly refused to accept that an organization of workers could be a "union" without striking or bargaining. In taking this stance, judges not only rejected what unions said they would do, but critically they ignored what public-sector unions were actually doing. . . .

———————

In this era, judges frequently upheld bans on public-sector *organizing* with harsh language that often referred to strikes even though the union had explicitly renounced the right to strike. Two separate court decisions in the 1940s, from Texas and New York, used the following quote: "To tolerate or recognize any combination of . . . employees of the government as a labor organization or union is not only incompatible with the spirit of democracy but inconsistent with every principle upon which our Government is founded." *CIO v. City of Dallas*, 198 S.W.2d 143, 145 (Tex.App. 1946), *quoting Railway Mail Ass'n v. Murphy, supra*, 44 N.Y.S.2d 601, 607 (1943). *City of Dallas* discounted the fact that the union's constitution and bylaws barred strikes and other "concerted economic weapons," and that the union was asking only to be allowed to organize, not to strike. The court stressed that strikes in the public service could never be allowed, and went on to uphold a ban on unionization, despite a state law generally protecting the right to join unions. 198 S.W.2d at 134–39, 144–45; Slater, Public Workers, *supra*, 82–85.

The fear that public-sector unions would strike, even when no evidence exists that the union would strike, continues to the modern times. In 2002, President George W. Bush issued Executive Order 13252, which barred collective bargaining in five subdivisions of the Department of Justice. White House spokesman Ari Fleischer explained, "There is a long tradition that presidents of both parties have honored about protecting the public by not allowing certain law enforcement or intelligence officials to strike." *See* Martin Malin, *The Paradox of Public-Sector Labor Law*, 84 Ind. L. J. 1369, 1377 (2009). The federal sector labor statute, which had previously covered these employees, barred strikes; and nobody had suggested that either the union that represented some of these employees or the employees themselves had ever struck, urged a strike, or urged that the law be changed such that they could strike.

In the mid-20th century, despite hostile courts, public workers continued to organize unions even though the unions had no formal legal right to represent them. The American Federation of State, County, & Municipal Employees (AFSCME) was formed in the 1930s. From the 1930s to the 1960s, public-sector union density ranged from 9 to 13 percent. Public-sector unions did what they could to represent their members. They participated in various political campaigns, supporting sympathetic candidates and lobbying for laws. Most important here were civil service laws which provided for "merit" in public employment to combat political patronage (which featured both unqualified political cronies being given public jobs as rewards and related wholesale firings and replacement of lower-level public employees when a candidate of a new party took power). These laws typically provided some basic rights not to be discharged for certain bad reasons (*e.g.*, not being a member of the right political party). Ultimately, such laws began to have general "just cause" rules for discipline and discharge, as well as civil service tests for hiring to assure minimal competency for public servants. Second, unions represented workers in civil service hearings and under other laws which gave rights to workers. Third, they provided training and information for their members. Fourth, some participated in "informal" bargaining, which did sometimes lead to agreements with employers over wages, hours, and working conditions. Although no laws authorized such agreements, in 1946, a study found that ninety-seven cities had written agreements with employee organizations. Such agreements were far short of modern union contracts, both in their limited scope and their dubious enforceability. Public-sector unionists were keenly aware that their lack of institutional rights greatly limited what they could accomplish. *See* Slater, Public Workers, *supra*, Ch. 4.

C. The Long History of Yellow Dog Contracts in the Public Sector

From the early 20th century to early 1960s, public employers often used "yellow dog" contracts or otherwise forbade their employees from joining unions on pain of discharge. The Norris-LaGuardia Act as well as the NLRA did not cover public employees. Courts routinely upheld such rules.

AFSCME Local 201 v. City of Muskegon

Supreme Court of Michigan
369 Mich. 384, 120 N.W.2d 197 (1963)

CARR, C.J.

The question at issue in this litigation concerns the validity of a rule adopted by the chief of police of the city of Muskegon on March 16, 1961. Such action was taken pursuant to Sections 2-103 and 2-104 of the municipal code of ordinances which, insofar as material here, read as follows:

> ... Section 2-104 *Chief of police; powers and duties.* — (1) He shall be the director of the police department subject to these rules and regulation. ...
>
> (2) He shall be responsible for the government, efficiency and general good conduct of the police department. ...
>
> (3) He shall have the power to prescribe, promulgate and enforce rules and regulations for the government of the members and employees of the department, which shall be approved by the city manager. ...

The rule in question was duly approved by the city manager. ... It reads as follows:

> Section 101: No police officer of the city of Muskegon police department shall hereafter be, or become a member of any organization in any manner identified with any federation or labor union which admits to membership persons who are not members of the Muskegon police department, or which would in any way exact prior consideration and prevent such officer from performing full and complete police duty at any time. Any police officer now a member of such unions shall disassociate himself within 30 days from this date. Failure to comply will constitute reason for immediate dismissal.

The situation to which the rule was intended to apply obviously had been under consideration by municipal officers prior to the adoption of the rule. Under date of March 14, 1961, the Muskegon city commission took the action indicated by the following statement and resolution:

> 61-165. *Resolution on banning of union affiliation by police officers adopted.* Certain of the police officers of the city of Muskegon police department are dues paying members of Local No. 201, Muskegon County and Municipal Employees Union affiliated with the American Federation of State, County and Municipal Employees, AF of L-CIO.
>
> This commission, as well as past commissions, have seriously questioned whether a police officer can be a member of such a union and still enforce,

impartially and without prejudice the laws of our city, county and State of Michigan.

Every police officer who joins the Muskegon police department must take an oath of office to support the Constitution and bear allegiance to his city and State and its Constitution and laws and to the best of ability, skill and judgment, diligently and faithfully, without partiality or prejudice, execute his office. Police officers are invested with broad powers, few of which are given to any other government employee. They have the legal right to carry a weapon, their powers of restraint, arrest, and control of moral and physical behaviour of others are grave and serious. A police officer is required by law and invariably becomes a neutralizer in controversies involving the right of public assemblage, neighborhood disputes, domestic difficulties and strikes, between labor and management. Again, his actions in these instances must be governed by his oath of office. He must recognize certain rights of people among which is the right of collective bargaining on the part of labor. Yet, at the same time, he must protect the rights and the property of management. In this instance, again, his neutrality must be the watchword of his every activity in the effort to protect the life and property of all those involved and to preserve peace and order during periods of such difficulty.

This commission subscribes to this statement of responsibility and, as such, cannot further condone police officers of the city of Muskegon to continue to be members of a union.

In the belief that we are acting in the best interest of all of the citizens of the city of Muskegon, the following resolution is presented.

Commissioner Carlson offered the following resolution and moved its adoption:

No police officer of the city of Muskegon police department shall hereafter be, or become, a member of any organization in any manner identified with any federation or labor union which admits to membership persons who are not members of the Muskegon police department, or which would in any way exact prior consideration and prevent such officer from performing full and complete police duty at any time. Any police officer now a member of such unions shall disassociate himself within 30 days from this date. Failure to comply will constitute reason for immediate dismissal.

It is apparent that the rule promulgated by the chief of police was designed to carry out the purpose expressed by the resolution of the legislative body of the city. . . .

[P]laintiffs filed suit in equity seeking injunctive relief against the enforcement of the commission's action and of the rule or regulation adopted by the chief of police. On the filing of the suit a temporary injunction was issued. . . . On behalf of plaintiffs it was contended in the trial court that the regulation in question was uncertain in its provisions in that the word "federation" created an ambiguity, that the municipal action was arbitrary and unreasonable, and that it operated to deprive plaintiffs, and members of the police force of the city of Muskegon who were also members of the plaintiff union, of rights protected by State and Federal Constitutions. The trial court agreed with the contentions of the plaintiffs and entered a decree accordingly. Defendants have appealed.

We are unable to agree with the contention that the rule as adopted by the chief of police of defendant city is ambiguous because of the inclusion of the word "federation" therein. A reading of the entire rule leaves no question as to its purpose and intent. The reference therein to "such unions" indicates clearly the meaning to be ascribed to the expression "federation or labor union." A reading of the record suggests the absence of any question as to the application of the rule, if otherwise valid, to the plaintiffs herein.

The basic question at issue is whether the defendant city may through its duly constituted authorities prescribe a regulation of the character here involved for the members of its police department. It may be assumed that in taking the action in question due consideration was given to local conditions and to the protection of the public interest generally. That a municipality maintaining a police department may adopt reasonable rules in connection therewith is not open to question. Opinions may perhaps differ as to what may be regarded as reasonable, or as the converse thereof. In the instant case the presumption of validity attaches to the regulation adopted by the chief of police pursuant to the code of ordinances of the city, and the burden rests on those assailing it to establish that there is an unwarranted, and therefore arbitrary, interference with rights protected by constitutional guaranties. If the municipality has acted within the scope of its powers, the regulation must be sustained.

Basically the question at issue is whether the city may exercise over the members of its police department the right of control asserted by the rule in question, rather than the effect of such rule on those employees who are within its scope. The restriction imposed is not directed at a class as such but, rather, solely at those who have sought and obtained employment in the police department of the defendant city. Decisions cited by counsel for plaintiffs relating to racial discrimination are not in point. . . .

State Lodge of Michigan, Fraternal Order of Police, v. City of Detroit, 318 Mich. 182 (1947) . . . involved a regulation of the police commissioner of defendant city forbidding members of the police force from being members of a fraternal order allowing other citizens to become associate members. The Court quoted with approval from the opinion in *Carter v. Thompson*, 164 Va. 312, (1935), as follows:

> Police and fire departments are in a class apart. Both are at times charged with the preservation of public order, and for manifold reasons they owe to the public their undivided allegiance. The power in the city of complete control is imperatively necessary if discipline is to be maintained.

In accord with prior holdings of this Court is the decision in *Perez v. Board of Police Commissioners of the City of Los Angeles*, 78 Cal.App.2d 638 (1947). At issue there was a resolution of the board of police commissioners of Los Angeles forbidding police officers of the city to become members of any organization identified with "any trade association, federation or labor union which admits to membership persons who are not members of the Los Angeles police department, or whose membership is not exclusively made up of employees of the city of Los Angeles." The action of the trial court in sustaining the resolution was upheld. It was specifically held that there was no violation of the 14th amendment to the Federal Constitution, and that the order of the defendant board was not arbitrary or unreasonable. In reaching the determination indicated, it was said in part:

> Whether a rational connection exists between union membership and lack of competency as a police officer, obviously, is a matter of opinion. And the question was solely one for the board of police commissioners to determine. Regardless of what the constitution and bylaw of any organization might provide for or against, it is idle to argue that such constitution and bylaw cannot be changed by amendment. Moreover, it was for the board of police commissioners, as the representatives, agents and servants of the people, to determine what the first duties, indeed, all of the duties, of a police officer should be. It should be noted also, that the board of police commissioners probably took into account the fact that labor unions are active politically, whereas civil service employees are prevented by law and as a condition of employment, from taking an active part in politics while on official duty or during working hours and, that means would be thus provided for doing indirectly and with impunity, that which the law specifically prohibits.

The Court also quoted from the opinion of the trial judge as follows:

> "In *Hayman v. City of Los Angeles*, 17 Cal.App.2d 674 (1936), in considering a question whether the discharge of a civil service employee was in violation of his rights to freedom of speech and of the press, and arbitrary, the court said:

> "The right which is involved here is not that which petitioner thinks has been denied him, but is the right of respondents to exercise a reasonable supervision over city employees, to the end that proper discipline may be maintained and that activities among employees be not allowed to disrupt or impair the public service. Such is not only the right but the duty of the city and its several departments. In the exercise of this duty they must be allowed a wide discretion and their acts are not subject to review by the courts until they have reached the point of illegality.

> "The rule adopted by the resolution here in question does not on its face appear unreasonable or arbitrary in the light of the foregoing authorities. Nor is it in violation of any constitutional right of police officers. If the rule is necessary and reasonable it cannot be charged with wrongfully depriving the police members of any constitutional right. All such rights are relative. Nor does the rule amount to a bill of attainder, nor does it produce or inflict

any of the incidents of such a legislative act. It was the result of a decision by the board in the exercise of that wide discretion which is accorded to them. Neither this court nor any judge thereof has the power to substitute its or his contrary views as to the propriety, necessity, desirability or reasonableness of the rule. The rule having been created by the board under and within its charter powers, and no appearance of unreasonableness or arbitrariness or unconstitutionality manifesting itself therein, it must be concluded that such rule cannot have reached the point of illegality and subject to review and annulment by the courts either by direct action or by means of injunction against enforcement thereof.

The regulation involved in the instant case is limited in its application to members of the police department of the city of Muskegon and it applies to them solely in their capacity as such members. As this Court pointed out in *City of Detroit v. Division 26 of the Amalgamated Association of Street, Electric Railway & Motor Coach Employees of America*, 332 Mich. 237, 51 (1952), there is no provision of either State or Federal Constitution which gives to individuals the right to be employed in government service or the right to continue therein. In said case the constitutionality of the so-called Hutchinson Act was upheld as applied to the Detroit transportation system and the employees thereof. In disposing of the issues raised it was said, in part:

> There is ample authority to the effect that public employment does not vest in such employees any fixed or permanent rights of employment. As individuals or in groups public employees may discontinue their employment, but, having done so, such public employees have no vested right to insist upon their re-employment on terms or conditions agreeable to the employees, or even without compliance with such conditions. To hold otherwise would result in public agencies being powerless to render public service and to effectively administer public affairs; and the public would thereby be deprived of its right to efficient government. For example, if the members of a fire department or of a police department collectively refuse to continue to serve except upon conditions insisted upon by them, unless their employer supinely yielded, the public, which by taxation pays therefor, would be deprived of fire or of police protection; and the right or power to exercise essential governmental affairs nullified. There seems to be ample reason and authority for holding that the right of public employees to collectively refuse to render the service for which they are employed differs in legal point of view from the right of private employees to strike, and hence the classification of 'public employees' for the purpose of applicable legislation is valid.

Plaintiffs herein have not borne the burden of proof of showing that members of the police department of Muskegon are deprived by the enforcement of the regulation in question of any constitutional rights to which they are entitled. As before suggested, they cannot claim a constitutional right to be appointed as members of said department, or to continue therein. They are subject to the authority of the municipality, granted by the Constitution and laws of the State, to manage its local affairs and to regulate the departments of municipal government. The duly consti-tuted authorities of the city have concluded that the regulation here under attack is reasonably required in the interests of a fair and impartial administration of the law by those entrusted with its enforcement, without discrimination or partiality. The basic principles recognized in the prior decisions of this Court and by courts in other States as well are applicable here. On the record before us it may not be said that the rule is unreasonable or arbitrary in its application. . . .

The decree of the circuit court of Muskegon county is reversed. . . .

Notes

1. Some of the language in this decision implies that it is more reasonable to bar police from unionizing (or affiliating with the broader labor movement) than to apply such bars to other types of public workers. However, up through the time of this decision, courts had uniformly upheld all employer bars on all types of public employee organizing. *See* SLATER, PUBLIC WORKERS, *supra*, Ch. 3.

2. Should police and fire employees be treated differently regarding the right to organize or to affiliate with the labor movement? If so, how and why? Again, police today have one of the highest unionization rates of any occupation, and some states grant collective bargaining rights to public safety workers but not other types of public workers. *See* KEARNEY & MARESCHAL, LABOR RELATIONS IN THE PUBLIC SEC-TOR, *supra*, 65–66. In 2011, a new Wisconsin law (discussed further below) stripped almost all collective bargaining rights from all types of public-sector workers *except* police and firefighters. Are there reasons to allow public safety workers *more* rights under a state collective bargaining law than other types of public employees?

D. The End of the Pre-Collective Bargaining Era and Public-Sector Unions After 1960

1. The First Public-Sector Labor Laws

The end of the old era began when, in 1959, Wisconsin became the first state to pass a statute authorizing public-sector collective bargaining. Supporters of such a rule had introduced bills regularly beginning in 1951. The 1959 Municipal Employee Relations Act gave employees of local governments the basic right to organize and bargain collectively. As amended in 1962, the law provided that if bar-gaining reached an impasse, a state agency could conduct mediation at the request of both parties and fact-finding at the request of either party. The agency (then the Wisconsin Employment Relations Board, later the Wisconsin Employment Rela-tions Commission) was also authorized to supervise elections. Later, the law was amended to provide, among other things, for binding arbitration. SLATER, PUBLIC WORKERS, *supra*, Ch. 6.

A wave of public-sector labor laws followed. Federal employees won the right to bargain collectively soon after in 1962, when President Kennedy issued Executive

Order 10988. By 1966, sixteen states had enacted laws granting organizing and bargaining rights to at least some public workers. SLATER, PUBLIC WORKERS, *supra*, 191. By the end of the 1970s, a majority of states had adopted such laws. Also, the Urban Mass Transit Act of 1964 required that the collective bargaining rights of transit employees be preserved when transit systems were converted from the private to the public sector. In 1978, President Carter signed the Federal Service Labor Management Relations Act, which provides bargaining rights and binding arbitration at impasse for most federal employees.

These developments had various causes. By the 1960s, the U.S. had considerable experience with private-sector unions, and the violence and radicalism associated with labor relations and some unions in the past was more of a distant memory. Also, in Wisconsin and other states, public-sector unions had organized, represented their members, and even informally bargained without striking or otherwise creating the parade of horribles that opponents of public-sector unions had predicted. Further, during the 1960s, public-sector employment expanded greatly, due in part to the Vietnam War, the Great Society programs of the day, and the increased population brought about by the baby boom. Also, public-sector pay began to lag private-sector pay more significantly.

In addition, the 1960s was a decade of activism and agitation, and public workers were not immune. For decades after the Boston police strike, with the exception of a handful of strikes in 1946 (still mostly small), public-sector strikes were rare and short. But the later 1960s and 1970s saw a sharp uptick in illegal strikes. Some were in states with public-sector labor laws, but some were in states that did not give public-sector unions any rights. Some of these strikes were successful, some were not. Beginning in the early 1980s, however, the number of illegal strikes by public workers decreased considerably.

Public-sector unionization increased rapidly in the 1960s and 1970s. AFSCME went from 99,000 members in 1955 to more than 250,000 members in 1969, and then to more than a million members by 1978. In 1955, all the public-sector unions put together had a combined membership of around 400,000; by the 1970s, the total was more than 4,000,000. SLATER, PUBLIC WORKERS, *supra*, 193; *History of AFSCME*, available at http://www.afscme.org/about/1028.cfm. Also, many organizations that previously had been outside the AFL-CIO either joined it or, like the National Education Association, began behaving more like a tradition union and less like a "professional association."

2. The First Amendment Right to Organize

Further helping public-sector unions in this period, in the late 1960s courts finally accepted an argument they had made for decades: the First Amendment of the Constitution prevents a public employer from firing or otherwise discriminating against a public employee because of membership in or support of a union. This was a major departure from the precedent of the first half of the 20th century.

In those decades, courts routinely rejected challenges to employer bans on unions based in the First Amendment. In so doing, they cited Justice Oliver Holmes's oft-quoted line in a Massachusetts Supreme Judicial Court opinion rejecting a free speech claim by a police officer: "[t]he petitioner may have a constitutional right to talk politics but he has no constitutional right to be a policeman." *McAuliffe v. New Bedford*, 155 Mass. 216, 219 (1892); *see* Slater, *The Court Does Not Know "What a Labor Union Is," supra*, 1006.

The beginning of the erosion of this concept came with *Garrity v. New Jersey*, 385 U.S. 493 (1967). *Garrity* held that public employees enjoyed certain rights under the Fifth Amendment (essentially, that a government employer cannot compel a confession to what could be a crime under threat of discharge and then use that confession in a criminal proceeding). "We conclude that policemen, like teachers and lawyers, are not relegated to a watered-down version of constitutional rights," the Court explained. 385 U.S. 493, 500. In the same term, *Keyishian v. Board of Regents*, 385 U.S. 589 (1967), held that a New York regulation requiring college teachers to certify that they were not communists violated the First Amendment. *Keyishian* rejected prior precedent and held that public employment could not "be conditioned upon the surrender of constitutional rights which could not be abridged by direct government action." 385 U.S. 589, 605.

A year after *Keyishian*, in *Pickering v. Board of Education*, 391 U.S. 563 (1968), the Supreme Court held that a school board had violated the First Amendment when it fired a public school teacher for writing a letter to a newspaper criticizing the school board's handling of a revenue measure and its allocation of funds between educational and athletic programs. The court established a "balancing test" for public employee speech cases which would later be refined in *Connick v. Myers*, 461 U.S. 138 (1983) and *Garcetti v. Ceballos*, 547 U.S. 410 (2006).

The early cases which held that public employment cannot be subject to unconstitutional conditions raised the question: do public employees have a First Amendment right to associate in unions such that they may not be disciplined or discharged for such activities?

Atkins v. City of Charlotte

District Court for the Western District of North Carolina
296 F. Supp. 1068 (1969)

CRAVEN, J.

This is a civil action brought to obtain a declaratory judgment and injunctive relief declaring unconstitutional and preventing enforcement of Sections 95-97, 95-98 and 95-99 of the General Statutes of North Carolina. We hold G.S. 95-97 unconstitutional on its face. We hold G.S. § 95-98 a valid and constitutional exercise of the legislative authority of the General Assembly of North Carolina. As for G.S. § 95-99, we hold it to be so related to G.S. § 95-97 that it cannot survive the invalidation of that section. . . .

The statutes sought to be invalidated are these:

N.C.G.S. §95-97: Employees of units of government prohibited from becoming members of trade unions or labor unions. — No employee of the State of North Carolina, or of any agency, office, institution or instrumentality thereof, or any employee of a city, town, county, or other municipality or agency thereof, or any public employee or employees of an entity or instrumentality of government shall be, become, or remain a member of any trade union, labor union, or labor organization which is, or may become, a part of or affiliated in any way with any national or international labor union, federation, or organization, and which has as its purpose or one of its purposes, collective bargaining with any employer mentioned in this article with respect to grievances, labor disputes, wages or salary, rates of pay, hours of employment, or the conditions of work of such employees. Nor shall such an employee organize or aid, assist or promote the organization of any such trade union, labor union, or labor organization, or affiliate with any such organization in any capacity whatsoever. The terms "employee," "public employee" or "employees" whenever used in this section shall mean any regular and full-time employee engaged exclusively in law enforcement or fire protection activity.

N.C.G.S. §95-98: Contracts between units of government and labor unions, trade unions or labor organizations concerning public employees declared to be illegal. — Any agreement, or contract between the governing authority of any city, town, county, or other municipality, or between any agency, unit, or instrumentality thereof, or between any agency, instrumentality, or institution of the State of North Carolina, and any labor union, trade union, or labor organization, as bargaining agent for any public employees of such city, town, county or other municipality, or agency or instrumentality of government, is hereby declared to be against the public policy of the State, illegal, unlawful, void and of no effect.

N.C.G.S. §95-99: Penalty for violation of article. — Any violation of the provisions of this article is hereby declared to be a misdemeanor, and upon conviction, plea of guilty or plea of nolo contendere shall be punishable in the discretion of the court.

All of the plaintiffs are members of the Charlotte Fire Department, and the gist of the complaint is that the statutes are overbroad and prohibit constitutionally guaranteed rights of the plaintiffs in violation of the First Amendment and the Due Process and Equal Protection Clauses of the Fourteenth Amendment to the Constitution of the United States. Specifically, plaintiffs want to become dues paying members of a Local which would become affiliated with International Association of Fire Fighters, the intervenor, Affidavits of some 400 fire fighters of the Charlotte Fire Department have been put into evidence to the effect that, if allowed to do so by law, affiants would join the Union.

The City of Charlotte is a municipal corporation which operates and maintains the Charlotte Fire Department pursuant to the City Charter. . . .

The Department has approximately 438 employees, consisting of the Chief, two assistant chiefs, 14 deputy chiefs, 60 fire captains, and 56 fire lieutenants, with the remainder being fire fighters, inspectors, fire alarm personnel and office personnel. The plaintiffs consist of deputy chiefs, captains, lieutenants and fire fighters and range in service with the department from two to 40 years.

For many years prior to the enactment in 1959 of the North Carolina General Statutes complained of, the International Association of Fire Fighters operated or maintained a union made up of Charlotte Fire Department members and designated as Local 660, an affiliate of the International Association of Fire Fighters. A number of Fire Department members paid dues to that organization which was engaged in collective bargaining activity. Further, the City checked off dues for union membership.

During 1959, the North Carolina Legislature enacted General Statutes §§ 95-97 through 95-99. Following the enactment of these statutes, Local 660 terminated its affiliation with the International Association of Fire Fighters and became, or took the name, Charlotte Fire Fighters Association. This organization continued the activities and representations very much as had been the practice with Local 660. The Fire Fighters Association continued to negotiate with the City and to represent the Charlotte firemen with respect to wages, grievances, and other conditions of employment, and the City continued its recognition of the association and permitted dues check-off. This practice continued from 1959 until 1962. On January 29, 1962, the City Council received and approved a report compiled by the City Manager. One of the recommendations of this report as it was approved established as a condition of continued employment in the Fire Department non-membership in the Fire Fighters Association or in any successor thereto. The City Council approved this report after having been advised by the City Attorney that the Fire Fighters Association was not illegal per se under the statutes complained of, but that the association and its recognition by the City was in violation of public policies of the State. Sometime after this action on the part of the City Council, the Fire Fighters Association terminated its activities and the City discontinued its recognition and dues check-off. A grievance procedure was established to allow individual employees to process grievances, but no provisions were made for group grievance procedure or for collective bargaining with respect to grievances, wages, and conditions of employment.

During March of 1967, members of the Charlotte Fire Department, the plaintiffs herein, organized the Charlotte Firemen's Assembly. This organization has as its purpose collective bargaining with the City of Charlotte with respect to wages, grievances, hours of employment and other conditions of employment. It would like to become a local affiliate of intervenor but is prevented by the statutes. The Firemen's Assembly has not been recognized by the City as a representative of firemen. . . .

We think N.C.G.S. §95-97 is void on its face as an abridgment of freedom of association protected by the First and Fourteenth Amendments of the Constitution of the United States. The flaw in it is an intolerable "overbreadth" unnecessary to the protection of valid state interests.... The Supreme Court of the United States has accorded "freedom of association" full status as an aspect of liberty protected by the Due Process Clause of the Fourteenth Amendment and by the rights of free speech and peaceful assembly explicitly set out in the First Amendment. In *NAACP v. Alabama ex rel. Patterson*, the Court said:

> "It is beyond debate that freedom to engage in association for the advancement of beliefs and ideas is an inseparable aspect of the 'liberty' assured by the Due Process Clause of the Fourteenth Amendment, which embraces freedom of speech.... Of course, it is immaterial whether the beliefs sought to be advanced by association pertain to political, economic, religious or cultural matters, and state action which may have the effect of curtailing the freedom to associate is subject to the closest scrutiny." 357 U.S. 449, 460–61 (1958).

The Court had previously noted the close connection between the freedoms of speech and assembly. In *De Jonge v. Oregon*, 299 U.S. 353, 364 (1937), the Court held that the right of peaceable assembly is a right cognate to those of free speech and free press and equally fundamental. It was said that the right is one that cannot be denied without violating fundamental principles of liberty and justice which lie at the base of all civil and political institutions. The Court made a careful distinction between the proper exercise of legislative power to protect against abuse of the right of assembly and legislative infringement per se of that right, holding that the latter is not permissible. Especially pertinent to the problem confronting us is the following:

> "[Consistently] with the Federal Constitution, peaceable assembly for lawful discussion cannot be made a crime. The holding of meetings for peaceable political action cannot be proscribed. Those who assist in the conduct of such meetings cannot be branded as criminals on that score. The question, if the rights of free speech and peaceable assembly are to be preserved, is not as to the auspices under which the meeting is held but as to its purpose...." *De Jonge v. Oregon*, 2999 U.S. 353, 365.

We would make the same distinction here. It matters not, we think, whether the firemen of the City of Charlotte meet under the auspices of the intervenor, a national labor union, but whether their proposed concerted action, if any, endangers valid state interests. We think there is no valid state interest in denying firemen the right to organize a labor union—whether local or national in scope. It is beyond argument that a single individual cannot negotiate on an equal basis with an employer who hires hundreds of people. Recognition of this fact of life is the basis of labor-management relations in this country. Charlotte concedes in its brief that the rights of public employees to join labor unions is becoming increasingly recognized[2] (with the exception of firemen and policemen) and even admits that collective bargaining might be beneficial in many situations in the case of municipal firemen. But Charlotte insists that the State has a valid interest in forbidding membership in a labor union to firemen. It is said that fire departments are quasi-military in structure, and that such a structure is necessary because individual firemen must be ready to respond instantly and without question to orders of a superior, and that such military discipline may well mean the difference between saving human life and property, and failure. The extension of this argument is, of course, that affiliation with a national labor union might eventuate in a strike against the public interest which could not be tolerated, and the very existence of which would imperil lives and property in the City of Charlotte. This is the only state interest that can be validly asserted for N.C.G.S. § 95-97. The thought of fires raging out of control in Charlotte while firemen, out on strike, Neroicly watch the flames, is frightening. We do not question the power of the State to deal with such a contingency.[3] We do question the overbreadth of G.S. § 95-97, which quite unnecessarily, in our opinion, goes far beyond the valid state interest that is suggested to us, and strikes down indiscriminately the right of association in a labor union — even one whose policy is opposed to strikes.

Since the only valid state interest suggested by defendants in support of the constitutionality of G.S. § 95-97 is the quite legitimate fear that fire protection for the people of Charlotte might be disrupted by violence or by strike, it seems quite clear that the statute must be invalidated for "overbreadth."

The Supreme Court "has repeatedly held that a governmental purpose to control or prevent activities constitutionally subject to state regulation may not be achieved by means which sweep unnecessarily broadly and thereby invade the area of protected freedoms." *NAACP v. Alabama ex rel. Flowers*, 377 U.S. 288, at 307 (1964).

---

2. The Charlotte Observer currently reports that city employees, including sanitation workers, have joined a national labor union.

3. Although the question is not before us, we note the position of plaintiffs ... on the power of the State to prevent strikes and/or violent conduct on the part of a labor union engaged in vital public employment. The following Article 22 was recommended as of January 10, 1968, for incorporation in the intervenor's constitution:

> "The International Association of Fire Fighters is a law abiding organization. Because of the public character of the work of its members and the protection of the lives and property of citizens and communities in case of fire and other hazard, no subordinate union or its members shall withhold fire protection services where collective bargaining, conciliation, mediation, fact finding with recommendations or voluntary binding conciliation or arbitration is available for resolution of disputes involving grievances, wages, hours or conditions of work. Where such procedures for resolving disputes are not available the subordinate union shall not withhold fire protection service but shall refer the matter to the International President and the International Executive Board for such further handling as may be available or necessary to secure an acceptable settlement of the dispute."

From the plaintiffs' brief: The State "may quite properly prohibit employees from striking or using violence in the settlement of disputes." ...

Again, "even though the governmental purposes are legitimate and substantial, that purpose cannot be pursued by means that broadly stifle fundamental personal liberties when the end can be more narrowly achieved." *Shelton v. Tucker*, 364 U.S. 479, 488 (1960). As previously indicated, the plaintiffs and intervenor do not question the power of the State to prohibit strikes against the public interest.

What we have said thus far supports our ultimate conclusion: that the firemen of the City of Charlotte are granted the right of free association by the First and Fourteenth Amendments of the United States Constitution; that that right of association includes the right to form and join a labor union—whether local or national; that membership in such a labor organization will confer upon the firemen no immunity from proper state regulation to protect valid state interests which are, in this case, the protection of property and life from destruction by fire. We think such a conclusion flows inevitably from the enunciations of the United States Supreme Court set out above. Our decision is consistent with that of the Seventh Circuit according the same right to teachers. *McLaughlin v. Tilendis*, 398 F.2d 287 (7th Cir. 1968). We do not think the McLaughlin decision is distinguishable on the asserted ground that the State in that case had not undertaken to prohibit membership in a teachers' labor union. The court's recitation that there was no such state legislation went to the question of whether there was a valid state interest. It held that there was no such state interest, and that the right of a teacher to join a labor union rested upon the First Amendment to the United States Constitution. In our case, we hold that the valid state interest may be served by more narrowly drawn legislation so as not to infringe the First Amendment.

We find nothing unconstitutional in G.S. § 95-98. It simply voids contracts between units of government within North Carolina and labor unions and expresses the public policy of North Carolina to be against such collective bargaining contracts. There is nothing in the United States Constitution which entitles one to have a contract with another who does not want it. It is but a step further to hold that the state may lawfully forbid such contracts with its instrumentalities. The solution, if there be one, from the viewpoint of the firemen, is that labor unions may someday persuade state government of the asserted value of collective bargaining agreements, but this is a political matter and does not yield to judicial solution. The right to a collective bargaining agreement, so firmly entrenched in American labor-management relations, rests upon national legislation and not upon the federal Constitution. The State is within the powers reserved to it to refuse to enter into such agreements and so to declare by statute. . . .

Entry of a declaratory judgment decreeing G.S. § 95-97 and § 95-99 invalid because in violation of the First and Fourteenth Amendments of the United States Constitution seems to us, on the facts of this case, a fully sufficient remedy. . . .

Notes

1. Compare the language in this case with the language from *Local 201, AFSCME v. City of Muskegon, supra*, and other cases in which courts voiced concern that

allowing unionization of public safety employees would lead to strikes by these employees.

2. The Eighth Circuit Court issued a similar opinion the same year as *Atkins*, holding that firing public employees for joining a union violated the First Amendment. *American Federation of State, County & Municipal Employees, AFL-CIO v. Woodward*, 406 F.2d 137 (8th Cir. 1969).

> Union membership is protected by the right of association under the First and Fourteenth Amendments. *Thomas v. Collins*, 323 U.S. 516, (1945). . . . The Court commented in *Thomas*:
>
> > . . . "in the circumstances of our times the dissemination of information concerning the facts of a labor dispute must be regarded as within that area of free discussion that is guaranteed by the Constitution. . . . Free discussion concerning the conditions in industry and the causes of labor disputes appears to us indispensable to the effective and intelligent use of the processes of popular government to shape the destiny of modern industrial society."
>
> . . . The right . . . to discuss, and inform people concerning, the advantages and disadvantages of unions and joining them is protected not only as part of free speech, but as part of free assembly. 406 F.2d 137,139–40.

3. Importantly, though, the First Amendment right found in *Atkins* and similar cases does not include the right to bargain collectively. Indeed, the Supreme Court has held that this right does not even include the right of a union member to have a grievance presented to his or her employer by the union. *Smith v. Arkansas State Highway Employees Local 1315*, 441 U.S. 463 (1979). The Court explained that "the First Amendment is not a substitute for the national labor relations laws." 441 U.S. 463, 464. "The public employee surely can associate and speak freely and petition openly, and he is protected by the First Amendment from retaliation for doing so. . . . But the First Amendment does not impose any affirmative obligation on the government to listen, to respond or, in this context, to recognize the association and bargain with it." *Id.* at 465.

4. Some state constitutions include a right to bargain collectively that covers public employees. The Florida Constitution, Art. I, §6 states: "The right of employees, by and through a labor organization, to bargain collectively shall not be denied or abridged." This has been applied to government employees. *Chiles v. United Faculty of Florida*, 615 So. 2d 671 (Fla. 1993). Hawaii's Constitution, Art. XIII, §2, provides: "Persons in public employment shall have the right to organize for the purpose of collective bargaining as provided by law." Missouri's Constitution, Art. I, §29, states that "employees shall have the right to bargain collectively through representatives of their own choosing." In 2007, the Missouri Supreme Court reversed precedent dating back to 1947 and held that this provision applies to public employees. *Independence-National Education Association v. Independence School District*, 223 S.W.3d 131 (Mo. 2007).

5. Thus, by the late 1960s, while some public employees were still without a legal right to bargain collectively, all had a Constitutional right to join unions.

3. Public-Sector Labor Law in the 21st Century

Public-sector labor laws today have many rules that are similar or identical to the NLRA. For example, all public-sector labor statutes make it a ULP to fire a covered employee because the employee supports a union; all public-sector jurisdictions impose a duty of fair representation on unions with the same or similar requirements as under the NLRA (*see* Chapter 14). Generally, public-sector jurisdictions have adopted many rules, either in whole or in large part, from the private sector.

But public-sector law also features significant differences from private-sector law, and considerable variation exists among public-sector laws. Major differences include whether public workers have a right to bargain at all, what topics they have a right to bargain about, and what methods can or must be used to resolve bargaining impasses. By the year 2007, twenty-eight states and the District of Columbia allowed collective bargaining for all major groups of public employees; thirteen states allowed only one to four types of public workers to bargain (most commonly police, teachers and/or firefighters); and seven did not allow any public workers to bargain. Two had only more limited "meet and confer" rights. The scope of bargaining is generally more restricted in the public sector than in the private—sometimes much more restricted. Also, in 2007, only twelve states allowed any public workers to strike; thirty-eight states and the District of Columbia provided alternative procedures to resolve bargaining impasses, generally involving some combination of mediation, fact-finding, and/or interest arbitration. *See* Chapter 11. And as various sections of this book discuss, there are other significant differences (*e.g.*, some public-sector laws cover at least some supervisors).

The portions of this book dedicated to the public sector will focus on those areas in which public-sector labor rules diverge the most from private-sector rules with potentially important consequences. It will also discuss the policy choices in forming public-sector labor law, including but not limited to the question of the extent to which private-sector rules should simply be imported to the public sector.

Also, unlike private-sector law, even in the 21st century, the very right of public workers to bargain collectively remains a live issue. In 2004, governors of Indiana and Missouri withdrew executive orders permitting state employees to bargain collectively. After 9/11, the Bush administration insisted that the bill creating the Department of Homeland Security (DHS) removed DHS employees from coverage under the existing federal sector statute and allowed creation of a new system that could drastically reduce union rights.

Even more dramatically, 2011 saw an unprecedented wave of laws significantly restricting—and in some cases, effectively eliminating—public-sector bargaining rights. The following captures the highlights of this relatively recent wave of restrictions on public-sector bargaining rights. For a more complete description, *see* Martin Malin, *The Legislative Upheaval in Public-Sector Labor Law: A Search for Common Elements*, 27 A.B.A. J. Lab. & Emp. L. 149 (2012).

Prior to 2011, Wisconsin had two fairly similar public-sector labor statutes, one covering local and county government employees (Wis. Stat. Ann. § 111.70, *et seq.*), and the other state employees (Wis. Stat. Ann. § 111.81, *et seq.*). As discussed above, the former was the first state law permitting public-sector collective bargaining in country, enacted in 1959. Act 10, the "Budget Repair Bill" signed by Governor Scott Walker in 2011, made sweeping revisions to these laws (except for certain employees in "protective occupations," mainly police and fire). It eliminated collective bargaining rights entirely for some employees: University of Wisconsin (UW) system employees, employees of the UW Hospitals and Clinics Authority, and certain home care and child care providers. It generally limited collective negotiations to bargaining over a percentage increase in total base wages, and even this could be no greater than any increase in the consumer price index. No other issues could be negotiated. It imposed "right to work" rules, meaning that it would be illegal for unions and employers to agree to "fair share" union security clauses obligating members of a union bargaining unit to pay the portion of their dues used to represent the bargaining unit in matters related to collective bargaining (*see* Chapter 14). The bill also limits the duration of collective bargaining agreements to one year, which is very unusual in labor law.

The new Wisconsin law also requires an unprecedented mandatory recertification system under which every union must face a recertification election every year and will only be recertified if 51 percent of the employees in the collective bargaining unit — not merely those voting — vote for recertification. So, if a bargaining unit had 400 members and the recertification vote was 201 favoring union representation and 100 against, the union would be decertified (because 201 is less than 51 percent of 400). This is a change from the prior system under which (consistent with the NLRA and other public-sector laws) a request from 30 percent of the bargaining unit was required to schedule a decertification election, decertification elections could not take place during the terms of valid union contracts (except that there had to be a "window period" every three years allowing a decertification election), and the majority of those voting determined the outcome. Further, the law makes it illegal for an employer to agree to automatic dues deduction, even for employees who voluntarily wish to pay dues.

In the spring of 2012, a lower court, while upholding most of Act 10, enjoined the recertification provision and the bar on dues check-off. *Wisconsin Educ. Ass'n Council v. Walker*, 824 F. Supp. 2d 856 (W.D. Wis. 2012). The court enjoined these provisions on both equal protection and First Amendment grounds, finding no rational basis for distinguishing between "protective occupations" and other public employees for these purposes, at least none that did not offend the First Amendment (the court noted that those exempted from Act 10 disproportionately supported the Scott Walker in the 2010 election).

However, the Seventh Circuit reversed this decision and upheld Act 10 in full in *Wisconsin Educ. Ass'n Council v. Walker*, 705 F.3d 640 (7th Cir. 2013). The court noted that while all five unions that had endorsed Governor Walker were excluded from Act 10 as "public safety unions," some of other excluded unions had not endorsed Governor Walker. 705 F.3d 640, 643. The court added:

> Admittedly, the Unions do offer some evidence of viewpoint discrimina-tion in the words of then-Senate Majority Leader Scott Fitzgerald suggest-ing Act 10, by limiting unions' fundraising capacity, would make it more difficult for President Obama to carry Wisconsin in the 2012 presidential election. While Senator Fitzgerald's statement may not reflect the highest of intentions, his sentiments do not invalidate an otherwise constitutional, viewpoint neutral law. Consequently, Act 10's prohibition on payroll dues deduction does not violate the First Amendment. 705 F.3d at 645.

The court went on to hold that the distinctions Act 10 makes between "public safety" unions and other public-sector unions survive rational basis scrutiny. This was mainly because of the state's claimed concern that if public safety officers were denied the rights Act 10 denies most public-sector unions, public safety officers might strike. 705 F.3d at 653–57. Given the rules involved (dues check-off and recer-tification requirements), is this convincing?

The Seventh Circuit later rejected another challenge to Act 10. In *Laborers Local 236 v. Walker*, 749 F.3d 628 (7th Cir. 2014), two unions claimed that Act 10 violated their rights under the First Amendment and the Equal Protection Clause. The court held that barring covered unions from negotiating over topics other than base wages did not violate the unions' First Amendment right of association or their right to petition the government. It also rejected the argument that Act 10 violated the Equal Protection clause because unionized employees can only discuss base wages with their employers, while non-unionized employees are not so limited. Citing *Smith v. Arkansas State Highway Employees Local 1315*, *supra*, the court reasoned that the First Amendment right to petition does not mean that the government must listen. It found unconvincing the unions' attempt to distinguish *Smith* on the grounds that Act 10 essentially bars government actors from discussing certain topics even if they wish to do so. As to the right of association, the court agreed that Act 10 would likely make things more challenging for unions, but added that the Constitution did not prohibit that effect. Finally, the court rejected a related Equal Protection claim, reasoning that the state was not treating public employees differently based on their exercise of associational rights.

The Wisconsin Supreme Court also rejected challenges to Act 10 based on, among other theories, the First Amendment and Equal Protection Clause, in *Madi-son Teachers, Inc. v. Walker*, 851 N.W.2d 337 (Wis. 2014). In *Walker*, the Dane County Circuit Court had struck down certain sections of Act 10 as violating the free speech, association, and equal protections provisions of the Wisconsin state Constitution. But the Wisconsin Supreme Court, over a dissent by two justices, reversed.

Ohio, in the early 1980s, enacted a public-sector labor law applicable to most public employees; it even allowed most public workers to strike. OHIO REV. CODE Ch. 4117.1-24. In 2011, Governor John Kasich signed SB-5, which was designed to greatly restrict the rights this law. However, SB-5 never went into effect. It was put on hold pending a voter referendum in November 2011, and in that referendum, the voters overwhelmingly rejected SB-5.

Among other things, SB-5 would have eliminated collective bargaining rights for certain employees, including at least most college and university faculty, lower level supervisors in police and fire departments, and employees of charter schools. For employees who could bargain, SB-5 would have eliminated both the right to strike for those who have that right (all covered employees except police, fire, and a few other small categories), and eliminated the right to binding interest arbitration at impasse for employees who cannot strike. Instead, the parties would have been left to mediation and fact-finding, and if those did not lead to an agreement, the governing legislative body could have, essentially, simply chosen to adopt the employer's final offer. SB-5 also would have imposed "right to work" rules and barred public employers from agreeing to provide payroll deductions for any contributions to a political action committee without written authorization from the individual employee. It would also have greatly restricted the scope of bargaining.

While Ohio and Wisconsin were the most radical and most publicized cases, other states (generally where Republicans controlled most or all of state government) also passed bills in or around 2011 limiting the collective bargaining rights of public workers.

Idaho enacted SB 1108, which limited collective bargaining by teachers to "compensation" (defined, essentially, as wages and benefits). The law also limited collective bargaining agreements to one year, and it eliminated the requirement of fact-finding (only mediation remained). However, in the November 2012 elections, voters in Idaho, via three ballot proposals, rejected the changes made by SB 1108. *See* Amy Linn, *Idaho Voters Say No to GOP-Backed School Overhaul, Anti-Union Measures*, 50 GERR (BNA) 1402 (Nov. 20, 2012).

Illinois, in SB 10, amended its Educational Labor Relations Act such that in the Chicago Public Schools, the length of the school day and school year are permissive, not mandatory subjects of bargaining. The law also made minor adjustments to the right to strike for most public education employees and imposed more significant restrictions on that right for Chicago public school employees. For example, such a union cannot strike unless at least 75% of the bargaining unit authorizes the strike. *Id.* § 13(b)(2.10).

Indiana, in 2011, enacted SB 575, which limited the scope of bargaining for teachers to wages and benefits, explicitly barring other subjects (including binding arbitration of grievances). Even as to wages and benefits, contracts that would put a school district in a deficit are forbidden.

Massachusetts Acts 2011, Ch. 69, made it easier for local government employers to make changes in health insurance plans for their employees, by making a tripartite committee the final decision-maker as to proposed changes.

In 2011, MICH. P.A. 103, limited the scope of bargaining for teachers. Among other things, educational employers and employees cannot bargain over placement of teachers, reductions in force and recalls, performance evaluation systems, the content and implementation of policies regarding employee discharge or discipline, and how performance evaluation is used to determine employee compensation.

In 2012, Michigan enacted P.A. 53, which provides that union dues for employees of public schools may no longer be collected through payroll deductions. In *Bailey v. Callaghan*, 715 F.3d 956 (6th Cir. 2013), the Sixth Circuit, in a 2–1 decision, reversed a district court order halting implementation of P.A. 53, rejecting First Amendment and Equal Protection claims on three grounds. First, it found a rational basis (ostensibly, saving public school resources) for P.A. 53. Second, it reasoned that unions lacked an affirmative right to use government payroll mechanisms for the purpose of obtaining funds for expression. Third, because the court found that P.A. 53 did not restrict speech, it therefore could not involve viewpoint discrimination. The dissent argued that viewpoint discrimination existed because the law was impermissibly motivated by a desire to suppress a particular point of view. In a separate bill, P.A. 45, Michigan removed collective bargaining rights from graduate assistants at Michigan public universities. This rule was then struck down by *Toth v. Callaghan*, 995 F. Supp. 2d 774 (E.D. Mich. 2014, *appeal dismissed*, No. 14-1351 (6th Cir. July 8, 2014), on the grounds that it violated Article IV § 24 of the Michigan Constitution, which bars changing the original purpose of a bill during the enactment process. In yet another 2012 law, S.B. 1018 ended collective bargaining for home healthcare workers funded by the state by declaring that they were not public employees. In 2014, Michigan Public Act 414 specifically excluded student-athletes at Michigan's public universities and colleges from the state's public-sector labor statute.

In Nebraska, Legis. Bill 397 changed its interest arbitration rules to be more favorable to public employers. In Nebraska, interest arbitration is performed by the Commission of Industrial Relations (CIR). The new Nebraska law provides detailed criteria for selecting an array of comparable communities for interest arbitrations. *See* Chapter 11. Also, it mandates that if the employer at issue pays compensation between 98 and 102 percent of the average of the comparables, then the CIR must leave compensation as it is. If the employer's compensation is below 98 percent of the average, then the CIR must order it raised to 98 percent, and if it is above 102 percent, the CIR must order it lowered to 102 percent. The targets are reduced to 95-100 percent during periods of recession.

Nevada enacted S.B. 98, which reduces the number of public employee supervisors eligible for collective bargaining. It also mandates that labor contracts contain clauses that would reopen the contract during fiscal emergencies (this law applies to local governments, as state employees in Nevada do not have collective bargaining rights).

New Hampshire enacted SB-1, which eliminates the requirement that the terms of a collective bargaining agreement automatically continue if an impasse is not resolved at the time of the expiration of such agreement. It also enacted HB-589, which repealed a 2007 law that provided for mandatory card check recognition (*i.e.*, mandatory certification of a union when a majority of the employees in a bargaining unit sign cards indicating they want that union to represent them, *see* Chapter 8).

In late December 2010, New Jersey enacted N.J. Laws 2010, ch. 105, which capped wage increases at 2 percent for New Jersey police and firefighter arbitration awards for contracts expiring between Jan. 1, 2011 and April 1, 2014. Further, this law placed serious restrictions on interest arbitrators. Arbitrators will now be randomly selected (as opposed to the previous process of mutual selection); arbitrator compensation is limited to $1,000 per day and $7,500 per case; and arbitrators will be penalized $1,000 per day for failing to issue an award within forty-five days of a request for interest arbitration. In 2011, in N.J. Pub. L. Ch. 78, the state suspended bargaining over health care benefits for four years while a new statute, which will control the issue, is phased in.

New York Bill A. 8086, passed in June 2013, requires interest arbitration panels (*see* Chapter 11) to give 70 percent weight in their decisions to the public employer's ability to pay.

Oklahoma, in H.B. 1593, repealed a 2004 law that required cities with populations of at least 35,000 to bargain collectively with unions. As in Wisconsin, though, this change does not affect police and firefighters, who, in Oklahoma, are covered by a separate statute.

Tennessee, in H.B. 130/S.B. 113, repealed a 1974 law that authorized collective bargaining for public school teachers. Teachers are now permitted only "collaborative conferencing." Teachers now will be represented by groups that receive 15 percent or more of votes in a confidential poll rather than by a particular union. The law also prohibits the discussion of certain issues during such conferences, including but not limited to various matters relating to pay, evaluations, staffing decisions, assignments, certain "innovative educational programs," and payroll deductions for political activities. Even on the issues the parties are permitted to "conference" about, the parties are not required to reach any agreement, and if no agreement is reached, the school board will set the terms and conditions of employment through school board policy.

In 2012 and early 2013, a number of states passed or proposed legislation limiting or eliminating the use of dues check-off for public-sector unions. For example, Kansas House Bill 2022, signed into law in April 2013, bars public-sector unions from using money deducted from paychecks for political activities. *See generally*, Ann C. Hodges, *Maintaining Union Resources in an Era of Public Sector Bargaining Retrenchment*, 16 Empl. Rts. & Empl. Pol'y J. 599 (2012).

This trend has continued in some places. In 2017, Iowa enacted House File 291, which is largely modeled after Wisconsin Act 10. Among other things, HF 291's severe restrictions apply to most public-sector unions, specifically all bargaining units that consist of less than 30 percent public safety employees. For the employees it covers, this amendment limits contract negotiations to "base wages and other matters mutually agreed upon." Further, affected unions must undergo mandatory recertification elections and will only be recertified if a majority of the entire bargaining unit votes to do so; automatic dues-deduction is barred; and interest arbitrators cannot grant wage increases in excess of whichever is lower, 3 percent or the increase in the cost of living. The Iowa Supreme Court upheld this law against various constitutional challenges in *AFSCME Iowa Council 61 v. State*, 928 N.W.2d 21 (2019).

In 2018, Missouri enacted H.B. 1413, which, among other things, requires public-sector unions to undergo a mandatory recertification election every three years and requires unions to obtain annual permission from members before having dues or fees deducted from their paychecks. However, a lower court has enjoined this law. *Missouri National Education Association v. Missouri Department of Labor and Industrial Relations*, Case. No. 18SL-CC03310 (Cir. Ct. St. Louis, March 8, 2019).

In 2018, Florida enacted CS/HB 7055. Among other things, this requires unions of public-school employees to seek recertification if a majority of bargaining unit members are not dues-paying members. After the decision in *Janus v. AFSCME* (discussed in Chapter 14), this rule has added significance.

In contrast, in recent years, four states have expanded collective bargaining rights to public employees. First, in 2017, California Senate Bill 201 amended its Higher Education Employer-Employee Relations Act to include student employees whose employment is contingent upon their status as students. Then in 2019, California House Bill 378 extended collective bargaining rights to in-home childcare providers.

Second, in 2013, Colorado enacted the Colorado Firefighter Safety Act, Senate Bill 13-025. This law allows local governments to allow collective bargaining for firefighters if certain requirements are met. It also requires public employers to at least "meet and confer" with firefighters regarding safety issues. Then in 2020, Colorado enacted HB20-1153, which grants collective bargaining rights to employees of the state government.

Third, in 2017, Nevada Senate Bill 493 extended collective bargaining rights to school administrators, including school principals. Then in 2019, Nevada Senate Bill 135 granted collective bargaining rights to employees of the state's government (local government employees already had such rights). This law, which covers approximately 20,000 employees, was hailed as the largest expansion of collective bargaining rights in the U.S. in sixteen years. *See* Jake Johnson, *"Massive Win for Working People": Nevada Governor Signs Bill Giving Over 20,000 State Employees Collective Bargaining Rights*, Common Dreams, (Jun. 13, 2019) at https://www.commondreams.org/news/2019/06/13/massive-win-working-people-nevada-governor-signs-bill-giving-over-20000-state.

Fourth, in 2020, Virginia enacted House Bill 582, which permits local governments to adopt ordinances permitting collective bargaining. Before this law, Virginia had outlawed all public sector collective bargaining, even if a union and employer wished to engage in it voluntarily.

Thus, public-sector labor law is still changing rather dramatically (evolving or regressing, depending on one's perspective). The "history" continues to be volatile. Consider, as you go through these materials, which legal rules you think are best. If you practice in this area, always keep your eyes open for new developments.

Chapter 2

Labor Law's Subjects: "Employees" and "Employers"

I. Introduction

The National Labor Relations Act (NLRA) and public-sector labor laws are principally concerned with worker protest, union organizing, bargaining between employers and organized workers, the economic weapons both may use during bargaining, and the enforcement of labor contracts. As shown in later chapters, these statutes expressly protect workers' rights to organize, engage in "concerted activity," and bargain collectively. They also impose a long list of responsibilities on unions, employers, and others, and establish administrative processes for enforcing the rights and responsibilities that they codify.

Labor laws establish the rights and responsibilities only of *covered* workers, unions, and employers, and only these workers, unions, and employers have access to the administrative processes established to vindicate and enforce those rights and responsibilities. The NLRA's § 7 lists the rights of "employees." Similarly, §§ 8(a) and 8(b), along with other sections of the NLRA, regulate "employers" ("It shall be an unfair labor practice for an employer . . .") and "labor organizations" ("It shall be an unfair labor practice for a *labor organization* or its agents . . ."). But not everyone who engages in compensated work, or every organization that purports to represent those engaged in compensated work, or every person or entity compensating others for their work, is "covered" by the NLRA or a public-sector labor law. Thus, the definitions of "employee" and "employer" are critical to understanding the scope of the NLRA and public-sector labor laws.

Workers who are not covered by the NLRA or a public-sector labor law may turn to other laws for protection of their organizing and protest activities. The Constitution, other local, state or federal statutes, and states' common law regimes may provide various protections for workers. Still, the NLRA and public-sector labor laws offer protections and processes that other laws do not and cannot (among other reasons, see Chapter 16 on preemption relating to private-sector labor law). Labor laws, therefore, are central to workers, unions, and employers with respect to organizing and labor-management relations. This chapter examines the coverage provisions of the NLRA (as amended) and public-sector labor laws, and how they have been interpreted by courts, the National Labor Relations Board (NLRB or Board), and state labor relations agencies.

Congress originally defined "employee" very broadly in the Wagner Act, presumably extending coverage close to the boundaries established by the Commerce Clause. Ever since, the scope of the NLRA's coverage has been a subject of sometimes heated debate in Congress, the courts, and the Board. In most cases in the private sector, the result has been a narrowed interpretation of the NLRA's coverage provisions—in some cases, significantly narrower. *See generally* Anne Marie Lofaso, *The Vanishing Employee: Putting the Autonomous Dignified Union Worker Back to Work*, 5 F.I.U. L. Rev. 495 (2010). Some changes are the product of evolving views of "employment" and collective bargaining in American society. Other changes reflect the political battles that often underlie the legal struggles that define and redefine labor law. In the end, the question of which workers are protected by the NLRA remains unsettled even eight decades after it became law.

In the public sector, questions of which government employees, if any, labor laws should cover have been even more controversial. Even today, state laws vary tremendously. As Chapter 1 explained, beginning in the late 1960s, courts have held that most public employees have a First Amendment right to organize into unions. But courts have not found a constitutional right for public employees to bargain collectively or to engage in most of the other activities that labor laws typically protect or allow. Thus, the right to bargain collectively in the public sector depends on whether a specific public-sector law covers a specific set of employees.

There are two issues specific to public-sector labor law in this regard. First, which, if any, *occupations* in the public sector are covered by the labor law. In other words, are public employees generally granted bargaining rights, generally denied bargaining rights, or are some employees in some occupations and categories (e.g., police, firefighters, teachers, and/or state employees) granted bargaining rights while other public employees are not? Second, if an occupation or category of public employees is granted bargaining rights, which types of workers within covered categories are still excluded.

As to the first issue, as of 2014, twenty-seven states and the District of Columbia allowed collective bargaining for at least most major groups of public workers; eight allowed only one to four types of public workers to bargain (most commonly, police, firefighters, educational employees, and/or state employees); four allowed "meet and confer" rights (discussed in Chapter 9), and eleven did not allow any public workers to bargain. Richard Kearney & Patrice Mareschal Labor Relations in the Public Sector 65–66 (5th ed. 2014).

As to the second issue, while public-sector labor statutes typically exclude managerial and confidential employees in the same way private-sector law does, many public-sector labor laws contain significantly different rules regarding supervisors. Some jurisdictions have a narrower definition of "supervisor," either for certain occupations or for public employees generally. Further, some public-sector labor laws do not exclude supervisors from their coverage at all. There are also other types of employees (faculty members in institutions of higher education, for example), who are generally excluded under the NLRA, but not excluded under many public-sector statutes. This raises some interesting practical and policy issues.

II. "Employees" Under the NLRA and Public-Sector Labor Laws

A. The Wagner Act's Definition and Exemptions

The Wagner Act's §2(3) offered only a circular definition of "employee": "The term 'employee' shall include any employee, and shall not be limited to the employees of a particular employer, unless the Act explicitly states otherwise." Section 2(3)'s ambiguity largely delegated the question of which workers would be covered by the Act to the Board and the courts that review its work. Of course, Congress reserved its power to determine whom the NLRA covers, and, as will be discussed below, exercised this power to reshape §2(3) when enacting the Taft-Hartley Act.

The Commerce Clause, U.S. Const., Art. 1, Sec. 8, Cl. 3—the source of Congress' power to enact the NLRA—has not been a meaningful limitation on the definition of "employee." NLRA §§10(a) and 9(c)(1) extend the Board's jurisdiction to cases "affecting commerce," as that phrase is defined in §2(7). As noted in Chapter 1, the Supreme Court held in *NLRB v. Jones & Laughlin Steel Corp.*, 301 U.S. 1 (1937), that the Board's authority over private-sector labor relations extended to the boundaries of Congress' power under the Commerce Clause. *See also NLRB v. Fainblatt*, 306 U.S. 601, 607 (1939). Thus, while the Supreme Court and the Board have found constitutional limits on the definition of "employee," see discussion *infra*, those limits do not arise out of the Commerce Clause.

The Wagner Act expressly excluded three categories of "employees": "any individual employed as an agricultural laborer"; "any individual . . . employed in the domestic service of any family or person at his home"; and "any individual employed by his parent or spouse." Professor Marc Linder has argued that agricultural laborers were excluded from New Deal programs and laws like the NLRA and the Fair Labor Standards Act (FLSA) as part of a deal between President Franklin D. Roosevelt and southern Congressmen. Roosevelt agreed in order to pass his New Deal legislation through Congress. The southern political and economic elite struck the deal to preserve the racial caste and plantation systems that would have been threatened had former slaves been given a legally enforceable right to organize. Marc Linder, *Farm Workers and the Fair Labor Standards Act: Racial Discrimination in the New Deal*, 65 Tex. L. Rev. 1335 (1987). The collapse of *de jure* segregation in the United States did not, however, change the legal status of farm workers. As a result, today's agricultural laborers, many of whom are migrant or immigrant workers from Mexico and Central America, remain excluded from the NLRA's coverage.

Since 1947, Congress has required the Board to define "agricultural laborer" using the definition of "agriculture" found in FLSA §3(f). 29 U.S.C. §203(f); *see also* Pub.

L. No. 79–549, 60 Stat. 679 (1946) ("rider" requiring the Board to rely on the FLSA's definition beginning with this 1947 appropriations bill). This definition limits the exclusion to workers who are either (1) directly engaged in farming: cultivating, tilling, growing, harvesting, "dairying," raising animals or insects; or (2) other practices performed by a farmer or on a farm incident to these farming operations. 29 C.F.R. § 780.105 (2007) (regulations explaining and implementing § 3(f)). Thus, the Board, with the Supreme Court's deference, has interpreted § 2(3) *not* to exclude, among others, fertilizer manufacturers, *Mississippi Chemical Corp.*, 110 N.L.R.B. 826 (1954); processors, *Nephi Processing Plant, Inc.*, 107 N.L.R.B. 647 (1953); haulers, *NLRB v. Kent Bros. Transp. Co.*, 458 F.2d 480 (9th Cir. 1972); lumberjacks, *NLRB v. Scott Paper Co.*, 440 F.2d 625 (1st Cir. 1971); surveyors, *NLRB v. Design Sciences*, 573 F.2d 1103 (9th Cir. 1978); irrigation workers, *Farmers Reservoir & Irrigation Co. v. McComb*, 337 U.S. 755 (1949); apiary workers, *Hubbard Apiaries*, 116 N.L.R.B. 1468 (1956); seafood raisers, *Aquacultural Research Corp.*, 215 N.L.R.B. 1 (1974); grain elevator operators, *Davis Grain Corp.*, 203 N.L.R.B. 319 (1973); nursery workers, *Kelly Bros. Nurseries, Inc.*, 140 N.L.R.B. 82 (1962); individuals employed by farms, livestock companies, and dairies working as salespeople, *Shoenberg Farms*, 132 N.L.R.B. 1331 (1961); gas station attendants, *Alta-Dena Dairy*, 150 N.L.R.B. 1537 (1965); construction workers, *NLRB v. Monterey County Building & Construction Trades Council*, 335 F.2d 927 (9th Cir. 1964); and mechanics, *McElrath Poultry Co., Inc.*, 206 N.L.R.B. 354 (1973). *See also Holly Farms Corp. v. NLRB*, 517 U.S. 392 (1996) (deferring to the Board); *Bayside Enterprises, Inc. v. NLRB*, 429 U.S. 298 (1977) (same).

Stepping into the breach created by the "agricultural laborer" exemption, several states have enacted labor laws for agricultural workers patterned on the NLRA. *See, e.g.*, Agricultural Employment Relations, Ariz. Rev. Stat. Ann. §§ 23-1381–23-1395 (2015); Agricultural Labor Relations Cal. Lab. Code §§ 1140–1167 (2014); Agricultural Labor Relations, Kan. Stat. Ann. §§ 44-818–44-830 (2014); Agricultural Laborers' Right to Work Law, La. Rev. Stat. Ann. §§ 23:881–23:889 (2013); Agricultural Labor Law, Idaho Code Ann. §§ 22-4101–22-4113 (repealed 2003); *see also Int'l B'hood of Teamsters, Local No. 863 v. Seaboard Farms*, 214 N.J. Super. 425 (App. Div. 1986) (agricultural workers' right to organize and collectively bargain is guaranteed by the New Jersey Constitution). But farm worker organizing began in many states even before these labor laws were enacted. *See* Anne Marie Lofaso, *Leveraging Secondary Activity Within and Outside Legal Boundaries, in* The Cambridge Handbook of U.S. Labor Law For the Twenty-First Century (Richard Bales & Charlotte Garden eds. 2019); Jennifer Gordon, *Law, Lawyers, and Labor: The United Farm Workers' Legal Strategy in the 1960s and 1970s and the Role of Law in Union Organizing Today*, 8 U. Pa. J. Lab. & Emp. L. 1, 10–20 (2005). In addition, thousands of farm workers have organized without the benefit of state or federal labor laws. *See, e.g.*, Mischa Gaus, *The Coalition of Immokalee Workers Turns "Corporate Social Responsibility" from Oxymoron into Reality*, In These Times, May 14, 2007, at 33; Somini Sengupta, *Farm Union Takes Aim at a Big Pickle Maker*, N.Y. Times, Oct. 26, 2000, at A22.

Like agricultural workers, "workers in domestic service" were excluded from most labor and employment laws enacted during the Progressive Era and the New Deal, including the NLRA. *See* Peggie Smith, *Regulating Paid Household Work: Class, Gender, Race, and Agendas of Reform*, 48 Am. U. L. Rev. 851 (1999). Domestic workers had begun organizing in the absence of legal protection from federal or state labor laws even before the Wagner Act was passed, and their organizing efforts continue. *See generally* Jennifer Gordon, Suburban Sweatshops 94–104 (2005); Peggie Smith, *Organizing the Unorganizable: Private Paid Household Workers and Approaches to Employee Representation*, 79 N.C. L. Rev. 45 (2000); *Think Tank: Dignifying Work That's Never Done*, N.Y. Times, Feb. 28, 1998, at B11. By contrast, workers employed to provide "housekeeping" services for corporations like hotels, condominiums, or maintenance contractors—that is, work that is essentially identical to that performed by domestic workers—are "employees" covered by the NLRA and many of these workers have organized. *See, e.g., Shore Club Condominium Association, Inc. v. NLRB*, 400 F.3d 1336 (11th Cir. 2005). The apparent justification for this exemption is that domestic workers work in a family's home and, therefore, including them within the NLRA's coverage might create tension with familial privacy interests. The implication is that the relationship between a domestic worker and his or her employer more closely resembles familial relations than a traditional employer-employee relationship. Since § 2(3) also expressly denies coverage to "any individual . . . employed by his parent or spouse," Congress seemingly found the analogy to workers in domestic service sufficient to justify excluding them from the NLRA's coverage. Katharine Silbaugh, *Turning Labor into Love: Housework and the Law*, 91 Nw. U. L. Rev. 1, 74–76 (1996).

B. "Economic Realities" and Deference to the Board: *NLRB v. Hearst Publications*

Section 2(3)'s structure—an open-ended definition of "employee" with a few specifically enumerated exclusions—was interpreted in the Wagner Act's early days to suggest that Congress intended broad coverage. *See, e.g., NLRB v. Blount*, 131 F.2d 585 (8th Cir. 1942). The Board's decisions were generally consistent with the philosophy that led Senator Robert Wagner to drive the NLRA to passage and President Franklin Roosevelt to acquiesce in Wagner's efforts. Professor Mark Barenberg described Senator Wagner as a firm believer in "social plasticity" and the omnipresence of "[o]pportunities for intentionally guiding the trajectory of social change." Thus, he would have had little concern for traditional definitional boundaries. Rather, Wagner's goal, shared by President Roosevelt, was to quell the rising labor unrest that was perceived as a threat to the nation's hopes of recovery from the Depression by constructing a system of industrial democracy. Mark Barenberg, *The Political Economy of the Wagner Act: Power, Symbol, and Workplace Cooperation*, 106 Harv. L. Rev. 1379 (1993). Senator Wagner would have wanted the legislation which bears his name to cover anyone or anything relevant to accomplishing these goals.

The Supreme Court's decision in **NLRB v. Hearst Publications**, 322 U.S. 111 (1944), took seriously Wagner's and Roosevelt's goal of redressing industrial unrest and ratified the Board's approach to achieving those goals in its early decisions. The Supreme Court was asked whether newsboys selling newspapers on the streets of Los Angeles were "employees" of those newspapers and, therefore, covered by the NLRA. The newspapers' publishers argued that, because Congress did not explicitly define "employee" in §2(3), its meaning should be determined according to common-law standards—that is, the common-law test found in the Restatement of the Law of Agency, which held that a worker is a "servant" in any situation "in which the [worker's] physical activities and his time are surrendered to the control of the master." Restatement of Agency §220 (1933).

The Restatement lists several factors for determining employee status, including: the master controls the details of the servant's work; the servant is not employed in a distinct occupation or business; the servant's work does not require special skill; the master supplies the instrumentalities, tools, and place of the servant's work; the relationship with the master is permanent; and the servant's work a regular part of the master's business. *Id.* At the time, and even today, the common-law test was principally designed for determining whether an employer should be held liable for the tortious acts of its employees pursuant to the doctrine of *respondeat superior.* See Restatement (Third) of Agency §7.07(3) (2007) (defining "employee" for the purpose of establishing vicarious liability); Restatement (Third) of Agency §7, comment f (2007) (using the same factors as the First Restatement to define "employee"); *see also* Richard Carlson, *Why the Law Still Can't Tell an Employee When It Sees One and How It Ought to Stop Trying*, 22 Berkeley J. Emp. & Lab. L. 295, 304–06 (2001).

Justice Rutledge, writing for the *Hearst Publications* Court, rejected the newspapers' reliance on the common-law test to define "employee" under the NLRA. Because the common-law control test could, and often did, lead to widely varying and unpredictable results, Rutledge predicted that the Board and courts interpreting §2(3) would be forced to resolve disputes over the definition of "employee" in either of two ways: reference to state law precedents, or distilling a "pervading general essence . . . from state law." *Hearst Publications*, 322 U.S. at 122. Congress intended neither result, according to Rutledge. The Wagner Act was federal legislation intended to solve a national problem on a national scale, said Rutledge.

Rather than relying on common law, wrote Rutledge, the question of

> [w]hether . . . the term "employee" includes such workers as these newsboys must be answered primarily from the history, terms and purposes of the legislation. The word "is not treated by Congress as a word of art having a definite meaning. . . ." Rather "it takes color from its surroundings . . . (in) the statute where it appears," and derives meaning from the context of that statute, which "must be read in the light of the mischief to be corrected and the end to be attained."

322 U.S. 111, 124. Looking to the NLRA's purposes, Rutledge found that Congress

sought to find a broad solution, one that would bring industrial peace by substituting, so far as its power could reach, the rights of workers to self-organization and collective bargaining for the industrial strife which prevails where these rights are not effectively established. . . .

The Act, as its first section states, was designed to avert the "substantial obstructions to the free flow of commerce" which result from "strikes and other forms of industrial strife or unrest" by eliminating the causes of that unrest. It is premised on explicit findings that strikes and industrial strife themselves result in large measure from the refusal of employers to bargain collectively and the inability of individual workers to bargain successfully for improvements in their "wages, hours, or other working conditions" with employers who are "organized in the corporate or other forms of ownership association." . . .

Interruption of commerce through strikes and unrest may stem as well from labor disputes between some who, for other purposes, are technically "independent contractors" and their employers as from disputes between persons who, for those purposes, are "employees" and their employers. Inequality of bargaining power in controversies over wages, hours and working conditions may as well characterize the status of the one group as of the other. . . . In short, when . . . the economic facts of the relation make it more nearly one of employment than of independent business enterprise with respect to the ends sought to be accomplished by the legislation, those characteristics may outweigh technical legal classification for purposes unrelated to the statute's objectives and bring the relation within its protections.

322 U.S. at 125–28.

Rutledge interpreted the NLRA as evidencing congressional intent to subject the Board's assessments only to deferential judicial review:

It is not necessary in this case to make a completely definitive limitation around the term "employee." That task has been assigned primarily to the agency created by Congress to administer the Act. . . . Everyday experience in the administration of the statute gives it familiarity with the circumstances and backgrounds of employment relationships in various industries, with the abilities and needs of the workers for self organization and collective action, and with the adaptability of collective bargaining for the peaceful settlement of their disputes with their employers. . . . Resolving that question, like determining whether unfair labor practices have been committed, "belongs to the usual administrative routine" of the Board.

In making that body's determinations as to the facts in these matters conclusive, if supported by evidence, Congress entrusted to it primarily the decision whether the evidence establishes the material facts. Hence in reviewing the Board's ultimate conclusions, it is not the court's function to substitute its own inferences of fact for the Board's, when the latter have support in the record.

Id. at 130.

Accordingly, after concluding that the evidence supported the Board's finding that the newsboys were "employees," the Court upheld the Board's order requiring the newspapers to bargain with the newsboys' union.

Notes

1. In a decision three years after *Hearst Publications*, the Supreme Court described this approach to defining "employee" as the "economic realities" test. *Bartels v. Birmingham*, 332 U.S. 126, 130 (1947) (interpreting the Social Security Act). Judge Learned Hand has been credited with introducing this test in *Lehigh Valley Coal Co. v. Yensavage*, 218 F. 547 (2d Cir. 1914), *cert. denied*, 235 U.S. 705 (1915).

2. Does the economic realities test necessarily assure more expansive NLRA coverage than the common-law test? Richard Carlson has suggested that the newsboys whose status was at issue in *Hearst Publications* might also have been "employees" if the Board had applied the common-law test. Carlson, *supra* at 316. What evidence would an employer have introduced in a Board hearing to prove that a worker was not an "employee"?

3. *Hearst Publications* took one side in a struggle over how best to interpret the NLRA that continues to this day. *Hearst Publications* is a classic example of "purposive statutory interpretation." *See* Seth Harris, *Conceptions of Fairness and the Fair Labor Standards Act*, 18 HOFSTRA LAB. & EMP. L.J. 19 (2000). Courts employing "purposivism" interpret phrases in statutes to serve Congress' general intent — that is, its "purpose" for enacting the statute. Purposivism was "a conceptual hallmark of the New Deal." WILLIAM N. ESKRIDGE ET AL., LEGISLATION AND STATUTORY INTERPRETATION 221 (2d ed. 2007). "Textualism," a competing interpretive strategy, holds that fealty to congressional intent requires interpreters to rely only on text-based sources (*e.g.*, dictionaries available when the law was enacted), not legislative history or broad statements of a statute's purpose. *Id.* at 227–28. The struggle between purposive statutory interpretation and textualist statutory interpretation will be an important subtext throughout this casebook. Does Justice Rutledge adequately explain why purposive interpretation was the superior methodology? How would a textualist have decided *Hearst Publications*?

4. Another important subtext of U.S. labor law is courts' relationship with the NLRB. At its core, this is a separation of powers question, although it more commonly manifests as a statutory interpretation issue. Congress created the Board to be the independent, expert agency administering private-sector labor relations pursuant to authority delegated by Congress. Thus, courts risk treading on Congress' authority if they second-guess the Board's work. The general rule is that, when a statute does not directly answer a question presented, the administrative agency's reasonable constructions of the Act "are given controlling weight unless they are

arbitrary, capricious, or manifestly contrary to the statute." *Chevron, U.S.A., Inc. v. Natural Res. Def. Council, Inc.*, 467 U.S. 837, 844 (1984); *see also U.S. v. Mead Corp.*, 533 U.S. 218 (2001) (clarifying when deference is due in the absence of an express delegation of regulatory authority to the agency). In the particular case of the Board, the rule is that "[c]ourts must defer to the requirements imposed by the Board if they are 'rational and consistent with the Act,' and if the Board's 'explication is not inadequate, irrational, or arbitrary.'" *Allentown Mack Sales & Serv., Inc. v. NLRB*, 522 U.S. 359, 364 (1998). Accordingly, the question arises in every judicial opinion reviewing a Board decision, is the Board's decision entitled to "*Chevron* deference"? The *Hearst Publications* Court was highly deferential to the Board's interpretation of §2(3). Was this deference appropriate considering the subsequently adopted *Chevron* standard?

C. "Employees" vs. "Independent Contractors"

1. Private Sector: The Taft-Hartley Act and "Independent Contractors"

The seemingly expansive scope of the Wagner Act's coverage, particularly after *Hearst Publications*, proved to be politically unsustainable in the post-war era. In the aftermath of President Roosevelt's death, Harry S. Truman's ascension to the presidency, the end of World War II, the perception that the Soviet Union posed a rising threat in Europe and beyond, spreading fear of purported "communist influence" at home, and the beginnings of the McCarthy Era and its "Red Scare," the progressive New Deal coalition was replaced by a new conservative majority in Congress. President Truman prepared for an election campaign in 1948 that most observers predicted, incorrectly as it turns out, would complete the conservative takeover of the federal government's political branches by transferring the White House to Republican control.

One of the first legislative targets for the new Republican congressional majority and their allies in the business community was the Wagner Act and, with it, the expansive growth of unions it had fostered. *See* Chapter 1. Among other things, the Taft-Hartley Act amended §2(3) to exclude "independent contractors" from the scope of the Act's coverage: "the term 'employee' . . . shall not include . . . any individual having the status of an independent contractor." This amendment legislatively overturned *Hearst Publications'* adoption of the economic realities test and ordered the Board and courts to use the common-law test to define the employer-employee relationship. H.R. Rep. No. 245 (1947) (Conf. Rep.) *reprinted in* I Legislative History of the Labor-Management Relations Act, 1947, at 292, 309 (1985); 93 Cong. Rec. 6593, 6599 (1947) *reprinted in* II Legislative History of The Labor Management Relations Act, 1947, at 1537, 1947 (1985).

Hearst Publications implied that the common-law test would not serve the Wagner Act's purposes. The Taft-Hartley Act amended the Act's purpose section, but only by adding a paragraph focusing on union activities which Congress wanted to rein in rather than the scope of the Act's coverage. It made no mention of coverage.

Some scholars have argued that the common-law test amounts to "purposeless" or "anti-purposive" determinations of which workers are and should be covered by the NLRA. *See, e.g.,* Marc Linder, *Dependent and Independent Contractors in Recent U.S. Labor Law: An Ambiguous Dichotomy Rooted in Simulated Statutory Purposelessness,* 21 Comp. Lab. L. & Pol'y J. 187, 197–205 (1999). Nonetheless, Congress had mandated a new (or, perhaps, old) means of determining which workers are "employees" under the NLRA.

National Labor Relations Board v. United Insurance Co.

Supreme Court of the United States
390 U.S. 254, 88 S. Ct. 988, 19 L. Ed. 2d 1083 (1968)

Black, J.

[United Insurance Company used "debit agents" to perform various insurance business functions. The Insurance Workers International Union won a certification election and sought to represent the debit agents. United Insurance refused to recognize the union claiming that the agents were "independent contractors" rather than "employees." The Union filed an unfair labor practice charge. The [NLRB] held that the agents were employees and ordered the company to bargain collectively with the Union. The Court of Appeals found that the agents were independent contractors and refused to enforce the Board's order. The Supreme Court granted certiorari.]

. . . [T]he question before us is whether these agents are "employees" who are protected by the [NLRA] or "independent contractors" who are expressly exempted from the Act. . . .

Initially this Court held in *NLRB v. Hearst Publications,* that "Whether . . . the term 'employee' includes (particular) workers . . . must be answered primarily from the history, terms and purposes of the legislation." Thus the standard was one of economic and policy considerations within the labor field. Congressional reaction to this construction of the Act was adverse and Congress passed an amendment specifically excluding "any individual having the status of an independent contractor" from the definition of "employee" contained in section 2(3) of the Act. The obvious purpose of this amendment was to have the Board and the courts apply general agency principles in distinguishing between employees and independent contractors under the Act. And both [the Union] and [United Insurance] agree that the proper standard here is the law of agency. . . .

. . . [United Insurance] has district offices in most States which are run by a manager who usually has several assistant managers under him. Each assistant manager has a staff of four or five debit agents. . . . New agents are hired by district managers, after interviews; they need have no prior experience and are assigned to a district office under the supervision of an assistant district manager. Once he is hired, a debit agent is issued a debit book which contains the names and addresses of the company's existing policyholders in a relatively concentrated geographic area. This book is company property and must be returned to the company upon termination of the agent's service. The main job of the debit agents is to collect premiums from the policyholders listed in this book. They also try to prevent the lapsing of policies and sell new insurance when time allows. The company compensates the agents as agreed to in the "Agent's Commission Plan" under which the agent retains 20% of his weekly premium collections on industrial insurance and 10% from holders of ordinary life, and 50% of the first year's premiums on new ordinary life insurance sold by him. The company plan also provides for bonuses and other fringe benefits for the debit agents. . . . At the beginning of an agent's service an assistant district manager accompanies the new agent on his rounds to acquaint him with his customers and show him the approved collection and selling techniques. The agent is also supplied with a company "Rate Book," which the agent is expected to follow, containing detailed instructions on how to perform many of his duties. An agent must turn in his collected premiums to the district office once a week and also file a weekly report. At this time the agent usually attends staff meetings for the discussion of the latest company sales techniques, company directives, etc. . . . The district manager submits a weekly report to the home office, specifying, among other things, the agents whose records are below average; the amounts of their debits; their collection percentages, arrears, and production; and what action the district manager has taken to remedy the production "letdown." If improvement does not follow, the company asks such agents to "resign," or exercises its rights under the "Agent's Commission Plan" to fire them "at any time."

There are innumerable situations which arise in the common law where it is difficult to say whether a particular individual is an employee or an independent contractor, and these cases present such a situation. . . . In such a situation as this there is no shorthand formula or magic phrase that can be applied to find the answer, but all of the incidents of the relationship must be assessed and weighed with no one factor being decisive. What is important is that the total factual context is assessed in light of the pertinent common-law agency principles. When this is done, the decisive factors in these cases become the following: the agents do not operate their own independent businesses, but perform functions that are an essential part of the company's normal operations; they need not have any prior training or experience, but are trained by company supervisory personnel; they do business in the company's name with considerable assistance and guidance from the company and its managerial personnel and ordinarily sell only the company's policies; the "Agent's Commission Plan" that contains the terms and conditions under which they operate is promulgated and changed unilaterally by the company; the agents account to the company for the funds they collect under an elaborate and regular reporting procedure; the agents receive the benefits of the company's vacation plan and group insurance and pension fund; and the agents have a permanent working arrangement with the company under which they may continue as long as their performance is satisfactory. Probably the best summation of what these factors mean in the reality of the actual working relationship was given by the chairman of the board of [the employer] in a letter to debit agents about the time this unfair labor practice proceeding arose:

> if any agent believes he has the power to make his own rules and plan of handling the company's business, then that agent should hand in his resignation at once, and if we learn that said agent is not going to operate in accordance with the company's plan, then the company will be forced to make the agents final (sic) . . .

The Board examined all of these facts and found that they showed the debit agents to be employees. . . . [T]he Board's determination was a judgment made after a hearing with witnesses and oral argument had been held and on the basis of written briefs. . . . Here the least that can be said for the Board's decision is that it made a choice between two fairly conflicting views, and under these circumstances the Court of Appeals should have enforced the Board's order. It was error to refuse to do so.

———————

United Insurance left open difficult questions about the common-law test: how should the Board and reviewing courts weigh the test's many factors in a particular case? Were some factors more important than others? Is there a fundamental core or "essence" to the test? In the aftermath of *United Insurance*, several Courts of Appeals answered this question by focusing on those factors that emphasized the employer's "right to control" the details of the worker's employment. Other Courts of Appeals rejected this approach. *Compare, e.g., Labor Relations Div. of Constr. Indus. v. Int'l B'hood of Teamsters, Local #379*, 29 F.3d 742 (1st Cir. 1994) (using the "right to control" test), *and NLRB v. Fugazy Continental Corp.*, 603 F.2d 214 (2d Cir. 1979) (same), *with Speen v. Crown Clothing Corp.*, 102 F.3d 625 (1st Cir. 1996) (rejecting the focus on "right to control" and using the balancing test), *and Pepsi-Cola Buffalo Bottling Co. v. NLRB*, 409 F.2d 676 (2d Cir. 1969) (same).

In *Federal Express Home Delivery v. NLRB*, 563 F.3d 492 (D.C. Cir. 2009), the U.S. Court of Appeals for the District of Columbia disagreed with its sister circuit courts on the importance of the "right to control" in the common-law test. The International Brotherhood of Teamsters had won elections among FedEx package delivery drivers at two terminals in Wilmington, Massachusetts. The employer refused to bargain with the union, instead arguing that the drivers were "independent contractors" who could not organize a union under the Act. The D.C. Circuit agreed and overturned the elections after concluding that the common-law test should not focus on "control":

> For a time, when applying this common law test, we spoke in terms of an employer's right to exercise control, making the extent of actual supervision of the means and manner of the worker's performance a key consideration in the totality of the circumstances assessment. Though all the common law factors were considered, the meta-question, as it were, focused on the sorts of controls employers could use without transforming a contractor

into an employee. . . . Gradually, however, a verbal formulation emerged that sought to identify the essential quantum of independence that separates a contractor from an employee . . . where we used words like control but struggled to articulate exactly what we meant by them. "Control," for instance, did not mean all kinds of controls, but only *certain* kinds. [citation omitted.]

[B]oth this court and the Board, while retaining all of the common law factors, "shift[ed the] emphasis" away from the unwieldy control inquiry in favor of a more accurate proxy: whether the "putative independent contractors have 'significant entrepreneurial opportunity for gain or loss.'" [citation omitted.] This subtle refinement was done at the Board's urging in light of a comment to the Restatement that explains a "'full-time cook is regarded as a servant'"—and not "an independent contractor"—"'although it is understood that the employer will exercise no control over the cooking.'" [citation omitted quoting RESTATEMENT (SECOND) OF AGENCY § 220(1) cmt. d]. Thus, while all the considerations at common law remain in play, an important animating principle by which to evaluate those factors in cases where some factors cut one way and some the other is whether the position presents the opportunities and risks inherent in entrepreneurialism. [citation omitted.]

Id. at 496–97. With this understanding of the common-law test, the D.C. Circuit reviewed the record for indicia of "entrepreneurial opportunities for gain or loss":

[T]he Regional Director found the contractors signed a Standard Contractor Operating Agreement that specifies the contractor is not an employee of FedEx "for any purpose" and confirms the "manner and means of reaching mutual business objectives" is within the contractor's discretion, and FedEx "may not prescribe hours of work, whether or when the contractors take breaks, what routes they follow, or other details of performance"; "contractors are not subject to reprimands or other discipline"; contractors must provide their own vehicles, although the vehicles must be compliant with government regulations and other safety requirements; and "contractors are responsible for all the costs associated with operating and maintaining their vehicles." [Citation omitted.] They may use the vehicles "for other commercial or personal purposes . . . so long as they remove or mask all FedEx Home logos and markings" and, . . . in the past "Alan Douglas[] used his FedEx truck for his 'Douglas Delivery' delivery service, in which he delivered items such as lawn mowers for a repair company." [Citation omitted.] Contractors can independently incorporate, and at least two in Wilmington have done so. At least one contractor has negotiated with FedEx for higher fees. [Citation omitted.]

Tellingly, contractors may contract to serve multiple routes or hire their own employees for their single routes; more than twenty-five percent of contractors have hired their own employees at some point. [Citation omitted.]

> "The multiple route contractors have sole authority to hire and dismiss their drivers"; they are responsible for the "drivers' wages" and "all expenses associated with hiring drivers, such as the cost of training, physical exams, drug screening, employment taxes, and work accident insurance." [Citation omitted.] The drivers' pay and benefits, as well as responsibility for fuel costs and the like, are negotiated "between the contractors and their drivers." In addition, "both multiple and single route contractors may hire drivers" as "temporary" replacements on their own routes; though they can use FedEx's "Time Off Program" to find replacement drivers when they are ill or away, they need not use this program, and not all do. [Citation omitted.] ... [C]ontractors do not need to show up at work every day (or ever, for that matter); instead, at their discretion, they can take a day, a week, a month, or more off, so long as they hire another to be there. "FedEx [also] is not involved in a contractor's decision to hire or terminate a substitute driver, and contractors do not even have to tell FedEx [] they have hired a replacement driver, as long as the driver is 'qualified.'" [Citation omitted.] "Contractors may also choose to hire helpers" without notifying FedEx at all; at least six contractors in Wilmington have done so. [Citation omitted.] This ability to hire "others to do the Company's work" is no small thing in evaluating "entrepreneurial opportunity." [Citation omitted.]

Id. at 498–99. The court also noted that drivers were permitted to assign their contractual rights to routes without FedEx's permission or involvement. These factors established entrepreneurial opportunity, in the court's view.

The court was not persuaded of the existence of an employment relationship by other facts found by the Regional Director: drivers were required to wear a FedEx uniform and conform to grooming standards; vehicles were required to be a particular color, a specific size range, and insured, while displaying FedEx's logo; drivers were required to complete a driving course or have commercial driving experience; FedEx "conducted two customer service rides per year" to audit performance and provided incentive pay and occasional fuel reimbursements and vehicle availability allotments, and required drivers to have a vehicle and driver available for deliveries Tuesday through Saturday. FedEx also kept control over routes. "[T]hose distinctions," said the court, "though not irrelevant, reflect differences in the type of service the contractors are providing rather than differences in the employment relationship. In other words, the distinctions are significant but not sufficient. . . ."

> The Regional Director also emphasized that these "contractors perform a function that is a regular and essential part of FedEx Home's normal operations, the delivery of packages," and that few have seized any of the alleged entrepreneurial opportunities. [Citation omitted.] While the essential nature of a worker's role is a legitimate consideration, it is not determinative in the face of more compelling countervailing factors [citation omitted] otherwise companies like FedEx could never hire delivery drivers who are independent contractors ... "[I]t is the worker's retention of the right

to engage in entrepreneurial activity rather than his regular exercise of that right that is most relevant for the purpose of determining whether he is an independent contractor." [Citation omitted.]

Id. at 502.

One of the Board precedents relied upon in *Federal Express Home Delivery* was *Dial-A-Mattress*, 326 N.L.R.B. 884 (1998). The Board issued its decision in *Dial-A-Mattress* along with a companion case, **Roadway Package System Inc.**, 326 N.L.R.B. 842 (1998), in an effort to clarify how the common-law test should be applied by contrasting the facts in the two cases. The cases were argued together and issued on the same day, but they reached opposite results. Roadway Package System's delivery truck drivers were "employees," while Dial-A-Mattress's delivery truck operators were "independent contractors."

In *Roadway Package System*, the Board rejected the employer's argument that the common-law test amounted to a "right to control" test and that factors relating to "control" were most important:

> The Supreme Court has clearly stated that "all of the incidents of the relationship must be assessed and weighed with no one factor being decisive." See *United Insurance*. . . . While we recognize that the common-law agency test described by the Restatement ultimately assesses the amount or degree of control exercised by an employing entity over an individual, we find insufficient basis for the proposition that those factors which do not include the concept of "control" are insignificant when compared to those that do. Section 220(2) of the Restatement [(Second) of Agency] refers to 10 pertinent factors as "among others," thereby specifically permitting the consideration of other relevant factors as well, depending on the factual circumstances presented. In addition, Comment c to Section 220(1) of the Restatement states that "[t]he factors in Subsection (2) are *all* considered in determining the question [of employee status], and it is for the triers of fact to determine whether or not there is *a sufficient group of favorable factors* to establish the employee relationship." (Emphasis added.) Thus, the common-law agency test encompasses a careful examination of all factors and not just those that involve a right of control. . . . 326 N.L.R.B. at 850.

Having seemingly resolved the legal question left open by *United Insurance*, the Board applied the common-law test to the facts of each case. In *Roadway Package System*, the Board found:

> [a]s in *United Insurance*, the drivers here do not operate independent businesses, but perform functions that are an essential part of one company's normal operations; they need not have any prior training or experience, but receive training from the company; they do business in the company's name with assistance and guidance from it; they do not ordinarily engage in outside business; they constitute an integral part of the company's business under its substantial control; they have no substantial proprietary

interest beyond their investment in their trucks; and they have no significant entrepreneurial opportunity for gain or loss. All these factors weigh heavily in favor of employee status. . . . *Id.* at 851.

By contrast, in *Dial-A-Mattress*, the Board found that:

Dial has structured its relationship with the owner-operators to allow them (with very little external controls) to make an entrepreneurial profit beyond a return on their labor and their capital investment. The owner-operators arrange their own training, hire their own employees, and have sole control over and complete responsibility for their employees, including setting their terms and conditions of employment. Dial also plays no part in the selection, acquisition, ownership, financing, inspection, or maintenance of the vehicles used by the owner-operators. There is no minimum compensation guaranteed the owner-operators to minimize their risk of performing deliveries for Dial, and they can decline orders without penalty. The owner-operators are not required to provide delivery services each scheduled workday. In short, their separateness from Dial is manifested in many ways, including significant entrepreneurial opportunity for gain or loss. *Dial-A-Mattress*, 326 N.L.R.B. at 891.

The Board also noted the factual differences between the companies' delivery truck operations:

Unlike [Dial-A-Mattress], Roadway provides its drivers with a vast array of support plans to reduce risk in the performance of their deliveries and pickups for Roadway. The amount of income for the Roadway drivers is based, inter alia, on a "guaranteed" [compensation scheme] determined by Roadway's estimate of what is a "normal" level of packages and pickup and deliveries for the drivers. The Roadway drivers' pay is also curtailed by the operation of Roadway's "flex" program where overflow work in a driver's service area is transferred to other drivers. Thus, the elements of Roadway's compensation plan, in effect, result in both minimum guarantees and effective ceilings for its drivers.

In contrast to Dial's indifference about the size, color, or type of vehicles used by the owner-operators, Roadway provides its drivers with assistance in acquiring new or leased custom designed specialty vans. . . . Roadway also eases its drivers' burden of obtaining a used vehicle from former Roadway drivers. To meet these initial vehicle costs, Roadway offers a startup loan to its new drivers. The Roadway drivers also have a "business support package" to help ensure that their vehicles are properly maintained and covered by specific warranties.

Roadway also exercises more control over its drivers' manner and means of accomplishing their work than Dial does here. The Roadway drivers are required to provide delivery services each scheduled workday. They cannot refuse to deliver or pick up packages in their primary service area without being subject to possible termination of their operating agreement with Roadway. Roadway also controls the appearance of its drivers and their vehicles. For instance, Roadway drivers are required to wear a specified uniform of a certain type and color, displaying the Roadway logo. Furthermore, the Roadway drivers do not have the attributes of entrepreneurship possessed by the Dial owner-operators. The Roadway drivers do not use multiple trucks or hire helpers or drivers to allow them to pursue other business ventures and opportunities. There is no evidence that the Roadway drivers can negotiate the type of special deals acquired by [three trucking enterprises working for Dial-A-Mattress]. *Id.* at 893.

Notes

1. Is the common-law test practicable? In *United Insurance*, Justice Black suggests it could have produced "two fairly conflicting views" and admits that "innumerable situations . . . arise in the common law where it is difficult to say whether a particular individual is an employee or an independent contractor." If applying the standard could produce opposing, yet equally reasonable results, how should the Board choose between these results? Is the outcome strictly a consequence of the political makeup of the Board when the case is reviewed? *Compare Stamford Taxi, Inc.*, 332 N.L.R.B. 1372 (2000) (Clinton Board holding that taxi drivers are "employees"), *with AAA Cab Services*, 341 N.L.R.B. 462 (2004) (Bush II Board holding that taxi drivers are not "employees"). *But compare also Philadelphia Newspapers, Inc.*, 1999 N.L.R.B. LEXIS 617 (Mar. 11, 1999) (Clinton Board holding that newspaper delivery drivers are "independent contractors") *with St. Joseph News-Press*, 345 N.L.R.B. 474 (2005) (Bush II Board holding same) (overturned in *FedEx Home Delivery v. N.L.R.B.*, *supra*; *Ridgewell's Inc.*, 334 N.L.R.B. 37 (2001) (Bush II Board holding that restaurant wait staff are "employees"). Further, the outcome may be determined by the choice of forum in which the Board's decision is reviewed. *Compare FedEx Home Delivery, supra, with Wells v. FedEx Ground Package Sys.*, 979 F. Supp. 2d 1006 (E.D. Mo. 2013) (refusing to follow the D.C. Circuit's reasoning).

2. How do *Roadway Package System* and *Dial-A-Mattress* answer the question left open by *United Insurance*: how should the factors from the common-law test be weighed? Relying on these two cases, how would you articulate a test that the Board and courts could apply in future cases? Does the concept of "control" give us a justiciable standard that serves the Act's goals? *See, e.g., St. Joseph News-Press*, 345 N.L.R.B. 474 (2005); *Pennsylvania Academy of the Fine Arts*, 343 N.L.R.B. 846 (2004); *Pan American Grain Co.*, 343 N.L.R.B. 318 (2004). Can *Federal Express Home Delivery* be reconciled with the different outcomes in *Dial-A-Mattress* and *Roadway Package Systems*?

3. Justice Rutledge apparently considered "independent contractor" to be synonymous with "independent business enterprise": an independent businessperson whose bargaining power is roughly equivalent to that of the "employer." Is *Federal Express Home Delivery* establishing the same "independent business enterprise"

test? Is this test the best way to resolve the ambiguities that arise when the common-law test is applied in many cases? Is there a meaningful difference, either in substance or with respect to outcomes, between the "independent business enterprise" approach and the "control" approach?

4. The Railway Labor Act (RLA), 45 U.S.C. §§ 151–188, was enacted in 1926 to establish a national system for administering and regulating the relationships between labor and management in the railroad industry that was later applied to the airline industry. The RLA's definition of "employee" differs from the NLRA's definition: "every person in the service of a [rail or airline] carrier (subject to its continuing authority to supervise and direct the manner of rendition of his service) who performs any work defined as that of an employee or subordinate official. . . ." 45 U.S.C. § 151, Fifth. Because of the specificity of this definition, courts have held that job applicants and trainees are excluded from RLA coverage because they are not yet "employees." *See Nelson v. Piedmont Aviation*, 750 F.2d 1234 (4th Cir. 1984), *cert. denied*, 471 U.S. 1116 (1985) (applicants); *IFFA v. Trans World Airlines*, 819 F.2d 839 (8th Cir. 1987), *rev'd on other grounds*, 489 U.S. 426 (1989).

5. The Board and reviewing courts continue to struggle with whether certain workers are statutory employees, who have rights under the NLRA, or independent contractors, who do not have such rights. To clarify this area, the Obama-era NLRB's Division of Advice issued an Advice memo in *Pacific 9 Transportation., Inc.*, Case 21-CA-150875 (Dec. 18, 2015), describing a theory of a Section 8(a)(1) violation based on misclassification of employees as independent contractors. However, since then, the courts have issued the following decisions reviewing Board decisions: *FedEx Home Delivery v. NLRB*, 849 F.3d 1123 (D.C. Cir. 2017) (denying enforcement to *FedEx Home Delivery*, 361 N.L.R.B. 610 (2014)) (*FedEx II*); *Lancaster Symphony Orchestra v. NLRB*, 822 F.3d 563 (D.C. Cir. 2016); and *Crew One Productions, Inc. v. NLRB*, 811 F.3d 1305 (11th Cir. 2016). Significantly, *FedEx II* expressly relied on *FedEx Home Delivery v. NLRB*, 563 F.3d 492 (D.C. Cir. 2009) (*FedEx I*), which had held that FedEx delivery drivers are independent contractors and not FedEx employees. In both cases, the D.C. Circuit reversed the Board's legal conclusion that the FedEx drivers were employees. The *FedEx II* court further noted that the records of the two cases were "materially indistinguishable." *FedEx II*, 849 F.3d at 1124.

The Trump Board recently switched directions in *SuperShuttle DFW, Inc.*, 367 N.L.R.B. No. 75 (Jan. 25, 2019). There, in the context of franchisees who operate shared-ride vans for SuperShuttle Dallas-Fort Worth, the Board brought the test for differentiating employees from independent contractors into line with the D.C. Circuit's view, and overturned the Board's decision in *FedEx II*, 361 N.L.R.B. 610 (2014), *enft. denied*, 849 F.3d 1123 (D.C. Cir. 2017).

FedEx drivers across the country generally have the same job duties, and state law governing independent contractor status is often based on the Restatement (Second) of Agency § 220(2), as is Board law. You might expect that tribunals throughout the sundry U.S. jurisdictions would reach the same conclusion about drivers' status, but this has not been the case. Compare the courts' analyses of the Board cases in *FedEx I* and *FedEx II* with that of the Ninth Circuit interpreting California law in *Alexander v. FedEx Ground Package System, Inc.*, 765 F.3d 981, 987 (9th Cir. 2014). These different analyses demand the question — Why? In thinking about this question, consider whether the following makes a difference: The D.C. Circuit (and now the Board) focuses on entrepreneurial opportunity and California law has developed with a focus on right of control.

This issue was once again tested in the D.C. Circuit in *Pennsylvania Interscholastic Athletic Association, Inc.*, 366 N.L.R.B. No. 10 (2018), *enft. denied*, 926 F.3d 837 (D.C. Cir. 2019), which presented the question whether the Board's holding — that lacrosse referees are statutory employees — was consistent with the D.C. Circuit's decision in *FedEx II*. The court acknowledged, in agreement with the Board's factual findings, that the referees had little entrepreneurial opportunity and that the employer, PIAA, controlled significant aspects of the referee's jobs. The court, however, refused to enforce the Board's order on the well-established principle that reviewing courts do not owe *Chevron* deference to the Board on this particular question of law. The court therefore drew its own conclusion based on its own balancing of the independent contractor factors.

Relatedly, on February 18, 2018, the Trump Board — perhaps in an effort to reject the theory described in the *Pacific 9 Transportation* Advice memo — issued a Notice and Invitation to File Briefs in *Velox Express*, Case 15-CA-184006, addressing the question: "Under what circumstances, if any, should the Board deem an employer's act of misclassifying statutory employees as independent contractors a violation of Section 8(a)(1) of the Act?" Applying its recent decision in *SuperShuttle DFW*, the Board found that the drivers there were independent contractors, thereby avoiding the question presented in the Obama-era Advice Memo. *See* 368 N.L.R.B. No. 61 (Aug. 29, 2019).

Problem 2.1

NetWorld is one of the world's largest software companies. It employs a core staff of permanent employees which it categorizes as "regular employees." NetWorld offers "regular employees" a wide variety of benefits, including group health and life insurance and pensions. It supplements its workforce with a pool of individuals NetWorld categorizes as "independent contractors" or "freelancers." They are not provided any of these benefits. Rather, NetWorld pays them a flat monthly fee for their services. Prior to beginning their work for NetWorld, "freelancers" sign "Independent Contractor Copyright Assignment and Non-Disclosure Agreements" and "Independent Contractor/Freelancer Information Forms." The agreements include a provision stating that the undersigned "agrees to be responsible for all federal and state taxes, withholding, social security, insurance and other benefits." The information document likewise states that "as an Independent Contractor, you are self-employed and are responsible for paying for all your own insurance and benefits."

NetWorld's International Division employed roughly fifty regular employees and seven "freelancers." Although hired to work on specific projects, these seven "freelancers" had worked on successive projects for a minimum of two years each in that division. Like the regular employees, the "freelancers" worked as software testers, production editors, proofreaders, formatters and indexers. They work on teams with regular employees, share the same supervisors, perform identical functions, and work the same hours. They use NetWorld's office equipment and supplies. However, unlike regular employees, "freelancers" are not given admittance keys and must be "buzzed in" every day when they arrive at work. "Freelancers" also wear badges of a different color, have different electronic-mail addresses, and attend a less formal orientation than that provided to regular employees. They cannot assign their work to others. They are not invited to official company functions or paid overtime wages. In addition, they are not paid through NetWorld's payroll department. Instead, they submit invoices for their services, documenting their hours and the projects on which they worked, and are paid through the accounts receivable department.

You are counsel to the International Software Workers Union. Your union's organizers have been collecting authorization cards from the regular employees in the international division, but it has become apparent that it will be difficult for the union to win an election in that division without the support of the "freelancers." What advice would you give the organizers regarding whether the "freelancers" are covered by the Act?

2. Public Sector "Employees"

Public-sector labor laws also typically exclude independent contractors, using similar rules. *Chief Judge of the Circuit Court of Cook County and Chicago Newspaper Guild, Local #34071*, 18 PERI ¶ 2016 (Ill. Lab. Bd. 2002), offers an illustration:

Section 3(n) [of the relevant Illinois statute] defines public employee as "any individual employed by a public employer . . . but excluding independent contractors." In *County of Will*, the then-State Board held that the existence of an employment relationship, as opposed to that of an independent contractor, depends upon whether the principal has retained the right to control the manner and means by which a result is to be accomplished by the individual performing the service. Where the control is limited to the results sought, the relationship between the individual performing the service and the principal is that of independent contractor. In determining whether an individual is an independent contractor, all of the incidents of the relationship must be assessed and weighed with no one factor being decisive. *County of Will*, citing *NLRB v. United Insurance Co., supra.*

The Board has considered a variety of factors when applying this test. These include whether the individuals at issue have other employment; the amount of time they spend performing duties for the employer; how their work is assigned; whether they can refuse work; whether and to what extent the employer supervises and directs their work; whether they exercise independent discretion in performing their work or deciding what work they will do; whether the employer provides any training or evaluates their performance; whether the employer provides them with an office, secretarial assistance and/or equipment, or pays any expenses for the same; whether they determine the hours they will work for the employer and whether they are required to record their hours worked; the extent of the employer's authority to discipline them; whether they receive a flat salary regardless of the amount of work they perform; whether taxes are withheld or other deductions made from their paychecks; and whether the employer provides them with any fringe benefits, such as health insurance or paid vacation leave.

In addition to the aforementioned factors, the [NLRB], when examining independent contractor status, has also considered whether the individuals at issue operate independent businesses; whether they perform functions that are an essential part of the employer's normal operations; whether prior training or experience is required; and whether they have significant entrepreneurial opportunity for gain or loss. *See, e.g., BKN., Inc.*; *Dial-A-Mattress Operating Corp.; Roadway Package System, Inc.*

Some public-sector cases have hinted that they could deviate more from private-sector precedent on this issue. ***New Jersey State Judiciary and Communications Workers of America***, 29 NJPER ¶ 76 (PERC 2002), rejected a claim that free-lance interpreters ("FLIs") working for courts should be excluded from a bargaining unit as independent contractors. The New Jersey Commission noted that the relevant statutory language, from N.J. Stat. Ann. § 34:13A-5.3 and N.J. Stat. Ann. § 34:13A-3(d), contained no specific exclusion for independent contractors (in a list of exclusions that did include, e.g., managerial and confidential employees). Rather, it contained the following language: "The term 'employee' shall include . . . any public employee, i.e., any person holding a position, by appointment or contract, or employment in the service of a public employer, except elected officials, members of boards and commissions, managerial executives and confidential employees."

The New Jersey Commission explained the significance of this difference as follows:

> It is undisputed that none of the statutory exclusions apply and that the Judiciary is a public employer. The question, therefore, is whether the FLIs . . . hold their positions "by appointment or contract, or employment in the service of a public employer." . . .

> The NLRA's definition of "employee" expressly excludes "independent contractors" whereas the [New Jersey] Act's definition of "employee" does not. The judiciary argues, however, that the definition of "public employee" under our Act implicitly contains the same "independent contractor" exclusion as under the NLRA. We will thus examine that difference in greater detail. . . .

Effective July 1, 1968, the New Jersey Legislature expanded the definition of "employee" in N.J. Stat. Ann. § 34:13A-3(d) to encompass any "public employee." The Legislature . . . did not copy the NLRA's exclusion of "independent contractors." *See State of New Jersey*, E.D. No. 67, 1 NJPER 2 (1975) (contrasting NLRA exclusion, Executive Director finds that independent contractors are not, per se, excluded from the Act's coverage). In addition, the Legislature decided that "employment" is but one of three ways to hold a position in the service of a public employer — the other ways are by "appointment" or "contract." Given the definitional differences between the NLRA and our Act, common law agency cases should not be applied mechanistically, regardless of the context in which they arose, in determining whether individuals performing services for a public employer are public employees. We will consider common law agency cases, but with an emphasis on the labor relations cases applying those principles and the labor relations policies informing our Act.

. . . Moreover, the coverage of remedial laws should be construed broadly; an employer-employee relationship may be found under such laws even though one might not be found under common law principles. . . . Our Act is remedial legislation and should be liberally construed to effectuate its purposes of reducing workplace strife and improving morale and efficiency.

In sum, common law agency principles are relevant to determining whether FLIs are public employees entitled to seek union representation, but so are the policies of our Act. We will consider the principles first and then the policies.

The Commission went on to use a test that incorporated the thirteen factors listed in the Restatement of Agency (Second) § 220 (1958), and also two other factors: "whether or not the parties believe they are creating the relationship of 'master and servant'" and whether the putative independent contractor has "a significant entrepreneurial opportunity for gain or loss." Is this test actually different from the NLRA test? Is it supported by the relevant statutory language?

While government agencies sometimes use independent contractors, the more common issue in the public sector is "contracting out" work formerly done by public employees to private firms. In such cases, the people performing the work for the contracting firm are not covered by the relevant public-sector labor law because they are employees of a private company. Further, as will be discussed in more detail, some cases raise interesting questions about the actual identity of the employer.

D. Supervisors

1. Taft-Hartley Act: "Supervisors" and "Professional Employees"

The Wagner Act did not mention supervisors directly. As the Supreme Court held in *Hearst Publications*, the Wagner Act defined "employee" expansively to "include any employee." 322 U.S. at 135. Consistent with this broad reading of § 2(3), the Court held that supervisors were protected by the Act in *Packard Motor Car Co. v. NLRB*, 330 U.S. 485 (1947) over Justice William Douglas's dissent. Douglas was concerned that allowing supervisors to organize would be inconsistent with the Act's background understanding of industrial organization:

> [The decision that supervisors are covered "employees"] tends to emphasize that the basic opposing forces in industry are not management and labor but the operating group on the one hand and the stockholder and bondholder group on the other. . . . The struggle for control or power between management and labor becomes secondary to a growing unity in their common demands on ownership. . . . 330 U.S. at 494. (Douglas, J., dissenting).

In 1947, Congress codified Justice Douglas's reasoning and a class divide between "supervisors," as representatives of management, and non-supervisory employees in the Taft-Hartley Act: "When Congress passed the Labor Act, we were concerned . . . with the welfare of 'workers' and 'wage earners,' not of the boss. It was to protect workers and their unions against foremen, not to unionize foremen, that Congress passed the act." H.R. Rep. No. 245 (1947) (Conf. Rep.) *reprinted in* I Legislative History of the Labor-Management Relations Act, 1947, 304 (1985).

At the same time, it exempted "supervisors," Congress clarified that "professional employees" are covered by the Act. 29 U.S.C. § 152(12) (2006), *amended by* Labor Management Relations Act, Pub. L. No. 80-101, 61 Stat. 136 (1947). Although many supervisors are not professional employees, some professional employees' jobs involve supervising other workers. Thus, the overlapping definitions of "supervisor" and "professional employee" in the Taft-Hartley Act created a tension which the Supreme Court would be asked to resolve. Congress did not foresee the tension it had created by adding these two sections to the Act and, therefore, offered no guidance regarding how to proceed.

In *NLRB v. Health Care and Retirement Corp.*, 511 U.S. 571 (1994), the Supreme Court considered the potential conflict between § 2(11)'s exemption of supervisors and § 2(12)'s definition of professional employees. The issue was whether a worker exercises her authority "in the interest of the employer," as § 2(11) requires, when "exercis[ing] professional judgment incidental to the treatment of patients." 511 U.S. 571 at 574. Heartland Nursing Home disciplined four licensed practical nurses who, in turn, filed unfair labor practice (ULP) charges. Heartland responded by arguing that the nurses were exempt supervisors because they had "responsibility to ensure adequate staffing; to make daily work assignments; to monitor the aides' work to ensure proper performance; to counsel and discipline aides; to resolve aides' problems and grievances; to evaluate aides' performances; and to report to management." *Id.* at 575. According to the employer, these activities constituted "responsibly directing" other employees—one of the supervisory activities listed in § 2(11). The Board adopted the Administrative Law Judge's rejection of the employer's argument on the grounds that, even if the nurses responsibly directed other employees, they did not do so "in the interest of the employer." Rather, "the nurses' focus is on the well-being of the residents rather than of the employer." *Id.*

The Supreme Court disagreed:

> [t]he Board has created a false dichotomy—in this case, a dichotomy between acts taken in connection with patient care and acts taken in the interest of the employer. That dichotomy makes no sense. Patient care is the business of a nursing home, and it follows that attending to the needs of the nursing home patients, who are the employer's customers, is in the interest of the employer. We thus see no basis for the Board's blanket assertion that supervisory authority exercised in connection with patient care is somehow not in the interest of the employer. . . .
>
> Consistent with the ordinary meaning of the phrase, . . . acts within the scope of employment or on the authorized business of the employer are in the interest of the employer. 511 U.S. at 577–78.

The Court also directly confronted the tension between §§ 2(11) and 2(12): "The Act does not distinguish professional employees from other employees for purposes of the definition of supervisor in § 2(11). The supervisor exclusion applies to 'any individual' meeting the statutory requirements, not to 'any non-professional employee.'" *Id.* at 581.

Health Care resolved one potential conflict between the "supervisor" exclusion and the inclusion of "professional employees." The Supreme Court addressed a closely related conflict a few years later.

NLRB v. Kentucky River Community Care, Inc.

Supreme Court of the United States
532 U.S. 706, 121 S. Ct. 1861, 149 L. Ed. 2d 939 (2001)

SCALIA, J.

Under the [NLRA], employees are deemed to be "supervisors" and thereby excluded from the protections of the Act if, *inter alia*, they exercise "independent judgment" in "responsibly . . . direct[ing]" other employees "in the interest of the employer." This case presents two questions: which party in an unfair-labor-practice proceeding bears the burden of proving or disproving an employee's supervisory status; and whether judgment is not "independent judgment" to the extent that it is informed by professional or technical training or experience.

I

. . . Kentucky River Community Care, Inc., operates a care facility for residents who suffer from mental retardation and mental illness. The facility, named the Caney Creek Developmental Complex (Caney Creek), employs approximately 110 professional and nonprofessional employees in addition to roughly a dozen concededly managerial or supervisory employees. In 1997, the Kentucky State District

Council of Carpenters petitioned the [NLRB] to represent a single unit of all 110 potentially eligible employees at Caney Creek.

At the ensuing representation hearing, respondent objected to the inclusion of Caney Creek's six registered nurses in the bargaining unit, arguing that they were "supervisors" under § 2(11) of the Act, and therefore excluded from the class of "employees" subject to the Act's protection and includable in the bargaining unit. See § 2(3). The Board's Regional Director . . . placed the burden of proving supervisory status on [Caney Creek,] found that respondent had not carried its burden, and therefore included the nurses in the bargaining unit. The Regional Director accordingly directed an election to determine whether the union would represent the unit. . . . [T]he union won the election and was certified as the representative of the Caney Creek employees.

[Caney Creek refused to bargain with the union. The Board granted summary judgment to the union on its ULP charge and ordered Caney Creek to bargain. Caney Creek petitioned for review in the United States Court of Appeals for the Sixth Circuit and the Board cross-petitioned. The Court of Appeals refused to enforce the bargaining order holding that the Board erred in placing the burden of proving supervisory status on Caney Creek rather than on the Board's General Counsel. It also rejected the Board's definition of "independent judgment" for determining whether the nurses were "supervisors." The Court granted the Board's petition for a writ of certiorari.]

II

The Act expressly defines the term "supervisor" in § 2(11), which provides:

> "The term 'supervisor' means any individual having authority, in the interest of the employer, to hire, transfer, suspend, lay off, recall, promote, discharge, assign, reward, or discipline other employees, or responsibly to direct them, or to adjust their grievances, or effectively to recommend such action, if in connection with the foregoing the exercise of such authority is not of a merely routine or clerical nature, but requires the use of independent judgment."

The Act does not, however, expressly allocate the burden of proving or disproving a challenged employee's supervisory status. The Board therefore has filled the statutory gap with the consistent rule that the burden is borne by the party claiming that the employee is a supervisor. For example, when the General Counsel seeks to attribute the conduct of certain employees to the employer by virtue of their supervisory status, this rule dictates that he bear the burden of proving supervisory status. Or, when a union challenges certain ballots cast in a representation election on the basis that they were cast by supervisors, the union bears the burden. . . .

[The Court unanimously upheld the Board's rule for assigning the burden and held that the Board properly placed the burden on Caney Creek both when it sought to exclude the nurses from the bargaining unit prior to the election and in the ULP hearing.]

III

. . . .

Employees are statutory supervisors if (1) they hold the authority to engage in any 1 of the 12 listed supervisory functions, (2) their "exercise of such authority is not of a merely routine or clerical nature, but requires the use of independent judgment," and (3) their authority is held "in the interest of the employer." *NLRB v. Health Care & Retirement Corp. of America*, supra. The only basis asserted by the Board . . . for rejecting respondent's proof of supervisory status with respect to directing patient care was the Board's interpretation of the second part of the test — to wit, that employees do not use "independent judgment" when they exercise "ordinary professional or technical judgment in directing less-skilled employees to deliver services in accordance with employer-specified standards." The Court of Appeals rejected that interpretation, and so do we.

Two aspects of the Board's interpretation are reasonable, and hence controlling on this Court. First, it is certainly true that the statutory term "independent judgment" is ambiguous with respect to the *degree* of discretion required for supervisory status. See *NLRB v. Health Care & Retirement Corp. of America*, supra. Many nominally supervisory functions may be performed without the "exercis[e of] such a degree of . . . judgment or discretion . . . as would warrant a finding" of supervisory status under the Act. It falls clearly within the Board's discretion to determine, within reason, what scope of discretion qualifies. Second, as reflected in the Board's phrase "in accordance with employer-specified standards," it is also undoubtedly true that the degree of judgment that might ordinarily be required to conduct a particular task may be reduced below the statutory threshold by detailed orders and regulations issued by the employer. . . .

The Board, however, argues further that the judgment even of employees who are permitted by their employer to exercise a sufficient *degree* of discretion is not "independent judgment" if it is a particular *kind* of judgment, namely, "ordinary professional or technical judgment in directing less-skilled employees to deliver services." The first five words of this interpretation insert a startling categorical exclusion into statutory text that does not suggest its existence. The text, by focusing on the "clerical" or "routine" (as opposed to "independent") nature of the judgment, introduces the question of degree of judgment that we have agreed falls within the reasonable discretion of the Board to resolve. But the Board's categorical exclusion turns on factors that have nothing to do with the degree of discretion an employee exercises. Let the judgment be significant and only loosely constrained by the employer; if it is "professional or technical" it will nonetheless not be independent. The breadth of this exclusion is made all the more startling by virtue of the Board's extension of it to judgment based on greater "experience" as well as formal training. What supervisory judgment worth exercising, one must wonder, does not rest on "professional or technical skill or experience"? If the Board applied this aspect of its test to every exercise of a supervisory function, it would virtually eliminate "supervisors" from the Act.

As it happens, though, only one class of supervisors would be eliminated in practice, because the Board limits its categorical exclusion with a qualifier: Only professional judgment that is applied "in directing less-skilled employees to deliver services" is excluded from the statutory category of "independent judgment." This second rule is no less striking than the first, and is directly contrary to the text of the statute. *Every* supervisory function listed by the Act is accompanied by the statutory requirement that its exercise "requir[e] the use of independent judgment" before supervisory status will obtain, but the Board would apply its restriction upon "independent judgment" to just 1 of the 12 listed functions: "responsibly to direct." There is no apparent textual justification for this asymmetrical limitation, and the Board has offered none. Surely no conceptual justification can be found in the proposition that supervisors exercise professional, technical, or experienced judgment only when they direct other employees. Decisions "to hire, . . . suspend, lay off, recall, promote, discharge, . . . or discipline" other employees, must often depend upon that same judgment, which enables assessment of the employee's proficiency in performing his job. Yet in no opinion that we were able to discover has the Board held that a supervisor's judgment in hiring, disciplining, or promoting another employee ceased to be "independent judgment" because it depended upon the supervisor's professional or technical training or experience. When an employee exercises one of these functions with judgment that possesses a sufficient degree of independence, the Board invariably finds supervisory status.

The Board's refusal to apply its limiting interpretation of "independent judgment" to any supervisory function other than responsibly directing other employees is particularly troubling because just seven years ago we rejected the Board's interpretation of part three of the supervisory test that similarly was applied only to the same supervisory function. See *NLRB v. Health Care & Retirement Corp. of America* [*Health Care*], *supra.* . . .

The Board contends, however, that Congress incorporated the Board's categorical restrictions on "independent judgment" when it first added the term "supervisor" to the Act in 1947. We think history shows the opposite. . . . The Labor Management Relations Act, 1947 (Taft-Hartley Act) expressly excluded "supervisors" from the definition of "employees" and thereby from the protections of the Act. §2(3) (The term 'employee' . . . shall not include . . . any individual employed as a supervisor"); Taft-Hartley Act §14(a), as amended, ([N]o employer [covered by the Act] shall be compelled to deem individuals defined herein as supervisors as employees for the purpose of any law, either national or local, relating to collective bargaining").

Well before the Taft-Hartley Act added the term "supervisor" to the Act, however, the Board had already been defining it, because while the Board agreed that supervisors were protected by the 1935 Act, it also determined that they should not be placed in the same bargaining unit as the employees they oversaw. To distinguish the two groups, the Board defined "supervisors" as employees who "supervise or direct the work of [other] employees . . . , *and* who have authority to hire, promote, discharge, discipline, or otherwise effect changes in the status of such employees." *Douglas Aircraft Co.*, (emphasis added). The "and" bears emphasis because it was a true conjunctive: The Board consistently held that employees whose only supervisory function was directing the work of other employees were not "supervisors" within its test....

When the Taft-Hartley Act added the term "supervisor" to the Act in 1947, it largely borrowed the Board's definition of the term, with one notable exception: Whereas the Board required a supervisor to direct the work of other employees *and* perform another listed function, the Act permitted direction alone to suffice. "The term 'supervisor' means any individual having authority ... to hire, transfer, suspend, lay off, recall, promote, discharge, assign, reward, or discipline other employees, *or* responsibly to direct them, or to adjust their grievances." Taft-Hartley Act § 2(11) (emphasis added). Moreover, the Act assuredly did *not* incorporate the Board's current interpretation of the term "independent judgment" as applied to the function of responsible direction, since the Board had not yet developed that interpretation. It had had no reason to do so, because it had limited the category of supervisors more directly, by requiring functions *in addition* to responsible direction. It is the Act's alteration of precisely that aspect of the Board's jurisprudence that has pushed the Board into a running struggle to limit the impact of "responsibly to direct" on the number of employees qualifying for supervisory status — presumably driven by the policy concern that otherwise the proper balance of labor-management power will be disrupted.

It is upon that policy concern that the Board ultimately rests its defense of its interpretation of "independent judgment." In arguments that parallel those expressed by the dissent in *Health Care*, and which are adopted by Justice Stevens in this case, the Board contends that its interpretation is necessary to preserve the inclusion of "professional employees" within the coverage of the Act. See § 2(12). Professional employees by definition engage in work "involving the consistent exercise of discretion and judgment." § 2(11)(a)(ii). Therefore, the Board argues (enlisting dictum from our decision in *NLRB v. Yeshiva Univ.* that was rejected in *Health Care*), if judgment of that sort makes one a supervisor under § 2(11), then Congress's intent to include professionals in the Act will be frustrated, because "many professional employees (such as lawyers, doctors, and nurses) customarily give judgment-based direction to the less-skilled employees with whom they work." The problem with the argument is not the soundness of its labor policy. It is that the policy cannot be given effect through this statutory text. See *Health Care, supra* ("[T]here may be 'some tension between the Act's exclusion of [supervisory and] managerial employees and its inclusion of professionals,' but we find no authority for 'suggesting that that tension can be resolved' by distorting the statutory language in the manner proposed by the Board") (quoting *NLRB v. Yeshiva Univ.*). Perhaps the Board could offer a limiting interpretation of the supervisory function of responsible direction by distinguishing employees who direct the manner of others' performance of discrete *tasks* from employees who direct other *employees*, as § 2(11) requires. Certain of the Board's decisions appear to have drawn that distinction in the past, see, *e.g., Providence Hospital.* We have no occasion to consider it here, however, because the Board has carefully insisted that the proper interpretation of "responsibly to direct" is not at issue in this case.

What is at issue is the Board's contention that the policy of covering professional employees under the Act justifies the categorical exclusion of professional judgments from a term, "independent judgment," that naturally includes them. And further, that it justifies limiting this categorical exclusion to the supervisory function of responsibly directing other employees. These contentions contradict both the text and structure of the statute, and they contradict as well the rule of *Health Care* that the test for supervisory status applies no differently to professionals than to other employees. We therefore find the Board's interpretation unlawful. . . .

We may not enforce the Board's order by applying a legal standard the Board did not adopt, and, as we noted above, the Board has not asked us to do so. Hence, the Board's error in interpreting "independent judgment" precludes us from enforcing its order. . . . "Our conclusion that the Court of Appeals was correct to find the Board's test inconsistent with the statute . . . suffices to resolve the case." *Health Care,* supra. The judgment of the Court of Appeals is affirmed.

STEVENS, J., SOUTER, J., GINSBURG, J., and BREYER J., concurring in part and dissenting in part.

In my opinion, the [NLRB] correctly found that respondent, Kentucky River Community Care, Inc., failed to prove that the six registered nurses employed at its facility in Pippa Passes, Kentucky, are "supervisors" within the meaning of the [NLRA]. . . .

I

. . . .

[T]he only additional responsibility shouldered by the RNs when serving as building supervisors was that of contacting other employees if a shift was not fully staffed according to preestablished ratios not set by the RNs. However, the RNs had no authority to compel an employee to stay on duty or to come to work to fill a vacancy under threat of discipline.

With respect to the RNs' regular duties, while they might "occasionally request other employees to perform routine tasks," they had no "authority to take any action if the employee refuse[d] their directives." In their routine work, they had no "authority to hire, fire, reward, promote or independently discipline employees or to effectively recommend such action. They did not evaluate employees or take any action which would affect their employment status." Indeed, the RNs, even when serving as "building supervisors," for the most part "work[ed] independently and by themselves without any subordinates." . . . .

II

. . . .

[T]he NLRB interprets the term "independent judgment" as not including the exercise of ordinary professional or technical judgment in directing less-skilled employees to deliver services in accordance with employer-specified standards. . . . The Board's interpretation is a familiar one, which has been routinely applied in other employment contexts. Applying that interpretation, the NLRB has concluded that in some cases the employees in question are supervisors, and that in others they are not.

The term "independent judgment" is indisputably ambiguous, and it is settled law that the NLRB's interpretation of ambiguous language in the [NLRA] is entitled to deference.[6] Such deference is particularly appropriate when the statutory ambiguity is compounded by the use of one ambiguous term — "independent judgment" — to modify another, equally ambiguous term — namely, "responsibly to direct."

Moreover, since Congress has expressly provided that professional employees are entitled to the protection of the Act, there is good reason to resolve the ambiguities consistently with the Board's interpretation. At the same time that Congress acted to exclude supervisors from the NLRA's protection, it explicitly extended those same protections to professionals, who, by definition, engage in work that involves "the consistent exercise of discretion and judgment in its performance." § 152(12)(a)(ii). As this Court has acknowledged, the inclusion of professional employees and the exclusion of supervisors necessarily gives rise to some tension in the statutory text. Accordingly, if the term "supervisor" is construed too broadly, without regard for the statutory context, then Congress' inclusion of professionals within the Act's protections is effectively nullified. *See Health Care* (Ginsburg, J., dissenting). In my opinion, the Court's approach does precisely what it accuses the Board of doing — namely, reading one part of the statute to the exclusion of the other.

. . . .

[I]n a *tour de force* supported by little more than *ipse dixit*, the Court concludes that *no* deference is due the Board's evaluation of the "kind of judgment" that professional employees exercise. Thus, under the Court's view, it is impermissible for the Board to attach a different weight to a nurse's judgment that an employee should be reassigned or disciplined than to a nurse's judgment that the employee should take a patient's temperature, even if nurses routinely instruct others to take a patient's temperature but do not ordinarily reassign or discipline employees. The

---

6. The majority suggests that the Board's interpretation of the term "independent judgment" is particularly problematic in light of this Court's decision in *NLRB v. Health Care & Retirement Corp. of America*, 511 U.S. 571 (1994) *(HCR)*. But in *HCR*, this Court concluded that the terms "independent judgment" and "responsibly to direct" were ambiguous, while the term at issue in that case, "in the interest of the employer," was not. *Id.* at 579.

Court's approach finds no support in the text of the statute, and is inconsistent with our case law.

The Court further argues that the Board errs by not applying its limiting interpretation of the term "independent judgment" to all 12 functions identified by the statute as supervisory in nature. But of those 12, it is only "responsibly to direct" that is ambiguous and thus capable of swallowing the whole if not narrowly construed. The authority to "promote" or to "discharge," to use only two examples, is specific and readily identifiable. In contrast, the authority "responsibly to direct" is far more vague. Thus, it is only logical for the term "independent judgment" to take on different contours depending on the nature of the supervisory function at issue and its comparative ambiguity.

Simply put, these are quintessential examples of terms that the expert agency should be allowed to interpret in the light of the policies animating the statute. Because the Board's interpretation is fully consistent both with the statutory text and with the policy favoring collective bargaining by professional employees, this Court is obligated to uphold it.

III

. . . .

Accordingly, while I join Part II of the Court's opinion, I respectfully dissent from its holding. I would reverse the judgment of the Court of Appeals.

———————

The majority opinions in *Health Care* and *Kentucky River* both acknowledged that the terms "independent judgment" and "responsibly to direct" in § 2(11)'s definition of "supervisor" were ambiguous. Ordinarily, textual ambiguity gives the administrative agency charged with administering the statute broad discretion to define those terms. Yet, in *Health Care* and *Kentucky River*, the Supreme Court held that the Board's interpretations extended beyond the scope of its discretion because they were inconsistent with the statutory language.

Providence Hospital, 320 N.L.R.B. 717 (1996), was decided after *Health Care* but before *Kentucky River*. In *Providence Hospital*, the Board took up but offered no final answer to the questions of how to interpret "independent judgment," "responsibly to direct," "assign," and "routine." The Board acknowledged a need to "harmonize" the provisions of § 2(11) and (12), but failed to offer definitions accomplishing that result. A decade later, in three decisions nicknamed the "Oakwood Trilogy" — *Oakwood Healthcare Inc.*, 348 N.L.R.B. 686 (2006); *Croft Metals, Inc.*, 348 N.L.R.B. 717 (2006); and *Golden Crest Health Care Center*, 348 N.L.R.B. 727 (2006) — the Board revisited the definitions of "independent judgment," "responsibly to direct," and "assign," and provided specific definitions drawn, at least in part, from dictionaries. This methodology suggested a textualist approach to this statutory interpretation task.

The Board construed "assign" to "[refer] to 'the act of designating an employee to a place (such as a location, department, or wing), appointing an employee to a time (such as a shift or overtime period), or giving significant overall duties, i.e., tasks, to an employee." *Oakwood Healthcare Inc.*, 348 N.L.R.B. at 717, 721. The Board interpreted "responsibly to direct," as several Courts of Appeals had, to require "accountability": "the employer delegated to the putative supervisor the authority to direct the work and the authority to take corrective action, if necessary. It also must be shown that there is a prospect of adverse consequences for the putative supervisor if he/she does not take these steps." *Id.* at 721. The Board's more elaborate exposition of "independent judgment" included employee decision-making untethered to "detailed instructions, whether set forth in company policies or rules, the verbal instructions of a higher authority, or in the provisions of a collective-bargaining agreement." *Id.* at 721.

In *Oakwood Healthcare Inc.*, 348 N.L.R.B. at 694, the Board also explained that an employee must spend a "regular and substantial portion of his/her time performing supervisory functions" in order to be excluded from the Act's coverage. "'[R]egular' means according to a pattern or schedule, as opposed to sporadic substitution." *Id.* "Substantial" means at least 10 percent to 15 percent of the employee's total work time, although the Board expressly disclaimed the adoption of any "strict numerical definition of substantiality." *Id.*

The Taft-Hartley Act, and Justice Douglas's dissent in *Packard Motor* which provided the rationale for § 2(11), assume a certain hierarchical structure in the workplace which was common during the immediate post-war period. However, in the 1980s, management theory and practice (particularly among large employers) embraced efforts to engage both unionized and non-union employees in employee participation programs of various kinds. President Bill Clinton's Secretaries of Labor and Commerce established the Commission on the Future of Worker-Management Relations, under the leadership of former Secretary of Labor John Dunlop, to study these changes, among other things. The "Dunlop Commission" found that these programs, which ranged from "quality circles" and "total quality management" to team-based production and "self-directed work teams," flattened hierarchies and engaged front-line workers directly in decision-making. Some workers were able to make recommendations to senior management regarding workplace safety and health. Others assumed decision-making responsibilities about production processes and product quality, among other topics. Some entities were ad hoc and lasted only for a period of months. Other employers had expansive and long-lasting worker-management committees. John Thomas Dunlop et. al., *Commission on the Future of Worker-Management Relations, Fact Finding Report 2-14*, 29–42 (May 1994) [*hereinafter* Fact Finding Report], *available at* http://digitalcommons.ilr.cornell.edu /key_workplace/276/; *see also* U.S. Department of Labor, *Commission on the Future of Worker-Management Relations, Report and Recommendations 61–62* (Dec. 1994).

As the Dunlop Commission's Report described it, "some employee participation processes that begin as production or quality focused problem-solving groups evolve over time to take on issues and responsibilities that in the past would have been handled by a supervisor or manager." Fact Finding Report at 39; *see also* KATH-ERINE V.W. STONE, FROM WIDGETS TO DIGITS: EMPLOYMENT REGULATION FOR THE CHANGING WORKPLACE 87–116 (2004). In the process, front-line workers stepped into the traditional roles of supervisors and other white collar workers whose jobs, in turn, were frequently eliminated. PETER CAPPELLI, THE NEW DEAL AT WORK (1999); PAUL OSTERMAN, SECURING PROSPERITY 90–93, 146–48 (1999). The Dunlop Commission focused on how these employee participation programs were regulated by § 8(a)(2) (*see* Chapter 5), but the Commission's findings may also be relevant to the scope of the Act's coverage. In light of the broad definition of "supervisor" adopted in *Health Care* and *Kentucky River*, are the employees who participate in some or all of these employee participation programs exempt from the Act's coverage? Should the definition of "supervisor" be adjusted to reflect the realities of modern management practice that could not have been known to Justice Douglas when he wrote his dissent in *Packard Motor* or Congress when it enacted the Taft-Hartley Act? Does § 2(11) allow for such an adjustment?

Notes

1. The Democratic minority in the U.S. House of Representatives objected to the definition of "supervisor" in the House's version of the Taft-Hartley Act, in part, on the grounds that "supervisors play only a minor role in this definition, which clearly includes all persons having only slight authority such as pushers, gang bosses, leaders, second hands, and a host of similarly placed persons with no actual supervisory status. It is sufficiently broad to cover a carpenter with a helper." H.R. REP. No. 245 (1947) (CONF. REP.) *reprinted in* I LEGISLATIVE HISTORY OF THE LABOR-MANAGEMENT RELATIONS ACT, 1947, at 362 (1985). The report on the Senate's version of the supervisor exemption—the version that Congress ultimately adopted—seemingly responded to this criticism: "the committee has not been unmindful of the fact that certain employees with minor supervisory duties have problems which may justify their inclusion in the act. It has therefore distinguished between straw bosses, leadmen, set-up men, and other minor supervisory employees, on the one hand, and the supervisor vested with genuine management prerogative." S. REP. No. 105 (1947) *reprinted in* I LEGISLATIVE HISTORY OF THE LABOR-MANAGEMENT RELATIONS ACT, 1947, at 410 (1985). Is the result in *Kentucky River* consistent with this legislative history? Should it matter whether it is?

2. One of the principal disagreements between the majority in *Kentucky River* and the dissent was the propriety of deferring to the Board's decisions. Did the majority correctly deny *Chevron* deference to the Board's decisions in *Health Care* and *Kentucky River*?

3. Do the definitions propounded by the Board in *Oakwood Health Care* "harmonize" §§ 2(11) and 2(12)? How would a Board member employing a purposivist approach have defined these terms?

4. *Health Care, Kentucky River*, and all three cases in the *Oakwood Trilogy* involved nurses and a health care setting; however, as Problem 2.1 suggests, these

cases apply to workers in other settings as well. *See, e.g., Pub. Serv. Co. v. NLRB*, 405 F.3d 1071 (10th Cir. 2005) (revenue-protection analyst and investigators); *NLRB v. Dole Fresh Vegetables, Inc.*, 334 F.3d 478 (6th Cir. 2003) (maintenance employees); *Entergy Mississippi, Inc.*, 367 N.L.R.B. No. 109 (2019) (dispatchers); *Riverboat Serv. of Ind., Inc.*, 345 N.L.R.B. 1286 (2005) (Assistant Chief Engineers); *Dynamic Sci., Inc.*, 334 N.L.R.B. 391 (2001) (artillery testers).

5. The Railway Labor Act does not categorically exclude supervisors from coverage. Rather, "subordinate officials" are covered while more senior managers are not. *See* 45 U.S.C. §§ 151, Fifth, 181. As the National Mediation Board explained in *Air Florida, Inc.*, 7 N.M.B. No. 89 at 166 (1979), "[t]he LMRA provides a detailed list of power, stated in the disjunctive, which indicate supervisory status, and provides that employer cannot be compelled to recognize supervisor representatives. On the other hand, the RLA excludes only those who are officials of the carrier permitting many first-line supervisors and leads to enjoy the rights granted by the Act. Only after the Board determines that the duties and authority of a supervisor attain a minimum level of responsibility will the supervisor be excluded."

6. Under the NLRA, supervisors may be protected from certain actions by their employers when covered employees' § 7 rights would be infringed by the employers' actions. For example, an employer may not discharge a supervisor for testifying against the employer at an NLRB or grievance proceeding or discharge a supervisor for refusing to commit ULPs or failing to prevent unionization. But supervisors are not protected when they engage in protected concerted activity alongside covered employees. *See Parker-Robb Chevrolet, Inc.*, 262 N.L.R.B. 402 (1982).

Problem 2.2

Alassippi Power & Light (APL) is a privately-owned utility providing gas and electric services to residential and commercial customers. Since 1946, the Utility Workers Union has represented APL's Operations, Production and Maintenance (OPM) employees and, in a separate bargaining unit, its meter readers. The union now seeks to represent three workers in APL's "revenue protection unit" (RPU): one revenue-protection analyst and two revenue-protection investigators. This unit responds to revenue losses caused by the use of energy for which APL has not been paid. The collective-bargaining agreements covering the OPM employees and meter readers provide bonuses for employees who find unauthorized energy diversions. Bonuses are capped at $15,000.00 per revenue loss. The RPU employees do not share in the bonus; rather, each receives a fixed annual salary. They are supervised by their parent company's personnel in another state.

An employee who discovers an apparent energy diversion enters a report into the company's computer system. The RPU analyst reviews these reports daily. If the computer system determines that the energy use was unauthorized, but there has not been a significant revenue loss, the analyst records a $10 bonus for the employee who found the energy diversion. When there has been a significant revenue loss, the analyst refers the case to the billing department which decides whether to add charges to the customer's bill. The analyst has discretion to decide whether the revenue loss is "significant." If it is, then the analyst records a bonus for the employee who found the diversion equal to the greater of $10 or 10 percent of the additional charge to the customer. If further investigation is required, the analyst assigns the case to one of the two RPU investigators who prepared a report for the analyst. The RPU investigators visit the site with a meter reader who verifies any theft or equipment malfunction and corrects the problem. The RPU investigator collects and preserves any physical evidence of theft. If the meter reader's findings correspond with the report of the employee who found the energy diversion, then the RPU investigator determines the size of that employee's bonus using the same formula described above. The RPU analyst reviews the investigator's report, indicates whether the reporting employee is eligible for a bonus in a cover note, and then forwards the note and report to the billing department.

OPM employees and meter readers can file grievances if they believe that they were improperly denied a bonus or that the amount of a bonus should have been higher. The RPU investigators and analyst report to APL managers how they determined bonus eligibility or how they calculated the amount of energy used. They may be asked to review the matter based on information from the employee, and an adjustment may be made.

You are APL's labor counsel. The general counsel has asked you whether the three RPU employees are protected by the Act. What is your best advice?

2. The Supervisory Exemption in the Public Sector

Some public-sector labor statutes have a supervisory exception which uses language identical or substantially identical to that in the private sector. *See, e.g., State, Dept. of Personnel v. Iowa Public Employment Rel. Bd.*, 560 N.W.2d 560 (Iowa 1997) (definition of "supervisory employee" in state public-sector labor statute excluding supervisory employees was taken from the NLRA, and thus federal interpretations of the NLRA are persuasive as to interpretations of statute); *Bd. of Tr., Robert H. Champlin Mem'l Library v. Rhode Island*, 694 A.2d 1185 (R.I. 1997) (both statutory language of Rhode Island statute covering municipal employees and policy concerns indicate that private-sector precedent should be used in determining who is an excluded "supervisor").

Often, however, public-sector jurisdictions have significantly different rules regarding supervisors and collective bargaining. First, some states have statutory language which excludes supervisors but uses a narrower definition of "supervisor" than the NLRA, thus excluding fewer employees from the statute's coverage. For example, the Illinois Public Relations Act excludes supervisors, but defines "supervisor" as follows:

> "Supervisor" is an employee whose principal work is substantially different from that of his subordinates and who has authority, in the interest of the employer, to hire, transfer, suspend, lay off, recall, promote, discharge,

direct, reward, or discipline employees, or to adjust their grievances, or to effectively recommend such action, if the exercise of such authority is not of a merely routine or clerical nature, but requires the consistent use of independent judgment. Except with respect to police employment, the term "supervisor" includes only those individuals who devote a preponderance of their employment time to exercising [such] authority . . . 5 ILL. COMP. STAT. 315/3(r) (2001).

How might this language limit who could be found to be a "supervisor"? *See City of Freeport v. Illinois State Labor Relations Bd.*, 554 N.E.2d 155 (Ill. 1990). Also, can you think of a justification, or at least a reason, why this statute contains a somewhat different test to determine whether police employees, unique among all public workers, are supervisors?

The Ohio statute, OHIO REV. CODE §4117.01(C)(10), explicitly excludes supervisors and, in defining supervisors in §4117.01(F), gives as the general rule the text from the NLRA exclusion. But §4117.01(C)(10) then adds some exceptions, including the following:

(1) Employees of school districts who are department chairpersons or consulting teachers shall not be deemed supervisors; (2) with respect to members of a police or fire department, no person shall be deemed a supervisor except the chief of the department or those individuals who, in the absence of the chief, are authorized to exercise the authority and perform the duties of the chief of the department; and (3) with respect to faculty members of a state institution of higher education, heads of departments or divisions are supervisors; however, no other faculty member or group of faculty members is a supervisor solely because the faculty member or group of faculty members participate in decisions with respect to courses, curriculum, personnel, or other matters of academic policy.

What do you think the practical effects of these exceptions are? Also, are there good reasons to ensure these employees are not excluded as supervisors under the public-sector labor law?

Additionally, the statute applicable to federal employees, the Federal Service Labor Management Relations Statute, 5 U.S.C.A. §7101 (2007), generally uses NLRA rules to determine supervisor status, but if a bargaining unit includes nurses or firefighters, an employee is a supervisor only if the employee spends a preponderance of employment time exercising supervisory authority. 5 U.S.C. §7103(a)(10). Again, what is the purpose of such an exception to the general rule, and is it a good idea?

Second, as shown below, some states go further and do not exclude supervisors at all from their public-sector labor statutes. Are there policy or practical concerns which distinguish public-sector and private-sector employment in this regard? Consider the discussion in the following case.

New Jersey Turnpike Authority v. American Federation of State, County and Municipal Employees, Council 73

Supreme Court of New Jersey
150 N.J. 331, 696 A.2d 585 (1997)

STEIN, J.

... Chapter 303 provided public employees with the right, freely and without fear of penalty or reprisal, to form, join and assist any employee organization or to refrain from any such activity. *L.* 1968, *c.* 303, §7 (codified as amended at *N.J.S.A.* 34A:13A-5.3). Negotiating units formed pursuant to Chapter 303 were to be defined with due regard for the community of interest among the employees concerned. ... *Ibid.* Supervisors having the power to hire, discharge, discipline, or to effectively recommend the same could generally organize so long as supervisory units did not admit nonsupervisory personnel. *Ibid.* ...

In 1972, the Legislature attempted to amend Chapter 303 by enacting Assembly Bill No. 520, in part to define PERC's authority to decide unfair labor practice questions. Governor Cahill conditionally vetoed the bill. The Governor's veto message included several proposed definitions intended to broaden the exclusions to the Act to make those exclusions more consistent with private sector labor law. The Legislature finally amended Chapter 303 in 1974. ... Those amendments, popularly known as Chapter 123, either rejected or modified Governor Cahill's proposed definitions.

The Governor had proposed that supervisors, whom he recommended not be permitted to organize, be defined as follows:

> The term supervisor means any individual having authority, in the interest of the public employer, to hire, transfer, suspend, lay off, recall, evaluate, promote, discharge, assign, reward, or discipline other employees, or responsibly to direct them, or to adjust their grievances or effectively to recommend such action, if in connection with the foregoing the exercise of such authority is not of a merely routine or clerical nature, but requires the use of independent judgment.

The Legislature rejected that proposal, retained the following clause from Chapter 303, and continued to permit supervisors to organize so long as supervisory and non-supervisory employees were not in the same unit:

> [A] supervisor [has] the power to hire, discharge, discipline, or to effectively recommend the same ... (codified at *N.J.S.A.* 34:13A-5.3). ...

Finally, Chapter 303 had provided that the term employee included [any] public employee ... except elected officials, *heads and deputy heads of departments and agencies*, and members of boards and commissions. ... *L.* 1968, *c.* 303, §4 (emphasis added). In enacting Chapter 123, the Legislature interpreted employee to exclude elected officials, members of boards and commissions, *managerial executives and confidential employees. L.* 1984, *c.* 123, § 2 (codified at *N.J.S.A.* 34:13A-3(d)). . . .

Although we recognize, as did the Appellate Division, that a public employer is entitled to a loyal management team, the concerns facing a public employer differ somewhat from those facing a private employer. A private employer's interest focuses primarily on the maximization of profit; the employees' interests emphasize the enhancement of their compensation and benefits. To the extent that private employers can reduce wages, the profits available to business owners increase. A private sector employer must have the undivided loyalty of a relatively large group of employees, including supervisors. The size of that management group becomes particularly important if private non-supervisory workers exercise their legal right to strike; an employer should have a workforce sufficient to sustain at least a minimal level of operation. For those reasons, federal private sector labor law specifically excludes supervisors from its definition of employee and does not permit supervisors to unionize. . . .

A somewhat different labor relations dynamic prevails in the public sector. Although public sector labor negotiations over compensation and other terms and conditions of employment frequently are protracted and adversarial, the elimination of the right to strike exerts a restraining influence on the negotiation process. Moreover, in comparison to the private sector, our impression is that public employers and public employees generally share a stronger common interest in the mission of the organization. In affording supervisors organizational rights under the Act, we infer that the Legislature appropriately took into account the differences between private and public sector labor negotiations.

The Legislature also recognized several other distinctions between private and public sector labor law. As noted, public employees may not strike. Furthermore, the scope of negotiations in the public sector is narrower than that in the private sector. *See N.J.S.A.* 34:13A-5.3 (referring to public employees' negotiating rights concerning rules governing working conditions . . . grievances, disciplinary disputes, and other terms and conditions of employment). In *Township of West Windsor v. PERC*, this Court held that

> employee proposals seeking to influence the actions of a public employer when it acts in a governmental capacity — rather than as an employer — are most appropriately presented through the political process and not through the labor relations process.
>
> [T]he preferred access for public employees resulting from the statutory requirement of mandatory good faith negotiation and compulsory grievance presentation, with its consequent enhancement of the effectiveness of their voice in governmental decision-making, is inappropriate with respect to matters which do not affect the terms and conditions of public employment. Only when government acts in the capacity of an employer, as opposed to discharging governmental policy-making functions, is

such preferred access necessary to protect the legitimate interests of public employees in the determination of the terms and conditions of their employment. *[Id.]*. . . .

The Appellate Division notes that, under Chapter 303, supervisors, defined as those having the power to hire, discharge, discipline, or effectively recommend the same, were permitted to organize. The court concluded that "[s]uch supervisors, we think, refer to those persons commonly understood as on-line supervisors." The court acknowledged that the Legislature had rejected Governor Cahill's broad definition of supervisors together with his recommendation that supervisors be excluded from membership in negotiating units. The court found it significant, however, that the Legislature, when it enacted Chapter 123, did not alter its definition of supervisors beyond that found in Chapter 303. Based on that analysis, the Appellate Division apparently found that only on-line supervisors, a term that presumably includes only first-level supervisors, may join a negotiating unit. We find that conclusion to be inconsistent with the statutory scheme. Higher-level supervisors who are not elected officials or members or boards or commissions and who do not fall within the managerial executive or confidential employee exclusions may organize; in the event that an actual or potential substantial conflict of interest exists between different levels of supervisors, separate supervisory units should be formed. . . .

Problem 2.3

A number of states do not exclude supervisors from their public-sector labor laws (*e.g.*, Alaska, California, Florida, Michigan, Minnesota, New Hampshire, and New Jersey). What are the strongest arguments for and against the proposition that public-sector labor laws should generally cover, rather than exclude, supervisors? Alternatively, should public-sector labor laws cover some but not all supervisors, as in Illinois and Ohio? If so, which supervisors should be allowed to bargain collectively? Finally, if you believe that at least some supervisors in the public sector should be covered under labor laws, should some or all supervisors in the private sector be given bargaining rights, or is there something generally different about the public sector?

Notes

1. States which allow supervisors to bargain collectively typically do not allow supervisors to be in the same bargaining unit as the employees the supervisors supervise (although a few states permit police and firefighter supervisors, such as sergeants, in the same bargaining unit as those they supervise). *See, e.g., In re New Hampshire Retirement System*, 203 L.R.R.M. (BNA) 3231 (NH, May 21, 2015) (individuals in a bargaining unit given genuine supervisory powers had to be excluded from bargaining unit containing employees the individuals supervised). For more on bargaining unit issues, see Chapter 7.

2. In New Hampshire, while supervisors are protected under the state public-sector labor law, not only must they be in a separate unit from the bargaining unit

which represents employees they supervise, but also the supervisors' bargaining unit cannot be affiliated with the same parent union as the bargaining unit of the supervised employees. *Appeal of Manchester Board of School Committee*, 129 N.H. 151, 523 A.2d 114 (1987) (school principals could not be represented by the Manchester Education Association [MEA] because the teachers they supervised were represented by the MEA, and this could lead, for example, to commingling on the same negotiating teams). For a Michigan decision reaching the opposite result, see *City of Highland Park*, 6 MPER ¶ 24062 (Mich. Emp. Rel. Comm. 1993) ("[W]e have long held that a union which represents nonsupervisory employees is not barred from representing a separate unit of supervisory employees of the same employer as long as the union maintains separate locals or other separate organizational structures . . . the potential conflict of interest inherent in a union representing both supervisors and nonsupervisors of the same employer must be balanced against the right of the employees to freely select their representative."). Which is the better approach?

3. Assuming supervisors are allowed to bargain in a bargaining unit separate from that which represents the employees they supervise, there is still the question of how "supervisor" is defined. Some states allow supervisors to bargain collectively in separate bargaining units and use the private-sector definition to determine who is a supervisor. *See, e.g., City of Adrian and AFSCME Michigan Council 25*, 16 MPER ¶ 61 (Mich. Emp. Rel. Comm. 2003) ("Although [the Public Employment Relations Act] contains no definition of the term 'supervisor,' we have often utilized the definition contained in the [NLRA]."); *Detroit Public Schools and International Union of Operating Engineers, Local 547*, 18 MPER ¶ 33 (Mich. Emp. Rel. Comm. 2005) ("hub supervisors" shared a community of interest with a supervisory bargaining unit as opposed to a non-supervisory unit). California uses the same approach for educational employees. *See East Whittier City Elem. Sch. Dist. and East Whittier Administrators and Supervisors Ass'n*, 30 PERC ¶ 2 (Cal. PERB 2005) (using private-sector definition of supervisor, but allowing supervisors to form separate bargaining units under the relevant statute).

4. In contrast, Missouri both allows supervisors to form unions *and* uses a narrower definition of "supervisor" than is used in the private sector. In *Central County Emergency 911 v. IAFF Local 2665*, 967 S.W.2d 696 (Mo. Ct. App. 1998), the court held that it was not bound by private-sector definitions of "supervisor" and instead, applying a "seven factor" test, held that certain employees were not supervisors. While the employees involved, titled "shift supervisors," did "have a role in disciplining, evaluating and hiring, they were not empowered to hire, fire and promote employees on their own volition." 976 S.W.2d 696, 701. Also, the shift supervisors and the dispatchers they supervised "performed the same duties at least fifty percent of the time." *Id.* The "shift supervisors" performed "incidentally to their work, a number of supervisory functions. Specifically, they are in charge of the facility on the second and third shifts, ensure proper staffing, monitor the dispatch work . . . to ensure proper performance, issue verbal and written warnings without prior

approval, conduct performance evaluations, and may be consulted in matters of hiring. However, the factors just listed are not enough to make them supervisors." *Id.* at 701–02. Thus, the shift supervisors could be included in a "rank and file" union and would not have to be separated into a separate, supervisory unit.

5. Are the concerns about how narrowly or broadly "supervisor" is defined the same in a state that allows supervisors to bargain as in a state which excludes supervisors from its bargaining law? Why or why not?

6. Other variations exist. Pennsylvania's Public Employee Relations Act uses the private-sector definition of supervisor, excludes supervisors from bargaining, but gives limited "meet and confer" rights to "first line" supervisors. *See Curley v. Bd. of Sch. Dir. of Greater Johnstown Sch. Dist.*, 641 A.2d 719 (Pa. Commw. Ct. 1994); 43 Pa. Cons. Stat. Ann. § 1101.301(6) (using a definition of "supervisor" substantively the same as in the NLRA).

Problem 2.4

Review the facts of Problem 2.2 above. Now, assume that Alassippi Power is owned and operated by the State of Alassippi. Assume also that this state generally allows public-sector employees, including employees of the state government, to bargain, unless the state public-sector labor statute specifically excludes them from coverage. Should the employees described above be treated differently because they are public employees?

E. Non-Statutory Exemptions

The Taft-Hartley Act required use of the common-law test to determine whether workers are "employees" and expressly exempted "independent contractors" and "supervisors," as well as "any individual employed by an employer subject to the Railway Labor Act . . . or by any other person who is not an employer as [defined by § 2(2)]." 29 U.S.C. § 152(3), *amended by* Labor Management Relations Act, Pub. L. No. 80-101, 61 Stat. 136 (1947). After the Taft-Hartley Act, workers would be forced to prove their way into a protected class of individuals entitled to the Act's protections and access to the Board's processes.

Congress did not give an explicit answer to the question of whether there are any further limits on the definition of "employee." The Supreme Court has suggested at times that workers are included within the scope of § 2(3)'s coverage unless specifically excluded by the statute. *See, e.g., Sure-Tan, Inc. v. NLRB*, 467 U.S. 883, 891–92 (1984). But the Board and the Supreme Court have also, at times, read the Taft-Hartley Act as impliedly rejecting *Hearst Publications'* broadly inclusive understanding of the NLRA in general and § 2(3) in particular—that is, they have interpreted the Taft-Hartley Act's silence to exclude still more categories of workers from the Act's coverage. This section will consider the non-statutory exemptions that have been created or confirmed by the Board and reviewing courts since Congress enacted the Taft-Hartley Act.

1. "Managerial" and "Confidential" Employees in the Public and Private Sectors

Before the Taft-Hartley Act and Justice Douglas's dissent in *Packard Motor*, the Board had excluded "managerial employees" from bargaining units of non-managerial employees. *See, e.g., Consolidated Vultee Aircraft Corp. (Downey, Cal.)*, 69 N.L.R.B. 860 (1946); *Pacific Gas & Elec. Co.*, 69 N.L.R.B. 258 (1946); *Pennsylvania Power & Light Co.*, 64 N.L.R.B. 874 (1945). The Board defined "managerial employees" to include all "who are in a position to formulate, determine, and effectuate management policies . . . [because] they express and make operative the decisions of management." *Ford Motor Co.*, 66 N.L.R.B. 1317, 1322 (1946). Yet, the Taft-Hartley Act made no mention of "managerial employees" in § 2(11)'s exclusion of "supervisors." Nonetheless, after the Taft-Hartley Act, the Board went farther and excluded managerial employees from coverage for any purpose. *See generally Minneapolis Soc. of Fine Arts*, 194 N.L.R.B. 371 (1971); *White Cross Stores, Inc.*, 186 N.L.R.B. 492 (1970); *G.K. Chevrolet, Inc.*, 176 N.L.R.B. 416 (1969). The Board subsequently reconsidered and limited the exclusion only to those managerial employees involved in the creation or implementation of the employer's labor relations policies. *See NLRB v. North Arkansas Elec. Cooperative, Inc.*, 412 F.2d 324 (8th Cir. 1969).

The Supreme Court disagreed. In **NLRB v. Bell Aerospace**, 416 U.S. 267 (1974), the Court held that managerial employees are entirely excluded from the Act's coverage. Although the Court acknowledged the Taft-Hartley Act's silence on "managerial employees," it explained this silence as resulting from Congress' conclusion that managers are "so clearly outside the Act that no specific exclusionary provision was thought necessary"—that is, they were "impliedly excluded." 416 U.S. 267, 283–84. In essence, the Court adopted Justice Douglas's assertion that covering managerial employees would effect a fundamental change in industrial philosophy inconsistent with the Act's purposes. *Id.*; *see also* Marion G. Crain, *Building Solidarity Through Expansion of NLRA Coverage: A Blueprint for Worker Empowerment*, 74 MINN. L. REV. 953 (1990) (critiquing this rationale, among others). As a result, employees who are in a position to formulate, determine, and effectuate management policies are generally excluded from NLRA coverage. *Bell Aerospace*, 416 U.S. at 288. For similar reasons, "confidential employees" with a "labor nexus"—those "who assist and act in a confidential capacity to persons who formulate, determine, and effectuate management policies in the field of labor relations" by expressing and making operative the decisions of their employer, and who have discretion in the performance of their jobs—are excluded from collective-bargaining units, although other employees with access to confidential information are not. *NLRB v. Hendricks Rural Elec. Membership Corp.*, 454 U.S. 170 (1981). The Court did not address the question of whether "confidential employees" are exempt from the Act's coverage for all purposes.

In **NLRB v. Yeshiva University**, 444 U.S. 672 (1980), the Supreme Court concluded that a private university's full-time faculty members were exempt "managerial employees." The Board had certified faculty bargaining units for almost a decade on the theory that academics are "professional employees" whose coverage is assured by § 2(12). The *Yeshiva University* Court rejected this conclusion based on the same reasoning later employed in *Kentucky River*: professionals are no less subject to exclusion as managerial employees than are other workers. 444 U.S. 672, 684. Given Yeshiva faculty members' "absolute authority" over academic affairs like course offerings, scheduling, and teaching assignments, their ability to determine teaching methods, grading policies, and matriculation standards, and their power to decide which students would be admitted, retained, and graduated, among other things, the Court observed that "it is difficult to imagine decisions more managerial than these." *Id.* at 686.

The Board reconsidered and modified the rule of *Yeshiva University* in *Pacific Lutheran University*, 361 N.L.R.B. No. 157 (2014) "to answer the question whether faculty in a university setting actually or effectively exercise control over decision making pertaining to central policies of the university such that they are aligned with management." *Id.* at 14. According to the Board, the overarching determination in the Court's decision in *Yeshiva University* was that "the faculty in question 'substantially and pervasively' operated the university by exercising extensive control over decision-making and playing a 'crucial role . . . in determining . . . central policies of the institution.'" *Id.* at 16. Thus, the Board announced that it would examine "the breadth and depth of the faculty's authority at the university" giving more weight to "those areas of policy making that affect the university as a whole, such as the product produced, the terms on which it is offered, and the customers served," and whether "the faculty actually exercise control or make effective recommendations over those areas of policy." *Id.* at 17. The Board applied its modified test for managerial status in *University of Southern California. See* 365 N.L.R.B. No. 89 (2017). The D.C. Circuit refused to enforce the Board's order based on its conclusion that *Pacific Lutheran*'s actual majority control rule conflicted with *Yeshiva. See University of Southern California v. NLRB*, 918 F.3d 126, 127 (D.C. Cir. 2019). The case has been remanded to the Board for further consideration.

Notes

1. Public-sector labor laws also routinely exclude confidential and managerial employees. As to confidential employees, public-sector laws tend to follow private-sector rules and definitions. *See, e.g. Metropolitan Alliance of Police, Chapter 294 v. Illinois Labor Relations Board*, No. 1-17-1322 (Sept. 28, 2018) (investigators at the Illinois Central Management Services and Department of Corrections properly excluded as confidential employees, because, among other things, investigators had access to emails that might contain confidential collective bargaining information).

A rare exception is *Central County Emergency 911, infra*, which stated that Missouri was not bound by NLRA precedent in defining "confidential," and articulated a somewhat broader definition (can you think of a policy reason supporting that approach?). The managerial exclusions in public-sector laws often require the employee to be truly high up in the public employer's hierarchy. For example,

§ 201(7)(a) of New York's law excludes as managers only those "(i) who formulate policy or (ii) who may reasonably be required on behalf of the public employer to assist directly in the preparation for and conduct of collective negotiations or to have a major role in the administration of agreements or in personnel adminis-tration provided that such role is not of a routine or clerical nature and requires the exercise of independent judgment." Further, "employees may be designated as confidential only if they are persons who assist and act in a confidential capacity to managerial employees described in clause (ii)." N.Y. Civ. Serv. Law § 201.

2. Also, a number of public-sector jurisdictions reject *Yeshiva University* and cover most college and university faculty. For example, Ohio Rev. Code §§ 4117.01(F)(3) and 4117.01(L) explicitly state, respectively, that faculty members in state institu-tions of higher learning are not supervisors solely because they participate in deci-sions with respect to courses, curriculum, personnel, or other matters of academic policy; and they are not managers because they are involved in the formulation or implementation of academic or institution policy. Are there principled reasons why labor laws should treat faculty members in public universities differently from those in private universities? If so, what are those reasons? If not, should labor laws cover most college and university faculty or not?

3. For a general discussion of the interaction between the exclusion of "manage-rial employees" and § 2(12)'s treatment of "professional employees," *see* David Rab-ban, *Distinguishing Excluded Managers from Covered Professionals Under the NLRA*, 89 Colum. L. Rev. 1775 (1989).

4. Can the reasoning of *Bell Aerospace* and *Yeshiva University* be summarized as follows: if the worker's loyalty is owed to the owners of the enterprise, then Congress intended that they be excluded from the Act as de facto "employers," while other workers who would not face a conflict of interest may organize based on loyalties shared with their co-workers? *See* George Feldman, *Unions, Solidarity, and Class: The Limits of Liberal Labor Law*, 15 Berkeley J. Emp. & Lab. L. 187, 217–19 (1994); *see also* Crain, *supra* (critiquing the "loyalty" and "conflict of interest" rationales for the "managerial" and "supervisory" exemptions). Archibald Cox questioned this rea-soning soon after the Taft-Hartley Act passed: "One may wonder . . . whether union activity by foremen was not itself a reaction to the failure of management to follow the teachings on which it has so strenuously insisted. If top management has learned from its recent experience that the foremen's problems are its own and accords fore-men a status and measure of individual dignity commensurate with the functions that it theoretically assigns them, there should be little occasion to seek recognition and bargaining rights by economic strength." Archibald Cox, *Some Aspects of the Labor Management Relations Act of 1947*, 61 Harv. L. Rev. 1, 5 (1947). As Cox noted, some supervisory personnel wanted the Act's protections before the Taft-Hartley Act excluded them. Do supervisors and managers need the Act's protections? Would coverage serve the Act's purposes? Do owners owe managers and supervisors the same loyalty which the Supreme Court concluded these workers owe to owners? If so, does the Act have anything to say about the nature of this relationship? Should it?

5. *Bell Aerospace* and *Yeshiva University* are both predicated on an understanding of industrial organization that is many decades old. As noted above, industrial organization has changed dramatically in the intervening years. As *Pacific Lutheran University* seems to acknowledge, the role of some faculty members in university and college decision-making has changed, as well, with the advent of more contingent and adjunct faculty members teaching in these institutions. Even before *Pacific Lutheran* University, but following *Yeshiva University*, the Board found some faculty-member bargaining units appropriate. *See, e.g., Bradford College*, 261 N.L.R.B. 565 (1982). Should the changes to academic institutions' and industrial employers' organizational structures cause us to reconsider the treatment of managers, and perhaps supervisors, in private-sector labor law?

6. Is the reasoning in *Bell Aerospace* consistent with Justice Scalia's textualist account in *Kentucky River, supra*, of how to resolve the tension between §§ 2(11) and 2(12)? Justice Scalia argued that the text of § 2(11) cannot bear an interpretation giving special treatment to professional employees in the context of determining who is a "supervisor" despite § 2(12). In contrast, the *Bell Aerospace* Court excluded "managerial employees" from coverage even though § 2(11) makes no mention of managers who do not engage in any of the 12 supervisory activities it lists. Is *Bell Aerospace* a purposive interpretation of § 2(3)? How would a textualist justice determine whether managerial employees are exempt?

Problem 2.5

Crown, Cork & Seal operates an aluminum can manufacturing facility with 150 employees in Sugar Land, Texas. It uses a management system which delegates to employees substantial authority to operate the plant. There are four "production teams" which involve every non-supervisory employee (thirty-two employees per team plus one manager). The teams have "decide and do" authority on subjects including production, quality, training, attendance, safety, maintenance, and discipline short of suspension or discharge. For example, the teams administer the plant's absenteeism program, decide safety issues, and can call back product if it is below their quality standards. All decisions are reached by consensus.

Three committees are organizationally superior to the production teams: (1) the Organizational Review Board monitors plant policies, suggests to the Management Team modifications to plant rules, and reviews discipline decisions; (2) the Advancement Certification Board certifies workers' levels of skills and recommends pay increases; and (3) the Safety Committee. Each of these committees consists of two employees from each production team and management representatives. The Management Team consists of fifteen managers and it is organizationally superior to the three committees. The Plant Manager oversees the entire system, but most decisions have been made and implemented before reaching him.

The authority exercised by the committees and the production teams is comparable to that of the front-line supervisor in the traditional plant setting. They do not have final and absolute decision-making power. Like supervisors and managers elsewhere, they forward recommendations to a higher level of authority. Are the employees who participate in the production teams and the committees exempt from the Act's coverage? Should they be?

2. Students in the Public and Private Sectors

Ever since it asserted jurisdiction over private, non-profit universities and colleges in *Cornell University*, 183 N.L.R.B. 329 (1970), the Board has struggled with the question whether students who work for their university or college can be "employees" covered by the Act. In several early cases, the Board excluded student laboratory or teaching assistants who were still pursuing graduate degrees from faculty bargaining units; however, these decisions did not categorically exclude students from the Act's coverage. They were premised on the lack of a "community of interest" between faculty and graduate assistants. *See, e.g., Long Island University (Brooklyn Center)*, 189 N.L.R.B. 909 (1971); *Adelphi University*, 195 N.L.R.B. 639 (1972). In *C. W. Post Center of Long Island University*, 189 N.L.R.B. 904 (1971), the Board held that a research associate who had completed his doctoral degree and was eligible for tenure should be included in a professionals' bargaining unit again, without deciding the coverage question.

In *Leland Stanford Junior University*, 214 N.L.R.B. 621 (1974), the Board held that graduate research assistants were not covered by the Act. Payments made in return for work were "in the nature of stipends or grants to permit them to pursue their advanced degrees and are not based on the skill or function of the particular individual or the nature of the research performed. Accordingly, we conclude that the payments are not wages and the RA's are not 'employees' as defined in § 2(3) of the Act." 214 N.L.R.B. 621, 621. The Board concluded that the research for which the students were paid was "part of the course of instruction, a part of the learning process, with the nature of the research depending on the point to which each candidate for the doctorate has advanced. Thus, the doctorate is a research degree, and independent investigation is required in order to earn it." 214 N.L.R.B. at 621–22. In sum, a "student" relationship with an institution of higher education is mutually exclusive of an employment relationship with that institution. Grant M. Hayden, *"The University Works Because We Do": Collective Bargaining Rights for Graduate Assistants*, 69 FORDHAM L. REV. 1233 (2001) (critiquing the purported dichotomy between "employee" and "student").

In *Boston Medical Center*, 330 N.L.R.B. 152 (1999), however, the Board overruled several prior decisions regarding medical education and asserted jurisdiction over interns, residents, and fellows. These post-graduate "students" had completed their medical degrees but were enrolled in a hospital's on-the-job training program that provided the education and experience needed for a license to practice medicine and to earn specialty certifications. 330 N.L.R.B. 152, 153. Thus, post-graduate medical "students" could be "employees" under § 2(3) while other students could not. In *New York University*, 332 N.L.R.B. 1205 (2000), the Board addressed the apparent contradiction in the differential treatment of students pursuing a medical education and those pursuing other post-graduate studies by overruling *Leland Stanford Junior University.* The Board held that NYU's graduate assistants, including teaching and research assistants, were analogous to the interns, residents, and fellows in *Boston Medical Center.* Under a straightforward application of the common-law test which governs coverage determinations under § 2(3), they were "employees."

Four short years later, after a new political party had taken control of the White House, the Board overruled *NYU* in **Brown University**, 342 N.L.R.B. 483 (2004). Returning to the reasoning in *Leland Stanford Junior University,* the *Brown* decision explained:

> We look to the underlying fundamental premise of the Act, viz. the Act is designed to cover economic relationships. The Board's longstanding rule that it will not assert jurisdiction over relationships that are "primarily educational" is consistent with these principles. . . .

> [T]he student-teacher relationship is based on the "mutual interest in the advancement of the student's education," while the employer-employee relationship is "largely predicated on the often conflicting interests" over economic issues. Because the collective-bargaining process is fundamentally an economic process, . . . subjecting educational decisions to such a process would be of "dubious value" because educational concerns are largely irrelevant to wages, hours, and working conditions. In short, . . . collective bargaining is not particularly well suited to educational decision making and that any change in emphasis from quality education to economic concerns will "prove detrimental to both labor and educational policies." 342 N.L.R.B. 483, 489.

As the Board had suggested in *Leland Stanford Junior University,* the money paid to Brown's graduate teaching assistants, research assistants, and proctors was "not 'consideration for work.' It is financial aid to a student." 342 N.L.R.B. at 488. Accordingly, the students were not "employees."

Intriguingly, the *Brown* majority brushed aside the dissent's argument, and *NYU*'s central premise, that the Taft-Hartley Act required application of the common-law test to students and all other workers:

> Our colleagues argue that graduate student assistants are employees at common law. Even assuming *arguendo* that this is so, it does not follow that they are employees within the meaning of the Act. The issue of employee status under the Act turns on whether Congress intended to cover the individual in question. The issue is not to be decided purely on the basis of older common-law concepts. 342 N.L.R.B. at 491.

Equally interesting, the Board expressly eschewed any suggestion that its decision in *Brown University* necessarily overturned *Boston Medical Center. Id.* at 491. Yet, the Board's heavy reliance on the precedents which *Boston Medical Center* overturned raises some doubts as to its continuing vitality.

Indeed, in 2016, the Board once again reversed course and overturned *Brown University*. In *The Trustees of Columbia University in the City of New York*, 364 N.L.R.B. No. 90, the Board revisited the question "whether students who perform services at a university in connection with their studies are statutory employees within the meaning of Section 2(3)." In answering that question, the *Columbia University* Board, noting both the broad language of Section 2(3)'s definition of employee and that the NLRA "does not speak directly to the issue posed here," decided to return to its interpretation of Section 2(3) as clarified in *New York University*, 332 N.L.R.B. 1205 (2000), on grounds that the *NYU* Board's construction of Section 2(3) better reflected both the breadth of that definition and the policies of the Act. The Board explained:

> The unequivocal policy of the Act . . . is to "encourag[e] the practice and procedure of collective bargaining" and to "protect[] the exercise by workers of full freedom of association, self-organization, and designation of representatives of their own choosing." Given this policy, coupled with the very broad statutory definitions of both "employee" and "employer," it is appropriate to extend statutory coverage to students working for universities covered by the Act unless there are strong reasons not to do so. We are not persuaded by the *Brown University* Board's self-described "fundamental belief that the imposition [sic] of collective bargaining on graduate students would improperly intrude into the educational process and would be inconsistent with the purposes and policies of the Act." This "fundamental belief" is unsupported by legal authority, by empirical evidence, or by the Board's actual experience.

In rejecting *Brown University*'s assertion that graduate assistants cannot be statutory employees because they "are primarily students and have a primarily educational, not economic, relationship with their university," the Board observed that it had "the statutory authority to treat student assistants as statutory employees, where they perform work, at the direction of the university, for which they are compensated. Statutory coverage is permitted by virtue of an employment relationship; it is not foreclosed by the existence of some other, additional relationship that the Act does not reach."

On September 23, 2019, the Trump Board issue its proposed rule on Jurisdiction—Nonemployee Status of University and College Students Working in Connection with Their Studies. *See* NPRM, 84 F.R. 49691 (Sept. 23, 2019), amended by NPRM, 84 F.R. 55265 (Oct. 16, 2019). The comment period, which had been extended to December 2019 with rebuttal until February 2020, is now closed. The Board's current proposed rule would overrule *Columbia University* and return to the rule in *Brown University*.

The issue also arose when, with support from a labor organization known as the College Athletes Players Association, a group of scholarship football players from Northwestern University petitioned for a representation election. In a lengthy analysis of the football players' relationship with their university, the Board's Regional Director concluded that the student-athletes were "employees" and ordered an election. *Nw. Univ. Employer & Coll. Athletes Players Ass'n (CAPA)*, 198 L.R.R.M. (BNA) ¶ 1837 (N.L.R.B. 2014). The election was held on April 25, 2014, but the ballots were impounded until the full Board could review the Regional Director's legal decision. *See Nw. Univ. Employer & Coll. Athletics Players Ass'n (Capa) Petitioner*, 198 L.R.R.M. (BNA) 1837 (N.L.R.B. 2014). The Regional Director distinguished *Brown University* using its four-part test. He found that: (1) the football players were not "primarily students" like the Brown graduate assistants; (2) the players' football activities were not integral to their education; (3) the academic faculty did not supervise Northwestern's football activities as part of a degree program; and (4) the players' scholarships were not similar to the student financial aid that Brown provided to teaching and non-teaching graduate assistants alike. While the Regional Director was bound to follow or distinguish *Brown University*, the Board originally signaled that its review of the Regional Director's decision could include a reconsideration of that precedent. *See Nw. Univ. Employer & Coll. Athletes Players Ass'n (Capa) Petitioner*, 13-RC-121359 (N.L.R.B. 2014). Yet, after an extended delay, the Board unanimously declined to assert jurisdiction after concluding that "it would not effectuate the policies of the Act to assert jurisdiction in this case, even if we assume, without deciding, that the grant-in-aid scholarship players are employees within the meaning of Section 2(3)" and "asserting jurisdiction in this case would not serve to promote stability in labor relations." *Nw. Univ. Employer & Coll. Athletes Players Ass'n (Capa) Petitioner*, 204 L.R.R.M. (BNA) 1001 (N.L.R.B. 2015) (Decision on Review and Order).

The Board had previously invited briefs on the question whether it should reverse or modify *Brown University* in two cases involving New York University. *See New York University*, Case 2-RC-23481 (June 22, 2012); *Polytechnic Institute of New York University*, Case 29-RC-12054 (June 22, 2012). In addition, in February 2015, graduate assistants at Columbia University and the New School University filed requests for review of orders dismissing their petitions to organize unions on their campuses. Resolving these cases likely will require the Board to address *Brown University*'s continuing vitality.

The Board's decision in these cases would apply only to the private-sector colleges and universities that make up only a part of the intercollegiate sports universe. Public universities are home to many high-profile football (and other sports) programs with scholarship athletes. Whether any of these public schools' athletes are employees for the purposes of labor law would be a matter of state law.

———————

In the public sector, however, the rule is often more inclusive. According to the AFL-CIO's brief filed in *Brown University*, bargaining relationships had been established between graduate assistants and the University of California, the University of Florida, the University of South Florida, the University of Iowa, the University of Kansas, the University of Massachusetts, Michigan State University, the University of Michigan, Rutgers, the City University of New York, New York University, the State University of New York, the University of Oregon, Temple University, the University of Wisconsin, and Wayne State University. "Brief for AFL-CIO as Amici Curiae Supporting Petitioner," *Brown University*, 342 N.L.R.B. 483, at 36. *Coalition of Graduate Workers v. Curators of the University of Missouri*, 585 S.W.3d 809 (Mo. 2019), held that a wide variety of graduate assistants in a public university were "employees" for purposes of Missouri's state constitutional right to bargain collectively.

Not all public-sector jurisdictions are so inclusive. In Illinois, students whose assistantships are "significantly connected to their status as students" are not covered. Thus, most research assistants would not be covered employees, although graduate students who receive a stipend to answer phones would be. *Graduate Employees' Organization v. Illinois Educational Labor Relations Bd.*, 733 N.E.2d 759 (Ill. App. Ct. 2000). More typical, though, is *In the Matter of the Employees of Temple University*, 32 PPER ¶ 32164 (Pa. Lab. Rel. Bd. 2001), which held that graduate assistants were covered employees. *Temple* University noted that *Graduate Employees' Organization* represented a small minority rule. The Pennsylvania Board cited numerous public-sector precedents holding that graduate assistants were covered, and it held that the Pennsylvania law covered them as well.

Toth v. Callaghan, 995 F. Supp. 2d 774 (E.D. Mich. 2014), held that a recently enacted Michigan law, which barred graduate assistants from collective bargaining (H.B. 4246, P.A. 45), violated the Michigan Constitution. Article IV, §24 of the Michigan Constitution prohibits alterations to legislation that would "change its original purpose." Here, the court found that the bill's original purpose was to expand the powers of emergency managers—specifically, giving them the power to void or modify CBAs in jurisdictions where such managers had control. Altering the bill such that it generally eliminated the union rights of graduate students changed the original purpose of the bill, and thus that modification was invalid.

Problem 2.6

If you believe there is no significant policy or practical reason why private-sector and public-sector graduate assistants should be treated differently under labor laws, what effect should the NLRB's changing positions have on public-sector law? *Temple University* relied in part on the NLRB's *New York University* decision. Now that the NLRB has overturned that decision, should the Pennsylvania Board reconsider?

This raises a recurring question in public-sector labor law. Public-sector labor boards often simply adopt private-sector rules, where the statutory language is the same and the Board finds that the public-sector context does not dictate a different result. It is certainly more efficient and makes the law more predictable if public-sector boards, when interpreting broad language that comes from the NLRA, simply adopt NLRB rules, at least where no significant distinction between public-sector and private-sector employment is apparent. The NLRB has been around much longer than any public-sector board and has a much larger jurisdiction, so private-sector law is significantly more developed than the public-sector law of any state. State boards thus conclude that often, there is no need to reinvent the wheel. But should public-sector boards shift their rules every time the NLRB reverses itself? More broadly, what are the advantages and disadvantages of public-sector labor boards rejecting private-sector rules, not because of differences in statutory language or policy differences between the private and public sectors, but rather because of the public-sector board's view of what constitutes good labor law in general?

Notes

1. In *Brown University*, the Board's majority noted in a footnote that Member Schaumber, who joined the majority, disagreed with the dissenters that the graduate assistants at issue in *Brown University* were "employees" according to the common-law test. 342 N.L.R.B. at 495. Review the facts of *Brown University*. Who has the better argument regarding the common-law test: Schaumber or the dissenters?

2. *Hearst Publications* relied on a purposive interpretation of the Act to reach its conclusion. Yet, the Taft-Hartley Act legislatively overruled *Hearst Publications*. Should the Board have read this legislative reversal as a rejection of purposive interpretations of the Act? *Brown University* relies upon extra-textual purposive interpretation to reach its result. Is this approach consistent with the Taft-Hartley Act? How would a textualist have decided *Brown University*?

3. For a discussion of factors graduate students consider when deciding whether to try to organize a union or not, *see* Joel Chanvisanuruk et al., *Graduate Student Employees and Their Propensity to Unionize: Part 1, A Heuristic Approach*, 31 J. Collective Negotiations 173 (2007) (noting that since 1969, 25 student organizing drives at universities have resulted in union representation, including 12 formed "just in the past few years, tripling graduate student union representation to almost 40,000").

3. Undocumented Workers

The Board has held consistently that undocumented workers — non-citizens working in the United States who do not have immigration documents authorizing their presence and/or their work — can be "employees" under NLRA § 2(3). *See, e.g., County Window Cleaning Co.*, 328 N.L.R.B. 190 (1999) (overruling a challenge to an undocumented worker voting in a representation election). In *Sure-Tan, Inc. v. NLRB*, 467 U.S. 883, 891–92 (1984), the Supreme Court upheld the Board's interpretation:

> extending the coverage of the Act to such workers is consistent with the Act's avowed purpose of encouraging and protecting the collective-bargaining process. As this Court has previously recognized: "[Acceptance] by illegal aliens of jobs on substandard terms as to wages and working conditions can seriously depress wage scales and working conditions of citizens and legally

admitted aliens; and employment of illegal aliens under such conditions can diminish the effectiveness of labor unions." If undocumented alien employees were excluded from participation in union activities and from protections against employer intimidation, there would be created a sub-class of workers without a comparable stake in the collective goals of their legally resident co-workers, thereby eroding the unity of all the employees and impeding effective collective bargaining. 467 U.S. at 892.

However, the Supreme Court's subsequent decision in *Hoffman Plastic Compounds v. NLRB*, 535 U.S. 137 (2002) undercut some aspects of *Sure-Tan*. The majority in *Hoffman Plastic* stated in a footnote that "[o]ur first holding in *Sure-Tan* is not at issue here and does not bear at all on the scope of Board remedies with respect to undocumented workers." 535 U.S. 137, 149 n.4; *see also NLRB v. Concrete Form Walls, Inc.*, 2007 U.S. App. LEXIS 11981 (11th Cir. May 22, 2007) (upholding the NLRB's conclusion that undocumented workers remain statutory employees under the NLRA after IRCA); *NLRB v. Kolkka*, 170 F.3d 937, 941 (9th Cir. 1999) (holding that the NLRA continues to define undocumented aliens as employees after IRCA); *Del Rey Tortilleria, Inc. v. NLRB*, 976 F.2d 1115, 1121 (7th Cir. 1992) (same). Yet, *Hoffman Plastic* held that awarding back pay to an undocumented worker as a remedy for his employer's ULPs would be inconsistent with the "comprehensive scheme prohibiting the employment of illegal aliens in the United States" enacted in the Immigration Reform and Control Act of 1986 (IRCA). 535 U.S. at 147; *see also* Immigration Reform and Control Act of 1986, 8 U.S.C. § 1324 (2006).

Notes

1. The tensions between *Sure-Tan* and *Hoffman Plastic* are illustrated well by *Agri Processor Co., Inc. v. NLRB*, 514 F. 3d 1 (D.C. Cir. 2008). A three-judge panel produced three conflicting opinions about how to resolve those tensions. The employer intentionally committed ULPs by refusing to bargain with a union in order to secure judicial review of a bargaining unit that included a large number of undocumented workers. Judge Tatel, writing for the majority, agreed with the other Courts of Appeals that had addressed this issue: neither *Hoffman Plastic* nor IRCA impliedly overruled *Sure-Tan*; therefore, undocumented aliens can be "employees" and the Board's conclusion that the employer committed ULPs should be upheld. Judge Henderson concurred, but only because she felt herself bound by *Sure-Tan* and the lack of any explicit statement overruling it in IRCA or *Hoffman Plastic*. She seemingly agreed in principle with Judge Kavanaugh's dissenting view that an undocumented worker cannot be an "employee" under the NLRA because IRCA made it illegal for these workers to be "employees" in the United States at all. Who has the better argument?

2. As a practical matter, does *Hoffman Plastic* make *Sure-Tan* irrelevant? For example, if an employer can fire undocumented workers who support a union organizing drive in their workplace, and there is no risk that these workers will be reinstated to their former jobs, does it matter that they are "employees" under § 2(3)? Several

commentators have asked why the Supreme Court concluded in *Hoffman Plastic* that the NLRA's purposes must yield to IRCA's purposes rather than the immigration law yielding to labor law's imperatives. *See, e.g.*, Michael C. Duff, *Days without Immigrants: Analysis and Implications of the Treatment of Immigration Rallies under the National Labor Relations Act*, 85 DENV. U. L. REV. 93 (2007); María Pabón López, *The Place of the Undocumented Worker in the United States Legal System after Hoffman Plastic Compounds: An Assessment and Comparison with Argentina's Legal System*, 15 IND. INT'L & COMP. L. REV. 301 (2005); Michael J. Wishnie, *Prohibiting the Employment of Unauthorized Immigrants: The Experiment Fails*, 2007 U. CHI LEGAL F. 193 (2007). If union organizing efforts can be sabotaged by obedience to immigration law, should immigration law yield instead?

3. Courts and administrative agencies have also addressed how *Hoffman Plastic* should influence the interpretation of labor and employment laws other than the NLRA. The widely held view is consistent with the court's decision in *Agri Processor*. The U.S. Department of Labor has stated that it would enforce the Fair Labor Standards Act and the Migrant and Seasonal Agricultural Worker Protection Act regardless of an employee's immigration status. U.S. Department of Labor Employment Standards Administration Wage and Hour Division, *Fact Sheet #48: Application of U.S. Labor Laws to Immigrant Workers: Effect of* Hoffman Plastics *decision on laws enforced by the Wage and Hour Division*, July 2008, *available at* http://www .dol.gov/whd/regs/compliance/whdfs48.pdf. The U.S. Equal Employment Opportunity Commission also stated that *Hoffman Plastic* does not prevent the agency from protecting undocumented workers from workplace discrimination. Several federal courts have agreed. *See, e.g., Rivera v. NIBCO*, 364 F.3d 1057 (9th Cir. 2004) ("serious doubt" that *Hoffman Plastic* is relevant to Title VII actions); *Martinez v. Mecca Farms, Inc.*, 213 F.R.D. 601 (S.D. Fla. 2002) (Agricultural Worker Protection Act applies regardless of immigration status); *Liu v. Donna Karan Int'l Inc.*, 207 F. Supp. 2d 191 (S.D.N.Y. 2002) (immigration status is irrelevant to FLSA claims for time actually worked).

4. The Special Case of Public-Sector Attorneys

Attorneys in the private sector rarely try to organize unions, but public-sector attorneys have done so more frequently. Attorneys fairly high up in an agency may be excluded as managers or as supervisors (if the state statute excludes supervisors). But if these exceptions do not apply, as a matter of policy, should public-sector labor laws cover government lawyers? *City of Newark v. Ass'n of Government Attorneys*, 788 A.2d 776 (N.J. Super. Ct. App. Div. 2002) rejected claims that covering lawyers created an "appearance of impropriety" under ethical rules or otherwise violated the duty of loyalty that lawyers owe their clients. Other cases finding that labor statutes covered public-sector attorneys include *Santa Clara County Counsel Attorneys Ass'n v. Woodside*, 869 P.2d 1142 (Cal. 1994); *Chiles v. State Employees Attorneys Guild*, 734 So. 2d 1030 (Fla. 1999); and *City of Philadelphia v. Pennsylvania Labor Relations Bd.*, 641 A.2d 709 (Pa. Commw. Ct. 1994).

A minority of jurisdictions, however, exclude most or all public sector lawyers. *See, e.g.,* N.Y. Civ. Serv. Law § 201(7)(b) (excluding as managers, "assistant attorneys general, assistant district attorneys, and law school graduates employed in titles which promote to assistant district attorneys upon admission to the bar." In Illinois, courts have held that most public-sector lawyers are not covered under the state's Public Labor Relations Act. *See, e.g., Chief Judge v. Illinois State Labor Relations Bd.*, 687 N.E.2d 795 (Ill. 1997) (assistant public defenders not covered); *Cook County State's Attorney v. Illinois Local Labor Relations Bd.*, 652 N.E.2d 301 (Ill. 1995) (assistant state's attorneys not covered). *But see Illinois Dept. of Central Mgmt. Servs. v. Illinois Labor Relations Bd.*, 388 Ill. App. 3d 319, 902 N.E.2d 1122 (2009) (staff attorneys in the Department of Healthcare, Family Services, Office of Inspector General, were not managers); and *AFSCME Council 31 and State of Illinois, Dept. of Central Mgmt. Services*, 26 PERI ¶ 40 (Ill. Lab. Bd. 2010) (administrative law judges in the Illinois Commerce Commission are not managers).Can these Illinois decisions be reconciled?

Ohio has reversed position on this issue twice. The original public-sector labor statute did not exclude attorneys; in 2004, the law was amended to exclude all employees "who must be licensed to practice law in this state to perform their duties as employees"; and then in 2006, the law was again amended to delete this clause. *See* H.R. 516, 125th Leg. (Ohio 2004); H.R. 530, 126th Leg. (Ohio 2006); Ohio Rev. Code § 4117.01(C).

Can you think of any special concerns about granting lawyers the right to bargain collectively? Does it matter what they can bargain about? Does it matter whether they can strike?

III. "Employers" in the Private and Public Sectors, and in Between

A. "Employers" in the Private and Public Sectors

NLRA § 2(2), which purports to define "employer," actually offers little insight into which entities are "employers": "The term 'employer' includes any person acting as an agent of an employer, directly or indirectly." Yet, § 2(2) does expressly exclude certain categories of employers from coverage: "the United States or any wholly owned Government corporation"; "any Federal Reserve Bank"; "any State or political subdivision thereof"; "any person subject to the Railway Labor Act"; and "any labor organization (other than when acting as an employer), or anyone acting in the capacity of officer or agent of such labor organization." In 1974, Congress expanded the scope of § 2(2)'s coverage by eliminating the exemption for not-for-profit hospitals and "health care institutions." Pub. L. No. 93-360 (1974); *see also* 29 U.S.C. § 152(14) (2006) (defining "health care institutions").

As discussed above, public-sector labor laws tend to define who is a covered employer together with who is a covered employee by listing the occupations or category of employees covered: e.g., teachers, police, fire, municipal employees generally, state employees generally, or public employees generally. Often, as to municipal employers, there is a minimum size defined by population. For example, Ohio's statute, § 4177.01, in defining "employer" requires that a municipal corporation must have a population of at least 5,000 according to the most recent federal decennial census. Ohio Rev. Code § 4117.01(B).

In the private sector, despite the broad scope of the language in § 2(2), three limitations have been imposed for reasons external to that provision's text. The first limitation has been practical: the Board has never had sufficient resources to regulate every employer in the United States. As a result, the Board has traditionally declined to assert jurisdiction over certain employers based on the annual dollar volume of business they conduct.

A partial list of these standards, which the NLRB established in 1958 and remain in effect today, holds that the Board will generally assert jurisdiction over: non-retail enterprises with gross annual revenue of at least $50,000; retail establishments (including taxi cab companies) with gross annual revenue of at least $500,000 and substantial purchases from or sales to other states; office buildings and shopping centers with gross annual revenue of at least $100,000 of which at least $25,000 comes from entities that meet any of these standards; newspapers with a gross annual business volume of at least $200,000; hotels, motels, apartments, and condominiums with gross annual revenue of at least $500,000; transit systems with gross annual volume of at least $250,000; restaurants and country clubs with gross annual volume of at least $500,000; hospitals with at least $250,000 in gross annual revenue, nursing homes and related facilities with at least $100,000 in gross annual revenue, all other health care institutions with at least $250,000 in gross annual revenue, and child care institutions with at least $250,000 in gross annual revenue; museums, cultural centers, and libraries with at least $1 million in gross annual revenue; and law firms and legal assistant programs with at least $250,000 in gross annual revenue. John E. Higgins, Jr., ed., The Developing Labor Law 2307–20 (5th ed. 2006).

The Landrum-Griffin Act added § 14(c) in 1959 to give the Board express authorization to decline jurisdiction by rule or decision "over any labor dispute involving any class or category of employers, where, in the opinion of the Board, the effect of such labor dispute on commerce is not sufficiently substantial to warrant exercise of its jurisdiction." Landrum-Griffin Act, Pub. L. No. 86-257, 73 Stat. 519 (1959) (codified as amended at 29 U.S.C. §§ 151–169 (2006)). However, this same section prohibits the Board from declining jurisdiction "over any labor dispute over which it would assert jurisdiction" when the Landrum-Griffin Act was enacted. *Id.*

The second limitation is constitutional. Courts are unlikely to permit the Board to assert jurisdiction over entities where asserting jurisdiction raises a constitutional question. This principle of constitutional avoidance has been specifically played out in the context of the U.S. Constitution's First Amendment, which limits the scope of the Act's coverage of religious institutions. The concern is that coverage would excessively, and therefore unconstitutionally, entangle the NLRB in religious decision-making. After the Board asserted jurisdiction over private, not-for-profit schools in *Cornell University, supra*, the Board regulated both secular and religious-affiliated schools. In ***NLRB v. Catholic Bishop of Chicago***, 440 U.S. 490 (1979), however, the Supreme Court applied a longstanding principle of statutory interpretation to hold that Congress did not intend the Act to cover religious schools: "an Act of Congress ought not to be construed to violate the Constitution if any other possible construction remains available." *Id.* at 500. In the face of "abundant evidence that the Board's exercise of jurisdiction over teachers in church-operated schools would implicate the guarantees of the [First Amendment's] Religion Clauses," and "in the absence of a clear expression of Congress' intent to bring teachers in church-operated schools within the jurisdiction of the Board," the Court restrained the Board from asserting jurisdiction over teachers in church-operated schools. *Id.* at 507.

The Board subsequently extended *Catholic Bishop* to refuse jurisdiction over religious schools run by lay directors rather than a church, *Jewish Day School of Greater Washington*, 283 N.L.R.B. 757 (1987), and employees other than teachers, *St. Edmunds Roman Catholic Church*, 337 N.L.R.B. 1260 (2002) (dismissing a representation petition covering custodians). However, the Board has asserted jurisdiction over religiously affiliated institutions that were not engaged in inculcating religious values, including hospitals. *See, e.g., Salvation Army*, 345 N.L.R.B. 550 (2005) (community correctional center); *Bon Secours Hospital*, 248 N.L.R.B. 115 (1980) (religiously affiliated hospital).

In *Pacific Lutheran University, supra*, the Board reconsidered the question whether it has jurisdiction over religiously affiliated universities and colleges. After *Catholic Bishop*, the Board explained, it used case-by-case analyses to assess whether a school had a "substantial religious character" such that Board jurisdiction risked infringement of the employer's First Amendment rights to free exercise of religion. *See Pacific Lutheran University*, 361 N.L.R.B. at 4 (citing *Jewish Day School*, 283 N.L.R.B. 757 (1987); *Livingstone College*, 286 N.L.R.B. 1308 (1987)). But the First and D.C. Circuits rejected this approach as amounting to little more than a test of whether the school is sufficiently religious. *See Pacific Lutheran*, at 5 (citing *Universidad Central de Bayamon v. NLRB*, 793 F.2d 383 (1st Cir. 1985) (*en banc*); *University of Great Falls v. NLRB*, 278 F.3d 1335 (D.C. Cir. 2002)). The courts preferred a three-part test allowing jurisdiction to be asserted unless a school "(a) holds itself out to students, faculty and the community as providing a religious educational environment; (b) is organized as a nonprofit; and (c) is affiliated with, or owned, operated or controlled, directly or indirectly, by a recognized religious organization, or with an entity, membership of which is determined, at least in part, with reference to religion." *Pacific Lutheran*, at 4 (citing *Great Falls*). Plainly influenced by the courts' adoption of this rule, the *Pacific Lutheran University* Board adopted a similar test:

> The Act permits jurisdiction over a unit of faculty members at an institution of higher learning unless the university or college demonstrates, as a

threshold matter, that it holds itself out as providing a religious education environment, and that it holds out the petitioned-for faculty members as performing a specific role in creating or maintaining the school's religious educational environment.

Id. at 6. Thus, the character of the institution would not be at issue; rather, the institution's own representations regarding the faculty members in the petitioned-for unit would be determinative. In that case, the Board found that the university did not specify a role for contingent faculty members in creating or maintaining the religious educational environment; therefore, the Board asserted jurisdiction. *Id.*

Employers have argued that the *Pacific Lutheran* test is inconsistent with *Catholic Bishop* and *Great Falls*, as well as the Religious Freedom Restoration Act, 42 U.S.C. §§ 2000bb to 2000bb-4, and the First Amendment. In *Duquesne University of the Holy Spirit v. NLRB*, 947 F.3d 824 (D.C. Cir. 2020), the D.C. Circuit applied its decision in *Great Falls* to hold that Duquesne was not required to bargain collectively with the union elected by its adjunct faculty, refusing to enforce the Board's application of *Pacific Lutheran*.

The third limitation is comity with foreign governments and sovereign Indian tribes within the United States. While Congress can enact laws that apply beyond the territorial boundaries of the United States, the Supreme Court has adopted a general presumption against application of American laws in foreign territory in the absence of express congressional intent favoring it. The goal of this interpretive canon is to avoid unintended clashes with the laws of other nations. *See Equal Employment Opportunity Comm'n v. Arabian American Oil Co.*, 499 U.S. 244 (1991). The Board has adopted an "effects" test to determine whether conduct is truly extraterritorial: the conduct must occur outside the United States and cause no effects within the United States. *California Gas Transport, Inc.*, 347 N.L.R.B. 1314 (2006) (relying on *Asplundh Tree Expert Co.*, 336 N.L.R.B. 1106 (2001), *enforcement denied*, 365 F.3d 168 (3d Cir. 2004)). For example, ULPs committed on foreign territory that have the effect of depriving employees in the United States of their rights under the Act are not extraterritorial and the employer committing the violations is a covered "employer." 347 N.L.R.B. 1314, 1315–17. Foreign entities doing business in the United States, if they are not sovereigns or treated as sovereigns, are covered employers. *See Benz v. Compania Naviera Hidalgo, S. A.*, 353 U.S. 138 (1957); *see also* International Organization Immunities Act, 22 U.S.C. § 288 (2006) (granting sovereign immunity to the World Bank and like institutions).

The Supreme Court has taken a similar approach with respect to the NLRA's coverage of Native American tribes. A statute can be construed to impair tribal sovereignty only if express congressional intent authorizes it. *San Manuel Indian Bingo and Casino v. NLRB*, 475 F.3d 1306, 1311 (D.C. Cir. 2007) (collecting cases). However, tribes frequently engage in commercial activities on and off their reservations that might be regulated without implicating the tribes' sovereignty. The Board has adopted a general rule that the Act applies to tribal activities, except in situations where: (1) the law touches exclusive rights of self-governance in purely intramural matters; (2) the application of the law to the tribe would abrogate rights guaranteed by treaties; or (3) there is proof by legislative history or some other means that Congress intended the law not to apply to Native Americans on their reservations. *Id.* at 1310 (quoting *Donovan v. Coeur d'Alene Tribal Farm*, 751 F.2d 1113 (9th Cir.1985)). In *San Manuel Indian Bingo*, the D.C. Circuit, without expressly endorsing the Board's approach, upheld the Board's assertion of jurisdiction over a tribe's casino on its reservation that employed and marketed to people who were not Native Americans. 475 F.3d 1306, 1315–17. The court also deferred to the Board's conclusion that "employer" in §2(2) encompassed tribes and tribal businesses. *Id.* at 1318. The Ninth Circuit recently enforced the Board's assertion of jurisdiction over a tribal enterprise in *Casino Pauma v. NLRB*, 888 F.3d 1066 (9th Cir. 2018) (enforcing *Casino Pauma*, 363 N.L.R.B. No. 60).

B. Multiple Employers

The Board has long encountered circumstances where more than one entity may be the employer of a group of employees engaged in protected concerted activity or seeking to organize and bargain collectively. In other words, more than one entity may satisfy the tests described earlier in this chapter for establishing an employment relationship between an entity and workers providing it with compensable services. These circumstances can take many forms. For example, an employer may engage a temporary help agency like Manpower Inc. or Kelly Services to supply clerical employees who will supplement the employer's existing administrative work force at the employer's work site. Or a franchisor can exercise control over decisions of its franchisees relating to the wages and terms of conditions of employment of employees in the franchisees' establishments. Or entire categories of work, like janitorial services or information technology support, may be outsourced by one employer to another, but still conducted on the premises of the outsourcing employer.

In each of these circumstances, and others, the Board must determine whether two or more employing entities are "joint employers"—that is, jointly and severally responsible for carrying out the obligations the Act imposes on employers. This case establishes the standard for "joint employment."

As with many other areas of labor law, this area has oscillated. The earliest Board cases to find joint employer status did so without discussion, where the two entities both "control[]ed] ... employment and labor relations." *Canisteo Mining Co.*, 39 N.L.R.B. No. 2 (1942). As this was the common law definition, these issues were rarely disputed and garnered little attention. Indeed, even in *Boire v. Greyhound Corp.*, which presented the question whether the Board had acted outside its jurisdictional bounds when it determined that both Greyhound and another company were joint employers, the Supreme Court skipped over the Board's joint employer analysis, holding that however the Board found, it acted within its authority. *See* 376 U.S. 473, 476, 481 (1964). Another twenty years passed before this issue raised eyebrows again. In *NLRB v. Browning-Ferris Industries of Pennsylvania, Inc.*, the court endorsed the Board's long-standing test for determining joint employer status grounded in the common law control test. *See* 691 F.2d 1117 (3d Cir. 1982), *enforcing*, 259 N.L.R.B. 148 (1981).

Shortly thereafter, in *TLI, Inc.*, 271 N.L.R.B. 798 (1984), *enfd. mem.* 772 F.2d 894 (3d Cir. 1985), and *Laerco Transportation*, 269 N.L.R.B. 324 (1984), the Reagan Board began to impose additional requirements before finding joint employer status. This continued for another thirty years until *Browning-Ferris Industries of California, Inc., d/b/a BFI Newby Island Recyclery (BFI Newby Island)*, where the Obama Board stated that it was returning to:

> the standard articulated by the Third Circuit in *Browning-Ferris* decision. Under this standard, the Board may find that two or more statutory employers are joint employers of the same statutory employees if they "share or codetermine those matters governing the essential terms and conditions of employment." In determining whether a putative joint employer meets this standard, the initial inquiry is whether there is a common-law employment relationship with the employees in question. If this common-law employment relationship exists, the inquiry then turns to whether the putative joint employer possesses sufficient control over employees' essential terms and conditions of employment to permit meaningful collective bargaining.

BFI Newby Island, 362 N.L.R.B. 1599, 1600 (2015).

In *Hy-Brand I*, the newly minted Trump Board overruled *BFI Newby Island*, thereby returning to its prior legal standard for determining whether two employers are joint employers under the NLRA. *See Hy-Brand I*, 365 N.L.R.B. No. 156 (Dec. 14, 2017). Shortly thereafter, the Board issued an order vacating *Hy-Brand I* and granting partial reconsideration. *Hy-Brand II*, 366 N.L.R.B. No. 26 (Feb. 26, 2018). The Trump Board's willingness to reconsider *Hy-Brand I* was not, however, a decision on the merits. Rather, the Trump Board vacated that decision based on the Board's Designated Agency Ethics Official determination that "Member Emanuel [whose former law firm represented Leadpoint, the joint-employer of Browning-Ferris] is, and should have been, disqualified from participating in this proceeding." Accordingly, "[a]fter careful consideration, and exercising the Board's authority under Section 102.48(c) of the Board's Rules and Regulations and Section 10(d) of the Act, [the Board] . . . decided to grant the Charging Parties' motion in part and to vacate and set aside the Board's December 14, 2017 Decision and Order." Thereafter, the Board unanimously denied the employer's motion for reconsideration of *Hy-Brand II*. *See Hy-Brand III*, 366 N.L.R.B. No. 93 (Jun. 6, 2018).

On September 14, 2018, the Board issued a Notice of Proposed Rulemaking and Request for Comments on "The Standard for Determining Joint-Employer Status." The proposed rule would require that, to be deemed a joint employer, an employer must possess and actually exercise substantial direct and immediate control over the essential terms and conditions of employment of another employer's employees in a manner that is not limited and routine.

The D.C. Circuit put a potential wrench in the rulemaking works, however, when it issued, on December 28, 2018, its decision reviewing *BFI Newby Island*, 362 N.L.R.B. 1599 (2015). *See Browning-Ferris Industries of California Inc.*, 911 F.3d 1195 (D.C. Cir. 2018). The court held that: "to the extent that the Board's joint-employer standard is predicated on interpreting the common law . . . [t]he content and meaning of the common law is a pure question of law that we review de novo without deference to the Board." Regarding the pending rulemaking, the court opined: "The policy expertise that the Board brings to bear on applying the [NLRA] to joint employers is bounded by the common-law's definition of a joint employer. The Board's rulemaking, in other words, must color within the common-law lines identified by the judiciary."

Turning to the Board's application of its joint employer standard as articulated in *BFI Newby Island*, the court stated that the question in the case was: "whether the common-law analysis of joint-employer status can factor in both (i) an employer's authorized but unexercised forms of control, and (ii) an employer's indirect control over employees' terms and conditions of employment." On that question, the court held: "We conclude that the Board's right-to-control standard is an established aspect of the common law of agency. The Board also correctly determined that the common-law inquiry is not woodenly confined to indicia of direct and immediate control; an employer's indirect control over employees can be a relevant consideration." However, the court determined that, in addressing an employer's exercise of indirect control, the Board had failed "to distinguish evidence of indirect control that bears on workers' essential terms and conditions from evidence that simply documents the routine parameters of company-to-company contracting" and remanded the case for the Board to address that issue.

The Trump Board thereafter issued its rule, taking account of the D.C. Circuit's opinion. The final rule took effect on April 27, 2020. *See* 85 Fed. Reg. 11184, 11188, 11235–11236, to be codified 29 C.F.R. § 103.40(a) *et seq.* The rule states as follows:

> (a) An employer, as defined by Section 2(2) of the National Labor Relations Act (the Act), may be considered a joint employer of a separate employer's employees *only if the two employers share or codetermine the employees' essential terms and conditions of employment.* To establish that an entity shares or codetermines the essential terms and conditions of another employer's employees, the entity must possess and exercise such substantial direct and immediate control over one or more essential terms or conditions of their employment as would warrant finding that the entity meaningfully affects matters relating to the employment relationship with those employees. Evidence of the entity's indirect control over essential terms and conditions of employment of another employer's employees, the entity's contractually reserved but never exercised authority over the essential terms and conditions of employment of another employer's employees, or the entity's control over mandatory subjects of bargaining other than the essential terms and conditions of employment is probative of joint-employer status, but only to the extent it supplements and reinforces evidence of the entity's

possession or exercise of direct and immediate control over a particular essential term and condition of employment. Joint-employer status must be determined on the totality of the relevant facts in each particular employment setting. The party asserting that an entity is a joint employer has the burden of proof. (Emphasis added.)

The rule further defines the following terms:

- "'Essential terms and conditions of employment' means wages, benefits, hours of work, hiring, discharge, discipline, supervision, and direction."

- "'Substantial direct and immediate control' means direct and immediate control that has a regular or continuous consequential effect on an essential term or condition of employment of another employer's employees. Such control is not 'substantial' if only exercised on a sporadic, isolated, or de minimis basis."

- "'Indirect control' means indirect control over essential terms and conditions of employment of another employer's employees but not control or influence over setting the objectives, basic ground rules, or expectations for another entity's performance under contract."

- "'Contractually reserved authority over essential terms and conditions of employment' means the authority that an entity reserves to itself, under the terms of a contract with another employer, over the essential terms and conditions of employment of that other employer's employees, but that has never been exercised."

Notes

1. On December 19, 2014, the General Counsel's office issued thirteen complaints involving seventy-eight charges against McDonald's USA and its franchisees as joint employers responsible for ULPs associated with their response to fast-food workers' protests seeking higher wages and improved working conditions. *See* NLRB, *McDonald's Fact Sheet, available at* www.nlrb.gov/news-outreach/fact-sheets/mcdonalds -fact-sheet (last visited Oct. 12, 2015). According to the General Counsel's office, its investigation found that "McDonald's, USA, LLC, through its franchise relationship and its use of tools, resources and technology, engaged in sufficient control over its franchisees' operations, beyond the protection of the brand, to make it a putative joint employer with its franchisees. . . ." *Id.* While *Browning-Ferris* did not directly involve a franchisor-franchisee relationship like those maintained by McDonald's, there was concern among large franchisors that the Board would apply the joint-employer doctrine to these relationships. The Board ultimately settled this case, without deciding the issue. *McDonald's USA, LLC*, 368 N.L.R.B. No. 134 (2019).

2. Did the Board make the correct decision when, in *BFI Newby Island*, it overturned precedents that had been in place for decades? Do employers and temporary staffing agencies have a legitimate complaint that they have relied on the law in constructing and organizing their business relationships? Does the Board risk disrupting business relationships? What standard, if any, should the Board satisfy to justify

a change of this magnitude after this period of time? Do these same arguments apply now that the Board has once again reversed itself through rulemaking? In any event, which is the better rule? Is there much difference between the rules?

3. Professor David Weil, in his book The Fissured Workplace: Why Work Became So Bad for So Many and What Can Be Done About It (2014), describes and explains the shift in many American workplaces from traditional employment relationships to "fissured" structures like outsourcing, the use of temporary workers, and franchising. Although Dr. Weil does not view the avoidance of legal liability under employment, labor, and tax laws as the only motivating factor behind these fissured work relationships, it is one relevant factor for some employers. Is the Board's decision in *Browning-Ferris* an appropriate response to the fissuring of work relationships? Is it appropriate for the Board to respond to large economic trends in this way? Will the Board's decision interfere with relationships that some believe are efficient, cost-saving, and flexible?

C. Joint Employment and the Borderline Between the Private and Public Sectors

Some cases involve the interplay between public- and private-sector employers. Most importantly, government agencies often "contract out" work to private employers that the public body might otherwise do with its own employees. Contracting out work is a significant and growing practice, involving hundreds of billions of dollars of government money. *See, e.g.,* Ellen Dannin, *Crumbling Infrastructure, Crumbling Democracy: Infrastructure Privatization Contracts and Their Effect on State and Local Governance,* 6 Nw. J.L. & Soc. Pol'y 47 (2011).

Contracting out raises a number of political and economic issues and also some specific questions for labor lawyers. Notably, when both public and private employers have some control over wages, hours, and working conditions of a set of employees, the already-fraught issue of "joint employment" is made even more complicated by the question of what labor board should exercise jurisdiction over the employees.

Management Training Corporation

National Labor Relations Board
317 N.L.R.B. 1355 (1995)

Gould, Chair

. . . .

In *Res-Care,* the Board held that, in deciding whether it would assert jurisdiction over an employer with close ties to an exempt government entity, it would examine the control over essential terms and conditions of employment retained by both the employer and the exempt entity to determine whether the employer in issue is capable of engaging in meaningful collective bargaining. After careful consideration of *Res-Care* and its progeny and for the reasons set forth below, we have decided that the test set forth in *Res-Care* is unworkable and unrealistic. Rather, we think that whether there are sufficient employment matters over which unions and employers can bargain is a question better left to the parties at the bargaining table and, ultimately, to the employee voters in each case.

The [International Brotherhood of Teamsters] filed the instant petition seeking to represent all of the Employer's Senior Residential Advisors and Residential Advisors, approximately 125 employees, at the Clearfield Job Corps Center, Clearfield, Utah. The Clearfield Job Corps Center is managed by the Employer pursuant to a contract with the United States Department of Labor (DOL).

The Employer contended that the Board should decline jurisdiction under *Res-Care* because DOL exercises the same degree of control over its employment terms and conditions as DOL exercised over *Res-Care's*. In support of this contention, the Employer submitted an affidavit from Sam T. Hunter, Executive Vice President, Training Programs, who is responsible for the preparation of proposals, negotiations, and oversight of the Employer's Job Corps contracts with DOL.[2]

According to Hunter's testimony, the Employer, like *Res-Care*, operates a job corps facility pursuant to a contract with the DOL. In both cases, the employers were required to include in their contract proposals (1) staffing tables listing job classifications and organizational charts as well as labor-grade schedules and salary schedules showing wage ranges, including the minimum and maximum wages for each grade and (2) a description of their personnel policies concerning compensatory time, overtime, severance pay, holidays, vacations, probationary employment, sick leave, raises, and equal employment opportunity. In both instances, the proposed salary structure and fringe benefits had to be supported by a wage and benefit comparability study to assure DOL that the proposals conformed to prevailing wage rates and benefits for persons providing substantially similar services in the area in which the job corps facility was located. In addition, the Employer's contract, like *Res-Care's*, required that any proposed changes to the approved staffing tables, labor grade schedules, salary schedules, personnel policies, or employee benefits must be submitted to DOL for approval. Both contracts also gave DOL the authority to deny reimbursement for any costs in excess of those allowed in the contract. The contracts further required the employers to follow DOL-approved policies in the hiring, firing, promotion, demotion, or transfer of any employee.

. . . .

[I]n view of the numerous and substantial similarities between this case and *Res-Care*, the Regional Director found *Res-Care* controlling and dismissed the petition.

Res-Care was an effort by the Board to clarify its prior decision in *National Transportation* in which it held that the Board would assert jurisdiction over an employer

---

2. The Job Corps is a Federal employment and training program authorized by the Job Training Partnership Act. The Employer, under its contract with DOL, operates 14 job corps centers, but only the Clearfield Job Corps Center is involved here.

if it met the definition of "employer" in Section 2(2) of the Act and if the employer had sufficient control over the employment conditions of its employees to enable it to bargain effectively with a labor organization as their representative. . . . [T]he Board stated that it would not only examine the control over essential terms and conditions of employment retained by the employer, but also the scope and degree of control exercised by the exempt entity over the employer's labor relations. Applying that rationale, the Board examined the relationship between *Res-Care* and DOL and determined that meaningful bargaining was not possible.

. . . .

Because the contract between *Res-Care* and DOL spelled out the precise ranges of wages and benefits that *Res-Care's* employees would receive, and DOL had the authority to approve those wage ranges and benefit levels as well as any changes thereto, the Board reasoned that *Res-Care* lacked the ultimate authority to determine economic terms and conditions of employment and thus lacked the ability to engage in meaningful bargaining. In reaching this conclusion, the Board discounted *Res-Care's* theoretical ability to absorb increases that were not approved by the DOL, noting that *Res-Care* had not chosen to increase employee compensation from its own funds and that all the money for the job corps program came from DOL.

Since then, the Board has summarily declined jurisdiction over job corps centers. The Board has also declined jurisdiction in a handful of non-job corps cases where the facts paralleled those in *Res-Care* in that the employers' contracts also spelled out wage ranges and benefits, and the exempt entity had to approve any changes to the contract. . . . [T]he Board's approach in this area has been far from uniform. In fact, by asserting jurisdiction in situations where the employer's contract sets out wages which must be approved by the exempt entity and where the employer did not have control over the "entire package of employee compensation," our decisions have eroded much of the basis for the *Res-Care* decision. . . .

In view of the varied and confusing approaches in these cases, we have reconsidered *Res-Care* and have decided that jurisdiction should no longer be determined on the basis of whether the employer or the Government controls most of the employee's terms and conditions of employment. Nor should the Board be deciding as a jurisdictional question which terms and conditions of employment are or are not essential to the bargaining process.

In retrospect, we think the emphasis in *Res-Care* on control of economic terms and conditions was an oversimplification of the bargaining process. While economic terms are certainly important aspects of the employment relationship, they are not the only subjects sought to be negotiated at the bargaining table. Indeed, monetary terms may not necessarily be the most critical issues between the parties. In times of downsizing, recession, low profits, or when economic growth is uncertain or doubtful, economic gains at the bargaining table are minimal at best. Here the focus of negotiations may be upon such matters as job security, job classifications, employer flexibility in assignments, employee involvement or participation and the like. Consequently, in those circumstances, it may be that the parties' primary interest is in the noneconomic area. It was shortsighted, therefore, for the Board to declare that bargaining is meaningless unless it includes the entire range of economic issues.

Moreover, it is unrealistic to characterize such topics as disciplinary procedure, including arbitration; strike provisions; management-rights clauses; and employee promotions, evaluations, and transfers as unimportant to the bargaining process. They are matters which have traditionally been fought over by both parties during contract negotiations. To treat them as inconsequential demeans the very bargaining process we are entrusted to protect.

In fact, successful and effective bargaining already occurs on a large scale in circumstances where economic benefits play a small role, i.e., bargaining under the Federal Services Labor Management Relations Statute, as well as public sector bargaining on the state and local level. Moreover, meaningful bargaining has even occurred in the *Res-Care* context. In those cases where we asserted jurisdiction, bargaining proceeded despite the fact that the employer's ability to respond to union demands was restricted by its contract with the exempt entity....

In *Res-Care*, by requiring the employer to have control of economic terms before it would assert jurisdiction, the Board seems to have made a judgment, either directly or indirectly, that not only were certain contract terms of higher priority than others, but that such terms must be a part of contract negotiations. This, we think, amounts to the Board's entrance into the substantive aspects of the bargaining process which is not permitted under [various Supreme Court precedents]....

. . . .

Consequently, ... we have decided that it is not proper for the Board to decide whether to assert jurisdiction based on the Board's assessment of the quality and/or quantity of factors available for negotiation. The Employer in question must, by hypothesis, control some matters relating to the employment relationship, or else it would not be an employer under the Act. In our view, it is for the parties to determine whether bargaining is possible with respect to other matters and, in the final analysis, employee voters will decide for themselves whether they wish to engage in collective bargaining under those circumstances.[16]

In light of the above, in determining whether the Board should assert jurisdiction, the Board will only consider whether the employer meets the definition of

---

16. We do, however, continue to find, as in *Res-Care* that we will not employ a joint employer analysis to determine jurisdiction. Whether the private employer and the exempt entity are joint employers is irrelevant. The fact that we have no jurisdiction over governmental entities and thus cannot compel them to sit at the bargaining table does not destroy the ability of private employers to engage in effective bargaining over terms and conditions of employment within their control. The holding in *Ohio Inns, Inc.* that it would not effectuate the policies of the Act to assert jurisdiction over a private employer because the state is a joint employer is hereby overruled.

"employer" under Section 2(2) of the Act, and whether such employer meets the applicable monetary jurisdictional standards. . . .

We find it unnecessary to consider specifically the circumstances under which the Board would or would not find that an employer had committed an unfair labor practice by failing to bargain over a matter asserted to be beyond the employer's control, as it is well settled that such issues are not relevant to the Board's jurisdiction. . . . [W]ithout question, an employer's voluntary decision to contract away some of its authority over terms and conditions of employment should not be determinative of the Board's jurisdiction. . . .

The Regional Director found, based on the testimony of Executive Vice President Hunter, that the Employer is a for-profit Delaware corporation engaged in the operation of a job corps center in Clearfield, Utah. The Regional Director further found that the Employer received at least $500,000 in gross revenue during the past 12 months and received at least $50,000 in goods or services directly from outside the State of Utah as well as shipped goods or furnished services in the same amount directly outside the State. Accordingly, we find that the Employer is engaged in commerce within the meaning of the Act.

Based on the foregoing, the Regional Director's administrative dismissal of the instant petition is reversed. Therefore, we shall reinstate the petition and remand the case to the Regional Director for further appropriate action. . . .

While the Board took jurisdiction in *Management Training Corp.*, footnote 16 of this case raised an important and difficult question: what if there is a joint employment relationship in these situations?

American Federation of State, County and Municipal Employees, Council 31 v. Illinois State Labor Relations Board, State Panel

Supreme Court of Illinois
216 Ill. 2d 569, 839 N.E.2d 479, 298 Ill. Dec. 156 (2005)

FREEMAN, J.

This case arises from a decision of the Illinois State Labor Relations Board, State Panel (Board), dismissing a certification petition and a related unfair labor practice claim filed by the American Federation of State, County, and Municipal Employees, Council 31 (AFSCME). The appellate court . . . set aside the Board's decision. We granted leave to appeal and now reverse the judgment of the appellate court.

Background

The Illinois Department of Corrections (DOC) is required by law to provide medical care to the inmates incarcerated in its facilities. By law, it may do so by contracting with private vendors. . . .

Pursuant to this process, the DOC has contracted with three private vendors to provide medical services at 34 correctional facilities. Wexford Health Sources, Inc. (Wexford), is one such vendor and provides medical services at 19 DOC facilities. . . .

The contracts between the DOC and Wexford[1] identify Wexford as an independent contractor and provide that neither Wexford nor its employees are agents of the DOC. . . .

Pursuant to procedures under the [NLRA], AFSCME became the exclusive bargaining representative of Wexford's bargaining unit employees in 1997. Subsequently, AFSCME and Wexford negotiated a collective-bargaining agreement. . . . Wexford employs approximately 375 individuals at the Illinois facilities it services, of which approximately 275 to 280 are members of AFSCME. The DOC was not represented at any of the negotiations, nor is it a party to the collective-bargaining agreement. The collective-bargaining agreement between AFSCME and Wexford outlines a grievance procedure for employees and addresses issues such as the appointment of Wexford employees to various DOC committees. The agreement also covers employees' hours of work, temporary assignments, seniority, layoff and recall, vacancies, leaves of absence, discipline, personnel files, evaluation, terminations, personal time off, wages, and benefits.

On November 27, 2000, AFSCME filed a representation/certification petition with the Board. In the petition, AFSCME noted that the DOC is a public employer under the Illinois Public Labor Relations Act (5 ILCS 315/1 *et seq.*). AFSCME sought to represent, under that Act, certain employees of Wexford, who work at the DOC facilities. AFSCME admitted that it already represented these same employees under the [NLRA], and that a collective-bargaining agreement existed between them. AFSCME contended, however, that the DOC was a joint employer of these employees. Also on that same date, AFSCME filed an unfair labor practice charge with the Board against Wexford, alleging that a registered nurse had been suspended by Wexford because of her position as a union officer. . . .

[Wexford and The Illinois Department of Central Management Services, which represents the state in labor issues, filed motions to dismiss claiming the NLRA preempted the Board's jurisdiction. The Board denied the motions.]

. . . .

The Board held that a hearing before one of its administrative law judges (ALJ) was necessary in order to determine whether the DOC is a joint employer of the employees involved. Further, the Board held that, if it determined that the DOC

---

1. Wexford and the DOC have separate vendor contracts for each DOC facility. The general provisions of the contracts are the same, but each contract sets forth the particularized staffing needs of each facility. For example, a contract might state that Wexford must provide a certain type of medical worker for 30 hours per week in a given facility. Wexford chooses how to staff the position, whether it be with one full-time employee or two part-time employees who work 15 hours a week.

was a joint employer, the Board would then file a petition with the [NLRB] asking whether the Board's assertion of jurisdiction would violate principles of federal preemption.

At the hearing, extensive testimony was offered by the parties regarding the degree of control which Wexford exercised over its employees. At the conclusion of the hearing, the ALJ issued a recommended decision and order. Based on the evidence, the ALJ found that the DOC did not control and was not involved in the recruiting or hiring of Wexford's employees. Nor does the DOC control Wexford employees' wages, benefits, paid time off, overtime, scheduling, and termination. Further, although Wexford employees are subject to the DOC's security regulations, the ALJ ruled that those regulations did not constitute control for purposes of imposing employer status on the DOC. In light of all of these factors, the ALJ concluded that the DOC was not a joint employer of the Wexford bargaining unit employees. The ALJ further reasoned that the state's presence at the bargaining table was not necessary to establish an effective bargaining relationship, noting that Wexford and AFSCME had entered into a collective-bargaining agreement under federal law. Accordingly, the ALJ recommended that the Board dismiss the representation/certification petition. Several weeks later, the Board's executive director dismissed the unfair labor practice charge regarding the registered nurse. The director believed that the clear implication of the ALJ's recommended order was that the Wexford employees were not public employees. The director maintained that if the Board concluded that the ALJ's recommended order did not resolve the issue of whether the nurse was a public employee, the charge should be set for a hearing. . . .

[The Board] . . . agreed with the ALJ's recommendations. Specifically, the Board found that the DOC exercised little meaningful control over any aspect of the employment of the Wexford bargaining unit employees, including hiring, instruction, evaluation, wages, benefits, and overall direction. Accordingly, the Board dismissed AFSCME's representation/certification petition and affirmed the Director's dismissal of the related unfair labor practice charge.

[The Appellate Court] . . . set aside the Board's decision, concluding that the Board clearly erred in finding that the DOC was not a joint employer of the Wexford employees. According to the appellate court, the record evidence demonstrates that the DOC possesses and exercises significant control over the supervision, retention, and discipline of Wexford employees. The Board's conclusion that the DOC's role is limited to oversight to ensure compliance with the vendor contract is not supported by the record. . . . Rather, the court held that the DOC and Wexford were joint employers who share authority over the training, retention, daily direction, rules compliance, discipline, and discharge of employees. CMS, on behalf of the DOC, thereafter petitioned this court for leave to appeal, which we allowed. See 177 Ill.2d R. 315. Additional pertinent facts will be discussed further in the context of our analysis of the issues.

Analysis

. . . .

Wexford maintains . . . that this matter has been preempted by . . . the [NLRA]. Wexford points out that AFSCME, in this action, is attempting to organize a group of employees that it acknowledges is already covered by a collective-bargaining agreement negotiated under the [NLRA]. Put another way, AFSCME seeks the right to bargain with two employers, a private company and a state governmental agency, under two different labor relations statutes with respect to one group of employees. As such, AFSCME is asking to be the employees' sole bargaining representative under our state labor relations act just as it already is under the [NLRA]. Wexford maintains that such simultaneous or concurrent jurisdiction has never been recognized by any agency or judicial opinion. . . .

CMS . . . maintains that the issue need not be addressed in resolving this appeal. Indeed, at oral argument in this case, all of the parties agreed, including Wexford, that this court need not address the question of federal preemption because if the appellate court's conclusion that the DOC is a joint employer were to be upheld, the Board would seek an advisory opinion from the [NLRB] on the matter. See 29 C.F.R. pt. 100, § 101.39 (2003).

Thus, while we believe that the question of whether it is possible for both the Board and the [NLRB] to assert concurrent jurisdiction over a single group of employees is both novel and interesting, given the arguments and representations of the parties at oral argument, we decline to address the issue of federal preemption. We therefore proceed to the question of whether the Board's decision, that the DOC is not a joint employer of the petitioned-for employees, should be confirmed. . . .

The question of whether the DOC is a joint employer under the Illinois Public Labor Relations Act is a mixed question of law and fact. . . . Thus, we review the Board's decision under the clearly erroneous standard. . . .

AFSCME maintains that the Board erred by overlooking the significant amount of control the DOC has retained for itself over the terms and conditions of the Wexford employees' employment. Citing to both federal and state labor relations cases, AFSCME argues that it is the DOC's theoretical, indirect control over the terms and conditions of employment and not its actual exercise of (or lack thereof) control over those terms and conditions that is dispositive. We disagree.

Contrary to AFSCME's contentions, joint employer status does not turn on theoretical control over the terms and conditions of employment. In *Village of Winfield v. Illinois State Labor Relations Board*, this court considered whether two entities were joint employers under the Illinois Labor Relations Act. In so doing, we enunciated the following test to be used when undertaking a joint employer assessment:

> The test for the existence of joint employers is whether two or more employers exert significant control over the same employees—where from the evidence

it can be shown that they share or co-determine those matters governing essential terms and conditions of employment. Relevant factors to consider in making this determination include the putative joint employer's role in hiring and firing; promotions and demotions; setting wages, work hours, and other terms and conditions of employment; discipline; and actual day-to-day supervision and direction of employees on the job. An important consideration in determining whether a particular entity is an employer is the extent to which that entity is necessary to create an effective bargaining relationship. *Village of Winfield.*

We note that the above citation reveals that the standard set forth in *Winfield* was predicated upon the same standard utilized under federal law with respect to joint employer status. This is so because, in labor cases, the rulings of the National Labor Relations Board (NLRB) and the Federal courts when these bodies construe the [NLRA] are persuasive authority for similar provisions in the State Act.

The test enunciated in *Winfield* remains consistent with that utilized in federal cases addressing joint employer status. Indeed, the [NLRB] has recently noted:

> [T]he Board's test for determining whether two separate entities should be considered to be joint employers with respect to a specific group of employees has been a matter of settled law for approximately 20 years. In determining whether a joint employer relationship exists under this test, the Board analyzes whether putative joint employers share or co-determine those matters governing essential terms and conditions of employment. The essential element in this analysis is whether a putative joint employer's control over employment matters is direct and immediate.

> Thus, approximately 20 years ago, the Board, with court approval, abandoned its previous test in this area, which had focused on a putative joint employer's *indirect* control over matters relating to the employment relationship.

Thus, under federal law, theoretical control is not dispositive to the determination of joint employer status. . . .

[T]he Board in this case employed the correct legal standard to assess whether the DOC was a joint employer of the Wexford employees. Accordingly, we turn our analysis to the question of whether the Board's conclusion that the DOC was not a joint employer is clearly erroneous.

In this case, the ALJ found, and the Board agreed, that Wexford's control over matters governing the essential terms and conditions of employment was direct and substantial and that the DOC's involvement did not rise to the level of sharing meaningful control. We agree and do not believe that the Board's decision was clearly erroneous. Uncontroverted facts entered into evidence at the Board hearing included consideration of all of the relevant terms and conditions of employment, which we address in turn.

With respect to hiring, Wendy Milner, Wexford's director of Human Resources in Risk Management, testified that the DOC has no control or involvement in the recruitment and hiring of Wexford employees. Wexford solely assesses its recruiting needs, identifies candidates, accepts applications and resumes, and conducts interviews. Wexford then makes the hiring decision without consultation with or any input from the DOC. Although testimony revealed that the DOC does conduct a background check of Wexford employees, such a check exists for security purposes only and is unrelated to hiring considerations made by Wexford. The background check is required of all DOC employees, contract employees, consultants, interns, volunteers and anyone allowed regular access to a DOC facility.

Another term and condition of employment is wages. Theodore R. Sucher III, Wexford's executive vice president for operations, testified that the wages paid to Wexford employees are the result of negotiations memorialized in the binding collective-bargaining agreement between Wexford and AFSCME. Although the vendor contracts between Wexford and the DOC are based upon a certain hourly rate for each staff position, it is done so to calculate the total amount of compensation to be provided to Wexford under their vendor contract. It does not bind Wexford to adhere to those calculations in deciding what to pay its own employees. Rather, Wexford is bound by the terms of its collective-bargaining agreement with AFSCME. Evidence established at the hearing revealed that those wages can and do differ from the rates delineated in the vendor contracts. . . .

[The Court also found that Wexford controlled overtime and time-off issues.]

With respect to performance evaluations, the record reflects that such evaluations are conducted by Wexford managers. These evaluations are recorded on a standard Wexford evaluation sheet which is different from the evaluation sheet used by the DOC for its employees. . . . On rare occasions, particularly where there is no on-site Wexford supervisor, an HCUA may provide input into the evaluation. However, this input may or may not be incorporated into the formal evaluation based on Wexford's judgment and does not affect an employee's wages. . . .

[As to discipline] Wexford employees are subject to Wexford rules and regulations. . . . The process and any resulting disciplinary measures which are taken are initiated and ultimately decided by Wexford supervisors or managers. Disciplinary issues may be raised by an HCUA or medical director, but they are directed to the Wexford officials who then determine an appropriate course of action. All discipline issued by Wexford between January 2000 and the date of the hearing (approximately 100 occasions) was the independent decision of Wexford, not the DOC. In fact, testimony revealed that DOC employees do not have the authority to discipline any Wexford employees. . . .

We note at this juncture that both the appellate court and AFSCME put emphasis on the HCUA's involvement with Wexford employees in matters such as the paid-time-off and disciplinary measures as an example of joint employer control

in that the DOC is responsible for the day-to-day direction of Wexford employees. In contrast, the Board ruled that the HCUA's participation in these activities
was limited solely to their capacity as a monitor of the vendor contract between the
DOC and Wexford and to ensure compliance therewith. . . . We agree and note that
the Board's approach to this question is consistent with that of the [NLRB] in similar circumstances. For example, in *Local 254, Service Employees International Union*,
the National Board found that the direct supervision by the putative joint employer
over the employees for purposes of assuring that it received contracted services was
not sufficient to impose a joint employer status. The Board, in our view, did not
clearly err in characterizing the HCUAs' involvement as being one related to mere
contractual compliance as opposed to control over the day-to-day direction of the
Wexford employees.

Further testimony at the hearing by Thomas Page, deputy director of the DOC,
revealed that wardens at any of the DOC facilities have the authority to issue a stop
order barring an individual from access to that facility. . . . Although AFSCME contends that the warden's power to issue a stop order is tantamount to control over
firing, evidence at the hearing established that Wexford has the sole ability to discharge any of its employees without input or approval from the DOC. The state cannot and has never discharged a Wexford employee.

Notwithstanding the above evidence, both AFSCME and the appellate court
assign great weight to the warden's power to issue a stop order and equate it with
control over termination, which both maintain raises the DOC to the level of joint
employer. We disagree. . . .

[T]he Board's approach to this question, *i.e.*, whether the ability to enforce prison
security rules renders a prison the employer of those who fall within the ambit of
the security directive, finds support in judicial opinions where the ability to deny
access to a prison has been claimed to render a prison an employer. . . . [In] *Hojnacki
v. Klein-Acosta*, . . . plaintiff was an employee of a private company that contracted
services to the DOC. The court held that the State was not plaintiff's employer for
purposes of her Title VII claims. [Relevant here] is the court's conclusion that "[t]he
fact that Hojnacki (contract employee) was subject to the prison's security regulations . . . does not make her an employee of the DOC." . . . On appeal, the United
States Court of Appeals for the Seventh Circuit affirmed, stating one can control the
conduct of another contracting party by setting out in detail his obligations; this is
nothing more than the freedom of contract. This sort of one-time control is significantly different than the discretionary control an employer daily exercises over its
employees' conduct. . . .

We . . . hold that the Board did not clearly err in finding that the control that
DOC may exert over Wexford employees with respect to prison security and safety
does not rise to the level of control for purposes of determining employer status
under the Illinois Labor Relations Act. . . . [S]top orders apply to everyone entering
the facility, including visitors, employees, volunteers, chaplains, vendors or contract
employees. . . .

After carefully reviewing all of the evidence adduced, we cannot say that the Board clearly erred in ruling that the Wexford employees were not jointly employed by the DOC. With respect to hiring and firing, promotions, and demotions, setting wages, work hours, discipline, and actual day-to-day supervision and direction of employees on the job, the evidence supports the Board's finding that the DOC did not share or codetermine control over these matters so as to be considered a joint employer. Moreover, we agree with the sentiment expressed by the Board at the conclusion of its written decision:

The Board's lack of jurisdiction over [the Wexford] employees does not completely remove them from the purview of collective bargaining. Rather, it simply removes them from the jurisdiction of the [Illinois State Labor Relations] Act. However, these employees are currently represented by AFSCME and are covered by the [NLRA]. They are thus not in the collective bargaining no-man's land in which many subcontracted employees of a public sector entity find themselves. . . . AFSCME may seek redress for any disruption or potential unfair labor practice in its bargaining relationship with Wexford from the [NLRB]. That is, if Wexford has relied on its connection with the State to justify an alleged refusal to bargain over certain terms and conditions of employment, or if AFSCME has been unable to process grievances under the collective bargaining agreement's grievance procedure because the State has denied its stewards access to the employees workplaces, AFSCME can pursue resolution of those matters with the [NLRB] pursuant to the [NLRA]'s unfair labor practice provisions.

. . . In light of our resolution of the joint employer status question, the Board's dismissal of the related unfair labor practice charge was correct.

Notes

1. Had the court found a joint employer relationship, there would indeed have been a difficult preemption question and related practical complications. Imagine a case in which a public employer and a private employer were joint employers. How should the state board and NLRB deal with such a situation?

2. This case relied on private-sector precedent that existed before *Browning-Ferris*, *supra*, holding that "potential" control of wages, hours, and working conditions was always insufficient to create a joint employer relationship. As the private-sector materials in this chapter show, *Browning-Ferris* held that "potential" control could be enough to create such a relationship, but the Trump Board has since sought to reinstate the pre-*Browning-Ferris* approach. Again, to what extent should changes in private-sector precedent be automatically adopted in cases involving the public sector? In this area specifically, does it matter that joint employment rules existed before the NLRA and are used in a variety of legal contexts beyond labor law (including, but not limited to, employment law matters)?

3. In *Mosaica Acad. of Saginaw v. Michigan Educ. Ass'n*, Case No. 230332 (unpublished) (Mich. Ct. App. June 25, 2002), Mosaica Academy, a public school

academy under Michigan law, contracted with a private entity to provide educational services. The Michigan Education Association filed a petition with the Michigan Employment Relations Commission (MERC) to represent certain Academy employees. MERC held that the Academy was a public school subject to state regulation and that it exercised ultimate control over all terms and conditions of employment. The Court of Appeals, however, disagreed and found that the case should be deferred to the NLRB, both because a public and a private entity were involved in the school's operation and because it was unclear which entity was the actual employer. *Accord Cesar Chavez Academy, and the Leona Group, L.L.C., and Michigan Association of Public Employees*, 19 MPER ¶ 66 (Mich. Emp. Rel. Comm. 2006).

More broadly, charter schools will be considered public employers (and therefore their employees are public employees) if one of two factors is present: (1) the school is created directly by the state, so as to constitute an arm of government; or (2) the school is administered by individuals who are responsible to public officials or to the general electorate. *Chicago Mathematics & Science Academy Charter School, Inc.*, 359 N.L.R.B. No. 41 (2012) (holding the employees in question were private-sector employees). For more recent examples of the NLRB taking jurisdiction over charter schools, see *Pennsylvania Virtual Charter School*, 364 N.L.R.B. No. 87 (2016), and *Hyde Leadership Charter School—Brooklyn*, 364 N.L.R.B. No. 68 (2016) (rejecting objections by, respectively, the employer and the union). In *Voices for International Business v. NLRB*, 905 F.3d 770 (5th Cir. 2018), the Fifth Circuit upheld the NLRB taking jurisdiction over an "independent public school" (a type of charter school) in Louisiana, as the school was not a "political subdivision" of Louisiana, it was not controlled by political actors, and there was no public control over any charter school policies.

In *KIPP Academy Charter School*, 369 N.L.R.B. No. 48, *1 (2020), the Board declined requests to (i) reverse *Hyde Leadership Charter School* and *Pennsylvania Virtual Charter School*, and (ii) exercise its discretion to decline jurisdiction over charter schools as a class.

4. Although some close cases exist, usually when a public employer "contracts out" work to a private-sector company, it is clear that company's employees are private-sector employees covered by private-sector labor law. Sometimes, the employees of private contractors are themselves unionized, but often they are not. Public-sector union leaders worry that governments use privatization in part as a union-avoidance strategy (since the private sector has a much lower union density). More broadly, there is a heated debate over the utility and desirability of privatizing public services. Some criticize the practice on the grounds that private contractors are politically unaccountable, not infrequently corrupt, and ultimately less efficient. Others claim that privatization will bring market efficiency to government services. *Compare* Ellen Dannin, *Red Tape or Accountability: Privatization, Publicization, and Public Values*, 15 CORNELL J.L. & PUB. POL'Y 111 (2005) (skeptical of privatization), *with* Margaret Thatcher, et al., *Transforming Government Through*

Privatization (Reason Foundation 2006), *available at* http://reason.org/files/d76731
7fa4806296191436e95f68082a.pdf (pro-privatization).

5. One recent case involving privatization had the opposite effect. After the terrorist attacks on the World Trade Center buildings on September 11, 2001, the federal government took over the task of performing security screening in airports across the country through a new federal agency, the Transportation Safety Administration (TSA). Unlike most employees of the federal government, TSA employees (at that time) were not allowed to bargain collectively, pursuant to an order by then-TSA Secretary James Loy. *See* Joseph Slater, *Homeland Security vs. Workers' Rights? What the Federal Government Should Learn from History and Experience, and Why*, 6 U. Pa. J. Lab. & Emp. L. 295, 314–15 (2004). The TSA then, pursuant to its authorizing statute, contracted out screening work at the Kansas City International Airport to a private employer, Firstline. In 2005, a union sought to organize the Firstline employees at the Kansas City airport under NLRA procedures. Firstline acknowledged that it met the NLRB's normal statutory and discretionary jurisdictional standards. Still, it argued it was not subject to the Board's jurisdiction. It first asserted that the NLRB was statutorily barred from asserting jurisdiction because of Secretary Loy's order. Second, it argued that the Board should decline to assert jurisdiction in the interest of national security. ***Firstline Transp. Sec., Inc. and Int'l Union, Sec. Police & Fire Professionals***, 347 N.L.R.B. 447 (2006).

The Board rejected both claims. First, the Board noted that the statute creating the TSA was not dispositive on bargaining rights; it merely permitted the TSA Secretary to prohibit collective bargaining with TSA employees. But the Secretary had no such authority regarding the employees of private contractors. Second, it stressed that coverage by a labor law was not inconsistent with security concerns.

> The Board has been confronted with issues concerning national security and national defense since its early days. . . . [F]or over 60 years, in times of both war and peace, the Board has asserted jurisdiction over employers and employees that have been involved in national security and defense. We can find no case in which our protection of employees' Section 7 rights had an adverse impact on national security or defense. Our jurisprudence establishes that with regard to national security and defense, employee "[s]elf-organization for collective bargaining is not incompatible with efficient and faithful performance of duty." 347 N.L.R.B. 447, 453 (citing *Dravo Corp.*, 52 N.L.R.B. 322, 327 (1943)).

If that is correct, is there a defensible rationale for denying TSA employees collective bargaining rights? Is it incongruous to deny such employees such bargaining rights while employees of private contractors doing airport screening work have such rights? Consider that the NLRA generally provides more rights to employees and their unions than does the general federal sector labor relations statute (*see, e.g.,* Chapter 10 regarding scope of bargaining). In 2011, TSA employees were granted some limited bargaining rights, but are still not covered by the federal sector labor statute, and this came only after considerable political wrangling and controversy.

See TSA Director John Pistole, Determination: Transportation Security Officers and Collective Bargaining, Feb. 4, 2011, *available at* http://www.tsa.gov/sites/default/files/assets/pdf/determination_tso_and_collective_bargaining.pdf.

IV. The Structure and Operation of the National Labor Relations Board⃰

A. The National Labor Relations Board (NLRB) Is an Independent Federal Agency to Which Congress Delegated the Authority to Administer Private-Sector Labor Relations

Independent agencies, such as the NLRB, are created by acts of Congress, in this case, the National Labor Relations Act (NLRA) of 1935 as amended, 29 U.S.C. § 151 et seq. All of the NLRB's authority is derived from the NLRA and its progeny. The NLRB operates outside the federal executive branch and, technically speaking, is not directly subject to the President's control. However, the President appoints the NLRB's Chair and all of its members to staggered five-year terms with the advice and consent of the U.S. Senate. 29 U.S.C. § 153(a). Further, a majority of Board members may be members of the President's political party. So, the President has a means of indirectly influencing the Board's decision-making through the exercise of his appointments power. Nonetheless, the NLRB is independent of, and should not be confused with, the U.S. Department of Labor or any other department in the President's Cabinet.

Although the NLRB's jurisdiction is co-extensive with the Commerce Clause of the United States Constitution, *see NLRB v. Jones & Laughlin Steel Corp.*, 301 U.S. 1 (1937), the Board has declined to assert its jurisdiction to the fullest extent. For example, the Board will only assert jurisdiction over retail enterprises that have at least $500,000 total annual volume of business and over nonretail businesses that have at least $50,000 annual outflow (direct sales of goods to out-of-state consumers) or inflow (direct purchases of goods from out-of-state suppliers). Accordingly, very small businesses are effectively exempt from complying with the NLRA. Nor does the NLRB have jurisdiction over the railway and airline industries or most of its workers who are covered by the Railway Labor Act.

B. The NLRB Has a Bifurcated Institutional Organization — the General Counsel and the Board

The NLRB is divided into two "sides": the General Counsel side and the Board side.

⃰ Portions of this section are adapted from Anne Marie Lofaso, *NLRB Primer and the Boeing Complaint*, http://www.lerachapters.org/OJS/ojs-2.4.4-1/index.php/LERAMR/article/view/1790.

1. The General Counsel or GC-side Investigates and Prosecutes Employer and Union Unlawful Conduct (Known as Unfair Labor Practices)

The GC-side, which is led by the General Counsel, has the following three main divisions: (1) the Division of Operations Management, which oversees the regional offices, (2) the Division of Advice, which advises the regional offices, and (3) the Division of Enforcement Litigation. The General Counsel's staff investigates and prosecutes ULP cases and conducts secret-ballot elections through its fifty-two offices located throughout the United States. These offices include twenty-six regional offices, three subregional offices, and sixteen resident offices. These offices are headed by a Regional Director.

2. The Board or Board-side Reviews Cases Prosecuted by the General Counsel

The National Labor Relations Board is a five-member Board, led by a Chair, and which acts as a quasi-judicial administrative body. The Board decides cases based on formal records in administrative proceedings typically heard first by administrative law judges. Accordingly, the Board itself tends to act as an administrative appellate tribunal. The Board plays no role in the investigation of charges or the issuance of complaints.

C. The NLRB Is Tasked by Congress with Prosecuting (GC-side) and Remedying (Board-side) Unlawful Conduct by Employers and Unions (Unfair Labor Practices)

When Congress enacted the NLRA in 1935, it created the NLRB and charged that agency with prosecuting and remedying the unlawful conduct of employers and unions. 29 U.S.C. § 158. Such unlawful conduct is known as unfair labor practices (ULPs).

There are five basic employer ULPs, all of which are described in §§ 8(a)(1) through 8(a)(5) of the NLRA. Under those subsections, it is an unfair labor practice for an employer to:

(1) "interfere with, restrain, or coerce employees in the exercise of the rights guaranteed in section 7;"

(2) "dominate or interfere with the formation or administration of any [union] or contribute financial or other support to it . . . ;"

(3) "discriminat[e] in regard to hire or tenure of employment or any term or condition of employment to encourage or discourage membership in a [union] . . . ;"

(4) "discharge or otherwise discriminate against an employee because he has filed charges or given testimony under this Act;"

(5) "refuse to bargain collectively with the representatives of his employees. . . ."

There are two main types of cases processed by the Board—unfair labor practice (ULP) cases and representation cases. The Board follows this process for ULP cases:

Step 1. Charge. All ULP cases start with a charge that is filed with the appropriate regional office. Any person can file a charge. For example, an employee or a union could file a charge regarding employer conduct. The charge alleges that an employer or a union has acted unlawfully by engaging in one of several ULPs.

Step 2. Investigation. The regional office investigates the charge and recommends to the Regional Director whether or not there is reasonable cause to believe that an employer or a union has committed a violation of the NLRA. If there is no such reasonable cause, the Regional Director will refuse to issue a complaint. That refusal may be appealed to the General Counsel. At any time during the investigation, the parties may settle the case.

Step 3. Complaint and Answer. If after the investigation there is reasonable cause to believe that an employer or union has committed a violation of the law, the Regional Director, under the General Counsel's authority, issues a complaint and a notice of hearing. The respondent-employer or union must file an answer within ten days.

Step 4. Hearing. An administrative law judge presides over an administrative hearing. At that hearing, counsel for the General Counsel presents testimonial and documentary evidence to show that the respondent has committed the ULPs as alleged. Other parties of interest—such as a charged employer or union—may present evidence including cross-examination of the General Counsel's witnesses. At any time before, during, or after the hearing, the parties may settle the case.

Step 5. The Administrative Law Judge's Decision and Recommended Order. After the close of the hearing, the judge issues a decision (ALJD) and order, recommending one of two courses of action to the Board. First, the judge may simply dismiss the complaint. Second, the judge may find that there is merit to all or some of the allegations. If so, he/she will recommend that the Board order the respondent to cease and desist from the unlawful conduct and take appropriate affirmative action. For example, if an employee is found to have been discharged for undertaking protected activity, the employer could be ordered to rehire the employee with back pay and to refrain from interfering with protected activity in the future.

Step 6. Exceptions. Parties may file exceptions (objections) to the ALJD within a specified time period. If the parties fail to file timely exceptions, then the ALJD becomes the Board's order. If, however, the parties file exceptions then the entire record, including the judge's decision and recommended order, is transferred to the Board for review.

Step 7. Board Review. The Board and its staff review the entire record and the ALJD. In most cases, the Board acts as a panel of three members. In exceptional circumstances the entire Board will review the case. Oral argument is rarely granted.

After each Board member reviews the case, the panel makes a decision and issues a final decision and order (D&O).

The Board need not agree with either the administrative law judge's opinion or the General Counsel's litigation position. The Board's review is independent of the judge's and the General Counsel's legal analysis and its review may result in a variety of orders. For example, the Board may dismiss the complaint, or it may find merit to some or all of the allegations. If the Board finds merit to any of the allegations, it will order the respondent to cease and desist from the unlawful conduct and to take appropriate affirmative action necessary to remedy the ULP. Occasionally, the Board may remand the case to the administrative law judge for additional findings.

Step 8. Court Review. At this stage, the losing party (known as the aggrieved party) may take one of three courses of action. First, it may try to settle the case with the Regional Office. Second, it may petition a United States court of appeals for review of the Board's D&O. Third, it can do nothing and wait for the Board to apply to a court of appeals to enforce its D&O. If the case goes to a court of appeals for review, then attorneys in the NLRB's Division of Enforcement (Section C.1. above) represent the Board in court. The court may make several types of decisions. It may decide (1) to enforce the Board's order, (2) to enforce the Board's order with some modifications; (3) to grant the petition for review and deny enforcement of the Board's order, (4) to enforce the Board's order in part and to grant the petition for review in part, or (5) to dismiss the complaint. In rare cases, the Supreme Court may review the case. Less than one NLRB case per year goes to the Supreme Court.

Step 9. Enforcement. Once the Board's order has been enforced by a federal court the parties are under court order to comply with any part of the Board's order that has been enforced. A party's failure to comply with a court-enforced Board order may result in contempt proceedings.

D. The General Counsel Is Also Tasked with Administering the Process by Which Workers Choose Whether to Organize a Union with an Appeal to the Board

The NLRA's §9(a) empowers a majority of workers in a "bargaining unit" to "designate" or "select" a representative "for the purposes of collective bargaining." The General Counsel, through the regional director and regional offices, administers this process. The usual means by which workers select a bargaining representative is through a NLRB-managed election.

The Board follows this process in election cases:

Step 1. To start the election process, a petition must be filed with the nearest NLRB regional office showing interest in the union from at least thirty percent of employees. Agents from the regional office investigate to make sure the Board has jurisdiction and there is nothing barring an election.

Step 2. The Board's agents typically seek an agreement between the employer and union setting the time and place for the election, the ballot language, the size and shape of the "bargaining unit" in which the election will be held, and a means of determining who is eligible to vote. Once an agreement is in place, the parties authorize the NLRB Regional Director to conduct the election. If no agreement is reached, the Regional Director can schedule a hearing and then order the election and set the conditions in accordance with the Board's rules and its decisions.

Step 3. Elections are expected to be held within thirty days of an election order by the regional director or authorization from the employer and union, but they can be delayed by ULP charges alleging conduct that would interfere with employee free choice in the election.

When a union is already in place, a competing union may file an election petition if the labor contract has expired or is about to expire, and it can show interest by at least thirty percent of the employees. This would normally result in a three-way election, with the choices being the incumbent union, the challenging union, and "none." If none of the three receives a majority vote, a runoff will be conducted between the top two vote-getters. In runoff election and when there is only one union participating, elections are decided by a majority of votes cast.

Step 4. Any party may file objections with the regional director within seven days of the vote count. The regional director's ruling may be appealed to the Board. The Board's decisions on these appeals are not subject to judicial review except indirectly: a party may commit a ULP—for example, by refusing to bargain—as a means of seeking to adjudicate the regional director's decisions associated with the election. Can you see why this process permits employers to appeal Board representation case decisions to court in a way that unions, practically speaking, cannot? Results of an election also may be set aside if the employer or the union engaged in conduct that interfered with the employees' freedom of choice.

Step 5. The Board will certify a union that receives a majority of the votes cast as the employees' bargaining representative. An employer's failure to bargain with the union at this point is a ULP.

As an alternative to an NLRB-conducted elections, a union may persuade an employer to voluntarily recognize a union that can demonstrate majority support from employees, for example, by asking them to sign cards authorizing the union to serve as their representative. The NLRB does not play a role in the voluntary recognition process.

Chapter 3

Union Organizing and Employer Speech

I. Introduction

Section 7 of the NLRA provides, in relevant part, that:

> Employees shall have the right to self-organization, to form, join, or assist labor organizations, to bargain collectively through representatives of their own choosing, and to engage in other concerted activities for the purpose of collective bargaining or other mutual aid or protection. . . .

In turn, §8(a)(1) provides that it shall be a ULP for an employer "to interfere with, restrain, or coerce employees in the exercise of the rights guaranteed in section 7."

This chapter discusses §7 protections, primarily in the context of union organizing. It examines what types of organizing activities are protected, what rules employers may and may not legally enforce as to organizing on their property, and what types of speech and other propaganda the two sides may legally use. It also considers proposals for reform in this area.

Rules in the public sector are often similar, although the Constitution can add further wrinkles, especially regarding access to property. Over the last several decades, private-sector employers have generally tended to oppose union organizing much more vigorously and vehemently than their public-sector counterparts. That, however, may be changing.

II. Organizing on an Employer's Property in the Private Sector

A. Employee Solicitation Rights on the Employer's Property

1. Solicitation and Distribution in the Physical World

Republic Aviation Corp. v. NLRB

Supreme Court of the United States
324 U.S. 793, 65 S. Ct. 982, 89 L. Ed. 1372 (1945)

REED, J.

In the *Republic Aviation Corporation* case, the employer, a large and rapidly growing military aircraft manufacturer, adopted, well before any union activity at the plant, a general rule against soliciting which read as follows:

"Soliciting of any type cannot be permitted in the factory or offices."

The Republic plant was located in a built-up section of Suffolk County, New York. An employee persisted after being warned of the rule in soliciting union membership in the plant by passing out application cards to employees on his own time during lunch periods. The employee was discharged for infraction of the rule and, as the [NLRB] found, without discrimination on the part of the employer toward union activity.

Three other employees were discharged for wearing UAW-CIO union steward buttons in the plant after being requested to remove the insignia. The union was at that time active in seeking to organize the plant. The reason which the employer gave for the request was that as the union was not then the duly designated representative of the employees, the wearing of the steward buttons in the plant indicated an acknowledgment . . . of the authority of the stewards to represent the employees in dealing with the management and might impinge upon the employer's policy of strict neutrality in union matters and might interfere with the existing grievance system of the corporation.

The Board [found] that wearing union steward buttons by employees did not carry any implication of recognition of that union . . . where, as here, there was no competing labor organization in the plant. The discharges of the stewards, however, were found not to be motivated by opposition to the particular union, or . . . to unionism.

The Board determined that the promulgation and enforcement of the "no solicitation" rule violated Section 8(1) of the [NLRA] as it interfered with, restrained and coerced employees in their rights under Section 7 and discriminated against the discharged employee under Section 8(3). It determined also that the discharge of the stewards violated Section 8(1) and 8(3). As a consequence of its conclusions as to the solicitation and the wearing of the insignia, the Board entered the usual cease and desist order and directed the reinstatement of the discharged employees with back pay and also the rescission of "the rule against solicitation in so far as it prohibits union activity and solicitation on company property during the employees' own time." ... The [Second Circuit affirmed] ... and we granted certiorari ... because of conflict with the decisions of other circuits.

In the case of *Le Tourneau Company of Georgia*, two employees were suspended two days each for distributing union literature or circulars on the employees' own time on company owned and policed parking lots, adjacent to the company's fenced in plant, in violation of a long standing and strictly enforced rule, adopted prior to union organization activity about the premises, which read as follows:

> "In the future no Merchants, Concern, Company or Individual or Individuals will be permitted to distribute, post or otherwise circulate handbills or posters, or any literature of any description on Company property without first securing permission from the Personnel Department."

The rule was adopted to control littering and petty pilfering from parked autos by distributors. The Board determined that there was no union bias or discrimination by the company in enforcing the rule. ...

The Board found that the application of the rule to the distribution of union literature by the employees on company property which resulted in the lay-offs was an unfair labor practice under Section 8(1) and 8(3). ... The [Fifth Circuit] reversed ... and we granted certiorari because of conflict with the [*Republic Aviation*] case. ...

These cases bring here for review the action of the [NLRB] in working out an adjustment between the undisputed right of self-organization assured to employees under the Wagner Act and the equally undisputed right of employers to maintain discipline in their establishments. Like so many others, these rights are not unlimited in the sense that they can be exercised without regard to any duty which the existence of rights in others may place upon employer or employee. Opportunity to organize and proper discipline are both essential elements in a balanced society.

The Wagner Act did not undertake the impossible task of specifying in precise and unmistakable language each incident which would constitute an unfair labor practice. On the contrary that Act left to the Board the work of applying the Act's general prohibitory language in the light of the infinite combinations of events which might be charged as violative of its terms. Thus a "rigid scheme of remedies" is avoided and administrative flexibility within appropriate statutory limitations obtained to accomplish the dominant purpose of the legislation. ... So far as we are here concerned that purpose is the right of employees to organize for mutual aid without employer interference. This is the principle of labor relations which the Board is to foster.

The gravamen of the objection of both Republic and Le Tourneau to the Board's orders is that they rest on a policy formulated without due administrative procedure. To be more specific it is that the Board cannot substitute its knowledge of industrial relations for substantive evidence. The contention is that there must be evidence before the Board to show that the rules and orders of the employers interfered with and discouraged union organization in the circumstances and situation of each company. Neither in the *Republic* nor the *Le Tourneau* cases can it properly be said that there was evidence or a finding that the plant's physical location made solicitation away from company property ineffective to reach prospective union members. Neither of these is like a mining or lumber camp where the employees pass their rest as well as their work time on the employer's premises, so that union organization must proceed upon the employer's premises or be seriously handicapped. . . .

The [NLRA] creates a system for the organization of labor with emphasis on collective bargaining by employees with employers in regard to labor relations which affect commerce. An essential part of that system is the provision for the prevention of unfair labor practices by the employer which might interfere with the guaranteed rights. The method for prevention of unfair labor practices is for the Board to hold a hearing on a complaint which has been duly served upon the employer who is charged with an unfair labor practice. At that hearing the employer has the right to file an answer and to give testimony. This testimony, together with that given in support of the complaint, must be reduced to writing and filed with the Board. The Board upon that testimony is directed to make findings of fact and dismiss the complaint or enter appropriate orders to prevent in whole or in part the unfair practices which have been charged. Upon the record so made as to testimony and issues, courts are empowered to enforce, modify or set aside the Board's orders, subject to the limitation that the findings of the Board as to facts, if supported by evidence, are conclusive.

Plainly this statutory plan for an adversary proceeding requires that the Board's orders on complaints of unfair labor practices be based upon evidence which is placed before the Board by witnesses who are subject to cross-examination by opposing parties. . . . One of the purposes which lead to the creation of such boards is to have decisions based upon evidential facts under the particular statute made by experienced officials with an adequate appreciation of the complexities of the subject which is entrusted to their administration. . . .

[In *Republic Aviation*] . . . petitioner felt that it would violate its neutrality in labor organization if it permitted the display of a steward button by an employee. From its point of view, such display represented to other employees that the union already was recognized.

No evidence was offered that any unusual conditions existed in labor relations, the plant location or otherwise to support any contention that conditions at this plant differed from those occurring normally at any other large establishment.

The *Le Tourneau Company of Georgia* case also is barren of special circumstances. . . .

The Intermediate Report in the *Republic Aviation* case set out the reason why the rule against solicitation was considered inimical to the right of organization.[6]

---

6. "Thus, under the conditions obtaining in January 1943, the respondent's employees, working long hours in a plant engaged entirely in war production and expanding with extreme rapidity, were entirely deprived of their normal right to 'full freedom of association' in the plant on their own time, the very time and place uniquely appropriate and almost solely available to them therefor. The respondent's rule is therefore in clear derogation of the rights of its employees guaranteed by the Act."

This was approved by the Board. . . . The Board's reasons for concluding that the petitioner's insistence that its employees refrain from wearing steward buttons [are as follows]:[7]

In [*Le Tourneau*], the discussion of the reasons underlying the findings was much more extended . . .[8]

The Board has fairly, we think, explicated in [*Peyton Packing Co.*, 49 N.L.R.B. 828 (1943) and other cases] the theory which moved it to its conclusions in these cases. The excerpts from its opinions just quoted show this. The reasons why it has decided as it has are sufficiently set forth. We cannot agree, as Republic urges, that in these present cases reviewing courts are left to "sheer acceptance" of the Board's conclusions or that its formulation of policy is "cryptic." . . .

Not only has the Board in these cases sufficiently expressed the theory upon which it concludes that rules against solicitation or prohibitions against the wearing of insignia must fall as interferences with union organization but in so far as rules against solicitation are concerned, it had theretofore succinctly expressed the requirements of proof which it considered appropriate to outweigh or overcome the presumption as to rules against solicitation. In [*Peyton Packing Co.*, at 843, 844] . . . the presumption adopted by the Board is set forth.[10]

---

7. We do not believe that the wearing of a steward button is a representation that the employer either approves or recognizes the union in question as the representative of the employees, especially when, as here, there is no competing labor organization in the plant. Furthermore, there is no evidence in the record herein that the respondent's employees so understood the steward buttons or that the appearance of union stewards in the plant affected the normal operation of the respondent's grievance procedure. On the other hand, the right of employees to wear union insignia at work has long been recognized as a reasonable and legitimate form of union activity, and the respondent's curtailment of that right is clearly violative of the Act.

8. As the [Second Circuit] has held, "It is not every interference with property rights that is within the Fifth Amendment and . . . inconvenience or even some dislocation of property rights, may be necessary in order to safeguard the right to collective bargaining." The Board has frequently applied this principle in decisions involving varying sets of circumstances, where it has held that the employer's right to control his property does not permit him to deny access to his property to persons whose presence is necessary there to enable to employees effectively to exercise their right to self-organization and collective bargaining, and in those decisions which have reached the courts, the Board's position has been sustained. Similarly, the Board has held that, while it was "within the province of an employer to promulgate and enforce a rule prohibiting union solicitation during working hours," it was "not within the province of an employer to promulgate and enforce a rule prohibiting union solicitation by an employee outside of working hours, although on company property," the latter restriction being deemed an unreasonable impediment to the exercise of the right to self-organization.

10. "The Act, of course, does not prevent an employer from making and enforcing reasonable rules covering the conduct of employees on company time. Working time is for work. It is therefore within the province of an employer to promulgate and enforce a rule prohibiting union solicitation during working hours. Such a rule must be presumed to be valid in the absence of evidence that it was adopted for a discriminatory purpose. It is no less true that time outside working hours, whether before or after work, or during luncheon or rest periods, is an employee's time to use as he wishes without unreasonable restraint, although the employee is on company property. It is

. . . We perceive no error in the Board's adoption of this presumption. The Board had previously considered similar rules in industrial establishments and the definitive form which the *Peyton Packing Company* decision gave to the presumption was the product of the Board's appraisal of normal conditions about industrial establishments. Like a statutory presumption or one established by regulation, the validity, perhaps in a varying degree, depends upon the rationality between what is proved and what is inferred.

In the Republic Aviation case, petitioner urges that irrespective of the validity of the rule against solicitation, its application in this instance did not violate Section 8(3) . . . because the rule was not discriminatorily applied against union solicitation but was impartially enforced against all solicitors. It seems clear, however that if a rule against solicitation is invalid as to union solicitation on the employer's premises during the employee's own time, a discharge because of violation of that rule discriminates within the meaning of Section 8(3) in that it discourages membership in a labor organization.

Republic Aviation Corp. v. NLRB is affirmed. . . .

NLRB v. Le Tourneau Co. is reversed.

Notes

1. *Republic Aviation* recognized that the workplace is "uniquely appropriate" for union organizing activities and thus is central to the exercise of § 7 rights. The Eleventh Circuit has similarly acknowledged that the workplace "is the one place where [employees] traditionally seek to persuade fellow workers in matters affecting their union organizational life and other matters related to their status as employees." *Southern Services, Inc. v. NLRB*, 954 F.2d 700 (11th Cir. 1992). As the Supreme Court has further observed, the right of self-organization depends in part on the ability of employees to learn the advantages of self-organization from others. *See NLRB v. Babcock & Wilcox Co.*, 351 U.S. 105, 113 (1956).

2. Organizing in the workplace also implicates employer rights and interests. To what extent are § 7 rights in conflict with owners' property rights, and what is the source of those rights? Re-read footnote 8 of *Republic Aviation*. There the Court acknowledges, but limits, the employer's property rights in this context.

3. The balance between employer and employee rights is embodied in the "*Peyton Packing* presumption," adopted by the Court in *Republic Aviation*. Under this presumption, a facially neutral rule prohibiting solicitation during *working time* is presumptively *valid* absent proof that the rule was enacted for a discriminatory purpose. On the other hand, a facially neutral rule prohibiting all soliciting on the employer's

---

therefore not within the province of an employer to promulgate and enforce a rule prohibiting union solicitation by an employee outside of working hours, although on company property. Such a rule must be presumed to be an unreasonable impediment to self-organization and therefore discriminatory in the absence of evidence that special circumstances make the rule necessary in order to maintain production or discipline."

property during *non-working* time is presumptively *invalid* absent evidence that special circumstances make the rule necessary for production or discipline. In adopting this rule, *Republic Aviation* found that these presumptions strike the appropriate balance between the managerial rights of employers and the § 7 rights of workers.

4. Thus, to be presumptively valid, a rule restricting solicitation must state with reasonable clarity that the rule does not apply during periods when employees are not scheduled to be working (*i.e.*, lunch and break periods, before and after work, etc.). For example, in *Our Way, Inc.*, 268 N.L.R.B. 394 (1983), the Board held that, although *Republic Aviation* and *Peyton Packing* used the term "working hours," restrictions on distribution or solicitation during "working hours," as opposed to "working time," are overly broad. The Board reasoned that employees could reasonably construe the term "working hours" to connote the time period running from the beginning to the end of a work shift, including breaks and lunch. *See also St. George Warehouse, Inc.*, 331 N.L.R.B. 454 (2000) ("In this regard, 'work hours' as opposed to 'working time,' connotes all hours of the workday including break and lunch times.").

5. The Board has distinguished between oral solicitations and distributing union literature. In distribution cases, the Board has held that a facially neutral rule restricting distribution to non-working areas of a workplace is presumptively valid regardless of whether the distribution of union literature occurs during working time. *See Stoddard-Quirk Mfg. Co.*, 138 N.L.R.B. 615 (1962). Why the distinction? What employer interests are implicated by the distribution of physical materials that are not implicated in oral solicitation?

For purposes of this distinction, the Board has held that handing out union cards is a form of solicitation. Similarly, the Board has found circulating a petition to garner employee signatures in protest of a management action was a form of solicitation. *See National Semiconductor Corp.*, 272 N.L.R.B. 973 (1984). On the other hand, handbilling is a classic example of distribution. *Stoddard-Quirk, supra*.

6. *Republic Aviation* noted that wearing union insignia at work had long been recognized as "a legitimate form of union activity." Courts have held that this right is "near-absolute." *See Meijer, Inc. v. NLRB*, 130 F.3d. 1209 (6th Cir. 1997). *Republic Aviation* held that, absent special circumstances, disciplining employees for wearing union buttons or insignia was an unfair labor practice. Examples of special circumstances include: maintenance of productivity and discipline, safety, preventing alienation of customers, preventing violence between employees, and promotion of patient care. *See, e.g., Eckert Fire Protection, Inc.*, 332 N.L.R.B. 198 (2000). Contact with customers in and of itself is not a special circumstance that automatically validates a ban on insignia. *See Flamingo Hilton-Laughlin*, 330 N.L.R.B. 287 (1999); *Albertsons, Inc.*, 300 N.L.R.B. 1013 (1990). However, an employer may ban large, brightly colored, potentially provocative union buttons. *See Virginia Elec. & Power Co. v. NLRB*, 703 F.2d 79 (4th Cir. 1983); *see also S. New England Tele. Co. v. NLRB*, 793 F.3d 93 (D.C. Cir. 2015) (special circumstances doctrine applied, and employer phone company did not violate NLRA by banning employees who interacted with the public from wearing union shirts that said "Inmate" or "Prisoner of AT$T").

7. Still, the Board has recognized that, given practical constraints inherent in certain industries, broader restrictions on solicitation, distribution, and the wearing of union insignia may be necessary. In a recent decision, the NLRB upheld a Wal-Mart rule banning associates from wearing large buttons (including those with union insignia) while in store areas to which customers had access. *Wal-Mart Stores, Inc.,* 368 N.L.R.B. No. 146 (2019). The Board deferred to Wal-Mart's explanation that larger buttons might make it harder for customers and "asset protection" employees to distinguish store employees from others, stating that it "must not second-guess the Respondent's decisions as to how it should run its business—provided, of course, that those decisions do not unreasonably interfere with the exercise of Section 7 rights."

However, in another recent decision, the Fifth Circuit affirmed the Board's conclusion that a fast-food chain violated the NLRA by maintaining a rule prohibiting employees from wearing "any type of pin or sticker" on their uniform. The case arose after employees of In-N-Out were told that they could not wear "Fight for $15" pins during work time. The Board emphasized that the "special circumstances" defense is narrow, and that employers cannot qualify for it simply by pointing to the fact that employees are required to wear a uniform. Further, the fact that In-N-Out occasionally required employees to wear specific promotional pins undermined its argument that the "no buttons" rule was necessary to maintain In-N-Out's public image. *In-N-Out Burger v. NLRB,* 894 F.3d 707 (5th Cir. 2018).

The Board generally permits non-working time bans on insignia, solicitation, and distribution in "immediate patient care" areas of hospitals such as patients' rooms, operating rooms, and other treatment areas. *See Cooper Health Systems,* 327 N.L.R.B. 1159 (1999); *Doctors' Hospital of Staten Island,* 325 N.L.R.B. 730 (1998). However, the Board will presume that such bans are invalid if they apply during non-working time in "patient access" or "visitor access" areas (*i.e.,* cafeterias, gift shops, and entrances). In *Beth Israel Hospital v. NLRB,* 437 U.S. 483 (1978), the Supreme Court approved this distinction. What constitutes an "immediate patient care area"? For instance, what about a visitor's room that is located near patient rooms? Finally, note that selective enforcement of such policies can also render them invalid. *Healthbridge Mgmt., LLC,* 360 N.L.R.B. 937 (2014).

8. Even presumptively valid bars on solicitations may still violate §8(a)(1) if they are applied in a discriminatory manner, *i.e.,* to prohibit employees from distributing union literature but not to prohibit other similar kinds of solicitation. In *NLRB v. J. P. Stevens & Co.,* 563 F.2d 8, 15 (2d Cir. 1977), the court found such a violation when the supervisor asked employees to stop distributing union literature on company property. The court found that the company routinely tolerated the distribution of other literature and enforced its no distribution rule only when union activity was involved. The court held that the employer violated §8(a)(1) in this context merely by asking the employees to distribute the union literature off the property. It observed that §8(a)(1) does not require the employer to discipline employees, only that the employer interferes with the employee's exercise of §7 rights. *See also Cooper Health System,* 327 N.L.R.B. 1159 (1999) (employer committed ULP by strictly

enforcing its facially valid no-solicitation/no-distribution rule against union solici-tation while permitting solicitations for Tupperware, Avon products, Girl Scout Cookies, Christmas gifts and gift baskets, cheesecakes, candles, decorations, and birdhouses in the same hospital areas).

What constitutes "discrimination" against a union can be a murky area, how-ever. For example, the Board has rejected discrimination claims in the context of a *de minimis* charitable contribution. *Hammary Mfg. Corp.*, 265 N.L.R.B. 57 (1982). After *Hammary*, the General Counsel issued a memo clarifying the *de minimis* exception. The memo explains that an employer may permit "a small number of isolated 'beneficent acts'" as exceptions to a no solicitation rule, but it may not permit frequent charitable solicitations and/or charitable solicitations over a long period of time, while simultaneously enforcing a rule against union solicitation.

9. Otherwise presumptively valid bars on solicitation may also violate § 8(a)(1) if they were adopted for a discriminatory purpose. It can be difficult to prove an employer's discriminatory intent, but timing that suggests the rules were adopted in response to union organizing can be probative evidence. *See Waste Mgmt. of Palm Beach*, 329 N.L.R.B. 198 (1999).

10. Further complicating matters, courts sometimes have a narrower view than the Board of what constitutes discrimination. In *6 West Ltd. Corp. v. NLRB*, 237 F.3d 767 (7th Cir. 2001), the court refused to defer to the Board's finding that the employer had violated § 8(a)(1) when it allowed solicitations for Girl Scout Cookies, Christmas ornaments, and hand-painted bottles, but not for union membership. The court explained:

> We are at a loss to comprehend how a restaurant could maintain positive relations with its employees and customers if it failed to allow an activity as innocent as the sale of girl scout cookies or the sale of hand-blown Christmas ornaments during the yuletide season. In short, the examples listed by the ALJ can be seen as beneficial to all employees, whereas the union solicitation by the three disciplined employees obviously, according to the record, made some of the employees uncomfortable enough to complain to management. A restaurant in the United States of America should be free to prohibit solicita-tions on the premises that interfere with or bother employees or customers, and allow those solicitations which neither interfere with nor bother employ-ees or customers. In this case, the record is barren of any evidence that . . . management allowed other unwanted solicitation in its restaurant. . . . Tucci was not in violation of the NLRA when it issued written warnings to three employees for union solicitation on the company's premises. 237 F.3d 767, 780.

The Court assumes that the sale of Christmas ornaments is "beneficial to all employees." Would the sale of such items necessarily be beneficial to Jewish or athe-ist employees? Second, it distinguishes between unwanted and wanted solicitations and then concludes that it was not discriminatory to discipline union solicitations because the employer never permitted other unwanted solicitations. Under that reasoning, would an employer always be permitted to suppress union solicitation so long as the employer suppresses any solicitation it finds distasteful?

11. *Republic Aviation* found a violation of §8(a)(3) as well as a violation of §8(a) (1). Section 8(a)(3) bars, among other things, discrimination to discourage union membership. Chapter 5 discusses this section in detail, but for now note that, ordinarily, an employer must possess anti-union animus to violate §8(a)(3). However, per the Board's findings, neither *Republic Aviation* nor *Le Tourneau* was motivated by anti-union animus when adopting the policies in question. Given this, how did the Court justify and uphold the Board's finding of a §8(a)(3) violation?

12. Given §8(a)(1)'s broader prohibition, was it necessary for the *Republic Aviation* Court to analyze the §8(a)(3) issue? *Compare NLRB v. Burnup & Sims, Inc.*, 379 U.S. 21 (1964). There, the employer fired two employees during a union organizing campaign after the employer was told that the employees had threatened to use dynamite to gain recognition. The Board found that this threat was untrue, but also that the employer had reasonably believed that such a threat existed. Nevertheless, the Board held that the employer's good-faith belief was not a defense to either a §8(a)(1) or a §8(a)(3) violation and ordered reinstatement and back pay. The Court affirmed the Board's order solely on the basis of §8(a)(1), indicating:

> We find it unnecessary to reach the questions raised under §8(a)(3) for we are of the view ... §8(a)(1) was plainly violated, whatever the employer's motive.... A protected activity acquires a precarious status if innocent employees can be discharged while engaging in it, even though the employer acts in good faith. It is the tendency of [such] discharges to weaken or destroy the §8(a)(1) right that is controlling. We are not in the realm of managerial prerogatives.... Had the alleged dynamiting threats been wholly disassociated from §7 activities quite different considerations might apply.

Given this "strict liability" under §8(a)(1), how can an employer, faced with the potential threat of violent organizing tactics, protect itself?

13. *Republic Aviation* explained that it was the Board's role to apply the broad language of the NLRA to "the infinite combinations of events which might be charged as violat[ing] ... its terms." The Court further observed that such a division of labor is sensible, as "experienced officials with an adequate appreciation of the complexities of the subject" are better situated to determine what constitutes unlawful conduct. 324 U.S. 793, 800. Do you agree with the Court that the Board should be given wide latitude in adjudicating these cases? How does this approach conform to the approach subsequently articulated in *Chevron U.S.A. Inc. v. Natural Resources Defense Council, Inc.*, 467 U.S. 837 (1984)?

2. Electronic Solicitation and Distribution

What if solicitation or distribution takes place via email? This could involve use of the employer's equipment—for example, workers may send or receive email from their work computers, or they may use their work email addresses, meaning the resulting messages will be stored on the employer's server. In recent years, the Board has taken different approaches to this question.

The Board's current approach distinguishes communications that use employer resources from those that do not. In *Caesars Entertainment d/b/a Rio All-Suites Hotel and Casino*, 368 N.L.R.B. No. 143 (2019), the Board held that employer property rights trumped employees' interests in using the employer's computer equipment to engage in protected concerted activity. The Board analogized employees' use of an employer's computers and server space to "employer-owned televisions, bulletin boards, copy machines, telephones, or public-address systems." This analogy was important, because the Board has generally held that §7 does not protect employees' use of employers' finite resources, although employers may not discriminate by, for example, allowing employees to use the office photocopier to create anti-union fliers but not pro-union ones. Further, the *Caesars Entertainment* Board reasoned that traditional methods of communication, such as those discussed in *Republic Aviation*, were adequate to allow workers to decide whether and how to exercise their §7 rights. Thus, the Board wrote that:

> The teaching of [*Republic Aviation*] regarding the times when and places where employers may restrict Section 7 activity has little relevance to an employer's email system, which creates a virtual space in which the distinction between working and nonworking areas is meaningless, and in which solicitation may and often would take place asynchronously—i.e., where Section 7-related communications may be composed, sent, and read at different times. We need not reach the issue of whether, as numerous amici contend, employers have no practical means of restricting nonwork emails to nonworking time under *Purple Communications* [361 N.L.R.B. No. 126 (2014)]. We simply observe that *Republic Aviation* was premised on the principle that "working time is for work" and involved circumstances in which the line separating working from nonworking time could be clearly perceived and understood by employers and employees alike, which is not the case with emails.

> More fundamentally, *Republic Aviation* does not support the proposition, embraced by a Board majority in *Purple Communications,* that if an employer grants employees access to its email system, it must allow them to use it for Section 7 activity absent special circumstances. To the contrary, even with respect to on-premises solicitation and literature distribution, any limitation imposed by the Act on "the employer's normal and legitimate property rights . . . is to be determined by the nature of the need." Moreover, "[w]here there is no necessary conflict neither right should be abridged. By the same [token], where conflict does exist, the abridgement of either right should be kept to a minimum." It necessarily follows that the scope of any limitation on employer property rights in equipment must likewise "be determined by the nature of the need" and, where necessary to accommodate Section 7 rights, "kept to a minimum."

Properly understood, then, *Republic Aviation* stands for the twin propositions that employees must have "*adequate* avenues of communication" in order to meaningfully exercise their Section 7 rights and that employer property rights must yield to employees' Section 7 rights when necessary to avoid creating an "*unreasonable* impediment to the exercise of the right to self-organization." In the typical workplace, however, oral solicitation and face-to-face literature distribution provide more than "adequate avenues of communication."

Caesars Entertainment was a return to the position that the Board initially took in 2007. *Register Guard*, 351 N.L.R.B 1110 (2007). However, in the interim, the Obama Board had adopted a different approach, applying a modified version of the *Republic Aviation* presumptions to employees' electronic communications. In the case that *Caesars Entertainment* overruled, the Board wrote that:

> [W]e adopt a presumption that employees who have been given access to the employer's email system in the course of their work are entitled to use the system to engage in statutorily protected discussions about their terms and conditions of employment while on nonworking time, absent a showing by the employer of special circumstances that justify specific restrictions.

Purple Communications, 361 N.L.R.B. No. 126 (2014).

The Obama Board reached its decision in *Purple Communications* based in part on its assessment of the importance of email to workplace interpersonal communications, characterizing email as a "natural gathering place" for workers to converse. *Id.* at *8. In addition, the Board concluded that the equipment involved in sending emails was far less likely to encounter capacity problems than bulletin boards or copy machines, meaning that the employer's proprietary interests receded. *Id.* at *9–*10.

At the same time, the Board did note some differences between in-person solicitation or distribution and email:

> Indeed, an email system is substantially different from any sort of property that the Board has previously considered, other than in *Register Guard* itself. Accordingly, we apply *Republic Aviation* and related precedents by analogy in some but not all respects. In particular, we do not find it appropriate to treat email communication as either solicitation or distribution per se. Rather, an email system is a forum for communication, and the individual messages sent and received via email may, depending on their content and context, constitute solicitation, literature (*i.e.*, information) distribution, or—as we expect would most often be true—merely communications that are neither solicitation nor distribution, but that nevertheless constitute protected activity. We also find it unnecessary to characterize email systems as work areas or nonwork areas. In the vast majority of cases, an employer's email system will amount to a mixed-use area, in which the work-area restrictions permitted on literature distribution generally will not apply. *Id.* at *13.

In reasoning later endorsed by the *Caesars Entertainment* Board, two dissenting Board members in *Purple Communications* emphasized concerns such as the costs to the employer of storing and maintaining these emails, the difficulty of discouraging employees from emailing about non-work subjects during working time, the risk of computer viruses, the possibility that recipients of messages sent from an employer-issued email account would believe the employer endorsed the message, and the risk that employers that routinely monitor employee email messages will violate the NLRA's prohibition on surveillance of protected activity. Conversely, they noted that many workers bring their own Internet-enabled devices to work with them, making it easy for them to send and receive emails on the personal accounts.

B. Non-Employee Solicitation Rights on the Employer's Private Property

Republic Aviation involved organizing activities by employees of the employer being organized. Eleven years after *Republic Aviation*, the Supreme Court addressed the question of whether employers were required to give union organizers who were not employees of the company being organized (typically paid union organizers) access to employer property for the purpose of union solicitation. In *NLRB v. Babcock & Wilcox Co.*, 351 U.S. 105 (1956) the Court held that, absent discrimination or alternative means of communication, the employees' right to learn about the benefits of union representation from non-employee union organizers were outweighed by the employer's property rights. The Court based its decision on the "distinction between rules of law applicable to employees and those applicable to nonemployees." The Court added:

> The distinction is one of substance. No restriction may be placed on the employees' right to discuss self-organization among themselves, unless the employer can demonstrate that a restriction is necessary to maintain production or discipline. *Republic Aviation Corp. v. NLRB*, 324 U.S. 793, 803 (1945). But no such obligation is owed nonemployee organizers. Their access to company property is governed by a different consideration. The right of self-organization depends in some measure on the ability of employees to learn the advantages of self- organization from others. Consequently, if the location of a plant and the living quarters of the employees place the employees beyond the reach of reasonable union efforts to communicate with them, the employer must allow the union to approach his employees on his property. No such conditions are shown in these records. 351 U.S. 105, 113.

Twenty years after *Babcock & Wilcox*, the Court took up the question of whether a property owner's threat to have union members engaged in peaceful picketing removed from its property and charged with criminal trespass violated either the constitution or the NLRA. In *Hudgens v. NLRB*, 424 U.S. 507 (1976), the Court held that such a threat is not unconstitutional where the pickets were trespassing on private property, and remanded the case to the Board to decide the appropriate statutory standard for analyzing such a case.

The question remanded by *Hudgens* concerned the role the Board should play in regulating non-employee union representatives who are engaged in § 7 activity. Quoting *Babcock & Wilcox, Hudgens* observed that the Board has primary responsibility to "accommodat[e] . . . § 7 rights and private property rights 'with as little destruction of one as is consistent with the maintenance of the other.' The locus of that accommodation, however, may fall at differing points along the spectrum depending on the nature and strength of the respective § 7 rights and private property rights asserted in any given context." 424 U.S. 507, 522.

The Board developed a test for the rights of non-employees engaged in union solicitation in *Jean Country*, 291 N.L.R.B. 11, 14 (1988). That test was challenged in the following case.

Lechmere, Inc. v. NLRB

Supreme Court of the United States
502 U.S. 527, 112 S. Ct. 841, 117 L. Ed. 2d 79 (1992)

Thomas, J.

. . . This case stems from the efforts of Local 919 of the United Food and Commercial Workers Union, AFL-CIO, to organize employees at a retail store in Newington, Connecticut, owned and operated by petitioner Lechmere, Inc. The store is located in the Lechmere Shopping Plaza, which occupies a roughly rectangular tract measuring approximately 880 feet from north to south and 740 feet from east to west. Lechmere's store is situated at the Plaza's south end, with the main parking lot to its north. A strip of 13 smaller "satellite stores" not owned by Lechmere runs along the west side of the Plaza, facing the parking lot. To the Plaza's east (where the main entrance is located) runs the Berlin Turnpike, a four-lane divided highway. The parking lot, however, does not abut the Turnpike; they are separated by a 46-foot-wide grassy strip, broken only by the Plaza's entrance. The parking lot is owned jointly by Lechmere and the developer of the satellite stores. The grassy strip is public property (except for a 4-foot-wide band adjoining the parking lot, which belongs to Lechmere).

The union began its campaign to organize the store's 200 employees, none of whom was represented by a union, in June 1987. After a full-page advertisement in a local newspaper drew little response, nonemployee union organizers entered Lechmere's parking lot and began placing handbills on the windshields of cars parked in a corner of the lot used mostly by employees. Lechmere's manager immediately confronted the organizers, informed them that Lechmere prohibited solicitation or handbill distribution of any kind on its property, and asked them to leave. They did so, and Lechmere personnel removed the handbills. The union organizers renewed this handbilling effort in the parking lot on several subsequent occasions; each time they were asked to leave and the handbills were removed. The organizers then relocated to the public grassy strip, from where they attempted to pass out handbills to cars entering the lot during hours (before opening and after closing) when the drivers were assumed to be primarily store employees. For one month, the union organizers returned daily to the grassy strip to picket Lechmere; after that, they picketed intermittently for another six months. They also recorded the license plate numbers of cars parked in the employee parking area; with the cooperation of the Connecticut Department of Motor Vehicles, they thus secured the names and addresses of some 41 nonsupervisory employees (roughly 20% of the store's total). The union sent four mailings to these employees; it also made some attempts to contact them by phone or home visits. These mailings and visits resulted in one signed union authorization card.

Alleging that Lechmere had violated the NLRA by barring the nonemployee organizers from its property, the union filed an unfair labor practice charge with respondent National Labor Relations Board (Board).... [A]n Administrative Law Judge (ALJ) ruled in the union's favor ... He recommended that Lechmere be ordered, among other things, to cease and desist from barring the union organizers from the parking lot....

The Board affirmed the ALJ's judgment and adopted the recommended order, applying the analysis set forth in its opinion in *Jean Country*, 291 N.L.R.B. 11 (1988) .... [T]he First Circuit denied Lechmere's petition for review and enforced the Board's order....

II

A

Section 7 of the NLRA provides in relevant part that "[e]mployees shall have the right to self-organization, to form, join, or assist labor organizations." ... Section 8(a)(1) of the Act, in turn, makes it an unfair labor practice for an employer "to interfere with, restrain, or coerce employees in the exercise of the rights guaranteed in [§ 7]." ... By its plain terms, thus, the NLRA confers rights only on *employees*, not on unions or their nonemployee organizers. In *NLRB v. Babcock & Wilcox Co.*, 351 U.S. 105 (1956), however, we recognized that insofar as the employees' "right of self-organization depends in some measure on [their] ability ... to learn the advantages of self-organization from others," ... § 7 of the NLRA may, in certain limited circumstances, restrict an employer's right to exclude nonemployee union organizers from his property. It is the nature of those circumstances that we explore today.

Babcock arose out of union attempts to organize employees at a factory located on an isolated 100-acre tract. The company had a policy against solicitation and distribution of literature on its property, which it enforced against all groups. About 40% of the company's employees lived in a town of some 21,000 persons near the factory; the remainder were scattered over a 30-mile radius. Almost all employees drove to work in private cars and parked in a company lot that adjoined the fenced-in plant area. The parking lot could be reached only by a 100-yard-long driveway connecting it to a public highway. This driveway was mostly on company-owned land, except where it crossed a 31-foot-wide public right-of-way adjoining the highway. Union organizers attempted to distribute literature from this right-of-way. The union also secured the names and addresses of some 100 employees (20% of the total) and sent them three mailings. Still other employees were contacted by telephone or home visit.

The union successfully challenged the company's refusal to allow nonemployee organizers onto its property before the Board. While acknowledging that there were alternative, nontrespassory means whereby the union could communicate with employees, the Board held that contact at the workplace was preferable. . . . "[T]he right to distribute is not absolute, but must be accommodated to the circumstances. Where it is impossible or unreasonably difficult for a union to distribute organizational literature to employees entirely off of the employer's premises, distribution on a nonworking area, such as the parking lot and the walkways between the parking lot and the gate, may be warranted." . . . Concluding that traffic on the highway made it unsafe for the union organizers to distribute leaflets from the right-of-way and that contacts through the mails, on the streets, at employees' homes, and over the telephone would be ineffective, the Board ordered the company to allow the organizers to distribute literature on the company's parking lot and exterior walkways. . . .

The [Fifth Circuit] refused to enforce the Board's order . . . and this Court affirmed. While recognizing that "the Board has the responsibility of 'applying the Act's general prohibitory language in the light of the infinite combinations of events which might be charged as violative of its terms,'" 351 U.S. at 111–12 . . . we explained that the Board had erred by failing to make the critical distinction between the organizing activities of employees (to whom §7 guarantees the right of self-organization) and nonemployees (to whom §7 applies only derivatively). Thus, while "[n]o restriction may be placed on the employees' right to discuss self-organization *among themselves*, unless the employer can demonstrate that a restriction is necessary to maintain production or discipline," 351 U.S. at 113 (emphasis added) (citing *Republic Aviation Corp. v. NLRB*, 324 U.S. 793, 803 (1945)), "no such obligation is owed nonemployee organizers," 351 U.S. at 113. As a rule, then, an employer cannot be compelled to allow distribution of union literature by nonemployee organizers on his property. As with many other rules, however, we recognized an exception. Where "the location of a plant and the living quarters of the employees place the employees beyond the reach of reasonable union efforts to communicate with them," *ibid.*, employers' property rights may be "required to yield to the extent needed to permit communication of information on the right to organize," *id.* at 112.

Although we have not had occasion to apply *Babcock's* analysis in the ensuing decades, we have described it in cases arising in related contexts. Two such cases, *Central Hardware Co. v. NLRB*, 407 U.S. 539 (1972), and *Hudgens v. NLRB*, 424 U.S. 507 (1976), involved activity by union supporters on employer-owned property. The principal issue in both cases was whether, based upon *Food Employees v.*

Logan Valley Plaza, Inc., 391 U.S. 308 (1968), the First Amendment protected such activities. In both cases we rejected the First Amendment claims, and in *Hudgens* we made it clear that *Logan Valley* was overruled. Having decided the cases on constitutional grounds, we remanded them to the Board for consideration of the union supporters' § 7 claims under *Babcock*. In both cases, we quoted approvingly *Babcock's* admonition that accommodation between employees' § 7 rights and employers' property rights "must be obtained with as little destruction of one as is consistent with the maintenance of the other," 351 U.S., at 112. See *Central Hardware*, 407 U.S. at 544; *Hudgens*, 424 U.S. at 521, 522. There is no hint in *Hudgens* and *Central Hardware*, however, that our invocation of *Babcock's* language of "accommodation" was intended to repudiate or modify *Babcock's* holding that an employer need not accommodate nonemployee organizers unless the employees are otherwise inaccessible. Indeed, in *Central Hardware* we expressly noted that nonemployee organizers cannot claim even a limited right of access to a nonconsenting employer's property until "[a]fter the requisite need for access to the employer's property has been shown." 407 U.S. at 545. . . .

B

Jean Country . . . represents the Board's latest attempt to implement the rights guaranteed by § 7. It sets forth a three-factor balancing test:

> [I]n all access cases our essential concern will be [1] the degree of impairment of the Section 7 right if access should be denied, as it balances against [2] the degree of impairment of the private property right if access should be granted. We view the consideration of [3] the availability of reasonably effective alternative means as especially significant in this balancing process." . . .

. . . Citing its role "as the agency with responsibility for implementing national labor policy," the Board maintains in this case that *Jean Country* is a reasonable interpretation of the NLRA entitled to judicial deference. . . .

Before we reach any issue of deference to the Board, however, we must first determine whether *Jean Country*—at least as applied to nonemployee organizational trespassing—is consistent with our past interpretation of § 7. "Once we have determined a statute's clear meaning, we adhere to that determination under the doctrine of *stare decisis*, and we judge an agency's later interpretation of the statute against our prior determination of the statute's meaning." . . .

In *Babcock*, as explained above, we held that the Act drew a distinction "of substance," 351 U.S. at 113, between the union activities of employees and nonemployees. In cases involving *employee* activities, we noted with approval, the Board "balanced the conflicting interests of employees to receive information on self-organization on the company's property from fellow employees during nonworking time, with the employer's right to control the use of his property." *Id.*, at 109–10. In cases involving *nonemployee* activities . . . , however, the Board was not permitted to engage in that same balancing. . . . By reversing the Board's interpretation of the statute for failing to distinguish between the organizing activities of employees and nonemployees, we were saying, in *Chevron* terms, that § 7 speaks to the issue of nonemployee access to an employer's property. *Babcock's* teaching is straightforward: § 7 simply does not protect nonemployee union organizers *except* in the rare case where "the inaccessibility of employees makes ineffective the reasonable attempts by nonemployees to communicate with them through the usual channels," *Id.* at 112. Our reference to "reasonable" attempts was nothing more than a commonsense recognition that unions need not engage in extraordinary feats to communicate with inaccessible employees—*not* an endorsement of the view . . . that the Act protects "reasonable" trespasses. Where reasonable alternative means of access exist, § 7's guarantees do not authorize trespasses by nonemployee organizers, *even* . . . "under . . . reasonable regulations" established by the Board.

Jean Country, which applies broadly to "all access cases," . . . misapprehends this critical point. Its principal inspiration derives not from *Babcock*, but from the following sentence in *Hudgens:* "[T]he locus of th[e] accommodation [between § 7 rights and private property rights] may fall at differing points along the spectrum depending on the nature and strength of the respective § 7 rights and private property rights asserted in any given context." 424 U.S. at 522. From this sentence the Board concluded that it was appropriate to approach every case by balancing § 7 rights against property rights, with alternative means of access thrown in as nothing more than an "especially significant" consideration. As explained above, however, *Hudgens* did not purport to modify *Babcock*, much less to alter it fundamentally in the way *Jean Country* suggests. To say that our cases require accommodation between employees' and employers' rights is a true but incomplete statement, for the cases also go far in establishing the *locus* of that accommodation where nonemployee organizing is at issue. So long as nonemployee union organizers have reasonable access to employees outside an employer's property, the requisite accommodation has taken place. It is *only* where such access is infeasible that it becomes necessary and proper to take the accommodation inquiry to a second level, balancing the employees' and employers' rights as described in the *Hudgens* dictum. . . . At least as applied to nonemployees, *Jean Country* impermissibly conflates these two stages of the inquiry—thereby significantly eroding *Babcock's* general rule that "an employer may validly post his property against nonemployee distribution of union literature," 351 U.S. at 112. We reaffirm that general rule today, and reject the Board's attempt to recast it as a multifactor balancing test.

C

The threshold inquiry in this case, then, is whether the facts here justify application of *Babcock's* inaccessibility exception. The ALJ below observed that "the facts herein convince me that reasonable alternative means [of communicating with Lechmere's employees] *were* available to the Union". . . . Reviewing the ALJ's decision under *Jean Country*, however, the Board reached a different conclusion on this point, asserting that "there was no reasonable, effective alternative means available for the Union to communicate its message to [Lechmere's] employees." . . .

We cannot accept the Board's conclusion, because it "rest[s] on erroneous legal foundations," *Babcock*, 351 U.S. at 112. . . . As we have explained, the exception to *Babcock's* rule is a narrow one. It does not apply wherever nontrespassory access to employees may be cumbersome or less-than-ideally effective, but only where "the *location of a plant and the living quarters of the employees* place the employees *beyond the reach* of reasonable union efforts to communicate with them," *Id.* at 113 (emphasis added). Classic examples include logging camps, . . . mining camps, . . . and mountain resort hotels. . . . *Babcock's* exception was crafted precisely to protect the §7 rights of those employees who, by virtue of their employment, are isolated from the ordinary flow of information that characterizes our society. The union's burden of establishing such isolation is . . . "a heavy one". . . . and one not satisfied by mere conjecture or the expression of doubts concerning the effectiveness of nontrespassory means of communication.

The Board's conclusion in this case that the union had no reasonable means short of trespass to make Lechmere's employees aware of its organizational efforts is based on a misunderstanding of the limited scope of this exception. Because the employees do not reside on Lechmere's property, they are presumptively not "beyond the reach," *Babcock*, 351 U.S. at 113, of the union's message. Although the employees live in a large metropolitan area (Greater Hartford), that fact does not in itself render them "inaccessible" in the sense contemplated by *Babcock*. . . . Their accessibility is suggested by the union's success in contacting a substantial percentage of them directly, via mailings, phone calls, and home visits. Such direct contact, of course, is not a necessary element of "reasonably effective" communication; signs or advertising also may suffice. In this case, the union tried advertising in local newspapers; the Board said that this was not reasonably effective because it was expensive and might not reach the employees. . . . Whatever the merits of that conclusion, other alternative means of communication were readily available. Thus, signs (displayed, for example, from the public grassy strip adjoining Lechmere's parking lot) would have informed the employees about the union's organizational efforts. (Indeed, union organizers picketed the shopping center's main entrance for months as employees came and went every day.) *Access* to employees, not *success* in winning them over, is the critical issue — although success, or lack thereof, may be relevant in determining whether reasonable access exists. Because the union in this case failed to establish the existence of any "unique obstacles," *Sears*, 436 U.S. at 205–06, n. 41, that frustrated access to Lechmere's employees, the Board erred in concluding that Lechmere committed an unfair labor practice by barring the nonemployee organizers from its property. . . . The judgment of the First Circuit is therefore reversed, and enforcement of the Board's order is denied.

Dissent of WHITE J., joined by BLACKMUN J., and STEVENS J.

. . . *Babcock* is at odds with modern concepts of deference to an administrative agency charged with administering a statute. See *Chevron U.S.A. Inc. v. Natural Resources Defense Council, Inc.*, 467 U.S. 837 (1984). When reviewing an agency's construction of a statute, we ask first whether Congress has spoken to the precise question at issue. *Id.*, at 842. If it has not, we do not simply impose our own construction on the statute; rather, we determine if the agency's view is based on a permissible construction of the statute. *Id.*, at 843. *Babcock* did not ask if Congress had specifically spoken to the issue of access by third parties and did not purport to explain how the NLRA specifically dealt with what the access rule should be where third parties are concerned. If it had made such an inquiry, the only basis for finding statutory language that settled the issue would have been the language of § 7, which speaks only of the rights of employees; *i.e.*, the Court might have found that § 7 extends no access rights at all to union representatives. But *Babcock* itself recognized that employees have a right to learn from others about self-organization, 351 U.S., at 113, and itself recognized that in some circumstances, §§ 7 and 8 required the employer to grant the union access to parking lots. So have later Courts, and so does the Court today.

Notes

1. The Court majority construed the NLRA as "plain[ly]" "confer[ring] rights only on *employees*, not on unions or their nonemployee organizers." Examine the text of §§ 7 and 8(a)(1). Note also § 2(3), which defines an "employee" as "any employee, and shall not be limited to the employees of a particular employer." Is the Court's construction correct? Or is the statutory language ambiguous? If ambiguous, should the Board's or the Court's interpretation govern?

2. Alternatively, the Court seems to be saying the Board's approach was inconsistent with the Court's decision in *Babcock & Wilcox*. Notably, that case came before *Chevron* and more modern ideas of deference to agencies. Does this use of *stare decisis* make sense in light of *Chevron*, which was decided in the years between *Babcock & Wilcox* and *Lechmere*? Justice White, dissenting, thought not. *See also Nat'l Cable & Telecomm. Ass'n v. Brand X Internet Servs.*, 545 U.S. 967, 982 (2005) ("A court's prior judicial construction of a statute trumps an agency construction otherwise entitled to *Chevron* deference only if the prior court decision holds that its construction follows from the unambiguous terms of the statute itself and thus leaves no room for agency discretion.").

3. *Lechmere* cites mining and logging camps and resort hotels as situations that fit within the exception it describes. *See Nabors Alaska Drilling, Inc.*, 325 N.L.R.B. 574 (1998) (no alternative means of communication where employees resided on an oil drilling rig, in employer-owned camps, and on an offshore oil platform). Can you think of other employers to which the exception could apply?

4. Does the "no alternative means of communication" exception make sense in a technologically advanced society? To what extent does a union need access to employer property in light of resources—like Facebook or Twitter—that streamline targeted mass communications? Before giving a final answer to this question, consider the materials below describing when and if the union has a right to learn all the names and addresses of the employees it is seeking to organize.

5. The employer in *Lechmere* did not permit any non-employee solicitation on its property. What if the employer had permitted other types of non-employee groups to solicit on its property, but not unions? What if the employer merely permitted some solicitation by charitable organizations? Notably, in *Babcock*, the Court limited its holding to situations where "the employer . . . does not discriminate against the union by allowing other [solicitation or] distribution."

As with discrimination involving employee use of company property for solicitation and distribution, the issue is somewhat murky, and the Board has sometimes been more willing to find discrimination than the courts. The main question concerns what activities are similar enough to union organizing to treat as comparators. For example, if an employer permits girl scouts to sell cookies, must it also allow a union to solicit petition signatories? What if the employer allows the Salvation Army to request donations, or supporters of ballot initiatives to solicit signatures? *Compare* **Be-Lo Stores v. NLRB**, 126 F.3d 268 (4th Cir. 1997) (doubting that the *Babcock* non-discrimination principle applies where non-organizational activity is involved), *with* **Sandusky Mall Co.**, 329 N.L.R.B. 618 (1999) (mall owner who had permitted substantial promotional activities committed ULP by preventing union solicitation); *enforcement denied*, Sandusky Mall Co. v. NLRB, 242 F.3d 682, 692 (6th Cir. 2001) (holding discrimination analysis requires union to point to comparable groups engaging in comparable activities that were allowed access to the employer's property). On charitable solicitation, *Compare Albertson's, Inc.*, 332 N.L.R.B. 1132 (2000) (employer who allows frequent nonemployee solicitation may not discriminate against unions regardless of whether the solicitation is charitable in nature), *with Cleveland Real Estate Partners v. NLRB*, 95 F.3d 457 (6th Cir. 1996) ("no relevant labor policies are advanced" by forcing an employer to prohibit charitable solicitation in order to avoid running afoul of *Babcock*'s nondiscrimination policy).

As the citations in the previous paragraph suggest, the courts have tended to treat a smaller class of activities as comparable to union organizing than has the Board. More recently, the Trump Board has also adopted this narrow approach, overruling *Sandusky Mall*. In **Kroger Ltd. P'Ship**, 368 N.L.R.B. No. 64 (2019), the Board considered whether Kroger discriminated against union organizers who were distributing handbills and circulating a petition that asked consumers to boycott the store. The crux of the case was that the store ejected the organizers from its parking lot, even though it had a policy of permitting "anything civic, like the local fire departments, military veterans, the Lions Club" to solicit donations, sell items, and distribute literature. Citing circuit court precedent and "[a]n employer's right to exclude from its property uses it finds objectionable," the Board adopted the following test:

> [A]n employer may deny access to nonemployees seeking to engage in protest activities on its property while allowing nonemployee access for a wide range of charitable, civic, and commercial activities that are not similar in nature to protest activities. Additionally, an employer may ban

nonemployee access for union organizational activities if it also bans comparable organizational activities by groups other than unions.

As an example of a situation that would reflect unlawful discrimination by the employer, the Board offered an employer that granted "access to nonemployee handbillers urging a boycott of the employer for environmental reasons while denying access to nonemployer handbillers urging a boycott in connection with a labor dispute." Likewise, the Board wrote that employers cannot allow access to supporters of one union but not another; or to outside union opponents but not supporters.

In another 2019 case, the Board held that a hospital was free to eject union organizers from a public cafeteria. *UPMC*, 368 N.L.R.B. No. 2 (2019). The organizers were speaking with employees, and union fliers and pins were displayed at the table they shared with employees. The Board wrote that an employer that opens space up to the public "does not have a duty to allow the use of its facility by nonemployees for promotional or organizational activity."

6. *Lechmere* held that employer property rights almost always outweigh the rights of non-employee union representatives. But this rule is not applicable when an employer does not have the right to exclude others from its property. For instance, if an employer merely has an easement or a license, it likely cannot exclude nonemployee union organizers from its property. Similarly, the California State Constitution is unusual in that it grants a right of access for persons engaging in expressive speech in shopping malls. *See Pruneyard Shopping Center v. Robins*, 447 U.S. 74 (1980) (upholding a California Supreme Court determination that shopping centers are the functional equivalent of "miniature downtowns" and should be treated as public forums from which expressive activity cannot be excluded).

The California rule has prompted litigation on the question of what constitutes a "shopping center" under *Pruneyard*. For instance, in *Waremart Foods v. NLRB*, 354 F.3d 870 (D.C. Cir. 2004), the Court reversed the Board and held (after the Supreme Court of California refused to answer a certified question) that *Pruneyard* does not apply to stand-alone grocery stores.

Compare *Fashion Valley Mall, LLC v. NLRB*, 172 P.3d 742 (Cal. 2007). In *Fashion Valley*, the California Supreme Court reached the opposite conclusion with respect to a large shopping mall in San Diego. In that case, approximately 40 union members stood outside one of Fashion Valley's many department stores and distributed leaflets to customers. Mall officials tried to stop the leafleting, relying on mall rules requiring permission before engaging in expressive activity on mall property. Citing *Pruneyard*, the Board held that California law permits expressive speech in a shopping mall. Accordingly, it found that the rules under which the union members were ejected violated §8(a)(1). After considering both California and federal free speech law, the California Supreme Court agreed. More recently, in *Ralphs Grocery Co. v. United Food & Commercial Workers Union Local 8*, 290 P.3d 1116 (Cal. 2012), the California Supreme Court held that "within a shopping center or mall, the areas outside the individual stores' customer entrances and exits, at least as typically configured, are not public forums" under the California Constitution.

7. Should courts be permitted to balance the strength of the employer's interests and the extent to which union access would impair those interests? In other words, should it matter that distributing handbills on a mall parking lot that is already open to the public likely has little to no effect on the actual functioning of the businesses in the mall or on employee discipline? Under the now-defunct *Jean Country* analysis, the Board could have considered the extent to which an employer's property was publicly accessible when assessing the degree of impairment of an employer's rights. After *Lechmere*, this is no longer the case. And in *Kroger*, the Board approvingly quoted the Fourth Circuit's statement that "an employer 'has a strong interest in preventing the use of its property for conduct which directly undermines its purposes, i.e., the sale of goods and services to [its] customers,' and that protest and boycott activities undermine that strong interest, unlike charitable, civic, and commercial activities (which, in fact, may promote its business interests)." (Quoting *Riesbeck Food Markets v. NLRB*, 91 F.3d 132 (1996).)

8. Does *Lechmere* mean that an employer may legally discipline employees for talking to non-employee union organizers who are wrongfully on the employer's property? In *North Hills Services, Inc.*, 345 N.L.R.B. 1262 (2005), the Board held it was not a ULP for an employer to order an employee to stop talking to a union organizer who was trespassing on company property. Could the employer discipline the employee if he or she failed to follow that order?

9. What alternatives do unions have? One option is "salting." In **NLRB v. Town & Country Electric, Inc.**, 516 U.S. 85 (1995), the Court held that salts — paid union organizers who apply and are hired as employees of the company being organized — are protected as employees under the NLRA. The employer argued that salts should not be protected for two reasons: (1) under agency law, a worker could not simultaneously be a servant of both the union and employer, and (2) salts are prone to quit at inopportune times or otherwise deliberately act to sabotage the company.

The Court rejected both arguments. As to divided loyalties, the Court reasoned that, "union organizing, when done for pay but during non-work hours, would seem equivalent to simple moonlighting, a practice wholly consistent with a company's control over its workers as to their assigned duties." Regarding the sabotage argument, the Court noted (a) salts are no more likely than other workers to quit early or sabotage a company, and (b) alternative remedies (*i.e.* term of employment contracts and employee discipline for unlawful conduct) were available to address employer concerns. *See also* Anne Lofaso, *The Persistence of Union Repression in an Era of Recognition*, 62 ME. L. REV. 199 (2010) (arguing that management views salts as a "Trojan Horse" strategy of "infiltrating the enemy from within").

10. The Bush II Board attempted to make "salting" more difficult. *Toering Elec. Co.*, 351 N.L.R.B. 225 (2007) held that salts are not statutory employees in circumstances where the salt is not "genuinely interested" in establishing an employment

relationship with the employer. What, specifically, does that mean? At a minimum, it would exclude "salts" who apply for jobs they do not want in order to develop evidence of an employer's discriminatory practices. Note that the General Counsel bears the burden of proving "genuine interest."

11. Sometimes it is unclear whether or not a union organizer qualifies as an employee. For instance:

a. Which rule should apply to off-duty employees? *See Tri-County Medical Center, Inc.*, 222 N.L.R.B. 1089 (1976) (off-duty employees are protected as long as their organizational activity is conducted outside "the interior of the plant and other working areas"); *see also Automotive Plastic Technologies, Inc.*, 313 N.L.R.B. 462 (1993) (affirming *Tri-County* post-*Lechmere*); *NLRB v. Pizza Crust Co. of Penn., Inc.*, 862 F.2d 49 (3rd Cir. 1988) (accord).

b. Does this rule change if the soliciting employees work at another one of the employer's facilities in a different location (*i.e.* off-site employees)? *See ITT Indus. v. NLRB*, 413 F.3d 64 (D.C. Cir. 2005) (upholding Board's treatment of off-duty, off-site employees as employees, as long as consideration is given to any special legitimate employer concerns such as security or traffic); *accord First Healthcare Corp. v. NLRB*, 344 F.3d 523 (6th Cir. 2003).

c. Which rule applies to employees of onsite contractors? This is another area where the Board has taken varying positions.

In *New York, New York Hotel & Casino*, 356 N.L.R.B. No. 119 (2011), the Board considered a dispute between the New York, New York Hotel and Casino, and the employees of its food service contractor, Ark Las Vegas. Several Ark Las Vegas employees had engaged in organizational, customer-directed handbilling outside the casino's main entrance and outside the two Ark Las Vegas restaurants inside the casino. The Board decided that it would balance the §7 rights of the employees with the employer's property and management interests on a case-by-case basis. As a guide for later cases, the Board held that contractor employees should only be excluded where exclusion is justified by a legitimate business interest of the employer. Applying that guide, the Court found that the casino had not articulated a legitimate business reason to bar the contractor employees from handbilling on-site. Accordingly, the Board found that the casino had violated §8(a)(1) by excluding the handbilling Ark employees from its property.

However, in **Bexar Cty. Performing Arts Center Fdn.**, 368 N.L.R.B. No. 46 (2019), the Board overruled *New York, New York*, and held that "contractor employees are not generally entitled to the same Section 7 access rights as the property owner's own employees." As in *Kroger*, discussed above, the Board based its decision on a desire to protect employers' property rights:

The contractor employees' right to access the property is derivative of their employer's right of access to conduct business there. Off-duty employees of a contractor are trespassers and are entitled to access for

Section 7 purposes only if the property owner cannot show that they have one or more reasonable alternative nontrespassory channels of communicating with their target audience. If there is at least one such channel, the Board will not compel the property owner to permit the contractor employees to infringe upon its property rights. Instead, the property owner will be free to assert its fundamental property right to exclude without conflicting with Federal labor law.

d. An employer's otherwise-lawful decision to bar a non-employee from a property may violate the NLRA if it discriminates against protected concerted activity. Thus, the Board held that an employer violated § 8(a)(1) when it barred an ex-employee from its premises because she had filed a collective action alleging wage and hour violations, where ex-employees were typically allowed access to the property on the same basis as the general public. *MEI-GSR Holdings, LLC*, 365 N.L.R.B. No. 76 (2017).

12. Most of the cases in this section involve non-union workplaces. But union organizers will want access to unionized workplaces as well, to speak with represented employees. To facilitate this, unions will often negotiate the conditions under which they can access employer property in a CBA. "When employees and/ or their exclusive collective-bargaining representative exercise rights embodied in their collective-bargaining agreement, the exercise of those rights is protected." *Fred Meyer Stores, Inc.*, 368 N.L.R.B. No. 6 (June 18, 2019). In *Fred Meyer Stores*, the NLRB found that union organizers exceeded the scope of the access rights granted in the CBA. Accordingly, the employer did not commit a ULP when a supervisor ordered the organizers to leave the premises and called the police when they did not.

C. Access to Employee Home and E-mail Addresses

In *Excelsior Underwear Inc.*, 156 N.L.R.B. 1236 (1966), the Board reviewed two cases in which a union had objected to an election because the employer had refused to supply the union with a list of employees and their addresses. In *Excelsior*, the union alleged that the employer had made material misstatements about the union, threatened plant closings and violence, refused to bargain with an elected union, promised benefits if the employees voted against the union, and more. Further, the employer impeded the union from responding to any of these statements by refusing to provide a list of employee names and addresses. Similarly, in *Kellogg*, the union alleged that the employer "sent to each employee letters containing certain false and coercive material," while refusing to give the union a list of employee names and addresses for the purpose of responding.

Because the unions lost both elections, the issue was "whether an employer's refusal to provide a union with the names and addresses of employees eligible to vote in a representation election should be grounds on which to set that election aside." 156 N.L.R.B. 1236, 1239. The Board issued the following rule:

> We are persuaded . . . that higher standards of disclosure than we have heretofore imposed are necessary, and that prompt disclosure of the information here sought by the Petitioners should be required in all representation elections. Accordingly, we now establish a requirement that will be applied in all election cases. That is, within 7 days after the Regional Director has approved a consent-election agreement . . . or after the Regional Director or the Board has directed an election . . . the employer must file with the Regional Director an election eligibility list, containing the names and addresses of all the eligible voters. The Regional Director, in turn, shall make this information available to all parties in the case. Failure to comply with this requirement shall be grounds for setting aside the election whenever proper objections are filed. 156 N.L.R.B. at 1239–40.

The Board's reasons for requiring employers to provides names and addresses to unions was to ensure that "employees have the opportunity to cast their ballots for or against representation under circumstances that are free not only from interference, restraint, or coercion violative of the Act, but also from other elements that prevent or impede a free and reasoned choice." *Id.* at 1240. The Board reasoned that providing unions with the names and addresses of employees would make it more likely that an employee would have "an effective opportunity to hear the arguments concerning representation" and therefore that the employee would be "in a better position to make a more fully informed and reasonable choice." *Id.* The Board viewed its *Excelsior* rule as "remov[ing an] impediment to communication." *Id.*

In reaching its holding, the Board rejected the Employer's argument that it had a property interest in its employee's names and addresses:

> [W]e are able to perceive no substantial infringement of employer interests that would flow from such a requirement. A list of employee names and addresses is not like a customer list, and an employer would appear to have no significant interest in keeping the names and addresses of his employees secret (other than a desire to prevent the union from communicating with his employees—an interest we see no reason to protect). Such legitimate interest in secrecy as an employer may have is, in any event, plainly outweighed by the substantial public interest in favor of disclosure where, as here, disclosure is a key factor in insuring a fair and free electorate.

Id. at 1243. However, the Board nonetheless certified the results of the two elections. First, the Board held that the various employer statements "could clearly be evaluated by the employees as partisan electioneering." As to the employers' failure to provide employee names and addresses, the Board held that "the rule we have here announced is to be applied prospectively only. It will not apply in the instant cases but only in those elections that are directed, or consented to, subsequent to 30 days from the date of this Decision. We impose this brief period of delay to insure that all parties to forthcoming representation elections are fully aware of their rights and obligations as here stated." *Id.* at 1240 n.5.

Notes

1. In *Trustees of Columbia University*, 350 N.L.R.B. 574 (2007), the employees the union sought to organize were working on a ship that was expected to be away from any port for more than three months. The union requested, as part of the *Excelsior* information, the on-board e-mail addresses for employees. The employer refused, insisting this was beyond what *Excelsior* required. The Board held for the employer. Is that the correct result under *Excelsior*?

2. In 2014, the Board amended its elections procedures via rulemaking. 79 FR 74308-01 (Dec. 15, 2014). Under the new rule, employers must include email addresses (and phone numbers) with the *Excelsior* list. *Id.* at 74310. Some employers maintain that this requirement violates employees' privacy. Is that persuasive from the employees' point of view? Is requiring e-mail addresses more or less intrusive than requiring home addresses? And from the point of view of union organizers, are home visits, emails, or a mix of the two likely to be the most productive approach to persuading employees?

3. As an administrative agency, the Board has both quasi-legislative (rulemaking) and quasi-judicial (adjudicatory) functions. Which method did the Board employ in *Excelsior*?

In *NLRB v. Wyman-Gordon*, 394 U.S. 759 (1969), the Supreme Court took up this question, considering whether *Excelsior*'s prospective rule was invalid because the Board did not follow the rulemaking procedures set out in the Administrative Procedures Act (APA). A divided Court decided that, despite the Board's unorthodox process, a subpoena requiring production of the *Excelsior* list was valid. Writing for the plurality, Justice Fortas explained that, although the determination in *Excelsior* was effectively a rulemaking (and thus subject to the APA), the subpoena issued in *Wyman-Gordon* was "unquestionably valid" because it was properly issued by the Board as an exercise of its authority to direct union elections. Concurring only in the judgment, three justices took issue with the plurality's characterization of *Excelsior*, writing that it was a valid adjudication by the Board despite the prospective application, and thus was not subject to the APA rule-making requirements. Finally, two dissenting justices would have held that the Board's prospective rule was improperly promulgated, and the subpoena premised on that rule was unenforceable.

Given that the *Wyman-Gordon* Court enforced the Board's subpoena, does it matter that six Justices also thought that the Board violated the APA by promulgating a prospective rule through adjudication? Note that the Board still issues prospective rules via adjudication. *See, e.g., Babcock & Wilcox Constr. Co.*, 361 N.L.R.B. No. 132 (2014) (applying new standard regarding Board deferral to decisions of labor arbitrators prospectively only).

4. Consider when, in the course of a union organizing drive, the *Excelsior* list is available. Typically, a union must attempt to organize employees for a significant period of time (often months) before the NLRB will schedule an election. That is because a union cannot petition for an election legally until it has support from at

least 30 percent of the bargaining unit, and practically it will want a much higher percentage before asking for an election. The *Excelsior* list is not available during this time.

D. Employer Regulation of Employee Speech

Employers often create (and enforce) rules of employee conduct, and it is possible for employer rules to violate the NLRA on their face. For example, a rule that stated "no employee may complain about their pay or treatment at work" would plainly violate §7 by barring activity that—so long as the "concerted" requirement is met—is at core of what the Act protects. Similarly, a rule that barred employees from revealing their salary to anyone else would also violate §7, because it would prohibit employees from discussing whether the employer was paying them fairly. But sometimes it is less obvious whether a rule violates the Act. For example, a rule that is aimed at protecting trade secrets might be drafted so broadly that it also prohibits protected concerted activity. Alternatively, such a rule might be drafted using vague language that an employee might reasonably interpret as prohibiting protected concerted activity, even if the employer did not mean the rule to go that far. In either of these cases, the rule might chill protected concerted activity.

In recent years, employer work rules have received a lot of Board attention. This section explains two approaches to assessing when work rules violate the NLRA. (Remember, a work rule that is permissible on its face might still violate the Act if it is applied in an unlawful way.)

One approach was set forth in *Martin Luther Memorial Home, Inc.*, 343 N.L.R.B. 646 (2004) ("*Lutheran Heritage*"). The Board explained that work rules violate §8(a)(1) when they "reasonably tend[] to chill employees in the exercise of their Section 7 rights." The Board then set out a list of circumstances under which work rules will unlawfully chill employees, before ultimately holding that the employer's rule was facially lawful:

> In determining whether a challenged rule is unlawful, the Board must, however, give the rule a reasonable reading. It must refrain from reading particular phrases in isolation, and it must not presume improper interference with employee rights. . . . Consistent with the foregoing, our inquiry into whether the maintenance of a challenged rule is unlawful begins with the issue of whether the rule *explicitly* restricts activities protected by Section 7. If it does, we will find the rule unlawful.
>
> If the rule does not explicitly restrict activity protected by Section 7, the violation is dependent upon a showing of one of the following: (1) employees would reasonably construe the language to prohibit Section 7 activity; (2) the rule was promulgated in response to union activity; or (3) the rule has been applied to restrict the exercise of Section 7 rights.

The work rule at issue in *Lutheran Heritage* prohibited the use of abusive or profane language. To understand why this rule raised questions, you need to know that employees who use profanity while engaging in protected concerted activity do not necessarily lose NLRA protection. Instead, the Board adopted a four-factor balancing test in *Atlantic Steel Co.*, 245 N.L.R.B. 814, 816 (1979): "(1) the place of the discussion; (2) the subject matter of the discussion; (3) the nature of the employee's outburst; and (4) whether the outburst was, in any way, provoked by the employer's unfair labor practice." This rule recognizes that labor disputes can be heated and stressful. *See, e.g., Plaza Auto Ctr., Inc.*, 360 N.L.R.B. 972 (2014) (considering factors and deciding employee did not lose NLRA protection when, in the course of a dispute over compensation, he called his boss a "fucking mother fuck[er]," a "fucking crook," and an "asshole," and told him that he was stupid, that nobody liked him, and that everyone talked about him behind his back).

Despite the fact that some uses of profane language are protected by § 7, the *Lutheran Heritage* Board upheld the employer's work rule, writing that the rules "serve legitimate business purposes: they are designed to maintain order in the workplace and to protect the Respondent from liability by prohibiting conduct that, if permitted, could result in such liability." Two Board members dissented from this holding, with Member Liebman proposing that the employer should have included a caveat that the rule did not apply to activity protected by § 7.

The Obama Board applied the *Lutheran Heritage* standard relatively strictly, meaning that it was likely to conclude that work rules impermissibly chilled § 7-protected activity. In a 2015 memo, former NLRB General Counsel (and co-author of this book) Richard Griffin, Jr. listed several categories of work rules that — in his view — would be likely to violate the Act. These included: (1) rules that broadly prohibit any disclosure of information about employees or the employer; (2) rules prohibiting criticism of the employer, such as that employees must "be respectful to the company"; (3) rules suggesting that employees may not discuss controversial topics with each other; (4) rules prohibiting employees from discussing anything concerning the company with third parties; (5) rules prohibiting fair use of the employer's intellectual property; (6) rules prohibiting employees from "walking off the job."

The Trump Board has taken a different approach. In *The Boeing Co.*, 365 N.L.R.B. No. 154 (Dec. 14, 2017), the Board criticized *Lutheran Heritage*'s "reasonably construe" test for failing to "tak[e] into account any legitimate justifications associated with policies, rules and handbook provisions," for requiring too much precision of employers, and for allowing too little consideration of workplace context. Instead, the Board adopted a new test, which it explained as follows:

> Under the standard we adopt today, when evaluating a facially neutral policy, rule or handbook provision that, when reasonably interpreted, would potentially interfere with the exercise of NLRA rights, the Board will evaluate two things: (i) the nature and extent of the potential impact on NLRA rights, *and* (ii) legitimate justifications associated with the rule. We emphasize that *the Board* will conduct this evaluation, consistent with the Board's "duty to strike the *proper balance* between . . . asserted business

justifications and the invasion of employee rights in light of the Act and its policy," focusing on the perspective of employees, which is consistent with Section 8(a)(1). As the result of this balancing, in this and future cases, the Board will delineate three categories of employment policies, rules and handbook provisions (hereinafter referred to as "rules"):

- *Category 1* will include rules that the Board designates as lawful to maintain, either because (i) the rule, when reasonably interpreted, does not prohibit or interfere with the exercise of NLRA rights; or (ii) the potential adverse impact on protected rights is outweighed by justifications associated with the rule. Examples of Category 1 rules are the no-camera requirement in this case, the "harmonious interactions and relationships" rule that was at issue in *William Beaumont Hospital*, and other rules requiring employees to abide by basic standards of civility.

- *Category 2* will include rules that warrant individualized scrutiny in each case as to whether the rule would prohibit or interfere with NLRA rights, and if so, whether any adverse impact on NLRA-protected conduct is outweighed by legitimate justifications.

- *Category 3* will include rules that the Board will designate as *unlawful* to maintain because they would prohibit or limit NLRA-protected conduct, and the adverse impact on NLRA rights is not outweighed by justifications associated with the rule. An example of a Category 3 rule would be a rule that prohibits employees from discussing wages or benefits with one another.

We emphasize that Category 1 consists of two subparts: (a) rules that are lawful because, when reasonably interpreted, they would have no tendency to interfere with Section 7 rights and therefore no balancing of rights and justifications is warranted, and (b) rules that are lawful because, although they do have a reasonable tendency to interfere with Section 7 rights, the Board has determined that the risk of such interference is outweighed by the justifications associated with the rules. Of course, as reflected in Categories 2 and 3, if a particular type of rule is determined to have a potential adverse impact on NLRA activity, the Board may conclude that maintenance of the rule is *unlawful*, either because individualized scrutiny reveals that the rule's potential adverse impact outweighs any justifications (Category 2), or because the type of rule at issue predictably has an adverse impact on Section 7 rights that outweighs any justifications (Category 3). Again, even when a rule's *maintenance* is deemed lawful, the Board will examine circumstances where the rule is *applied* to discipline employees who have engaged in NLRA-protected activity, and in such situations, the discipline may be found to violate the Act.

Later, in *LA Specialty Produce Co.*, 368 N.L.R.B. No. 93 (2019), the Board modified some aspects of *Boeing*. First, the Board stated that whether a rule is lawful under *Boeing* "should be determined by reference to the perspective of an objectively reasonable employee who is 'aware of his legal rights but who also interprets work rules as they apply to the everydayness of his job. The reasonable employee does not view every employer policy through the prism of the NLRA.'" Then, the Board adjusted the initial showing required of the General Counsel:

> First, it is the General Counsel's initial burden in all cases to prove that a facially neutral rule *would* in context be interpreted by a reasonable employee, as defined above, to potentially interfere with the exercise of Section 7 rights. . . . Second, if the General Counsel meets the initial burden of proving that a reasonable employee would interpret a rule to potentially interfere with the exercise of Section 7 rights, the *Boeing* analysis will require a balancing of that potential interference against the legitimate justifications associated with the rule.

Note

One important species of work rule concerns confidentiality requirements. As discussed above, employers may not prohibit employees from sharing their own salaries. In *Flex Frac Logistics, L.L.C. v. NLRB*, 746 F.3d 205 (5th Cir. 2014), the Board considered non-union Flex Frac Logistics' rule prohibiting employees from sharing certain information outside the company, including information related to company "financial information, including costs, prices. . . ." In the absence of an explicit ban on wage discussions, the Board (applying *Lutheran Heritage*) asked whether "(1) employees would reasonably construe the language to prohibit §7 activities; (2) the rule was promulgated in response to a union organizing activity; or (3) the rule has been applied to restrict the exercise of §7 rights." The Board held (and the Fifth Circuit later affirmed) that Flex Frac's policy was overbroad and employees could reasonably construe it as restricting their §7 right to engage in concerted activities for mutual aid or protection—in particular, speaking with one another about their wages.

However, in *National Indemnity Co.*, 368 N.L.R.B. No. 96 (2019), the Board applied *Boeing* to uphold an employer's Code of Conduct that required employees to "maintain the confidentiality of confidential information entrusted to them," including "all non-public information that might be of use to competitors or harmful to the Company or its customers if disclosed." Whereas the ALJ applied *Lutheran Heritage* (which was the governing standard at the time) to hold that the policy violated the NLRA, the Board held that the rule fell under *Boeing* category one because it could not be "reasonably interpreted" to interfere with §7 rights. The Board added that all "rules that require employees to maintain the confidentiality of non-public information that, if disclosed outside the company, could harm the company or its customers or benefit its competitor" fall in category one, provided they either do not cover information about wages or working conditions, or else makes clear that covered personnel information "is limited to data maintained and only accessible in the employer's confidential records."

A different confidentiality issue arises in the context of workplace investigations, such as those that might occur if one employee accuses another of harassment. In *Apogee Retail*, 368 N.L.R.B. No. 144 (2019), the Board held that rules requiring employees to keep confidential information about workplace investigations were generally lawful/*Boeing* category one rules. This decision overruled *Banner Estrella Medical Ctr*, 362 N.L.R.B. 1108 (2015), which allowed employers to require confidentiality about workplace investigations only when there was a particular need, such as when disclosure could lead to evidence being destroyed.

Problem 3.1

Suppose an employer's rule provides the following: "We honor confidentiality. We recognize and protect the confidentiality of any information concerning the company, its business plans, its employees, customers, and financial matters." Does this rule violate § 7? *See Cintas Corp. v. NLRB*, 482 F.3d 463, 465 (D.C. Cir. 2007).

III. Losing § 7 Protection: Disloyal Employee Speech

As the previous section indicates, speech and actions that would otherwise be protected by § 7 (because, *e.g.*, they involve organizing or are "concerted" and for "mutual aid and protection") may not be protected by § 7 if they are sufficiently abusive. A group of employees threatening a supervisor with weapons to try to get a raise is "concerted" and arguably "for mutual aid and protection," but for obvious reasons, an employer could legally discipline or discharge employees engaged in such activity without running afoul of § 8(a)(1).

More difficult questions arise when an employer argues employees should lose § 7 protection because they have been "disloyal." In the following case, the Supreme Court sought to draw a line between protected and unprotected concerted activity.

NLRB v. Local Union No. 1229, Int'l B'hood of Electrical Workers (Jefferson Standard)

Supreme Court of the United States
346 U.S. 464, 74 S. Ct. 172, 98 L. Ed. 195 (1953)

BURTON, J.

The issue before us is whether the discharge of certain employees by their employer constituted an unfair labor practice, within the meaning of §§ 8(a)(1) and 7 of the Taft-Hartley Act, justifying their reinstatement by the [NLRB]. For the reason that their discharge was "for cause" within the meaning of § 10 (c) of that Act, we sustain the Board in not requiring their reinstatement.

In 1949, the Jefferson Standard Broadcasting Company (here called the company) . . . operated, at Charlotte, North Carolina, a 50,000-watt radio station, with call letters WBT. It broadcast 10 to 12 hours daily by radio and television. The television service, which it started July 14, 1949, representing an investment of about $500,000, was the only such service in the area. Less than 50% of the station's programs originated in Charlotte. The others were piped in over leased wires, generally from New York, California or Illinois from several different networks. . . .

The company employed 22 technicians. In December 1948, negotiations to settle the terms of their employment after January 31, 1949, were begun between representatives of the company and of the respondent Local Union No. 1229, International Brotherhood of Electrical Workers, American Federation of Labor (here called the union). The negotiations reached an impasse in January 1949, and the existing contract of employment expired January 31. The technicians, nevertheless, continued to work for the company and their collective-bargaining negotiations were resumed in July, only to break down again July 8. The main point of disagreement arose from the union's demand for the renewal of a provision that all discharges from employment be subject to arbitration and the company's counterproposal that such arbitration be limited to the facts material to each discharge, leaving it to the company to determine whether those facts gave adequate cause for discharge.

On July 9, 1949, the union began daily peaceful picketing of the company's station. Placards and handbills on the picket line charged the company with unfairness to its technicians and emphasized the company's refusal to renew the provision for arbitration of discharges. The placards and handbills named the union as the representative of the WBT technicians. The employees did not strike. They confined their respective tours of picketing to their off-duty hours and continued to draw full pay. There was no violence or threat of violence and no one has taken exception to any of the above conduct.

But on August 24, 1949, a new procedure made its appearance. Without warning, several of its technicians launched a vitriolic attack on the quality of the company's television broadcasts. Five thousand handbills were printed over the designation "WBT TECHNICIANS." These were distributed on the picket line, on the public square two or three blocks from the company's premises, in barber shops, restaurants and busses. Some were mailed to local businessmen. The handbills made no reference to the union, to a labor controversy or to collective bargaining. They read:

"IS CHARLOTTE A SECOND-CLASS CITY?

"You might think so from the kind of Television programs being presented by the Jefferson Standard Broadcasting Co. over WBTV. Have you seen one of their television programs lately? Did you know that all the programs presented over WBTV are on film and may be from one day to five years old. There are no local programs presented by WBTV. You cannot receive the local baseball games, football games or other local events because WBTV does not have the proper equipment to make these pickups. Cities like New York, Boston, Philadelphia, Washington receive such programs nightly. Why doesn't the Jefferson Standard Broadcasting Company purchase the needed equipment to bring you the same type of programs enjoyed by other leading American cities? Could it be that they consider Charlotte a second-class community and only entitled to the pictures now being presented to them?

"WBT TECHNICIANS"

This attack continued until September 3, 1949, when the company discharged ten of its technicians, whom it charged with sponsoring or distributing these handbills.

. . . [T]he union filed with the Board a charge that the company, by discharging the above-mentioned ten technicians, had engaged in an unfair labor practice. The General Counsel for the Board filed a complaint based on those charges and, after hearing, a trial examiner made detailed findings and a recommendation that all of those discharged be reinstated with back pay. The Board found that one of the discharged men had neither sponsored nor distributed the "Second-Class City" handbill and ordered his reinstatement with back pay. It then found that the other nine had sponsored or distributed the handbill and held that the company, by discharging them for such conduct, had not engaged in an unfair labor practice. The Board, accordingly, did not order their reinstatement. [The Court of Appeals remanded to the Board.] We granted certiorari because of the importance of the case in the administration of the Taft-Hartley Act.

In its essence, the issue is simple. It is whether these employees, whose contracts of employment had expired, were discharged "for cause." They were discharged solely because, at a critical time in the initiation of the company's television service, they sponsored or distributed 5,000 handbills making a sharp, public, disparaging attack upon the quality of the company's product and its business policies, in a manner reasonably calculated to harm the company's reputation and reduce its income. The attack was made by them expressly as "WBT TECHNICIANS." It continued ten days without indication of abatement. . . . The company's letter [discharging the employees] shows that it interpreted the handbill as a demonstration of such detrimental disloyalty as to provide "cause" for its refusal to continue in its employ the perpetrators of the attack. We agree.

Section 10(c) of the Taft-Hartley Act expressly provides that "No order of the Board shall require the reinstatement of any individual as an employee who has been suspended or discharged, or the payment to him of any back pay, if such individual was suspended or discharged for cause." There is no more elemental cause for discharge of an employee than disloyalty to his employer. It is equally elemental that the Taft-Hartley Act seeks to strengthen, rather than to weaken, that cooperation, continuity of service and cordial contractual relation between employer and employee that is born of loyalty to their common enterprise.

. . . The legal principle that insubordination, disobedience or disloyalty is adequate cause for discharge is plain enough. The difficulty arises in determining whether, in fact, the discharges are made because of such a separable cause or because of some other concerted activities engaged in for the purpose of collective bargaining or other mutual aid or protection which may not be adequate cause for discharge.

. . . Assuming that there had been no pending labor controversy, the conduct of the "WBT TECHNICIANS" from August 24 through September 3 unquestionably would have provided adequate cause for their disciplinary discharge within the meaning of § 10(c). Their attack related itself to no labor practice of the company. It made no reference to wages, hours or working conditions. The policies attacked were those of finance and public relations for which management, not technicians, must be responsible. The attack asked for no public sympathy or support. It was a continuing attack, initiated while off duty, upon the very interests which the attackers were being paid to conserve and develop. Nothing could be further from the purpose of the Act than to require an employer to finance such activities. Nothing would contribute less to the Act's declared purpose of promoting industrial peace and stability.

The fortuity of the coexistence of a labor dispute affords these technicians no substantial defense. While they were also union men and leaders in the labor controversy, they took pains to separate those categories. In contrast to their claims on the picket line as to the labor controversy, their handbill of August 24 omitted all reference to it. The handbill diverted attention from the labor controversy. It attacked public policies of the company which had no discernible relation to that controversy. The only connection between the handbill and the labor controversy was an ultimate and undisclosed purpose or motive on the part of some of the sponsors that, by the hoped-for financial pressure, the attack might extract from the company some future concession. A disclosure of that motive might have lost more public support for the employees than it would have gained, for it would have given the handbill more the character of coercion than of collective bargaining. Referring to the attack, the Board said "In our judgment, these tactics, in the circumstances of this case, were hardly less 'indefensible' than acts of physical sabotage." In any event, the findings of the Board effectively separate the attack from the labor controversy and treat it solely as one made by the company's technical experts upon the quality of the company's product. As such, it was as adequate a cause for the discharge of its sponsors as if the labor controversy had not been pending. The technicians, themselves, so handled their attack as thus to bring their discharge under § 10(c).

The Board stated "We . . . do not decide whether the disparagement of product involved here would have justified the employer in discharging the employees responsible for it, had it been uttered in the context of a conventional appeal for support of the union in the labor dispute." This underscored the Board's factual conclusion that the attack of August 24 was not part of an appeal for support in the pending dispute. It was a concerted separable attack purporting to be made in the interest of the public rather than in that of the employees.

Accordingly, the order of the Court of Appeals remanding the cause to the [NLRB] is set aside. . . .

FRANKFURTER, J., with whom BLACK, J., and DOUGLAS J. join, dissenting.

. . . The issue is whether we should reverse the Court of Appeals . . . because that court . . . found that the Board employed an improper standard as the basis for its decision. The Board judged the conduct in controversy by finding it "indefensible." The Court of Appeals held that by "giving 'indefensible' a vague content different from 'unlawful,' the Board misconceived the scope of the established rule." . . .

On this central issue—whether the Court of Appeals rightly or wrongly found that the Board applied an improper criterion—this Court is silent. It does not support the Board in using "indefensible" as the legal litmus nor does it reject the Court of Appeals' rejection of that test. This Court presumably does not disagree with the assumption of the Court of Appeals that conduct may be "indefensible" in the colloquial meaning of that loose adjective, and yet be within the protection of § 7.

Instead, the Court, relying on § 10(c) which permits discharges "for cause," points to the "disloyalty" of the employees and finds sufficient "cause" regardless of whether the handbill was a "concerted activity" within § 7. Section 10(c) does not speak of discharge "for disloyalty." If Congress had so written that section, it would have overturned much of the law that had been developed by the Board and the courts in the twelve years preceding the Taft-Hartley Act. The legislative history makes clear that Congress had no such purpose but was rather expressing approval of the construction of "concerted activities" adopted by the Board and the courts. Many of the legally recognized tactics and weapons of labor would readily be condemned for "disloyalty" were they employed between man and man in friendly personal relations. . . .

To suggest that all actions which in the absence of a labor controversy might be "cause"—or, to use the words commonly found in labor agreements, "just cause"—for discharge should be unprotected, even when such actions were undertaken as "concerted activities, for the purpose of collective bargaining," is to misconstrue legislation designed to put labor on a fair footing with management. Furthermore, it would disregard the rough and tumble of strikes, in the course of which loose and even reckless language is properly discounted. . . .

Notes

1. What is the rule of *Jefferson Standard*? It cannot be analogized to threatening a supervisor with harm, or to picket-line violence, because the employees' conduct in *Jefferson* was not illegal. The statements made by the technicians did not amount to defamation, other tort, or crime. *See generally* DAN DOBBS, THE LAW OF TORTS 1117–67 (2000). Justice Frankfurter, dissenting, disparaged the majority's rationale that employee speech loses its protection because it is "indefensible" or "disloyal" in part because, in Frankfurter's view, neither phrase offers a coherent justiciable standard. Was he correct? Another possibility is that *Jefferson Standard* means that union speech during organizing or bargaining disputes must be closely related, or at least related, to the content of that dispute in order to be protected by § 7. Finally, it

could be that the dispositive factor in *Jefferson Standard* was that there was no way for the public to know that the handbilling was related to a labor dispute.

2. How could the picketers in *Jefferson Standard* have modified their communications to make as many of the same points as possible but not be "disloyal"?

3. Various cases have held that disparaging the employer's product is disloyal and therefore unprotected, if "unnecessary to carry on the workers' legitimate concerted activities." *NLRB v. Washington Aluminum Co.*, 370 U.S. 9, 17 (1962). *Elko General Hospital*, 347 N.L.R.B. 1425 (2006), found unprotected, disloyal activity when an employee (during a captive audience meeting) stated that her husband had had a bad experience at the employer's hospital and that she wished the hospital was still run by the county.

What if the claim is that striker replacements are producing inferior products? *See Patterson-Sargent Co.*, 115 N.L.R.B. 1627 (1956) (finding disloyal conduct). How could a striking employee support a boycott of the employer's product without being found disloyal (and thus losing whatever right to reinstatement the employee would otherwise have)? *See George A. Hormel and Co. v. NLRB*, 962 F.2d 1061 (D.C. Cir. 1992) (stating that "[a]s a rule, an employee who supports a boycott of his employer's product violates his duty of loyalty to the employer. . . . There is an exception to that rule, however: supporting a boycott is protected § 7 activity if it (1) is related to an ongoing labor dispute and (2) does not disparage the employer's product.")

It is not always clear whether an employee protest disparages a product—or would be understood by the public to disparage a product—at all. In *Micklin Enters., Inc. v. NLRB*, 861 F.3d 812 (8th Cir. 2017), the Eighth Circuit, *en banc*, held that fast food employees lost NLRA protection when they created posters that suggested that—because workers did not receive paid sick days—sick workers might be preparing food for customers. The posters included the sentence, directed at customers, "we hope your immune system is ready because you're about to take the sandwich test." Although the protest was clearly connected to a labor dispute related to sick leave, it was unprotected, because it "target[ed] the food product itself." In contrast, in *Medco Health Solutions of Las Vegas, Inc.*, 364 N.L.R.B. No. 115 (2016), the Board applied *Republic Aviation* and *Martin Luther* instead of *Jefferson Standard* when an employer disciplined an employee for wearing a shirt that disparaged an employee incentive system rather than a product.

4. Should it matter whether disparaging statements are truthful? In ***MasTec Technologies***, 357 N.L.R.B. 103 (2011), an employer fired employee technicians because of their negative statements, made on a news broadcast, about their employer (which installed DirecTV). Among other things, the technicians, in uniform, said they were told to lie to customers and that if they failed to convince customers to buy services they did not need, money would be taken out of their paychecks.

MasTec set out a two-part test for determining when concerted activity loses its protection under *Jefferson Standard* and related precedent. "[E]mployee communications to third parties in an effort to obtain their support are protected where the communication indicated it is related to an ongoing dispute between employees and the employer and the communication is not so disloyal, reckless or maliciously untrue as to lose the Act's protection." 357 N.L.R.B. at 107. The Board then held that the technicians' statements were protected because they were not maliciously untrue or sufficiently disloyal or reckless. The terminations, therefore, violated §8(a)(1). The D.C. Circuit enforced the Board's decision. *DirecTV, Inc. v. NLRB*, 837 F.3d 25 (D.C. Cir. 2016).

5. The preceding materials illustrate an important way that employers and employees are situated differently under the NLRA. While employees can lose NLRA protections for "disloyalty" to the employer, there is no equivalent requirement that employers owe to employees (much less their unions). Would it be possible to design a labor law regime in which the employer and the employees owed reciprocal duties of loyalty?

IV. Regulating Employer and Union Speech During Organizing

A. Employers May Engage in Noncoercive Campaign Speech

NLRB v. Virginia Electric and Power Co.

Supreme Court of the United States
314 U.S. 469, 62 S. Ct. 344, 86 L. Ed. 348 (1941)

MURPHY, J.

... For years prior to the events in this case the Virginia Electric and Power Company [the Company] was hostile to labor organizations.... On April 26, 1937, shortly after the Act was upheld ... and an A.F. of L. organizer had appeared, the Company posted a bulletin throughout its operations appealing to the employees to bargain with the Company directly without the intervention of an "outside" union, and thereby coerced its employees. In response to this bulletin several requests for increased wages and better working conditions were received. The Company decided to withhold action on those requests and directed its employees to select representatives to attend meetings at which Company officials would speak on the Wagner Act. These representatives met in Norfolk and Richmond on May 24 and were addressed by high Company officials who read identical speeches stressing the desirability of forming a bargaining agency. At the Richmond meeting it was announced that any wage increase granted would be retroactive to June 1. By the substance of the speeches and the mechanics of the meetings the Company gave impetus to and assured the creation of an "inside" organization and coerced its employees in the exercise of their rights guaranteed by section 7 of the Act. Meetings, arranged with the cooperation of Company supervisors, on Company property and, in some instances on Company time, followed, at which the May 24 speeches were reported to the men who voted to form an "inside" organization and selected committees for that purpose. These committees met on Company property until June 15 when the constitution of the Independent was adopted. . . .

Upon the basis of these findings [and other findings] . . . the Board concluded that the Company had committed unfair labor practices within the meaning of section 8(1), (2) and (3) of the Act. Its order directed the Company to cease and desist from its unfair labor practices . . . and to post appropriate notices. [The court of appeals denied enforcement of the Board's order]. . . .

The Company is engaged in the business of generating and distributing electrical energy in eastern Virginia and northeastern North Carolina. It also furnishes illuminating gas to customers in the vicinity of Norfolk, Virginia, and operates transportation services in Richmond, Norfolk, Portsmouth and Petersburg. . . .

The Board specifically found that the bulletin of April 26 and the speeches of May 24 "interfered with, restrained and coerced" the Company's employees in the exercise of their rights guaranteed by section 7 of the Act. The Company strongly urges that such a finding is repugnant to the First Amendment. Neither the Act nor the Board's order here enjoins the employer from expressing its view on labor policies or problems, nor is a penalty imposed upon it because of any utterances which it has made. The sanctions of the Act are imposed not in punishment of the employer but for the protection of the employees. The employer in this case is as free now as ever to take any side it may choose on this controversial issue. But certainly conduct, though evidenced in part by speech, may amount in connection with other circumstances to coercion within the meaning of the Act. If the total activities of an employer restrain or coerce his employees in their free choice, then those employees are entitled to the protection of the Act. And in determining whether a course of conduct amounts to restraint or coercion, pressure exerted vocally by the employer may no more be disregarded than pressure exerted in other ways. . . .

If the Board's order here may fairly be said to be based on the totality of the Company's activities during the period in question, we may not consider the findings of the Board as to the coercive effect of the bulletin and the speeches in isolation from the findings as respects the other conduct of the Company. If the Board's ultimate conclusion is based upon a complex of activities, such as the anti-union background of the Company, the activities of [company managers'] warning to the employees that they would be discharged for "messing with the C.I.O.," the discharge of [an employee], the quick formation of [an employer-dominated labor organization], that conclusion would not be vitiated by the fact that the Board considered what the Company said in conjunction with what it did. The mere fact that language merges into a course of conduct does not put that whole course without the range of otherwise applicable administrative power. In determining whether the Company actually interfered with, restrained, and coerced its employees the Board has a right to look at what the Company has said as well as what it has done. . . .

The Board was of the view that the speeches delivered in the meetings of May 24 provided the impetus for the formation of a system-wide organization, that they re-emphasized the Company's distaste for "outside" organizations by referring to the bulletin, and that, after quoting the provision of the Act forbidding employer domination of labor organizations, they suggested that the employees select their "own" officers, and adopt their "own" by-laws and rules. The Board's finding was: "We find that at the May 24 meetings the respondent urged its employees to organize and to do so independently of 'outside' assistance, and that it thereby interfered with, restrained, and coerced its employees in the exercise of the rights guaranteed in Section 7 of the Act."

It is clear that the Board specifically found that those utterances were unfair labor practices, and it does not appear that the Board raised them to the stature of coercion by reliance on the surrounding circumstances. If the utterances are thus to be separated from their background, we find it difficult to sustain a finding of coercion with respect to them alone. The bulletin and the speeches set forth the right of the employees to do as they please without fear of retaliation by the Company. Perhaps the purport of these utterances may be altered by imponderable subtleties at work which it is not our function to appraise. Whether there are sufficient findings and evidence of interference, restraint, coercion, and domination without reference to the bulletin and the speeches, or whether the whole course of conduct evidenced in part by the utterances was aimed at achieving objectives forbidden by the Act, are questions for the Board to decide upon the evidence.

Here we are not sufficiently certain from the findings that the Board based its conclusion . . . upon the whole course of conduct revealed by this record. Rather it appears that the Board rested heavily upon findings with regard to the bulletin and the speeches the adequacy of which we regard as doubtful. We therefore remand the cause to the Circuit Court of Appeals with directions to remand it to the Board for a redetermination of the issues in the light of this opinion. We do not mean to intimate any views of our own as to whether the Independent was dominated or suggest to the Board what its conclusion should be when it reconsiders the case. Since the Board rested the remainder of its order in large part on its findings with respect to the domination of the Independent, we do not at this time reach the other parts of the Board's order, including the command that the checked-off dues and assessments should be refunded. . . . Reversed and remanded.

Notes

1. In *Virginia Electric*, the Board used employer speech as evidence of several ULPs. The Court rejected the employer's argument that the First Amendment protected its speech and remanded the case for the Board to make further findings as to whether the facts showed unlawful coercion. On remand, based on more "elaborate" findings of fact, the Board drew the same conclusions: the employer had violated § 8(a)(1), (2) and (3). *Virginia Elec. & Power Co. v. NLRB*, 319 U.S. 533, 534 (1943). The Supreme Court heard the case a second time and upheld that Board's findings that the Company had violated § 8(a)(2) and (1) by dominating and interfering with a so-called "Independent" union. The Court observed that the Board's

"findings and conclusions [were] not subject to the infirmities of the original [decision and order]. . . . While the bulletin . . . and the speeches . . . are still stressed, they are considered not in isolation but as part of a pattern of events adding up to the conclusion of domination and interference." *Id.* at 539.

Shortly after these cases were decided, the Taft-Hartley Act added § 8(c) to the NLRA. This section provides:

> The expressing of any views, argument, or opinion, or the dissemination thereof, whether in written, printed, graphic, or visual form, shall not constitute or be evidence of an unfair labor practice under any of the provisions of this Act [subchapter], if such expression contains no threat of reprisal or force or promise of benefit.

Section 8(c) does not create a general right protecting all employer speech in the organizing context. Rather, it privileges employer and union "view[s], argument[s], or opinion[s]" from constituting or evidencing a ULP.

2. In *General Shoe Corp.*, 77 N.L.R.B. 124 (1948), *enforced,* 192 F.2d 504 (6th Cir. 1951), the Board famously held that "laboratory conditions" were required for a free and fair election. The Board explained its new rule as follows:

> Conduct that creates an atmosphere which renders improbable a free choice will sometimes warrant invalidating an election, even though that conduct may not constitute an unfair labor practice. An election can serve its true purpose only if the surrounding conditions enable employees to register a free and untrammeled choice for or against a bargaining representative. . . . When a record reveals conduct so glaring that it is almost certain to have impaired employees' freedom of choice, we have set an election aside and directed a new one. Because we cannot police the details surrounding every election, and because we believe that in the absence of excessive acts employees can be taken to have expressed their true convictions in the secrecy of the polling booth, the Board has exercised this power sparingly. The question is one of degree.

Accordingly, the *General Shoe* Board ordered a new election based on the employer's disruption of "laboratory conditions." Specifically, shortly before the election, the employer brought groups of 20–25 employees into his office, "the very room which each employee must have regarded as the locus of final authority in the plant," where he "read every small group the same intemperate anti-union address." In addition, the employer instructed foremen to visit employees at home for the purpose of campaigning against the union.

Why do you think the Board is especially concerned about conduct that occurs right before the election? Moreover, how accurate is the "laboratory conditions" metaphor? Is it possible for a union election to accurately capture employees' views, free of undue employer or union influence?

3. *General Shoe* held that employer speech that does not constitute a ULP because it is protected under § 8(c) may still sufficiently interfere with the laboratory conditions

to require a re-run election. Along these lines, the Board has repeatedly held that conduct which violates § 8(a)(1) is "*a fortiori*, conduct which interferes with the exercise of a free and untrammeled choice in an election . . . because the test of conduct which may interfere with the 'laboratory conditions' for an election is considerably more restrictive than the test of conduct which amounts to interference, restraint, or coercion which violates Section 8(a)(1)." *Dal-Tex Optical Co.*, 137 N.L.R.B. 1782, 1786–87 (1962); *accord IRIS U.S.A., Inc.*, 336 N.L.R.B. 1013, 1013 (2001).

4. In *General Shoe*, the union initially filed both election objections and ULP charges. Parties are free to file either or both, based on the same conduct. There are, however, three significant differences between the two proceedings. First, election objections must be filed within seven days after the election, whereas ULP charges can be filed up to six months after the conduct was committed. Second, as indicated above, some conduct might be objectionable under *General Shoe*, yet not constitute a ULP. Third, the remedies differ. The Board typically remedies objections by ordering a new election. In contrast, the Board remedies ULPs with cease-and-desist orders and appropriate affirmative action within its § 10(c) authority. See Chapter 6 for a full discussion of remedies.

B. "Threats of Reprisal" and "Promises of Benefits"

Section 8(c) protects expressive speech from constituting or being evidence of a ULP "if such expression contains no threat of reprisal or promise of benefit." The materials below discuss what constitutes unlawful threats and promises.

1. Distinguishing Illegal Threats from Permissible Predictions

The excerpt of *Gissel* below deals with the distinction between (lawful) employer predictions as to the effect unionization will have on employment and (unlawful) employer threats. Chapter 8 contains another portion of *Gissel* (dealing with the validity of bargaining orders based on authorization cards and employer ULPs).

NLRB v. Gissel Packing Co.

Supreme Court of the United States
395 U.S. 575, 89 S. Ct. 1918, 23 L. Ed. 2d 547 (1969)

WARREN, C.J.

. . . When [the president of one of the four companies involved in this case] first learned of the Union's drive in July, he talked with all of his employees in an effort to dissuade them from joining a union. He particularly emphasized the results of the long 1952 strike, which he claimed "almost put our company out of business," and expressed worry that the employees were forgetting the "lessons of the past." He emphasized, secondly, that the Company was still on "thin ice" financially, that the Union's "only weapon is to strike," and that a strike "could lead to the closing of the plant," since the parent company had ample manufacturing facilities elsewhere.

He noted, thirdly, that because of their age and the limited usefulness of their skills outside their craft, the employees might not be able to find re-employment if they lost their jobs as a result of a strike. Finally, he warned those who did not believe that the plant could go out of business to "look around Holyoke and see a lot of them out of business." The president sent letters to the same effect to the employees in early November, emphasizing that the parent company had no reason to stay in Massachusetts if profits went down.

During the two or three weeks immediately prior to the election on December 9, the president sent the employees a pamphlet captioned: "Do you want another 13-week strike?" stating, inter alia, that: "We have no doubt that the Teamsters Union can again close the Wire Weaving Department and the entire plant by a strike. We have no hopes that the Teamsters Union Bosses will not call a strike. . . . The Teamsters Union is a strike happy outfit." Similar communications followed in late November, including one stressing the Teamsters' "hoodlum control." Two days before the election, the Company sent out another pamphlet that was entitled: "Let's Look at the Record," and that purported to be an obituary of companies in the Holyoke-Springfield, Massachusetts, area that had allegedly gone out of business because of union demands, eliminating some 3,500 jobs; the first page carried a large cartoon showing the preparation of a grave for the Sinclair Company and other headstones containing the names of other plants allegedly victimized by the unions. Finally, on the day before the election, the president made another personal appeal to his employees to reject the Union. He repeated that the Company's financial condition was precarious; that a possible strike would jeopardize the continued operation of the plant; and that age and lack of education would make re-employment difficult. The Union lost the election 7–6, and then filed both objections to the election and unfair labor practice charges. . . .

[T]he Board made a finding, left undisturbed by the First Circuit, that the employer's threats of reprisal were so coercive that, even in the absence of a §8(a)(5) violation, a bargaining order would have been necessary to repair the unlawful effect of those threats. The Board therefore did not have to make the determination . . . that the risks that a fair rerun election might not be possible were too great to disregard the desires of the employees already expressed through the cards. The employer argues, however, that its communications to its employees were protected by the First Amendment and §8(c) of the Act (29 U.S.C. §158(c)), whatever the effect of those communications on the union's majority or the Board's ability to ensure a fair election. . . .

. . . [T]he question raised here most often arises in the context of a nascent union organizational drive, where employers must be careful in waging their antiunion campaign. As to conduct generally, the above-noted gradations of unfair labor practices, with their varying consequences, create certain hazards for employers when they seek to estimate or resist unionization efforts. But so long as the differences involve conduct easily avoided, such as discharge, surveillance, and coercive interrogation, we do not think that employers can complain that the distinctions are unreasonably difficult to follow. Where an employer's antiunion efforts consist of speech alone, however, the difficulties raised are not so easily resolved. [W]e do note that an employer's free speech right to communicate his views to his employees is firmly established and cannot be infringed by a union or the Board. Thus, §8(c) ... merely implements the First Amendment by requiring that the expression of "any views, argument, or opinion" shall not be "evidence of an unfair labor practice," so long as such expression contains "no threat of reprisal or force or promise of benefit" in violation of §8(a)(1). Section 8(a)(1), in turn, prohibits interference, restraint or coercion of employees in the exercise of their right to self-organization.

Any assessment of the precise scope of employer expression, of course, must be made in the context of its labor relations setting. Thus, an employer's rights cannot outweigh the equal rights of the employees to associate freely, as those rights are embodied in §7 and protected by §8(a)(1) and the proviso to §8(c). And any balancing of those rights must take into account the economic dependence of the employees on their employers, and the necessary tendency of the former, because of that relationship, to pick up intended implications of the latter that might be more readily dismissed by a more disinterested ear. Stating these obvious principles is but another way of recognizing that what is basically at stake is the establishment of a nonpermanent, limited relationship between the employer, his economically dependent employee and his union agent, not the election of legislators or the enactment of legislation whereby that relationship is ultimately defined and where the independent voter may be freer to listen more objectively and employers as a class freer to talk. *Cf. New York Times Co. v. Sullivan*, 376 U.S. 254 (1964).

Within this framework, we must reject the Company's challenge to the decision below. . . . The standards used below for evaluating the impact of an employer's statements are not seriously questioned by petitioner and we see no need to tamper with them here. Thus, an employer is free to communicate to his employees any of his general views about unionism or any of his specific views about a particular union, so long as the communications do not contain a "threat of reprisal or force or promise of benefit." He may even make a prediction as to the precise effects he believes unionization will have on his company. In such a case, however, the prediction must be carefully phrased on the basis of objective fact to convey an employer's belief as to demonstrably probable consequences beyond his control or to convey a management decision already arrived at to close the plant in case of unionization. *See Textile Workers v. Darlington Mfg. Co.*, 380 U.S. 263, 274, n. 20 (1965). If there is any implication that an employer may or may not take action solely on his own initiative for reasons unrelated to economic necessities and known only to him, the statement is no longer a reasonable prediction based on available facts but a threat of retaliation based on misrepresentation and coercion, and as such without the protection of the First Amendment. We therefore agree with the court below that "[c]onveyance of the employer's belief, even though sincere, that unionization will or may result in the closing of the plant is not a statement of fact unless, which is most improbable, the eventuality of closing is capable of proof." . . . As stated elsewhere, an employer is free only to tell "what he reasonably believes will be the likely economic consequences of unionization that are outside his control," and not "threats of economic reprisal to be taken solely on his own volition." *NLRB v. River Togs, Inc.*, 382 F.2d 198, 202 (2d Cir. 1967).

Equally valid was the finding by the court and the Board that petitioner's statements and communications were not cast as a prediction of "demonstrable 'economic consequences,'" *NLRB v. Sinclair Co.*, 397 F.2d 157, 160 (1st Cir. 1968), but rather as a threat of retaliatory action. The Board found that petitioner's speeches, pamphlets, leaflets, and letters conveyed the following message: that the company was in a precarious financial condition; that the "strike-happy" union would in all likelihood have to obtain its potentially unreasonable demands by striking, the probable result of which would be a plant shutdown, as the past history of labor relations in the area indicated; and that the employees in such a case would have great difficulty finding employment elsewhere. In carrying out its duty to focus on the question: "[W]hat did the speaker intend and the listener understand?" (A. Cox, Law and the National Labor Policy 44 (1960)), the Board could reasonably conclude that the intended and understood import of that message was not to predict that unionization would inevitably cause the plant to close but to threaten to throw employees out of work regardless of the economic realities. In this connection, we need go no further than to point out (1) that petitioner had no support for its basic assumption that the union, which had not yet even presented any demands, would have to strike to be heard, and that it admitted at the hearing that it had no basis for attributing other plant closings in the area to unionism; and (2) that the Board has often found that employees, who are particularly sensitive to rumors of plant closings, take such hints as coercive threats rather than honest forecasts.

Petitioner argues that the line between so-called permitted predictions and proscribed threats is too vague to stand up under traditional First Amendment analysis and that the Board's discretion to curtail free speech rights is correspondingly too uncontrolled. It is true that a reviewing court must recognize the Board's competence in the first instance to judge the impact of utterances made in the context of the employer-employee relationship, *see NLRB v. Virginia Electric & Power Co.*, 314 U.S. 469, 479 (1941). But an employer, who has control over that relationship and therefore knows it best, cannot be heard to complain that he is without an adequate guide for his behavior. He can easily make his views known without engaging in "brinkmanship" when it becomes all too easy to "overstep and tumble [over] the brink," *Wausau Steel Corp. v. NLRB*, 377 F.2d 369, 372 (7th Cir. 1967). At the least he can avoid coercive speech simply by avoiding conscious overstatements he has reason to believe will mislead his employees. For the foregoing reasons, we affirm the judgment of . . . the First Circuit.

Notes

1. Does the test set forth in *Gissel* effectively distinguish between threats and predictions? Does it essentially require an employer to offer proof that its statement

is based on "objective fact" before the Board will uphold that statement as a non-threatening prediction?

2. In *Crown Cork & Seal Co.*, 308 N.L.R.B. 445 (1992), *enforcement denied, Crown Cork & Seal Co. v. NLRB*, 36 F.3d 1130 (D.C. Cir. 1994), the Board held unlawful, among other things, an employer's statements threatening employees with job loss if the union won the election. The D.C. Circuit denied enforcement. The Court explained that, in applying the *Gissel* threat/prediction distinction:

> [T]he Board may penalize two types of statements without encroaching on the employer's First Amendment rights. First, it may condemn a "threat of reprisal." Second, it may sanction at least some predictions of adverse economic consequences: predictions that may be understood by workers as threats, because they *suggest* that the action will occur not because of the ordinary operations of a market economy ("economic necessities"), but because the employer, for reasons of labor strategy, will seek to penalize concerted activity. 36 F.3d 1130, 1134.

Applying *Gissel*, the Court held that the following statement could not be read as a threat to close the plant in retaliation for unionization: "your job security depends on our being able to provide Progresso with the best product and the best service at the best price. *Union or no union*, if we can continue to do that your job is secure. And—*union or no*—if we cannot continue to do that, your job is on [the] line." *Id.*

3. Compare the pre-*Gissel* case, *Trane Co.*, 137 N.L.R.B. 1506 (1962). There, the employer sent three separate letters, each containing phrases like:

> The Company is continually reviewing the benefit program in effect at Clarksville now. This has been our policy, and will continue to be our policy . . . *union or no union*. What, then, can the union organizers offer you but more promises . . . a chance to pay dues for benefits you'll receive anyway? 137 N.L.R.B. 1506, 1509–10.

Is this distinguishable from *Crown Cork & Seal? Trane* found that these letters were "reasonably calculated to have a coercive effect on employees" who, like most people, "are [disinclined] to indulge in futile acts." The Board continues to hold that statements indicating that joining a union would be futile violate §8(a)(1), at least when they are not supported with objective facts. *See, e.g., Matros Automated Elect. Constr. Corp.*, 353 N.L.R.B. 569 (2008) (violation of §8(a)(1) for employer to tell employees that it "would never sign a contract" with the union and that "hell will freeze over" before it recognizes the union).

4. What about statements along the lines of "bargaining will begin from scratch"? Does it matter if the employer adds, "you could lose the benefits you have"? *Compare Federated Logistics & Operations v. NLRB*, 340 N.L.R.B. 255, *enforced* 400 F.3d 920 (D.C. Cir. 2005), *with Wild Oats Mkts., Inc.*, 344 N.L.R.B. 717 (2005).

A recent high-profile case asks whether Tesla CEO Elon Musk violated labor law when he tweeted the following: "Nothing stopping Tesla team at our car plant from voting union. Could do so tmrw if they wanted. But why pay union dues & give up stock options for nothing? Our safety record is 2X better than when plant was UAW & everybody already gets healthcare." Given the other cases in this section, how should the Board decide this case? *See Tesla, Inc.*, NLRB Case No. 32-CA-197020, 2019 WL 4795430 (Sept 27, 2019).

5. *Eldorado Tool*, 325 N.L.R.B. 222 (1997) featured a less subtle threat. There, the Board found that an employer's decision to construct a mock graveyard depicting manufacturing plants allegedly "killed" by the United Auto Workers constituted an implicit threat in violation of §8(a)(1). The employer also displayed a banner with "PLANT CLOSURES: UAW WALL OF SHAME" written on the top. Beneath the headline, the employer placed a series of paper tombstones, each of which had "RIP" along with the name of a closed UAW plant written on it. The employer added one such tombstone each day during the organizing campaign. On the final day of the campaign, the employer added a final tombstone reading "ELDORADO?" In holding that this tactic violated §8(a)(1) violation, the Board explained, "the logical inference to be drawn from the expanding cemetery of UAW-represented plants is that the same fate of plant closure and job loss awaited Eldorado." 325 N.L.R.B. 222, 223. Also, Eldorado had not articulated any specific economic consequences of unionization that might threaten to close the plant.

6. In *Be-Lo Stores*, 318 N.L.R.B. 1 (1995), *enforcement denied. in relevant part*, 126 F.3d 268 (4th Cir. 1997), the Board found that an employer who delivered a mock "pink slip" to employees in advance of an election had violated §8(a)(1). The case arose during a United Food and Commercial Workers (UFCW) campaign to organize a 30-store chain of Be-Lo's grocery stores. The "pink slip" read: "Dear Unionized Employees: I regret to inform you that because we have lost our ability to compete in this extremely competitive market, we shall be forced to close this store and put you out of work." It contained the names and logos of three other stores that had recently closed after being organized by the UFCW. It also came with a cover letter which read "[w]e will do everything we can to prevent this from happening to you . . . but you should consider what the union has DELIVERED in the past before you believe what they PROMISE in the future." 126 F.3d at 286, 291. The Board concluded that the "pink slip" amounted to a threat because Be-Lo employees could reasonably have inferred that the employer was intending to convey that the pink slip would be addressed to them if the store unionized. In part, the Board based its decision on the surrounding circumstances, noting that the employer had made similar statements to the employees on several other occasions.

The Fourth Circuit, however, reversed, holding that the employer did not "take action solely on [its] own initiative for reasons unrelated to economic necessities." Instead, the court found that the "pink slip" and cover letter simply represented the employer's prediction as to the "probable economic consequences" of unionization based upon the "experiences of similarly situated stores." 126 F.3d 268, 286 (4th Cir. 1997). Which decision in this case is more convincing?

7. In *Spring Industries, Inc.*, 332 N.L.R.B. 40 (2000), the Board held that if an employer makes a threat to a small group of employees (in this case, in a break

room), the Board will presume that the threat was disseminated throughout the entire plant. *Spring Industries* based this rule on the fact that a "hallmark" violation of § 8(a)(1) (*e.g.*, a threat to close a plant to spite a union) has far-reaching implications for the entire workforce. Thus, the Board found it is "all but inevitable" that an employee will discuss such a threat with other employees.

In *Crown Bolt, Inc.*, 343 N.L.R.B. 776 (2004), the Board overruled *Spring Industries* and reversed this presumption. The Board relied on several considerations. Most notably, it found that: (a) in practice, the *Spring Industries* presumption had become too difficult to rebut; (b) if the presumption is accurate and dissemination is "all but inevitable," then the presumption is unnecessary and proving dissemination would be relatively easy; and (c) there was no data lending credence to *Spring Industries*' inevitability claim.

8. What about language that is simply insulting? In *Trailmobile Trailer*, 343 N.L.R.B. 95 (2004), the Board rejected an ALJ's determination that an employer's vituperative remarks regarding union workers amounted to threats in violation of § 8(a)(1). There, the employer, a trailer manufacturer, told a group of welders that he could teach monkeys to weld in 10 minutes. Similarly, a week before the election, the same employer remarked that the "fat ass [union organizer was] living it up at the Holiday Inn on the employees' dues." *Id.* at 95. In finding this speech was protected by § 8(c), the Board held "[w]ords of disparagement alone concerning a union or its officials are insufficient for finding a violation of Section 8(a)(1)." *Id.* Generally, "'flip and intemperate' remarks that are mere expressions of personal opinion are protected by the free speech provisions of § 8(c) of the Act." *Id.* Is this contrary to the principle in *Jefferson Standard, supra*?

9. Along these lines, in *Sears, Roebuck & Co.*, 305 N.L.R.B. 193 (1991), the employer's Employee Relations Manager told employees that the union might send someone out to break their legs in order to collect dues. The Board refused to find a § 8(a)(1) violation. Can you think of why this might not be considered a "threat" under *Gissel* and § 8(c)?

2. Promises of Benefits

NLRB v. Exchange Parts Co.

Supreme Court of the United States
375 U.S. 405, 84 S. Ct. 457, 11 L. Ed. 2d 435 (1964)

Harlan, J.

This case presents a question concerning the limitations which § 8(a)(1) of the [NLRA], places on the right of an employer to confer economic benefits on his employees shortly before a representation election. The precise issue is whether that section prohibits the conferral of such benefits, without more, where the employer's purpose is to affect the outcome of the election. . . .

The respondent, Exchange Parts Company, is engaged in the business of rebuilding automobile parts in Fort Worth, Texas. Prior to November 1959 its employees were not represented by a union. On November 9, 1959, the International Brother-hood of Boilermakers, Iron Shipbuilders, Blacksmiths, Forgers and Helpers, AFL-CIO, advised Exchange Parts that the union was conducting an organizational campaign at the plant and that a majority of the employees had designated the union as their bargaining representative. On November 16 the union petitioned the Labor Board for a representation election. The Board conducted a hearing on December 29, and on February 19, 1960, issued an order directing that an election be held. The election was held on March 18, 1960.

At two meetings on November 4 and 5, 1959, C. V. McDonald, the Vice-President and General Manager of Exchange Parts, announced to the employees that their "floating holiday" in 1959 would fall on December 26 and that there would be an additional "floating holiday" in 1960. On February 25, six days after the Board issued its election order, Exchange Parts held a dinner for employees at which Vice-President McDonald told the employees that they could decide whether the extra day of vacation in 1960 would be a "floating holiday" or would be taken on their birthdays. The employees voted for the latter. McDonald also referred to the forth-coming representation election as one in which, in the words of the trial examiner, the employees would "determine whether . . . [they] wished to hand over their right to speak and act for themselves." He stated that the union had distorted some of the facts and pointed out the benefits obtained by the employees without a union. He urged all the employees to vote in the election.

On March 4 Exchange Parts sent its employees a letter which spoke of "the Empty Promises of the Union" and "the fact that it is the Company that puts things in your envelope. . . ." After mentioning a number of benefits, the letter said: "The Union can't put any of those things in your envelope—only the Company can do that." Further on, the letter stated: ". . . [I]t didn't take a Union to get any of those things and . . . it won't take a Union to get additional improvements in the future." Accompanying the letter was a detailed statement of the benefits granted by the company since 1949 and an estimate of the monetary value of such benefits to the employees. Included in the statement of benefits for 1960 were the birthday holiday, a new sys-tem for computing overtime during holiday weeks which had the effect of increas-ing wages for those weeks, and a new vacation schedule which enabled employees to extend their vacations by sandwiching them between two weekends. Although Exchange Parts asserts that the policy behind the latter two benefits was established earlier, it is clear that the letter of March 4 was the first general announcement of the changes to the employees. In the ensuing election the union lost.

The Board, affirming the findings of the trial examiner, found that the announce-ment of the birthday holiday and the grant and announcement of overtime and vacation benefits were arranged by Exchange Parts with the intention of inducing the employees to vote against the union. It found that this conduct violated § 8(a) (1). . . . [T]he Court of Appeals . . . denied enforcement of the Board's order. It believed that it was not an unfair labor practice under § 8(a)(1) for an employer to grant benefits to its employees in these circumstances. . . .

We think the Court of Appeals was mistaken in concluding that the conferral of employee benefits while a representation election is pending, for the purpose of inducing employees to vote against the union, does not "interfere with" the protected right to organize.

The broad purpose of § 8(a)(1) is to establish "the right of employees to organize for mutual aid without employer interference." *Republic Aviation Corp. v. NLRB*, 324 U.S. 793, 798. We have no doubt that it prohibits not only intrusive threats and promises but also conduct immediately favorable to employees which is undertaken with the express purpose of impinging upon their freedom of choice for or against unionization and is reasonably calculated to have that effect. In *Medo Photo Supply Corp. v. NLRB*, 321 U.S. 678, 686, this Court said: "The action of employees with respect to the choice of their bargaining agents may be induced by favors bestowed by the employer as well as by his threats or domination." Although in that case there was already a designated bargaining agent and the offer of "favors" was in response to a suggestion of the employees that they would leave the union if favors were bestowed, the principles which dictated the result there are fully applicable here. The danger inherent in well-timed increases in benefits is the suggestion of a fist inside the velvet glove. Employees are not likely to miss the inference that the source of benefits now conferred is also the source from which future benefits must flow and which may dry up if it is not obliged.[3] The danger may be diminished if, as in this case, the benefits are conferred permanently and unconditionally. But the absence of conditions or threats pertaining to the particular benefits conferred would be of controlling significance only if it could be presumed that no question of additional benefits or renegotiation of existing benefits would arise in the future; and, of course, no such presumption is tenable.

. . . It is true, as the court below pointed out, that in most cases of this kind the increase in benefits could be regarded as "one part of an overall program of interference and restraint by the employer," . . . and that in this case the questioned conduct stood in isolation. Other unlawful conduct may often be an indication of the motive behind a grant of benefits while an election is pending, and to that extent it is relevant to the legality of the grant; but when as here the motive is otherwise established, an employer is not free to violate § 8(a)(1) by conferring benefits simply because it refrains from other, more obvious violations. We cannot agree with the Court of Appeals that enforcement of the Board's order will have the "ironic" result of "discouraging benefits for labor." . . . The beneficence of an employer is likely to be ephemeral if prompted by a threat of unionization which is subsequently

---

3. The inference was made almost explicit in Exchange Parts' letter to its employees of March 4, already quoted, which said: "The Union can't put any of those . . . (benefits) in your envelope — *only the Company can do that.*" (Original italics.) We place no reliance, however, on these or other words of the respondent dissociated from its conduct. Section 8(c) provides that the expression or dissemination of "any views, argument, or opinion" "shall not constitute or be evidence of an unfair labor practice under any of the provisions of this Act, if such expression contains no threat of reprisal or force or promise of benefit."

removed. Insulating the right of collective organization from calculated good will of this sort deprives employees of little that has lasting value. Reversed.

Notes

1. Justice Harlan famously said of benefits conferred on employees during an election campaign: "The danger inherent in well-timed increases in benefits is the suggestion of a fist inside the velvet glove." How does this analogy describe the effect of benefits conferred on employees during an election campaign?

2. The typical remedy for a § 8(a)(1) violation is a cease-and-desist order and affirmative action. What affirmative action could the Board order the employer to take in this case? Would the Board have to order the employer to rescind the benefits? *See Hogan Transps., Inc.*, 363 N.L.R.B. No. 196 (2016) (holding that employer violated 8(a)(1) "by blaming the Union for attempting to take away [an] unlawful wage increase" after the union filed an unfair labor practice charge alleging an *Exchange Parts* violation, and observing that "the Board does not typically require a company to rescind a wage increase" offered in violation of *Exchange Parts*).

3. The Board "will infer that an announcement or grant of benefits during the critical period [between the date of the filing of a representation petition and the date of the election] is coercive, but the employer may rebut the inference by establishing an explanation other than the pending election for the time of the announcement or bestowal of the benefit. . . . In making a determination, the Board will examine the size of the benefit conferred, the number of employees receiving it, the timing of the benefit, and how employees reasonably would view the purpose of the benefit." *Star, Inc.*, 337 N.L.R.B. 962, 962–63 (2002) (finding that the employer could not show that year-end bonuses of up to $400 conformed to its past practice). The employer bears the burden of establishing that "[the timing of the] actions were governed by factors other than the pend[ency of the] election." *American Sunroof Corp.*, 248 N.L.R.B. 748 (1980), *modified on other grounds*, 667 F.2d 20 (6th Cir. 1981). In *Waste Management of Palm Beach*, 329 N.L.R.B. 198 (1999), the Board held that an announcement of a benefit increase at an employer-sponsored dinner party violated § 8(a)(1). There, the employer hosted the party for employees three days before a union election. At the party, the employer announced an increase in its matching contribution to the employees' § 401(k) plan. The Board found that, although the dinner itself was a non-coercive and legitimate campaign device, the announcement at the party was an unfair labor practice.

What if an employer grants a new benefit to its workers who are not eligible to unionize, but refuses to extend that benefit to union-eligible employees? At least where the employer cites the pendency of a union election as its reason, the Board has held (and the D.C. Circuit has affirmed) that this too violates the Act. *Care One at Madison Avenue, LLC v. NLRB*, 832 F.3d 351 (D.C. Cir. 2016).

4. Unions can also run afoul of rules prohibiting benefits during an organizing campaign. In *NLRB v. Savair Mfg. Co.*, 414 U.S. 270 (1973), the union promised to waive union initiation fees for employees who signed representation cards. While

the Board held this practice was not a violation, the Supreme Court disagreed, explaining that it "allows the union to buy endorsements and paint a false portrait of employee support during its election campaign[s]." 414 U.S. 270, 277.

5. A recurring issue in this regard has been unions providing employees with legal representation in employment law suits (*e.g.*, under the Fair Labor Standards Act) around the time of a union representation election. In some cases, courts have found this to be an improper benefit, especially (but not necessarily exclusively) if it occurred in the "critical period" leading up to an election. *See, e.g., Freund Baking Co. v. NLRB*, 165 F.3d 928 (D.C. Cir. 1999).

The Board announced the following new rule for these cases in *Stericycle, Inc.*, 357 N.L.R.B. 582 (2011).

> [A] union does not engage in objectionable conduct by funding employment-related litigation on behalf of employees so long as the litigation is commenced prior to the filing of an election petition. Unions typically learn about employees' workplace concerns in the earliest stages of organizing, prior to the filing of an election petition, as we observed above. Based on the voicing of these concerns, the union may investigate and discover during this prepetition period colorable claims of violation of the FLSA or other employment laws. These circumstances constitute a legitimate justification for seeking legal redress prepetition akin to an employer's legitimate business justification for the grant of a wage increase during that time period. This is particularly so when the passage of time will bar or reduce the employees' claim. *Id.* at 586.

What are the competing concerns in this type of case? Does the rule in *Stericycle* properly balance these concerns?

C. Material Misrepresentations

The Board has oscillated several times on the question of whether misrepresentations during an election campaign justify holding a re-run election. In *Hollywood Ceramics Co.*, 140 N.L.R.B. 221, 224 (1962), the Board held that it would set aside an election where "a misrepresentation or other similar campaign trickery, which involves a substantial departure from the truth, at a time which prevents the other party or parties from making an effective reply, so that the misrepresentation, whether deliberate or not, may reasonably be expected to have a significant impact on the election." Fifteen years later, the Board abandoned this approach in *Shopping Kart Food Mkt., Inc.*, 228 N.L.R.B. 1311 (1977). *Shopping Kart* concluded that employees do not need the Board's "'protection' from campaign misrepresentations," and held that it would "no longer set elections aside on the basis of misleading campaign statements" except "where a party has engaged in such deceptive campaign practices as improperly involving the Board and its processes, or the use of forged documents which render the voters unable to recognize the propaganda for what it is." 228 N.L.R.B. 1311, 1313. That rule was short-lived. *See General Knit of California*, 239 N.L.R.B. 619 (1978) (returning to *Hollywood Ceramics*). In *General Knit*, the Board based its decision not on the naiveté of the employee electorate, but rather on its view that some misrepresentations "may materially affect an election" and therefore that a re-run election remedy was necessary to "preserve[] the integrity of [the Board's] electoral processes." 239 N.L.R.B. 619, 620–21.

In the following case, the Board shifted its position again.

Midland National Life Insurance Co.

National Labor Relations Board
263 N.L.R.B. 127 (1982)

[The Board conducted a secret-ballot election on March 2, 1978 (first election), which the union lost. The union filed objections to conduct affecting the results of the election and a § 8(a)(1) charge. After a hearing on the union's objections consolidated with the representation and ULP hearing, the ALJ found that the employer had engaged in objectionable conduct affecting the results of the election and had committed the alleged ULPs. The judge recommended that a second election be held, the Board affirmed, and the Eighth Circuit enforced the Board's order. The Board conducted the second election on October 16, 1980. Of approximately 239 eligible voters, 107 cast ballots for the union, 107 cast ballots against the union, 1 ballot was void, and 20 ballots were challenged, a number sufficient to affect the results. The union timely filed election objections. A hearing was held, where the parties agreed that the workers casting the 20 challenged ballots were ineligible solely for the purposes of the October 16, 1980, election, and the Hearing Officer recommended that the challenges be sustained. The Hearing Officer also recommended that the Board direct a third election because the employer had engaged in objectionable conduct. The employer timely filed exceptions to the Hearing Officer's report; the union filed a response.]

The Board has reviewed the rulings made by the Hearing Officer at the hearing and finds that no prejudicial error was committed. The rulings are hereby affirmed. The Board has considered the record . . . and, for the reasons discussed below, finds merit in the Employer's exceptions.

I.

. . . On the afternoon of October 15, 1980, the day before the election, the Employer distributed campaign literature to its employees with their paychecks. One of the distributions was a six-page document which included photographs and text depicting three local employers and their involvements with the Petitioner. The document also contained a reproduction of a portion of the Petitioner's 1979 financial report (hereinafter LMRDA report) submitted to the Department of Labor pursuant to the provisions of the Labor Management Reporting and Disclosure Act of

1959. The Petitioner learned of the document the next morning, 3-1/2 hours before the polls were to open.

The first subject of the document, Meilman Food, Inc., was portrayed in "recent" pictures as a deserted facility, and was described in accompanying text as follows: "They too employed between 200 and 300 employees. This Local 304A struck this plant—violence ensued. *Now all of the workers are gone!* What did the Local 304A do for them? Where is the 304A union job security?" Jack Smith, the Petitioner's business representative, testified that Local 304A, the Petitioner, had been the representative of Meilman's employees, but that neither the Petitioner nor Meilman's employees had been on strike when the plant closed. He added that the employees had been working for at least 1 1/2 years following the strike and prior to the closure of the facility.

The second and third employers pictured and discussed in the document were Luther Manor Nursing Home and Blue Cross/Blue Shield. The text accompanying the pictures of Luther Manor explained that:

> [a]lmost a year ago this same union that tells you they will "make job security" (we believe you are the only ones who can do that) and will get you more pay, told the employees of LUTHER MANOR (again, here in Sioux Falls) . . . the union would get them a contract with job security and more money. Unfortunately Local 304A did not tell the Luther Manor employees what year or century they were talking about. Today the employees have no contract. Most of the union leaders left to work elsewhere. Their job security is the same (depends upon the individual as it always has). There has been no change or increase in wages or hours. The union has sent in three different sets of negotiators. Again, promises and performance are two different things. All wages, fringes, working conditions are remaining the same while negotiations continue.

The text accompanying the pictures of Blue Cross stated that "this same Local union won an election at Blue Cross/Blue Shield after promising less restrictive policies, better pay and more job security. Since the election a good percentage of its former employees are no longer working there. Ask them! The employees have been offered a wage increase—*next year* of 5%. . . ."

Smith testified that the Petitioner took over negotiations at Luther Manor and at Blue Cross on or about July 1, 1980, after the Petitioner had merged with Retail Clerks, Local 1665, and that Retail Clerks, Local 1665, not the Petitioner, had conducted the prior negotiations and won the election at Blue Cross.

Assessing the statements concerning these local employers, the Hearing Officer concluded that, in its description of Meilman Food, the Employer intended to instill in the minds of its employees the false impression that the Petitioner had conducted a strike at Meilman, that violence had ensued, and that, as a direct result of the strike, all of the employees at Meilman were terminated. Evaluating the statements about Luther Manor and Blue Cross, the Hearing Officer found that the Employer had misrepresented the labor organization involved, and had implied that the Petitioner was an ineffectual and inefficient bargaining representative who would cause employees to suffer.

The Employer's distribution also included a portion of the Petitioner's 1979 LMRDA report which listed information concerning the Petitioner's assets, liabilities, and cash receipts and disbursements for the reporting period. Three entries on the reproduced page were underlined: total receipts, reported at $508,946; disbursements "On Behalf of Individual Members," reported at zero; and total disbursements, reported at $492,701. Other entries on the reproduced page showed disbursements of $93,185 to officers, and $22,662 to employees. The accompanying text stated that $141,000 of the Petitioner's funds went to "union officers and officials and those who worked for them," and that "NOTHING—according to the report they filed with the U.S. Government was spent 'on behalf of the individual members.' [sic]"

The Hearing Officer found that the report actually showed that the Petitioner disbursed only $115,847 to its officers and employees, a difference of $25,000, and that the Employer's statement attributed 19 percent more in income to the officials and employees than was actually received. He further found that, while the report showed that no sums had been spent "on behalf of the individual members," the instructions for the LMRDA report require that entry to reflect disbursements for "other than normal operating purposes," and that the Employer failed to include this fact in its distribution.

[T]he Hearing Officer concluded that the document distributed by the Employer contained numerous misrepresentations of fact of a substantial nature designed to portray the Petitioner as an organization staffed by highly paid officials and employees who were ineffectual as bargaining representatives, and that as a consequence employees would suffer with respect to job security and compensation. The Hearing Officer also determined that the document was distributed on the afternoon before the election, that the Petitioner did not become aware of it until approximately 10 a.m. election day, 2-1/2 hours before the preelection conference and 3-1/2 hours before the polls were to open, and that, owing to the nature of the misrepresentations, the Petitioner did not have sufficient time to respond effectively. Applying the standard found in *General Knit of California, Inc.*, 239 N.L.R.B. 619 (1978) and *Hollywood Ceramics Company, Inc.*, 140 N.L.R.B. 221 (1962), the Hearing Officer accordingly recommended that the objection be sustained and that a third election be directed.

We have decided to reject the Hearing Officer's recommendations and to certify the results of the election. We do so because, after painstaking evaluation and careful consideration, we have resolved to return to the sound rule announced in *Shopping Kart Food Market, Inc.*, 228 N.L.R.B. 1311 (1977) and to overrule *General Knit* and *Hollywood Ceramics.* Before discussing the controlling factors which underlie our decision, we believe it would be instructive to review briefly the Board's past treatment of this troublesome area.

II.

During the years under the Wagner Act, the Board made no attempt to regulate campaign propaganda, and concerned itself solely with conduct which might tend to coerce employees in their election choice. As the Board stated in *Maywood Hosiery Mills, Inc.*, 64 N.L.R.B. 146, 150 (1945), "we cannot censor the information, misinformation, argument, gossip, and opinion which accompany all controversies of any importance and which, perceptively or otherwise, condition employees' desires and decisions; nor is it our function to do so." "[E]mployees," as the Board acknowledged even then, "undoubtedly recognize [campaign] propaganda for what it is, and discount it." *Corn Products Refining Company*, 58 N.L.R.B. 1441, 1442 (1944).

Following the enactment of the Taft-Hartley amendments, the Board continued to disregard issues concerning the truth or falsity of campaign propaganda. . . . Again relying on the ability of employees to recognize and assess campaign propaganda for what it is, the Board entrusted these matters to the "good sense" of the voters. . . . In an apparent effort to remove itself further from controversies of this nature, the Board also imposed a duty upon the parties to correct "inaccurate or untruthful statements by any of them." . . .

Even as it was refusing to consider the truth or falsity of campaign propaganda, the Board announced its "laboratory conditions" standard. *General Shoe Corporation*, 77 N.L.R.B. 124 (1948). . . . However, as was subsequently explained in *The Liberal Market, Inc.*, 108 N.L.R.B. 1481, 1482 (1954), the Board had a realistic recognition that elections did "not occur in a laboratory where controlled or artificial conditions may be established," and that, accordingly, the Board's goal was "to establish ideal conditions insofar as possible," and to assess "the actual facts in the light of realistic standards of human conduct." *Id.*

Exhibiting the understanding and realism espoused in *Liberal Market*, the Board recognized a limited exception to its general rule barring an examination of the effect of the truth or falsity of campaign propaganda upon the election results. Thus, where it appeared that employees were deceived as to the source of campaign propaganda by trickery or fraud, and that they could therefore neither recognize nor evaluate propaganda for what it was, the Board set aside the election. *United Aircraft Corporation*, 103 N.L.R.B. 102 (1953). . . . In those situations, the Board found that election standards had been "lowered . . . to a level which impaired the free and informed atmosphere requisite to an untrammeled expression of choice by the employees." *United Aircraft Corporation*, 103 N.L.R.B. at 105.

It was not until 20 years after the Board began establishing standards for elections that it deviated from its practice of refusing to consider the truth or falsity of campaign propaganda. In *The Gummed Products Company*, 112 N.L.R.B. 1092 (1955), the Board set aside an election where the union deliberately misrepresented wage rates it had negotiated with another employer. . . .

The Board refined this standard 7 years later in *Hollywood Ceramics Company, Inc.*, 140 N.L.R.B. 221 (1962). [The Board then reviewed the history of its election rules governing misrepresentation from *Hollywood Ceramics* to *Shopping Kart* to *General Knit* discussed above.]

Many lessons and conclusions can be drawn from this summary of the Board's past practice regarding the role of misrepresentations in Board elections and, no doubt, many will be. However, one lesson which cannot be mistaken is that reasonable, informed individuals can differ, and indeed have differed, in their assessment of the effect of misrepresentations on voters and in their views of the Board's proper role in policing such misrepresentations. No one can or does dispute the ultimate purpose of this controversy that is the necessity of Board procedures which insure the fair and free choice of a bargaining representative. The sole question facing us is how that "fair and free choice" is best assured.

III.

We begin with the recognition that Congress has entrusted a wide degree of discretion to the Board to establish the procedures necessary to insure the fair and free choice of bargaining representatives by employees. . . .

Although the Board's exercise of discretion must be consistent with the principle of majority rule, the Supreme Court has held that the Board is not precluded from making "practical adjustments designed to protect the election machinery from the ever-present dangers of abuse and fraud." *Id.* In making these rules, the Board must weigh and accommodate not only the principle of majority rule, but several other conflicting factors, such as preserving the secrecy of the ballot, insuring the certainty and finality of election results, and minimizing unwarranted and dilatory claims by those opposed to the election results. *Id.*

Accordingly, a Board rule governing a representation proceeding need not be an "absolute guarantee" that the election will, without exception, reflect the choice of a majority of the voting employees. Rather, the rule simply must be "consistent with" and constitute a "justifiable and reasonable adjustment of the democratic process." *Id.* at 332, 333.

For numerous reasons, we find that the rule we announce today constitutes just such a "justifiable and reasonable adjustment" of our democratic electoral processes. By returning to the sound principles espoused in *Shopping Kart*, not only do we alleviate the many difficulties attending the *Hollywood Ceramics* rule, but we also insure the certainty and finality of election results, and minimize unwarranted and dilatory claims attacking those results.

As was discussed earlier, an election would be set aside under *Hollywood Ceramics*

> . . . only where there has been a misrepresentation or other similar campaign trickery, which involves a substantial departure from the truth, at a time which prevents the other party . . . from making an effective reply, so that the misrepresentation, whether deliberate or not, may reasonably be expected to have a significant impact on the election.

As an initial matter, it is apparent that reasonable, informed individuals can differ on the multitude of subjective issues encompassed in this rule. When does a particular statement involve a "substantial" departure from the "truth"? Under what conditions has there been time for an "effective reply"? May the misrepresentation "reasonably be expected" to have a "significant impact" upon the election? As Professor Derek C. Bok concluded in his classic work on the Board's election procedures, restrictions on the content of campaign propaganda requiring truthful and accurate statements "resist every effort at a clear formulation and tend inexorably to give rise to vague and inconsistent rulings which baffle the parties and provoke litigation."

The Board's experience under the *Hollywood Ceramics* rule bears this out. As was found in *Shopping Kart*, although the adoption of the *Hollywood Ceramics* rule "was premised on assuring employee free choice its administration has in fact tended to impede the attainment of that goal. The ill effects of the rule include extensive analysis of campaign propaganda, restriction of free speech, variance in application as between the Board and the courts, increasing litigation, and a resulting decrease in the finality of election results."

In sharp contrast to the *Hollywood Ceramics* standard, *Shopping Kart* "draws a clear line between what is and what is not objectionable." Thus, "elections will be set aside 'not on the basis of the *substance* of the representation, but the deceptive *manner* in which it was made.' . . . As long as the campaign material is what it purports to be, i.e., mere propaganda of a particular party, the Board would leave the task of evaluating its contents solely to the employees." Where, due to forgery, no voter could recognize the propaganda "for what it is," Board intervention is warranted. Further, unlike *Hollywood Ceramics*, the rule in *Shopping Kart* lends itself to definite results which are both predictable and speedy. The incentive for protracted litigation is greatly reduced, as is the possibility of disagreement between the Board and the courts. Because objections alleging false or inaccurate statements can be summarily rejected at the first stage of Board proceedings, the opportunity for delay is almost nonexistent. Finally, the rule in *Shopping Kart* "furthers the goal of consistent and equitable adjudications" by applying uniformly to the objections of both unions and employers.

In addition to finding the *Hollywood Ceramics* rule to be unwieldy and counterproductive, we also consider it to have an unrealistic view of the ability of voters to assess misleading campaign propaganda. As is clear from an examination of our treatment of misrepresentations under the Wagner Act, the Board had long viewed employees as aware that parties to a campaign are seeking to achieve certain results and to promote their own goals. Employees, knowing these interests, could not help but greet the various claims made during a campaign with natural skepticism. The "protectionism" propounded by the *Hollywood Ceramics* rule is simply not warranted. On the contrary, as we found in *Shopping Kart*, "we believe that Board rules in this area must be based on a view of employees as mature individuals who are capable of recognizing campaign propaganda for what it is and discounting it."

This fact is apparently recognized to a certain extent even under *Hollywood Ceramics*. Thus, although the Board determined that a substantial misrepresentation had been made, the election would not be set aside if it also appeared that there had been ample time to respond. This result would obtain no matter how egregious the error or falsity, and regardless of whether in fact a response had been made. . . .

In sum, we rule today that we will no longer probe into the truth or falsity of the parties' campaign statements, and that we will not set elections aside on the basis of misleading campaign statements. We will, however, intervene in cases where a party has used forged documents which render the voters unable to recognize propaganda for what it is. Thus, we will set an election aside not because of the substance of the representation, but because of the deceptive manner in which it was made, a manner which renders employees unable to evaluate the forgery for what it is. As was the case in *Shopping Kart*, we will continue to protect against other campaign conduct, such as threats, promises, or the like, which interferes with employee free choice.

Accordingly, inasmuch as the Petitioner's objection alleges nothing more than misrepresentations, it is hereby overruled. Because the tally of ballots shows that the Petitioner failed to receive a majority of the valid ballots cast, we shall certify the results.

[Dissent of MEMBERS FANNING and JENKINS omitted.]

Notes

1. In *Van Dorn Plastic Mach. Co. v. NLRB*, 736 F.2d 343 (6th Cir. 1984), the Court refused to endorse the Board's *Midland* doctrine. It explained:

> Though we have no hesitation in upholding the Board's decision on the issue of misrepresentation in the present case we [are] reluctan[t] to be bound by the *Midland National Life* rule in every case. There may be cases where no forgery can be proved, but where the misrepresentation is so pervasive and the deception so artful that employees will be unable to separate truth from untruth and where their right to a free and fair choice will be affected. We agree with the Board that it should not set aside an election on the basis of the substance of representations alone, but only on the deceptive manner in which representations are made.

2. In *Formco, Inc.*, 233 N.L.R.B. 61 (1977), the Board created the "forgery exception" to the *Midland* doctrine. There, the Board held—in the context of a union distribution of a document claiming that Formco had been "'found guilty of engaging in [an] unfair labor practice[]'"—that "any substantial mischaracterization or misuse of a Board document for partisan election purposes is a serious misrepresentation warranting setting an election aside." 233 N.L.R.B. at 61. Is this more of a forgery exception or a protection of the Board's processes exception? Note, though, that it remains illegal for one party (union or employer) to forge material to give the false impression that the material originated with the other party. *See, e.g., Albertson's, Inc.*, 344 N.L.R.B. 1357 (2005).

3. Could the Board have used a different theory to find that at least some of the employer's statements in this case were objectionable and indeed constituted a ULP?

This question raises a larger issue: how should one reconcile *Midland National* with the cases in the earlier part of this chapter? On one hand, the Board will not police statements that are merely misleading. On the other, coercive statements are a ULP and/or a violation of laboratory conditions. In *Didlake, Inc.*, the Board attempted to parse the line between these two categories. 367 NLRB No. 125 (2019). The employer told employees in part that, if a union drive was successful, "[f]irst thing they will require you to do is join the Union. . . . And if you don't, you will not be able to work here. . . . If they win, you will have to join as a condition of your employment to be here, and you will be paying union dues. . . . All the other things will become negotiation."

The employer's statement was wrong as a matter of law — as discussed in Chapter 14, union security clauses are not imposed automatically when a union wins an election, and in any event, employees cannot be required to join the union that represents them. But was the statement also coercive? The Board majority concluded that the best way to read the statement was as a non-coercive prediction based on the employer's experience with the union at another location. The dissent disagreed and would have read the statement as a threat of job loss if the union was elected.

4. One part of the debate in *Midland National* and other aspects of labor law is the extent to which a union representation election is similar to a political election. Can you think of ways in which the two types of elections are different that arguably might call for different rules? Consider this also in the following section.

D. Inflammatory Appeals to Prejudice

The Board will also set aside elections where the parties make inflammatory remarks that appeal to certain prejudices. In *Sewell Mfg. Co.*, 138 N.L.R.B. 66 (1962), the Board took this action for an election in Georgia. In the months leading up to the election, the employer had regularly linked unions to racial integration. This included mailing pictures featuring an African American man and a white woman dancing, distributing materials linking unions to "race mixing," and citing contributions labor groups had made to the Congress of Racial Equality. The Board held that, unlike in a political election, in a union election, the Board must insure "that the voters have the opportunity of exercising a reasoned, untrammeled choice," and the election must be free from "elements which prevent or impede a reasoned choice." *Id.* at 69–70. The Board stressed that "prejudice based on color is a powerful emotional force" and "a deliberate appeal to such prejudice is not intended or calculated to encourage the reasoning faculty." *Id.* at 71.

Under *Sewell*, minor or isolated references to race may be tolerated, but only if truthful, relevant, and non-inflammatory (*e.g.*, discussions of the union's position on civil rights). *Id.* at 71–72. In the *Sewell* case itself, the employer's actions failed this test. Nonetheless, the Board observed that in some instances, employers would be permitted to inform employees of the union's position on integration, even if it did so to appeal to workers' prejudices:

> We would be less than realistic if we did not recognize that such statements, even when moderate and truthful, do in fact cater to racial prejudice. Yet we believe that they must be tolerated because they are true and because they pertain to a subject concerning which employees are entitled to have knowledge — the union's position on racial matters. . . . [N]o one would suggest that Negro employees were not entitled to know that the union which seeks to represent them practices racial discrimination. *Id.* at 71.

This rule has been enforced against unions as well as employers. *See, e.g., YKK (USA)*, 269 N.L.R.B. 82 (1984) (union election victory at a company with Japanese ownership and management set aside due to union references to "beating [the] 'Japs' at Pearl Harbor"). On the other hand, union appeals to racial pride are treated differently. *See, e.g., Archer Laundry Co.*, 150 N.L.R.B. 1427 (1965) (upholding an election when the union had urged employees to "[b]e a free person — not a 'Handkerchief-head Uncle Tom'"). Why is this distinguishable? What if the union predicts that if it loses an election, black employees will be disproportionately hurt by layoffs — and does it matter if the prediction is honest or accurate? *See NLRB v. Bancroft Mfg. Co.*, 516 F.2d 436 (5th Cir. 1975). What if union appeals to black employees as a group are antagonistic to white employees as a group? *See Carrington South Health Care Center v. NLRB*, 76 F.3d 802 (6th Cir. 1996).

This rule has also been applied to inflammatory appeals to prejudice against religion, but as with race, more than minor or isolated references are required. *See, e.g., Honeyville Grain v. NLRB*, 444 F.3d 1269 (10th Cir. 2006) (enforcing Board decision that comments at a union meeting that the employer was "run by Mormons" and was "giving its money to the Mormon church," among others, did not justify rerunning the election). What about prejudice against women or people who identify as LBGT? Should the presence of Title VII (which had not yet been passed when *Sewell* was decided) make a difference? If so, how and why? Title VII creates a cause of action against employers for, among other things, creating or permitting a hostile work environment based on race, sex, color, religion, or national origin. It covers unions, but only to the extent they act as employers. Do the remedies available under the different statutes matter?

Compare the restrictions in the inflammatory appeal cases to the speech that *Midland National* allows. Certainly, appeals to racial prejudice may be harmful and interfere with the reasoning facility. Still, is allowing the parties to promulgate intentionally deceptive materials about what the union or employer has done or is capable of doing, as was done in *Midland National*, arguably even more problematic in terms of employees exercising a reasoned choice in a union election?

E. "Captive Audience" Meetings

A "captive audience" meeting is a mandatory meeting that an employer calls during the work day, even during working time, in which the employer discusses its views on unionization. Could a union, facing a solicitation rule otherwise valid under *Republic Aviation*, argue that the employer is violating its own rule with such a meeting? Would the union therefore be entitled to "equal time"?

NLRB v. United Steelworkers of America (Nutone, Inc. and Avondale Mills)

Supreme Court of the United States
357 U.S. 357, 78 S. Ct. 1286, 2 L. Ed. 2d 1383 (1958)

FRANKFURTER, J.

These two cases . . . are controlled by the same considerations and will be disposed of in a single opinion. In one case the [NLRB] ruled that it was not an unfair labor practice for an employer to enforce against his employees a no-solicitation rule, in itself concededly valid, while the employer was himself engaged in anti-union solicitation in a context of separate unfair labor practices. This ruling was reversed by a Court of Appeals. In the second case the Board on the basis of similar facts, except that the employer's anti-union solicitation by itself constituted a separate unfair labor practice, found the enforcement of the rule to have been an unfair labor practice, but another Court of Appeals denied enforcement of the Board's order. . . .

Employer rules prohibiting organizational solicitation are not in and of themselves violative of the Act, for they may duly serve production, order and discipline. See *Republic Aviation Corp. v. NLRB*, 324 U.S. 793; *NLRB v. Babcock & Wilcox Co.*, 351 U.S. 105. In neither of the cases before us did the party attacking the enforcement of the no-solicitation rule contest its validity. Nor is the claim made that an employer may not, under proper circumstances, engage in non-coercive anti-union solicitation; indeed, his right to do so is protected by the so-called "employer free speech" provision of § 8(c) of the Act. . . . The very narrow and almost abstract question here derives from the claim that, when the employer himself engages in anti-union solicitation that if engaged in by employees would constitute a violation of the rule — particularly when his solicitation is coercive or accompanied by other unfair labor practices — his enforcement of an otherwise valid no-solicitation rule against the employees is itself an unfair labor practice. We are asked to rule that the coincidence of these circumstances necessarily violates the Act, regardless of the way in which the particular controversy arose or whether the employer's conduct to any considerable degree created an imbalance in the opportunities for organizational communication. For us to lay down such a rule of law would show indifference to the responsibilities imposed by the Act primarily on the Board to appraise carefully the interests of both sides of any labor-management controversy in the diverse circumstances of particular cases and in light of the Board's special understanding of these industrial situations.

. . . Certainly the employer is not obliged voluntarily and without any request to offer the use of his facilities and the time of his employees for pro-union solicitation. He may very well be wary of a charge that he is interfering with, or contributing support to, a labor organization in violation of § 8(a)(2) of the Act.

No attempt was made in either of these cases to make a showing that the no-solicitation rules truly diminished the ability of the labor organizations involved to carry their message to the employees. Just as that is a vital consideration in determining the validity of a no-solicitation rule, *see Republic Aviation Corp. v. NLRB*, 324 U.S. at 797–98; *NLRB v. Babcock & Wilcox Co.*, 351 U.S. at 112, it is highly relevant in determining whether a valid rule has been fairly applied. Of course the rules had the effect of closing off one channel of communication; but the Taft-Hartley Act does not command that labor organizations as a matter of abstract law, under all circumstances, be protected in the use of every possible means of reaching the minds of individual workers, nor that they are entitled to use a medium of communication simply because the employer is using it. *Cf. Bonwit Teller, Inc., v. NLRB*, 197 F.2d 640, 646 (2 Cir.); . . . If, by virtue of the location of the plant and of the facilities and resources available to the union, the opportunities for effectively reaching the employees with a pro-union message, in spite of a no-solicitation rule, are at least as great as the employer's ability to promote the legally authorized expression of his anti-union views, there is no basis for invalidating these "otherwise valid" rules. The Board, in determining whether or not the enforcement of such a rule in the circumstances of an individual case is an unfair labor practice, may find relevant alternative channels, available for communications on the right to organize. When this important issue is not even raised before the Board and no evidence bearing on it adduced, the concrete basis for appraising the significance of the employer's conduct is wanting.

We do not at all imply that the enforcement of a valid no-solicitation rule by an employer who is at the same time engaging in anti-union solicitation may not constitute an unfair labor practice. All we hold is that there must be some basis, in the actualities of industrial relations, for such a finding. The records in both cases—the issues raised in the proceedings—are barren of the ingredients for such a finding. . . .

Notes

1. This consolidated case is best known as *Nutone* and/or *Avondale*. In *Nutone*, the Court approved the Board's principle that captive audience meetings are not *per se* ULPs, and that employers can hold them without having to give unions an equal opportunity to present their views. The Board articulated this principle in *Livingston Shirt Corp.*, 107 N.L.R.B. 400, 409 (1953), where the Board reversed *Bonwit Teller, Inc.*, 96 N.L.R.B. 608 (1951) (which had held that an employer violates the

NLRA when it does not grant a union's request to respond to a captive-audience speech).

2. Employers can bar questions during captive audience speeches and exclude employees who are union supporters from the meetings. *F.W. Woolworth Co.*, 251 N.L.R.B. 1111 (1980); *Luxuray of New York*, 185 N.L.R.B. 100 (1970).

3. One special rule for captive audience meetings exists: an employer is not permitted to hold one within 24 hours of the vote in a union election. *Peerless Plywood*, 107 N.L.R.B. 427 (1953). Note that this rule does not apply to other non-coercive forms of communication. Speeches and other forms of propaganda (including misleading materials protected by *Midland National Life*) are permitted within the 24-hour period. *See AWB Metal, Inc.*, 306 N.L.R.B. 109 (1992), *enforced*, 4 F.3d 993 (6th Cir. 1993) (refusing to create a rule that would bar misleading materials in this period). Why only bar captive audience meetings?

F. Empirical Evidence Regarding Campaign Tactics and Worker Free Choice

Effective April 2015, the NLRB adopted a rule intended to streamline certain aspects of how union elections are conducted. 79 Fed. Reg. 74307 (2014). (This rule, along with a subsequent rule adopted by the Trump NLRB, is discussed in Chapter 7.)

On July 18 and 19, 2011, the NLRB conducted public hearings regarding the proposed rules. The affected parties—employers, unions, and employees—gave differing views. Employers expressed concerns about having sufficient time to give their views on union representation; unions voiced concerns about tactical delay used to engage in coercive misconduct sufficient to chip away at employee support for the union. Pro-union employees described harassment, whereas anti-union employees (and the National Right to Work Organization) stressed employees' right to hear both sides of the debate. Excerpts of the testimony of two academics on the effects of employer anti-union campaigns follow.

Testimony of Dr. Dorian Warren
Assistant Professor, Columbia University

. . . [S]everal weeks ago, Columbia University released the study I coauthored with Professor Kate Bronfenbrenner of Cornell University entitled, *The Empirical Case for Streamlining the NLRB Certification Process: The Role of Date of Unfair Labor Practice Occurrence*. Our research is directly relevant to the proposed rule changes to streamlining representation election procedures. Simply put, our findings, using a unique dataset of unfair labor practices and representation elections, indicate the need for streamlining and modernizing the NLRB certification process. Our data show[] that employer opposition or what's been called communication in these hearings begins much earlier than expected and continues every day all the way through to the election.

... [F]irst, on methodology, the data for analysis originate from a thorough review of primary NLRB documents, starting from a random sample of 1,000 NLRB elections that took place between 1999 and 2003. Using the Freedom of Information Act process, we requested all unfair labor practice documents for every case in our sample from the Board with a response rate of 99 percent. ... [T]he data I'm presenting today is only for the last year of our sample of 2003.

... [W]e have systematic and not anecdotal evidence about when the employer campaign begins, and from this evidence, we can make valid and generalizable claims about the NLRB election process ... [W]e have heard hyperbolic claims from those opposing the proposed rule changes that employers do not have the opportunity to express their views to workers. They're ambushed suddenly when workers file a petition for an election, and that the proposed rule changes would eviscerate workers' ability to make an informed choice. And, in fact, one witness even claimed yesterday that employers do not know about a union campaign until petitioners present their cards. All of these claims are empirically false. Our ULP documents show that some of the most egregious employer opposition starts long before employees have even filed a petition. Some numbers: 47 percent of serious allegations are filed before the petition, and 86 percent are filed before the election. Sixty-seven percent of all serious allegations are filed within two weeks after the petition is filed. Forty-seven percent of all serious allegations won by employees, through Board or court decisions or settlements, occurred before the petition was filed. And 89 percent are won before the election. Sixty percent of allegations of interrogation and harassment are filed before the petition. Fifty-four percent of allegations of coercive statements and threats are filed before the petition. And finally 39 percent of allegations for discharges for union activity are filed before the petition, while 76 percent of these are filed before the election. The punch line is this. Contrary to previous witnesses who claim that employers have little or no ability to communicate effectively with employees, the voicing of employer opposition to union representation begins from the moment employees begin talking about the union and continues day after day, week after week, leading up to the election. Our study reveals the pervasiveness, consistency, and intensity of employer opposition to workers' exercising their rights to union representation, and we'll submit the full study as part of our written testimony. ...

Testimony of Kate Bronfenbrenner

Director of Labor Education Research, Cornell University

... For the last ... two days, we've heard many voices, some coming from the employer's side who are outraged that you would tamper with a system that has served them so well for so many decades. Unions are winning, they say, in NLRB elections. But as the workers who testified here made clear, those numbers only include the fewer than 50,000 workers a year who manage to survive the gauntlets of threats, harassment, intimidation, coercion, retaliation they have to endure first to even get to a petition, much less get to an election or win. We have heard multiple employer representatives state that employers first learn of campaigns after the petition is filed, and if the campaign process were streamlined, they wouldn't have enough time to prepare for their campaign and communicate with their employees. And this lack of communication would have an impact on election turnout that would bias in favor of unions. Last, they repeatedly mentioned that the streamlining proposals, such as giving the union the e-mail addresses, are an unprecedented invasion of privacy.

But my past research along with the NLRB's own documents as summarized in the study I conducted with my co-author Dorian Warren say otherwise. As Professor Warren explained earlier, before our research, no one knew exactly when employer campaigns began because they were using the only variable at their disposal, the date unfair labor practices were filed. But by going through the painstaking process of searching through FOIA NLRB documents for each unfair labor practice allegation in our sample . . . we were able to develop and add a new variable to our already unique dataset of ULP allegations occurred. This allowed us to examine the relationship between petition date, election date, and when the most serious allegations of employer opposition actually occurred during the representation campaign. It also allowed me to . . . make sure that the allegations were indeed election-related allegations and were tied to the specific election that occurred. Our data not only show that nearly half of all serious allegations occur before the petition, but the percentage is the same for serious ULP allegations won. And that many occur many, many months before the petition and for most continue straight up through the elections and beyond. Thus, contrary to employer testimony, for a significant number of employers, opposition starts long before the filing of the petition and continues on after the petition, while workers wait for the election to be certified and persist still after that.

This mission is accomplished through multiple tactics at the employer's disposal. They're the building blocks of employer campaigns that I've seen in my research for the last 20 years. These include threats, interrogations, surveillance, fear, coercion, violence, retaliation, harassment for union activity, promises and bribes, and interference with the election process itself. It is notable that threats, interrogation, and surveillance are especially concentrated before the petition is filed. For example, with 72 percent of surveillance allegations occurring before the petition filed, it is difficult to take employer concerns about privacy seriously. As for their ability to communicate with employees, they have a host of legal means of communicating with employees, such as captive audience meeting, supervisor one-on-ones, letters, leaflets, videos, and e-mails that our data show they use early in campaigns. Ninety percent of campaigns that did weekly supervisor meetings, 67 percent that did 5 or more captive audience meetings, and 57 percent that did 5 or more letters had at least one serious allegation occur 150 days before the election took place.

If they can communicate that well before the petition, they should have no trouble communicating afterwards. Nor will lessening the delay impact turnout. Turnout is averaged above 85 percent in NLRB elections regardless of delay because both employers and unions know that every vote matters, and they work very hard to get their voters to turn out. But the finding that is most relevant to the issue of timing of elections is this. Employer opposition to unions is constant and cumulative. I stand here at the close of the hearing process to reassure you that the streamlining of the election process matters. Timing matters. . . . [T]he time between when the employer campaign starts, when the petition is filed, and when the election is held matters very much to whether workers are able to withstand the intense opposition that the majority of employers routinely engage in today, long enough to file a petition, stay through the election, through the challenges, and then certification. The proposed rule change will be a step closer in ending the process of having workers winnowed out at each stage for no other reason than delay and the employer opposition to continue one day longer than the workers could bear. . . .

V. Other Common Employer Unfair Labor Practices During Organizing: Interrogation, Polls, Surveillance, and Solicitating/Remedying Grievances

A. Overview

This section covers other employer ULPs during organizing campaigns that have not yet been discussed. The most common of these are interrogations, polls, surveillance, and solicitation and remedying of the grievances that brought the union on the scene.

B. Unlawful Interrogations, Polls, and Solicitations

Employers have both valid and invalid reasons to ask employees whether or not they support the union. The most obvious valid reason is to determine whether a request for voluntary recognition is in fact based on majority support of the union. The most obvious invalid reason is to attempt to intimidate employees. What legal rules should govern employer polling of employees in the organizing context?

In *Struksnes Constr. Co.*, 165 N.L.R.B. 1062, 1063 (1967), the Board set out the following rule for employer polling in this context, and the reasons for the rule.

> Absent unusual circumstances, the polling of employees by an employer will be violative of Section 8(a)(1) . . . unless the following safeguards are observed: (1) the purpose of the poll is to determine the truth of a union's claim of majority, (2) this purpose is communicated to the employees, (3) assurances against reprisal are given, (4) the employees are polled by secret ballot, and (5) the employer has not engaged in unfair labor practices or otherwise created a coercive atmosphere.

> The purpose of the polling in these circumstances is clearly relevant to an issue raised by a union's claim for recognition and is therefore lawful.

The requirement that the lawful purpose be communicated to the employees, along with assurances against reprisal, is designed to allay any fear of discrimination which might otherwise arise from the polling, and any tendency to interfere with employees' Section 7 rights. Secrecy of the ballot will give further assurance that reprisals cannot be taken against employees because the views of each individual will not be known. And the absence of employer unfair labor practices or other conduct creating a coercive atmosphere will serve as a further warranty to the employees that the poll does not have some unlawful object, contrary to the lawful purpose stated by the employer. In accord with presumptive rules applied by the Board with court approval in other situations, this rule is designed to effectuate the purposes of the Act by maintaining a reasonable balance between the protection of employee rights and legitimate interests of employers.

On the other hand, a poll taken while a petition for a Board election is pending does not, in our view, serve any legitimate interest of the employer that would not be better served by the forthcoming Board election. In accord with long-established Board policy, therefore, such polls will continue to be found violative of Section 8(a)(1) of the Act.

Be sure to distinguish this type of polling—during an organizing campaign—from polling the employer is sometimes, but not always, permitted to do when there is an incumbent union. See Chapter 15 for rules on polling in that context.

Employers may also engage in a more direct method of questioning their employees that is usually referred to as "interrogation." The following is a seminal interrogation case in which the Board set aside a tie-vote secret-ballot election on the basis of the employer's coercive interrogation of its employees. The case then reached the D.C. Circuit.

Timsco, Inc. v. NLRB

United States Court of Appeals for the D.C. Circuit
819 F.2d 1173 (1987)

Mikva, C.J.:

[The Board reviewed the following seven allegedly coercive interrogations during the election campaign, to which the union objected.]

1) On November 10, 1984, during the election campaign, Keith Pritchard, Timsco's general manager and the son of its president, approached John Marhefka, a maintenance employee, and asked, "What's going on?" Marhefka responded, "What?" K. Pritchard then said to him, "You know, who's ever behind this organizing is going to screw up a lot of jobs for a lot of people."

2) On November 20, 1984 Marhefka approached K. Pritchard outside of K. Pritchard's office to discuss an anticipated leave of absence. Marhefka followed K. Pritchard into his office, and following the discussion about the leave of absence,

K. Pritchard said, "Since you asked me a question, I would like to ask you a question. I know the Union is well organized and they have told you not to say anything. I would like to know why the people want to start a union. We pay them a good wage." Pritchard prefaced this portion of the conversation by asking Marhefka to keep it "in confidence"; Marhefka agreed.

3) During the week of November 23–30, K. Pritchard approached Marhefka at his work area and asked, "What do these people want? Is it money?" Marhefka responded, "What I would like to have is hospitalization." K. Pritchard replied, "If you wanted this, why didn't you come to me when you had your evaluation and ask for it? Like Vince, because Vince came to me and-during review time and wasn't satisfied, and he was given an increase."

4) During the week of December 3, 1984 K. Pritchard and Marhefka had an exchange about whether the Union would challenge the vote of maintenance employee David Ehrenfried at the scheduled election. K. Pritchard said, "I heard that they are going to challenge Dave's vote." Marhefka responded, "I don't know." K. Pritchard then asked, "You know, what grounds do they have to challenge Dave's vote?" Marhefka responded, "I think Dave can vote." K. Pritchard then asked, "Would you hate Dave if he voted no [against representation]?" Marhefka responded, "No. . . ."

5) On December 6, 1984 Walter Pritchard, Keith's father and president of Timsco, approached Marhefka and asked, "Weren't you a union member?" W. Pritchard also asked where Marhefka had been employed and what union he had belonged to. Marhefka responded that while employed at U.S. Steel's Clairton Works he had been a member of the United Steelworkers of America. W. Pritchard told Marhefka that he didn't think that the Union was good for the Company and that he would like Marhefka's support.

6) On December 6, 1984 W. Pritchard approached Dorothea Green, a graphic artist for the company, and said, "I understand that you are active in organizing getting the Union in." Green responded, "You mean, you're discounting my vote." W. Pritchard told her that he was disappointed that she felt she had to contact the Union and that he would much rather have her come in to see him, that his door was always open.

7) After lunch on the same day, December 6, 1984, W. Pritchard again approached Green and said to her, "I'm surprised at you Dorothea. How did you come about contacting the Union?" Green responded that she had telephoned the Union after finding it listed in the telephone directory. W. Pritchard told Green that he was surprised that Green had done this and that he didn't think she had it in her.

[The Board upheld the Hearing Officer's conclusion that each of these conversations constituted unlawful interrogation. The Board added that "'because there were numerous occasions of coercive employee interrogations that occurred in a small unit of approximately 22 eligible voters, and because the election resulted in a tie-vote, the cumulative effect of the interrogations amount to sufficient objectionable conduct to interfere with the results of the election.'"]

All recent significant precedent on coercive questioning begins with a discussion of *Bourne v. NLRB*, 332 F.2d 47 (2d Cir.1964), which articulated criteria for assessing the legality of employer questioning under the [NLRA]. The "*Bourne* standards" require that we consider:

(1) The background, i.e. is there a history of employer hostility and discrimination?

(2) The nature of the information sought. . . .

(3) The identity of the questioner, i.e. how high was he in the company hierarchy?

(4) Place and method of interrogation. . . .

(5) Truthfulness of the reply.

. . . The Board clearly acted reasonably in deeming coercive the first conversation between K. Pritchard and Marhefka, in which K. Pritchard said that the union organizers were "going to screw up a lot of jobs for a lot of people." The Hearing Officer found this statement to be a threat, all the more effective because directed at an employee who was not an open and active union supporter. . . . More significantly, the line between prediction and threat is a thin one, and in the field of labor relations that line is to be determined by context and the expertise of the Board. Given the context here (small workplace, interrogator was general manager, employee was maintenance worker and not active union supporter), we accept the Board's conclusion that Marhefka was threatened in this first conversation.

This threat impacts the next three conversations between Marhefka and K. Pritchard. Repeated questioning about union sympathies in light of the early threat of jobs being "screwed up" can reasonably be deemed coercive even if any *single* exchange, taken out of context, could not itself support a finding of coercion. Moreover, the exchanges between Marhefka and K. Pritchard exhibited many of the characteristics earmarked as coercive by *Bourne*. For example, the November 20 conversation took place in K. Pritchard's office, where Pritchard extracted a promise of confidentiality from Marhefka. *Bourne* identified the importance of the place of interrogation, and clearly the employer's office is "the locus of authority." . . . The promise of confidentiality extracted by Pritchard, the Board could reasonably conclude, added to the coerciveness of the closed-door chat by increasing Marhefka's isolation in the face of managerial pressure. In addition, K. Pritchard sought information from Marhefka about the Union's plans to challenge another employee's vote. In light of the circumstances, the Board could reasonably conclude that the questions were motivated by the purpose-improper under *Bourne* -to elicit specific information concerning union strategy so that the Company could better plan its own antiunion strategy.

The last three incidents of questioning involved W. Pritchard, the president of Timsco, and his involvement by itself has a coercive air under the *Bourne* standards because he is the highest ranking officer in the Company hierarchy. Although the smallness of the unit in this case might suggest that a conversation with the president is not a particularly unusual or intimidating event, the record reveals that the president's previous contacts with employees were limited to conversations about the weather. . . . The impact of the president's involvement was heightened by the fact that he began his questioning on the day immediately preceding the election, approaching employees a total of three times that day. The president first questioned Marhefka about his past union membership . . . [I]n the instant case, the Board could reasonably conclude that a private interrogation by the president of the company of an employee who was not an open union supporter in the context of prior questionings and a threat from the general manager is another thing entirely.

Similarly, the exchanges between the president and Dorothea Green about her role in the union organizing campaign could reasonably be understood as coercive in light of the rank of the interrogator, the fact that Green's support of the Union was not openly acknowledged at the workplace, and the timing of the questioning (twice the same day on the day before the election). These particular factors distinguish these exchanges from those in other cases that the Company cites. *See J. J. Newberry, Inc. v. NLRB*, 442 F.2d 897 (2d Cir.1971) (single incident, not on eve of election); *NLRB v. Welsh Industries, Inc.*, 385 F.2d 538 (6th Cir.1967) (single incident, early in union campaign). In light of these factors, the Board's finding of coercion is reasonable.

We grant that with the exception of the first threatening conversation between Marhefka and K. Pritchard, none of the exchanges, taken individually and out of context, sounds especially coercive on its face. But it is the Board's job, not ours, to assess the cumulative effect of the seven exchanges—the "totality of the circumstances." Our task is not to reassess independently the coerciveness of the questions, but rather to assess the reasonableness of the Board's conclusion. . . . Given that the voting pool was so small (22 voters) and the vote so close (tied), *any* coercion resulting from the questioning would be strongly felt throughout the voting pool and easily could have affected the outcome of the first election. We find reasonable the Board's conclusion that the questioning was coercive enough to disrupt laboratory conditions so as to require a rerun election. . . .

Notes

1. Interrogation continues to be an issue. In *Newlonbro, LLC (Connecticut's Own) Milford*, 332 N.L.R.B. 1559 (2000), the union filed a complaint against a Mazda dealership following a failed election to unionize the dealership's sales force. The employer had fired two employees—the only ones who voted for the union in the election—shortly after the dealership was notified of the attempt to unionize. The Board held that the employer violated § 8(a)(1) for improper surveillance, unlawful interrogation, and threatening that working conditions would worsen. These violations stemmed from a conversation between one of the employees and a manager. In that conversation, the manager indicated that the employer knew that the terminated employees were the only two who attended meetings with union officials. The manager then interrogated the employee about the meetings, why the employee

supported unionization, and if he was the new employee union representative. This conversation took place after the other pro-union employee had already been fired. The manager then threatened that conditions at the dealership would worsen if the employees voted in a union.

The employer asserted a legitimate reason for the discharge, but the ALJ found it lacking.

> Finally, I note that the asserted reason for Sachs' termination does not withstand even minimal scrutiny. The Respondent claimed that Sachs was conducting personal business on "company time" even though the June 17 telephone call from his tenant, the 34 messages left for Sachs on the Respondent's voicemail overnight and the fax received at the dealership from his insurance agent on June 18 all occurred at times when Sachs was not even working! 332 N.L.R.B. 1559, 1568.

2. A recurring issue in this area is employers taking pictures or videotapes of employees engaged in protected activity. *See, e.g., F.W. Woolworth Co.*, 310 N.L.R.B. 1197, 1197 (1993): "[T]he Board has long held that absent proper justification, the photographing of employees engaged in protected concerted activities violates the Act because it has a tendency to intimidate." Suppose an employer makes a video designed to show how content employees are without a union. What, if anything, should the employer be required to ask or tell the employees it wants to be in the video? Is this analogous to polling? *See Allegheny Ludlum Corp. v. NLRB*, 301 F.3d 167 (3d Cir. 2002).

3. Should similar rules apply to unions? *Mike Yurosek & Son, Inc.*, 292 N.L.R.B. 1074 (1989) held that a union representative taking photos of anti-union employees constituted improper surveillance. In addition, the union representative told an anti-union employee, "[w]e've got it on film; we know who you guys are . . . after the Union wins the election some of you may not be here." 292 N.L.R.B. 1074, 1074. The Board found illegal intimidation and ordered a new election. What if the union wants to make a videotape of its supporters gathering signatures on a pro-union petition? *See Randell Warehouse of Arizona, Inc. v. NLRB*, 347 N.L.R.B. 591 (2006).

4. More generally, unions are allowed to do certain things in this context that employers are not. For example, union representatives can ask individual employees if they support the union. Indeed, the point of the *Excelsior* list is to allow union organizers to visit individual employees at their homes. Assuming this is done in a non-coercive manner, it is entirely legal. Unions are not bound by the *Struksnes* polling rules. Why should the rules be different for unions? *See Louis-Allis Co. v. NLRB*, 463 F.2d 512 (7th Cir. 1972); *Kusan Mfg. Co. v. District Lodge 155*, 267 N.L.R.B. 740 (1983).

5. It may also be improper for an employer, in reaction to a union organizing campaign, to suddenly express a desire to solicit and remedy employee grievances. For example, in *DTR Industries*, 311 N.L.R.B. 833 (1993), *enforced in rel. part*, 39 F.3d 106 (6th Cir. 1994), the employer created a free "employee hotline" and employee

"suggestion boxes" during the election period. The employer had not done anything similar previously. The Board held that these acts were an implied promise to remedy employee grievances, and thus they violated § 8(a)(1). Why? What doctrine in the cases above justifies this result? Should it matter if the employer solicits, but does not imply it will remedy employee grievances? *See Airport 2000 Concessions*, 346 N.L.R.B. 958 (2006).

6. Surveillance techniques that are available to employers are becoming much more sophisticated. Companies have long had the capacity to log employees' keystrokes, meaning employers can easily track which websites their employees are visiting from their work computers. But the rise of big data analysis means that companies can now use the information gleaned from keystroke loggers in a much more nuanced (and arguably intrusive) way. For example, one company offers to scan and analyze employees' email to develop a portrait of how employee "sentiment changes over time." Other companies promise similar analyses based on employees' movements throughout the day, or even their conversations, recorded via microphones that employees wear or that are placed throughout the workplace.

Routine employer surveillance typically does not violate the NLRA. Thus, the fact that an employer happens to monitor the workplace with closed-circuit cameras to deter theft does not give rise to a ULP charge, even if the presence of those cameras also deters union organizing. (In contrast, if a workplace is already unionized, the employer would be obligated to bargain over the installation of new surveillance technology.) Is this rule — which dates from the earliest days of the NLRA — adequate to the challenges of modern employer surveillance techniques? For an argument that it is not, see Charlotte Garden, *Labor Organizing in the Age of Surveillance*, 63 St. Louis U. L.J. 55 (2018).

VI. Organizing and Employee Speech in the Public Sector

A. Generally

Most of the rules discussed in this chapter have been adopted in the public sector. Public-sector labor statutes typically (although not always) have language identical or substantively quite similar to, NLRA §§ 7 and 8(a)(1), and under these rules, public-sector jurisdictions have generally adopted, for example, the rules from *Republic Aviation, Exchange Parts*, and *Excelsior Underwear*. *See, e.g., Temple Univ. Hospital Nurses Ass'n & Temple Univ. Hospital Allied Health Professionals v. Temple Univ. Health System & Temple Univ. Hospital*, 42 Pa. Pub. Emp. Rep. ¶ 55 (LRB Hearing Examiner 2011) (*Republic Aviation* and *Beth Israel* rules apply to employer ban on union buttons in a hospital); *SEIU Local 1021 v. Sonoma County Superior Court*, 32 Cal. Pub. Emp. Rep. for Cal. ¶ 155 (PERB ALJ 2008) (California public-sector rule is a "carbon copy" of *Republic Aviation*); *Canaveral Port Authority*, 24

Fla. Pub. Emp. Rep. ¶ 29083 (PERC 1998) (applying *Exchange Parts* and finding no violation); *Borough of Neptune City*, 22 N.J. Pub. Emp. Rep. ¶ 27179 (PERC 1996) (applying *Exchange Parts* and finding a violation); *Calhoun County Medical Care Facility and SEIU Health Care Michigan*, 25 Mich. Pub. Emp. Rep. ¶ 3 (MERC 2011) (Michigan Rule 147(2) modeled on *Excelsior Underwear*); *Township of North Bergen and Teamsters Local 701*, 36 N.J. Pub. Emp. Rep. ¶ 77 (PERC 2010) (New Jersey adopted *Excelsior Underwear* in 1982).

Of course, when using similar rules, similar issues arise. Consider *East Whittier Education Association v. East Whittier School District*, 29 P.E.R.C. ¶ 40 (Cal. PERB 2004). In this case, during contract negotiations, teachers wore buttons stating, "It's Double Digit Time," (referring to percentage of wage increase). The school board had a rule barring teachers from wearing any buttons or other objects referring to matters being negotiated when the teacher was in instructional areas in the presence of students. The California Board held that the employer's bar was a ULP. Could bars on wearing buttons that contained other sorts of messages (concerning union-related matters) in a classroom be treated differently?

Also, the email issue has also arisen in the public sector, with similar results. *City of Saginaw v. Police Officers Ass'n of Michigan*, 23 Mich. Pub. Emp. Rep. ¶ 106 (MERC 2010) found that an employee's use of his employer's e-mail system to send an e-mail complaining about the employer's conduct was protected activity. It explained:

> We recognize that an employee's right to use his employer's e-mail system for union or other protected communication under Section 9 of PERA is not unlimited. Instead, the Commission has adopted the NLRB's holding in *Lockheed Martin Skunk Works*, 331 N.L.R.B. 852 (2000) that an employer may restrict the use of its equipment to work-related purposes and prohibit any personal use of e-mail, telephones, copiers, and other office equipment. See, *Oakland Co.*, 2001 MERC Lab Op 385, 391, where we stated, however, that an employer may not exercise its discretion in a content-discriminatory fashion, such as by allowing non-work related e-mails as long as they do not contain union-related information. In the present case, it is clear from reading Respondent's policy that Respondent did not intend to prohibit all personal e-mail. The fact that Kuhn's e-mail was singled out because he complained that his employer was not bargaining in good faith makes this action discriminatory.

Accord City of Clearwater, 32 Fla. Pub. Emp. Rptr. ¶ 210 (PERC 2006). Compare the case cited by *City of Saginaw, Oakland County*, 15 Mich. Pub. Emp. Rptr. ¶ 33018 (MERC 2001) (following private-sector precedent and finding no violation where an employer enforced a policy barring all non-business-related emails in a non-discriminatory manner).

These cases were all decided before the NLRB set out a new approach for emails in *Purple Communications*, *supra*, but later reversed itself in *Caesars Entertainment*, *supra*. This raises a recurring question in public-sector labor law. When the relevant statutory language in a public-sector statute and the NLRA is the same, should public-sector labor boards follow NLRB interpretations of such language, even when the NLRB rule changes dramatically? Consider this further after reading *Broadlawns Medical Center, infra*.

A small handful of variations on the rules discussed in the private-sector portion of this chapter exist. Courts or legislators can decide that certain rules developed under broad statutory language in the private sector are not appropriate in the public sector. Also, as shown in the next section, public employment may implicate constitutional concerns.

In addition to legal rules, however, the practice of the parties is very significant. Public-sector employers are, generally, not nearly as willing as private-sector employers are, generally, to engage in border-line illegal to clearly illegal conduct in anti-union campaigns. One important reason for this is political constraints (at least in some times and places). Also, many public employers may not feel the pressures of economic competition the way private employers do—although in times of tax-cutting and budget difficulties, public-sector managers feel analogous pressures more often. Further, most public employees covered by labor statutes are also covered by civil service laws (or other laws, such as tenure laws) that provide "just cause" discipline and discharge protection. Thus, it is more difficult to fire or discipline public employees for trumped-up reasons, and therefore they are probably more difficult to intimidate than private-sector employees. Consider the practical impact of these factors as you read the following materials.

B. Access of Non-Employee Union Organizers

Does the fact that a government employer is on public, as opposed to private, property change anything about, or add anything to, the *Lechmere* calculus?

Service Employees International Union Local 73 and Palatine Community Consolidated School District No. 15

Illinois Educational Labor Relations Board
18 P.E.R.I. ¶ 1043 (2002)

... The ALJ concluded that the District violated Section 14(a)(1) of the Act by ... restricting non-employee union organizer access to public property during a union campaign. ...

In its exceptions, the District contends that the ALJ erred in finding that it could not bar non-employee union organizers from its property, unless doing so was necessary to prevent disruption of the educational process. ...

This case arises out of the Union's attempt to organize the District's bus drivers. The District's bus drivers begin work at approximately 5:30 a.m. when they conduct a safety inspection of the bus, make their first run and then return to the bus garage at approximately 9:30 a.m. Upon returning to the bus garage, the drivers punch out for their break and remain on break until their next run.

Drivers routinely discuss work and non-work related issues while both on and off the clock. The District has no written policy regarding what the drivers are allowed to discuss when they are either on or off the clock. However, bus drivers routinely engage in various types of solicitation while both on and off the clock, including Tupperware sales, craft item sales, wrapping paper and candy sales and other fund-raising sales.

In spring 1999, two bus drivers, Sue Hernandez and Marge Hunn, contacted the Union because they were dissatisfied with the District's treatment of the bus drivers. On October 31, 1999, the Union began organizing the bus drivers at the District's bus garage. Cathy Nicosia, union business representative, and Joseph Richert, a union representative, talked to bus drivers about the Union and handed out literature and doughnuts to the drivers as they came in to work. Later, in fall 1999, Nicosia, Richert and Bill Silver, a union representative, went to a District school to speak with bus drivers as they waited in their empty busses for children to be released from school. The bus drivers told the Union representatives that, when they stepped on District property, the drivers were instructed to call dispatch, and someone from the District would come and ask them to leave.

On December 7, 1999, Assistant Superintendent for Personnel and Human Services Linda Vass issued a memorandum to the bus drivers in response to complaints she received about the Union organizing campaign. The memorandum informed drivers that they did not have to talk to the Union representatives and that the Union had no right to interfere with the driver's work time. Vass also sent a copy of the memorandum to Nicosia with a letter stating that the Union was not to conduct business on school property during work time.

Nicosia responded in writing to Vass's memo stating that the Union was not interfering with the bus driver's work time and that the Union was willing to reach a compromise with the District regarding the organizing campaign. Subsequently, on January 5, 2000, Nicosia and Vass met informally and agreed that Union representatives would not enter school grounds to distribute leaflets, but would be allowed to distribute information and talk to the bus drivers at the bus garage during non-work periods. However, shortly thereafter, the District informed the Union representatives that they were only allowed to hand out leaflets on the public sidewalk across the street from the area where the drivers came in to work or while standing in the road. . . .

On March 9, 2000, Union organizer Joseph Richert stood on the sidewalk next to the driveway leading into the school grounds and talked to the drivers as they came down the driveway on the way to their cars. Vass told Richert that he must leave the sidewalk because he was intimidating drivers. Richert responded that he was standing on a public sidewalk and that he had a right to be there. Vass said that if Richert did not leave, she would call the police, and then left. Vass and Director of Transportation Bill Willetts then went to the parking lot behind the school and asked another union official, Bill Silver, to leave District property.

> In March, 2000, the District issued a memorandum to the bus drivers which stated that

> . . . An agreement has been reached with the union organizers that they will remain off school property to hand out information and talk to employees.

Under Section 14(a)(1) of the Act, an employer is prohibited from "interfering, restraining or coercing employees in the exercise of the rights guaranteed under this Act." 115 ILCS 5/14(a)(1). The right to organize and choose a collective bargaining representative is a fundamental right under the Act. . . .

In *Lechmere, Inc. v. NLRB*, 502 U.S. 527 (1992) the Supreme Court . . . held that Section 7 of the [NLRA] confers rights on employees, not unions or their non-employee organizers. The Court reaffirmed the general rule of *NLRB v. Babcock & Wilcox Co.*, 351 U.S. 105 (1956) that an employer may validly prohibit non-employee distribution of union literature on its property. According to the Court, it is only where access to employees outside of the employer's property is not feasible that employers' private property rights are balanced against employees' rights under Section 7. . . . Thus, except under extremely limited circumstances, a private employer may prohibit non-employee access to its premises for the purposes of union organizing. . . .

Lechmere, however, only applies to private employers. In the case of a public employer, the public owns the property. Non-employee union organizers, like other individuals, are members of the public. The adverse private ownership interest that was present in *Lechmere* is absent. Thus, *Lechmere* does not apply to situations involving public property.

In *Perry Education Ass'n v. Perry Local Educators' Ass'n*, 460 U.S. 37 (1983), the Supreme Court held that public property can be identified as either a public forum or non-public forum. In a non-public forum, distinctions in access may be drawn if "they are reasonable in light of the purpose which the forum at issue serves," and are not an attempt to suppress expression merely because public officials disagree with it. In *Perry*, the Court determined that a school's internal mail system was not a public forum. Thus, school property that has not been opened to public communication is a non-public forum, as opposed to streets and parks, which are considered public forums. Because school property is generally a non-public forum, schools may reasonably regulate certain types of speech and restrict access to their premises. For example, a school may allow access to organizations "that engage in activities of interest and educational relevance to students," without being required to permit access to organizations concerned with terms and conditions of employment.

Here, the District banned all non-employee union organizers from access to school property. Under *Perry*, a school may restrict access to its premises because the school is a non-public forum. In this case, the District did not open its doors to the public, as it would have for a school play or basketball game. If the District had opened its doors to the public, then arguably it could be considered a public forum at those times. However, the District was conducting its normal operations and did not open its doors to the public. Thus, it was reasonable for the District to prohibit the expression of views which would interfere with the District's normal operations in a non-public forum.

Union representatives stood in the parking lot in front of the bus garage and on school grounds at busses waiting to pick up children. These locations were reserved for the District's transportation functions and were not devoted to the public expression of views. Similarly, although union organizer Richert was standing on a sidewalk, he was speaking to employees who were on a driveway devoted to the District's transportation functions.

Because the District's schools and the specific locations where non-employee organizing activity occurred were non-public forums, the District acted lawfully by restricting non-employee union access to its premises. Accordingly, based on the above analysis, the District did not violate Section 14(a)(1) of the Act by prohibiting all non-employee union organizer access to school property that was not a public forum. . . .

Notes

1. In contrast to this rejection of *Lechmere*, *Temple University*, 23 Penn. Pub. Emp. Rep. ¶ 23118 (Pa. LRB 1992), in upholding a ban on picketing by a faculty union on a college campus, cited *Lechmere* approvingly (in general and with regard to non-employees who wished to join the picketing).

2. As a practical matter, what is the difference between the rule in *Lechmere* and the constitutional test in *Palatine* as to where a non-employee union organizer has a right to go? Consider a parking lot owned by a public employer but open to the public under both approaches. What about a basketball game, open to the public, at a public high school?

3. As in the private sector, public-sector employer bars on access and solicitation that would otherwise be legal will be illegal if they are applied in a manner which discriminates against the union. *See, e.g., Staff Association of Waubonsee Community College and Waubonsee Community College*, 24 Pub. Emp. Rptr. Ill. 63 (Ill. Educ. LRB 2008) (discrimination where employer allows various school groups and outside organizations, but not a union organizing committee, to rent its rooms).

C. Misstatements of Material Fact

Most public-sector jurisdictions follow the private-sector rule from *Midland National Life* that significant misstatements of material facts are not ULPs or grounds to overturn an election. *See, e.g., Poway Unified Sch. Dist.*, 26 Pub. Emp. Rep. for Cal. ¶ 33003 (PERB 2001); *Saginaw County Mental Health*, 9 Mich. Pub.

Emp. Rep. ¶ 27103 (MERC 1996). However, some jurisdictions take a different approach.

Broadlawns Medical Center and AFSCME Iowa Council 61

Iowa Public Employment Relations Board
Case No. 5944 (Mar. 20, 2000)

. . . [T]he ALJ sustained an objection to a representation election filed by AFSCME Iowa Council 61 (AFSCME) pursuant to PERB subrule 621 IAC 5.4(2), and ordered that a new election be conducted. Broadlawns Medical Center (BMC) appealed the ALJ's decision to the full Board.

. . . The relevant facts are essentially uncontroverted.

On December 3, 1998, AFSCME filed a bargaining representative determination petition seeking certification as the exclusive collective bargaining representative of a previously determined bargaining unit of BMC employees. . . .

Two hundred twelve (212) ballots were cast for representation by AFSCME, 349 ballots were cast for "no representative," and there were 13 unresolved challenged ballots. . . .

During the period beginning with the filing of AFSCME's election petition with the Board and ending with the conclusion of the election (the February 17, 1999 ballot count), both AFSCME and BMC distributed a substantial amount of printed campaign material to employees. In some of those documents, both AFSCME and BMC accused each other of distorting facts, telling half-truths, stretching the truth, or lying to employees in various campaign materials.

On approximately February 1, 1999, BMC distributed a letter and flyer to employees which represented that PERB had decided to hold the election by mail ballot because the parties could not agree on a location for an on-site election. BMC claimed it had offered any conference room at its main premises other than the Ingersoll room, but that AFSCME had insisted on the Ingersoll room.

Part of AFSCME's campaign effort involved visiting the residences of eligible voters to provide them with information and encourage them to support AFSCME. AFSCME made such visits prior to February 1, 1999, and issued a flyer on February 1 in an attempt to recruit additional home visitors. The flyer provided:

AFSCME-Broadlawns Medical Center
Organizing Committee needs your
HELP!!!

What: Homevisits to BMC employees

When: Starting February 1, 1999

Monday-Friday: Noon to 8pm

Saturday: 10am to 8pm

Sunday: 11am to 8pm

Where: AFSCME Council 61 4320 NW 2nd Ave.

For those of you who have not done homevisits before there will be training beginning 1 hour prior to each shift.

If you have questions or special requests for training please contact R.A. Caraway at 246-0700.

Any time you can spare during these shifts will help Broadlawns' employees be successful in gaining Union representation.

Thank you in advance.

In Solidarity: AFSCME-BMC Organizing Committee

In accordance with the previously established schedule, PERB mailed ballots to all eligible voters' home addresses on Thursday, February 4, 1999.

On Friday, February 5, 1999, BMC posted and distributed the following one-page document to BMC employees:

FRAUD ALERT FRAUD ALERT FRAUD ALERT

Broadlawns has learned that the AFSCME organizers are now in the process of recruiting people to visit the homes of our employees over the weekend. It is obvious that the purpose of these home visits is to "assist" employees in filing out their secret ballots. This is yet another AFSCME desperation tactic which insults our intelligence and invades our privacy.

The election is supposed to be by secret ballot. Therefore, you have the absolute right to reject any attempts by the union organizers and operatives to influence your right to vote in secret. You have the absolute right to say NO! to them. You do not have to answer any of their questions, and you should not let them even touch your ballot. If they offer you any additional ballots or offer to fill out your ballot for you, refuse and write down their name and a summary of what they said. We will then report this conduct to PERB.

You have the right to demand that they leave your property. If they refuse, the police should be called.

We regret that Broadlawns employees continue to be subject to this deplorable harassment.

AFSCME representatives and organizers were upset about BMC's "Fraud Alert," and met over the weekend to compose another campaign flyer, which included the following paragraph:

Supervisors Try to Influence Votes

In fact, it was supervisors, not the union, who told employees they would help them "fill out" their secret ballot. We wanted a mail ballot so your vote would remain secret. Don't submit to this pressure.

This flyer was distributed on or about Monday, February 8.

AFSCME organizers who conducted home visits received a much colder reception from eligible voters during home visits after the "fraud alert" came out than they had before, with more voters reluctant or refusing to talk to them after the "fraud alert" was posted and distributed. . . .

AFSCME filed its objection to the election with PERB on February 26, 1999.

Conclusions of Law

Iowa Code section 20.15(4) provides, in relevant part:

[I]f the board finds that misconduct or other circumstances prevented the public employees eligible to vote from freely expressing their preferences, the board may invalidate the election and hold a second election for the public employees.

Consistent with section 20.15(4), the Board promulgated subrule 5.4(2), providing for the filing of objections to elections, and subrule 5.4(3), which provides:

5.4(3) *Objectionable conduct during election campaigns.* The following types of activity, if conducted during the period beginning with the filing of an election petition with the board and ending at the conclusion of the election, and if determined by the board that such activity could have affected the results of the election, shall be considered to be objectionable conduct sufficient to invalidate the results of the election: . . .

> *b.* Misstatements of material facts by any party to the election or its representative without sufficient time for the adversely affected party to adequately respond; . . .

> *g.* Any other misconduct or other circumstance which prevents employees from freely expressing their preferences in the election.

In its objection to the election, AFSCME alleges BMC engaged in objectionable conduct within the meaning of this rule as follows:

. . . a) On Feb. 5, 1999, after the mail election had commenced, informed BMC voters that AFSCME was committing the crime of voter fraud and violating the right of secret ballot by going to workers' homes with ballots. This conduct is libel per se and a reckless disregard for the truth. These false statements of material fact adversely affected the election and AFSCME did not have sufficient time to respond for the reason that over 300 ballots were mailed in during the weekend of Feb. 6, 7, and 8 and there was no adequate time to respond until Feb. 8, 1999.

b) The Employer misled the voters by informing them that the Employer had made all meeting rooms in the basement available for the on-site election on Feb. 17, 18, or 19, 1999, with the exception of the Ingersoll Room, when the fact is the employer refused to make any meeting rooms available in the basement for an on-site election on Feb. 17, 18 or 19, 1999, when AFSCME had requested all meeting rooms as well as the library, rec room or gym to be used as ballot rooms. These false statements of material facts by the Employer or its representative adversely affected the election and the union did not have adequate time to respond.

The leading Iowa public-sector case concerning allegations of objectionable conduct during a representation election campaign is *Mount Pleasant Community School District v. Public Employment Relations Board*, 343 N.W.2d 472 (Iowa 1984). In that case, the Iowa Supreme Court agreed with PERB that certain statements made by management in a notice to employees concerning such matters as the meaning of "good faith bargaining" and the effect of unionization on job security, salaries and benefits, were not misrepresentations but were instead substantially true statements and, thus, not objectionable under subrule 5.4(3)(b). The court also found, contrary to PERB's view, that the statements did not constitute "threats" which prevented employees from freely expressing their preferences in the election and, thus, that the employer did not violate subrule 5.4(3)(g).

In discussing the "misrepresentation" issue in *Mount Pleasant*, the court recognized that subrule 5.4(3)(b) is a restatement of the [NLRB]'s holding in *Hollywood Ceramics Co.*, 140 N.L.R.B. 221 (1962), in which the NLRB invalidated the result of an election because the union had made misrepresentations concerning comparative wage rates on the eve of the election. [The Iowa Board then recounted the NLRB's shifting positions on this issue].

... The *Shopping Kart/Midland National Life* approach is still followed by the NLRB, although not without controversy and criticism by some appellate courts.

In the present case, BMC argues that PERB, like the NLRB, should abandon the *Hollywood Ceramics* standard and utilize the *Shopping Kart/Midland National* approach of refusing to overturn elections in cases where misrepresentations have occurred. However, unlike the NLRB, which has vacillated over the years while dealing with the issue in the context of case law, PERB long ago embodied the *Hollywood Ceramics* standard in an administrative rule, formally adopted pursuant to the provisions of Iowa Code chapter 17A, which has not changed over the years. We are bound by our own valid administrative rule, and are not free to change it in the context of an individual case, even were we convinced that it would be wise to do so, which we are not. Any such change must be made, instead, pursuant to the rulemaking process specified in Iowa Code section 17A.4 (either by amending the rule, or by repealing it so as to allow for the making of such policy declarations in the context of case law, as does the NLRB).

Having concluded that the *Hollywood Ceramics* standard embodied in PERB subrule 5.4(3)(b) is applicable here, we further conclude that the distribution and posting of the "fraud alert" by BMC constituted objectionable conduct sufficient to invalidate the results of the election.

The "fraud alert" involved a substantial departure from the truth. Webster's New Collegiate Dictionary defines "fraud" as:

1 a : deceit, trickery; *specif*: intentional perversion of truth in order to induce another to part with something of value or to surrender a legal right b : an act of deceiving or misrepresenting: trick. G. & C. Merriam Co. (1975) p. 457.

Viewed objectively, the title "fraud alert," together with the language employed in the body of the document, conveyed the message that AFSCME was conducting home visits in order to engage in deceit or trickery concerning the employees' ballots, possibly by attempting to mark the voter's ballot or perhaps by replacing it with one of the "additional ballots" the "fraud alert" suggested AFSCME might have in its possession.

BMC argues that the document "merely expresses BMC's well-founded opinion as to its suspicions regarding the timing and purpose of the Union's last minute home visits, and an accurate statement of employees' rights in the event of any improper conduct." However, the document in fact flatly asserts, rather than merely opining, that "the purpose of these home visits is to 'assist' employees in filling out their secret ballots." The "fraud alert" goes on to suggest that AFSCME might attempt to touch or mark the voter's ballot, and that it might have additional (and thus counterfeit) ballots available for its or a voter's use.

There is simply no evidence to suggest that BMC's representations ascribing an improper purpose to AFSCME's visits were "well-founded" or based on any facts, or that AFSCME at any time had engaged, attempted to engage or intended to engage in any improper conduct during home visits. The "fraud alert" came from BMC, a supposedly authoritative source which employees would presume would be aware and knowledgeable about the campaign tactics being employed by AFSCME. The offending document was posted and distributed the day after ballots were mailed to employees' homes—a time when AFSCME had insufficient opportunity to adequately respond. (. . . many employees voted and returned their ballots very soon after receiving them). . . .

BMC argues that any misrepresentation involved here did not involve a material fact. Although *Mount Pleasant* and many of the cases decided by the NLRB under the *Hollywood Ceramics* standard deal with alleged misrepresentations concerning facts more directly related to actual bargaining issues, such as wage comparisons, job security matters and benefits, some involve broader misrepresentations similar in nature to those involved here.

In *Buddies Supermarkets, Inc.*, 192 N.L.R.B. 1004 (1971), the NLRB invalidated an election where the employer posted "Wanted" posters shortly before the election, displaying pictures of union organizers with inaccurate information about their criminal records. The NLRB determined that, although the exhibition of the posters did not amount to an unfair labor practice, the conduct nonetheless interfered with the laboratory conditions required for a free and untrammeled election and warranted vacating the election results. . . .

In *Tunica Manufacturing Company*, 182 N.L.R.B. 729 (1970), the NLRB overturned an election where the employer had given employees a letter approximately two weeks prior to the election misrepresenting the purpose of the so-called "Excelsior list" and frightening employees so as to cause them to refuse to receive union solicitors at their homes. . . .

In our view, BMC's "fraud alert," although more subtle, accomplished the purposes found objectionable by the NLRB in *Buddies Supermarkets* and *Tunica Manufacturing*. It depicted AFSCME organizers as unsavory characters engaged in "fraud" which, even if not criminal, is certainly reprehensible and seriously improper conduct. It created an unsubstantiated atmosphere of distrust and fear . . . of being victimized in their homes . . . by AFSCME's deceit and trickery. This atmosphere of suspicion, distrust and fear could reasonably be expected to impede communications between AFSCME and the employees. The "fraud alert" exceeded the limits of legitimate campaign rhetoric or propaganda and lowered the standards of campaigning to a level which impaired the free and untrammeled expression of choice by the employees. It could reasonably be expected to have impacted the election results. . . .

BMC also argues that the "fraud alert" is simply an exercise of its right of free speech, protected by Iowa Code section 20.10(4), which provides

> The expressing of any views, argument, or opinion, or the dissemination thereof, whether in written, printed, graphic, or visual form, shall not constitute or be evidence of any unfair labor practice under any of the provisions of this chapter, if such expression contains no threat of reprisal or force or promise of benefit.

Iowa Code section 20.10(4) is virtually identical to section 8(c) of the federal statute, 29 U.S.C. § 158(c). It is well settled that section 8(c) applies only to unfair labor practice determinations, and does not limit the discretion of the NLRB in determining whether an election was conducted under "laboratory conditions." *Bausch & Lomb, Inc. v. NLRB*, 451 F.2d 873, 877 (2d Cir. 1971). Likewise, Iowa Code section 20.10(4) is, by its express terms, limited in its application to unfair labor practice cases brought pursuant to the Iowa Act. This objection proceeding is not such a case.

Although the strictures of the first amendment must be considered in all cases, including representation cases, the first amendment is not violated by application of the *Hollywood Ceramics* standard. In *Bausch & Lomb* the second circuit determined that pre-election misrepresentations are not constitutionally protected. 451 F.2d at 878. The court stated:

> We recognize that the Board's laboratory standards may have a minimal chilling effect on both the speech of the employer and the union. The parties vying for the votes of the employees may be reluctant to express themselves fully, fearing that an unintentionally false statement will be seized upon later in overturning an election. But the incidental effects of regulation on the rights of employer and union must be weighed against the interest of employees and the public at large in free, fair and informed representation elections.

... In the highly charged atmosphere which surrounds representation elections, election-eve lies can have a devastating effect. It would be intolerable for this Court to condone misstatements by employer or union on the eve of an election. To do so would be to sanction free-for-all-anything-goes conduct. Such a sorry state of affairs would undermine the policies of the National [NLRA] and bring chaos, not peace to employer-employee relations. *Id.* at 879.

We conclude that the distribution of the "fraud alert" constituted objectionable conduct . . . which could have affected the results of the election. This objectionable conduct is sufficient to warrant invalidation of the election which concluded on February 17, 1999.

With regard to AFSCME's objection that BMC misrepresented what had occurred during the abortive attempt to arrange for an on-site election, we do not find merit in this objection. We need not decide whether BMC's statement constituted a misrepresentation since, even if a misrepresentation was made, we do not believe it concerned a matter of such significance as could reasonably be expected to have an impact on the outcome of the election. . . .

Notes

1. Is this a better rule than the rule in *Midland National Life*? Does the public-sector context make a difference in your answer?

2. This case again raises the issue of the extent to which public-sector labor boards should adopt private-sector interpretations of the same statutory language. Even today, it is not unusual in public-sector labor law to find that a particular state labor board has not yet addressed certain NLRB rules and doctrines. This is because individual state boards cover many fewer employers and employees than the NLRB does, and because the NLRB has been around significantly longer than state public-sector laws (the Ohio law was enacted in 1983, 46 years after the NLRA). In such situations, it would make some sense for state labor boards to use a default presumption that they will adopt private-sector rules where the relevant statutory language is the essentially the same and nothing about the public-sector context makes the rule inappropriate. This would make the law more predictable, and individual state boards would not have reinvent the wheel of decades of NLRA law.

But *Broadlawns Medical Center* raises a recurring issue with that approach. When the NLRB shifts positions—as it has on a number of issues, including but not limited to the rule in *Midland National Life*—should public-sector labor boards follow these shifts in NLRB doctrine automatically? If not, how should they decide what their rule should be (assuming different statutory language does not determine the result)?

Chapter 4

Protection of Workers' Protests and "Concerted Activities"

I. Introduction

Labor law is often misunderstood as relating exclusively to the protection of workers who are organizing for the purpose of bargaining collectively with their employers and the rules governing bargaining. While these may be principal functions of American labor law, they are not its exclusive functions. To the contrary, labor law can also operate as something more like a form of employment law regulating the relationship between an employer and an individual worker or a group of workers. In particular, workers may engage in protests and representative or organizing activities regardless of whether their ultimate goal is to form a union. If opposed by their employers, the workers may turn to the NLRA's §7 to secure protection from employer interference with some of these activities. In some cases, protection will be available. In others, it will not. This chapter examines the law governing these circumstances.

Many observers also associate the NLRA, as amended, with traditional majority unions—that is, unions that win an election among a group of employees, or voluntary recognition of their majority status from an employer, and bargain with those employees' bosses. Again, majority unions are a principal focus of the NLRA, but not its exclusive focus. Labor law can protect and regulate other forms of worker organizing and the organizations that have risen up to support them. These developments have proven to be especially important in recent years as private-sector union density has declined and workers and organizers sought new strategies that do not necessarily depend on traditional labor law mechanisms or union organizing.

This chapter begins by reviewing the expansion and retraction of constitutional protections for labor picketing. (Statutory rules for picketing and other forms of collective economic weapons are examined in Chapter 12.) The chapter continues with materials addressing §7's protection of concerted activities in unionized workplaces that do not necessarily constitute traditional union organizing or collective bargaining. It then discusses the NLRA's protection of workers' right to engage in "concerted activities" outside the union context and invites a comparison of §7's protections in unionized and non-union environments. (Chapter 8 addresses the related issue of "members' only" or "minority" unions) Finally, this chapter examines the rise of non-traditional (*i.e.*, non-union) methods of worker organizing.

These models include immigrant worker centers, the Freelancers Union, the Industrial Areas Foundation, and the AFL-CIO's non-union affiliate Working America.

The chapter includes a short section on public-sector law governing worker protest and organizing that discusses similar, but not always identical, rules and fact patterns. It also covers union activity and organization in the public sector in jurisdictions where unions have no collective-bargaining rights.

II. The U.S. Constitution and Worker Protest

A. Government as Speech Regulator

In *Thornhill v. Alabama*, the Supreme Court examined the constitutionality of §3448 of the Alabama State Code, a statute designed to inhibit the speech of labor unions. The statute read as follows:

> Loitering or picketing forbidden. Any person or persons, who, without a just cause or legal excuse therefor[e], go near to or loiter about the premises or place of business of any other person, firm, corporation, or association of people, engaged in a lawful business, for the purpose, or with intent of influencing, or inducing other persons not to trade with, buy from, sell to, have business dealings with, or be employed by such persons, firm, corporation, or association, or who picket the works or place of business of such other persons, firms, corporations, or associations of persons, for the purpose of hindering, delaying, or interfering with or injuring any lawful business or enterprise of another, shall be guilty of a misdemeanor; but nothing herein shall prevent any person from soliciting trade or business for a competitive business.

If applied to a state prosecution of a labor organizer, does this statute pass constitutional muster? The Supreme Court addressed this issue in the following decision:

Thornhill v. Alabama

Supreme Court of the United States
310 U.S. 88, 60 S. Ct. 736, 84 L. Ed. 1093 (1940)

MURPHY, J.

The complaint against petitioner . . . is phrased substantially in the very words of the statute. . . . Petitioner demurred to the complaint on the grounds . . . that Section 3448 was [unconstitutional under the First Amendment] in that it deprived him of "the right of peaceful assemblage," "the right of freedom of speech," and "the right to petition for redress." The demurrer . . . was not ruled upon, and petitioner pleaded not guilty. The Circuit Court then proceeded to try the case without a jury. . . . At the close of the case for the State, petitioner moved to exclude all the testimony taken at the trial on the ground that Section 3448 was [unconstitutional].

The Circuit Court overruled the motion, found petitioner "guilty of Loitering and Picketing as charged in the complaint," and entered judgment accordingly. The judgment was affirmed by the Court of Appeals, which considered the constitutional question and sustained the section on the authority of two previous decisions in the Alabama courts. . . . A petition for certiorari was denied by the Supreme Court of the State. The case is here on certiorari granted because of the importance of the questions presented. . . .

The proofs consist of the testimony of two witnesses for the prosecution. It appears that petitioner on the morning of his arrest was seen "in company with six or eight other men" "on the picket line" at the plant of the Brown Wood Preserving Company. Some weeks previously a strike order had been issued by a Union, apparently affiliated with [the A.F.L.], which had as members all but four of the approximately one hundred employees of the plant. Since that time a picket line with two picket posts of six to eight men each had been maintained around the plant twenty-four hours a day. The picket posts appear to have been on Company property, "on a private entrance for employees, and not on any public road." One witness explained that practically all of the employees live on Company property and get their mail from a post office on Company property and that the Union holds its meetings on Company property. No demand was ever made upon the men not to come on the property. There is no testimony indicating the nature of the dispute between the Union and the Preserving Company, or the course of events which led to the issuance of the strike order, or the nature of the efforts for conciliation.

The Company scheduled a day for the plant to resume operations. One of the witnesses, Clarence Simpson, who was not a member of the Union, on reporting to the plant on the day indicated, was approached by petitioner who told him that "they were on strike and did not want anybody to go up there to work." None of the other employees said anything to Simpson, who testified: "Neither Mr. Thornhill nor any other employee threatened me on the occasion testified to. Mr. Thornhill approached me in a peaceful manner, and did not put me in fear; he did not appear to be mad." "I then turned and went back to the house, and did not go to work." The other witness, J. M. Walden, testified: "At the time Mr. Thornhill and Clarence Simpson were talking to each other, there was no one else present, and I heard no harsh words and saw nothing threatening in the manner of either man." For engaging in some or all of these activities, petitioner was arrested, charged, and convicted as described.

First. The freedom of speech and of the press, which are secured by the First Amendment against abridgment by the United States, are among the fundamental personal rights and liberties which are secured to all persons by the Fourteenth Amendment against abridgment by a state.

The safeguarding of these rights to the ends that men may speak as they think on matters vital to them and that falsehoods may be exposed through the processes of education and discussion is essential to free government. Those who won our independence had confidence in the power of free and fearless reasoning and communication of ideas to discover and spread political and economic truth. Noxious doctrines in those fields may be refuted and their evil averted by the courageous exercise of the right of free discussion. Abridgment of freedom of speech and of the press, however, impairs those opportunities for public education that are essential to effective exercise of the power of correcting error through the processes of popular government. . . . Mere legislative preference for one rather than another means for combatting substantive evils, therefore, may well prove an inadequate foundation on which to rest regulations which are aimed at or in their operation diminish the effective exercise of rights so necessary to the maintenance of democratic institutions. It is imperative that, when the effective exercise of these rights is claimed to be abridged, the courts should "weigh the circumstances" and "appraise the substantiality of the reasons advanced" in support of the challenged regulations. *Schneider v. State*, 308 U.S. 147, 161, 162 (1939).

Second. The section in question must be judged upon its face.

The finding against petitioner was a general one. It did not specify the testimony upon which it rested. The charges were framed in the words of the statute and so must be given a like construction. The courts below expressed no intention of narrowing the construction put upon the statute by prior State decisions. In these circumstances, there is no occasion to go behind the face of the statute or of the complaint for the purpose of determining whether the evidence, together with the permissible inferences to be drawn from it, could ever support a conviction founded upon different and more precise charges. . . .

There is a further reason for testing the section on its face. . . . The existence of such a statute [which does not aim specifically at evils within the allowable area of State control but . . . sweeps within its ambit other activities that in ordinary circumstances constitute an exercise of freedom of speech or of the press], readily lends itself to harsh and discriminatory enforcement by local prosecuting officials, against particular groups deemed to merit their displeasure, results in a continuous and pervasive restraint on all freedom of discussion that might reasonably be regarded as within its purview. It is not any less effective or, if the restraint is not permissible, less pernicious than the restraint on freedom of discussion imposed by the threat of censorship. An accused, after arrest and conviction under such a statute, does not have to sustain the burden of demonstrating that the State could not constitutionally have written a different and specific statute covering his activities as disclosed by the charge and the evidence introduced against him. . . . Where regulations of the liberty of free discussion are concerned, there are special reasons for observing the rule that it is the statute, and not the accusation or the evidence under it, which prescribes the limits of permissible conduct and warns against transgression. . . .

Third. Section 3448 has been applied by the State courts so as to prohibit a single individual from walking slowly and peacefully back and forth on the public sidewalk in front of the premises of an employer, without speaking to anyone, carrying a sign or placard on a staff above his head stating only the fact that the employer did not employ union men affiliated with the [A.F.L.]; the purpose of the described activity was concededly to advise customers and prospective customers of the relationship existing between the employer and its employees and thereby to induce such customers not to patronize the employer. The statute as thus authoritatively construed and applied leaves room for no exceptions based upon either the number of persons engaged in the proscribed activity, the peaceful character of their demeanor, the nature of their dispute with an employer, or the restrained character and the accurateness of the terminology used in notifying the public of the facts of the dispute. . . .

Fourth. We think that Section 3448 is invalid on its face.

The freedom of speech and of the press guaranteed by the Constitution embraces at the least the liberty to discuss publicly and truthfully all matters of public concern without previous restraint or fear of subsequent punishment. . . . The importance of this consists, besides the advancement of truth, science, morality, and arts in general, in its diffusion of liberal sentiments on the administration of Government, its ready communication of thoughts between subjects, and its consequential promotion of union among them, whereby oppressive officers are shamed or intimidated, into more honourable and just modes of conducting affairs.' . . . Freedom of discussion, if it would fulfill its historic function in this nation, must embrace all issues about which information is needed or appropriate to enable the members of society to cope with the exigencies of their period.

In the circumstances of our times the dissemination of information concerning the facts of a labor dispute must be regarded as within that area of free discussion that is guaranteed by the Constitution. . . . [S]atisfactory hours and wages and working conditions in industry and a bargaining position which makes these possible have an importance which is not less than the interests of those in the business or industry directly concerned. The health of the present generation and of those as yet unborn may depend on these matters, and the practices in a single factory may have economic repercussions upon a whole region and affect widespread systems of marketing. The merest glance at State and Federal legislation on the subject demonstrates the force of the argument that labor relations are not matters of mere local or private concern. Free discussion concerning the conditions in industry and the causes of labor disputes appears to us indispensable to the effective and intelligent use of the processes of popular government to shape the destiny of modern industrial society. The issues raised by regulations, such as are challenged here, infringing upon the right of employees effectively to inform the public of the facts of a labor dispute are part of this larger problem. We concur in the observation of Mr. Justice Brandeis [*Senn v. Tile Layers Protective Union, Local No. 5*, 301 U.S. 468 (1937)]: "Members of a union might, without special statutory authorization by a state, make known the facts of a labor dispute, for freedom of speech is guaranteed by the Federal Constitution."

It is true that the rights of employers and employees to conduct their economic affairs and to compete with others for a share in the products of industry are subject to modification or qualification in the interests of the society in which they exist.

This is but an instance of the power of the State to set the limits of permissible contest open to industrial combatants. . . . It does not follow that the State in dealing with the evils arising from industrial disputes may impair the effective exercise of the right to discuss freely industrial relations which are matters of public concern. A contrary conclusion could be used to support abridgment of freedom of speech and of the press concerning almost every matter of importance to society.

The range of activities proscribed by Section 3448, whether characterized as picketing or loitering or otherwise, embraces nearly every practicable, effective means whereby those interested—including the employees directly affected—may enlighten the public on the nature and causes of a labor dispute. The safeguarding of these means is essential to the securing of an informed and educated public opinion with respect to a matter which is of public concern. It may be that effective exercise of the means of advancing public knowledge may persuade some of those reached to refrain from entering into advantageous relations with the business establishment which is the scene of the dispute. Every expression of opinion on matters that are important has the potentiality of inducing action in the interests of one rather than another group in society. But the group in power at any moment may not impose penal sanctions on peaceful and truthful discussion of matters of public interest merely on a showing that others may thereby be persuaded to take action inconsistent with its interests. Abridgment of the liberty of such discussion can be justified only where the clear danger of substantive evils arises under circumstances affording no opportunity to test the merits of ideas by competition for acceptance in the market of public opinion. We hold that the danger of injury to an industrial concern is neither so serious nor so imminent as to justify the sweeping proscription of freedom of discussion embodied in Section 3448.

The State urges that the purpose of the challenged statute is the protection of the community from the violence and breaches of the peace, which, it asserts, are the concomitants of picketing. The power and the duty of the State to take adequate steps to preserve the peace and to protect the privacy, the lives, and the property of its residents cannot be doubted. But no clear and present danger of destruction of life or property, or invasion of the right of privacy, or breach of the peace can be thought to be inherent in the activities of every person who approaches the premises of an employer and publicizes the facts of a labor dispute involving the latter. We are not now concerned with picketing en masse or otherwise conducted which might occasion such imminent and aggravated danger to these interests as to justify a statute narrowly drawn to cover the precise situation giving rise to the danger. . . . Section 3448 . . . does not aim specifically at serious encroachments on these interests and does not evidence any such care in balancing these interests against the interest of the community and that of the individual in freedom of discussion on matters of public concern.

It is not enough to say that Section 3448 is limited or restricted in its application to such activity as takes place at the scene of the labor dispute. "[The] streets are natural and proper places for the dissemination of information and opinion;

and one is not to have the exercise of his liberty of expression in appropriate places abridged on the plea that it may be exercised in some other place." *Schneider v. State*, 308 U.S. 147, 161; *Hague v. C.I.O.*, 307 U.S. 496, 515, 516. The danger of breach of the peace or serious invasion of rights of property or privacy at the scene of a labor dispute is not sufficiently imminent in all cases to warrant the legislature in determining that such place is not appropriate for the range of activities outlawed by Section 3448. Reversed.

───────────

In the following case, the Court reviewed the path of its systematic retreat from the seemingly comprehensive protection of labor picketing defined in *Thornhill*.

Teamsters Local 695 v. Vogt, Inc.

Supreme Court of the United States
354 U.S. 284, 77 S. Ct. 1166, 1 L. Ed. 2d 1347 (1957)

Frankfurter, J.

This is one more in the long series of cases in which this Court has been required to consider the limits imposed by the Fourteenth Amendment on the power of a State to enjoin picketing. . . . Respondent owns and operates a gravel pit in Oconomowoc, Wisconsin, where it employs 15 to 20 men. Petitioner unions sought unsuccessfully to induce some of respondent's employees to join the unions and commenced to picket the entrance to respondent's place of business with signs reading, "The men on this job are not 100% affiliated with the A.F.L." "In consequence," drivers of several trucking companies refused to deliver and haul goods to and from respondent's plant, causing substantial damage to respondent. Respondent thereupon sought an injunction to restrain the picketing.

The trial court did not make the finding, requested by respondent, "That the picketing of plaintiff's premises has been engaged in for the purpose of coercing, intimidating and inducing the employer to force, compel, or induce its employees to become members of defendant labor organizations, and for the purpose of injuring the plaintiff in its business because of its refusal to in any way interfere with the rights of its employees to join or not to join a labor organization." It nevertheless held that by virtue of Wis.Stat. § 103.535, prohibiting picketing in the absence of a "labor dispute," the petitioners must be enjoined from maintaining any pickets near respondent's place of business, from displaying at any place near respondent's place of business signs indicating that there was a labor dispute between respondent and its employees or between respondent and any of the petitioners, and from inducing others to decline to transport goods to and from respondent's business establishment.

On appeal, the Wisconsin Supreme Court at first reversed, relying largely on *A.F.L. v. Swing*, 312 U.S. 321, to hold § 103.535 unconstitutional, on the ground that picketing could not constitutionally be enjoined merely because of the absence of a "labor dispute." . . .

Upon reargument . . . however, the court withdrew its original opinion. . . . [T]he Supreme Court . . . canvassed the whole circumstances surrounding the picketing and held that "One would be credulous, indeed, to believe under the circumstances that the union had no thought of coercing the employer to interfere with its employees in their right to join or refuse to join the defendant union." Such picketing, the court held, was for "an unlawful purpose," since Wis.Stat. § 111.06(2)(b) made it an unfair labor practice for an employee individually or in concert with others to "coerce, intimidate or induce any employer to interfere with any of his employees in the enjoyment of their legal rights . . . or to engage in any practice with regard to his employees which would constitute an unfair labor practice if undertaken by him on his own initiative." Relying on *Building Service Employees v. Gazzam*, 339 U.S. 532, and *Pappas v. Stacey*, 151 Me. 36, the Wisconsin Supreme Court therefore affirmed the granting of the injunction on this different ground. . . .

We are asked to reverse the judgment of the Wisconsin Supreme Court, which to a large extent rested its decision on that of the Supreme Judicial Court of Maine in *Pappas v. Stacey*. . . .

It is not too surprising that the response of States—legislative and judicial—to use of the injunction in labor controversies should have given rise to a series of adjudications in this Court relating to the limitations on state action contained in the provisions of the Due Process Clause of the Fourteenth Amendment. It is also not too surprising that examination of these adjudications should disclose an evolving, not a static, course of decision.

The series begins with *Truax v. Corrigan*, 257 U.S. 312, in which a closely divided Court found it to be violative of the Equal Protection Clause—not of the Due Process Clause—for a State to deny use of the injunction in the special class of cases arising out of labor conflicts. The considerations that underlay that case soon had to yield, through legislation and later through litigation, to the persuasiveness of undermining facts. Thus, to remedy the abusive use of the injunction in the federal courts . . . the Norris-LaGuardia Act . . . withdrew, subject to qualifications, jurisdiction from the federal courts to issue injunctions in labor disputes to prohibit certain acts. Its example was widely followed by state enactments.

Apart from remedying the abuses of the injunction in this general type of litigation, legislatures and courts began to find in one of the aims of picketing an aspect of communication. This view came to the fore in *Senn v. Tile Layers Union*, 301 U.S. 468 (1937), where the Court held that the Fourteenth Amendment did not prohibit Wisconsin from authorizing peaceful stranger picketing by a union that was attempting to unionize a shop and to induce an employer to refrain from working in his business as a laborer.

Although the Court had been closely divided in the *Senn* case, three years later, in passing on a restrictive instead of a permissive state statute, the Court made sweeping pronouncements about the right to picket in holding unconstitutional a statute that had been applied to ban all picketing, with "no exceptions based upon either the number of persons engaged in the proscribed activity, the peaceful character of their demeanor, the nature of their dispute with an employer, or the restrained character and the accurateness of the terminology used in notifying the public of the facts of the dispute." *Thornhill v. Alabama*, 310 U.S. 88, 99. As the statute dealt at large with all picketing, so the Court broadly assimilated peaceful picketing in general to freedom of speech, and as such protected against abridgment by the Fourteenth Amendment.

These principles were applied by the Court in *A.F.L. v. Swing*, 312 U.S. 321, to hold unconstitutional an injunction against peaceful picketing, based on a State's common-law policy against picketing when there was no immediate dispute between employer and employee. On the same day, however, the Court upheld a generalized injunction against picketing where there had been violence because "it could justifiably be concluded that the momentum of fear generated by past violence would survive even though future picketing might be wholly peaceful." *Milk Wagon Drivers U. v. Meadowmoor Dairies*, 312 U.S. 287, 294.

Soon, however, the Court came to realize that the broad pronouncements, but not the specific holding, of *Thornhill* had to yield "to the impact of facts unforeseen," or at least not sufficiently appreciated. . . . Cases reached the Court in which a State had designed a remedy to meet a specific situation or to accomplish a particular social policy. These cases made manifest that picketing, even though "peaceful," involved more than just communication of ideas and could not be immune from all state regulation. "Picketing by an organized group is more than free speech, since it involves patrol of a particular locality and since the very presence of a picket line may induce action of one kind or another, quite irrespective of the nature of the ideas which are being disseminated." *Bakery and Pastry Drivers Local v. Wohl*, 315 U.S. 769, 776 (concurring opinion); see *Carpenters and Joiners U. v. Ritter's Café*, 315 U.S. 722, 725–28.

These latter two cases required the Court to review a choice made by two States between the competing interests of unions, employers, their employees, and the public at large. In [*Ritter's Café*], Texas had enjoined as a violation of its antitrust law picketing of a restaurant by unions to bring pressure on its owner with respect to the use of nonunion labor by a contractor of the restaurant owner in the construction of a building having nothing to do with the restaurant. The Court held that Texas could, consistent with the Fourteenth Amendment, insulate from the dispute a neutral establishment that industrially had no connection with it. This type of picketing certainly involved little, if any, "communication."

In *Bakery and Pastry Drivers Local v. Wohl*, 315 U.S. 769, in a very narrowly restricted decision, the Court held that because of the impossibility of otherwise publicizing a legitimate grievance and because of the slight effect on "strangers" to the dispute, a State could not constitutionally prohibit a union from picketing bakeries in its efforts to have independent peddlers, buying from bakers and selling to small stores, conform to certain union requests. Although the Court in *Ritter's Cafe* and *Wohl* did not question the holding of *Thornhill*, the strong reliance on the particular facts in each case demonstrated a growing awareness that these cases involved not so much questions of free speech as review of the balance struck by a State between picketing that involved more than "publicity" and competing interests of state policy. . . .

The implied reassessments of the broad language of the *Thornhill* case were finally generalized in a series of cases sustaining injunctions against peaceful picketing, even when arising in the course of a labor controversy, when such picketing was counter to valid state policy in a domain open to state regulation. The decisive reconsideration came in *Giboney v. Empire Storage & Ice Co.*, 336 U.S. 490 (1949). A union, seeking to organize peddlers, picketed a wholesale dealer to induce it to refrain from selling to nonunion peddlers. The state courts, finding that such an agreement would constitute a conspiracy in restraint of trade in violation of the state antitrust laws, enjoined the picketing. This Court affirmed unanimously.

> It is contended that the injunction against picketing adjacent to Empire's place of business is an unconstitutional abridgment of free speech because the picketers were attempting peacefully to publicize truthful facts about a labor dispute. . . . But the record here does not permit this publicizing to be treated in isolation. For according to the pleadings, the evidence, the findings, and the argument of the appellants, the sole immediate object of the publicizing adjacent to the premises of Empire, as well as the other activities of the appellants and their allies, was to compel Empire to agree to stop selling ice to nonunion peddlers. Thus all of appellants' activities . . . constituted a single and integrated course of conduct, which was in violation of Missouri's valid law. In this situation, the injunction did no more than enjoin an offense against Missouri law, a felony. *Id.* at 497–498.

The Court therefore concluded that it was "clear that appellants were doing more than exercising a right of free speech or press. . . . They were exercising their economic power together with that of their allies to compel Empire to abide by union rather than by state regulation of trade." *Id.* at 503.

The following Term, the Court decided a group of cases applying and elaborating on the theory of *Giboney.* In *Hughes v. Superior Court*, 339 U.S. 460, the Court held that the Fourteenth Amendment did not bar use of the injunction to prohibit picketing of a place of business solely to secure compliance with a demand that its employees be hired in percentage to the racial origin of its customers. "We cannot construe the Due Process Clause as prohibiting California from securing respect for its policy against involuntary employment on racial lines by prohibiting systematic picketing that would subvert such policy." *Id.* at 466. The Court also found it immaterial that the state policy had been expressed by the judiciary rather than by the legislature.

On the same day, the Court decided *Teamsters v. Hanke*, 339 U.S. 470, holding that a State was not restrained by the Fourteenth Amendment from enjoining picketing of a business, conducted by the owner himself without employees, in order to secure compliance with a demand to become a union shop. Although there was no one opinion for the Court, its decision was another instance of the affirmance of an injunction against picketing because directed against a valid public policy of the State.

A third case, *Building Service Emp. Intern. Union v. Gazzam*, 339 U.S. 532, was decided the same day. Following an unsuccessful attempt at unionization of a small hotel and refusal by the owner to sign a contract with the union as bargaining agent, the union began to picket the hotel with signs stating that the owner was unfair to organized labor. The State, finding that the object of the picketing was in violation of its statutory policy against employer coercion of employees' choice of bargaining representative, enjoined picketing for such purpose. This Court affirmed, rejecting the argument that "the *Swing* case, *supra*, is controlling. . . . In that case this Court struck down the State's restraint of picketing based solely on the absence of an employer-employee relationship. An adequate basis for the instant decree is the unlawful objective of the picketing, namely, coercion by the employer of the employees' selection of a bargaining representative. Peaceful picketing for any lawful purpose is not prohibited by the decree under review." *Id.* at 539.

A similar problem was involved in *Local Union No. 10, United Ass'n of Journeymen, Plumbers and Steamfitters v. Graham*, 345 U.S. 192, where a state court had enjoined, as a violation of its "Right to Work" law, picketing that advertised that nonunion men were being employed on a building job. This Court found that there was evidence in the record supporting a conclusion that a substantial purpose of the picketing was to put pressure on the general contractor to eliminate nonunion men from the job and, on the reasoning of the cases that we have just discussed, held that the injunction was not in conflict with the Fourteenth Amendment.

This series of cases, then, established a broad field in which a State, in enforcing some public policy, whether of its criminal or its civil law, and whether announced by its legislature or its courts, could constitutionally enjoin peaceful picketing aimed at preventing effectuation of that policy.

In the light of this background, the Maine Supreme Judicial Court in 1955 decided, on an agreed statement of facts, the case of *Pappas v. Stacey*, 151 Me. 36, 42. From the statement, it appeared that three union employees went on strike and picketed a restaurant peacefully "for the sole purpose of seeking to organize other employees of the Plaintiff, ultimately to have the Plaintiff enter into collective bargaining and negotiations with the Union. . . ." Maine had a statute providing that workers should have full liberty of self-organization, free from restraint by employers or other persons. The Maine Supreme Judicial Court drew the inference from the agreed statement of facts that "there is a steady and exacting pressure upon the employer to interfere with the free choice of the employees in the matter of organization. To say that the picketing is not designed to bring about such action is to forget an obvious purpose of the picketing—to cause economic loss to the business during noncompliance by the employees with the request of the union." It therefore enjoined the picketing, and an appeal was taken to this Court.

The whole series of cases discussed above allowing, as they did, wide discretion to a State in the formulation of domestic policy, and not involving a curtailment of free speech in its obvious and accepted scope, led this Court . . . to grant appellee's motion to dismiss the appeal in that it no longer presented a substantial federal question. 350 U.S. 870.

The *Stacey* case is this case. As in *Stacey*, the present case was tried without oral testimony. As in Stacey, the highest state court drew the inference from the facts that the picketing was to coerce the employer to put pressure on his employers to join the union, in violation of the declared policy of the State. (For a declaration of similar congressional policy, see § 8 of the [NLRA].) The cases discussed above all hold that, consistent with the Fourteenth Amendment, a State may enjoin such conduct.

Of course, the mere fact that there is "picketing" does not automatically justify its restraint without an investigation into its conduct and purposes. State courts, no more than state legislatures, can enact blanket prohibitions against picketing. *Thornhill v. Alabama* and *A.F.L. v. Swing*. The series of cases following *Thornhill* and *Swing* demonstrate that the policy of Wisconsin enforced by the prohibition of this picketing is a valid one. In this case, the circumstances set forth in the opinion of the Wisconsin Supreme Court afford a rational basis for the inference it drew concerning the purpose of the picketing. No question was raised here concerning the breadth of the injunction, but of course its terms must be read in the light of the opinion of the Wisconsin Supreme Court, which justified it on the ground that the picketing was for the purpose of coercing the employer to coerce his employees. "If astuteness may discover argumentative excess in the scope of the (injunction) beyond what we constitutionally justify by this opinion, it will be open to petitioners to raise the matter, which they have not raised here, when the (case) on remand (reaches) the (Wisconsin) court." *Teamsters v. Hanke*, 339 U.S. at 480–81.

Therefore, having deemed it appropriate to elaborate on the issues in the case, we affirm.

DOUGLAS, J., THE CHIEF JUSTICE and BLACK, J. concurring, dissenting.

The Court has now come full circle. In [*Thornhill*], we struck down a state ban on picketing on the ground that "the dissemination of information concerning the facts of a labor dispute must be regarded as within that area of free discussion that is guaranteed by the Constitution." Less than one year later, we held that the First Amendment protected organizational picketing on a factual record which cannot be distinguished from the one now before us. *A.F.L. v. Swing*. Of course, we have always recognized that picketing has aspects which make it more than speech. *Bakery and Pastry Drivers Local v. Wohl*, 315 U.S. 769, 776–77 (concurring opinion). That difference underlines our decision in *Giboney v. Empire Storage & Ice Co.* There, picketing was an essential part of "a single and integrated course of conduct, which was in violation of Missouri's valid law." *Id.* at 498. *And see NLRB v. Virginia Elec. & Power Co.*, 314 U.S. 469, 477–78. We emphasized that "there was clear danger, imminent and immediate, that unless restrained, appellants would succeed in making [the state] policy a dead letter. . . ." 336 U.S. at 503. Speech there was enjoined because it was an inseparable part of conduct which the State constitutionally could and did regulate.

But where, as here, there is no rioting, no mass picketing, no violence, no disorder, no fisticuffs, no coercion—indeed nothing but speech—the principles announced in *Thornhill* and *Swing* should give the advocacy of one side of a dispute First Amendment protection.

The retreat began when, in *Teamsters v. Hanke*, 339 U.S. 470, four members of the Court announced that all picketing could be prohibited if a state court decided that that picketing violated the State's public policy. The retreat became a rout in *Local Union No. 10, United Ass'n of Journeymen, Plumbers and Steamfitters. v. Graham*, 345 U.S. 192. It was only the "purpose" of the picketing which was relevant. The state court's characterization of the picketers' "purpose" had been made well nigh conclusive. Considerations of the proximity of picketing to conduct which the State could control or prevent were abandoned, and no longer was it necessary for the state court's decree to be narrowly drawn to prescribe a specific evil. *Id.* at 201–05 (dissenting opinion).

Today, the Court signs the formal surrender. State courts and state legislatures cannot fashion blanket prohibitions on all picketing. But, for practical purposes, the situation now is as it was when *Senn v. Tile Layers Union*, 301 U.S. 468, was decided. State courts and state legislatures are free to decide whether to permit or suppress any particular picket line for any reason other than a blanket policy against all picketing. I would adhere to the principle announced in *Thornhill*. I would adhere to the result reached in *Swing*. I would return to the test enunciated in *Giboney*—that this form of expression can be regulated or prohibited only to the extent that it forms an essential part of a course of conduct which the State can regulate or prohibit. I would reverse the judgment below.

Notes

1. What is left of *Thornhill* and *A.F.L. v. Swing* after *Vogt*? Is *Vogt* simply a return to *Senn*, as the dissent suggests, or can they be distinguished in a manner that is more protective of labor picketing than *Senn* was? These issues are revisited in Chapter 12, *infra*.

2. Suppose that the dictatorial nation of Freedonia decides to invade a neighboring country and then puts that country's people to work at exceedingly low wages in factories designed to manufacture goods for export. The United States condemns the invasion as an act of war but continues to trade with Freedonia. The President of the longshoremen's union, in an act of patriotism, orders all union members to refuse to handle cargo arriving from or going to Freedonia. That order, which is accompanied by longshoremen picketing all along the Pacific coast, effectively stops all trade to and from Freedonia—a blockade that harms many American

companies that import cheap manufactured goods from Freedonia for resale in the United States. A federal district court, at the urging of some of those American companies, enjoins the longshoremen union's protests. On appeal, the longshoremen argue that the federal ban on its picketing violates the First Amendment. What result? *Cf. Int'l Longshoremen's Ass'n v. Allied Int'l, Inc.*, 456 U.S. 212 (1982) (NLRA § 8(b)(4)(b) prohibited union's refusal to load and unload cargo from the Soviet Union in protest of the Soviet Union's invasion of Afghanistan and such bans do not violate the First Amendment). The Court wrote:

> Application of § 8(b)(4) to the ILA's activity in this case will not infringe upon the First Amendment rights of the ILA and its members. We have consistently rejected the claim that secondary picketing by labor unions in violation of § 8(b)(4) is protected activity under the First Amendment. . . . It would seem even clearer that conduct designed not to communicate but to coerce merits still less consideration under the First Amendment. The labor laws reflect a careful balancing of interests. There are many ways in which a union and its individual members may express their opposition to Russian foreign policy without infringing upon the rights of others. 456 U.S. 212, 226–27.

In so holding, the Court relied (*id.* at 226 n.26) in part on *NLRB v. Retail Store Employees*, 447 U.S. 607, 619 (1980) ("The statutory ban in this case affects only that aspect of the union's efforts to communicate its views that calls for an automatic response to a signal, rather than a reasoned response to an idea.") (Stevens, J., concurring); and *United States v. O'Brien*, 391 U.S. 367, 376 (1968) ("This Court has held that when 'speech' and 'nonspeech' elements are combined in the same course of conduct, a sufficiently important governmental interest in regulating the nonspeech element can justify incidental limitations on First Amendment freedoms."). Do these distinctions between reaction and reason or nonspeech and speech make sense?

3. In *Madsen v. Women's Health Ctr., Inc.*, 512 U.S. 753 (1994), the Supreme Court evaluated a Florida state court injunction issued against antiabortion protesters, which established a 36-foot buffer zone around an abortion clinic, from which the abortion protesters were excluded, to ensure that those protesters were not impeding access to an abortion clinic. The Court rejected the argument that injunctions such as these are content-based because to accept that argument would be "to classify virtually every injunction as content or viewpoint based. An injunction, by its very nature, applies only to a particular group (or individuals) and regulates the activities, and perhaps the speech, of that group. It does so, however, because of the group's past actions in the context of a specific dispute between real parties." The Court held that "when evaluating a content-neutral injunction, standard time, place, and manner analysis is not sufficiently rigorous. We must ask instead whether the challenged provisions of the injunction burden no more speech than necessary to serve a significant government interest." Justice Scalia dissented, arguing that injunctions are content-based and therefore should be evaluated under the strict scrutiny test.

In *Hill v. Colorado*, 530 U.S. 703 (2000), the Court, applying *Madsen*, held that a criminal statute barring any person within 100 feet of a health care facility from "knowingly approach[ing]" within eight feet another person without that person's consent was a constitutionally permissible, narrowly tailored, content-neutral, time-place-and-manner regulation. The statute effectively limited sidewalk counselors from protesting, educating, or counseling women about having an abortion inside the clinic. The Court found the statute to be content neutral, stressing that the state legislature adopted the restriction based not on the message spoken by one person to another but rather on conduct that may result in physical or emotional harm to those seeking medical treatment at the health care facility. *Id.* at 718.

However, in *McCullen v. Coakley*, 573 U.S. 464 (2014), the Court struck down amendments to a Massachusetts law that made it a crime to knowingly stand on a "public way or sidewalk" within 35 feet of an entrance or driveway to any "reproductive health care facility." Reiterating the "special position in terms of First Amendment protection" of public ways and sidewalks, the Court found that the amendments unconstitutionally restricted access to these traditional public fora. *Id.* Even though content neutral, the restrictions were required to be narrowly tailored to serve a significant government interest. In this case, the Court found that a substantial portion of the burdens imposed by the amendments to Massachusetts' law did not advance the state's goals of patient and public safety and access to reproductive health care, but they did burden the efforts of anti-abortion "counselors" to communicate with women entering clinics for abortions or other health care services. Accordingly, the Court invalidated the 35-foot "buffer zone."

In another context, the Court held that picketers associated with the Westboro Baptist Church could not be held liable for intentional infliction of emotional distress resulting from their display of patently offensive messages near a military funeral. *Snyder v. Phelps*, 562 U.S. 443 (2011). The Court relied heavily on the fact that the picketing related to matters of public concern, defined as follows: "'Speech deals with matters of public concern when it can 'be fairly considered as relating to any matter of political, social, or other concern to the community,' or when it 'is a subject of legitimate news interest; that is, a subject of general interest and of value and concern to the public.'" *Id.* at 1216 (citation omitted). The Court did not suggest that the fact that Westboro chose to convey its message via picket signs decreased the level of First Amendment protection applicable to its speech; if anything, the Court implied that picketing is more likely to qualify as "public concern" speech than other forms of speech that reach only a more limited audience. *Id.* at 1217 (observing that "[t]he signs certainly convey Westboro's position on those issues, in a manner designed . . . to reach as broad a public audience as possible.").

How should these cases inform the jurisprudence of labor-picketing injunctions? Would the balancing of interests differ? If the state can constitutionally protect women seeking abortions by restricting protestors' access to them, in some circumstances, can it also protect consumers by restricting unwanted messages about labor unions?

B. Is There a Constitutional Right to Organize in the Private Sector?

The following article by Professor James Gray Pope accepts the challenge posed by the Supreme Court's First Amendment jurisprudence by arguing that the courts engage in unconstitutional content regulation to discriminate against worker organizing. For this reason, he argues for public and worker protest in support of a constitutional right to organize based on the Thirteenth Amendment's prohibition against involuntary servitude. While his approach does not express a majority view of the best path to labor law reform among labor law scholars, Professor Pope's scholarship on this topic, *see also* James Gray Pope, *The Thirteenth Amendment Versus the Commerce Clause: Labor and the Shaping of American Constitutional Law: 1921–1957*, 102 Colum. L. Rev. 1 (2002), has garnered support from other scholars also offering arguments relating to labor law that rely on the Thirteenth Amendment. *See, e.g.*, Rebecca E. Zietlow, *Free At Last! Anti-Subordination and the Thirteenth Amendment*, 90 B.U.L. Rev. 255 (2010).

James Gray Pope, *The First Amendment, the Thirteenth Amendment, and the Right to Organize in the Twenty-First Century*
51 Rutgers L. Rev. 941 (1999)[*]

II. The Neutrality Principle, or Insisting that Workers and Unions Be Accorded the Same First Amendment Rights Enjoyed by Other Groups

I want to consider two possible strategies of constitutional transformation. The first would apply the First Amendment principle of content-neutrality to protect workers and unions against content-based restrictions on organizing and protest. This approach easily passes the straight-faced test, and it could conceivably improve the law. The current state of the law is shameful—reflecting judicial prejudice against workers no less virulent than in the days of government by injunction—and should be vulnerable to a determined attack. However, the main point of this Part is not to ask whether asserting the neutrality principle is a good tactic, but whether the principle can serve as the centerpiece of a long-term strategy for establishing a meaningful right to organize.

A. The Labor Black Hole and the Strategy of Neutrality

Back in the 1980s, some of the most forward-looking labor strategists thought that the movement could make major gains by engaging in corporate campaigns and building labor-community alliances. It seemed to many people then that the traditional strike was a dying tactic, and that the labor movement needed to look outside the workplace for new allies and forms of pressure. The legal side of this strategy focused on the First Amendment principle of neutrality. If the same

---

protective doctrines that are applied to corporate speech, civil rights protest, and—more recently—hate speech were also applied to labor protest, some onerous restrictions on worker protest would be declared unconstitutional. This is because most restrictions on labor expression burden only speech that advocates a boycott or strike, while leaving opponents free to use precisely the same methods of communication to oppose the boycott or strike—viewpoint discrimination in its most basic form—and because those restrictions apply only to unions and workers, leaving others free to engage in the same activities.

Recall, for example, the Furby—a walking, talking, computerized toy that every American child just had to have last Christmas. The only problem was that the Furby was made in Asia, apparently under slave labor conditions. Now, imagine two people with signs standing in front of a store called Toy Town. A unionist holds the first sign, which asks consumers to boycott Toy Town because it sells Furbies, and Furbies are produced by non-union slave labor. A store employee holds the second sign, which invites consumers to shop at Toy Town, where Furbies sell for the low price of $35. Under section 8(b)(4)(ii) of the [NLRA], the unionist—but not the store—is engaging in illegal secondary boycott activity. This is a textbook example of viewpoint discrimination. The unionist's message is illegal because it criticizes the store's policy of selling Furbies and urges consumers to express their disapproval by taking their patronage elsewhere, while the store's message is legal because it approves the sale of Furbies and urges consumers to patronize the store and take advantage of the low price no doubt made possible by the use of slave labor. Outside the labor sphere, viewpoint discrimination calls for strict judicial scrutiny. [*See, e.g., Texas v. Johnson*, 491 U.S. 397, 410, 412 (1989) (holding that restrictions on flag burning are content-based).] But section 8(b)(4)(ii) has been upheld under minimum rationality review. [*NLRB v. Retail Store Employees U., Local 1001*, 447 U.S. 607, 614–15 (1980).]

Now suppose that there is a third person standing in front of the store, also carrying a sign. This person is an international human rights activist, and her sign urges customers to boycott Toy Town because it sells Furbies, and the Furby company exploits Asian workers. Like the unionist, the human rights activist is urging a secondary boycott of the store. However, her activity is not illegal under the Act because section 8(b)(4)(ii) applies only to unionists, leaving others free to engage in precisely the same activities. This violates the First Amendment principle of neutrality among speakers. [*See, e.g., First Nat'l Bank v. Bellotti*, 435 U.S. 765, 776–77 (1978).] . . .

In short, the First Amendment principle of neutrality does not apply in the labor sphere. . . . [T]he Supreme Court's [bizarre and indefensible] treatment of labor speech amount[s] to a black hole in the Constitution—a place where all the usual principles of First Amendment law were strangely reversed. With the exception of one decision [*Edward J. DeBartolo Corp. v. Florida Gulf Coast Bldg. & Constr. Trades Council*, 485 U.S. 568 (1988)], however, the Supreme Court has not disturbed this black hole. In fact, the hole is much deeper today than it was when the scholarly criticism was pouring forth. In *R.A.V. v. City of St. Paul*, the Court applied the principles of viewpoint and subject-matter neutrality to trigger strict scrutiny of a law that regulated fighting words—unprotected speech. After *R.A.V.*, labor speech bears the distinction of having somehow managed to find a place in First Amendment jurisprudence where it is worse off even than unprotected speech in terms of its vulnerability to government censorship. It would seem, then, that the obvious strategy for labor would be to use *R.A.V.* to challenge restrictions on labor protest. The black hole seems more vulnerable than ever. Statements in recent cases suggest that the Court would not defend it if forced to confront the issue. In [*DeBartolo*], for example, the Court opined that union leaflets urging a secondary boycott did not appear to be "typical commercial speech" because they "pressed the benefits of unionism to the community and the dangers of inadequate wages to the economy and the standard of living of the populace." But there are at least two reasons to question the sufficiency of the neutrality approach, the first of which is apparent in DeBartolo itself.

B. Lawmaking from Below and the Limits of Neutrality

The "victory" in *DeBartolo* was achieved by making a kind of argument that—in the long-term—is debilitating to the point of self-destruction. [T]he Court was convinced to protect consumer boycott leafleting by unions because it was "'much less effective than labor picketing.'" Obviously, First Amendment protection that hinges on the ineffectiveness of expression will not be of great use to the labor movement. If this were the extent of the Court's reasoning, the reference to ineffectiveness could be dismissed as itself a departure from the principle of neutrality; certainly, the expression of other groups does not lose protection merely because it is effective. [See *Bellotti*, 435 U.S. at 776–77 (rejecting argument that corporate speech may be restricted because corporations "are wealthy and powerful and their views may drown out other points of view").] But the Court went on to explain that picketing was more potent than leafleting because leaflets "'depend entirely on the persuasive force of the idea'" while picketing exerts "'influences, and it produces consequences, different from other modes of communication.'" The idea here is that labor speech is distinctive because—rather than persuading autonomous individuals to act on the merits of a particular issue—it "signals" adherence to pre-existing loyalties and principles. [See *NLRB v. Retail Store Employees*, 447 U.S. at 619 (Stevens, J., concurring) (picketing "calls for an automatic response to a signal, rather than a reasoned response to an idea").] In effect, much labor speech is—in the words of the Supreme Court—part and parcel of an effort "to compel [employers] to abide by union rather than by state regulation of trade." [*Giboney*, 336 U.S. at 503.]

Now, much of the neutrality-based scholarship . . . has been directed at demonstrating that no such signaling or unofficial regulating goes on in consumer boycott picketing by unions (or at least that whatever signaling or regulating that does go on is no worse when unions are involved than when they are not). But this is—from a long-term perspective — little different from conceding that labor speech should be protected only when it is ineffective. . . . Ultimately, the movement must be able to deploy its core source of power — the ability to withhold labor — if it is to overcome determined employer resistance. And that, in turn, depends on the vitality of the unofficial law of solidarity. Consider the much-touted defeat of employer resistance at the Frontier Hotel in Las Vegas. While the union's brilliant corporate campaign has received much attention, the ultimate success probably depended at least as much on the solidarity of the strikers. Over the course of the six-month strike, not a single one of the 550 striking workers crossed the picket line. One hundred percent solidarity like that achieved by the Frontier strikers does not come about through autonomous calculations of individual costs and benefits, but through the experience of collectively legislating and enforcing rules of solidarity.

In short, the labor movement does engage in lawmaking from below, and speech plays an essential role in that process. As John R. Commons observed nearly eight decades ago, the structure of industrial relations is shaped by conflicting normative orders. Workers construct their own "common law of labor" grounded in the principle of solidarity. Arrayed against the workers' law is the common law of business, grounded in the principle of individual competition. Since Commons' day, collective bargaining has restructured this process, but — especially at times of conflict — the basic clash of individualistic and solidaristic norms remains the same. A First Amendment doctrine that leaves speech unprotected merely because it is connected to unofficial lawmaking and enforcement will be of little use. . . .

III. A Constitutional Right to Organize In the 21st Century?

If the preceding analysis is correct, then any meaningful theory of constitutional labor liberty must include two ingredients. First, it must provide a legal justification for the labor movement's unofficial lawmaking from below. Second, it must find a constitutional source for labor liberty outside the First Amendment.

A. Constitutional Protection for Lawmaking from Below

The obvious source for a constitutional right to engage in lawmaking from below is the assembly clause of the First Amendment. The American colonists initially asserted the right of assembly in response to British efforts to suppress their unofficial lawmaking. During the resistance to the Stamp Act of 1765, numerous associations and congresses passed resolutions . . . directing Americans to boycott British goods[] and threatening to "Expose to shame and Contempt" all offenders. When the British attempted to suppress the movement, the Americans replied that they had the right to assemble peaceably. Nevertheless, Parliament enacted a law prohibiting Americans from calling meetings without permission from the governor, and chastised them for passing "many dangerous and unwarrantable resolves." The Continental Congress promptly responded by proclaiming that the people enjoyed the right "peaceably to assemble, consider of their grievances, and petition the King."

After the Declaration of Independence and the formation of revolutionary state governments, unofficial popular assemblies continued to convene and pass legislation, a practice justified by Samuel Adams as an exercise of the people's right "to assemble upon all occasions to consult measures for promoting liberty and happiness." The defeat of the British did not bring a halt to unofficial lawmaking. Americans continued to invoke the right of assembly to justify insurgent conventions and assemblies, the most famous of which culminated in Shays' Rebellion of 1786. Some Americans contended that the right of assembly was no longer necessary now that the country had "a constitution of our own chusing," but the "right of the people peaceably to assemble" was nevertheless included in the Bill of Rights. Consistently with the limiting term "peaceably," the available evidence indicates that assemblies crossed the line from legality to illegality in the eyes of most Americans not when they purported to pass binding legislation, or when they enforced their legislation through economic or social coercion, but when they engaged in physical violence. . . .

Reviewing the cases, it is immediately apparent that — notwithstanding original meaning — the courts have never recognized any general right to engage in lawmaking from below. . . .

It is equally clear, however, that at times courts have extended First Amendment protection to lawmaking from below. The boycott involved in *NAACP v. Claiborne Hardware*, for example, displayed all the elements of unofficial lawmaking and enforcement. Several hundred black citizens of Port Gibson, Mississippi met at a church and voted unanimously to boycott white businesses in protest of private and governmental race discrimination. They picketed white-owned stores and organized a group known as the "Deacons" or "Black Hats" to enforce the boycott. Violators were publicly exposed as "traitors" to the black community, socially ostracized, occasionally threatened with violence, and, on a few occasions, physically attacked. The target businesses suffered extensive financial losses. Nevertheless, the Supreme Court held that all but the physical attacks themselves were constitutionally protected.

A second example has special relevance for the labor movement. Taking their cue from the sit-down strikers of the 1930s, black and white civil rights activists launched a campaign of "sit-ins" at segregated establishments. Convicted of trespassing, the protesters maintained that they were exercising their rights under the First and Fourteenth Amendments. Although the Supreme Court managed to overturn the convictions without reaching the merits, some Justices went further. In a concurring opinion, Justice Harlan concluded that the sit-ins were "as much a part of the 'free trade in ideas' . . . as is verbal expression," and hence that they were protected under the First Amendment. . . .

The boycott and sit-in cases suggest that Judges are sometimes willing to protect unofficial lawmaking and enforcement under the First Amendment, at least where there is a convergence of First and Fourteenth Amendment values. This brings us to the second requirement for a meaningful constitutional right to organize: a constitutional source for labor liberty outside the First Amendment. . . .

B. The Thirteenth Amendment and the Right to Organize

. . . .

First, the legal case for a Thirteenth Amendment right to organize is simple, straightforward, and well within the range of argumentative strategies typically deployed to justify transformations in constitutional doctrine. Although the Thirteenth Amendment's immediate purpose was the abolition of African slavery, the use of the term "involuntary servitude" in addition to the more limited and historically fixed term "slavery" . . . suggests that the former should be considered among those "vague and elastic" concepts "purposely left to gather meaning from experience." [*National Mut. Ins. Co. v. Tidewater Transfer Co.*, 337 U.S. 582, 646 (1946) (Frankfurter, J., dissenting).] Accordingly, the Supreme Court has long held that the Amendment mandates a "basic system of free labor" [*Pollock v. Williams*, 322 U.S. 4, 17 (1944)] for "all persons, of whatever race, color or estate, under the flag." [*Bailey v. Alabama*, 219 U.S. 219, 241 (1911).] . . .

A majority of courts addressing the issue have held that the constitutionally mandated system of free labor amounts to nothing more than the individual right to quit. The Supreme Court has, however, stated that that right is not an end in itself, but a "defense against oppressive hours, pay, working conditions or treatment." [*Pollock v. Williams*, 322 U.S. at 17.] The Amendment had the broad purpose of making "labor free by prohibiting that control by which the personal service of one man is disposed of or coerced for another's benefit." [*Bailey*, 219 U.S. at 241.] From a labor viewpoint, it seems obvious that the freedom to organize is an essential means of accomplishing that purpose. On occasion, the Court has said as much, opining—for example—that collective action is the worker's "means of putting himself on an equality with his employer." [*Charles Wolff Packing Co. v. Court of Indus. Relations*, 262 U.S. 522, 540 (1923).] Never has the Court squarely rejected the proposition that the Amendment encompasses rights of self-organization and collective action. . . . Moreover—unlike many previous trips down the path (such as the invalidation of de jure segregation and the extension of heightened equal protection scrutiny to sex classifications)—there is no on-point legislative history or Supreme Court precedent standing in the way.

Second, the Thirteenth Amendment is the only rights-granting constitutional provision that has been judicially limited to individual—as opposed to collective—rights. Organized group property, in the form of the corporation, enjoys constitutional property rights. Individuals have gained the right to associate in the exercise of advocacy rights, and advocacy organizations enjoy the full protection of the First Amendment. Yet, the Thirteenth Amendment has yet to be extended beyond the individual right to quit. From this perspective, it is the judicial denial of a Thirteenth Amendment right to organize—not the proposal to recognize one—that is out of line with current doctrine. . . .

Finally, and most importantly, the Thirteenth Amendment theory of collective labor rights originated not in the heads of lawyers or legal scholars, but in the thought and action of workers. Through the 1940s, worker activists and union leaders held that the rights to organize and strike meant the difference between slavery and freedom. Not only did they declare labor injunctions and anti-strike laws to be unconstitutional under the First and Thirteenth Amendments, but they also endeavored to strike them down through non-compliance and direct action. The American Federation of Labor maintained that a worker confronted with an unconstitutional injunction had an imperative duty to "refuse obedience and take whatever consequences may ensue." During the 1930s, unionists upheld the constitutionality of federal statutes granting labor rights. They defended the Norris-LaGuardia Anti-Injunction Act as an exercise of Congress' power to enforce the Thirteenth Amendment. And, while the Supreme Court struck down the National Industrial Recovery Act on commerce clause grounds and lower courts invalidated the Wagner Act on the same grounds, worker activists and labor leaders defended those statutes not primarily as an exercise of the commerce power, but as legislation designed to enforce human rights. With government enforcement stymied by the courts, they proceeded to enforce first section 7(a) of the NIRA and then the Wagner Act themselves. Examples of this self-help enforcement include the general strikes of 1934–35 and the sit-down strikes of 1936–37.

Although a few judges endorsed the theory that the Thirteenth Amendment encompassed protection for the right to strike, the issue was not squarely presented to the Supreme Court during the time that the labor movement was committed to the theory. This was, however, the period during which worker activists played a role in expanding First Amendment rights similar to that played by the civil rights movement in the 1960s. Just as civil rights activists combined the constitutional values of racial equality and free speech, so did worker activists combine the constitutional values of labor liberty and free speech. Instead of appealing to abstract principles of First Amendment law, worker activists defended their protest activities as essential to the attainment of labor freedom. In the first draft of the Supreme Court's opinion in *Thornhill v. Alabama*, the decision that established constitutional protection for labor picketing, Justice Murphy suggested that labor protest had special constitutional value because "satisfactory hours and wages and working conditions in industry and a bargaining position which makes these possible have an importance which transcends the interests of those in the business or industry directly concerned." Although Murphy toned down this language in response to criticism from Justices Stone and Hughes, it hinted at the existence of a relationship between the constitutional value of labor liberty and the extent of free speech protection. In *AFL v. Swing*, the highwater mark of protection for labor picketing, the Court held that a state could not prohibit workers employed by one company in an industry from picketing at another company in the same industry. Instead of relying on abstract principles of First Amendment law, the Court reasoned that the "interdependence of economic interest of all engaged in the same industry has become a commonplace." Although such forthright assertions of the value of labor protest were rare in judicial opinions, the Court's practice suggests that it was pushing the boundaries of the First Amendment outward not solely because of general free speech concerns but because workers and unions were pursuing the objective of labor freedom. In addition to the labor picketing cases, the Supreme Court also broke new ground when it held — in cases brought by labor unions — that government could not censor speech in public spaces or impose onerous licensing requirements on organizers.

This history suggests that First Amendment rights tend to be expanded not on the basis of free speech values alone, but when there is a convergence of free speech values with other constitutional values. The two examples we have discussed — the labor cases of the 1930s and 1940s, and the civil rights cases of the 1960s — arguably stand as the two most dramatic expansions of free speech protection in the history of the United States. . . .

C. Government as Employer

As Chapter 1 explained, beginning in the 1960s, courts for the first time accepted the argument that government employment constituted state action sufficient to trigger constitutional protections: notably here, that the First Amendment protected the right of government employees to organize unions. Relevant to Professor Pope's thesis, public-sector unions had argued that interpretation of the First Amendment — and in many cases, acted in accordance with that interpretation — for over half a century before courts accepted it. *See* Joseph Slater, Public Workers, Chs. 1–3. Still, as Chapter 1 also noted, this First Amendment doctrine has not been extended beyond the right to organize. Courts have not found a (federal) constitutional right for public employees to strike or even bargain collectively. What does this history mean (if anything) for Professor Pope's arguments?

III. The NLRA And Concerted Activities in the Union Context

A. Protests in a Unionized Environment

This section addresses "concerted activities" outside the context of organizing and collective bargaining with a particular focus on protests and unions' representation activities on behalf of union members and others. Strikes and other "concerted activities" that are economic weapons used in the context of collective bargaining are addressed in Chapter 11.

NLRB v. City Disposal Systems, Inc.

Supreme Court of the United States
465 U.S. 822, 104 S. Ct. 1505, 79 L. Ed. 2d 839 (1984)

BRENNAN, J.

James Brown, a truck driver employed by respondent, was discharged when he refused to drive a truck that he honestly and reasonably believed to be unsafe because of faulty brakes. Article XXI of the collective-bargaining agreement between respondent and Local 247 of the International Brotherhood of Teamsters, Chauffeurs, Warehousemen and Helpers of America, which covered Brown, provides:

> "[t]he Employer shall not require employees to take out on the streets or highways any vehicle that is not in safe operating condition or equipped with safety appliances prescribed by law. It shall not be a violation of the Agreement where employees refuse to operate such equipment unless such refusal is unjustified."[1]

The question to be decided is whether Brown's honest and reasonable assertion of his right to be free of the obligation to drive unsafe trucks constituted "concerted activit[y]" within the meaning of § 7 of the [NLRA]. The [NLRB] held that Brown's refusal was concerted activity within § 7, and that his discharge was, therefore, an unfair labor practice under § 8(a)(1) of the Act. . . . The Court of Appeals disagreed and declined enforcement. At least three other Courts of Appeals, however, have accepted the Board's interpretation of "concerted activities" as including the assertion by an individual employee of a right grounded in a collective-bargaining agreement. We granted certiorari to resolve the conflict, and now reverse.

I

The facts are not in dispute. . . . Respondent, City Disposal System, Inc. (City Disposal), hauls garbage for the City of Detroit. Under the collective-bargaining agreement with Local Union No. 247, respondent's truck drivers haul garbage from Detroit to a land fill about 37 miles away. Each driver is assigned to operate a particular truck, which he or she operates each day of work, unless that truck is in disrepair.

James Brown was assigned to truck No. 245. On Saturday, May 12, 1979, Brown observed that a fellow driver had difficulty with the brakes of another truck, truck No. 244. As a result of the brake problem, truck No. 244 nearly collided with Brown's truck. After unloading their garbage at the land fill, Brown and the driver of truck No. 244 brought No. 244 to respondent's truck-repair facility, where they were told that the brakes would be repaired either over the weekend or in the morning of Monday, May 14.

---

1. Article XXI also provides that "[t]he Employer shall not ask or require any employee to take out equipment that has been reported by any other employee as being in an unsafe operating condition until same has been approved as being safe by the mechanical department."

Early in the morning of Monday, May 14, while transporting a load of garbage to the land fill, Brown experienced difficulty with one of the wheels of his own truck—No. 245—and brought that truck in for repair. At the repair facility, Brown was told that, because of a backlog at the facility, No. 245 could not be repaired that day. Brown reported the situation to his supervisor, Otto Jasmund, who ordered Brown to punch out and go home. Before Brown could leave, however, Jasmund changed his mind and asked Brown to drive truck No. 244 instead. Brown refused, explaining that "there's something wrong with that truck. . . . [S]omething was wrong with the brakes . . . there was a grease seal or something leaking causing it to be affecting the brakes." Brown did not, however, explicitly refer to Article XXI of the collective-bargaining agreement or to the agreement in general. In response to Brown's refusal to drive truck No. 244, Jasmund angrily told Brown to go home. At that point, an argument ensued and Robert Madary, another supervisor, intervened, repeating Jasmund's request that Brown drive truck No. 244. Again, Brown refused, explaining that No. 244 "has got problems and I don't want to drive it." Madary replied that half the trucks had problems and that if respondent tried to fix all of them it would be unable to do business. He went on to tell Brown that "[w]e've got all this garbage out here to haul and you tell me about you don't want to drive." Brown responded, "Bob, what you going to do, put the garbage ahead of the safety of the men?" Finally, Madary went to his office and Brown went home. Later that day, Brown received word that he had been discharged. He immediately returned to work in an attempt to gain reinstatement but was unsuccessful.

On May 15, the day after the discharge, Brown filed a written grievance, pursuant to the collective-bargaining agreement, asserting that truck No. 244 was defective, that it had been improper for him to have been ordered to drive the truck, and that his discharge was therefore also improper. The union . . . found no objective merit in the grievance and declined to process it.

On September 7, 1979, Brown filed an unfair labor practice charge with the NLRB, challenging his discharge. The Administrative Law Judge (ALJ) found that Brown had been discharged for refusing to operate truck No. 244, that Brown's refusal was covered by § 7 of the NLRA, and that respondent had therefore committed an unfair labor practice under § 8(a)(1) of the Act. The ALJ held that an employee who acts alone in asserting a contractual right can nevertheless be engaged in concerted activity within the meaning of § 7:

> "[W]hen an employee makes complaints concerning safety matters which are embodied in a contract, he is acting not only in his own interest, but is attempting to enforce such contract provisions in the interest of all the employees covered under the contract. Such activity we have found to be concerted and protected under the Act, and the discharge of an individual for engaging in such activity to be in violation of Section 8(a)(1) of the Act." . . .

The NLRB adopted the findings and conclusions of the ALJ and ordered that Brown be reinstated with backpay.

. . . [T]he Court of Appeals disagreed with the ALJ and the Board. Finding that Brown's refusal to drive truck No. 244 was an action taken solely on his own behalf, the Court of Appeals concluded that the refusal was not a concerted activity within the meaning of § 7. This holding followed the court's prior decision in *ARO, Inc. v. NLRB*, 596 F.2d 713 (6th Cir. 1979), in which the Court of Appeals had held:

> "For an individual claim or complaint to amount to concerted action under the Act it must not have been made solely on behalf of an individual employee, but it must be made on behalf of other employees or at least be made with the object of inducing or preparing for group action and have some arguable basis in the collective bargaining agreement." *Id.*, at 718.

II

. . . .

The NLRB's decision in this case applied the Board's longstanding "Interboro doctrine," under which an individual's assertion of a right grounded in a collective-bargaining agreement is recognized as "concerted activit[y]" and therefore accorded the protection of § 7. *See Interboro Contractors, Inc.*, 157 N.L.R.B. 1295, 1298 (1966), *enf'd*, 388 F.2d 495 (2d Cir. 1967). . . . The Board has relied on two justifications for the doctrine: First, the assertion of a right contained in a collective-bargaining agreement is an extension of the concerted action that produced the agreement . . . ; and second, the assertion of such a right affects the rights of all employees covered by the collective-bargaining agreement. . . .

We have often reaffirmed that the task of defining the scope of § 7 "is for the Board to perform in the first instance as it considers the wide variety of cases that come before it," *Eastex, Inc. v. NLRB*, 437 U.S. 556, 568 (1978), and, on an issue that implicates its expertise in labor relations, a reasonable construction by the Board is entitled to considerable deference. . . . The question for decision today is thus narrowed to whether the Board's application of § 7 to Brown's refusal to drive truck No. 244 is reasonable. Several reasons persuade us that it is.

A

Neither the Court of Appeals nor respondent appears to question that an employee's invocation of a right derived from a collective-bargaining agreement meets § 7's requirement that an employee's action be taken "for purposes of collective bargaining or other mutual aid or protection." As the Board first explained in the *Interboro* case, a single employee's invocation of such rights affects all the employees that are covered by the collective-bargaining agreement. *Interboro Contractors, Inc., supra*, at 1298. This type of generalized effect, as our cases have demonstrated, is sufficient to bring the actions of an individual employee within the "mutual aid or protection" standard, regardless of whether the employee has his own interests most immediately in mind. *See, e.g., Weingarten v. NLRB*, 420 U.S. 251, 260–61 (1975).

The term "concerted activit[y]" is not defined in the Act but it clearly enough embraces the activities of employees who have joined together in order to achieve common goals. See, *e.g., Meyers Industries*, 268 N.L.R.B. No. 73, at 3 (1984). What is not self-evident from the language of the Act, however, and what we must elucidate, is the precise manner in which particular actions of an individual employee must be linked to the actions of fellow employees in order to permit it to be said that the individual is engaged in concerted activity. We now turn to consider the Board's analysis of that question as expressed in the *Interboro* doctrine.

Although one could interpret the phrase, "to engage in concerted activities," to refer to a situation in which two or more employees are working together at the same time and the same place toward a common goal, the language of § 7 does not confine itself to such a narrow meaning. In fact, § 7 itself defines both joining and assisting labor organizations—activities in which a single employee can engage—as concerted activities. Indeed, even the courts that have rejected the *Interboro* doctrine recognize the possibility that an individual employee may be engaged in concerted activity when he acts alone. They have limited their recognition of this type of concerted activity, however, to two situations: (1) that in which the lone employee intends to induce group activity, and (2) that in which the employee acts as a representative of at least one other employee. See, *e.g., Aro, Inc. v. NLRB*, 596 F.2d, at 713, 717 (6th Cir. 1979); *NLRB v. Northern Metal Co.*, 440 F.2d 881, 884 (3rd Cir. 1971). The disagreement over the *Interboro* doctrine, therefore, merely reflects differing views regarding the nature of the relationship that must exist between the action of the individual employee and the actions of the group in order for § 7 to apply. We cannot say that the Board's view of that relationship, as applied in the *Interboro* doctrine, is unreasonable.

The invocation of a right rooted in a collective-bargaining agreement is unquestionably an integral part of the process that gave rise to the agreement. That process—beginning with the organization of a union, continuing into the negotiation of a collective-bargaining agreement, and extending through the enforcement of the agreement—is a single, collective activity. Obviously, an employee could not invoke a right grounded in a collective-bargaining agreement were it not for the prior negotiating activities of his fellow employees. Nor would it make sense for a union to negotiate a collective-bargaining agreement if individual employees could not invoke the rights thereby created against their employer. Moreover, when an employee invokes a right grounded in the collective-bargaining agreement, he does not stand alone. Instead, he brings to bear on his employer the power and resolve of all his fellow employees. When, for instance, James Brown refused to drive a truck he believed to be unsafe, he was in effect reminding his employer that he and his fellow employees, at the time their collective-bargaining agreement was signed, had extracted a promise from City Disposal that they would not be asked to drive unsafe trucks. He was also reminding his employer that if it persisted in ordering him to drive an unsafe truck, he could rehearness the power of that group to ensure the enforcement of that promise. It was just as though James Brown was reassembling his fellow union members to reenact their decision not to drive unsafe trucks. A lone employee's invocation of a right grounded in his collective-bargaining agreement is, therefore, a concerted activity in a very real sense.

Furthermore, the acts of joining and assisting a labor organization, which § 7 explicitly recognizes as concerted, are related to collective action in essentially the same way that the invocation of a collectively bargained right is related to collective action. When an employee joins or assists a labor organization, his actions may be divorced in time, and in location as well, from the actions of fellow employees. Because of the integral relationship among the employees' actions, however, Congress viewed each employee as engaged in concerted activity. The lone employee could not join or assist a labor organization were it not for the related organizing activities of his fellow employees. Conversely, there would be limited utility in forming a labor organization if other employees could not join or assist the organization once it is formed. Thus, the formation of a labor organization is integrally related to the activity of joining or assisting such an organization in the same sense that the negotiation of a collective-bargaining agreement is integrally related to the invocation of a right provided for in the agreement. In each case, neither the individual activity nor the group activity would be complete without the other.

The *Interboro* doctrine is also entirely consistent with the purposes of the Act, which explicitly include the encouragement of collective bargaining and other "practices fundamental to the friendly adjustment of industrial disputes arising out of differences as to wages, hours, or other working conditions." 29 U.S.C. § 151. Although, as we have said, there is nothing in the legislative history of § 7 that specifically expresses the understanding of Congress in enacting the "concerted activities" language, the general history of § 7 reveals no inconsistency between the *Interboro* doctrine and congressional intent. That history begins in the early days of the labor movement, when employers invoked the common law doctrines of criminal conspiracy and restraint of trade to thwart workers' attempts to unionize. . . . As this Court recognized in *NLRB v. Jones & Laughlin Steel Corp.*, 301 U.S. 1, 33 (1937), a single employee at that time "was helpless in dealing with an employer; . . . he was dependent ordinarily on his daily wage for the maintenance of himself and his family; . . . if the employer refused to pay him the wages that he thought fair, he was nevertheless unable to leave the employ and resist arbitrary and unfair treatment; . . . union was essential to give laborers opportunity to deal on an equality with their employer."

Congress's first attempt to equalize the bargaining power of management and labor, and its first use of the term "concert" in this context, came in 1914 with the enactment of §§ 6 and 20 of the Clayton Act, which exempted from the antitrust laws certain types of peaceful union activities. There followed, in 1932, the Norris-LaGuardia Act, which declared that "the individual . . . worker shall be free from the interference, restraint, or coercion, of employers . . . in self-organization or in *other concerted activities for the purpose of collective bargaining or other mutual aid or protection.*" (emphasis added). This was the source of the language enacted in § 7. It was adopted first in § 7(a) of the National Industrial Recovery Act and then, in 1935, in § 7 of the NLRA. . . .

Against this background, it is evident that, in enacting § 7 of the NLRA, Congress sought generally to equalize the bargaining power of the employee with that of his employer by allowing employees to band together in confronting an employer regarding the terms and conditions of their employment. There is no indication that Congress intended to limit this protection to situations in which an employee's activity and that of his fellow employees combine with one another in any particular way. Nor, more specifically, does it appear that Congress intended to have this general protection withdrawn in situations in which a single employee, acting alone, participates in an integral aspect of a collective process. Instead, what emerges from the general background of § 7—and what is consistent with the Act's statement of purpose—is a congressional intent to create an equality in bargaining power between the employee and the employer throughout the entire process of labor organizing, collective bargaining, and enforcement of collective-bargaining agreements.

The Board's *Interboro* doctrine, based on a recognition that the potential inequality in the relationship between the employee and the employer continues beyond the point at which a collective-bargaining agreement is signed, mitigates that inequality throughout the duration of the employment relationship, and is, therefore, fully consistent with congressional intent. Moreover, by applying § 7 to the actions of individual employees invoking their rights under a collective-bargaining agreement, the *Interboro* doctrine preserves the integrity of the entire collective-bargaining process; for by invoking a right grounded in a collective-bargaining agreement, the employee makes that right a reality, and breathes life, not only into the promises contained in the collective-bargaining agreement, but also into the entire process envisioned by Congress as the means by which to achieve industrial peace.

To be sure, the principal tool by which an employee invokes the rights granted him in a collective-bargaining agreement is the processing of a grievance according to whatever procedures his collective-bargaining agreement establishes. No one doubts that the processing of a grievance in such a manner is concerted activity within the meaning of § 7. . . . Indeed, it would make little sense for § 7 to cover an employee's conduct while negotiating a collective-bargaining agreement, including a grievance mechanism by which to protect the rights created by the agreement, but not to cover an employee's attempt to utilize that mechanism to enforce the agreement.

In practice, however, there is unlikely to be a bright-line distinction between an incipient grievance, a complaint to an employer, and perhaps even an employee's initial refusal to perform a certain job that he believes he has no duty to perform. It is reasonable to expect that an employee's first response to a situation that he believes violates his collective-bargaining agreement will be a protest to his employer. Whether he files a grievance will depend in part on his employer's reaction and in part upon the nature of the right at issue. In addition, certain rights might not be susceptible of enforcement by the filing of a grievance. In such a case, the collective-bargaining agreement might provide for an alternative method of enforcement, as did the agreement involved in this case . . . or the agreement might be silent on the matter. Thus, for a variety of reasons, an employee's initial statement to an employer to the effect that he believes a collectively bargained right is being violated, or the employee's initial refusal to do that which he believes he is not obligated to do, might serve as both a natural prelude to, and an efficient substitute for, the filing of a formal grievance. As long as the employee's statement or action is based on a reasonable and honest belief that he is being, or has been, asked to perform a task that he is not required to perform under his collective-bargaining agreement, and the statement or action is reasonably directed toward the enforcement of a collectively bargained right, there is no justification for overturning the Board's judgment that the employee is engaged in concerted activity, just as he would have been had he filed a formal grievance.

The fact that an activity is concerted, however, does not necessarily mean that an employee can engage in the activity with impunity. An employee may engage in concerted activity in such an abusive manner that he loses the protection of § 7. . . . Furthermore, if an employer does not wish to tolerate certain methods by which employees invoke their collectively bargained rights, he is free to negotiate a provision in his collective-bargaining agreement that limits the availability of such methods. No-strike provisions, for instance, are a common mechanism by which employers and employees agree that the latter will not invoke their rights by refusing to work. In general, if an employee violates such a provision, his activity is unprotected even though it may be concerted. *Mastro Plastics Corp. v. NLRB*, 350 U.S. 270 (1956). Whether Brown's action in this case was unprotected, however, is not before us.

B

Respondent argues that the *Interboro* doctrine undermines the arbitration process by providing employees with the possibility of provoking a discharge and then filing an unfair labor practice claim. . . . This argument, however, misses the mark for several reasons. First, an employee who purposefully follows this route would run the risk that the Board would find his actions concerted but nonetheless unprotected, as discussed above.

Second, the *Interboro* doctrine does not shift dispute resolution from the grievance and arbitration process to NLRB adjudication in any way that is different from the alternative position adopted by the Court of Appeals, and pressed upon us by respondent. . . . [T]he Court of Appeals would allow a finding of concerted activity if two employees together invoke a collectively bargained right, if a lone employee represents another employee in addition to himself when he invokes the right, or if the lone employee invokes the right in a manner that is intended to induce at least one other employee to join him. In each of these situations, however, the underlying substance of the dispute between the employees and the employer is the same as when a single employee invokes a collectively bargained right by himself. In each case the employees are claiming that their employer violated their collective-bargaining agreement, and if the complaining employee or employees in those situations are discharged, their unfair labor practice action would be identical to an action brought by an employee who has been discharged for invoking a collectively bargained right by himself. Because the employees in each of these situations are equally well positioned to go through the grievance and arbitration process, there is no basis for singling out the *Interboro* doctrine as undermining that process any more than would the approach of respondent and the Courts of Appeals that have rejected the doctrine.

Finally, and most importantly, to the extent that the factual issues raised in an unfair labor practice action have been, or can be, addressed through the grievance process, the Board may defer to that process. See *Collyer Insulated Wire*, 192 N.L.R.B. 837 (1971). . . . There is no reason, therefore, for the Board's interpretation of "concerted activit[y]" in § 7 to be constrained by a concern for maintaining the integrity of the grievance and arbitration process.

III

[T]he Board found that James Brown's refusal to drive truck No. 244 was based on an honest and reasonable belief that the brakes on the truck were faulty. Brown explained to each of his supervisors his reason for refusing to drive the truck. Although he did not refer to his collective-bargaining agreement in either of these confrontations, the agreement provided not only that "[t]he Employer shall not require employees to take out on the streets or highways any vehicle that is not in safe operating condition," but also that "[i]t shall not be a violation of the Agreement where employees refuse to operate such equipment, unless such refusal is unjustified." . . . There is no doubt . . . that by refusing to drive truck No. 244, Brown was invoking the right granted him in his collective-bargaining agreement to be free of the obligation to drive unsafe trucks. Moreover, there can be no question but that Brown's refusal to drive the truck was reasonably well directed toward the enforcement of that right. Indeed, it would appear that there were no other means available by which Brown could have enforced the right. If he had gone ahead and driven truck No. 244, the issue may have been moot.

Respondent argues that Brown's action was not concerted because he did not explicitly refer to the collective-bargaining agreement as a basis for his refusal to drive the truck. . . . The Board, however, has never held that an employee must make such an explicit reference for his actions to be covered by the *Interboro* doctrine, and we find that position reasonable. . . .

Respondent further argues that the Board erred in finding Brown's action concerted based only on Brown's reasonable and honest belief that truck No. 244 was unsafe. . . . Respondent bases its argument on the language of the collective-bargaining agreement, which provides that an employee may refuse to drive an unsafe truck "unless such refusal is unjustified." In the view of respondent, this language allows a driver to refuse to drive a truck only if the truck is objectively unsafe. Regardless of whether respondent's interpretation of the agreement is correct, a question as to which we express no view, this argument confuses the threshold question whether Brown's conduct was concerted with the ultimate question whether that conduct was protected. The rationale of the *Interboro* doctrine compels the conclusion that an honest and reasonable invocation of a collectively bargained right constitutes concerted activity, regardless of whether the employee turns out to have been correct in his belief that his right was violated. . . . No one would suggest, for instance, that the filing of a grievance is concerted only if the grievance turns out to be meritorious. As long as the grievance is based on an honest and reasonable belief that a right had been violated, its filing is a concerted activity because it is an integral part of the process by which the collective-bargaining agreement is enforced. The same is true of other methods by which an employee enforces the agreement. On the other hand, if the collective-bargaining agreement imposes a limitation on the means by which a right may be invoked, the concerted activity would be unprotected if it went beyond that limitation.

[B]ecause Brown reasonably and honestly invoked his right to avoid driving unsafe trucks, his action was concerted. It may be that the collective-bargaining agreement prohibits an employee from refusing to drive a truck that he reasonably believes to be unsafe, but that is, in fact, perfectly safe. If so, Brown's action was concerted but unprotected. As stated above, however, the only issue before this Court and the only issue passed upon by the Board or the Court of Appeals is whether Brown's action was concerted, not whether it was protected.

IV

The NLRB's *Interboro* doctrine recognizes as concerted activity an individual employee's reasonable and honest invocation of a right provided for in his collective-bargaining agreement. We conclude that the doctrine constitutes a reasonable interpretation of the Act. Accordingly, we accept the Board's conclusion that James Brown was engaged in concerted activity when he refused to drive truck No. 244. We therefore reverse the judgment of the Court of Appeals and remand the case for further proceedings consistent with this opinion, including an inquiry into whether respondent may continue to defend this action on the theory that Brown's refusal to drive truck No. 244 was unprotected, even if concerted.

[The dissenting opinion of O'CONNOR, J., joined by THE CHIEF JUSTICE, POWELL, J. AND REHNQUIST, J. is omitted.]

Notes

1. Justice Brennan, one of the Supreme Court's leading purposivist interpreters of statutes, engages in something like a textualist analysis of §7 to explain that the statutory phrase "to engage in concerted activities" does not refer only to situations in which two or more employees are working together at the same time and the same place toward a common goal. In *Mushroom Transportation Co. v. NLRB*, 330 F.2d 683 (3d Cir. 1964), regarding employee conversations, the Court observed that:

> It is not questioned that a conversation may constitute a concerted activity although it involves only a speaker and a listener, but to qualify as such, it

must appear at the very least that it was engaged in with the object of initiating or inducing or preparing for group action or that it had some relation to group action in the interest of the employees. . . . Activity which consists of mere talk must, in order to be protected, be talk looking toward group action. *Id.* at 685.

The Board thereafter reaffirmed, with court approval, that the "activity of a single employee in enlisting the support of his fellow employees for their mutual aid and protection is as much 'concerted activity' as is ordinary group activity." *Owens-Corning Fiberglas Corp. v. NLRB*, 407 F.2d 1357, 1365 (4th Cir. 1969).

2. Is water cooler griping concerted activity under § 7? Apparently not, noted the Court in *City Disposal*, 465 U.S. at 833 n.10 (citing *Capital Ornamental Concrete Specialties, Inc.*, 248 N.L.R.B. 851 (1980)):

> Of course, at some point an individual employee's actions may become so remotely related to the activities of fellow employees that it cannot reasonably be said that the employee is engaged in concerted activity. For instance, the Board has held that if an employer were to discharge an employee for purely personal "griping," the employee could not claim the protection of § 7.

In *Alstate Maintenance, LLC & Trevor Greenidge*, the Board considered the line between concerted activity and griping. 367 N.L.R.B. No. 68 (2019). Employee Trevor Greenidge was working as a skycap at JFK Airport when he was asked by Lufthansa Airlines to assist with a soccer team's equipment. Greenidge responded that "[w]e did a similar job a year prior and we didn't receive a tip for it." (The Board noted that "[t]he bulk of skycaps' compensation comes from passengers' tips.") When the van containing the team's equipment arrived, four skycaps walked away. Later, all four skycaps were fired, and Greenidge's letter stated that he was fired for his comments about the (lack of) tip the previous year.

The Board concluded that Greenidge's comment did not qualify as concerted activity. It found that Greenidge was neither "bringing a truly group complaint to the attention or management," nor did "the statement in and of itself . . . demonstrate that Greenidge was seeking to initiate or induce group action." (Unhelpfully to his cause, Greenidge "testified that his remark was 'just a comment' and was not aimed at changing the Respondent's policies or practices.")

In reaching this conclusion, the NLRB also overruled *WorldMark by Wyndham*, 356 N.L.R.B. 765 (2011), which held that "an employee who protests publicly in a group meeting is engaged in initiating group action." Instead, the *Alstate* Board emphasized that whether a complaint is voiced on behalf of multiple employees or aimed at initiating collective action is a fact-bound inquiry.

3. For a more recent example of the *Interboro* doctrine, see *S. Freedman & Sons, Inc. v. NLRB*, 713 F. App'x 152 (4th Cir. 2017) (employee's refusal to work overtime was protected when he "plainly referred to the CBA when refusing the additional driving assignment, and the record contains evidence that at least three junior

drivers were available to take the truck to the repair facility," and employee did not lose NLRA protection by using profanity during his exchange with his employer). *See also St. Paul Park Refining Co., LLC v. NLRB*, 929 F.3d 610 (8th Cir. 2019) (affirming Board's finding that employer committed ULP when it suspended an employee who invoked safety procedures described in CBA, which included stopping work to call for a safety review).

Problem 4.1

Suppose plant supervisor Andy incessantly asks one of the female factory workers, Mary, on dates. Mary always says no. One night, as Andy is walking past Mary and her friend Rose on their way to their cars in the company parking lot, Andy grabs Mary's buttocks as she walks by. A fearful Rose claims to have seen nothing. The following day, Mary files an EEOC complaint with the EEO office. Later that day, the employer fires Mary. Is Mary's activity protected under §7?

Now assume the same facts as above, but before filing the EEOC complaint, Mary talks about the incident during her lunch period in the break room with her co-workers. Her co-workers encourage her to file a complaint with the EEO. Mary does and is later fired. Is Mary's conduct protected under §7?

Now assume the same facts as in the first paragraph. But this time, when Mary enters the break room, she and her co-workers are reluctant to file the complaint. Becky stands up, slaps her hand on the break room table and exclaimed, "Come on, are we going to let that pervert Andy get away with this? We need to file that complaint." Unbeknownst to Becky, Andy overhears her plea and fires her later that afternoon. Is Becky's conduct protected under §7?

Eastex, Inc. v. NLRB

Supreme Court of the United States
437 U.S. 556, 98 S. Ct. 2505, 57 L. Ed. 2d 428 (1978)

POWELL, J.

Employees of petitioner sought to distribute a union newsletter in nonworking areas of petitioner's property during nonworking time urging employees to support the union and discussing a proposal to incorporate the state "right-to-work" statute into the state constitution and a Presidential veto of an increase in the federal minimum wage. The newsletter also called on employees to take action to protect their interests as employees with respect to these two issues. The question presented is whether petitioner's refusal to allow the distribution violated [§8(a)(1)], by interfering with, restraining, or coercing employees' exercise of their right under [§7], to engage in "concerted activities for the purpose of . . . mutual aid or protection."

I

Petitioner is a company that manufactures paper products in Silsbee, Tex. Since 1954, petitioner's production employees have been represented by Local 801 of the United Paperworkers International Union. It appears that many, although not all, of petitioner's approximately 800 production employees are members of Local 801. Since Texas is a "right-to-work" State by statute, Local 801 is barred from obtaining an agreement with petitioner requiring all production employees to become union members.

In March 1974, officers of Local 801, seeking to strengthen employee support for the union and perhaps recruit new members in anticipation of upcoming contract negotiations with petitioner, decided to distribute a union newsletter to petitioner's production employees. The newsletter was divided into four sections. The first and fourth sections urged employees to support and participate in the union and, more generally, extolled the benefits of union solidarity. The second section encouraged employees to write their legislators to oppose incorporation of the state "right-to-work" statute into a revised state constitution then under consideration, warning that incorporation would "weake[n] Unions and improv[e] the edge business has at the bargaining table." The third section noted that the President recently had vetoed a bill to increase the federal minimum wage from $1.60 to $2.00 per hour, compared this action to the increase of prices and profits in the oil industry under administration policies, and admonished: "As working men and women we must defeat our enemies and elect our friends. If you haven't registered to vote, please do so today."

On March 26, 1974, Hugh Terry, an employee of petitioner and vice president of Local 801, asked Herbert George, petitioner's assistant personnel director, for permission to distribute the newsletter to employees in the "clock alley" [a 6 or 7 foot-wide passageway, flanked by administrative offices, that contains an employee bulletin board, petitioner's time clocks, and benches and chairs for those waiting to transact business in the offices]. George doubted whether management would allow employees to "hand out propaganda like that," but agreed to check with his superiors. Leonard Menius, petitioner's personnel director, confirmed that petitioner would not allow employees to distribute the newsletter in clock alley. A few days later George communicated this decision to Terry, but gave no reasons for it.

On April 22, 1974, Boyd Young, president of Local 801, together with Terry and another employee, asked George whether employees could distribute the newsletter in any nonworking areas of petitioner's property other than clock alley. After conferring again with Menius, George reported that employees would not be allowed to do so and that petitioner thought the union had other ways to communicate with employees. Local 801 then filed an unfair practice charge with the [NLRB], alleging that petitioner's refusal to allow employees to distribute the newsletter in nonworking areas of petitioner's property during nonworking time interfered with, restrained, and coerced employees' exercise of their §7 rights in violation of §8(a)(1).

At a hearing on the charge, Menius testified that he had no objection to the first and fourth sections of the newsletter. He had denied permission to distribute the newsletter because he "didn't see any way in which [the second and third sections were] related to our association with the Union." . . . The Administrative Law Judge held that although not all of the newsletter had immediate bearing on the relationship between petitioner and Local 801, distribution of all its contents was protected under §7 as concerted activity for the "mutual aid or protection" of employees. Because petitioner had presented no evidence of "special circumstances" to justify a ban on the distribution of protected matter by employees in nonworking areas during nonworking time, the Administrative Law Judge held that petitioner had violated §8(a)(1) and ordered petitioner to cease and desist from the violation. The Board affirmed the Administrative Law Judge's rulings, findings, and conclusions, and adopted his recommended order. . . .

The [Fifth Circuit] enforced the order. . . . It rejected petitioner's argument that the "mutual aid or protection" clause of §7 protects only concerted activity by employees that is directed at conditions that their employer has the authority or power to change or control. Without expressing an opinion as to the full range of §7 rights "when exercised off the employer's property," . . . the court purported to balance those rights against the employer's property rights and concluded that "whatever is reasonably related to the employees' *jobs* or to their status or condition as employees in the plant may be the subject of such handouts as we treat of here, distributed on the plant premises in such a manner as not to interfere with the work. . . ." The court further held that all of the material in the newsletter here met this test. . . . We affirm.

II

Two distinct questions are presented. The first is whether, apart from the location of the activity, distribution of the newsletter is the kind of concerted activity that is protected from employer interference by §§7 and 8(a)(1) of the [NLRA]. If it is, then the second question is whether the fact that the activity takes place on petitioner's property gives rise to a countervailing interest that outweighs the exercise of §7 rights in that location. . . .

A

. . . .

Petitioner contends that the activity here is not within the "mutual aid or protection" language [of §7] because it does not relate to a "specific dispute" between employees and their own employer "over an issue which the employer has the right or power to affect." . . . In support of its position, petitioner asserts that the term "employees" in §7 refers only to employees of a particular employer, so that only activity by employees on behalf of themselves or other employees of the same employer is protected. . . . Petitioner also argues that the term "collective bargaining" in §7 "indicates a direct bargaining relationship whereas 'other mutual aid or protection' must refer to activities of a similar nature. . . ." Thus, in petitioner's view, under §7 "the employee is only protected for activity within the scope of the employment relationship." . . . Petitioner rejects the idea that §7 might protect any activity that could be characterized as "political," and suggests that the discharge of an employee who engages in any such activity would not violate the Act.

We believe that petitioner misconceives the reach of the "mutual aid or protection" clause. The "employees" who may engage in concerted activities for "mutual aid or protection" are defined by § 2(3) of the Act . . . to "include any employee, and shall not be limited to the employees of a particular employer. . . ." This definition was intended to protect employees when they engage in otherwise proper concerted activities in support of employees of employers other than their own. In recognition of this intent, the Board and the courts long have held that the "mutual aid or protection" clause encompasses such activity. Petitioner's argument on this point ignores the language of the Act and its settled construction.

We also find no warrant for petitioner's view that employees lose their protection under the "mutual aid or protection" clause when they seek to improve terms and conditions of employment or otherwise improve their lot as employees through channels outside the immediate employee-employer relationship. The 74th Congress knew well enough that labor's cause often is advanced on fronts other than collective bargaining and grievance settlement within the immediate employment context. It recognized this fact by choosing, as the language of § 7 makes clear, to protect concerted activities for the somewhat broader purpose of "mutual aid or protection" as well as for the narrower purposes of "self-organization" and "collective bargaining." Thus, it has been held that the "mutual aid or protection" clause protects employees from retaliation by their employers when they seek to improve working conditions through resort to administrative and judicial forums, and that employees' appeals to legislators to protect their interests as employees are within the scope of this clause. To hold that activity of this nature is entirely unprotected—irrespective of location or the means employed—would leave employees open to retaliation for much legitimate activity that could improve their lot as employees. As this could "frustrate the policy of the Act to protect the right of workers to act together to better their working conditions," *NLRB v. Washington Aluminum Co.*, 370 U.S. 9, 14 (1962), we do not think that Congress could have intended the protection of § 7 to be as narrow as petitioner insists.

It is true, of course, that some concerted activity bears a less immediate relationship to employees' interests as employees than other such activity. We may assume that at some point the relationship becomes so attenuated that an activity cannot fairly be deemed to come within the "mutual aid or protection" clause. It is neither necessary nor appropriate, however, for us to attempt to delineate precisely the boundaries of the "mutual aid or protection" clause. That task is for the Board to perform in the first instance as it considers the wide variety of cases that come before it. . . . To decide this case, it is enough to determine whether the Board erred in holding that distribution of the second and third sections of the newsletter is for the purpose of "mutual aid or protection."

The Board determined that distribution of the second section, urging employees to write their legislators to oppose incorporation of the state "right-to-work" statute into a revised state constitution, was protected because union security is "central to the union concept of strength through solidarity" and "a mandatory subject of bargaining in other than right-to-work states." ... The newsletter warned that incorporation could affect employees adversely "by weakening Unions and improving the edge business has at the bargaining table." The fact that Texas already has a "right-to-work" statute does not render employees' interest in this matter any less strong, for, as the Court of Appeals noted, it is "one thing to face a statutory scheme which is open to legislative modification or repeal" and "quite another thing to face the prospect that such a scheme will be frozen in a concrete constitutional mandate." ... We cannot say that the Board erred in holding that this section of the newsletter bears such a relation to employees' interests as to come within the guarantee of the "mutual aid or protection" clause. ...

The Board held that distribution of the third section, criticizing a Presidential veto of an increase in the federal minimum wage and urging employees to register to vote to "defeat our enemies and elect our friends," was protected despite the fact that petitioner's employees were paid more than the vetoed minimum wage. It reasoned that the "minimum wage inevitably influences wage levels derived from collective bargaining, even those far above the minimum," and that "concern by [petitioner's] employees for the plight of other employees might gain support for them at some future time when they might have a dispute with their employer." ... We think that the Board acted within the range of its discretion in so holding. Few topics are of such immediate concern to employees as the level of their wages. The Board was entitled to note the widely recognized impact that a rise in the minimum wage may have on the level of negotiated wages generally, a phenomenon that would not have been lost on petitioner's employees. The union's call, in the circumstances of this case, for these employees to back persons who support an increase in the minimum wage, and to oppose those who oppose it, fairly is characterized as concerted activity for the "mutual aid or protection" of petitioner's employees and of employees generally.

In sum, we hold that distribution of both the second and the third sections of the newsletter is protected under the "mutual aid or protection" clause of § 7.

B

The question that remains is whether the Board erred in holding that petitioner's employees may distribute the newsletter in nonworking areas of petitioner's property during nonworking time. Consideration of this issue must begin with the Court's decisions in [*Republic Aviation Corp. v. NLRB* and *NLRB v. Babcock & Wilcox Co.*]. In *Republic Aviation* the Court upheld the Board's ruling that an employer may not prohibit its employees from distributing union organizational literature in nonworking areas of its industrial property during nonworking time, absent a showing by the employer that a ban is necessary to maintain plant discipline or production. This ruling obtained even though the employees had not shown that distribution of the employer's property would be ineffective. 324 U.S. at 798–799, 801. In the Court's view, the Board had reached an acceptable "adjustment between the undisputed right of self-organization assured to employees under the Wagner

Act and the equally undisputed right of employers to maintain discipline in their establishments." *Id.* at 797–98.

In *Babcock & Wilcox*, on the other hand, nonemployees sought to enter an employer's property to distribute union organizational literature. The Board applied the rule of *Republic Aviation* in this situation, but the Court held that there is a distinction "of substance" between "rules of law applicable to employees and those applicable to nonemployees." 351 U.S. at 113. The difference was that the nonemployees in *Babcock & Wilcox* sought to trespass on the employer's property, whereas the employees in *Republic Aviation* did not. Striking a balance between § 7 organizational rights and an employer's right to keep strangers from entering on its property, the Court held that the employer in *Babcock & Wilcox* was entitled to prevent "nonemployee distribution of union literature [on its property] if reasonable efforts by the union through other available channels of communication will enable it to reach the employees with its message. . . ." *Id.* at 112. The Court recently has emphasized the distinction between the two cases: "A wholly different balance was struck when the organizational activity was carried on by employees already rightfully on the employer's property, since the employer's management interests rather than his property interests were there involved." *Hudgens v. NLRB*, 424 U.S. at 521–22, n.10; *see also Central Hardware Co. v. NLRB*, 407 U.S. at 543–45.

It is apparent that the instant case resembles *Republic Aviation* rather closely. . . . The only possible ground of distinction is that part of the newsletter in this case does not address purely organizational matters, but rather concerns other activity protected by § 7. The question, then, is whether this difference required the Board to apply a different rule here than it applied in *Republic Aviation*.

Petitioner contends that the Board must distinguish among distributions of protected matter by employees on an employer's property on the basis of the content of each distribution. Echoing its earlier argument, petitioner urges that the *Republic Aviation* rule should not be applied if a distribution "does not involve a request for any action on the part of the employer, or does not concern a matter over which the employer has any degree of control. . . ." In petitioner's view, distribution of any other matter protected by § 7 would be an "unnecessary intrusio[n] on the employer's property rights" . . . in the absence of a showing by employees that no alternative channels of communication with fellow employees are available.

We hold that the Board was not required to adopt this view in the case at hand. In the first place, petitioner's reliance on its property right is largely misplaced. Here, as in *Republic Aviation*, petitioner's employees are "already rightfully on the employer's property," so that in the context of this case it is the "employer's management interests rather than [its] property interests" that primarily are implicated. *Hudgens*, at 521–22, n.10. As already noted, petitioner made no attempt to show that its management interests would be prejudiced in any way by the exercise of § 7 rights proposed by its employees here. Even if the mere distribution by employees of material protected by § 7 can be said to intrude on petitioner's property rights in any meaningful sense, the degree of intrusion does not vary with the content of the material. Petitioner's only cognizable property right in this respect is in preventing employees from bringing literature onto its property and distributing it there — not in choosing which distributions protected by § 7 it wishes to suppress.

On the other side of the balance, it may be argued that the employees' interest in distributing literature that deals with matters affecting them as employees, but not with self-organization or collective bargaining, is so removed from the central concerns of the Act as to justify application of a different rule than in *Republic Aviation*. Although such an argument may have force in some circumstances, see *Hudgens*, at 522, the Board to date generally has chosen not to engage in such refinement of its rules regarding the distribution of literature by employees during nonworking time in nonworking areas of their employers' property. We are not prepared to say in this case that the Board erred in the view it took. . . .

Petitioner concedes that its employees were entitled to distribute a substantial portion of his newsletter on its property. In addition, as we have held above, the sections to which petitioner objected concern activity which petitioner, in the absence of a countervailing interest of its own, is not entitled to suppress. Yet petitioner made no attempt to show that its management interests would be prejudiced in any manner by distribution of these sections, and in our view any incremental intrusion on petitioner's property rights from their distribution together with the other sections would be minimal. Moreover, it is undisputed that the union undertook the distribution in order to boost its support and improve its bargaining position in upcoming contract negotiations with petitioner. Thus, viewed in context, the distribution was closely tied to vital concerns of the Act. In these circumstances, we hold that the Board did not err in applying the *Republic Aviation* rule to the facts of this case. The judgment of the Court of Appeals therefore is *affirmed*.

Rehnquist, J., with whom The Chief Justice joins, dissenting.

It is not necessary to determine the scope of the "mutual aid or protection" language of § 7 of the [NLRA] to conclude that Congress never intended to require the opening of private property to the sort of political advocacy involved in this case. Petitioner's right as a property owner to prescribe the conditions under which strangers may enter its property is fully recognized under Texas law. "'A licensee who goes beyond the rights and privileges granted by the license becomes a trespasser.'" . . . Thus, the employees' effort to distribute their leaflet in defiance of petitioner's wishes would clearly be a trespass infringing upon petitioner's property right. . . . So far as appears, a Texas property owner may admit certain leaflets onto his property and exclude others, as it pleases him. The Court can only mean that the Board need not take cognizance of any greater property right because the Congress has clearly and constitutionally said so.

From its earliest cases construing the [NLRA] the Court has recognized the weight of an employer's property rights, rights which are explicitly protected from federal interference by the Fifth Amendment to the Constitution. The Court has not been quick to conclude in a given instance that Congress has authorized the displacement of those rights by the federally created rights of the employees. . . .

An employer's property rights must give way only where necessary to effectuate the central purposes of the Act: "to safeguard the rights of self-organization and collective bargaining, and thus by the promotion of industrial peace to remove obstructions to the free flow of commerce as defined in the Act." *NLRB v. Fansteel Metallurgical Corp.*, 306 U.S. 240, 257 (1939). . . .

The Court today cites no case in which it has ever held that anyone, whether an employee or a nonemployee, has a protected right to engage in anything other than organizational activity on an employer's property. The simple question before us is whether Congress has authorized the Board to displace an employer's right to prevent the distribution on his property of political material concerning matters over which he has no control. In eschewing any analysis of this question, in deference to the supposed expertise of the Board, the Court permits a "'yielding' of property rights" which is certainly not "temporary"; and I cannot conclude that the deprivation of such a right of property can be dismissed as "minimal." It may be that Congress has power under the Commerce Clause to require an employer to open his property to such political advocacy, but, if Congress intended to do so, "such a legislative intention should be found in some definite and unmistakable expression." *Fansteel*, 306 U.S. at 255. Finding no such expression in the Act, I would not permit the Board to balance away petitioner's right to exclude political literature from its property.

Notes

1. In *Eastex*, 437 U.S. at 565, the Supreme Court endorsed the Board's view that § 7's "mutual aid or protection" clause protects employees when they seek to "improve their lot as employees through channels outside the immediate employee-employer relationship." The Court, in *dicta*, mused about the limits of this clause: "at some point the relationship [between employees' interests as employees and their concerted activity] becomes so attenuated that an activity cannot fairly be deemed to come within the 'mutual aid or protection' clause." *Id.* at 567–68. The question for the Board is where to draw that line.

a. Employee appeals to legislators and government agencies are protected so long as the substance of those appeals is related to working conditions. In one case, for example, an engineer wrote to Congress on behalf of his colleagues opposing a competitor company's efforts to obtain resident visas for foreign engineers. The Board, with court approval, concluded that the engineer, who was motivated by a concern that an influx of foreign labor would threaten the job security of American engineers, was engaged in protected concerted activity. *Kaiser Engineers*, 213 N.L.R.B. 752 (1974), *enforced*, 538 F.2d 1379, 1384–85 (9th Cir. 1976).

b. Employee complaints to government overseers regarding working conditions are also considered concerted activities for mutual aid and protection. Employees of a casino boat operator sent letters to the Coast Guard asking it to reverse its decision to lower licensing requirements for engineers and requesting it to reinstate the original certificate of inspection that required all engineers to possess unlimited licenses. That action would tend to ensure a wage floor—engineers with unlimited licenses generally make greater wages than engineers with limited licenses—and greater safety. The Board held that these employees were engaged in protected concerted activity because they were "attempt[ing] to better their terms and conditions of employment." *Riverboat Servs. of Indiana, Inc.*, 345 N.L.R.B. 1286, 1297 (2005). *See also Misericordia Hosp. Med. Ctr.*, 246 N.L.R.B. 351, 356 (1979), *enforced*, 623 F.2d 808 (2d Cir. 1980) (nurse's report to hospital accrediting agency critical of hospital operations and staffing policies was protected activity).

c. Employee complaints to administrative agencies are treated similarly. For example, in *Petrochem Insulation, Inc.*, 330 N.L.R.B. 47 (1999), *enforced*, 240 F.3d 26 (D.C. Cir. 2001), the Board found that a union's intervention before state environmental proceedings to "'force construction companies to pay their employees a living wage, including health and other benefits,'" was a form of "area-standards activity" that was "undisputedly protected" because the union had legitimate interests in "expand[ing] union job opportunities for current union members," "improv[ing] their ability to bargain for higher wages by mitigating employer resistance based on concerns about being undercut by nonunion competitors," and furthering "the safety and health of all employees who would eventually be employed at a particular worksite." Generally, "public appeals [are] protected when they appear[] necessary to effectuate the employees' lawful aims." *NLRB v. Mount Desert Island Hosp.*, 695 F.2d 634, 640 (1st Cir. 1982).

d. Employee complaints to administrative agencies that raise only generalized safety concerns may not be sufficient to constitute protected activity. For example, in *Five Star Transportation, Inc.*, 349 N.L.R.B. 42, 44–45 (2007), the Board found that §7 protected those school bus drivers who raised—in letters written to the school committee about a bus company that was taking over school bus transportation services for the school district—employment-related safety concerns but not those who raised general safety concerns on behalf of the children. *See also Waters of Orchard Park*, 341 N.L.R.B. 642, 643–44 (2004) (holding that a telephone call to a state health department patient care hotline to report excessive heat was unprotected because the conduct did not relate to a term or condition of the employees' employment).

2. Is distributing pro-union appeals to employees after the union has won an election protected activity? *See Old Dominion Branch No. 496, Nat'l Ass'n of Letter Carriers v. Austin*, 418 U.S. 264, 279 (1974) ("Unions have a legitimate and substantial interest in continuing organizational efforts after recognition. Whether the goal is merely to strengthen or preserve the union's majority, or is to achieve 100% employee membership—a particularly substantial union concern where union security agreements are not permitted, as they are not here . . . —these organizing efforts are equally entitled to the protection of §7."). What about the distribution of

anti-union literature by dissident employees? *See NLRB v. Magnavox Co.*, 415 U.S. 322, 326–27 (1974) (union cannot waive the §7 right of dissident employees to distribute anti-union literature).

3. Would the concerted protests of several employees who honestly believe that their union is not fairly representing the workers' interests be protected? In *Emporium Capwell Co. v. Western Addition Community Organization*, 420 U.S. 50 (1975), the Court held unprotected the conduct of a group of minority employees who picketed and attempted to bargain with the employer over issues of employment discrimination, explaining that the minority employees' conduct circumvented the union as the exclusive bargaining representative.

Problem 4.2

a. Suppose Tea Party members of Congress had successfully blocked congressional efforts to raise the debt. As a result, Congress drastically cut all "entitlement programs," including social security, welfare, and Medicaid. It also defunded the NLRB and other agencies the Tea Party deemed "useless" because they believed the mission of those agencies harmed the free market. To protest, AFL-CIO unions ask all of their members to distribute the following leaflet at the workplace during break times and in break areas:

> We, the People, are being blackmailed by a group of traitors known as the Tea Party. They claim, ironically, to have their roots in those patriotic Americans who poured tea into the Boston Harbor to protest British taxation *without* representation. Now they wish to destroy our great country and the last vestiges of the middle class by lowering taxes for the rich and cutting the budgets of important government programs that support the working poor.
>
> Be a patriot! Fight for your country! Write to the President and ask him to veto this bill. Contact your member of Congress and ask him or her to tax the rich. Ask your member of Congress to support unions, which are essential to rebuilding the middle class. Ask your member of Congress to fund the NLRB.

Daniele Smith, President of a UAW local union, receives a copy of this leaflet and distributes it during her lunch break. Her boss is a Tea Party supporter. The following day, Daniele is fired. Was Daniele's action protected?

b. Local 23 President Daniele Smith takes her actions one step further. She decides to distribute campaign literature at her workplace (during her lunch break and in the break room) in favor of the Democratic Party congressional candidate. In response, her employer promulgates a rule that says "no distribution of political literature at the workplace." Daniele, thinking her activity is protected (see *Republic Aviation, supra*, Chapter 3), distributes the literature in violation of the new work rule. Is Daniele's conduct protected? *See Ford Motor Co.*, 221 N.L.R.B. 663, 666 (1975), *enforced*, 546 F.2d 418 (3d Cir. 1976) (distribution on employer's premises of a "purely political tract" unprotected even though "the election of any political candidate may have an ultimate effect on employment conditions"); *cf. Ford Motor Co. (Rouge Complex)*, 233 N.L.R.B. 698, 705 (1977) (ALJ decision) (concession of General Counsel that distributions on employer's premises of literature urging participation in Revolutionary Communist Party celebration, and of Party's newspaper, were unprotected). What if Daniele were distributing literature for the New Labor Party, a political party dedicated exclusively to improving the plight of the middle and working classes? *See Eastex*, 437 U.S. at n.18 (noting that "[t]he Board has not yet made clear whether it considers distributions like those in the above-cited [*Ford Motor*] cases to be unprotected altogether, or only on the employer's premises.").

c. Shortly after President Trump's inauguration, protests such as the Day Without Immigrants and Day Without Women called on employees to skip work to demonstrate support for issues such as civil rights, immigration, raising the minimum wage, and preserving the Affordable Care Act. Would the NLRA cover participation in such a protest? How would you analyze whether an employer could lawfully fire an employee who missed work to participate? And, given that analysis, is there anything an employee could do to increase the likelihood that her participation would be protected by the NLRA? You may want to re-consider your answers to these questions after you have read *Washington Aluminum* in the next section of this chapter. For more on this, see General Counsel Memo No. 08-10 (July 22, 2008), and Advice Memo No. 07-CA-193475 (Aug. 30, 2017).

NLRB v. J. Weingarten, Inc.

Supreme Court of the United States
420 U.S. 251, 95 S. Ct. 959, 43 L. Ed. 2d 171 (1975)

BRENNAN, J.

The [NLRB] held . . . that respondent employer's denial of an employee's request that her union representative be present at an investigatory interview which the employee reasonably believed might result in disciplinary action constituted an unfair labor practice in violation of § 8(a)(1) of the [NLRA], because it interfered with, restrained, and coerced the individual right of the employee, protected by § 7 of the Act, "to engage in . . . concerted activities for . . . mutual aid or protection. . . ." . . . The [Fifth Circuit] held that this was an impermissible construction of § 7 and refused to enforce the Board's order that directed respondent to cease and desist from requiring any employee to take part in an investigatory interview without union representation if the employee requests representation and reasonably fears disciplinary action. . . . We granted certiorari and set the case for oral argument with . . . *Garment Workers v. Quality Mfg. Co.*, 420 U.S. 276, 416 U.S. 969 (1974). We reverse.

I

Respondent operates a chain of some 100 retail stores with lunch counters at some, and so-called lobby food operations at others, dispensing food to take out or eat on the premises. Respondent's sales personnel are represented for collective-bargaining purposes by Retail Clerks Union, Local 455. Leura Collins, one of the sales personnel, worked at the lunch counter at Store No. 2 from 1961 to 1970 when she was transferred to the lobby operation at Store No. 98. . . . [A store manager told "Loss Prevention Specialist" Hardy that] a fellow lobby employee of Collins had just reported that Collins had purchased a box of chicken that sold for $2.98, but had placed only $1 in the cash register. Collins was summoned to an interview with Specialist Hardy and the store manager, and Hardy questioned her. The Board found that several times during the questioning she asked the store manager to call the union shop steward or some other union representative to the interview, and that her requests were denied. Collins admitted that she had purchased some chicken, a loaf of bread, and some cake which she said she paid for and donated to her church for a church dinner. She explained that she purchased four pieces of chicken for which the price was $1, but that because the lobby department was out of the small-size boxes in which such purchases were usually packaged she put the chicken into the larger box normally used for packaging larger quantities. Specialist Hardy left the interview to check Collins' explanation with the fellow employee who had reported Collins. This employee confirmed that the lobby department had run out of small boxes and also said that she did not know how many pieces of chicken Collins had put in the larger box. Specialist Hardy returned to the interview, told Collins that her explanation had checked out, that he was sorry if he had inconvenienced her, and that the matter was closed.

Collins thereupon burst into tears and blurted out that the only thing she had ever gotten from the store without paying for it was her free lunch. This revelation surprised the store manager and Hardy because, although free lunches had been provided at Store No. 2 when Collins worked at the lunch counter there, company policy was not to provide free lunches at stores operating lobby departments. In consequence, the store manager and Specialist Hardy closely interrogated Collins about violations of the policy in the lobby department at Store No. 98. Collins again asked that a shop steward be called to the interview, but the store manager denied her request. Based on her answers to his questions, Specialist Hardy prepared a written statement which included a computation that Collins owed the store approximately $160 for lunches. Collins refused to sign the statement. The Board found that Collins, as well as most, if not all, employees in the lobby department of Store No. 98, including the manager of that department, took lunch from the lobby without paying for it, apparently because no contrary policy was ever made known to them. Indeed, when company headquarters advised Specialist Hardy by telephone during the interview that headquarters itself was uncertain whether the policy against providing free lunches at lobby departments was in effect at Store No. 98, he terminated his interrogation of Collins. The store manager asked Collins not to discuss the matter with anyone. . . . Collins, however, reported the details of the interview fully to her shop steward and other union representatives, and this unfair labor practice proceeding resulted.

II

The Board's construction that § 7 creates a statutory right in an employee to refuse to submit without union representation to an interview which he reasonably fears may result in his discipline was announced . . . in *Quality Mfg. Co.*, 195 N.L.R.B. 197 (1972), considered in *Garment Workers v. Quality Mfg. Co.*, 420 U.S. 276. In its opinions in that case and in *Mobil Oil Corp.*, 196 N.L.R.B. 1052 (1972) . . . the Board shaped the contours and limits of the statutory right.

First, the right inheres in § 7's guarantee of the right of employees to act in concert for mutual aid and protection. In *Mobil Oil*, the Board stated:

> An employee's right to union representation upon request is based on Section 7 of the Act which guarantees the right of employees to act in concert for "mutual aid and protection." The denial of this right has a reasonable tendency to interfere with, restrain, and coerce employees in violation of Section 8(a)(1) of the Act. Thus, it is a serious violation of the employee's individual right to engage in concerted activity by seeking the assistance of his statutory representative if the employer denies the employee's request and compels the employee to appear unassisted at an interview which may put his job security in jeopardy. Such a dilution of the employee's right to act collectively to protect his job interests is, in our view, unwarranted interference with his right to insist on concerted protection, rather than individual self-protection, against possible adverse employer action. *Ibid.*

Second, the right arises only in situations where the employee requests representation. In other words, the employee may forgo his guaranteed right and, if he prefers, participate in an interview unaccompanied by his union representative.

Third, the employee's right to request representation as a condition of participation in an interview is limited to situations where the employee reasonably believes the investigation will result in disciplinary action. Thus the Board stated in *Quality*:

> "We would not apply the rule to such run-of-the-mill shop-floor conversation as, for example, the giving of instructions or training or needed corrections of work techniques. In such cases there cannot normally be any reasonable basis for an employee to fear that any adverse impact may result from the interview, and thus we would then see no reasonable basis for him to seek the assistance of his representative." . . .

Fourth, exercise of the right may not interfere with legitimate employer prerogatives. The employer has no obligation to justify his refusal to allow union representation, and despite refusal, the employer is free to carry on his inquiry without interviewing the employee, and thus leave to the employee the choice between having an interview unaccompanied by his representative, or having no interview and forgoing any benefits that might be derived from one. As stated in *Mobil Oil*:

> "The employer may, if it wishes, advise the employee that it will not proceed with the interview unless the employee is willing to enter the interview

unaccompanied by his representative. The employee may then refrain from participating in the interview, thereby protecting his right to representation, but at the same time relinquishing any benefit which might be derived from the interview. The employer would then be free to act on the basis of information obtained from other sources." . . .

Fifth, the employer has no duty to bargain with any union representative who may be permitted to attend the investigatory interview. The Board said in *Mobil*, "we are not giving the Union any particular rights with respect to prediscipinary discussions which it otherwise was not able to secure during collective-bargaining negotiations." 196 N.L.R.B. at 1052 n. 3. The Board thus adhered to its decisions distinguishing between disciplinary and investigatory interviews, imposing a mandatory affirmative obligation to meet with the union representative only in the case of the disciplinary interview. . . . The employer has no duty to bargain with the union representative at an investigatory interview. "The representative is present to assist the employee, and may attempt to clarify the facts or suggest other employees who may have knowledge of them. The employer, however, is free to insist that he is only interested, at that time, in hearing the employee's own account of the matter under investigation." . . .

The Board's holding is a permissible construction of "concerted activities for . . . mutual aid or protection" by the agency charged by Congress with enforcement of the Act, and should have been sustained.

The action of an employee in seeking to have the assistance of his union representative at a confrontation with his employer clearly falls within the literal wording of § 7 that "[e]mployees shall have the right . . . to engage in . . . concerted activities for the purpose of . . . mutual aid or protection. . . ." This is true even though the employee alone may have an immediate stake in the outcome; he seeks "aid or protection" against a perceived threat to his employment security. The union representative whose participation he seeks is, however, safeguarding not only the particular employee's interest, but also the interests of the entire bargaining unit by exercising vigilance to make certain that the employer does not initiate or continue a practice of imposing punishment unjustly. The representative's presence is an assurance to other employees in the bargaining unit that they, too, can obtain his aid and protection if called upon to attend a like interview. Concerted activity for mutual aid or protection is therefore as present here as it was held to be in *NLRB v. Peter Cailler Kohler Swiss Chocolates Co.*, 130 F.2d 503, 505–506 (2d Cir. 1942) . . . :

> "When all the other workmen in a shop make common cause with a fellow workman over his separate grievance, and go out on strike in his support, they engage in a 'concerted activity' for 'mutual aid or protection,' although the aggrieved workman is the only one of them who has any immediate stake in the outcome. The rest know that by their action each of them assures himself, in case his turn ever comes, of the support of the one whom they are all then helping; and the solidarity so established is 'mutual aid' in the most literal sense, as nobody doubts."

The Board's construction plainly effectuates the most fundamental purposes of the Act. In § 1 . . . the Act declares that it is a goal of national labor policy to protect "the exercise by workers of full freedom of association, self-organization, and designation of representatives of their own choosing, for the purpose of . . . mutual aid or protection." To that end the Act is designed to eliminate the "inequality of bargaining power between employees . . . and employers." Ibid. Requiring a lone employee to attend an investigatory interview which he reasonably believes may result in the imposition of discipline perpetuates the inequality the Act was designed to eliminate, and bars recourse to the safeguards the Act provided "to redress the perceived imbalance of economic power between labor and management." . . . Viewed in this light, the Board's recognition that § 7 guarantees an employee's right to the presence of a union representative at an investigatory interview in which the risk of discipline reasonably inheres is within the protective ambit of the section "read in the light of the mischief to be corrected and the end to be attained. . . ."

The Board's construction also gives recognition to the right when it is most useful to both employee and employer. A single employee confronted by an employer investigating whether certain conduct deserves discipline may be too fearful or inarticulate to relate accurately the incident being investigated, or too ignorant to raise extenuating factors. A knowledgeable union representative could assist the employer by eliciting favorable facts, and save the employer production time by getting to the bottom of the incident occasioning the interview. Certainly his presence need not transform the interview into an adversary contest. Respondent suggests nonetheless that union representation at this stage is unnecessary because a decision as to employee culpability or disciplinary action can be corrected after the decision to impose discipline has become final. In other words, respondent would defer representation until the filing of a formal grievance challenging the employer's determination of guilt after the employee has been discharged or otherwise disciplined. At that point, however, it becomes increasingly difficult for the employee to vindicate himself, and the value of representation is correspondingly diminished. The employer may then be more concerned with justifying his actions than re-examining them.

IV

. . . .

The responsibility to adapt the Act to changing patterns of industrial life is entrusted to the Board. The Court of Appeals impermissibly encroached upon the Board's function in determining for itself that an employee has no "need" for union assistance at an investigatory interview. . . . It is the province of the Board, not the courts, to determine whether or not the "need" exists in light of changing industrial practices and the Board's cumulative experience in dealing with labor-management relations. . . . Reviewing courts are of course not "to stand aside and rubber stamp" Board determinations that run contrary to the language or tenor of the Act . . . But the Board's construction here, while it may not be required by the Act, is at least permissible under it. . . . In sum, the Board has reached a fair and reasoned balance upon a question within its special competence, its newly arrived at construction of §7 does not exceed the reach of that section, and the Board has adequately explicated the basis of its interpretation.

The statutory right confirmed today is in full harmony with actual industrial practice. Many important collective-bargaining agreements have provisions that accord employees rights of union representation at investigatory interviews. Even where such a right is not explicitly provided in the agreement a "well-established current of arbitral authority" sustains the right of union representation at investigatory interviews which the employee reasonably believes may result in disciplinary action against him. . . .

The judgment is reversed and the case is remanded with direction to enter a judgment enforcing the Board's order.

Notes

1. Remedies for violations of an employee's *Weingarten* rights differ depending upon the quality of the violation. In *Weingarten*, the Supreme Court made clear that an employee could not be disciplined for refusing to answer questions posed during an investigatory interview for which he was denied union representation, although the employer could proceed with its investigation and forego interviewing the unrepresented employee. 420 U.S. 251 (1975). Similarly, in *Ralphs Grocery Company*, 361 N.L.R.B. 80 (2014), the Board ordered the reinstatement of an employee who had been discharged for refusing to take a drug test without having had an opportunity to consult with his union representative. However, in *Taracorp Indus.*, 273 N.L.R.B. 221 (1984), the Board did not order reinstatement for an employee who had been disciplined as the result of a meeting in which he was denied union representation because the discharge was solely motivated by the employee's refusal to perform a task, not by the employee's invocation of his *Weingarten* rights.

2. Do employees have *Weingarten* rights when voluntarily attending a meeting or hearing? The Board recently answered "yes," but the D.C. Circuit reversed. In *Midwest Div.—MMC*, the Board held that two nurses' §7 rights were violated when their employer refused their requests for a union representative to accompany them to a "peer review" meeting that they reasonably expected could result in discipline. However, the D.C. Circuit reversed, because the nurses were not required to attend the peer review meeting at all, writing that "absent compulsory attendance, the right to union representation recognized in *Weingarten* does not arise." *Midwest Div.—MMC v. NLRB*, 867 F.3d 1288 (D.C. Cir. 2017).

3. When do *Weingarten* rights attach? In *Ozburn-Hessey Logistics, LLC*, the Board held that they attach as soon as the union wins a representation election, rather than when the union is certified by the Board. 366 N.L.R.B. No. 177 (2018). Thus, an employer that denies employees their *Weingarten* rights while it contests the results of a union election will have committed a ULP if its challenge ultimately fails.

IV. The NLRA and "Concerted Activities" in the Non-Union Context

A central element in many of the cases finding concerted activity in a unionized environment is what might be called a "chain of concerted activities" that begins with workers organizing a union and continues with bargaining and administering a collective bargaining agreement. This uninterrupted chain of activities establishes a link between the individual action of one employee with the protection of a group of employees and prior collective action by those employees. But what happens when there is not chain of concerted activities because no union has been organized and no agreement bargained collectively?

NLRB v. Washington Aluminum Co.

Supreme Court of the United States
370 U.S. 9, 82 S. Ct. 1099, 8 L. Ed. 2d 298 (1962)

BLACK, J.

The [Fourth Circuit] refused to enforce an order of the [NLRB] directing the respondent Washington Aluminum Company to reinstate and make whole seven employees whom the company had discharged for leaving their work in the machine shop without permission on claims that the shop was too cold to work in. Because that decision raises important questions affecting the proper administration of the [NLRA], we granted certiorari. . . .

January 5, 1959, was an extraordinarily cold day for Baltimore, with unusually high winds and a low temperature of 11 degrees followed by a high of 22. When the employees on the day shift came to work that morning, they found the shop bitterly cold, due not only to the unusually harsh weather, but also to the fact that the large oil furnace had broken down the night before and had not as yet been put back into operation. As the workers gathered in the shop just before the starting hour of 7:30, one of them, a Mr. Caron, went into the office of Mr. Jarvis, the foreman, hoping to warm himself but, instead, found the foreman's quarters as uncomfortable as the rest of the shop. As Caron and Jarvis sat in Jarvis' office discussing how bitingly cold the building was, some of the other machinists walked by the office window "huddled" together in a fashion that caused Jarvis to exclaim that "(i)f those fellows had any guts at all, they would go home." When the starting buzzer sounded a few moments later, Caron walked back to his working place in the shop and found all the other machinists "huddled there, shaking a little, cold." Caron then said to these workers, ". . . Dave (Jarvis) told me if we had any guts, we would go home. . . . I am going home, it is too damned cold to work." Caron asked the other workers what they were going to do and, after some discussion among themselves, they decided to leave with him. One of these workers, testifying before the Board, summarized their entire discussion this way: "And we had all got together and thought it would be a good idea to go home; maybe we could get some heat brought into the plant that way." As they started to leave, Jarvis approached and persuaded one of the workers to remain at the job. But Caron and the other six workers on the day shift left practically in a body in a matter of minutes after the 7:30 buzzer.

When the company's general foreman arrived between 7:45 and 8 that morning, Jarvis promptly informed him that all but one of the employees had left because the shop was too cold. The company's president came in at approximately 8:20 a.m. and, upon learning of the walkout, immediately said to the foreman, "[I]f they have all gone, we are going to terminate them. . . ."

On these facts the Board found that the conduct of the workers was a concerted activity to protest the company's failure to supply adequate heat in its machine shop, that such conduct is protected under the provision of § 7 of the [NLRA] which guarantees that "Employees shall have the right . . . to engage in . . . concerted activities for the purpose of collective bargaining or other mutual aid or protection," and that the discharge of these workers by the company amounted to an unfair labor practice under § 8(a)(1). . . . Acting under the authority of § 10(c) . . . the Board then ordered the company to reinstate the discharged workers to their previous positions and to make them whole for losses resulting from what the Board found to have been the unlawful termination of their employment.

In denying enforcement of this order, the majority of the Court of Appeals took the position that because the workers simply "summarily left their place of employment" without affording the company an "opportunity to avoid the work stoppage by granting a concession to a demand," their walkout did not amount to a concerted activity protected by § 7. . . . On this basis, they held that there was no justification for the conduct of the workers in violating the established rules of the plant by leaving their jobs without permission and that the Board had therefore exceeded its power in issuing the order involved here because § 10(c) declares that the Board shall not require reinstatement or back pay for an employee whom an employer has suspended or discharged "for cause."

We cannot agree that employees necessarily lose their right to engage in concerted activities under § 7 merely because they do not present a specific demand upon their employer to remedy a condition they find objectionable. The language of § 7 is broad enough to protect concerted activities whether they take place before, after, or at the same time such a demand is made. To compel the Board to interpret and apply that language in the restricted fashion suggested by the respondent here would only tend to frustrate the policy of the Act to protect the right of workers to act together to better their working conditions. Indeed, as indicated by this very case, such an interpretation of § 7 might place burdens upon employees so great that it would effectively nullify the right to engage in concerted activities which that section protects. The seven employees here were part of a small group of employees who were wholly unorganized. They had no bargaining representative and, in fact, no representative of any kind to present their grievances to their employer. Under these circumstances, they had to speak for themselves as best they could. As pointed out above, prior to the day they left the shop, several of them had repeatedly complained to company officials about the cold working conditions in the shop. These had been more or less spontaneous individual pleas, unsupported by any threat of concerted protest, to which the company apparently gave little consideration and which it now says the Board should have treated as nothing more than "the same sort of gripes as the gripes made about the heat in the summertime." The bitter cold of January 5, however, finally brought these workers' individual complaints into concert so that some more effective action could be considered. Having no bargaining representative and no established procedure by which they could take full advantage of their unanimity of opinion in negotiations with the company, the men took the most direct course to let the company know that they wanted a warmer place in which to work. So, after talking among themselves, they walked out together in the hope that this action might spotlight their complaint and bring about some improvement in what they considered to be the "miserable" conditions of their employment. This we think was enough to justify the Board's holding that they were not required to make any more specific demand than they did to be entitled to the protection of §7.

Although the company contends to the contrary, we think that the walkout involved here did grow out of a "labor dispute" within the plain meaning of the definition of that term in §2(9) . . . , which declares that it includes "any controversy concerning terms, tenure or conditions of employment. . . ." The findings of the Board, which are supported by substantial evidence and which were not disturbed below, show a running dispute between the machine shop employees and the company over the heating of the shop on cold days—a dispute which culminated in the decision of the employees to act concertedly in an effort to force the company to improve that condition of their employment. . . .

Nor can we accept the company's contention that because it admittedly had an established plant rule which forbade employees to leave their work without permission of the foreman, there was justifiable "cause" for discharging these employees, wholly separate and apart from any concerted activities in which they engaged in protest against the poorly heated plant. Section 10(c) of the Act does authorize an employer to discharge employees for "cause" and our cases have long recognized this right on the part of an employer. But this, of course, cannot mean that an employer is at liberty to punish a man by discharging him for engaging in concerted activities which §7 of the Act protects. And the plant rule in question here purports to permit the company to do just that for it would prohibit even the most plainly protected kinds of concerted work stoppages until and unless the permission of the company's foreman was obtained.

It is of course true that §7 does not protect all concerted activities, but that aspect of the section is not involved in this case. . . .

We hold therefore that the Board correctly interpreted and applied the Act to the circumstances of this case and it was error for the Court of Appeals to refuse to enforce its order. The judgment of the Court of Appeals is reversed and the cause is remanded to that court with directions to enforce the order in its entirety.

Washington Aluminum posits a powerful interpretation of § 7: unorganized employees who act concertedly for "mutual aid or protection" are protected from retaliation by their employers. Perhaps the bigger implication of *Washington Aluminum* is that the NLRA protects not only the small percent of the private-sector workforce that is unionized, but all private-sector workers, so long as they meet the definition of "employee" set forth in § 2(3). Another example of the application of this principle is *Trompler, Inc.*, 335 N.L.R.B. 478, 478–79 (2001), *enforced*, 338 F.3d 747 (7th Cir. 2003), in which the Board, with court approval, found that the NLRA's § 7 protected the activity of six employees of a non-union workshop who had walked off the job in protest of their supervisor's performance. In particular, the employees disapproved of the supervisor's failure to prevent a male worker from harassing a female worker, insensitive treatment of another worker's drug problem for which she was being treated, and incompetence as a machine operator. In this case, only two workers—the supervisor and the one accused of harassment—did not join in the walkout.

A good way of understanding that "mutual aid or protection" does not require a union or union organizing drive can be found in an old Second Circuit case, *NLRB v. Peter Cailler Kohler Swiss Chocolates Co.*, 130 F.2d 503, 505–06 (2d Cir. 1942), where Judge Learned Hand wrote:

> [N]othing . . . in the act limits the scope of the language to "activities" designed to benefit other "employees"; and its rationale forbids such a limitation. When all the other workmen in a shop make common cause with a fellow workman over his separate grievance, and go out on strike in his support, they engage in a "concerted activity" for "mutual aid or protection," although the aggrieved workman is the only one of them who has any immediate stake in the outcome. The rest know that by their action each one of them assures himself, in case his turn ever comes, of the support of the one whom they are all then helping; and the solidarity so established is "mutual aid" in the most literal sense.

1. When "Concerted" Means Concerted: Walkouts, Lawsuits, Grievances, and Social Media

Unlike in *NLRB v. City Disposal Systems*, the employees in *Washington Aluminum* and *Trompler* could not claim that they were engaged in "concerted activities" because of a connection between their walkouts and earlier collective activities of organizing a union, bargaining with their employer, and agreeing to a collective bargaining agreement. In these cases, there is no union, and so there is no "chain of collective activity" upon which these workers may rely to gain the protection of § 7. So, what makes their activity "concerted"? Apparently, it is "concerted" in the colloquial sense of that term: joint action in support of a common cause, even if expressed through an individual grievance, as Judge Hand suggested. There are a number of examples in which this definition of "concerted" could apply:

Concerted Litigation and Alternative Dispute Resolution: Groups of employees bringing joint, class-, or collective-action lawsuits against their employers under various employment laws, or collective grievances under employers' dispute resolution and arbitration policies, would seem to fit comfortably within the colloquial definition of "concerted." In *D.R. Horton, Inc.*, 357 N.L.R.B. No. 184 (2012), *enforcement denied*, 737 F.3d 344 (5th Cir. 2013), the Board agreed and held that an employer commits a ULP if it requires its employees to sign clauses requiring the employees to resolve all employment disputes through individual arbitration — that is, agreements precluding employees from filing class actions or collective claims against the employer in any forum. According to the Board, § 7's protection of employees' right "to engage in . . . concerted activities for the purpose of . . . mutual aid or protection" extends to employees filing class claims and pursuing class litigation to improve their working conditions in administrative, judicial, and arbitral forums.

The Board repeatedly affirmed *D.R. Horton*'s rule — that employees must have at least one forum (either arbitral or judicial) in which they can bring joint or class or collective claims. But circuit courts split as to whether the Board's rule was permissible, and the Supreme Court agreed to hear a trio of cases presenting this issue. *Lewis v. Epic Sys.*, 823 F.3d 1147 (7th Cir. 2016); *Morris v. Ernst & Young, LLP*, 834 F.3d 975 (9th Cir. 2016); and *Murphy Oil USA, Inc., v. NLRB*, 808 F.3d 1013 (5th Cir. 2013). In *Epic Systems* and *Ernst & Young*, the lower courts held that the NLRA's language clearly supported the Board's rule. But in *Murphy Oil*, the Fifth Circuit relied on its earlier analysis rejecting the Board's *D.R. Horton* decision, which held that the Board's rule was inconsistent with the requirement of the Federal Arbitration Act (FAA) that arbitration agreements "shall be valid, irrevocable, and enforceable. . . ." 9 U.S.C. § 2.

The Supreme Court granted *certiorari* shortly before President Trump's inauguration and consolidated the three cases for briefing and oral argument. Although the Board and the Solicitor General jointly filed the *Murphy Oil cert.* petition on behalf of the Board, the Trump Administration's Acting Solicitor General did an about-face, filing an amicus brief on behalf of the employers, arguing that the NLRB's rule was inconsistent with the FAA. The NLRB represented itself before the Supreme Court, defending the *Murphy Oil/D.R. Horton* rule.

In a 5–4 decision written by Justice Gorsuch, *Epic Systems Corp. v. Lewis*, 138 S. Ct. 1612 (2018), the Supreme Court held that the individual arbitration agreements were enforceable under the FAA and neither the FAA's savings clause nor the provisions of the NLRA required a different result. The Court harmonized the FAA and the NLRA by reading § 7's protection of employees' right "to engage in . . . concerted activities for the purpose of . . . mutual aid or protection" narrowly, stating that: "where, as here, a general term follows more specific terms in a list, the general term is usually understood to 'embrace only objects similar in nature to those objects enumerated by the preceding specific words' . . . . All of which suggests that the term 'other concerted activities' should, like the terms that precede it, serve to protect things employees 'just do' for themselves in the course of exercising their right to free association in the workplace, rather than the 'highly regulated, courtroom-bound "activities" of class and joint litigation.'" *Id.* at 12 (citations omitted). Justice Ginsberg dissented, contending that "the Court's decision is egregiously wrong" and explaining "why the Arbitration Act, sensibly read, does not shrink the NLRA's protective sphere."

The majority's interpretation of concerted activities for other mutual aid or protection is at least in tension with the *Eastex* Court's statement that Congress chose "to protect concerted activities for the somewhat *broader* purpose of 'mutual aid or protection' as well as for the *narrower* purposes of 'self-organization' and 'collective bargaining.' *Eastex* at 565 (emphasis added). Justice Gorsuch did not address this prior understanding of the language he was interpreting.

A different issue is presented when an employer demands that an employee waive their right to make an administrative complaint, such as by filing an NLRB charge—this is an unfair labor practice. In a recent case, the Board confronted the intersection of this rule and *Boeing Corp.*, which was discussed in Chapter 3. The Board found that a clause requiring that "all claims or controversies for which a federal or state court would be authorized to grant relief" be resolved by arbitration would reasonably be interpreted by employees in a way that would interfere with their right to file Board charges. The Board then held that the employer lacked a sufficient justification for the rule, because "as a matter of law, there is not and cannot be any legitimate justification for provisions, in an arbitration agreement or otherwise, that restrict employees' access to the Board or its processes." *Prime Healthcare Paradise Valley, LLC*, 368 N.L.R.B. No. 10 (2019).

Employee Information Sharing: Refer back to the discussion of *Flex Frac Logistics, L.L.C. v. NLRB*, 746 F.3d 205 (5th Cir. 2014) in Chapter 3. Recall that this case involved a non-union employer and information exchange between employees that did not relate to organizing a union. The Fifth Circuit agreed with the Board that this information exchange was concerted activity, and employees could reasonably construe Flex Frac's rule as restricting their § 7 right to engage in concerted activities for mutual aid or protection.

Use of Social Media: The Board has applied its longstanding test for determining whether an employer has illegally retaliated against employees for engaging in "concerted activities" to the use of the social networking site Facebook. In *Hispanics United of Buffalo, Inc.*, 359 N.L.R.B. No. 37 (2012), the Board held that four co-workers' negative comments posted on Facebook about a fifth co-worker's criticism of their performance constituted protected concerted activity. The Board, applying its rule from *Meyers Industries, Inc.*, 268 N.L.R.B. 493 (1984), held that the employer violated § 8(a)(1) by discharging the four Facebook-using co-workers because commenting on Facebook is a "concerted activity." In a later case, the Board found, and the Second Circuit affirmed, that "liking" a post on Facebook could also constitute concerted activity. *Three D, LLC v. NLRB*, 629 F. App'x 33 (2d Cir. 2015).

2. When Acting Alone is "Concerted Activity"

What happens when an employee acts alone, like in *City Disposal Systems*, but in the absence of a union and a collective bargaining agreement? The broadest reading of §7 in this context was ***Alleluia Cushion Co.***, 221 N.L.R.B. 999 (1975), where the Board held that the individual assertion of a matter of common concern to other employees constitutes concerted activity. In that case, Jack Henley, a maintenance worker at a carpet manufacturing and wholesale distribution company, complained "about safety conditions, including the lack of instruction regarding chemicals used in production, the absence of protective guards on machines, his inability to communicate safety instructions to the majority of employees who were Spanish-speaking, and the absence of first aid stations, eyewash stations, and an overall safety program." Henley was thereafter transferred to another facility where he made similar complaints. When he found his employer's response unsatisfactory, he wrote a letter of complaint to the state OSHA office. Henley was discharged the day after an OSHA inspection of the workplace. The Board rejected the company's argument that the employer was privileged to discharge Henley because his complaints did not constitute concerted activity and therefore were not protected under the NLRA:

> While it is undisputed that Henley acted alone in protesting Respondent's lack of safety precautions, the absence of any outward manifestation of support for his efforts is not, in our judgment, sufficient to establish that Respondent's employees did not share Henley's interest in safety or that they did not support his complaints regarding the safety violations. Safe working conditions are matters of great and continuing concern for all within the work force. Indeed, occupational safety is one of the most important conditions of employment. Recent years have witnessed the recognition of this vital interest by Congress through enactment of the Occupational Safety and Health Act, and by state and local governments through the passage of similar legislation. The [NLRA] cannot be administered in a vacuum. The Board must recognize the purposes and policies of other employment legislation, and construe the Act in a manner supportive of the overall statutory scheme.

> Section 7 provides that employees have the right to engage in concerted activities for the purpose of mutual aid and protection. Henley's filing of the complaint with the California OSHA office was an action taken in furtherance of guaranteeing Respondent's employees their rights under the California Occupational Safety and Health Act. It would be incongruous with the public policy enunciated in such occupational safety legislation (i.e., to provide safe and healthful working conditions and to preserve the nation's human resources) to presume that, absent an outward manifestation of support, Henley's fellow employees did not agree with his efforts to secure compliance with the statutory obligations imposed on Respondent for their benefit. Rather, since minimum safe and healthful employment conditions for the protection and well-being of employees have been legislatively declared to be in the overall public interest, the consent and concert of action emanates from the mere assertion of such statutory rights.

Accordingly, where an employee speaks up and seeks to enforce statutory provisions relating to occupational safety designed for the benefit of all employees, in the absence of any evidence that fellow employees disavow such representation, we will find an implied consent thereto and deem such activity to be concerted.

The circumstances of this case bear out such an implication. The complaint filed by Henley sought to compel Respondent to comply with a state statute concerning occupational safety. While his own personal safety may have been one motivation, it is clear from the nature and extent of the safety complaints registered that Henley's object encompassed the well-being of his fellow employees. Most of the conditions he sought to remedy, i.e., live electrical wires in work areas, lack of instruction regarding chemicals used in production, and inadequate ventilation, involved work areas and potential hazards that Henley was unlikely to encounter. In fact, the one specific safety improvement the protests accomplished—the installation of eye-wash stands—directly benefits the employees within the rebonding process and only marginally affects Henley.

In light of the above, we find Henley was engaged in protected concerted activity when he filed the complaint with the California OSHA office. 221 N.L.R.B. 999, 1000–01.

The Board backtracked from the *Alleluia Cushion* doctrine in a series of cases that remain protective of concerted activity. In *Meyers Indus.*, 268 N.L.R.B. 493, 497 (1984) (*Meyers I*), *remanded sub nom. Prill v. NLRB*, 755 F.2d 941 (D.C. Cir. 1985), *reaffirmed*, 281 N.L.R.B. 882 (1986) (*Meyers II*), *enforced sub nom. Prill v. NLRB*, 835 F.2d 1481 (D.C. Cir. 1987), the Board held that "in general, to find an employee's activity to be 'concerted,' we shall require it to be engaged in with or on the authority of other employees, and not solely by and on behalf of the employee himself." *Meyers I* and *Meyers II* thereby overruled *Alleluia Cushion Co.* The Board nevertheless recognized that even under the *Meyers* test, "the question of whether an employee engaged in concerted activity is, at its heart, a factual one." *Meyers I*, 268 N.L.R.B. at 496–97. Furthermore, in both *Meyers I*, 268 N.L.R.B. at 494, and *Meyers II*, 281 N.L.R.B. 882, the Board reaffirmed *Root-Carlin, Inc.*, 92 N.L.R.B. 1313, 1314 (1951), which held that "the guarantees of §7 of the Act extend to concerted activity which in its inception involves only a speaker and a listener, for such activity is an indispensable preliminary step to employee self-organization."

The Board has found that an employee, acting alone, engages in concerted activity where the conduct has "some relation to group action in the interest of employees." *Frank Briscoe, Inc. v. NLRB*, 637 F.2d 946, 949 (3rd Cir. 1981). For example, in *NLRB v. Mount Desert Island Hospital*, 695 F.2d 634 (1st Cir. 1982), the Board concluded that a hospital employee who wrote a letter to a newspaper that documented poor working conditions and understaffing was engaged in concerted activity where the evidence showed that, prior to writing the letter, the employee had extensively discussed working conditions with other employees, where the letter itself referred to "the plight of fellow workers at the Hospital," and where the letter prompted other employees to sign a petition circulated by that employee. The court, upholding the Board's conclusion, noted that the employee's "action, even if not endorsed in advance by other employees, clearly had the 'welfare of other workers in mind.'" 695 F.2d 634, 640. The examples offered in Note #2 following *Eastex, supra,* also fit this "individual action on behalf of the group" definition, regardless of whether there is a union present in the workplace.

3. "*Weingarten* Rights" in the Non-Union Workplace

In *Weingarten,* the employee was a member of a union bargaining unit. Should "*Weingarten* rights" apply to employees covered by the NLRA, but employed in a non-union workplace? The Board has oscillated on this topic. *See Materials Research Corp.,* 262 N.L.R.B. 1010 (1982) (holding *Weingarten* covers employees in nonunion workplaces); *Sears, Roebuck & Co.,* 274 N.L.R.B. 230 (1985) (reversing *Materials Research Corp.*); *Epilepsy Fdn. of Northeast Ohio,* 331 N.L.R.B. 676 (2000) (reinstating *Weingarten* rights for non-union employees); *IBM Corp.,* 341 N.L.R.B. 1288 (2004) (reversing *Epilepsy Fdn.*).

In *Materials Research Corp.* and *Epilepsy Foundation,* the Board identified the following reasons for its conclusion that non-union employees have a right under the NLRA to bring a co-worker representative to disciplinary meetings.

- *Weingarten* rights derive from the text of § 7; employees have a collective interest in ensuring that the employer does not impose unjust discipline. The scope of § 7 rights do not depend on the presence of a union. Further, because an employer can always forego disciplinary meetings, the existence of *Weingarten* rights in non-union settings does not require an employer to deal with an unelected employee representative.

- Even if a non-union employee representative has a greater likelihood of ineffectiveness than a union representative, § 7 rights do not depend on the predicted effectiveness of the collective action. Further, employees may always choose to forego collective action if they think it will be ineffective.

- While the presence of a co-worker representative might make an employer investigation less efficient in some sense, that is because § 7 is functioning in this context to provide a fairer process for employees

Conversely, the Board relied on the following alternative considerations in *Sears* and *IBM:*

- The scope of § 7 rights can vary depending on whether or not a group of employees is represented by a union, and so the presence of *Weingarten* rights for union employees is not dispositive of the rights of non-union employees.

- *Weingarten* rights for non-union employees would interfere with a non-union employer's right to deal with employees on an individual basis. They could also make it more difficult for employers to investigate wrongdoing if, for example, an employee chose their "co-conspirator" as their representative, or if the representative publicized confidential information about the disciplinary process.

- Employee representatives in a non-union setting are not bound by the duty of fair representation, and so might not represent the interests of the workforce as a whole.

- A non-union representative will not necessarily have the training or skills required to make their presence in a disciplinary meeting meaningful or workable. Further, employee representatives who lack a union's backing will have less ability to "level the playing field" or exert influence on the employer's decision.

- If employers decide to forego disciplinary meetings because of the likelihood that the non-union employees would invoke their *Weingarten* rights, then the employees might lose their only chance to explain their side of the story. (In contrast, a unionized worker would have access to a grievance mechanism in the event that an employer disciplines or fires the worker.)

- Non-union employers might not be aware of *Weingarten*.

Notes

1. In *IBM Corp.*, the Board majority asserted that it had not held that "a non-union employee lacks a §7 right to seek mutual aid and assistance from a fellow employee . . . [or that] a nonunion employee is incapable of representing a fellow employee . . . [or that] nonunion employees lack the legal right to seek to stand up for each other. . . . [E]mployees have the right to seek such representation; they cannot be disciplined for asserting those rights. . . . Our only holding is that the non-union employer has no obligation to *accede* to the request, i.e., to deal collectively with the employees." 341 N.L.R.B. 1288, 1294. Thus, a non-union employee cannot be discharged for *requesting* the presence of a co-worker at an investigatory hearing but the non-union employer can refuse that request and compel the employee to attend the meeting without a witness. The non-union employer can also discharge for insubordination the employee who refuses to attend that interrogation.

2. Which definition of "concerted" is at play in the Board's *Weingarten-IBM* line of cases? Is it the colloquial definition of multiple parties working together toward a common cause? Or did *Weingarten*'s reliance on the role of the union representative in enforcing the collective bargaining agreement and protecting the interests of other employees in the bargaining unit essentially doom non-union employees' right to have a representative present during an investigative interview? Should *IBM* have come out differently if the Board considered the colloquial definition of "concerted"?

3. The history of the *Weingarten* rule is a good example of several principles of administrative law. First, administrative agencies, like the NLRB, may use adjudicatory proceedings to develop rules and make policy choices. *See SEC v. Chenery Corp.*, 332 U.S. 194 (1947) (*Chenery II*). *Weingarten*'s progeny show the Board doing

just that—developing and redeveloping rules by adjudication. Second, the history of the *Weingarten* rule is also a good example of administrative policy oscillation—the permissible practice of administrative agencies reversing through adjudication rules originally created by adjudication. Samuel Estreicher, *Policy Oscillation at the Labor Board: A Plea for Rulemaking*, 37 ADMIN. L. REV. 163 (1985). *Cf. Perez v. Mortgage Bankers Ass'n*, Nos. 13-1041, 13-1052 (Mar. 9, 2015) (agencies may change non-legislative regulations without proceeding through the Administrative Procedure Act's notice and comment process). Oscillation in the NLRB context is particularly common when a new political party takes over the White House and appoints new Board members, switching the Board's majority from one party to another.

There are, however, limits to policy oscillation. Applying the principle that "[a]n administrative order cannot be upheld unless the grounds upon which the agency acted in exercising its powers were those upon which its action can be sustained," *SEC v. Chenery Corp.*, 318 U.S. 80, 95 (1943) (*Chenery I*), reviewing courts will set aside Board cases that are not supported by adequate reasoning. The Board must apply the prior-adopted rule consistently until it articulates in a subsequent decision reasons for changing its policy. *See* Estreicher, 37 ADMIN. L. REV. at 166 (explaining that "[a]dministrative law requires the Labor Board to adopt a consistent rule at any given point in time"). Further, when an agency makes policy through adjudication, it must wait for a case presenting the issue in order to change its approach.

V. Protection of Public-Sector Workers' Protest

As Chapter 1 indicated, government employees are covered by a range of statutes and constitutional provisions, and these can offer some protections to public-sector employee protestors that are not available to private-sector employees. As to statutes, most importantly, civil service rules often require just cause for discipline or discharge, and many teachers have some form of tenure (which typically also requires good cause for discipline or discharge). These protections are broader than that labor law affords, in that they do not require that the employee be engaged in concerted activity for mutual aid and protection. As Chapter 1 also noted, individual public employees enjoy First Amendment protections for some (but not all) types of speech entirely outside the workplace context. *See Garcetii v. Ceballos*, 547 U.S. 410 (2006). All these protections, however, tend not to focus on workers organizing or protesting as a group. Rather, cases in these areas typically involve one individual employee. Chapter 10 revisits these laws in the context of their effect on the scope of bargaining in the public sector.

This section will first use "concerted activity for mutual aid and protection" to focus on a recurring issue in the public sector: how language in public-sector labor statutes that is similar to, but somewhat different from, language in the NLRA, should be interpreted. Specifically, these materials exam *Weingarten* rights in this context. Second, this section will discuss what unions of public workers do in states without collective-bargaining laws. In other words, how do public workers act collectively to further their interests in the workplace where they lack the right to bargain collectively?

A. *Weingarten* and Concerted Activity in the Public Sector

1. *The Significance of Statutory Language*

Most public-sector labor statutes have simply copied and or essentially incorporated the language of NLRA §7. *See, e.g.,* Ohio Rev. Code §4117.03(A)(1)–(2) (Public employees have the right to: "Form, join, assist, or participate in, or refrain from forming, joining, assisting or participating in . . . any employee organization of their own choosing; engage in other concerted activities for the purpose of collective bargaining or other mutual aid and protection.").

A few states have somewhat narrower statutory language. For example, §3515 of the California State Employer-Employee Relations Act provides that "state employees shall have the right to form, join, and participate in the activities of employee organizations of their own choosing for the purpose of representation on all matters of employer-employee relations" and "shall have the right to refuse to join or participate in the activities of employee organizations." Cal. Gov't Code §3515. Similarly, §202 of New York's Taylor Law provides that "employees shall have the right to form, join and participate in, or to refrain from forming, joining, or participating in, any employee organization of their own choosing." N.Y. Civ. Serv. Law §202.

What is the significance of a definition of employee rights that is narrower than that in NLRA §7? In *New York City Transit Authority v. Public Employment Relations Bd.*, 864 N.E.2d 56 (N.Y. 2007), the New York Court of Appeals held that the different language in the New York statute meant that *Weingarten* should not be adopted for New York public workers covered by the statute. The court explained:

> Civil Service Law §202 provides: "Public employees shall have the right to form, join and participate in, or to refrain from forming, joining, or participating in, any employee organization of their own choosing."

> This statutory language is in some ways similar to, but in more relevant ways different from, that of the statute interpreted in *Weingarten*, section 7 of the NLRA. . . .

> While some of the rights given by section 7 ("to form, join, or assist labor organizations, to bargain collectively through representatives of their own choosing") have close counterparts in section 202 ("to form, join and participate in . . . any employee organization of their own choosing"), those are not the rights that the Supreme Court relied on in *Weingarten*. Rather, *Weingarten* upheld the NLRB's decision that the right to "engage in . . . concerted activities for the purpose of . . . mutual aid or protection" included a right to have union representatives present at disciplinary interviews. Since the "mutual aid or protection" language is absent from section 202,

Weingarten does not support a holding that section 202 creates a *Weingarten* right. . . . 864 N.E.2d 56, 57–58.

Chief Judge Kaye, dissenting, would have adopted the *Weingarten* rule despite the difference in statutory language. She focused on the term "participate" in the New York law.

> The majority today reverses PERB's determination essentially because the words, "concerted activities for the purpose of . . . mutual aid or protection" are not found in the Taylor Law. That section 202 of the Taylor Law omits these words, however, does not contravene an interpretation that the word "participate" in its "natural signification" in the Taylor Law manifests a legislative intent to allow public employees the right to union representation at an investigatory interview when the employee seeks that representation.
>
> . . . Issues concerning union representation on disciplinary matters for bargaining unit members are part of the employment relationship in the public sector. Thus, a proper interpretation of the Taylor Law is that it incorporates the right to have representation relating to informal investigations of employee conduct. . . . To "participate" means to take part in something, usually in common with others. Seeking advice from a union representative when a bargaining unit member is most vulnerable certainly is encompassed in the plain language of "participate."

After this decision, the New York legislature amended the statute to provide a *Weingarten* right. Section 209-a(1)(g) of the Taylor Law made it an "improper practice" for an employer:

> to fail to permit or refuse to afford a public employee the right, upon the employee's demand, to representation by a representative of the employee organization, or the designee of such organization, which has been certified or recognized under this article when at the time of questioning by the employer of such employee it reasonably appears that he or she may be the subject of a potential disciplinary action. If representation is requested, and the employee is a potential target of disciplinary action at the time of questioning, a reasonable period of time shall be afforded to the employee to obtain such representation. . . .

2. Weingarten *and Public-Sector Employees and Unions Without the Right to Bargain Collectively*

As shown earlier in this chapter, the NLRB has on several occasions changed its position as to whether private-sector employees in non-unionized workplaces have *Weingarten* rights. Consider a recurring theme in public-sector law here: if a public-sector labor board is inclined to follow private-sector precedent, what should it do when private-sector case law changes back and forth, as it did with *Epilepsy Foundation* and then *IBM Corp.*? Change with the private-sector changes? Make an independent determination as to which rule is the best labor policy?

In the specific case of whether a *Weingarten*-type rule should apply to public employees, does the public-sector context matter? In *Commonwealth v. Pennsylvania Labor Rel. Bd.*, 916 A.2d 541 (Pa. 2007), the Court upheld a Pennsylvania Labor Relations Board decision which rejected an argument that *Weingarten* rights were unnecessary for public employees because most such employees are covered by civil service and other laws which provide specific procedures employers must follow in serious discipline cases.

Further complicating matters, it is not uncommon in the public sector for employees to be unionized, yet have no right to bargain collectively. Should *Weingarten* rights be extended to such employees?

City of Round Rock v. Rodriguez

Texas Supreme Court
399 S.W.3d 130 (Tex. 2013)

GREEN, J., joined by JOHNSON, J., WILLETT, J., GUZMAN, J., BOYD, J., and DEVINE, J.

In this statutory construction case, we are asked to decide whether section 101.001 of the Texas Labor Code grants unionized public-sector employees in Texas the right to, upon request, have union representation during an internal investigatory interview when the employee reasonably believes the interview may result in disciplinary action. The court of appeals held that section 101.001 confers such a right. Although private sector employees and federal public-sector employees both possess such a representation right, we hold that the Texas Legislature has not granted that right to public-sector employees in Texas. . . .

I. Factual Background

In July 2008, Round Rock Fire Chief Larry Hodge called fire fighter Jaime Rodriguez into a meeting in Chief Hodge's office. In the room, Chief Hodge was joined by the assistant fire chief and Rodriguez's battalion chief. Chief Hodge told Rodriguez that the purpose of the meeting was to conduct an internal interview of Rodriguez regarding a personnel complaint that Chief Hodge had filed against him. Chief Hodge alleged that Rodriguez had misused his sick leave earlier that month to get a physical examination to pursue employment with the Austin Fire Department. The complaint stated, "Since this is an Internal Interview you may not be represented during our meeting; however, if a pre disciplinary meeting is set following our meeting you would be eligible for representation at that time." The complaint also prohibited Rodriguez from discussing the complaint with anyone other than Rodriguez's attorney, including union leadership and other union members.

Before the interview began, Rodriguez asserted the right to union representation, requesting to have a representative from the Round Rock Fire Fighters Association (the Association) present during the interview. Chief Hodge denied Rodriguez's request and interviewed him without Association representation. In October 2008 . . . Chief Hodge allowed Rodriguez to choose between being discharged and accepting a five-day suspension without right of appeal. A few days later, Rodriguez executed an agreement that opted for the five-day suspension.

Three months later, Rodriguez and the Association filed a declaratory judgment action, alleging that Chief Hodge and the City of Round Rock violated Rodriguez's right to union representation, and asserting that such a right is conferred by section 101.001 of the Texas Labor Code. . . . In its final judgment, the trial court declared that Rodriguez was denied his right to union representation under section 101.001 of the Labor Code, and enjoined Chief Hodge and the City from further denying fire fighters the right to, upon request, be represented by the Association at investigatory interviews they reasonably believe might result in discipline. The court of appeals affirmed the decision.

II. The *Weingarten* Decision

The right to union representation in an investigatory interview derives from the United States Supreme Court's decision in *NLRB v. Weingarten*, 420 U.S. 251 (1975), the seminal case regarding private sector employee representation rights. In that case, an employer challenged the National Labor Relations Board's (NLRB) determination that Section 7 of the National Labor Relations Act (NLRA) granted private sector employees the right to have a union representative present at an investigatory interview when the employee reasonably believes that the interview could result in disciplinary action. The NLRB determined that this right inhered in Section 7's guarantee of the right of employees to engage in "concerted activities for . . . mutual aid or protection." The Supreme Court held that the NLRB permissibly construed Section 7 to confer the representation right, noting that the NLRB's construction may not be required by the statute's text. In doing so, the Supreme Court explained that the NLRB's decisions are "subject to limited judicial review" because of the NLRB's "special function" in interpreting Section 7 and its "special competence" in the field of labor management relations. Following *Weingarten*, Congress extended the representation right to federal public-sector employees. 5 U.S.C. §7101(b). . . .

III. Statutory Construction

. . . A. The Plain Language of Section 101.001 Does Not Confer the Representation Right Asserted by Rodriguez

Section 101.001, captioned "Right to Organize," provides: "All persons engaged in any kind of labor may associate and form trade unions and other organizations to protect themselves in their personal labor in their respective employment." . . . While the statute is broad, we do not read it as conferring, by its plain language, the specific right to have a union representative present at an investigatory interview that an employee reasonably believes might result in disciplinary action. In fact, on its face, the statute confers only one explicit right: the right to organize into a trade union or other organization. . . .

Indeed, this Court has previously recognized this construction of section 101.001 when discussing the joint purpose of a former codification of section 101.001 and section 101.002 of the Labor Code, which addresses the rights of individuals to influence others in employment matters. . . . We clearly delineated the specific roles of each statute: Section 101.001 confers the right to organize into a union, and section 101.002 then provides substance to that right by allowing employees to influence other employees to enter, refuse, or quit employment. . . .

This reading of section 101.001 comports with other labor related provisions in the Texas statutes, which are premised on section 101.001's right to form unions. While section 101.001 protects the right of employees to organize into labor unions, section 101.052 of the Labor Code protects the "right-to-work." . . . This Court has recognized that the "intent [of the right-to-work statute] seems obvious to protect *employees in the exercise of the right* of free choice of joining or not joining a union." . . .

Similarly, our construction of section 101.001 "as conferring the right to organize into unions" is in accord with Chapter 617 of the Texas Government Code, which defines specific rights of Texas public sector labor unions. *See* Tex. Gov't Code §§ 617.001–.003 (expressly disarming public-sector unions of rights usually enjoyed in the private sector, such as striking and collective bargaining); *id.* § 617.005 (granting public sector unionized employees the limited right "to present grievances concerning their wages, hours of employment, or conditions of work either individually or through a representative that does not claim the right to strike"); *see also* Tex. Att'y Gen. Op. No. H_422 (1974) (determining that implicit in section 617.005 "is the notion that public officials should meet with public employees or their representatives at reasonable times and places to hear their grievances concerning wages, hours of work, and conditions of work"). Chapter 617, while conferring the right to present grievances, does not confer the right to union representation during investigatory interviews.

B. Section 7 of the NLRA Differs Significantly from Section 101.001

Although we look to federal statutes and case law when a Texas statute and federal statute are "animated in their common history, language, and purpose," key differences between the NLRA and the state statutes here compel a different result from that reached by the United States Supreme Court in *Weingarten*.

Section 7 of the NLRA states, in relevant part:

Employees shall have the right to self-organization, to form, join, or assist labor organizations, to bargain collectively through representatives of their own choosing, and to engage in other concerted activities for the purpose of collective bargaining or other mutual aid or protection. . . .

In contrast, section 101.001 provides:

All persons engaged in any kind of labor may associate and form trade unions and other organizations to protect themselves in their personal labor in their respective employment.

Although Rodriguez and the dissent argue that the language is "substantially similar," we read the statutes as substantially dissimilar.

Section 7 confers four rights that union members can invoke for their protection: (1) "self-organization"; (2) "form, join, or assist labor organizations"; (3) "bargain collectively through representatives of their own choosing"; and (4) "engage in other concerted activities for the purpose of collective bargaining or other mutual aid or protection." The *Weingarten* right recognized by the Supreme Court is rooted in that fourth right, "the individual right of the employee, protected by [Section] 7 of the Act, 'to engage in . . . concerted activities for . . . mutual aid or protection.'" Because Section 7 guarantees private sector employees the specific right to collective bargaining and the more general right to engage in other concerted activity toward collective bargaining or some other sort of aid or protection–rights that attach once unions are formed–the Supreme Court concluded that the language of Section 7 could include the *Weingarten* right. While section 101.001 mirrors Section 7 in conferring the first right–a right to organize–and part of the second–a right to form unions and other organizations–granted to private-sector employees, nothing in section 101.001 allows us to reach the same conclusion. Just as the Fifth Circuit declined to find a representation right for railway employees because the Railway Labor Act lacks the "concerted activities" language found in the NLRA, see *Johnson v. Express One Int'l Inc.*, 944 F.2d 247, 251 (5th Cir.1991), we cannot find a representation right in section 101.001 without similar "concerted activities" language. *See id.* (warning against applying NLRA case law to statutes with language that "differs substantially" from the NLRA). *Cf. N.Y.C. Transit Auth. v. N.Y. State Pub. Emp't Relations Bd.*, 8 N.Y.3d 226,(2007) (holding that a state statute that differed materially from the text of NLRA Section 7 and lacked "concerted activities for . . . mutual aid or protection" language did not give a representation right to public-sector employees).

The dissent suggests that the mere inclusion of the word "protect" in the statute indicates the Legislature's intent to grant unionized public-sector employees specific rights to enable them to seek protection in their employment, including the right to union representation during investigatory interviews. But, as explained above, there is nothing in the statute to indicate such an intent. We read "protect" as describing the purpose around which individuals would organize and form unions, pursuant to the right conferred under section 101.001. The Legislature grants and denies rights to unionized public-sector employees by specific enactment. *See, e.g.,* TEX. GOV'T CODE § 617.002(a) (denying public-sector employees the right to bargain collectively); *id.* § 617.003 (denying public-sector employees the right to strike); *id.* § 617.005 (granting public-sector employees the right to present their grievances concerning wages, hours, or conditions of work through a union representative). At most, the inclusion of "protect" serves as a limitation on the type of union or organization—those formed to protect employees in their employment—whose members are subject to those specific enactments that grant rights, such as the right to present work related grievances, and deny rights, such as collective bargaining and the right to strike. This reading does not deprive section 101.001 of meaning; rather, when read in connection with the grants and denials of specific rights, it gives section 101.001 precisely the meaning the plain language indicates the Legislature intended: Texas public employees have the right to band together and form labor unions.

C. The Supreme Court's Analysis in *Weingarten* Does Not Apply

Weingarten provides little guidance for important reasons. First, there is no question that Section 7 of the NLRA and the *Weingarten* decision apply only to private sector employees. . . . In the thirty-eight years since *Weingarten* was decided, the Texas Legislature has declined to enact similar legislation.

Second, Section 7 does not expressly confer the *Weingarten* right, and the Supreme Court recognized that. In *Weingarten*, the Court merely determined that the NLRB had permissibly construed Section 7 to find the *Weingarten* right rooted in the "concerted activities" portion of that statute, although the language of Section 7 may not actually grant the right. *See* [420 U.S. at 266–67] (stating that even though the NLRB's construction "may not be required by [Section 7, it] is at least permissible under it"). The Court afforded the NLRB's construction considerable deference because, with its "special competence," the NLRB is entrusted with "responsibility to adapt the [NLRA] to changing patterns of life," and its construction of the NLRA is therefore "subject to limited judicial review." *See id.* at 264–68. . . . In Texas, we have no NLRB equivalent. Instead, labor policy and regulation is determined exclusively by the Texas Legislature and the language of its legislative enactments. And, unlike the United States Congress, the Texas Legislature has not enacted legislation to confer the right to union representation on Texas public-sector employees during investigatory interviews.

Third, as explained above, the *Weingarten* decision was based on language in Section 7 that is absent from section 101.001. Without anything resembling Section 7's "concerted activities" language, section 101.001 cannot confer on Texas public-sector employees a right to have union representation during investigatory interviews they reasonably believe may result in disciplinary action.

D. Related State and Federal Statutory Enactments Support This Construction of Section 101.001

. . . .

The Legislature enacted the first codification of section 101.001 in 1899, long before Congress enacted the NLRA or the Supreme Court decided the Weingarten case. . . . The original 1899 provision stated:

> [I]t shall be lawful for any and all persons engaged in any kind of work or labor, manual or mental, or both, to associate themselves together and form trade unions and other organizations for the purpose of protecting themselves in their personal work, personal labor, and personal service, in their respective pursuits and employments.

At the time this provision was enacted, unions were attempting to clarify their position under recent state and federal antitrust legislation. . . . In 1890, Congress passed the landmark Sherman Antitrust Act, which included language broad enough to consider labor unions to be trusts. . . . By 1889, Texas had enacted similar comprehensive antitrust legislation, and the Legislature amended Texas antitrust laws in 1899. . . . Two days after passing those amendments, the Legislature enacted the 1899 right to organize statute, which included language clarifying labor's role under Texas's antitrust laws. . . .

Courts of appeals have acknowledged this historical context when discussing the former codification of section 101.001. For example, the Seventh Court of Appeals surmised:

> It was probably the purpose of this legislation to make it clear that the early English decisions, which held labor unions under certain circumstances to be unlawful, and our own laws against trusts and combinations in restraint of trade, did not apply to labor unions. The act merely announced that there was no prohibition of law against such unions. [*McNatt v. Lawther*, 223 S.W. 503, 505 (Tex. Civ. App. 1920)].

. . . In this historical context, it is clear that the 1899 right to organize statute aligns more closely with the Clayton Act of 1914, which partially exempted labor unions from violating federal antitrust laws, than with Section 7 of the NLRA, which was not enacted until much later.

. . . .

E. If Representation Rights Are to Be Conferred on Texas Public-Sector Employees, the Legislature Must Make That Policy Determination

We recognize, as the dissent does, that there are good reasons for Texas public-sector employees to have the same access to union representation in investigatory interviews as private sector employees and federal public-sector employees. In Texas, however, the Legislature must make this policy determination. . . . Our role in statutory construction is merely to give effect to the Legislature's intent by examining the plain meaning of the statute. . . . Here, we must give effect to the statute's silence on this issue and the Legislature's decision not to confer representation rights akin to *Weingarten* rights on Texas public-sector employees. . . .

Although it seems an anomaly for Texas public-sector employees to have to face investigatory interviews alone, we note that the Legislature may have good reasons for treating public-sector employees in Texas differently from private-sector employees. *See, e.g., Cong. of Indust. Org. v. City of Dallas*, 198 S.W.2d 143, 144 (Tex. Civ.App.-Dallas 1946, writ ref'd n.r.e.) ("[T]he status of governmental employees, National, State and Municipal, is radically different from that of employees in private business or industry"); *see also Headquarters Nat'l Aeronautics & Space Admin.*, 50 F.L.R.A. 601, 608 n. 5 (1995) ("noting Congress'[s] recognition that the [Weingarten] right to representation might evolve differently in the private and Federal sectors"). For example, the Legislature may have decided not to extend such a representation right to Texas public-sector employees because unions in Texas lack authority to engage in collective bargaining, unlike the union in Weingarten.

JEFFERSON, J., joined by HECHT, J., and LEHRMANN, J., dissenting:

Fire fighter Jaime Rodriguez learned that his employer, the City of Round Rock, planned to interview him about a personnel complaint his chief had filed against him. The chief told Rodriguez that, at best, his alleged misreporting of 2.5 hours of sick leave could result in discipline, including termination of his employment. At worst, Rodriguez could face criminal charges. The battalion chief ordered Rodriguez not to discuss the investigation with his union president or any of its members; if Rodriguez did so, he would be subject to disciplinary action for violating a direct order. The chief ordered Rodriguez to appear in person, unrepresented, for an interview in the fire chief's office. At that interview, the chief, the assistant fire chief, and the battalion chief interrogated Rodriguez for forty-five minutes. Rodriguez asked that a union representative be permitted to attend the meeting, but the chief refused. Later, the chief met once more with Rodriguez (still unrepresented) and told him that he either had to agree to a five shift suspension and waive appellate and grievance rights, or be discharged. Rodriguez chose the former.

A Texas statute guarantees employees the right to unionize for job protection. We must decide whether that includes a "representation right," which permits an employee to have a union representative accompany him when his employer conducts an interview that foreshadows disciplinary action. For decades, private and federal employees have exercised this right, as have Texas public sector employees acting under our statute and the only existing precedent.[5] But in Texas, after today, state and local government employees must go it alone. The Court concedes that the statute permits unionization, but precludes a prime attribute that makes the union worthwhile. Precedent does not compel this anomaly. Nor does a proper reading of the relevant law. . . .

I. The Labor Code grants public employees the right, upon request, to union representation at an interview at which the employee reasonably believes he may be subject to discipline.

Largely unchanged since its passage more than a century ago, Labor Code section 101.001 states that "[a]ll persons engaged in any kind of labor may associate and form trade unions and other organizations to protect themselves in their personal labor in their respective employment." The statute does not state that employees have the right, upon request, to have a union representative participate in an internal interview when the employee reasonably believes that the interview may lead to disciplinary action. The question is whether such a right inheres in an employee's freedom to "associate and form trade unions . . . to protect themselves in their personal labor in their respective employment." *Id.*

---

5. *See Glen v. Tex. State Emps. Union-CWA/AFL-CIO,* No. 13,723 (Tex.App.-Austin Sept. 1, 1982, no writ) (not designated for publication).

Despite the statute's age, only two Texas cases have answered this question — the court of appeals' decision in this case and an earlier, unpublished decision from the same court. Both held that the statute gives an employee the right to union representation during internal interviews that might have disciplinary repercussions. . . .

Of course, we are not bound by *Weingarten*. Our statute was not based on the NLRA, nor does this case involve an appeal of an administrative decision, as *Weingarten* did. Nonetheless, the Supreme Court's interpretation of a statute very similar to our own is instructive. *See, e.g., Sayre v. Mullins*, 681 S.W.2d 25, 28 (Tex. 1984) (applying Supreme Court's interpretation of "condition of work" in NLRA to Texas statute governing grievance rights); *Lunsford v. City of Bryan*, 156 Tex. 520 (1957) (interpreting Texas's "right to work" statute in light of the Supreme Court's determination that NLRA prohibited firing employees because of union membership). . . .

The Court [In *Weingarten*] held that the right "*clearly falls within the literal wording* of [the statute] that '[employees] shall have the right . . . to engage in . . . concerted activities for the purpose of . . . mutual aid or protection.'" [420 U.S.] at 260 (emphasis added). It reasoned that although the employee's predicament may not implicate collective rights, he nevertheless seeks "aid or protection" against a perceived threat to his job. *Id.* The union representative protects not only the particular employee's interest but that of the "entire bargaining unit by exercising vigilance to make certain that the employer does not initiate or continue a practice of imposing punishment unjustly." *Id.* at 260–61 The Court noted that "the right inheres in [the statute's] guarantee of the right of employees to act in concert for mutual aid and protection." *Id.* at 256 The Court also emphasized the right's limited nature. It arises only when the employee requests representation and is a member of a labor union. Moreover, the employee's right to do so is limited to situations that he reasonably believes will lead to disciplinary action and when exercising the right does not interfere with legitimate employer prerogatives. . . .

The Court observed that union representation, much like legal representation, may advance both parties' interests. The representative can help an employee form a defense, because employees "may be too fearful or inarticulate to relate accurately the incident being investigated, or too ignorant to raise extenuating factors." *Id.* at 263. Representation at the interview is preferable to pursuing a grievance afterwards, as "it becomes increasingly difficult for the employee to vindicate himself, and the value of representation is correspondingly diminished. The employer may then be more concerned with justifying his actions than re-examining them." *Id.* at 263–64. The employer may benefit as well, because a knowledgeable representative can streamline the investigation and may promote a more informed decision.

. . . .

Our statute says employees may unionize for "protect[ion]." Tex. Lab. Code § 101.001. This case asks what that word describes. Statutes omitting that concept have been held not to convey the right to union participation in employer interviews;[10] laws that include it do.[11]

I am perplexed by the Court's conclusion that "Section 7 [of the NLRA] does not expressly confer the *Weingarten* right, and the Supreme Court recognized that." In fact, the Supreme Court held that the right *"clearly falls within the literal wording of § 7* that "[employees] shall have the right . . . to engage in . . . concerted activities for the purpose of . . . mutual aid or protection." *Weingarten*, 420 U.S. at 260 (emphasis added). Here, the Court declines to recognize a representation right in part because the Labor Code does not include the NLRA's "'concerted activities' language." But Texas has given employees not just the ability to unionize–already a constitutional right–but the right to do so *to protect themselves in their personal labor in their respective employment.*" TEX. LAB. CODE § 101.001 (emphasis added). How can unions protect employees' jobs if they cannot engage in conduct to protect employees' jobs? Rodriguez was not only denied representation during the meeting; his employer prohibited him from even seeking his union's advice, *before the meeting*, about how to defend against a disciplinary matter that could culminate in termination of his employment and criminal proceedings. To Rodriguez, the union is an oasis; to the Court, only a mirage. The *Weingarten* court agreed with Rodriguez's view, holding that the employee may bring a union representative to the meeting for "'aid or protection' against a perceived threat to his employment security." *Weingarten*, 420 U.S. at 260. I would hold, as the court of appeals did, that the Texas statute, whose language is substantially similar to the federal law, conveys the same right that *Weingarten* recognized.

The City and the chief suggest that a representation right is inconsistent with more recent legislative restrictions on Texas public employees' collective activity.

---

10. *See, e.g., Johnson v. Express One Int'l, Inc.*, 944 F.2d 247, 251 (5th Cir.1991) (holding that "the absence of the explicit right 'to engage in other concerted activities for the purpose of . . . other mutual aid or protection' in the [Railway Labor Act] proves fatal" to petitioner's claim that the Act granted the *Weingarten* right); *N.Y. City Transit Auth. v. N.Y. State Pub. Employment Relations Bd.*, 8 N.Y.3d 226 (2007) (holding that New York statute that gave public employees the right to "form, join, and participate in . . . any employee organization of their own choosing" did not confer the *Weingarten* right; "Since the 'mutual aid or protection' language is absent from [the New York statute], *Weingarten* does not support a holding that [the statute] creates a *Weingarten* right").

11. *See, e.g., City of Clearwater v. Lewis*, 404 So. 2d 1156, 1161–63 (Fla. Dist. Ct. App. 1981) (applying *Weingarten* and holding that Florida statute granting public employees the right to engage in concerted activities for "mutual aid or protection," contained language "similar" to NLRA § 7); *Town of Hudson v. Labor Relations Comm'n*, 870 N.E.2d 618, 620–21 & n.4 (Mass. 2007) (applying *Weingarten* to Massachusetts statute that granted employees the right to "engage in lawful, concerted activities for the purpose of . . . mutual aid or protection"); *Wayne-Westland Educ. Ass'n v. Wayne-Westland Community Schools*, 439 N.W.2d 372, 373 (Mich. App. 1989) (affirming state labor commission's application of *Weingarten* right under Michigan statute granting public employees the right to engage in "lawful concerted activities for the purpose of. . . . mutual aid and protection"); *Office of Admin. v. Pa. Labor Relations Bd.*, 916 A.2d 541, 548–49 (Pa. 2007) (holding that Pennsylvania statute authorizing "lawful concerted activities for the purpose of collective bargaining or other mutual aid and protection" granted the *Weingarten* right).

Texas, for example, forbids public employees from striking or bargaining collectively.[13] Tex. Gov't Code §§ 617.002, .003. But in enacting those restrictions, the Legislature also specified that it did not intend to "impair the right of public employees to present grievances concerning . . . conditions of work either individually or through a representative that does not claim the right to strike." Id. § 617.005. Rather than eliminating the representation right, these restrictions (passed decades after section 101.001) demonstrate that the Legislature knows how to limit public employee union activity when it wants to. Instead, it left Labor Code section 101.001 untouched, even in the face of a decision from the United States Supreme Court that thoroughly dissected the scope of the representation right. . . . The Court suggests—and the dissent below agreed—that *Weingarten* was premised on the employee's right to bargain collectively. . . . They assert that because Texas public employees lack that ability, our statute's right to protection should not be interpreted in the same manner. I disagree.

Weingarten was grounded not in the employee's collective bargaining rights but in "§ 7's guarantee of the right of employees to act in concert for mutual aid and protection." Although the *Weingarten* court used the phrase "bargaining unit" to describe the employees at that particular workplace, it did so because they were parties to a collective bargaining agreement, not because the phrase itself had special legal significance.

Federal courts of appeals applying *Weingarten* have rejected the notion that it was founded on the right to bargain collectively. The Third Circuit held "it . . . plain beyond cavil that the *Weingarten* right is rooted in [the NLRA's] protection of concerted activity, not [the statute's] guarantee of the right to bargain collectively." *Slaughter v. NLRB*, 794 F.2d 120, 126 (3d Cir.1986). Conversely, the Fifth Circuit concluded that a statute granting the right to bargain collectively but not the right "to engage in other concerted activities for the purpose of . . . other mutual aid or protection" did not convey the *Weingarten* right. Johnson, 944 F.2d at 251 (holding that "[t]he omission of that language is critical because the rule of *Weingarten* . . . is grounded upon it"). The Texas collective bargaining ban does not affect a public employee's right to unionize for protection, and it does not provide a basis for denying the representation right. . . .

II. Conclusion

The Texas statute was passed in 1899, a time of national labor upheaval and organized activity. Between 1881 and 1900, more than 22,000 labor strikes occurred throughout the country. . . . Five hundred seventy-four were in Texas. Of those,

---

13. There are exceptions to the ban on collective bargaining. Cities (and other political subdivisions) may authorize their fire fighters and police officers to bargain collectively. *See* Tex. Loc. Gov't Code §§ 174.023, .051. The City of Round Rock has not authorized the Fire Fighter's Association to collectively bargain, although it adopted Local Government Code chapter 143, which allows the Association to negotiate with the City. *See id.* §§ 142.101, .110.

forty involved workers striking "[a]gainst being compelled to sign [an] agreement to deal with employers as individuals instead of through [a] union"—the third most common complaint, following wage and hour disputes. Rodriguez, the Association, and a number of amici provide extensive historical detail about Texas labor relations at that time. Without repeating the specifics here, it is clear that the Legislature was aware of the right to union representation when it granted employees the ability "to associate themselves together and form trades unions and other organizations for the purpose of protecting themselves in their personal work." I would not eliminate that protection today. Because the Court does so, I respectfully dissent.

Notes

1. The majority and dissent disagree on the significance of the differences in the statutory language between the NLRA and the Texas statute. Who is more convincing on this point? Note that both opinions cite for support the *Johnson* case interpreting the Railway Labor Act.

2. This disagreement is based in significant part on differing readings of the Supreme Court's decision in *Weingarten*. Which opinion has the better reading of that case?

3. The majority also states that "the Legislature may have good reasons for treating public-sector employees in Texas differently from private sector employees," citing *Cong. of Indust. Org. v. City of Dallas*, 198 S.W.2d 143, 144 (Tex. Civ. App. 1946), for the proposition that the "status of governmental employees, National, State and Municipal, is radically different from that of employees in private business or industry." *City of Dallas* upheld a requirement that city employees sign a "yellow dog" contract agreeing not to join a union as a condition of employment. This was in the era before courts had found a constitutional right for public workers to associate in unions. For a discussion of this case and similar cases of this era, see SLATER, PUBLIC WORKERS, *supra*, 73–79. Is this case persuasive precedent that public employees today should not have *Weingarten* rights?

4. The majority came to the same conclusion as the dissent in the court of appeals decision in this case below, but not for all the same reasons. Notably, the dissent below relied in part on the reasoning of *IBM Corporation*, and the majority here did not. Again, the employees in *City of Round Rock* occupy a category that does not exist in the private sector: they are represented by a union for some purposes, but they do not have formal collective bargaining rights. Do the arguments in *IBM Corporation* about the practical inefficacy of "representatives" in a non-union environment apply to public employees who are represented for some purposes by a union but who lack collective bargaining rights? While the employees here did not have a collective bargaining agreement, the union representatives in *City of Round Rock* were experienced in representing them in other contexts. Consider this further after you've read the excerpt from the article by Professor Ann Hodges, *infra*.

VI. Diverse Models of Worker Organization

In this article, Professor Alan Hyde offers a helpful taxonomy of non-union worker advocacy organizations in support of his argument that the law should be agnostic about what kind of organizations workers choose to advance their own interests. From his descriptions, it appears that the activities of almost all of the worker organizations he identifies are engaged in forms of "concerted activity" that may be protected by the NLRA.

Alan Hyde, *New Institutions for Worker Representation in the United States: Theoretical Issues*

50 N.Y.L. Sch. L. Rev. 385 (2005)*

Labor union membership continues to decline in the United States, especially in the private sector. Meanwhile, in the last decade or so, several new organizations that advocate for working people have emerged. I will discuss many of these groups, using the term Alternative Worker Organization (AWO) to refer to all of them. The common feature that sets AWOs apart from traditional labor unions is that they function more like social movements than traditional unions. Although influential, no one type of AWO is numerically large or dominant, even in a particular industry or firm. . . .

This article proposes that all of these organizations contribute something important to the labor and organizing movements, and that these contributions will need to be considered by policymakers. The same will be true of even newer organizations that have yet to emerge. . . .

Based on the achievements of AWOs to date, there does not appear to be any compelling policy reason for the law to channel workers into one type of organization rather than another, or provide incentives such as a representational monopoly to particular types or forms of organizations — as opposed to any organization that enrolls a majority. The guiding legal principles should be tolerance of organizational diversity and pluralism, and the maintenance of basic values of democracy and organizational responsiveness.

II. The Current Organizational Landscape in the United States

It is difficult to present a coherent picture of emerging nonunion institutions of worker advocacy since many forms compete; there are no legal definitions of any, and no scholarly consensus about how to define or classify them. This article will deal with eight types of AWOs; however, this list should not be considered complete because the groups will change over time. . . .

---

1. Membership Organizations Affiliated with Labor Unions

. . . .

Unions have recently developed several affiliated organizations that directly enroll members but do not bargain for them collectively or otherwise deal with employers on their behalf. These have been organized by the national federation itself (AFL-CIO); international unions (Communication Workers); a central labor council (Working Partnerships); and a local union (Hotel and Restaurant Workers in New York City). All attempted to create different types of movements that will remain affiliated with the sponsoring labor union.

The AFL-CIO has created Working America, "A Community Affiliate of the AFL-CIO." Working America is a membership organization of individuals who affiliate with the labor movement but are not members of any particular union or represented by one for purposes of collective bargaining. Until now, Working America has only been used as a get-out-the-vote vehicle. . . . Early efforts have been successful at registering members and mobilizing them to vote for the Democratic Party. Working America has not yet tried to mobilize its members for other projects. It does not arrange face-to-face meetings among its members. Working America is directed by the central AFL-CIO; it is not controlled by its members. . . .

The Communication Workers of America (CWA) is an established union that represents workers at traditional telephone companies. CWA has set up two innovative projects to advance the interests of information professionals without representing them for purposes of collective bargaining. These have been described as "virtual unions." . . .

In some ways the most interesting AWO attempts self-consciously to form a movement for workers who are unquestionably defined as employees and could be represented through traditional union representation. Restaurant Opportunities Center New York (ROC-NY), was asked by Local 100, Hotel and Restaurant Employees (HERE), to start an independent organization to work with displaced workers after the destruction of the World Trade Center on September 11, 2001. ROC-NY was asked to coordinate social services for the surviving staff of the Windows on the World restaurant. With charitable donations coming in, the union found it convenient for accounting and disclosure purposes to create a separate entity, organized, not as a labor organization, but as a charity. Such a nonunion structure soon proved potentially useful as an organizing vehicle, particularly after the hiring of executive director Saru Jayaraman. . . .

ROC-NY has now engaged in six successful organizing campaigns at groups of fancy "white tablecloth" restaurants [which] have culminated in the signing of a contract, enforceable not as a collective bargaining agreement—since ROC-NY claims not to be a statutory "labor organization"—but as a contract under state law. The employers commit to increases in wages and benefits, settle claims of discrimination and failure to pay minimum wage or overtime, and pledge job security, including a pledge not to discharge employees without notice to ROC-NY. These agreements have been signed following lengthy campaigns marked by public demonstrations, "dinner theater" performances by students who gain admission to the restaurant as patrons, and similar media events.

I asked Saru Jayaraman why, in light of this success, it was important for ROC-NY that it not be a "labor organization," since these employers might well have recognized HERE as an exclusive representative. She mentioned three legal advantages that ROC-NY believes it gains from being a charity rather than a labor organization. First, ROC-NY does not service contracts. It does not expend resources on arbitrating grievances or owe a duty of fair representation. Second, the charity does not face the same limitations and restrictions that unions may face [such as organizational picketing]. Third, ROC-NY opened the worker-owned restaurant COLORS in Greenwich Village in January 2006. Although unions have helped organize employee trusts to own companies, the legal picture is not entirely clear, and Jayaraman thinks that it is possible that an organization that is not a labor organization might have more freedom to own a business or facilitate such employee ownership. A possible drawback that might offset the positive aspects of ROC-NY not being a labor organization might be that unions have greater freedom of political action under federal law than do charities. ROC-NY also litigates claims for restaurant workers under employment statutes, lobbies and advocates for restaurant workers, and provides classes on immigration rights and other subjects.

2. Employee Caucuses

Many large United States employers, otherwise nonunion, permit or even encourage caucuses in which African-American, Latino/a, Asian, female, or gay and lesbian employees meet to discuss common interests, assist the employer in recruiting or community efforts, and otherwise provide mutual support. Such groups are known only when individual employers permit research about them. There is no data on how widespread they are and no formal definition of them. These employee groups apparently restrict themselves to mutual support and assisting management. They rarely make any formal demands on management.

3. Benefits Provider: Working Today

Working Today . . . is a membership organization not affiliated with any union. It aspires to become a movement or lobbying organization speaking for everyone who works. Its particular focus is on independent contractors, freelancers, frequent job-changers, part-time workers, and others who fall outside the model of work often assumed by employment law and labor unions. Its current strategy of organization, typical of worker organizations of the past two centuries, is to sell health insurance and other portable benefits as a way of building membership. When reviewed by Joni Hersch in 2003, the package appeared fairly expensive, offering little advantage over plans available directly from insurance companies. "It remains to be seen whether a participatory or democratic employee organization will have any advantage over the private sector in the marketing of benefits such as health insurance. . . ."

4. Immigrants' Rights Organizations

Some organizations that provide services and advocacy for immigrant workers also speak for them on issues at work. Casa Mexico played a supporting role in attempts to organize employees of greengrocers in New York State, nearly all of whom are Mexican immigrants. The Immigrants Support Network (ISN) lobbies to protect the interest of workers in the United States under the H-1B visa program, which issues three-year visas for skilled professionals. Since advocacy organizations of this type are not statutory labor organizations, they may and do (as in the case of ISN) receive support from employers.

5. Immigrant Worker Centers

Another immigrants' advocacy organization deserves separate treatment because of the more intense level of participation it generates. At least 133 immigrant worker centers provide advocacy and social services targeted to workers of particular ethnic groups, in specific geographic communities. While such centers vary, nearly all introduce members to social services; research and report on working conditions; lobby for legal changes; advocate with government agencies; build organizations, often in coalition with other groups; and offer classes integrated with organizing. Some provide legal services and sue employers. All occasionally advocate with employers on behalf of individual workers.

6. Legal Advocacy Groups

Numerous legal advocacy groups provide representation on issues of employment law. [The article continues to discuss particular groups, such as the National Employment Law Project, that were active in organizing campaigns in New York.]

7. Government Bodies

. . . .

The [former] Attorney General of the State of New York, Eliot Spitzer, has actively used his office to challenge corporate fraud and other white-collar crimes that in the United States are often left to be prosecuted by the federal government. . . . Among his accomplishments is a bureau that is actively litigating violations of labor standards, particularly for low-wage, immigrant workers without other representation.

8. Internet and Intranet Protest

Finally, the United States has enough experience with electronic protest by employees to permit inclusion of Internet and Intranet-based protest as an eighth AWO; indeed, it is the only AWO available to most well-paid professionals.

Notes

1. As discussed in Chapter 1, the union membership rate in the private sector has been falling over the past several decades. *See* Press Release, U.S. Dep't of Labor, Union Members Summary (Jan. 23, 2015), *available at* http://www.bls.gov/news .release/union2.nr0.htm. Do these data help explain why workers might be organizing in non-traditional ways? Or are these data the result of some other social,

economic, or political force that is also channeling workers into AWOs for mutual aid and protection?

2. Are the activities of these AWOs, or the workers involved in them, protected as "concerted activity" by the NLRA's § 7? After reviewing Chapter 5's discussion of § 8(a)(2), assess whether the activities of any of these AWOs could constitute ULPs under § 8(a)(2).

3. Marion Crain and Ken Matheny argue that "[t]he best hope for a revived labor movement appears to lie with new actors such as workers' centers, community and occupational groups, and identity caucuses that can work in partnerships with established unions; class action plaintiffs' firms dedicated to enforcing workplace rights; and government agencies and attorneys general." In turn, the success of these groups' efforts depends upon "more robust constitutional protection for group action in its many forms" built on the First Amendment's freedom of assembly. Marion Crain & Ken Matheny, *Beyond Unions, Notwithstanding Labor Law*, 4 UC IRVINE L. REV. 561, 564 (2014). Are Crain and Matheny correct with respect to both parts of their argument? First, does the union movement's revival in the United States depend upon the success and expansion of AWOs? Can these non-union work organizations mature into vehicles for the exercise of aggregated worker economic power in the workplace like exclusive majority unions? And second, does the First Amendment provide the requisite protection for this success and growth? Refer back to Prof. Jim Pope's argument that the First Amendment offers a starting place, but that it must be supplemented by some additional source of constitutional protection, which he argues should be the 13th Amendment.

B. Public-Sector Organizing Without Collective Bargaining Rights

Ann Hodges, *Lessons from the Laboratory: The Polar Opposites on the Public Sector Labor Law Spectrum*
18 CORNELL J.L. & PUB. POL'Y 735 (2009)*

One of the widely touted advantages of the multiple public sector labor law regimes is that the jurisdictions serve as laboratories for experimentation and evaluation of various approaches to the complex issues involved in the field. In order for the laboratory approach to work most effectively, it is necessary to analyze the law and its impact in various jurisdictions. This Article conducts such an analysis with respect to two of the jurisdictions at opposite ends of the legal spectrum, Illinois and Virginia. . . . Illinois has a long history of public sector bargaining and has enacted two comprehensive bargaining statutes which took effect in 1984. . . . By contrast, Virginia outlawed public sector collective bargaining by court decision in

---

1977 and later confirmed the decision by statute in 1993. A comparison of the two approaches and the resulting realities in the two states provides lessons for both the remainder of the public sector and the private sector. . . .

An examination of Illinois and Virginia law and labor relations, and comparisons to the private sector, reveal that state labor law strongly affects public sector labor relations. Whether law is the cause or the effect, or more likely both, where the law is more favorable to unions and collective bargaining, unions are more prevalent and more active, and where unions are more prevalent and more active, the law is more favorable to unionization and bargaining. This conclusion provides support for those advocates and lawmakers who contend that changing the law will positively affect unionization rates and bargaining.

Equally important, however, this Article shows that parties operating in different legal regimes adapt their strategies to fit their environment. . . . The representational strategies used in Virginia's hostile legal environment share similarities with strategies that some unions and other employee advocacy groups are beginning to use in the private sector. The constant organizing done out of necessity in Virginia could also benefit unions in more traditional legal environments. Finally, more flexible and cooperative relationships may flourish in less traditional settings. The labor relations field is, and will continue to be, in a state of flux. Those that explore alternatives (lawmakers and participants in the systems alike) are more likely to have surviving and even thriving labor relations systems and relationships, and accordingly, more successful governmental and business operations.

. . . Although collective bargaining in the public sector was extensive in Illinois prior to the enactment of its labor statutes, passage of the legislation increased unionization substantially. As of 2008, 50.3% of public employees in the state were union members and 52.8% were covered by collective bargaining agreements. Average hourly earnings are $23.32 for unionized public sector workers in Illinois and $21.61 for nonunion public sector workers. . . . In terms of overall unionization, Illinois ranks third in the nation in the total number of union members in the state and tenth in the nation in percentage of workers who are union members.

A review of the law, history, and reality in Virginia shows dramatic differences from Illinois and the private sector.

As far back as 1946, the Virginia General Assembly expressed its opposition to collective bargaining for public employees in the form of a joint resolution. Nevertheless, like Illinois, Virginia has a history of collective bargaining in the public sector, at least at the local level. However, legal collective bargaining came to an abrupt halt in 1977 with the decision of the Virginia Supreme Court in Virginia v. Arlington County [holding that local public employers in Virginia lacked the power to enter into agreements with unions, even voluntarily]. . . .

Prior to this decision, nearly one-third of Virginia's teachers were covered by collective bargaining agreements, along with thousands of police officers, firefighters, and other government employees. Shortly after the Arlington County decision, the Virginia Supreme Court struck another blow to the state's teachers, ruling that binding arbitration for disputes between school boards and their employees was an unconstitutional delegation of power. . . .

Subsequent to the Arlington County decision, there were additional efforts to legalize public employee collective bargaining, but none were successful. . . .

The change in the legal climate had a dramatic effect on public sector union membership in Virginia. Between 1972 and 1978, union membership dropped from 38.5% to 19.5% of public sector workers. Despite the judicial and legislative decisions to ban binding collective bargaining, however, unions still play an active role in Virginia's public sector, albeit a much smaller role than Illinois unions play. The current percentage of public employees who are union members in Virginia is 9.3%, while 11.7% are covered by collective bargaining agreements. The average earnings of unionized public sector workers in the state are $28.81 per hour, while nonunion public sector workers average $27.29 per hour. In terms of overall union membership, Virginia ranks twenty-sixth in the number of union members and forty-eighth, very near the bottom, in the percentage of workers who are union members. The unions that are most active in Virginia's public sector are predominantly the same unions that are most active in Illinois, including affiliates of the NEA, the AFT, the International Association of Firefighters (IAFF), and AFSCME.

What options are available for unions that cannot negotiate binding collective bargaining agreements? As noted previously, employees have a constitutional right to join labor unions and these unions represent employees in a number of forums. Unions in the public sector promote legislation that favors public employees and oppose legislation that they identify as detrimental to public employees. These unions speak before legislative commissions, county boards, city councils, school boards, and other governmental bodies to advocate for employee rights. Unions also represent employees in the existing grievance procedures established by [a state] law. Such representation may obviate the need for legal representation, which can be costly for employees. The existence of the grievance procedure, while it may have been intended to forestall unionization and substitute in part for collective bargaining, provides a vehicle for unions to prove their value to current and potential members. Unions also represent employees in other legal proceedings related to their employment. In some jurisdictions, employees have even engaged in concerted activities such as "working to the rule" or taking down from the classroom all items paid for by the teachers. In short, public sector unions in Virginia, like public sector unions in Illinois and nationwide, serve as a voice for the workers they represent. In addition to representation in various legislative, judicial, and administrative forums, unions provide other value-added benefits to their members such as insurance, educational workshops, and support for families of members who have been killed or injured. Unions also engage in charitable endeavors to benefit their communities. These activities can generate support for the union. When the union needs political support, it may contact those who have benefited from union largesse to make calls and write letters to political leaders in support of union objectives.

The limits on Virginia unions, however, preclude them from negotiating binding collective bargaining agreements. Once a union in Illinois is certified as an employee representative, the focus shifts to negotiating successive contracts governing terms and conditions of employment, and administering those agreements by representing employees in the grievance and arbitration procedure. Illinois statutes allow the union to negotiate fair share provisions requiring nonmembers to pay the costs of collective bargaining, contract administration, and other activities affecting wages, hours, and conditions of employment through payroll deduction. In Virginia, by contrast, the unions must convince employees to join the union and pay dues despite the inability to negotiate a binding agreement. Unions must convince members to continue to pay dues, whereas in states like Illinois the typical contract provides for dues to be deducted from the employee's paycheck and remitted to the union. Union leaders in Virginia describe a continual need to organize the workforce. The organizing campaign does not end with certification, as it often does in states with collective bargaining and fair share rights.

Furthermore, because any agreements that are reached are nonbinding, unions in Virginia must also work continually to sustain relationships with employers and legislative bodies that control the terms and conditions of employment. Even in the absence of collective bargaining rights, however, several unions in Virginia have negotiated nonbinding memoranda of agreement with employers. According to the unions, employers generally comply with such agreements. Employers and unions in some areas of Virginia have reported healthy, productive relationships where they work together on a regular basis. . . .

Those unions that operate most effectively in Virginia are concentrated in firefighting and education—areas with strong national organizations and a strong history of organizational activity. Further, public sector unions have an advantage that private sector unions lack, as public sector unions can play a role in electing their employers through the exertion of political influence in campaigns for the same public offices that are responsible for negotiating with unions. Thus, they can mobilize political power to help them accomplish their goals by supporting candidates that are more sympathetic to unions' positions. . . .

All is not rosy for unions in Virginia, however. The unions that are thriving represent workers primarily in local government in large metropolitan areas. . . . It has been more difficult for unions to organize effectively at the state level and in smaller localities. While unions that have been able to build effective, politically savvy organizations have prospered, many employees remain without any union representation. Although some employees would not choose union representation regardless of the state of the law, there are likely other employees who would prefer union representation, yet currently have none. In addition, a downside to the lack of collective bargaining and the reliance on personal relationships to uphold agreements is, in most cases, the absence of formal written documentation of agreements. When union leadership changes, institutional memory may be lost and the status of agreements may be cast into doubt. . . .

It is clear that there are significant difficulties for unions in states where bargaining is outlawed. Union membership in such states is significantly lower than in more favorable legal environments, and the wages for many of the same positions in those states are lower as well. Nevertheless, some unions have survived in hostile legal climates such as Virginia, and some have even prospered. For example, it is interesting that public sector union membership in Virginia is higher than national private sector union membership although federal law is less hostile to collective bargaining. . . .

As indicated above, unions in Virginia are largely in the same place today as public sector unions generally were in an era when the courts and legislatures, not to mention at least some members of the public, were hostile to public sector unionization. . . .

There is a longstanding debate among scholars and legislators about the role that the law has played in the decline of unionization in the private sector. While the law is certainly not the only contributing factor in unions' loss of membership in the private sector, the comparison of Virginia and Illinois suggests that the law does have an effect on unionization rates. In Illinois, where the law is more favorable, unions have thrived in the public sector, whereas in Virginia they have struggled. However, higher unionization rates also lead to more favorable laws. Thus, where the law is not favorable, successful efforts to spread unionization may later lead to changes in the law, as unionized employees gain political power. The analysis also demonstrates that while legislation that authorizes bargaining may encourage and promote unionization, unions can succeed in representing employees without favorable legislation. Given the decline of legal protection for unionization in the private sector and the ineffectiveness of the NLRA, can the success of some unions in Virginia's public sector provide a blueprint for private sector unions, helping them to reverse the long decline in union density?

First, it must be noted that there are significant differences between the public sector and the private sector. Most public sector employees have some legal protection against termination, while most private sector employees are terminable at-will. Thus, the risks of termination for attempting to unionize are greater in the private sector and the fear of job loss may be a greater deterrent to unionization. Furthermore, public employers in general tend to be less hostile to unionization than private employers, although, as noted above, negative attitudes toward unionization in Virginia are widespread. Nevertheless, those employers that deal with unions in Virginia in the absence of legal requirements have concluded that the benefits outweigh the costs. These differences may help explain the fact that unionization is now higher in Virginia's public sector, where bargaining is outlawed, than it is in the private sector.

Second, much of the success of public sector unions in Virginia has come through the political process. While private sector employees and unions can obtain important benefits through the political process as well, the process is far less direct. Employees in the private sector can rarely directly influence their employers with political activity, while public sector employees have the potential to do so because their employers are almost always elected. At the local level, the influence is far more direct for groups like teachers, firefighters, and police officers who can participate actively in campaigns for school board members, city council representatives, county board members, and mayors. . . .

In recent years, there have been substantial efforts to organize and empower low-wage workers, who often are immigrants, outside the bounds of traditional labor unions. While these efforts have been supported by traditional unions in some cases, much of the work has been done by worker advocacy organizations and attorneys. One can scarcely imagine a group with less job security and political clout than low-wage, immigrant, and in some cases, undocumented workers. They are easily replaced, may risk deportation, do not have money to contribute to political candidates, and in some cases, cannot even vote. Yet, these organizing efforts have not been without success. . . .

These campaigns illustrate several different models of combining legal strategies with organizing to achieve protection for workers. Like the worker centers, public sector unions in Virginia, without the ability to strike or to negotiate binding collective bargaining agreements, use similar strategies of lobbying, service (including legal actions), and organizing to accomplish their goals. Traditional unions utilizing these strategies have some advantages over the worker centers. One of the major issues facing the worker centers is financing. Traditional unions can rely on member dues for financial stability if they are able to organize workers effectively or can lawfully negotiate a union security clause requiring payment of dues by bargaining unit members.

Worker centers and the most successful Virginia unions share an additional characteristic. The most successful unions in Virginia are primarily those in workplaces where the employees share not only an employer, but a profession. Many worker centers focus on employees from particular ethnic groups. Thus, both groups organize employees with shared characteristics that create bonds which may aid in organizing. . . .

Despite these differences between the public and private sectors, the Virginia experience may provide further support for alternative union strategies in the private sector. Professor [Kenneth] Dau-Schmidt has suggested that traditional collective bargaining may continue to be effective only where international competition is not a threat. The success of some Virginia public sector unions suggests that unions can survive, and in some cases thrive, without traditional bargaining. Virginia provides a model for unionization in an uncertain or even hostile legal environment. . . .

One factor that Virginia union leaders have stressed is the need for continual organizing in situations where there is no collective bargaining agreement and no union security clause. These leaders distinguished their unions from those in states which authorize bargaining in this regard, suggesting that their counterparts in other states relied on the contracts more heavily and did not feel the same need to engage in constant organizing and political activity. . . . Under this model, the union is not a servicing organization for the members; rather the union is driven by the members themselves and its members' activism leads to more successful results in disputes with management. The experience of some Virginia unions supports the conclusion that this model can be successful even where formal bargaining is not permitted. . . .

This is not to suggest the repeal of existing collective bargaining laws, nor to promote the legal approach adopted by the Virginia legislature . . . But where no collective bargaining law exists, the savvy union will seize the opportunity for employee involvement in decision-making that the union can achieve through a combination of political pressure and emphasis on the lack of risk to the employer.

Notes

1. Imagine you were a union leader or union lawyer in a state such as Virginia that barred formal collective-bargaining. What strategies and actions would you propose the union undertake to further its goals?

2. Imagine you were the head of a local public employer or a lawyer for such an employer in a state such as Virginia, and a majority of your employees (or a majority of employees in a particular job category) had joined a union. How (if at all) would you deal with the union, and why? Would it depend on certain facts? If so, which facts, and how?

3. How important is labor law? Professor Hodges points out that in Virginia, public-sector union density is much lower than in Illinois (which has a strong public-sector labor law), but Virginia's public-sector union density is higher than private-sector union density in the U.S. as a whole under the NLRA. How does she account for these numbers? How would you?

4. Professor Hodges compares some public-sector union activity in Virginia to the workers' centers and other alternative forms of worker organizing that Professor Hyde discussed in his article earlier. Are the comparisons valid? Can the private-sector groups Professor Hyde describes and the public-sector unions Professor Hodges describes learn anything useful from each other? If so, what?

5. When this article was written, it was legal for public-sector unions in many states, including Illinois, to negotiate "union security clauses" that, as in the private sector, required members of union bargaining units to pay at least some dues to the union. In 2018, the Supreme Court in *Janus v. AFSCME Council 31*, 38 S. Ct. 2448 (2018), ruled for the first time that all union security clauses in the public sector violate the First Amendment. Chapter 14 discusses this issue in detail. Consider, as you go through the public-sector materials in this book, the extent to which *Janus* limits the advantages to unions of having collective bargaining rights.

6. In 2007, the International Labor Organization (ILO), an agency of the United Nations, called on North Carolina to eliminate its bar on public-sector

collective-bargaining because it violates international labor standards regarding freedom of association and collective bargaining. Note, though, that the U.S. is not a party to the three international conventions on collective bargaining and freedom of association relied on by the ILO. Still, should the fact that the U.S. is out of step on this issue with, essentially, all other industrial democracies matter to U.S. policy-makers?

Chapter 5

Protection and Prohibition: Other Employer Responses to Organizing

I. Introduction

This chapter addresses various ways in which employers respond to union organizing drives other than through speech. It begins with the concept of exclusive, majority representation, then it discusses "company unions" and related issues under §8(a)(2). The chapter then turns to anti-union discrimination under §8(a)(3), including substantive and procedural rules, and court review of NLRB decisions. All these issues have analogs in the public sector, where the rules are often, but not always, very similar.

II. The Exclusivity Principle, "Company Unions," and Improper Employer Assistance to Unions

A. The Exclusivity Principle: The Majority Union Is the Sole and Exclusive Employee Representative

1. In the Private Sector

In the following case, the Supreme Court endorsed the view that a union, as the chosen representative of a majority of a group of employees, is the sole and exclusive representative of those employees.

J.I. Case Co. v. NLRB

The Supreme Court of the United States
321 U.S. 332, 64 S. Ct. 576, 88 L. Ed 762 (1944)

JACKSON, J.

. . . The petitioner, J. I. Case Company . . . , from 1937 offered each employee an individual contract of employment. The contracts were uniform and for a term of one year. The Company agreed to furnish employment as steadily as conditions permitted, to pay a specified rate, which the Company might redetermine if the job changed, and to maintain certain hospital facilities. The employee agreed to accept the provisions, to serve faithfully and honestly for the term, to comply with factory rules, and that defective work should not be paid for. About 75% of the employees accepted and worked under these agreements.

[T]he execution of the contracts was not a condition of employment, nor was the status of individual employees affected by reason of signing or failing to sign the contracts. It is not found or contended that the agreements were coerced, obtained by any unfair labor practice, or that they were not valid under the circumstances in which they were made.

While the individual contracts executed August 1, 1941 were in effect, a C.I.O. union petitioned the Board for certification as the exclusive bargaining representative of the production and maintenance employees. [A] hearing was held, at which the Company urged the individual contracts as a bar to representation proceedings. The Board, however, directed an election, which was won by the union. The union was . . . certified as the exclusive bargaining representative of the employees. . . .

The union then asked the Company to bargain. It refused, declaring that it could not deal with the union in any manner affecting rights and obligations under the individual contracts while they remained in effect. It offered to negotiate on matters which did not affect rights under the individual contracts, and said that upon the expiration of the contracts it would bargain as to all matters. Twice the Company sent circulars to its employees asserting the validity of the individual contracts. . . .

The Board held that the Company had refused to bargain collectively, in violation of § 8(5) . . . ; and that the contracts had been utilized . . . to impede employees in the exercise of [§ 7] rights . . . , [therefore] the Company [violated] § 8(1). . . . It ordered the Company to cease and desist from giving effect to the contracts, from extending them or entering into new ones, from refusing to bargain and from interfering with the employees; and it required the Company to give notice accordingly and to bargain upon request.

The [Seventh Circuit], with modification not in issue here, granted . . . enforcement. The issues are unsettled ones important in the administration of the Act, and we granted certiorari. . . .

. . . Collective bargaining between employer and the representatives . . . results in an accord as to terms which will cover hiring and work and pay in that unit. The result is not, however, a contract of employment except in rare cases; no one has a job by reason of it and no obligation to any individual ordinarily comes into existence from it alone. The negotiations between union and management result in what often has been called a trade agreement, rather than in a contract of employment. . . . [T]he agreement may be likened to the tariffs established by a carrier, to standard provisions prescribed by supervising authorities for insurance policies, or to utility schedules of rates and rules for service, which do not of themselves establish any relationships but which do govern the terms of the shipper or insurer or customer relationship whenever and with whomever it may be established. Indeed, in some European countries, contrary to American practice, the terms of a collectively negotiated trade agreement are submitted to a government department and if approved become a governmental regulation ruling employment in the unit.

After the collective trade agreement is made, the individuals who shall benefit by it are identified by individual hirings. The employer, except as restricted by the collective agreement itself and except that he must engage in no unfair labor practice or discrimination, is free to select those he will employ or discharge. But the terms of the employment already have been traded out. There is little left to individual agreement except the act of hiring. This hiring may be by writing or by word of mouth or may be implied from conduct. In the sense of contracts of hiring, individual contracts between the employer and employee are not forbidden, but indeed are necessitated by the collective bargaining procedure.

[A]n employee becomes entitled by virtue of the [NLRA] . . . as a third party beneficiary to all benefits of the collective trade agreement, even if on his own he would yield to less favorable terms. The individual hiring contract is subsidiary to the terms of the trade agreement and may not waive any of its benefits, any more than a shipper can contract away the benefit of filed tariffs, the insurer the benefit of standard provisions, or the utility customer the benefit of legally established rates.

Concurrent existence of these two types of agreement raises problems as to which the [NLRA] makes no express provision. . . . [I]ndividual contracts obtained as the result of an unfair labor practice may not be the basis of advantage to the violator . . . nor of disadvantage to employees. *Nat'l Licorice Co. v. NLRB*, 309 U.S. 350. But it is urged that where, as here, the contracts were not unfairly or unlawfully obtained, the court indicated a contrary rule in [other cases]. Without reviewing those cases in detail, it may be said that their decision called for nothing and their opinions contain nothing which may be properly read to rule the case before us. The court . . . did not undertake to define it or to consider the relations between lawful individual and collective agreements, which is the problem now before us.

Care has been taken in the opinions of the Court to reserve a field for the individual contract. . . . The conditions for collective bargaining may not exist; thus a majority of the employees may refuse to join a union or to agree upon or designate bargaining representatives, or the majority may not be demonstrable by the means prescribed by the statute, or a previously existent majority may have been lost without unlawful interference by the employer and no new majority have been formed. As the employer in these circumstances may be under no legal obligation to bargain collectively, he may be free to enter into individual contracts.

Individual contracts no matter what the circumstances that justify their execution or what their terms, may not be availed of to defeat or delay the procedures prescribed by the [NLRA] looking to collective bargaining, nor to exclude the contracting employee from a duly ascertained bargaining unit; nor may they be used to forestall bargaining or to limit or condition the terms of the collective agreement. 'The Board asserts a public right vested in it as a public body, charged in the public interest with the duty of preventing unfair labor practices.' *Nat'l Licorice Co. v. NLRB*, 309 U.S. at 364. Wherever private contracts conflict with its functions, they obviously must yield or the Act would be reduced to a futility.

It is equally clear since the collective trade agreement is to serve the purpose contemplated by the Act, the individual contract cannot be effective as a waiver of any benefit to which the employee otherwise would be entitled under the trade agreement. The very purpose of providing by statute for the collective agreement is to supersede the terms of separate agreements of employees with terms which reflect the strength and bargaining power and serve the welfare of the group. Its benefits and advantages are open to every employee of the represented unit, whatever the type or terms of his pre-existing contract of employment.

But it is urged that some employees may lose by the collective agreement, that an individual workman may sometimes have, or be capable of getting, better terms than those obtainable by the group and that his freedom of contract must be respected on that account. We are not called upon to say that under no circumstances can an individual enforce an agreement more advantageous than a collective agreement, but we find the mere possibility that such agreements might be made no ground for holding generally that individual contracts may survive or surmount collective ones. The practice and philosophy of collective bargaining looks with suspicion on such individual advantages. Of course, where there is great variation in circumstances of employment or capacity of employees, it is possible for the collective bargain to prescribe only minimum rates or maximum hours or expressly to leave certain areas open to individual bargaining. But except as so provided, advantages to individuals may prove as disruptive of industrial peace as disadvantages. They are a fruitful way of interfering with organization and choice of representatives; increased compensation, if individually deserved, is often earned at the cost of breaking down some other standard thought to be for the welfare of the group, and always creates the suspicion of being paid at the long-range expense of the group as a whole. Such discriminations not infrequently amount to unfair labor practices. The workman is free, if he values his own bargaining position more than that of the group, to vote against representation; but the majority rules, and if it collectivizes the employment bargain, individual advantages or favors will generally in practice go in as a contribution to the collective result. We cannot except individual contracts generally from the operation of collective ones because some may be more individually advantageous. Individual contracts cannot subtract from collective ones, and whether under some circumstances they may add to them in matters covered by the collective bargain, we leave to be determined by appropriate forums under the laws of contracts applicable, and to the Labor Board if they constitute unfair labor practices.

It also is urged that such individual contracts may embody matters that are not necessarily included within the statutory scope of collective bargaining. . . . We know of nothing to prevent the employee's, because he is an employee, making any contract provided it is not inconsistent with a collective agreement or does not amount to or result from or is not part of an unfair labor practice. But in so doing the employer may not incidentally exact or obtain any diminution of his own obligation or any increase of those of employees in the matters covered by collective agreement. . . .

As so modified the decree is . . . [a]ffirmed.

Roberts, J. is of opinion that the judgment should be reversed.

Notes

1. This case stands for the principle that the "[r]epresentatives designated or selected for the purposes of collective bargaining by the majority of employees in a unit appropriate for such purposes, shall be the exclusive representative of all the employees in such unit for the purposes of collective bargaining in respect to rates of pay, wages, hours of employment, or other conditions of employment." 29 U.S.C. § 159(a). In other words, the "majority" representative is also the "exclusive" representative. According to Thomas Kohler, *Individualism and Communitarianism at Work*, 1993 B.Y.U. L. Rev. 727, 733–34:[*]

> The so-called exclusivity principle bottoms the American model of collective bargaining. It also marks one of the starkest differences between the American and Continental industrial-relations systems. The exclusivity principle rests on the idea of majority rule. The principle establishes the association formed by a majority of employees in the affected workplace unit as the exclusive representative of them all. The principle prohibits an employer from attempting to bypass the majority-designated representative by unilaterally changing the terms or conditions of employment, or by dealing with individuals or groups of employees independently of the union. The preferred status the majority-representative enjoys in this scheme carries with it the legally enforceable obligation to represent all employees fairly and even-handedly, regardless of their support for or membership in the union.

> The exclusivity doctrine prevents the fragmentation and dissolution of the strength employees achieve through collective action. It thereby acts to protect the principles of majoritarianism that underpin the Act's scheme. The exclusivity principle reflects the fact that American workers generally organize and bargain on a workplace or employer basis, and not at an industry-wide or national level. To a substantial degree, the principle is a function of the emphasis in American-style collective bargaining on local, "bottoms-up" law-making. The centrality of exclusivity to the Act's scheme reveals the statute's preoccupation with the removal of impediments to the free formation of autonomous, self-organized employee associations.

2. By the time this case arrived in the Supreme Court, the individual contracts would have expired. Why then was this case not moot? The Court concluded that the case was not moot "[i]n view of the continuing character of the obligation imposed by the Board's order." What did the Court mean by that?

---

3. The Court explains that collective-bargaining agreements do not result in a contract of employment. Instead, the Court observes that a collective-bargaining agreement is more like a trade agreement than an employment contract. What does the Court mean by drawing this analogy? *Cf. Spearfish Educ. Ass'n v. Spearfish School Dist.*, 780 N.W.2d 481 (S.D. 2010) ("'[N]o one has a job by reason of [a collective-bargaining agreement] and no obligation to any individual ordinarily comes into existence from it alone.'" The trade agreement is a contract between the union and the organization. "'After the collective trade agreement is made, the individuals who shall benefit by it are identified by individual hiring.'") (quoting *Sisseton Educ. Ass'n v. Sisseton Sch. Dist. No. 54-8*, 516 N.W.2d 301, 303 (S.D. 1994) (internal citations omitted).)

4. Assuming that not all workers are equally skilled, union critics claim that middling workers most benefit from a collective-bargaining agreement. These critics argue that unions create mediocrity. According to this view, because higher-skilled workers could have negotiated a better deal on their own, and lower-skilled workers could not have negotiated as good a deal, the higher-skilled workers essentially have surrendered some of what they could have negotiated in exchange for solidarity. If this is true, why would higher-skilled workers do that (as opposed to, say, seeking out non-union employers)? *See Collins v. City of Manchester*, 797 A.2d 132, 135 (N.H. 2002) (noting that, while more favorable contracts for higher-skilled workers may be permissible under *J.I. Case*, such contracts might be undesirable as they prove divisive and threaten worker solidarity) (citing *J.I. Case Co.*, 321 U.S. at 338–39). For an example of this potential conflict playing out in the context of the United Auto Workers representation of skilled trades, see https://bit.ly/2B28Mdt. Could this issue be addressed with separate bargaining units for the more skilled and lesser skilled workers? (For a discussion of bargaining units, see Chapter 8.)

5. This case cements the idea that individual contracts may have different meanings in the unionized context. For example, the Court in *J.I. Case* holds that collective-bargaining agreements, like tariff agreements, essentially override individual contracts. There are several corollaries of this holding.

a. The most prominent of these corollaries is the bar on direct dealing: Employers may not deal directly with their employees, thereby bypassing the employees' union as representative. As reviewing courts have repeatedly recognized:

> [T]he prohibition on direct dealing is nearly as old as the Act itself. The Supreme Court made clear . . . that an employer cannot bypass the union on matters at the very core of mandatory bargaining: "[I]t is a violation of the essential principle of collective bargaining and an infringement of the Act for the employer to disregard the bargaining representative by negotiating with individual employees . . . with respect to wages, hours and working conditions." *Retlaw Broadcasting Co. v. NLRB*, 172 F.3d 660, 667 (9th Cir. 1999) (quoting *Medo Photo Supply Corp. v. NLRB*, 321 U.S. 678, 684 (1944) (reiterating rule of *J.I. Case Co. v. NLRB*, 321 U.S. 332 (1944))).

b. The Act's prohibition on direct dealing is another way of stating the "exclusivity principle": Unions are the exclusive bargaining representatives of those in the bargaining unit. (For a discussion of bargaining units, see Chapter 8.)

c. Collective-bargaining agreements thereby create a floor of rights below which employers and individuals may not agree to dip. Does this mean that collective-bargaining agreements create both a floor and a ceiling of rights? Consider the relationship between professional baseball players' agents and the Major League Baseball Players Association. In that scenario, an individual player is permitted to hire an agent to secure more favorable terms and conditions of employment so long as the Association authorizes the agent to act for such purposes. *See 2017–2021 Basic Agreement*, Art. IV, A, https://www.mlbplayers.com/cba ("A player, if he so desires, may designate an agent to conduct on his behalf, or to assist him in, the negotiation of an individual salary and/or Special Covenants to be included in his Uniform Player's Contract . . . provided such agent has been certified to the Clubs by the Association as authorized to act as a Player Agent for such purposes.") What part of the *J.I. Case* permits this type of relationship?

d. Employees are not protected when they seek to bypass the union to deal directly with the employer. In *Emporium Capwell Co. v. W. Addition Cmty. Org.*, 420 U.S. 50 (1975), several African-American workers sought to bypass the union by bargaining directly with the employer over racial discrimination in the workplace. The Court, in an opinion by the greatest civil rights lawyer in American history, Justice Thurgood Marshall, noted that, because the employees' collective-bargaining agreement contained a clause prohibiting racial discrimination, the employees' proper course of action was to pursue the collective-bargaining agreement's grievance-arbitration procedures. The Court thereby held that the employer did not violate the Act when it discharged the employees for ignoring the grievance-arbitration machinery and picketing the employer's premises to publicize the employer's racist policies. The Court explained:

> National labor policy has been built on the premise that by pooling their economic strength and acting through a labor organization freely chosen by the majority, the employees of an appropriate unit have the most effective means of bargaining for improvements in wages, hours, and working conditions. The policy therefore extinguishes the individual employee's power to order his own relations with his employer and creates a power vested in the chosen representative to act in the interests of all employees. 'Congress has seen fit to clothe the bargaining representative with powers comparable to those possessed by a legislative body both to create and restrict the rights of those whom it represents. . . .' *Emporium Capwell*, 420 U.S. at 63 (quoting *Steele v. Louisville & Nashville R.R. Co.*, 323 U.S. 192, 202 (1944)).

The *Emporium Capwell* Court further reiterated that "only the union may contract the employee's terms and conditions of employment, and provisions for processing his grievances. . . ." *Id.* at 64 (citing *NLRB v. Allis-Chalmers Mfg. Co.*, 388 U.S. 175, 180 (1967)).

In reaching these conclusions, the Court dismissed in a footnote the contention that the African-American workers could rely on the proviso to § 9(a), 29 U.S.C. § 159(a). That proviso states: "Provided, That any individual employee or a group of employees shall have the right at any time to present grievances to their employer and to have such grievances adjusted, without the intervention of the bargaining representative, as long as the adjustment is not inconsistent with the terms of the collective-bargaining contract or agreement then in effect: Provided further, That the bargaining representative has been given opportunity to be present at such adjustment." The Court noted:

> Respondent clearly misapprehends the nature of the "right" conferred by this section. The intendment of the proviso is to permit employees to present grievances and to authorize the employer to entertain them without opening itself to liability for dealing directly with employees in derogation of the duty to bargain only with the exclusive bargaining representative, a violation of 8(a)(5) .... The Act nowhere protects this "right" by making it an unfair labor practice for an employer to refuse to entertain such a presentation, nor can it be read to authorize resort to economic coercion.... If the employees' activity in the present litigation is to be deemed protected, therefore, it must be so by reason of the reading given to the main part of 9(a), in light of Title VII and the national policy against employment discrimination, and not by burdening the proviso to that section with a load it was not meant to carry. *Emporium Capwell*, 420 U.S. at 61, note 12.

6. The bar on direct dealing applies regardless of whether the employer or the employees initiated the dealing. In *Medo Photo Supply Corp. v. NLRB*, 321 U.S. 678 (1944), the Court held that the employer "was not relieved from its obligations [to bargain with the union] because the employees asked that they be disregarded." There, the employer was engaged in wage negotiations with a properly designated union. The parties had set a meeting date at which those negotiations were to take place. Prior to the meeting, several employees approached the employer and requested a wage increase for all employees. The company agreed and thereafter refused to negotiate with the union. In finding a violation of the Act, the Supreme Court held that "[t]he statute was enacted in the public interest for the protection of the employees' right to collectively bargain and it may not be ignored by the employer, even [with] the employees' consent...." *Id.* at 687 (citations omitted).

Courts have routinely applied *Medo* to prohibit direct dealings between employers and represented employees. *See, e.g., Hajoca Corp. v. NLRB*, 872 F.2d 1169, 1176 (3d Cir.1989) ("An employer who attempts an end run around a certified union's bargaining representatives and negotiates directly with employees violates section 8(a)(5) and (1)."); *Szabo v. U.S. Marine Corp.*, 819 F.2d 714, 718 (7th Cir.1987) ("[T]he employer is not to go behind the union's back and negotiate with individual workers, nor otherwise to undermine the union's status as exclusive bargaining representative."); *Queen Mary Restaurants Corp. v. NLRB*, 560 F.2d 403, 407–08 (9th Cir. 1977) (employer who held a meeting and granted increased seniority to employees in attendance without consulting properly authorized union violated *Medo*); *NLRB v. General Elec. Co.*, 418 F.2d 736, 755 (2d Cir.1969) ("The vice that *Medo* sought to avoid was the practice of undermining the authority of the union's bargaining representatives through direct dealings with the locals or employees they represented.").

7. *J.I. Case* recognizes that, under normal circumstances, when employers increase wages or confer more favorable terms of employment on some employees for certain reasons, it can create adverse effects on a group of employees as a whole. Does this logic apply to entire industries? If so, does this highlight a need for industry-wide unionization? *See* L. Hamburger, *The Extension of Collective Agreements to Cover Entire Trade and Industries*, 40 INT'L LABOR REV. 153, 154–57 (1939). For a current discussion of this issue *see Clean Slate for Worker Power: Building a Just Economy and Democracy* (at 37–45), available at https://bit.ly/37XSdLJ (discussing sectoral representation and bargaining).

8. In *International Ladies' Garment Workers' Union v. NLRB* (*Bernhard-Altmann Texas Corp.*), 366 U.S. 731 (1961), discussed further in Chapter 8, the Court held that an employer violates §8(a)(2) and (1) and a union violates §8(b)(1)(A) when the employer recognizes the union as the exclusive bargaining representative before the union enjoys majority support. This is so even in cases where the union obtains majority support before the parties enter into a collective-bargaining agreement. See Chapter 8 for a broader discussion of this issue.

2. In the Public Sector

The majority, exclusive representative model is ubiquitous in the public sector. "The principle of exclusive representation is considered fundamental in our labor law. . . . The principle has been carried over from the private sector to the public sector. . . ." Clyde Summers, *Bargaining in the Government's Business: Principles and Politics*, 18 U. TOL. L. REV. 265, 269 (1987). *See, e.g.*, OHIO REV. CODE ANN. §§4117.04, 4117.05. Where public workers lack the statutory authority to bargain collectively, unions and employers might be able to deal with each other on a different basis. But statutes that provide for public-sector collective bargaining use the exclusive, majority model. As in the private sector, this principle implicates issues of employer domination (discussed in subsection II-B, *infra*), and the duty of fair representation (discussed in Chapter 14).

The public-sector context did raise a constitutional issue. Does an exclusive representation system for bargaining or other forms of negotiation violate the First Amendment right of individuals or groups excluded from such negotiations? In *Minnesota State Board for Community Colleges v. Knight*, 465 U.S. 271 (1984), the Supreme Court held that it did not. The case involved Minnesota's statutory authorization of a "meet and confer" negotiation system for professional employees (for more on "meet and confer" in the public sector, see Chapter 10). This system relied on an exclusive, majority representation system. The Court explained this did not violate the First Amendment. "The Constitution does not grant to members of the public generally a right to be heard by public bodies making decisions of policy." 465 U.S. 271, 283. The voice of the union may have been "amplified" through the exclusive representative process, but such amplification "is inherent in government's freedom to choose its advisors. A person's right to speak is not infringed when government simply ignores that person while listening to others." *Id.* at 288. (New lawsuits challenging public-sector exclusive representation under the First Amendment are discussed in Chapter 14.)

Also, a possible exception may be emerging in Missouri. As Chapter 1 explained, in *Independence Nat'l Educ. Ass'n v. Independence Sch. Dist.*, 223 S.W.3d 131 (Mo. 2007), the Missouri Supreme Court interpreted a clause in the state's constitution to mean that public workers had a right to "collective bargaining." But this case did not define what "collective bargaining" meant, and as of this writing, the Missouri legislature has not defined it in a statute. Missouri does have a public-sector labor statute, enacted in the 1960s, but it excludes significant groups of public employees (*e.g.*, police and teachers). Thus, many public employees in Missouri have a constitutional right to bargain collectively with no definition of that right.

Relevant here, in *Springfield Nat'l Educ. Ass'n v. Springfield Bd. of Educ.*, Case No. 0931-CV08322 (Cir. Ct. Greene Cty, MO, Sept. 10, 2009), a school board in Missouri created a system for union recognition in which teachers could choose to have more than one union represent them at the same time. This was not a "minority union" system in which multiple unions could represent different teachers within a school system. This option would have been a departure from the "majority" part of "exclusive majority representative" and the "exclusive" part. The court rejected the union's challenge to this option, but this decision was effectively mooted after the teachers, in the subsequent representation election, chose the option of a single, exclusive majority union representative. Still, the case allowing multiple representation is still good law. How do you think such a system would function, in practice?

In contrast, in *Bayless Educ. Ass'n v. Bayless School Dist.*, Case No. 09SL-CC01481 (Cir. Ct. St. Louis, Feb. 10, 2010), a union successfully challenged a different process. There the employer required employees in each school in the district to select two individual representatives and two alternates; these representatives, plus one representative designated by the union with the largest employee membership, would then be allowed, as a group, to bargain with the employer. *Bayless* held this did not satisfy the constitutional right to bargain collectively. The court distinguished *Springfield* by noting that in *Springfield*, employees were at least permitted to choose a traditional exclusive representative. Further, the system in *Bayless* "mandates collaborative bargaining, not collective bargaining through a union representative."

Are alternative forms of employee representation superior to exclusive representation, or are some at least worth a try? Recall from Chapter 1 that in 2011, Tennessee revised its statute regarding teachers to change from "collective bargaining" to "collaborative conferencing," and under this new process, teachers can be represented in the "conferencing" process by any group that receives support of at least 15 percent of a group of teachers. What are the pros and cons of such a system?

Consider it both with and without the additional restrictions Tennessee puts on the collaborative conferencing process described in Chapter 1. Consider the broader issue of alternative forms of representation further when you read Chapter 8.

B. Interference and Domination — The Company Union

1. In the Private Sector

In this section, we examine the extent to which an employer violates §8(a)(2) when it consciously sets up an employee group, often in response to employee grievances about workplace issues. This issue has its origins in the "company union" problem in the pre-NLRA era. As Chapter 1 discussed, before the NLRA was passed, many employers created "company unions" (often called "employee representation plans"). These were employee organizations which the employer created and controlled, at least often to avoid unionization by independent labor organizations, especially those affiliated with the AFL. Employers often hand-picked the leaders of these groups, and they had no legally enforceable rights. For an example of this surviving into the NLRA era, see *Edward G. Budd Manufacturing Co. v. NLRB*, 138 F.2d 86 (3d Cir. 1943), *infra*.

Senator Wagner made it clear that a principle purpose of the NLRA was to outlaw company unions. "The development of the company-dominated union has been one of the great obstacles to genuine freedom of organization." 1 NLRB LEGISLATIVE HISTORY OF THE NLRA, 1935, at 1416. The relevant Senate Committee explained:

> The so-called "company union" features of the bill are designed to prevent interference by employers with organizations of their workers that serve or might serve as collective bargaining agencies. Such interference exists when employers actively participate in framing the constitution or bylaws of labor organizations. . . . It exists when they participate in the internal management or elections of a labor organization. . . . It is impossible to catalog all the practices that might constitute interference, which may rest upon subtle but conscious economic pressure exerted by virtue of the employment relationship. The question is one of fact in each case. . . . REPORT OF THE SENATE COMMITTEE ON EDUCATION AND LABOR, S. REP. 573, (74th Cong., 1st Sess., 1935), at 9–11.

The specific section of the NLRA addressing this issue is §8(a)(2), originally, §8(2). Section 8(a)(2), in relevant part, makes it an unfair labor practice for an employer "to dominate or interfere with the formation or administration of any labor organization or contribute financial or other support to it."

This means that there are two issues in many §8(a)(2) cases. First, is the group a "labor organization" within the meaning of the NLRA? Second, if the group is a statutory labor organization, did the employer dominate or interfere with its formation or administration, or contribute prohibited aid to it under the facts presented by the case?

Section 2(5) defines a "labor organization" as:

> any organization of any kind, or any agency or employee representation committee or plan, in which employees participate and which exists for the purpose, in whole or in part, of dealing with employers concerning grievances, labor disputes, wages, rates of pay, hours of employment, or conditions of work. 29 U.S.C. § 152(5).

The Supreme Court has long held that the Board must be given great latitude in constructing this statutory definition. *See Marine Engineers Beneficial Ass'n v. Interlake S.S. Co.*, 370 U.S. 173, 181–82 (1962); *NLRB v. Cabot Carbon Co.*, 360 U.S. 203, 211 & n.7 (1959). The Board has determined that an employee group or committee constitutes a statutory labor organization if that committee involves: "(1) employee participation, (2) a purpose to *deal with* employers, (3) concerning itself with conditions of employment or other statutory subjects, and (4) if an 'employee representation committee or plan' is involved, evidence that the committee is in some way representing the employees." *Electromation, Inc.*, 309 N.L.R.B. 990, 996 (1992) (emphasis added), *enf'd*, 35 F.3d 1148 (7th Cir. 1994).

While the type of company unions that existed before the NLRA are mostly a thing of the past, § 8(a)(2) has considerable importance in modern labor law, primarily because of certain management theories which became popular beginning in the 1980s. Specifically, employers started to promote mechanisms for group employee input (called, *e.g.*, "employee participation programs" or "quality circles"). The motivations in some cases were, as in the past, to avoid unionization by true, independent unions affiliated with the labor movement. In other cases, however, the motivation was to seek some type of collective employee input (albeit typically in a manner that the employer could ignore if it wished).

Proponents of these groups make the following three arguments. First, the economy and the workplace in America has changed dramatically such that a greater percentage of the workforce now needs more skills and has more responsibility. In this environment, it is important to be able to communicate with employees and encourage their input. Second, a decreasing minority of private-sector workers are represented by unions, so another model for employee input is needed. Third, the model of labor relations in the Wagner Act is too adversarial. Workers and managers should not think of each other as opponents; instead the two sides should focus on cooperation, which would be good for everyone and the economy as a whole.

Unions and some others remain skeptical. They argue that there already is a method for worker input: collective bargaining under the NLRA. This model would work well in more cases if private-sector employers had not taken such an adversarial stance toward unions and were not acting so aggressively against them (*see* Chapter 3 and Chapter 11). Moreover, these aggressive anti-union tactics cast doubt on employer claims that they really seek genuine cooperation. Finally, skeptics argue that these new participation groups will be like the old company unions: they will have leaders the employer hand-picks and no enforceable rights.

These competing concerns, and § 8(a)(2), came to a head in the following, leading modern case on the issue.

Electromation, Inc. v. NLRB

The United States Court of Appeals for the Seventh Circuit
35 F.3d 1148 (7th Cir. 1994)

WILL, DISTRICT JUDGE, sitting by designation.

[W]e consider a petition to set aside and a cross-petition to enforce an [NLRB] order . . . , which found that the petitioner employer, Electromation, Inc. (the "company"), violated Section 8(a)(2) and (1) of the [NLRA] through its establishment and administration of "action committees" consisting of employees and management. . . . [W]e . . . [enforce] the Board's order. . . .

Electromation manufactures . . . small electrical and electronic components and related products . . . primarily for the automobile industry and for power equipment manufacturers. . . . Electromation's approximately 200 employees, most of whom were women, [are] not represented by any labor organization. To minimize . . . financial losses . . . , the company in late 1988 decided to cut expenses by revising its employee attendance policy and replacing the 1989 scheduled wage increases with lump sum payments based on the length of each employee's service at the company. Electromation informed its employees of these changes at the 1988 employee Christmas party.

In January 1989, the company received a handwritten request signed by 68 employees expressing their dissatisfaction with and requesting reconsideration of the revised attendance bonus/wage policy. After meeting with the company's supervisors, the company President, John Howard, decided to meet directly with employees to discuss their concerns. [Thereafter], the company met with eight employees—three randomly selected high-seniority employees, three randomly selected low-seniority employees, and two additional employees who had requested that they be included—to discuss a number of matters, including wages, bonuses, incentive pay, tardiness, attendance programs, and bereavement and sick leave policy, all normal collective bargaining issues.

Following this meeting, Howard met again with the supervisors and concluded that management had "possibly made a mistake in judgment in December in deciding what we ought to do." Because Howard concluded that "it was very unlikely that further unilateral management action to resolve these problems was going to come anywhere near making everybody happy . . . [and] that the better course of action would be to involve the employees in coming up with solutions to these issues," the company determined that "action committees" would be an appropriate way to involve employees in the process. . . . [T]he company met again [on January 18] with the same eight employees and Howard explained that the management had distilled the employees' complaints, which had addressed approximately 20–25 areas of concern, into five categories and proposed the creation of action committees to "meet and try to come up with ways to resolve these problems; and that if they came up with solutions that . . . we believed were within budget concerns and they generally felt would be acceptable to the employees, that we would implement these suggestions or proposals."

The employees at the January 18 meeting initially reacted negatively to the concept of action committees. . . . Howard then explained to them that because "the business was in trouble financially . . . we couldn't just put things back the way they were . . . we don't have better ideas at this point than to sit down and work with you on them." According to Howard, as the meeting progressed, the employees "began to understand that [the action-committees proposal] was far better than leaving things as they were, and we weren't going to just unilaterally make changes. And so they accepted it." At the employees' suggestion, Howard agreed that . . . sign-up sheets for each action committee would be posted.

On the next day, the company posted [sign-up sheets and] a memorandum to all employees announcing the formation of the following five action committees: (1) Absenteeism/Infractions; (2) No Smoking Policy; (3) Communication Network; (4) Pay Progression for Premium Positions; and (5) Attendance Bonus Program. . . . Each committee was to consist of up to six employees and one or two members of management, as well as the company's Employee Benefits Manager, Loretta Dickey, who was in charge of the coordination of all the committees. . . . Dickey's role was primarily to facilitate the discussions between the company and its employees. Although the sign-up sheets also stated the goals of each action committee, no employees were involved in the drafting of any aspect of the memorandum or the statement of subjects that the committees were to consider.

The company also unilaterally decided that two employees who had signed up for more than one committee would be limited to participation on only one committee. . . .

Shortly thereafter, the company posted a memorandum announcing the members of each committee and dates of the initial committee meetings. . . . Dickey apparently made the final determination of which employees would participate on each committee. Five employees were eventually chosen to serve on each committee. The employees were not given an opportunity to vote on Dickey's selection of employee committee members. Each committee also included at least one supervisor or manager in addition to Dickey.

The No Smoking Policy Committee was never organized and apparently held no meetings. In late January and early February 1989, each of the other action committees began to meet. All committee meetings took place [weekly] on company premises. . . . Each committee elected a secretary to take notes. The company paid employees for their time spent in committee meetings and provided all necessary materials and supplies, such as files, pencils, paper, and telephones. . . . [M]anagement expected that the employee members of the committees would "kind of talk back and forth" with the other employees in the plant because "anyone

[who] wanted to know what was going on, they [could] go to these people." . . . [A]t least one update memorandum was posted which described the activities of the action committees. . . . The update memorandum was drafted by management without consultation with the employee members of each committee.

During the Attendance Bonus Committee's first meeting, Dickey and Electromation's Controller, Dan Mazur, solicited employee ideas regarding a good employee attendance award program. Their goal was to develop an attendance program which would be both affordable to the company and satisfactory to the employees. Through the discussions, the committee developed a proposal, which was declared by Mazur to be too costly and was not pursued further for that reason. Because the first proposal had been rejected, the committee developed a second proposal, which was deemed fiscally sound by Mazur. However, due to the intervening demand for union recognition, the second proposal was never presented to Howard and no responsive action by the company was ever taken.

On February 13, 1989, the International Brotherhood of Teamsters, Local Union No. 1049 (the "union") demanded recognition from the company. . . . In late February, Howard informed Dickey of the union's demand for recognition. . . . Dickey announced at the next meeting of each committee that, due to the union demand, the company could no longer participate in the committees, but that the employee members could continue to meet if they so desired.

The Absenteeism/Infraction and the Communication Network Committees continued to meet. The Pay Progression Committee disbanded. The Attendance Bonus Committee decided to write up its second proposal and then to disband. Finally, on March 15, 1989, Howard formally announced to the employees that "due to the Union's campaign, the Company would be unable to participate in the [committee] meetings and could not continue to work with the committees until after the [union] election." The union election took place on March 31, 1989; the employees voted 95 to 82 against union representation. On April 24, 1989, a regional director of the Board issued a complaint alleging that Electromation had violated the Act. . . .

The Board . . . found that the action committees constituted labor organizations within the meaning of Section 2(5) . . . , and that the company had dominated and assisted them within the meaning of Section 8(a)(2) and (1). . . .

The Board also concluded that the employee committee members acted in a representational capacity within the meaning of the Act. . . . Noting that (1) the employer initiated the idea to create the committees, (2) the employer unilaterally drafted the written purposes and goals statements of the committees, (3) the employer unilaterally determined how many members would compose each committee and that an employee could serve on only one committee at a time, and (4) the employer appointed management representatives to the committees to facilitate the discussions, the Board found that the company had violated Section 8(a)(2) and (1) of the Act by dominating the formation and administration of, and contributing financial and other support to, the action committees. . . .

The Board concluded . . . that the committees were the creation of the employer and that the impetus for their continued existence rested solely with Electromation. . . . [T]he purpose of the action committees was not to enable management and employees to cooperate to improve quality or efficiency, but rather to create in employees the impression that their disagreements with management had been resolved bilaterally, where in fact the employer had imposed on its employees a unilateral form of bargaining in violation of Sections 8(a)(2) and (1). . . .

An allegation that Electromation has violated Section 8(a)(2) and (1) . . . raises two distinct issues: first, whether the action committees in this case constituted "labor organizations" within the meaning of Section 2(5); and second, whether the employer dominated, influenced, or interfered with the formation or administration of the organization or contributed financial or other support to it, in violation of Section 8(a)(2) and (1) of the Act. Each issue will be examined in turn.

A. The Action Committees Constituted Labor Organizations

. . . Under th[e] statutory definition [of § 2(5)], the action committees would constitute labor organizations if: (1) the Electromation employees participated in the committees; (2) the committees existed, at least in part, for the purpose of "dealing with" the employer; and (3) these dealings concerned "grievances, labor disputes, wages, rates of pay, hours of employment, or conditions of work."

[T]he Board . . . noted that "if the organization has as a purpose the representation of employees, it meets the statutory definition of 'employee representation committee or plan' under Section 2(5) and will constitute a labor organization if it also meets the criteria of employee participation and dealing with conditions of work or other statutory subjects." . . . Because the Board found that the employee members of the action committees had acted in a representational capacity, it did not decide whether an employee group could ever be found to constitute a labor organization in the absence of [such] a finding. . . .

With respect to the first factor, there is no question that the Electromation employees participated in the action committees. Turning to the second factor, which is the most seriously contested on appeal, the Board found that the activities of the action committees constituted "dealing with" the employer. [T]he company primarily argues that the Board erred in finding that Section 8(a)(2) was violated. [In the] alternative . . . , the company contends that there is not substantial evidence to support the finding that at least three of the action committees—the Absenteeism/Infractions Committee, the Communication Network Committee, and the Pay Progression for Premium Positions Committee—existed for the purpose of "dealing with" Electromation. [T]he company concedes . . . that there is enough evidence to support a finding that the fourth committee—the Attendance Bonus Program Committee—existed for the purpose of dealing with the company. . . . The company argues that the other three action committees existed only as simple communication devices not engaged in collective bargaining of any sort, so they are not labor organizations under the statutory definition.

Although the company admits that one action committee constituted a labor organization, it argues that each committee must be considered separately under Section 2(5). Given the facts surrounding the formation and administration of all the action committees in this case, we cannot treat each committee separately. First, in their formation and administration, the individual committees were constituted as part of a single entity or program. They were initially conceived as an integrated employer response to deal with growing employee dissatisfaction. It was not until later that individual committee subject areas were identified and categorized by management. Also, a single management representative, Loretta Dickey, was assigned the responsibility for coordinating all action committee activities. The interrelatedness of these committees is further demonstrated by the company's determination that an employee could serve on only one committee at a time.

The company in fact posted only a single announcement identifying the members of each committee. Without consulting each committee individually, Dickey drafted a single statement summarizing the contemplated activities of all the committees. We agree with the Board that the action committees can be differentiated only in the specific subject matter with which each dealt. Each committee had an identical relationship to the company: the purpose, structure, and administration of each committee was essentially the same.

. . . [I]n addition, . . . even if the committees are considered individually, there exists substantial evidence that each was formed and existed for the purpose of "dealing with" the company. [T]he shared similarities among the committee structures . . . compel[] unitary treatment of them for the purposes of the issues raised in this appeal.

The company argues in favor of a narrow construction of "labor organization" under the Act. However, as the Board noted, Congress phrased the statutory definition of labor organizations "very broadly." . . . This Court has interpreted this definition very broadly as well. For example, relying on congressional intent, we have previously held that a labor organization need not have officers, a constitution, bylaws, dues, or a treasury in order to fit the statutory definition. . . .

We have previously noted that the broad construction of labor organization applies not only with regard to the "absence of formal organization, [but also to] the type of interchange between parties which may be deemed 'dealing'" with employers. . . . [A]n organization may satisfy the statutory requirement that it exist for the purpose in whole or in part of dealing with employers even if it has not engaged in actual bargaining or concluded a bargaining agreement. . . .

In *Cabot Carbon*, the Supreme Court expressly rejected the contention that "dealing with" means "bargaining with," noting that Congress had declined to accept a proposal to substitute the phrase "bargaining with" for "dealing with" under Section 2(5). . . .

First, the [*Cabot Carbon*] Court found that nothing in the plain words of Section 2(5), its legislative history, or the decisions construing it, supported the contention that an employee committee which does not "bargain with" employers in the usual concept of collective bargaining does not engage in "dealing with" employers and, therefore, is not a labor organization. . . . [T]he legislative history of Section 2(5) "strongly confirms that Congress did not understand or intend those terms to be synonymous." . . . [W]hen the original print of the Wagner bill . . . was being considered in the Senate, the then Secretary of Labor proposed an amendment to Section 2(5), which sought to substitute the term "bargaining collectively" for "dealing." . . . [B]y adopting the broader term "dealing with" and rejecting the more limited term "bargaining collectively," Congress clearly did not intend that the broad term "dealing with" should be limited to and mean only "bargaining with." . . .

The Court further noted that, with full knowledge of the terms of Section 2(5) . . . , as well as its legislative history and judicial construction, Congress in the 1947 Taft-Hartley Act re-enacted Section 2(5) without change. The Court observed that several courts . . . had uniformly held that employee committees . . . were labor organizations. . . . Because the employee committees "made proposals and requests respecting such matters as seniority, job classification, job bidding, working schedules, holidays, vacations, sick leave, a merit system, wage corrections, and improvement of working facilities and conditions," the Court concluded that they existed for the purpose of "dealing with" the employer. . . .

[T]he [*Cabot Carbon*] Court also considered whether Congress by its 1947 amendment of Section 9(a) eliminated employee participation committees from the term "labor organization" as defined in Section 2(5) and used in Section 8(a) (2). In concluding that it did not, the Court rejected the argument that Congress intended by its amendment to Section 9(a), which provided in pertinent part that "any individual employee or a group of employees shall have the right at any time to present grievances to their employer," . . . to approve inferentially what was expressly rejected by the House. The proposed new section, to be designated Section 8(d)(3), if adopted, would have permitted an employer to form or maintain "a committee of employees and discuss[ ] with it matters of mutual interest, including grievances, wages, hours of employment, and other working conditions, if the Board has not certified or if the employer has not recognized a representative as their representative under section 9." . . . Such an argument . . . overlooks the facts (1) . . . that "[t]he conference agreement does not make any change" in the definition of "labor organization," . . . and (2) that the conferees specifically rejected all attempts to "amend[ ] the provisions in subsection 8(2) relating to company-dominated unions . . ." and had left its prohibitions "unchanged," . . .

The Supreme Court in *Cabot Carbon* clearly held that the later amendment of Section 9(a) provided only that any individual employee or group of employees should have the right personally to present their own grievances to their employer, and to have such grievances adjusted, without the intervention of any bargaining representative, as long as the adjustment was not inconsistent with the terms of any collective bargaining contract then in effect, and the bargaining representative, if there was one, was given the opportunity to be present. . . . Taft-Hartley . . . thus failed to change the meaning of "labor organization" under Sections 2(5) and 8(a) (2) . . . .

Relying in large part on these principles, the Board here explained that "dealing with" is a bilateral mechanism involving proposals from the employee organization concerning the subjects listed in Section 2(5), coupled with real or apparent consideration of those proposals by management. . . . While the Board further suggested that unilateral mechanisms such as suggestion boxes, brainstorming conferences, and other information exchanges do not constitute dealing, it is not necessary for us to reach that question.

Given the Supreme Court's holding in *Cabot Carbon* that "dealing with" includes conduct much broader than collective bargaining, the Board did not err in determining that the Electromation action committees constituted labor organizations within the meaning of Sections 2(5) and 8(a)(2) of the Act. Although it is true that Howard made no guarantees as to the results regarding the employee recommendations, the activities of the action committees nonetheless constituted "dealing with" the employer. Finally, with respect to the third factor, the subject matter of that dealing—for example, the treatment of employee absenteeism and employee bonuses—obviously concerned conditions of employment. . . . [T]he purpose of the action committees was not limited to the improvement of company efficiency or product quality, but . . . were designed to function and in fact functioned in an essentially representative capacity. . . . [G]iven the statute's traditionally broad construction, there is substantial evidence to support the Board's finding that the action committees constituted labor organizations. . . .

B. The Company Violated Section 8(a)(2) and (1) of the Act

Having concluded that each of the action committees constituted a labor organization under Section 2(5) of the Act, we must next consider whether, through their creation and administration of the action committees, the company acted unlawfully in violation of Section 8(a)(2) and (1) of the Act. . . .

Electromation argues that the Board wrongly interpreted Section 8(a)(2) solely from the perspective of an employer's conduct and incorrectly attempted to develop an objective list of employer actions which constitute illegal domination or interference under the Act. . . . To support its contention . . . the company addresses statutory construction, legislative history, legislative policy, and judicial precedent.

1. Statutory Construction

Both sides concede that the analysis of Section 8(a)(2) cannot be limited to the statutory language since its terms are not all self-defining. However, the company argues that the statutory language of Section 8(a)(2) supports its contention that the proper focus of the Board's inquiry should be the subjective will of the employees.

[T]he statute declares it an [unfair] labor practice for an employer "to dominate or interfere with the formation or administration of any labor organization or contribute financial or other support to it. . . ." . . . The proviso to this section adds that "an employer shall not be prohibited from permitting employees to confer with him during working hours without loss of time or pay." . . .

Relying especially on the proviso, the company argues that, in adopting Section 8(a)(2), Congress plainly did not mean to prohibit all contacts or cooperation between employers and employees. Without a doubt, this is true. However, the Board's determination neither disputes nor rejects this principle. Rather, the Board found that the activities of the company in this case constituted more than mere cooperation. *See* 309 N.L.R.B. at 997–98 ("There can be no doubt that the Respondent's conduct vis à vis the Action Committees constituted 'domination' in their formation and administration. . . . [The] employees essentially were presented with the Hobson's choice of accepting the status quo, which they disliked, or undertaking a bilateral 'exchange of ideas' within the framework of the Action Committees, as presented by the Respondent.").

The company also suggests that the words "dominate" and "interfere with" in Section 8(a)(2) are relational terms, which require consideration of both the subject and the object for their complete meaning. In other words, you cannot find that X dominates Y simply by looking at the actions of X; to so find, you must evaluate X's conduct *and its effect upon Y's rights and wishes.* Under this theory, the same conduct of X, if viewed from an objective standpoint, can be construed as either illegal domination or lawful cooperation, depending entirely upon what Y's rights and wishes are.

We agree with Electromation that the relevant terms in Section 8(a)(2) are relational, but disagree that the Board failed to comprehend this principle in its interpretation of that section's language. Indeed, the Board focused its analysis on the relationship between Electromation's actions in creating and administering the action committees and the resulting effect upon its employees' rights under the Act. The Board did not, as the company suggests, base its decision solely on "a list of objective practices . . . that are *per se* unlawful." . . .

Nowhere in the Board's decision can we find evidence that the company's objective acts were considered outside of the context of the employees' rights and wishes. The Board in fact considered the totality of the employer's conduct in finding company domination of the action committees. The Board correctly focused on management's participation in the action committees and its effect on the employees and found domination in that the company defined the committee structures and committee subject matters, appointed a manager to coordinate and monitor the committee meetings, structured each committee to include one or two management representatives, and permitted those managers to review and reject committee proposals before they could be presented to upper level management. The Board's interpretation of Section 8(a)(2) simply does not contravene the statutory language.

2. Legislative History

Electromation next argues that the legislative history supports its interpretation of Section 8(a)(2). It essentially argues that, in drafting Section 8(a)(2), Congress mandated that the proper focus of inquiry should be on the subjective wishes of the employees rather than the conduct of the employer. . . .

The Board found that the legislative history . . . supports its interpretation and application of Section 8(a)(2) to the facts of this case. We agree. While it is true that the thrust of Section 8(a)(2) is designed to protect the free will of the employees, the legislative history reveals that the coverage of that section is broad indeed. As Senator Wagner emphasized throughout the Senate's deliberations on the Act, "[c]ollective bargaining becomes a sham when the employer sits on both sides of the table or pulls the strings behind the spokesman of those with whom he is dealing." . . .

Moreover, the legislative history reflects that Congress was well aware of both the usefulness and the popularity of employee committees at the time that it drafted the provisions of the Wagner Act. . . . Congress heard extensive testimony from employees who expressed great satisfaction with their employee representation plans and committees. . . .

Congress nonetheless enacted a broad proscription of employer conduct in Section 8(a)(2). Addressing the type of conduct proscribed by this section, the Report of the Senate Committee on Education and Labor provided an illustrative, but non-exhaustive, list of illegal employer domination or interference:

> The so-called "company-union" features of the bill are designed to prevent interference by employers with organizations of their workers that serve or might serve as collective bargaining agencies. Such interference exists when employers actively participate in framing the constitution or bylaws of labor organizations; or when, by provisions in the constitution or by laws [sic], changes in the structure of the organization cannot be made without the consent of the employer. It exists when they participate in the internal management or elections of a labor organization or when they supervise the agenda or procedure of meetings. It is impossible to catalog all the practices that might constitute interference, which may rest upon subtle but conscious economic pressure exerted by virtue of the employment relationship. The question is one of fact in each case. And where several of these interferences exist in combination, the employer may be said to dominate the labor organization by overriding the will of the employees. . . .

This language illustrates the broad proscription on employer interference that Section 8(a)(2) was designed to provide. In this case, Electromation actually engaged in several of the activities included in this non-exhaustive list of proscribed employer conduct: it "participate[d] in the internal management . . . of a labor organization," it "supervise[d] the agenda or procedure of meetings," and, although the action committees did not have formal constitutions or by laws [sic], the company "actively participate[d] in framing . . . [the purposes and goals statements] of labor organizations." Moreover, as is discussed in greater detail below, courts have consistently interpreted Section 8(a)(2) as a broad proscription against employer formation of or participation of almost any kind in employee committees or organizations which function in a representational capacity.

3. Congressional Policies

In further support of its position, the company identifies two congressional policies underlying Section 8(a)(2): first, the protection of employees' freedom of choice; and second, the promotion of cooperation between employers and employees. We agree that both constitute legitimate goals of this section. . . .

. . . The company claims that, in light of the twin goals of freedom of choice and cooperation, Section 8(a)(2) must be construed to allow employers and employees to discuss matters of mutual interest concerning the employment relationship as long as the employees' choice about how to discuss such matters is not overridden. Even accepting that contention, it is far from clear that the Electromation employees' choice was not overridden in this case. In fact, the company "supported" the action committees in such a way that it possessed an unacceptable degree of control and influence. The company's involvement and control of membership, subjects, and decisions of the committees cannot fairly be characterized as "mere cooperation." . . .

C. Substantial Evidence Supports the Board's Factual Findings

. . . [S]ubstantial evidence supports the finding of company domination of the action committees. First, the company proposed and essentially imposed the action committees upon its employees as the only acceptable mechanism for resolution of their acknowledged grievances regarding the newly announced attendance bonus policies. In response to perceived employee dissatisfaction with working conditions and a petition signed by 68 workers specifically protesting the changes in Electromation's attendance policy, the company unilaterally developed the concept of action committees. . . .

The record also clearly shows that the employees were initially reluctant to accept the company's proposal of the action committees as a means to address their concerns; their reaction was "not positive." Nonetheless, the company continued to press the idea until the employees eventually accepted. Moreover, although the company informed the employees that they could continue to meet on their own, shortly after Electromation removed its management representatives from the committees due to the union recognition demand and announced that it would not work with the committees until after the union election, several of the committees disbanded. It was on this basis that the Board reasonably concluded that the company created the action committees and provided the impetus for their continued existence. . . .

The company played a pivotal role in establishing both the framework and the agenda for the action committees. Electromation unilaterally selected the size, structure, and procedural functioning of the committees; it decided the number of committees and the topic(s) to be addressed by each. The company unilaterally drafted the action committees' purposes and goal statements, which identified from the start the focus of each committee's work. . . . [D]espite the fact that the employees were seriously concerned about the lack of a wage increase, no action committee was designated to consider this specific issue. In this way, Electromation actually controlled which issues received attention by the committees and which did not. . . .

Although the company acceded to the employees' request that volunteers form the committees, it unilaterally determined how many could serve on each committee, decided that an employee could serve on only one committee at a time, and determined which committee certain employees would serve on, thus exercising significant control over the employees' participation and voice at the committee meetings. Also, . . . the initial sign-up sheets indicated that the employer would decide which six employees would be chosen as committee members where more than six expressed interest in a particular committee. Ultimately, the company limited membership to five and determined the five to serve. . . .

Also, the company designated management representatives to serve on the committees. Employee Benefits Manager Dickey was assigned to coordinate and serve on all committees. In the case of the Attendance Bonus Program Committee, the management representative—Controller Mazur—reviewed employee proposals, determined whether they were economically feasible, and further decided whether they would be presented to higher management. This role of the management committee members effectively put the employer on both sides of the bargaining table, an avowed proscription of the Act. . . .

Finally, the company paid the employees for their time spent on committee activities, provided meeting space, and furnished all necessary supplies for the committees' activities. While such financial support is clearly not a violation of Section 8(a)(2) by itself, . . . in the totality of the circumstances . . . such support may reasonably be characterized to be in furtherance of the company's domination of the action committees. We therefore conclude that there is substantial evidence to support the Board's finding of unlawful employer domination and interference in violation of Section 8(a)(2) and (1). . . .

The Supreme Court has explained that domination of a labor organization exists where the employer controls the form and structure of a labor organization such that the employees are deprived of complete freedom and independence of action as guaranteed to them by Section 7 . . . , and that the principal distinction between an independent labor organization and an employer-dominated organization lies in the unfettered power of the independent organization to determine its own actions. . . . The Electromation action committees, which were wholly created by the employer, whose continued existence depended upon the employer, and whose functions were essentially determined by the employer, lacked the independence of action and free choice guaranteed by Section 7. This is not to suggest that Howard and the other management representatives were anti-union or had devious intentions in proposing the creation of the committees. But, even assuming they acted from good intentions, their procedure in establishing the committees, their control of the subject matters to be considered or excluded, their membership and participation on the committees, and their financial support of the committees all combined to make the committees labor organizations dominated by the employer in violation of the Act.

Accordingly, because we find that substantial evidence supports the Board's factual findings and that its legal conclusions have a reasonable basis in the law, we affirm the Board's findings and enforce the Board's order.

Notes

1. Professor Robert Moberly characterizes *Electromation* as "the vehicle for a national struggle between competing visions of worker participation and company unions, involving the [NLRB], the federal courts, Congress, and the President of the United States." Robert B. Moberly, *The Story of Electromation: Are Employee Participation Programs a Competitive Necessity or a Wolf in Sheep's Clothing?, in* Labor Law Stories 315, 315 (Laura J. Cooper & Catherine L. Fisk eds., 2005). In examining the note questions, keep in mind Professor Moberly's description of this debate.

2. In *Electromation*, the Board explained that "dealing with" contemplates "a bilateral mechanism involving proposals from the employee committee concerning the subjects listed in Section 2(5), coupled with real or apparent consideration of those proposals by management." *Electromation, Inc.*, 309 N.L.R.B. 990, 995 n.21 (1992), *enf'd*, 35 F.3d 1148 (7th Cir. 1994). The Board subsequently explained that "'bilateral mechanism' ordinarily entails a pattern or practice in which a group of employees, over time, makes proposals to management, [and] management responds to these proposals by acceptance or rejection by word or deed...." *E.I. du Pont & Co.*, 311 N.L.R.B. 893, 894 (1993).

3. If an employer delegates final authority (or essentially final authority) to an "employee participation" type of organization, should that change the analysis under *Electromation*? If so, why? In *Crown, Cork & Seal Company*, 334 N.L.R.B. 699 (2001), the Board held that the company's delegation of such authority meant that it was not "dealing with" a labor organization; rather, it was engaging in lawful chain-of-command management. Thus, the Board found that § 8(a)(2) was not violated.

4. The Board has closely examined the statutory concept of "dealing." In *Keeler Brass Co.*, for example, the Board found "dealing" where an employee committee and the company "went back and forth explaining themselves until an acceptable result was achieved." 317 N.L.R.B. 1110, 1114 (1995). There, the company discharged an employee under its "no-call, no-show" policy. The employee committee determined that the punishment was too harsh and recommended that the company reinstate the employee and reexamine the policy. After considering the committee recommendation, the company changed its policy, but upheld the discharge as justified by past practice. Thereafter, the grievance committee heard testimony on the past-practice issue but denied the grievance. By contrast, in *General Foods Corp.*, the Board found no "dealing" where a company "flatly delegated [managerial functions] to employees" involved in a "job enrichment program" designed "to enlarge

the powers and responsibilities of all its rank-and-file employees and to give them certain powers or controls over their job situations which are normally not assigned to manual laborers." 231 N.L.R.B. 1232, 1232–33, 1235 (1977). The Board further explained (*id.* at 1235):

> While the employer could withdraw the powers delegated to employees to perform these functions on its behalf, the withdrawal of authority would be wholly unilateral on its part just as was Respondent's original delega-tion. There was no dealing between employer and employee (or employee group) involved in these matters. These functions were just other assign-ments of job duties, albeit duties not normally granted to rank-and-file personnel.

5. The Board has also closely examined the concept of domination under of § 8(a) (2). *See, e.g., NLRB v. Cabot Carbon Co.*, 360 U.S. 203, 213 (1959). In *Electromation*, the Board reaffirmed its view that employer domination occurs "when the impetus behind the formation of an organization of employees emanates from an employer and the organization has no effective existence independent of the employer's active involvement." *Electromation, Inc.*, 309 N.L.R.B. 990, 996 (1992).

6. *Electromation* drew criticism from the business community. In response, con-gressional Republicans introduced the Teamwork for Employees and Management Act (TEAM Act), which would have amended the NLRA to allow labor-management groups made unlawful under the Board's construction of § 8(a)(2) in *Electromation*. Business communities warned that the TEAM Act was necessary to permit labor-management cooperation to improve economic competitiveness in the United States. Unions argued the TEAM Act would have permitted employers to circum-vent employee representatives of the employees' own choosing thereby eroding the NLRA's protection of worker self-governance. President Clinton vetoed the bill.

Problem 5.1

The law faculty of a large private university hires visiting assistant professors (VAPs). These positions are two-year contract positions, renewable once only. Orig-inally, the faculty hired the VAPs as an inexpensive way of meeting course cover-age. The VAPs were given teaching but no committee or other service assignments; other than teaching one or two courses per semester, VAPs were free to work on their own scholarship. The Dean received numerous complaints from the perma-nent faculty that the VAPs were not doing their share of faculty governance. To rem-edy that issue, the Dean decided to assign committee work to the VAPs. Each VAP was placed on at least one of the following committees: librarian search committee, staff search committee, health and safety committee, sustainability committee. The sustainability committee recommended to the faculty as a whole various measures to adopt to make the law school a more green-friendly community. The law school installed water-filtered fountains, distributed water bottles to all students, faculty and staff, and installed low-flush toilets throughout the school, following a full fac-ulty vote, which included VAP participation for the first time. The health and safety committee never met. The search committees met, reviewed resumes, interviewed candidates, and recommended candidates for hire to the full faculty.

Did the university violate §8(a)(2) by placing the VAPs on these committees? Does this hypothetical turn on whether the VAPs are statutory employees? Or is the university free to give the VAPs additional job duties thereby converting their position to a managerial one? *See* Chapter 2, especially *NLRB v. Yeshiva Univ.*, 444 U.S. 672 (1980). Does your answer depend on whether the VAPs were attempting to organize at the time they were asked to serve on these committees?

―――――――――

In *Electromation*, the company responded to employee grievances in a way that gave voice to its employees. This observation leads to the question: Is there tension between an employer voluntarily giving employees a say in their own work lives and conduct that is unlawful under §8(a)(2)? Think about the policies underlying the NLRA in determining the purpose of §8(a)(2)'s prohibition on company unions. Does the Board's *Electromation* test sweep too broadly?

Problem 5.2

A nonunion company, engaged in the business of manufacturing and selling cameras, creates an employee committee (EC) comprised of nonsupervisory employees of all ranks — mechanics, maintenance worker, machine operators, financial analysts, camera-model makers, and research and development technicians. These EC representatives are elected by their peers to two-year terms. During that time, the company pays the EC reps their normal salary, but their main job is to serve on the EC.

The EC reps serve as grievance representatives. Whenever an employee has a complaint, the employee may approach their EC rep, who will then try to informally resolve the grievance with the employee's supervisor. If the grievance cannot be resolved informally, then the EC rep can file a formal complaint with the lowest level supervisor (step one). If the complaint is not resolved at step one, then the EC rep can take the complaint to the manager (step two). If the complaint is not resolved at step two, then the EC rep can take the complaint to the Director of Human Resources (step three). If the complaint is not resolved at step three, then the EC rep can take the complaint directly to the President of the company. If the complaint is not resolved at the final step, then the EC rep can ask the company to arbitrate the dispute. Although it is the company's decision whether or not to arbitrate the dispute, if the company decides to arbitrate the dispute, it will pay for the arbitration. At arbitration, the grievant may ask the EC rep to represent him/her or he/she may pay for an attorney. If the company decides not to take the case to arbitration then the employee can litigate the case.

Does the EC violate §8(a)(2)? As written, the EC does not appear to violate §8(a)(2). However, this arrangement could violate §8(a)(2) if management has sufficient control over how the elections are run and when it has authority to remove reps. Consider whether the EC is "dealing with" the employer. Is there a bilateral relationship?

Board Member Oviatt's concurrence in *Electromation* suggested that certain issues, such as productivity, efficiency, and production quality, do not come within the mandatory subjects of bargaining, and therefore, management programs established to discuss such subjects do not violate § 8(a)(5).

2. In the Public Sector

As Chapter 1 showed, "company unions" had a much longer history in the public sector, as employers routinely barred employee organizations that were affiliated with the broader labor movement. Decades after NLRA § 8(a)(2) banned this practice in the private sector, such groups continued to exist in the public sector.

When public-sector labor statutes began being passed, however, they typically barred employer-dominated labor organizations. *See, e.g.,* OHIO REV. CODE ANN. § 4117.11(A)(2) (making it an employer unfair labor practice to "Initiate, create, dominate, or interfere with the formation or administration of any employee organization"); PENNSYLVANIA PUBLIC EMPLOYMENT RELATIONS ACT § 1201(a)(2) (as *SEPTA (Victory District)*, 40 PPER 87 (PLRB 2009) explained, "it is well-settled that Section 1201(2) prohibits 'company unions' and is directed at employer domination of, or assistance to, employee organizations,"); Illinois Educational Labor Relations Act § 14(a)(2); FLA. STAT. § 447.501.

Where such laws were passed, some groups that had traditionally been dominated by employers (or at least by administrators and supervisors) withered away; others (most notably the National Education Association) began behaving more like traditional unions.

C. Employer in the Middle: Competing Unions

As touched upon in *J.I. Case*, an employer may recognize and bargain with a union as the exclusive bargaining representative of the employees in an appropriate bargaining unit only if the union has earned the support of a majority of those employees. Employer bargaining with minority unions may run afoul of § 8(a)(2), however. For example, in *International Ladies' Garment Workers' Union v. NLRB*, 366 U.S. 731 (1961), the Court held that the employer violated § 8(a)(2) and that the union violated § 8(b)(1)(A) when the employer recognized the union and the parties bargained for a collective-bargaining agreement at a time when the union did not enjoy majority support — even though the union gained majority support by the time the collective-bargaining agreement had been executed and the parties at all relevant times harbored a bona fide belief that the union did enjoy majority support. For a fuller discussion, see Chapter 8. The following case focuses on initial organizing situations involving two or more rival labor organizations.

Abraham Grossman D/B/A Bruckner Nursing Home

National Labor Relations Board

262 N.L.R.B. 955 (1982)

... In the spring of 1974, Local 144, Hotel, Hospital, Nursing Home & Allied Health Services Union, S.E.I.U., AFL-CIO [Local 144], and Local 1115, Joint Board, Nursing Home and Hospital Employees Division [Local 1115], began organizational activities at Respondent Employer's nursing home facility in New York, New York. In early September 1974, Local 144 notified the Employer that it possessed a majority of signed authorization cards, and a date was set for a card count. Shortly thereafter, Local 1115 sent a mailgram to the Employer which stated that it was engaged in organizational activity among the Employer's employees and that the Employer should not extend recognition to any other labor organization. On September 23, 1974, Local 1115 filed charges against the Employer and Local 144 alleging violations of Sections 8(a)(1) and 8(b)(1)(A) through interference with the employees' right to select a union of their choice.

The card count was conducted on September 27, 1974, by an extension specialist of the New York State School of Industrial and Labor Relations. Thereafter, the extension specialist informed the Employer that Local 144 represented a majority of its employees. Local 144 subsequently requested negotiations, but the Employer refused pending the outcome of the unfair labor practice charges filed by Local 1115.

[In November], the unfair labor practice charges filed by Local 1115 were dismissed. ... Negotiations between Local 144 and the Employer commenced shortly thereafter and culminated in the execution of a collective-bargaining agreement [in December]. Local 1115 then filed ... the charges at issue in this proceeding.

On September 27, 1974, the date of the card check, Respondent Employer had approximately 125 people in its employ. At that time, Local 1115 had two authorization cards, while Local 144 possessed signed authorization cards from approximately 80 to 90 percent of the Employer's employees. No representation petition was filed on behalf of either labor organization in this proceeding.

... [T]he Administrative Law Judge found that Local 1115 possessed a "colorable claim" to representation herein based on its continuous efforts to obtain employee support during the fall of 1974, and the fact that it had actually obtained a few authorization cards. The [ALJ] concluded that the Employer "by executing a collective-bargaining agreement ... in the face of a real question concerning representation which had not been settled [by] the special procedures of the Act" had rendered unlawful assistance to Local 144 in violation of Section 8(a)(2). ... In what has become a standard remedy in this type of setting, the [ALJ] ordered that the Employer cease giving effect to the collective-bargaining agreement with Local 144, and further ordered the Employer to withdraw and withhold recognition from Local 144 unless and until it has been certified in a Board-conducted election.

In this and a companion case, *RCA del Caribe, Inc.*, 262 N.L.R.B. No. 116 (1982) . . . , we undertake a reevaluation of what has come to be known as the *Midwest Piping* doctrine (*Midwest Piping & Supply Co.*, 63 N.L.R.B. 1060 (1945) . . . .

As originally formulated, the "*Midwest Piping* doctrine" was an attempt by the Board to insure that, in a rival union situation, an employer would not render "aid" to one of two or more unions competing for exclusive bargaining representative status through a grant of recognition in advance of a Board-conducted election. In *Midwest Piping* itself, the Board found that an employer gave unlawful assistance to a labor organization when the employer recognized one of two competing labor organizations, both of which had filed representation petitions, and both of which had campaigned extensively for the mantle of exclusive bargaining representative. In the context of that case, we held that the employer had arrogated the resolution of the representation issue, and that a Board-conducted election was the "best" means of ascertaining the true desires of employees. We further stated that employers presented with rival claims from competing unions (in the form of representation petitions) should follow a course of strict neutrality with respect to the competing unions until such time as the "real question concerning representation" had been resolved through the mechanism of a Board-conducted election.

In cases that followed soon thereafter, we applied the principle that the duty of strict employer neutrality and the necessity of a Board-conducted election were operative only when a representation petition had been filed with the Board, and further noted that the "doctrine" should be "strictly construed" and "sparingly applied." *Ensher, Alexander & Barsoom, Inc.*, 74 N.L.R.B. 1443 (1947).

In subsequent decisions, the Board removed the requirement that a representation petition actually be filed, stating that a petition was not a prerequisite to the finding of a "real" or "genuine" question concerning representation. *Pittsburgh Valve Company*, 114 N.L.R.B. 193 (1955), *enforcement denied*, 234 F.2d 565 (4th Cir. 1956). The removal of the prerequisite of a petition stemmed in part from the need to recognize the existence of a rival union contest even before formal invocation of the Board's election procedures so as to insure that those procedures would be available. If more than one union enjoyed at least some employee support, we perceived a Board-conducted election as the best way, often the only way, to guarantee employees a fair and free opportunity to make the final choice of a bargaining representative. Although often unstated, another reason for removing the petition requirement in a rival union setting was to preclude the serious possibility of employer abuse where no petition had been filed. Often we were faced with the scenario of a union presenting a substantial showing of majority support based on cards which the employer would reject while invariably professing a preference for the Board's election procedures. A short time thereafter, the employer would recognize another union and, typically, sign a contract in a remarkably accelerated bargaining process. This scenario was played once too often, so we determined that in order to protect the democratic right of employees to their own collective-bargaining representative, and to prevent employer abuse, we would require an election whenever there were two or more unions on the scene, and each had some support or organizational interest in the unit sought. We defined the "interest" that a union must have to trigger the operation of the *Midwest Piping* doctrine as a "colorable claim," a claim that was not "clearly unsupportable," or a claim that was not "naked." *Playskool, Inc.*, 195 N.L.R.B. 560 (1972), *enforcement denied*, 477 F.2d 66 (7th Cir. 1973). Thus, we held that the original *Midwest Piping* requirement of strict employer neutrality would be operative where a question concerning representation existed even though no petition had been filed unless and until a Board-conducted election had been held and the results certified.

Difficulties with this modification of the original *Midwest Piping* decision arose in defining precisely what was meant by the terms "naked claim," "clearly unsupportable claim," and "colorable claim." Inevitably we were called upon to make close judgments as to whether 8 cards in a unit of over 90 employees made a colorable claim, whether prior organizational activity constituted a clearly unsupportable claim, or whether an expressed interest in organizing a certain group of employees was simply a naked claim. While attempting to maintain flexibility and to decide these questions on a case-by-case basis, we were unable to provide employers, unions, and employees alike with clear standards that would enable them to discern the fine line between a colorable claim and a naked one.

Extending the *Midwest Piping* doctrine frequently allowed a minority union possessing a few cards to forestall the recognition of a majority union in an effort either to buy time to gather more support for itself or simply to frustrate its rivals. For instance, here, where one union enjoys overwhelming support and the other has but a few cards, collective bargaining would be delayed until the 8(a)(2) charge has been resolved and the results of a later Board-conducted election have been certified. This delay would occur simply because an employer has done what in the absence of a rival claimant it may (but by no means has to) do in recognizing a majority union based on authorization cards. Ironically, in this factual setting, invoking "employee free choice" to justify Board intervention would clearly impede and frustrate the expression of employee preference, as well as the collective-bargaining process. For here, where employees have made a free choice and the employer has recognized that choice, the ultimate aim of that choice—the establishment of a collective-bargaining relationship and the benefits flowing therefrom—could not be achieved because another union has a "colorable claim" to representation.

Meanwhile, circuit courts refused to enforce many of our decisions based on "modified" *Midwest Piping* violations. The courts took a distinctly different approach to the problems presented by the rival union situation. Whereas the Board viewed the matter in terms of protecting employee free choice and the integrity and efficacy of our election process, the courts took the view that the question concerning representation was resolved whenever an employer recognized a bona fide majority claimant and had not actually aided, in the traditional 8(a)(2) sense of that word, the recognized labor organization. At the point an unassisted majority union had been recognized, the courts considered the matter settled, and the question concerning representation resolved. *Air Master Corporation*, 142 N.L.R.B. 181 (1963), *enforcement denied*, 339 F.2d 553 (3d Cir. 1964). However, reiterating its concern for the Section 7 rights of employees and employer manipulation of the recognition process, the Board held to the view that our election machinery was still the optimum means of resolving the rival union representation question. Just as often as the Board reaffirmed its adherence to the now "modified" *Midwest Piping* doctrine, however, the courts of appeals refused to enforce our decisions finding 8(a)(2) violations on this basis.

We have reviewed the Board's experience with *Midwest Piping* with a desire to accommodate the view of the courts of appeals in light of our statutory mandate to protect employees' freedom to select their bargaining representatives and in harmony with our statutory mandate to encourage collective bargaining. Having identified the difficult problems in this area, it is the Board's task to reconcile the various interests of policy and law involved in fashioning a rule which will give, as far as possible, equal consideration to each of those interests in the light of industrial reality. We have concluded that this task has not been accomplished through the modified *Midwest Piping* doctrine. Accordingly, we will no longer find 8(a)(2) violations in rival union, initial organizing situations when an employer recognizes a labor organization which represents an uncoerced, unassisted majority, before a valid petition for an election has been filed with the Board. However, once notified of a valid petition, an employer must refrain from recognizing any of the rival unions. Of course, we will continue to process timely filed petitions and to conduct elections in the most expeditious manner possible, following our normal procedures with respect to intervention and placement of parties on the ballot.

Making the filing of a valid petition the operative event for the imposition of strict employer neutrality in rival union, initial organizing situations will establish a clearly defined rule of conduct and encourage both employee free choice and industrial stability. Where one of several rival labor organizations cannot command the support of even 30 percent of the unit, it will no longer be permitted to forestall an employer's recognition of another labor organization which represents an uncoerced majority of employees and thereby frustrate the establishment of a collective-bargaining relationship. Likewise, an employer will no longer have to guess whether a real question concerning representation has been raised but will be able to recognize a labor organization unless it has received notice of a properly filed petition.

On the other hand, where a labor organization has filed a petition, both the Act and our administrative experience dictate the need for resolution of the representation issue through a Board election rather than through employer recognition. When a union has demonstrated substantial support by filing a valid petition, an active contest exists for the employees' allegiance. This contest takes on special significance where rival unions are involved since there an employer's grant of recognition may unduly influence or effectively end a contest between labor organizations. As long ago as 1938, the Supreme Court noted that, in enacting Section 8(a)(2) and (1) of the Act, Congress had been influenced by "data showing that once an employer has conferred recognition on a particular organization it has a marked advantage over any other in securing the adherence of employees, and hence in preventing the recognition of any other." *NLRB. v. Pennsylvania Greyhound Lines, Inc.,* 303 U.S. 261 (1938). Without questioning the reliability of authorization cards or unduly exalting election procedure, we believe the proper balance will be struck by prohibiting an employer from recognizing any of the competing unions for the limited period during which a representation petition is in process even though one or more of the unions may present a valid card majority.

In addition to avoiding potential undue influence by an employer, our new approach provides a satisfactory answer to problems created by execution of dual authorization cards. It is our experience that employees confronted by solicitations from rival unions will frequently sign authorization cards for more than one union. Dual cards reflect the competing organizational campaigns. They may indicate shifting employee sentiments or employee desire to be represented by either of two rival unions. In this situation, authorization cards are less reliable as indications of employee preference. When a petition supported by a 30-percent showing of interest has been filed by one union, the reliability of a rival's expression of a card majority is sufficiently doubtful to require resolution of the competing claims through the Board's election process.

Our reevaluation of the *Midwest Piping* doctrine to find the proper balance between statutory purposes is entirely consistent with the judicial acceptance of authorization cards as at least one reliable indicator of employee sentiment. At the time of the original *Midwest Piping* decision and even up until 1969, reliance on authorization cards as an appropriate measure of employee support had not received the sanction of the Supreme Court. After *NLRB v. Gissel Packing Co., Inc.,* 395 U.S. 575 (1969), and *Linden Lumber Div., Summer & Co. v. NLRB,* 419 301 (1974), it was settled that, while a Board-conducted election was still the optimum vehicle for ascertaining employee preferences, it was certainly not the sole means to that end. The phenomenon of dual cards in a rival union organizational setting must be taken into account, but can no longer solely justify our absolute refusal to rely on cards in *Midwest Piping* situations, particularly since we regard them as a reliable means of ascertaining the wishes of a majority of employees in other organizational settings. However, while some courts of appeals have expressed the view that an employer may lawfully recognize one of two or more competing labor organizations even in the face of a pending petition, our view continues to be that, once a properly supported petition is filed, the employer may not circumvent an election by granting recognition to one of the competing unions.

In sum, under our new formulation, the duty of strict employer neutrality and the necessity for a Board-conducted election attach only when a properly supported petition has been filed by one or more of the competing labor organizations. Where no petition has been filed, an employer will be free to grant recognition to a labor organization with an uncoerced majority, so long as it does not render assistance of the type which would otherwise violate Section 8(a)(2) of the Act.

Applying the principles outlined above to the facts of the instant case, it is clear that no petition was filed by either of the rival unions and that the Employer recognized a clear majority claimant in extending recognition to Local 144. Accordingly, inasmuch as no petition was filed and recognition was granted to a labor organization with an uncoerced, unassisted majority, we shall dismiss the instant complaint in its entirety. . . . [The NLRB] hereby orders that the complaint in the instant case be . . . dismissed.

Notes

1. *Bruckner* deals with the situation in which rival unions are competing for majority support within the same bargaining unit. Under the Board's *Midwest Piping* rule, in those circumstances, an employer was prohibited from recognizing union A, even if union A had majority support, where union B had a "colorable claim" of support. In such cases, the question concerning representation had to be resolved by a Board-conducted, secret-ballot election. This approach proved problematic, because minority opposition could delay recognition, and what constituted a "colorable claim" was unclear. In *Bruckner*, the Board resolved that problem by creating a bright-line rule: an employer is prohibited from voluntarily recognizing a majority union only where the rival union has filed a valid election petition. What balance is the Board attempting to strike here?

2. What result if there is a challenge to an *incumbent* union by a rival union? May the employer voluntarily recognize the rival union if presented with a majority of cards without running afoul of § 8(a)(2)? In *RCA del Caribe, Inc.*, 262 N.L.R.B. 963 (1982), the company and the incumbent union were in the midst of bargaining over a successor agreement when the incumbent authorized the employees to strike. The strike lasted about seven weeks during which time the rival union filed a representation petition. The company cut off recognition of, and bargaining with, the incumbent union. The incumbent responded by submitting to the company a petition signed by 157 of the 227 bargaining unit employees. After the company verified the signatures by comparing them with its employment records, the parties recommenced bargaining. Soon thereafter, the parties reached agreement. The question presented is whether the employer violated § 8(a)(2) by engaging in the post-petition bargaining.

The Board held:

> . . . [R]equiring an employer to withdraw from bargaining after a petition has been filed is not the best means of assuring employer neutrality, thereby facilitating employee free choice. Unlike initial organizing situations, an employer in an existing collective- bargaining relationship cannot observe strict neutrality. In many situations, as here, the incumbent challenged by an outside union is in the process of—perhaps close to completing—negotiation of a contract when the petition is filed. If an employer continues to bargain, employees may perceive a preference for the incumbent union, whether or not the employer holds that preference. . . . [I]f

an employer withdraws from bargaining, particularly when agreement is imminent, this withdrawal may more emphatically signal repudiation of the incumbent and preference for the rival. . . . [I]t may be of little practical consequence to the employees whether the employer actually intended this signal or was compelled by law to withdraw from bargaining. We further recognize that an employer may be faced with changing economic circumstances which could require immediate response and commensurate changes in working conditions. . . . [T]o prohibit negotiations until the Board has ruled on the results of a new election might work an undue hardship on employers, unions, and employees. Under the circumstances, . . . preservation of the status quo through an employer's continued bargaining with an incumbent is the better way to approximate employer neutrality.

For [these] reasons, . . . the mere filing of a representation petition by an outside, challenging union will no longer require or permit an employer to withdraw from bargaining or executing a contract with an incumbent union. Under this rule, an employer will not violate Section 8(a)(2) by postpetition negotiations or execution of a contract with an incumbent, but an employer will violate Section 8(a)(5) by withdrawing from bargaining based solely on the fact that a petition has been filed by an outside union.

This new approach affords maximum protection to the complementary statutory policies of furthering stability in industrial relations and of insuring employee free choice. . . . [O]ur new rule does not have the effect of insulating incumbent unions from a legitimate outside challenge. . . . [A] timely filed petition will put an incumbent to the test of demonstrating that it still is the majority choice for exclusive bargaining representative. Unlike before, however, even though a valid petition has been filed, an incumbent will retain its earned right to demonstrate its effectiveness as a representative at the bargaining table. An outside union and its employee supporters will now be required to take their incumbent opponent as they find it—as the previously elected majority representative. Consequently, in the ensuing election, employees will no longer be presented with a distorted choice between an incumbent artificially deprived of the attributes of its office and a rival union artificially placed on an equal footing with the incumbent.

. . . [T]he Board will continue to process valid petitions timely filed by outside unions and to conduct the election as expeditiously as possible. . . . If the incumbent prevails in the election held, any contract executed with the incumbent will be valid and binding. If the challenging union prevails, however, any contract executed with the incumbent will be null and void.

3. *Bruckner* illustrates that neutrality agreements and card check agreements are lawful. Under these agreements, employers agree to remain neutral during an organizing drive and to recognize a union when presented with a majority of cards. *See* Chapter 8, especially James Brudney, "Neutrality Agreements and Card Check Recognition: Prospects for Changing Labor Relations Paradigms," ACS Issue Brief

(Feb. 2007). This ruling presents the following question: How extensive can such agreements be before an employer will be found to have improperly assisted a union?

4. Articles XX and XXI of the AFL-CIO Constitution provide for an internal dispute resolution (mediation/arbitration) process for resolving fights between competing unions. One purpose of this process is to protect the collective-bargaining relationships that AFL-CIO affiliates have developed. *See* Art. XX, § 2. Another aspect is that affiliates "actively engaged in organizing a group of employees and seeking to become their exclusive representative may invoke [the procedures in Article XXI] to seek a determination affirming its ability to do so without being subject to ongoing competition by any other AFL-CIO affiliate." *See* Art. XXI, § 2. The Board has normally deferred to the AFL-CIO's internal dispute resolution proceedings where two or more affiliates are involved in a representation battle. *See Irvin H. Whitehouse & Sons Co., Inc. v. Local Union No. 118 of Intern. Broth. of Painters and Allied Trades, AFL-CIO*, 1992 WL 19472, at *5 (6th Cir. 1992) (citing NLRB Casehandling Manual Part II (Representation Proceedings) § 11052.1). These sections are now found at NLRB Casehandling Manual Part II (Representation Proceedings) §§ 11017–11019.

III. Discrimination

In this section, we move from examining the question of what constitutes unlawful company assistance to a union under § 8(a)(2) to what constitutes discrimination under § 8(a)(3).

A. The Intent Requirement

Edward G. Budd Manufacturing Co. v. NLRB

United States Court of Appeals for the Third Circuit
138 F.2d 86 (1943)

BIGGS, CIRCUIT JUDGE.

[Upon the passage of the National Industrial Recovery Act of 1933, some of the petitioner's employees desired to form a labor organization. Some employees tried unsuccessfully to form a union under the American Federation of Labor. Shortly thereafter, the company's President Edward G. Budd established the Budd Employee Representation Association. On September 7, nineteen employee representatives were elected to the Association by an election held on company property on company time and paid with company funds.]

The case of Walter Weigand[, a former Association representative,] is extraordinary. [While he was a representative, the Company never disciplined him.] If ever a workman deserved summary discharge it was he. He was under the influence of liquor while on duty. He came to work when he chose and he left the plant and his shift as he pleased. In fact, a foreman on one occasion was agreeably surprised to find Weigand at work and commented upon it. Weigand amiably stated that he was enjoying it. [Weigand stated that he was carried on the payroll as a 'rigger'. He was asked what was a rigger. He replied: 'I don't know; I am not a rigger.'] He brought a woman (apparently generally known as the 'Duchess') to the rear of the plant yard and introduced some of the employees to her. He took another employee to visit her and when this man got too drunk to be able to go home, punched his time-card for him and put him on the table in the representatives' meeting room in the plant in order to sleep off his intoxication. Weigand's immediate superiors demanded again and again that he be discharged, but each time higher officials intervened on Weigand's behalf because as was naively stated he was 'a representative.' In return for not working at the job for which he was hired, the petitioner gave him full pay and on five separate occasions raised his wages. One of these raises was general; that is to say, Weigand profited by a general wage increase throughout the plant, but the other four raises were given Weigand at times when other employees in the plant did not receive wage increases

The petitioner contends that Weigand was discharged because of cumulative grievances against him. But about the time of the discharge it was suspected by some of the representatives that Weigand had joined the complaining CIO union [a rival union to the Association]. One of the representatives taxed him with this fact and Weigand offered to bet a hundred dollars that it could not be proved. On July 22, 1941 Weigand did disclose his union membership to the vice-chairman (Rattigan) of the Association and to another representative (Mullen) and apparently tried to persuade them to support the union. Weigand asserts that the next day he with Rattigan and Mullen, were seen talking to CIO organizer Reichwein on a street corner. The following day, according to Weigand's testimony, Mullen came to Weigand at the plant and stated that Weigand, Rattigan and himself had been seen talking to Reichwein and that he, Mullen, had just had an interview with Personnel Director McIlvain and Plant Manager Mahan. According to Weigand, Mullen said to him, 'Maybe you didn't get me in a jam.' And, 'We were seen down there.' The following day Weigand was discharged.

As this court stated in *NLRB v. Condenser Corp.*, 128 F.2d at 75 (3 Cir.), an employer may discharge an employee for a good reason, a poor reason or no reason at all so long as the provisions of the [NLRA] are not violated. It is, of course, a violation to discharge an employee because he has engaged in activities on behalf of a union. Conversely an employer may retain an employee for a good reason, a bad reason or no reason at all and the reason is not a concern of the Board. But it is certainly too great a strain on our credibility to assert, as does the petitioner, that Weigand was discharged for an accumulation of offenses. We think that he was discharged because his work on behalf of the CIO had become known to the plant manager. That ended his sinecure at the Budd plant. The Board found that he was discharged because of his activities on behalf of the union. The record shows that the Board's finding was based on sufficient evidence. . . . The order of the Board will be enforced.

Notes

1. *Edward G. Budd* demonstrates the intent requirement of § 8(a)(3). In that case, the Board, with court approval, explained that employers may not simply fire "bad" employees whose conduct they had tolerated when the employees' union sympathies were aligned with management's. Here, the Board found that the company only discharged employee Budd when he supported the CIO union over the company union, the Budd Employee Representation Association. This conclusion foreshadows the Board's later *Wright Line* doctrine, in which the Board permits the employer to offer the affirmative defense that, although union animus was a substantial motivating factor in the adverse employment action, the employer would have (not could have) taken the adverse action anyway.

2. It's hard to imagine a worse employee than Weigand in *Edward G. Budd*—until you've read *Mueller Brass Co. v. NLRB*, 544 F.2d 815 (5th Cir. 1977). In that case, James Roy Rogers had been a known union adherent for 18 months but was only discharged after he displayed "a mechanized artificial male sex organ" to a female coworker, followed by "an indecent and offensive proposition" to another female coworker the following night during his shift. After an investigation in which Rogers admitted to the conduct, the company discharged Rogers for violating a plant rule, which forbade employees from "engag[ing] in disorderly, immoral, indecent or illegal conduct." The court reversed the Board's finding that the company's reason for discharging Rogers was pretextual. Although there was ample evidence that the company harbored union animus and even discriminated against Rogers in the past because of his status as a union supporter, the court could not agree that substantial evidence supported the Board's finding that the company merely latched onto a convenient excuse when it discharged him pursuant to the plant rule. *Id.* at 818–19. The dissent would have upheld the Board's conclusion on substantial evidence grounds, based primarily on evidence that the company tolerated a general level of sexual horseplay in the workplace without subjecting the workers to discipline. What is the difference between Weigand and Rogers? Is there a way to reconcile these cases? Return to these cases after you read *NLRB v. Transportation Management, infra.*

But first, consider **Radio Officers' Union v. NLRB**, 347 U.S. 17 (1954). This case discusses the circumstances in which the Board may infer that an employer had the required intent to "encourage or discourage membership in any labor organization" in violation of § 8(a)(3).

Radio Officers' is really three consolidated cases: **Teamsters**, **Radio Officers'**, and **Gaynor**. In **NLRB v. Int'l Bhd. of Teamsters**, 196 F.2d 1 (8th Cir. 1952) (*Teamsters*), the Eighth Circuit, following a Third Circuit decision (*NLRB v. Reliable Newspaper Delivery, Inc.*, 187 F.2d 547 (3d Cir. 1951)) "held that express proof that employer discrimination had the effect of encouraging or discouraging employees in their attitude toward union membership is an essential element to establish violation of this section."

That holding conflicted with the holdings of several circuits upholding the Board's contrary view. *See **Radio Officers' Union of Commercial Telegraphers U. v. NLRB**,* 196 F.2d 960 (2d Cir. 1952) (*Radio Officers*); *NLRB v. Gaynor News Co., Inc.,* 197 F.2d 719 (2d Cir. 1952) (*Gaynor*). "[I]n *Gaynor,* the Second Circuit also rejected the contention ... that there can be no violation of § 8(a)(3) unless it is shown by specific evidence that the employer intended his discriminatory action to encourage or discourage union membership. The Second Circuit determined that the employer intended the natural result of his discriminatory action. ... Moreover, *Radio Officers* and *Teamsters* present conflicting views by Courts of Appeals as to the scope of the phrase 'membership in any labor organization' in § 8(a)(3). The Eighth Circuit restricts this phrase to 'adhesion to membership,' i.e., joining or remaining on a union's membership roster; the Second Circuit, on the other hand, interprets it to include obligations of membership, i.e., being a good union member. ... *Radio Officers* also raises subsidiary questions regarding the interrelationship of § 8(a)(3) with § 8(b)(2) ...."

The Supreme Court ultimately upheld the Board's view. The facts of the three cases are as follows:

Teamsters. The union operated a hiring hall that referred truck drivers to the company based on a seniority list that included both union members and non-members. The agreement maintained that all seniority disputes were to be referred to the union. Frank Boston, a truck driver and union member, was placed at the bottom of the list because he was one year in arrears in paying his union dues. The company denied work to Boston for which he would have received compensation had he maintained his position on the list. The complaint alleged that the union violated §§ 8(b)(1)(A) and 8(b)(2) by causing the company to discriminate against Boston by reducing his seniority standing because of Boston's delinquency in paying his union dues. The Board held that the union unlawfully discriminated against Boston. The Eighth Circuit denied the Board's application for enforcement. The court held that the evidence supported the Board's finding of discrimination but that "discrimination alone is not sufficient" to support the conclusion that the union's actions "did or would encourage or discourage membership in any labor organization."

Radio Officers. The complaint alleged that the Radio Officers' Union of the Commercial Telegraphers Union, A.F.L., caused the A. H. Bull Steamship Company to discriminatorily refuse to employ William Christian Fowler in violation of §§ 8(b)(1)(A) and 8(b)(2). No complaint was issued against the company because no charge was against it. The Board held that the union violated the Act. The Second Circuit enforced the Board's order. The court held that the union's refusal to clear Fowler for work "caused the company to unlawfully discriminate against Fowler. Without the necessary clearance it could not accept him as an employee. The result was to encourage membership in the union. Such conduct displayed to all non-members the union's power and the strong measure it was prepared to take to protect union members."

Gaynor. The complaint alleged that the company, a wholesale newspaper and periodical distributor, violated §§ 8(a)(1), (2), and (3), by agreeing with the union to grant retroactive wage increase and vacation payments to employees who were union members (Newspaper and Mail Deliverers' Union of New York and Vicinity) and refusing such benefits to other employees because they were not union members. The Board concluded that "the contract affords no defense to the allegation that the Respondent engaged in disparate treatment of employees on the basis of union membership or lack of it," and held that the company had violated the Act as alleged. The Board rejected the company's arguments that its actions had not violated § 8(a)(3) because "the record is barren of any evidence that the discriminatory treatment of non-union employees encouraged them to join the union" or had such purpose. Further, there could be no such evidence because all the non-union employees had previously sought membership in the union and been denied because of the union's closed-shop policy. The Board held that "it is obvious that the discrimination with respect to retroactive wages and vacation benefits had the natural and probable effect not only of encouraging non-union employees to join the union, but also of encouraging union employees to retain their union membership." The Second Circuit enforced. The court found that the union "represented the majority of employees and was the exclusive bargaining agent for the plant. Accordingly, it could not betray the trust of non-union members, by bargaining for special benefits to union members only, thus leaving the non-union members with no means of equalizing the situation." The court rejected as irrelevant the company's contention that its action "had neither the purpose nor the effect required by § 8(a)(3)": "discriminatory conduct, such as that practiced here, is inherently conducive to increased union membership. [T]here can be little doubt that it 'encourages' union membership, by increasing the number of workers who would like to join and/or their quantum of desire."

Below is an excerpt from the Court's reasoning.

Radio Officers' Union v. NLRB

The Supreme Court of the United States
347 U.S. 17 (1954)

Reed, J.

. . . In past cases we have been called upon to clarify the terms 'discrimination' and 'membership in any labor organization'. Discrimination is not contested in these cases: involuntary reduction of seniority, refusal to hire for an available job, and disparate wage treatment are clearly discriminatory. But the scope of the phrase 'membership in a labor organization' is in issue here. Subject to limitations, we have held that phrase to include discrimination to discourage participation in union activities as well as to discourage adhesion to union membership.

Similar principles govern the interpretation of union membership where encouragement is alleged. The policy of the Act is to insulate employees' jobs from their [§ 7] organizational rights. Thus §§ 8(a)(3) and 8(b)(2) were designed to allow employees to freely exercise their right to join unions, be good, bad, or indifferent members, or abstain from joining any union without imperiling their livelihood. . . .

. . . [T]he Eighth Circuit too restrictively interpreted the term 'membership' in *Teamsters*. Boston was discriminated against by his employer because he was delinquent in a union obligation. Thus he was denied employment to which he was otherwise entitled for no reason other than his tardy payment of union dues. The union caused this discrimination by applying a rule apparently aimed at encouraging prompt payment of dues. The union's action was not sanctioned by a valid union security contract, and . . . the union did not choose to terminate Boston's membership for his delinquency. Thus the union by requesting such discrimination, and the employer by submitting to such an illegal request, deprived Boston of the right guaranteed by the Act to join in or abstain from union activities without thereby affecting his job. [T]he Second Circuit correctly concluded in *Radio Officers* that such encouragement to remain in good standing in a union is proscribed. Thus that union in causing the employer to discriminate against Fowler by denying him employment in order to coerce Fowler into following the union's desired hiring practices deprived Fowler of a protected right. . . .

The language of § 8(a)(3) is not ambiguous. The unfair labor practice is for an employer to encourage or discourage membership by means of discrimination. Thus this section does not outlaw all encouragement or discouragement of membership in labor organizations; only such as is accomplished by discrimination is prohibited. Nor does this section outlaw discrimination in employment as such; only such discrimination as encourages or discourages membership in a labor organization is proscribed.

. . . .

That Congress intended the employer's purpose in discriminating to be controlling is clear. The Senate Report on the Wagner Act said: 'Of course nothing in the bill prevents an employer from discharging a man for incompetence; from advancing him for special aptitude; or from demoting him for failure to perform.' . . .

But it is also clear that specific evidence of intent to encourage or discourage is not an indispensable element of proof of violation of § 8(a)(3). . . . Both the Board and the courts have recognized that proof of certain types of discrimination satisfies the intent requirement. This recognition that specific proof of intent is unnecessary where employer conduct inherently encourages or discourages union membership is but an application of the common law rule that a man is held to intend the foreseeable consequences of his conduct. . . . Thus an employer's protestation that he did not intend to encourage or discourage must be unavailing where a natural consequence of his action was such encouragement or discouragement. Concluding that encouragement or discouragement will result, it is presumed that he intended such consequence. In such circumstances intent to encourage is sufficiently established. Our decision in *Republic Aviation Corp. v. NLRB*, 324 U.S. 79, relied upon by the Board to support its contention that employers' motives are irrelevant under § 8(a)(3), applied this principle. That decision dealt primarily with the right of the Board to infer discouragement from facts proven for purposes of proof of violation of § 8(3). In holding that discharges and suspensions of employees under company 'no solicitation' rules for soliciting union membership, in the circumstances disclosed, violated § 8(3), we noted that such employer action was not 'motivated by opposition to the particular union, or we deduce, to unionism' and that 'there was no union bias or discrimination by the company in enforcing the rule.' But we affirmed the Board's holding that the rules involved were invalid when applied to union solicitation since they interfered with the employees' right to organize. Since the rules were no defense and the employers intended to discriminate solely on the ground of such protected union activity, it did not matter that they did not intend to discourage membership since such was a foreseeable result.

In *Gaynor*, the Second Circuit also properly applied this principle. The court there held that disparate wage treatment of employees based solely on union membership status is 'inherently conducive to increased union membership.' In holding that a natural consequence of discrimination, based solely on union membership or lack thereof, is discouragement or encouragement of membership in such union, the court merely recognized a fact of common experience — that the desire of employees to unionize is directly proportional to the advantages thought to be obtained from such action. No more striking example of discrimination so foreseeably causing employee response as to obviate the need for any other proof of intent is apparent than the payment of different wages to union employees doing a job than to nonunion employees doing the same job. . . .

In *Gaynor* it was conceded that the sole criterion for extra payments was union membership. . . .

. . . We . . . hold that in the circumstances of this case, the union being exclusive bargaining agent for both member and nonmember employees, the employer could not, without violating § 8(a)(3), discriminate in wages solely on the basis of such membership. . . . [T]he legislative history of the [NLRA] emphasize[s] that exclusive bargaining agents are powerless 'to make agreements more favorable to the majority than to the minority.' Such discriminatory contracts are illegal and provide no defense to an action under § 8(a)(3). . . .

Petitioners in *Gaynor* and *Radio Officers* contend that the Board's orders in these cases should not have been enforced by the Second Circuit because the records do not include 'independent proof that encouragement of Union membership actually occurred.' The Eighth Circuit subscribed to this view that such independent proof is required in *Teamsters* when it denied enforcement of the Board's order in that proceeding on the ground that it was not supported by substantial evidence of encouragement. The Board argues that actual encouragement need not be proved but that a tendency to encourage is sufficient, and 'such tendency is sufficiently established if its existence may reasonably be inferred from the character of the discrimination.'

We considered this problem in [*Republic Aviation*]. To the contention 'that there must be evidence before the Board to show that the rules and orders of the employers interfered with and discouraged union organization in the circumstances and situation of each company' we replied that the statutory plan for an adversary proceeding 'does not go beyond the necessity for the production of evidential facts, however, and compel evidence as to the results which may flow from such facts. . . . An administrative agency . . . may infer . . . from the proven facts such conclusions as reasonably may be based upon the facts proven. One of the purposes which lead to the creation of such boards is to have decisions based upon evidential facts under the particular statute made by experienced officials with an adequate appreciation of the complexities of the subject which is entrusted to their administration. . . .'

. . . In these cases we but restated a rule familiar to the law and followed by all factfinding tribunals—that it is permissible to draw on experience in factual inquiries.

[The Court rejected the contention that these cases ceased to be good law after the Taft-Hartley amendments.]

Encouragement and discouragement are 'subtle things' requiring 'a high degree of introspective perception.' . . . But . . . it is common experience that the desire of employees to unionize is raised or lowered by the advantages thought to be attained by such action. Moreover, the Act does not require that the employees discriminated against be the ones encouraged for purposes of violations of § 8(a)(3). Nor does the Act require that this change in employees' 'quantum of desire' to join a union have immediate manifestations.

Obviously, it would be gross inconsistency to hold that an inherent effect of certain discrimination is encouragement of union membership, but that the Board may not reasonably infer such encouragement. We have held that a natural result of the disparate wage treatment in *Gaynor* was encouragement of union membership; thus it would be unreasonable to draw any inference other than that encouragement would result from such action. . . .

The circumstances in *Radio Officers* and *Teamsters* are nearly identical. In each case the employer discriminated upon the instigation of the union. The purposes of the unions in causing such discrimination clearly were to encourage members to perform obligations or supposed obligations of membership. . . . Both Boston and Fowler were denied jobs by employers solely because of the unions' actions. Since encouragement of union membership is obviously a natural and foreseeable consequence of any employer discrimination at the request of a union, those employers must be presumed to have intended such encouragement. It follows that it was eminently reasonable for the Board to infer encouragement of union membership, and the Eighth Circuit erred in holding encouragement not proved.

[*Radio Officers* is affirmed. *Teamsters* is reversed. *Gaynor* is affirmed.]

Notes

1. *Radio Officers* stands for the principle that the General Counsel need not prove the specific intent to discriminate between union and nonunion status where the discrimination naturally results in the encouragement or discouragement of union membership. *B.G. Costich & Sons, Inc. v. NLRB*, 613 F.2d 450 (2d Cir. 1980) demonstrates the principle that the General Counsel must show unlawful intent unless the employer's conduct inherently encourages or discourages union membership. In that case, the Board held that an employer violated § 8(a)(3), notwithstanding the fact that no affirmative evidence of intent was proffered, where the employer made payments to a pension fund on behalf of union casual workers but not on behalf of nonunion casual workers in a state where workers had to join the union within 30 days. The Court rejected as speculative the Board's conclusion that workers would have been encouraged to join the union sooner by a desire to receive 30 days of benefits 15 years from the date of hire.

2. In the context of remanding a case as inconsistent with *Radio Officers'* progeny, one court recently articulated the requirement as follows:

> The Supreme Court has held, time and again, that a violation of § 8(a)(3) normally turns on an employer's antiunion purpose or motive. "That Congress intended the employer's *purpose in discriminating* to be controlling is clear." [*Radio Officers'*] . . . .
>
> However, under certain circumstances, actual proof of an improper antiunion motive has been held to be unnecessary. Specifically, "two categories of § 8(a)(3) violations . . . do not require *proof* of motive." . . . . "First, if an employer's conduct is 'inherently destructive' of important employee rights, no proof of anti-union motivation is needed and the Board can find an unfair labor practice even if the employer introduces evidence that his conduct was motivated by business considerations." . . . . "Second, if the employer's conduct could have adversely affected employee rights to some extent[,] the employer must establish that [it] was motivated by legitimate objectives," and, if [it] does not, "the conduct constitutes an unfair labor practice 'without reference to intent.'" . . . . If the employer does proffer a substantial and legitimate business justification for the different treatment, however, it can be overcome by proof of antiunion motive, notwithstanding an otherwise legitimate justification.

800 River Rd. Operating Co. LLC v. NLRB, 784 F.3d 902, 908–09 (3d Cir. 2015).

Other cases have gone farther than *Radio Officers*. In *NLRB v. Erie Resistor Corp.*, 373 U.S. 221, 228, 231 (1963), in the context of concluding that an employer's grant of super-seniority to strikebreakers violated § 8(a)(3), the court observed that some conduct "carries with it unavoidable consequences which the employer not only foresaw but which he must have intended" and thus bears "its own indicia of intent." In *NLRB v. Great Danes Trailers, Inc.*, 388 U.S. 26, 34 (1967), in the context of concluding that an employer's refusal to grant vacation benefits to strikers violated § 8(a)(3), the Supreme Court explained that "if it can reasonably be concluded that the employer's discriminatory conduct was 'inherently destructive' of important employee rights, no proof of an antiunion motivation is needed and the Board can find an unfair labor practice even if the employer introduces evidence that the conduct was motivated by business considerations." In *Great Dane*, the Court never decided the question whether the employer's conduct was inherently destructive of employees' rights because the employer never came forward with any business justification for its action. Accordingly, the employer's conduct violated § 8(a)(3) because the employer failed to meet its burden of producing evidence of another motivation. For more on this topic, see Chapter 11.

3. What result if the practice of granting super-seniority rights to union officials has become an industry standard? In *NLRB v. American Can Co.*, 658 F.2d 746 (10th Cir. 1981), the court upheld the Board's finding that the union violated § 8(b)(1)(A) and the employer violated § 8(a)(3) when the parties applied a super-seniority clause to a union trustee and a union guard. The court refused to pass on the Board's practice of finding such clauses presumptively valid when limited to layoff and recall of stewards.

4. What result if the employer has an honest but mistaken belief that an employee has engaged in misconduct? In *NLRB v. Burnup & Sims, Inc.*, 379 U.S. 21 (1964), the employer discharged two pro-union employees (Davis and Harmon) when employee Pate advised the Superintendent that Davis and Harmon, while soliciting Pate, allegedly told him that the union would use dynamite to get the union in if the union did not obtain majority cards. The court held those discharges unlawful in light of two Board findings: the allegations were untrue and the employer honestly believed them to be true. How can an employer protect itself in such a case? Could it conduct an investigation of the allegations before jumping to conclusions? Do you think that this case turns on the reasonableness of the employer's honest belief?

5. In *Teamsters*, is the union encouraging nonmembers to join the union or discouraging union membership? Does it matter?

Problem 5.3

An employer and union enter into the following agreement (which happens to be the wording of the agreement in *American Can Co.*):

> super-seniority shall apply to a total of not more than ten local union officers and grievance committeemen who, notwithstanding their positions on the seniority roster, shall have preferential seniority in case of layoff or recall, provided there is work available which they can perform.

Do the parties violate the NLRA when they apply that clause to union stewards? In *NLRB v. Milk Drivers & Dairy Employees, Local 338, Teamsters*, 531 F.2d 1162, 1166–67 (2d Cir. 1976), the court upheld the Board's finding that the union violated § 8(b)(1)(A) and (2) and the employer violated § 8(a)(3) when the parties entered into an agreement providing that the union's shop steward shall be deemed the most senior employee in the plant even if other workers have accumulated far more years of service. In rejecting the union's asserted justification, the court observed:

> If a union finds that it must offer incentives to attract qualified stewards, it may pay a salary to the stewards, or may give them other non-job benefits. The policy of §§ 8(a)(3) and 8(b)(2) is to insulate employees' jobs from their organizational rights. . . . For the union to employ job-related benefits to maintain its own organization would, thus, fly in the face of this statutory purpose.

Could the union have prevailed if it had proffered additional evidence showing that alternative inducements were insufficient to attract quality stewards?

B. Burdens and Proof

1. In the Private Sector

NLRB v. Transportation Management Corp.

Supreme Court of the United States
462 U.S. 393, 103 S. Ct. 2469, 76 L. Ed. 2d 667 (1983)

White, J.

The [NLRA] makes unlawful the discharge of a worker because of union activity, but employers retain the right to discharge workers for any number of other reasons unrelated to the employee's union activities. When the [NLRB] General Counsel . . . [issues] a complaint alleging that an employee was discharged because of his union activities, the employer may assert legitimate motives for his decision. In *Wright Line*, 251 N.L.R.B. 1083 (1980), *enforced*, 662 F.2d 899 (1st Cir. 1981), *cert. denied*, 455 U.S. 989 (1982), the [NLRB] reformulated the allocation of the burden of proof in such cases. It determined that the General Counsel carried the burden of persuading the Board that an anti-union animus contributed to the employer's decision to discharge an employee, a burden that does not shift, but that the employer, even if it failed to meet or neutralize the General Counsel's showing, could avoid the finding that it violated the statute by demonstrating by a preponderance of the evidence that the worker would have been fired even if he had not been involved with the Union. The question presented in this case is whether the burden placed on the employer in *Wright Line* is consistent with §§ 8(a)(1) and 8(a)(3), as well as with § 10(c) of the NLRA, 29 U.S.C. § 160(c), which provides that the Board must prove an unlawful labor practice by a "preponderance of the evidence."

Prior to his discharge, Sam Santillo was a bus driver for respondent Transportation Management Corp. On March 19, 1979, Santillo talked to officials of the [Teamsters] about organizing the drivers who worked with him. Over the next four days Santillo discussed with his fellow drivers the possibility of joining the Teamsters and distributed authorization cards. On the night of March 23, George Patterson, who supervised Santillo and the other drivers, told one of the drivers that he had heard of Santillo's activities. Patterson referred to Santillo as two-faced, and promised to get even with him.

Later that evening Patterson talked to Ed West, who was also a bus driver for respondent. Patterson asked, "What's with Sam and the Union?" Patterson said that he took Santillo's actions personally, recounted several favors he had done for Santillo, and added that he would remember Santillo's activities when Santillo again asked for a favor. On Monday, March 26, Santillo was discharged. Patterson told Santillo that he was being fired for leaving his keys in the bus and taking unauthorized breaks.

Santillo filed a [charge] . . . alleging that he had been discharged because of his union activities, contrary to §§ 8(a)(1) and 8(a)(3) of the NLRA. The General Counsel issued a complaint. The administrative law judge (ALJ) determined by a preponderance of the evidence that Patterson clearly had an anti-union animus and that Santillo's discharge was motivated by a desire to discourage union activities. The ALJ also found that the asserted reasons for the discharge could not withstand scrutiny. Patterson's disapproval of Santillo's practice of leaving his keys in the bus was clearly a pretext, for Patterson had not known about Santillo's practice until after he had decided to discharge Santillo; moreover, the practice of leaving keys in buses was commonplace among respondent's employees. Respondent identified two types of unauthorized breaks, coffee breaks and stops at home. With respect to both coffee breaks and stopping at home, the ALJ found that Santillo was never cautioned or admonished about such behavior, and that the employer had not followed its customary practice of issuing three written warnings before discharging a driver. The ALJ also found that the taking of coffee breaks during working hours was normal practice, and that respondent tolerated the practice unless the breaks interfered with the driver's performance of his duties. In any event, said the ALJ, respondent had never taken any adverse personnel action against an employee because of such behavior. While acknowledging that Santillo had engaged in some unsatisfactory conduct, the ALJ was not persuaded that Santillo would have been fired had it not been for his union activities.

The Board affirmed, adopting with some clarification the ALJ's findings and conclusions and expressly applying its *Wright Line* decision. It stated that respondent had failed to carry its burden of persuading the Board that the discharge would have taken place had Santillo not engaged in activity protected by the Act. The [First Circuit], relying on its previous decision rejecting the Board's *Wright Line* test, *NLRB v. Wright Line*, 662 F.2d 899 (1st Cir. 1981), refused to enforce the Board's order and remanded for consideration of whether the General Counsel had proved by a preponderance of the evidence that Santillo would not have been fired had it not been for his union activities. . . . We granted certiorari, . . . because of conflicts on the issue among the Courts of Appeals. We now reverse [the First Circuit]. . . .

Under these provisions it is undisputed that if the employer fires an employee for having engaged in union activities and has no other basis for the discharge, or if the reasons that he proffers are pretextual, the employer [violates §8(a)(3) and (1)]. He does not violate the NLRA, however, if any anti-union animus that he might have entertained did not contribute at all to an otherwise lawful discharge for good cause. Soon after the passage of the Act, the Board held that it was an unfair labor practice for an employer to discharge a worker where anti-union animus actually contributed to the discharge decision. . . . In *Consumers Research*, 2 N.L.R.B. 57, 73 (1936), the Board rejected the position that "antecedent to a finding of violation of the Act, it must be found that the sole motive for discharge was the employee's union activity." It explained that "[s]uch an interpretation is repugnant to the purpose and meaning of the Act, and . . . may not be made." *Ibid.* In its Third Annual Report, the Board stated, "Where the employer has discharged an employee for two or more reasons, and one of them is union affiliation or activity, the Board has found a violation [of §8(a)(3)]." . . . In the following year in *Dow Chemical Co.*, 13 N.L.R.B. 993, 1023 (1939), *enforced in relevant part*, 117 F.2d 455 (6th Cir. 1941), the Board stated that a violation could be found where the employer acted out of anti-union bias "whether or not the [employer] may have had some other motive . . . and without regard to whether or not the [employer's] asserted motive was lawful." . . . . This construction of the Act — that to establish an unfair labor practice the General Counsel need show by a preponderance of the evidence only that a discharge is in any way motivated by a desire to frustrate union activity — was plainly rational and acceptable. The Board has adhered to that construction of the Act since that time.

At the same time, there were decisions indicating that the presence of an anti-union motivation in a discharge case was not the end of the matter. An employer could escape the consequences of a violation by proving that without regard to the impermissible motivation, the employer would have taken the same action for wholly permissible reasons. . . .

The Courts of Appeals were not entirely satisfied with the Board's approach to dual-motive cases. The Board's *Wright Line* decision in 1980 was an attempt to restate its analysis in a way more acceptable to the Courts of Appeals. The Board held that the General Counsel . . . had the burden of proving that the employee's conduct protected by §7 was a substantial or a motivating factor in the discharge. Even if this was the case, and the employer failed to rebut it, the employer could avoid being held in violation of §§8(a)(1) and 8(a)(3) by proving by a preponderance of the evidence that the discharge rested on the employee's unprotected conduct as well and that the employee would have lost his job in any event. It thus became clear, if it was not clear before, that proof that the discharge would have occurred in any event and for valid reasons amounted to an affirmative defense on which the employer carried the burden of proof by a preponderance of the evidence. "The shifting burden merely requires the employer to make out what is actually an affirmative defense. . . ." *Wright Line, supra*, at 1088, n. 11; see also *id.* at 1084, n. 5.

The [First Circuit] refused enforcement of the *Wright Line* decision because in its view it was error to place the burden on the employer to prove that the discharge would have occurred had the forbidden motive not been present. The General Counsel, the [court] held, had the burden of showing not only that a forbidden motivation contributed to the discharge but also that the discharge would not have taken place independently of the protected conduct of the employee. The [court] was quite correct, and the Board does not disagree, that throughout the proceedings, the General Counsel carries the burden of proving the elements of an unfair labor practice. Section 10(c) . . . expressly directs that violations may be adjudicated only "upon the preponderance of the testimony" taken by the Board. The Board's rules also state "the Board's attorney has the burden of pro[ving] violations of Section 8." . . . We are quite sure, however, that the [court] erred in holding that § 10(c) forbids placing the burden on the employer to prove that absent the improper motivation he would have acted in the same manner for wholly legitimate reasons.

As we understand the Board's decisions, they have consistently held that the unfair labor practice consists of a discharge or other adverse action that is based in whole or in part on anti-union animus — or as the Board now puts it, that the employee's protected conduct was a substantial or motivating factor in the adverse action. The General Counsel has the burden of proving these elements under § 10(c). But the Board's construction of the statute permits an employer to avoid being adjudicated a violator by showing what his actions would have been regardless of his forbidden motivation. It extends to the employer what the Board considers to be an affirmative defense but does not change or add to the elements of the unfair labor practice that the General Counsel has the burden of proving under § 10(c). We assume that the Board could reasonably have construed the Act in the manner insisted on by the [court]. We also assume that the Board might have considered a showing by the employer that the adverse action would have occurred in any event as not obviating a violation adjudication but as going only to the permissible remedy, in which event the burden of proof could surely have been put on the employer. The Board has instead chosen to recognize, as it insists it has done for many years, what it designates as an affirmative defense that the employer has the burden of sustaining. We are unprepared to hold that this is an impermissible construction of the Act. "[T]he Board's construction here, while it may not be required by the Act, is at least permissible under it . . . ," and in these circumstances its position is entitled to deference. *NLRB v. Weingarten, Inc.*, 420 U.S. 251, 266–267 (1975); *NLRB v. Erie Resistor Corp.*, 373 U.S. 221, 236 (1963).

The Board's allocation of the burden of proof is clearly reasonable in this context, for the reason stated in *NLRB v. Remington Rand*, 94 F.2d 862, 872 (2d Cir.), *cert. denied*, 304 U.S. 576 (1938), a case on which the Board relied when it began taking the position that the burden of persuasion could be shifted. . . . The employer is a wrongdoer; he has acted out of a motive that is declared illegitimate by the statute. It is fair that he bear the risk that the influence of legal and illegal motives cannot be separated, because he knowingly created the risk and because the risk was created not by innocent activity but by his own wrongdoing.

In *Mount Healthy City Board of Education v. Doyle*, 429 U.S. 274 (1977), we found it prudent, albeit in a case implicating the Constitution, to set up an allocation of the burden of proof which the Board heavily relied on and borrowed from in its *Wright Line* decision. There, we held that the plaintiff had to show that the employer's disapproval of his First Amendment protected expression played a role in the employer's decision to discharge him. If that burden of persuasion were carried, the burden would be on the defendant to show by a preponderance of the evidence that he would have reached the same decision even if, hypothetically, he had not been motivated by a desire to punish plaintiff for exercising his First Amendment rights. The analogy to *Mount Healthy* drawn by the Board was a fair one.

For these reasons, we conclude that the Court of Appeals erred in refusing to enforce the Board's orders, which rested on the Board's *Wright Line* decision.

The Board was justified . . . in concluding that Santillo would not have been discharged had the employer not considered his efforts to establish a union. At least two of the transgressions that purportedly would have in any event prompted Santillo's discharge were commonplace, and yet no transgressor had ever before received any kind of discipline. Moreover, the employer departed from its usual practice in dealing with rules infractions; indeed, not only did the employer not warn Santillo that his actions would result in being subjected to discipline, it never even expressed its disapproval of his conduct. In addition, Patterson, the person who made the initial decision to discharge Santillo, was obviously upset with Santillo for engaging in such protected activity. It is thus clear that the Board's finding that Santillo would not have been fired even if the employer had not had an anti-union animus was "supported by substantial evidence on the record considered as a whole". . . . [T]he judgment is *Reversed*.

Notes

1. An employer unlawfully discriminates against an employee where it takes an adverse employment action because of that employee's union activity. *See* 29 U.S.C. §§ 158(a)(3) and (1). Under the Board's *Wright Line* test, the Board focuses on the employer's motive. If union animus is a substantial motivating factor in the employer's decision, then the employer acted unlawfully unless it can be shown that the employer would have taken the same action even in the absence of the employee's union activity.

2. The question of an employer's motivation is a question of fact. The Board may properly rely on circumstantial evidence. *Hosp. Cristo Redentor, Inc. v. NLRB*, 488 F.3d 513, 518 (1st Cir. 2007); *NLRB v. Link-Belt Co.*, 311 U.S. 584, 602 (1941). In particular, the Board may reasonably rely on the following in drawing an inference of unlawful motive:

The employer's knowledge of employees' union activities, *Tasty Baking Co. v. NLRB*, 254 F.3d 114, 125 (D.C. Cir. 2001) (finding that a Philadelphia bakery violated § (8)(a)(3) where it admitted that its adverse employment action was motivated by its knowledge of employees union activity outside factory);

The coincidence in timing between the adverse employment action and onset of the employer's knowledge of union activity, *Healthcare Employees Union, Local 399, Affiliated With Serv. Employees Int'l Union, AFL-CIO v. NLRB*, 463 F.3d 909, 919 (9th Cir. 2006) (supporting the Board's finding that an employer's decision to look into outsourcing employee work nine days after employees' filing of a petition for a representative election supported "a powerful inference of anti-union animus");

The employer's expressed hostility toward union activities, *Traction Wholesale Ctr. Co., Inc. v. NLRB*, 216 F.3d 92, 99 (D.C. Cir. 2000) (employer's unrefuted, anti-union statements supported finding of anti-union animus);

The employer's failure to investigate fully the purported reason for the adverse action, *Conley v. NLRB*, 520 F.3d 629, 643–44 (6th Cir. 2008) (employer's lack of investigation into terminated employee's absence record and productivity statistics demonstrated that the employer's listing of these grounds for termination was merely the development of post hoc rationale);

The employer's disparate treatment of employees on the basis of union activities, *NLRB v. Aquatech, Inc.*, 926 F.2d 538, 547 (6th Cir. 1991) (employer had not demonstrated a "discriminatory application or lax administration of policies" in its termination of employees weeks after a probationary period, as other disciplinary actions had been taken well after a week from the time of probation); and

The employer's reliance on pretextual reasons to justify the adverse action, *Shamrock Foods Co. v. NLRB*, 346 F.3d 1130, 1136 (D.C. Cir. 2003) (an employer's proper application of a "but for" rationale to the termination of one employee did not apply to the termination of another). For an interesting recent discussion of pretext, see *Electrolux Home Products, Inc.*, 368 N.L.R.B. No. 34 (2019).

3. In *W&M Properties of Conn., Inc. v. NLRB*, 514 F.3d 1341 (D.C. Cir. 2008), the court concluded that substantial evidence supported the Board's finding that W&M Properties violated § 8(a)(3) when it declined to rehire employees of Trizechahn, a union company it had just purchased. Here, the General Counsel demonstrated that union animus was a substantial motivating factor in the employer's decision to refuse to rehire. The employer was unable to support its claim that it failed to rehire the unionized engineers because the property at which they worked was in disrepair. However, W&M went on to express interest in hiring the non-unionized manager at the property who would have been primarily responsible for the property's disrepair. This fact, combined with statements of union animus, showed that W&M's reasoning for failing to rehire the previously unionized engineers was pre-textual and would have not arose had the engineers not been unionized.

4. Notwithstanding the protections afforded by §8(a)(3), Congress clarified in §10(c) that §8(a)(3) does not bar an employer from discharging an employee "for cause." What result if:

a. An employer, who is about to fire an employee because of his union activity, suddenly learns that the employee has been stealing large sums of money from the cash register. The employer changes the letter of termination to read: "Reason for termination: theft."

b. Does the result change if the employer learns that the employee has been bringing company pencils home?

c. Does the result change if the employer learns that the employee had been tardy to work three times that month? What if the employer has a policy of not firing employees for tardiness that is less than 15 minutes?

d. For a recent example of the Board's discussion of employer affirmative defenses to §8(a)(3) charges, *see Preferred Building Services*, 366 N.L.R.B. No. 159 (2018) (holding that an employer may justifiably discharge employees engaged in unprotected picketing).

5. Several courts have attempted to clarify the differences between Title VII's burden-shifting analysis and the Board's *Wright Line* test. Under Title VII's famous burden-shifting test, the plaintiff-employee must show that he or she (1) belongs to a group protected under Title VII; (2) applied for and was qualified for a job for which the employer was seeking applicants; (3) was rejected for (fired from) the position; and (4) the position was filled or the position remained open and the employer continued to seek applicants of the same qualifications. This is called the "prima facie case." *See McDonnell Douglas Corp. v. Green*, 411 U.S. 792, 802 (1973). Once the plaintiff meets the relatively light burden of the prima facie case, the burden shifts to the employer to produce a legitimate, nondiscriminatory reason for the adverse employment action. The burden then switches to the plaintiff-employee to show that the employer's legitimate, nondiscriminatory reason is pretextual. The Supreme Court in *Furnco Const. Corp. v. Waters*, 438 U.S. 567, 577 (1978), explained the purpose of this burden-shifting analysis:

> A prima facie case under *McDonnell Douglas* raises an inference of discrimination only because we presume these acts, if otherwise unexplained, are more likely than not based on the consideration of impermissible factors. . . . And we are willing to presume this largely because we know from our experience that more often than not people do not act in a totally arbitrary manner, without any underlying reasons, especially in a business setting. Thus, when all legitimate reasons for rejecting an applicant have been eliminated as possible reasons for the employer's actions, it is more likely than not the employer, who we generally assume acts only with *some* reason, based his decision on an impermissible consideration such as race.

While there are many similarities between *McDonnell Douglas* and *Wright*, the differences are significant. The court in *Valmont Indus., Inc. v. NLRB*, 244 F.3d 454 (5th Cir. 2001) explained that:

> ... the term "*prima facie* case" is inappropriate in this context. ... The term "*prima facie* case" is more often used for the allocation of burdens of proof in Title VII cases. However, the General Counsel's burden is not the same as that of the plaintiff in a Title VII case. The General Counsel must do more than simply support an inference that protected conduct is a motivating factor in the employer's decision. The General Counsel's burden is to persuade the Board that the employer acted out of antiunion animus. "Because of the continuing confusion surrounding the nature of the General Counsel's burden, we agree with those courts who have suggested that the Board no longer use the term '*prima facie* case,' in the *Wright Line* context." *NLRB v. CWI of Maryland, Inc.*, 127 F.3d 319, 330 n.7 (4th Cir.1997) (collecting cases).

Why do you think the federal government, through the interpretation of federal legislation, has created two different types of tests for proving discrimination—one for proving discrimination based on race, color, gender, national origin, or religion (Title VII protected categories), and the other based on union activity?

6. Another important distinction between Title VII and *Wright Line* is that, under *Wright Line*, an employer can escape liability if the Board is persuaded that the employer *would have* taken the adverse employment action even in the absence of union animus. Under the 1991 amendments to Title VII, an employer cannot escape liability in these circumstances. If an employer is found to have taken an adverse employment action because of a person's Title VII protected category, the employer remains liable even if it would have taken such action in the absence of the person's Title VII protected category. The employer can, however, limit its damages in such cases.

7. Technically, an employer does not violate §8(a)(3) when it adversely affects an employee's employment because of his nonunion concerted activity—for example, concerted activity for mutual aid or protect that is not union-related. *See, e.g., Washington Aluminum, supra*, Chapter 4. In such cases, the employer does, however, violate §8(a)(1).

2. In the Public Sector

A clear majority of public-sector jurisdictions have adopted the *Wright-Line* "but-for" test. *See, e.g., Wissahickon Educ. Support Personnel Ass'n v. Wissahickon Sch. Dist.*, 35 PPER ¶ 9.35 (PLRB Hearing Officer, 2014); *Hardin County Educ. Ass'n v. IELRB*, 174 Ill. App. 3d 168 (1988); *McPherson v. PERB*, 189 Cal. App. 3d 293 (1987); *Michigan Educational Support Personnel Ass'n v. Evart Public Schools*, 336 N.W.2d 235 (Mich. Ct. App. 1983). But exceptions exist.

State Employment Relations Board v. Adena Local School District Board of Education

Supreme Court of Ohio
66 Ohio St. 3d 485, 613 N.E.2d 605 (1993)

Resnick, J.

[Daniel Kelley began employment as a vocational agriculture teacher at Adena High School on July 1, 1976. The Adena Local School District Board of Education (Board) employed Kelley under a series of limited contracts, including a five-year limited contract which expired in 1984. In April 1984, the Board issued Kelley a two-year probationary contract, and declined to issue the continuing contract for which he was eligible. Kelley claimed the employer made this decision because of Kelley's involvement with the union. SERB found a ULP.]

For the reasons which follow . . . [we] reverse the judgment of the court of appeals and reinstate the judgment of the trial court upholding SERB's order that appellee board of education offer appellant reinstatement and award him back pay. . . .

II

The trial court in this case, after examining the evidence, determined that the board of education's decision to nonrenew appellant was motivated both by legitimate and illegitimate reasons. The trial court then applied what was SERB's approach at that time in "mixed motive" cases, the "in part" test. . . . Because the employer's action was motivated at least in part by a desire to retaliate for the participation in a protected activity (filing a grievance), the trial court found that a ULP had occurred, and upheld SERB's order.

Upon appeal, the appellate court found that the trial court erred in applying the "in part" test, because that test cannot reasonably be reconciled with R.C. Chapter 4117. In ordering this cause remanded to SERB, the court of appeals noted that SERB has announced that it will now apply the so-called "but for" test, which has been applied by the [NLRB] since 1980. . . . The court of appeals determined that the "in part" test can lead to absurd results, because a ULP can be found under that test when an employer's actions are motivated mainly by legitimate reasons, and only in small part by discriminatory ones. Thus, the appellate court found that the "but for" test is mandated by R.C. Chapter 4117.

We do not accept the conclusions drawn by the court of appeals. We therefore examine the "in part" and "but for" causation tests in light of R.C. Chapter 4117. We seek to determine which test, if either, comports with the goals of the General Assembly when it enacted those statutes, particularly R.C. 4117.11 (which defines ULPs) and R.C. 4117.12 (which guides SERB in its disposition of ULP charges).

The motivation behind an employer's decision to take an action regarding an employee is the central question that must be resolved in a ULP case. R.C. Chapter 4117 makes it SERB's responsibility to evaluate the factual situation surrounding a ULP charge, and to determine whether a ULP has in fact occurred. Determining the motivation underlying an employer's decision almost always presents difficulties which are not easily overcome. Motivation is rarely clear. An employer charged with a ULP will almost always claim that the particular action was taken for sound business reasons, totally unrelated to the employee's participation in protected activities. The employee will almost always claim that the action was taken to retaliate for his or her exercise of protected rights. Since evidence of the employer's motivation is rarely direct, SERB must rely on a good deal of circumstantial evidence in arriving at its conclusion. To facilitate consideration of ULP cases, administrative agencies (*e.g.*, SERB and the NLRB) utilize causation tests to provide some uniformity in evaluating ULP charges and to give a reviewing court a framework for determining if substantial evidence supports the agency's decision. The "in part" and "but for" approaches are two examples of such causation tests.

A

R.C. Chapter 4117's treatment of ULP cases is modeled to a large extent on the federal statutes that empower the NLRB to resolve ULP charges in cases within its jurisdiction. . . . Thus, consideration of the NLRB's experience in applying the "in part" and "but for" tests can be instructive in resolving which test, if either, best accomplishes the goals embodied in Ohio's statutes regarding ULPs.

Between the 1930s and 1980, the NLRB, when evaluating ULP charges, applied the "in part" test. The NLRB construed the [NLRA] to provide that a ULP has occurred when the NLRB finds that an employer's action was taken at least in part to discriminate against an employee for engaging in protected activities, regardless of other reasons for the action. . . .

In 1980, in *Wright Line, Div. of Wright Line, Inc.* (1980) the NLRB changed the analysis it applied in resolving ULP cases. In *Wright Line*, the NLRB adopted a causation test commonly called the "but for" test, in an attempt to alleviate dissatisfaction over the "in part" test expressed by several federal courts of appeals. . . .

The *Wright Line* test allows the employer to present its alleged legitimate reasons for its actions as an affirmative defense. This causation test is commonly called the "but for" test because it establishes that a ULP has occurred when the evidence shows that "but for" the exercise of protected activity, the employer's action (*e.g.*, a discharge) regarding the employee would not have been taken.

The *Wright Line* test was not uniformly embraced by the federal courts of appeals. . . . However, in *Natl. Labor Relations Bd. v. Transp. Mgt. Corp.* (1983), 462 U.S. 393, the United States Supreme Court held that the NLRB's *Wright Line* test was a permissible construction of the NLRA, and was entitled to deference. The court also found that the "in part" test applied before *Wright Line* "was plainly rational and acceptable." *Transp. Mgt.*, 462 U.S. at 399.

B

As we have said, the ULP provisions of Ohio's R.C. Chapter 4117 are modeled in many respects upon the NLRA. Since the General Assembly enacted R.C. Chapter 4117 to be effective in 1984, we may safely assume that that body was aware of the controversy in the federal courts concerning the NLRB's application of the "in part" and "but for" tests, and of *Wright Line* and *Transp. Mgt.* Both appellant and the board of education in this case argue that the General Assembly intended to codify a causation test in R.C. Chapter 4117, although they of course disagree as to which test was adopted. . . .

Appellant reads R.C. Chapter 4117, and particularly R.C. 4117.12(B)(4), as requiring the "in part" test to determine causation in ULP cases. The board of education urges that R.C. Chapter 4117 mandates the *Wright Line* "but for" method of analysis. The trial court in this case found that appellant's interpretation was correct. The court of appeals, in reversing the trial court, held that the "in part" test is not a reasonable interpretation. . . .

Initially, we cannot agree with the court of appeals that the "in part" test is not a reasonable interpretation of R.C. Chapter 4117. The "in part" test, because it focuses on the employer's motivation and requires a finding that a ULP has been committed when it is established that the motivation is improper, obviously comports with R.C. Chapter 4117. Clearly, when a preponderance of the evidence supports a finding that an employer acted at least in part to discriminate against an employee for the exercise of protected rights, SERB's finding of a ULP is a reasonable interpretation of the statutory directive.

We also do not agree with the court of appeals that R.C. Chapter 4117, and in particular R.C. 4117.12(B)(4), call for the "but for" test. In our view, the *Wright Line* "but for" method cannot be reconciled with R.C. Chapter 4117. Allowing the employer to present, as an affirmative defense, all the alleged legitimate reasons supporting the action against the employee turns the focus of the inquiry away from the employer's motivation. The inquiry instead then becomes focused on the employee's work record, and SERB's factual consideration becomes subsumed by both the employer's and employee's evidence on that question. Even though SERB has necessarily already concluded that the employer was motivated by improper reasons before the employer needs to present this evidence, the employer's improper motivation is sanctioned so long as the employer can convince the factfinder to accept its view of the employee's work history.

Contrary to the assertions of the board of education, R.C. 4117.12(B)(4) does not authorize the "but for" test. That statute provides that SERB may not order the reinstatement of any individual "if the suspension or discharge was for just cause not related to rights provided in section 4117.03 of the Revised Code. . . ." We find that this statute, by limiting SERB's order when the employer's action was "not related to" protected rights, further emphasizes that a ULP must be found when an employer's motivation is improper. The "but for" test, because it turns the inquiry away from the employer's motivation, is not a reasonable interpretation of R.C. Chapter 4117.

Even though we have found the "but for" approach to be inconsistent with R.C. Chapter 4117, we also find that, unless the employer is given an opportunity to counter the evidence presented by the employee, the "in part" approach will not be the most accurate test. When, for example, it is determined that antiunion animus played a minuscule part in the employer's decision regarding an employee, a literal application of the "in part" test would appear to mandate a finding that the employer committed a ULP. We find that R.C. Chapter 4117 does not require SERB to conclude that a ULP occurred in that circumstance. The "in part" test must not be applied so narrowly. Rather, the "in part" approach must be broad enough to take into account the actual or true motive of the employer. Thus, only when the employer's decision regarding the employee was actually motivated by antiunion animus must a ULP be found. In determining actual motivation in the context of the "in part" test, the requirements of R.C. Chapter 4117 are best fulfilled when SERB considers the evidence before it in the framework of a single inquiry, focusing on intent of the employer.

Hence, we hold that the "in part" test to determine the motivation of an employer charged with a ULP is mandated by R.C. Chapter 4117. We further hold that under the "in part" test to determine the actual motivation of an employer charged with a ULP, the proponent of the charge has the initial burden of showing that the action by the employer was taken to discriminate against the employee for the exercise of rights protected by R.C. Chapter 4117. Where the proponent meets this burden, a prima facie case is created which raises a presumption of antiunion animus. The employer is then given an opportunity to present evidence that its actions were the result of other conduct by the employee not related to protected activity, to rebut the presumption. SERB then determines, by a preponderance of the evidence, whether a ULP has occurred.

When the "in part" test is properly applied it results in a determination of the actual motive of the employer in taking the action. This approach allows SERB to consider the employee's work history, but only as circumstantial evidence of the employer's motivation, and not as a separate inquiry characterized as an affirmative defense. Thus, application of the "in part" test in this manner allows SERB, in resolving ULP charges, to focus on the important inquiry-the motivation of the employer. The problems associated with the "but for" test and its burden-shifting, wrongly focused, bifurcated inquiry are avoided.

We realize that recognizing actual motivation to be a component of the "in part" test will not necessarily make SERB's task in determining employer motivation an easy one. SERB must still evaluate the evidence presented to determine if antiunion animus actually motivated the employer to take the action against the employee. However, we are confident that this causation analysis will allow SERB to comport more closely with the requirements of R.C. Chapter 4117 in resolving ULP cases. . . .

Judgment reversed.

WRIGHT, J., joined by MOYER, J., concurring in part and concurring in the judgment.

. . . There is simply no support in R.C. Chapter 4117 for the majority's conclusion that the chapter "mandate[s]" the use of the "in part" test. Moreover, the majority deviates from this court's precedent and the scheme of R.C. Chapter 4117 by substituting its judgment for SERB's. . . . This court's precedent holds that in the adjudication of unfair labor practice ("ULP") charges, SERB's interpretation of the Act is to be given broad deference by the courts. . . .

Thus, when SERB construes the Act in a *permissible* fashion, the courts should not interfere. It is only when the agency makes a decision that is without support under the law that we may impose our construction of the statute. . . .

The majority admirably sets forth the terms of the debate over the "in part" and the "but for" tests. In my view, however, its discussion of the law leads inexorably to the conclusion that *both* tests are permissible under R.C. Chapter 4117 and *neither* is "mandated." It is precisely on this point that the majority errs. . . .

In *Natl. Labor Relations Bd. v. Transp. Mgt. Corp.* the United States Supreme Court considered whether the [NLRB]'s use of the *Wright Line* "but for" test was proper under the [NLRA]. The court deferred to the board; it held that the *Wright Line* test would not be disturbed because it is not "an impermissible construction of the Act." This court should now adopt the same position with regard to both the "in part" and the "but for" tests as used by SERB.

R.C. Chapter 4117 neither mandates nor prohibits the use of either the "in part" or the "but for" tests. The Act is worded broadly enough to easily accommodate both approaches and I believe that this is just what the General Assembly intended. The majority, in fact, does not hold that the language of the Act leads to the conclusion it reaches.

The majority, instead, treats its decision as a labor policy choice—a political choice. And, of course, it is. The majority has made the essentially political decision that "the requirements of R.C. Chapter 4117 are *best fulfilled*" when SERB uses the "in part" test. (Emphasis added.) But the judgment as to what "best fulfill[s]" the requirements of the Act has been vested by the General Assembly in SERB-not this court. Our inquiry in ULP cases should begin, and end, with the question of whether what SERB did was *permissible*—not whether it was "best."

Moreover, there are serious questions in my mind as to whether SERB will be able to apply the test promulgated by the majority. The test amounts to the "in part" test with a caveat: the antiunion animus must be more than a "minuscule part" of the employer's motivation. The majority writes that "only when the employer's decision regarding the employee was *actually motivated* by antiunion animus must a ULP be found." (Emphasis added.) This sounds to me as much like the "but for" test as the "in part" test. Under the "but for" test a ULP occurs if the employee would not have been disciplined but for his or her protected activities. Under the majority's test, SERB is charged with finding whether the employer was "actually motivated" by the employee's exercise of protected activities. These two inquiries seem much the same to me and my concern is that SERB will be as confused as I am and will not be able to effectively apply the majority's test. Of course, this problem would not arise if SERB, instead of this court, was allowed to formulate and follow its own permissible tests. . . .

I express no opinion as to which of the two tests I prefer or believe to "best fulfill" the goals of the Act. I would merely hold that both the "in part" and "but for" tests are permissible under R.C. Chapter 4117 and that the court of appeals erred by mandating the "but for" test.

Notes

1. As a matter of law and statutory interpretation, who is more convincing, the majority or the partial concurrence? Note that because of this decision, the Ohio SERB went back to using the "in part" test, which it has used ever since. *See, e.g., State Employment Relations Board v. Sylvania Twp. Trustees, Lucas County*, 26 OPER ¶ 91 (Oh SERB ALJ, 91 2009) (using the "in part" test as described by *Adena*).

2. As a matter of policy, which do you prefer, the "but for" test or the "in part" test? In what types of cases would the two tests yield different results? Note that the dissent in *Adena* concurred in the result that the employer had committed an unfair labor practice in that case.

3. For another case using the minority "in part" test, see *Wisconsin Dept. of Employment Relations v. WERC*, 122 Wis. 2d 132 (1985). Among other things, the court reasoned that:

> the "in part" test recognizes the practical difficulty that a discharged employee may have in proving a violation of SELRA and refuting an allegation of misconduct. The discharged employee and the employer do not stand on equal footing in cases alleging unfair labor practice, because of the employer's advantage of being able to monitor the employee's work performance and document any *bona fide* basis for discipline. 122 Wis. 2d 132, 142.

The court also suggested that the evidence of legitimate reasons to discharge the employee could go to the remedy, citing approvingly the decision by the WERC in the case at bar to reinstate the employee, but deny backpay (due to evidence of failure to comply with work rules). *Id.* at 143.

C. Discrimination in an Employer's Capital Decisions

In general, employers may close their plants, relocate, or contract out work if objectively motivated by economic reasons. The following case explains what happens when an employer's decision is motivated in part by anti-union animus.

Textile Workers Union v. Darlington Mfg. Co.

Supreme Court of the United States
380 U.S. 263, 85 S. Ct. 994, 13 L. Ed. 2d 827 (1965)

HARLAN, J.

We here review judgments of the Court of Appeals setting aside and refusing to enforce an order of the [NLRB] which found respondent Darlington guilty of an unfair labor practice by reason of having permanently closed its plant following petitioner union's election as the bargaining representative of Darlington's employees.

Darlington Manufacturing Company was a South Carolina corporation operating one textile mill. A majority of Darlington's stock was held by Deering Milliken, a New York 'selling house' marketing textiles produced by others. Deering Milliken in turn was controlled by Roger Milliken, president of Darlington, and by other members of the Milliken family. The [NLRB] found that the Milliken family, through Deering Milliken, operated 17 textile manufacturers, including Darlington, whose products manufactured in 27 different mills, were marketed through Deering Milliken.

In March 1956 petitioner Textile Workers Union initiated an organizational campaign at Darlington which the company resisted vigorously in various ways, including threats to close the mill if the union won a representation election. [For example, the Board found that Darlington had interrogated employees and threatened to close the mill if the union won the election. After the decision to liquidate was made, Darlington employees were told that the decision to close was caused by the election, and they were encouraged to sign a petition disavowing the union. These practices violated NLRA § 8(a)(1); that part of the Board decision is not challenged here.] . . . [T]he union won an election by a narrow margin. When Roger Milliken was advised of the union victory, he decided to call a meeting of the Darlington board of directors to consider closing the mill. Mr. Milliken testified before the [NLRB]:

> 'I felt that as a result of the [union] campaign . . . and the promises and statements made in these letters that had been distributed (favoring unionization), that if before we had had some hope, possible hope of achieving competitive (costs) . . . by taking advantage of new machinery that was being put in, that this hope had diminished as a result of the election because a majority of the employees had voted in favor of the union. . . .'

The board of directors met on September 12 and voted to liquidate the corporation, action which was approved by the stockholders on October 17. The plant ceased operations entirely in November, and all plant machinery and equipment were sold piecemeal at auction in December.

The union filed charges with the [NLRB] claiming that Darlington had violated §§ 8(a)(1) and (3) . . . by closing its plant. . . . The Board . . . found that Darlington had been closed because of the antiunion animus of Roger Milliken, and held that to be a violation of § 8(a)(3). The Board also found Darlington to be part of a single integrated employer group controlled by the Milliken family through Deering Milliken; therefore Deering Milliken could be held liable for the unfair labor practices of Darlington. Alternatively, since Darlington was a part of the Deering Milliken enterprise, Deering Milliken had violated the Act by closing part of its business for a discriminatory purpose. The Board ordered back pay for all Darlington employees until they obtained substantially equivalent work or were put on preferential hiring lists at the other Deering Milliken mills. Respondent Deering Milliken was ordered to bargain with the union in regard to details of compliance with the Board order. . . .

On review, the Court of Appeals, sitting en banc, set aside the order and denied enforcement. . . . The Court of Appeals held that even accepting arguendo the Board's determination that Deering Milliken had the status of a single employer, a company has the absolute right to close out a part or all of its business regardless of antiunion motives. The court therefore did not review the Board's finding that Deering Milliken was a single integrated employer. We granted certiorari . . . to consider the important questions involved. We hold that so far as the [NLRA] is concerned, an employer has the absolute right to terminate his entire business for any reason he pleases, but disagree with the Court of Appeals that such right includes the ability to close part of a business no matter what the reason. We conclude that the case must be remanded to the Board for further proceedings.

[T]he Board was correct in treating the closing only under § 8(a)(3). Section 8(a)(1) provides that it is an unfair labor practice for an employer 'to interfere with, restrain, or coerce employees in the exercise of' § 7 rights. Naturally, certain business decisions will, to some degree, interfere with concerted activities by employees. But it is only when the interference with § 7 rights outweighs the business justification for the employer's action that § 8(a)(1) is violated. *See, e.g., NLRB v. United Steelworkers*, 357 U.S. 357; *Republic Aviation Corp. v. NLRB*, 324 U.S. 793. A violation of § 8(a)(1) alone therefore presupposes an act which is unlawful even absent a discriminatory motive. Whatever may be the limits of § 8(a)(1), some employer decisions are so peculiarly matters of management prerogative that they would never constitute violations of § 8(a)(1), whether or not they involved sound business judgment, unless they also violated § 8(a)(3). Thus it is not questioned in this case that an employer has the right to terminate his business, whatever the impact of such action on concerted activities, if the decision to close is motivated by other than discriminatory reasons. But such action, if discriminatorily motivated, is encompassed within the literal language of § 8(a)(3). We therefore deal with the Darlington closing under that section. . . .

We consider first the argument, advanced by the petitioner union but not by the Board, and rejected by the Court of Appeals, that an employer may not go completely out of business without running afoul of the [NLRA] if such action is prompted by a desire to avoid unionization. Given the Board's findings on the issue of motive, acceptance of this contention would carry the day for the Board's conclusion that the closing of this plant was an unfair labor practice, even on the assumption that Darlington is to be regarded as an independent unrelated employer. A proposition that a single businessman cannot choose to go out of business if he wants to would represent such a startling innovation that it should not be entertained without the clearest manifestation of legislative intent or unequivocal judicial precedent so construing the [NLRA]. We find neither.

So far as legislative manifestation is concerned, it is sufficient to say that there is not the slightest indication in the history of the Wagner Act or of the Taft-Hartley Act that Congress envisaged any such result under either statute.

As for judicial precedent, the Board recognized that '(t)here is no decided case directly dispositive of Darlington's claim that it had an absolute right to close its mill, irrespective of motive.' . . .

The courts of appeals have generally assumed that a complete cessation of business will remove an employer from future coverage by the Act. Thus the Court of Appeals said in these cases: The Act 'does not compel a person to become or remain an employee. It does not compel one to become or remain an employer. Either may withdraw from that status with immunity, so long as the obligations of any employment contract have been met.' . . . The Eighth Circuit, in *NLRB v. New Madrid Mfg. Co.*, 215 F.2d 908, 914, was equally explicit:

> 'But none of this can be taken to mean that an employer does not have the absolute right, at all times, to permanently close and go out of business . . . for whatever reason he may choose, whether union animosity or anything else, and without his being thereby left subject to a remedial liability under the Labor Management Relations Act for such unfair labor practices as he may have committed in the enterprise, except up to the time that such actual and permanent closing . . . has occurred.'

. . . We are not presented here with the case of a 'runaway shop,' whereby Darlington would transfer its work to another plant or open a new plant in another locality to replace its closed plant. Nor are we concerned with a shutdown where the employees, by renouncing the union, could cause the plant to reopen. Such cases would involve discriminatory employer action for the purpose of obtaining some benefit in the future from the employees in the future. We hold here only that when an employer closes his entire business, even if the liquidation is motivated by vindictiveness toward the union, such action is not an unfair labor practice. . . .

While we thus agree with the Court of Appeals that viewing Darlington as an independent employer the liquidation of its business was not an unfair labor practice, we cannot accept the lower court's view that the same conclusion necessarily follows if Darlington is regarded as an integral part of the Deering Milliken enterprise.

The closing of an entire business, even though discriminatory, ends the employer-employee relationship; the force of such a closing is entirely spent as to that business when termination of the enterprise takes place. On the other hand, a discriminatory partial closing may have repercussions on what remains of the business, affording employer leverage for discouraging the free exercise of § 7 rights among remaining employees of much the same kind as that found to exist in the 'runaway shop' and 'temporary closing' cases. . . . [A] possible remedy open to the Board in such a case, like the remedies available in the 'runaway shop' and 'temporary closing' cases, is to order reinstatement of the discharged employees in the other parts of the business. No such remedy is available when an entire business has been terminated. By analogy to those cases involving a continuing enterprise we are constrained to hold, in disagreement with the Court of Appeals, that a partial closing is an unfair labor practice under § 8(a)(3) if motivated by a purpose to chill unionism in any of the remaining plants of the single employer and if the employer may reasonably have foreseen that such closing would likely have that effect.

While we have spoken in terms of a 'partial closing' in the context of the Board's finding that Darlington was part of a larger single enterprise controlled by the Milliken family, we do not mean to suggest that an organizational integration of plants or corporations is a necessary prerequisite to the establishment of such a violation of § 8(a)(3). If the persons exercising control over a plant that is being closed for antiunion reasons (1) have an interest in another business, whether or not affiliated with or engaged in the same line of commercial activity as the closed plant, of sufficient substantiality to give promise of their reaping a benefit from the discouragement of unionization in that business; (2) act to close their plant with the purpose of producing such a result; and (3) occupy a relationship to the other business which makes it realistically foreseeable that its employees will fear that such business will also be closed down if they persist in organizational activities, we think that an unfair labor practice has been made out.

Although the Board's single employer finding necessarily embraced findings as to Roger Milliken and the Milliken family which, if sustained by the Court of Appeals, would satisfy the elements of 'interest' and 'relationship' with respect to other parts of the Deering Milliken enterprise, that and the other Board findings fall short of establishing the factors of 'purpose' and 'effect' which are vital requisites of the general principles that govern a case of this kind.

Thus, the Board's findings as to the purpose and foreseeable effect of the Darlington closing pertained only to its impact on the Darlington employees. No findings were made as to the purpose and effect of the closing with respect to the employees in the other plants comprising the Deering Milliken group. It does not suffice to establish the unfair labor practice charged here to argue that the Darlington closing necessarily had an adverse impact upon unionization in such other plants. We have heretofore observed that employer action which has a foreseeable consequence of discouraging concerted activities generally does not amount to a violation of § 8(a)(3) in the absence of a showing of motivation which is aimed at achieving the prohibited effect. . . . In an area which trenches so closely upon otherwise legitimate employer prerogatives, we consider the absence of Board findings on this score a fatal defect in its decision. The Court of Appeals for its part did not deal with the question of purpose and effect at all, since it concluded that an employer's right to close down his entire business because of distaste for unionism, also embraced a partial closing so motivated. . . .

In these circumstances, we think the proper disposition of this cause is to require that it be remanded to the Board so as to afford the Board the opportunity to make further findings on the issue of purpose and effect. . . . This is particularly appropriate here since the cases involve issues of first impression. If such findings are made, the cases will then be in a posture for further review by the Court of Appeals on all issues. Accordingly, without intimating any view as to how any of these matters should eventuate, we vacate the judgments of the Court of Appeals and remand the cases to that court with instructions to remand them to the Board for further proceedings consistent with this opinion. It is so ordered. . . .

Notes

1. An employer's decision to shut down part of its business for legitimate business reasons does not typically violate the NLRA. For example, in *NLRB v. Lassing*, 284 F.2d 781 (6th Cir. 1960) (per curiam), in the context of an employer decision to shut down the trucking portion of its business shortly after its truck drivers voted for a union, the court in disagreement with the Board held that the employer's decision was not motivated by union animus but based on a legitimate analysis of the cost of operations that was undertaken months before the union was even on the scene. *Accord Dayton Newspapers, Inc. v. NLRB*, 402 F.3d 651, 665–66 (6th Cir. 2005) (holding that employer did not violate §8(a)(3) when it expedited its plan to move locations, which resulted in layoffs, shortly after the employees engaged in a strike); *NLRB v. Rapid Bindery Inc.*, 293 F.2d 170 (2d Cir. 1961) (no violation where employer's decision was required by economic necessity). Do you think that the court would have enforced the Board's order had the employer's decision coincided with the union campaign? What if the employer's decision was motivated by the union campaign but it would have relocated for legitimate business reasons anyway? *See Dorsey Trailers, Inc. v. NLRB*, 233 F.3d 831 (4th Cir. 2000) (holding lawful employer's decision to relocated even though partially motivated by union animus where employer proved that it would have taken the same action based on legitimate economic reasons).

2. *Darlington* takes this analysis one step further. Here, the Supreme Court held that an employer does not per se violate the NLRA when it closes a plant for anti-union reasons. Instead, the Court put forth a three-part test for determining whether persons who exercises control over such a plant engaged in an unfair labor practice:

> (1) [they] have an interest in another business, whether or not affiliated with or engaged in the same line of commercial activity as the closed plant, of sufficient substantiality to give promise of their reaping a benefit from the discouragement of unionization in that business; (2) act to close their

plant with the purpose of producing such a result; and (3) occupy a relationship to the other business which makes it realistically foreseeable that its employees will fear that such business will also be closed down if they persist in organizational activities, we think that an unfair labor practice has been made out.

The Court remanded this case because the Board had not made sufficient findings on each of these elements. On remand, the Board summarized its conclusions as follows:

> We find . . . that such a chilling purpose [discouraging unionism at other mills], at least in part, lay behind the decision to close the Darlington mill; those exercising control over Darlington, especially in the person of Roger Milliken, had other business interests of sufficient substantiality to give promise of their reaping benefits from the discouragement of unionization in those businesses; the relationship of the persons closing Darlington to the other businesses was such as to make it realistically foreseeable that employees of the latter would fear that their mills also would be closed if they engaged in organizational activity; the persons exercising control over Darlington did in fact foresee and intend this effect; and a number of these employees were, in all likelihood, so affected. *Darlington Manufacturing Co.*, 165 N.L.R.B. 1074, 1087 (1967).

3. When a plant closes, the employer must discharge all the employees from their jobs at that plant. Those discharges also violate the NLRA if it is found that the employer violated § 8(a)(3) for closing the plant in the first place.

4. What if the employer, motivated by union animus, merely closed a department in its business and transferred the work to nonunion independent contractors? In *NLRB v. Amber Delivery Service, Inc.*, 651 F.2d 57 (1st Cir. 1981), the employer converted its employee drivers to independent contractors in response to its drivers' organizing efforts. Then-Judge Stephen Breyer wrote:

> It is clear that Amber is free, in the sincere and justifiable exercise of business judgment unrelated to its employees' union activity, to convert its workers to independent contractors notwithstanding that such action has the incidental effect of excluding these persons from the Act's coverage. It is equally clear, however, that Amber is not at liberty to effect such a conversion, or attempt to do so, as an artifice or device for depriving its employees of their statutory right to union representation. "The conversion of employees to independent contractor status is an unfair labor practice when motivated by anti-union animus." . . . Were changes for this sort of reason permissible, an employer might forestall union organizing simply by announcing that, if its employees organize, it will convert them into independent contractors thus leaving them, should the threat prove effective, with the worst of both worlds. "The critical fact," . . . "is the underlying motive for the respondent's change of business practice." 651 F.2d at 65.

5. What about a mere threat to close a plant? The Board has repeatedly held, with court approval, that an employer may not threaten to close its plant if a union wins an election. *See NLRB v. Gissel Packing Co.*, 395 U.S. 575 (1969), *supra* Chapter 3. This is so even though, as *Darlington* illustrates, that very same employer may go out of business if the union wins the election.

———————

The tension between employer actions motivated for legitimate economic reasons and motivated by union animus recently played out in the Boeing case. There, Boeing decided to move its Dreamliner production lines from unionized operations in Washington and Oregon to nonunion operations in South Carolina. If prompted by legitimate business reasons to relocate, this case would have never made it past first base. But upon investigating charges that Boeing's decision was motivated by union animus, the NLRB Regional Office alleged that it uncovered smoking guns — publicized statements by Boeing officials that it was relocating because of Boeing's employees' strike activity. Although the case was settled before the hearing, the Board was publicly ridiculed by Republican politicians for interfering with Boeing's entrepreneurial decisions. In the excerpt below, written before the case was settled, Professor Lofaso argues that, if the facts as alleged were true, then this case would be a textbook example of a § 8(a)(3) violation. What do you think?

Anne Marie Lofaso, *NLRB Primer and the Boeing Complaint*[*]

. . .

VIII. The Boeing Case: The Facts and Procedural History

<u>Undisputed Facts.</u> The Boeing Company manufactures and produces military and commercial aircraft at facilities throughout the United States, including facilities in Washington state and Portland, Oregon. . . .

The [Union] . . . has represented the Company's production and maintenance employees in Washington State (the Puget Sound Unit) and the Company's production and maintenance employees in the Portland, Oregon, area (the Portland Unit) since at least 1975. . . . [T]he Company has a legal obligation . . . to bargain with the Union over wages, hours, and other terms and conditions of employment of the employees in those units. Since 1975, throughout the course of the Company's and the Union's bargaining relationship, the Union engaged in strikes in 1977, 1989, 1995, 2005, and 2008. In late October 2009, the Company decided to place a second assembly line for the 787 Dreamliner in North Charleston, South Carolina. It is the nature of that decision and comments made by company agents about that decision that is the subject of this labor dispute. . . .

[T]he Union filed a charge, alleging that the Company had engaged in several unfair labor practices related to its decision to place a second production line for the

———————

[*] Copyright © 2011. Reprinted by permission. Available at https://bit.ly/2BrDigP.

787 Dreamliner airplane in a non-union facility. . . . The NLRB's Seattle regional office investigated that charge.

. . . On April 20, 2011, the Regional Director, Richard L. Ahearn, acting under the General Counsel's authority, issued the complaint and notice of hearing. That complaint alleges that the Boeing Company violated Section 8(a)(1) of the NLRA by making "coercive statements to its employees that it would remove or had removed work from the Unit because employees had struck and Respondent threatened or impliedly threatened that the unit would lose additional work in the event of future strikes." Since the NLRA protects the right to strike, such threats could be construed as interference with that right. The complaint further alleges that the Boeing Company violated Section 8(a)(3) of the NLRA by deciding to transfer work from union facilities (the Units) to nonunion facilities in South Carolina. The Boeing Company, as respondent, filed an answer, denying those allegations. . . .

Detailed Account of the Complaint and Answer, Including the Disputed Facts

The General Counsel alleges . . . that company representatives made several statements that, if true, would violate Section 8(a)(1) of the law. In particular, the General Counsel alleges that Company President James McNerney stated that the Company was moving 787 Dreamliner production work from Seattle to South Carolina because of "strikes happening every three to four years in Puget Sound." The General Counsel further alleges that company agents made several other statements indicating that it would be moving production from Seattle to South Carolina. Many of these statements appeared in newspapers or have been videotaped. The Company admits that the newspapers printed these statements but denies either that the statements were made or, if made, that they were unlawfully coercive. Affirmatively, the Company contends that these statements are protected both by Section 8(c) of the NLRA and under the First Amendment of the United States Constitution. . . .

The General Counsel also alleges several violations of Section 8(a)(3) . . . . First, . . . the Company's decision to transfer its second 787 Dreamliner production line of three planes per month from the Puget Sound and Portland Units to a non-union site in South Carolina violates Section 8(a)(3) because of the Company's motives in making that decision and because of the effect that decision has on protected Section 7 activity. In particular, . . . the Company decided to transfer work from union sites to a nonunion site because the employees at the union sites had engaged in lawful strikes. The General Counsel alleges that the Company's decision had the purpose of discouraging union activity and is inherently destructive of the rights of employees in the Puget Sound and Portland Units. Second, the General Counsel alleges . . . that the Company's decision to transfer a sourcing supply program for its 787 Dreamliner production line from the Units to a non-union facility in South Carolina or to subcontractors also violated Section 8(a)(3) for the same reasons. The Company's main defense to the Section 8(a)(3) violations is that its decisions were not motivated by anti-union animus but by legitimate business reasons. Alternatively, the Company contends that the Union contractually waived its employees' rights to the work. . . .

To remedy the violations it alleges Boeing committed, the General Counsel has asked for a cease and desist order and the following affirmative action: (1) that an appropriate remedial notice be read to its Unit employees and posted on the Company's intranet; and (2) that the disputed work be maintained in the Puget Sound and Portland Units. The Company contends that this second remedy is unduly punitive and that it effectively requires the Company to shut down operations in South Carolina. . . .

IX. The Legal Principles Involved in the Boeing Case

A. An Employer Violates Section 8(a)(1) by Making Statements that Have a Reasonable Tendency to Chill Employees' Section 7 Activity

Section 7 of the NLRA grants "employees the right to self-organization, to form, join, or assist labor organizations, to bargain collectively through representatives of their own choosing, and to engage in other concerted activities for the purpose of collective bargaining or other mutual aid or protection, and shall also have the right to refrain from any or all such activities . . ." Section 13 of the NLRA provides that "[n]othing in this Act . . . shall be construed so as either to interfere with or impede or diminish in any way the right to strike or to affect the limitations or qualifications of that right." The right to strike is protected under both Section 7 and Section 13. Section 8(a)(1) of the NLRA makes it an unfair labor practice for an employer to interfere with, restrain, or coerce employees in the exercise of the rights guaranteed in section 7." Section 8(c) of the NLRA provides that the "expressing of any views, argument, or opinion, or the dissemination thereof . . . shall not constitute or be evidence of an unfair labor practice . . . *if such expression contains no threat of reprisal or force or promise of benefit.*"

An employer's conduct violates Section 8(a)(1) if it has a reasonable tendency to coerce employees or interfere with their Section 7 rights. In examining such violations, the Board considers "the economic dependence of the employees on their employers, and the necessary tendency of the former . . . to pick up intended implications of the latter that might be more readily dismissed by a more disinterested ear." [*NLRB v. Gissel Packing Corp.*, 395 U.S. 575, 617 (1969).] The critical inquiry is what the employee reasonably could have inferred from the employer's statements or actions—not what the employer intended to imply. . . .

Under the facts alleged, the Board could find that statements that the Company transferred work from the Puget Sound and Portland Units to a non-union facility because of the Unit employees striking activity are coercive and have a reasonable tendency to chill employees' Section 7 activity, namely strikes. Those statements, if found to be true, send a message to the Units' employees that if they want to keep enough work to sustain their jobs, they should refrain from engaging in future strikes. Moreover, coercive speech is neither protected by Section 8(c) nor protected by the First Amendment's Free Speech Clause. [T]he NLRB may remedy employer speech that is coercive without running afoul of either Section 8(c) or the First Amendment.

B. An Employer Violates Section 8(a)(3) by Taking Actions that Discourage Employee Participation in Union Activity, Such as Strikes

Section 8(a)(3) . . . makes it an unfair labor practice for an employer "by discrimination in regard to hire or tenure of employment or any term or condition of employment to encourage or discourage membership in any labor organization." The Board has found that retaliation against employees' for having engaged in striking activity constitutes a Section 8(a)(3) violation. If the complaint allegations are true, that the Company decided to transfer work from the Units to a non-union facility, then the Board could reasonably find that the employer's conduct was unlawfully motivated by a desire to retaliate against employees for participating in past strikes.

C. The Board Has Broad Statutory Authority to Remedy an Unfair Labor Practice

Section 10(c) of the NLRA authorizes the Board, upon finding a violation of the NLRA, to order the violator not only to cease and desist from the unlawful conduct but also "to take such affirmative action . . . as will effectuate the policies of th[e] Act." The purpose of the Board's remedial order is "to restore, so far as possible, the status quo that would have obtained but for the wrongful act." [*NLRB v. J.H. Rutter-Rex Mfg. Co.*, 396 U.S. 258, 265 (1969).] Here, if the Board finds that the Company acted unlawfully as alleged, then the Board would be required "to restore, so far as possible, the status quo that would have obtained but for the wrongful act." In this case, the status quo ante could be to return the work to the Puget Sound and Portland Units. However, how the administrative law judge or the NLRB might rule, and what remedy might be proposed if Boeing is found to have committed an unfair labor practice, is unknown at this time.

Conclusion: The Boeing Complaint Is Routine

This primer demonstrates the following key points. First, despite news reports that the Boeing Complaint is unprecedented, the complaint has firm grounding in the law, including statutory and Supreme Court precedent. Second, the Boeing Case is still in the early stages of litigation. The dispute may be settled at any time. And most importantly, the Board had nothing to do with the issuance of the complaint against Boeing, nor has the Board reviewed this case yet.

The NLRB General Counsel-side has exclusive authority to issue complaints. The purpose of issuing complaints is to enforce the law. Here, the General Counsel issued a complaint after an investigation of the facts and an understanding of the law as it applied to those facts. If the General Counsel can prove these facts at the administrative hearing then the General Counsel can prove the unfair labor practices alleged. Assuming that the General Counsel acted in good faith during the investigation, the General Counsel acted properly in his prosecutorial role by choosing to prosecute this case. As yet, no remedy, if the complaint is found to have validity, has been determined.

IV. Judicial Review of Unfair Labor Practice Determinations

A. Judicial Review of the Board's Findings of Fact: The Substantial Evidence Test

Section 10(e) of the NLRA states that "findings of the Board with respect to questions of fact if supported by substantial evidence on the record considered as a whole shall be conclusive." 29 U.S.C. § 160(e). The Supreme Court has defined substantial evidence as "more than a mere scintilla. It means such relevant evidence as a reasonable mind might accept as adequate to support a conclusion." *Consolidated Edison Co. v. NLRB*, 305 U.S. 197 (1938). The court has further explained that substantial evidence "must do more than create a suspicion of the existence of the fact to be established. . . . It must be enough to justify, if the trial were to a jury, a refusal to direct a verdict when the conclusion sought to be drawn from it is one of fact for the jury." *NLRB v. Columbian Enameling & Stamping Co.*, 306 U.S. 292, 300 (1939). In *Universal Camera Corp. v. NLRB*, 340 U.S. 474, 488 (1951), the Court further added that the "substantiality of evidence must take into account whatever in the record fairly detracts from its weight."

Nevertheless, court review of the Board's factual findings remains "highly deferential." *W&M Properties of Conn., Inc. v. NLRB*, 514 F.3d 1341, 1348 (D.C. Cir. 2008). As the Supreme Court explained:

> [T]he requirement for canvassing "the whole record" . . . to ascertain substantiality does not furnish a calculus of value by which a reviewing court can assess the evidence. Nor was it intended to negative the function of the [NLRB] as one of those agencies presumably equipped or informed by experience to deal with a specialized field of knowledge, whose findings within that field carry the authority of an expertness which courts do not possess and therefore must respect. *Nor does it mean that even as to matters not requiring expertise a court may displace the Board's choice between two fairly conflicting views, even though the court would justifiably have made a different choice had the matter been before it de novo.* Congress has merely made it clear that a reviewing court is not barred from setting aside a Board decision when it cannot conscientiously find that the evidence supporting that decision is substantial, when viewed in the light that the record in its entirety furnishes, including the body of evidence opposed to the Board's view. *Universal Camera Corp.*, 340 U.S. at 488 (emphasis added).

Accord Vincent Indus. Plastics, Inc. v. NLRB, 209 F.3d 727, 734 (D.C. Cir. 2000) ("This court will uphold the Board's decision upon substantial evidence even if we would reach a different result upon *de novo* review."). The D.C. Circuit, the appellate court that hears more administrative cases than any other circuit court, has explained the substantial evidence test in this way in *Traction Wholesale Center Co. v. NLRB*, 216 F.3d 92, 99 (D.C. Cir. 2000):

> Our review of Board unfair labor practice determinations is quite narrow. "The Board's findings of fact, if supported by substantial evidence, are conclusive." . . . In reviewing the Board's conclusions, "[w]e ask not whether [petitioner's] view of the facts supports its version of what happened, but rather whether the Board's interpretation of the facts is reasonably defensible." . . . Moreover, "we must accept the ALJ's credibility determinations, as adopted by the Board, unless they are patently insupportable." . . . . "We are even more deferential when reviewing the Board's conclusions regarding discriminatory motive, because most evidence of motive is circumstantial." . . .

B. Judicial Review of the Board's Construction of the NLRA: *Chevron* Deference

Below is an excellent explication of the law on *Chevron* deference from the "*Standard of Review*" section of the Seventh Circuit's opinion in *Electromation, supra*, 35 F.3d 1148, 1155–56:

> We have jurisdiction to consider the parties' petitions under 29 U.S.C. § 160(e) and (f). . . . However, our role in reviewing Board decisions is sharply limited. We must uphold the Board's determinations if its factual findings are supported by substantial evidence and its legal conclusions have a reasonable basis in the law. . . .
>
> The Board's findings of fact are conclusive if they are supported by substantial evidence on the record as a whole, even if this Court would have reached different conclusions had the matter been before it *de novo*. . . . Substantial evidence is such relevant evidence that a reasonable mind might accept as adequate to support the Board's determination. . . .
>
> We must also consider whether the Board's construction of the Act is reasonable in light of its language and purposes, as determined by controlling decisions of the Supreme Court. *Local 1384, United Auto., Aerospace and Agric. Implement Workers of America, UAW v. NLRB*, 756 F.2d 482, 492 (7th Cir.1985) (appellate court's enforcement of Board decision "reflects only a determination by the court of appeals that the rule is rational and consistent with the Act, not that it is the uniquely correct rule"); *International Ass'n of Bridge, Structural, and Ornamental Ironworkers, AFL-CIO, Local No. 111 v. NLRB*, 946 F.2d 1264, 1267 (7th Cir.1991) (*quoting Chevron U.S.A. Inc. v. Natural Resources Defense Council, Inc.*, 467 U.S. 837, 844 (1984)) (where Board's interpretation of the Act is not "precluded by

statutory language or clear congressional intent, we must honor it if not 'arbitrary, capricious, or manifestly contrary to the statute'"). *See also Shelby Memorial Hosp.*, 1 F.3d at 554 (citation omitted) . . . .

In reaching our determination in this case, we recall the Supreme Court's observation in *Beth Israel Hospital v. NLRB*, 437 U.S. 483, 500–01 (1978) (citation omitted): "[i]t is the Board on which Congress conferred the authority to develop and apply fundamental national labor policy. . . . 'The function of striking [the balance between conflicting legitimate interests] to effectuate national labor policy is often a difficult and delicate responsibility, which the Congress committed primarily to the [NLRB], subject to limited judicial review.'" *See also Local No. 111*, 946 F.2d at 1267 (citing *NLRB v. Manitowoc Eng'g Co.*, 909 F.2d 963, 971 n. 10 (7th Cir.1990)) ("[o]ur standard of review is deferential in recognition of Congress' delegation to the NLRB of primary responsibility for national labor policy").

Notes

1. In *Chevron U.S.A. Inc. v. Natural Resources Defense Council*, 467 U.S. 837, 842–43 (1984), the Supreme Court announced the standard for reviewing an agency's interpretation of law:

When a court reviews an agency's construction of the statute which it administers, it is confronted with two questions. First, always, is the question whether Congress has directly spoken to the precise question at issue. If the intent of Congress is clear, that is the end of the matter; for the court, as well as the agency, must give effect to the unambiguously expressed intent of Congress. If, however, the court determines Congress has not directly addressed the precise question at issue, the court does not simply impose its own construction on the statute, as would be necessary in the absence of an administrative interpretation. Rather, if the statute is silent or ambiguous with respect to the specific issue, the question for the court is whether the agency's answer is based on a permissible construction of the statute.

Chevron thereby creates a two-step process by which courts review agency interpretations of the statute which it is charged by Congress with administering. Under *Chevron* prong one, the court must determine whether the language is plain and clear. In such circumstances, "[t]he judiciary is the final authority on issues of statutory construction and must reject administrative constructions which are contrary to clear congressional intent. . . . If a court, employing traditional tools of statutory construction, ascertains that Congress had an intention on the precise question at issue, that intention is the law and must be given effect." 467 U.S. at 843, n.9. Under *Chevron* prong two, if the court under prong one determines that the statute is silent or ambiguous, then it must defer to the agency's "permissible construction of the statute." *Id.* at 843. Here, it is important to note, as the Court did, that a reviewing "court need not conclude that the agency construction was the only one it permissibly could have adopted to uphold the construction, or even the reading the court would have reached if the question initially had arisen in a judicial proceeding." *Id.* at 843, n.11.

2. *Chevron* deference does not apply to an agency's construction of a statute outside its administration. *See* **Hoffman Plastics Compounds, Inc. v. NLRB**, 535 U.S. 137, 144 (2002) (explaining that the NLRB is entitled to no particular deference when interpreting immigration laws). Nevertheless, in cases where there is a potential conflict between the NLRA and a federal law, the NLRB is not compelled to "abandon an independent inquiry into the requirements of its own statute." *Carpenters Local 1976 v. NLRB*, 357 U.S. 93, 111 (1958). In such cases, the Court will determine which statute will prevail under the particular circumstances of that case. For example, in *Southern S.S. Co. v. NLRB*, 316 U.S. 31, 40–47 (1942), in the context of determining whether seamen, who conducted a strike aboard a docked vessel, were engaged in lawful concerted activity or an unlawful mutiny, the Court concluded that the seamen lost §7 protection when their otherwise protected activity turned into unlawful mutiny. In that case, the Court observed that "the Board has not been commissioned to effectuate the policies of the [NLRA] so single-mindedly that it may wholly ignore other and equally important Congressional objectives." 316 U.S. at 47. *See also* **Epic Systems Corp. v. Lewis**, 584 U.S. ___, 138 S. Ct. 1612 (2018) (addressing conflict between the NLRA and the Federal Arbitration Act).

3. The Supreme Court has also noted that the Board's interpretation of the NLRA is entitled to deference even if it is one of many reasonable interpretations. Accordingly, it is not for the Court to choose which of those interpretations it prefers but to review whether the interpretation that the Board chose is reasonable. For example, in *IBM Corp.*, 341 N.L.R.B. 1288, 1289–905 (2004), the Board chose between two permissible interpretations of the NLRA when it decided not to extend *Weingarten* rights to nonunion employees, thereby overturning *Epilepsy Foundation*, 331 N.L.R.B. 676 (2000), *enf'd in relevant part*, 268 F.3d 1095 (D.C. Cir. 2001) (excerpted below).

4. The Board's interpretation of the NLRA must be "permissible." Unconstitutional interpretations of the NLRA are not permissible. For example, in *NLRB v. Catholic Bishop of Chicago*, 440 U.S. 490 (1979), the Supreme Court rejected the Board's policy to decline jurisdiction over employees of a religiously sponsored organization "only when they are completely religious, not just religiously associated." *Id.* at 493 (quoting *Roman Catholic Archdiocese of Baltimore*, 216 N.L.R.B. 249, 250 (1975)). There, in the context of reviewing the Board's conclusion that a private religious school violated the NLRA, the Court observed:

> That there are constitutional limitations on the Board's actions has been repeatedly recognized by this Court even while acknowledging the broad scope of the grant of jurisdiction. The First Amendment, of course, is a limitation on the power of Congress. Thus, if we were to conclude that the Act granted the challenged jurisdiction over these teachers we would be required to decide whether that was constitutionally permissible under the Religion Clauses of the First Amendment. 440 U.S. at 499.

With these principles in mind, the Court determined that the Board's attempt to distinguish between "completely religious" and "just religiously associated" organizations necessarily raised Establishment Clause concerns under the First Amendment. *Id.* at 499–02 (finding that the Board's test inevitably would lead to excessive entanglement issues under *Lemon v. Kurtzman*, 403 U.S. 602 (1971)).

5. In cases where a reviewing court has determined that the Board's construction of the NLRA is irrational or otherwise impermissible, the court does not have authority to interpret the NLRA in the first instance. Rather the court must remand the case to the Board with instructions to construe the NLRA in a manner not inconsistent with the court's decision.

6. Although the Board has broad discretion to interpret § 2(3)'s definition of employee, it does not have any discretion to choose the definition of "independent contractor." As explained in Chapter 2, the Board must apply the common law test, and typically applies the ten-factor test found in the RESTATEMENT (SECOND) OF AGENCY § 220(2).

7. The courts are split as to whether they should defer to the Board's interpretation of labor contracts. *Compare NLRB v. Local 32B-32J SEIU*, 353 F.3d 197, 199 (2d Cir. 2003) (we give "deference to the Board's reasonable interpretation of labor contracts, in light of its expertise"), *with Titanium Metals Corp. v. NLRB*, 392 F.3d 439, 446 (D.C. Cir. 2004) ("we accord no deference to the Board's interpretation of labor contracts"). Which do you think is the better rule?

8. *Chevron* deference has come under broad attack. Chief among its critics is current Supreme Court Justice Neil Gorsuch, who, while a judge on the 10th Circuit, characterized *Chevron* as permitting "executive bureaucracies to swallow huge amounts of core judicial and legislative power and concentrate federal power in a way that seems more than a little difficult to square with the Constitution of the framers' design." *Gutierrez-Brizuela v. Lynch*, 834 F.3d 1142, 1149 (10th Cir. 2016) (Gorsuch, J., concurring). Is Justice Gorsuch's critique correct? Are there aspects of the NLRA that distinguish the decisions of the NLRB from the acts of other administrative agencies for deference purposes?

C. Judicial Review of Arguments Not Presented to the Board: Section 10(e) Waiver

NLRA § 10(e) provides that "[n]o objection that has not been urged before the Board . . . shall be considered by the court, unless the failure or neglect to urge such objections shall be excused because of extraordinary circumstances." That statutory provision thus creates a jurisdictional bar against judicial review of issues not raised before the Board. *See Woelke & Romero Framing, Inc. v. NLRB*, 456 U.S. 645, 665–66 (1982). For example, in *ILGWU v. Quality Mfg. Co.*, 420 U.S. 276, 281 n.3 (1975), the Court held that § 10(e) precluded judicial consideration of a party's contention that the Board denied it due process by basing its order on a theory neither charged nor litigated, because that party failed to urge its objection on the Board through a motion for reconsideration, rehearing, or reopening of the record. Moreover, § 10(e) requires objection to the Board—not mere discussion by the Board. *See Woelke & Romero Framing, Inc.*, 456 U.S. at 665–66 (although the Board discussed the issue, judicial review is barred because party failed to object through a motion for reconsideration).

The Court has explained that the purpose of this rule is to ensure that parties do not engage in judicial end-run of administrative adjudication. Permitting a party to present its arguments directly to the court would not only directly contradict the plain language of § 10(e) but also contravene the "salutary policy" embodied in that section of "affording the Board the opportunity to consider on the merits questions to be urged upon review of its order." *Marshall Field & Co. v. NLRB*, 318 U.S. 253, 256 (1943) (per curiam). As the Court has explained, "[s]imple fairness . . . requires as a general rule that courts should not topple over administrative decisions unless the administrative body not only has erred but has erred against objection made at the time appropriate under its practices." *U.S. v. L.A. Tucker Truck Lines, Inc.*, 344 U.S. 33, 37 (1952).

Section 10(e) does allow the requirement that a party must raise an objection before the Board to be excused "because of extraordinary circumstances." For a discussion of a particular example of such "extraordinary circumstances," see *Noel Canning v. NLRB*, 705 F.3d 490 (D.C. Cir. 2013), *aff'd on different grounds*, 573 U.S. 513 (2014) (extraordinary circumstances test met in case involving constitutional challenge to President's authority to recess appoint NLRB Board Members).

Epilepsy Foundation of N.E. Ohio v. NLRB

United States Court of Appeals for the District of Columbia Circuit
268 F.3d 1095 (D.C. Cir. 2001)

Edwards, J.

Petitioner, the Epilepsy Foundation of Northeast Ohio ("the Foundation"), challenges a[n] [NLRB] decision finding that the Foundation committed unfair labor practices when it discharged Ashraful Hasan and Arnis Borgs in violation of § 8(a)(1) of the [NLRA]. In reaching this result, the NLRB first interpreted § 7 of the Act to extend the rule of *NLRB v. J. Weingarten, Inc.*, 420 U.S. 251 (1975), to nonunion workplaces. The Board then applied the new rule retroactively in holding the Foundation liable for Borgs' discharge. . . . The NLRB also found that the Foundation committed an unfair labor practice in firing Hasan for engaging in protected concerted activity. . . .

In its brief to this court, the Foundation asserts for the first time that the Board's interpretation of the NLRA places an unconstitutional restriction on employer speech. And at oral argument before the court, counsel for the Foundation argued for the first time that, even if *Weingarten* rights are applicable in a nonunionized workplace, the facts of this case do not implicate *Weingarten*. Neither claim is properly before the court, because neither was raised with the Board in the first instance. Under § 10 of the Act, "[n]o objection that has not been urged before the Board . . . shall be considered by the court, unless the failure or neglect to urge such objection shall be excused because of extraordinary circumstances." 29 U.S.C. § 160(e); *see Exxel/Atmos, Inc. v. NLRB*, 147 F.3d 972, 978 (D.C. Cir. 1998). There are no extraordinary circumstances here. Although the Foundation could not challenge the Board's findings regarding the factual predicates supporting the application of *Weingarten* until after the issuance of the Board's decision, it could have objected to the Board's decision in a petition for rehearing. "The failure to do so prevents consideration of the question by the courts." *Woelke & Romero Framing, Inc. v. NLRB*, 456 U.S. 645, 666 (1982).

Finally, the Foundation argues that the Board has not provided an adequate explanation for its decision. We need not tarry long over this claim, for it is plainly meritless. Apart from the detailed discussions recited above, the Board also relied heavily on its prior decision in *Materials Research* to support the judgment that *Weingarten* rights are applicable in nonunion workplaces. . . . The Board's conclusion obviously is debatable (because the Board has "changed its mind" several times in addressing this issue); but the rationale underlying the decision in this case is both clear and reasonable. That is all that is necessary to garner deference from the court. "When a challenge to an agency construction of a statutory provision, fairly conceptualized, really centers on the wisdom of the agency's policy, rather than whether it is a reasonable choice within a gap left open by Congress, the challenge must fail." *Chevron U.S.A. Inc. v. Natural Res. Def. Council, Inc.*, 467 U.S. 837, 866 (1984). The Foundation's challenge here is merely an attack on the wisdom of the agency's policy, and, therefore, the challenge must fail.

Chapter 6

Remedies for Unlawful Interference with Concerted Activity

I. Introduction

This chapter describes the remedies available to the Board and state labor relations boards for ULPs involving worker protests, speech regulation, or conduct regulation in the context of a union organizing campaign. These include injunctions to prevent or immediately remedy ULPs designed to hamper organizing. The chapter also discusses the extensive debate over remedies in private-sector law, including the opinion — strongly held in some quarters — that NLRA remedies for employer ULPs during organizing are insufficient to deter unlawful behavior. This debate relates to a broader theme of modern labor relations: the trend of some private-sector unions abandoning traditional NLRA mechanisms. In contrast, public-sector remedies for ULPs have generally not been controversial or seen as inadequate even though those remedies are almost always the same as private-sector remedies. Consider why that might be as you read this chapter. Other chapters cover remedies for other types of ULPs (*e.g.*, Chapter 9 describes remedies for the failure to bargain in good faith).

II. The Scope of the Board's Authority to Remedy Unfair Labor Practices During Organizing

A. The Board's Remedial Authority

1. *The Board Generally Has Broad Remedial Discretion to Remedy and to Prevent Unfair Labor Practices*

Section 10(c) of the NLRA expressly authorizes the Board, on finding a violation of the NLRA, to order the wrongdoer not only to cease and desist from the unlawful conduct, but also "to take such affirmative action . . . as will effectuate the policies of this Act." The basic purpose of a Board remedial order is "to restore, so far as possible, the status quo that would have obtained but for the wrongful act." *NLRB v. J.H. Rutter-Rex Mfg. Co.*, 396 U.S. 258, 265 (1969). The Board's authority to fashion appropriate orders to prevent and remedy the effects of unfair labor practices is "a broad discretionary one, subject to limited judicial review." *Fibreboard*

Paper Prods. Corp. v. NLRB, 379 U.S. 203, 216 (1964). The Board's choice of remedy "should stand unless it can be shown that the order is a patent attempt to achieve ends other than those which can fairly be said to effectuate the policies of the Act." *Virginia Elec. & Power Co. v. NLRB*, 319 U.S. 533, 540 (1943). "Because the relation of remedy to policy is peculiarly a matter for administrative competence, courts must not enter the allowable area of the Board's discretion and must guard against the danger of sliding unconsciously from the narrow confines of law into the more spacious domain of policy." *Phelps Dodge Corp. v. NLRB*, 313 U.S. 177, 194 (1941).

There are, however, limits to the Board's broad remedial discretion. Section 10(c) expressly preserves an employer's right under common law to discharge employees "for cause," thereby placing limits on the Board's power to reinstate employees: "No order of the Board shall require the reinstatement of any individual as an employee who has been suspended or discharged, or the payment to him of any back pay, if such individual was suspended or discharged for cause." In *NLRB v. Local U. No. 1229, IBEW*, 346 U.S. 464 (1953) (*Jefferson Standard*), the Court agreed with the Board's conclusion that § 10(c) permits an employer to discharge an employee "for cause" in some cases where the employee's misconduct might have constituted protected activity. It is important to note, however, that the holding of this case has been narrowly read as permitting employers to discharge employees who engage in misconduct such as product disparagement that is unlinked to a labor dispute. *See id.* at 468–72 (holding that employer permissibly fired "for cause" employees who distributed handbills "making a sharp, public, disparaging attack upon the quality of the company's product and its business policies, in a manner reasonably calculated to harm the company's reputation and reduce its income" while making no reference to the labor dispute). A broader construction of § 10(c)'s for-cause-discharge clause would swallow up most concerted activity. After all, an employer could reasonably view most concerted activity as disloyal to the employer.

All Board orders are bifurcated into the cease-and-desist order and the affirmative order. Section 10(c) expressly authorizes "reinstatement" and "back pay" as appropriate affirmative orders. The Supreme Court has echoed that authority: "The legitimacy of back pay as a remedy for unlawful discharge or unlawful failure to reinstate is beyond dispute." *NLRB v. J.H. Rutter-Rex Mfg. Co.*, 396 U.S. 258, 262–63 (1969).

2. The Basic ULP Remedies Are Cease-and-Desist and Affirmative Orders

The Board issues two types of remedial orders: (a) cease-and-desist orders; and (b) affirmative relief orders.

a. Cease-and-Desist Orders

A cease-and-desist order typically commands the respondent, as an adjudicated labor-law violator, to "cease and desist from" engaging in the particular unfair labor practices found. For example, the Board might order the violator to cease and desist from:

- threatening employees with termination if they refuse to act against the union;
- promising employees benefits in exchange for voting against the union;
- soliciting grievances directly from employees;
- discharging employees because they form, join, or assist the union, or any other labor organization, or engage in concerted activities;
- failing and refusing to recognize and bargain with the union, as the exclusive collective-bargaining representative of the employees in the bargaining unit;
- failing and refusing to meet and bargain collectively and in good faith with the union as the exclusive collective-bargaining representative of the employees in the following appropriate unit;
- failing and refusing to furnish the union with requested information that is necessary for, and relevant to, the performance of its duties as the exclusive collective-bargaining representative;
- unilaterally changing a term or condition of employment.

The Board will also issue a catchall cease-and-desist order, which comes in two varieties—narrow or broad. Although both types of orders are fairly broad, the Board and courts use these terms to distinguish between ordinary cease-and-desist orders and extremely broad ones. In most cases, the Board will issue a *narrow* cease-and-desist order, which enjoins the respondent, in "any like or related manner," from "interfering with, restraining, or coercing employees in the exercise of the rights guaranteed them by Section 7 of the Act." In cases where "a respondent is shown to have a proclivity to violate the [NLRA] or has engaged in such egregious or widespread misconduct as to demonstrate a general disregard for the employees' fundamental statutory rights," the Board will issue a *broad* cease-and-desist order. *Hickmott Foods, Inc.*, 242 N.L.R.B. 1357, 1357 (1979). A broad cease-and-desist order commands the NLRA violator not only to cease and desist from engaging in misconduct in "any like or related manner," but also to cease and desist from engaging in misconduct "[i]n any other manner interfering with, restraining, or coercing employees in the exercise of the rights guaranteed them by Section 7 of the [NLRA]." *Federated Logistics & Operations v. NLRB*, 400 F.3d 920, 928–29 (D.C. Cir. 2005) (upholding broad cease-and-desist order where employer "ha[s] a proclivity to violate the [NLRA], or has engaged in such egregious or widespread misconduct as to demonstrate a general disregard for the employees' fundamental statutory rights") (internal quotation marks omitted).

Notes

1. The Board finds that an employer violated the Act by committing several § 8(a)(1) violations. The employer petitions the court of appeals to review the Board's order but the court denies the employer's petition and enforces the Board's order in full. Less than one month after the court enforces the Board's order, the employer engages in additional ULPs. Assuming that the Board finds that the employer's

conduct is unlawful under the NLRA, under what circumstances should the Board issue a broad remedial order? *See, e.g., NLRB v. Regency Grande Nursing & Rehabilitation Ctr.*, 2011 U.S. App. LEXIS 16505, at *9–*12 (3d Cir. Aug. 9, 2011) (upholding Board's broad order where employer resumed unlawful conduct, albeit in a different manner, only weeks after a court of appeals enforced the Board's decision and order).

2. The Board finds that an employer engages in several ULPs. Under what circumstances should the Board issue the broad cease-and-desist order? *See, e.g., U.F.C.W. Local 204 v. NLRB*, 447 F.3d 821, 828 (D.C. Cir. 2006) (upholding broad cease-and-desist order where employer engaged in a long laundry list of unfair labor practices).

b. Affirmative Relief Orders

An affirmative (relief) order goes hand-in-hand with a cease-and-desist order. As the name suggests, an affirmative order is one in which the Board orders the NLRA violator to take some sort of affirmative or positive action to remedy the unfair labor practice that it committed. The Board typically orders the violator to "[t]ake . . . affirmative action necessary to effectuate the policies of the Act," and then enumerates the type of action that must be taken. For example, the Board will typically order the violator to post—in a conspicuous place for 60 days—copies of a remedial notice confessing to having committed the violation. The violator must post this notice within 14 days after service by the Regional Office. Although the deterrence value of this limited remedy has been questioned, the Supreme Court has approved the remedy as "sufficient to effectuate national labor policy," *Sure-Tan, Inc. v. NLRB*, 467 U.S. 883, 904 (1984), and, more controversially, as "significant." *Hoffman Plastic Compounds, Inc. v. NLRB*, 535 U.S. 137, 152 (2002). An example of a remedial notice can be found in the Supplement.

An employer engages in a laundry list of ULPs. Under what circumstances should the Board order adjudicated violators of the NLRA not only to post a remedial notice but also to read that notice to its employees? *See, e.g., Federated Logistics & Operations v. NLRB*, 400 F.3d 920, 929 (D.C. Cir. 2005) (upholding Board order directing that either a management official or an NLRB agent in the presence of a management official read the notice to employees where many of the ULPs were committed by high-level management officials).

In addition to notice posting, the Board issues other types of affirmative relief. Some common forms of affirmative relief include:

- back pay and reinstatement to remedy a § 8(a)(3) or (1) unlawful discharge;
- instatement to remedy a § 8(a)(3) or (1) unlawful refusal to hire;
- making discriminatees whole for lost earnings and other benefits resulting from unlawful discrimination;
- removal of unlawful items (*e.g.*, unlawful warnings or references to unlawful discipline) from employees' personnel files;

- preservation of payroll records for inspection by the Regional Office;

- an order to recognize a union to remedy a § 8(a)(5) unlawful refusal to recognize a union;

- an order to bargain with the union on request to remedy a § 8(a)(5) unlawful refusal to bargain;

- overturning an election result and ordering a new election;

- disclosing information requested by the union to remedy a § 8(a)(5) unlawful refusal to furnish information;

- rescinding a § 8(a)(5) unlawful unilateral cancelation of benefits, restoring the status quo, and making employees whole for any lost earnings and other benefits.

Additionally, the Board may, in rare cases, require an employer to recognize and bargain with a union in the face of "substantial unfair labor practices," even before an election or after a union has lost an election. *NLRB v. Gissel Packing Co.*, 395 U.S. 575, 615 (1969). Chapter 8 discusses such "*Gissel* bargaining orders" at length, but it is important to recognize here that additional remedies are available when extraordinary circumstances are present.

Below is a deeper review of some of the more common remedies.

3. A Closer Look at "Cease-and-Desist" Orders to Remedy § 8(a)(1) Violations: How to Remedy Employer "Bribes"

Section 8(a)(1) makes it unlawful for an employer to "interfere with, restrain or coerce employees" in the exercise of their § 7 rights. The only relief typically available for a § 8(a)(1) violation is a cease-and-desist order, requiring the employer to refrain from engaging in the particular unfair labor practice. This remedy is problematic in the context of employer benefits to employees, which could be viewed as a bribe for voting against union representation.

Problem 6.1

An employer unilaterally raises wages one week before a union election, and the Board finds that this conduct violates § 8(a)(1) (recall *NLRB v. Exchange Parts Co.*, 375 U.S. 405 (1964) from Chapter 3). Should the Board order the employer to rescind the wage increase and compel the employees to return the wages?

Unlike most orders that the Board issues to remedy unilateral changes, the Board does not generally require rescission of the unlawfully bestowed benefits. Why not?

4. "Make-Whole Relief" to Remedy § 8(a)(3) Violations

Section 8(a)(3) makes it a ULP for an employer to discriminate against employees "in regard to hire or tenure of employment or any term or condition of employment" because of their affiliation with a union. Reinstatement with back pay is the conventional remedy for such violations. Reinstatement, however, can take a long time, during which the employer's ULPs remain unremedied. In the meantime, back pay alone may not be a sufficient make-whole remedy. In the following case, the Supreme Court explained the Board's broad discretion to order reinstatement.

Phelps Dodge Corp. v. NLRB
Supreme Court of the United States
313 U.S. 177, 61 S. Ct. 845, 85 L. Ed. 1271 (1941)

FRANKFURTER, J.

The dominating question which this litigation brings here for the first time is whether an employer subject to the [NLRA] may refuse to hire employees solely because of their affiliations with a labor union. Subsidiary questions grow out of this central issue relating to the means open to the Board to "effectuate the policies of this Act (chapter)," if it finds such discrimination in hiring an "unfair labor practice." Other questions touching the remedial powers of the Board are also involved....

It is no longer disputed that workers cannot be dismissed from employment because of their union affiliations. Is the national interest in industrial peace less affected by discrimination against union activity when men are hired? The contrary is overwhelmingly attested by the long history of industrial conflicts, the diagnosis of their causes by official investigations, the conviction of public men, industrialists and scholars.... Such a policy is an inevitable corollary of the principle of freedom of organization. Discrimination against union labor in the hiring of men is a dam to self organization at the source of supply. The effect of such discrimination is not confined to the actual denial of employment; it inevitably operates against the whole idea of the legitimacy of organization. In a word, it undermines the principle which ... is recognized as basic to the attainment of industrial peace.

... [A]n embargo against employment of union labor was notoriously one of the chief obstructions to collective bargaining through self-organization. Indisputably the removal of such obstructions was the driving force behind the enactment of the [NLRA]. The prohibition against "discrimination in regard to hire" must be applied as a means towards the accomplishment of the main object of the legislation. We are asked to read "hire" as meaning the wages paid to an employee so as to make the statute merely forbid discrimination in one of the terms of men who have secured employment. So to read the statute would do violence to a spontaneous textual reading of § 8(3) in that "hire" would serve no function because, in the sense which is urged upon us, it is included in the prohibition against "discrimination in regard to ... any term or condition of employment." Contemporaneous legislative history, and, above all, the background of industrial experience forbid such textual mutilation....

Since the refusal to hire Curtis and Daugherty solely because of their affiliation with the Union was an unfair labor practice under §8(3), the remedial authority of the Board under §10(c) became operative. Of course it could issue, as it did, an order "to cease and desist from such unfair labor practice" in the future. Did Congress also empower the Board to order the employer to undo the wrong by offering the men discriminated against the opportunity for employment which should not have been denied them?

Reinstatement is the conventional correction for discriminatory discharges. Experience having demonstrated that discrimination in hiring is twin to discrimination in firing, it would indeed be surprising if Congress gave a remedy for the one which it denied for the other. . . . [i]f §10(c), had empowered the Board to "take such affirmative action . . . as will effectuate the policies of this Act (chapter)," the right to restore to a man employment which was wrongfully denied him could hardly be doubted. . . . Attainment of a great national policy through expert administration in collaboration with limited judicial review must not be confined within narrow canons for equitable relief deemed suitable by chancellors in ordinary private controversies. . . . To differentiate between discrimination in denying employment and in terminating it, would be a differentiation not only without substance but in defiance of that against which the prohibition of discrimination is directed. . . . To attribute such a function to the participial phrase introduced by "including" is to shrivel a versatile principle to an illustrative application. We find no justification whatever for attributing to Congress such a casuistic withdrawal of the authority which, but for the illustration, it clearly has given the Board. The word "including" does not lend itself to such destructive significance. . . .

There remain for consideration the limitations upon the Board's power to undo the effects of discrimination. Specifically, we have the question of the Board's power to order employment in cases where the men discriminated against had obtained "substantially equivalent employment". . . .

Denial of the Board's power to order opportunities of employment in this situation derives wholly from an infiltration of a portion of §2(3) into §10(c). The argument runs thus: §10(c) specifically refers to "reinstatement of employees"; the latter portion of §2(3) refers to an "employee" as a person "who has not obtained any other regular and substantially equivalent employment"; therefore, there can be no reinstatement of an employee who has obtained such employment. The syllogism is perfect. But this is a bit of verbal logic from which the meaning of things has evaporated. . . .

To deny the Board power to neutralize discrimination merely because workers have obtained compensatory employment would confine the "policies of this Act" to the correction of private injuries. The Board was not devised for such a limited function. . . . To be sure, reinstatement is not needed to repair the economic loss of a worker who, after discrimination, has obtained an equally profitable job. But to limit the significance of discrimination merely to questions of monetary loss to workers would thwart the central purpose of the Act, directed as that is toward the achievement and maintenance of workers' self-organization. That there are factors other than loss of wages to a particular worker to be considered is suggested even by a meager knowledge of industrial affairs. Thus, to give only one illustration, if men were discharged who were leading efforts at organization in a plant having a low wage scale, they would not unnaturally be compelled by their economic circumstances to seek and obtain employment elsewhere at equivalent wages. In such a situation, to deny the Board power to wipe out the prior discrimination by ordering the employment of such workers would sanction a most effective way of defeating the right of self-organization.

Therefore, the mere fact that the victim of discrimination has obtained equivalent employment does not itself preclude the Board from undoing the discrimination and requiring employment. But neither does this remedy automatically flow from the Act itself when discrimination has been found. A statute expressive of such large public policy as that on which the [NLRB] is based must be broadly phrased and necessarily carries with it the task of administrative application. There is an area plainly covered by the language of the Act and an area no less plainly without it. But in the nature of things Congress could not catalogue all the devices and stratagems for circumventing the policies of the Act. Nor could it define the whole gamut of remedies to effectuate these policies in an infinite variety of specific situations. Congress met these difficulties by leaving the adaptation of means to end to the empiric process of administration. The exercise of the process was committed to the Board, subject to limited judicial review. Because the relation of remedy to policy is peculiarly a matter for administrative competence, courts must not enter the allowable area of the Board's discretion and must guard against the danger of sliding unconsciously from the narrow confines of law into the more spacious domain of policy. On the other hand, the power with which Congress invested the Board implies responsibility—the responsibility of exercising its judgment in employing the statutory powers. . . .

Note

What arguments support the claim that reinstatement and back pay are ineffective ways of remedying illegal dismissals? Professor West has argued that reinstatement is an ineffective remedy because it occurs a long time after the unlawful discharge. *See* Martha West, *The Case Against Reinstatement in Wrongful Discharge*, 1988 U. ILL. L. REV. 1, 28–32 (arguing that back pay "only compensates for a portion of the loss employees have suffered").

5. Limits on Make-Whole Relief

As noted in Chapter 2, undocumented workers are treated as employees under the NLRA. *Sure-Tan, Inc. v. NLRB*, 467 U.S. 883 (1984). But the Supreme Court, in the following case, greatly limited the remedies available to such workers in cases where their employer violated their § 7 rights.

Hoffman Plastics Compounds v. NLRB

Supreme Court of the United States
535 U.S. 137, 122 S. Ct. 1275, 152 L. Ed. 2d 271 (2002)

Rehnquist, C.J.

[The Board found that the employer, Hoffman laid off Jose Castro for supporting a union organizing effort. At the Board hearing, Castro admitted that he was not legally authorized to work in the U.S., and indeed had used fraudulent documents to obtain employment. The Board held that Castro was not entitled to reinstatement because he lacked legal authorization to work in the U.S., but the Board awarded backpay, explaining in part that "the most effective way to accommodate and further the immigration policies embodied in" the Immigration Reform and Control Act [IRCA] was "to provide the protections and remedies of the [NLRA] to undocumented workers in the same manner as to other employees."]

Since the Board's inception, we have consistently set aside awards of reinstatement or backpay to employees found guilty of serious illegal conduct in connection with their employment. In *Fansteel*, the Board awarded reinstatement with backpay to employees who engaged in a "sit down strike" that led to confrontation with local law enforcement officials. We set aside the award, saying: "We are unable to conclude that Congress intended to compel employers to retain persons in their employ regardless of their unlawful conduct,—to invest those who go on strike with an immunity from discharge for acts of trespass or violence against the employer's property, which they would not have enjoyed had they remained at work." 306 U.S. at 255.

Though we found that the employer had committed serious violations of the NLRA, the Board had no discretion to remedy those violations by awarding reinstatement with backpay to employees who themselves had committed serious criminal acts. Two years later, in *Southern S.S. Co.*, supra, the Board awarded reinstatement with backpay to five employees whose strike on shipboard had amounted to a mutiny in violation of federal law. We set aside the award, saying: "It is sufficient for this case to observe that the Board has not been commissioned to effectuate the policies of the Labor Relations Act so single-mindedly that it may wholly ignore other and equally important [c]ongressional objectives." 316 U.S. at 47.

Although the Board had argued that the employees' conduct did not in fact violate the federal mutiny statute, we rejected this view, finding the Board's interpretation of a statute so far removed from its expertise merited no deference from this Court. *Id.*, at 40–46. Since *Southern S.S. Co.*, we have accordingly never deferred to the Board's remedial preferences where such preferences potentially trench upon federal statutes and policies unrelated to the NLRA. Thus, we have precluded the Board from enforcing orders found in conflict with the Bankruptcy Code, . . . and precluded the Board from selecting remedies pursuant to its own interpretation of the Interstate Commerce Act, *Carpenters v. NLRB*, 357 U.S. 93, 108–110 (1958). . . .

The *Southern S.S. Co.* line of cases established that where the Board's chosen remedy trenches upon a federal statute or policy outside the Board's competence to administer, the Board's remedy may be required to yield. Whether or not this was the situation at the time of *Sure-Tan*, it is precisely the situation today. In 1986, two years after *Sure-Tan*, Congress enacted IRCA, a comprehensive scheme prohibiting the employment of illegal aliens in the United States. §8 U.S.C. §1324a. As we have previously noted, IRCA "forcefully" made combating the employment of illegal aliens central to "[t]he policy of immigration law." *INS v. National Center for Immigrants' Rights, Inc.*, 502 U.S. 183, 194 & n. 8 (1991). It did so by establishing an extensive "employment verification system," §1324a(a)(1), designed to deny employment to aliens who (a) are not lawfully present in the United States, or (b) are not lawfully authorized to work in the United States, §1324a(h)(3). This verification system is critical to the IRCA regime. To enforce it, IRCA mandates that employers verify the identity and eligibility of all new hires by examining specified documents before they begin work. §1324a(b). If an alien applicant is unable to present the required documentation, the unauthorized alien cannot be hired. §1324a(a)(1).

Similarly, if an employer unknowingly hires an unauthorized alien, or if the alien becomes unauthorized while employed, the employer is compelled to discharge the worker upon discovery of the worker's undocumented status. . . . IRCA also makes it a crime for an unauthorized alien to subvert the employer verification system by tendering fraudulent documents. §1324c(a). It thus prohibits aliens from using or attempting to use "any forged, counterfeit, altered, or falsely made document" or "any document lawfully issued to or with respect to a person other than the possessor" for purposes of obtaining employment in the United States. §§1324c(a)(1)–(3). Aliens who use or attempt to use such documents are subject to fines and criminal prosecution. 18 U.S.C. §1546(b). There is no dispute that Castro's use of false documents to obtain employment with Hoffman violated these provisions.

Under the IRCA regime, it is impossible for an undocumented alien to obtain employment in the United States without some party directly contravening explicit congressional policies. Either the undocumented alien tenders fraudulent identification, which subverts the cornerstone of IRCA's enforcement mechanism, or the employer knowingly hires the undocumented alien in direct contradiction of its IRCA obligations. The Board asks that we overlook this fact and allow it to award backpay to an illegal alien for years of work not performed, for wages that could not lawfully have been earned, and for a job obtained in the first instance by a criminal fraud. We find, however, that awarding backpay to illegal aliens runs counter to policies underlying IRCA, policies the Board has no authority to enforce or administer. Therefore, as we have consistently held in like circumstances, the award lies beyond the bounds of the Board's remedial discretion. . . .

Indeed, awarding backpay in a case like this not only trivializes the immigration laws, it also condones and encourages future violations. The Board admits that had the INS detained Castro, or had Castro obeyed the law and departed to Mexico, Castro would have lost his right to backpay. . . . Castro thus qualifies for the Board's award only by remaining inside the United States illegally. . . . Similarly, Castro cannot mitigate damages, a duty our cases require. . . .

We therefore conclude that allowing the Board to award backpay to illegal aliens would unduly trench upon explicit statutory prohibitions critical to federal immigration policy, as expressed in IRCA. It would encourage the successful evasion of apprehension by immigration authorities, condone prior violations of the immigration laws, and encourage future violations. However broad the Board's discretion to fashion remedies when dealing only with the NLRA, it is not so unbounded as to authorize this sort of an award.

Lack of authority to award backpay does not mean that the employer gets off scot-free. The Board here has already imposed other significant sanctions against Hoffman-sanctions Hoffman does not challenge. . . . These include orders that Hoffman cease and desist its violations of the NLRA, and that it conspicuously post a notice to employees setting forth their rights under the NLRA and detailing its prior unfair practices. . . . Hoffman will be subject to contempt proceedings should it fail to comply with these orders. *NLRB v. Warren Co.*, 350 U.S. 107 (1955) (Congress gave the Board civil contempt power to enforce compliance with the Board's orders). We have deemed such "traditional remedies" sufficient to effectuate national labor policy regardless of whether the "spur and catalyst" of back pay accompanies them. *Sure-Tan*, 467 U.S. at 904. *See also id.*, at 904 n. 13 ("This threat of contempt sanctions . . . provides a significant deterrent against future violations of the [NLRA]"). As we concluded in *Sure-Tan*, "in light of the practical workings of the immigration laws," any "perceived deficienc[y] in the NLRA's existing remedial arsenal" must be "addressed by congressional action," not the courts. *Id.*, at 904. In light of IRCA, this statement is even truer today. . . .

Breyer J., joined by Stevens, J., Souter, J., and Ginsberg, J., dissenting

I cannot agree that the backpay award before us "runs counter to," or "trenches upon," national immigration policy. . . . Rather, it reasonably helps to deter unlawful activity that *both* labor laws *and* immigration laws seek to prevent. Consequently, the order is lawful. . . .

The Court does not deny that the employer in this case dismissed an employee for trying to organize a union — a crude and obvious violation of the labor laws. And it cannot deny that the Board has especially broad discretion in choosing an appropriate remedy for addressing such violations. *NLRB v. Gissel Packing Co.*, 395 U.S. 575, 612, n. 32. Nor can it deny that in such circumstances backpay awards serve critically important remedial purposes. *NLRB v. J.H. Rutter-Rex Mfg. Co.*, 396 U.S. 258 (1969). Those purposes involve more than victim compensation; they also include deterrence, *i.e.*, discouraging employers from violating the Nation's labor laws. . . .

Without the possibility of the deterrence that backpay provides, the Board can impose only future-oriented obligations upon law-violating employers — for it has no other weapons in its remedial arsenal. And in the absence of the backpay weapon, employers could conclude that they can violate the labor laws at least once with impunity. See *A.P.R.A. Fuel Oil Buyers Group, Inc.*, 320 N.L.R.B. 408, 415, n. 38 (1995) (without potential backpay order employer might simply discharge employees who show interest in a union "secure in the knowledge" that only penalties were requirements "to cease and desist and post a notice"). . . .

The immigration statutes say that an employer may not knowingly employ an illegal alien, that an alien may not submit false documents, and that the employer must verify documentation. . . . But the statutes' language itself does not explicitly state how a violation is to effect the enforcement of other laws, such as the labor laws. What is to happen, for example, when an employer hires, or an alien works, in violation of these provisions? Must the alien forfeit all pay earned? May the employer ignore the labor laws? More to the point, may the employer violate those laws with impunity, at least once—secure in the knowledge that the Board cannot assess a monetary penalty? The immigration statutes' language simply does not say.

Nor can the Court comfortably rest its conclusion upon the immigration laws' purposes. For one thing, the general purpose of the immigration statute's employment prohibition is to diminish the attractive force of employment, which like a "magnet" pulls illegal immigrants toward the United States. H.R.Rep. No. 99–682, pt. 1, p. 45 (1986). To permit the Board to award backpay could not significantly increase the strength of this magnetic force, for so speculative a future possibility could not realistically influence an individual's decision to migrate illegally. . . .

To *deny* the Board the power to award backpay, however, might very well increase the strength of this magnetic force. That denial lowers the cost to the employer of an initial labor law violation (provided, of course, that the only victims are illegal aliens). It thereby increases the employer's incentive to find and to hire illegal-alien employees. Were the Board forbidden to assess backpay against a *knowing* employer—a circumstance not before us today . . . this perverse economic incentive, which runs directly contrary to the immigration statute's basic objective, would be obvious and serious. But even if limited to cases where the employer did not know of the employee's status, the incentive may prove significant—for, as the Board has told us, the Court's rule offers employers immunity in borderline cases, thereby encouraging them to take risks, *i.e.*, to hire with a wink and a nod those potentially unlawful aliens whose unlawful employment (given the Court's views) ultimately will lower the costs of labor law violations. . . .

Notes

1. Who has the better argument, the majority or the dissent? Does *Hoffman Plastics* strike the appropriate balance between labor and immigration policy (to the extent they are in tension)?

2. According to one amicus brief submitted on behalf of employers and employer organizations (Brief Amici Curiae of Employers and Employer Organizations in Support of Respondents, *Hoffman Plastics Compounds, Inc. v. NLRB*, Docket No. 00-1525):

Fundamental principles of economics and fair competition weigh heavily against the creation of an exemption for employers of undocumented workers from ordinary backpay liability. Although estimates vary, there may be as many as thirteen million undocumented persons in the United States today, nearly all of working age, and the NLRA should apply uniformly to all companies that employ them. . . . Basic economics teaches that a firm with a lower cost structure, over time, will be more successful than a firm with a relatively higher cost structure (all other factors being equal), in any price-competitive industry. With a lower cost structure, the successful firm will choose between matching the prices of the higher-cost firm (and achieving a lower overall market share) or undercutting prices (and achieving a higher overall market share). Either choice will result in higher revenues/profits for the low-cost firm relative to the high-cost firm. . . . This economic principle holds true whether the successful firm achieves lower costs through greater efficiency or by evading costs of regulatory compliance. As one commentator has explained, the "[d]irect benefits [of avoiding regulatory compliance] may be retained with the [firm]; alternatively they may be passed on [to] the customers in the form of lower prices. Either way they may produce indirect benefits in terms of product enhancement, increased market share, or other factors that affect profitability." . . . When one firm gains a cost advantage by avoiding regulations, other existing competitors will suffer a systemic competitive disadvantage as a result, and will be forced either to exit the market or to adopt similar illegal tactics to replicate the lower cost structure of the successful firm in a perverse "race to the bottom" scenario.

Why would a group representing employers file an amicus brief taking the position that the Board should order back pay to discriminatees in these circumstances?

3. More recently, the Board held that *Hoffman* precluded back pay as a remedy even against employers who *knowingly* employed undocumented workers. *Mezonos Maven Bakery Inc.*, 357 N.L.R.B. 376 (2011). In a concurring opinion, then-Chair Liebman and Member Pearce noted that they believed that "the policy arguments for awarding backpay to undocumented workers are compelling. They conclude, however, that *Hoffman* forecloses that remedy." *Id.*, at 379, n. 26. What incentives does this rule create for employers? For unions? For undocumented workers? For a summary of how the General Counsel's office approaches this difficult issue, see GC 15-03, "Updated Procedures in Addressing Immigration Status Issues That Arise During ULP Proceedings."

4. The question of the availability of other remedies for undocumented workers—unpaid wages for time actually worked for example—remains open. *See, e.g.,* Michael Wishnie, *Emerging Issues for Undocumented Workers*, 6 U. Pa. J. Lab. & Emp. L. 497, 509 (2004). Also, it appears that an employer reporting its own undocumented workers to the former Immigration and Naturalization Service (now U.S. Immigration and Customs Enforcement or ICE) to retaliate for union organizing

efforts can be subject to a range of penalties outside the typical labor law realm. *Id.* at 503–05.

5. In *We Are In This Together: The Rule of Law, the Commerce Clause, and the Enhancement of Liberty Through Mutual Aid* (2013), Professor Anne Marie Lofaso criticized the Supreme Court's holding in *Hoffmann Plastics*, calling for a bipartisan legislative solution that would discourage employers from taking advantage of undocumented workers while contributing—in a symbolic way—to federal-budget fiscal responsibility by authorizing treble damages to be paid into the United States Treasury:

> The administration should suggest legislation authorizing back pay in these cases. The Board could collect the back pay and rather than distributing it to the undocumented workers, it could distribute the award to the general treasury minus an administrative fee, which would go toward paying agency expenses. In cases where the Board finds that the employer knowingly hired undocumented workers, the amendment could authorize treble damages, which could be used for funding nonmilitary, discretionary expenses.

——————

The Board bifurcates its proceedings into two stages. In the liability stage, the Board determines whether the employer or the union has engaged in an unfair labor practice. If so, it issues a cease-and-desist order and orders affirmative relief. To the extent that relief needs to be liquidated, the parties participate in the compliance stage. ***ABF Freight Sys., Inc. v. NLRB***, 510 U.S. 317 (1994) (discussed in *Hoffman Plastics, supra*), presents the question whether an employee forfeits the remedy of reinstatement with back pay after an administrative law judge finds that the employee purposefully testified falsely during the administrative hearing. Although the administrative hearing in this case occurred during the liability stage, these questions may also arise in the compliance phase.

In *ABF*, the Board found that employee Michael Manso was fired in violation of his § 7 rights. The Board also found that Manso had lied to his employer about why he was late to work and repeated that lie under oath at the NLRB hearing on the matter. The employer, ABF, argued that this fact alone should defeat any claim for reinstatement or back pay. While the Court stated that "false testimony in a formal proceeding is intolerable," 510 U.S. 317, 323, it upheld the Board's award of reinstatement and back pay.

> The Act expressly authorizes the Board "to take such affirmative action including reinstatement of employees with or without back pay, as will effectuate the policies of [the Act]." 29 U.S.C. § 160(c). Only in cases of discharge for cause does the statute restrict the Board's authority to order reinstatement. This is not such a case.
>
> When Congress expressly delegates to an administrative agency the authority to make specific policy determinations, courts must give the agency's decision controlling weight unless it is "arbitrary, capricious, or

manifestly contrary to the statute." *Chevron U.S.A. Inc. v. Natural Resources Defense Council, Inc.*, 467 U.S. 837, 844 (1984). Because this case involves that kind of express delegation, the Board's views merit the greatest deference. This has been our consistent appraisal of the Board's remedial authority throughout its long history of administering the Act. As we explained over a half century ago:

> Because the relation of remedy to policy is peculiarly a matter for administrative competence, courts must not enter the allowable area of the Board's discretion and must guard against the danger of sliding unconsciously from the narrow confines of law into the more spacious domain of policy. *Phelps Dodge Corp. v. NLRB*, 313 U.S. 177, 194 (1941).

> Notwithstanding our concern about the seriousness of Manso's ill-advised decision to repeat under oath his false excuse for tardiness, we cannot say that the Board's remedial order in this case was an abuse of its broad discretion or that it was obligated to adopt a rigid rule that would foreclose relief in all comparable cases. Nor can we fault the Board's conclusions that Manso's reason for being late to work was ultimately irrelevant to whether antiunion animus actually motivated his discharge and that ordering effective relief in a case of this character promotes a vital public interest. . . . 510 U.S. 317, 324–25.

ABF's policy argument in this case relied on several decisions refusing to enforce reinstatement orders where the employee had engaged in serious misconduct. *See, e.g., Precision Window Mfg. v. NLRB*, 963 F.2d 1105, 1110 (8th Cir. 1992) (employee lied about extent of union activities and threatened to kill supervisor); *NLRB v. Magnusen*, 523 F.2d 643, 646 (9th Cir. 1975) (employee padded time card and lied about it under oath); *NLRB v. Commonwealth Foods, Inc.*, 506 F.2d 1065, 1068 (4th Cir. 1974) (employees stole from employer); *NLRB v. Breitling*, 378 F.2d 663, 664 (10th Cir. 1967) (employee confessed to stealing from employer). Are these cases good law after *ABF*? Or is there a significant distinction between these cases and instances in which an employee lies in an administrative hearing? Can an argument be made for the proposition that lying in an administrative hearing is worse, at least in some instances, than engaging in serious misconduct?

Given that the Court stated that it was deferring to the Board in this matter, would it also defer to the Board if it had adopted ABF's position that any employee who lied in a Board hearing should be precluded from reinstatement and/or back pay? Would such a rule be better policy? Why or why not?

B. Judicial Interpretation of the Board's § 10(c) Authority as Remedial, Not Punitive

In a series of cases between 1938 and 1941, the Supreme Court held that the NLRB's statutory authority to remedy ULPs was remedial, not punitive. When reading about these cases, consider whether the Court's reasoning is consistent with the language of § 10(c) and best serves the purposes of the Act.

In *Consolidated Edison Co. v. NLRB*, 305 U.S. 197 (1938), the Court interpreted § 10(c) in the context of the Board's authority to invalidate contracts between an employer and a union to remedy a § 8(2) [now § 8(a)(2)] violation. *See supra* Chapter 5 for a discussion of § 8(a)(2). The Court explained:

> The Act gives no express authority to the Board to invalidate contracts with independent labor organizations. That authority, if it exists, must rest upon the provisions of Section 10(c). That section authorizes the Board, when it has found the employer guilty of unfair labor practices, to require him to desist from such practices "and to take such affirmative action, including reinstatement of employees with or without back pay, as will effectuate the policies of this Act." 305 U.S. 197, 235.

The Court then declared that:

> We think that this authority to order affirmative action does not go so far as to confer a punitive jurisdiction enabling the Board to inflict upon the employer any penalty it may choose because he is engaged in unfair labor practices, even though the Board be of the opinion that the policies of the Act might be effectuated by such an order. *Id.* at 235–36.

The Court continued: "[t]he power to command affirmative action [is] remedial, not punitive, and is to be exercised in aid of the Board's authority to restrain violations and as a means of removing or avoiding the consequences of violation where those consequences are of a kind to thwart the purposes of the Act." *Id.* at 236. The Court then held that:

> The continued existence of a company union established by unfair labor practices or of a union dominated by the employer is a consequence or violation of the Act whose continuance thwarts the purposes of the Act and renders ineffective any order restraining the unfair practices. . . . Here, there is no basis for a finding that the contracts with the Brotherhood and its locals were a consequence of the unfair labor practices found by the Board or that these contracts in themselves thwart any policy of the Act or that their cancellation would in any way make the order to cease the specified practices any more effective. *Id.*

In *NLRB v. Fansteel Metallurgical Corp.*, 306 U.S. 240, 257 (1939), the Court extended its holding in *Consolidated Edison*—that the Board was without authority to affect the rights of unions who were not parties to the underlying litigation—to additional cases, holding that the Board was without authority to order reinstatement of workers who engaged in a sit-down strike, a type of strike that is unprotected under the Act (*see* Chapter 11). The Court wrote:

> The authority to require affirmative action to "effectuate the policies" of the Act is broad but it is not unlimited. It has the essential limitations

which inhere in the very policies of the Act which the Board invokes. Thus in *Consolidated Edison Co.*, . . . we held that the authority to order affirmative action did not go so far as to confer a punitive jurisdiction enabling the Board to inflict upon the employer any penalty it may choose because he is engaged in unfair labor practices, even though the Board is of the opinion that the policies of the Act may be effectuated by such an order. We held that the power to command affirmative action is remedial, not punitive, and is to be exercised in aid of the Board's authority to restrain violations and as a means of removing or avoiding the consequences of violation where those consequences are of a kind to thwart the purposes of the Act.

In this context, the Court held that "to provide for the reinstatement or reemployment of employees guilty of the acts which the Board finds to have been committed in this instance would not only not effectuate any policy of the Act but would directly tend to make abortive its plan for peaceable procedure." *Id.* at 258.

Professor Ellen Dannin has been at the forefront in arguing that the Court's interpretation of the NLRB's remedial authority to exclude punitive damages constitutes judicial amendment of the NLRA. *See* ELLEN DANNIN, TAKING BACK THE WORKERS' LAW (2006).

C. Injunctive Relief

1. The Board's Decision to Seek Injunctive Relief Under 10(j)

In 1947, Congress amended the NLRA to authorize the NLRB to seek temporary injunctions against employers and unions in federal district courts to stop serious ULPs while a case proceeds through the Board's processes. 29 U.S.C. § 160(j). The court may issue a temporary restraining order or a preliminary injunction. These § 10(j) injunctions are sometimes necessary to protect employees' rights under the NLRA, safeguard the collective-bargaining process, and ensure that, when the Board decides a case, those decisions will be meaningful rather than moot. *See* Catherine Hodgman Helm, *The Practicality of Increasing the Use of NLRA Section 10(j) Injunctions*, 7 INDUS. REL. L. J. 599, 600–07 (1985).

Under the Board's procedures, the Regional Offices identify potential cases for review by the General Counsel who must obtain Board authorization before proceeding to court. The Board has created the following fourteen categories of labor disputes in which § 10(j) injunctions may be appropriate:

1. Interference with organization campaign (no [union] majority)

   a. Includes traditional "nip in the bud" [ULPs], such as threats, coercive interrogations, surveillance . . . , improper grant of benefits, and unlawful employee discipline . . .

2. Interference with organizational campaign (majority)

   a. Includes *Gissel* cases . . .

   b. . . . [I]ncludes ULPs [from] Category 1

3. Subcontracting or other change to avoid bargaining obligation

    a. ... [I]nclude[s] shutdown or relocation of operations [and other business transformations]

    b. [Includes] [c]hanges [that are] discriminatorily motivated . . .

4. Withdrawal of recognition from incumbent [union]. Undermining of bargaining representative . . .

5. Minority union recognition [§ 8(a)(2) violations]

6. Successor refusal to recognize and bargain

    a. Includes discriminatory refusal to hire predecessor's employees

7. Conduct during bargaining

    a. Includes refusal to provide relevant information, delay or refusal to meet, insistence to premature impasse or impasse on permissive or illegal subjects of bargaining, unlawful course of conduct in bargaining, or surface bargaining

8. Mass picketing and violence . . .

9. Notice requirements for strikes or picketing under Section 8(d) and 8(g) . . .

10. Refusal to permit protected activity on property . . .

11. Union coercion to achieve unlawful objective . . .

12. Interference with access to Board processes

    a. [Includes] . . . retaliation against employees for having resorted to the processes of the Board

    b. Retaliation may include threats, discharges, the imposition of internal union discipline or the institution of groundless lawsuits

13. Segregating assets

    a. Includes an alienation of assets which may require a protective order to preserve respondent's assets for backpay

14. Miscellaneous

    a. Includes injunction against certain lawsuits, employer violence, interference with employee activities for mutual aid and protection.

See generally Section 10(j) Categories, https://www.nlrb.gov/sites/default/files/attachments/pages/node-174/redacted10jmanual50reduced.pdf.

For over 15 years, NLRB General Counsels Meisburg, Solomon, Griffin, and now Robb have issued a series of memos prioritizing first contract bad faith bargaining, nip-in-the-bud discipline in organizing, and successorship refusal to hire cases for 10(j) relief. *See* G.C. Memo 18-05 for the latest memo.

2. Judicial Review of the Board's 10(j) Petition

To obtain an injunction, the Board must petition a U.S. district court. As the case below demonstrates, a court may grant injunctive relief under § 10(j) when "just and proper." *See* 29 U.S.C. § 160(j) (2012) (awarding an injunction when "just and proper"). Although the standard for what is "just and proper" differs slightly from circuit to circuit, district courts typically apply the same equitable criteria used for granting a preliminary injunction. These criteria are discussed in *Frankl v. HTH Corp.*, excerpted below.

Frankl v. HTH Corp.

United States Court of Appeals for the Ninth Circuit
650 F.3d 1334 (2011)

... The ... question is whether the [§ 10(j)] injunction should be affirmed on its merits. We have little difficulty concurring in the District Court's assessment that the NLRB was likely to determine ... that appellants (the "Hotel") engaged in violations of § 8(a)(1), (3) and (5) ... by refusing to bargain in good faith and excluding five union activists from the workforce. The District Court likewise did not abuse its discretion in concluding that the other requisites for § 10(j) relief were met. ...

When the General Counsel ... issues a complaint alleging an unfair labor practice and commences proceedings before the Board, it takes considerable time — sometimes years — for the administrative process to conclude. But "[t]ime is usually of the essence [in labor disputes]." *Miller v. Cal. Pac. Med. Ctr.*, 19 F.3d 449, 455 n. 3 (9th Cir. 1994) (en banc) (quoting S.Rep. No. 80-105, at 8 (1947). As a result of "the relatively slow procedure of Board hearing and order, followed many months later by an enforcing decree of the circuit court of appeals ... [i]t [may be] possible for persons violating the act to accomplish their unlawful objective before being placed under any legal restraint and thereby to make it impossible or not feasible [for the Board] to restore ... the status quo." ...

To remedy this problem, Congress added § 10(j) to the NLRA, as part of a comprehensive labor law reform in 1947. ... The purpose of a § 10(j) injunction is "to protect the integrity of the collective bargaining process and to preserve the Board's remedial power while it processes" an unfair labor practice complaint. ...

The circumstances ... in this case are as follows: In 2002, the International Longshore and Warehouse Union, Local 142 (the "Union") began to organize employees at the Pacific Beach Hotel in Waikiki, Honolulu. A representation election was held ... but the Board set it aside, finding that the Hotel had "engaged in objectionable conduct by coercively interrogating employees and maintaining an overly broad no-solicitation policy." ... After a second election, preceding which ... the Hotel again engaged in objectionable conduct ... the Union was certified, prevailing by a one-vote margin.

Bargaining between the Union and the Hotel did not go well. ... [T]he Union filed numerous unfair labor practice charges. ... The [Regional] Director investigated the charges and issued an unfair labor practice complaint.

[A] Board Administrative Law Judge ("ALJ") determined that the Hotel had violated § 8(a)(1), (3) and (5) ... and recommended that the Board order the Hotel

to cease and desist from various unfair labor practices and to take other remedial actions. The Hotel filed extensive exceptions to the ALJ's ruling. . . . The case
remains pending before the Board.

On January 7, 2010, the Director filed a petition in the District Court for injunctive relief under § 10(j) . . . . [T]he District Court issued an injunction requiring
the Hotel to bargain with the Union, to reinstate certain discharged employees,
to rescind unilateral changes to the bargaining unit members' terms and conditions of employment, and to take various other remedial measures. . . . The Hotel
appealed. . . .

Section 10(j) permits a district court to grant relief "it deems just and proper." . . .
"To decide whether granting a request for interim relief under Section 10(j) is 'just
and proper,' district courts consider the traditional equitable criteria used in deciding whether to grant a preliminary injunction." . . . Thus, when a Regional Director
seeks § 10(j) relief, he "must establish that he is likely to succeed on the merits, that
he is likely to suffer irreparable harm in the absence of preliminary relief, that the
balance of equities tips in his favor, and that an injunction is in the public interest."
Winter v. Nat. Res. Def. Council, 555 U.S. 7 (2008). "'[S]erious questions going to the
merits' and a balance of hardships that tips sharply towards the [Regional Director]
can support issuance of a preliminary injunction, so long as the [Regional Director]
also shows that there is a likelihood of irreparable harm and that the injunction is
in the public interest." . . . In all cases, however, the Regional Director "must establish that irreparable harm is likely, not just possible, in order to obtain a preliminary injunction." . . . "[T]he court must evaluate the traditional equitable criteria
through the prism of the underlying purpose of section 10(j), which is to protect the
integrity of the collective bargaining process and to preserve the Board's remedial
power." . . .

The District Court determined that the Director was likely to succeed on the
merits and likely to suffer irreparable harm; that the balance of hardships tipped in
the Director's favor; and that a preliminary injunction would be in the public interest. The District Court therefore enjoined the Hotel from various activities that, in
its view, the Board would likely determine, and be affirmed by the Ninth Circuit in
so determining, are unfair labor practices. . . .

We may reverse the grant of a § 10(j) preliminary injunction "only where the district court abused its discretion or based its decision on an erroneous legal standard
or on clearly erroneous findings of fact." . . . "Where the district court is alleged to
have relied on erroneous legal premises, review is plenary." . . . Applying these standards, we affirm.

A. Likelihood of Success on the Merits

Legal Standards

On a § 10(j) petition, likelihood of success is a function of the probability that the
Board will issue an order determining that the unfair labor practices alleged by the
Regional Director occurred and that this Court would grant a petition enforcing

that order, if such enforcement were sought. . . . We have explained that when the General Counsel, and not the Board, gives final approval to file a § 10(j) petition, "we do not presume that the Regional Director's position will ultimately be adopted by the Board." . . . Because the Board did not approve the petition here, we do not accord significance to the fact of the petition's filing in evaluating the Director's likelihood of success.

Nonetheless, in evaluating the likelihood of success, "it is necessary to factor in the district court's lack of jurisdiction over unfair labor practices, and the deference accorded to NLRB determinations by the courts of appeals." *Miller*, 19 F.3d at 460. It is, after all, the Board and not the courts, which "has primary responsibility for declaring federal labor policy." *Id.* Additionally, and for similar reasons, "even on an issue of law, the district court should be hospitable to the views of the General Counsel, however novel." *Id.* Given these considerations, it remains the case — whether or not the Board itself approved the filing of the § 10(j) petition — that the regional director in a § 10(j) proceeding "can make a threshold showing of likelihood of success by producing some evidence to support the unfair labor practice charge, together with an arguable legal theory." *Id.*; *see also Scott*, 241 F.3d at 662 ("[T]o satisfy the 'likelihood of success' prong of the traditional equitable test, [the Director] need only show a better than a negligible chance of success"). But if the Director does not show that success is likely, and instead shows only that there are serious questions going to the merits, then he must show that the balance of hardships tilts sharply in his favor, as well as showing that there is irreparable harm and that the injunction is in the public interest. . . .

Underlying facts

[The Hotel engaged in multiple ULPs, including bargaining in bad faith, effectively discharging five union supporters, improperly withdrawing recognition from the union, unilaterally granting wage increases to certain employees, and unilaterally changing the work schedules and responsibilities of employees.]

Likelihood of success: § 8(a)(3)

The District Court determined that the Director was likely to succeed in showing that the Hotel violated § 8(a)(3) by terminating five Union leaders, all long-term Hotel employees and all members of the Union's negotiation team when it reclaimed management responsibilities from PBHM. The Hotel limits its challenge to this determination to arguing that the District Court applied the wrong legal standard, maintaining the Hotel did not terminate but only refused to *rehire* the employees on December 1, 2007. The theory is that PBHM was a distinct employer from the Hotel, so that the latter was hiring afresh as of December 2007.

The District Court found that the Hotel decided not to continue the employment of the five long-term employees because of their leadership roles in the Union. The Hotel does not now argue that this finding was clearly erroneous. Refusing to hire new employees because of their prior union involvement is as much an unfair labor practice as is firing current employees for that reason. . . . While the General

Counsel must in the hiring context prove "that there was at least one available opening for the applicant," the Hotel does not contest that there were such openings here. As to union animus, the burden is on the Regional Director to demonstrate its role in motivating the employment decision with regard to either a termination or a failure to hire, and both the ALJ and District Court found that the Regional Director had met that burden for each of the five excluded employees.

[The Court also found a likelihood of success on the § 8(a)(5) charge.]

B. Likelihood of Irreparable Harm

. . . [W]hile a district court may not presume irreparable injury with regard to likely unfair labor practices generally, irreparable injury is established if a likely unfair labor practice is shown along with a present or impending deleterious effect of the likely unfair labor practice that would likely not be cured by later relief. In making the latter determination, inferences from the nature of the particular unfair labor practice at issue remain available.

. . . "[T]he discharge of active and open union supporters risks a serious adverse impact on employee interest in unionization and can create irreparable harm to the collective bargaining process." *Pye v. Excel Case Ready*, 238 F.3d 69, 74 (1st Cir. 2001); *see id.* (observing that other employees' "fear of employer retaliation after the firing of union supporters is exactly the 'irreparable harm' contemplated by § 10(j)"). For these reasons, a likelihood of success as to a § 8(a)(3) violation with regard to union activists that occurred during contract negotiations or an organizing drive largely establishes likely irreparable harm, absent unusual circumstances. . . .

[The Court also found a likelihood of irreparable harm on the § 8(a)(5) charge.]

C. Balance of the Hardships

The District Court determined that the balance of the hardships weighed in the Director's favor. The primary hardship the Hotel had advanced was the protection of its employees from the Union, which, the Hotel claims, the employees did not want to represent them. The Hotel renews that hardship argument before us. We also reject it.

"[I]n considering the balance of hardships, the district court must take into account the probability that declining to issue the injunction will permit the alleged[ ] unfair labor practices to reach fruition and thereby render meaningless the Board's remedial authority." . . . [For that reason], by establishing a strong likelihood of success on the merits of the alleged § 8(a)(3) . . . violations, the Regional Director showed that it was more likely than not that the Hotel had committed pervasive unfair labor practices. As the Board's case law indicates, in the context of pervasive unremedied unfair labor practices, it becomes impossible to know if employees truly no longer want representation by the elected union, as their expressed preferences are generally tainted by the effects of the unfair labor practices. In all likelihood, it will only be possible accurately to gauge union support after the Hotel ceases and desists from its allegedly unfair labor practices and resumes bargaining with the

Union—precisely the relief the Regional Director sought and the District Court granted. The District Court, therefore, had no reason to give significant weight to the Hotel's assertions concerning support for the Union, and so properly assessed the balance of the hardships.

D. Public Interest

"In § 10(j) cases, the public interest is to ensure that an unfair labor practice will not succeed because the Board takes too long to investigate and adjudicate the charge." *Miller*, 19 F.3d at 460. Ordinarily then, when, as here, the Director makes a strong showing of likelihood of success and of likelihood of irreparable harm, the Director will have established that preliminary relief is in the public interest.

The Hotel contests that conclusion as applied here, objecting that the Director "was literally asking the District Court to grant the Board's remedy, before the Board itself even has a chance to decide the case." But, in most bad-faith bargaining cases, a § 10(j) remedy *will* be identical, or at least very similar, to the Board's final order. This precept follows from the nature of interim § 10(j) relief and of the Board's final remedial power.

The purpose of § 10(j) relief is "to preserve the Board's remedial power." . . . The task of the Board in devising a final remedy is "to take measures designed to recreate the conditions and relationships that would have been had there been no unfair labor practice." *Franks v. Bowman Transp. Co.*, 424 U.S. 747, 769 (1976). Very often, the most effective way to protect the Board's ability to recreate such relationships and restore the status quo will be for the court itself to order a return to the status quo. *See Scott*, 241 F.3d at 660 (observing that "injunctive relief under section 10(j) is intended to preserve the status quo pending final action by the Board"). So the District Court cannot have abused its discretion just because it entered an order similar to the one the Board was likely to enter in this case. We have thus no reason to disturb the District Court's determination that injunctive relief was in the public interest.

Notes

1. The Regional Director sought injunctive relief about two years after the events of this case took place. The court concluded that the delay did not cut against issuance of the injunction. Do you agree? What caused this delay? To what was the court referring when it stated: "Because the Board did not approve the petition here . . ."?

2. What standard does the Ninth Circuit use to determine whether to affirm the issuance of a § 10(j) injunction? While the standards in other circuits are similar, they are not the same. For example, the Seventh Circuit applies the following "four traditional criteria that a party must demonstrate in order to obtain injunctive relief: (1) no adequate remedy at law, (2) irreparable harm absent an injunction that exceeds the harm suffered by the other party as a result of the injunction, (3) a reasonable likelihood of success on the merits, and (4) 'harm to the public interest stemming from the injunction that is tolerable in light of the benefits achieved by

the relief.'" *NLRB v. Electro-Voice, Inc.*, 83 F.3d 1559, 1566–67 (7th Cir. 1996). The Eighth Circuit applies a similar four-part test: "Whether a preliminary injunction should issue involves consideration of (1) the threat of irreparable harm to the movant; (2) the state of the balance between this harm and the injury that granting the injunction will inflict on other parties litigant; (3) the probability that movant will succeed on the merits; and (4) the public interest." *Dataphase Sys., Inc. v. C L Sys., Inc.*, 640 F.2d 109, 113 (8th Cir. 1981) (en banc), relied upon in *Osthus v. Whitesell Corp.*, 639 F.3d 841, 845 (8th Cir. 2011) (applying the traditional four factors in the 10(j) context).

3. This case also involved a §8(a)(5) (failure to bargain in good faith) claim. For more on the substantive law and remedies available under §8(a)(5), *see infra* Chapter 9.

4. Requests for injunctions for all *employer* ULPs, including §8(a)(1) and §8(a)(3) ULPs during organizing, and §8(a)(5) ULPs during negotiations, are *discretionary* for the Board: the NLRB may choose to seek injunctions in such cases "upon issuance of a complaint" by the Regional Director, but is not required to. NLRA §10(j), 29 U.S.C. §160(j). In contrast, cases where the Board "has reasonable cause to believe" that a charge concerning certain *union* ULPs (notably, violations of the secondary boycott provisions of §8(b)(4) or recognitional picketing in violation of §8(b)(7)) "is true and that a complaint should issue," the Board is *required* to seek an injunction under NLRB §10(l). *See* Chapter 12; *see generally* Richard Lapp, *A Call for a Simpler Approach: Examining the NLRA's Section 10(j) Standard*, 3 U. Pa. J. Lab. & Emp. L. 251, 262–63 (2001). Why would Congress make this distinction? Consider this question further—and whether this distinction is good policy—after reading Chapter 12.

5. Injunctions against employers that commit serious ULPs during organizing campaigns remain controversial. Employers and their advocates argue that injunctive relief in labor cases, as in other areas of the law is "extraordinary" relief which should be used sparingly, especially because the parties will not have had the opportunity to fully litigate the case. Unions and their advocates insist that remedies limited to posting, back pay, and reinstatement, often after many years of litigation, are not sufficient to deter employer ULPs during organizing, and thus employers faced with organizing campaigns will, predictably, violate the law, preferring these penalties to unionization. In the mid-1990s, under President Clinton, the Board was briefly more aggressive in seeking injunctions: in fiscal year 1994, the Board sought 83 injunctions, and in 1995, it sought 104. Under President G. W. Bush, these numbers declined dramatically. For a description of how hard it can be for the Board to obtain a §10(j) injunction, see William Lubbers, *Discretionary Injunction Authority Under Section 10(j)*, 35 Lab. L.J. 259 (1984).

6. If you believe that, at least in some cases, remedies for employer ULPs during organizing campaigns are inadequate, to what extent would that problem be alleviated by increased use of injunctions? What are the pros and cons of this remedy?

7. In *Ohr ex rel. NLRB v. Latino Exp., Inc.*, 776 F.3d 469, 479 (7th Cir. 2015), the court ordered attorneys' fees in conjunction with injunctive relief:

> The district court ordered the payment of the Board's costs and expenses, including reasonable attorney's fees, reasoning that "[t]axpayers should not bear the cost of the respondent's willful disregard of our Order." *Latino Express, Inc.*, 2012 U.S. Dist. LEXIS 90907, 27 (N.D. Ill. July 2, 2012). The district court was well within its discretion to do so. Latino Express and Gardunio intractably recycled the same baseless argument that a decertification petition affected the proceedings before the district court in the preliminary injunction hearing, in a motion to reconsider, in the contempt proceedings, and again in this court on appeal. The [NLRB Regional] Director correctly points out that given the respondent's contumacy, it was necessary to continue to monitor compliance and seek relief before the court even after the respondent's claimed they had complied with certain aspects of the order. Although we agree that the Director is entitled to costs and attorneys' fees, we decline to make any further rulings, as to do so would be premature. The district court has yet to assess the amount of those fees and costs. *Ohr ex rel. Nat'l Labor Relations Bd. v. Latino Exp., Inc.*, 776 F.3d 469, 479 (7th Cir. 2015).

When does fee-shifting make sense? Must the respondent be in contempt of the Board's order?

Notwithstanding *Latino Express*, the Board is without inherent authority to award attorneys' fees in an administrative proceeding. *See Unbelievable, Inc. v. NLRB*, 118 F.3d 795, 804–06 (D.C. Cir. 1997). Following that line of reasoning, the court in *Camelot Terrace, Inc. v. NLRB*, 824 F.3d 1085 (D.C. Cir. 2016), refused to award attorneys' fees to pay the union's and the NLRB General Counsel's litigation costs incurred in the Board's *administrative* proceedings. The court nevertheless enforced the Board's award of the union's bargaining costs as a remedy for the Section 8(a)(5) violation. Specifically, it held that, in a bad-faith refusal to bargain case, "the Board may require an employer to reimburse a union's bargaining expenses pursuant to its remedial authority under section 10(c) of the Act." *Id.* at 1087.

Although the Board may not award attorneys' fees in an administrative proceeding as a punishment, it may award attorneys' fees where the litigation itself is the unlawful act. In *Road Sprinkler Fitters Local Union 669*, 365 N.L.R.B. No. 83 (2017), the union filed a grievance and lawsuit to enforce a CBA predicated on a reading of that agreement which would convert it into an unlawful agreement under Section 8(e). The Board therefore concluded that using "the grievance procedure and the court system in this manner constitute[d] unlawful means pursuant to Section 8(b)(4)(A)." As part of the remedy, the Board awarded attorneys' fees that the employer had to incur to fight the illegal lawsuit. The D.C. Circuit agreed and enforced the Board's order. *See Road Sprinkler Fitters Local Union 669 v. NLRB*, 2018 WL 3040513, at *4 (D.C. Cir. 2018) (explaining that "[t]he Local misconceives the reason for the award of attorney's fees. It is not because the Local's behavior is particularly egregious but rather because the litigation itself is the illegal act. Since, as the Board determined, the Local's [grievance and suit were] illegal ab initio, . . . costs . . . are therefore the logical measure of damages.") (citing *Local 32B-32J, Service Employees Intern. Union, AFL-CIO v. NLRB*, 68 F.3d 490, 496 (D.C. Cir. 1995).

III. Proposals for Reform

Although interested parties have attempted to amend the NLRA several times, no substantial changes have been passed since the 1947 Taft-Hartley amendments—the Health Care Amendments of 1974 targeted one industry. Two attempts—the Labor Law Reform Act and the Employee Free Choice Act—stand out for their efforts to strengthen NLRA remedies and the Board's power to enforce the Act. A recent effort, the Protecting the Right to Organize Act (PRO Act), proposes a more comprehensive reform, but also would significantly strengthen the Act's remedial provisions.

The Labor Law Reform Act of 1977

The Labor Law Reform Act of 1977, H.R. 77, sought significantly to amend the NLRA. Some of those changes would have directly strengthened remedies, for example, by doubling back pay awards without regard to damages mitigation. Other changes would have indirectly strengthened remedies. In the excerpt below, Professor Weiler analyzes some of the reforms of the 1977 proposal in the context of the NLRA's current remedial scheme. Although nearly four decades have passed since the publication of this article, many of the problems and issues remain the same.

Paul C. Weiler, *Promises to Keep: Securing Workers' Rights to Self-Organization Under the NLRA*

96 Harv. L. Rev. 1769 (1983)*

A. Current Remedies Under the NLRA

1. The Remedial Philosophy of the NLRA. — A tacit assumption of American labor law is that regulation is the appropriate means of containing coercive employer actions. Certain forms of harmful and illegitimate behavior are prohibited on pain of legal measures imposed through the administrative procedures of the NLRB. . . . [T]he failure of the system to prevent unfair practices is generally attributed to the weakness of the sanctions for even the crudest forms of retaliation against union supporters, and to delays in the administration of the law. Remedying these problems, it is supposed, will cure the ills of the entire system.

Before we consider proposals for beefing up NLRA remedies or reducing administrative delay, we must be clear about the function such remedies are meant to serve. Section 10(c) . . . authorizes the Board "to take such affirmative action, including

---

reinstatement of employees with or without back pay, as will effectuate the policies" of the Act. The basic right created by the Wagner Act is the employees' right "to self-organization, to form, join, or assist labor organizations, to bargain collectively through representatives of their own choosing." This right is to be protected through a ban on employer "discrimination in regard to hire or tenure of employment . . . to encourage or discourage membership in any labor organization." It would seem logical, then, that a major aim of Board action should be the prevention of employer interference with the employees' collective right to self-organization. The remedial philosophy as it has evolved, however, is heavily oriented toward the repair of harm inflicted on individual victims of antiunion action by employers.

Consider, as an illustration of the difference between protecting a group right to self-organization and repairing the harms done to individuals, the case of an employee discharged in response to his union organizing activities. The law might repair the harm to this individual by restoring him to his job and making up the income that he has lost. If the employer's purpose had simply been to punish the worker for supporting the union, the fact that the law would effectively undo this damage at the employer's expense might discourage the use of the tactic in the future.

But the real purpose of such discharges is to break the momentum of the union's organizing campaign. By the time the discharged employee has been reinstated, much of the union's support may have melted away, and the election may thus have been lost. Unlike the discharged employee's loss of wages, this setback to the employees' quest for a collective voice in their workplace cannot easily be repaired. To protect the employees' group rights, the NLRA must rely on the preventive force of its sanctions. But the traditional remedies for discriminatory discharge—backpay and reinstatement—simply are not effective deterrents to employers who are tempted to trample on their employees' rights.

2. The Backpay Award.—At first blush, the backpay award might seem to serve both remedial and deterrent functions. Although from the employees' point of view the award is merely compensation for what has been lost, from the employer's point of view it is a financial penalty: the employer is required to pay for services it has not received. The problem is that this "fine"—paid to the worker rather than the state—is far too small to be a significant deterrent. . . . [T]he average backpay award in 1980 was only $2000. The small size of the average award is partly attributable to cases in which employers settle quickly and reinstate the employees to limit the monetary loss. But even in troublesome cases in which reinstatement is not forthcoming for months or years, the employer's potential liability is inherently limited. Early [on], the principle was settled that the proper measure of the backpay award is not the wages the guilty employer failed to pay, but rather the net loss suffered by the employee after the deduction of any wages earned in the interim in another job. Indeed, the law requires the employee to take all reasonable steps necessary to mitigate his loss by finding another job. If he fails to take such steps, his potential earnings may be deducted from the backpay award even if they are not actually earned.

The combination of the net loss and mitigation doctrines is the most telling illustration of the supremacy of the reparative policy over the deterrent policy in American labor law. If the backpay remedy were designed to deter the employer's unlawful conduct, there would be no reason to deduct any wages that the employee earned, or could have earned, in another job. By minimizing the employer's potential liability, such a deduction removes most of the deterrent effect of the backpay award.

Because of the ineffectiveness of the current reparative remedies in containing the incidence of employer unfair labor practices, many critics and legislators have sought to reorient the remedial philosophy of the NLRA to emphasize prevention as an independent objective. Among such reformers there is little sentiment for using criminal sanctions for this purpose. Instead, a favorite proposal is a multiple damage award, such as those used in fair labor standards and antitrust law. One key provision of the Labor Reform Act would have directed the Board to award to employees who had been discriminatorily discharged during an organizational campaign double the wages they would have earned had they not been fired, with no setoff for wages earned elsewhere. Thus, for example, if an employer illegally fired two union supporters, each earning $20,000 a year, and refused to take them back until a decision was rendered by an administrative law judge a year later, the employer's liability would total $80,000. This is a substantial sum for the kind of small firm that is the target of much union organizing activity.

One should not, however, overestimate the deterrent effect of even such an exemplary award. Suppose a firm has just twenty-five employees in a unit that is the target of a union organization drive, and suppose these employees receive an average of $20,000 per year in wages and benefits at a total annual cost to the employer of $500,000. Assuming an average union wage effect of 20%, the employer can predict that, if the union succeeds, the firm's wage bill for the first year alone will jump by $100,000, a sum exceeding the penalty for illegally firing two employees. To the extent that discriminatory discharges are effective in forestalling union organizing campaigns, the potential liability for a multiple backpay award (which itself would have to be discounted by the difficulty of proving the charge) may be a sensible investment in long-term labor cost containment.

Nevertheless, the double-backpay remedy with no mitigation requirement was too "punitive" to survive in Congress. The House amended the bill to provide for deduction of wages actually earned, and the Senate Committee went on to reduce the award to one-and-one-half times backpay. The assumption that NLRB remedies should be reparative rather than punitive was so pervasive that even the Labor Reform Act's supporters defended the measure as a means of compensating discharged workers for actual harms suffered over and above lost pay.

3. Reinstatement.—What about reinstatement, the other standard form of relief? In principle, such an in-kind remedy seems nicely designed to play both a reparative and a preventive role. The dismissed employee gets his job back, and his fellow workers see the power of collective action and labor law protection. Not only is the employer deprived of the fruits of its illegal behavior, but it also suffers a serious erosion of its hitherto absolute sway within its own plant. The prospect of such a result would seem to be a major disincentive to flouting the law in the first place.

The reinstatement remedy, however, has proved to be far less effective in practice than in theory. It is one thing for the NLRB to calculate the amount of wages lost and see that this sum is paid to the discharged employee. It is quite another thing for an outside agency to try to reconstruct an enduring employment relationship. An employer that is sufficiently antiunion to break the law by firing a union supporter is also likely to feel quite vindictive when forced to take the employee back, and may well start looking for an excuse to get rid of him again. The employee, fully aware of this attitude, will often be reluctant to return, especially if returning means giving up another job that he has obtained in the interim.

There have been two systematic studies of the efficacy of the reinstatement remedy, one from New England in the early 1960's and the other from Texas in the early 1970s. Both studies reached remarkably similar conclusions. First, only about 40% of the employees for whom reinstatement was ordered actually took their jobs back. The major reason given by employees for declining reinstatement was fear of employer retaliation, a factor that may well also have affected some of those who said that they had simply found better jobs. The employees' fears were apparently well founded; of employees who did go back, nearly 80% were gone within a year or two, and most blamed their departure on vindictive treatment by the employer. If the reinstatement remedy is judged by its ability to reestablish an enduring employment relationship, the verdict is clear: this goal is achieved in only about 10% of the meritorious cases. Small wonder that the prospect of a reinstatement order does not loom large for the antiunion employer making a coldblooded assessment of the legal sanctions it faces.

Time is the crucial variable in reinstatement cases. If the Board can secure reinstatement quickly, the wrongfully discharged employee is likely to accept the offer. In time, however, the employee generally obtains another job, which he will be reluctant to leave for the bleak prospects at his old position. Thus, he becomes progressively less likely to assert his reinstatement rights. Only about 5% of reinstatement offers obtained after six months are in fact accepted.

The timing of reinstatement is even more significant insofar as this remedy is designed to undo the chilling effect of a discriminatory discharge on the group impulse toward collective bargaining. If the dismissed employee were returned to his job immediately, the employer's attempt at intimidation would likely backfire. The message the employees would receive instead would be a demonstration of how effective a trade union could be in asserting and defending employees' rights against oppressive management. But if that lesson is to be at all influential, reinstatement must come before the representation election is actually conducted—normally about two months after the union has filed its petition. Although delay is unfortunate for the individual worker, he usually finds another job and will eventually receive all his lost pay. But delay is fatal to the viability of a union organizing drive. If the law is to have any chance of vindicating the employees' group right to "bargain collectively through representatives of their own choosing," the reinstatement it promises must come quickly. . . .

B. Delay in Unfair Labor Practice Cases

1. Delay Under the NLRA. — We have seen that time is of the essence in implementing NLRB remedies. If . . . a reinstatement order . . . is to be effective, it must come quickly. The question that arises, then, is how long an employer can forestall an enforceable order in an unfair labor practice proceeding. The answer is distressing: nearly 1000 days as of 1980.

[There are various stages at which the employer can effectuate delay.] In the first stage, someone files an unfair labor practice charge with one of the Board's regional offices, where charges are investigated and spurious complaints are screened out. If the charge is found to be meritorious, the Board staff will try to settle the case; the regional office will issue a formal complaint if settlement efforts are unsuccessful. In 1980, this first stage typically took a month and a half. . . .

In the second stage, formal complaints are tried before an administrative law judge (ALJ). The independent, tenured ALJ conducts a full-scale evidentiary hearing near the location of the complaint, analyzes the transcript and posthearing briefs, and ultimately produces a lengthy written opinion. All of this takes another ten months or more. The ALJ, however, does not have the authority to make a legally binding ruling. If any party takes exceptions to the ALJ's preliminary ruling, the final decision must be made by the Board itself.

The third stage, in which the ALJ's ruling is reviewed by the Board . . . , consumes another four to five months. But even the painstaking process within the NLRB structure does not end the arduous journey of an unfair labor practice charge. Without an enforcement order from a federal court of appeals, a Board order is entirely without teeth. The enforcement proceeding in the court of appeals provides an employer who is prepared to spend the requisite legal fees an opportunity to obtain extensive review of the Board's conclusions and to put off for another sixteen months the point at which the employer is finally faced with a legal directive that it must obey under penalty of sanctions for contempt of court. . . .

2. Reducing Delay: Enforcement Before Appeal. — In order to make effective such in-kind remedies as reinstatement and bargaining orders, would-be reformers of the NLRA have sought to reduce drastically the time required to obtain them. The natural starting point for minimizing delay is at the review stage. Procedures before the Board and in the circuit courts were the subject of a number of measures proposed in the Labor Reform Act. These reforms, however, would at best have made only a minor dent in the 1000-day period required for the current adjudicative process.

The most effective way to accelerate the review process would be to confer on the ALJ the power to make binding decisions. For example, reinstatement orders, perhaps subject to sparingly granted discretionary stays, could go into effect even as they were being appealed. But however reasonable such a reform might be, it is politically untenable and, more importantly, unlikely to be effective. . . . [D]elegation of real authority to the ALJ is not the solution to the problem of delay, because the ALJ phase is itself a major part of that problem. The ALJ stage now lasts 316 days. Even if the politically improbable were to happen and ALJ orders were made immediately enforceable, it would still take a full year to get a reinstatement order in a typical discriminatory discharge case. The remedy would continue to be utterly ineffacious. As discussed above, if a reinstatement order is not forthcoming within two or three months, it is unlikely to be accepted by the discharged employee or to make any difference in the representation contest.

3. Reducing Delay: Interim Relief. — No one suggests that a trial-type procedure could produce a final decision in fewer than two or three months in even a fraction of the tens of thousands of unfair labor practice cases processed annually under the NLRA. Recognition of the delay inherent in such a procedure has led to a different proposal: providing interim relief from unfair labor practices committed during the organizational campaign.

The present NLRA authorizes, but does not require, the use of an expedited remedy for unfair labor practices committed by employers. Section 10(j) empowers the Board to petition a federal district court for an interim order restraining an unfair labor practice pending the Board's own leisurely proceedings toward a final verdict. In contrast with this permissive provision is section 10(l), which was enacted in 1947 and applies only to certain unfair labor practices committed by unions. Section 10(l) requires the Board to petition for interim relief when it has reasonable cause to believe that a union has violated the provisions of the Act limiting organizational picketing and prohibiting secondary boycotts — two traditional union weapons — and assigns first priority to the investigation of such charges. The theory behind section 10(l) is that a union must be immediately restrained from using self-help to force recognition by an employer, because such "top-down organizing" obviously threatens employee self-determination. But if the law acts quickly to protect employees from illegal coercion by the union — as, in my view, it should — should it not respond with the same alacrity when the coercion is by the employer?

The actual practice under section 10(j) has been startlingly different from that under section 10(l). . . . Even in the most recent period, when the General Counsel of the NLRB was firmly committed to the use of immediate relief under section 10(j) as an antidote to the acceleration of unfair labor practices and when the pace at which section 10(j) petitions were filed more than doubled to an average of about fifty a year, the employer's risk of facing a section 10(j) petition in connection with a section 8(a)(3) complaint was still just one-fiftieth of the union's exposure under section 10(l). Only one section 10(j) proceeding was instituted for every 1700 section 8(a)(3) charges of antiunion discrimination by employers. The Board thus failed to use what was and still is, for preventive as well as for reparative purposes, the most effective weapon in its arsenal. Perhaps the most important proposal in the Labor Reform Act was one intended to change this pattern by including discriminatory discharge during an organizational campaign or first contract negotiation in the category of offenses that merit priority in investigation and give rise to mandatory injunctive proceedings under section 10(*l*) . . .

But however compelling may be the substantive principle of subjecting employer coercion of workers to the same remedial regime that applies to coercion by unions, it is an institutional reform of dubious value to shift the basic responsibility for administering section 8(a)(3) from the NLRB to the federal district courts. Section 8(a)(3) cases differ significantly in number, complexity, and stakes from those now subject to section 10(*l*). Currently, sections 10(j) and 10(*l*) together generate fewer than 300 cases annually in the federal district courts. The Board estimated in 1978 that, under the LRA, it would receive each year approximately 17,000 complaints of discriminatory discharges during organizational campaigns or first contract negotiations, and that these complaints would require it to file about 3500 petitions for injunctions. If the Board's estimates were correct, the NLRA caseload of the federal district courts would increase by more than ten times.

Moreover, the typical section 8(a)(3) case is far more complex than are the picketing complaints that are now brought under section 10(*l*). Whether picketing is taking place at a particular location is a simple factual question that can be decided on the basis of a photograph. By contrast, the legality of a discharge under section 8(a)(3) is always open to dispute, because it depends on the employer's intent. The judgment whether an employer acted with a discriminatory motive requires delicate inference from a mosaic of circumstantial evidence regarding such matters as the employee's involvement in the union's campaign and the likelihood that the employer knew of this involvement, the kind of infraction for which the employee was dismissed and the way comparable infractions were handled when no union was present, the employer's degree of opposition to the union, and so on. . . .

Professor Weiler then discussed the possibility of card check as a method for remedying the problem of election delay.

The Employee Free Choice Act

With the failure of the 1977 bill, labor statutory reform remained on the back burner until the early 21st century, when the Employee Free Choice Act (EFCA) was introduced into both houses of Congress. H.R. 1409 and S. 560. The bill's stated purpose was "[t]o amend the [NLRA] to establish an efficient system to enable employees to form, join, or assist labor organizations, to provide for mandatory injunctions for unfair labor practices during organizing efforts, and for other purposes." Bill Text, H.R. 1409 IH (2009–10) (https://www.govtrack.us/congress/bills/111/hr1409).

EFCA had initially been introduced in 2007 (H.R. 800) and resubmitted after the 2008 elections seemed to give Democrats a filibuster-proof 60 votes in the Senate. EFCA never passed, however. It was unclear whether all of the Democrats would have voted to stop a filibuster of EFCA. With the death of leading EFCA advocate Senate Edward Kennedy and his replacement by a Republican pledged to oppose labor law reform, EFCA was no longer a viable option for reform supporters.

Much of the debate around EFCA focused on its §4, the card-card certification provision, which would have required the Board to certify unions that obtained cards authorizing union representation from a majority of employees in an appropriate bargaining unit. Chapter 8 discusses this "mandatory card check" provision further. But EFCA's section on "Strengthening Enforcement" set forth three significant changes to the NLRA's enforcement scheme, which harkened back to the 1977 bill:

(1) EFCA would have compelled the Board to seek injunctions against employers who had committed §8(a)(1) or 8(a)(3) violations;

(2) EFCA would have authorized the Board to order employers to pay treble damages in back pay; and

(3) EFCA would have authorized the Board to issue civil penalties up to $20,000 per violation against "any employer who willfully or repeatedly commits any unfair labor practice."

Much like the 1977 Act, these changes would have significantly strengthened the NLRB's power to punish employers who violate the NLRA, perhaps especially during organizing campaigns. The addition of meaningful financial penalties to the NLRB's enforcement structure would, in theory, more greatly deter employer misconduct.

The PRO Act

Introduced in the House of Representatives on May 2, 2019, and passed in the House by a 224 to 196 vote on February 6, 2020, the Protecting the Right to Organize Act (PRO Act) provides for comprehensive reform of the NLRA. Its remedial provisions would: (1) provide for backpay without any reduction for interim earnings, front pay, consequential damages, and an additional amount as liquidated damages equal to two times the amount of damages awarded; (2) make Board orders self-enforcing, and, if a party refuses to comply, allow the Board to initiate contempt proceedings in the federal district courts; (3) require the Board to seek temporary injunctive relief whenever there is reasonable cause to believe an employer unlawfully terminated an employee or significantly interfered with an employee's rights; (4) provide for civil penalties of $500 per violation if a party fails to post certain required notices; and (5) provide for civil penalties not exceed $50,000 for unlawful discharge or serious unfair labor practices, and also authorize the Board to hold corporate officers and directors personally liable and impose the civil penalty on them. *See* Bill Text, H.R. 2474-116th Congress (2019–2020) (https://congress.gov /bill/116th-congress/house-bill/2474/text).

Notes

1. Review the various proposed changes in the 1977 bill, in the EFCA, and in the PRO Act. In your opinion, which are good ideas, and which are bad ideas, and why?

2. In his article, Professor Weiler goes on to argue that the representation campaign needs to be dismantled in favor of instant elections. Do you agree? What

details about how the system would work would you want to know? To the extent that the goal is to prevent improper employer coercion, which is a better solution, revising the election process or adding more penalties for ULPs?

3. Two common features of the proposed statutory reforms are increased injunction power and additional financial penalties. Which is more likely to prevent an employer from violating the NLRA? Do they serve the same purpose, or different purposes?

4. In *Jackson Hospital v. NLRB*, 356 N.L.R.B. 6 (2010), the Board held that it would "adopt a policy under which interest on backpay will be compounded on a daily basis, using the established methods for computing backpay and for determining the applicable rate of interest." 356 N.L.R.B. 6, 6. The Board explained that its decision to adopt this policy is reasonable because "the daily compounding of interest is used under other comparable legal regimes (including the Internal Revenue Code, which the Board has followed in other respects related to awards of interest), and it will better serve the remedial policies of the [NLRA]." *Id.* Will compounding interest significantly impact employer behavior by encouraging, for example, settlement due to the length of the average NLRB case?

IV. In the Public Sector

In the public sector, remedies for ULPs analogous to NLRA §8(a)(1) and (a)(3) violations during organizing are generally the same as under the NLRA: reinstatement, back pay, and posting a notice. *See, e.g.,* Ohio Rev. Code §4117.12(B)(4) (providing for reinstatement and back pay, except for employees discharged for just cause), and §4117.12(C) (providing for discretionary requests for injunctive relief). But, as noted in the Introduction to this Chapter, such remedies have not been nearly as controversial as they are in the private sector.

Joseph Slater, *The "American Rule" That Swallows the Exceptions*
11 Emp. Rts. & Emp. Pol'y J. 53 (2007)*

Scholars and union advocates often claim that the NLRA provides inadequate responses to employer unfair labor practices, especially for employers simply firing union supporters. Studies confirm that private-sector employers routinely fire or discipline workers for supporting unions. A recent report estimated that one in three employers in the U.S. faced with union organizing drives engages in this practice. This replicates an earlier study, which found that from 1992–95, more than a third of employers fired workers for union activity during NLRB elections. Another report found that one of four employers illegally fired workers for union activity during organizing campaigns, and on average, these employers fired four workers per election campaign. A study in the late 1990s concluded that employers illegally fired or otherwise retaliated against one of every eighteen private-sector workers who supported a union during a union organizing campaign. Employees get the message: a poll found that 79 percent of workers thought it was either "somewhat" or "very" likely that employees "will get fired if they try to organize a union."

Of course, it violates the NLRA to fire an employee for supporting a union. But usually the only relief wrongfully discharged employees can receive is reinstatement and back-pay, minus whatever the employee earned or should have earned after being illegally fired. No emotional or punitive damages are available, as there are in Title VII cases of disparate treatment, nor are there double damages, as the Fair Labor Standards Act (FLSA) provides, nor do successful plaintiffs receive attorneys' fees, as they typically do in Title VII, FLSA, and other types of employment law cases. Under the NLRA, it is possible, but in practice quite difficult, to get injunctions against employer discrimination during organizing campaigns. Beyond that, the only remedies are cease and desist orders and orders that employers post notices that they have violated the NLRA. . . .

Not only are remedies weak, but they are often seriously delayed. In 2003, the median wait for an unfair labor practice case pending an NLRB ruling was nearly three years from the filing of a charge, and employer appeals of NLRB rulings to federal courts often add years of further delay. In the context of an organizing campaign, this typically means that the status quo of no union is maintained. Further, the reinstatement remedy is problematic in practice. The majority of workers discriminated against decline reinstatement. One can imagine why a reasonable worker would not wish to return to a company that had illegally fired her, but lengthy delays make this attitude even more likely and thus make this remedy worth even less.

The incentives this creates are troubling. James Pope notes that "[f]rom a cost-benefit point of view, it is often profitable to fire union advocates." Gordon Lafer explains that "[b]eyond the delays . . . there are virtually no penalties for those ultimately found guilty." Thus, "[r]ational employers might well decide that the modest penalty for firing a few union supporters was worth the benefit of scaring hundreds more into abandoning the cause of unionization. Similarly, Kenneth Roth, the Executive Director of Human Rights Watch, writes that "[l]abor law is so weak that companies often treat the minor penalties as a routine cost of doing business, not a deterrent against violations."

Real world experiences support these critiques. Former NLRB General Counsel Leonard Page describes "outrageous and pervasive violations" by employers which took place "on a regular basis" during his tenure in the 1990s, noting that the weak remedies problem was "clearly exemplified" by employer unfair labor practices during union organizing campaigns. Another former NLRB General Counsel, Fred Feinstein, discussing the aggressive and not infrequently illegal tactics of Wal-Mart in opposing unions, explained that "even when the board charged companies like Wal-Mart with illegal actions, the remedies often could not salvage an organizing drive crippled by employer illegalities," and even Business Week agreed that Wal-Mart's illegal activities "carry insignificant penalties." . . .

C. Lessons from the Public Sector.

. . . Weak remedies . . . certainly hurt private-sector unions. But . . . public-sector labor laws provide the same weak remedies for employees fired for supporting unions, and still public workers have organized at a rate nearly five times that of private workers.

One key difference in the public sector is the absence of a background employment at-will rule. . . . Most public workers eligible to join unions are covered by civil service rules that require some form of "just cause" for discharge. Also, the constitution gives public employees some substantive and procedural protections in discharge cases. Thus, their employers may not fire them with relative impunity at the first sign of union organizing, as happens too frequently in the private sector. . . .

As to remedies, most public-sector statutes simply copy the NLRA's language, and public-sector agencies generally use the NLRB's interpretation of that language. Thus, the standard remedy for illegal discharge is, as in the private sector, reinstatement with backpay, minus whatever the employee earned or should have earned. Punitive and emotional damages are not available in public-sector unfair labor practice cases, and generally neither are attorneys' fees. . . .

2. The Difference: Just Cause in the Public Sector Instead of At-Will

Given that the same weaknesses appear in private and public-sector labor law, why is union density so much higher in the public sector? A large part of the reason is that public employers are not able to fire public workers engaged in union organizing as easily. This is because public employees generally are not employees at will due to civil service and related rules, and are given substantive and procedural protections by the Constitution. In short, there is no underlying rule of at-will to swallow the exception that the labor law is designed to create.

Civil service laws date from the late nineteenth century and are designed to protect merit principles: public workers should be hired, fired, promoted, or demoted because of their abilities, not as favors or punishments by political machine bosses. Thus, civil service rules typically require some form of just cause to fire a covered employee. While not all public officials are covered by just cause rules (policy-making officials typically are not, and there is often a probationary period for lower-level workers), the vast majority of public employees eligible to form unions are covered by such rules.

Additionally, the Constitution provides public workers with substantive and procedural protections. As to substance, for example, it violates the First Amendment for public employers to discriminate against their employees because of union membership. . . .

Many public employees also have constitutionally-protected procedural rights when their discharge is proposed. Civil service just cause rules (among other things) can create a property interest in a job which cannot be taken away without due process. The Supreme Court has held that an employee with a property interest in a job is entitled to both a relatively brief hearing prior to a proposed discharge and a more formal hearing after the discharge. These rules make it more difficult for a public employer to discharge union supporters summarily in an attempt to thwart a union organizing campaign. No such protections exist for private-sector employees wishing to unionize.

Further, under civil service just cause rules, the burden is on the employer to prove that a valid reason existed for a discharge. In contrast, in a private-sector unfair labor practice case, the burden is on the employee to prove anti-union motivation. This has several significant effects. First, in the public sector, it is more difficult for employers to win simply by asserting a whole host of reasons . . . for the discharge, hoping the fact-finder will credit them sufficiently to defeat plaintiff's attempt to carry her burden of proof. In contrast, government employers in civil service hearings must carry the burden to show that a particular, plausible, legitimate reason was in fact the real reason. This makes it more difficult for the employer to discharge employees for illegitimate reasons.

Second, for related reasons, this burden makes it less fruitful for public-sector employers to engage in multiple, time-wasting appeals, a process that can undercut organizing even if the fired worker ultimately prevails. Thus, delays in remedies, a serious problem under the NLRA, are not a serious problem in the public sector. . . .

3. Non-Legal Factors: Employer Hostility

Legal rules, of course, are not the only factors that affect union density. In response to the thesis above, it could be suggested that private-sector employers can be much more aggressively hostile toward unions than are their public-sector counterparts. Indeed, some have argued that what makes U.S. private-sector labor relations unique among industrialized democracies is the level of employer hostility toward unions. In addition to firing employees for organizing, many private employers convincingly threaten to close or move their shops in response to unionization. According to one survey, while only 1 percent of private-sector companies actually close up shop after their employees vote to unionize, 71 percent of manufacturing employers threaten to close during a union election campaign. Although privatization is a real threat to public-sector unions, equivalent threats of moving the work are more routine in the private sector.

Some public employers do in fact resist unions vigorously. And while private-sector employers are much more aggressive much more frequently, the reasons for that difference need to be unpacked.

First, opposition to unions by public employers is more common than the conventional wisdom would have it. One study notes that "the evidence suggests the majority of employers in both sectors" oppose unionization. In the past few years, some large and influential public employers have taken very aggressive actions against unions. The creation of the Department of Homeland Security (DHS) was delayed for months due to the Bush administration's insistence that the tens of thousands of workers in the new, merged department be denied collective bargaining rights they had enjoyed in predecessor agencies. . . . Such attacks are not limited to the federal government: governors of Indiana and Missouri recently revoked the collective bargaining rights of state employees in those states.

Still, the situation is worse in the private sector. One study found that private-sector employers were six times more likely to engage in unfair labor practices, including discharges for union activity, than public-sector employers during union organizing campaigns. While a rate even one-sixth of that in the private sector is still distressingly high, the difference is significant.

The question is, what causes this difference in behavior? The traditional answers are that public employers are less concerned with competition through lower wages than are private employers, and that political pressure inhibits public employers from expensive quasi-legal anti-union campaigns. While there is some truth to both those points, budget problems in a political environment sympathetic to tax cutting and unsympathetic to "bureaucrats" have given public employers incentives to fight unions for financial reasons and a political rhetoric to do so.

Most importantly here, the legal context in the private sector allows opposition and hostility to be turned into action more frequently and effectively. The background at-will rule significantly facilitates the use of quasi-legal to illegal tactics against unions. In contrast, in the public sector, the lack of this rule that swallows the exception inhibits such tactics by making them less effective. Protections against arbitrary dismissals based in civil service or other rules take away a "union avoidance" tool of easily firing union supporters, a tool that is too often used in the private sector. . . .

Notes

1. Is Professor Slater convincing that remedies in the public sector are much less of an issue than in the private sector because public employees are generally not "at-will" employees? Or are other reasons as or more important (*e.g.*, the differences in levels of employer opposition to unionization in the private and public sectors and/ or political concerns)?

2. Traditionally, most public employers have been less willing to run the sort of extremely aggressive anti-union campaigns that are often seen in the private sector. Are the laws of 2011 restricting the rights of public-sector unions (*see* Chapter 1) a counter-example? Harbingers of a trend that may continue? If so, will remedies for violations of labor laws become a more significant issue in the public sector? Or will the issue be broader: whether public workers in some jurisdictions will continue to have a right to bargain collectively at all?

Chapter 7

Electing a Union Representative

I. Introduction

This chapter describes the law governing the representation election process, as administered by the NLRB and state public-sector labor boards. It discusses requirements for and bars to elections, bargaining unit determinations, and methods to test an incumbent union's majority status. This chapter also explains how the law regulates efforts by employers and employees to test whether and how long after a representation election a union is presumed to have majority support and therefore authority to represent a group of employees.

While public-sector rules often track NLRA rules in these areas, this chapter will also describe some differences. For example, most public-sector jurisdictions prefer larger units, while the NLRB generally prefers smaller, single-location units.

II. Preconditions for an NLRA Representation Election

A. Overview of Private-Sector Elections — NLRA and RLA

Congress vested the NLRB with the power to safeguard employees' rights to organize and to decide whether a union would serve as their bargaining representative. Section 9(a) of the NLRA provides that employee representatives that have been "designated or selected for the purposes of collective bargaining by the majority of the employees in a unit appropriate for such purposes, shall be the exclusive representatives of all the employees in such unit for the purposes of collective bargaining." In *NLRB v. Gissel Packing Co.*, 395 U.S. 575 (1969), the Supreme Court endorsed the Board's view that although "secret elections are generally the most satisfactory — indeed the preferred — method of ascertaining whether a union has majority support,'" *id.* at 602, "an employer had a duty to bargain whenever the union representative presented 'convincing evidence of majority support,'" *id.* at 596. *Gissel Packing* further explained that employees may also organize for the purpose of collective bargaining through a "card check" process in which a union seeks voluntary recognition from an employer after collecting authorization cards from a majority of employees in a bargaining unit in the employer's workplace. Chapter 8 discusses the law governing this means of organizing a union. This chapter focuses on the Board's certification process through Board-conducted secret ballot elections.

To invoke the NLRB's authority in a representation proceeding, employees or unions must file a petition with the Regional Office in the area where the unit of employees is located. 29 U.S.C. § 159(c)(1). Section 9(c)(1)(B) further provides that, when a petition is filed, "the Board shall investigate such petition and if it has reasonable cause to believe that a question of representation affecting commerce exists shall provide for an appropriate hearing upon due notice." *Id.* The purpose of the investigation is to determine, among other things: (1) whether the Board has jurisdiction to conduct an election; (2) whether there is a sufficient showing of employee interest to justify an election; (3) whether a question of representation exists; (4) whether the election is sought in an appropriate unit of employees; (5) whether the representative named in the petition is qualified; and (6) whether there are any barriers to an election in the form of existing contracts or prior elections. *See* NLRB, *Basic Guide to the NLRA*, 8, *available at* http://www.nlrb.gov/sites/default/files /documents/224/basicguide.pdf.

If the Board finds from the proffered evidence that "a question of representation exists," § 9(c)(1) authorizes the Board to direct a secret-ballot election and to "certify the results" of that election. A question concerning representation exists if the employer refuses the union's request for bargaining after a sufficient showing of interest has been made. The Board's investigatory standards for jurisdictional questions, "showing of interest," and qualified representatives are set forth below. The remaining preconditions for an election are taken up in the following sections.

The Board has jurisdiction only over "employers" and "employees" as those terms are defined in NLRA §§ 2(2) and 2(3). *See* Chapter 2. Although the NLRA extends the Board's jurisdiction over cases "affecting commerce," which the Supreme Court has construed as being co-extensive with the U.S. Constitution's commerce clause, *see NLRB v. Jones & Laughlin Steel Corp.*, 301 U.S. 1 (1937), the Board has a policy of declining to assert jurisdiction over very small businesses. *See* Anne Marie Lofaso, *The Persistence of Union Repression in an Era of Recognition*, 62 Me. L. Rev. 199, 204–10 (2010) (describing those self-imposed limits).

Board policy requires a petitioner requesting an election for certification of representatives to make a "showing of interest": at least thirty percent of the employees in a proposed bargaining unit favor an election. The NLRA also requires that a petition for a union decertification election be filed by thirty percent or more of the employees in the unit covered by the agreement.

Section 2(4) broadly provides that the employee representative for the purposes of collective bargaining can be "any individual or labor organization." 29 U.S.C § 152(4). In determining a labor organization's qualifications to serve as bargaining representative, the Board takes into account that organization's willingness to represent the employees. *See Sierra Vista Hosp.*, 241 N.L.R.B. 631, 631 (1979). Nevertheless, a labor organization dominated by supervisors or managers does not qualify as a collective-bargaining representative. *See NLRB v. Annapolis Emergency Hosp. Ass'n*, 561 F.2d 524, 535 (4th Cir. 1977) (collecting cases).

Lengthy litigation of many issues had become a significant concern in representation election cases, with some arguing that the Board's election investigations had themselves become a barrier to workers exercising their rights to organize and bargain collectively. *See, e.g.,* Wilma Liebman, *Decline and Disenchantment: Reflections on the Aging of the National Labor Relations Board*, 28 Berkeley J. Emp. & Lab. L. 569, 584–87 (2007); James Brudney, *Neutrality Agreements and Card Check Recognition: Prospects for Changing Paradigms*, 90 Iowa L. Rev. 819, 863–77 (2005). To address these concerns, the Board issued a rare final regulation in December 2014, effective in April 2015, making several changes to its representation case procedures. Representation Case Procedures, 79 Fed. Reg. 74,307 (Dec. 15, 2014) (codified at 29 C.F.R. pts. 101–03).

Some changes effected by the rule merely recognized the availability and value of email. Parties were permitted to file petitions and other documents electronically rather than by fax or mail. *Id.* at 74,309. Similarly, employers' *Excelsior* lists of eligible voters provided to the union and the Board (see discussion in Chapter 3) had to include employees' personal email addresses and phone numbers. *Id.* at 74,310. The rule also required faster distribution of the election petition and other information to all of the involved parties, and more rapid answers from those parties to those documents. *Id.* It also required the employer to post a Notice of Petition for Election for its employees informing them of the filing and their rights within two business days of the Regional Director's service of the petition on the parties. *Id.* at 74,362.

Changes to procedures for litigating representation case issues proved to be even more controversial, however. For example, under the rule, the Regional Director could permit pre-election litigation only of issues that were necessary to determine whether an election should be conducted. Eligibility and inclusion issues affecting a small percentage of the bargaining unit typically were addressed in post-election litigation when those issues did not have to be resolved in order to determine if an election should be held. *Id.* at 74,309. Those issues could not be litigated at all if they would have no effect on the results of the election. Further, both pre-election and post-election hearings occurred on an expedited scheduled. *Id.* While the involved parties could seek post-election review of the Regional Director's rulings in a representation case (when the election results had not made the issues moot), the election ordinarily was not stayed after the Regional Director issued a decision and direction of election. Also, the Board had the discretion to deny review of regional director post-election rulings. *Id.*

Facial challenges to the NLRB's final representation procedures rule were raised in *Chamber of Commerce v. NLRB*, 118 F. Supp. 3d 171 (D.D.C. 2015), and *Associated Builders and Contractors of Texas, Inc. v. NLRB*, 826 F.3d 215 (5th Cir. 2016), and the rule was upheld in both instances.

On December 14, 2017, the Board, now with a majority of three Republican Members, published a Request For Information (RFI), asking for public input regarding whether the Board should retain the 2014 Representation Election Rule without change, or with modifications, or should rescind the 2014 Rule. The Board's two Democrats dissented. The Board received nearly 7,000 submissions in response to the RFI.

On December 13, 2019, without notice and comment and without relying on any of the comments received in response to the RFI, the Board, with a lengthy dissent by Member McFerran, issued a new representation procedure rule, largely rolling back the changes made by the 2014 rule. Representation Case Procedures, 84 Fed. Reg. 69,524 (Dec. 18, 2019). The Board acknowledged that the 2014 rule had resulted in elections being conducted more quickly, and had not changed the results of elections; the Board's experience under the 2014 rule was that unions won elections at the same rate under the 2014 rule as they had before. However, the Board held that its changes would advance the interests of efficiency, uniformity, transparency, finality, and the reduction of litigation.

The Board made a number of specific changes, almost all designed to slow the representation election process down considerably. In addition to extending almost all the time frames in the election process and making all time calculations based on business days rather than calendar days, the Board made the following changes: at the pre-election hearing, parties were given the right to litigate most voter eligibility and inclusion issues prior to the election; petitioning parties were also required to file a statement of position in advance of the hearing; post-hearing briefs could once again be filed as a matter of right; a party's selection of election observers was limited to individuals who are current members of the voting unit whenever possible; for pre-election requests for review, if filed within ten days of the direction of election, and if the Board either does not rule on a request for review or grants the request before the election, ballots will be impounded and remain unopened pending a decision by the Board, while post-election, parties may still wait to file a request for review of a direction of election until after the election has been conducted and the ballots counted; and the Regional Director will no longer issue certifications following elections if a request for review is pending or before the time has passed during which a request for review could be filed.

The AFL-CIO filed suit in the District of Columbia contending that the 2019 Representation Rule violated the Administrative Procedure Act because: 1) it was not procedural, and therefore had to be promulgated pursuant to notice and comment; 2) it was arbitrary and capricious as a whole, because in promulgating the rule, the Board ignored its own experience under the 2014 rule and the 7,000 comments it received in response to the RFI; 3) certain specific aspects of the rule were arbitrary and capricious; and 4) certain specific aspects of the rule were contrary to explicit provisions of the NLRA. *AFL-CIO v. NLRB*, Case No. 20-cv-00675-KBJ (March 6, 2020). In her initial ruling on the case, Judge Ketanji Brown Jackson vacated five specific aspects of the rule—litigating eligibility issues at pre-election hearings, the setting of the election date, the timing of providing the voter eligibility list, election observer eligibility, and the timing of the Regional Director's issuance of the certification of representative—as not procedural and requiring notice and comment prior to promulgation, but allowed those aspects to be severed. She did not reach the AFL-CIO's arbitrary and capricious or statutory claims. The Board voted to proceed with implementing the rest of the rule, and the AFL-CIO sought reconsideration of Judge Jackson's ruling, asking her to reach the other contentions in its suit. On July 1, 2020, Judge Jackson granted reconsideration, but then found against the AFL-CIO on its remaining claims, granting summary judgment to the NLRB and upholding the rest of the rule.

Unit determination under the Railway Labor Act operates somewhat differently from the NLRA system and offers an interesting contrast. Like the NLRB, the National Mediation Board (NMB) has exclusive jurisdiction over representation questions. It plays a "referee" role subject to strictly limited judicial review of its decisions. *See Switchmen's Union of North America v. NMB*, 320 U.S. 297 (1943). The NMB has consistently held that all union representation under its authority must be system-wide (e.g., an entire rail system) for a craft or class of employees of a single employer rather than local or regional. The concern is that a work stoppage by one local bargaining unit would have the effect of shutting down an entire carrier, and so forcing system-wide bargaining brings all of the affected parties to the bargaining table. *See Summit Airlines v. Teamsters Local No. 295*, 628 F.2d 787 (2d Cir. 1980); *In re Northeast Illinois Regional Commuter R.R. Corp.*, 16 N.M.B. 175 (1989).

Unlike the NLRB, however, the NMB does not have the authority to establish an "appropriate unit." *See In re Air Florida, Inc.*, 7 N.M.B. 162, 166 (1979). From very early in its existence, the NMB has held that "craft or class" is determined by looking to the historical classes and crafts in the industry, *see Chicago & N.W. Ry. Co.*, 1 N.M.B. 52 (1937), although it has begun looking at "composite crafts" as the rail industry restructured in recent years. *See, e.g., In re Kansas City Southern Ry. Co.*, 29 N.M.B. 410 (2002). What constitutes a "system," particularly when two railroads or airlines have merged, is decided by looking at several factors, including the commonality of schedules and routes, uniforms, and marketing; integration of essential operations; centralization of labor and personnel operations; and combined or common workforce, ownership, management, board members, and/or corporate officers. *See National Mediation Board Representation Manual*, § 19.501 (June 12, 2018).

Under the RLA, a "showing of interest" requires signed authorization cards from fifty percent of the workforce. 29 CFR § 1206.2 (2013). Prior to 2010, a union could win an election only by securing the votes of a majority of eligible voters, rather than those actually casting votes. The NMB changed this rule by regulation so that eligible employees could choose union representation with a majority of those voting. 75 Fed. Reg. 26,062–89 (May 11, 2010).

B. Bars to a NLRB-Administered Election

1. Certification-Year and Voluntary-Recognition Bars

If a union wins a representation election by receiving a majority of valid votes, then the Regional Director (or the Board) must certify that union as the exclusive representative of the employees in the bargaining unit by issuing a "certification of representative." If the union has lost the election, then the Regional Director (or Board) will typically issue a "certification of results." A certification-year bar arises in cases where the NLRB has certified the union.

Brooks v. NLRB

Supreme Court of the United States
348 U.S. 96, 75 S. Ct. 176, 99 L. Ed. 125 (1954)

FRANKFURTER, J.

The [NLRB] conducted a representation election in petitioner's [the Company's] Chrysler-Plymouth agency on April 12, 1951. [The Machinists, Local No. 727], won by a vote of eight to five, and the [NLRB] certified it as the exclusive bargaining representative on April 20. A week after the election and the day before the certification, [the Company] received a handwritten letter signed by 9 of the 13 employees in the bargaining unit stating: "We, the undersigned majority of the employees . . . are not in favor of being represented by Union Local No. 727 as a bargaining agent."

Relying on this letter . . . , [the Company] refused to bargain with the union. The [NLRB] found . . . that [the Company] had thereby committed an unfair labor practice in violation of §§ 8(a)(1) and 8(a)(5) . . . and . . . the Ninth Circuit enforced the Board's order to bargain. . . . In view of the conflict between the Circuits, we granted certiorari. . . .

The issue before us is the duty of an employer toward a duly certified bargaining agent if, shortly after the election which resulted in the certification, the union has lost, without the employer's fault, a majority of the employees from its membership.

Under [§ 9(c) of] the original Wagner Act, the [NLRB] was given the power to certify a union as the exclusive representative of the employees in a bargaining unit when it had determined by election or "any other suitable method," that the union commanded majority support. . . . In exercising this authority the Board evolved a number of working rules, of which the following are relevant to our purpose:

(a) A certification, if based on a Board-conducted election, must be honored for a "reasonable" period, ordinarily "one year," in the absence of "unusual circumstances."

(b) "Unusual circumstances" were found in at least three situations: (1) the certified union dissolved or became defunct; (2) as a result of a schism, substantially all the members of officers of the certified union transferred their affiliation to a new local or international; (3) the size of the bargaining unit fluctuated radically within a short time.

(c) Loss of majority support after the "reasonable" period could be questioned in two ways: (1) employer's refusal to bargain, or (2) petition by a rival union for a new election. . . .

The Board uniform[ly] found an unfair labor practice where, during the so-called "certification year," an employer refused to bargain on the ground that the certified union no longer possessed a majority. While the courts in the main enforced the Board's decisions, they did not commit themselves to one year as the determinate content of reasonableness. The Board and the courts proceeded along this line of reasoning:

(a) In the political and business spheres, the choice of the voters in an election binds them for a fixed time. This promotes a sense of responsibility in the electorate and needed coherence in administration. These considerations are equally relevant to healthy labor relations.

(b) Since an election is a solemn and costly occasion, conducted under safeguards to voluntary choice, revocation of authority should occur by a procedure no less solemn than that of the initial designation. A petition or a public meeting—in which those voting for and against unionism are disclosed to management, and in which the influences of mass psychology are present—is not comparable to the privacy and independence of the voting booth.

(c) A union should be given ample time for carrying out its mandate on behalf of its members, and should not be under exigent pressure to produce hothouse results or be turned out.

(d) It is scarcely conducive to bargaining in good faith for an employer to know that, if he dillydallies or subtly undermines, union strength may erode and thereby relieve him of his statutory duties at any time, while if he works conscientiously toward agreement, the rank and file may, at the last moment, repudiate their agent.

(e) In situation[s], not wholly rare, where unions are competing, raiding and strife will be minimized if elections are not at the hazard of informal and short-term recall.

Certain aspects of the [NLRB's] representation procedures came under Taft-Hartley Act in 1947. . . . Congress was mindful that, once employees had chosen a union, they could not vote to revoke its authority and refrain from union activities, while if they voted against having a union in the first place, the union could begin at once to agitate for a new election. The [NLRA] was amended to provide that (a) employees could petition the Board for a decertification election, at which they would have an opportunity to choose no longer to be represented by a union, . . . § 9(c)(1)(A)(ii); (b) an employer, if in doubt as to the majority claimed by a union without formal election or beset by the conflicting claims of rival unions, could likewise petition the Board for an election, . . . § 9(c)(1)(B); (c) after a valid certification or decertification election had been conducted, the Board could not hold a second election in the same bargaining unit until a year had elapsed, . . . § 9(c)(3); (d) Board certification could only be granted as the result of an election, . . . § 9(c)(1), though an employer would presumably still be under a duty to bargain with an uncertified union that had a clear majority. . . .

The Board continued to apply its "one-year certification" rule after the Taft-Hartley Act came into force, except that even "unusual circumstances" no longer left the Board free to order an election where one had taken place within the preceding 12 months. Conflicting views became manifest in the Courts of Appeals when the Board sought to enforce orders based on refusal to bargain in violation of its rule. . . .

The issue is open here. . . . In [*Franks Bros. Co. v. NLRB*, 321 U.S. 702], we held that where a union's majority was dissipated after an employer's unfair labor practice in refusing to bargain, the Board could appropriately find that such conduct had undermined that prestige of the union and require the employer to bargain with it for a reasonable period despite the loss of majority. And in [*NLRB v. Mexia Textile Mills, Inc.*, 339 U.S. 563], we held that a claim of an intervening loss of majority was no defense to a proceeding for enforcement of an order to cease and desist from certain unfair labor practices.

[The Company] contends that whenever an employer is presented with evidence that his employees have deserted their certified union, he may forthwith refuse to bargain. In effect, he seeks to vindicate the rights of his employees to select their bargaining representative. If the employees are dissatisfied with their chosen union, they may submit their own grievance to the Board. If an employer has doubts about his duty to continue bargaining, it is his responsibility to petition the Board for relief, while continuing to bargain in good faith at least until the Board has given some indication that his claim has merit. Although the Board may, if the facts warrant, revoke a certification or agree not to pursue a charge of an unfair labor practice, these are matters for the Board; they do not justify employer self-help or judicial intervention. The underlying purpose of this statute is industrial peace. To allow employers to rely on employees' rights in refusing to bargain with the formally designated union is not conducive to that end, it is inimical to it. Congress has devised a formal mode for selection and rejection of bargaining agents and has fixed the spacing of elections, with a view of furthering industrial stability and with due regard to administrative prudence.

We find wanting the arguments against these controlling considerations. In placing a nonconsenting minority under the bargaining responsibility of an agency selected by a majority of the workers, Congress has discarded common-law doctrines of agency. . . .

To be sure, what we have said has special pertinence only to the period during which a second election is impossible. But the Board's view that the one-year period should run from the date of certification rather than the date of election seems within the allowable area of the Board's discretion in carrying out congressional policy. . . . Otherwise, encouragement would be given to management or a rival union to delay certification by spurious objections to the conduct of an election and thereby diminish the duration of the duty to bargain. Furthermore, the Board has ruled that one year after certification the employer can ask for an election or, if he has fair doubts about the union's continuing majority, he may refuse to bargain further with it. . . . This, too, is a matter appropriately determined by the Board's administrative authority.

We conclude that the judgment of the Court of Appeals enforcing the Board's order must be affirmed.

Notes

1. According to *Brooks*, when does the certification year commence? *See also Mallinckrodt Chem. Works*, 84 N.L.R.B. 291, 292 (1949) (rejecting the company's construction of § 9(c)(3) that "the 12-month period within which a second election may not follow an earlier election for the same unit . . . begin[s] to run . . . from the date on which the Board finally determines the results of the balloting"); *Sec. Alum. Co.*, 149 N.L.R.B. 581, 582 (1964) (holding that the prior election must be a valid election). Does the Board's court-approved holding—that the certification-year runs from the date of balloting—square with the plain language of § 9(c)(3)? What policies are promoted by this rule?

2. In *Brooks*, the Court noted that "[t]he cases in which the Board found 'unusual circumstances' were all representation cases in which a rival union sought a new election less than a year after certification." 348 U.S. 96, 97 n.2. Should the question of who seeks the new election make a difference?

3. The Court, in summarizing the Board's certification-year bar and the policies supporting it, discussed the Board's analogy to political and business elections. How persuasive is that reasoning? What are its pitfalls?

4. The Court ultimately rejected the Company's argument that, "whenever an employer is presented with evidence that his employees have deserted their certified union, he may forthwith refuse to bargain. In effect, he seeks to vindicate the rights of his employees to select their bargaining representative." Forty-two years later, in *Auciello Iron Works, Inc. v. NLRB*, 517 U.S. 781, 790 (1996), Justice Souter, writing for a unanimous Court, held that the Board reasonably concluded that an employer acts unlawfully when it disavows a collective-bargaining agreement based on a good-faith doubt of the union's majority status that the employer failed to raise during contract negotiations. Justice Souter noted:

> The Board is accordingly entitled to suspicion when faced with an employer's benevolence as its workers' champion against their certified union, which is subject to a decertification petition from the workers if they want to file one. There is nothing unreasonable in giving a short leash to the employer as vindicator of its employees' organizational freedom.

What policies is the Board balancing in these cases?

5. For many years, the Board held that an employer's voluntary recognition of a union affords the parties "a reasonable time to bargain and to execute the contracts resulting from such bargaining." *Keller Plastics Eastern, Inc.*, 157 N.L.R.B. 583, 587 (1966). The Board added that "[s]uch negotiations can succeed, however, and the

policies of the Act can thereby be effectuated, only if the parties can normally rely on the continuing representative status of the lawfully recognized union for a reasonable period of time." *Id.* at 587.

In *Dana Corp.*, 351 N.L.R.B. 434, 434 (2007), the Board modified its rule in *Keller Plastics* and removed the "voluntary recognition bar [to decertification]" for the first 45 days following employer recognition. The *Dana* rule also required employers and unions to notify employees of their new right to file a decertification petition or election petition within 45 days of receiving notice that their employer has recognized the union under a neutrality or card-check agreement. Under the new rules, a recognition bar was created only if "45 days pass from the date of notice without the filing of a valid petition." *Id.* at 434.

In 2011, the Board overturned *Dana Corp.* and returned to the rule of *Keller Plastics* in **Lamons Gasket Co.**, 357 N.L.R.B. 739 (2011). The Board also refined its definition of a "reasonable period." "Reasonable" means no less than six months and no more than one year. Within that range, the Board will determine reasonableness by looking at five factors: "(1) whether the parties are bargaining for an initial contract; (2) the complexity of the issues being negotiated and of the parties' bargaining processes; (3) the amount of time elapsed since bargaining commenced and the number of bargaining sessions; (4) the amount of progress made in negotiations and how near the parties are to concluding an agreement; and (5) whether the parties are at impasse." *Id.* at 748 & n.34.

On August 12, 2019, the Board proposed rules to change the law on the blocking charge policy, the voluntary recognition bar, and § 9(a) recognition in the construction industry. The Board issued a final rule on these topics on April 1, 2020, 85 Fed. Reg. 18,366 (April 1, 2020), and subsequently extended the effective date of the rule until July 31, 2020. With respect to the voluntary recognition bar, the Board overruled *Lamons Gasket* and returned to the rule of *Dana Corp.*, 351 N.L.R.B. 434 (2007). For voluntary recognition under § 9(a) of the act to bar a subsequent representation petition—and for a post-recognition collective bargaining agreement to have contract-bar effect—the rule provides that unit employees must receive notice that voluntary recognition has been granted, and employees are given a 45-day open period within which to file an election petition. The rule applies to a voluntary recognition on or after the effective date of the rule.

2. The Contract Bar to Elections

The Board's contract-bar doctrine generally prohibits an election among employees covered by a valid collective-bargaining agreement. *Hexton Furniture Co.*, 111 N.L.R.B. 342 (1955); *J.P. Sand & Gravel Co.*, 222 N.L.R.B. 83, 84 (1976) (the agreement must be collective); *Frank Hager, Inc.*, 230 N.L.R.B. 476, 477 (1977) (the agreement must be the result of free collective bargaining). The Board designed the contract-bar doctrine to balance industrial stability with employee free choice. Under the Board's contract-bar doctrine, an employer may not lawfully withdraw recognition while a collective-bargaining agreement is in effect, because an incumbent union enjoys a conclusive presumption of majority status during the life of the contract (up to three years). *Auciello Iron Works, Inc. v. NLRB*, 517 U.S. 781, 786 (1996).

a. Requirements, Duration, Window Periods, and Insulation Periods

Because the contract bar restricts the free choice of at least some employees, before an agreement may bar an election it "must meet certain formal and substantive requirements." *Waste Mgmt. of Md., Inc.*, 338 N.L.R.B. 1002, 1002 (2003). For a contract to operate as a bar to an election, "it must have been reduced to writing and signed prior to the filing of the petition sought to be barred." *J. Sullivan & Sons, Mfg. Corp.*, 105 N.L.R.B. 549, 550 (1953); *see also Empire Screen Printing, Inc.*, 249 N.L.R.B. 718, 718 (1980) (holding that an oral wage agreement does not constitute a bar to a decertification election). The contract must contain substantial terms and conditions of employment sufficient to establish a stable bargaining relationship, and it must clearly and by its terms encompass those employees for whom an election is sought and cover an appropriate unit. *See, e.g., Hotel Emp'rs Ass'n of San Francisco*, 159 N.L.R.B. 143, 147 (1966); *Appalachian Shale Prods. Co.*, 121 N.L.R.B. 1160, 1161–64 (1958). An agreement limited to wages alone will not be sufficient to meet the "substantial terms and conditions" requirement. *Appalachian Shale Prods.*, 121 N.L.R.B. at 1163. The Board has limited its inquiry to "the four corners of the document or documents alleged to bar an election and has excluded the consideration of extrinsic evidence." *Waste Mgmt. of Md.*, 338 N.L.R.B. 1002, 1003 (2003).

The contract-bar doctrine does not require a formal document, however. *Hotel Emp'rs Ass'n of San Francisco*, 159 N.L.R.B. 143 (1966). Rather, "[a]n informal document or series of documents, such as a written proposal and a written acceptance, which nonetheless contain substantial terms and conditions of employment, are sufficient if signed." *De Paul Adult Care Cmtys., Inc.*, 325 N.L.R.B. 681, 681 (1998); *American Suppliers, Inc.*, 98 N.L.R.B. 692, 694 n.3 (1952); *Standard Brands, Inc.*, 81 N.L.R.B. 1311, 1312 (1949).

In *General Cable Corp.*, 139 N.L.R.B. 1123, 1125 (1962), the Board announced that "[c]ontracts of definite duration for terms up to 3 years will bar an election for their entire period; contracts having longer fixed terms will be treated for bar purposes as 3-year agreements and will preclude an election for only their initial 3 years." The three-year contract rule applies only to petitions filed by rival unions and employees. Petitions filed by the parties—the employer and the certified union—are barred for the duration of the contract. *Montgomery Ward & Co.*, 137 N.L.R.B. 346, 347–49 (1962).

Could a union thus remain in power, notwithstanding a lost majority, so long as it is able to negotiate successor agreements? To create a finer balance between industrial stability and employee free choice, the Board created "window" (or "open") periods and "insulated" periods. For most industries, the Board has adopted a rule requiring that a decertification petition must be filed more than 60 days but less than 90 days before contract expiration. *Leonard Wholesale Meats, Inc.*, 136 N.L.R.B.

1000, 1001 (1962). The 60 days prior to contract expiration is the insulation period, during which time the Board will not entertain a petition to decertify the union. In the health care industry, the window period is 90 to 120 days, with a 90-day insulation period. *Trinity Lutheran Hosp.*, 218 N.L.R.B. 199, 199 (1975). Parties cannot waive window or insulation periods. *Empire Screen Printing, Inc.*, 249 N.L.R.B. 718, 718–19 (1980).

b. Representative Status of the Contracting Union

A contract does not bar an election in cases where there is a union schism or where the union is defunct. *Hershey Chocolate Corp.*, 121 N.L.R.B. 901 (1958), *enforcement denied*, 297 F.2d 286 (3d Cir. 1961). The Board has determined that a union schism exists only if the following three conditions are met: (1) there exists "a basic intraunion conflict over policy resulting in a disruption of existing intraunion relationships," *Clayton & Lambert Mfg. Co.*, 128 N.L.R.B. 209, 210–11 (1960); (2) "the employees involved shall have had an opportunity to exercise their judgment on the merits of the basic intraunion conflict at an open meeting with due notice to the members in the unit," *William Wolf Bakery, Inc.*, 122 N.L.R.B. 1163, 1164 (1959); and (3) the employees involved must take action within "a reasonable time after the alleged intraunion conflict arose," *Great Atl. & Pac. Tea Co.*, 126 N.L.R.B. 580, 582, n.1 (1960).

The Board has also held that "a representative is defunct, and its contract is not a bar, if it is unable or unwilling to represent the employees." *Hershey Chocolate Corp.*, 121 N.L.R.B. at 911. This is a narrow exception. For example, "mere temporary inability to function does not constitute defunctness; nor is the loss of all members in the unit the equivalent of defunctness if the representative otherwise continues in existence and is willing and able to represent the employees." *Id.*

The principle in these cases is that "the contract, which would normally be a bar, is no longer a stabilizing force and there is therefore no warrant for denying to the employees the immediate exercise of their right to select their representative, and because it is only through the medium of an election that stability can be restored to the disrupted relationship." *Id.* at 910. It is interesting to note that there is no contract bar doctrine under the RLA. *Metro North R.R.*, 10 N.M.B. 345 (1983). Rather, if a new union takes over representation of an existing bargaining unit, the new union simply administers the collective bargaining agreement, which remains in effect. *See, e.g., Bensel v. Allied Pilots Ass'n*, 387 F.3d 298 (3d. Cir. 2004).

c. Limited Exceptions to the Contract Bar Doctrine

In limited and particular circumstances, a collective bargaining agreement may not establish a contract bar to a new election. For example, where one company (the successor) purchases another company (the predecessor) that has a collective-bargaining agreement, an agreement bargained between the predecessor and a union will not serve as a bar to an election absent an express written assumption by the successor. *NLRB v. Burns Int'l Sec. Servs., Inc.*, 406 U.S. 272 (1972). Nor does a contract "bar an election if executed (1) before any employees had been hired or (2) prior to a substantial increase in personnel." *Gen. Extrusion Co.*, 121 N.L.R.B. 1165, 1167 (1958).

Also, citing *Brown* v. *Board of Education*, 349 U.S. 294 (1955) and related cases, the Board has held that racially discriminatory contracts will not serve as a bar to an election:

> Consistent with clear court decisions in other contexts which condemn governmental sanctioning of racially separate groupings as inherently discriminatory . . . where the bargaining representative of employees in an appropriate unit executes separate contracts, or even a single contract, discriminating between Negro and white employees on racial lines, the Board will not deem such contracts as a bar to an election. *Pioneer Bus Co.*, 140 N.L.R.B. 54, 55 & n.3 (1963).

On the other hand, a contract that contains an unlawful clause may still bar an election. *Compare Food Hauler, Inc.*, 136 N.L.R.B. 394, 395–96 (1962) (contract containing a hot cargo clause unlawful under § 8(e), would bar an election because such a clause "does not in any sense act as a restraint upon an employee's choice of a bargaining representative") *with In re C. Hager & Sons Hinge Mfg. Co.*, 80 N.L.R.B. 163, 165 (1949) (holding that a contract containing an unlawful union-security clause would not bar an election because the "mere existence of such a provision acts as a restraint upon those desiring to refrain from union activities within the meaning of Section 7").

C. The Blocking Charge

Almost from its inception, the Board has maintained a "blocking charge" policy that plays an important role in the conduct of representation elections. *See U. S. Coal & Coke Co.*, 3 N.L.R.B. 398, 399 (1937). Under this policy, the Board "hold[s] in abeyance the processing of a[n election] petition where a concurrent unfair labor practice charge is filed by a party to the petition and the charge alleges conduct that, if proven, would interfere with employee free choice in an election, were one to be conducted." NLRB Casehandling Manual (CHM), Part Two, § 11730, *et seq.*

On August 12, 2019, the Board proposed rules to change the law on the blocking charge policy, the voluntary recognition bar, and § 9(a) recognition in the construction industry. The Board issued a final rule on these topics on April 1, 2020, 85 Fed. Reg. 18,366 (April 1, 2020), and subsequently extended the effective date of the rule until July 31, 2020. With respect to the blocking charge policy, the rule completely revised the procedure such that the conduct of an election will no longer be stopped by pending unfair labor practice charges, while, depending on the nature of and outcome of such charges, charges may put off the counting of the ballots or the certification of the results of the election. Under the new rule, to be codified at 29 C.F.R § 103.20(a), whenever any party to a representation case files an unfair labor practice charge together with a request that the charge block the election, or whenever any party requests that its previously filed unfair labor practice charge block the election, the party shall simultaneously file with the Region a written offer of proof in support of the charge. The offer of proof shall provide the names of the witnesses who will testify in support of the charge and a summary of their anticipated testimony, and the party proffering the witnesses shall promptly make the witnesses available to the regional office. 85 Fed. Reg. at 18,399.

Paragraph (b) of the final rule baldly states that if the charges filed allege unfair labor practices other than those specified in paragraph (c), "the ballots will be opened and counted at the conclusion of the election." *Id.* Paragraph (c) provides that, if charges are filed that allege violations of §8(a)(1) and §8(a)(2) or §8(b)(1)(A) and that challenge the circumstances surrounding the petition or the showing of interest submitted in support of the petition, or a charge is filed that an employer has dominated a union in violation of §8(a)(2) and seeks to disestablish a bargaining relationship, the regional director shall impound the ballots for up to 60 days from the conclusion of the election if the charge has not been withdrawn or dismissed; if a complaint issues with respect to the charge at any point prior to the expiration of the 60-day post-election period, then the ballots shall continue to be impounded until there is a final determination regarding the charge and its effect on the election petition. If the charge is withdrawn or dismissed at any time during the 60-day period or if the 60-day period ends without a complaint issuing, then the ballots shall be promptly opened and counted. The 60-day period will not be extended, even if more than one unfair labor practice is filed serially. *Id.*

Finally, paragraph (d) of the new rule provides that, for all unfair labor practice charges described in paragraphs (b) and (c), the certification of results, including, where appropriate, a certification of representative, shall not issue until there is a final disposition of the charge. *Id.*

Under this new rule, is there any occasion where unfair labor practices meritoriously alleging a mass discharge of union supporters in violation of §8(a)(3) will hold off the conduct of a pending representation election? If the answer to this question is "no," what does that say about the Board's commitment to hold representation elections under "laboratory conditions" or about the wise use of the Agency's limited resources?

Charges that taint an incumbent union's loss of majority support tend to raise a causal connection between the alleged violations and subsequent employee disaffection with the incumbent union. *See id.* §11730.3(c); *Williams Enters.*, 312 N.L.R.B. 937, 939 (1993) (finding a §8(a)(1) violation in a statement that tainted a decertification petition; remedy is to dismiss the petition and issue an affirmative bargaining order). One of the most common is known as a tainted decertification case. In a tainted decertification case, the employer's unlawful conduct—coercion, illegal discharges, discriminatory conduct toward union members—results in employee disaffection and the union's subsequent loss of majority status. To determine whether there is a causal connection between these unfair labor practices and subsequent employee disaffection, the Board applies the following factors:

(1) The length of time between the unfair labor practices and the withdrawal of recognition; (2) the nature of the illegal acts, including the possibility of their detrimental or lasting effect on employees; (3) any possible
tendency to cause employee disaffection from the union; and (4) the effect
of the unlawful conduct on employee morale, organizational activities, and
membership in the union.*Master Slack Corp.*, 271 N.L.R.B. 78, 84 (1984).

Below is a typical *Master Slack* case.

Vincent Industrial Plastics, Inc. v. NLRB

U.S. Court of Appeals for the District of Columbia
209 F.3d 727 (D.C. Cir. 2000)

EDWARDS, C.J.

Vincent Industrial Plastics, Inc. ("Vincent" or "the Company") operates a plastics manufacturing plant in Henderson, Kentucky. On February 19, 1993, a majority
of Vincent's full- and part-time production and maintenance employees . . . selected
the International Chemical Workers Union, AFL-CIO, Local 1032 ("the Union") as
the employees' bargaining representative. The Board certified the Union on September 29, 1993, and Company and Union officials commenced collective bargaining negotiations in January 1994. The negotiations continued for more than a year,
but the parties were unable to reach a final agreement. On February 16, 1995, after
receiving a decertification petition from unit employees, the Company withdrew
its recognition of the Union and declined to participate in any further collective
bargaining negotiations. Between July 5, 1994 and April 20, 1995, the Union filed
several unfair labor practice charges ("ULPs") alleging that Vincent violated the
[NLRA §§ 8(a)(1), (3), and (5)] by unilaterally implementing material changes in
working conditions, coercively interrogating an employee, disciplining and terminating employees on account of their support for the Union, and unlawfully withdrawing its recognition of the Union. The Board issued complaints on all of the
charges.

Following a hearing on the complaints, an Administrative Law Judge ("ALJ")
concluded that the Company was guilty of ULPs on all but one charge. . . . The
[NLRB] subsequently held that Vincent was guilty of ULPs on all charges. The
Board specifically rejected the ALJ's finding that Vincent had not violated the Act
in unilaterally changing the Company's attendance policy. . . . The Board issued a
cease-and-desist order (including a remedy of reinstatement and back pay for the
employees who were unlawfully fired) and a "*Gissel*" bargaining order requiring the
Company to recognize the Union and to resume collective bargaining negotiations.

Vincent petitions for review of the Board's order, and the Board cross-petitions
for enforcement. We grant the Board's petition for enforcement, with one significant exception. The Board, inexplicably, has once again defied the law of this
circuit and failed to offer an adequate justification for the bargaining order sanction imposed against Vincent. We therefore find ourselves in the all-too-familiar

position of having to remand this case to the Board for adequate justification of the proposed affirmative bargaining order. . . .

I. Background

A. Factual Background

. . . .

Between July and December, 1994, Vincent unilaterally promulgated four policy changes relating to attendance, work duties, working hours, and time-keeping. We review each of these briefly.

On July 1, 1994, Vincent changed the policy by which it disciplined employees for attendance problems. . . .

Between October and December 1994, Vincent instituted three additional policy changes without first proposing them to the Union during ongoing collective bargaining sessions. First, in October, Vincent relieved quality control employees of their weighing and labeling duties, which comprised 25% of their workday, and transferred the duties to press operators. Then, in mid-November, Vincent instituted a shift extension requiring quality control employees to work an extra 15 minutes at the end of each shift. Finally, on December 9, 1994, Vincent eliminated the use of time cards and instituted a team system in which employees check in at the beginning of their shift with their "team leader," and the team leader then keeps track of the hours worked by each team member. Vincent alleged that the new system was precipitated by its observation that time cards were often lost or stolen, that employees clocked in without reporting immediately to work, and that employees clocked in for one another.

In addition to the foregoing changes in working conditions, the Union also filed ULP charges related to Vincent's treatment of four Union members. First, in December 1994, Mark Coomes, a supervisor, called Robert Ferguson away from his machine and asked him whether he had heard anything about the Union going on strike. . . . Mr. Ferguson testified that Mr. Coomes inquired as to a possible strike a second time that day, in the break room. The Union alleged that Mr. Coomes' conduct constituted coercive interrogation in violation of the Act.

In January 1995, Vincent disciplined Gloria Chester, the Union's designated observer at the 1993 election and its plant steward until October 1993, for alleged insubordination and disrespectful actions toward a supervisor. . . . The Union claimed that Vincent disciplined Ms. Chester on account of her Union affiliation.

The third ULP related to Vincent's treatment of Union members involves the allegedly discriminatory termination of Mr. Early, Union President, in February 1995. . . .

The day Mr. Early was terminated, employees circulated a petition to decertify the Union. Over two days, on February 15 and 16, 1995, a majority (82 out of 128) of the maintenance and production employees signed the petition. Management at Vincent verified the signatures and informed the Union that the Company would no longer engage in bargaining. After withdrawing its recognition of the Union,

Vincent granted wage increases, implemented a 401(k) plan, and denied the Union's request for information regarding bargaining unit employees.

About a month later, on March 20, Vincent terminated Wanda Nantz, a press operator and Union supporter (she was, in fact, among those who did not sign the petition to decertify the Union). . . .

B. Board Proceedings

The ALJ found that Vincent violated the Act by unilaterally implementing all of the policy changes except for the attendance policy. . . . As for the other policy changes, the ALJ found both that, in each case, Vincent failed to present the proposed changes to the Union during contract negotiations, thereby giving the Union no opportunity to bargain over the issues, and that none of the changes was necessitated by economic hardship. . . .

In addition, the ALJ found the questioning of Mr. Ferguson, the termination of Mr. Early and Ms. Nantz, and the disciplining of Ms. Chester to constitute violations of § 8(a)(1) and (3) of the Act. . . .

On review of the ALJ's decision, the Board affirmed all of the ALJ's ULP findings save one. The Board reversed the ALJ on the attendance policy issue . . . finding that Vincent had "failed to prove that its attendance problem constituted an economic exigency." . . . Therefore, the Board found that the change in attendance policy violated § 8(a)(1) and (5) of the Act.

On its own analysis, the Board found that Vincent's withdrawal of recognition was a violation of § 8(a)(1) and (5) of the Act, applying the so-called "*Master Slack*" factors, *see Master Slack Corp.*, 271 N.L.R.B. 78 (1984), to evaluate the causal connection between the unremedied ULPs and subsequent employee expression of dissatisfaction with a union. The Board cited the following factors in finding a causal connection between the ULPs and the decertification movement: (1) the unremedied ULPs continued until the day before the employees began signing the decertification petition; (2) the unilateral changes and disciplining of Union supporters were "likely to have a long lasting effect on the bargaining unit and to discourage employees from supporting the Union"; and (3) the disciplining and termination of Union supporters "convey to employees the notion that any support for the Union may jeopardize their employment." . . . The Board also imposed an affirmative bargaining order as a remedy for the Company's violations of the Act. No justification was offered to support the bargaining order. . . .

II. Analysis

. . . .

We review Board ULP findings under a deferential standard. This court will uphold the Board's decision upon substantial evidence even if we would reach a different result upon *de novo* review. . . .

Furthermore, when the Board, as it did here, concludes that unremedied ULPs tainted a decertification petition, this court requires it to offer a reasoned explanation, based on substantial evidence, in support of its finding. . . . Finally, to justify the imposition of an affirmative bargaining order, we require the Board to explicitly balance three considerations: (1) the employees' §7 rights; (2) whether other purposes of the Act override the rights of employees to choose their bargaining representatives; and (3) whether alternative remedies are adequate to remedy the violations of the Act. . . .

A. The Board's ULP Findings

The Board's holding that Vincent's unilateral actions changing established working conditions constituted ULPs is easily upheld. An employer may not unilaterally impose material changes in terms or conditions of employment that are mandatory subjects of bargaining without first negotiating to impasse. . . . There are two exceptions to this general rule: An employer may impose unilateral terms if the union engages in dilatory tactics to delay bargaining. . . . And an employer may act unilaterally if faced with an economic exigency justifying the change. . . . An economic exigency must be a "heavy burden" and must require prompt implementation. . . . The employer must additionally demonstrate that "the exigency was caused by external events, was beyond the employer's control, or was not reasonably foreseeable." . . .

Vincent imposed all of the changes save one without presenting a proposal to the Union during bargaining sessions. Vincent can mount no argument that any of the disputed changes were made due to an economic exigency. . . . All of the changes involved mandatory subjects of bargaining, they raised material issues, and the Union cannot be held to have waived the right to bargain over an issue that was never proposed during bargaining sessions. . . .

The Board's findings that Vincent fired two employees and disciplined another in violation of the Act are also supported by substantial evidence in the record. . . .

The ALJ found, and the Board affirmed, that Vincent violated the Act in three instances when it took adverse employment actions against its employees on account of their Union affiliation: (1) when Vincent disciplined Gloria Chester; (2) when Vincent terminated Michael Early; and (3) when Vincent terminated Wanda Nantz. With respect to all three findings, there is substantial evidence to support the Board's determination. . . .

The ALJ, with whom the Board agreed, relied on Ms. Chester's position as a Union supporter, the fact that she received discipline at a time when Vincent had taken several unlawful unilateral actions, and the "significant aberrant circumstances surrounding issuance of the warning" to conclude that the discipline would not have occurred but for Ms. Chester's Union involvement. . . . There is substantial evidence to support this conclusion. . . .

The ALJ and the Board relied on similar factors to conclude that the Company discharged Mr. Early in violation of the Act. [The court held that the ALJ's finding that Mr. Early's status of Union President influenced Vincent's actions against him was not unreasonable.]

With respect to Vincent's justification for disciplining Ms. Nantz, . . . there was substantial evidence for the ALJ and Board to conclude that Vincent's purported reason for disciplining Ms. Nantz was pretextual.

The Board's finding that Vincent supervisor Mark Coomes violated the Act by coercively interrogating Robert Ferguson is less easily upheld. . . . Here the ALJ relied on the following facts to conclude that Mr. Coomes compromised Mr. Ferguson's right to "keep private his sentiments as to the Union and his knowledge of its affairs": Mr. Coomes pulled Mr. Ferguson away from his work area to initiate questioning; and Mr. Ferguson had not previously identified with the Union. . . . The ALJ inferred that Mr. Coomes' purpose, to test the strength of the Union, was clear. Given the substantial evidence in the record, we cannot say that this conclusion is unreasonable. . . .

The Board's findings that several unremedied ULPs tainted the decertification petition is unassailable. For the first year after a successful certification election, a union enjoys an irrebuttable presumption of majority support, after which the employer may withdraw recognition if it has a good faith, reasonable basis to doubt majority support for the union. . . . When a majority of unit employees signs a petition in support of decertification, an employer may reasonably doubt that there exists majority support for the union. . . . Nonetheless, if the Board determines that unremedied ULPs contributed to the erosion of support for the union, the employer may commit an unfair labor practice by withdrawing its recognition of the union. *See, e.g., Lee Lumber & Bldg. Material Corp. v. NLRB*, 117 F.3d 1454, 1458–60 (D.C.Cir.1997) (per curiam). . . .

The Board's traditional four-factor test for determining whether there is a causal connection between unremedied ULPs and a petition for decertification consists of the following elements: "(1) [t]he length of time between the unfair labor practices and the withdrawal of recognition; (2) the nature of the illegal acts, including the possibility of their detrimental or lasting effect on employees; (3) any possible tendency to cause employee disaffection from the union; and (4) the effect of the unlawful conduct on employee morale, organizational activities, and membership in the union." *Master Slack Corp.*, at 84. Vincent argues that the explanation offered by the Board does not satisfy the *Master Slack* requirements. We reject this contention.

The Board adequately explained its decision on the basis of all four *Master Slack* factors, in more than conclusory language. The Board noted the close temporal link between the unremedied ULPs and the decertification petition. The Board additionally explained that the unilateral implementation of changes in working conditions has the tendency to undermine confidence in the employees' chosen collective-bargaining agent. The Board finally reasonably concluded that the discipline and termination of public supporters of the Union "convey to employees the notion that any support for the Union may jeopardize their employment." The Board's conclusion that Vincent's practices contributed to the decertification petition are reasonably justified and supported by substantial evidence. *See NLRB v.*

Williams Enters., Inc., 50 F.3d 1280, 1288–89 (4th Cir.1995) (upholding finding of causation where four months passed between company's anti-union statements and decertification petition); *Columbia Portland Cement Co.,* 303 N.L.R.B. 880, 882 (1991), *enforced,* 979 F.2d 460, 464–65 (6th Cir.1992) (upholding Board's finding of causation where justification offered by Board was simply that the unremedied ULPs "are likely to have undermined the Union's authority generally and influenced [the Union's] employees to reject the Union as their bargaining representative"). . . .

B. The Board's Remedies

The Board's remedies on behalf of the Union and the unit employees who were adversely affected by Vincent's ULPs included a cease-and-desist order, reinstatement and back pay for the employees who were unlawfully terminated, and an affirmative bargaining order. The Company challenges all of the remedies imposed by the Board on the grounds that the employer did not commit any ULPs. As noted above, we reject this contention as meritless. The Company argues further, however, that even if the Board did not err in finding the aforecited ULPs, there was no basis for the Board to issue an affirmative bargaining order against Vincent. The Company's argument on this point is well taken.

The Board approved the ALJ's recommended remedy of an affirmative bargaining order with little explanation. The closest the ALJ came to justifying the order was to observe that the "serious and egregious misconduct shown here [ ] demonstrates a general disregard for fundamental rights guaranteed employees by Section 7 of the Act." This will not do. This court repeatedly has reminded the Board that an affirmative bargaining order is an extreme remedy that must be justified by a reasoned analysis that includes an explicit balancing of three considerations: (1) the employees' §7 rights; (2) whether other purposes of the Act override the rights of employees to choose their bargaining representatives; and (3) whether alternative remedies are adequate to remedy the violations of the Act. There is no such reasoned analysis in the instant case.

Instead, the Board's counsel was forced to conjure up an argument in an effort to bolster the Board's unsupported position. According to counsel, the Board need not justify the imposition of a bargaining order in two types of cases: where the employer has unlawfully withdrawn recognition from the Union; and, as a subset of the first class, where there are explicit *Master Slack* findings demonstrating a causal connection between unremedied ULPs and a withdrawal of recognition. Counsel's argument in defense of this position was inspired and thoughtful, albeit in vain. The problem here is that counsel's argument is nowhere to be found in the orders under review, so we cannot ascribe it to the Board. The argument therefore constitutes a *post hoc* rationalization, which carries no weight on review.

The Board's stubborn refusal to accept this circuit's position on affirmative bargaining orders is perplexing, for it merely undermines the Board's purported goal of protecting workers against employer violations of the Act. Board decisions, like those from other administrative agencies, are entitled to deference. However, once a court has issued a legal ruling on a disputed issue, the Board is bound to follow the court's judgment unless and until it is reversed by the Supreme Court. The Board, no doubt, will plead innocence, claiming that circuit courts often take different positions on certain legal issues, so the Board is free to adopt a course most to its liking within a maze of disparate courts of appeals judgments. In addition, as counsel pointed out during oral argument in this case, the Board sometimes has no clear idea where a petition for review will be filed, so it cannot always guess right in deciding what circuit law to follow. This latter point is a fair rebuttal, but it is short-sighted in a case such as the instant one. What is so troubling about this case, and others like it, is that the Board could easily follow the law of the D.C. Circuit — *i.e.*, give a reasoned analysis to support an affirmative bargaining order — without ever transgressing the law of any other circuit. Some other circuits may not require as much as does the D.C. Circuit with respect to what is required to justify an affirmative bargaining order, but no circuit will reject a bargaining order if the Board justifies it as this court requires.

. . . .

As a result of the Board's failure to justify the imposition of an affirmative bargaining order, relief for the employees represented by the Union will be that much further delayed. Three years passed between the ALJ's decision and the Board's decision upholding the ALJ. Another year has passed since the issuance of the Board decision here on review. We now remand to the Board for an undetermined amount of time. As the Board well knows, in the context of employee representation and collective bargaining, relief delayed under the Act may be relief denied. This makes little sense where, as here, the Board can easily satisfy the commands of this circuit's law without running amok because of a split in the law of the circuits.

———————

On remand, the Board provided a three-part explanation for why an affirmative bargaining order was justified in this case:

> 1. An affirmative bargaining order in this case vindicates the Section 7 rights of the unit employees who were denied the benefits of collective bargaining by the Employer's unlawful withdrawal of recognition. In contrast, an affirmative bargaining order, with its attendant bar to raising a question concerning the Union's continuing majority status for a reasonable time, does not unduly prejudice the Section 7 rights of employees who may oppose continued union representation because the duration of the order is no longer than is reasonably necessary to remedy the ill effects of the violation.
>
> Moreover, . . . the Respondent's numerous and serious unfair labor practices were of the type that would cause employee disaffection from the union. Indeed, during the course of the parties' negotiations for an initial collective-bargaining agreement, the Respondent committed the first in a series of unfair labor practices that undermined the employees' support

for the Union. The Respondent first violated Section 8(a)(5) by unilaterally changing the employee attendance policy in July 1994, only 6 months after the parties began contract negotiations, and less than a year after the Union's certification as the unit employees' collective-bargaining representative. The Board has long recognized that a newly certified union needs a year to establish itself in the eyes of the employees it represents. . . . The Board has also recognized that bargaining for an initial contract is especially difficult.

The Respondent's unilateral change to the employee attendance policy was soon followed by more unilateral changes to employees' terms and conditions of employment . . . These changes were made without any notice or opportunity to bargain with the Union. Thus, in complete disregard for its collective-bargaining obligation, the Respondent compounded the acknowledged difficulty in negotiating an initial collective-bargaining agreement, and deprived the employees of the use of their chosen bargaining representative free of unlawful interference by the Respondent.

In addition . . . the Respondent violated Section 8(a)(3) both by disciplining a member of the Union's negotiating team, who was also a former union steward and, more significantly, by discharging the union president. It is hardly surprising that, on the same day as the union president was discharged, this series of unfair labor practices culminated with the employees circulating a decertification petition and obtaining, by the next day, 82 of 128 unit employees' signatures. Because the only demonstrated dissatisfaction with the Union appears to have been unlawfully fomented by the Respondent's own actions, a temporary decertification bar would trench very little on genuine employee desire (if there is any) to remove the Union as the bargaining representative. At the same time it would protect the countervailing desire to be represented by the Union initially expressed by a majority of the employees, as reflected in the earlier certification, by giving the Union a reasonable time in which to reestablish the bargaining relationship and its status with the employees, and get on with contract negotiations.

The Respondent did not cease its unlawful conduct with the withdrawal of recognition. To the contrary, it continued to make unilateral changes to the unit employees' terms and conditions of employment. . . . Further, the Respondent unlawfully disciplined and discharged another union official. By this conduct, the Respondent demonstrated to employees that support for the Union would be punished, while rejection of the Union would be rewarded, and thereby further derogated the Union's status and interfered with the collective-bargaining process. It is clear that only an affirmative bargaining order will provide the necessary opportunity for the Union to prove itself to the unit employees and, likewise, for the unit employees to assess for themselves the merits of collective-bargaining representation by the Union.

[The] decertification petition did not reflect employee free choice under Section 7, but rather the effect of the Respondent's most serious prewithdrawal unfair labor practices described above. We find that these additional circumstances support giving greater weight to the Section 7 rights that were infringed by the Respondent's unlawful withdrawal of recognition.

2. The affirmative bargaining order also serves the policies of the Act by fostering meaningful collective bargaining and industrial peace. That is, it removes the Respondent's incentive to delay bargaining or to engage in any other conduct designed to further discourage support for the Union. It also ensures that the Union will not be pressured, by the possibility of a decertification petition, to achieve immediate results at the bargaining table following the Board's resolution of its unfair labor practice charges and issuance of a cease-and-desist order. Thus, the affirmative bargaining order, and the temporary decertification bar that it would provide, would restore to the Union and the majority who selected the Union a benefit that the Respondent's violations deprived them of, namely a period of repose during which the bargaining relationship will have a genuine opportunity to bear fruit.

3. A cease-and-desist order, without a temporary decertification bar, would be inadequate to remedy the Respondent's violations because it would permit a decertification petition to be filed before the Respondent had afforded the employees a reasonable time to regroup and bargain through their representative in an effort to reach a collective-bargaining agreement. Such a result would be particularly unfair in circumstances such as those here, where many of the Respondent's unfair labor practices were of a continuing nature and were likely to have a continuing effect, thereby tainting any employees' disaffection from the Union arising during that period or immediately thereafter. We find that these circumstances outweigh the temporary impact the affirmative bargaining order will have on the rights of any employees who oppose continued union representation for reasons that do not result from the Respondent's unlawful undermining of the bargaining process. . . .

Vincent Industrial Plastics, Inc., 336 N.L.R.B. 697 (2001).

Notes

1. *Vincent Industrial Plastics* involves a decertification petition presented to an employer who subsequently withdrew recognition. The case does not state whether the petition was filed with the Board as an RD (decertification) petition. If it were, how, under the new rule described above, how would the Board have treated the unfair labor practice charges here? Would the charges have blocked the conduct of the decertification election or the regional director's issuance of a certification of the results of that election?

2. The remedy in cases such as these, where the employer's withdrawal of recognition is based on a tainted decertification petition, is an affirmative bargaining order. The court, however, cites *NLRB v. Gissel Packing Co.*, 395 U.S. 575 (1969) as the relevant authority. After you review *Gissel* in Chapter 8, evaluate whether the court is correct or whether it is confusing affirmative bargaining orders with *Gissel* bargaining orders.

3. The RLA election process does not include blocking charges because the NMB is not a law enforcement agency like the NLRB. *See American West Airlines v. NMB*, 969 F.2d 777 (9th Cir. 1992). Illegal conduct under the RLA is remedied by the federal courts, not the NMB. However, the NMB has the authority to invalidate an election and require a new election when a carrier engages in conduct to "interfere . . . influence or coerce" employees in their decision with respect to representation. 45 U.S.C. § 152, Fourth. The NMB's standards for conduct that constitutes interference, influence, or coercion can be stricter than those imposed by the NLRB. *See, e.g., US Air, Inc.*, 17 N.M.B. 377 (1990) (finding a poster criticizing past experiences with the union to be a violation of the RLA).

III. Bargaining Unit Determinations

A. Overview

Section 9(b) of the NLRA empowers the Board to "decide in each case . . . the unit appropriate for the purposes of collective bargaining." Further, "[t]he selection of an appropriate bargaining unit lies largely within the discretion of the Board whose decision, if not final, is rarely to be disturbed." *So. Prairie Constr. v. Operating Eng'rs Local 627*, 425 U.S. 800, 805 (1976).

There are, however, some statutory limitations on the Board's discretion. First, the Board must determine that each appropriate unit "assure[s] to employees the fullest freedom in exercising the rights guaranteed by this Act." NLRA § 9(b); 29 U.S.C. § 159(b); *see P. Ballantine & Sons*, 141 N.L.R.B. 1103, 1106 (1963). Those rights include, of course, the rights to self-organization and to collective bargaining. Second, the Act's plain language does not require that the bargaining unit be the *only* appropriate unit or the *most* appropriate unit. The Act requires only that the unit be "appropriate." Accordingly, "the Board generally attempts to select a unit that is the smallest appropriate unit encompassing the petitioned-for employees." *Bartlett Collins Co.*, 334 N.L.R.B. 484, 484 (2001).

There are also four express statutory limitations on unit appropriateness, those pertaining to professional employees (§ 9(b)(1)); craft representation (§ 9(b)(2)); plant guards (§ 9(b)(3)); and the extent of organization (§ 9(c)(5)). *See* Section III-C.

There are two major types of issues concerning appropriate bargaining units. The first relates to scope of the unit and involves questions such as whether the unit should be plant-wide rather than employer-wide, or single-employer rather than multiemployer (*see* Sections III-D and III-E). The second relates to the composition of the unit and involves questions regarding the inclusion or exclusion of disputed employees (*see* Section III-C).

B. Appropriate Bargaining Units: General Considerations

The central question in the unit determination is whether a group of employees, should they choose a union to be their bargaining representative, will be able to work together successfully to bargain an agreement with their employer on their terms and conditions of employment. Of course, the election unit is also going to serve as the bargaining unit, so the decision about which employees can vote in the election is tightly bound up with the question of whether those employees can form a successful bargaining unit. *See Pittsburgh Plate Glass Co. v. NLRB*, 313 U.S. 146, 165 (1941). Several factors go into the Board's decision as to whether the unit is "an appropriate unit." These factors include the employees' "community of interest" and the collective-bargaining history of the proposed unit. The history of the proposed unit offers a shortcut to the employees' likelihood of success as a bargaining unit in the future — that is, the Board assumes that prior success as a bargaining unit means likely future success.

Determining whether employees have a community of interest — that is, will they have common goals and interests when their union represents them in bargaining — requires the Board to consider several factors: the degree to which unit members' jobs are functionally integrated; whether the employees are subject to common supervision; the nature of the employees' skills and functions; interchangeability and contact among employees; whether they work in a single location or several; general working conditions; and fringe benefits. *See* NLRB, An Outline of Law and Procedure In Representation Cases § 12-210 (Aug. 2008). In *Blue Man Vegas, LLC v. NLRB*, 529 F.3d 417, 421 (D.C. Cir. 2008), the court explained that under the community of interest standard, "[t]here is no hard and fast definition or an inclusive or exclusive listing of the factors to consider . . . Those factors include whether, in distinction from other employees, the employees in the proposed unit have 'different methods of compensation, hours of work, benefits, supervision, training and skills; if their contact with other employees is infrequent; if their work functions are not integrated with those of other employees; and if they have historically been part of a distinct bargaining unit.'"

The language of § 9(b) suggests that there are certain presumptively appropriate bargaining units: "the unit appropriate for purposes of collective bargaining shall be the employer unit, craft unit, plant unit, or subdivision thereof." 29 U.S.C. § 159(b). The Board has held that units consisting of all employees of an employer, all employees in a particular craft, or all employees at a particular plant are presumptively appropriate. *See, e.g., Kroger Ltd. P'ship*, 348 N.L.R.B. 1200 (2006); *Greenhorne & O'Mara, Inc.*, 326 N.L.R.B. 514 (1998); *Mallinckrodt Chemical Works*, 162 N.L.R.B.

387 (1966). In addition, over time, the Board has established additional presumptions that certain units are appropriate. *See, e.g., Groendyke Transport*, 171 N.L.R.B. 997 (1968) (holding that a single-terminal unit is presumptively appropriate); *Colorado Interstate Gas Co.*, 202 N.L.R.B. 847 (1973) (suggesting a presumption that a systemwide unit is appropriate for public utilities). However, in *Specialty Healthcare & Rehabilitation Center of Mobile*, 357 N.L.R.B. 934 (2011) (*Specialty Healthcare*), *enfd. sub nom. Kindred Nursing Centers East, LLC v. NLRB*, 727 F.3d 552 (6th Cir. 2013), the Board held that "[a] party petitioning for a unit other than a presumptively appropriate unit . . . bears no heightened burden to show that the petitioned-for unit is also an appropriate unit. . . . [Rather] they merely shift the burden to the party arguing that a petitioned-for and presumptively appropriate unit is inappropriate." 357 N.L.R.B. 934, 940 (2011).

The Board's procedure for determining an appropriate unit is:

> to examine first the petitioned-for unit. If that unit is appropriate, then the inquiry into the appropriate unit ends. If the petitioned-for unit is not appropriate, the Board may examine the alternative units suggested by the parties, but it also has the discretion to select an appropriate unit that is different from the alternative proposals of the parties.

Boeing Co., 337 N.L.R.B. 152, 153 (2001). At their core, the broadly stated standards for unit determination do not operate as inflexible rules defining what is "appropriate." Instead, unit determination is a fact-based, case-by-case inquiry by the Board. *See NLRB v. Yeshiva Univ.*, 444 U.S. 672, 691 (1980).

There is no rule requiring inclusion of all employees with a community of interest in one bargaining unit; a smaller unit of employees with a community of interest also may be appropriate. *See Blue Man Vegas LLC*, 529 F.3d at 421; *see also Dunbar Armored, Inc. v. NLRB*, 186 F.3d 844 (7th Cir. 1999). When employees in a petitioned-for unit share a community of interest, the Board's rule was that the opposing party arguing that this smaller unit is inappropriate can succeed only by satisfying the heightened burden of showing that the employees in a larger unit share an "overwhelming community of interest." *In re Specialty Healthcare*, 357 N.L.R.B. at 11–13.

However, in *PCC Structurals, Inc.*, 365 N.L.R.B. No. 160 (2017), the Board overruled *Specialty Healthcare* and "reinstate[d] the traditional community-of interest standard as articulated in . . . *United Operations, Inc.*, 338 N.L.R.B. 123 (2002). The Board further stated that "the correct standard for determining whether a proposed bargaining unit constitutes an appropriate unit for collective bargaining when the employer contends that the smallest appropriate unit must include additional employees" is not, as *Specialty Healthcare* held, whether the employer could show that the additional employees "share an overwhelming community of interest with the petitioned-for employees, such that there is no legitimate basis upon which to exclude certain employees from the petitioned-for unit because the traditional community-of-interest factors overlap almost completely." *Id.* at *1 (internal quotation marks and citations omitted). Instead, the Board reinstated its traditional community of interest test.

The Board further "clarified" the *PCC Structurals* test in *The Boeing Co.*, 368 N.L.R.B. No. 67 (2019). In *Boeing*, the Machinists Union had petitioned for an election in a unit of 178 employees whose job was to assure the flightworthiness of Boeing's planes after they came off Boeing's assembly line in North Charleston, South Carolina. After a lengthy hearing, the Board's Regional Director found the unit appropriate, an election was held, and the union won the election by a substantial margin. After the election, Boeing filed a request for review with the Board and contended that the bargaining unit was not appropriate; Boeing argued that the appropriate unit would have combined the petitioned-for employees with the more than 2,000 production and maintenance workers at the North Charleston facility. The Board agreed and vacated the election results. In so doing, the Board stated that: "*PCC Structurals* contemplates a three-step process for determining an appropriate bargaining unit under our traditional community-of-interest test. First, the proposed unit must share an internal community of interest. Second, the interests of those within the proposed unit and the shared and distinct interests of those excluded from that unit must be comparatively analyzed and weighed. Third, consideration must be given to the Board's decisions on appropriate units in the particular industry involved." *Boeing*, sl. op. at 3.

If the test for an appropriate bargaining unit is whether the petitioned-for employees share a community of interest, and the first step of the test articulated in *Boeing* is that the petitioned-for employees share an "internal community of interest," why has the Board added two additional steps to the test? What purpose do those steps serve? How do they fulfill the Board's obligation to "encourage[e] the practice and procedure of collective bargaining"?

While there may be principled reasons for unions or employers to prefer larger or smaller bargaining units where either would be appropriate, these parties' advocacy for particular bargaining units typically focuses on a strategic concern: in which proposed unit is the union or the employer most likely to win an election? At the margins, unions tend to petition for smaller, less comprehensive units because they believe they are more likely to be able to control and predict the results of the election when fewer employees are involved. However, if they find overwhelming support in a larger unit, the union is more likely to petition for the larger unit.

Apart from the Board's investigation of prior bargaining history and its assessment of community of interest, there are few objective standards the Board and the parties must follow in unit determination in most industries. The following case examines bargaining unit determinations in a different context: where the Board has issued a specific rule regarding an entire industry.

American Hospital Ass'n v. NLRB

Supreme Court of the United States
499 U.S. 606, 111 S. Ct. 1539, 113 L. Ed. 2d 675 (1991)

STEVENS, J.

For the first time since the NLRB was established in 1935, the Board has promulgated a substantive rule defining the employee units appropriate for collective bargaining in a particular line of commerce. The rule is applicable to acute care hospitals and provides, with three exceptions, that eight, and only eight, units shall be appropriate in any such hospital. The three exceptions are for cases that present extraordinary circumstances, cases in which nonconforming units already exist, and cases in which labor organizations seek to combine two or more of the eight specified units. The extraordinary circumstances exception applies automatically to hospitals in which the eight-unit rule will produce a unit of five or fewer employees. See 29 CFR § 103.30 (1990).

Petitioner, American Hospital Association, brought this action challenging the facial validity of the rule on three grounds: First, petitioner argues that § 9(b) of the NLRA requires the Board to make a separate bargaining unit determination "in each case" and therefore prohibits the Board from using general rules to define bargaining units; second, petitioner contends that the rule that the Board has formulated violates a congressional admonition to the Board to avoid the undue proliferation of bargaining units in the health care industry; and, finally, petitioner maintains that the rule is arbitrary and capricious.

The [District Court] agreed with petitioner's second argument and enjoined enforcement of the rule. The Court of Appeals found no merit in any of the three arguments and reversed. Because of the importance of the case, we granted certiorari. We now affirm.

I

Petitioner's first argument is a general challenge to the Board's rulemaking authority in connection with bargaining unit determinations based on the terms of the NLRA, as originally enacted in 1935. In § 1 of the NLRA Congress made the legislative finding that the "inequality of bargaining power" between unorganized employees and corporate employers had adversely affected commerce and declared it to be the policy of the United States to mitigate or eliminate those adverse effects "by encouraging the practice and procedure of collective bargaining and by protecting the exercise by workers of full freedom of association, self-organization, and designation of representatives of their own choosing, for the purpose of negotiating the terms and conditions of their employment or other mutual aid or protection." The central purpose of the Act was to protect and facilitate employees' opportunity to organize unions to represent them in collective-bargaining negotiations.

Sections 3, 4, and 5 of the Act created the Board and generally described its powers. §§ 153–155. Section 6 granted the Board the "authority from time to time to make, amend, and rescind . . . such rules and regulations as may be necessary to carry out the provisions" of the Act. § 156. This grant was unquestionably sufficient to authorize the rule at issue in this case unless limited by some other provision in the Act.

Petitioner argues that § 9(b) provides such a limitation because this section requires the Board to determine the appropriate bargaining unit "in each case." § 159(b). We are not persuaded. Petitioner would have us put more weight on these three words than they can reasonably carry.

Section 9(a) of the Act provides that the representative "designated or selected for the purposes of collective bargaining by the majority of the employees in a unit appropriate for such purposes" shall be the exclusive bargaining representative for all the employees in that unit. This section, read in light of the policy of the Act, implies that the initiative in selecting an appropriate unit resides with the employees. Moreover, the language suggests that employees may seek to organize "a unit" that is "appropriate"—not necessarily *the* single most appropriate unit. . . . Thus, one union might seek to represent all of the employees in a particular plant, those in a particular craft, or perhaps just a portion thereof.

Given the obvious potential for disagreement concerning the appropriateness of the unit selected by the union seeking recognition by the employer—disagreements that might involve rival unions claiming jurisdiction over contested segments of the work force as well as disagreements between management and labor—§ 9(b) authorizes the Board to decide whether the designated unit is appropriate. . . . Section 9(b) provides:

> "The Board shall decide *in each case* whether, in order to insure to employees the full benefit of their right to self-organization and to collective bargaining, and otherwise to effectuate the policies of this Act, the unit appropriate for the purposes of collective bargaining shall be the employer unit, craft unit, plant unit, or subdivision thereof." (Emphasis added.)

Petitioner reads the emphasized phrase as a limitation on the Board's rulemaking powers. Although the contours of the restriction that petitioner ascribes to the phrase are murky, petitioner's reading of the language would prevent the Board from imposing any industry-wide rule delineating the appropriate bargaining units. We believe petitioner's reading is inconsistent with the natural meaning of the language read in the context of the statute as a whole.

The more natural reading of these three words is simply to indicate that whenever there is a disagreement about the appropriateness of a unit, the Board shall resolve the dispute. Under this reading, the words "in each case" are synonymous with "whenever necessary" or "in any case in which there is a dispute." Congress chose not to enact a general rule that would require plant unions, craft unions, or industry-wide unions for every employer in every line of commerce, but also chose not to leave the decision up to employees or employers alone. Instead, the decision "in each case" in which a dispute arises is to be made by the Board.

In resolving such a dispute, the Board's decision is presumably to be guided not simply by the basic policy of the Act but also by the rules that the Board develops to circumscribe and to guide its discretion either in the process of case-by-case adjudication or by the exercise of its rulemaking authority. The requirement that the Board exercise its discretion in every disputed case cannot fairly or logically be read to command the Board to exercise standardless discretion in each case. As a noted scholar on administrative law has observed: "[T]he mandate to decide 'in each case' does not prevent the Board from supplanting the original discretionary chaos with some degree of order, and the principal instruments for regularizing the system of deciding 'in each case' are classifications, rules, principles, and precedents. Sensible men could not refuse to use such instruments and a sensible Congress would not expect them to." K. Davis, Administrative Law Text § 6.04, p. 145 (3d ed. 1972). . . .

We simply cannot find in the three words "in each case" any basis for the fine distinction that petitioner would have us draw. Contrary to petitioner's contention, the Board's rule is not an irrebuttable presumption; instead, it contains an exception for "extraordinary circumstances." Even if the rule did establish an irrebuttable presumption, it would not differ significantly from the prior rules adopted by the Board. As with its prior rules, the Board must still apply the rule "in each case." For example, the Board must decide in each case, among a host of other issues, whether a given facility is properly classified as an acute care hospital and whether particular employees are properly placed in particular units. . . .

In sum, we believe that the meaning of § 9(b)'s mandate that the Board decide the appropriate bargaining unit "in each case" is clear and contrary to the meaning advanced by petitioner. Even if we could find any ambiguity in § 9(b) after employing the traditional tools of statutory construction, we would still defer to the Board's reasonable interpretation of the statutory text. . . . We thus conclude that § 9(b) does not limit the Board's rulemaking authority under § 6.

II

[The Court then considered the legislative history of the 1974 amendments to the NLRA that applied the Act to acute care hospitals]. . . .

Both the House and the Senate Committee Reports on the legislation contained this statement: . . . "Due consideration should be given by the Board to preventing proliferation of bargaining units in the health care industry.". . . .

[P]etitioner's primary argument is that the admonition, when coupled with the rejection of a general rule imposing a five-unit limit, evinces Congress' intent to emphasize the importance of the "in each case" requirement in § 9(b).

We find this argument no more persuasive than petitioner's reliance on § 9(b) itself. Assuming that the admonition was designed to emphasize the requirement that the Board determine the appropriate bargaining unit in each case, we have already explained that the Board's rule does not contravene this mandate. See Part I, *supra*.

Petitioner also suggests that the admonition "is an authoritative statement of what Congress intended when it extended the Act's coverage to include nonproprietary hospitals." . . . Even if we accepted this suggestion, we read the admonition as an expression by the Committees of their desire that the Board give "due consideration" to the special problems that "proliferation" might create in acute care hospitals. Examining the record of the Board's rulemaking proceeding, we find that it gave extensive consideration to this very issue. . . .

In any event, we think that the admonition in the Committee Reports is best understood as a form of notice to the Board that if it did not give appropriate consideration to the problem of proliferation in this industry, Congress might respond with a legislative remedy. So read, the remedy for noncompliance with the admonition is in the hands of the body that issued it. . . . If Congress believes that the Board has not given "due consideration" to the issue, Congress may fashion an appropriate response.

III

Petitioner's final argument is that the rule is arbitrary and capricious because "it ignores critical differences among the more than 4,000 acute-care hospitals in the United States, including differences in size, location, operations, and work-force organization." . . . Petitioner supports this argument by noting [earlier Board comments on the diverse character of the health care industry].

The Board responds to this argument by relying on the extensive record developed during the rulemaking proceedings, as well as its experience in the adjudication of health care cases during the 13-year period between the enactment of the health care amendments and its notice of proposed rulemaking. Based on that experience, the Board formed the "considered judgment" that "acute care hospitals do not differ in substantial, significant ways relating to the appropriateness of units." . . . Moreover, the Board argues, the exception for "extraordinary circumstances" is adequate to take care of the unusual case in which a particular application of the rule might be arbitrary. . . .

The Board's conclusion that, absent extraordinary circumstances, "acute care hospitals do not differ in substantial, significant ways relating to the appropriateness of units," . . . was based on a "reasoned analysis" of an extensive record. . . .

In this opinion, we have deliberately avoided any extended comment on the wisdom of the rule, the propriety of the specific unit determinations, or the importance of avoiding work stoppages in acute care hospitals. We have pretermitted such discussion not because these matters are unimportant but because they primarily concern the Board's exercise of its authority rather than the limited scope of our review of the legal arguments presented by petitioner. Because we find no merit in any of these legal arguments, the judgment of the Court of Appeals is affirmed.

Notes

1. The rule at issue in *American Hosp. Ass'n* was the Board's first use of substantive rulemaking in its history. Section 6 authorizes the Board to engage in rulemaking

in accordance with the Administrative Procedure Act. NLRA §6; 29 U.S.C. §156. *See* Mark Grunewald, *The NLRB's First Rulemaking: An Exercise in Pragmatism*, 41 Duke L. J. 274, 294 (1991) (stating in the context of *American Hosp. Ass'n*, "Section 6 of the NLRA expressly grants the Board rulemaking authority. Thus, the general authority of the Board to engage in rulemaking was not in doubt."); *cf.* Thomas Merrill & Kathryn Tongue Watts, *Agency Rules with the Force of Law: The Original Convention*, 116 Harv. L. Rev. 467, 511, 526 (1991) (arguing Congress did not originally intend the NLRA's general rulemaking grant in §6 to authorize the Board, or other agencies, to issue rules beyond procedural matters).

2. In *American Hosp. Ass'n*, the Board's hospital rule was challenged in a U.S. district court. Board unfair labor practice decisions are normally reviewable only in the courts of appeal, NLRA §§10(e)–(f); 29 U.S.C. §§160(e)–(f), and its decisions in representation cases are ordinarily unreviewable by the courts. *American Federation of Labor v. NLRB*, 308 U.S. 184 (1940). Why does the procedural posture differ if the Board issues a rule through notice-and-comment rulemaking? *See* 5 U.S.C. §702 ("A person suffering legal wrong because of agency action, or adversely affected or aggrieved by agency action within the meaning of a relevant statute, is entitled to judicial review thereof. . . .").

3. The Board has attempted to issue other rules affecting bargaining unit determinations. In 1995, for example, the Board proposed a rule to govern the appropriateness of single location bargaining units in most industries. *See* Notice of Proposed Rulemaking: Appropriateness of Requested Single Location Bargaining Units in Representation Cases, 60 Fed. Reg. 50,146 (1995), *withdrawn*, 63 Fed. Reg. 8890 (1998). This rule was blocked by Congress before a final rule could be promulgated using successive "riders" (*i.e.*, policy proscriptions) added to the Board's annual appropriations bills that fund the agency.

4. In 2011, the Board issued a rule mandating covered employers, regardless of whether their employees are represented by a union, to post notices informing their employees of their rights to act together to improve wages and working conditions, to form, join and assist a union, to bargain collectively with their employer, and to refrain from any of these activities. The notice provided examples of unlawful employer and union conduct and tells employees how to contact the NLRB. *See* https://www.nlrb.gov/news/board-issues-final-rule-require-posting-nlra-rights. However, the rule was struck down by two U.S. Courts of Appeals. *Nat'l Ass'n of Mfrs. v. NLRB*, 717 F.3d 947 (D.C. Cir. 2013); *Chamber of Commerce v. NLRB*, 721 F.3d 152 (4th Cir. 2013).

5. *American Hospital Ass'n* applies to acute health care facilities. What about bargaining units in non-acute facilities, such as nursing homes and rehabilitation centers? Originally, in *Park Manor Care Center*, 305 N.L.R.B. 872 (1991), a case that dealt specifically with a nursing home, the Board indicated that in non-acute health care facilities, the Board would apply a "pragmatic" or "empirical" community-of-interest test under which it would consider traditional community-of-interest factors, as well as factors considered relevant during the Health Care

Rulemaking and prior cases involving either the type of facility in dispute or the type of unit sought. The Board subsequently made clear that *Park Manor* applied to all health care facilities not covered by the Health Care Rule. *McLean Hospital Corp.*, 309 N.L.R.B. 564, 564 fn. 1 (1992). In *Specialty Healthcare & Rehabilitation Center of Mobile*, 357 N.L.R.B. 934, 938 (2011), *enfd. sub nom. Kindred Nursing Centers East, LLC v. NLRB*, 727 F.3d 552 (6th Cir. 2013) — another nursing home case — the Board overruled *Park Manor* and stated that it would henceforth "apply our traditional community-of-interest standards in this case and others like it." The Board subsequently overruled *Specialty Healthcare* in *PCC Structurals,* 365 N.L.R.B. No. 160 (2017), and, in doing so, reinstated the standard established in *Park Manor Care Center* for unit determinations in non-acute care facilities. *PCC Structurals*, sl. op. at 1 and fn. 3.

C. Statutory Limitations on Unit Determinations

In addition to the Board's obligation to determine appropriate units to "assure to employees the fullest freedom in exercising the rights guaranteed by this Act," there are four express statutory limitations on unit appropriateness. Three are in §9(b): those pertaining to professional employees, craft representation, and plant guards. The fourth limitation, the extent of organization, is in §9(c)(5). 29 U.S.C. §159(c)(5).

Under §9(b), "the Board shall not decide that any unit is appropriate . . . if such unit includes both professional employees and employees who are not professional employees unless a majority of such professional employees vote for inclusion in such unit." 29 U.S.C. §159(b). Section 2(12) defines professional employee to mean employees engaged in work that is predominantly intellectual and varied in character; involving the consistent exercise of discretion and judgment; where the output or result cannot be standardized in relation to a given period of time; requiring knowledge of an advanced type in a field of science or learning customarily acquired by a prolonged course of specialized intellectual instruction and study in an institution of higher learning or hospital; or employees who have completed certain specialized instruction and are performing related work under the supervision of a professional. 29 U.S.C. §152(12). For procedures for the vote professional employees must take before being included with non-professionals, see *In re Sonotone Corp.*, 90 N.L.R.B. 1236, 1241(1950).

Under §9(b), "the Board shall not decide that any craft unit is inappropriate . . . on the ground that a different unit has been established by a prior Board determination, unless a majority of the employees in the proposed craft unit votes against separate representation." 29 U.S.C. §159. The Board has defined a craft unit as "one consisting of a distinct and homogeneous group of skilled journeymen craftsmen, who, together with helpers or apprentices, are primarily engaged in the performance of tasks which are not performed by other employees and which require the use of substantial craft skills and specialized tools and equipment." *Burns & Roe Servs.*

Corp., 313 N.L.R.B. 1307, 1308 (1994). In *Mallinckrodt Chemical Works*, 162 N.L.R.B. 387, 397 (1967), the Board declared that it would evaluate all factors normally considered in bargaining unit determinations in determining whether craft employees should be severed from a larger unit.

Under § 9(b), "the Board shall not decide that any unit is appropriate . . . if it includes, together with other employees, any individual employed as a guard to enforce against employees and other persons rules to protect property of the employer or to protect the safety of persons on the employer's premises"; also, "no labor organization shall be certified as the representative of employees in a bargaining unit of guards if such organization admits to membership, or is affiliated directly or indirectly with an organization which admits to membership, employees other than guards." 29 U.S.C. § 159(b). *See also, e.g., Wackenhut Corp. v. NLRB,* 178 F.3d 543 (D.C. Cir. 1999). The purpose of § 9(b)(3) is to avoid potential conflicts of interests for unions that might represent nonguards and guards. Simply, the latter group may be required to enforce an employer's work rules against the former. In light of that purpose, the Board has determined that "[i]ndirect affiliation between a guard union and a nonguard union is established when 'the extent and duration of [the guard union's] dependence upon [the nonguard union] indicates a lack of freedom and independence in formulating its own policies and deciding its own course of action.'" *U.S. Corr. Corp.*, 325 N.L.R.B. 375, 376 (1998).

The Board's authority is also limited by § 9(c)(5), which provides that "[i]n determining whether a unit is appropriate . . . the extent to which the employees have organized shall not be controlling." 29 U.S.C. § 159(c). In amending the NLRA to include § 9(c)(5), "Congress intended to overrule Board decisions where the unit determined could only be supported on the basis of the extent of organization." *NLRB v. Metro. Life Ins. Co.*, 380 U.S. 438, 441 (1965). The language and legislative history of § 9(c)(5), however, "demonstrate that the provision was not intended to prohibit the Board from considering the extent of organization as one factor, though not the controlling factor, in its unit determination." *Id.* at 442.

Notes

1. Bargaining units also must not include employees who are not covered by the NLRA, including agricultural laborers, supervisors, managers, and confidential employees. *See* Chapter 2.

2. The Board has developed numerous rules regarding the appropriateness of units that include both plant clericals and office clericals, as well as units that include both technical workers and other workers. For example, in determining whether it is appropriate to include technical workers in a unit with production and maintenance workers, the Board makes a "pragmatic judgment" based on the following considerations: (a) the desires of the parties, (b) bargaining history, (c) similarity of skills and job functions, (d) common supervision, (e) contracts or interchange with other employees, (f) similarity of working conditions, (g) type of industry, (h) organization of the plant, (i) whether the technical employees work in

separately situated and separately controlled areas, and (j) whether any union seeks to represent technical employees separately. *See Sheffield Corp.*, 134 N.L.R.B. 1101, 1103–04 (1962); *Virginia Mfg. Co.*, 311 N.L.R.B. 992, 993 (1993).

3. The Board has interpreted the NLRA as permitting and in some cases requiring self-determination elections: "A self-determination election is typically held where (1) the several units proposed by competing labor organizations are equally appropriate, as in the case of a separate unit vis-à-vis a comprehensive unit; (2) craft or traditional departmental severance is involved; (3) such an election is instrumental in effectuating a statutory requirement as in the case of an election under § 9(b)(1) involving professional employees; or (4) the issue is the inclusion of a group in an existing unit as against continued nonrepresentation." *See* Outline of Law and Procedure in Representation Cases, § 21-100, *et seq.* (citing *In re Globe Mach. & Stamping Co.*, 3 N.L.R.B. 294 (1937).

D. Employers with Multiple Locations

NLRB v. Chicago Health & Tennis Clubs, Inc.

U.S. Court of Appeals for the Seventh Circuit
567 F.2d 331 (7th Cir. 1977)

SWYGERT, J.

In the two cases before us, the [NLRB or Board] petitions for enforcement of its orders directing each of the respondents to cease and desist from refusing to bargain collectively with the union which had been certified as the exclusive bargaining representative. These two cases have been consolidated for this opinion because they present the identical legal issue: whether the Board abused its discretion in certifying a single retail store as an appropriate unit for collective bargaining where such store constitutes only one of a chain of stores owned and operated by the company in the Chicago metropolitan area. For the reasons set forth, we grant the petition in Chicago Health Clubs and deny enforcement in Saxon Paint.

I

(A) Parties

No. 77-1227. Chicago Health & Tennis Clubs is an Illinois corporation engaged in the sale of club memberships and providing services of exercise training and weight loss counseling for its members. It operates sixteen clubs in the Chicago metropolitan area . . . and all clubs are within a 28-mile radius of [its central] office [in Chicago].

No. 77-1504. Saxon Paint & Home Care Centers is an Illinois corporation engaged in the retail sale of paint, wallpaper, and home decorating supplies. It owns and operates twenty-one stores in the Chicago metropolitan area [and] has seven other stores in Illinois, Indiana, and Wisconsin. Although these seven stores are operated by separate corporate entities, they are owned in part by the same stockholders and are operated through a single managerial hierarchy. All of the Chicago metropolitan area stores are within a 30-mile radius of each other.

(B) Procedural History

[In both cases, a local of the Retail Clerks Union petitioned for an election in a unit limited to the employees of a single store in the company's chain of stores. In both cases, the Regional Director found the proposed unit appropriate, and the Board denied review. In both cases, the union won a representation election, the employer refused to bargain (claiming the unit was inappropriate), the Board found an 8(a)(5) violation, and the Board petitioned for enforcement].

II

The primary responsibility for determining the appropriateness of a unit for collective bargaining rests with the Board. It is given broad discretion in determining bargaining units "to assure to employees the fullest freedom in exercising the rights guaranteed by (the Act)." 29 U.S.C. s 159(b). The Board is not required to select the most appropriate bargaining unit in a given factual situation; it need choose only an appropriate unit within the range of appropriate units. . . . It follows that Board unit determinations are rarely to be disturbed. South Prairie Construction Co. v. Local No. 627, International Union, 425 U.S. 800, 805 (1976). . . .

Although Board determinations are subject to limited review, they are not immune from judicial scrutiny . . . Indeed, the Supreme Court has held that we are not "'to stand aside and rubber-stamp' Board determinations that run contrary to the language or tenor of the Act." *NLRB v. Weingarten, Inc.*, 420 U.S. 251, 256 (1975). . . . [W]e have the responsibility of determining whether the Board's unit determinations were unreasonable, arbitrarily or capriciously made . . . , or unsupported by substantial evidence. . . .

In making unit determinations, the Board must effect the policy of the Act to assure employees the fullest freedom in exercising their rights, yet at the same time "respect the interest of an integrated multi-unit employer in maintaining enterprise-wide labor relations." *NLRB v. Solis Theatre Corp.*, 403 F.2d 381, 382 (2d Cir. 1968). . . . In reaching its decision, the Board considers several criteria, no single factor alone being determinative. . . . These factors include: (a) geographic proximity of the stores in relation to each other . . . ; (b) history of collective bargaining or unionization . . . ; (c) extent of employee interchange between various stores . . . ; (d) functional integration of operations . . . ; and (e) centralization of management, particularly in regard to central control of personnel and labor relations. . . .

As the geographic proximity of the stores in the two cases before us is almost identical, our decision whether to grant the petitions for enforcement must rest on an analysis of the other factors.

. . . .

. . . [The Board has] adopted the administrative policy that a single store is "presumptively an appropriate unit for bargaining." *Haag Drug Corp.*, 169 N.L.R.B. 877,

877–78 (1968). That presumption, however, is not conclusive and "may be overcome where factors are present in a particular case which would counter the appropriateness of a single store unit. . . ." *Id.* at 878.

We turn now to the two cases before us.

(A) Saxon Paint, No. 77-1504

Although the Board recognized that the Chicago area Saxon stores exhibited "a high degree of centralized administration," it nevertheless found a single store unit appropriate. In large part, the Board based its unit determination on the role of the local store manager, adopting the Regional Director's finding that "substantial responsibility is invested in the Employer's store managers." We believe that the Board exaggerated the control exercised by the store manager over labor and administrative matters and hold that the Board's finding that the store manager possesses autonomy and authority is not supported by substantial evidence.

The evidence in the record clearly establishes that Saxon is a highly integrated operation. Each Saxon store is similar in all respects to each of the other Saxon stores in Cook County. All of the stores are open on the same days and at the same times. They sell the same merchandise at the same price and the physical layout of each store is similar. Special sales and promotions are held at the same time in each store with the same sale prices being charged. Advertising covers the entire metropolitan area and is prepared by headquarters as are store signs and window displays. The stores are "as much alike in this respect as peas in a pod." *NLRB v. Frisch's Big Boy Ill-Mar, Inc.*, 356 F.2d 895, 896 (7th Cir. 1966).

Personnel and labor relations policies for the Saxon stores are also centrally administered, being formulated by the personnel director who maintains his office at corporate headquarters. Payrolls, accounts, personnel files, and other records are maintained at the general office. Employee job classifications are the same at each store, and employees within a particular classification perform the same duties and are required to have the same skills and experience. Employees within the same classification, experience, and seniority receive the same wages. A uniform fringe benefit program is maintained at each store, and store employees enjoy company-wide seniority.

The actual operations of the Cook County stores are also highly centralized. Under the vice president of operations are three district managers who are responsible for assuring that all stores within their respective districts are being operated in full compliance with the policies and procedures formulated at headquarters, including personnel and labor relations policies. These district managers visit the stores within their district on the average of every two days and maintain further contact with the individual stores through frequent telephone calls and written memoranda. In addition, the company maintains a messenger service which visits each metropolitan area store daily.

At the store level and below the district managers, the company employs fourteen store managers in all three districts. Seven of these managers are assigned to single stores, the remaining seven managers are each assigned to two stores. The evidence establishes that, contrary to the Board's conclusion, these store managers have limited involvement in the store's non-labor business activities. The individual store managers have no authority to commit the employer's credit, purchase or order merchandise and supplies, arrange for repair or maintenance work, change prices, or resolve customer complaints. At best it can be said that it is the responsibility of the store managers to implement the company's policies and procedures within the individual stores.

The store managers' involvement in labor relations and personnel matters is also severely limited. They have no authority to do any of the following: (a) hire new employees; (b) grant promotions, wage increases or changes in job classifications; (c) discharge or suspend employees for disciplinary reasons; (d) lay-off employees; (e) handle employee grievances; (f) grant requests for vacations or leaves of absence; (g) permanently or temporarily transfer employees between any of the stores; and (h) post the weekly work schedule without prior approval by the district manager. While the store manager may offer recommendations in certain of these areas, the record shows that these recommendations, even in such key areas as employee discharge, may not be followed. Furthermore, in certain areas such as promotion and wage increases, the store manager may not even be consulted before a decision is made. As the Second Circuit noted in *NLRB v. Solis Theatre Corp.*, 403 F.2d 381, 383 (2d Cir. 1968): "It appears, therefore, that instead of being in a decision making position, the 'manager' has little or no authority on labor policy but is subject to detailed instructions from the central office."

That Saxon is completely integrated functionally is best illustrated by its hiring and training practices. Hiring is done almost exclusively through the corporate offices. Job applications are taken and interviews are held at the personnel office. The store manager may interview an applicant only after the applicant has first interviewed with the personnel director and then the district manager. Applicants may be rejected and new employees hired, however, without prior consultation with or participation by the store manager.

Similarly, the training of new employees comes under the primary jurisdiction of the central personnel department. The company issues manuals to all new employees and provides them with formal training, lasting from one to two weeks, at its corporate headquarters. In sum, it is apparent that there is no local autonomy among the individual stores and that the store managers lack the authority to resolve issues which would be subject to collective bargaining. . . .

That Saxon's business is both centralized and integrated and that the individual stores lack meaningful identity as a self-contained unit is further supported by the numbers of employee transfers, both temporary and permanent, among the metropolitan area stores. During a thirteen month period and discounting employees not covered in the unit, eighteen percent of all employees were transferred permanently among the Chicago stores. Additional testimony showed that temporary transfers frequently occur, almost on a daily basis. While this alone may be insufficient to negate a single store unit, we cannot agree with the Board's finding that "the degree of employee interchange (was) too inconsequential and insubstantial to rebut the appropriateness of a single store unit," particularly when this factor is considered in light of all of the other factors. . . .

That a single store is inappropriate here is further shown by the history of collective bargaining. The pattern of unionization both at stores in other regions and at stores within the Chicago metropolitan area has always been district wide. Since 1966, the employees at the company's two Hammond, Indiana stores have been represented by another local of the Retail Clerks Union. These employees are covered by one collective bargaining agreement between the union and the company. Both present and past agreements have stated that the unit it covers is "all present and future retail establishments of the Company situated within the Gary, Indiana metropolitan area, including the County of Lake." A similar clause was contained in the agreement with the employees from the company's store in Rockford, Illinois. . . .

[W]e conclude that the Board's determination that a single Saxon store was an appropriate bargaining unit is not supported by substantial evidence and therefore is arbitrary and unreasonable. Accordingly, the Board's order is set aside and enforcement is denied.

(B) Chicago Health Clubs, No. 77-1227

Chicago Health Clubs is, at first sight, quite similar factually to Saxon Paint. The company's sixteen stores (clubs) are in a similar geographic proximity to each other. Many of its operations and procedures are centralized.

Other similarities are readily apparent. Chicago Health Clubs has two area supervisors (similar to Saxon's district managers) who oversee its sixteen clubs. These supervisors visit their respective clubs two or three times a week and maintain frequent telephone contact. Despite these similarities, we conclude that substantial evidence supports the Board's finding that a single club is an appropriate bargaining unit.

Notably absent in this case is any prior history of collective bargaining. In addition, the extent of employee interchange among the various clubs is minimal [and involved only sales trainees]. Furthermore, there are significant differences in the functional integration of the clubs, the extent to which the company is centralized, and the degree of autonomy of the local club managers.

Unlike the Saxon stores which are virtually identical with each other, Chicago Health Clubs operates at least three types of clubs. Some clubs exclusively serve women, others serve men on one day and women on another. Still others serve men and women on the same day. The clubs also differ in the type of facilities available. Some have handball courts, others have swimming pools. One has a tennis court.

Although many aspects of the company's operations and procedures are centralized, they are not as highly centralized as in Saxon Paint. For example, even though official personnel and payroll records are maintained at the central office, each club manager also maintains records detailing needed information about the club employees. Similarly, the central office controls the advertising for all sixteen clubs, but the advertising may be directed at only one geographical area or may be on behalf of only one of the clubs.

Also unlike the store managers in Saxon Paint, the club managers exercise a marked degree of control over personnel and labor relations matters. Applicants apply at the individual clubs and are interviewed by the club manager without further interview by the area supervisor. Part-time employees, a large number if not a majority of all employees, are hired and fired by the club manager without consultation with the area supervisor. Although full-time employees are hired with the approval of the area supervisor, the decision is based on the applicant's interview with the club manager. In hiring, the club manager sets the wage rate for new employees within the perimeters determined by the area supervisor.

Additionally, unlike the store managers in Saxon Paint, the club managers here exercise considerable disciplinary authority over rank-and-file employees. A club manager may reprimand employees without prior approval. Moreover, in extreme cases, the club manager has the authority to discharge or suspend employees without prior consultation with the area supervisor.

The club manager exercises control over the working conditions of employees in many other respects. For example, the club manager handles employee complaints and grievances about wages and hours, schedules vacations, grants or denies overtime, decides whether employees may take their lunch break on or off the premises, administers the local payroll system, and trains employees in exercise instruction and sales. Thus, unlike Saxon Paint and like Walgreen, much of the day-to-day employment activities are supervised directly by the local club manager "without significant interference" by the central corporate organization.

Based on the autonomy of the club manager, the insubstantial amount of employee interchange among the metropolitan clubs, and the absence of any collective bargaining history, we conclude that the Board's determination that a single store was an appropriate bargaining unit is reasonable in light of all the facts presented in this case. Since Chicago Health Clubs has admitted its refusal to bargain with the union representing this single club, we accordingly enforce the Board's order. . . .

In cases involving chain stores and other multi-facility employers, the NLRB applies a presumption that a single store is "presumptively an appropriate unit for bargaining." *Haag Drug Co., Inc.*, 169 N.L.R.B. 877, 878. In **Friendly Ice Cream v. NLRB**, 705 F.2d 570, 576 (1st Cir. 1983), the court explained that, "this rebuttable presumption is consistent with the Act, has a rational foundation, and reflects the Board's expertise." The court continued.

We have recently upheld the Board determination that a single store constitutes an appropriate unit for collective bargaining. In *NLRB v. Living and*

Learning Centers, Inc., 652 F.2d 209 (1st Cir.1981), the Board had ordered a representation election to be held at one day care center which was part of a twenty-nine unit chain operating in Massachusetts. While each center had a director who could hire, fire, schedule vacations and resolve work-related disputes, the director was bound by central management's specification of curriculum, wages and benefits. In reviewing the Board's unit determination, we acknowledged the high "degree of the Employer's control of personnel policies and the extent of integration of the Massachusetts centers." Yet, we felt that these factors were insufficient to overcome the presumptive appropriateness of the single center unit. As we explained: "It [one center] immediately seems to be *an* appropriate unit because there is apt to be a bond of interest among all the persons employed by the same employer in connection with the same enterprise at the same locus" (emphasis in original). . . . 705 F.2d 570, 576–77.

In the context of a retail chain operation, one of the most weighty factors in determining the appropriateness of a single store unit is the degree of control vested in the local store manager. . . .

[T]he Board had ample grounds for concluding that the Store Manager was, in fact, autonomous. . . . Employees at the Weymouth restaurant perform their day-to-day work under the immediate supervision of the Store Manager. The Store Manager is usually the only company official who interviews prospective applicants for employment. On his own, the Store Manager can decide not to grant a second interview. Job applicants receive a conditional offer of employment from the Store Manager and, in some cases, an immediate offer following the first interview.

Once hired, employees receive most of their training from the Store Manager or his designee. He regularly reviews their work and fills out quarterly written evaluations which are used as the basis for recommending wage increases. According to company policy, the District Manager must approve all wage increases, but, in practice, the Store Manager, at times, grants wage increases on the spot.

The Store Manager schedules employees' hours and tasks, within guidelines established by the company. On his own initiative he can allow an employee to leave early or take a day off. Also, on a day-to-day basis he can decide to call in more or less than the scheduled number of employees to meet changing business needs. In matters of employee discipline, the Store Manager has the authority to issue oral warnings and suspend employees. The Store Manager can recommend that written warnings be given or that an employee be terminated. And, in cases of gross misconduct, the Store Manager can discharge an employee without prior approval. The Store Manager plays a central role in the resolution of grievances, since the company's Open Door policy calls for every effort to be made to settle problems on the local level.

Generally, the party favoring the multi-facility unit bears the burden of rebutting the single-unit presumption. *J&L Plate, Inc.*, 310 N.L.R.B. 429, 429 (1993). To determine whether the presumption has been rebutted, the Board examines these factors: (1) degree of central control over daily operations and labor relations, including extent of local autonomy; (2) similarity of employee skills, functions, and working conditions; (3) degree of employee interchange; (4) distance between locations; and (5) bargaining history, if any. *Id.* The single-facility presumption is inapplicable where the petitioning union seeks a multi-facility unit. *Capital Coors Co.*, 309 N.L.R.B. 322 (1992) (citing *NLRB v. Carson Cable TV*, 795 F.2d 879 (9th Cir. 1986)).

Notes

1. Under the RLA, the issue of multi-employer bargaining units generally does not arise. The RLA favors system-wide bargaining units by craft or class.

2. As noted, in 1995, the Board proposed a rule on the appropriateness of single location bargaining units in almost all industries subject to its jurisdiction (excluding public utilities, construction, and crews on ocean-going vessels). Under the proposed rule, a petitioned-for, single-location unit would be appropriate if, absent "extraordinary circumstances," "(a) [at least 15] employees were employed [at the single location]; (b) "no other facility of the employer was located within [1 mile]; and (c) a statutory supervisor . . . was located at the site." According to the proposed rule, a "showing of extraordinary circumstances would render the rule inapplicable, and refer the case to adjudication, such as where a set percentage of the employees in the unit sought performed work at another location for a set percentage of the time." The Board asserted that the proposed rule would reduce litigation costs, increase predictability in this area of the law, and save agency resources. What are the arguments against such a rule?

3. Cases such as *Chicago Health & Tennis Clubs* are known as "technical 8(a)(5)" cases. In such cases, the employer admits that it has refused to bargain but argues that it is privileged to do so because the bargaining unit is invalid in scope or in composition. The issue is not the factual question of whether the employer refused to bargain but rather the legal question of whether the employer's refusal to bargain violated §8(a)(5) and (1). The answer to that legal question typically turns on whether the bargaining unit is appropriate. Thus, employers have an effective opportunity to obtain judicial review of representation decisions in the context of their petition for review of the related §8(a)(5) unfair labor practice decision, despite the fact that the NLRA does not provide for direct appeal of representation cases. Are unions able to gain effective appeals of representation matters through a similar tactic?

4. Theoretically, one other way to obtain judicial review of a Board representation decision exists. In **Leedom v. Kyne**, 358 U.S. 184 (1958), the Supreme Court heard a challenge to the Board's actions after it held an election for a unit that contained professionals and non-professionals without first holding an election among

the professionals to see if they agreed to such a unit. This ignored the statutory rule in §9(b)(2) discussed above. The professional employees brought suit in Federal District Court, which set aside the Board's determination of the bargaining unit, the result of the election, and the Board's certification of the union representing the unit. The Court of Appeals held that the District Court lacked jurisdiction, but the Supreme Court reversed and reinstated the judgment of the District Court. Notably, the Supreme Court stressed that it was not reviewing the case under the provisions of the NLRA; rather, the Court held that this was a case of an agency acting in excess of its delegated powers and the suit was cognizable by a district court under the original jurisdiction granted by 28 U.S.C § 1337 of "any civil action or proceeding arising under any Act of Congress regulating commerce." Thus, in cases where the Board is alleged to have acted truly without authority and there is no other opportunity for judicial review, a district court has jurisdiction. *See Detroit Newspaper Agency v. NLRB*, 286 F.3d 391, 400 (6th Cir. 2002) (holding that the district court was without jurisdiction where plaintiff-employer would ultimately have the opportunity to petition for review under §10(f)). The court does not, however, decide the underlying issue — only whether the Board has acted outside the scope of its authority.

This avenue of appeal is rarely available. "The *Kyne* exception is a narrow one, not to be extended to permit plenary District Court review of Board orders in certification proceedings whenever it can be said that an erroneous assessment of the particular facts before the Board has led it to a conclusion which does not comport with the law." *Boire v. Greyhound Corp.*, 376 U.S. 473, 481 (1964).

E. Private-Sector Units Encompassing Multiple Employers

1. Multiple Employers in an Industry

Organizing efforts in some industries raise the question of whether bargaining units should comprise a single-employer or multi-employer unit. The Board applies a single-employer presumption: "A single employer unit is presumptively appropriate and a party urging a multiemployer unit must demonstrate a controlling history of bargaining on a multiemployer basis and an unequivocal intent by the employer to participate in and be bound by the results of group bargaining." *Centra, Inc.*, 328 N.L.R.B. 407, 408 (1999). The essence of multiemployer bargaining is that it is based on "a voluntary arrangement, dependent upon the real consent of the participants to bind themselves to each other for bargaining purposes." *Van Eerden Co.*, 154 N.L.R.B. 496, 499 (1965). Therefore, "[t]he Board will find a multiemployer bargaining unit appropriate when the employers involved have evidenced a clear intent to participate in multiemployer bargaining and to be bound by the actions of the bargaining agent." *Hunts Point Recycling Corp.*, 301 N.L.R.B. 751, 752 (1991). The members of the multiemployer association must exhibit an "unequivocal intention to be bound in collective bargaining by group rather than individual action" *J.D. Consulting, LLC*, 345 N.L.R.B. 1298, 1299 (2005). That agreement may be based on "either participation in the group bargaining or delegation of authority to another to engage in such bargaining." *Architectural Contractors Trade Ass'n*, 343 N.L.R.B. 259, 260 (2004).

The case below discusses the conditions under which a multiemployer association member can lawfully withdraw from a multi-employer bargaining unit and, in the process, discloses the history, logic, and operation of such units.

Charles D. Bonanno Linen Serv., Inc. v. NLRB

Supreme Court of the United States
454 U.S. 404, 102 S. Ct. 720, 70 L. Ed. 2d 656 (1982)

WHITE, J.

The issue here is whether a bargaining impasse justifies an employer's unilateral withdrawal from a multiemployer bargaining unit. The [Board] concluded that an employer attempting such a withdrawal commits an unfair labor practice in violation of §§ 8(a)(5) and 8(a)(1) of the [NLRA], by refusing to execute the collective-bargaining agreement later executed by the union and the multiemployer association. The Court of Appeals for the First Circuit enforced the Board's order. . . . We granted certiorari to resolve the conflict among the Circuits on this important question of federal labor law. We affirm the judgment of the Court of Appeals.

I

The factual findings of the Administrative Law Judge were affirmed by the Board and are undisputed. Petitioner, Charles D. Bonanno Linen Service, Inc. (Bonanno), is a Massachusetts corporation engaged in laundering, renting, and distributing linens and uniforms. Teamsters Local No. 25 (Union) represents its drivers and helpers as well as those of other linen supply companies in the area. For several years, Bonanno has been a member of the New England Linen Supply Association (Association), a group of 10 employers formed to negotiate with the Union as a multiemployer unit and a signatory of the contracts negotiated between the Union and the Association. On February 19, 1975, Bonanno authorized the Association's negotiating committee to represent it in the anticipated negotiations for a new contract. Bonanno's president became a member of the committee.

The Union and the Association held 10 bargaining sessions during March and April. On April 30, the negotiators agreed upon a proposed contract, but four days later the Union members rejected it. By May 15, according to the stipulations of the parties, the Union and the Association had reached an impasse over the method of compensation: the Union demanded that the drivers be paid on commission, while the Association insisted on continuing payment at an hourly rate.

Several subsequent meetings failed to break the impasse. On June 23, the Union initiated a selective strike against Bonanno. In response, most of Association members locked out their drivers. Despite sporadic meetings, the stalemate continued throughout the summer. During this period two of the employers met secretly with the Union, presumably in an effort to reach a separate settlement. These meetings, however, never reached the level of negotiations.

Bonanno hired permanent replacements for all of its striking drivers. On November 21, it notified the Association by letter that it was "withdrawing from the Association with specific respect to negotiations at this time because of an ongoing impasse with Teamsters Local 25." . . . Bonanno mailed a copy of its revocation letter to the Union and read the letter over the phone to a Union representative.

Soon after Bonanno's putative withdrawal, the Association ended the lockout. It told the Union that it wished to continue multiemployer negotiations. Several negotiating sessions took place between December and April, without Bonanno participating. In the middle of April, the Union abandoned its demand for payment on commission and accepted the Association's offer of a revised hourly wage rate. With this development, the parties quickly agreed on a new contract, dated April 23, 1976, and given retroactive effect to April 18, 1975.

Meanwhile, on April 9, 1976, the Union had filed the present action, alleging that Bonanno's purported withdrawal from the bargaining unit constituted an unfair labor practice. In a letter dated April 29, the Union informed Bonanno that because the Union had never consented to the withdrawal, it considered Bonanno to be bound by the settlement just reached. In a reply letter, Bonanno denied that it was bound by the contract.

An Administrative Law Judge concluded, after a hearing, that no unusual circumstances excused Bonanno's withdrawal from the multiemployer bargaining unit. The Board affirmed, ordering Bonanno to sign and implement the contract retroactively. In a supplemental decision, the Board explained the basis of its decision that Bonanno's attempt to withdraw from the multiemployer unit was untimely and ineffective. . . . The Court of Appeals enforced the Board's order. . . .

II

The standard for judicial review of the Board's decision in this case was established by *NLRB v. Truck Drivers*, 353 U.S. 87 (1957) (*Buffalo Linen*). There, the Union struck a single employer during negotiations with a multiemployer bargaining association. The other employers responded with a lockout. Negotiations continued, and an agreement was reached. The Union, claiming that the lockout violated its rights under §§ 7 and 8 of the Act, then filed charges with the Board. The Board rejected the claim, but the Court of Appeals held that the lockout was an unfair practice.

This Court in turn reversed. That the Act did not expressly authorize or deal with multiemployer units or with lockouts in that context was recognized. Nonetheless, multiemployer bargaining had "long antedated the Wagner Act" and had become more common as employers, in the course of complying with their duty to bargain under the Act, "sought through group bargaining to match increased union strength." 353 U.S. at 94–95 (footnote omitted). Furthermore, at the time of the debates on the Taft-Hartley amendments, Congress had rejected a proposal to limit or outlaw multiemployer bargaining. The debates and their results offered "cogent evidence that in many industries multiemployer-bargaining basis was a vital factor in the effectuation of the national policy of promoting labor peace through strengthened collective bargaining." *Id.* at 95.[3] Congress' refusal to intervene indicated that it intended to leave to the Board's specialized judgment the resolution of conflicts between union and employer rights that were bound to arise in multiemployer bargaining. In such situations, the Court said:

> "The ultimate problem is the balancing of the conflicting legitimate interests. The function of striking that balance to effectuate national labor policy is often a difficult and delicate responsibility, which the Congress committed primarily to the [NLRB], subject to limited judicial review." *Id.* at 96.

Thus, the Court of Appeals' rejection of the Board's justification of the lockout as an acceptable effort to maintain the integrity of the multiemployer unit and its refusal to accept the lockout as a legitimate response to the whipsaw strike had too narrowly confined the exercise of the Board's discretion. *Id.* at 97.

Multiemployer bargaining has continued to be the preferred bargaining mechanism in many industries, and as *Buffalo Linen* predicted, it has raised a variety of problems requiring resolution. One critical question concerns the rights of the union and the employers to terminate the multiemployer bargaining arrangement. Until 1958, the Board permitted both employers and the Union to abandon the unit even in the midst of bargaining. . . . But in *Retail Associates, Inc.,* 120 N.L.R.B. 388 (1958), the Board announced guidelines for withdrawal from multiemployer units. These rules, which reflect an increasing emphasis on the stability of multiemployer units, permit any party to withdraw prior to the date set for negotiation of a new contract or the date on which negotiations actually begin, provided that adequate notice is given. Once negotiations for a new contract have commenced, however, withdrawal is permitted only if there is "mutual consent" or "unusual circumstances" exist. *Id.* at 395.

---

3. As the Court of Appeals explained in this case:
"Multiemployer bargaining offers advantages to both management and labor. It enables smaller employers to bargain 'on an equal basis with a large union' and avoid 'the competitive disadvantages resulting from nonuniform contractual terms.' *NLRB v. Truck Drivers Local 449*, 353 U.S. 87, 96 (1957). At the same time, it facilitates the development of industry-wide, worker benefit programs that employers otherwise might be unable to provide. More generally, multiemployer bargaining encourages both sides to adopt a flexible attitude during negotiations; as the Board explains, employers can make concessions 'without fear that other employers will refuse to make similar concessions to achieve a competitive advantage,' and a union can act similarly 'without fear that the employees will be dissatisfied at not receiving the same benefits which the union might win from other employers.' . . . Finally, by permitting the union and employers to concentrate their bargaining resources on the negotiation of a single contract, multiemployer bargaining enhances the efficiency and effectiveness of the collective bargaining process and thereby reduces industrial strife."

The Board's approach in *Retail Associates* has been accepted in the courts, as have its decisions that unusual circumstances will be found where an employer is subject to extreme financial pressures or where a bargaining unit has become substantially fragmented. But as yet there is no consensus as to whether an impasse in bargaining in a multiemployer unit is an unusual circumstance justifying unilateral withdrawal by the Union or by an employer. After equivocating for a time, the Board squarely held that an impasse is not such an unusual circumstance. *Hi-Way Billboards, Inc.*, 206 N.L.R.B. 22 (1973). The [Fifth Circuit] refused enforcement of that decision, although it has since modified its views and now supports the Board. Similar decisions by the Board were also overturned by the Courts of Appeals in three other Circuits. . . . After again considering the question in this case, the Board issued its decision reaffirming its position that an impasse is not an unusual circumstance justifying withdrawal. Its decision was sustained and enforced by [the First Circuit].

III

We agree with the Board and with the Court of Appeals. The Board has recognized the voluntary nature of multiemployer bargaining. It neither forces employers into multiemployer units nor erects barriers to withdrawal prior to bargaining. At the same time, it has sought to further the utility of multiemployer bargaining as an instrument of labor peace by limiting the circumstances under which any party may unilaterally withdraw during negotiations. Thus, it has reiterated the view expressed in *Hi-Way Billboards* that an impasse is not sufficiently destructive of group bargaining to justify unilateral withdrawal. As a recurring feature in the bargaining process, impasse is only a temporary deadlock or hiatus in negotiations "which in almost all cases is eventually broken, through either a change of mind or the application of economic force." 243 N.L.R.B., at 1093–94. Furthermore, an impasse may be "brought about intentionally by one or both parties as a device to further, rather than destroy, the bargaining process." *Id.* at 1094. Hence, "there is little warrant for regarding an impasse as a rupture of the bargaining relation which leaves the parties free to go their own ways." *Ibid.* As the Board sees it, permitting withdrawal at impasse would as a practical matter undermine the utility of multiemployer bargaining.

Of course, the ground rules for multiemployer bargaining have not come into being overnight. They have evolved and are still evolving, as the Board, employing its expertise in the light of experience, has sought to balance the "conflicting legitimate interests" in pursuit of the "national policy of promoting labor peace through strengthened collective bargaining." *Buffalo Linen*, 353 U.S. at 95, 96. The Board might have struck a different balance from the one it has, and it may be that some or all of us would prefer that it had done so. But assessing the significance of impasse and the dynamics of collective bargaining is precisely the kind of judgment that *Buffalo Linen* ruled should be left to the Board. We cannot say that the Board's current resolution of the issue is arbitrary or contrary to law.

If the Board's refusal to accept an impasse, standing alone, as an unusual circumstance warranting withdrawal were the only issue in this case, we would affirm without more. But several Courts of Appeals have rejected *Hi-Way Billboards* on the grounds that impasse may precipitate a strike against one or all members of the unit and that upon impasse the Board permits the union to execute interim agreements with individual employers. These Courts of Appeals consider the possibility of such events as sufficient grounds for any employer in the unit to withdraw.

In *Beck Engraving Co.*, for example, [the Third Circuit] held that an impasse followed by a selective strike justified unilateral withdrawal from the bargaining unit. Because at that juncture labor relations law, as interpreted by the Board, would permit the union to execute an interim agreement with the struck employer, the Court of Appeals concluded that the union and the employer entering into such an agreement would be given unfair advantage against other employers if the latter were not permitted to withdraw from the unit. The Court of Appeals thought the employer's right to withdraw and the union's privilege of executing interim contracts should mature simultaneously. It concluded that the Board's approach too drastically upset the bargaining equilibrium to be justified in the name of maintaining the stability of the bargaining unit.

The Board's reasons for adhering to its *Hi-Way Billboards* position are telling. They are surely adequate to survive judicial review. First, it is said that strikes and interim agreements often occur in the course of negotiations prior to impasse and that neither tactic is necessarily associated with impasse. Second, it is "vital" to understand that the Board distinguishes "between interim agreements which contemplate adherence to a final unitwide contract and are thus not antithetical to group bargaining and individual agreements which are clearly inconsistent with, and destructive of, group bargaining." 243 N.L.R.B., at 1096. In *Sangamo Construction Co.*, 188 N.L.R.B. 159 (1971), and *Plumbers and Steamfitters Union No. 323 (P. H. C. Mechanical Contractors)*, 191 N.L.R.B. 592 (1971), the agreements arrived at with the struck employers were only temporary: both the union and the employer executing the interim agreement were bound by any settlement resulting from multiemployer bargaining. "[I]n both cases, since the early signers maintained a vested interest in the outcome of final union-association negotiations, the multiemployer unit was neither fragmented nor significantly weakened," 243 N.L.R.B., at 1096, and unilateral withdrawal was not justified.

On the other hand, where the union, not content with interim agreements that expire with the execution of a unitwide contract, executes separate agreements that will survive unit negotiations, the union has so "effectively fragmented and destroyed the integrity of the bargaining unit," *ibid.*, as to create an "unusual circumstance" under *Retail Associates* rules. . . .

The Board therefore emphatically rejects the proposition that the negotiation of truly interim, temporary agreements, as distinguished from separate, final contracts, is "inconsistent with the concept of multiemployer bargaining units." 243 N.L.R.B., at 1096. Although interim agreements establish terms and conditions of employment for one or more employer members of the unit pending the outcome of renewed group bargaining, all employers, including those executing interim agreements, have an "equivalent stake" in the final outcome because the "resulting group agreement would then apply to all employers, including each signer of an interim agreement." *Ibid.* Such interim arrangements "preclude a finding that the early signers had withdrawn from the unit." *Ibid.* Although the Board concedes that interim agreements exert economic pressure on struck employers, this fact should no more warrant withdrawal than the refusal of one employer to join with others in a lockout. In any event, the Board's view is that interim agreements, on balance, tend to deter rather than promote unit fragmentation since they preserve a continuing mutual interest by all employer members in a final associationwide contract.

The Board also rests on this Court's admonition that the Board should balance "conflicting legitimate interests" rather than economic weapons and bargaining strength. Its conclusion is that the interest in unit stability, recognized as a major consideration by both *Buffalo Linen* and *NLRB v. Brown*, 380 U.S. 278 (1965), adequately justifies enforcement of the obligation to bargain despite the execution of a temporary agreement.

Of course, no interim or separate agreements were executed in this case. But neither did the impasse initiate any right to execute an agreement inconsistent with the duty to abide by the results of group bargaining. Some Courts of Appeals, taking a different view of the interests involved, question the legitimacy of enforcing the duty to bargain where impasse has occurred and interim agreements have been or may be executed. We think the Board has confined itself within the zone of discretion entrusted to it by Congress. The balance it has struck is not inconsistent with the terms or purposes of the Act, and its decision should therefore be enforced. . . .

Notes

1. The Board found that impasse did not amount to sufficiently unusual circumstances to justify withdrawal from the multi-employer bargaining unit in part because

> if withdrawal were permitted at impasse, the parties would bargain under the threat of withdrawal by any party who was not completely satisfied with the results of the negotiations. That is, parties could precipitate an impasse in order to escape any agreement less favorable than the one expected. In addition, it is precisely at and during impasse, when bargaining is temporarily replaced by economic warfare, that the need for a stable, predictable bargaining unit becomes acute in order that the parties can weigh the costs and possible benefits of their conduct. 454 U.S. 404, 412, n.8.

The *Bonanno* Court approved of this reasoning. *Id.* at 412. As a result, it is not easy for an employer to exit a multi-employer group once bargaining has begun by claiming "unusual circumstances." *See, e.g., El Cerrito Mill & Lumber Co.*, 316 N.L.R.B. 1005 (1995). Is the *Bonanno* Board's rationale persuasive? On the other hand, multi-employer bargaining units are entirely voluntary and yet are not uncommon. Consider the reasons why employers would agree to enter into such units, particularly given the difficulty of exiting this kind of bargaining relationship.

2. The *Bonanno* Court also noted the Board's adherence to the view that "'the uneven application of economic pressure per se is not inconsistent with multi-employer bargaining.'" *Id.* at 415 n.9. The Court, describing the Board's position, added that:

> [T]he employer also has additional weapons at its disposal for exerting eco-nomic pressure. It can engage in a lockout, make unilateral changes in work-ing conditions if they are consistent with the offers the union has rejected, hire replacements to counter the loss of striking employees, and try to blunt the effectiveness of an anticipated strike by stockpiling inventories, read-justing contract schedules, or transferring work from one plant to another. The Board further notes that interim agreements do not always have the effect the Union desires. The signing of an interim agreement may not weaken the association's determination to resist the union's demands . . . and the eventual contract settlement may have terms more favorable to the employers than the interim agreements, requiring the union to give up its temporary gains. *Id.*

What values underlay the Board's and the Court's view of economic weapons?

2. Leased Employees

Chapter 3 discussed the difficult problem of determining whether two entities could be "joint employers" of employees and thereby subject to the legal respon-sibilities assigned by the Act to "employers." A closely related issue is whether so-called "leased employees"—that is, employees of a temporary help agency or other labor outsourcing entity (the lessor)—should be included in a bargaining unit that includes the lessee's employees. The following case discusses this modern challenge to the traditional employment relationship.

Miller & Anderson

National Labor Relations Board
Case 05-RC-079249, 364 N.L.R.B. No. 39 (July 11, 2016)

I. Introduction

The fundamental issue raised by the Petitioner's request for review is whether under [the Act] the employees who work for a user employer—both those employ-ees the user alone employs and those employees it jointly employs (along with a sup-plier employer)—must obtain employer consent if they wish to be represented for purposes of collective bargaining in a single unit, even if both groups of employees share a community of interest with one another under the Board's traditional test for determining appropriate units.

Anyone familiar with the Act's history might well wonder why employees must obtain the consent of their employers in order to bargain collectively. After all, Congress passed the Act to compel employers to recognize and bargain with the designated representatives of appropriate units of employees, even if the employers would prefer not to do so. But most recently in *Oakwood Care Center*, 343 N.L.R.B. 659 (2004) ("*Oakwood*"), the Board held that bargaining units that combine employees who are solely employed by a user employer and employees who are jointly employed by that same user employer and an employer supplying employees to the user employer constitute multi-employer units, which are appropriate only with the consent of the parties. . . . The *Oakwood* Board thereby overruled *M.B. Sturgis, Inc.*, 331 N.L.R.B. 1298 (2000) ("*Sturgis*"), which had held that the Act permits such units without the consent of the user and supplier employers, provided the employees share a community of interest. . . .

The Petitioner requests that the Board overturn *Oakwood* and return to the rule of *Sturgis* in its request for review of the Regional Director's administrative dismissal of its petition seeking to represent a unit of all sheet metal workers employed by Miller & Anderson, Inc. and/or Tradesmen International as either single employers or joint employers on all job sites in Franklin County, Pennsylvania.

We granted review to consider the important issue raised. . . . Following our grant of review, we issued a Notice and Invitation to File Briefs ("NIFB"). The NIFB invited the parties and interested amici to address one or more of the following questions:

> 1. How, if at all, have the Section 7 rights of employees in alternative work arrangements, including temporary employees, part-time employees and other contingent workers, been affected by the Board's decision in *Oakwood Care Center*, 343 N.L.R.B. 659 (2004), overruling *M.B. Sturgis*, 331 N.L.R.B. 1298 (2000)?
>
> 2. Should the Board continue to adhere to the holding of *Oakwood Care Center*, which disallows inclusion of solely employed employees and jointly employed employees in the same unit absent the consent of the employers?
>
> 3. If the Board decides not to adhere to *Oakwood Care Center*, should the Board return to the holding of *Sturgis*, which permits units including both solely employed employees and jointly employed employees without the consent of the employers? Alternatively, what principles, apart from those set forth in *Oakwood* and *Sturgis*, should govern this area?

. . . .

After carefully considering the briefs of the parties and amici and the views of our dissenting colleague, we conclude that *Sturgis* is more consistent with our statutory charge. Accordingly, we overrule *Oakwood* and return to the holding of *Sturgis*. Employer consent is not necessary for units that combine jointly employed and solely employed employees of a single user employer. Instead, we will apply the traditional community of interest factors to decide if such units are appropriate. . . . We also agree with the *Sturgis* Board's clarification that there is no statutory impediment to processing petitions that seek units composed only of the employees supplied to a single user, or that seek units of all the employees of a supplier employer and name only the supplier employer. . . . We remand the case to the Regional Director for further proceedings consistent with this Decision.

II. Overview of Precedent

A. Board Precedent Prior to Sturgis

A review of Board precedent demonstrates that units combining employees solely employed by a user employer and employees jointly employed by that same user employer and a supplier employer are not novel. In the early years of the Act's administration and continuing for 4 decades, the Board routinely found units of the employees of a single employer appropriate, regardless of whether some of those employees were jointly employed by other employers. The Board used its traditional community of interest test to decide whether such units were appropriate. Significantly, the Board identified no statutory impediment to such units, and the issue of employer consent was neither raised nor discussed.

Thus, in the 1940's, the Board included employees who worked for concessionaires in a unit of the employees of the retail department store where the concessions were located. . . . Although these concessionaires operated whole departments, the Board included the employees in these departments in the unit with the solely employed department store employees where the evidence demonstrated that the department store possessed sufficient control over the former to be deemed their employer, and where those employees shared a community of interest with the store's solely employed employees. On the other hand, the Board excluded employees in the departments operated by the concessionaires pursuant to lease or similarly-styled arrangements if they were solely employed by the concessionaires. In these cases, the Board noted that they did not share "sufficient interests" with the employees in the other departments to be joined for collective bargaining. . . . In the 1950s, the Board continued to include the employees in the leased departments in units with the store's employees. . . .

In the 1960s, the Board recognized that control over employees in leased departments may be shared between user and supplier employers and, hence, the employees may be jointly employed. . . . With this shared employment relationship, the Board continued to sanction units combining solely employed department store employees with jointly employed employees working in the leased departments, applying the community of interest test to decide whether jointly employed employees should be included in the unit. . . .

In 1969, the [Sixth Circuit] rejected an employer's challenge to a storewide unit that included jointly employed employees supplied by several employers in a unit with Kresge's employees. *S.S. Kresge Co. v. NLRB*, 416 F.2d 1225 (6th Cir. 1969), *enfg. in relevant part*, *S.S. Kresge Co.*, 169 N.L.R.B. 442 (1968). The employer contended that "to compel unwilling employers to bargain as joint employers will disrupt the collective bargaining process because each licensee may have independent ideas about appropriate labor policy." . . . The court specifically rejected this contention, relying on a similar case from the [Ninth Circuit] which rejected an employer's contention that a userwide (storewide) unit would have a "highly disruptive effect upon the store's operation, [and] will prejudice the licensees and not produce sound and stable collective bargaining relationships." *See Gallenkamp Stores Co. v. NLRB*, 402 F.2d 525, 531 (9th Cir. 1968). The *Gallenkamp* court also had rejected the employer's contention that the jointly employed employees of one the licensees "lack[ed] a sufficient community of interest" with the store employees to be included in the unit. . . .

In short, as of the end of the 1960s, no Board or court decision had barred, absent employer consent, units combining solely employed employees and jointly employed employees. To the contrary, the Board and the courts perceived no statutory impediments to units combining solely employed employees and jointly employed employees. Inclusion of the jointly employed employees was subject only to the Board's traditional community of interest standards.

During the next 2 decades, the Board continued to find appropriate collective bargaining units that combined employees solely employed by a single user employer and employees jointly employed by that same user employer and a supplier employer, provided the employees shared a community of interest under the Board's traditional test for determining unit appropriateness. . . .

Similarly, [one court] found no impediment to bargaining in units of these mixed groups of employees absent employer consent. Thus, in *NLRB v. Western Temporary Services, Inc.*, 821 F.2d 1258, 1265 (7th Cir. 1987), the court found that a user employer, Classic, was not prejudiced by the inclusion—in a unit with Classic's solely employed employees—of the part-time employees supplied to it by Western Temporary Services ("Western") whom Classic jointly employed (along with Western).

However, the Board's treatment of units combining jointly employed and solely employed user employees abruptly changed in *Lee Hospital*, 300 N.L.R.B. 947 (1990), without any explanation or even so much as an acknowledgement from the Board that it was breaking with precedent. The issue arose there in a convoluted manner. The petitioner sought a unit limited to certified registered nurse anesthetists (CRNAs) who worked in a department operated by Anesthesiology Associates, Inc. (AAI) for the hospital. The Regional Director found that CRNAs did not constitute an appropriate unit separate from other hospital professionals, because under the then applicable "disparity of interest" test applied to health care institutions, the CRNAs possessed no sharper than usual differences from the other professionals employed by the hospital. Accordingly, the Regional Director dismissed the petition. The petitioner sought review of this decision arguing, among other things, that the CRNAs were jointly employed by Lee Hospital and AAI, and that this joint employer relationship further evidenced a disparity of interest between the CRNAs and the other hospital professionals who were not jointly employed.

On review, the Board, unlike the Regional Director, concluded that the joint employer issue had to be resolved to determine whether a separate CRNA unit was appropriate. This was so because, according to the Board, "as a general rule, the

Board does not include employees in the same unit if they do not have the same employer, absent employer consent[.] Thus, if AAI is a joint employer, the CRNAs could be included in the unit with other professionals employed by Lee Hospital only with the hospital's consent[,] and [i]t is clear that Lee Hospital does not consent to such an arrangement." ...

In announcing this "general rule," however, *Lee Hospital* entirely ignored the Board's routine practice of finding appropriate units that combined employees solely employed by a user employer and employees jointly employed by that same user employer and a supplier employer. *Lee Hospital* also failed to offer any rationale in support of its supposed general rule. Instead, it simply cited in a footnote ... a single case — *Greenhoot, Inc.*, 205 NLRB 250 (1973) — in support of the supposed general rule.

The Board's decision in *Greenhoot*, however, had left undisturbed — indeed it had said nothing about — the Board's long-standing practice of finding appropriate units that combined employees solely employed by a user employer and employees jointly employed by that same user employer and a supplier employer absent employer consent. Instead, *Greenhoot* addressed the entirely different situation where a union seeks to represent a unit of employees who perform work for, and who are employed by, different user employers.

Subsequently, the Board applied the "rule" of *Lee Hospital* to prohibit any unit that would combine jointly employed employees with solely employed employees of one of the joint employers, absent consent of both employers. .... These cases applying *Lee Hospital* did not discuss, explain, or rationalize the "rule."

B. Sturgis

A decade later, the Board reexamined *Lee Hospital* in *Sturgis*. The Regional Director ... had issued a Decision and Direction of Election in *M.B. Sturgis, Inc.*, Case 14-RC-11572, in which he found appropriate a petitioned-for unit consisting of all employees employed by M.B. Sturgis, with the exception of 10–15 "temporary" employees used by Sturgis and supplied by Interim, Inc. The Regional Director found that the temporary employees were jointly employed by Sturgis and Interim, but that under *Lee Hospital*, they could not be included in the same unit with employees employed solely by Sturgis absent the consent of both Sturgis and Interim. ...

On review, the Board concluded that *Lee Hospital* had improperly extended the multi-employer analysis in *Greenhoot* to situations where a single user employer obtains employees from a supplier employer and a union is seeking to represent both those jointly employed employees and the user's solely employed employees in a single unit. The Board rejected the "faulty logic" of *Lee Hospital* that a user employer and a supplier employer — both of which employ employees who perform work on behalf of the same user employer pursuant to the user's arrangement with the supplier — are equivalent to the completely independent user employers in multi-employer bargaining units. .... The Board found that employer consent is not required for a unit combining the employees solely employed by a user employer and the employees jointly employed by that same user employer and a supplier employer, because such a unit is an "employer unit" given that all the employees in such a unit perform work for the user employer and all are employed by the user employer.... The Board held that it would apply traditional community of interest factors to decide if such units are appropriate.... Accordingly, the Board remanded the cases to the Regional Directors to decide the unit questions without regard to the restriction imposed by *Lee Hospital*....

C. Oakwood

Four years later, however, the Board changed course. In *Oakwood*, the Regional Director ... had ... found appropriate a petitioned-for unit of nonprofessional employees at *Oakwood*'s residential care facility.... The petitioned-for unit included both the employees who were solely employed by *Oakwood* and the employees who were jointly employed by *Oakwood* and its supplier employer, a personnel staffing agency. The parties stipulated that under *Sturgis*, the petitioned-for unit of the employees solely employed by *Oakwood* and the jointly employed supplier employees (who wore identification tags that were issued by *Oakwood* and that identified them as employees of *Oakwood*'s facility) was appropriate. However, *Oakwood* urged the Board to reverse *Sturgis*, contending that it was wrongly decided....

After granting review, the Board concluded that *Sturgis* was misguided both as a matter of statutory interpretation and sound national labor policy.... The Board concluded that Congress had not authorized the Board to direct elections in units encompassing the employees of more than one employer, and that the bargaining structure contemplated by *Sturgis* gives rise to significant conflicts among the various employers and groups of employees participating in the process....

III. Discussion

With the foregoing review of the Board's and the courts' historical treatment of combined units of jointly employed and solely employed employees in mind, we turn to our own analysis of the issue. We begin, as we must, with the statute itself. Section 1 of the Act sets forth the Congressional findings that the denial by some employers of the right of employees to organize and bargain collectively and the inequality of bargaining power between employers and employees, who do not possess full freedom of association, lead to industrial strife that adversely affects commerce. Congress therefore declared it to be the policy of the United States to mitigate or eliminate those adverse effects by "encouraging the practice and procedure of collective bargaining and by protecting the exercise by workers of full freedom of association, self-organization, and designation of representatives of their own choosing, for the purpose of negotiating the terms and conditions of their employment or other mutual aid or protection." 29 U.S.C. § 151. In short, the central purpose of the Act is "to protect and facilitate employees' opportunity to organize unions to represent them in collective bargaining negotiations." *American Hospital Assn. v. NLRB*, 499 U.S. 606, 609 (1991). Thus, Section 7 ... grants employees "the right to self-organization, to form, join, or assist labor organizations, to bargain collectively through representatives of their own choosing, and to engage in other concerted activities for the purpose of collective bargaining or other mutual aid or protection[.]" . . .

Section 9 . . . speaks to the implementation of employees' right to bargain collectively through representatives of their own choosing. Section 9(a) thus provides that representatives "designated or selected for the purposes of collective bargaining by the majority of the employees in a unit appropriate for such purposes, shall be the exclusive representatives of all the employees in such unit for the purposes of collective bargaining in respect to rates of pay, wages, hours of employment, or other conditions of employment[.]" . . . And Section 9(b) relevantly provides that "[t]he Board shall decide in each case whether, in order to assure to employees the fullest freedom in exercising the rights guaranteed by this Act, the unit appropriate for the purposes of collective bargaining shall be the employer unit, craft unit, plant unit, or subdivision thereof[.]" . . . But neither Section, nor any other portion of Section 9 or the Act itself, explicitly addresses whether the Board may find appropriate a unit that combines employees solely employed by a user employer and employees jointly employed by that same user employer and a supplier employer.

That circumstance establishes two important foundations for our consideration of the employer-consent issue. First, the Act does not compel *Oakwood*'s holding that bargaining units combining solely employed and jointly employed employees are appropriate only with the consent of the user and supplier employers. Second, precisely because the Act does not dictate a particular rule, we may find that another rule is not only a permissible interpretation of the statute, but also that it better serves the purposes of the Act. For the reasons explained below, we find that the *Sturgis* rule, not requiring employer consent to units combining jointly employed and solely employed employees of a single user employer, meets both of those criteria.

A. Sturgis Is Consistent with Section 9(b)

The "exact limits of the Board's powers" under Section 9 and "the precise meaning" of the term "employer unit" are not defined by the statute. *Pittsburgh Plate Glass Co. v. NLRB*, 313 U.S. 146, 165 (1941). Notably, however, the statutory definition of the terms "employer" and "employee" . . . are very broad, and, as described, Congress's "statutory command" to the Board, in deciding whether a particular bargaining unit is appropriate, is "to assure to employees the fullest freedom in exercising the rights guaranteed by th[e] Act[.]" [*Gallenkamp Stores Co. v. NLRB*]. In that context, we are persuaded that a unit combining employees solely employed by a user employer and employees jointly employed by that same user employer and a supplier employer logically falls within the ambit of a 9(b) employer unit. All the employees in such a unit are performing work for the user employer and are employed within the meaning of the common law by the user employer. Thus, the user employer and the supplier employer are joint employers of the employees referred by the supplier to the user for the latter's use. The employees solely employed by the user employer likewise plainly perform work for the user employer and are employed by the user within the meaning of the common law. In sum, a *Sturgis* unit comprises employees who, working side by side, are part of a common enterprise.

As *Sturgis*[, 331 N.L.R.B. at 1304–05] explained,

> That a unit of all of the user's employees, both those solely employed by the user and those jointly employed by the user and the supplier, is an "employer unit" within the meaning of Section 9(b), is logical and consistent with precedent. The scope of a bargaining unit is delineated by the work being performed for a particular employer. In a unit combining the user employer's solely employed employees with those jointly employed by it and a supplier employer, all of the work is being performed for the user employer. Further, all of the employees in the unit are employed, either solely or jointly, by the user employer. Thus, it follows that a unit of employees performing work for one user employer is an "employer unit" for purposes of Section 9(b). . . .

The restrictive view that the *Oakwood* Board and our dissenting colleague place on Section 9(b) is based on the erroneous conception that bargaining in a *Sturgis* unit constitutes multi-employer bargaining, which requires the consent of all parties. However, in the traditional multi-employer bargaining situation, the employers are entirely independent businesses, with nothing in common except that they operate in the same industry. They are often in competition for work with each other, operate at separate locations on different work projects, and hire their own employees. Multi-employer bargaining units are created without regard for any preexisting community of interest among the employees of the various separate employers. In fact, the Board developed the consent requirement in such cases precisely because the employers at issue were physically and economically separate from each other, their operations were not intermingled, and their employees were not jointly controlled.

In multi-employer bargaining, the unrelated employers on their own initiative decide to join an employer association and bargain through a mutually selected agent to match union strength and to avoid the competitive disadvantages resulting from nonuniform contractual terms. As an agency relationship cannot be compelled, multi-employer bargaining is voluntary in nature; unions may not coerce employers into joining associations which negotiate labor contracts on behalf of their members . . . Indeed, by conceding that employer consent is not required when a petition names two employers and seeks a unit composed of the employees jointly employed by the two employers, *Oakwood* itself recognized that a bargaining unit involving more than one employer is not ipso facto a "multi-employer bargaining unit."

There plainly is a distinction of substance between a *Sturgis* unit and a multi-employer bargaining unit. Put simply, as shown, in a *Sturgis* unit, all of the employees are employed by the user employer. . . . After all, the employees who are solely employed by the user employer share an employer (the user employer) with the contingent employees who are jointly employed by that same user employer and a supplier employer. Thus, a *Sturgis* unit fits comfortably within 9(b)'s sanctioning of an "employer unit." By contrast, although a multi-employer bargaining unit also involves more than one employer, there is no common user employer for all the employees in such a unit.

The legislative history relied on in *Oakwood*, which indicates that "Congress included the phrase 'or subdivision thereof' [in Section 9(b)] to authorize other units 'not as broad as "employer unit," yet not necessarily coincident with the phrases "craft unit" or "plant unit,"'" does not persuade us that a single user employer unit is inappropriate. That Congress sought to authorize the Board to find appropriate employer subunits hardly establishes that Congress sought to disallow units of employees of a user employer combined with employees who the user jointly employs with a supplier. Indeed, our dissenting colleague . . . cites no legislative history expressing disapproval of such units. The only concern expressed by either the Wagner Act Congress or the Taft-Hartley Congress with respect to bargaining units that included more than one employer was focused on industrywide or anticompetitive bargaining units and on multiple-worksite situations.

Tradesmen, several amici, and our dissenting colleague nevertheless contend that the Board is precluded from returning to *Sturgis*, relying on the following single phrase from Section 9(b) . . . .

The Board shall decide in each case whether, in order to assure to employees the fullest freedom in exercising the rights guaranteed by this Act, *the unit appropriate for the purposes of collective bargaining shall be the employer unit, craft unit, plant unit, or subdivision thereof*[.]

. . . Citing *Oakwood*, they reason that because the broadest permissible unit category listed in Section 9(b) is the "employer unit," with each of the other delineated types of appropriate units representing subgroups of the work force of an employer, "the text of the Act reflects that Congress has not authorized the Board to direct elections in units encompassing the employees of more than one employer." . . .

However, the proponents of this argument put more weight on those few words than they can reasonably carry. As we have explained, given the broad definition of "employer" and "employee" in Sections 2(2) and 2(3) of the Act, along with our statutory charge to afford employees "the fullest freedom" in exercising their right to bargain collectively, a combined unit of employees solely employed by a user employer and employees jointly employed by that same user employer and a supplier employer does not fall outside the ambit of a Section 9(b) "employer unit," because all work is performed for the user employer and all employees are employed, either solely, or jointly, by the user employer. And . . . finding such a unit to be appropriate is responsive to Section 9(b)'s statutory command and effectuates fundamental policies of the Act. Accordingly, we conclude that the Act does not preclude us from returning to *Sturgis*.

B. Sturgis Effectuates Fundamental Policies of the Act that Oakwood Frustrates

Sturgis is manifestly more responsive than *Oakwood* to Section 9(b)'s "statutory command" to the Board, in deciding whether a petitioned-for bargaining unit is appropriate, "'to assure to employees the fullest freedom in exercising the rights guaranteed' by th[e] Act[.]" [*Gallenkamp Stores Co. v. NLRB*]. The Board has recognized that "[a] key aspect of the right to 'self-organization' is the right to draw the boundaries of that organization—to choose whom to include and whom to exclude." . . . The *Sturgis* approach honors that principle because it does not require employees to obtain employer permission before they may organize in their desired unit. Nor does *Sturgis* mandate any particular bargaining unit for the contingent employees (who are jointly employed by a user employer and a supplier employer) and the employees solely employed by that same user employer. Rather, *Sturgis* leaves the employees free to choose the unit they wish to organize, provided their desired unit is appropriate under the Board's traditional test for determining unit appropriateness. Thus, *Sturgis* permits the jointly employed contingent employees to organize in bargaining units with their coworkers who are solely employed by the user employer if they share the requisite community of interest, while also leaving both groups free to organize separately if they would prefer to do so.

In contrast, *Oakwood* denies employees in an otherwise appropriate unit full freedom of association. Thus, even if the jointly employed employees and their coworkers who are solely employed by the user employer wish to be represented for purposes of collective bargaining in the same unit, and even if both groups share a community of interest with one another, *Oakwood* prevents them from so organizing unless the employers consent. Requiring employees to obtain employer permission to organize in such a unit is surely not what Congress envisioned when it instructed the Board, in deciding whether a particular bargaining unit is appropriate, "to assure to employees the fullest freedom in exercising the rights guaranteed by th[e] Act." 29 U.S.C. § 159(b). In fact, by requiring employer consent to an otherwise appropriate bargaining unit desired by employees, *Oakwood* has upended the Section 9(b) mandate and allowed employers to shape their ideal bargaining unit, which is precisely the opposite of what Congress intended.

Oakwood also potentially limits the contingent employees' opportunity for workplace representation. Under *Oakwood*, the contingent employees cannot organize in the same unit as the employees solely employed by the user employer unless the user and supplier employers consent. Some amici argue that *Oakwood* does not deprive the contingent employees of their Section 7 rights to organize because a union does not need employer consent if it files a petition that names just the supplier employer and seeks a unit of just the supplier employees or if it files a petition that names both the user and supplier employers and seeks a unit limited to the jointly employed employees. However, *Oakwood* would appear to deny employees and unions the first option in cases where the supplier employer establishes that the petitioned-for employees are jointly employed by a user employer. . . . Moreover, many supplier employers do not just serve one client; rather they serve many clients simultaneously, and accordingly, the supplier employees may be scattered among various locations. Given their isolation from one another, those employees may face near-insurmountable challenges in attempting to organize, and even if they do, it may prove extremely difficult for them to have their collective voice heard by their referring employer. As for the second option, there may be no union that wishes to name the user and supplier employers on a petition that seeks to represent a unit limited to the jointly employed contingent employees.

In any event, limiting the contingent employees to these options, by definition, deprives them of the full ability to associate for collective bargaining purposes with their coworkers who are solely employed by the user employer. It also deprives the solely employed employees of their full ability to associate with their contingent coworkers. And . . . it dilutes the bargaining power of both groups. In short, *Oakwood*'s interjection of a consent requirement in workplaces utilizing contingent workers creates an obstacle to workers' freedom to organize and bargain collectively as they see fit even when the contingent workers share a broad community of interest with the user's solely employed employees they work alongside.

Sturgis is also more consistent with the premise upon which national labor policy is based, because it permits employees in an otherwise appropriate unit to pool their economic strength and act through a union freely chosen by the majority so that they can effectively bargain for improvements in their wages, hours and working conditions. *See NLRB v. Allis-Chalmers Manufacturing Co.*, 388 U.S. 175, 180 (1967) (our national labor policy "has been built on the premise that by pooling their economic strength and acting through a labor organization freely chosen by the majority, the employees of an appropriate unit have the most effective means of bargaining for improvements in wages, hours, and working conditions."). . . . On the other hand, by requiring the two groups of employees to engage in parallel organizing drives and then parallel bargaining relationships, despite their shared community of interest and desire to bargain in a single unit, the *Oakwood* approach diminishes the bargaining power of both the employees solely employed by the user employer and the employees jointly employed by that same user employer and a supplier employer.

These deleterious effects of the *Oakwood* rule requiring employer consent are all the more troubling because of changes in the American economy over the last several decades. [The Board describes the modern fragmented workforce, which it had previously described in *Browning Ferris (BFI)*, 362 N.L.R.B. 1599 (2015).]

In *BFI*, we concluded that given our "responsibility to adapt the Act to the changing patterns of industrial life," this change in the nature of the workforce was reason enough to revisit the Board's then current joint-employer standard. . . . Just as was the case with respect to that standard, *Oakwood* imposes additional requirements that are disconnected from the reality of today's workforce and are not compelled by the Act. We correspondingly conclude that to fully protect employee rights, the Board should return to the standard articulated in *Sturgis*.

C. The Policy Arguments Advanced by Sturgis' Opponents Are Unpersuasive

Tradesmen, several amici, and our dissenting colleague also argue that returning to *Sturgis* would be unwise as a policy matter because it would hinder meaningful bargaining, threaten labor peace, and harm employee rights. They argue that this is so because *Sturgis* permits a bargaining structure that allegedly gives rise to significant conflicts both among the various employers and among the groups of employees participating in the process, thereby making agreement much less likely and increasing the chances for labor strife.

However, the specter of conflicts posited by *Sturgis'* opponents did not materialize during the many decades before *Sturgis* that the Board had "routinely found units of the employees of a single employer appropriate, regardless of whether some of those employees were jointly employed by other employers." . . . And *Sturgis'* opponents do not demonstrate that those problems materialized in the years between *Sturgis* and *Oakwood*.

Moreover, the amici and our dissenting colleague fail to show that collective bargaining involving a *Sturgis* unit is significantly more complicated than if the jointly and solely employed employees were in separate bargaining units, as envisioned by *Oakwood*. . . .

Accordingly, the claim that *Sturgis* gives rise to an unworkable bargaining structure—because there may be disputes on the employer side of the table over who has the responsibility to bargain over or pay for certain items—is unconvincing, because the potential for such disputes could be said to exist in every case involving joint employer bargaining, which has long been sanctioned by the Board and the courts. After all, in every joint employer bargaining case, more than one employer must sit at a bargaining table and bargain with the union that represents the unit employees.

Not surprisingly, the appellate courts have also rejected claims that inclusion of jointly employed employees in a unit of solely employed employees over the objections of one or more of the joint employers is inimical to effective collective bargaining. . . . [I]n *S.S. Kresge Co. v. NLRB*, the Sixth Circuit rejected the claim that "to compel unwilling employers to bargain as joint-employers will disrupt the collective bargaining process" because each of the joint employers may have independent ideas about appropriate labor policy. . . . The court explained: "Whether [this] asserted practical difficult[y] will occur is speculative." The court also agreed with the Ninth Circuit that just as the different entities have managed to resolve any differences between them in agreeing to do business with one another, so too should they be able to resolve any differences between them when it comes to bargaining. . . .

As for employee interests, to the extent that the user and supplier employers are unable or unwilling to give both the solely employed and the jointly employed employees everything they want, tradeoffs may have to be made. But the same would be true regardless of whether the bargaining takes place in two parallel units or one *Sturgis* combined unit. And, as *Sturgis* noted, "Even in units composed only of solely employed employees, it is common for groups of employees to have differing, even competing, interests. Unions and employers are routinely called upon to handle such differences, and do so successfully." . . . In *S.S. Kresge Co. v. NLRB*, the Sixth Circuit rejected a similar claim that the rights of the licensees' employees would be impaired if they were included in the same unit as the employees solely employed by Kresge because the solely employed employees would outnumber the others and therefore dominate union policy. . . . The court explained:

> There is the possibility that the employees in the departments operated by Kresge will dominate union policy. This, however, is a problem which is germane to all units encompassing different departments with divergent interests. Indeed, the same problem could arise if the appropriate unit consisted solely of Kresge employees, because employees in larger Kresge departments could impose their decisions on employees in smaller departments. Such a result does not mean that the unit is inappropriate, particularly when, as in the present case, there is a sufficient community of interest among the employees in the unit to suggest the problem will not be serious if it does occur.

Contrary to amici, *Sturgis* does not encourage a tyranny of the majority over minority interests. Under [*Sturgis*], the Board will not find a combined unit appropriate for the purposes of collective bargaining unless the two groups share a community of interest; moreover, by virtue of the union's status as exclusive representative of the unit, the union has a duty to fairly and in good faith represent the interests of *all* the unit employees, including in collective bargaining. . . .

Nor are we persuaded by the other policy arguments opposing a return to *Sturgis*. For example, some amici argue that the Board would harm contingent workers and the economy as a whole if it were to return to *Sturgis*. They reason that if the Board were to . . . return to *Sturgis*, it would discourage employers from entering into, or maintaining, alternative staffing arrangements because user employers will wish to avoid the costs, uncertainty and inherent difficulties presented by the prospect of bargaining in *Sturgis* units. But this employer wish runs counter to the Act's stated policy of encouraging the practice of collective bargaining. In any event, *Sturgis* leaves employers free to enter into, or maintain, such arrangements. In other words, we have decided to return to *Sturgis*, not to prevent employers from entering into, or maintaining user-supplier arrangements, but rather to better effectuate the policies of the Act if the employees affected by such arrangements choose to exercise their Section 7 rights.

The Chamber of Commerce . . . cautions that . . . returning to *Sturgis* would be bad for unions seeking to organize just the employees solely employed by the user employer, because "employers may use *Sturgis* as a weapon to dilute a union's support" and to preclude employees solely employed by a user employer "from being represented at all." The Chamber adds, "If the temporary [supplier] employees out-number the employees solely employed by the user, this possibility may well become likely." In our view, rather than undermining the case for returning to *Sturgis*, the suggestion that employers might choose which positions to take regarding the inclusion of the supplier employees based solely on tactical considerations relating to the election, contradicts their claims that combined units hinder collective bargaining, foster labor strife, and undermine employee rights.

Nor . . . can it fairly be said that returning to *Sturgis* would undermine Section 8(b)'s prohibitions. For example, nothing in *Sturgis* permits a union in any way to restrain or coerce an employer in the selection of his collective bargaining representative or grievance adjustor. Nothing in *Sturgis* permits a union to strike or to threaten, coerce, or restrain an employer to join an employer organization. Nothing in *Sturgis* forces an employer to bargain with a labor organization before it has been certified. And nothing in *Sturgis* eliminates the prohibition on secondary boycott activity. . . .

D. Response to the Dissent

Our dissenting colleague offers both policy arguments and statutory arguments against a return to *Sturgis*, but . . . we are not persuaded.

We have explained that our interpretation of the Act is consistent with its text and supportive of its policies. Our dissenting colleague does not argue, nor could he, that Congress has spoken directly to the issue in this case. Instead, the dissent repeatedly—but mistakenly—characterizes the bargaining that takes place in a *Sturgis* unit as "multi-employer/non-employer bargaining." As discussed above, it is not "multi-employer" bargaining because all the employees in a *Sturgis* unit perform work for the user employer and all the employees are employed (either solely or jointly) by the user employer. By contrast, there is no common user employer for all the employees in a multi-employer bargaining unit.

The dissent's contention that under *Sturgis*, an employer is required to bargain with respect to non-employees—in contravention of Section 8(a)(5)—is likewise mistaken. . . . [I]n a *Sturgis* unit, each employer is obligated to bargain only over the employees with whom it has an employment relationship (and only with respect to such terms and conditions which it possesses the authority to control). [*Sturgis*]. Accordingly, no employer bargains regarding employees it does not employ, and so our colleague's use of the term "non-employer" bargaining is inaccurate. To the extent that multiple employers will be required, as a practical matter, to cooperate or coordinate in bargaining, that is a function of the freely chosen business relationship between user and supplier employers that defines all joint-employer situations.

Contrary to our dissenting colleague's suggestion, we are not, by returning to *Sturgis*, abdicating our responsibility to carefully review and make an appropriate bargaining unit determination in each case. As the *Sturgis* Board explained, "By our decision today, we do not suggest that every unit sought by a petitioner, which combines jointly employed and solely employed employees of a single user employer, will necessarily be found appropriate. As in the Board's pre-*Greenhoot* cases, application of our community of interest test may not always result in jointly employed employees being included in units with solely employed employees." . . . The Board continued to carefully examine the community of interest factors in determining the appropriateness of petitioned-for units while *Sturgis* was in effect. . . . And, as our order in this case makes clear, no election can be conducted in the combined unit sought by the petitioner here unless, among other things, it is established that the employees supplied by Tradesmen to Miller & Anderson (who are allegedly jointly employed by both entities) share a community of interest with the employees solely employed by Miller & Anderson.

Our dissenting colleague is mistaken in asserting that the return to *Sturgis*, coupled with *BFI*'s restatement of the joint-employer standard, somehow creates an unprecedented situation. In *BFI*, the Board returned to its traditional test, endorsed by the Third Circuit. . . . *BFI* merely represents a return to the Board's "earlier reliance on reserved control and indirect control as indicia of joint-employer status." . . . Indeed, *Sturgis* itself cited several cases that relied on such factors. . . . Before the Board's restrictive joint-employer decisions of 1984 (overruled in *BFI*) and before 1990's *Lee Hospital* decision, the Board followed the same approach we endorse today: a broad definition of joint employment and a practice of including jointly-employed and solely-employed employees of a single user employer in the same bargaining unit, where they shared a community of interest. There is no evidence of destabilized collective bargaining during that long period. In any event, for the reasons explained here and in *BFI*, both rules are based on permissible constructions of the Act and effectuate the Act's policies.

IV. Conclusion

We hold today that *Sturgis* is more consistent with our statutory charge than *Oakwood*. Accordingly, we overrule *Oakwood* and return to the holding of *Sturgis*. Employer consent is not necessary for units that combine jointly employed and solely employed employees of a single user employer. Instead, we will apply the traditional community of interest factors to decide if such units are appropriate. *Sturgis*, 331 N.L.R.B. at 1308. We likewise agree with the *Sturgis* Board's sanctioning of units of the employees employed by a supplier employer, provided the units are otherwise appropriate. *Ibid*.

Notes

1. In *Miller & Anderson*, the Obama Board overturned the Bush II Board's decision in *H.S. Care LLC (Oakwood Care Center)*, 343 N.L.R.B. 659 (2004), which itself had overturned the Clinton Board's decision in *M.B. Sturgis, Inc.*, 331 N.L.R.B. 1298 (2000) ("*Sturgis*"), which had overturned the Bush I Board's decision in *Lee Hospital*, 300 N.L.R.B. 947 (1990). The Board's decisions in *Miller & Anderson*, and *Sturgis* stand for the proposition that the Board will certify bargaining units that contain both solely and jointly employed employees without the employer's consent. This is a return to the Board's normal rule that employer consent is not required

for bargaining-unit certification. *See, e.g., S.S. Kresge Co.*, 169 N.L.R.B. 442 (1968), *enf'd*. 416 F.2d 1225 (6th Cir. 1969). Which is the better rule for deciding how and whether leased employees should be included in a bargaining unit? Do permanent and leased employees share a community of interest? Is there another circumstance under the NLRA in which the employer's permission is needed before a group of employees may be included in a bargaining unit?

2. Why do pro-business Boards tend to favor employer consent in these circumstances and more union-friendly Boards tend to favor leaving the employer out of the decision? Could it be that the *Sturgis* rule facilitated organizing temporary and contingent workers?

3. *Miller & Anderson* and *Oakwood* are examples of Board oscillation. Given the Republican majority on the Trump Board, is this rule likely to flip-flop once again?

4. In *Hy-Brand I*, 365 N.L.R.B. No. 156 (2017), discussed in Chapter 2, the Trump Board criticized the *Miller & Anderson* majority for "unnecessarily overrul[ing] existing law to find a petitioned-for bargaining unit appropriate despite unrebutted evidence that the bargaining unit had ceased to exist more than 3 years before the Board issued its decision." *Id.* at 2017 WL 6403496, at *52. Although the Trump Board vacated that decision in *Hy-Brand II*, 366 N.L.R.B. No. 26 (2018), *supra*, this critique of *Miller & Anderson* suggests that the Trump Board may be willing to revert position once again. In fact, in an October 31, 2019, unpublished decision denying the employer's request for review in *Stericycle of Puerto Rico, Inc.*, Case 12-RC-238280, a Board panel consisting of Chairman John Ring and Members Marvin Kaplan and William Emanuel stated: "We do not pass on whether *Miller & Anderson* was correctly decided and would be open to reconsidering it in a future appropriate case."

IV. Testing an Incumbent Union's Majority Status

Section I of this Chapter noted that unions may be decertified through elections just as they may be certified. That section discussed when decertification elections may be held, and when they may not. This section discusses a related topic: unilateral actions an employer may take when it believes that an incumbent union no longer enjoys majority support among its employees and no bar exists to such challenges (as discussed in section 1). This topic involves a balancing of risks. There is a risk that some employers may cease dealing with unions because they are motivated by improper anti-union animus. On the other hand, recall from Chapter 5 that employers risk violating § 8(a)(2) if they deal with unions that enjoy only minority support regardless of their motivations.

What can an employer do if it believes a union lacks majority support? Traditionally, it could do three things: take a poll of its employees to determine whether the union has majority support; file a decertification petition seeking an election administered by the Board; or stop negotiating with the union and respond to any ULP charge that might result. The circumstances under which employers could take any of these actions were limited, however. First, employers could take such actions only during periods when the union's majority status was subject to challenge, (*i.e.*, not during the first year after an election, nor during the term of a valid contract bar). Second, the Board required employers to demonstrate that they had some form of good-faith doubt that the union enjoyed majority support. For the most part, the legal rules in this area cannot be found in the text of the NLRA. Rather, the Board crafted them.

In *Allentown Mack Sales and Serv., Inc. v. NLRB*, 522 U.S. 359 (1998), the Supreme Court reviewed two important aspects of the Board's handling of these cases. First, the employer challenged the Board's rule that the same type of "good-faith doubt" was required for polling, decertification election petitions, and refusals to negotiate. The court acknowledged that polling was a significantly less drastic step than refusing to negotiate, and described the Board's choice of a unitary standard as "puzzling." But it upheld the unitary standard because it was not so irrational as to be arbitrary or capricious, and was therefore within the Board's authority. *Id.* at 364. Second, the Court found that the Board had interpreted its own standard improperly. While the Board had the power to require "good-faith doubt" for these employer actions, the court found that in the instant case, the Board had in fact required more than good-faith doubt: "disbelief" rather than "uncertainty" that the union lacked majority support. Justice Scalia, writing for the majority, analogized to the difference between agnosticism and atheism. *Id.* at 367. Thus, the Board had acted improperly because it had announced one legal standard but, in fact, applied a different legal standard. *Id.* at 372–78.

In sum, after *Allentown Mack*, an employer was required to show it had "good-faith doubt" about the union's majority support to poll, file a decertification election petition, or refuse to deal with a union when no bar to a challenge to majority status exists. And "good-faith doubt" means "uncertainty" (like an agnostic), not "disbelief" (like an atheist).

After *Allentown Mack*, the Board reconsidered its rules in *Levitz Furniture Co.*, 333 N.L.R.B. 717 (2001), where it held that "an employer may unilaterally withdraw recognition from an incumbent union only where the union has actually lost the support of the majority of the bargaining unit employees, and we overrule *Celanese* and its progeny insofar as they permit withdrawal on the basis of good-faith doubt. Under our new standard, an employer can defeat a postwithdrawal refusal to bargain allegation if it shows, as a defense, the union's actual loss of majority status." The Board further explained that "employers [may] obtain RM elections by demonstrating good-faith reasonable uncertainty (rather than disbelief) as to unions' continuing majority status. We adopt this standard to enable employers who seek to test a union's majority status to use the Board's election procedures—in our view the most reliable measure of union support—rather than the more disruptive process of unilateral withdrawal of recognition."

Although *Levitz* followed Justice Scalia's opinion in *Allentown Mack* and was issued during the George W. Bush years, that Board was still chaired by the moderate

John Truesdale, a career NLRB employee with a reputation for impartiality. *Levitz* was never popular with the ever-more conservative leaning management bar, which finally had a chance to overrule *Levitz* in the following case.

Johnson Controls, Inc.

National Labor Relations Board
Case 10–CA–151843, 368 N.L.R.B. No. 20 (July 3, 2019)

This case involves what happens when employees—with no improper influence or assistance from management—provide their employer with evidence that at least 50 percent of the bargaining unit no longer wishes to be represented by their union, the employer tells the union that it will withdraw recognition when the parties' labor contract expires, and the union subsequently claims that it has reacquired majority status before the employer actually withdraws recognition. Under extant precedent, the Board determines the union's representative status and the legality of the employer's action by applying a "last in time" rule, under which the union's evidence controls the outcome because it postdates the employer's evidence. As we shall explain, this framework has proven unworkable and does not advance the purposes of the Act. Today, we adopt a new framework that is fairer, promotes greater labor relations stability, and better protects § 7 rights by creating a new opportunity to determine employees' wishes concerning representation through the preferred means of a secret ballot, Board-conducted election.

Under well-established precedent, an employer that receives evidence, within a reasonable period of time before its existing CBA expires, that the union representing its employees no longer enjoys majority support may give notice that it will withdraw recognition from the union when the CBA expires, and the employer may also suspend bargaining or refuse to bargain for a successor contract.[2] This is called an "anticipatory" withdrawal of recognition.

When the contract expires, however, an employer that has made a lawful anticipatory withdrawal of recognition still withdraws recognition at its peril. [Under *Levitz Furniture Co.*, 333 NLRB 717, 725 (2001), i]f the union challenges the withdrawal of recognition in a ULP case, the employer will have violated § 8(a)(5) if it fails to establish that the union lacked majority status at the time recognition was actually withdrawn. In making this determination, the Board will rely on evidence that the union reacquired majority status in the interim between anticipatory and actual withdrawal, regardless of whether the employer *knew* that the union had reacquired majority status. As a result, an employer that properly withdraws recognition anticipatorily, based on evidence in its possession showing that the union has lost majority status, can unexpectedly find itself on the losing end of an 8(a)(5) charge when it withdraws recognition at contract expiration. Moreover, [under *Lee Lumber & Building Material Corp.*, 334 N.L.R.B. 399 (2001), *enforced*, 310 F.3d 209 (D.C. Cir. 2002)],

---

2. The employer, however, must comply with the existing contract in the interim.

the remedy for that violation will typically include an affirmative bargaining order, which precludes any challenge to the union's majority status for a reasonable period of time—at least 6 months, as long as 1 year. And if, within this insulated period, the parties reach agreement on a successor contract, the union's majority status will again be irrebuttably presumed for the duration of that contract, up to another 3 years [*see General Cable Corp.*, 139 N.L.R.B. 1123 (1962)].

The facts of this case and others like it highlight the crux of the problem. Where the union possesses evidence that it has reacquired majority status notwithstanding prior disaffection evidence showing that it had lost that status, some unit employees necessarily must be "dual signers." That is, some employees must have signed both the anti-union petition and, subsequently, a union authorization card or pro-union counter-petition. And where this happens, unions and employers are generally unwilling to disclose the identities of signers on their respective sides, for fear that the other party may retaliate against them. Although one may wish it were otherwise, we cannot say this mutual concern of retaliation is wholly groundless.

Further, we believe there are better ways to settle disputes over a union's post-contract majority status than by relying on the "last in time" rule. In what often may be a contentious and confusing time for employees who are being repeatedly asked to express their representational preference, the "last in time" rule strikes us as ill-suited for making such an important determination. Moreover, we are concerned that the union's ability to gather its counter-evidence secretly, together with the "peril" rule of *Levitz*, creates an opportunity, if not an actual incentive, for incumbent unions to take advantage of the "last in time" rule to extend the bar against challenges to its representative status for years to come, to the detriment of employees' § 7 right to choose a different bargaining representative or to refrain from union representation altogether.

The framework we announce today addresses all these concerns and creates a mechanism that settles questions concerning employees' representational preference in the anticipatory withdrawal context through a Board-conducted, secret-ballot election, the preferred means of resolving such questions. In doing so, we overrule *Levitz* and its progeny insofar as they permit an incumbent union to defeat an employer's withdrawal of recognition in a ULP proceeding with evidence that it reacquired majority status in the interim between anticipatory and actual withdrawal. Instead, we hold that proof of an incumbent union's actual loss of majority support, if received by an employer within 90 days prior to contract expiration, conclusively rebuts the union's presumptive continuing majority status when the contract expires. However, the union may attempt to reestablish that status by filing a petition for a Board election within 45 days from the date the employer gives notice of an anticipatory withdrawal of recognition. Consistent with the Board's usual practice, we shall apply our new holding retroactively in this case and in other pending cases. Accordingly, we will adopt the judge's recommended Order and dismiss the complaint.

Facts

Johnson Controls manufactures, distributes, and sells interior automobile components from its facility in Florence, South Carolina. Since August 18, 2010, the Union has represented a unit of production and maintenance employees employed at the Florence facility. The parties' most recent CBA was effective from May 7, 2012, through May 7, 2015. Negotiations for a successor agreement began on April 20. However, on April 21, Johnson Controls was presented with a union-disaffection petition circulated by employees Brenda Lynch and Anna Marie Grant. The petition, titled "Union Decertification Petition," was signed by 83 of the 160 bargaining-unit employees and stated, in pertinent part:

> WE, THE UNDERSIGNED, EMPLOYEES OF Johnson Controls, Florence facility, DO NOT WISH TO CONTINUE TO BE REPRESENTED BY THE United Auto Workers, LOCAL UNION NO. 3066 (Local 3066) FOR PURPOSES OF COLLECTIVE BARGAINING OR ANY OTHER PURPOSE ALLOWED BY LAW. WE UNDERSTAND THIS PETITION MAY BE USED TO OBTAIN AN ELECTION SUPERVISED BY THE NATIONAL LABOR RELATIONS BOARD OR TO SUPPORT WITHDRAWAL OF RECOGNITION OF THE UNION.

There is no allegation that any of the disaffection signatures were tainted by supervisory involvement.

Later that same day (April 21), Johnson Controls notified the Union that it had received the petition and would no longer recognize the Union as the employees' bargaining representative when the parties' CBA expired on May 7. Johnson Controls also stated that it was cancelling the previously scheduled bargaining sessions for a successor agreement. In its April 22 response, the Union stated that it had not received a petition or any verifiable evidence that it no longer enjoyed majority support, and it demanded that Johnson Controls return to the bargaining table. On April 24, Johnson Controls refused to provide the petition or to continue bargaining.

The Union thereafter began soliciting authorization cards from bargaining-unit employees. The authorization cards stated:

Uaw Authorization Card

Date:

It's Time!

I, _____ authorize the United Auto Workers to represent me in collective-bargaining.

The cards included signature lines for the employee and a witness. Between April 27 and May 7, the Union collected 69 signed authorization cards, six of which were signed by employees who had also signed the disaffection petition ("dual signers").

On May 5, Johnson Controls informed the Union that it had not received any evidence from the Union that the Union continued to enjoy majority support among the bargaining-unit employees and that, in the absence of such evidence, it would withdraw recognition upon expiration of the parties' current contract. Although not mentioned by the judge, the Union responded by letter the following day, advising Johnson Controls that it "ha[d] credible evidence" that it retained majority support and was "happy to meet" to compare evidence. By letter dated May 7, Johnson Controls acknowledged the Union's request to meet but stated that it was "not willing . . . to share the names of the employees who signed the [disaffection] petition." Johnson Controls further stated:

> You indicate that despite the evidence the [Johnson Controls] has received from our employees, the [U]nion has evidence it has not lost majority support. However, while the employees provided the [Johnson Controls] with their evidence, to date the [U]nion has not provided any substantiated evidence supporting its position. Absent contrary evidence, we must rely upon the evidence in our possession and proceed as previously indicated.

Johnson Controls withdrew recognition from the Union on May 8. Immediately thereafter, Johnson Controls announced improvements to the employees' terms and conditions of employment, including a 3-percent wage increase and a match to employees' 401(k) retirement contributions.

On August 28, Lynch filed a petition for a decertification election in Case 10-RD-158949. Processing of that petition has been blocked, however, by the ULP charge the Union filed in this case.

At the ULP hearing, four of the six dual signers testified that on May 8—the day Johnson Controls withdrew recognition from the Union—they did not want the Union to represent them, and the judge credited their testimony. Based on the disaffection petition and the credited testimony of the four dual signers, the judge concluded that at the time Johnson Controls withdrew recognition, the Union had actually lost majority support. That is, adding these four dual signers to the 77 bargaining-unit employees who signed only the disaffection petition, 81 employees out of the 160-employee unit no longer wished to be represented by the Union. On this basis, the judge found the withdrawal of recognition lawful and dismissed the complaint.

Discussion

The issue presented here is whether Johnson Controls demonstrated that the Union had lost its majority status as of May 8, the date Johnson Controls withdrew recognition. Under current law, and declining to rely on dual-signer testimony (unlike the judge), all six dual signers would be counted as supporting the Union because they signed union authorization cards after having signed the disaffection petition. In other words, their prior signatures on the disaffection petition would be disregarded. We believe there is a better way to resolve anticipatory withdrawal cases such as this one. Before we explain our new framework, however, we will first review the legal context within which this case and others like it arise.

I. The Legal Context

Under § 9(a), the bargaining representative of an appropriate unit of employees is the representative "designated or selected for the purposes of collective bargaining by the majority of the employees in [such] unit," and § 8(a)(5) requires the employer of the unit employees to recognize and bargain with their 9(a) representative.[12] Under longstanding precedent, once a union has been designated or selected as the § 9(a) representative of a bargaining unit, it enjoys a presumption of continuing majority status, which under certain conditions is irrebuttable. Specifically, a union "usually is entitled to a conclusive presumption of majority status for one year following Board certification as [the exclusive bargaining] representative" of a bargaining unit.[14] In addition, under the "contract bar" doctrine, a union is entitled to a conclusive presumption of majority status during the term of a CBA, up to 3 years.[15] As the Supreme Court has observed [in *Auciello*] , "[t]hese presumptions are based not so much on an absolute certainty that the union's majority status will not erode as on the need to achieve stability in collective-bargaining relationships." At the end of the certification year or upon expiration of the CBA, the policy-based presumption of majority status becomes factually rebuttable.

Prior to *Levitz*, an employer could rebut the incumbent union's presumption of majority status by establishing either that the union did not enjoy majority status at the time the employer refused to bargain, or the refusal to bargain was based on a good-faith reasonable doubt, supported by objective considerations, of the union's majority status. [*See Celanese Corp. of America*, 95 N.L.R.B. 664, 671–675 (1951).] In addition, under the "anticipatory withdrawal of recognition" doctrine, while an existing contract would bar a *present* withdrawal of recognition, an employer that established good-faith doubt of the union's majority status within a reasonable time prior to the expiration of a CBA could announce that it did not intend to negotiate

---

12. . . . [A]n employer violates § 8(a)(2) by recognizing or continuing to recognize a union that lacks majority support. *See International Ladies' Garment Workers' Union v. NLRB (Bernhard-Altmann) v. NLRB*, 366 U.S. 731, 738–739 (1961). In *Levitz*, however, the Board created a safe harbor from 8(a)(2) liability for employers with evidence of actual loss of majority status that elect to file an RM petition for an election rather than withdraw recognition. . . .

14. *Auciello Iron Works, Inc. v. NLRB*, 517 U.S. 781, 786 (1996). Certain "unusual circumstances" are recognized as exceptions to the otherwise irrebuttable presumption of majority status during the certification year: defunctness of the union, schism within the certified representative, and radical fluctuation of the size of the bargaining unit. . . .

15. . . . Additionally, an affirmative bargaining order precludes any challenge to a union's majority status for a reasonable period of time. *See Lee Lumber*, 334 N.L.R.B. at 399. And under the "successor bar" and "recognition bar" doctrines, majority status is similarly irrebuttable for a reasonable period of time. *See UGLUNICCO Service Co.*, 357 N.L.R.B. 801 (2011) (successor bar); *Lamons Gasket Co.*, 357 N.L.R.B. 739 (2011) (recognition bar). We express no view as to whether *UGL-UNICCO* and *Lamons Gasket* were correctly decided.

a successor agreement, and it could then lawfully withdraw recognition and implement unilateral changes when the existing contract expired.

The "good-faith reasonable doubt" standard came under scrutiny in the Supreme Court's decision in *Allentown Mack Sales and Service, Inc. v. NLRB*, 522 U.S. 359 (1998). . . . . [T]he Board had found that the employer failed to demonstrate that it harbored a reasonable doubt of the union's majority status. Before the Supreme Court, Allentown Mack contended that the Board had effectively abandoned the "reasonable doubt" standard and would recognize an employer's reasonable doubt "only if a majority of the unit employees renounce[d] the union." At oral argument, the Board maintained that "the word 'doubt' may mean either 'uncertainty' or 'disbelief'" and that its reasonable-doubt standard "use[d] the word only in the latter sense." The Court rejected the Board's position and held that *doubt* means "uncertainty." Accordingly, it held that under the Board's reasonable-doubt standard, properly construed, the question was whether Allentown Mack had "a genuine, reasonable uncertainty" about the union's continued majority status. The Court also held that the Board could permissibly maintain a unitary standard for withdrawal of recognition, filing an RM petition, and polling, but it could also rationally adopt different standards, including more stringent requirements for withdrawal of recognition.

Thereafter, in *Levitz*, the Board abandoned the "good-faith doubt" standard for withdrawal of recognition and held that, at times when an incumbent union's majority support is rebuttably presumed, an employer may withdraw recognition only "where the union has actually lost the support of the majority of the bargaining unit employees." *Id.* at 717; *see id.* at 725 ("[A]n employer may rebut the continuing presumption of an incumbent union's majority status, and unilaterally withdraw recognition, only on a showing that the union has, in fact, lost the support of a majority of the employees in the bargaining unit."). At the same time, the Board stressed "that an employer with objective evidence that the union has lost majority support . . . withdraws recognition at its peril." *Id.* at 725. This means that if the union challenges the withdrawal of recognition in a ULP proceeding, the employer will have violated § 8(a)(5) if it fails to establish actual loss of majority status at the time recognition was withdrawn. *Id.*

. . . Subsequent to *Levitz*, . . . the Board incorporated the "actual loss of majority status" standard into its statement of the anticipatory withdrawal doctrine. Thus, an employer that receives evidence, within a reasonable period of time before its existing CBA expires, that the union representing its employees no longer enjoys majority support may lawfully refuse to negotiate a successor agreement and announce that it will not recognize the union after the contract expires. It must, of course, continue to recognize the union and adhere to the terms of the existing contract in the interim, since until the contract expires the union enjoys an irrebuttable presumption of majority status under the "contract bar" doctrine. *Levitz*, 333 N.L.R.B. at 730 n. 70. But, under *Levitz*, when an employer follows its anticipatory withdrawal of recognition with actual withdrawal when the contract expires, it does so at its peril: if the union challenges the employer's claim of loss of majority status in a ULP case, the employer will be found to have violated § 8(a)(5) if it fails to establish loss of majority status at the time it withdrew recognition. *Id.* at 725.

In combination, the change from the *Celanese* "good-faith doubt" standard to the "actual loss of majority status" requirement, plus the *Levitz* "peril" rule, created an opportunity that unions reasonably seized. An employer's anticipatory withdrawal of recognition became a signal to the union to mount a counter-offensive. If, in the interim between anticipatory and actual withdrawal, a union were able to reacquire majority status, the employer's withdrawal of recognition would violate § 8(a)(5). The remedy for that violation would most likely include an affirmative bargaining order, which would insulate the union's majority status from challenge for up to one year. And if a successor contract could be concluded within that insulated period, a new contract bar would take effect, giving the union up to 3 more years during which its majority status would be irrebuttably presumed. Moreover, an incumbent union need not show the employer its evidence of reacquired majority status prior to contract expiration. From one perspective, this rule is justified by concern that an employer might retaliate against employees should their identities and preferences be revealed. But it is also true that the union's ability to *covertly* reacquire majority status increases the odds that the employer's withdrawal of recognition will unwittingly violate § 8(a)(5), potentially resulting in an affirmative bargaining order, concomitant decertification bar, successor contract, and another contract bar.

II. Need for a New Framework

The issue presented in this case and in prior similar cases is how best to determine the wishes of employees concerning representation where the employer has evidence that at least fifty percent of unit employees no longer desire to be represented by the union, and the union possesses evidence that it has reacquired majority status. In these situations, as in this case, some unit employees are necessarily "dual signers." In resolving this issue, the Board is required to "balance the statutory goal of promoting labor relations stability against its statutory responsibility to give effect to employees' wishes concerning representation." After careful consideration, we do not believe the existing framework effectively serves either goal.

First, existing precedent does not properly safeguard employee free choice. In determining the dual signers' wishes, extant precedent follows a "last in time" principle, giving controlling effect to the later signature. Thus, an employee's disaffection signature is automatically invalidated by his or her subsequent reauthorization signature. Such a rule ignores the fact that dual signers have expressed both support for *and* opposition to union representation within a brief period of time. Moreover, it is quite possible that some dual signers may fail to understand that when they sign a union card or counter-petition after having signed a union-disaffection petition, they are effectively revoking their prior signature on the disaffection petition.[31]

---

31. For example, in the instant case, employee Jefferson testified that he "didn't really know what [the union authorization card] meant." And employee McFadden testified that "they had

Parties have sometimes sought to ascertain dual signers' representational wishes by asking them, at ULP hearings, what their sentiments were on the date recognition was withdrawn. Here, for example, the judge allowed such questions and relied on the testimony of four dual signers to find actual loss of majority status notwithstanding the Union's documentary evidence to the contrary. We cannot endorse this practice. Employees' testimony about their representational wishes, given in the presence of the parties' representatives and bound to displease one of them, is an unreliable substitute for a secret ballot, cast within the safeguards of a Board-conducted election.[32]

Second, existing precedent does not effectively promote labor relations stability, either. A union is under no obligation to disclose to an employer that it has reacquired majority status prior to the employer's actual withdrawal of recognition. Thus, an employer possessed of numerically sufficient disaffection signatures, and unaware of the union's counter signatures, will likely withdraw recognition at contract expiration and make unilateral changes, only to discover that it has violated § 8(a)(5). This results in an unwarranted disruption of the bargaining relationship, which could have been avoided had the employer known that its disaffection evidence had been superseded. The union may obtain a decertification-barring affirmative bargaining order as a result, but the bargaining relationship has still been unlawfully and unnecessarily disrupted. In contrast, if the union were permitted to re-establish its majority status through an election, there would be no unlawful disruption of the bargaining relationship, and the union would receive a new certification year if it won the election.

---

already told us that the Union was out, so I felt like signing [the union authorization card], you know, wouldn't make a difference. So I just signed it anyway." In noting this evidence, we do not rely on after-the-fact testimony to ascertain these employees' representational sentiments. We merely observe that this testimony illustrates the fallibility of the "last in time" rule.

32. The question of how to resolve dual-signer situations has plagued the Board. Two past Board members proposed addressing this issue by requiring the union to present its evidence of reacquired majority status. . . . In addition to removing the risk of unfair surprise, such a requirement would also (as former Member Johnson noted) discourage gamesmanship and eliminate unwitting violations of Section 8(a)(5), which disrupt bargaining relationships and typically result in the decertification-barring issuance of an affirmative bargaining order.

Although this proposal has merit, we believe a Board-conducted, secret-ballot election provided under our new framework is the better solution. First, as this case illustrates, both employers and unions may be reluctant to disclose their evidence to each other, or they may dispute which side should "go first." In this regard, we note that the Union's offer to compare its evidence with Johnson Controls's evidence contemplated an exchange of evidence, as the dissent acknowledges. Unlike the dissent, we read the Union's offer to disclose its evidence as conditioned on reciprocity. Had the Union intended an unconditional offer, it would have provided its evidence even though Johnson Controls did not do likewise. Second, the mandated disclosure proposal of past Board members accepts the "last in time" rule, provided the union timely discloses its evidence to the employer. We would not apply the "last in time" rule. When, as here, a majority of employees have validly withdrawn support from the union, evidence that some of them may have subsequently recanted gives rise to a situation that is best resolved through an election.

Third, the treatment of dual signers under current precedent is analytically unsound . . . *Levitz* establishes an unjustified asymmetry: the Board only allows an employer to prove the dispositive fact—a union's loss of majority support—with evidence the employer actually possessed and relied on, but it permits the union, through the General Counsel, to challenge that evidence with after-acquired evidence the employer did not possess. There is the following asymmetry as well. An employee's union authorization card "cannot be effectively revoked in the absence of notification to the Union prior to the demand of recognition." But an employee's signature on a disaffection petition *is* effectively revoked by a pro-union countersignature in the absence of notification to the employer prior to its withdrawal of recognition. Nowhere in *Levitz* or its progeny is there any explanation why an employee's signature on a disaffection petition, presented to an employer for the purpose of securing an end to union representation, should be treated differently than his or her signature on a union authorization card.

Finally, the Board's current treatment of dual signers under current precedent was questioned in *Scomas of Sausalito, LLC v. NLRB*, 849 F.3d 1147 (D.C. Cir. 2017). There, unbeknownst to the employer, the union reacquired majority status by obtaining signed union authorization cards from dual signers 3 days before recognition was withdrawn. Although the majority affirmed the Board's finding that the employer unlawfully withdrew recognition, Judge Henderson questioned whether an employer violates the Act at all "when, in good faith, it withdraws recognition from a union as a result of the union's intentional nondisclosure of its restored majority status." Moreover, the court unanimously refused to enforce the Board's affirmative bargaining order, citing the unintentional nature of the employer's violation and the union's having withheld the evidence of its restored majority status. Instead, the court indicated that in these circumstances, the question concerning representation should be resolved through an election.

We agree. The determination of union majority status through ULP litigation in cases like these has proven to be unsatisfactory. A Board-conducted secret ballot election, in contrast, is the preferred means of resolving questions concerning representation. Under current representation law, both employers and employees can obtain a Board-conducted secret ballot election when, as here, a sufficient number of unit employees have indicated that they no longer wish to be represented by an incumbent union.[38] We conclude that unions, too, should have an electoral mechanism to determine the will of the majority following an anticipatory withdrawal of recognition, and we believe that such a mechanism is preferable to the current *Levitz* regime.

---

38. Section 9(c)(1)(A) provides for elections petitioned for by employees seeking to decertify an incumbent union ("RD" elections). Section 9(c)(1)(B) provides for employer-petitioned elections to determine majority support ("RM" elections).

III. The New Standard

a. Anticipatory Withdrawal and the 45-Day Window Period

We reaffirm the settled doctrine that if, within a reasonable time before an existing CBA expires, an employer receives evidence that the union has lost majority status, the employer may inform the union that it will withdraw recognition when the contract expires, and it may refuse to bargain or suspend bargaining for a successor contract. A union that receives such notice of anticipatory withdrawal has a variety of options. Assuming it has grounds to do so, it may file a ULP charge alleging that the employer initiated the union-disaffection petition or unlawfully assisted it, that the petition fails to make the employees' representational wishes sufficiently clear,[40] that the petition is tainted by serious unremedied ULPs,[41] or that the number of valid signatures on the disaffection petition fails to establish loss of majority status.[42] However, the Board will no longer consider, in a ULP case, whether a union has reacquired majority status as of the time recognition was actually withdrawn. Instead, if the union wishes to reestablish its majority status, it must file an election petition. The Board will process the petition without regard to whether the parties' contract is still in force at the time the petition is filed.[43]

We recognize that so long as the contract remains in effect, the union's majority status is irrebuttably presumed. The election, however, is to determine whether

---

40. *Compare Highlands Regional Medical Center*, 347 N.L.R.B. at 1406 (finding that petition denominated "a showing of interest for decertification" did not establish that employees no longer wanted union representation), *with Wurtland Nursing & Rehabilitation Center*, 351 N.L.R.B. 817, 817–18 (2007) (finding that petition evidenced loss of majority status given that it expressly referenced removal of union).

In overruling *Highlands Regional Medical Center* to the extent it is inconsistent with today's decision, we do not reach the question of whether a petition that describes itself as a showing of interest for decertification may be relied upon to evidence nonsupport of the union as well as support for a decertification election. *Id.* at 1406 fn. 15. Such a question may be considered in the context of a future representation proceeding.

41. *See, e.g., Mesker Door, Inc.*, 357 N.L.R.B. 591, 596–98 (2011) (concluding that unlawful threats by employer's attorney and plant manager were causally related to employees' disaffection petition and thus the employer's withdrawal of recognition based on the petition was unlawful) (citing cases).

42. Under current law, an employer is not obligated to provide the union with a copy of its disaffection evidence at the time it withdraws recognition anticipatorily. We do not change that precedent. We believe that a union on the receiving end of an anticipatory withdrawal may readily acquire sufficient relevant information from its stewards and/or other pro-union employees to determine whether an unfair labor practice charge would be warranted. The sufficiency of the employer's disaffection evidence will, of course, be evaluated by the Board's regional office in its investigation of any unfair labor practice charge that may be filed regarding the employer's anticipatory withdrawal and refusal to bargain for a successor contract.

43. Consistent with existing law, a union satisfies the requirement for a showing of interest to support its petition if it is the certified or currently recognized bargaining agent of the employees involved or a party to a current or recently expired collective-bargaining agreement covering the employees in whole or in part. *See* Casehandling Manual (Part II) Representation Cases § 11022.1.

a majority of unit employees wish the union to continue to represent them *after* the contract expires. Although a union typically enjoys a rebuttable presumption of majority support post-contract, the fact that at least fifty percent of the unit has signaled its nonsupport of the union rebuts the presumption.

Accordingly, we modify the "anticipatory withdrawal of recognition" doctrine in two respects. First, the "reasonable time" before contract expiration within which anticipatory withdrawal may be effected is defined as no more than 90 days before the contract expires. This change removes any uncertainty as to what constitutes a "reasonable time" before contract expiration, and it aligns the start of the "anticipatory withdrawal" period with the usual start of the 30-day open period during which decertification and rival union petitions may be filed. Second, if an incumbent union wishes to attempt to re-establish its majority status following an anticipatory withdrawal of recognition, it must file an election petition within 45 days from the date the employer announces its anticipatory withdrawal. The union has 45 days to file this petition regardless of whether the employer gives notice of anticipatory withdrawal more than or fewer than 45 days before the contract expires. . . .

If *no* post-anticipatory withdrawal election petition is timely filed, the employer, at contract expiration, may rely on the disaffection evidence upon which it relied to effect anticipatory withdrawal; that evidence—assuming it does, in fact, establish loss of majority status at the time of anticipatory withdrawal—will be dispositive of the union's loss of majority status at the time of actual withdrawal at contract expiration; and the withdrawal of recognition will be lawful if no other grounds exist to render it unlawful.[46] If a post-anticipatory withdrawal election petition *is* timely

---

46. Following anticipatory withdrawal, the union will now have an electoral means to re-establish its majority status. If it chooses not to employ that means, the employer's disaffection evidence will be dispositive because it will be the only cognizable evidence of the unit employees' representational desires.

[I]f the union believes the employer is bluffing and does not, in fact, have evidence that the union has lost majority status, it can call the employer's bluff by filing a charge alleging that the employer's refusal to bargain for a successor contract violated § 8(a)(5). It can also file a petition for an election and an 8(a)(5) charge, and the block example, if a union receives notice of anticipatory withdrawal and has sufficient information to believe that the employer solicited disaffection evidence, it may file an election petition and an 8(a)(5) charge with a simultaneous offer of proof, thereby blocking the election. *See* § 103.20 of the Board's Rules & Regulations. We clarify, however, that if a union opts to file a ULP charge rather than an election petition first, or at all, we will not toll the 45-day period. Thus, a union must file an election petition within 45 days of receiving notice of anticipatory withdrawal. If the union chooses to first pursue a ULP charge, it will have no election recourse if it does not file an election petition within the 45-day window period.

Under the blocking-charge policy, the pendency of a ULP—regardless of whether it is meritorious—may prevent an election from occurring for an extended period of time. For this reason, among others, the Board plans to revisit the blocking charge policy in a future rulemaking proceeding. As of the issuance of this decision, however, the Board has not yet revisited the policy. Thus, for institutional reasons, we continue to maintain extant law pertaining to blocking charges. . . .

filed, the employer may still withdraw recognition at contract expiration since the union's post-contract presumption of continuing majority status has been rebutted by the employer's disaffection evidence, and the employer may withhold recognition unless and until the union's majority status is reestablished electorally. Under certain circumstances, however, such an employer may permissibly continue to recognize the union, as explained below.

Thus, an employer's numerically sufficient and untainted evidence that an incumbent 9(a) representative has lost its majority status, upon which the employer relies to withdraw recognition anticipatorily, will be dispositive of the union's loss of majority status at contract expiration. Accordingly, an employer possessing such evidence *may* withdraw recognition when the contract expires: the union's irrebuttable presumption of majority status disappears when the contract expires; its post-contract presumptive majority status has been rebutted by evidence that at least fifty percent of the unit employees no longer support the union; and its majority status may only be re-established through an election that has yet to be held. In recognizing the right of an employer, thus situated, to withdraw recognition at contract expiration, we protect the §7 right of employees to refrain from union representation and collective bargaining. In the interest of promoting labor relations stability, however, we do not *require* such an employer to withdraw recognition at contract expiration if the 45-day window period remains open or a union election petition has been timely filed and the election remains pending.

We recognize . . . that where an incumbent union has lost majority status, permitting an employer to refrain from withdrawing recognition as described above implicates §8(a)(2). Therefore, just as the Board in *Levitz* created a safe harbor from 8(a)(2) liability for employers with evidence of actual loss of majority status that choose to file an RM petition rather than withdraw recognition, . . . so also we create a safe harbor from 8(a)(2) (and 8(b)(1)(A)) liability to the extent necessary to accommodate the legal structure we adopt today. No employer that permissibly refrains from withdrawing recognition from a minority union in conformity with this decision will violate §8(a)(2) . . . , and no union that accepts such recognition will violate §8(b)(1)(A).

There is, however, one exception to the foregoing "safe harbor" rule. That exception is when a rival union has filed an election petition or intervenes in the incumbent union's representation case. In that situation, the employer must withdraw recognition from the incumbent, since continued recognition of the incumbent union would give it an unfair advantage over its rival. The employer may lawfully express its *preference* for one of the competing unions, but it may not continue to recognize the incumbent union to the disadvantage of its rival.

b. Impact of the New Standard on Unilateral Changes

Whether an employer may or should take unilateral action following a lawful withdrawal of recognition depends on the situation. As noted, except in limited circumstances, unilateral action by the employer would entail substantial risk. . . .

1. Gap period between contract termination and union election

If there is a gap between the date the contract terminates and the date of the election, an employer that makes unilateral changes in unit employees' terms and conditions of employment during that intervening period would not violate §8(a)(5), since the unit employees' showing of disaffection will have rebutted the union's post-contract presumption of continuing majority status. However, unilateral changes made after the election petition has been filed—during the pre-election "critical period"—could constitute objectionable conduct where the changes would reasonably interfere with employee free choice (for example, a wage increase or grant of benefits), warranting a second election if the union were to lose the first one.

2. Unchallenged election loss by the Union

If the union loses a post-anticipatory withdrawal election, has not challenged a potentially outcome-determinative number of ballots, and does not file election objections, the employer must withdraw recognition (if it has not done so already), and it may proceed to act unilaterally.

3. Challenged election loss by the union

Assuming the employer refrains from making changes pre-election, if the union *loses* the election and either had challenged a potentially determinative number of ballots or files election objections, or both, the employer would make unilateral changes after the election at its peril. If the disposition of the union's ballot challenges were to change the outcome of the election and result in a union victory, the union's representative status would be established as of the date of the election, and the employer's unilateral changes made after that date would violate §8(a)(5). Assuming no outcome-changing ballot challenges, if the union were to prevail on its objections, a second election would be directed, and the employer's unilateral changes prior to that election could furnish grounds for the union—if it loses the second election—to file objections yet again and obtain a third election. Of course, if the union's outcome-determinative ballot challenges and/or objections are overruled, the employer must withdraw recognition (if it has not done so already), and it may proceed to act unilaterally.

4. Employer challenges union election win

Similar considerations are brought to bear if the union *wins* the post-anticipatory withdrawal election, and the employer either challenged a potentially determinative number of ballots or files election objections, or both. Again, the employer would make unilateral changes at its peril. If the disposition of the determinative challenged ballots results in the union preserving its election win, the union's representative status would be established as of the date of the election, and the employer's unilateral changes made after that date would violate §8(a)(5). If the employer's objections are sustained and a second election directed, its unilateral changes in unit employees' terms and conditions of employment would furnish the union grounds to file objections to the second election and obtain a third election in the event it loses the second election. In other words, if an employer wants to avoid interfering with its own efforts to secure an efficacious rerun election, it should refrain from making unilateral changes until post-election proceedings have run their course.

Accordingly, as a practical matter, whereas withdrawing recognition after the contract expires following a lawful anticipatory withdrawal will generally be a risk-free act, making unilateral changes poses considerable risks. An employer should take these risks into consideration in its decision making, although we are well aware that the exigencies of running a business may exert other pressures. . . .

IV. Retroactive Application

[In this section, the Board holds that it will not apply the new rule retroactively.]

V. Ruling on the Merits

. . . On April 21, Johnson Controls was presented with a disaffection petition signed by 83 of the 160 bargaining-unit employees, over 50 percent of the unit. Later on April 21, Johnson Controls notified the Union that it had received the petition and would no longer recognize the Union as the employees' bargaining representative when the parties' CBA expired on May 7. Consistent with this announcement, Johnson Controls withdrew recognition on May 8, and the Union did not file an election petition. Because a majority of unit employees no longer wished to be represented by the Union at the time Johnson Controls withdrew recognition, Johnson Controls acted lawfully. Although the Union had solicited authorization cards from 69 bargaining-unit employees, six of whom were "dual signers," we do not consider this evidence for the purpose of determining whether Johnson Controls's withdrawal of recognition was lawful for the reasons fully explained in this decision. We also do not consider the dual signers' testimony about their true sentiments concerning representation on the date recognition was withdrawn, or testimony concerning the sentiments of other employees who did not sign the disaffection petition.

VI. Response To Dissent

Our dissenting colleague contends that our decision is contrary to the foundational principle that an incumbent union is entitled to a continuing presumption of majority support, which must be measured solely as of the time the employer withdraws recognition. Our colleague also contends that the Board should consider prohibiting employers from ever withdrawing recognition unilaterally and should instead require them to seek a Board election. We respectfully disagree.

Our colleague's single-minded focus on the irrebuttable presumption of majority status during the first 3 years of a contract term turns a blind eye to a salient aspect of anticipatory-withdrawal precedent. Under well-settled law, both before and after *Levitz*, an employer that receives evidence, within a reasonable period of time (now defined as 90 days) before a CBA expires, may lawfully do two things. First, it may lawfully announce that it will withdraw recognition when the contract expires (and with it, the union's conclusive presumption of majority status under the contract-bar doctrine). Second—and this is the salient point—it may *immediately* refuse to bargain or suspend bargaining for a successor CBA, at a time when the union's majority status is otherwise irrebuttable. That such a refusal is lawful can only mean one thing: the Board recognizes, and has long recognized, that the irrebuttable presumption of majority status is a policy-based presumption of law, not a presumption of fact, and that there are policy-based circumstances warranting an exception to this presumption when an incumbent union has actually lost majority status within a reasonable period of time before the contract expires. The presumption—the legal fiction—of the union's continuing post-contract majority status has been rebutted in fact, and it's pointless to pretend otherwise. Our framework accepts this reality and furnishes an electoral mechanism for the union to seek to regain majority status even before the contract expires, or shortly thereafter, with a consequent renewal of the certification-year bar. The dissent disregards this reality and prefers legal fictions instead.

The dissent compounds her error by faulting Johnson Controls for following through on its anticipatory withdrawal of recognition announcement without post-expiration affirmation of the union's continued loss of majority status. In this respect, she relies on unsupported presumptions of fact to buttress her unsupported presumption of law. For our colleague, the only thing that matters is whether Johnson Controls could prove loss of majority status on the date it withdrew recognition, shackled by restrictive evidentiary rules that (1) conclusively presume dual signers were union supporters; (2) count pro-union evidence in the union's possession whether or not the employer knew of it; and (3) exclude all evidence detracting from the union's support not in the employer's possession. §7 . . . creates a right for employees to be represented by a union of their own choosing, and it also creates a right for employees to refrain from such representation. The dissent's restrictive evidentiary rules effectively privilege the former right over the latter . . .

We also reject the dissent's advocacy for a rule under which all withdrawals of recognition would be unlawful absent an election. . . . [T]hat position was fully considered and rejected in *Levitz* by a unanimous Board. . . . We adhere to the views there expressed. In addition, it would be anomalous to hold that an election is the only means by which a union's representative status under §9(a) may be ended when unions may achieve 9(a) status through voluntary recognition as well as by an election. Moreover, unilateral withdrawal of recognition has been a lawful means of terminating a union's 9(a) status for many decades—and although, since *Levitz*, such withdrawal requires a showing that the incumbent union has lost its majority status, for most of the Board's history recognition could be lawfully withdrawn based on a lesser showing of good-faith doubt of the union's continuing majority status. See *Celanese Corp.*, 95 N.L.R.B. 664 (1951). Although we do not here propose returning to the good-faith doubt standard, the dissent establishes no valid basis for running to the opposite extreme and abolishing withdrawal of recognition altogether.

Order

The [ALJ's] recommended Order . . . is adopted and the complaint is dismissed.

MEMBER McFERRAN, dissenting.

In the name of promoting employee free choice and preserving stability in collective bargaining, the majority does the opposite: It permits an employer unilaterally to withdraw recognition from an incumbent labor union, in the face of objective evidence that the union has *not* lost majority support among the employees it represents. It then requires the union to petition for and win an election to regain its representative status, which should never have been stripped from it. This result—reached by reversing precedent unasked and without briefing—violates two foundational principles under the [NLRA]: first, that a recognized union is entitled to a continuing presumption of majority support, and, second, that a Board-conducted election—not empowering unilateral employer action—is the preferred way to determine whether an incumbent union continues to enjoy majority support. Indeed, the majority has invented an entirely new scheme that flips these longstanding principles on their head. . . .

Today, the majority imposes a contrived solution on a nonexistent problem. Employers in cases like this one face no real dilemma. The situation is this: Presented with objective evidence that the union has lost majority support—but precluded (under the Board's "contract bar" doctrine) from withdrawing recognition because a collective-bargaining remains in effect the employer announces that it *will* withdraw recognition *when the contract expires* (under the "anticipatory withdrawal" doctrine). But before the contract expires, and so before withdrawal can be effectuated, the union gathers evidence showing that it has *not* lost majority support, and, though not required to do so, even offers to share that evidence with the employer. What is the employer to do? The answer under *Levitz* is obvious: petition for a Board election.

Instead of following sound precedent, the majority constructs an entirely new scheme for addressing cases like this one. Disregarding the union's continuing presumption of majority support and dismissing the union's rebuttal evidence as immaterial, the employer is now permitted to oust the union as the employees' bargaining representative the second the contract expires—and the union remains ousted, unless and until it seeks and wins a Board election.

The Supreme Court has observed that when it comes to employers who unilaterally withdraw recognition from incumbent unions, "[t]here is nothing unreasonable in giving a short leash to the employer as vindicator of its employees' organizational freedom." That is precisely what *Levitz* and the Board's "anticipatory withdrawal" cases have done, with the approval of the federal courts. In contrast, the majority's apparent aim is to let employers off the leash completely, even in cases like this one, where it is clear that the employer is vindicating not "employees' organizational freedom," but rather its own interest in ousting a Board-certified union without an election. Here, letting employers off the leash means that unions and the workers that support them will get bit. That result may not trouble the majority, but it is inimical to the NLRA. Accordingly, I dissent.

Notes

1. Reviewing courts had approved the Board's rule announced in *Levitz. See, e.g., NLRB v. B.A. Mullican Lumber & Mfg. Co.*, 535 F.3d 271, 273 (4th Cir. 2008) (applying *Levitz* and finding the employer met its burden of presenting objective evidence); *NLRB v. HQM of Bayside*, 518 F.3d 256, 261 (4th Cir. 2008) (applying *Levitz* and finding that employer failed to meet its burden of presenting objective evidence); *Parkwood Dev. Cntr., Inc. v. NLRB*, 521 F.3d 404, 408–10 (D.C. Cir. 2008) (same).

2. What is the remedy when an employer unlawfully withdraws recognition? In *Lee Lumber and Bldg. Material Corp. v. NLRB*, 310 F.3d 209 (D.C. Cir. 2002), after finding that an employer violated §§ 8(a)(1) and (5) by unlawfully assisting employees in circulating a decertification petition, withdrawing recognition, and making unilateral changes based on the tainted decertification petition, the court approved the Board's order that the employer bargain with the union for a reasonable period of time.

3. Does it matter if the employer uses evidence suggesting a lack of majority support that it gained during a period when the union enjoyed an irrebuttable presumption of majority support? Suppose, for example, that the employer came across some information indicating a lack of majority support during the first year after a union won a certification election. Then, after the first year had passed, the employer withdrew recognition, relying on that same information. Should that be lawful? *See Chelsea Indus., Inc.*, 331 N.L.R.B. 1648 (2000).

4. As to why an employer's unilateral withdrawal of recognition is not necessary to effectuate the policy of the Act that employees should be able to reject incumbent unions, *Levitz* explained:

> Employers' invocation of employee free choice as a rationale for withdrawing recognition has, with good reason, met with skepticism. As the Supreme Court observed in *Auciello Iron Works v. NLRB*, "The Board is accordingly entitled to suspicion when faced with an employer's benevolence as its workers' champion against their certified union, which is subject to a decertification petition from the workers if they want to file one. There is nothing unreasonable in giving a short leash to the employer as vindicator of its employees' organizational freedom." 517 U.S. at 790. *See also NLRB v. Cornerstone Builders, Inc.*, 963 F.2d at 1078 ("unilateral withdrawal is based on the subjective belief of an inherently biased party"). 333 N.L.R.B. 717, 725, n. 45.

5. *NLRB v. Curtin Matheson*, *supra*, raised a different issue regarding what types of evidence and assumptions could support an employer's good-faith belief that a union lacked majority support. The issue was whether the NLRB was required

to presume that striker replacements did not wish to be represented by a union. Prior to this case, the Board had adopted various positions on this point. It first adopted a presumption that replacements did not favor the union. *See Stoner Rubber Co.*, 123 N.L.R.B. 1440, 1444 (1959). Later, it presumed that striker replacements supported the union in the same proportion that all members of the bargaining unit supported the union (the same rule used for new hires). *See Cutten Supermarket*, 220 N.L.R.B. 507 (1975). By the time of *Curtin Matheson*, the Board had decided it would presume nothing from the status of striker replacement and would instead analyze each case on its own facts. *See Buckley Broadcasting Corp. of Ca.*, 284 N.L.R.B. 1339 (1987).

In *Curtin Matheson*, Justice Marshall, writing for a 6–3 majority, held that this approach (no presumption) was within the Board's discretion. Also, the majority cited evidence that replacements did not, in fact, always oppose the union. Justice Scalia's dissent (joined by Justices O'Connor and Kennedy) argued that the only permissible presumption was a good-faith doubt that replacement workers supported the union. Studies have, however, cast doubt on Justice Scalia's belief on this issue. *See, e.g.*, Michael LeRoy, *Strike Crossovers and Striker Replacements: An Empirical Test of the NLRB's No-Presumption Policy*, 32 Ariz. L. Rev. 291 (1991).

Consider the various reasons people might cross a picket line and act as replacement workers. What presumption about union support or lack thereof, if any, is most appropriate? What presumptions should the Board have the discretion to use? What sort of empirical evidence is relevant to these questions?

Under the current "no presumption" rule, what evidence should the Board use to determine whether an employer is justified in believing that replacements do not support the union? In the past, the Board has found picket line violence and union demands that replacements be discharged to be highly probative. *See, e.g.*, *Stormor, Inc.*, 268 N.L.R.B. 860, 866–867 (1984) (replacements' crossing a picket line in the face of continued violence, along with other evidence, overcame Board's former presumption that replacements supported the union in the same proportion as the bargaining unit as a whole); *IT Services*, 263 N.L.R.B. 1183, 1185–88 (1982) (picket-line violence, union's demand that replacements be discharged, and antiunion statements by most of replacements, overcame same presumption).

V. Public-Sector Rules

A. Representation Elections

Most public-sector jurisdictions use rules that are the same or similar to NLRA rules for union elections. For example, public-sector jurisdictions generally require (typically in the statute itself) a 30 percent showing of interest in support of a representation petition. *See, e.g.*, Oh. Rev. Code § 4117.07(A)(1).

B. Bars to Elections

Public-sector jurisdictions also tend to use the election bars that have developed under the NLRA. The main difference is that often (although not always) in the public sector, these rules are written explicitly into the statute. *See, e.g.,* Oh. Rev. Code § 4117.07(C) (essentially codifying the "contract bar" rule). The public-sector context, however, can raise some interesting wrinkles.

Appeal of State Employees Association of New Hampshire, Inc., SEIU Local 1984

Supreme Court of New Hampshire
158 N.H. 258, 965 A.2d 1103 (2009)

Dalianis, J.

The petitioner, the State Employees' Association of New Hampshire, Inc., SEIU, Local 1984 (SEA), appeals an order of the New Hampshire Public Employee Labor Relations Board (PELRB) denying SEA's motion to dismiss the certification petitions filed by the respondent, the New England Police Benevolent Association (NEPBA), in which NEPBA sought to represent a bargaining unit of certain officers employed by the New Hampshire Department of Corrections (DOC). In denying the motion to dismiss, the PELRB ruled that the 2007–2009 collective bargaining agreement between the State and SEA did not bar the certification petitions. *See* RSA 273-A:11, I(b) (1999). We reverse and remand.

. . . The most recent collective bargaining agreement (CBA) between the State and SEA was executed on July 19, 2007. . . .

The State and SEA began negotiating the 2007–2009 CBA in January 2007. After more than thirty bargaining sessions, they reached a tentative oral agreement on June 14, 2007, which was reduced to a writing the following day, and finalized on or before June 20, 2007. This tentative agreement was submitted to the joint committee on employee relations for approval . . . and, on June 27, 2007, its cost items were funded by the legislature. . . . The tentative agreement was submitted to union members on June 22, 2007; voting on ratification closed on July 5, 2007. On July 9, 2007, NEPBA filed the instant petitions. Later that evening, SEA officials counted union member votes and certified that the tentative agreement was ratified by a vote of 1607 to 1405. On July 19, 2007, the Governor and SEA President signed the 2007–2009 CBA. . . .

RSA 273-A:11, I(b), which governs the timing of representation elections, states:

> Public employers shall extend . . . to the exclusive representative of a bargaining unit . . . [t]he right to represent the bargaining unit exclusively and without challenge during the term of the collective bargaining agreement. Notwithstanding the foregoing, an election may be held not more than 180 nor less than 120 days prior to the budget submission date in the year such collective bargaining agreement shall expire.

Under this provision, referred to as the "contract bar rule," a CBA bars an election for a new representative unless the election occurs "not more than 180 nor less than 120 days prior to the budget submission date in the year such collective bargaining agreement shall expire." RSA 273-A:11, I(b).

While the statutory contract bar rule concerns actual elections, the PELRB has promulgated *New Hampshire Administrative Rules*, Pub. 301.01 (Rule 301.01), which applies to certification petitions. . . .

Under this rule, where, as here, an exclusive bargaining representative is in place, a certification petition may not be filed sooner than 210 days nor later than 150 days before the employer's budget submission date in the year that the agreement expires. "The purpose for creating such a window is to allow for the conduct of an orderly election and still leave sufficient time, deemed 120 days prior to the budget submission date, for the parties to negotiate a CBA. . . .

The parties' dispute centers upon the first sentence of RSA 273-A:11, I(b), which insulates a certified representative from challenge "during the term of the collective bargaining agreement." NEPBA contends that its petitions were not filed "during the term of the collective bargaining agreement," because by July 9, 2007, the 2005–2007 CBA had expired and the 2007–2009 CBA had not yet been executed. Relying upon decisions by the [NLRB] interpreting its contract bar rule, NEPBA asserts that, for a contract to act as a bar to a certification petition, it must be signed by the parties. *See Appalachian Shale Products Co.*, 121 N.L.R.B. 1160, 1162 (1958). Because the 2007–2009 CBA was not signed until after NEPBA filed its petitions, it did not bar them.

SEA counters that, even if we assume, without deciding, that the 2005–2007 CBA expired on June 30, 2007, the 2007–2009 CBA barred the petitions because before NEPBA filed them, this CBA had been reduced to a writing, the legislature had approved legislation to fund all of its cost items, and voting on ratification had closed. Under these circumstances, SEA urges, the 2007–2009 CBA barred NEPBA's petitions.

Based upon our review of the relevant statutory scheme, construed as a whole, we hold that SEA's position best comports with the legislature's intent as expressed in the plain meaning of the pertinent statutes. We conclude, therefore, that the PELRB erred when it ruled that the 2007–2009 CBA could not act as a bar to NEPBA's petitions because the CBA had not been executed when those petitions were filed.

RSA chapter 273-A governs collective bargaining for state employees. This chapter obligates the State to negotiate with the certified representative of its employees regarding all cost items and "terms and conditions of employment affecting state employees in the classified system." RSA 273-A:9; *see* RSA 273-A:3 (1999). A cost item, as defined by RSA 273-A:1, IV (1999), is "any benefit acquired through collective bargaining whose implementation requires an appropriation by the legislative body of the public employer with which negotiations are being conducted." Any party seeking to bargain must serve written notice of this intent at least 120 days before the State's budget submission date. *See* RSA 273-A:3, II(a). Bargaining must begin "not later than 120 days before the deadline for submission of the governor's proposed operating budget." *Id.*

Assuming that the parties reach agreement, they must then submit the cost items contained therein to the proper legislative body. RSA 273-A:3, II(b). CBAs negotiated between a public employer and the union representing its employees are unenforceable until the proper legislative body ratifies the agreement's cost items. A public employer commits an unfair labor practice by . . . failing to submit to the legislative body any negotiated cost item. RSA 273-A:5, I(e) (1999).

The New Hampshire legislature is the legislative body that approves the cost items in CBAs affecting state employees. *See* RSA 273-A:9, V(d). The joint committee on employee relations reviews the items first and then submits recommendations to the legislature. *See* RSA 273-A:9, V. If the legislature rejects any part of the submission or takes any action that would result in modifying the terms of the cost items submitted to it, "either party may reopen negotiations on all or part of the entire agreement." RSA 273-A:3, II(b). . . .

Nothing in this legislative scheme suggests that a CBA remains unenforceable until it is executed. While the scheme contemplates that such agreements will be signed, *see* RSA 273-A:16, it does not require that execution take place before they are enforceable. There is no requirement, for instance, that the legislature act only upon signed CBAs. . . . Execution, under these circumstances, is merely a ministerial act.

Given this legislative scheme, we conclude that the PELRB erred when it ruled that the 2007–2009 CBA could not bar NEPBA's petitions because it was unsigned when NEPBA filed them. The record shows that when NEPBA filed its petitions, not only was the CBA reduced to a writing, as required by RSA 273-A:4, but its cost items had been approved by the legislature, *see* RSA 273-A:3, II(b), and union members had completed voting on whether to ratify it. Under these circumstances, we hold that NEPBA's petitions were filed "during the term" of the 2007–2009 CBA, and, thus, that the 2007–2009 CBA could bar them despite the fact that it was unsigned.

NEPBA argues that the PELRB's decision is correct, in part, because it is consistent with decisions of the NLRB. . . .

[T]he NLRB has required that, to serve as a bar, the agreement "must contain substantial terms and conditions of employment deemed sufficient to stabilize the bargaining relationship," and be signed by the parties before a petition is filed, "even though the parties consider it properly concluded and put into effect some or all of its provisions." *Appalachian Shale Products, Co.*, 121 N.L.R.B. at 1162–63. . . .

The rule of *Appalachian Shale*, that only a written agreement will bar the processing of an election petition, is essentially an effort to avert the danger that unions and employers may collude to defeat employees' representational wishes on the basis of illusory or fabricated agreements." *YWCA of Western Massachusetts*, 349 N.L.R.B. 762, 764 (2007). . . .

Under the NLRB's contract bar rule, if a petition is filed before the execution date of a contract that is effective either immediately or retroactively and is otherwise timely, the contract subsequently entered into will not bar the processing of the petition and the holding of an election. *City Markets*, 273 N.L.R.B. at 469. If the incumbent union prevails in the election, any contract executed with the employer is valid and binding. *Id.* If, however, the incumbent union loses, the contract is null and void. *Id.* at 469–70.

Significantly, the NLRB's contract bar rule, unlike New Hampshire's contract bar rule, is not mandated by statute. Rather, it "is an administrative device early adopted by the [NLRB] in the exercise of its discretion as a means of maintaining stability of collective bargaining relationships." *Direct Press Modern Litho, Inc.*, 328 N.L.R.B. 860, 860–61 (1999). Because it is an administrative device, "[t]he [NLRB] has discretion to apply a contract bar or waive its application consistent with the facts of a given case, guided by [its] interest in stability and fairness in collective-bargaining agreements." *Id.* at 861. By contrast, the New Hampshire contract bar rule is a creature of statute, and the PELRB has no discretion to waive it. . . .

Given the NLRB's broad discretion to waive its own contract bar rule, including its self-imposed requirement that to act as a bar, a contract must be signed, we have no way of knowing whether, if faced with identical facts involving a private-sector employer, the NLRB would have ruled as the PELRB did. We, therefore, are not persuaded that the PELRB's decision is consistent with the NLRB's jurisprudence. Had the NLRB been faced with these facts—a statutory mandate that bargaining take place within a certain time frame and that all cost items be approved by a legislative body, approval by the legislature of the legislation necessary to fund the agreement's cost items, and a written CBA which union members had already voted to ratify—it may well have waived its own contract bar rule. Under these circumstances, the interest in stability in labor relations appears to outweigh the employees' interest in a change of bargaining representative. Collusion is not an issue under these circumstances. . . .

NEPBA argues as well that the PELRB's decision is correct because it is consistent with the decisions of other jurisdictions. NEPBA, however, has not directed us to any jurisdiction with a statutory scheme similar to New Hampshire's that has adopted the NLRB's requirement that a CBA be signed before it may bar a petition. To the contrary, the three jurisdictions to which NEPBA points, Maine, Massachusetts and Vermont, have statutory schemes that differ from ours.

Maine's contract bar rule, set forth by statute, *see* 26 Me.Rev.Stat. Ann. § 967(2) (West 2007), is expressly based upon the NLRB's rule. . . . Thus, the fact that Maine has adopted the NLRB's signature requirement is consistent with its overall intent to mirror the NLRB's contract bar rule.

By contrast, the Vermont contract bar rule is merely an administrative rule that the Vermont Labor Relations Board may apply or waive as the facts of a given case may demand. *See* Vt. Labor Relations Board, *Case Law Summary of Labor Relations Decisions.* . . .

Similarly, the Massachusetts rule is an administrative rule that the Massachusetts Division of Labor Relations may waive for good cause shown. . . . Moreover, the statutory scheme in Massachusetts expressly requires that a public-sector CBA be executed before it is submitted to the Massachusetts Labor Commission for review and to the legislature for approval of its cost items. *See* Mass. Gen. Laws ch. 150E, §§ 1, 7 (Supp.2008). Accordingly, that Massachusetts requires a collective bargaining agreement to be signed before it may act as a bar is consistent with the statutory scheme there.

Because we conclude that the PELRB erred when it ruled that the 2007–2009 CBA could not bar NEPBA's petitions because it was not signed before they were filed, we reverse its ruling and remand for further proceedings consistent with this opinion. . . .

Note

Should the public sector use different contract bar rules than the private sector? Consider, in this regard, that collective bargaining in the public sector often takes longer than in the private sector, and that tentative agreements in the public sector often must be submitted to the employer's governing body for approval.

C. Bargaining Unit Determinations

Rules for bargaining units in the public sector are often quite similar to NLRA rules, but some interesting differences exist. First, recall from Chapter 2 that where public-sector laws cover supervisors, supervisors are generally not permitted to be in the same bargaining unit as the employees they supervise.

The most common difference is that public-sector rules usually include a preference for fewer, larger bargaining units as opposed to more numerous, smaller units. This approach was established early in the development of public-sector labor rules. *See* Eli Rock, *The Appropriate Unit Question in the Public Service: The Problem of Proliferation*, 67 Mich. L. Rev. 1001 (1969). It remains an important part of many current public-sector laws, either explicitly in statutes or adopted in case law, often expressed as a concern about "over-fragmentation" of public-sector bargaining units.

One rationale for this preference is that public employers prefer, for obvious reasons, standardized rules to cover, *e.g.*, all the individual public schools in a school district. A related concern is that while in the private sector, authority to bargain can be delegated to the heads of relatively small subdivisions of the employer, in the public sector, that may not be as feasible or even legal, due to the practical need or formal requirements for standardized conditions within or even among agencies. Further, the comparatively lengthy negotiation process for public-sector contracts also makes multiple units within the same agency unwieldy. Smaller units also can lead to destructive internal competition. Rock at 1006–08.

A few other variations exist. For example, Ohio law, contrary to the NLRB rule, empowers the labor board to insist on a more appropriate unit, even if the union has petitioned for a unit that is "appropriate." Oh. Rev. Code §4117.06(c) ("the board may determine a unit to be the appropriate unit in a particular case, even though some other unit might be appropriate"). Thus, in *Piqua City School Dist. Bd. of Ed.*, 16 OPER ¶ 1125 (Oh. SERB 1999), a union proposed a bargaining unit in a school consisting of all non-teaching personnel except bus drivers. The employer objected and proposed a unit that included bus drivers (as an aside, why do you think the employer did that?). The state labor board held that while both units were appropriate, the employer's proposed unit was better. Therefore, it ordered that the employer's proposed unit be used. For more on this "more appropriate" unit issue, *see* Andrea Knapp, *Anatomy of a Public Sector Bargaining Unit*, 35 Case Western Reserve L. Rev. 395, 404–05 (1985).

The preference for larger, less "fragmented" units also runs contrary to the NLRB's presumption that a single location in a group of chain stores is an appropriate unit. This preference also played a role in the following case, in which the Alaska Labor Relations Agency considered whether the rule in *American Hospital Ass'n, supra*, should be adopted under the Alaska public-sector labor statute.

Alaska Nurses Ass'n v. Wrangell Medical Center

Alaska Labor Relations Agency
Case No. 10-1591-RC, Decision and Order No. 296 (Nov. 30, 2011)

Statement of the Case

The Alaska Nurses Association (the Association) filed a Petition for Certification of Representative on December 14, 2010, seeing representation of a unit of registered nurses at the Wrangell Medical Center. The Association's petition states that seven employees comprise the proposed unit. . . . The Association's petition describes the unit as follows:

> INCLUDED: Non-Supervisory, under 8 AAC 97.990(a)(5), nurses at Wrangell Medical Center.
>
> EXCLUDED: All other employees

The Medical Center objects to the appropriateness of the proposed bargaining unit, arguing that a unit consisting exclusively of non-supervisory nurses would result in unnecessary fragmentation in conflict with AS 23.40.090. Instead, the Medical Center asserts that a wall-to-wall unit consisting of all non-supervisory employees at the Medical Center is the appropriate bargaining unit under AS 23.40.090. The Association counters that unnecessary fragmentation is not relevant in this case. . . .

Issues

. . . 2. Should we apply the provisions of the [NLRA] for determining appropriate units in health care facilities?

3. Under AS 23.40.90, would a bargaining unit consisting exclusively of non-supervisory nurses by the unit appropriate for the purposes of collective bargaining at the Wrangell Medical Center?

Findings of Fact

. . . The Medical Center is a small medical facility that combines long-term and acute care treatment for patients. . . .

There are currently 12 supervisory positions and 54 non-supervisory "regular employees at the Medical Center. . . .

None of the non-supervisory employees at the Wrangell Medical Center is currently represented by a labor organization. . . .

All non-supervisory positions at the Medical Center are organized by category and job classification. The clinical services positions are under the overall supervision of the Director of Nursing and include the following:

a. Medical Technologist

b. Medical Technician

c. Radiology Technician

d. Registered Nurse

e. Medical Social Worker

f. Ward Clerk

g. Scope Tech

h. Activities Director

i. Certified Nursing Assistant

j. Nursing Assistant

The financial services positions, listed under the Chief Financial Officer, include the following:

k. Medical Records Tech

l. Patient Accounts Representative

m. Payroll/Accounts Payable

n. Visiting Physicians Clerk

o. Floating Clerical.

The support services positions are under the Director of Environmental Services and include the following:

p. Cook

q. Housekeeper

r. Laundry Worker

s. Dietary Aide. . . .

All employees at the Medical Center are paid an hourly wage. . . . Registered nurses . . . are paid the highest median and highest average hourly wage. . . .

Qualifications, skills, and licensing requirements vary substantially from one position to another at the Medical Center. . . .

Because the Medical Center is a small facility with a relatively small number of employees, there is a significant degree of functional integration among the employees. . . .

Analysis

. . . 2. Should we apply the provisions of the [NLRA] for determining appropriate units in health care facilities?

Among its arguments, the Association asks this Agency to consider the [NLRA] as guidance here, find that the Medical Center is an acute care hospital, and apply the NLRA's presumption that nurses should have their own separate unit. The Association argues that we should consider the provisions in the "[NLRB] and the courts" that . . . "[t]ime and again, professionals are permitted to be in a different unit than non-professionals. A review of the education, training, and job duties performed by the nurses establishes that they are professional employees and should be treated as such." Later in its brief, the Association asserts as follows:

> Moreover, an analogy should be made to the findings of the [NLRB] with regard to acute care facilities. The Board has found eight presumptively appropriate units: 1) physicians; 2) registered nurses; 3) other professionals; 4) technical employees; 5) skilled maintenance employees; 6) business office clerical; 7) guards; and 8) other nonprofessionals. Nurses are clearly treated differently from technical, maintenance, business office clerical, and other non-professional employees. For acute hospital care, courts and the Board have made a clear distinction between nursing and other types of work performed. The Board's rationale is based on registered nurses having an impressive history of exclusive representation and collective bargaining and finding that a separate RN unit is justified on traditional community of interest grounds. In other words, federal law supports the idea that registered nurses belong in their own unit. Although ALRA is not bound by NLRB precedent on this issue, the logic of the NLRB's approach should be considered.

The Association is correct that the [NLRB] has regulations providing for eight appropriate bargaining units in the health care industry, generally as it asserted in its brief. . . .

We agree that the nurses at the Medical Center are dedicated, hard-working professional employees. They perform a vital role in the medical care of patients at the Medical Center. The evidence in this case shows that the nurses at the Medical

Center are required to perform not only the duties of their own position but some-times the duties and tasks of other employees at the Medical Center. They direct and help provide medical care pursuant to the team health care approach taken by the Medical Center's employees.

However, this Agency and our predecessor agencies have not previously required or deemed essential that we separate professional employees from non-professional employees in determining an appropriate unit for collective bargaining, whether it be an initial petition for representation or a petition to sever a group from a rep-resented bargaining unit. In fact, the agency's decisional history shows a relatively common thread of combining professional and other employees into mixed units, at both the state level and the political subdivision level. See, e.g., *Public Safety Employees Association v. City of Wasilla*, Decision and Order No. 286 (June 3, 2008) (combining professional police officers with other employees in a mixed unit); *Alaska Vocational Technical Education Center Teachers Association v. State of Alaska*, Decision and Order No. 262 at 3 (Feb. 19, 2003) (noting that the statewide general government unit, representing nonsupervisory state employees, includes technical, professional, and clerical personnel). . . . To separate out professional and nonpro-fessional employees in bargaining units under our jurisdiction would be a radical departure from agency precedent. If we were to depart from this long line of deci-sional precedent and adopt or apply the NLRB's regulations by "analogy," we would upset stability in labor relations under the Public Employment Relations Act.

We decline to make such a change and follow NLRB precedent here. First, our regulation 8 AAC 97.450(c) provides that "[r]elevant decisions of the [NLRB] and federal courts will be given great weight in the decisions and orders made under this chapter and AS 23.40.070—23.40.260 . . . ." This regulation applies only to NLRB and court decisions, not NLRB regulations. We realize there are many decisions addressing disputes over this section, but in any event, we find the NLRB regulation irrelevant and inapplicable to the above agency regulation.

Finally, we have already addressed a request to analogize "to the findings of the [NLRB] with regard to acute care facilities." *Alaska Nurses Association v. Fairbanks North Star Borough School District*, Decision & Order No. 258 at 10 (January 30, 2002). We addressed the NLRB's presumption of appropriate units for eight differ-ent health care positions, including nurses. In declining to adopt the NLRB's regu-lations and case law, we stated:

> We find a marked difference between the [National Labor Relations Act] and Alaska Public Employment Relations Act (PERA) regarding the deter-mination of an appropriate bargaining unit for professional employees. PERA clearly departs from the NLRA and the other states in this respect. Unlike the NLRA, PERA does not distinguish between professional and non-professional employees, regarding composition of bargaining units or otherwise. Contrary to the NLRA, PERA does not contain a definition of "professional employee," nor does PERA provide for separate units of nurses or other professional employees. We find it would be inappropriate

for this Agency to mandate, by decision and order, that nurses and other public employees deemed "professional" should have separate units due to this status alone. Whether PERA should provide distinctions for employees based only on their professional or other status is a decision that should be left to the legislative process. Barring any future amendments to PERA, we will continue to apply the traditional factors contained in AS 23.40.090, in determining appropriate units. Accordingly, we will not give great weight to decisions of the NLRB or federal courts on this issue. 8 AAC 97.450(b). (Decision and Order No. 258 at 11 (citations omitted)).

As noted, this Agency has a long history of finding that mixed units of professional and 'nonprofessional' employees are appropriate. As in Decision and Order No. 258, we are not persuaded that we should depart from this substantial and consistent precedent under the facts of this particular case.

3. Under AS 23.40.090, would a bargaining unit consisting exclusively of supervisory nurses be the unit appropriate for the purposes of collective bargaining at the Wrangell Medical Center?

... Our regulations provide that "relevant decisions of the [NLRB] and federal courts will be given great weight in the decisions and orders made under this chapter and AS 23.40.070 — 23.40.260 ...." Federal courts have endorsed the notion of determining community of interest on a case-by-case basis. The "central test is whether the employees share a 'community of interest,' that is, 'substantial mutual interest in wages, hours and other conditions of employment.'" ...

Community of Interest. The Wrangell Medical Center is a small facility. Because of its small size both in terms of physical size of the facility, the relatively small number of patients, and the relatively small number of employees, there is frequent contact among its employees, including nurses and other employees. This frequent interaction supports a strong community of interest in a wall-to-wall unit at the Medical Center. While nurses play a vital role in the provision of medical care at the Medical Center, they are assisted by other employees, and the medical care is provided on a team basis.

[The agency found a sufficient community of interest among all the employees on the issues of wages, hours, and other working conditions, and that the lack of a history of collective bargaining did not argue for or against the proposed unit].

Desires of the Employees. Some employees expressed a desire to be represented, while others expressed a desire for no representation for collective bargaining. We find this factor does not support either a nurses'-only unit or a wall-to-wall unit.

Fragmentation. We next must examine, under AS 23.40.090, the statutory mandate that "[b]argaining units shall be as large as is reasonable, and unnecessary fragmenting shall be avoided." Under the facts in this petition, we find that unnecessary fragmenting would result if the 8 non-supervisory nurses were placed into their own, separate bargaining unit from the other 46 employees. As we have stated frequently, the Medical Center is a small, combined-care facility. Given the limited size of the employee population at the Medical Center, the high degree of functional integration among all 54 employees, and the close similarity of wages, hours, and other working conditions, we conclude that the unit appropriate is a wall-to-wall unit. To find otherwise here would risk unnecessary fragmenting.

Based on the factors in AS 23.40.090, such as community of interest, wages, hours, and other working conditions of the employees involved, the desires of the employees, and the concern for unnecessary fragmenting in a small medical facility like the Medical Center, we conclude that a wall-to-wall bargaining unit is the appropriate unit for employees at the Wrangell Medical Center. . . .

Notes

1. To what extent does the decision not to follow the NLRB rule turn on the different treatment of "professional" employees under the Alaska statute than under the private-sector law? To what extent does it turn on concerns of "over-fragmentation"?

2. Should it matter at all under Alaska law if a proposed unit mixes professional and non-professional employees? Footnote 4 of the decision (not reproduced above) states, "[t]his is not to say that the status of 'professional employee' carries no weight in unit determinations." Given Alaska's statutory language, what weight should it carry?

3. Is the Alaska approach of at least more easily mixing professionals and non-professionals in the same unit preferable to the NLRB approach generally? Is this approach more appropriate in the public sector than in the private sector? Why or why not?

Alaska's labor agency may be more willing to combine different types of employees into one bargaining unit than most. *Public Safety Employees Ass'n, AFSCME Local 803 v. City of Whittier*, 2018 WL 2561079 (Alaska Labor Relations Agency, May 7, 2018), approved a unit composed of all police, fire, and EMS service employees in the city. The agency rejected the city's objections (among others) that the unit combined law enforcement and non-law enforcement personnel and both temporary and permanent employees. Does this reflect an especially aggressive concern about over-fragmentation, or realities about public services in at least certain parts of Alaska? (In 2019, Whittier had a total population of 220.)

4. For another case taking the traditional and still-common view that public-sector bargaining units should avoid over-fragmentation, *see Michigan Education Ass'n v. Alpena Community College*, 457 Mich. 300 (1998).

5. In partial contrast, § 9(b) of the Illinois Public Sector Relations Act, while listing fragmentation as a factor to consider, states that "fragmentation shall not be the sole or predominant factor used by the Board in determining an appropriate bargaining unit." 5 ILCS 315/9(b). In *Illinois Council of Police v. Ill. Labor Relations*, 404 Ill. App. 3d 589 (1st Dist. 2010), the court upheld the labor board's finding that a small unit was appropriate, despite "over-fragmentation" objections. The court noted the labor board's "softening" position on the fragmentation issue, 404 Ill.

App. 3d 589, 596, quoting the board as follows: "in some of our previous decisions, excessive concern with avoiding fragmentation and promoting economy and efficiency in public bargaining and contract administration consumed not only the employees' right to organize, but also the criteria set forth in [s]ection 9(b)." 404 Ill. App. 3d 589, 599.

6. In public institutes of higher education, full-time, tenure-track faculty are usually not in the same bargaining unit as part-time, adjunct faculty, on the theory that the employees lack sufficient community of interest. *See, e.g., Tompkins Cortland Community College Adjuncts Ass'n*, 50 PERB ¶4001 (NY PERB, Feb. 8, 2017). For a contrary example holding that over-fragmentation concerns require one unit for both types of faculty, see *Employees of Beaver County Community College*, 47 Pa. Pub. Employee Rep. ¶ 78 (Pa. Lab. Rel. Bd., Feb. 16, 2016).

7. Sometimes, small units are unavoidable. Indeed, the Ohio labor agency has held that a bargaining unit could have literally just a single member (here, a city Records Clerk). *Ohio Labor Council Inc. v. City of Maple Heights*, 34 Ohio Pub. Employee Rep. ¶ 100 (SERB 2017). It rejected the employer's argument that the statute's use of the term "employees" necessarily required more than one employee in a bargaining unit.

———

Some public-sector statutes explicitly define bargaining units for at least many employees. Most sweepingly, HAWAII REV.STAT. § 89-6 provides:

Appropriate bargaining units. (a) All employees throughout the State within any of the following categories shall constitute an appropriate bargaining unit:

(1) Nonsupervisory employees in blue collar positions;

(2) Supervisory employees in blue collar positions;

(3) Nonsupervisory employees in white collar positions;

(4) Supervisory employees in white collar positions;

(5) Teachers and other personnel of the department of education under the same pay schedule, including part-time employees working less than twenty hours a week who are equal to one-half of a full-time equivalent;

(6) Educational officers and other personnel of the department of education under the same pay schedule;

(7) Faculty of the University of Hawaii and the community college system;

(8) Personnel of the University of Hawaii and the community college system, other than faculty;

(9) Registered professional nurses;

(10) Institutional health and correctional workers;

(11) Firefighters;

(12) Police officers; and

(13) Professional and scientific employees, who cannot be included in any of the other bargaining units.

(b) Because of the nature of work involved and the essentiality of certain occupations which require specialized training, supervisory employees who are eligible for inclusion in units (9) through (13) shall be included in units (9) through (13), respectively, instead of unit (2) or (4).

Oʜɪᴏ Rᴇᴠ. Cᴏᴅᴇ § 4117.06, takes the more traditional approach for most, but not all, employees. It first provides:

(B) The board shall determine the appropriateness of each bargaining unit and shall consider among other relevant factors: the desires of the employees; the community of interest; wages, hours, and other working conditions of the public employees; the effect of over-fragmentation; the efficiency of operations of the public employer; the administrative structure of the public employer; and the history of collective bargaining.

This statute continues with rules at least very similar to NLRA rules. In a small variation, professionals and non-professionals may not be included in the same unit unless a majority of both groups consents. *Id.*, § .06(D)(1). As with the NLRA, guards and corrections officers may not be mixed with other types of public employees. *Id.*, § 06(D)(2). Police, fire, and state highway patrol employees may not be mixed with other types of public employees. *Id.*, § .06(D)(3).

Still, the Ohio statute has some special rules for state employees. Bargaining units may not include more than one institution of higher education. *Id.* § .06(4), but the Ohio labor board divided all other state employees into fourteen bargaining units, by job category (*e.g.*, paraprofessional human services; food service, custodial, and laundry; maintenance and trades; administrative support; health care professionals; social services professionals; engineering and science; and administrative professionals). *See In re State of Ohio*, 2 OPER ¶ 2423 (SERB 1985).

Consider how these two approaches differ from each other and from the NLRA. Which approach do you think is best for the public sector?

D. Decertification Elections

Public-sector jurisdictions usually provide the same rules for decertification petitions as under the NLRA: where no bar exists, they may be filed either by employees (with 30 percent support), or employers (who possess "good faith doubt" about the union's majority support).

Ohio has two interesting variations. First, under Rule 4117-5-01 of the Ohio SERB, while employee decertification petitions requesting a different union to represent the employees requires support from 30 percent or more of the bargaining unit, a petition stating that the workers want no union to represent them requires support from at least 50 percent of the bargaining unit. In the private sector and most public-sector jurisdictions, 30 percent is required for both. What are the policy arguments for and against the distinction in Ohio's rule?

Second, Ohio departs even further from private-sector law in regard to what employers are permitted to do, as the following case shows.

SERB v. Miami University

Supreme Court of Ohio
71 Ohio St. 3d 351, 643 N.E.2d 1113 (1994)

RESNICK, J.

Under SERB's present policy, an Ohio public employer may not unilaterally withdraw recognition of and/or refuse to bargain collectively with a certified union, despite any good faith doubt the employer may have concerning the union's continuing majority support among the unit's employees. Instead, an employer may cease negotiations with a certified union only during the pendency of a decertification or rival union petition after the granting of a stay by SERB. Thus, an employer is guilty of committing a ULP in violation of R.C. 4117.11(A)(5) when it refuses to negotiate with a certified union following the dismissal of a pending petition. *In re Marion Cty. Children's Serv. Bd.* (Oct. 1, 1992). This case presents a challenge to that policy.

Miami contends, and the court of appeals held, that SERB's policy, reflected in *Marion Cty. Children's Services Bd.*, is fundamentally inconsistent with the statutory framework of R.C. Chapter 4117 (the Ohio Public Employees' Collective Bargaining Act), federal private-sector labor decisions and SERB's own past decisions. SERB and AFSCME, on the other hand, concede that SERB's present policy regarding good faith refusal to negotiate represents a departure from private-sector precedent, but argue that substantial differences between the Ohio and federal statutes clearly warrant a different result.

In assessing SERB's policy, this court must afford deference to SERB's interpretation of R.C. Chapter 4117.... Our review is limited to whether SERB's policy is unreasonable or in conflict with the explicit language of R.C. Chapter 4117....

It is also important to note the relationship that federal decisions bear to Ohio public-sector labor law. Since "R.C. Chapter 4117's treatment of ULP cases is modeled to a large extent on the federal statutes that empower the NLRB to resolve ULP charges in cases within its jurisdiction ... the NLRB's experience ... can be instructive...." *Adena Local School Dist. Bd. of Edn.* 66 Ohio St.3d at 495. It is not, however, conclusive. The prime focus must remain whether the federal approach "comports with the goals of the General Assembly when it enacted those statutes, particularly R.C. 4117.11 (which defines ULPs)...."

Once certified, the representative's exclusive status is maintained until the representative is displaced in accordance with the procedures set forth in R.C. 4117.07.

Displacement occurs following a four step process: (1) a decertification or rival union petition is filed; (2) SERB investigates the petition, and if it finds reasonable cause to believe that a question of representation exists, holds a hearing; (3) if, following the hearing, SERB finds that a question of representation does exist, it must direct an election; and (4) SERB must certify the results of the election. R.C. 4117.07(A).

Prior to the enactment of R.C. Chapter 4117, federal decisions had already embraced the "good faith doubt" doctrine in the private sector. Under this doctrine, an employer who withdraws recognition and refuses to bargain with an incumbent union is not guilty of a ULP if the employer had a good faith or reasonable doubt of the union's continuing majority status. . . .

SERB first addressed the issue of whether a public employer in Ohio may decline in good faith to bargain with an incumbent union in *In re Cleveland City School Dist. Bd. of Edn.* (Feb. 1, 1985). . . . SERB went on to establish the policy that an employer may justifiably refuse to bargain with an incumbent union where a decertification or rival union petition is filed and a stay is granted by SERB. *Id.* at syllabus; *In re N. Canton City Schools* (Aug. 2, 1985). . . .

Later, SERB clarified its policy in *Marion Cty. Children's Services Bd., supra*. In that case, as in this case, the employer refused to bargain with AFSCME based on its assertion of good faith doubt following the dismissal of a decertification petition. SERB found that the employer committed a ULP by refusing to resume negotiations with AFSCME after the decertification petition which had been pending was dismissed. SERB did "not agree . . . that good faith doubt may be established apart from a pending petition." . . . Instead, after acknowledging its departure from NLRB precedent, SERB offered the following explanation:

> "Chapter 4117 neither provides for voluntary recognition of bargaining representatives outside the certification process nor contemplates voluntary withdrawal of recognition. Even when an employer is willing to voluntarily recognize a bargaining agent, this agent must be certified by SERB. (O.R.C. § 4117.05(A)(2)). Clearly, under Ohio law, certification is the benchmark which triggers a bargaining obligation.

> "Only SERB has the power to certify an employee organization as the exclusive bargaining agent, and only SERB can take away such a certification. The duty to bargain in Ohio Revised Code § 4117.08(A) exists as long as a certified or deemed certified exclusive bargaining agent exists and may temporarily be stayed only by SERB action.

> "Accordingly, we do not believe the Ohio statute contemplates allowing an employer to decide unilaterally to terminate a bargaining relationship conferred by certification.

> "There is no statutory basis for such unilateral action, and moreover, such action flies in the face of any good labor policy.

"Further, a review of private sector law in the area of good faith doubt convinces us that allowing employers to suspend bargaining obligations on this basis undermines labor stability and proliferates litigation to an extent not warranted by any benefits it affords. . . . Allowing employers to suspend bargaining obligations based on good faith doubt creates a conflict between the termination of the collective bargaining process by the employer on one hand, and the statutory duty to bargain with the certified bargaining representative on the other hand. Such a conflict has a resolution in the private sector where the employer may petition the NLRB for a Board-conducted election under Section 9(c)(1)(B) of the NLRA (an RM election). However, this is not the case in the public sector. Chapter 4117 does not contemplate an employer-initiated election where no petition is pending before the Board. Thus, in the public sector, allowing an employer to act on its 'good faith doubt' without Board action leads to an irresolvable conflict, which does not encourage good and sensible public policy. . . ." *Id.* at 3-57 to 3-58.

In reviewing SERB's policy, we note that the absence of any provision relative to the "good faith doubt" doctrine in R.C. Chapter 4117,[14] in spite of the substantial body of pre-Act private sector law on the subject, evinces a legislative delegation of policy-making authority to SERB in this area. We cannot say that SERB's policy choice, as reflected in *Marion Cty. Children's Services Bd.*, is unreasonable. Instead, its choice strikes a balance between employee rights and the status of a certified union under the Ohio Act.

Moreover, R.C. Chapter 4117 clearly establishes SERB as the conduit through which Ohio public-sector bargaining relationships must pass. Unlike the federal statutes, "[t]he wording of the Ohio Act suggests that, except where the union has enjoyed 'historical' (pre-Act) recognition, a union achieves full status as an exclusive representative only when it has been formally certified by SERB." Drucker, Collective Bargaining Law in Ohio (1993) 243, § 6.02(B)(2). Concomitantly, that status can only be displaced by SERB. R.C. 4117.07. It is not inconsistent with this scheme for SERB to preclude the cessation of bargaining without SERB's involvement.

Accordingly, a public employer in Ohio commits a ULP in violation of R.C. 4117.11(A)(5) when it unilaterally terminates bargaining with an incumbent union, despite its good faith doubt as to the union's continued majority status. . . . *Judgment reversed.*

Notes

1. Is the primary reason for Ohio's alternative approach in this area the language in the Ohio statute? Or is it a perceived difference between the public and private

---

14. Contrast this with, *e.g.*, 43 Pa.Consol.Stat.Ann. 1101.607(ii), which specifically provides that "a public employer alleging a good faith doubt of the majority status of said representative may file a [decertification] petition. . . ."

sectors? A different view of what constitutes good labor policy generally? Some combination of the three?

2. Is the Ohio approach a good one? If so, would it also be a good approach in the private sector? Why or why not?

3. In contrast, it is easier than normal to decertify unions covered by Missouri's state constitutional right to bargain collectively. *St. Louis Police Leadership Org. v. City of St. Louis*, 484 S.W.3d 882 (Mo. App. 2016), involved a decertification process an employer set up that, among other things, had no provisions for a union to challenge decertification and allowed decertification via petition without any actual voting. The court held this system did not violate the state constitutional right to bargain collectively or any other legal rule.

Chapter 8

Organizing Without an Election

I. Introduction

As you saw in the last chapter, the primary way that a labor union becomes the designated bargaining agent for a group of employees is through an NLRB election. But that is not the only way; in fact, the trend in private-sector union organizing is away from Board-administered elections and toward private agreements between unions and employers to decide representation questions. Unions increasingly seek "card check" agreements in which the employer agrees to recognize the union as the representative of a group of employees if a majority of those employees (or some higher threshold) signs cards authorizing the union to bargain on their behalf (*i.e.*, "authorization cards"). This chapter explains the causes and effects of this trend as well as the cases and statutory provisions governing it. It also discusses several states in the public sector that have adopted mandatory card check recognition rules.

In addition to traditional NLRB elections and voluntary card checks, there are two other possible ways to create a bargaining relationship. First, the NLRB may issue mandatory "*Gissel* bargaining orders." In such orders, the Board requires an employer to recognize a union if: (1) the union had demonstrated majority support at one point, and (2) the employer has committed ULPs that "have the tendency to undermine majority strength and impede the election processes." *NLRB v. Gissel Packing Co.*, 395 U.S. 575, 614–15 (1969). These orders are rare; as you will see, they require years of litigation, and are also disfavored by courts.

The private-sector portion of this chapter ends with a discussion of whether minority "members only" unions should be permitted in the private sector—another alternative to current practices. The chapter concludes with a brief section on related rules in the public sector.

II. Bargaining Orders in the Private Sector

A fundamental purpose of the NLRA is to encourage collective bargaining based on the principles of majority rule and employee free choice. But an employer's conduct can sometimes make employee free choice impossible. The Supreme Court case, *NLRB v. Gissel Packing Co.*, excerpted below (as well as in Chapter 3, regarding the distinction between employer predictions and threats), consolidates four cases—*Gissel Packing Co.*, *Heck's*, *General Steel Products*, and *Sinclair*—all of which raised the same legal question in similar contexts. In this seminal case, the

Supreme Court set out the circumstances under which the employer's duty to bargain arises—even though a union has lost an election, or an election was never held—where the employer has committed pervasive ULPs. The Court held that, in some such cases, the Board is authorized to issue a remedial bargaining order, now known as the *Gissel* bargaining order.

NLRB v. Gissel Packing Co.

Supreme Court of the United States
395 U.S. 575, 89 S. Ct. 1918, 23 L. Ed. 2d 547 (1969)

WARREN, J.

These cases involve the extent of an employer's duty under the [NLRA] to recognize a union that bases its claim to representative status solely on the possession of union authorization cards, and the steps an employer may take, particularly with regard to the scope and content of statements he may make, in legitimately resisting such card-based recognition. The specific questions facing us here are whether the duty to bargain can arise without a Board election under the Act; whether union authorization cards, if obtained from a majority of employees without misrepresentation or coercion, are reliable enough generally to provide a valid, alternate route to majority status; whether a bargaining order is an appropriate and authorized remedy where an employer rejects a card majority while at the same time committing unfair practices that tend to undermine the union's majority and make a fair election an unlikely possibility; and whether certain specific statements made by an employer to his employees constituted such an election-voiding unfair labor practice and thus fell outside the protection of the First Amendment and §8(c) of the Act, 29 U.S.C. §158(c). For reasons given below, we answer each of these questions in the affirmative. . . .

In each of the cases from the Fourth Circuit, the course of action followed by the Union and the employer and the Board's response were similar. In each case, the Union waged an organizational campaign, obtained authorization cards from a majority of employees in the appropriate bargaining unit, and then, on the basis of the cards, demanded recognition by the employer. All three employers refused to bargain on the ground that authorization cards were inherently unreliable indicators of employee desires; and they either embarked on, or continued, vigorous antiunion campaigns that gave rise to numerous unfair labor practice charges. In *Gissel*, where the employer's campaign began almost at the outset of the Union's organizational drive, the Union (petitioner in No. 691), did not seek an election, but instead filed three unfair labor practice charges against the employer, for refusing to bargain in violation of §8(a)(5), for coercion and intimidation of employees in violation of §8(a)(1), and for discharge of Union adherents in violation of §8(a)(3). In *Heck*'s an election sought by the Union was never held because of nearly identical unfair labor practice charges later filed by the Union as a result of the employer's antiunion campaign, initiated after the Union's recognition demand. And in *General Steel*, an election petitioned for by the Union and won by the employer was set aside by the Board because of the unfair labor practices committed by the employer in the pre-election period. [Editors' note: specific descriptions of the employers' ULPs are set forth in the notes following this case.]

In each case, the Board's primary response was an order to bargain directed at the employers, despite the absence of an election in *Gissel* and *Heck's* and the employer's victory in *General Steel*. More specifically, the Board found in each case (1) that the Union had obtained valid authorization cards from a majority of the employees in the bargaining unit and was thus entitled to represent the employees for collective bargaining purposes; and (2) that the employer's refusal to bargain with the Union in violation of § 8(a)(5) was motivated, not by a "good faith" doubt of the Union's majority status, but by a desire to gain time to dissipate that status. The Board based its conclusion as to the lack of good faith doubt on the fact that the employers had committed substantial unfair labor practices during their antiunion campaign efforts to resist recognition. Thus, the Board found that all three employers had engaged in restraint and coercion of employees in violation of § 8(a)(1) — in *Gissel*, for coercively interrogating employees about Union activities, threatening them with discharge, and promising them benefits; in *Heck's*, for coercively interrogating employees, threatening reprisals, creating the appearance of surveillance, and offering benefits for opposing the Union; and in *General Steel*, for coercive interrogation and threats of reprisals, including discharge. In addition, the Board found that the employers in *Gissel* and *Heck's* had wrongfully discharged employees for engaging in Union activities in violation of § 8(a)(3). And, because the employers had rejected the card-based bargaining demand in bad faith, the Board found that all three had refused to recognize the Unions in violation of § 8(a)(5).

Only in *General Steel* was there any objection by an employer to the validity of the cards and the manner in which they had been solicited, and the doubt raised by the evidence was resolved in the following manner. The customary approach of the Board in dealing with allegations of misrepresentation by the Union and misunderstanding by the employees of the purpose for which the cards were being solicited has been set out in *Cumberland Shoe Corp.*, 144 N.L.R.B. 1268 (1963), and reaffirmed in *Levi Strauss & Co.*, 172 N.L.R.B. No. 57 (1968). Under the *Cumberland Shoe* doctrine, if the card itself is unambiguous (i.e., states on its face that the signer authorizes the Union to represent the employee for collective bargaining purposes and not to seek an election), it will be counted unless it is proved that the employee was told that the card was to be used solely for the purpose of obtaining an election. In *General Steel*, the trial examiner considered the allegations of misrepresentation at length and, applying the Board's customary analysis, rejected the claims with findings that were adopted by the Board and are reprinted in the margin.

Consequently, the Board ordered the companies to cease and desist from their unfair labor practices, to offer reinstatement and back pay to the employees who had been discriminatorily discharged, to bargain with the Unions on request, and to post the appropriate notices.

On appeal, . . . the Fourth Circuit, . . . in each of the three cases sustained the Board's findings as to the §§ 8(a)(1) and (3) violations, but rejected the Board's findings that the employers' refusal to bargain violated § 8(a)(5) and declined to enforce those portions of the Board's orders directing the . . . companies to bargain in good faith. The court based its § 8(a)(5) rulings on its 1967 decisions raising the same fundamental issues. . . . The court in those cases held that the 1947 Taft-Hartley amendments . . . , which permitted the Board to resolve representation disputes by certification under § 9(c) only by secret ballot election, withdrew from the Board the authority to order an employer to bargain under § 8(a)(5) on the basis of cards, in the absence of NLRB certification, unless the employer knows independently of the cards that there is in fact no representation dispute. The court held that the cards themselves were so inherently unreliable that their use gave an employer virtually an automatic, good faith claim that such a dispute existed, for which a secret election was necessary. Thus, these rulings established that a company could not be ordered to bargain unless (1) there was no question about a Union's majority status (either because the employer agreed the cards were valid or had conducted his own poll so indicating), or (2) the employer's §§ 8(a)(1) and (3) unfair labor practices committed during the representation campaign were so extensive and pervasive that a bargaining order was the only available Board remedy irrespective of a card majority. . . .

In No. 585 [the Teamsters attempted to organize the Sinclair Company]. . . . During the two or three weeks immediately prior to the election on December 9, the president sent the employees a pamphlet captioned: "Do you want another 13-week strike?" stating, inter alia, that: "We have no doubt that the Teamsters Union can again close the Wire Weaving Department and the entire plant by a strike. We have no hopes that the Teamsters Union Bosses will not call a strike. . . . The Teamsters Union is a strike happy outfit." Similar communications followed in late November, including one stressing the Teamsters' "hoodlum control." Two days before the election, the Company sent out another pamphlet that was entitled: "Let's Look at the Record," and that purported to be an obituary of companies in the Holyoke-Springfield, Massachusetts, area that had allegedly gone out of business because of union demands, eliminating some 3,500 jobs; the first page carried a large cartoon showing the preparation of a grave for the Sinclair Company and other headstones containing the names of other plants allegedly victimized by the unions. Finally, on the day before the election, the president made another personal appeal to his employees to reject the Union. He repeated that the Company's financial condition was precarious; that a possible strike would jeopardize the continued operation of the plant; and that age and lack of education would make re-employment difficult. The Union lost the election 7–6, and then filed both objections to the election and unfair labor practice charges which were consolidated for hearing before the trial examiner.

The Board agreed with the trial examiner that the president's communications with his employees, when considered as a whole, "reasonably tended to convey to the employees the belief or impression that selection of the Union in the forthcoming election could lead (the Company) to close its plant, or to the transfer of the weaving production, with the resultant loss of jobs to the wire weavers." Thus, the Board found that under the "totality of the circumstances" petitioner's activities constituted a violation of §8(a)(1) of the Act. The Board further agreed with the trial examiner that petitioner's activities, because they "also interfered with the exercise of a free and untrammeled choice in the election," and "tended to foreclose the possibility" of holding a fair election, required that the election be set aside. The Board also found that the Union had a valid card majority (the unambiguous cards . . . went unchallenged) when it demanded recognition initially and that the Company declined recognition, not because of a good faith doubt as to the majority status, but, as the §8(a)(1) violations indicated, in order to gain time to dissipate that status-in violation of §8(a)(5). Consequently, the Board set the election aside, entered a cease-and-desist order, and ordered the Company to bargain on request.

On appeal, the First Circuit sustained the Board's findings and conclusions and enforced its order in full. The court rejected the Company's proposition that the inherent unreliability of authorization cards entitled an employer automatically to insist on an election, noting that the representative status of a union may be shown by means other than an election; the court thus reaffirmed its stance among those circuits disavowing the Fourth Circuit's approach to authorization cards. . . . For reasons given below, we reverse the decisions of the [the Fourth Circuit] and affirm the ruling of [the First Circuit].

II.

In urging us to reverse the Fourth Circuit and to affirm the First Circuit, the [NLRB] contends that we should approve . . . its current practice, which is briefly as follows. When confronted by a recognition demand based on possession of cards allegedly signed by a majority of his employees, an employer need not grant recognition immediately, but may, unless he has knowledge independently of the cards that the union has a majority, decline the union's request and insist on an election, either by requesting the union to file an election petition or by filing such a petition himself under §9(c)(1)(B). If, however, the employer commits independent and substantial unfair labor practices disruptive of election conditions, the Board may withhold the election or set it aside, and issue instead a bargaining order as a remedy for the various violations. . . .

The traditional approach utilized by the Board for many years has been known as the *Joy Silk* doctrine. *Joy Silk Mills, Inc.*, 85 N.L.R.B. 1263 (1949), *enforced*, 185 F.2d 732 (1950). Under that rule, an employer could lawfully refuse to bargain with a union claiming representative status through possession of authorization cards if he had a "good faith doubt" as to the union's majority status; instead of bargaining, he could insist that the union seek an election in order to test out his doubts. The Board, then, could find a lack of good faith doubt and enter a bargaining order in one of two ways. It could find (1) that the employer's independent unfair labor practices were evidence of bad faith, showing that the employer was seeking time to dissipate the union's majority. Or the Board could find (2) that the employer had come forward with no reasons for entertaining any doubt and therefore that he must have rejected the bargaining demand in bad faith. . . .

The leading case codifying modifications to the Joy Silk doctrine was *Aaron Brothers*, 158 N.L.R.B. 1077 (1966). There the Board . . . shifted the burden to the General Counsel to show bad faith and that an employer "will not be held to have violated his bargaining obligation . . . simply because he refuses to rely upon cards, rather than an election, as the method for determining the union's majority." 158 N.L.R.B. at 1078. Two significant consequences were emphasized. The Board noted (1) that not every unfair labor practice would automatically result in a finding of bad faith and therefore a bargaining order; the Board implied that it would find bad faith only if the unfair labor practice was serious enough to have the tendency to dissipate the union's majority. The Board noted (2) that an employer no longer needed to come forward with reasons for rejecting a bargaining demand. The Board pointed out, however, that a bargaining order would issue if it could prove that an employer's "course of conduct" gave indications as to the employer's bad faith. . . .

Although the Board's brief . . . generally followed . . . [the *Aaron Brothers* approach,] the Board announced at oral argument that it had virtually abandoned the *Joy Silk* doctrine altogether. Under the Board's current practice, an employer's good faith doubt is largely irrelevant, and the key to the issuance of a bargaining order is the commission of serious unfair labor practices that interfere with the election processes and tend to preclude the holding of a fair election. Thus, an employer can insist that a union go to an election, regardless of his subjective motivation, so long as he is not guilty of misconduct; he need give no affirmative reasons for rejecting a recognition request, and he can demand an election with a simple "no comment" to the union. The Board pointed out, however, (1) that an employer could not refuse to bargain if he knew, through a personal poll for instance, that a majority of his employees supported the union, and (2) that an employer could not refuse recognition initially because of questions as to the appropriateness of the unit and then later claim, as an afterthought, that he doubted the union's strength. . . .

Because the employers' refusal to bargain in each of these cases was accompanied by independent unfair labor practices which tend to preclude the holding of a fair election, we need not decide whether a bargaining order is ever appropriate in cases where there is no interference with the election processes. . . .

III.

A.

The first issue . . . is whether a union can establish a bargaining obligation by means other than a Board election and whether the validity of alternate routes to majority status, such as cards, was affected by the 1947 Taft-Hartley amendments. The most commonly traveled route for a union to obtain recognition as the exclusive bargaining representative of an unorganized group of employees is through the Board's election and certification procedures under [§ 9(c)]; it is also, from the

Board's point of view, the preferred route. A union is not limited to a Board election, however, for, in addition to §9, the present Act provides in [§8(a)(5)], as did the Wagner Act in §8(5), that "[i]t shall be an unfair labor practice for an employer . . . to refuse to bargain collectively with the representatives of his employees, subject to the provisions of section 9(a)." Since §9(a), in both the Wagner Act and the present Act, refers to the representative as the one "designated or selected" by a majority of the employees without specifying precisely how that representative is to be chosen, it was early recognized that an employer had a duty to bargain whenever the union representative presented "convincing evidence of majority support." Almost from the inception of the Act, then, it was recognized that a union did not have to be certified as the winner of a Board election to invoke a bargaining obligation; it could establish majority status by other means under the unfair labor practice provision of §8(a)(5)—by showing convincing support, for instance, by a union-called strike or strike vote, or, as here, by possession of cards signed by a majority of the employees authorizing the union to represent them for collective bargaining purposes.

We have consistently accepted this interpretation of the . . . Act, particularly as to the use of authorization cards. [See, e.g., . . . *United Mine Workers v. Arkansas Flooring Co.*, 351 U.S. 62 (1956)]. Thus, in *United Mine Workers*, *supra*, we noted that a "Board election is not the only method by which an employer may satisfy itself as to the union's majority status," since §9(a), "which deals expressly with employee representation, says nothing as to how the employees' representative shall be chosen." We therefore pointed out in that case, where the union had obtained signed authorization cards from a majority of the employees, that "(i)n the absence of any bona fide dispute as to the existence of the required majority of eligible employees, the employer's denial of recognition of the union would have violated §8(a)(5) of the Act." We see no reason to reject this approach to bargaining obligations now, and we find unpersuasive the Fourth Circuit's view that the 1947 Taft-Hartley amendments, enacted some nine years before our decision in United Mine Workers, *supra*, require us to disregard that case. . . .

The employers rely finally on the addition to §9(c) of subparagraph (B), which allows an employer to petition for an election whenever "one or more individuals or labor organizations have presented to him a claim to be recognized the cards themselves may never be used section 9(a)." That provision was not added, as the employers assert, to give them an absolute right to an election at any time; rather, it was intended, as the legislative history indicates, to allow them, after being asked to bargain, to test out their doubts as to a union's majority in a secret election which they would then presumably not cause to be set aside by illegal antiunion activity. We agree with the Board's assertion here that there is no suggestion that Congress intended §9(c)(1)(B) to relieve any employer of his §8(a)(5) bargaining obligation where, without good faith, he engaged in unfair labor practices disruptive of the Board's election machinery. And we agree that the policies reflected in §9(c)(1)(B) fully support the Board's present administration of the Act . . . ; for an employer can insist on a secret ballot election, unless in the words of the Board, he engages "in contemporaneous unfair labor practices likely to destroy the union's majority and seriously impede the election." . . .

In short, we hold that the 1947 amendments did not restrict an employer's duty to bargain under §8(a)(5) solely to those unions whose representative status is certified after a Board election.

B.

We next consider the question whether authorization cards are such inherently unreliable indicators of employee desires that, whatever the validity of other alternate routes to representative status, the cards themselves may never be [used] to determine a union's majority and to support an order to bargain. In this context, the employers urge us to take the step the 1947 amendments and their legislative history indicate Congress did not take, namely, to rule out completely the use of cards in the bargaining arena. Even if we do not unhesitatingly accept the Fourth Circuit's view in the matter, the employers argue, at the very least we should overrule the *Cumberland Shoe* doctrine . . . and establish stricter controls over the solicitation of the cards by union representatives.

The objections to the use of cards voiced by the employers and the Fourth Circuit boil down to two contentions: (1) that, as contrasted with the election procedure, the cards cannot accurately reflect an employee's wishes, either because an employer has not had a chance to present his views and thus a chance to insure that the employee choice was an informed one, or because the choice was the result of group pressures and not individual decision made in the privacy of a voting booth; and (2) that quite apart from the election comparison, the cards are too often obtained through misrepresentation and coercion which compound the cards' inherent inferiority to the election process. Neither contention is persuasive, and each proves too much. The Board itself has recognized, and continues to do so here, that secret elections are generally the most satisfactory-indeed the preferred-method of ascertaining whether a union has majority support. The acknowledged superiority of the election process, however, does not mean that cards are thereby rendered totally invalid, for where an employer engages in conduct disruptive of the election process, cards may be the most effective-perhaps the only-way of assuring employee choice. As for misrepresentation, in any specific case of alleged irregularity in the solicitation of the cards, the proper course is to apply the Board's customary standards (to be discussed more fully below) and rule that there was no majority if the standards were not satisfied. It does not follow that because there are some instances of irregularity, the cards can never be used; otherwise, an employer could put off his bargaining obligation indefinitely through continuing interference with elections.

That the cards, though admittedly inferior to the election process, can adequately reflect employee sentiment when that process has been impeded, needs no extended discussion, for the employers' contentions cannot withstand close examination. The employers argue that their employees cannot make an informed choice because the card drive will be over before the employer has had a chance to present his side of the unionization issues. Normally, however, the union will inform the employer of its organization drive early in order to subject the employer to the unfair labor practice provisions of the Act; the union must be able to show the employer's awareness of the drive in order to prove that his contemporaneous conduct constituted unfair labor practices on which a bargaining order can be based if the drive is ultimately successful. . . .

Further, the employers argue that without a secret ballot an employee may, in a card drive, succumb to group pressures or sign simply to get the union "off his back" and then be unable to change his mind as he would be free to do once inside a voting booth. But the same pressures are likely to be equally present in an election, for election cases arise most often with small bargaining units where virtually every voter's sentiments can be carefully and individually canvassed. And no voter, of course, can change his mind after casting a ballot in an election even though he may think better of his choice shortly thereafter.

The employers' second complaint, that the cards are too often obtained through misrepresentation and coercion, must be rejected also in view of the Board's present rules for controlling card solicitation, which we view as adequate to the task where the cards involved state their purpose clearly and unambiguously on their face. We would be closing our eyes to obvious difficulties, of course, if we did not recognize that there have been abuses, primarily arising out of misrepresentations by union organizers as to whether the effect of signing a card was to designate the union to represent the employee for collective bargaining purposes or merely to authorize it to seek an election to determine that issue. And we would be equally blind if we did not recognize that various courts of appeals and commentators have differed significantly as to the effectiveness of the Board's *Cumberland Shoe* doctrine . . . to cure such abuses. . . .

We need make no decision as to the conflicting approaches used with regard to dual-purpose cards, for in each of the five organization campaigns in the four cases before us the cards used were single-purpose cards, stating clearly and unambiguously on their face that the signer designated the union as his representative. And even the view forcefully voiced by the Fourth Circuit below that unambiguous cards as well present too many opportunities for misrepresentation comes before us somewhat weakened in view of the fact that there were no allegations of irregularities in four of those five campaigns. . . . [and in the fifth, General Steel, the Board found no irregularities]. . . .

In resolving the conflict among the circuits in favor of approving the Board's *Cumberland* rule, we think it sufficient to point out that employees should be bound by the clear language of what they sign unless that language is deliberately and clearly canceled by a union adherent with words calculated to direct the signer to disregard and forget the language above his signature. There is nothing inconsistent in handing an employee a card that says the signer authorizes the union to represent him and then telling him that the card will probably be used first to get an election. . . . We cannot agree with the employers here that employees as a rule are too unsophisticated to be bound by what they sign unless expressly told that their act of signing represents something else. . . .

We agree, however, with the Board's own warnings in *Levi Strauss & Co.*, 172 N.L.R.B. No. 57 & n. 7 (1968), that in hearing testimony concerning a card challenge, trial examiners should not neglect their obligation to ensure employee free choice by a too easy mechanical application of the *Cumberland* rule. We also accept the observation that employees are more likely than not, many months after a card drive and in response to questions by company counsel, to give testimony damaging to the union, particularly where company officials have previously threatened reprisals for union activity in violation of § 8(a)(1). We therefore reject any rule that requires a probe of an employee's subjective motivations as involving an endless and unreliable inquiry. We nevertheless feel that the trial examiner's findings in General Steel . . . represent the limits of the *Cumberland* rule's application. We emphasize that the Board should be careful to guard against an approach any more rigid than that in General Steel. And we reiterate that nothing we say here indicates our approval of the *Cumberland Shoe* rule when applied to ambiguous, dual-purpose cards.

The employers argue as a final reason for rejecting the use of the cards that they are faced with a Hobson's choice under current Board rules and will almost inevitably come out the loser. They contend that if they do not make an immediate, personal investigation into possible solicitation irregularities to determine whether in fact the union represents an uncoerced majority, they will have unlawfully refused to bargain for failure to have a good faith doubt of the union's majority; and if they do make such an investigation, their efforts at polling and interrogation will constitute an unfair labor practice in violation of § 8(a)(1) and they will again be ordered to bargain. As we have pointed out, however, an employer is not obligated to accept a card check as proof of majority status, under the Board's current practice, and he is not required to justify his insistence on an election by making his own investigation of employee sentiment and showing affirmative reasons for doubting the majority status. . . . If he does make an investigation, the Board's recent cases indicate that reasonable polling in this regard will not always be termed violative of § 8(a) (1). . . . And even if an employer's limited interrogation is found violative of the Act, it might not be serious enough to call for a bargaining order. . . .

C.

Remaining before us is the propriety of a bargaining order as a remedy for a § 8(a)(5) refusal to bargain where an employer has committed independent unfair labor practices which have made the holding of a fair election unlikely or which have in fact undermined a union's majority and caused an election to be set aside. We have long held that the Board is not limited to a cease-and-desist order in such cases, but has the authority to issue a bargaining order without first requiring the union to show that it has been able to maintain its majority status. See *NLRB v.*

Katz, 369 U.S. 736, 748, n 16. . . . And we have held the Board has the same authority even where it is clear that the union, which once had possession of cards from
a majority of the employees, represents only a minority when the bargaining order
is entered. *Franks Bros. Co. v. NLRB,* 321 U.S. 702 (1944). We see no reason now
to withdraw this authority from the Board. If the Board could enter only a cease-
and-desist order and direct an election or a rerun, it would in effect be rewarding the employer and allowing him "to profit from (his) own wrongful refusal
to bargain," *Franks Bros., supra,* at 704, while at the same time severely curtailing the employees' right freely to determine whether they desire a representative.
The employer could continue to delay or disrupt the election processes and put
off indefinitely his obligation to bargain; and any election held under these circumstances would not be likely to demonstrate the employees' true, undistorted
desires.

The employers argue that the Board has ample remedies, over and above the
cease-and-desist order, to control employer misconduct. The Board can, they assert,
direct the companies to mail notices to employees, to read notices to employees
during plant time and to give the union access to employees during working time
at the plant, or it can seek a court injunctive order under §10(j) (29 U.S.C. §160(j))
as a last resort. In view of the Board's power, they conclude, the bargaining order
is an unnecessarily harsh remedy that needlessly prejudices employees' §7 rights
solely for the purpose of punishing or restraining an employer. Such an argument
ignores that a bargaining order is designed as much to remedy past election damage as it is to deter future misconduct. If an employer has succeeded in undermining a union's strength and destroying the laboratory conditions necessary for a
fair election, he may see no need to violate a cease-and-desist order by further
unlawful activity. The damage will have been done, and perhaps the only fair way
to effectuate employee rights is to re-establish the conditions as they existed before
the employer's unlawful campaign. There is, after all, nothing permanent in a bargaining order, and if, after the effects of the employer's acts have worn off, the
employees clearly desire to disavow the union, they can do so by filing a representation petition. . . .

Despite our reversal of the Fourth Circuit below in Nos. 573 and 691 on all
major issues, the actual area of disagreement between our position here and that
of the Fourth Circuit is not large as a practical matter. While refusing to validate
the general use of a bargaining order in reliance on cards, the Fourth Circuit nevertheless left open the possibility of imposing a bargaining order, without need of
inquiry into majority status on the basis of cards or otherwise, in "exceptional"
cases marked by "outrageous" and "pervasive" unfair labor practices. Such an
order would be an appropriate remedy for those practices, the court noted, if they
are of "such a nature that their coercive effects cannot be eliminated by the application of traditional remedies, with the result that a fair and reliable election cannot be had." . . . The Board itself, we should add, has long had a similar policy of

issuing a bargaining order, in the absence of a §8(a)(5) violation or even a bargaining demand, when that was the only available, effective remedy for substantial unfair labor practices. . . .

The only effect of our holding here is to approve the Board's use of the bargaining order in less extraordinary cases marked by less pervasive practices which nonetheless still have the tendency to undermine majority strength and impede the election processes. The Board's authority to issue such an order on a lesser showing of employer misconduct is appropriate, we should reemphasize, where there is also a showing that at one point the union had a majority; in such a case, of course, effectuating ascertainable employee free choice becomes as important a goal as deterring employer misbehavior. In fashioning a remedy in the exercise of its discretion, then, the Board can properly take into consideration the extensiveness of an employer's unfair practices in terms of their past effect on election conditions and the likelihood of their recurrence in the future. If the Board finds that the possibility of erasing the effects of past practices and of ensuring a fair election (or a fair rerun) by the use of traditional remedies, though present, is slight and that employee sentiment once expressed through cards would, on balance, be better protected by a bargaining order, then such an order should issue. . . .

We emphasize that under the Board's remedial power there is still a third category of minor or less extensive unfair labor practices, which, because of their minimal impact on the election machinery, will not sustain a bargaining order. There is, the Board says, no per se rule that the commission of any unfair practice will automatically result in a §8(a)(5) violation and the issuance of an order to bargain. . . .

With these considerations in mind, we turn to an examination of the orders in these cases. In Sinclair, No. 585, the Board made a finding, left undisturbed by the First Circuit, that the employer's threats of reprisal were so coercive that, even in the absence of a s 8(a)(5) violation, a bargaining order would have been necessary to repair the unlawful effect of those threats. The Board therefore did not have to make the determination called for in the intermediate situation above that the risks that a fair rerun election might not be possible were too great to disregard the desires of the employees already expressed through the cards. . . .

In the three cases in Nos. 573 and 691 from the Fourth Circuit, on the other hand, the Board did not make a similar finding that a bargaining order would have been necessary in the absence of an unlawful refusal to bargain. Nor did it make a finding that, even though traditional remedies might be able to ensure a fair election, there was insufficient indication that an election (or a rerun in General Steel) would definitely be a more reliable test of the employees' desires than the card count taken before the unfair labor practices occurred. . . .

[The Court's discussion of the threat/prediction distinction and §8(c) is in Chapter 3.]

[W]e affirm the judgment of [the First Circuit] in No. 585, and we reverse the judgments of [the Fourth Circuit] in Nos. 573 and 691 insofar as they decline enforcement of the Board's orders to bargain and remand those cases to that court with directions to remand to the Board for further proceedings in conformity with this opinion.

Notes

1. At first blush, a *Gissel* bargaining order might seem like an extraordinary remedy. And it is often described as such by judges, especially when refusing to enforce a bargaining order. *See, e.g.*, Peter Leff, *Failing to Give the Board Its Due: The Lack of Deference Afforded by the Appellate Courts in* Gissel *Bargaining Order Cases*, 18 Lab. Law. 93, 103 (2002) (reviewing judicial treatment of *Gissel* bargaining order cases and concluding that judges often disfavor the remedy and mischaracterize it as "extraordinary and drastic"); *Overnite Transp. Co. v. NLRB*, 280 F.3d 417, 436 (4th Cir. 2002) (characterizing the *Gissel* bargaining order as the "extraordinary and drastic remedy of forced bargaining . . . available only when traditional remedies are insufficient to make possible a 'fair and reliable election'"). Indeed, the Board is ordering an employer to bargain with a union that has not yet won an election (and in some cases has lost an election). In almost all *Gissel* cases, however, the Board has found that the employer's misconduct had dissipated the majority support that the union once enjoyed through a validated card check. The justification is that, in those circumstances, the Board is merely determining that the earlier card check is a better indication of the employees' true, undisturbed desires for representation.

2. To determine whether a *Gissel* bargaining order is an appropriate remedy, the basic questions are: first, did the union ever demonstrate majority support in the bargaining unit; and second, did the employer commit ULPs of the type that would undermine that support and make even a new election unreliable? More specifically, the following questions guide the Board and courts in deciding whether to issue a *Gissel* bargaining order: Was there an on-going union organizing campaign, and did the union petition for an election or seek majority status through a card check in an appropriate unit? Were authorization cards distributed, did the union receive signed cards from a majority of employees in the unit, and were the cards validated? Did the union ever request recognition? If so, when, and what was the employer's response? What ULPs did the employer commit? Were they "outrageous" and "pervasive"? If not, did they "have the tendency to undermine majority strength and impede the election processes"? Are "hallmark" violations present? How large is the bargaining unit and how many employees were affected? If there was an election, who won? If no election was held, why not? Finally, has enough time passed that the effect of the employer's conduct on employees' free choice is likely to have worn off?

3. Before discussing the development of the law in these areas, it is useful to deconstruct the complicated fact-pattern in the four *Gissel* cases to determine the

answers to the questions in note 2. Notice that in all four cases, the union had enjoyed majority support. Should any of the factual differences classified below make a difference in the outcome?

	Gissel Packing Co.	Heck's	General Steel Products	Sinclair Co.
Case No.	No. 691	No. 573	No. 573	No. 585
Did the Board issue a bargaining order?	Yes	Yes	Yes	Yes
Lower Court	Fourth Circuit enforced ULP findings but refused to enforce bargaining order	Fourth Circuit enforced ULP findings but refused to enforce bargaining order	Fourth Circuit enforced ULP findings but refused to enforce bargaining order	First Circuit enforced ULP findings and the Board's bargaining order
Supreme Court	Reversed judgment	Reversed judgment	Reversed judgment	Affirmed judgment
Petitioning Union	Food Stores Employees Union Local 347	International Brotherhood of Teamsters Local 175	Upholsterers' International Union of North America	International Brotherhood of Teamsters Local 404
Authorization Cards				
a. Majority	Yes. 31/47	Yes. 21/38	Yes. 120/207	Yes. 11/14
b. Valid	Yes	Yes	Yes	Yes
c. Appropriate unit	Yes	Yes	Yes	Yes
d. ER challenge	No	No	Yes, on the basis of misrepresentation	No
Union demand for recognition	Yes	Yes	Yes	Yes
Employer's response to Union's bargaining request	Refused to bargain Grounds: authorization cards are inherently unreliable indicators of employee desires	Refused to bargain Grounds: authorization cards are inherently unreliable indicators of employee desires	Refused to bargain Grounds: authorization cards are inherently unreliable indicators of employee desires	Refused to bargain Grounds: ER claimed a good-faith doubt of majority status based on inherent unreliability of authorization cards
Did the Union file ULP charges?	Yes	Yes	Yes	Yes

	Gissel Packing Co.	Heck's	General Steel Products	Sinclair Co.
Nature of employer ULPs as found by the Board	1. §8(a)(1) coercive interrogations, threats of discharge, promise of benefits;2. §8(a)(3) discharges3. §8(a)(5) refusal to recognize union	1. §8(a)(1) coercive interrogations, threats, promise of benefits, appearance of surveillance;2. §8(a)(3) discharges3. §8(a)(5) refusal to recognize union	1. §8(a)(1) coercive interrogations, threats, of discharge;2. §8(a)(5) refusal to recognize union	1. §8(a)(1) threats of plant closure; 2. §8(a)(5) refusal to recognize union
Election				
a. Did Union petition for election?	No	Yes	Yes	Yes
b. Did an election occur?	No	No	Yes	Yes
c. Election results	N/A	N/A	Union lost	Union lost
d. If no election, why not?	Rather than petitioning for an election, union filed ULP charges	Election never held because of employer's misconduct	N/A	N/A

4. In *Gissel*, the Court suggests that three types of cases exist. In what are known as *Gissel I* cases, the Board may impose a bargaining order "without need of inquiry into majority status on the basis of cards or otherwise, in 'exceptional' cases marked by 'outrageous' and 'pervasive' unfair labor practices." 395 U.S. at 613. A bargaining order "would be an appropriate remedy for those practices . . . if they are of 'such a nature that their coercive effects cannot be eliminated by the application of traditional remedies, with the result that a fair and reliable election cannot be had.'" *Id.* at 614 (citing with approval the Fourth Circuit and Board standard for issuing a bargaining order, where it is the "only available, effective remedy for substantial unfair labor practices.") Despite this language, it is very unusual for the Board or the courts to issue a *Gissel* bargaining order absent a majority showing of authenticated cards. In fact, the Board at one point held that *Gissel I* bargaining orders were inconsistent with the NLRA's majority-rule principle. *Gourmet Foods, Inc.*, 270 N.L.R.B. 578, 587 (1984). However, the Board has since reversed course, and has on occasion issued bargaining orders in cases in which there has been no showing of majority support. *See, e.g., Am. Directional Boring*, 355 N.L.R.B. 1020 (2010) (*Gissel I* order appropriate where employer ULPs included "repeated threats of plant closure and job loss, repeated statements that unionization would be futile, threats

of discipline, fabrication of evidence against union supporters, and discharge of 13 union supporters"). Still, *Gissel* I orders remain exceedingly rare.

In *Gissel II* cases, the Board may issue a "bargaining order in less extraordinary cases marked by less pervasive practices which nonetheless still have the tendency to undermine majority strength and impede the election processes." *Id.* at 614. The Court predicated "[t]he Board's authority to issue such an order on a lesser showing of employer misconduct" in cases "where there is also a showing that at one point the union had a majority; in such a case, of course, effectuating ascertainable employee free choice becomes as important a goal as deterring employer misbehavior." *Id.* The Court declared that the Board could "properly take into consideration the extensiveness of an employer's unfair practices in terms of their past effect on election conditions and the likelihood of their recurrence in the future" in fashioning such a remedy. *Id.* Significantly, the Court noted that "[i]f the Board finds that the possibility of erasing the effects of past practices and of ensuring a fair election (or a fair rerun) by the use of traditional remedies, though present, is slight and that employee sentiment once expressed through cards would, on balance, be better protected by a bargaining order, then such an order should issue. . . ." *Id.* at 614–15. The D.C. Circuit has rephrased category II cases as the following three-part test:

> In Category II cases, before we will enforce a bargaining order, we must find that substantial evidence supports three conclusions: (1) at some time, the union had majority support within the bargaining unit; (2) the employer's unfair labor practices have had the tendency to undermine majority strength and impede the election process; and (3) the possibility of erasing the effects of past unfair labor practices and of ensuring a fair rerun election by the use of traditional remedies is slight, and the once-expressed sentiment in favor of the union would be better protected by a bargaining order.

See, e.g., *Davis Supermkts, Inc. v. NLRB*, 2 F.3d 1162, 1171 (D.C. Cir. 1993); *see also id.* (explaining that "[t]here is no need to decide whether this case falls within Category I or Category II" because "[t]he case clearly satisfies the three-part inquiry applied to Category II cases").

Gissel III cases describe "a third category of minor or less extensive unfair labor practices, which, because of their minimal impact on the election machinery, will not sustain a bargaining order. There is, the Board says, no *per se* rule that the commission of any unfair practice will automatically result in a § 8(a)(5) violation and the issuance of an order to bargain." *Id.* at 615.

Which category best describes each of the four consolidated cases that make up the *Gissel* case before the Supreme Court?

5. In *Gissel*, the Court found that the employer in each of the four consolidated cases engaged in numerous ULPs. The Court affirmed the Board's authority to issue a bargaining order not only in "'exceptional' cases marked by 'outrageous' and 'pervasive' unfair labor practices," but also in cases where the employer committed the

type of ULPs that "have the tendency to undermine majority strength and impede the election processes." *Id.* at 613, 614. The Court held that the Board was authorized to issue a bargaining order in the latter case "[i]f the Board finds that the possibility of erasing the effects of past practices and of ensuring a fair election . . . by the use of traditional remedies . . . is slight and that employee sentiment once expressed through [union] cards would, on balance, be better protected by a bargaining order." *Id.* at 614–15.

The question for the Board and lower courts then is what constitutes the kind of "serious" employer misconduct that supports a *Gissel* bargaining order. In a series of cases, the D.C. Circuit has attempted to summarize those types of employer ULPs that could support a *Gissel* order. Noting that "the vast majority of bargaining order cases involve a series of unfair labor practices rather than a single act of illegality," the Court specified that *Gissel* bargaining orders are often justified in cases involving: (1) "an unfair labor practice that is viewed as 'deliberate' or 'calculated,'" (2) "employer[] statements or acts . . . [that] threaten[] . . . a significant economic interest, such as retention of jobs, or a fundamental legal right," (3) "acts of reprisal, particularly discharges," or (4) "promises to correct the grievance that led to union organization." *Skyline Distribs. v. NLRB*, 99 F.3d 403, 411 (D.C. Cir. 1996).

6. In *Gissel*, the Court found that the employer in each of the four consolidated cases engaged in numerous ULPs, as charted above. For example, the Court found that the Gissel company engaged in the following misconduct:

> At the outset of the Union campaign, the Company vice president informed two employees, later discharged, that if they were caught talking to Union men, "you God-damned things will go." . . . Rejecting the bargaining demand, the Company began to interrogate employees as to their Union activities; to promise them better benefits than the Union could offer; and to warn them that if the "union got in, (the vice president) would just take his money and let the union run the place," that the Union was not going to get in, and that it would have to "fight" the Company first. Further, when the Company learned of an impending Union meeting, it arranged . . . to have an agent present to report the identity of the Union's adherents. On the first day following the meeting, the vice president told the two employees referred to above that he knew they had gone to the meeting and that their work hours were henceforth reduced to half a day. Three hours later, the two employees were discharged. *Gissel*, 395 U.S. at 580 n.1.

In *Heck's*, the Court found that the Company engaged in the following misconduct:

> After responding "No comment" to the Union's repeated requests for recognition, the president assembled the employees and told them of his shock at their selection of the Union; he singled out one of the employees to ask if he had signed an authorization card. The next day the Union obtained the additional card necessary to establish a majority. That same day, the

leading Union supporter . . . was discharged, and another employee was interrogated as to his Union activities, encouraged to withdraw his authorization, and warned that a Union victory could result in reduced hours, fewer raises, and withdrawal of bonuses. A second demand for recognition was made two days later, and thereafter the president summoned two known Union supporters to his office and offered them new jobs at higher pay if they would use their influence to "break up the union."

The same pattern was repeated a year later at the Company's Ashland, Kentucky, store. . . . [T]he Company told the employees that an employee of another company store had been fired on the spot for signing a card, warned employees that the Company knew which ones had signed cards, and polled employees about their desire for Union representation without giving them assurances against reprisals. *Gissel*, 395 U.S. at 581 n.2.

Using the guidelines from *Skyline Distributors* described in note 5, how would you classify the type of ULPs in these cases? Do they justify a bargaining order?

7. The Board is unlikely to issue *Gissel* bargaining orders unless the employer has committed ULPs that are highly coercive of § 7 rights. Such ULPs are known as "hallmark" violations. The Board has stated that the severity of hallmark violations makes them likely to have "a lasting inhibitive effect on a substantial percentage of the work force," thereby making a fair re-run election unlikely. *NLRB v. Jamaica Towing, Inc.*, 632 F.2d 208, 213 (2d Cir. 1980). The following chart describes several hallmark violations.

Type of Violation	Case	Rationale
Plant closure or threat of plant closure	*NLRB v. Jamaica Towing, Inc.*, 632 F.2d 208, 213 (2d Cir. 1980)	This violation "is the one serious threat of economic disadvantage which is wholly beyond the influence of the union or the control of the employees."
	Gissel, 395 U.S. at 611 n.31.	This violation is "more effective to destroy election conditions for a longer period of time than others."
Discharge of union sympathizers	*M.J. Metal Products, Inc.*, 328 N.L.R.B. 1184, 1185 (1999) (quoting *NLRB v. Entwistle Mfg. Co.*, 120 F.2d 532, 536 (4th Cir. 1941)).	Such misconduct "'goes to the very heart of the Act' and is not likely to be forgotten . . . 'Such action can only serve to reinforce employees' fear that they will lose employment if they persist in union activity."
	NLRB v. Davis, 642 F.2d 350, 354 (9th Cir. 1981)	Employees are not likely "to miss the point that backpay and offers of reinstatement made some 9 to 11 months after the discharge does not necessarily compensate for the financial hardship and emotional and mental anguish apt to be experienced during an interim period of unemployment."

Type of Violation	Case	Rationale
Threats of discharge	*Garney Morris, Inc.,* 313 N.L.R.B. 101, 103 (1993), *enf'd mem.,* 47 F.3d 1161 (3d Cir. 1995)	
Granting benefits to employees	*NLRB v. Exchange Parts, Inc.,* 375 U.S. 405 (1964)	
	America's Best Quality Coatings Corp., 313 N.L.R.B. 470, 472 (1993), *enf'd,* 44 F.3d 516 (7th Cir. 1995)	Unlawfully granted benefits "are particularly lasting in their effect on employees and difficult to remedy by traditional means . . . not only because of their significance to the employees, but also because the Board's traditional remedies do not require the Respondent to withdraw the benefits from the employees."

8. In *Gissel*, the Board found that cards used in the organizing campaigns "unambiguously authorized the Union to represent the signing employee for collective bargaining purposes; there was no reference to elections." 395 U.S. at 583 n.4. Typical were the cards "used in the Charleston campaign in *Heck*'s," which stated, in relevant part:

> Desiring to become a member of the above Union of the International Brotherhood of Teamsters, Chauffeurs, Warehousemen and Helpers of America, I hereby make application for admission to membership. I hereby authorize you, your agents or representatives to act for me as collective bargaining agent on all matters pertaining to rates of pay, hours, or any other conditions of employment. *Id.*

Such cards are known as single-purpose cards. Single-purpose cards "stat[e] clearly and unambiguously on their face that the signer designated the union as his representative, are presumptively valid." *Id.* at 606. Single-purpose cards are typically distributed by employees or non-employee union organizers who may inform the worker "(1) that the card would be used to get an election (2) that he had the right to vote either way, even though he signed the card (3) that the card would be kept secret and not shown to anybody except to the Board in order to get an election." *Id.* at 584 n.5. The Court concluded, however, that such statements "do not foreclose use of the cards for the purpose designated on their face."

9. The Board's *Cumberland Shoe* doctrine, which the Supreme Court reaffirmed in *Gissel*, "holds that a signed single-purpose authorization card will be counted towards establishing a union majority unless it is proven that the employee was led to believe that his/her card would be used solely for the purpose of obtaining an election." *NLRB v. Horizon Air Servs., Inc.,* 761 F.2d 22, 29 (1st Cir. 1985). A card would be invalid only if the card's express terms were "deliberately and clearly canceled by a union adherent with words calculated to direct the signer to disregard and forget the language above his signature." *Gissel,* 395 U.S. at 606.

10. At the hearing before an ALJ, the General Counsel will typically put every authorization card into evidence as an exhibit. The General Counsel authenticates the cards in a variety of ways. One way is to compare the signatures on the cards with signatures on file with the employer. Sometimes a handwriting expert is used. The witness that is used to put the cards into evidence may be the person who signed the card, or it may be the person who solicited the worker's signature. The witness may be asked questions to determine whether any misrepresentations were made.

11. Are there any advantages to having a union certified by the Board? *Gissel*, at 598–99, noted that "[a] certified union has the benefit of numerous special privileges which are not accorded unions recognized voluntarily or under a bargaining order and which, Congress could determine, should not be dispensed unless a union has survived the crucible of a secret ballot election." Those privileges include:

> protection against the filing of new election petitions by rival unions or employees seeking decertification for 12 months (§ 9(c)(3)), protection for a reasonable period, usually one year, against any disruption of the bargaining relationship because of claims that the union no longer represents a majority (*see Brooks v. NLRB*, 348 U.S. 96 (1954)), protection against recognitional picketing by rival unions (§ 8(b)(4)(C)), and freedom from the restrictions placed in work assignments disputes by § 8(b)(4)(D), and on recognitional and organizational picketing by § 8(b)(7). *Id.* at 599 n.14.

12. *Gissel* bargaining order cases often show that employer coercion can be a serious obstacle to determining employee free choice. There have been several responses to counter the problem of employer coercion. First, some unions have begun to develop cooperative relationships with employers. These unions forego the organizing drive in favor of cooperative agreements with employers involving card checks. Under these agreements, employers voluntarily choose to recognize the union when presented with a majority of employee-signed cards authorizing union representation.

A second response is to pair these card-check procedures with neutrality agreements. "These voluntary pacts between employers and union representatives establish a code of conduct that prohibits each party from disparaging the other or using intimidating, coercive tactics on employees. Under this process, both parties work together to set rules that give workers a chance to freely decide to form a union without pressure or interference from either side." Adrienne Eaton & Jill Kriesky, *Fact Over Fiction: Opposition to Card Check Doesn't Add Up* (2006). "Card check and neutrality agreements are a long-standing, legitimate process of union formation that is recognized under labor law." *Id.* (citing James Brudney, *Neutrality Agreements and Card Check Recognition: Prospects for Changing Paradigms*, 90 Iowa L. Rev. 819 (2005)).

A third response to this coercion was the Employee Free Choice Act (EFCA), H.R. 1409. This bill was introduced in Congress several times (most recently on March 10, 2009) but failed to pass. EFCA would have, among other things, required the NLRB to develop procedures for validating signed authorization cards and would have required the NLRB to certify a union that presented a majority of such cards. EFCA met with fierce opposition from the business community, which wished to preserve its right to insist upon a secret-ballot election. *See infra, Linden Lumber* and accompanying notes. Do you see why card check elections are responsive to the problem of employer coercion?

13. Some employers have challenged *Gissel* bargaining orders on grounds that such orders infringe upon the § 7 rights of employees who voted against the union or in some cases did not have an opportunity to vote at all in a secret-ballot election. *Gissel* itself rejected that view. "Such an argument ignores that a bargaining order is designed as much to remedy past election damage as it is to deter future misconduct." 395 U.S. at 612. In other words, the earlier showing of majority status based on valid cards better reflects the uncoerced choice of employees than the later showing of lost union support through a tainted election. The Supreme Court in *Gissel* added:

> [E]mployee rights are affected whether or not a bargaining order is entered, for those who desire representation may not be protected by an inadequate rerun election, and those who oppose collective bargaining may be prejudiced by a bargaining order if in fact the union would have lost an election absent employer coercion. . . . Any effect will be minimal at best, however, for there "is every reason for the union to negotiate a contract that will satisfy the majority, for the union will surely realize that it must win the support of the employees, in the face of a hostile employer, in order to survive the threat of a decertification election after a year has passed." 395 U.S. at 613 n. 33.

Is *Vincent Industrial Plastics*, discussed in Chapter 7, consistent with this reasoning?

14. Employers have also challenged *Gissel* bargaining orders based on changed circumstances. The D.C. Circuit, for example, has "'repeatedly instructed the Board to determine the appropriateness of a *Gissel* bargaining order in light of the circumstances existing at the time it is entered' rather than at the time of the election." *Traction Wholesale Center Co. v. NLRB*, 216 F.3d 92, 108 (D.C. Cir. 2000); *see Novelis Corp. v. NLRB*, 885 F.3d 100 (2d Cir. 2018) (reversing bargaining order because Board did not account for effects of other Board-ordered remedies, including that employer posted and publicly read to employees a notice that it had engaged in unfair labor practices, and two years had elapsed). In *Novelis*, the Board on remand issued special remedies, including ordering the employer to (1) furnish "the names, addresses, telephone numbers and e-mail addresses of its current unit employees,"

so that the union could contact those employees "in an atmosphere relatively free of restraint and coercion"; and (2) give "reasonable access to its bulletin boards and all places where notices to employees are customarily posted." 367 N.L.R.B. No. 47, at *2 (2018).

The two types of changed circumstances most often cited are employee turnover and passage of time since the ULPs occurred. To preserve these objections, the employer must move the Board to reopen the record for consideration of these factors. *See, e.g., NLRB v. U.S.A. Polymer Corp.*, 272 F.3d 289, 293–98 (5th Cir. 2001) (noting that most circuits require the Board to take into consideration changed circumstances; explaining that "the NLRB is entitled to treat the facts as of the ALJ's decision as static until the parties provide the NLRB with evidence that the relevant circumstances have materially changed"; and holding that the company there failed to timely present such evidence to the NLRB). Although the Board typically denies such motions, it will often fully discuss the evidence as proffered and explain why such changes would not mitigate the need for the *Gissel* order. The Board will often consider whether the passage of time makes a fair rerun election possible; that can mean examining whether current employees are still aware of previous management's misconduct. This discussion allows the company to preserve the issue for appeal.

For example, in **Garvey Marine, Inc.**, 328 N.L.R.B. 991 (1999), *enf'd*, 245 F.3d 819 (D.C. Cir. 2001), the Board first explained why it does not consider turnover relevant:

> The Board traditionally does not consider turnover among bargaining unit employees in determining whether a bargaining order is appropriate, but rather assesses the appropriateness of this remedy based on the situation at the time the unfair labor practices were committed. . . . Otherwise, the employer that has committed unfair labor practices of sufficient gravity to warrant the issuance of a bargaining order would be allowed to benefit from the effects of its wrongdoing. These effects include the delays inherent in the litigation process as well as employee turnover, some of which may occur as a direct result of the unlawful conduct. Thus, the employer would be rewarded for, or at a minimum, relieved of the remedial consequences of, its statutory violations. . . . Such a result would permit employers, particularly in businesses like the Respondent's that experience significant turnover in normal circumstances, to disregard the requirements of the Act with impunity, with little expectation of incurring the legal consequences of their violations. In addition, the Board has noted that a bargaining order's impact on employee free choice is limited, because employees remain free to reject their bargaining representative after a reasonable period of time.

The Board then explained that, even when turnover is considered,

> a *Gissel* bargaining order remains an appropriate remedy when the Board finds that traditional alternatives are insufficient. . . . In the present

case . . . we find that the effects of the Respondent's unlawful conduct are not likely to be sufficiently dissipated by turnover to ensure a free second election. . . . Although a significant number of the employees who were employed at the time of the unlawful conduct surrounding the election may have left the facility for reasons related or unrelated to the Respondent's unfair labor practices, others remain who would recall these events. In addition, only one of the numerous supervisors involved in the unlawful conduct has left. We further find that the new employees may well be affected by the continuing influence of the Respondent's past unfair labor practices. As the Fifth Circuit has recognized, "Practices may live on in the lore of the shop and continue to repress employee sentiment long after most, or even all, original participants have departed." . . . In the present case, it is difficult to believe that the impression made by Respondent's barrage of serious unlawful conduct during the period before and after the Board election, and continuing to the time of the hearing, could have dissipated in the minds of those employees who were then employed, and that the virulence of the Respondent's response to the previous election campaign would not restrain employee free choice in a second election. Indeed, as noted above, the Respondent's violations are precisely the types of unfair labor practices that endure in the memories of those employed at the time and are most likely to be described in cautionary tales to later hires.

Compare *Intersweet, Inc.*, 321 N.L.R.B. 1 (1996), *enf'd*, 125 F.3d 1064, 1069 (7th Cir. 1997) (employer failed to show that employee turnover had eliminated effects of employer's mass discharge even where only nine of the thirty-one employees employed at the time of the terminations were still employed at the plant, the employer had hired 105 new workers, and the management official who had ordered the terminations had died), *with Douglas Foods Corp. v. NLRB*, 251 F.3d 1056 (D.C. Cir. 2001) (rejecting the Board's reasons for justifying the issuance of a *Gissel* bargaining order in light of changed circumstances), *and Be-Lo Stores v. NLRB*, 126 F.3d 268, 282 (4th Cir. 1997) (reversing *Gissel* bargaining order where an "inordinate amount of time ha[d] passed since [the company's ULPs] were committed and . . . the adverse effects of all but the most egregious [ULPs] . . . dissipated with the passage of time, particularly when that conduct amounted to insubstantial violations in the first place"), *and Sysco Grand Rapids, LLC*, 367 N.L.R.B. No. 111 (2019) (observing that, while it "would normally consider issuing a remedial bargaining order," the fact that four years had elapsed since the employer's ULPs and approximately thirty percent of the workforce had turned over meant that "a bargaining order would likely be unenforceable"; adding, "rather than engender further litigation and delay over the propriety of a bargaining order, [the Board decided] that employees' rights would be better served by proceeding directly to a second election."), and *Stern Produce Co.*, 368 N.L.R.B. No. 31 (2019) (declining to issue a bargaining order because of 3.5 year delay).

15. In cases where an employer acts unilaterally during an election campaign, the employer has violated § 8(a)(1) (and sometimes § 8(a)(3)). *See, e.g., NLRB v. Exchange Parts, Inc.*, 375 U.S. 405 (1964), discussed in Chapter 3. If, however, an employer acts unilaterally during an election campaign, the remedy for which is a *Gissel* bargaining order, those unilateral changes transform into derivative § 8(a)(5) violations as of the date that the union has a card majority and requested bargaining. *See, e.g., Parts Depot, Inc.*, 332 N.L.R.B. 670, 674 (2000), *enf'd*, 2001 U.S. App. LEXIS 27433 (D.C. Cir. Nov. 15, 2001) (employer's unilateral actions — general wage increases and layoffs — taken after the *Gissel* bargaining order attached violated § 8(a)(5)). See Chapter 9 for a more in-depth discussion of § 8(a)(5) violations.

16. In 1999, the Clinton-appointed Board General Counsel issued a Memorandum directing the Regions to consider injunctive relief in all *Gissel* complaint cases. Fred Feinstein, *Guideline Memorandum Concerning* Gissel, Memorandum GC 99-08 (Nov. 10, 1999). As the memo pointed out, NLRA § 10(j) empowers the Board to seek injunctive relief from the district courts upon issuance of a ULP complaint. Section 10(j) also grants jurisdiction on district courts to grant such relief. General Counsel Feinstein cited case law that had "accepted the propriety of interim *Gissel* bargaining orders under Section 10(j)." *Id.* By contrast, the Bush II Board rarely imposed *Gissel* bargaining orders let alone sought injunctive relief. Is there a principled reason for the difference in this policy? Return to this question after reading Professor Brudney's article in the next section.

17. Consider the law under the *Joy Silk* rule: an employer could refuse to bargain with a union that had a card majority only if the employer had a "good faith doubt" about the legitimacy of the proffered card majority. Without such a doubt, the employer would violate § 8(a)(5) if it refused to bargain. Does that represent better policy than current law? As *Gissel* notes, the lawyer for the Board did not defend this rule at oral argument. For an explanation of this and further background on *Gissel*, see Laura Cooper and Dennis Nolan, *The Story of* NLRB v. Gissel Packing, in Laura Cooper and Catherine Fisk, Eds., Labor Law Stories (2005).

III. Voluntary Recognition by the Employer in the Private Sector

A. Voluntary Recognition and the Minority Union

Gissel reaffirmed the long-standing principle that an employer may lawfully recognize a union that has achieved majority status through card check. The Court noted that:

> Cards have been used under the act for thirty years; (this) Court has repeatedly held that certification is not the only route to representative status; and the 1947 attempt in the House-passed Hartley Bill to amend section 8(a)

(5) ... was rejected by the conference committee that produced the Taft-Hartley Act. No amount of drum-beating should be permitted to overcome, without legislation, this history. *Gissel*, 395 U.S. at 600 n. 17 (quoting Lesnick, *Establishment of Bargaining Rights Without an NLRB Election*, 65 Mich.L.Rev. 851, 861–862 (1967)).

The Supreme Court in *Gissel* noted, however, the Board's preference for secret-ballot elections as the method to determine employee choice. In an article excerpted in the next section, Professor Brudney makes the case for why card checks should be the preferred method for determining uncoerced employee choice for or against representation.

Regardless of how one stands on these issues, it remains unlawful under § 8(a)(2) for an employer to recognize a minority union as the exclusive representative of a bargaining unit. As shown below, this is true even if the employer believed in good faith at the time of recognition that the union had majority support.

International Ladies' Garment Workers' Union v. NLRB (Bernhard-Altmann Texas Corp.)

Supreme Court of the United States
366 U.S. 731, 81 S. Ct. 1603, 6 L. Ed. 2d 762 (1961)

Clark, J.

We are asked to decide ... whether it was an unfair labor practice for both an employer and a union to enter into an agreement under which the employer recognized the union as exclusive bargaining representative of certain of his employees, although in fact only a minority of those employees had authorized the union to represent their interests. The Board found that by extending such recognition, even though done in the good-faith belief that the union had the consent of a majority of employees in the appropriate bargaining unit, the employer interfered with the organizational rights of his employees in violation of § 8(a)(1) of the [NLRA] and that such recognition also constituted unlawful support to a labor organization in violation of § 8(a)(2). In addition, the Board found that the union violated § 8(b)(1)(A) by its acceptance of exclusive bargaining authority at a time when in fact it did not have the support of a majority of the employees, and this in spite of its bona fide belief that it did. Accordingly, the Board ordered the unfair labor practices discontinued and directed the holding of a representation election. The Court of Appeals ... granted enforcement. ... We agree with the Board and the Court of Appeals that such extension and acceptance of recognition constitute unfair labor practices, and that the remedy provided was appropriate.

In October 1956 the petitioner union initiated an organizational campaign at Bernhard-Altmann Texas Corporation's knitwear manufacturing plant in San Antonio, Texas. No other labor organization was similarly engaged at that time.

During the course of that campaign, on July 29, 1957, certain of the company's Topping Department employees went on strike in protest against a wage reduction. That dispute was in no way related to the union campaign, however, and the organizational efforts were continued during the strike. Some of the striking employees had signed authorization cards solicited by the union during its drive, and, while the strike was in progress, the union entered upon a course of negotiations with the employer. As a result of those negotiations, held in New York City where the home offices of both were located, on August 30, 1957, the employer and union signed a "memorandum of understanding." In that memorandum the company recognized the union as exclusive bargaining representative of "all production and shipping employees." The union representative asserted that the union's comparison of the employee authorization cards in its possession with the number of eligible employees representatives of the company furnished it indicated that the union had in fact secured such cards from a majority of employees in the unit. Neither employer nor union made any effort at that time to check the cards in the union's possession against the employee roll, or otherwise, to ascertain with any degree of certainty that the union's assertion, later found by the Board to be erroneous, was founded on fact rather than upon good-faith assumption. The agreement, containing no union security provisions, called for the ending of the strike and for certain improved wages and conditions of employment. It also provided that a "formal agreement containing these terms" would "be promptly drafted . . . and signed by both parties within the next two weeks."

Thereafter, on October 10, 1957, a formal collective bargaining agreement, embodying the terms of the August 30 memorandum, was signed by the parties. The bargaining unit description set out in the formal contract, although more specific, conformed to that contained in the prior memorandum. It is not disputed that as of execution of the formal contract the union in fact represented a clear majority of employees in the appropriate unit. In upholding the complaints filed against the employer and union by the General Counsel, the Board decided that the employer's good-faith belief that the union in fact represented a majority of employees in the unit on the critical date of the memorandum of understanding was not a defense, "particularly where, as here, the Company made no effort to check the authorization cards against its payroll records." . . . Noting that the union was "actively seeking recognition at the time such recognition was granted," and that "the Union was (not) the passive recipient of an unsolicited gift bestowed by the Company," the Board found that the union's execution of the August 30 agreement was a "direct deprivation" of the nonconsenting majority employees' organizational and bargaining rights. . . .

The Court of Appeals found it difficult to "conceive of a clearer restraint on the employees' right of self-organization than for their employer to enter into a collective-bargaining agreement with a minority of the employees." . . . The court held that the bona fides of the parties was irrelevant except to the extent that it "was arrived at through an adequate effort to determine the true facts of the situation." . . .

At the outset, we reject as without relevance to our decision the fact that, as of the execution date of the formal agreement on October 10, petitioner represented a majority of the employees. As the Court of Appeals indicated, the recognition of the minority union on August 30, 1957, was "a fait accompli depriving the majority of the employees of their guaranteed right to choose their own representative." . . . It is, therefore, of no consequence that petitioner may have acquired by October 10 the necessary majority if, during the interim, it was acting unlawfully. Indeed, such acquisition of majority status itself might indicate that the recognition secured by the August 30 agreement afforded petitioner a deceptive cloak of authority with which to persuasively elicit additional employee support. . . .

In their selection of a bargaining representative, §9(a) of the Wagner Act guarantees employees freedom of choice and majority rule. . . . In short, as we said in *Brooks v. NLRB*, 348 U.S. 96, 103, the Act placed "a nonconsenting minority under the bargaining responsibility of an agency selected by a majority of the workers." Here, however, the reverse has been shown to be the case. Bernhard-Altmann granted exclusive bargaining status to an agency selected by a minority of its employees, thereby impressing that agent upon the nonconsenting majority. There could be no clearer abridgment of §7 of the Act, assuring employees the right "to bargain collectively through representatives of their own choosing" or "to refrain from" such activity. It follows, without need of further demonstration, that the employer activity found present here violated §8(a)(1) of the Act which prohibits employer interference with, and restraint of, employee exercise of §7 rights. Section 8(a)(2) of the Act makes it an unfair labor practice for an employer to "contribute . . . support" to a labor organization. The law has long been settled that a grant of exclusive recognition to a minority union constitutes unlawful support in violation of that section, because the union so favored is given "a marked advantage over any other in securing the adherence of employees," . . . In the Taft-Hartley Law, Congress added §8(b)(1)(A) to the Wagner Act, prohibiting, as the Court of Appeals held, "unions from invading the rights of employees under §7 in a fashion comparable to the activities of employers prohibited under §8(a)(1)." . . .

The petitioner, while taking no issue with the fact of its minority status on the critical date, maintains that both Bernhard-Altmann's and its own good-faith beliefs in petitioner's majority status are a complete defense. To countenance such an excuse would place in permissibly careless employer and union hands the power to completely frustrate employee realization of the premise of the Act-that its prohibitions will go far to assure freedom of choice and majority rule in employee selection of representatives. We find nothing in the statutory language prescribing scienter as an element of the unfair labor practices are involved. The act made unlawful by §8(a)(2) is employer support of a minority union. Here that support is an accomplished fact. More need not be shown, for, even if mistakenly, the employees' rights have been invaded. It follows that prohibited conduct cannot be excused by a showing of good faith.

This conclusion, while giving the employee only the protection assured him by the Act, places no particular hardship on the employer or the union. It merely requires that recognition be withheld until the Board-conducted election results in majority selection of a representative. The Board's order here, as we might infer from the employer's failure to resist its enforcement, would apparently result in similarly slight hardship upon it. We do not share petitioner's apprehension that holding such conduct unlawful will somehow induce a breakdown, or seriously impede the progress of collective bargaining. If an employer takes reasonable steps to verify union claims, themselves advanced only after careful estimate-precisely what Bernhard-Altmann and petitioner failed to do here-he can readily ascertain their validity and obviate a Board election. We fail to see any onerous burden involved in requiring responsible negotiators to be careful, by cross-checking, for example, well-analyzed employer records with union listings or authorization cards. Individual and collective employee rights may not be trampled upon merely because it is inconvenient to avoid doing so. Moreover, no penalty is attached to the violation. Assuming that an employer in good faith accepts or rejects a union claim of majority status, the validity of his decision may be tested in an unfair labor practice proceeding. If he is found to have erred in extending or withholding recognition, he is subject only to a remedial order requiring him to conform his conduct to the norms set out in the Act, as was the case here. No further penalty results. We believe the Board's remedial order is the proper one in such cases. . . .

MR. JUSTICE DOUGLAS, with whom MR. JUSTICE BLACK joins, concurring in part and dissenting in part.

I agree that, under the statutory scheme, a minority union does not have the standing to bargain for all employees. That principle of representative government extends only to the majority. But where there is no majority union, I see no reason why the minority union should be disabled from bargaining for the minority of the members who have joined it. Yet the order of the Board, now approved, enjoins petitioner union from acting as the exclusive bargaining representative "of any of the employees," and it enjoins the employer from recognizing the union as the representative of "any of its employees."

We have indicated over and again that, absent an exclusive agency for bargaining created by a majority of workers, a minority union has standing to bargain for its members. In *Virginian R. Co. v. System Federation No. 40*, 300 U.S. 515, 549, n.6, the Court quoted with approval a concession that "If the majority of a craft or class has not selected a representative, the carrier is free to make with anyone it pleases and for any group it pleases contracts establishing rates of pay, rules, or working conditions."

That case was under the Railway Labor Act. But it has been followed under the [NLRA]. In *Consolidated Edison Co. of New York v. NLRB*, 305 U.S. 197, a union, the

Brotherhood of Electrical Workers, was allowed to act as a bargaining representative for the employees who were its members, even though they were a minority. The Court said, ". . . in the absence of such an exclusive agency the employees represented by the Brotherhood, even if they were a minority, clearly had the right to make their own choice." *Id.* at 237. Maintenance of the status of a minority union, until an election was held, might well serve the purpose of protecting commerce "from interruptions and obstructions caused by industrial strife." *Id.* . . .

It was in that tradition that we recently sustained the right of a minority union to picket peacefully to compel recognition. *NLRB v. Drivers Local Union No. 639*, 362 U.S. 274. . . . To be sure, this Court recognized in that case that "tension exists between . . . (the) right to form, join or assist labor organizations and (the) right to refrain from doing so." *Id.* at 280. But when a minority union seeks only to represent its own, what provision of the Act deprives it of its right to represent them, where a majority ha[s] not selected another union to represent them?

Judge Learned Hand in [*Douds v. Local 1250*, 173 F.2d 764, 770 (2d Cir.)], stated that "the right to bargain collectively and the right to strike and induce others to do so, are derived from the common-law; it is only in so far as something in the Act forbids their exercise that their exercise becomes unlawful." In that case a minority union was recognized as having standing in a grievance proceeding outside the collective bargaining agreement, even where a majority had chosen another union. *See American Steel Foundries v. Tri-City Central Trades Council*, 257 U.S. 184.

Honoring a minority union — where no majority union exists or even where the activities of the minority union do not collide with a bargaining agreement — is being respectful of history. Long before the Wagner Act, employers and employees had the right to discuss their problems. In the early days the unions were representatives of a minority of workers. The aim — at least the hope — of the legislation was that majority unions would emerge and provide stabilizing influences. Yet I have found nothing in the history of the successive measures, starting with the Wagner Act, that indicates any purpose on the part of Congress to deny a minority union the right to bargain for its members when a majority ha[s] not in fact chosen a bargaining representative.

I think the Court is correct insofar as it sets aside the exclusive recognition clause in the contract. I think it is incorrect in setting aside the entire contract. First, that agreement secured valuable benefits for the union's members regarding wages and hours, work standards and distribution, discharge and discipline, holidays, vacations, health and welfare fund, and other matters. Since there was no duly selected representative for all the employees authorized in accordance with the Act, it certainly was the right of the employee union members to designate the union or any other appropriate person to make this contract they desired. To hold the contract void as to the union's voluntary members seems to me to go beyond the competency of the Board under the Act and to be unsupported by any principle of contract law. Certainly there is no principle of justice or fairness with which I am familiar that requires these employees to be stripped of the benefits they acquired by the good-faith bargaining of their designated agent. Such a deprivation gives no protection to the majority who were not members of the union and arbitrarily takes from the union members their contract rights.

Second, the result of today's decision is to enjoin the employer from dealing with the union as the representative of its own members in any manner, whether in relation to grievances or otherwise, until it is certified as a majority union. A case for complete disestablishment of the union cannot be sustained under our decisions. While the power of the Board is broad, it is "not limitless." . . . Thus a distinction has been taken between remedies in situations where a union has been dominated by the employer and where unions have been assisted but not dominated. . . .

I think this union is entitled to speak for its members until another union is certified as occupying the bargaining field. . . .

Notes

1. The dissent in this case is advocating for what is called a members-only union model of employee representation. Section IV of this chapter, *infra*, discusses this issue in more depth.

2. The dissent points out that while the collective bargaining agreement in *Bernhard-Altmann* made "the union 'the sole and exclusive bargaining representative' for all workers in the bargaining unit," that agreement also contained "a separability clause—that if 'any provision' is held 'invalid,' the remainder of the agreement is not affected." Should that have mattered to the majority?

B. The Union's Duty to Petition for Election

The Court in *Gissel*, 395 U.S. at 601 n.18, left open the following question:

> . . . whether, absent election interference by an employer's unfair labor practices, he may obtain an election only if he petitions for one himself; whether, if he does not, he must bargain with a card majority if the Union chooses not to seek an election; and whether, in the latter situation, he is bound by the Board's ultimate determination of the card results regardless of his earlier good faith doubts, or whether he can still insist on a Union-sought election if he makes an affirmative showing of his positive reasons for believing there is a representation dispute. In short, a union's right to rely on cards as a freely interchangeable substitute for elections where there has been no election interference is not put in issue here; we need only decide whether the cards are reliable enough to support a bargaining order where a fair election probably could not have been held. . . .

The answer to this question is significant. If the employer is obligated to file a petition for election once it rejects a union's bargaining demand based on a showing of cards signed by a majority, and the employer does not, then a union would be able to petition the Board for certification based on the card check alone. If, however, the union is obligated to file a petition for election once the employer rejects the union's bargaining demand, then the union would not be certified based on the card check. This question was at issue in the following case.

Linden Lumber Div., Summer & Co. v. NLRB

Supreme Court of the United States
419 U.S. 301, 95 S. Ct. 429, 42 L. Ed. 2d 465 (1974)

DOUGLAS, J.

These cases present a question expressly reserved in *NLRB v. Gissel Packing Co.*, 395 U.S. 575, 595, 601 n. 18 (1969).

In *Linden* respondent union obtained authorization cards from a majority of petitioner's employees and demanded that it be recognized as the collective-bargaining representative of those employees. Linden said it doubted the union's claimed majority status and suggested the union petition the Board for an election. . . . Respondent union thereupon renewed its demand for collective bargaining; and again Linden declined, saying that the union's claimed membership had been improperly influenced by supervisors. . . .

There is no charge that Linden engaged in an unfair labor practice apart from its refusal to bargain. The Board held that Linden should not be guilty of an unfair labor practice solely on the basis "of its refusal to accept evidence of majority status other than the results of a Board election."

[A companion case, Wilder, had a similar factual history and the Board made the same ruling] . . . On petitions for review the Court of Appeals reversed. We reverse the Court of Appeals.

In *Gissel* we held that an employer who engages in "unfair" labor practices "likely to destroy the union's majority and seriously impede the election" may not insist that before it bargains the union get a secret ballot election. 395 U.S. at 600. There were no such unfair labor practices here. . . .

We recognized in *Gissel* that while the election process had acknowledged superiority in ascertaining whether a union has majority support, cards may "adequately reflect employee sentiment." *Id.*, at 603.

. . . As we said, however, in *Gissel*, the Board had largely abandoned its earlier test that the employer's refusal to bargain was warranted, if he had a good faith doubt that the union represented a majority. A different approach was indicated. We said:

> "[A]n employer is not obligated to accept a card check as proof of majority status, under the Board's current practice, and he is not required to justify his insistence on an election by making his own investigation of employee sentiment and showing affirmative reasons for doubting the majority status. . . ."

In the present cases the Board found that the employers "should not be found guilty of a violation of Section 8(a)(5) solely upon the basis of (their) refusal to accept evidence of majority status other than the results of a Board election." . . . The question whether the employers had good reasons or poor reasons was not deemed relevant to the inquiry. . . .

To take the Board's position is not to say that authorization cards are wholly unreliable as an indication of employee support of the union. An employer concededly may have valid objections to recognizing a union on that basis. His objection to cards may, of course, mask his opposition to unions. On the other hand he may have rational, good-faith grounds for distrusting authorization cards in a given situation. He may be convinced that the fact that a majority of the employees strike and picket does not necessarily establish that they desire the particular union as their representative. Fear may indeed prevent some from crossing a picket line; or sympathy for strikers, not the desire to have the particular union in the saddle, may influence others. These factors make difficult an examination of the employer's motive to ascertain whether it was in good faith. To enter that domain is to reject the approval by *Gissel* of the retreat which the Board took from its "good faith" inquiries.

The union which is faced with an unwilling employer has two alternative remedies under the Board's decision in the instant cases. It can file for an election; or it can press unfair labor practice charges against the employer under *Gissel*. The later alternative promises to consume much time. In *Linden* the time between filing the charge and the Board's ruling was about 4 1/2 years; in *Wilder*, about 6 1/2 years. The Board's experience indicates that the median time in a contested case is 388 days. *Gissel*, 395 U.S. at 611 n. 30. On the other hand the median time between the filing of the petition for an election and the decision of the Regional Director is about 45 days. . . . In terms of getting on with the problems of inaugurating regimes of industrial peace, the policy of encouraging secret elections under the Act is favored. The question remains-should the burden be on the union to ask for an election or should it be the responsibility of the employer?

The Court of Appeals concluded that since Congress in 1947 authorized employers to file their own representation petitions by enacting § 9(c)(1)(B), the burden was on them. But the history of that provision indicates it was aimed at eliminating the discrimination against employers which had previously existed under the Board's prior rules, permitting employers to petition for an election only when confronted with claims by two or more unions. There is no suggestion that Congress wanted to place the burden of getting a secret election on the employer. . . .

The Board has at least some expertise in these matters and its judgment is that an employer's petition for an election, though permissible, is not the required course. It points out in its brief here that an employer wanting to gain delay can draw a petition to elicit protests by the union, and the thought that an employer petition would obviate litigation over the sufficiency of the union's showing of interest is in its purview apparently not well taken. A union petition to be sure must be backed by a 30% showing of employee interest. But the sufficiency of such a showing is not litigable by the parties.

In light of the statutory scheme and the practical administrative procedural questions involved, we cannot say that the Board's decision that the union should go forward and ask for an election on the employer's refusal to recognize the authorization cards was arbitrary and capricious or an abuse of discretion.

In sum, we sustain the Board in holding that, unless an employer has engaged in an unfair labor practice that impairs the electoral process, a union with authorization cards purporting to represent a majority of the employees, which is refused recognition, has the burden of taking the next step in invoking the Board's election procedure.

STEWART, J., with whom WHITE, J., MARSHALL, J., and POWELL, J., join, dissenting.

Under a recently adopted Board policy, an employer who does not commit independent unfair labor practices prejudicing the holding of a fair election has an absolute right to refuse to bargain with a union selected by a majority of his employees until that union petitions for and wins a Board-supervised election. I cannot agree with the Court's conclusion that this Board policy constitutes a permissible interpretation of §§ 8(a)(5) and 9(a) of the Act. . . .

Section 9(a) expressly provides that the employees' exclusive bargaining representative shall be the union "designated or selected" by a majority of the employees in an appropriate unit. Neither § 9(a) nor § 8(a)(5), which makes it an unfair labor practice for an employer to refuse to bargain with the representative of his employees, specifies how that representative is to be chosen. The language of the Act thus seems purposefully designed to impose a duty upon an employer to bargain whenever the union representative presents convincing evidence of majority support, regardless of the method by which that support is demonstrated. And both the Board and this Court have in the past consistently interpreted §§ 8(a)(5) and 9(a) to mean exactly that. A "union did not have to be certified as the winner of a Board election to invoke a bargaining obligation; it could establish majority status by other means under the unfair labor practice provision of § 8(a)(5) — by showing convincing support, for instance, by a union-called strike or strike vote, or, as here, by possession of cards signed by a majority of the employees authorizing the union to represent them for collective bargaining purposes." *NLRB v. Gissel Packing Co.*, 395 U.S. 575, 597 (footnote omitted). . . .

As the Court recognized in *Gissel*, the 1947 Taft-Hartley amendments strengthen this interpretation of the Act. One early version of the House bill would have amended the Act to permit the Board to find an employer unfair labor practice for refusing to bargain with a union only if the union was "currently recognized by the employer or certified as such [through an election] under section 9." § 8(a)(5) of H.R. 3020, 80th Cong., 1st Sess. The proposed change, which would have eliminated any method of requiring employer recognition of a union other than a Board-supervised election, was rejected in conference. H.R.Conf.Rep. No. 510, 80th Cong., 1st Sess., 41. After rejection of the proposed House amendment, the House Conference Report explicitly stated that § 8(a)(5) was intended to follow the provisions of "existing law." Ibid. And "existing law" unequivocally recognized that a union could establish majority status and thereby impose a bargaining obligation on an unwilling employer by means other than petitioning for and winning a Board-supervised election. [*Gissel, supra*, at 596–98.]

The 1947 amendments, however, did provide an alternative to immediate union recognition for an employer faced with a union demand to bargain on behalf of his employees. Section 9(c)(1)(B), added to the Act in 1947, provides that an employer, alleging that one or more individuals or labor organizations have presented a claim to be recognized as the exclusive representative of his employees, may file a petition for a Board-supervised representation election.

This section, together with §§ 8(a)(5) and 9(a), provides clear congressional direction as to the proper approach to the situation before us. When an employer is faced with a demand for recognition by a union that has presented convincing evidence of majority support, he may elect to follow one of four alternatives. First, he is free to recognize the union and thereby satisfy his § 8(a)(5) obligation to bargain with the representatives "designated or selected" by his employees. Second, he may petition for a Board-supervised election, pursuant to § 9(c)(1)(B). . . . Third, rather than file his own election petition, the employer can agree to be bound by the results of an expedited consent election ordered after the filing of a union election petition. *See* 29 C.F.R. § 102.62. Finally, the employer can refuse to recognize the union, despite its convincing evidence of majority support, and also refuse either to petition for an election or to consent to a union-requested election. In this event, however, the Act clearly provides that the union may charge the employer with an unfair labor practice under § 8(a)(5) for refusing to bargain collectively with the representatives of his employees. If the General Counsel issues a complaint and the Board determines that the union in fact represents a majority of the employees, the Board must issue an order directing the employer to bargain with the union. . . .

The Court offers two justifications for its approval of the new Board practice which, disregarding the clear language of §§ 8(a)(5) and 9(a), requires an employer to bargain only with a union certified as bargaining representative after a Board-supervised election conducted upon the petition of the union.

First, it is suggested that to require the Board under some circumstances to find a § 8(a)(5) violation when an employer refuses to bargain with the noncertified union supported by a majority of his employees would compel the Board to re-enter the domain of subjective "good faith" inquiries . . . This fear is unwarranted. . . .

The second ground upon which the Court justifies its approval of the Board's new practice is that it serves to remove from the employer the burden of obtaining a Board-supervised election. . . . Although I agree with the Court that it would be improper to impose such an obligation on an employer, the Board's new policy is not necessary to eliminate such a burden.

The only employer obligation relevant to this case, apart from the requirement that the employer not commit independent unfair labor practices that would prejudice the holding of a fair election, is the one imposed by §§ 8(a)(5) and 9(a) of the Act: an employer has a duty to bargain collectively with the representative designated or selected by his employees. When an employer is confronted with "convincing evidence of majority support," he has the option of petitioning for an election or consenting to an expedited union-petitioned election. As the Court explains, § 9(c)(1)(B) does not require the employer to exercise this option. If he does not, however, and if he does not voluntarily recognize the union, he must take the risk that his conduct will be found by the Board to constitute a violation of his § 8(a)(5) duty to bargain. In short, petitioning for an election is not an employer obligation; it is a device created by Congress for the employer's self-protection, much as Congress gave unions the right to petition for elections to establish their majority status but deliberately chose not to require a union to seek an election before it could impose a bargaining obligation on an unwilling employer. . . .

The language and history of the Act clearly indicate that Congress intended to impose upon an employer the duty to bargain with a union that has presented convincing evidence of majority support, even though the union has not petitioned for and won a Board-supervised election. "It is not necessary for us to justify the policy of Congress. It is enough that we find it in the statute. That policy cannot be defeated by the Board's policy." *Colgate-Palmolive-Peet Co. v. NLRB*, 338 U.S. 355, 363. Accordingly, I would affirm the judgment of the Court of Appeals remanding the case to the Board, but for further proceedings consistent with the views expressed in this opinion.

Notes

1. *Linden Lumber* upheld as permissible the Board's interpretation of the NLRA—that an employer can insist on a Board-conducted, secret-ballot election when presented with a card majority. The dissent contends that this construction of the NLRA is impermissible. Are both interpretations of the Act reasonable, and thus is this really just a matter of agency discretion under *Chevron*? Or is the dissent correct that the NLRA does not reasonably permit the Board's interpretation in this case?

2. As the dissent acknowledges, an employer who voluntarily recognizes a minority union believing in good faith that the union enjoyed majority support violates § 8(a)(1) and (2). The majority observed that "[t]his result, however, imposes no real hardship on the employer or the union since it merely requires that recognition be withheld until a Board conducted election results in majority selection of a representative. . . . In addition, an employer concerned about the possibility of recognizing a minority union may always petition for an election pursuant to § 9(c)(1)(B) prior to recognition." 419 U.S. at 313 n.3.

3. Notwithstanding § 8(a)(2), NLRA § 8(f) permits employers engaged primarily in the building and construction industry to enter into pre-hire collective-bargaining agreements before the union has demonstrated majority support. What policies—or distinctive facts about this industry—support treating the building and construction industry differently?

One difference between a regular collective bargaining agreement—one governed by §9(a)—and a pre-hire agreement is that when the latter expires, the employer is no longer obligated to bargain with the union. This difference is key to understanding *Colorado Fire Sprinkler, Inc. v. NLRB*, 891 F.3d 1031 (D.C. Cir. 2018). There, the company negotiated a series of pre-hire agreements with a union. When the last of those agreements expired, the company refused to continue bargaining. The union, backed by the Board, asserted that it had become the exclusive representative under §9(a), and the pre-hire agreements had been converted to regular CBAs. The basis for that assertion was that the union had previously offered to demonstrate to the employer that it had the support of a majority of employees, and several of the earlier agreements acknowledged the union's status as exclusive representative under §9(a). This was sufficient under NLRB precedent, *Staunton Fuel & Material, Inc.*, 335 N.L.R.B. 717 (2001), but the D.C. Circuit held that a union's offer to show proof of majority support was not sufficient to establish that the union was an exclusive representative of a group of employees under *Bernhard-Altmann*. Instead, the D.C. Circuit held that a §8(f) agreement could be converted into a §9(a) agreement only if the union had at some time produced proof of its majority status.

Based in part on *Colorado Fire Sprinkler*, the Board later issued a call for amicus briefs in a case presenting the question of whether *Staunton Fuel* should be overturned. However, the union later withdrew its charge, and the case ended. Instead, the Board turned to rulemaking. On April 1, 2020, the Board issued a Final Rule that took effect on July 31, 2020. The Final Rule, among other things, requires evidence of a majority-based §9(a) bargaining relationship between the employer and the union in the construction industry. In particular, the Final Rule's third amendment, "Proof of majority-based bargaining relationship between employer and labor organization in the construction industry" states as follows:

> (a) A voluntary recognition or collective-bargaining agreement between an employer primarily engaged in the building and construction industry and a labor organization will not bar any election petition filed pursuant to section 9(c) or 9(e) of the Act absent positive evidence that the union unequivocally demanded recognition as the section 9(a) exclusive bargaining representative of employees in an appropriate bargaining unit, and that the employer unequivocally accepted it as such, based on a contemporaneous showing of support from a majority of employees in an appropriate unit. Collective-bargaining agreement language, standing alone, will not be sufficient to provide the showing of majority support.

> (b) This section shall be applicable to an employer's voluntary recognition extended on or after the effective date of this rule and to any collective-bargaining agreement entered into on or after the date of voluntary recognition extended on or after the effective date of this rule.

This amendment overrules *Staunton Fuel & Material*.

4. The Employee Free Choice Act (EFCA), discussed *supra*, would have, among other things, required employers to recognize a union if it had collected a majority of authorization cards that the Board had authenticated. Some opponents of EFCA, including the Chamber of Commerce, claimed this would have removed the right of employees to a secret-ballot election. Do you see why that claim is misleading and arguably simply wrong? First, under *Linden Lumber* and related rules, assuming a majority of employees have signed cards requesting union representation, employees opposed to unionizing do not have a right to insist on a secret-ballot election; *employers*, however, can insist on an election. Second, *employees* would still be able to push for a secret-ballot election by refusing to sign the traditional single-purpose authorization cards and instead asking to sign a card authorizing a secret-ballot election. Because a union could not obtain certification without a majority, employees who prefer a secret-ballot could join forces with employees who prefer no union to force an election. Thus, it would have been more accurate to say that the card-check provision of EFCA would have taken away the *employer's* right to insist on an election.

C. Modern "Card Check," Neutrality, and Pre-Recognition Agreements

The following article by Professor James Brudney challenges the election model as the preferred model for workplace democracy. As you read this article, consider the arguments in favor of and against card check. Also, consider why an employer might agree to a card check election, even though it is not required by law to do so, and considering that the employer will have committed a violation of § 8(a)(2) if the card check yields an inaccurate result.

James J. Brudney, *Neutrality Agreements and Card Check Recognition: Prospects for Changing Labor Relations Paradigms*
90 Iowa L. Rev. 819 (2005)*

... The past decade has witnessed a growing challenge by organized labor to the validity of the election paradigm as a preferred approach in ascertaining which "representatives of their own choosing" employees want. A central component of unions' challenge is their success in negotiating agreements that provide for employers to remain neutral during an upcoming union organizing campaign. These neutrality agreements generally include language specifying that the employer will not exercise its right to demand a Board-supervised election, but will instead recognize the union as exclusive representative, and participate in collective bargaining, if a majority of its employees sign valid authorization cards.

. . . .

---

* Copyright © 2005. Reprinted by permission.

I. The Rise of Neutrality and Card Check Agreements
A. Bypassing NLRB Elections Since the Mid-1990s

A labor organizing campaign typically begins when a union is contacted by employees who . . . feel unfairly treated in their work environment. [During] its campaign, the union distributes authorization cards, providing supportive employees with the chance to designate the union as their bargaining representative. If the union has received card support from a majority of employees . . . , it ordinarily will request that the employer recognize the union and enter into a collective bargaining relationship. The employer may lawfully accede to this request (provided there is in fact uncoerced majority support for the union). Employers, however, usually decline the union's request and exercise their right to demand a representation election, in which they will urge their employees to vote against unionization; the election is thus a contest challenging the union's assertion that it enjoys majority support. After an employer refuses a request for recognition, the union files a petition with the NLRB, in order to schedule the election in which it can demonstrate its majority status.

Starting in the late 1970s, individual employers and unions began negotiating agreements that modified this traditional approach by providing for employers to remain neutral in future organizing campaigns. [One agreement] . . . specified that ". . . management will neither discourage nor encourage the Union's efforts in organizing production and maintenance employees traditionally represented by the Union elsewhere . . . , but will observe a posture of neutrality in these matters." Other early neutrality agreement language conditioned an employer's neutral stance on "responsible" union behavior, pledging that management would remain neutral in future organizing campaigns "providing the Union conducts itself in a manner which neither demeans the Corporation as an Organization nor its representatives as individuals."

By the late 1990s, as unions bargained for neutrality protection with greater frequency, these agreements had become a central component of the labor movement's organizing strategy. In an important empirical study, [*Union Organizing Under Neutrality and Card Check Agreements*, 55 INDUS. & LAB. REV. REV. 42, 45–52 (2001)] Professors Adrienne Eaton and Jill Kriesky collected and analyzed 132 neutrality agreements negotiated by twenty-three different national unions; approximately 80% of the agreements they examined were bargained during the 1990s. One-half of the neutrality agreements covered employees in the service sector, with the majority of these negotiated in the hospitality, gaming, and telecommunication areas. Within the manufacturing sector, most agreements were in the auto and steel industries.

. . . Professors Eaton and Kriesky found considerable variation in the substantive aspects of these agreements. Certain core provisions, however, were present in the vast majority of settings. Almost all agreements included an explicit employer commitment to neutrality (93%), and some two-thirds of the agreements (65%)

included both a statement of neutrality and a provision to recognize union majority status through card check procedures. Notably, card check provisions (with and even without neutrality statements) were associated with a substantial reduction in the numbers of employers running anti-union campaigns, and card check arrangements also reduced the intensity of such campaigns. The diminished levels of employer opposition presumably relate to unions' ability to recruit majority support in a shorter time span through authorization cards than under election arrangements and also to unions' ability to reach large numbers of workers before employers can begin to generate pressure against the organizing effort.

The Eaton and Kriesky study reported certain other common features that were typically included in these bargained-for organizing agreements. Some two-thirds of the agreements called for union access to the employer's physical property, thereby contracting around the access restrictions established in [*Lechmere, Inc. v. NLRB*, 502 U.S. 527 (1992)]. Nearly four-fifths of the agreements imposed certain limits on the union's behavior—most often the union agreed not to attack management during its campaign, but agreements also provided for organizing to occur during a specified period of time or for unions to notify management in advance of their intention to initiate a particular organizing campaign. Finally, more than 90% of the agreements called for some form of dispute resolution, most often arbitration, to address differences about unit determination or allegations of non-neutral conduct by one of the parties.

. . . [T]he proliferation of neutrality agreements that include card check provisions is part of a larger commitment on the part of unions to modify the NLRB election-based approach to organizing. . . . [N]eutrality combined with card check has become a major weapon in the arsenal of organized labor. . . .

The Eaton and Kriesky findings suggest a link between what provisions are included in a neutrality agreement and the ultimate success of union organizing efforts. Organizing campaigns that featured an employer neutrality statement without providing for card check resulted in recognition for the union 46% of the time. By contrast, organizing campaigns in which the parties agreed to both employer neutrality and card check ended with union recognition 78% of the time.

B. Why Unions Negotiate for Neutrality with Card Check

. . . The explanation for the success currently enjoyed under neutrality and card check relates in large part to the effects frequently associated with employer tactics in opposition to unions during election campaigns. Neutrality arrangements allow unions to avoid these effects—in particular to sidestep the intimidating consequences of employers' anti-union speech or conduct and to minimize the eviscerating impact of lengthy delays under the Board's legal regime.

. . . [N]umerous studies have demonstrated the adverse impact of employer speech and conduct opposing unionization. The greater the amount of employer communication during a campaign, the less likely a union is to prevail in the election. While one could posit that this adverse impact stems primarily from the countervailing educative aspects of employer speech, research in the past two decades strongly suggests that it is the aggressive and hierarchical nature of employer communication that generates increased management success.

When an employer delivers a series of forceful messages that unionization is looked upon with extreme disfavor, the impact upon employees is likely to reflect their perceptions about the speaker's basic power over their work lives rather than the persuasive content of the words themselves. Captive audience speeches, oblique or direct threats to act against union supporters, and intense personal campaigning by supervisors are among the lawful or borderline lawful techniques that have proven especially effective in diminishing union support or defeating unionization over the years. Employers' unlawfully discriminatory conduct during campaigns—particularly the firing of active or prominent union supporters—also has substantially curtailed unions' success rate in elections. By reducing or eliminating such tactics, neutrality agreements substantially improve unions' chances of securing majority support.

With regard to delay, there is again considerable evidence that unions fare less well as the period of time increases between the filing of an election petition and the actual election. The impact of delay seems linked in part to employer use of intimidating speech or conduct during the extended campaign period. In addition, some studies have found that employer challenges to the size or scope of the proposed election unit—which necessarily extend the period from petition to election by months if not years—are associated with decreased union chances for success. Neutrality agreements can avoid the NLRB elections process altogether by providing for card check recognition or for an election conducted by a third party other than the Board. . . . Either of these approaches, . . . shortens the time period within which the union attempts to secure majority support and be recognized as the exclusive bargaining representative. Of even greater importance, neutrality agreements—with or without card check—minimize the prospects for delay in the initiation of collective bargaining once a determination has been made that the union enjoys majority support.

C. Why Employers Agree to Neutrality with Card Check

At first glance, it is less obvious why employers would agree to negotiate neutrality and card check provisions with unions, provisions that make it far easier for their employees to become organized and pursue a collective bargaining relationship. . . . Eaton and Kriesky found that a majority of employers identified as their principal motive the costs they would incur if they did not agree to the neutrality and card check language; they also found, however, that a substantial minority of employers pointed primarily to the benefits derived from reaching such an agreement.

In terms of avoiding costs, most employers referred to the economic losses associated with a work stoppage, although many spoke of acting to avoid potentially damaging picketing by the union. . . . In addition, Eaton and Kriesky found that employers would agree to remain neutral if the union was able to impose (or threatened to impose) costs through the use of third parties—such as the withholding of financial support or investment by a municipality or union pension fund, or the withholding of customer business by religious or community groups. . . .

For many employers, neutrality agreements offer a marketing edge that is valuable in attracting new business. One auto supply firm studied by Eaton and Kriesky embraced neutrality because the UAW—which plays an important role in sourcing decisions made by Ford, Chrysler, and General Motors—then became its advocate in pushing the Big Three to increase dealings with unionized suppliers. Hotels wishing to attract substantial numbers of new visitors, and health providers seeking to expand their patient base, have made comparable decisions: the neutrality agreements negotiated include union commitments to advocate that their members purchase the products or services the employers are providing. Likewise, unions' ability to convince supermarkets that they should favor producers who pledge neutrality has encouraged agricultural producers to enter into such neutrality arrangements.

Neutrality agreements also give rise to union-management partnerships that can more effectively extract benefits from government. For instance, Eaton and Kriesky report that a group of residential care facilities in Massachusetts reached organizing agreements with SEIU in order to enhance prospects for state financial assistance. Further, employers have relied on the union support garnered from a neutrality agreement to assist them in passing or defeating legislation and in securing favorable regulatory results or judicial settlements. In addition, employers have been given incentives to maintain peaceful and largely non-adversarial labor relations during organizing campaigns in order to secure competitive advantages as suppliers of goods and services to local governments.

Apart from expanding their base of customers and angling for more favorable relations with government, employers have determined in certain instances that neutrality agreements may enhance their ability to attract qualified workers. . . .

II. The Business Critique: Defending Employee Free Choice

. . . [N]ot all employers or those sympathetic to the employer position have accepted organized labor's new approach. Concern or opposition has been expressed by a number of management attorneys and business lobbyists, by certain members of Congress, and by some labor relations scholars. Their challenges to the lawfulness of neutrality and card check revolve around the claim that such arrangements usurp or undermine the § 7 rights of individual employees. In essence, these critics contend that employees' § 7 right to choose "to form, join, or assist labor organizations . . . and . . . to refrain from any or all such activities" is appropriately realized or vindicated only through a spirited election campaign supervised by the NLRB, in which the employer and the union each seek to inform and persuade employees as to the merits of their respective positions.

A. . . . Congressional Opposition

In May 2002, seven Republican members of the House, including the majority leader, introduced a bill to prohibit card check recognition. A similar bill introduced in May 2004 garnered fifty-seven Republican cosponsors. The proposed legislation seeks to modify §8(a)(2) so as to make it unlawful for an employer to recognize or bargain collectively with a union that has not been selected through a Board-supervised election.

B. Basic Challenges to the Lawfulness of Neutrality and Card Check

There are . . . at least three distinct aspects to the argument that employer agreements to remain neutral and abandon the elections process are presumptively unlawful under the NLRA.

1. Neutrality Agreements and NLRA §8(a)(2)

Section 8(a)(2) makes it unlawful for an employer "to dominate or interfere with the formation or administration of any labor organization or contribute financial or other support to it." Some employer advocates have maintained that an employer's agreement to refrain from saying anything negative about the consequences of unionization, to allow union representatives to enter its facility and express pro-union views to its employees, and to accept authorization card signatures as convincing evidence of majority union backing, is tantamount to contributing unlawful support or assistance toward a labor organization's success. In essence, their argument is that such agreed-upon benefits, provided in advance of any showing of employee support, confer upon the union in question a favored status that operates to its continuing and unfair advantage in the organizing process.

Preliminarily, any contention that such favored status might unlawfully interfere with the rights of a rival union is problematic. In its 1945 *Midwest Piping & Supply Co.* decision, the Board determined that an employer violated §8(a)(2) by recognizing one of two competing unions after both had filed election petitions. However, this "strict" standard has since been softened when reviewing an employer's determination to choose between competing unions. . . .

Both the Board and the appellate courts have thus concluded that an employer's determination to recognize a union based on majority card support does not qualify as unlawful assistance against a minority union that is already on the scene. It would seem apparent that an employer's less intrusive decision—to remain neutral while a union seeks to garner such majority card support—is similarly not an unlawful preference for one union over another. . . .

In the absence of a competing union, there remains the contention that the favored status conferred by neutrality agreements directly undermines employee free choice. Critics maintain that a binding agreement to forego opposition effectively signals that the union enjoys a special status, and that the employer's contractual expression of deference subtly but inevitably constrains his employees in their decision about whether to support the union. This argument questions the very legitimacy of an employer's de facto willingness to facilitate arm's length union organizing. For several reasons, the argument cannot withstand analysis.

. . . Employers have the right to oppose unions in their facilities, but they do not have a duty to do so. The NLRA permits an employer to recognize a particular union voluntarily or to remain silent while that union campaigns among his employees, just as it allows employers to express vigorously their opposition to unionization. . . .

The Supreme Court in [*Bernhard-Altmann*] did refer to the possibility that a premature contractual agreement between employer and union might provide a "deceptive cloak of authority with which [the union could] persuasively elicit additional employee support." But in *Bernhard-Altmann*, the employer had actually granted exclusive representative status to a union supported by only a minority of employees. . . . By contrast, a neutrality agreement involves no deception at all: the employer is simply stating its readiness to allow union efforts to secure majority support, and its willingness to recognize and bargain with the union should those efforts succeed. Even if the neutrality agreement conveys by fair implication the employer's belief that a union contract would be "mutually beneficial," such predictive expression is surely no more inhibiting than protected employer statements that a union contract will impose costs and disharmony.

Moreover, from a practical standpoint the employees themselves are not bound by neutrality agreements between employers and unions. Employees who wish to express opposition to the union remain free to do so. Such opposition may on occasion trigger hostility from the union or its supporters, but instances of unlawful misrepresentation, pressure, or reprisal can be fully addressed through existing Board procedures. In addition, trade associations and interested groups like the Chamber of Commerce or the Human Resources Policy Association also are not covered by neutrality agreements. . . .

Accordingly, there is no basis for inferring that neutrality agreements systemically inhibit the expressive options of employees who wish to oppose unionization. Indeed, while Professors Eaton and Kriesky reported a substantial success rate for unions in campaigns featuring neutrality agreements, they also found that unions lost one out of five campaigns in which they relied on both neutrality and card check and lost some one-half of all campaigns involving neutrality agreements alone. Some of these results may be less favorable for union opponents than results obtained through Board elections, but they do suggest that employees resisting unions retain an effective voice.

Stepping back, the argument that an employer's formal neutrality stance compromises employee free choice seems to rest, at bottom, on the notion that § 8(a)(2) contemplates a fundamentally adversarial relationship between management and labor. If § 8(a)(2) is understood to condemn as "collusive" any form of union-management cooperation that eliminates management's expression of opposition, then neutrality agreements would indeed be troubling. In historical terms, however, it is worth recognizing the narrower or more focused setting in which § 8(a)(2) arose. The provision was self-consciously aimed at eliminating in-house labor organizations referred to as company unions, in order to permit the growth of truly autonomous organizations that would engage in collective bargaining. While company unions were characterized by a notable absence of adversarial relations, it does not follow that the provision banning them embraced such an adversarial stance.

... While there may be instances of abuse in terms of implementation, an employer's announced willingness to allow his employees to debate on their own the merits of whether to support these independent unions in their pursuit of collective bargaining is simply not the kind of "mischief" that §8(a)(2) was designed to address.

2. Neutrality Agreements and Waiver of the §8(c) Right to Communicate

Section 8(c) protects employers' freedom to speak out against unionization, so long as this sharing of views "contains no threat of reprisal or force or promise of benefit." ... It has been contended that neutrality agreements are incompatible with the letter and spirit of §8(c) because they amount to the waiver of a fundamental employer right, a waiver that runs contrary to federal labor policy. This subsidiary challenge to the lawfulness of neutrality provisions is without merit.

Accepting arguendo that employers' right to engage in noncoercive speech during a union campaign implicates First Amendment considerations, such a right may be waived if done "voluntarily, intelligently, and knowingly ... with full awareness of the legal consequences." [*D.H. Overmyer Co. v. Frick Co.*, 405 U.S. 174, 187 (1972) (setting forth standards for waiver of due process rights in civil context).] Neutrality agreements that are sufficiently explicit typically satisfy this standard without difficulty. ...

There remains the possibility that even a voluntary, knowing, and intelligent waiver may be invalid on public policy grounds. Here, it has been asserted that any agreement by an employer to remain silent during union organizing should be held to contravene federal labor policy, principally because it undermines the §7 rights of employees. The argument is that to permit the employer to be silent compels employees to choose for or against unionization without adequate information. The problem with this contention is that federal labor policy—as expressed in statutory and decisional law—does not command employers to resist unionization in order to educate employees about its vices or virtues. As the Ninth Circuit has succinctly observed, "[n]othing in the relevant statutes or NLRB decisions suggests employers may not agree to remain silent during a union's organizational campaign—something an employer is certainly free to do in the absence of such an agreement." [*Hotel Employees, Rest. Employees Union, Local 2 v. Marriott Corp.*, 961 F.2d 1464, 1470 (9th Cir. 1992).] If anything, neutrality agreements, as employer-sponsored communications, would seem themselves to be protected by §8(c). Moreover, honoring collectively bargained neutrality agreements actually promotes federal labor policy by respecting both parties' decisions to forego reliance on a potentially more divisive elections process and by signaling more generally a preference for voluntary (and peaceful) resolution of union-management differences.

Finally, the employer's waiver is of its own statutorily protected right to speak during a union campaign ... does not deny employees' §7 rights to organize or refrain from doing so. Section 7, of course, conveys no right to receive any particular information from one's employer; if it did, an employer's ad hoc decision not to participate in an organizing campaign would be suspect. Nothing in the Act requires an employer to oppose or speak against unions. That an employer is protected in doing so under § 8(c) is a response to congressional pressure to allow employers to speak, not employee demands to be informed.

3. Card Check Recognition and Actual or Presumptive Coercion

As noted earlier, roughly two-thirds of all neutrality agreements include a provision for recognizing union majority status through card check procedures. Critics have suggested that reliance on signed authorization cards to determine employee choice should be only a last resort because card signatures are obtained in presumptively unreliable circumstances. Unlike NLRB elections, there are no formal conditions or procedures that can help structure a card solicitation campaign. In particular, several attributes of Board elections—the privacy of the voting booth, the anonymity of a secret ballot, oversight by a federal agency—seem dedicated to protecting freedom of choice when compared with the group-oriented, face-to-face, and relatively open-ended nature of the card signature process.

Taking note of such differences, the Supreme Court in [Gissel] declared that cards were "admittedly inferior to the election process" as a means of reflecting employee choice. At the same time, the Gissel Court made clear that authorization card signatures may serve as an adequate reflection of employee sentiment. In reaching this conclusion, the Court relied in part on the fact that Congress—when enacting the Taft-Hartley amendments in 1947—had debated and deliberately rejected a proposal to eliminate the use of authorization cards. The Court also considered and dismissed claims that the card-signing process was inherently unreliable due to group pressure, lack of sufficient information being shared, or the presence of misrepresentation and coercion. Four years later, in *Linden Lumber Division, Summer & Co. v. NLRB*, the Court held that employers were not required to accede to a card majority showing, but could instead force the union to invoke the Board's election procedure. Employers, however, were still permitted to recognize a union based on its card majority. Indeed, the *Linden Lumber* Court emphasized the importance of "getting on with the problems of inaugurating regimes of industrial peace," and it implicitly viewed voluntary recognition as furthering that laudable objective. . . .

The well-settled line of authority holding card check agreements to be valid and enforceable is consistent with the broader principle that both labor and management should be held accountable for their contractual undertakings. Indeed, encouraging management and unions to resolve their differences on a voluntary and peaceful basis—through agreements that are individually tailored and privately enforceable—has long been a fundamental tenet of federal labor policy. This tenet reflects the special role that Congress assigned to collective entities under the NLRA. Unions (acting on behalf of a substantial number of employees) and management (responding to a group claim for recognition) have the power to invoke the Board's election machinery. They also may forego the exercise of this power and agree on other means for determining majority preferences. While card check agreements cannot waive individual employees' rights under § 7, those statutory rights do not include the right of an individual employee to demand a secret ballot election. . . .

The fact that recognition of valid card majorities—and contractual agreements to be bound by such majorities—are presumptively lawful does not mean that card majorities themselves are always lawfully obtained. Those soliciting employees' signatures may provide inaccurate information as to the content or import of the cards, they may exert considerable pressure on employees to sign, or they may promise benefits as an inducement for signatures. The Supreme Court, the circuit courts, and the Board have all been attentive to such concerns and have established that signed cards may be rejected based on sufficient showings of misrepresentation, coercion, or improper promise of benefits. . . .

More recently, courts reviewing the enforceability of neutrality and card check agreements have been sensitive to the importance of assuring employee freedom of choice. When deciding that such agreements are enforceable under § 301 of the LMRA, courts have been careful to consider whether an agreement provides employees with a fair opportunity to decide for themselves to accept or reject the union. . . .

As Part I indicated, however, reliance on neutrality and card check over the past decade has in practice gone well beyond the exceptional. The widespread use of a lawful approach predicated on contractually based cooperation rather than relatively unbridled competition thus presents a challenge to the long-prevailing notion that Board-supervised elections are the best and most accurate method of ascertaining what employees want. . . .

Note

As Professor Brudney pointed out, most courts have held that card check and neutrality agreements are consistent with labor law. However, in *Mulhall v. Unite Here Local 355*, 667 F.3d 1211 (11th Cir. 2012), the Eleventh Circuit cracked open the door to claims that neutrality agreements violate § 302 of the LMRA, which generally prohibits an employer from giving a union any "thing of value." Mulhall, an employee who opposed union representation, challenged the legality of a neutrality agreement in which his employer promised union organizers access to the job site, a list of employee names and contact information, and a neutrality pledge. In exchange, the union pledged to "lend financial support to a ballot initiative regarding casino gaming," and ultimately "spent more than $100,000 campaigning for the ballot initiative." *Id.* at 1213. Reversing the district court's order dismissing the case, the Eleventh Circuit wrote that:

> It is too broad to hold that all neutrality and cooperation agreements are exempt from the prohibitions in § 302. Employers and unions may set ground rules for an organizing campaign, even if the employer and union

benefit from the agreement. But innocuous ground rules can become illegal payments if used as valuable consideration in a scheme to corrupt a union or to extort a benefit from an employer. *Id.* at 1215–16.

Accordingly, the Eleventh Circuit would have remanded the case for further proceedings to determine why the union and employer entered into the neutrality agreement. *Id.* at 1216. But before that could happen, the Supreme Court granted *certiorari*. Had the Court decided *Mulhall*, it would have resolved a circuit split. *See Hotel Employees & Rest. Employees Union, Local 57 v. Sage Hospitality Res., LLC*, 390 F.3d 206 (3d Cir. 2004); *Adcock v. Freightliner LLC*, 550 F.3d 369, 371 (4th Cir. 2008). However, the Court did not decide the case, instead dismissing the writ of *certiorari* as improvidently granted after oral argument. *Unite Here Local 355 v. Mulhall*, 134 S. Ct. 594 (2013). Dissenting from that order, Justice Breyer, joined by Justices Sotomayor and Kagan, indicated that the dismissal was due to the Court's realization that serious justiciability problems plagued the case, including that the neutrality agreement had expired before the Eleventh Circuit issued its decision, and that it was unclear that Mulhall had standing. In addition, Justice Breyer wrote that it was an open question whether § 302 authorizes a private right of action. *See Ohlendorf v. UFCW Local 876*, 883 F.3d 636 (6th Cir. 2018) (holding that § 302 does not create a private right of action).

Notably, the position of the United States (signed off on by the Criminal Division of the Justice Department, the Department of Labor, and the NLRB), is that a card check recognition agreement is not a "thing of value" for Section 302 purposes, and that, in any event, there is not a private right of action under Section 302. The most recent iteration of this position is found in the Statement of Interest of the United States, filed in the federal district court action that the Right-to-Work committee brought seeking to set aside the Volkswagen-UAW neutrality agreement in Chattanooga. *See infra* for further discussion of that the Volkswagen case.

————————

The previous materials concerned card-check and neutrality agreements, which govern union and employer behavior during the organizing phase of their relationship. But what about agreements intended to reach forward into the bargaining phase? For over half a century, the Board has been dealing with the question whether, and the extent to which, unions attempting to organize an employer's workers may enter into an agreement about bargaining procedures and the terms of any future collective-bargaining agreements. As discussed in *Bernhard-Altmann*, an employer and a union violate § 8(a)(2) and § 8(b)(1)(A), respectively, if they bargain for and enter into a CBA before a union has obtained a majority. But to what extent may the parties lawfully shape the contents of a future CBA before the union obtains majority status? *Majestic Weaving* demonstrates when the parties go too far, and *Montague* demonstrates when the parties act lawfully close to, but not over, the line.

Majestic Weaving Co.

National Labor Relations Board
147 N.L.R.B. 859 (1964)

... The Trial Examiner found that the Respondent had not violated Section 8(a) (2).... [W]e reach a contrary result. The majority support which Local 815 had ... when the contract was signed, was an assisted majority. All cards signed up to that time were secured through the efforts of Felter, who during this critical period of initial hiring when the Respondent was starting its operation at this plant admittedly acted in a lead capacity for the general laborers then being hired and had the cooperation of the Respondent in his organizing efforts.... Felter's testimony indicates that when he was asked to solicit for Local 815, so shortly after being hired, he had no fear of incurring [the employer's] ill feeling..., and that Personnel Manager Thomson thereafter cooperated with him in this solicitation ... by pointing out new employees.... Based upon this solicitation by Felter, ... we find that the Respondent rendered unlawful assistance to Local 815 in violation of Section 8(a) (2) of the Act.

... [T]he Respondent ... negotiated with Local 815, despite its minority status, as the exclusive representative of its employees in a production and maintenance unit. As stated by the Supreme Court in [*Bernhard-Altmann Texas Corp. v. NLRB*, 366 U.S. 731], Section 9(a) ... "guarantees employees freedom of choice and majority rule." The Court also observed that there "could be no clearer abridgment" of the Section 7 rights of employees than impressing upon a nonconsenting majority an agent granted exclusive bargaining status. That is precisely what the Respondent did here, and the fact that it conditioned the actual signing of a contract with Local 815 on the latter achieving a majority at the "conclusion" of negotiations is immaterial. In the *Bernhard-Altmann* case an interim agreement without union-security provisions was the vehicle for prematurely granting a union exclusive bargaining status which was found objectionable ... ; in this case contract negotiation following an oral recognition agreement was the method. We see no difference between the two in the effect upon employee rights. Accordingly, we hold that the Respondent's contract negotiation with a nonmajority union constituted unlawful support within the meaning of Section 8(a)(2) of the Act. We also find that the resulting contract was an invalid union-security agreement in view of Local 815's assisted majority, and that the execution and maintenance of that contract have interfered with the Section 7 rights of employees in violation of Section 8(a)(1)....

In the following case, the court affirmed the Board's dismissal of a complaint, thereby finding that the union and the employer did not violate § 8(a)(2) by entering into a letter of agreement (LOA) setting forth ground rules for the organizing campaign, procedures for voluntary recognition, and topics that any subsequent CBA would address if the union obtained majority support and employer recognition.

Montague v. NLRB

United States Court of Appeals for the Sixth Circuit
698 F.3d 307 (2012)

ROGERS, C.J.

This case raises the question of whether—before employees officially recognize a union—a union and an employer may enter into a [LOA] setting forth general terms, including provisions related to health care benefits and future collective-bargaining agreements, that are subject to further negotiation but may become binding if arbitration is necessary. Because the [NLRB], which sets labor policy, reasonably determined that the agreement did not impermissibly restrict employee choice, we uphold the Board's dismissal of the petitioners' complaint.

Dana Companies, the employer . . . , is an automotive parts manufacturer with about 90 facilities throughout the United States, Canada, and 30 other countries. Dana entered into discussions with the International Union, United Automobile, Aerospace & Agricultural Implement Workers of America, AFL-CIO (UAW) about potentially representing approximately 305 employees at Dana's St. Johns, Michigan facility. Dana and the UAW had had a long-standing bargaining relationship before discussions about the St. Johns facility began, and the UAW already represented 2,200 to 2,300 Dana employees at various locations. . . .

On August 6, 2003, Dana and the UAW entered into the [LOA] that is at the heart of this appeal, which included various provisions intended to manage the relationship between the parties should the majority of St. Johns employees select the UAW as their exclusive collective-bargaining representative.

The LOA included a statement of purpose recognizing that the challenges of the automotive industry would "be more effectively met through a partnership [with the union] that is more positive, non-adversarial and with constructive attitudes." The statement of purpose also reiterated that an "[e]mployee's freedom to choose is a paramount concern of Dana as well as the UAW," and both parties agreed to "not allow anyone to be intimidated or coerced into a decision [when selecting their exclusive bargaining representative]." The LOA [Article 3.1] further stated that:

> The parties understand that the Company may not recognize the Union as the exclusive representative of employees in the absence of showing that a majority of the employees in an appropriate bargaining unit have expressed their desire to be represented by the Union. . . .

In the LOA Dana undertook to be neutral in the event of an organizing campaign, and to: (1) allow the employees to meet on company property, Article 2.1.3.5; (2) refrain from discussing any "potential negative effects or results of representation by the Union on the Company," Article 2.1.2.7; (3) provide the Union "with access to employees during the workday in non-workday areas," Article 2.1.3.5; and (4) provide the UAW with personal information about the employees targeted for unionization, Article 2.1.3.1. The LOA also provided for a card check process by a neutral third party as the procedure for recognizing when the union received the support of the majority of the employees, Article 3. In addition, the parties consented to a no strike/no lockout commitment, Article 6, at least until the first formal collective-bargaining agreement was finalized.

Most centrally to the issues in this case, the LOA also described certain principles that were to be included in future bargaining agreements between the parties. With regard to healthcare, Article 4 contained a commitment by the union that bargaining would not erode "current solutions and concepts already in place or scheduled to be implemented January 1, 2004," including "premium sharing, deductibles, and out of pocket maximums." The LOA [Article 4.2.4] also contained the parties' agreement "that in labor agreements bargained pursuant to this Letter, the following conditions must be included for the facility to have a reasonable opportunity to succeed and grow":

- Healthcare costs that reflect the competitive reality of the supplier industry and product(s) involved

- Minimum classifications

- Team-based approaches

- The importance of attendance to productivity and quality

- Dana's idea program (two ideas per person per month and 80% implementation)

- Continuous improvement

- Flexible Compensation

- Mandatory overtime when necessary (after qualified volunteers) to support the customer

... Dana and the union agreed that if they did not reach an agreement on any of the terms for the first formal contract, including those discussed in Article 4.2.4, within six months, they would submit the unresolved issues to arbitration with a neutral arbitrator according to Article 4.2.5–4.2.6. For any potential violations of the LOA itself, Article 5 established a dispute resolution procedure where a neutral arbitrator was empowered to issue "final and binding" decisions.

On August 13, 2003, Dana issued a press release that it had reached a "partnership agreement" with the UAW. According to the Board's decision, there is nothing in the record regarding to what extent the press release and the LOA were made available to Dana's employees. . . .

In December 2003, the UAW requested a list of employees working at the St. Johns facility, pursuant to Article 2.1.3.1. . . . Joseph Montague and Kenneth Gray . . . file[d] [ULP] charges. [T]he . . . complaint alleg[ed] that by entering into the LOA Dana had rendered unlawful assistance to the UAW in violation of § 8(a)(2) and (1) . . . , and that the UAW had restrained and coerced employees regarding their choice of exclusive bargaining representative in violation of § 8(b)(1)(A). At no time prior to or during the litigation of this case did the employees select the UAW as their exclusive bargaining representative.

The Administrative Law Judge (ALJ) . . . dismissed the complaint, ... The ALJ determined that Dana had not granted recognition to a minority union, which would have been an [ULP] under . . . *International Ladies' Garment Workers Union v. NLRB*, 366 U.S. 731 (1961) ("*Bernhard-Altmann*"). Nor did the LOA violate the corollary principle of *Majestic Weaving Co.*, 147 N.L.R.B. 859 (1964), *enf. denied*, 355 F.2d 854 (2d Cir.1966), that an employer could not negotiate a tentative contract with a union that had not yet achieved majority status, where the contract is conditioned on the union's gaining majority support. The ALJ reasoned that the LOA was "a far cry from a collective-bargaining agreement." . . . The ALJ also alternatively relied upon the fact that Dana already had [CBAs] with the UAW at other plants, and those agreements could have required Dana to recognize the union as the bargaining representative of additional, future facilities, and apply the [CBA] to those employees, once the unions achieved majority status, under the Board's precedent in *Houston Division of the Kroger Co.*, 219 N.L.R.B. 388 (1975).

According to Article 7.1 of the LOA, the Agreement expired on June 8, 2007. On December 30, 2007, after the ALJ's decision was announced but before the Board's opinion was made public, Dana sold its St. Johns, Michigan facility to MAHLE Engine Components USA, Inc.

After the sale, the Board issued a 2–1 opinion upholding the ALJ's dismissal of the complaint on the merits. The Board began by identifying the primary legislative purpose of the operative statutory language. An employer is prohibited by section 8(a)(2) . . . from "dominat[ing] or interfer[ing] with the formation or administration of any labor organization or contribut[ing] financial or other support to it," and the purpose of this language "was to eradicate company unionism, a practice whereby employers would establish and control in-house labor organizations in order to prevent organization by autonomous unions." . . .

Section 8(a)(2) is grounded in the notion that foisting a union on unconsenting employees and thus impeding employees from pursuing representation by outside unions are incompatible with "genuine collective bargaining." It is in this context that the statutory prohibition on "financial or other support" to unions must be understood. . . . The amount of employer cooperation that crosses the line and becomes unlawful support, according to the Board, "is not susceptible to precise measurement." . . . The Board then detailed its long recognition of the legality of various types of agreements and understandings between employers and unrecognized unions.

The Board acknowledged that employer recognition of a minority union as the exclusive bargaining representative crosses the line, as the Supreme Court held in *Bernhard-Altmann*, even if the employer in good faith believed that the union had majority support. The Board also acknowledged its extension of this principle in *Majestic Weaving* to bar negotiation of a [CBA] conditioned on the later attainment of majority status by a union. The Board did not read its own *Majestic Weaving* precedent, however, to create a rule that any negotiation with a union over substantive terms of employment is per se unlawful.

The Board distinguished *Majestic Weaving* on several grounds. *Majestic Weaving* involved an initial, oral grant of exclusive recognition, followed by the negotiation of a complete [CBA], consummated but for a ministerial act, whereas the LOA in this case "did no more than create a framework for future collective bargaining, if . . . the UAW were first able to provide proof of majority status." . . . Instead of an exclusive-representation provision[,] which was banned in *Bernhard-Altmann*, the LOA expressly prohibited Dana from recognizing the union without a showing of majority support. The Board reasoned:

> That the LOA set forth certain principles that would inform future bargaining on particular topics—bargaining contingent on a showing of majority support, as verified by a neutral third party—is not enough to constitute exclusive recognition. The UAW did not purport to speak for a majority of Dana's employees, nor was it treated as if it did. On the contrary, the LOA unmistakably disclaimed exclusive recognition by setting forth the process by which such status could be achieved. Nothing in the LOA affected employees' existing terms and conditions of employment or obligated Dana to alter them. Any potential effect on employees would have required substantial negotiations, following recognition pursuant to the terms of the Agreement. Nothing in the Agreement, its context, or the parties' conduct would reasonably have led employees to believe that recognition of the UAW was a foregone conclusion or, by the same token, that rejection of UAW representation by employees was futile.

. . . The Board found support for its conclusion in the policy underlying the NLRA. "The ultimate object of the [NLRA], as the Supreme Court has repeatedly stated, is 'industrial peace.'" . . . The Board expressed its reluctance to put "new obstacles" in the way of voluntary recognition of a union (e.g., recognition of a union's majority status by authorization cards rather than by election), and further noted that "[i]n practice, an employer's willingness to voluntarily recognize a union may turn on the employer's ability to predict the consequences of doing so." . . . The Board reasoned that, "[c]ategorically prohibiting prerecognition negotiations over substantive issues would needlessly preclude unions and employers from confronting workplace challenges in a strategic manner that serves the employer's needs, creates a more hospitable environment for collective bargaining, and—because no recognition is granted unless and until the union has majority support—still preserves employee free choice." . . .

Having rejected a categorical rule, the Board proceeded to determine that the LOA in this case was well within the boundaries of the NLRA:

> The LOA was reached at arm's length, in a context free of unfair labor practices. It disclaimed any recognition of the union as exclusive bargaining

representative, and it created, on its face, a lawful mechanism for determining if and when the union had achieved majority support. The LOA had no immediate effect on employees' terms and conditions of employment, and even its potential future effect was both limited and contingent on substantial future negotiations. As its statement of purpose makes clear, the LOA was an attempt to directly address certain challenges of the contemporary workplace. Considering the LOA as a whole, we find nothing that presents UAW representation as a fait accompli or that otherwise constitutes unlawful support of the UAW. Indeed, according to the General Counsel, employees here had no difficulty in rejecting the UAW's representation. . . .

One member of the Board dissented, arguing that the LOA included "substantive contract provisions" and that there were "no meaningful factual or legal distinctions" between the LOA at issue in this case and *Majestic Weaving Co.*, . . . According to the dissent, the majority "effectively overrule[d] *Majestic Weaving*," because "premature recognition is *not* a prerequisite for finding unlawful support in dealings between an employer and a minority union." . . .

At the heart of the dissent's argument was the concern that, in the context of the LOA, "employees could reasonably believe they had no choice but to agree to representation by the UAW without even knowing whether they approved or disapproved of the contract terms that union had negotiated for them." . . . The dissent rejected the majority's description of the LOA as merely a "framework" for future bargaining, finding instead that the LOA, specifically Article 4.2.4, included "substantive terms and conditions of employment" that "*had to be included* in any prospective future collective-bargaining agreement [s] covering these employees." . . . According to the dissent, the LOA "significantly limited the parameters" for negotiations on a number of other issues as well, including: future contract terms (4–5 years); healthcare cost initiatives; eight bargaining subjects; interest arbitration after six months of negotiation; and a waiver of strike rights prior to the final contract. . . . The dissent also dismissed the policy rationale put forth by the majority, arguing that even if employers and unions benefitted from negotiations, "the legality of negotiating such terms must turn on the statutory rights of employees, not on the commercial interests of unions and employers." . . .

The majority addressed the dissent's concerns in its opinion, noting that the Board's precedent does not "compel the categorical conclusion that an employer violates Section 8(a)(2) whenever it 'negotiates terms and conditions of employment with a union before a majority of unit employees . . . has designated the union as their bargaining representative.'" . . . Among other things, the majority countered the dissent's contention that the employees "could reasonably believe they had no choice but to agree to union representation," by pointing out that a majority of the employees *rejected* the UAW, and the UAW was never selected as the employees' exclusive bargaining representative. . . . In fact, according to the majority, agreements like the LOA "promote an informed choice by employees" because the employees "presumably will reject the union if they conclude or suspect that it has agreed to a bad deal or that it is otherwise compromised by the agreement from representing them effectively." . . .

Petitioners filed a timely petition for review of the Board's decision to dismiss the complaint, and Dana Companies, LLC and the UAW intervened. . . . [The court held, among other things, that the case is not moot because there continues to be an Article III case or controversy.]

The thoughtful majority and dissenting opinions of the Board members in this case show that reasonable minds could differ as to how the NLRA should be interpreted to further the underlying purposes of the NLRA in the context of employer negotiations with unions that do not have majority status. We must deny the petition for review, not because we find one position more persuasive than the other, but because Congress has given the Board the power to make industrial policy as long as it is doing so within the confines of the statutory language. . . . Indeed, the balancing of "conflicting legitimate interests" in pursuit of "the national policy of promoting labor peace through strengthened collective bargaining" is "precisely the kind of judgfment that . . . should be left to the Board." . . .

The Board reasonably held that the LOA did not include the type of an explicit recognition of a union that the Supreme Court determined to be unlawful in *Bernhard-Altmann*. In that case, the employer and the union signed a "memorandum of understanding" that "recognized the union as exclusive bargaining representative of all production and shipping employees." *Bernhard-Altmann*, 366 U.S. at 734. Even though the union in *Bernhard-Altmann* had achieved majority status by the time a formal [CBA] was reached, the Supreme Court held that the memorandum of understanding was still an unlawful form of pre-recognition bargaining because it granted the union "a deceptive cloak of authority with which to persuasively elicit additional employee support." *Id.* at 736.

In contrast, the pre-recognition agreement at issue in this case contains an explicit notice that Dana would *not* recognize the Union prior to the union's receiving a majority vote of the employees. Article 3.1 stated:

> The parties understand that the Company may not recognize the Union as the exclusive representative of employees in the absence of showing that a majority of the employees in an appropriate bargaining unit have expressed their desire to be represented by the Union.

In addition, the "Purpose" section of the LOA, which both parties agreed to communicate to the employees, Article 2.1.3.5, emphasized the fact that "[e]mployee's freedom to choose is a paramount concern of Dana as well as the UAW." In light of the differences between the memorandum of understanding in *Bernhard-Altmann* and the LOA at issue in this case, it was reasonable for the Board to hold that this agreement did not unlawfully recognize the union as the exclusive bargaining representative of Dana's employees.

The LOA was also not a form of "oral recognition" that the NLRB determined to be an unlawful form of pre-recognition bargaining in *Majestic Weaving Co.*,

147 N.L.R.B. 859 (1964). In that case, the Board held that even though the employer "conditioned the actual signing of a contract with Local 815 on the latter achieving a majority [of employees' support]," the fact that contract negotiations followed "an *oral recognition agreement*" constituted premature recognition of the union as the exclusive bargaining representative. *Majestic Weaving*, 147 N.L.R.B. at 860–61 (emphasis in the original). Not only did no such oral agreement occur in this case, but both parties explicitly agreed *not* to recognize the union until the union received the requisite show of support from the majority of Dana's employees.

The Board also reasonably found that the LOA was not a full [CBA] and required substantial negotiations, post-recognition, before it could become the employees' terms and conditions of employment. In *Bernhard-Altmann*, the Supreme Court held that an agreement that included "certain improved wages and conditions of employment," and that was simply waiting for execution of a "formal agreement *containing these terms* " was unlawful. *Bernhard-Altmann*, 366 U.S. at 734. While petitioners state that the LOA included "pre-negotiated concessions" and "contractual" obligations, . . . the Board determined that the LOA "did no more than create a framework for future collective bargaining," . . . , and was shy of the full agreements that required little more than formal execution and were held to be unlawful in *Bernhard-Altmann*. While some of the provisions in the LOA *may* have become binding if arbitration was necessary, the Board's interpretation of the NLRA and how the LOA relates to the statute is nonetheless still "a reasonable one." . . .

Petitioners argue that Article 4 contains the bulk of the problematic "contractual" obligations. . . . For instance, petitioners claim that Article 4.2.1 "compel[s] the UAW" because it specifies certain "premium sharing, deductibles, and out of pocket maximums" for healthcare costs to be maintained. Petitioners also argue that Article 4.2.4 includes examples of substantive terms that "contractually b[ind]" the employees of Dana. . . . These general terms included:

- Healthcare costs that reflect the competitive reality of the supplier industry and product(s) involved
- Minimum classifications
- Team-based approaches
- The importance of attendance to productivity and quality
- Dana's idea program (two ideas per person per month and 80% implementation)
- Continuous improvement
- Flexible Compensation
- Mandatory overtime when necessary (after qualified volunteers) to support the customer

At the heart of the dispute between the parties is the extent to which the terms in Article 4 are "substantive" because they are "binding." On their face, the terms in Article 4.2.4 are not specific, and would require further negotiations to reach any level of detail. However, Article 4.2.5 requires arbitration if both parties do not reach the first formal agreement within six months, and that agreement—according to the LOA—must include the provisions discussed in Article 4.2.4. In this way, terms regarding "mandatory overtime" or "compensation," for instance, could become binding. As the entity entrusted with maintaining "industrial peace," however, the Board was within its discretion to allow some substantive terms to be determined between the employer and union prior to recognition, as long as that agreement did not ultimately impact employees' choice regarding union representation. With the LOA in this case, employees may decide if they agree with the general principles that the agreement sets forth as well as if they are willing to risk being bound to any concessions that the union may make during negotiations of the first formal contract. If the employees are not willing to take that risk, then they do not have to select the union as their exclusive bargaining representative. In this instance, the employees at Dana did not select the UAW.

Petitioners also point to other LOA provisions as evidence of the substantive and binding nature of the LOA. These provisions fit even more comfortably within the Board's reasoning that some agreements short of a complete collective-bargaining agreement are acceptable. For instance, Article 4.2.2 states that any future agreements between the union and the company will be of a "minimum duration of ... four years." While contract duration is obviously important, the Board could conclude that it is part of the framework for negotiation that may be appropriately agreed upon before the employees choose whether to accept the union. Again, if employees felt hindered by this provision, they could reject any union that would make this concession on their behalf—and they ultimately did by not selecting UAW as their exclusive bargaining representative.

Petitioners also cite Article 6, the "No Strike/No Lockout" provision, as an infringement upon the rights of employees to select their own exclusive bargaining representative. . . . However, as the Board and Dana point out, this provision is only applicable until "the resolution of the first contract at each facility." Thus, this is an agreed-upon mechanism—one the employees can reject by not choosing the UAW—to ensure that bargaining moves forward in an attempt to achieve "industrial peace." . . . It is not a permanent forfeiture of the employees' rights.

Finally, petitioners point to provisions in the LOA that they argue "contractually b[ind]" Dana's employees, . . . such as Article 5's dispute resolution mechanism. While petitioners argue that Article 5 makes the LOA binding or enforceable, the dispute resolution mechanism is specifically intended to address any "violation(s) of this Agreement," which is limited to the process the parties will undergo *prior to reaching a full collective-bargaining agreement*. Thus, like the no strike/no lockout provision, this is a limited concession that employees were free to reject.

Though the petitioners rely heavily on the dissent's interpretation of Supreme Court and Board precedent, the Board majority's response to these concerns was reasonable. Again, our task is not to determine which NLRB members were more persuasive, but whether the majority's interpretation of the NLRA was reasonable.

Petitioner attempts to limit the degree of our deference to the Board by characterizing the issue before us as one of interpretation of the LOA. But there is no real issue presented to us as to the meaning of the LOA. The question is whether the LOA . . . violates the NLRA. It is the scope of the prohibitions of the NLRA—what constitutes unlawful interference—that is at issue, and this is clear from the arguments of both the majority and dissenting Board members. We are required to defer to the Board's reasonable interpretation of the statute.

For the foregoing reasons, we deny the petition to review.

Notes

1. In *Montague v. NLRB*, the court affirmed, under a different case name, the Board's dismissal of the complaint alleging that the parties violated § 8(a)(2) by entering into the LOA. *See Dana Corp.*, 356 N.L.R.B. 256 (2010), *aff'd*, *Montague v. NLRB*, 698 F.3d 307 (6th Cir. 2012). Accordingly, many labor lawyers still refer to this case as *Dana Corporation*. This decision should not be confused with *Dana Corp.*, 351 N.L.R.B. 434 (2007), discussed in Chapter 7, which involves the very different issue of the voluntary recognition bar.

2. In *Majestic Weaving*, *supra*, the Board held that an employer violates the NLRA when it begins to bargain with a minority union even though the parties expressly condition execution of the agreement on the union obtaining majority status. The *Dana Corp.* majority, as affirmed by the Sixth Circuit, distinguished *Majestic Weaving* on two grounds. First, the parties in that case negotiated a complete collective-bargaining agreement before the union had achieved majority status. In those circumstances the parties were legally required to execute that agreement under § 8(d). Second, the union's showing of majority support depended on a supervisor's solicitation of authorization cards. Are either of those grounds persuasive? To what extent has *Majestic Weaving* survived *Dana Corp./Montague*?

3. In *"Easy in, Easy Out": A Future for U.S. Workplace Representation*, 98 Minn. L. Rev. 1615 (2014), Professor Samuel Estreicher argues that framework agreements, such as the one found lawful in *Dana Corp./Montague*, could complement "easy in" methods for certifying unions seeking to represent employees. According to Estreicher:

> The "easy in" component would apply to workers not presently represented by a labor organization for collective bargaining purposes. On a limited showing of interest, workers would have an automatic right, once every two years—say, on the second Monday after Labor Day—to cast a secret-ballot vote on whether they wish to be represented by a union and whether they wish to be represented by one of the petitioning unions. The NLRB . . . would be empowered to promulgate rules establishing in advance, and without the requirement of a hearing, appropriate bargaining units for the election and at least initial bargaining. The electorate would be all full- and part-time employees on the payroll by, say, Labor Day. The election would be decided by a majority of the votes cast within the particular

unit. If a majority of the workers in the unit votes against union representation, the agency could not hold another election for a year. If the majority
of the workers in the unit votes for representation by one of the petitioning
unions, that union would be automatically certified as the bargaining agent
for a period of two years. The employer would be under a statutory duty to
bargain with the certified union, as it is under present law. A run-off election would be held if no choice won a majority on the first ballot. . . .

The "easy out" component would apply to any bargaining unit of workers covered by the NLRA . . . for whom a union has been certified as the
statutory bargaining agent, whether it achieved a collective bargaining
contract or not. The workers in the unit would be able after two years to
vote in an automatic secret-ballot election to decide whether they wished to
continue the representation of the certified bargaining agent, whether they
wanted no representation at all, or whether they wished to be represented
by another, petitioning union. As with the initial election, a majority vote
for no representation would preclude an NLRB election for another year; a
vote to continue representation by the certified agent or to be represented
by another union would preclude an election for a period of two years. Estreicher, 98 MINN. L. REV. at 1630–31.

In Estreicher's view, such easy-in methods for certifying unions are good policy,
especially when coupled with easy-out methods for decertifying unions, because
they lower the stakes involved in such elections. He argues that this, in turn, lowers
the risk of industrial strife.

4. Under the Board's contract-bar doctrine, *see* Chapter 7, a union enjoys an
irrebuttable presumption of majority support for the life of a collective-bargaining
agreement up to three years. The Board majority in *Dana* distinguished *Bernhard-
Altmann*, noting (n.18) that the contract at issue there would have been sufficient
to bar an election whereas the LOA would not be have been sufficient to serve as a
contract bar. *See Appalachian Shale Prods. Co.*, 121 N.L.R.B. 1160, 1163–64 (1958)
("[T]o serve as a bar, a contract must contain substantial terms and conditions of
employment deemed sufficient to stabilize the bargaining relationship; it will not
constitute a bar if it is limited to wages only, or to one or several provisions not
deemed substantial.").

5. The majority responded to the dissent's contention that the LOA provided the
union with a "'deceptive cloak of authority,'" (356 N.L.R.B. at 265) as follows:

The essential premise of the dissent is that employees, made aware of an
agreement like the one at issue here, "could reasonably believe they had
no choice but to agree to [union] representation." Our colleague offers no
evidence in support of this hypothesis—and the evidence here certainly
tends to refute it: a majority of the employees subsequently rejected the
UAW. Where, as in this case, an agreement expressly requires a showing of
majority support, as determined by a neutral third party, before the union

can be recognized, and where no unfair labor practices have been committed, it is hard to believe that a reasonable employee—a rational actor presumed by federal labor law to be capable of exercising free choice— would feel compelled to sign a union-authorization card simply because the agreement prospectively addresses some substantive terms and conditions of employment. If anything, such an agreement tends to promote an informed choice by employees. They presumably will reject the union if they conclude (or suspect) that it has agreed to a bad deal or that it is otherwise compromised by the agreement from representing them effectively. 356 N.L.R.B. at 264.

What do you think? How close to agreement do the parties have to get before their conduct constitutes an unfair labor practice?

D. After-Acquired Facilities

Kroger Co.

National Labor Relations Board
219 N.L.R.B. 388 (1975)

. . . .

The facts are not in dispute. Respondent has separate collective-bargaining agreements with Retail Clerks Local 455 and Meat Cutters Local 408. In each of these collective-bargaining agreements, Respondent has agreed to recognize the Union as the exclusive bargaining representative of employees in designated classifications at all stores operated by Respondent's Houston Division in the State of Texas. Recognition clauses of a similar nature have appeared in prior collective-bargaining agreements executed by the parties and, over the years, the parties' practice has been to treat stores newly added to the division as accretions to the contract units. The instant controversy had its beginning in March 1972, when Kroger Co. decided, for administrative purposes, to shift its stores at Nacogdoches and Lufkin, Texas, from its Dallas to its Houston Division. The Unions took the position that they were entitled to recognition as the bargaining representatives of these employees under the terms of their collective-bargaining agreements with Respondent. The Unions formally demanded recognition on March 22, 1972, and, although their claims were based on the recognition clauses in their respective contracts, both Unions offered to submit proof that they had card majorities among the employees at the stores in issue. Respondent rejected both the claim for recognition under the collective-bargaining agreements and the offer to prove majority status on the basis of cards. It is undisputed that, at the time the recognition requests were made, the Unions possessed valid card majorities among the employees sought.

. . . [T]he Board has held that "additional store clauses" are valid in situations where the Board is satisfied that the employees affected are not denied their right to have a say in the selection of their bargaining representative. Here . . . it is conceded that the Unions have a valid card majority in the units involved, which leaves no barrier to giving full effect to the contractual commitments of the parties. . . .

Interpreting these clauses to mean that an employer can voluntarily recognize a union or demand an election renders them totally meaningless and without effect, for unions need no contract authorization to establish their representation status in a Board-conducted election. However, these clauses can be read to require recognition upon proof of majority status by a union. . . . [T]here is no need to hold these clauses totally invalid simply because they do not contain an explicit condition that unions must represent a majority of the employees in a new store, inasmuch as the Board will impose such a condition as a matter of law. . . .

The court examined these clauses in the context of this case and found that they constituted a waiver by Kroger of its right to demand an election in these circumstances. Upon reconsideration we now adopt this view as the only reasonable interpretation which saves these clauses from meaninglessness or from impinging on functions reserved solely to the Board.

Finally, having concluded that these clauses are valid and constitute a waiver of the Employer's right to demand an election, we must consider the court's last question on remand, as to whether there exists any considerations of national labor policy which would require us to find these clauses illegal, not-withstanding our other findings. We not only find that no such negative considerations exist, but agree with the suggestion in the court's opinion that national labor policy favors enforcing their validity.

As we have interpreted them, these clauses are contractual commitments by the Employer to forgo its right to resort to the use of the Board's election process in determining the Unions' representation status in these new stores. To permit the Employer to claim the very right which it has forgone, perhaps in return for concessions in other areas, would violate the basic national labor policy requiring the Board to respect the integrity of collective-bargaining agreements. Since the Unions' majority is conceded by all concerned, there is no countervailing considerations of policy not to give effect to these agreements. . . . The Board has held that an employer may agree in advance of a card count to recognize a union on the basis of a card majority, and we can perceive of no reason why it may not contract with the union to do so in advance of the time the union has commenced organization. . . .

Note

In *Shaw's Supermarkets*, 343 N.L.R.B. 963 (2004), the Board created some doubt about the *Kroger* after-acquired facility doctrine. That case raised two issues: "(1) [w]hether the Employer clearly and unmistakably waived the right to a Board election; (2) if so, whether public policy reasons outweigh the Employer's private agreement not to have an election." *Id.* The Board stated it would "not resolve these issues at this stage"; instead, it would "merely hold that they are worthy of review." *Id.*

Although not resolved, these statements sparked the following defense of the *Kroger* doctrine by Board Member Dennis Walsh.

> [In *Kroger*] the Board adopted as "the only reasonable interpretation" the court's view that the contract clauses were waivers of the employer's right to demand an election. . . . Finally, the Board reasoned that "national labor policy favors enforcing [the clauses'] validity." . . .
>
> For nearly 30 years, the Board has repeatedly followed *Kroger* and found that an employer waives its right to an election by agreeing to an additional stores clause. . . . The fact that such a clause does not explicitly state that it constitutes a waiver is not determinative. . . .
>
> The Board has also applied *Kroger* to the very situation present here: an RM petition filed in response to a union's invocation of an after-acquired stores clause. In *Central Parking*, the union contended that its agreement with the employer contained an "after-acquired stores clause," pursuant to which the employer agreed, upon proof of majority status, to recognize the union as the bargaining representative of employees at after-acquired parking facilities in the San Francisco area. When the employer acquired another company that operated parking facilities in that area, the union sought recognition as the collective-bargaining representative of employees at those facilities. The employer denied recognition, and the union filed a grievance and sought arbitration. The employer refused to arbitrate and instead filed an RM petition for an election in a separate unit consisting of the newly acquired facilities. The Regional Director dismissed the petition, and the Board majority affirmed. . . .
>
> *Central Parking* therefore makes clear that under *Kroger*, an RM petition that is based on a demand to apply an after-acquired stores clause must be dismissed. *Id.* at 966.

What are the interests being protected by the *Kroger* doctrine? Is there a possibility that this doctrine might implicate concerns under §8(a)(2)? Should the Board revisit the issue of whether the NLRA even *permits* voluntary recognition? If so, what should it conclude?

IV. Members-Only Unions in the Private Sector

The traditional model of union representation is an exclusive, majority representative. But could "members' only" unions—unions that only represent dues-paying members, who could be only a minority of employees in bargaining unit—be lawful under the NRLA? And if so, would it be good policy? In the following excerpt, Professor Morris comments on Judge John True's review of Morris's book, The Blue Eagle at Work: Reclaiming Democratic Rights in the American Workplace (Blue Eagle).

Charles J. Morris, *Minority Union Collective Bargaining: A Commentary on John True's Review Essay on the Blue Eagle at Work, and a Reply to Skeptics Regarding Members-Only Bargaining Under the NLRA*

27 Berkeley J. Emp. & Lab. L. 179 (2006)[*]

[Blue Eagle's minority-union bargaining] thesis revives and reaffirms the legality of a long-forgotten industrial relations practice: workers organizing into minority labor unions and exercising the right to bargain with their employers on a members-only basis in workplaces where there is not yet a designated majority representative. This concept challenges and overrides the conventional wisdom—or, more accurately the habit—that has long supported the erroneous belief that the Act requires bargaining only with a union that represents a majority of the employees in an appropriate bargaining unit.

. . . Judge True agrees with the Blue Eagle's basic premise . . . that "[n]othing in the actual language of the NLRA, in its legislative history, in NLRB or court cases, in the constitution, in international law, or indeed in common sense or sound policy suggests that unions could not still use this 'members only' bargaining approach." . . .

Notwithstanding that insightful recognition of the broad scope of the bargaining requirement, his emphasis on the independent role of section 8(a)(1) fails to appreciate that the integrated structure of the Act determines that an employer's duty to bargain with a minority union on a members-only basis stands on two separate legs: One is section 8(a)(1) . . . and the other—of equal if not greater importance—is section 8(a)(5), which he virtually ignores or seems to suggest is applicable only to majority unions. The language of that section, however, contains no such limitation, and its legislative history shows conclusively that this belatedly added unfairlabor-practice . . . was intended to enhance rather than diminish the bargaining requirements of section 8(a)(1). . . . The provision was deliberately worded to avoid limiting an employer's bargaining duty to majority unions only. The "smoking gun" that revealed such deliberation . . . was the Senate's rejection of an alternative version of section 8(5) that would have confined the bargaining requirement to employee representatives "chosen as provided in section 9(a)"—in other words, only to majority representatives within appropriate bargaining units. Instead, Congress adopted the present generic language, which is not so limited.

. . . [F]our [former] NLRB General Counsels . . . proposed . . . that an employer was duty bound to deal with an ad hoc group of employees regarding group grievances, which would be a discretionary [under *Chevron*]—though highly desirable—reading of the second-track requirement of section 7, i.e., protected concerted activity for "mutual aid or protection." However, although the latter clause is closely related, it is not the statutory basis for the duty to bargain collectively with a

---

minority union, which relies primarily on the express grant of collective-bargaining rights for all employees contained in the first part of section 7 and is based on a mandatory reading of clear and specific language. . . .

II. A Response to the Doubters

. . . .

Regarding the underlying question—i.e., the validity of a members-only contract—it has been long established by both Supreme Court and NLRB authority that voluntary members-only bargaining and its resulting contracts are legal under the Act. The only noteworthy questions still open regarding this subject are: (1) whether an employer has a duty to engage in members-only non-majority bargaining where there is no section 9(a) majority representative and (2) to what extent, if any, benefits contained in member-only collective agreements may be granted exclusively to union members covered by such contracts—as to which there is a subsidiary question, to wit, whether the law requires the contracting employer to grant any or all of the same benefits to similarly-situated nonunion employees. . . . There is no open question under existing law, however, as to the legality of voluntary members-only minority-union bargaining where there is no section 9(a) representative; nor is there any reason to question the inherent validity of contracts resulting from such bargaining, though of course the parties could poison both the process and its contracts by engaging in otherwise unlawful conduct violative of sections 8(a)(1), 8(a)(2), 8(a)(3), 8(b)(1)(A), and/or 8(b)(2). Indeed, there have been a number of such cases involving various infractions of that nature, but their holdings should not be confused with the issue of untainted members-only bargaining.

A. The Legality of Members-Only Collective Bargaining Contracts: A Settled Issue

. . . [T]here are doubters who assert that these contracts must be deemed illegal because they represent a form of discrimination against nonunion employees—from which, they contend, it must logically follow that even voluntary members-only bargaining violates the Act, for such bargaining cannot be legal if its product is illegal. . . .

The obvious place to begin this process is with the skeptical conclusions of Julius Getman. . . . Here are Getman's positions and reasons quoted in full from his 2003 article, *The National Labor Relations Act: What Went Wrong; Can We Fix It?* [45 B.C. L. Rev. 125, 136–38 (2003)].

> We know that the concept of exclusivity together with § 8(a)(2) forbids an employer from bargaining with a minority union on behalf of a unit in which the union does not represent a majority. In other respects, questions abound. Does a union that seeks minority representation violate the NLRA? Is its activity protected? May a union seek to bargain for its members alone? At least two major legal scholars, Clyde Summers and Charles Morris, believe that minority unions may bargain for their own members . . . Despite the support of such distinguished scholars, this position is, in my view, wrong.

My basic reasons for disagreeing are first, that any agreement which applies to union members only would violate §8(a)(3). This proposition was established in 1952 when the U.S. Court of Appeals for the Second Circuit held in *NLRB v. Gaynor News Co.* that granting benefits to union members that were denied to nonunion members violated §8(a)(3) because it was "inherently conducive to increased union membership." The Supreme Court affirmed in 1954, stating, "[i]n holding that a natural consequence of discrimination, based solely on union membership or lack thereof, is discouragement or encouragement of membership in such union, the court merely recognized a fact of common experience." Second, any agreement that either overtly or tacitly applies more generally to the work force violates the concept of exclusivity and therefore violates §8(a)(2).

[Professor Morris then explains why, in his view, Professor Getman is wrong.] . . . In [*Consolidated Edison Co. v. NLRB*, [305 U.S. 197 (1938)], the Supreme Court unequivocally held that members-only collective bargaining agreements, "in the absence of [a section 9(a) majority-based] exclusive agency," were valid under the Act even if the covered employees "were a minority." Not only has that decision never been overruled, the Court reaffirmed its holding on two subsequent occasions, in *International Ladies Garment Workers v. NLRB (Bernhard-Altmann Texas Corp.)* [366 U.S. 731 (1961)] and *Retail Clerks International Association v. Lion Dry Goods, Inc.,* [369 U.S. 17 (1962)]. . . .

[I]n its original *Consolidated Edison* decision the Board expressly held that the involved companies "have not engaged in unfair labor practices within the meaning of section 8(2) of the Act." The Supreme Court's decision in that case thus addressed only the section 8(1) and 8(3) issues. Soon after, in *Solvay Process Co.,* 5 N.L.R.B. 330 (1938), the Board reaffirmed its dismissal of the section 8(2) charge in *Consolidated Edison* by expressly holding that an employer's recognition of a minority union "as the sole bargaining agency for its members only" was not a violation of section 8(2). And in *Consolidated Builders, Inc.,* 99 N.L.R.B. 972, 975, n.6 (1952), the Board again held that recognition of, and a collective agreement with, a members-only minority union does not violate section 8(a)(2). . . .

. . . [I]n *Bernhard Altmann*, the Court revisited the issue. That case concerned an employer's signing of a collective bargaining agreement with a minority union, thus recognizing it as the exclusive bargaining agent of all unit employees. This was the most significant of the "false majority" cases previously noted. Such conduct was deemed a section 8(a)(2) violation by the employer and a section 8(b)(1)(A) violation by the union. Although Justice Douglas' partial dissent has been cited for its clarity in depicting the nature of and rationale for members-only contracts and for its reminder of the long history validating such contracts, the majority opinion also favorably acknowledged the validity of those contracts. Not only did it not question the accuracy of Justice Douglas' observations—disagreeing only as to the appropriate remedy—it expressly explained that the section 8(a)(2) "violation which the

Board found was the grant by the employer of exclusive representation status to a minority union, as distinguished from an employer's bargaining with a minority union for its members only. Therefore the exclusive representation provision is the vice in the agreement. . . .

The Supreme Court thus reiterated, without qualification, that a members-only agreement with a minority union would not be deemed a violation of sections 8(a)(2) or 8(b)(1)(A). And a year later, in *Lion Dry Goods*, [369 U.S. 17, 29 (1962)] the Court again reconfirmed the validity of such a minority-union contract, reminding us that "members-only contracts have long been recognized."

. . . Getman simply asserts that minority unions cannot bargain for their members only because "any agreement which applies to union members only would violate § 8(a)(3)." He bases that over-broad conclusion on a single case, *Gaynor News Co.*, which was reviewed by the Supreme Court in *Radio Officers*. The fact situation there, however, was not one that involved representation of union-members only; rather, it was a case where a majority union purported to represent an entire bargaining unit, signed a contract containing an exclusive recognition clause to that effect, then proceeded to represent only its union members. . . . Accordingly, in no way is that case an indictment of members-only bargaining contracts where there is not a recognized section 9(a) exclusive bargaining agent. . . .

B. Unlawful or Irrelevant Majority-Union Bargaining for Union Members Only

1. Majority-Union Discrimination

Gaynor/Radio Officers was but one of several cases where the Board used rhetoric describing representation or bargaining for union members to portray scenarios where the recognized majority union and the employer were discriminating against nonunion employees. None of those cases concerned the issue of non-majority and non-exclusive unions bargaining on behalf of their members only. The vice in the parties' conduct in each of these cases was the employer's recognition of a union as the majority and exclusive representative of all the employees in the unit, when in fact the union was representing only its own members and the willing employer was intentionally not granting collectively-bargained benefits to the nonunion employees. These cases . . . were basically combinations of breach of the duty of fair representation (DFR) by the union, unlawful section 8(a)(2) favoring of the union by the employer, and discrimination against nonunion employees by both the union and the employer. . . .

C. Members-Only Bargaining v. Individual Bargaining: What Right, if any, do Nonunion Employees Have to Benefits Achieved Through Less-Than-Majority Members-Only Bargaining?

[T]he following questions have not yet been definitively answered: To what extent, if any, can benefits contained in a member-only collective agreement be granted exclusively to union members covered by such a contract? And, as a subsidiary question, does the law require the employer to grant any or all of the same benefits to similarly-situated nonunion employees, or is that a matter that may be left to the discretion of the employer?

[T]he answers to these questions do not affect the BLUE EAGLE's basic thesis, that the NLRA protects the right of less-than-majority employees to bargain collectively through a union of their own choosing wherever there is not an existing section 9(a) exclusive representative. What can be affected by the answers, however, is the impact that such bargaining might ultimately have on employees who are not members of the union.

[T]he statute and existing case law, coupled with simple logic and socially-desirable end results, point firmly in the direction of an affirmative answer to the first question, i.e., allowing collectively-bargained benefits under a members-only agreement to be granted exclusively to union employees without the employer being required to grant the same benefits to nonunion employees, who, by having refrained from joining the union, have chosen to bargain individually. . . .

[E]ven if it were determined that denying the benefits of such contracts to similarly-situated nonunion employees would be unlawful, it would not follow that either the bargaining process or the resulting contracts would be illegal per se. Such a determination would simply mean that the bargaining employer would be obligated to grant the same benefits to affected nonmember employees. Such benefits, however, would likely be economic benefits only, for benefits such as access to union stewards and grievance and arbitration procedures are inseparable parts of the union-representational process. Absent a DFR requirement—which is dependent on the concept of exclusive representation, not here present—a nonmajority union would have no obligation to provide the latter-type benefits to nonmembers who pay no dues. In other words, even if the Board or the courts were to decide (erroneously in my view) that denial of collective benefits to nonunion employees would constitute discrimination under section 8(a)(3)—and conceivably also under section 8(b)(2)—the only effect of such a ruling would be to require employers henceforth to grant those benefits, which many if not most employers would likely grant anyway without legal compulsion. Accordingly, the following excerpt from the BLUE EAGLE concerning the impact of providing such collectively-bargained benefits to nonunion employees is here pertinent:

> When a minority union succeeds in negotiating economic benefits for its members—as distinguished from noneconomic benefits, such as grievance procedures—it may be indirectly negotiating those same benefits on behalf of others, for the employer may choose to extend them to nonunion workers similarly situated. A non-majority union must be careful not to urge that such benefits be applicable to union members only, for it will want to avoid being charged with having caused the employer to discriminate against nonunion employees. On the other hand, if the employer on its own chooses not to extend the same benefits to nonunion employees, this would not violate the Act unless it can be shown that its purpose was to discriminate against those employees in order to encourage their joining the union, which

normally would be unlikely. The employer's purpose might simply be to save money, in which event, however, many nonunion workers would undoubtedly hasten to join the union to obtain the negotiated benefits. The more likely scenario is that the employer will extend those benefits to the other employees, but this will nevertheless represent a gain for the union in that it can now properly claim credit for the employer's action while exhorting the recipients of the windfall not to be free-riders. Significantly, as previously noted, such extended benefits will not be part of the collective agreement, hence not enforceable thereunder, either by arbitration or court action.

. . . The more appropriate resolution of the opening question, however, is that a disparity between benefits for union members and nonmembers does not violate the Act. This is not to say that the bargaining employer would necessarily want to withhold such benefits; but this should be the employer's own business decision, not one dictated by law, especially law that purports to encourage collective bargaining. Nevertheless, as noted in the foregoing excerpt from the Blue Eagle, the union should carefully avoid requesting, or even suggesting, that any economic benefits be withheld from nonmember employees, for such conduct might be misconstrued as evidence of the union "caus[ing] or attempting to cause an employer to discriminate against an employee in violation of subsection 8(a)(3)," thereby violating section 8(b)(2).

The key element that determines this issue, however, is the employer's purpose. . . .

Notes

1. This debate raises two separate issues. First, does the language of the NLRA, along with Board and Court precedent, require or at least permit the recognition and certification of "minority unions"? Morris argues, in The Blue Eagle at Work, that the language of § 7 gives workers this right: "employees shall have the right . . . to bargain collectively through representatives of their own choosing." This language, he notes, does not require or even refer to a representative chosen by a majority of workers in a given bargaining unit. Section 9(a) does refer to majority representatives, but Morris sees that as an *alternative* to the type of representation allowed under § 7, not a requirement for representation under § 7. Where a majority union existed there could be no minority union, Morris argues, but where no majority union exists, a minority union could. Morris and his critics have debated whether subsequent Board and court precedent have rejected the minority union interpretation. For a description of the arguments on both sides, see Joseph Slater, *Do Unions Representing a Minority of Employees Have the Right to Bargain Collectively? A Review of Charles Morris, The Blue Eagle at Work*, 9 Emp. Rts. & Emp. Pol'y J. 383 (2005).

2. The day before his NLRB term ended, Member Hirozawa issued a concurrence in *Children's Hospital & Research Center of Oakland*, 364 N.L.R.B. No. 114 (Aug. 26, 2016), endorsing Professor Morris's position. The case concerned whether the employer was required to arbitrate grievances with a union that had been replaced by another union, given that the grievance arose while the first union still enjoyed majority status. The Board answered "yes," reasoning that it was logical to require

the employer to arbitrate with the first union, because there was no other mechanism to redress violations of the contract between that union and the employer. However, Member Hirozawa would have gone farther, writing that:

> Section 8(a)(5) provides that it is an unfair labor practice for an employer "to refuse to bargain collectively with the representatives of [its] employees, subject to the provisions of section 9(a)." Section 9(a), in turn, provides that "[r]epresentatives designated or selected for the purposes of collective bargaining by the majority of the employees in a unit appropriate for such purposes, shall be the exclusive representatives of all the employees in such unit. . . ." The Board's decision in this case explains what the subject-to-Section-9(a) clause means and marshals powerful arguments in support of its interpretation of the statute. That holding alone fully justifies the result in this case.
>
> I think it is also useful, however, to consider what the subject-to-Section-9(a) clause does *not* mean. It does not mean that for an employer to have a duty to bargain with a union on behalf of its employees, the union must be a Section 9(a) exclusive representative. This reading finds ample support in the text of the Act.
>
> First, the Section 8(a)(5) clause at issue here simply says, "subject to the provisions of section 9(a)." It does not say, if such representative is "the representative of the employees as provided in section 9(a)." Clearly, the Wagner Act Congress, which drafted the language of Section 8(a)(5), knew how to impose such a requirement if it so intended. It imposed precisely that requirement, using precisely that language, in a parallel subsection of the same section of the Act, Section 8(a)(3). The absence of such a requirement from Section 8(a)(5) is a strong indication that no such requirement was intended by Congress.
>
> Second, the Act's statement of the right enforced by Section 8(a)(5) is unencumbered by any requirement of Section 9(a) status. That statement appears, of course, in Section 7: "Employees shall have the right . . . to bargain collectively through representatives of their own choosing. . . ." Again, there is no requirement that the representatives through which employees exercise their right to bargain have attained Section 9(a) status or otherwise demonstrated majority support. In my view, these provisions, in the light they shed on the intended scope of Section 8(a)(5), reinforce the Board's finding of a violation of that section for refusal to bargain with a superseded union, which by definition was no longer a Section 9(a) exclusive representative.

For a contrary view to that of Member Hirozawa, see the Advice Memo in *Dick's Sporting Goods*, Case 6-CA-34821 (June 22, 2006); *see also* Denial of Appeal in *SCA Tissue North America*, Case 03-CA-132930 (June 5, 2015).

3. Second, independent of whether current law permits or requires recognition of minority unions, would it be good policy? From the perspective of unions or pro-union employees, what would be the advantages of a minority union, and what

would be the disadvantages? From the perspective of the employer? Of employees who do not want a union? What would you want to know about how, exactly, such a system would work?

4. One of the most interesting and closely watched union representation elections in recent years was the United Auto Workers' (UAW) effort to organize the production and maintenance employees in Volkswagen Group of America's (VWGOA) manufacturing facility in Chattanooga, Tennessee. With foreign carmakers moving production facilities to the United States to gain readier access to the lucrative American market, the UAW launched a long-term effort to organize their workers, particularly in the southern United States where most foreign car companies sited their plants. The foreign carmakers have been competing with the heavily unionized "Big Three" American carmakers and expanding their market share in the U.S. The UAW's organizing effort was aimed at both preserving its existing membership's competitive position and expanding the UAW's membership, which had shrunk dramatically with the decline of the U.S. auto industry. *See generally* Jim Efstathiou, *UAW Vote at Volkswagen Confronts Union Aversion in South*, Bloomberg (Feb. 11, 2014, 2:21 p.m.), http://www.bloomberg.com/news/2014-02-11/uaw-vote -at-volkswagen-confronts-union-aversion-in-south.html.

The venue seeming likeliest to yield an organizing success for the UAW was Volkswagen's sole U.S. manufacturing facility. Volkswagen is seen as a worker- and union-friendly company. In particular, VWGOA's parent company, Volkswagen AG, has works councils—worker representation enterprises mandated by statute in Volkswagen's home country of Germany—in all of its plants around the world except for those located in the United States and China. Bernie Woodall & Andreas Cremer, *UAW president pushes for 'works council' at VW Tennessee plant*, Reuters (Sep. 3, 2013 10:22 p.m.), http://www.reuters.com/article/2013/09/04/us-autos-vw -uaw-idUSBRE98304E20130904. These works councils consist of representatives elected by all employees in a Volkswagen facility. Works council representatives are empowered to receive and review information from the company about production and other issues, consult with the employer about many managerial decisions, and engage in "co-determination" (*i.e.*, shared decisionmaking) with the employer on selected high-level issues. Betriebsverfassungsgesetz [BetrVG] [Works Constitution Act], May 15, 1972, Bundesgesetzblatt [BGBl] at I p. 2518, *as amended by* Art. 3 Abs. 4G V. 20.4.2013 I 868; *see also* Volkswagen Auto Group, Declaration on Social Rights and Industrial Relationships at Volkswagen (Jun. 6, 2002).

Both Volkswagen's global works council—a confederation of its plant-level works councils—and the unions that represent Volkswagen's German employees are represented on Volkswagen's governing board. *See* Stefan Rüb, World Works Councils and Other Forms of Global Employee Representation in Transnational Undertakings 20–26 (Pete Burgess trans., Hans-Böckler-Stiftung 2002). As a result, its employees have a great deal of influence over Volkswagen's decisionmaking.

Volkswagen entered into a neutrality agreement in which it promised not to oppose the UAW. The agreement also gave the UAW extensive access to bargaining-unit members in the Chattanooga plant, including allowing UAW officials to address employee meetings. Since both Volkswagen and the UAW had publicly taken the position that creating a works council in the United States requires a collective-bargaining relationship with a majority union, the election agreement included language committing both parties to bargaining over the creation of a works council if the UAW won the election. *See* Woodall & Cremer, *supra*. But the National Right to Work Committee and Americans for Tax Reform intervened in the election process by running aggressive anti-union campaigns and working with some employees in the Chattanooga plant and a local organization calling itself Southern Momentum. *See* Steven Greenhouse, *Outsiders, Not Auto Plant, Battle U.A.W. in Tennessee*, N.Y. Times, Jan. 29, 2014, at B1. In addition, important Tennessee elected officials expressed their strong opposition to the UAW. Just before bargaining-unit members were about to vote, two Republican state legislators announced they would oppose further tax incentives to Volkswagen to expand its plant if the UAW won the election. Documents revealed that then-Governor Bill Haslam (R-TN) proposed a $300 million subsidy for another production line at the Chattanooga plant, but would have required the unionization vote to be "satisfactory" to the state. *See* Steven Greenhouse, *In Bid for Revote, Union Claims Tennessee Officials Frightened Workers*, N.Y. Times, Apr. 5, 2014, at B3. And then-Senator Robert Corker (R-TN) announced a few days before the election that he had spoken with sources inside Volkswagen who had told him that the Chattanooga plant would expand only if the UAW lost the election. *See* Steven Greenhouse, *U.A.W. Asks U.S. Labor Board to Examine Vote at Tennessee Plant*, N.Y. Times, Feb. 22, 2014, at B3. The UAW lost the election by a vote of 712–626.

The UAW initially challenged the election on the grounds that the outside groups and the Tennessee politicians had destroyed the "laboratory conditions" necessary to employee free choice in an NLRB election. Objections to Conduct Affecting Election, No. 10-RM-121704 (N.L.R.B. 2014). After anti-union employees, aided by the National Right to Work Committee, intervened in the post-election hearing with the Board's permission, *Volkswagen Grp. of Am., Inc.*, 10-RM-121704 (N.L.R.B. 2014), the UAW withdrew its challenge and the election results were certified. Several employees, again assisted by the National Right to Work Committee, had also filed a challenge to the UAW-Volkswagen election agreement using the same arguments advanced in *Unite Here Local 355 v. Mulhall*, 667 F.3d 1211, 1213 (11th Cir. 2012), that the agreement was a violation of § 302 of the LMRA. The employees withdrew their lawsuit after the NLRB certified the election results, and all parties agreed that the certification bar prohibited a new election for one year. *See* Complaint, *Burton v. Auto Workers*, No. 14-CV-76 (E.D. Tenn. Mar. 12, 2014).

However, the UAW has continued organizing in Volkswagen's Chattanooga plant. In July 2014, the UAW announced it would establish Local 42 to operate as a members-only union representing workers in the Volkswagen plant. *See* Steven Greenhouse, *Despite Earlier Loss, U.A.W. Creates a Union at VW Plant*, N.Y. Times, July 11, 2014, at B4. In November 2014, Volkswagen announced a new policy to guide its interactions with its workers' representatives in Chattanooga. Under the policy, groups representing at least 15 percent of eligible workers would be entitled to meetings with management and other resources, with increased access for representatives that signed up 30 or 45 percent of workers. Mike Pare, *Labor Groups Support New VW Policy as Volkswagen Opens Way for Talks, Meetings with UAW and ACE*, Chattanooga Times Free Press, Nov. 13, 2014, http://bit.ly/1UeH4K2. Within one month, Local 42 had signed up at least 45 percent of eligible Volkswagen employees, entitling it to the highest level of access to VW management. Another group, the American Council of Employees ("ACE")—a group founded by workers who opposed UAW representation during the initial union drive—qualified for the lowest level of access. Lydia DePillis, *The Strange Case of the Anti-Union Union at Volkswagen's Plant in Tennessee*, Wash. Post (Nov. 19, 2014), http://wapo.st/11CE7wd. In May 2015, Local 42 announced that it represented 55 percent of the eligible workforce, and called for Volkswagen to voluntarily recognize it as exclusive bargaining representative; Volkswagen refused that request. Mark Clothier, *VW Denies UAW Request to be Sole Representative in Tennessee*, Bloomberg (May 7, 2015), http://bloom.bg/1CeQjEq.

Following these events, the UAW petitioned for—and won—a union election among the maintenance employees at the Chattanooga plant. Volkswagen opposed the union election on the grounds that more of the plant's employees should have been included in the unit. The Obama Board rejected Volkswagen's challenge in a decision applying the *Specialty Healthcare* standard discussed in Chapter 7. Volkswagen refused to bargain with the UAW in order to appeal the bargaining unit determination. However, the Trump Board then successfully moved the D.C. Circuit to remand the case in light of its decision in *PCC Structurals, Inc.*, 365 N.L.R.B. No. 160 (Dec. 15, 2017), which overruled *Specialty Healthcare*.

Months passed without a decision from the Board. Evidently tired of waiting for what would almost certainly be a loss, on April 9, 2019, the UAW filed a new petition seeking a plant-wide election. On April 17, 2019, it moved to withdraw its petition to represent the maintenance employees and dismiss the related ULP charge, and the Board granted that motion on May 3. But the Board found that this sequence of events was impermissible because of the certification bar. Recall that the Board bars new union election petitions from being filed for one year following a Board order certifying a union, and that period is tolled if there is a challenge to the certification. Therefore, the Board majority concluded, the certification bar was still in effect when the UAW filed its new election petition, and further, that problem was not cured by the UAW later disclaiming interest in representing the unit of maintenance workers. *See Volkswagen Group of America Chattanooga Operations, LLC*, 367 N.L.R.B. No. 138 (May 22, 2019).

Board Member McFerran issued a scathing dissent stating that, faced with VW's tactical invocation of the certification bar rule, the Board had "abandon[ed] our duty" to protect workers' §7 rights: "When the Union effectively conceded victory to the Employer by petitioning for the unit that the Employer had demanded, the Employer sought to block the new petition. And the employer now prevails. 'Heads the employer wins; tails the union loses' cannot be the Board's new motto."

Following the Board's decision, the UAW filed a new union election petition, which meant the election was further delayed. After employees voted over the course of three days in June 2019, the union lost, 833–776.

This potentially pathbreaking episode in labor relations history is likely to continue, with several legal questions still unanswered. First, should the UAW and its supporters in the Chattanooga plant have been entitled to a new election because of the behavior of the Tennessee elected officials and outside groups? Can the Board account for third-party enterprises' and individuals' behavior when deciding whether an election was valid? Can third parties commit ULPs? Second, can Volkswagen establish a works council in its Chattanooga plant absent a collective-bargaining relationship with a majority union? Or would Volkswagen's Chattanooga management, in its dealings with its local works council, necessarily commit ULPs under §§ 8(a)(1), (2), and (3)? Third, if the UAW becomes a majority representative, can Volkswagen and the UAW legally agree to a contract that delegates mandatory subjects of bargaining to a works council? Does the answer to this question change if the UAW represents the production and maintenance employees in the Chattanooga plant, but not other employees in the plant who are covered by the NLRA? Fourth, if the UAW establishes a members-only union, can Volkswagen bargain with it? Is Volkswagen legally required to bargain with it? Can Volkswagen agree to terms and conditions of employment with the UAW for its members without providing those same terms and conditions of employment to Volkswagen's other Chattanooga employees? Would that violate sections 8(a)(1) and (3)? Would providing terms and conditions agreed to with the UAW to non-UAW members violate sections 8(a)(1) and (2)? Is it possible that both options constitute violations of the law? Can it be that members-only unions, while theoretically consistent with the Act, are not practicable given the Act's constraints? Finally, does a neutrality agreement like the UAW-Volkswagen election agreement violate the LMRDA's section 302? The Supreme Court refused to answer this question in *Mulhall*, and the U.S. courts of appeals are split. What is the best answer?

V. In the Public Sector

A. Organizing Without an Election

Almost all public-sector jurisdictions provide for voluntary card-check recognition. Many have rules that are substantially similar to those under the NLRA. Some have rules that are more restrictive. Most importantly, a number of public-sector jurisdictions require employers to recognize unions on the basis of a legitimate card majority: a mandatory card-check recognition option not available in the private sector.

On the more restrictive side, Kansas requires a secret-ballot election before a public employer may recognize a union as exclusive bargaining agent, period. KAN. STAT. ANN. § 75-4327(d). Some other states permit voluntary recognition based on cards but add more procedural steps. For example, OHIO REV. CODE § 4117.05(a) requires that if an employer intends to voluntarily recognize a union, the employer must first post notice of the proposed recognition and allow other unions to intervene and oppose the voluntary recognition. It also requires the employer to submit evidence of the union's majority support to the labor board. What might be the purpose of those rules?

On the other hand, several states require recognition if the union shows a card majority. New York has had such a rule since 1967. Under this law, the New York PERB is empowered to:

> ascertain the public employees' choice of employee organization as their representative choice (in cases where the parties to a dispute have not agreed on the means to ascertain the choice, if any, of the employees in the unit) on the basis of dues deduction authorization and other evidences, or, if necessary, by conducting an election. N.Y. CIV. SERV. LAW § 207(2).

Indeed, in New York, certification based on dues deduction authorization and similar evidence, rather than election, is the preferred method for determining employee choice. *See Town of Islip*, 8 N.Y.P.E.R.B. ¶ 3049 (NY PERB 1975); *see generally* William Herbert, *Card Check Labor Certification: Lessons from New York*, 74 ALB. L. REV. 93 (2010–11).

More recently, Illinois, California, New Jersey, New Hampshire, Massachusetts, and Oregon added rules that provide for mandatory card-check recognition (although New Hampshire later revoked that rule, see Chapter 1). *See* Rafael Gely and Timothy Chandler, *Organizing Principles*: *The Significance of Card-Check Laws*, 30 ST. LOUIS U. PUB. L. REV. 475, 479 (2011). How do these laws work in practice?

County of Du Page v. Illinois Labor Relations Board

Supreme Court of Illinois
231 Ill. 2d 593, 900 N.E.2d 1095, 326 Ill. Dec. 848 (2008)

FITZGERALD, J.

. . .

Background

The Illinois Public Labor Relations Act (the Act) grants public employees "full freedom of association, self-organization, and designation of representatives of their own choosing for the purposes of negotiating wages, hours and other conditions of employment." 5 ILCS 315/2. . . . When the legislature enacted section 9(a-5) [in 2003], it provided public employees and labor organizations an alternative to the election process. Section 9(a-5) states:

> "The [Illinois Labor Relations] Board shall designate an exclusive representative for purposes of collective bargaining when the representative demonstrates a showing of majority interest by employees in the unit. If the parties to a dispute are without agreement on the means to ascertain the choice, if any, of employee organization as their representative,

the Board shall ascertain the employees' choice of employee organization, on the basis of *dues deduction authorization and other evidence*, or, if necessary, by conducting an election. If either party provides to the Board, before the designation of a representative, clear and convincing evidence that the dues deduction authorizations, and other evidence upon which the Board would otherwise rely to ascertain the employees' choice of representative, are fraudulent or were obtained through coercion, the Board shall promptly thereafter conduct an election. The Board shall also investigate and consider a party's allegations that the dues deduction authorizations and other evidence submitted in support of a designation of representative without an election were subsequently changed, altered, withdrawn, or withheld as result of employer fraud, coercion, or any other unfair labor practice by the employer. If the Board determines that a labor organization would have had a majority interest but for an employer's fraud, coercion, or unfair labor practice, it shall designate the labor organization as an exclusive representative without conducting an election." (Emphasis added.) 5 ILCS 315/9(a-5).

A union seeking to be certified under section 9(a-5) must file with the Board a "majority interest petition," *i.e.*, a representation petition "accompanied by a showing of interest evidencing that a majority of the employees in the petitioned-for bargaining unit wish to be represented by the labor organization." ... Under the Board's rules, the showing of interest in support of such a petition "may consist of *authorization cards, petitions, or any other evidence* that demonstrates that a majority of the employees wish to be represented by the union for the purposes of collective bargaining." ... The evidence of majority support must contain original, legible, signatures, which do not predate the filing of the petition by more than six months. ... In addition, the showing of interest "shall state that by signing the card the employee acknowledges that if a majority of his/her coworkers in an appropriate unit sign evidence of majority support, the card can be used by the petitioner to obtain certification as the employees' exclusive representative without an election." ... Evidence of majority support is not furnished to any of the parties. ...

The employer is required to submit signature exemplars for the employees in the proposed bargaining unit and is permitted an opportunity to respond to the petition. ... In addition to providing "clear and convincing evidence of any alleged fraud or coercion in obtaining majority support," the employer must set forth its "position with respect to the matters asserted in the petition, including, but not limited to, the appropriateness of the bargaining unit and, to the extent known, whether any employees sought by petitioner to be included should be excluded from the unit." ... "Any person aggrieved" by an order of the Board certifying a labor organization "may apply for and obtain judicial review. ...

The present legal dispute arose out of a majority interest petition filed by MAP [the Metropolitan Alliance of Police] ... in which MAP sought to be certified as the exclusive representative for a unit of Du Page County deputy sheriffs. The Employer objected to the petition on several grounds. . . . The Employer argued that section 9(a-5) required the Union to submit both dues deduction authorization evidence and some other evidence of majority support, and that the Board's rules to the contrary were invalid. The Employer also argued that it was entitled to copies of the Union's evidence and that the requested bargaining unit was inappropriate.

The Board rejected the Employer's arguments and, on March 23, 2006, certified MAP as the exclusive bargaining representative for the requested employee unit. The Board's tally indicated that 189 employees were in the unit; 111 valid cards were signed in support of MAP; no cards were found, or even alleged, to have been obtained through the use of fraud or coercion; and 14 cards were found invalid for other reasons (*e.g.*, the employee was not included in the unit, or the card was not signed or dated).

The Employer sought administrative review of the Board's decision, arguing that the word "and," as used in the statutory phrase "dues deduction authorization and other evidence" should be read in its conjunctive sense, and that the Board's rules contradict the statute and are therefore invalid. The Employer also argued that the Board likely applied the invalid regulations and did not require the Union to supply both dues deduction authorization and other evidence in support of its petition. . . .

The Board and the Union disagreed with the Employer's construction of section 9(a—5) and argued that the word "and," when construed in light of the entire section, should be read in its several, disjunctive sense. The Board and the Union also argued that the underlying evidence supporting a majority interest petition is confidential and that the employer does not have a right to review it. . . .

The appellate court vacated the Board's decision and remanded the matter to the Board for further proceedings. The appellate court determined that both constructions of section 9(a-5) advanced by the parties were reasonable and that the statute was therefore ambiguous. Ultimately, however, the appellate court agreed with the Employer: "[T]he majority interest provision requires that both dues deduction authorization and other evidence be submitted demonstrating that a majority of the employees support representation by the named organization." The appellate court also held that because the Board's regulations only require one form of evidence to support a majority interest showing, and do not require dues deduction authorization evidence, the Board's regulations conflict with the requirements of section 9(a-5) and, therefore, are invalid. The appellate court further held that the Board's decision on a majority interest petition is a final order, expressly subject to administrative review, and that meaningful review requires, at a minimum, that the reviewing court be able to ascertain that the evidence submitted to the Board was "the type and amount" sufficient to demonstrate a showing of interest by a majority of the eligible employees. The appellate court noted that there was no evidence of record to support the Board's decision, and inferred that MAP submitted evidence in conformance with the Board's invalid regulations, rather than the requirements of section 9(a-5). Accordingly, the appellate court held that the Board's decision certifying MAP was against the manifest weight of the evidence.

The appellate court also concluded that no reason existed to prohibit the Employer from reviewing the Union's evidence of majority interest, where the employees' identities are redacted. "Further, because the majority interest petition stands in lieu of an election, and to allow the meaningful review of the Board's decision, the Board must adopt some sort of regulation that provides for the submission of the evidence it relied upon to the reviewing court." . . .

Analysis

. . .

I. "Dues deduction authorization and other evidence"

. . . The Board argues that the word "and," as used in the phrase "dues deduction authorization and other evidence," when considered in the context of section 9(a-5) as a whole, should be read in the disjunctive. Under this reading, "dues deduction authorization and other evidence" establishes a range or category of evidence which will support a majority interest petition, but it does not require that the petition be supported by all such evidence. Rather, dues deduction authorization *or* other evidence, similar in kind to dues deduction authorizations, is sufficient. This interpretation is reflected in the Board's rules, which state in relevant part: "The showing of interest in support of a majority interest petition may consist of authorization cards, petitions, *or* any other evidence that demonstrates that a majority of the employees wish to be represented by the union for the purposes of collective bargaining." (Emphasis added.) . . .

The Employer argues that "and" typically "signifies and expresses the relation of addition," and thus is generally read in the conjunctive. The Employer disputes that reading "and" in this fashion creates an inconsistency in the statute, and adopts the reasoning of the appellate court that the term "otherwise," when given its ordinary meaning, can be reconciled with reading "and" in the conjunctive. . . .

In construing statutes, the strict meaning of words like "and" "is more readily departed from than that of other words." *John P. Moriarty, Inc. v. Murphy*, 387 Ill. 119, 129 (1944). Thus, if reading "and" in its literal sense would create an inconsistency in the statute or "render[ ] the sense of a statutory enactment dubious," we will read "and" as "or." . . .

We conclude that the basic premise underlying the Board's reading of the statute—that "and" does not necessarily mean "and"—and the basic premise underlying the Employer's reading of the statute—that "and" typically means "and"—both appear, at first blush, to be on solid ground. We conclude also that both interpretations can be harmonized, to a greater or lesser degree, with section 9(a-5) as a whole, including the "otherwise" clause. Accordingly, because section 9(a-5) is "'capable of being understood by reasonably well-informed persons in two or more different senses,'" we deem the statute ambiguous.

To resolve this ambiguity, we turn to the legislative history of section 9(a-5), which began its life as House Bill 3396. We find instructive the statements of Senator Martin Sandoval, who spoke in support of this bill:

"Under current law, workers must go through a difficult process to form a union. Workers must first sign union authorization cards stating that they want a union. Then, even though they've already said they want a union, they must file for a Labor Board-run election. The election process can be lengthy and cumbersome, as we all know, during which time the employer has control of the employers [*sic*] and can interfere with the employees' decision. And, in fact, employers routinely use this time to scare workers into voting against a union even if the workers want a union. Solution to this problem for public employees is to allow them to vote for a union through a process called card check." . . .

The senator's statements indicate that the legislature intended, through its adoption of House Bill 3396, to provide an alternative to the "lengthy and cumbersome" statutory election procedure, namely, a simple "card check" procedure. We therefore cannot agree with the Employer that the legislature would have complicated the card check procedure by requiring two forms of evidence: a dues checkoff card and some other unspecified form of evidence.

Support for this conclusion is also found in the statements of Representative Larry McKeon: "House Bill 3396 is modeled after a piece of legislation in New York that simplifies the manner in which elections may be held to certify a collective bargaining agent." . . .

The New York statute requires that for purposes of resolving disputes concerning representation status, the public employees' choice of representative shall be ascertained "on the basis of dues deduction authorization *and* other evidences." (Emphasis added.) N.Y. Civ. Serv. § 207. To implement the statute, New York's labor board adopted rules requiring a majority of the employees to indicate their choice of representative "by the execution of dues deduction authorization cards which are current *or* individual designation cards." (Emphasis added.) . . . We presume that our legislature, having modeled House Bill 3396 on the New York statute, was also aware of the corresponding administrative regulations, which were then in effect. Having adopted language that mirrors in pertinent part the language of the New York statute, we also presume that the legislature intended a similar result. The Board's reading of section 9(a-5), as reflected in its regulations, achieves that result. . . .

We hold that the word "and," as used in the phrase "dues deduction authorization and other evidence," was intended by the legislature to mean "or." The appellate court therefore erred in holding section 1210.80(d)(2)(A) of the Board's regulations, which do not require dues deduction authorization evidence, invalid. . . .

II. Employer Review of Majority Interest Evidence

. . . The Board's rules state that "[t]he Board shall maintain the confidentiality of the showing of interest," and that such evidence "shall not be furnished to any of the parties." . . . The Board argues that if the confidentiality of the evidence of majority support is not preserved, the basic purposes of the Act will be undermined. Relying upon federal case law analyzing the [NLRA], the Board contends that "employees have a strong privacy interest in their personal sentiments regarding union representation, and that this right to privacy is a right necessary to full and free exercise of the[ir] organizational rights" under the Act. *Pacific Molasses Co. v. NLRB Regional Office # 15*, 577 F.2d 1172, 1182 (5th Cir.1978). According to the Board, disclosure of authorization cards, which identify the signers, would chill the right of employees to express their union sentiments. *Pacific Molasses*, 577 F.2d at 1182. . . . The Board notes that even the attempted discovery of union authorization cards by an employer has been deemed an "illegal objective" . . . *Wright Electric, Inc. v. NLRB*, 200 F.3d 1162, 1167 (8th Cir.2000).

. . . [T]he appellate court attempted to address the Board's confidentiality concerns. The appellate court stated:

> "We note that respondents [the Board and the Union] raise concerns over breaching the anonymity protections of the employees who might be seeking to organize union representation, and the chilling effect on unionization that review of the majority interest petition might entail. We note further, however, that petitioners [the Employer] appear to be sensitive to such concerns and have requested only that they be allowed to review such redacted evidence that demonstrates majority interest on the part of the eligible deputies while maintaining the anonymity of the deputies. We certainly see no problems in providing for some sort of review of the redacted evidence in support of a majority interest petition. Further, because the majority interest petition stands in lieu of an election, and to allow the meaningful review of the Board's decision, the Board must adopt some sort of regulation that provides for the submission of the evidence it relied upon to the reviewing court and follows the mandates of section 9(a-5). We imagine that the submission of redacted dues authorization cards and other evidence will both preserve the employees' anonymity and allow the employer to have the same rights of review as provided in section 9(a) regarding the secret ballot election of a representative."

The Board questions the value of submitting redacted authorization cards. The Board notes that if all of the identifying information is redacted (name, signature, address, social security number, work unit), only the original preprinted card remains. Whatever the benefits, or burdens, in submitting redacted copies of the evidence of majority support, the submission of redacted evidence at least appears to address the confidentiality concerns raised by the Board.

The Board's disagreement with the appellate court opinion, however, goes beyond issues of confidentiality. The Board also disagrees with the appellate court's rationale for allowing an employer access to the evidence of majority support. The appellate court reasoned as follows. The Board's certification order is a final administrative decision and therefore subject to review by the appellate court. . . . Review must be meaningful, *i.e.*, the court must be able to ascertain that the union's evidence was the type and amount sufficient to demonstrate majority support. Therefore, the evidence of support must be submitted to the reviewing court and to the employer.

The Board argues that the appellate court's reasoning overlooks that the Act limits an employer's role in the determination of majority interest, and that except in narrow circumstances not present here, the Board's majority interest determination is not litigable. See 80 Ill. Adm.Code § 1210.80(e)(3) (providing that the showing of interest shall be determined administratively by the Board and is not subject to litigation, except for cases of fraud or coercion). We understand the Board's argument to be this. If, under the Act, an employer may not challenge the Board's determination of majority status, then this is not an issue that could be raised before the Board and not an issue that could be raised on administrative review. Therefore, no need exists to submit copies of the evidence of majority support (redacted or otherwise) to the employer. In evaluating this argument, we return to the language of the Act.

Section 9(a-5) mandates that "[t]he Board shall designate an exclusive representative for purposes of collective bargaining when the representative demonstrates a showing of majority interest by employees in the unit." Significantly, the legislature provided for minimal involvement by the employer in this procedure. Section 9(a-5) states: "If either party provides to the Board, before the designation of a representative, clear and convincing evidence that the dues deduction authorizations, and other evidence are fraudulent or were obtained through coercion, the Board shall promptly thereafter conduct an election." The legislature made no other provision for the employer to involve itself in the process by which the union seeks certification under section 9(a-5), or the process by which the Board determines whether a union has established majority support under section 9(a-5). We will not assume that the legislature intended a larger role for the employer than the language of section 9(a-5) allows. We thus agree with the Board that its determination of whether a union enjoys majority support may not be litigated.

This conclusion finds support in the fact that, at the time the legislature adopted section 9(a-5), the Board's rules provided that the showing of interest under section 9(a) would be determined administratively by the Board and would not be subject to litigation. If the legislature desired a different result when it adopted section 9(a-5), it could have included appropriate language in the statute. It did not do so.

To the extent section 9(a-5) could be considered ambiguous and the legislature's intent in doubt, we would defer to the Board's reasonable construction of the statute. The Board's construction, which limits the employer's ability to challenge a finding of majority support, is consistent with the legislative history . . . demonstrating that the General Assembly intended section 9(a-5) to limit an employer's ability to delay or interfere in the process of union recognition. . . . The legislature would not have provided a streamlined "card check" procedure for union recognition on the one hand, but on the other hand provide an employer the ability to delay a certification order by allowing a fishing expedition in the union's evidence of support. . . .

In sum, we hold that section 9(a-5) precludes an employer from litigating the Board's determination that a union enjoys majority status and, consequently, that an employer is not entitled to review the evidence of majority support. The appellate court erred in requiring the Board to make this evidence available to the employer. . . .

Notes

1. The court approved rules from the labor board that provide only a limited role for employers in the card-check certification process. Was the court convincing on that issue? Is this approach good policy?

2. In Illinois and in other states that provide for mandatory card-check certification, if fraud or coercion in obtaining evidence of majority support is shown, the state agency will order an election. How would one show fraud or coercion? Is this a sufficient protection for employees?

3. Opponents of mandatory card-check provisions often claim that such rules would lead to coercion by unions in gaining representation cards. What is the evidence from the public sector on this? One study of card-check petitions filed between 2003 and 2009 in Illinois, New Jersey, New York, and Oregon examined 1,073 orders of certification and over 1,300 petitions. In all these cases, there were only five allegations of union misconduct raised with the labor boards, and none of these allegations were sustained. Robert Bruno *et al., Majority Authorizations and Union Organizing in the Public Sector: A Four-State Perspective* (May 14, 2009), *available at* http://www.ler .illinois.edu/labor/images/Multi-State%20EFCA%20Report.pdf.

In *Great Futures Charter High School for the Health Sciences and Great Futures Educ. Ass'n*, 43 N.J. Pub. Employee Rep. ¶ 45 (2016), the New Jersey agency, in rejecting the employer's claim that the union had used coercion to obtain representation cards, stated the following:

> Since the Legislature authorized petitions for card check certification as the majority representative in 2005, we have only once ordered an election in addressing a challenge to the validity of authorization cards. *North Bergen Tp.*, 35 NJPER 244 (¶ 88 2009); aff'd at P.E.R.C. No. 2010-37, 35 NJPER 435 (¶ 143 2009). In *North Bergen Tp.*, the Commission upheld a decision by the Director to order an election since the validity of a significant number of authorization cards were called into question by numerous letters from employees to the Director describing threats, promises of benefits, and misleading statements causing them to sign cards. Specifically, ten (10) employees of a unit of forty (40) employees expressed in writing their desire to revoke their authorization cards.

Is this evidence suggestive of what would likely happen in the private sector if similar rules were adopted?

4. More broadly, should the experience with mandatory card-check recognition rules in some larger public-sector jurisdictions provide useful experience and evidence for policymakers considering whether to adopt a similar rule for the private sector? Or is such a rule more appropriate for the public sector than for the private sector?

5. States that provide for mandatory card-check recognition in the public sector typically have rules stating what type of language should appear on cards to be used for recognition purposes, and the duration for which cards will be valid (six months is typical; in Oregon, 90 days, in Massachusetts, one year). Assuming a state has adopted mandatory card-check recognition, what rules do you think should be in place to make the process work as fairly as possible?

B. The Exclusive, Majority Representation Model

The exclusive, majority representation model has been essentially ubiquitous in public-sector labor laws. But recall two recent alternatives to this model in the public sector mentioned in previous chapters. First, the 2011 Tennessee law for teachers, discussed near the end of Chapter 1, replaced "collective bargaining" with "collaborative conferencing," a process in which teachers may be represented by any organization that receives at least 15 percent support in a vote by the employees. Second, *Springfield Nat'l Educ. Ass'n v. Springfield Bd. of Educ.*, discussed in Chapter 5, held that employees in a teachers' bargaining unit could, in an initial ballot, choose to be represented by one union, multiple unions, or no union.

Are these good alternatives for unions? For employees? For employers? Why or why not? Note that in both of these cases, employers pushed for these alternatives, and unions opposed them. If you were to design a system of representation outside the exclusive, majority representation model, how exactly would it work? Consider this question again after you have read Chapter 14 and studied rules about the union's duty of fair representation and agency fees.

Chapter 9

The Duty to Bargain Collectively

I. Introduction

After workers have selected their representative, the employer and the union are required to engage in a process in which they will resolve important workplace issues. As the Supreme Court announced soon after the Wagner Act (the Act) was enacted, the Act's objective was to require of employers "the making of contracts with labor organizations." *Consolidated Edison Co. v. NLRB*, 305 U.S. 197, 236 (1938). Yet, collective bargaining is different from negotiations over ordinary commercial contracts. The relationship is a "bilateral monopoly"—that is, the parties are not free to seek out other contracting partners who might offer preferable terms. An employer must deal only with its employees' representative and vice versa. As a result, contract terms are not tested in a market. They are the product of the parties' relationship, dealings, and economic power. *See* Stewart J. Schwab, *Collective Bargaining and the Coase Theorem*, 72 Cornell L. Rev. 245, 268–69 (1987).

Nonetheless, the Wagner Act had little to say about the NLRB's role in helping to achieve the making of contracts. Section 8(5) required employers to bargain collectively with their employees' representatives, but the Act offered no further definition or guidance regarding this duty, even though it first appeared in the National War Labor Board's jurisprudence during World War I and many of the most difficult questions had already surfaced. *See* Archibald Cox, *The Duty to Bargain in Good Faith*, 71 Harv. L. Rev. 1401, 1404–05 (1958). In the Taft-Hartley Act, Congress added § 8(b)(3) to subject unions to the same risk of liability facing employers for failure to bargain collectively. It also added § 8(d) to define "bargain collectively":

> [T]o bargain collectively is the performance of the mutual obligation of the employer and the representative of the employees to meet at reasonable times and confer in good faith with respect to wages, hours, and other terms and conditions of employment, or the negotiation of an agreement, or any question arising thereunder, and the execution of a written contract incorporating any agreement reached if requested by either party, but such obligation does not compel either party to agree to a proposal or require the making of a concession. 29 U.S.C. § 158(d).

Thus, under §§ 8(a)(5) and 8(b)(3), conduct that is within § 8(d)'s definition of "bargain collectively" is subject to regulation by the Board through ULP proceedings. Conduct that is outside this definition cannot be reached by the Board, at least not through ULP proceedings under §§ 8(a)(5) and 8(b)(3). The meaning of "confer in good faith" was left to the Board and the courts to determine.

The legislative history of § 8(5), which became § 8(a)(5) after the Taft-Hartley Act, neatly presents the fundamental paradox that arises when assessing whether the parties have bargained in "good faith." The Senate Labor Committee gave the following explanation for its decision to add § 8(5) to Senator Wagner's original bill:

> The committee wishes to dispel any possible false impression that this bill is designed to compel the making of agreements or to permit governmental supervision of their terms. It must be stressed that the duty to bargain collectively does not carry with it the duty to reach an agreement, because the essence of collective bargaining is that either party shall be free to decide whether proposals made to it are satisfactory.

> But, after deliberation, the committee has concluded that this fifth unfair labor practice [8(5), now 8(a)(5)] should be inserted in the bill. It seems clear that a guarantee of the right of employees to bargain collectively through representatives of their own choosing is a mere delusion if it is not accompanied by the correlative duty on the part of the other party to recognize such representatives as they have been designated (whether as individuals or labor organizations) and to negotiate with them in a bona fide effort to arrive at a collective bargaining agreement. S. Rep. No. 573, 74th Cong., 1st Sess. 12 (1935) (quoted in *NLRB v. American National Insurance Co.*, 343 U.S. 395, 403 (1952)).

In sum, employers and unions are required to bargain collectively, but refusing to agree to any contract provision or failing to make any concessions during bargaining alone could not result in liability for failing to bargain. This two-part command raised the question, how can the Board know whether a party is bargaining in good faith if actually reaching agreement and making concessions are not measures?

As to the mechanics of bargaining, public-sector rules typically reflect the NLRA approach, due to statutory language or, more commonly, due to agency and court interpretation. But some rules corollary to the duty to bargain in good faith (e.g., rules relating to bargaining impasse) play out differently in the public sector. This chapter notes the similarities and describes the differences.

In the easiest "failure to bargain" cases, labor boards need only assess whether the parties are engaged in the objective functions of bargaining. While there are no per se standards, either the parties are meeting, as § 8(d) and its public-sector equivalents require, or they are not. Either they have executed a written contract or they have not. For example, in *Bryant & Stratton Business Inst., Inc. v. NLRB*, 140 F.3d 169 (2d Cir. 1998), the court upheld the NLRB's conclusion that the employer had breached its duty to bargain, among other things, because it refused to meet for bargaining sessions on consecutive days, scheduled meetings only for late afternoons, cancelled meetings because it was unprepared, and abruptly adjourned several sessions.

But these are the easiest cases. Many of the phrases in §8(d) do not lend themselves to objective measurement. Interpreting §§8(d), 8(a)(5), 8(b)(3), and their public-sector counterparts becomes far more difficult when the parties are engaged in the mechanical functions of collective bargaining—for example, they are meeting at reasonable times—but not in the true substance of bargaining. This behavior is sometimes called "surface bargaining." The question of whether a party has shown "good faith" while bargaining often requires an inquiry into the parties' substantive bargaining positions and their use of economic weapons to influence an agreement's substance. This inquiry raises fundamental questions about labor boards' role in collective bargaining.

The Board's intervention in the bargaining process through a ULP proceeding based on the parties' substantive bargaining *positions*, rather than their bargaining *behavior*, risks involving the government agency in the writing, or influencing the writing, of collective bargaining agreements. As this and other chapters explain, the NLRA does not contemplate the Board playing that role. Nor do public-sector laws contemplate public labor boards playing that role through ULP proceedings. The broadest exception to this general rule in both the public and private sectors is the determination of what topics are "mandatory subjects of bargaining." Parties are subject to a duty to bargain in good faith only with respect to "mandatory" subjects. *See* Chapter 10. In the public sector, a second exception is "interest arbitration," a type of impasse resolution procedure, which Chapter 12 discusses. Otherwise, the substance of collective bargaining is supposed to be left to the parties. *See* Seth Harris, *Coase's Paradox and the Inefficiency of Permanent Strike Replacements*, 80 Wash. U. L.Q.1185, 1270–72 (2002). As this chapter demonstrates, stating this principle has proved easier than implementing it.

Even before the Taft-Hartley Act became law, courts sought to articulate a standard for determining whether the parties had satisfied their duty to bargain in "good faith." In *Globe Cotton Mills v. NLRB*, the Fifth Circuit defined it as a duty "to enter into discussion with an open and fair mind, and a sincere purpose to find a basis of agreement." 103 F.2d 91, 94 (5th Cir. 1939) (endorsed after Taft-Hartley in *NLRB v. Herman Sausage Co.*, 275 F.2d 229, 231 (5th Cir. 1960)). In *NLRB v. Montgomery Ward & Co.*, the Ninth Circuit described it as "an obligation to participate actively in the deliberations so as to indicate a present intention to find a basis for agreement." 133 F.2d 676, 686 (9th Cir. 1943). After the Taft-Hartley Act was enacted, the same court stated that "[a]n unpretending, sincere intention and effort to arrive at an agreement is required by statute." *NLRB v. Stanislaus Implement and Hardware Co., Ltd.*, 226 F.2d 377, 380 (9th Cir. 1955). The First Circuit similarly interpreted §8(d) to hold that "the employer is obliged to make *some* reasonable effort in *some* direction to compose his differences with the union. . . ." *NLRB v. Reed & Prince Mfg. Co.*, 205 F.2d 131, 135 (1st Cir. 1953) (emphasis in original).

These courts' formulations strongly suggest that subjective intention matters most. Consider, throughout this chapter, whether subjective bad faith is a necessary element of the failure to bargain in good faith. Further, the Fifth Circuit stressed that these standards must not result in requiring either party to retreat from a firmly held view: "If the insistence is genuinely and sincerely held, if it is not mere window dressing, it may be maintained forever though it produce a stalemate. . . . The Government, through the Board, may not subject the parties to direction either by compulsory arbitration or the more subtle means of determining that the position is inherently unreasonable, or unfair, or impracticable, or unsound." *NLRB v. Herman Sausage Co., supra*, 275 F.2d 229, 231.

Public-sector labor laws often track private-sector rules on good-faith bargaining, but two significant differences can arise. First, some public-sector laws recognize only a more limited duty to "meet and confer." The duty to meet and confer simply obliges the employer to meet with the union and listen to its proposals; there are no obligations to go further (and no provisions for impasse resolution). This system is relatively rare today, but where it is used, "good faith bargaining" rules— which, under the NLRA and most public sector statutes, require bargaining in good faith to impasse—have little significance. This issue can be confusing, since some public-sector statutes which use the term "meet and confer" actually require something like "collective bargaining" as it is understood in other jurisdictions or the private sector (e.g., California). This chapter will contrast the duty to "meet and confer" with the "duty to bargain collectively."

The second difference is that, unlike the NLRA, most public-sector laws require parties to submit unresolved bargaining issues to a third-party dispute resolution procedure. Chapter 11 will address this in detail; however, the availability of these third-party processes changes the impact of public-sector labor boards' enforcement of the duty to bargain in good faith. In jurisdictions with mandatory, binding impasse resolution mechanisms, the law promises both a bargaining process and a decision-making process that will, one way or another, produce a result. In contrast, §8(d) of the NLRA does not promise a result; it promises only a process. Does this mean that the duty to bargain in good faith is less important in these public-sector jurisdictions than under the NLRA? In contrast, other public-sector jurisdictions lack impasse resolution procedures that are both mandatory and binding, and unions are not allowed to strike. Is the duty to bargain in good faith more important, at least to unions, in these jurisdictions than it is under the NLRA?

Further, impasse resolution procedures raise timing issues. As shown below, some actions by an employer do not violate the duty to bargain in good faith if and only if the employer and union are at "impasse." In the private sector, "impasse" is a creation of the parties: the question is whether or not the union and employer can make further progress bargaining by themselves. While public-sector jurisdictions often use the NLRA rule that certain acts are only permissible at impasse, the existence of third-party impasse dispute mechanisms—which have various stages and can take some time to complete—creates questions of when the parties should be considered "at impasse" for the purpose of these rules.

II. The Duty to Bargain in "Good Faith"

A. Defining "Good Faith" in the Private Sector

In the landmark article *Regulation of Collective Bargaining by the National Labor Relations Board*, 63 HARV. L. REV. 389 (1950),[*] labor law scholars Archibald Cox and John Dunlop (later Secretary of Labor) posed fundamental questions about how the Board and the courts should interpret §§ 8(d), 8(a)(5), and 8(b)(3). Do these provisions require the employer and union to share responsibility for all mandatory subjects of bargaining? Or may the employer bargain for a provision that will be the exclusive function of management? As Cox and Dunlop noted, "[n]othing in the statute furnishes a clear answer to these questions."

Cox and Dunlop posited two possible answers:

First. Section 8(a)(5) makes it an unfair labor practice "to refuse to bargain collectively" with the representative designated by a majority of the employees. Section 9(a) plainly declares that the representative's authority extends to "rates of pay, wages, hours of employment, or other conditions of employment." Therefore, the employer must bargain with respect to each such subject and . . . a refusal to discuss a subject covered by the quoted phrase is an unfair labor practice. . . . [A]lthough an employer must discuss every subject embraced within section 9(a), he complies with the duty to bargain if he negotiates in good faith any question as to whether a specific term or condition of employment (1) should be established by the collective agreement; or (2) should be fixed periodically by joint management-union determination within the framework of the contract; or (3) should be left to management's discretion or individual bargaining without the intervention of the bargaining agent.

Second . . . The essential policy of the statute is that industrial peace can be achieved by taking from management exclusive control over wages, hours, and the other aspects of the employment relationship defined by section 9(a). For that reason the Supreme Court and courts of appeals have repeatedly held that section 8(a)(5) makes unilateral action by an employer an unfair labor practice. The employer who insists upon unilateral control of any "condition of employment" is therefore guilty of an unfair labor practice even though he backs his position by argument and negotiates in good faith. *Id.* at 403–04.

---

[*] Copyright 1950. Reprinted by permission.

Cox and Dunlop justified their preference for the second interpretation on several grounds, but their principal argument rested on

> the difference between (a) taking unilateral action without consulting the bargaining representative on matters concerning which it may wish to bargain and (b) negotiating in good faith for the union's agreement to a contract provision granting management the power to act unilaterally in defined areas. The historical differences are obvious: the one has been a "union-busting" tactic, the other has been an accepted part of collective bargaining. The reasons for proscribing unilateral changes made in disregard of the representative are inapplicable to the exercise of functions assigned to management after collective negotiations. In the former case the employer's action, regardless of its motive, effectively tells the employees that they can without collective bargaining secure advantages as great as, or possibly greater than, those attainable through the intervention of a union. Unilateral changes while the representative is seeking to bargain also interfere with normal collective bargaining by weakening the union's bargaining position.... No such consequences result from an employer's adherence to procedures established by mutual consent.
>
> . . . .
>
> Every partnership allocates individual responsibilities to various members of the firm according to their special capabilities. When one partner takes action within the scope of his authority, the others accept it as the result of their own arrangement. The situation is the same when the employer acts unilaterally pursuant to the management clause of a collective bargaining agreement; its action too is founded on mutual consent.... The function of section 8(a)(5) was to bring about this change in the government of industrial life, not to prevent the negotiation of a mutually satisfactory distribution of functions between the three areas of responsibility. *Id.* at 420–21.

In *NLRB v. American National Insurance Co.*, 343 U.S. 395 (1952), the Supreme Court agreed with Cox and Dunlop. The Office Employees International Union, certified representative of American National Insurance's employees, met several times with the employer to negotiate a collective agreement. The union's initial offer included, among other things, a clause establishing a procedure for settling grievances arising under the contract by successive appeals to management with ultimate resort to an arbitrator. The employer objected to the provisions calling for unlimited arbitration and counter-proposed a management functions clause listing matters such as promotions, discipline and work scheduling as management's exclusive responsibility and thereby excluding such matters from arbitration. The union's representative took the position that the union would not agree to a management rights clause so long as it covered matters subject to the duty to bargain collectively.

The union continued to object to the employer's proposal for a management rights provision and filed a ULP charge based on the employer's alleged refusal to bargain. While the proceeding was pending, negotiations between the union and the employer continued with the management functions clause remaining an obstacle to agreement. The parties reached an agreement which contained a management functions clause that rendered nonarbitrable matters of discipline, work schedules and other matters covered by the clause. The subject of promotions and demotions was deleted from the clause and made the subject of a special clause establishing a union-management committee to pass upon promotion matters.

The Board agreed with the Trial Examiner that respondent had not bargained in a good faith effort to reach an agreement with the Union. But the Board rejected the Examiner's view that an employer may bargain for a management functions clause without committing a ULP. The Board found a ULP and ordered respondent in general terms to bargain collectively with the Union, but prohibited bargaining for any management functions clause covering a condition of employment.

The Supreme Court disagreed, beginning its analysis with a description of the NLRA's philosophy, design and history:

> The National Labor Relations Act is designed to promote industrial peace by encouraging the making of voluntary agreements governing relations between unions and employers. The Act does not compel any agreement whatsoever between employees and employers. Nor does the Act regulate the substantive terms governing wages, hours and working conditions which are incorporated in an agreement. The theory of the Act is that the making of voluntary labor agreements is encouraged by protecting employees' rights to organize for collective bargaining and by imposing on labor and management the mutual obligation to bargain collectively.

> Enforcement of the obligation to bargain collectively is crucial to the statutory scheme. And, as has long been recognized, performance of the duty to bargain requires more than a willingness to enter upon a sterile discussion of union-management differences. Before the [NLRA's] enactment, ... the duty of an employer to bargain collectively required the employer "to negotiate in good faith with his employees' representatives; to match their proposals, if unacceptable, with counter-proposals; and to make every reasonable effort to reach an agreement." The duty to bargain collectively, implicit in the Wagner Act as introduced in Congress, was made express by the insertion of the fifth employer unfair labor practice accompanied by an explanation of the purpose and meaning of the phrase "bargain collectively in a good faith effort to reach an agreement." This understanding of the duty to bargain collectively has been accepted and applied throughout the administration of the Wagner Act by the [NLRB] and the Courts of Appeal.

> . . . .

As amended in the Senate and passed as the Taft-Hartley Act, the good faith test of bargaining was retained and written into Section 8(d) of the [NLRA]. That Section contains the express provision that the obligation to bargain collectively does not compel either party to agree to a proposal or require the making of a concession.

Thus it is now apparent from the statute itself that the Act does not encourage a party to engage in fruitless marathon discussions at the expense of frank statement and support of his position. And . . . the Board may not, either directly or indirectly, compel concessions or otherwise sit in judgment upon the substantive terms of collective bargaining agreements. 343 U.S. 395, 402–04.

The Court then addressed the core question presented by Professors Cox and Dunlop: did the Board correctly conclude that any party seeking unilateral control over hours, wages, or terms and condition of employment has committed a ULP by failing to bargain in good faith?

Conceding that there is nothing unlawful in including a management functions clause in a labor agreement, the Board would permit an employer to "propose" such a clause. But the Board would forbid bargaining for any such clause when the Union declines to accept the proposal, even where the clause is offered as a counterproposal to a Union demand for unlimited arbitration. . . . [T]he Board [posits] that employers subject to the Act must agree to include in any labor agreement provisions establishing fixed standards for work schedules or any other condition of employment. An employer would be permitted to bargain as to the content of the standard so long as he agrees to freeze a standard into a contract. Bargaining for more flexible treatment of such matters would be denied employers even though the result may be contrary to common collective bargaining practice in the industry. The Board was not empowered so to disrupt collective bargaining practices. On the contrary, the term "bargain collectively" as used in the Act "has been considered to absorb and give statutory approval to the philosophy of bargaining as worked out in the labor movement in the United States."

Congress provided expressly that the Board should not pass upon the desirability of the substantive terms of labor agreements. Whether a contract should contain a clause fixing standards for such matters as work scheduling or should provide for more flexible treatment of such matters is an issue for determination across the bargaining table, not by the Board. If the latter approach is agreed upon, the extent of union and management participation in the administration of such matters is itself a condition of employment to be settled by bargaining.

Accordingly, we reject the Board's holding that bargaining for the management functions clause proposed by respondent was, per se, an unfair labor practice. . . . The duty to bargain collectively is to be enforced by application of the good faith bargaining standards of Section 8(d) to the facts of each case rather than by prohibiting all employers in every industry from bargaining for management functions clauses altogether. 343 U.S. at 408–09.

B. Surface Bargaining and Substantive Bargaining Positions

1. In the Private Sector

While *American National Insurance* seemingly resolved the question of whether private-sector bargaining partners must share responsibility for "wages, hours, and terms and conditions of employment," it did not prevent the Board from considering the parties' substantive bargaining positions in an effort to assess whether they are bargaining in good faith. In essence, it left open the question of whether and how the Board can assess the parties' intent (i.e., good faith vs. bad faith) by drawing inferences from proposals made at the bargaining table. Subsequent decisions have demonstrated that private-sector labor law's embrace of the Cox-Dunlop position may have loosened over time. The next case and the notes following it begin that discussion.

NLRB v. A-1 King Size Sandwich

United States Court of Appeals for the Eleventh Circuit
732 F.2d 872 (11th Cir. 1984)

DYER, J.

This case is before us upon the application of the [NLRB] pursuant to Section 10(e) of the [NLRA], for enforcement of its order issued against A-1 King Size Sandwiches, Inc.

The Hotel, Motel, Restaurant Employees & Bartenders Union, Local No. 737, filed an unfair labor practice charge against the Company, alleging that the Company failed to bargain in good faith, and, instead, engaged in surface bargaining. . . . [T]he [ALJ] issued a decision finding that the Company had violated Section 8(a) (1) and (5) of the Act, by engaging in surface bargaining with no intention of entering into a collective bargaining agreement. The Board affirmed the [ALJ]'s rulings, findings and conclusions.

The Company argues that its proposals were not so unusually harsh, vindictive or unreasonable that they were predictably unacceptable, and its bargaining was therefore in good faith. We disagree and enforce. [After the union won an election and Board certification, the Company unsuccessfully challenged certification by refusing to bargain. The court of appeals enforced the Board's bargaining order.]

There were eighteen bargaining sessions at agreed times and places during an eleven-month period. The negotiations did not result in a contract. The parties reached agreement on a recognition clause; plant visitation by Union representatives; the number, rights and duties of Union stewards; the Union's use of a bulletin board; pay for jury duty; leaves of absence; and a procedure for processing grievances and conducting arbitrations with respect to matters of interpretation or application of express provisions of the contract. As to all other subjects no agreement was reached. The [ALJ] properly found that the Company met at reasonable times and places, and that the Company bore no animus toward the Union. There is no evidence that the Company engaged in any conduct away from the bargaining table that might tend to show it would not conclude an agreement with the Union.

The well-settled principles bearing upon the issues here presented are easily stated but not so easily applied. Section 8(a)(5) of the Act, makes it an unfair labor practice for an employer to refuse to bargain collectively with the employees' representative. The Supreme Court . . . has said, "the Act does not compel any agreement whatsoever between employees and employers." *NLRB v. American Nat'l Ins.,* *supra.* "And it is equally clear that [under § 8(d) of the Act] the Board may not, either directly or indirectly, compel concessions or otherwise sit in judgment upon the substantive terms of collective bargaining agreements." *American Nat'l Ins.,* 343 U.S. at 404, 72 S. Ct. at 829. However, "[e]nforcement of the obligation to bargain collectively is crucial to the statutory scheme. And . . . performance of the duty to bargain requires more than a willingness to enter upon a sterile discussion of union-management differences." *Id.* Moreover,

> In evaluating the parties' good faith, the Board is not precluded from examining the substantive proposals put forth. Indeed . . . if the Board is not to be blinded by empty talk and by mere surface motions of collective bargaining, it must take some cognizance of the reasonableness of the positions taken by the employer in the course of bargaining negotiations. [citation omitted.]

And "[s]ometimes, especially if the parties are sophisticated, the only indicia of bad faith may be the proposals advanced and adhered to." [citation omitted]. . . .

The question to be decided is a narrow one: Whether the content of the Company's bargaining proposals together with the positions taken by the Company are sufficient to establish that it entered into bargaining with no real intention of concluding a collective bargaining agreement. We defer to the Board to make the initial determination, but we are required to review the proposals to determine whether the Board's findings are supported by substantial evidence on the record as a whole.

Wages

The Company's proposal on wages retained its historic method of paying each employee. Wage increases were to be determined solely on the basis of semi-annual merit wage reviews in which the Union would be given notice of each separate review and could participate in the process, but the Company would make the final decision as to any increases. Under the wage proposal the Company was barred from reducing the wages of any employee whose wages had once risen above that level. The Union proposed a specific wage schedule but the Company adhered to its original wage proposal.

The Company insisted that it remain in total control over wages. Its proposal to continue granting wage increases on the basis of semi-annual wage reviews, in which the Company would make the final decision, coupled with the Company's Management Rights clause, *infra*, under which it had the exclusive right to evaluate, reward, promote and demote employees, left the Union's "participation" in the process meaningless. The Union was foreclosed from introducing factors other than merit into the equation. It had no contractual remedies since the granting or withholding of merit increases would not be arbitrable. The Union could not strike and, in fact, it had no leverage to require its views to be taken into account. Moreover, once an employee's wage rate increased above the level of the rate existing at the time of the contract, the Company could unilaterally reduce that which had been given in a previous merit increase and the Union could not grieve such action. It could not strike, and under the Zipper Clause, *infra*, it could not even discuss the matter with the Company. Thus, the Company's unalterable position was that it remain in total control of this mandatory subject of bargaining.

Management Rights

The Company submitted a management rights clause which initially provided that the Company retained exclusively all of its normal inherent rights and exempted the Company's decisions concerning these rights from the grievance procedure. Later the Company proposed a new management rights clause, which was much broader than the first proposal, and which reserved exclusively to the Company all authority customarily exercised by Management and "each and every right, power and privilege that it had ever enjoyed, whether exercised or not, except insofar as [the Company] has, by express and specific terms of the agreement, agreed to limitations." It further provided that the Company was authorized to:

1. Determine the qualifications and select its employees.

2. Determine the size and composition of its work forces.

3. Determine work schedules and all methods of production.

4. Assign overtime work.

5. Determine the number and types of equipment.

6. Hire, retire, promote, demote, evaluate, transfer, suspend, assign, direct, lay off and recall employees.

7. Reward, reprimand, discharge or otherwise discipline employees.

8. Determine job content and minimum training qualifications for job classifications and the amounts and types of work to be performed by employees.

9. Establish and change working rules and regulations.

10. Establish new jobs and abolish or change existing jobs.

11. Increase or decrease the number of jobs or employees.

12. Determine whether and to what extent the work required in its operations should be performed by employees.

13. Have supervisors or other non-union employees perform work of the kind performed by employees of the Union.

14. Determine assignments of work.

15. Discontinue, transfer or assign all or any part of its functions, services or production or other operations.

16. Subcontract any part of the Company's work.

17. Expand, reduce, alter, combine, transfer, assign, cease or create any job, job classification, department or operation for business purposes.

18. Alter or vary practices.

19. Otherwise generally manage the business, direct the work force and establish terms and conditions of employment.

The new proposal further expanded the original by providing that the Company could exercise all of its reserved rights without advising the Union of any such proposed action, change or modification, and exempted the Company from any requirement to negotiate over the decision, or its effects on employees except as altered by the Agreement. The substituted proposal no longer contained a clause expressly excluding the Company's decisions from the grievance and arbitration procedure.

This proposal gave the Company the absolute right to subcontract work, assign it to supervisors, abolish jobs, and transfer, discontinue or assign any or all of its operations. It also required the Union to relinquish the employees' statutory right to notice and bargaining over such actions and their effects. Finally, the grievance and arbitration procedure was largely illusory because actions taken under this clause were subject to that procedure only if the right was limited by express contractual provision, and there was no such limitation.

Zipper Clause

The Company proposed a "zipper" clause under which "the parties [waived the] right to bargain during the life of the agreement regarding any subject or any matter referred to or covered in the agreement or any other subject matter which could be considered mandatory or permissive subject of bargaining under existing law." The Union offered to agree to the clause if the latter portion waiving the right to bargain over any other mandatory or permissive bargaining subject was deleted. The Company refused.

No Strike Clause

The Company proposed a no strike clause that prohibited both the Union and employees from calling, encouraging, ratifying, participating in or engaging in any primary or sympathy strike, slow down, boycott, picketing or any other work interruption for any reason, including but not limited to alleged or actual unfair labor practices, alleged or actual unfair employment practices under any anti-discrimination law, alleged or actual breaches of contract, and showing support or sympathy for other employees or Union or their activities. The Union, although conceding that any contract would contain a no-strike clause, objected to waiving employees' right to strike over unfair labor practices or unfair employment practices. The Company declined to change the proposal. This extremely broad "no strike" clause clearly prohibited any strike for any reason.

Discharge and Discipline

The Union proposed that the Company have the right to discipline an employee for any just or sufficient cause. The Company, citing meritless discrimination charges filed against it, refused the proposal because it would subject all of the discipline and discharge actions to grievance-arbitration. This is a common non-controversial clause. When considered with the rights expressly reserved in the management rights Clause, to suspend, reprimand, discharge, or otherwise discipline employees, the Company retained unfettered control over discharges and discipline.

Layoff and Recall

With respect to layoff and recall, the Company proposed that the layoff of employees would be at the Company's sole discretion. Company-wide seniority would be considered but not controlling. Selection for layoff would not be the subject of grievance or arbitration. Recall from layoff was to be at the discretion of the Company and it was not required to consider seniority. The Company insisted on the clause as presented because it wanted to make the decisions on the basis of productivity and not seniority and not make the ability question subject to grievance and arbitration.

This clause gave the Company absolute control over the selection of employees for layoff and recall and freed it from its statutory obligation to bargain over these subjects.

Dues Check-Off

The Union proposed a dues check-off clause which the Company rejected as being nothing more than a Union security device and because it made employees' earnings appear lower.

Non-Discrimination Clause

The Union proposed a non-discrimination clause. The Company rejected this proposal saying that it merely restated existing law. Further, the Company considered the Union trigger-happy about filing complaints and did not want such complaints to be arbitrable.

The Union finally proposed a "swap off." The Union would agree to some type of management rights, no strike and zipper clauses if the Company would agree to a just cause for discipline and discharge provision, and seniority for layoff and recall provision. The Company refused.

Deciding when a party has reached the "point when hard bargaining ends and obstructionist intransigence begins," is "an inescapably elusive inquiry." But it is clear from our extended recital of the proposals made over a ten-month period that the Company insisted on unilateral control over virtually all significant terms and conditions of employment, including discharge, discipline, layoff, recall, subcontracting and assignment of unit work to supervisors.

Its efforts were focused on requiring the employees to surrender statutory rights to bargain, or strike, without offering any real incentive for a surrender of such rights.

The Company refused to give the Union any voice whatsoever concerning employee work and safety rules, time studies, production quotas, overtime assignments, transfers, retirement, demotions and employee qualifications-all mandatory subjects of bargaining. Elimination of unit work, discipline or discharge of employees, layoff and recall were all exempted from the grievance and arbitration procedure.

The Company's rejection of the Union's dues check-off provision was not based on any legitimate business reason and does not satisfy the statutory obligation to bargain in good faith. Furthermore, we are unimpressed with the Company's rejection of a non-discriminatory clause because the Union "was trigger-happy" about filing complaints. The clause did no more than require the Company to abide by federal law to avoid discrimination against its employees on account of race, sex, age, national origin or union affiliation.

Finally, it is worthy of note that the Company responded to the Union's objections to the breadth of its original management rights and zipper clauses by submitting new proposals that were even broader. Such bargaining is clearly an indicia that the Company had little desire to work towards agreement of a contract.

The Board correctly inferred bad faith from the Company's insistence on proposals that are so unusually harsh and unreasonable that they are predictably unworkable. They would have left the Union and the employees with substantially fewer rights and less protection than they would have had if they had relied solely upon the Union's certification. . . .

Enforced.

———————

There is a fine and difficult-to-discern line between "hard bargaining" and a failure to bargain in good faith, particularly when the Board or a court is considering only the parties' behavior at the bargaining table. As the First Circuit observed:

> More than in most areas of labor law, distinguishing hard bargaining from surface bargaining calls for sifting a complex array of facts, which taken in isolation may often be ambiguous. "In every case, the basic question is

whether the employer acted like a man with a mind closed against agreement with the union. The Board can judge his subjective state of mind only
by asking whether a normal employer, willing to agree with a labor union,
would have followed the same course of action." Cox, *The Duty to Bargain
in Good Faith*, 71 Harv. L. Rev. 1401, 1419 (1958). The duty to bargain
"does not compel either party to agree to a proposal or require the making of a concession," 29 U.S.C. § 158(d). At the same time, "if the Board is
not to be blinded by empty talk and by the mere surface motions of collective bargaining, it must take some cognizance of the reasonableness of the
positions taken by an employer in the course of bargaining negotiations."
[citation omitted]. *Eastern Maine Medical Center v. NLRB*, 658 F.2d 1, 10
(1st Cir. 1981).

In *Pleasantview Nursing Home, Inc. v. NLRB*, 351 F.3d 747 (6th Cir. 2003), one
of the nursing home's negotiating goals was to significantly increase the pay of its
unionized employees to redress a labor shortage. Among other provisions, the nursing home offered to increase hourly wages, but also proposed a "buy back" provision
that would finance the increase, in part, by eliminating three paid holidays and the
company's contribution to union-managed pension and disability funds. In return,
employees would receive access to employer-sponsored investment and insurance
plans. The nursing home did not change its position on these issues throughout the
negotiations. During one negotiating session, the nursing home's negotiator stated
that its position was non-negotiable. Nonetheless, the court of appeals reversed the
Board's conclusion that the nursing home had failed to bargain in good faith:

> Pleasantview's ultimate refusal to change its position regarding the buy-
> backs does not constitute bad faith. "Good faith bargaining is all that is
> required. That the position of one party on an issue prevails unchanged
> does not mandate the conclusion that there was no collective bargaining
> over the issue." The 1947 "amendment [to the NLRA] makes it clear that
> the failure to reach an agreement because of the employer's refusal to make
> a concession to the Union does not, by itself, constitute lack of good faith."
> Where "[t]he failure to execute a contract was not because of a failure or
> refusal to negotiate, but in the final analysis was because the parties would
> not agree on one remaining issue, considered by both of them as basically
> important," no bad faith has been evinced. "To say that the Company
> should have accepted the Union's proposal on this issue is to ignore the
> language of the statute that the obligation to bargain collectively 'does not
> compel either party to agree to a proposal or require the making of a con-
> cession.'" Pleasantview's insistence on the buy-backs constituted no more
> than hard bargaining. . . . 351 F.3d 747, 758.

Similarly, in *NLRB v. Cummer-Graham Co.*, 279 F.2d 757 (5th Cir. 1960), the
employer's insistence on a no-strike provision in the collective bargaining agreement
coupled with its refusal to agree to an arbitration clause proposed by the union did
not constitute a failure to bargain in good faith. The court of appeals acknowledged

that the Supreme Court had opined in *Textile Workers Union of America v. Lincoln Mills*, 353 U.S. 448, 455 (1957), that "'[p]lainly the agreement to arbitrate grievance disputes is the quid pro quo for an agreement not to strike.'" Nonetheless, the court of appeals concluded that "[t]hese are matters for management and labor to resolve, if they can, at the bargaining table. If they cannot there be decided, then neither Board nor Court can compel an agreement or require a concession." 279 F.2d 757, 759. *See also, e.g., Coastal Electric Cooperative, Inc.*, 311 N.L.R.B. 1126 (1993) (employer holding firmly to its position on management rights, employment-at-will, arbitration, seniority, and wages was "hard bargaining" rather than a ULP); *Teamsters Local 287, International Brotherhood of Teamsters*, 347 N.L.R.B. No. 32 (2006) (applying § 8(b)(3) to a union in the same way it applies § 8(a)(5) to employers, holding that union failed to bargain in good faith by delaying a ratification vote on the final agreement reached with the employer), *enforced*, 293 Fed. App'x 518 (9th Cir. 2008).

"Regressive bargaining," where one party withdraws a bargaining proposal or returns to an earlier position that was unacceptable to the other party, is not a ULP per se. *See Telescope Casual Furniture, Inc.*, 326 N.L.R.B. 588 (1998). However, it presents the Board with the same challenge of assessing the bargainer's intent. In *Mead Corp. v. NLRB*, 697 F.2d 1013 (1983), the Eleventh Circuit suggested that "withdrawal of a proposal by an employer without good cause is evidence of a lack of good faith bargaining by the employer in violation of § 8(a)(5) where the proposal has been tentatively agreed upon or acceptance by the Union appears to be imminent." 697 F.2d 1013, 1021–22. The D.C. Circuit similarly stated that "the key issue in evaluating the propriety of regressive bargaining is whether it is designed to 'frustrate the bargaining process.'" *Graphic Communications Local 458-3M v. NLRB*, 206 F.3d 22, 32 (D.C. Cir. 2000). Thus, withdrawal of a proposal without adequate justification may be evidence of bad faith, but it may be consistent with good-faith bargaining where the employer adjusts its bargaining position to changed circumstances. *Compare, e.g., Valley Central Emergency Veterinary Hospital*, 349 N.L.R.B. 1126 (2007) (employer's withdrawal from agreement constitutes bad faith because union members' failure to ratify was not a condition precedent to agreement) *with Atlas Metal Parts Co., Inc. v. NLRB*, 660 F.2d 304 (7th Cir. 1981) (employer's change of bargaining position after union's strike failed did not evidence bad faith).

Notes

1. How can *A-1 King Size Sandwich* be reconciled with *Herman Sausage*'s command that the Board "may not subject the parties to direction [by] determining that the position is inherently unreasonable, or unfair, or impracticable, or unsound"? Is there any reason to believe A-1 King Size Sandwich's position was not "genuinely and sincerely held"? Did the employer exhibit subjective bad faith? Or did the court essentially hold that certain bargaining positions are per se ULPs? *See NLRB v. Cable Vision, Inc.*, 660 F.2d 1 (1st Cir. 1981) (employer clinging to bargaining positions it could have predicted would be unacceptable to the union, refusing to make meaningful concessions in nearly every area, and insisting on positions

unsupported by explanations—that is, failing to come close to agreement while refusing to make concessions—was evidence that the employer violated its duty to bargain in good faith); *Radisson Plaza Minneapolis v. NLRB*, 987 F.2d 1376 (8th Cir. 1993) (employer committed a ULP when its chief negotiator insisted that the collective bargaining agreement contain provisions relieving the employer of its obligation to bargain should either of the unions be found to be "dominated by organized crime" and that the employer's employee handbook form the basis for the agreement even though to do so would have allowed the employer to unilaterally amend, modify, or discontinue benefits or change working conditions).

2. Contrary to the suggestion in *A-1 King Size Sandwich*, but consistent with *American National Insurance*, courts of appeals have held that an employer's insistence on unilateral control over important aspects of the employment relationship that are mandatory subjects of bargaining—including wages—does not necessarily constitute a ULP. *See Cincinnati Newspaper Guild, Local 9 v. NLRB*, 938 F.2d 284 (D.C. Cir. 1991) (collecting and discussing cases); *but see McClatchy Newspapers, Inc. v. NLRB, infra.* Does the court's conclusion in *A-1 King Size Sandwich* turn on the number of subjects over which the employer sought unilateral control? Was it their importance? Was it the exclusivity of the employer's control?

3. *American National Insurance*, in its adoption of the Cox-Dunlop interpretation of §§ 8(d), 8(a)(5), and 8(b)(3), seemingly relies on a purposive interpretation of those provisions designed to strengthen the collective bargaining process. How would a textualist have interpreted these provisions of the Act, particularly in light of Cox and Dunlop's observation that "[n]othing in the statute furnishes a clear answer to these questions"?

2. "Good Faith" in the Public Sector

Public-sector jurisdictions that permit collective bargaining typically use the NLRA approach to the general obligation to bargain in good faith. In *West Hartford Ed. Ass'n v. Dayson DeCourcy*, 162 Conn. 566, 589–90 (Conn. 1972) the court was interpreting state statute § 10-153d, which required public employers to "confer in good faith" and was otherwise substantively the same as the NLRA. Citing private-sector precedent, it held that "[t]he duty to negotiate in good faith generally has been defined as an obligation to participate actively in deliberations so as to indicate a present intention to find a basis for agreement. . . . Not only must the employer have an open mind and a sincere desire to reach an agreement but a sincere effort must be made to reach a common ground. . . . This duty does not require an employer to agree to a proposal or require the making of a concession." In *Pasco County School Bd. v. Florida Public Emp. Rel. Comm.*, 353 So.2d 108,122–26 (Fla. App. 1977), the court was interpreting § 447.501(c) of the Florida statute, which barred employers from "failing to bargain collectively in good faith." The court cited numerous private-sector precedents as good law for the duty to bargain in good faith under the Florida statute (and the court specifically noted that a subjective showing of bad faith was not necessary to find a violation, *id.* at 125–26). *In the Matter of County of Morris v. Morris Council No. 6, NJCSA, IFPTE, AFL-CIO*, 852 A.2d 1126, 1131–32 (N.J. Super 2004), dealing with state statutory language barring an employer from "[r]efusing to negotiate in good faith," stressed that "[NLRA] precedents should guide our interpretation of the state act."

For an analog to *A-1 King Size Sandwich*, see *Oakland Community College and Teamsters Local 241*, 15 M.P.E.R. ¶ 33006 (Mich. Emp. Rel. Comm. 2001) (finding illegal "surface bargaining" mostly on the basis of the extreme substance of the employer's proposals). Also, *Kitsap County Deputy Sheriffs Guild v. Kitsap County*, Dec. 9623-A (Wash. Pub. Emp. Rel. Com. 2008), while finding no violation, explained that regressive bargaining could, in some cases, be the basis for a failure to bargain in good faith charge. "In order for a party to bargain regressively, a bad faith element must infect the collective bargaining process."

However, some public-sector decisions have refined the rules somewhat, and some issues are unique to the public sector.

Association of Oregon Corrections Employees v. State of Oregon, Department of Corrections

Oregon Court of Appeals
213 Or. App. 648, 164 P.3d 291 (2007)

WOLLHEIM, J.

Following the dot-com boom years of the late 1990s and the early 2000s, this state faced a serious recession. As a result of that recession, revenue to the state fell far short of previous revenue forecasts. This case arose from state employee salary freezes during the 2003–2005 biennium and involves a dispute between two labor organizations and two state agencies under the Public Employees Collective Bargaining Act (PECBA), ORS 243.650 to 243.782. The Association of Oregon Corrections Employees (AOCE) filed an unfair labor practice complaint against the Oregon Department of Corrections (DOC), and the Oregon State Police Officers' Association (OSPOA) filed an unfair labor practice complaint against the Oregon State Police (OSP). Both complaints alleged that the state agencies committed unfair labor practices during the course of negotiating new contracts. . . . [T]he Employment Relations Board (the board) . . . dismissed the complaints, and both unions (collectively, petitioners) seek judicial review. For the reasons explained below, we affirm.

    . . . .

When the new Governor took office in January 2003, the state was in the midst of a recession; forecasted revenues for the 2003–2005 biennium showed a budgetary shortfall of more than $1 billion. As a result, the Governor proposed a budget to the legislature that included a salary freeze for all state employees during the entire 2003–2005 biennium. That is, no money was included in the budget for either cost-of-living adjustments (COLAs) or increases based on advancement on salary schedule steps (step increases), which are annual salary increases for merit and longevity that are received by many state employees. The legislature approved a 2003–2005 budget that provided that no state employee would receive a COLA or a step increase.

. . . .

The state's chief negotiator for collective bargaining understood that, in light of the budgetary constraints, she had virtually no flexibility in bargaining over salaries. . . . In February 2003, the state began negotiations with the Service Employees International Union Local 503, Oregon Public Employees Association (SEIU), which represents about 65 percent of the state's employees. . . . After months of bargaining, the state and SEIU reached tentative agreement on a 2003–2005 CBA. Under the agreement, wages for bargaining unit members would be frozen for the 2003–2005 biennium. There would be no COLAs or step increases. However, each employee who worked for the state from July 1, 2003 through January 2005 would receive a one-time "workload adjustment" payment of $350.

Gary Weeks, then administrator of the Department of Administrative Services . . . was present at the bargaining session in which the state and SEIU reached their tentative agreement providing for a wage freeze and work adjustment payment of $350. At that time, Weeks spoke with Leslie Frane, the head of the SEIU bargaining unit. Frane noted that SEIU was the first union to reach agreement with the state, and she expressed concern that other unions might receive more favorable contract terms. Weeks said that the Governor's position would remain consistent, *viz.*, that no money was available for salary increases. Weeks told Frane that the state would take the same position with all other unions as it had taken with SEIU and that other unions also would receive wage freezes because there was no money for COLAs or step increases. . . .

AOCE is the exclusive representative of a mixed bargaining unit of DOC employees. In January 2003, AOCE and DOC began negotiations for a new CBA that was to replace the CBA that would expire on June 30, 2003. The parties participated in seven collective bargaining sessions between January and June 2003. At a June bargaining session, DOC proposed a two-year wage freeze; it also proposed increases in the dollar amount of the employer-paid health insurance subsidy, but did not offer to guarantee that DOC employees would incur no out-of-pocket health insurance costs. In response, AOCE proposed to continue COLAs and step increases. . . .

AOCE and DOC did not reach voluntary agreement, and the matter proceeded to mediation and then arbitration. . . . DOC's final offer provided that the parties could agree in writing to begin the suspension of step increases at a later date, but that the freeze would be in effect for 24 months. In regard to health insurance, DOC's proposal was the same as its earlier one. AOCE's final offer included a proposal to provide a COLA on July 1, 2005. AOCE also provided a counter-proposal regarding step increases and proposed that DOC pay the full cost of the medical, dental, and disability plans selected by employees. . . .

In January 2004, the parties submitted their last best offers before arbitration. . . . DOC's last best offer included a proposal that suspended all step increases for a period of "up to 24 months" from the date on which the arbitrator's award was issued. . . .

Ultimately, the arbitrator selected DOC's last best offer. With respect to the parties' negotiations over the 2003–2005 CBA, the board found:

> AOCE and DOC offered concessions on a variety of proposals and exchanged counterproposals on a number of subjects. As part of this process, DOC proposed increases in health insurance, an adjustment to the pay differential received by certain non-security employees, and a choice for each employee between accepting a one-time "workload adjustment" payment of $350 or accepting additional leave.

> During the negotiations process, the parties reached agreement on a number of contract articles and proposals and signed off on these agreements.

OSPOA is the exclusive representative of a mixed bargaining unit of OSP employees. Its bargaining history regarding the 2003–2005 CBA with OSP largely paralleled AOCE's experience with DOC. . . .

On judicial review, petitioners argue that . . . the board erred in concluding that the state did not engage in so-called "surface bargaining" in violation of the duty to bargain in good faith imposed by ORS 243.672(1)(e). . . .

Under ORS 243.672(1)(e), it is an unlawful labor practice for a public employer to "[r]efuse to bargain collectively in good faith with the exclusive representative." Surface bargaining has been described as "going through the motions of negotiating, without any real intent to reach an agreement. It violates the [National Labor Relations] Act's requirement that parties negotiate in good faith." *K-Mart Corp. v. NLRB*, 626 F.2d 704, 706 (9th Cir.1980).[2]

According to petitioners, "[a]ny time an employer makes a deal with a bargaining unit that no other bargaining unit will receive a better economic package it commits a *per se* violation of its duty to bargain in good faith with the other units." In petitioners' view, once the state promised SEIU that no other bargaining unit would get a better deal than it had gotten, the state's negotiations with petitioners were—as a matter of law—not conducted in good faith. Petitioners go on to argue that, even if the state's behavior did not constitute a *per se* violation of the duty to bargain in good faith, under the "totality-of-conduct" standard applied by the board, the state did not bargain in good faith.

---

2. In *Portland Assn. Teachers v. Mult. Sch. Dist. No. 1*, 171 Or.App. 616, 631 n. 6 (2000), we explained:

> Oregon's Public Employees Collective Bargaining Act (PECBA), including ORS 243.672, was adopted to model the [NLRA]. . . . We therefore may look to cases decided under the federal act—and particularly to cases decided before 1973, the year in which PECBA was adopted—for guidance in interpreting PECBA.

The state responds that it was budget constraints, not the promise to SEIU, that dictated the state's position in bargaining with petitioners. In light of the state constitutional requirement of a balanced budget and the economic conditions at the time, the state asserts, the legislature could not have intended that the duty to bargain in good faith precluded the state from taking the positions that it did. "[I]n enacting ORS 243.672(1)(e)," the state contends, "the legislature could not have intended that the state's decision during collective bargaining to remain within the funds available would constitute a *per se* violation of the duty to bargain in good faith." Finally, the state argues, under the board's "totality-of-conduct" standard, the state's actions did not amount to a failure to bargain in good faith. As did the board, we agree with the state.

. . . In this case, we defer—as we consistently have—to the board's methodology for determining whether parties have bargained in good faith. . . .

The board's case law interpreting that provision posits two categories of violations of the duty to bargain in good faith. The first is a *per se* violation, premised on the idea that some conduct is "so inimical to the bargaining process that it amounts to a *per se* violation of the duty to bargain in good faith." Examples of conduct that the board has concluded amounts to a *per se* violation include (1) an employer's unilateral implementation of a change in a mandatory subject of bargaining; (2) submitting a new proposal at the mediation stage; and (3) submitting a new proposal in a final offer.

The second way in which any party may violate its duty to bargain in good faith is where "the totality of that party's conduct during the period of negotiations . . . indicates an unwillingness on the part of the charged party to reach a negotiated agreement." *School Employees Local Union 140 v. School District No. 1, Multnomah County*, 20 PECBR 420, 431 (2003). In its order in this case, the board explained how it applies that test:

> In applying this "totality-of-conduct" standard, this Board analyzes the following factors to determine whether an employer's conduct indicates an unwillingness to reach agreement: (1) dilatory tactics—whether the employer used tactics that unreasonably impeded negotiation; (2) contents of the proposals—whether the employer made unduly harsh or unreasonable proposals; (3) behavior of the spokesperson—whether the negotiator's behavior was extremely discourteous; (4) concessions—whether the employer made some 'reasonable effort' to settle differences with the union; (5) failure to explain bargaining positions—whether the employer adequately explained its proposals; and (6) course of negotiations—whether the employer "rushes through the negotiation process mandated by the PECBA," demonstrating a lack of serious intention to reach agreement.

Petitioners argued to the board that the state's conduct—in promising SEIU that no other union would receive a better contract offer than SEIU received—was a *per se* violation of the duty to bargain in good faith. The board, describing the state's promise to SEIU as a kind of "reverse parity clause," rejected petitioners' argument. On appeal, petitioners reiterate their argument. . . . In response, the state argues:

> In light of the constitutional balanced-budget requirement, and the intent stated in ORS 291.232(1),[5] the legislature could not have intended that where it deliberately includes no money in the budget for cost-of-living or step increases, a state agency's decision to stand firm in collective bargaining and not grant such increases constitutes a *per se* violation of the duty to bargain in good faith. Such a construction would mean that, by complying with ORS 291.232(1)—electing to spend moneys appropriated in accordance with the legislatively adopted budget and the agency's enabling statutes—an agency would, *as a matter of law*, violate ORS 243.672(1)(e).

We agree with that analysis and reject petitioners' argument that the state's conduct was a *per se* violation of the good faith bargaining requirement. We turn, accordingly, to petitioners' alternative argument that the state's actions constituted a failure to bargain in good faith under the board's totality-of-conduct test.

Applying the three relevant factors from its six-factor test—contents of the proposals, concessions, and course of the negotiations—the board concluded that the state had not violated the good faith bargaining requirement by refusing to budge on the salary freeze issue. The board reasoned that, although the state's wage freeze proposals were "obviously unacceptable" to petitioners, those salary freeze proposals must be viewed in the totality of the circumstances surrounding the negotiations—specifically, the budget constraints under which the state was operating. And viewing the content of the salary freeze proposals, the board concluded that the state's harsh position was not a refusal to bargain in good faith. We agree. Given the economic hand it was dealt, the state's wage freeze proposals cannot be said to have been "unduly harsh or unreasonable."

Regarding the second relevant factor—any concessions—the board found, as set out above, that all parties offered concessions on a variety of proposals and exchanged counterproposals on a number of subjects. And some concessions ultimately were made. For example, DOC agreed to provide fully paid health insurance benefits for 2004 and agreed to provide each employee with a choice of a $350 "workload adjustment" payment or paid leave. OSP made similar concessions regarding the workload adjustment and health insurance. In short, although the state never

---

5. ORS 291.232(1) provides:

It is declared to be the policy and intent of the Legislative Assembly that:

(a) The legislatively adopted or approved budget for a state agency constitutes a determination by the Legislative Assembly of the amount needed by the agency for the biennium to meet the responsibilities imposed on the agency through the budget and through statutes governing the agency; and

(b) Except as provided in subsections (2) and (3) of this section, appropriations from the General Fund to a state agency constitute a direction to the agency to spend the amount of moneys appropriated in order to meet the responsibilities imposed on the agency through the budget and through statutes governing the agency.

wavered in its position that it could not afford to provide COLAs and step increases, the state made concessions where it could. That factor, like the first, does not support petitioners' argument that the state refused to bargain in good faith.

Finally, examination of the course of the negotiations between the state and petitioners establishes that the state did not rush through the negotiation process mandated by PECBA, "demonstrating a lack of a serious intention to reach agreement." The board found that AOCE and DOC "participated in seven collective bargaining sessions between January 22 and June 24, 2003" and at least four mediation sessions, findings that AOCE does not challenge on review. Similarly, OSPOA and OSP participated in a number of collective bargaining and mediation sessions. As noted above, the last best offers by the state differed from its initial proposals. PECBA's definition of "collective bargaining" notes: "The obligation to meet and negotiate does not compel either party to agree to a proposal or require the making of a concession." ORS 243.650(4). The state met regularly with petitioners, made concessions, and agreed to some of petitioners' proposals. . . .

Looking at the course of negotiations, the nature of the state's proposals (in light of the strict budgetary constraints under which it was operating), and the concessions made by the state, we conclude that the state did not violate its duty under ORS 243.672(1)(e) to bargain in good faith by insisting on a salary freeze like that agreed to by SEIU.[6]

In summary, the board did not err in concluding that the state's hard-line bargaining position regarding the 2003–2005 CBAs was dictated, not by a promise made to SEIU, but by the real budgetary constraints facing the state in difficult economic times. . . . Affirmed.

Notes

1. Should unions worry that other public employers will follow the lead of the employer in *Association of Oregon Corrections Employees*, passing rules or statutes which, by imposing specific budget requirements, essentially forbid pay increases? Are such measures prudent, reasonable, or at least necessary responses to tough economic times, or are they an improper end-run around collective bargaining rights, unfairly disadvantaging one particular constituency?

2. *Association of Oregon Corrections Employees* makes a brief reference to "parity clauses," another issue that often arises in the public sector. A "parity" clause is a provision in a collective bargaining agreement that requires the employer and union to enter into the same or similar terms that the employer and another union have agreed to: for example, a city agrees with a firefighters' union that salary increases

---

6. Regarding the other factors, the parties stipulated that no party engaged in dilatory tactics; that, during the course of the negotiations, the parties "behaved appropriately and professionally towards each other"; and that the parties "engaged in a reasonable period of negotiations, a reasonable number of mediation sessions . . . and following mediation continued to negotiate up to interest arbitration."

for firefighters will be the same percentage as salary increases that the city negotiates with its police union. Such clauses have advantages in that they prevent competition (and perhaps jealousy) among different types of city employees. Also, they provide a measure of predictability to employers. Further, a smaller bargaining unit that negotiates parity clauses with regard to a larger unit may benefit due to the greater bargaining power of the larger unit.

But such clauses raise a duty to bargain in good faith issue. The union used as the parity comparison (*e.g.*, the police union in the above example) is arguably unfairly burdened in its bargaining, because the employer will be aware that the consequence of giving, say, a significant raise to the police union will be that the employer is also obligated to give the same raise to firefighters, employees outside the police union with which the employer is currently bargaining.

For these reasons, courts and labor boards in some jurisdictions have held that parity agreements always violate the duty to bargain in good faith. For example, in *Local 1650, IAFF v. City of Augusta*, No. 04-14 (M.L.R.B., Aug. 10, 2004), the Maine Board held that the city of Augusta violated its duty to bargain in good faith with one union, Local 1650, because the city had entered into parity agreements with other unions regarding the terms of Local 1650's contracts. The Board reasoned that parity agreements subvert the bargaining process by burdening the bargaining agent and making it unable to fully avail itself of the opportunities granted by the state public sector labor statute. It concluded that "parity agreements are inherently destructive of collective bargaining rights and are therefore a *per se* violation of [the statute]."

On the other hand, some jurisdictions take a case-by-case approach with parity clauses. For example, in *Whatcom County Deputy Sheriff's Guild v. Whatcom County*, Decision 8512-A (PECB 2005) the Washington Public Employment Relations Commission dismissed a charge by a union, the Guild, which had complained that the employer had impaired negotiations with the Guild by entering into parity clauses with other unions regarding the Guild contract's provision of medical benefits. The Commission held that parity clauses are not *per se* violations of the duty to bargain in good faith; rather, the charging party has the burden of proving that the parity clause(s) did in fact burden its negotiations. Here, while the employer had taken a hard stance on the issue of medical benefits, no evidence showed that the parity clauses were the reason for that stance. *See also TWU Local 106 and New York City Transit Auth.*, 39 NY PERB 2006) (an illegal parity agreement is one that trespasses on the negotiation rights of a union that is not a party to the agreement, and here there was no illegal burden).

3. Constraints imposed through the political process are part of the territory of public-sector labor law. But is it a failure to bargain in good faith if a public employer lobbies for a change in the law that would limit its obligations to bargain? An Ohio court considered this issue in *SERB v. Queen Lodge No. 69*, 174 Oh. App. 3d 570 (2007). In *Queen Lodge*, the employer had supported a successful ballot amendment to Cincinnati's civil charter which altered rules governing certain promotions in

city employment, including in the city's unionized police department. 174 Oh. App. 3d 570, 572–73. The police union challenged the city's refusal to bargain about these changes and specifically charged that the city, by promoting a ballot amendment that would change the terms of a collective bargaining agreement it had signed, had failed to bargain in good faith.

Judge Painter, writing for the majority, held that while the city would normally be required to bargain over changes to the promotion process, bargaining was not required here because of a rule (found in Ohio and elsewhere) that public employers are not obligated to bargain where a higher-level legislative authority imposes a rule through legislative action. The court explained that while it would violate the duty to bargain in good faith if a city council signed a collective bargaining agreement but then passed an ordinance abrogating the agreement, this had not happened here. Rather, the city had merely placed the charter amendment on the ballot nearly a year after signing its agreement with the union. The court found that the "voting public" qualified as a "higher-level legislative authority," and thus the employer had no duty to bargain in good faith about the promotion issue. *Id.* at 578–80.

Judge Hildebrandt, dissenting, argued that there was "substantial evidence that the city had acted in bad faith by placing the charter amendment on the ballot." *Id.* at 581. City officials "publicly acknowledged that the CBA would have to be renegotiated if the charter amendment passed. But instead of requesting [bargaining], the city chose to unilaterally implement the charter amendment, which changed the terms and conditions of employment . . . the city had originally agreed upon." This did not demonstrate "good faith." *Id.* Further, the "higher-level legislative body" exception "contemplates a situation where a superior legislative or executive authority acts beyond the control of the public entity that is the party to the labor agreement in such a way that it frustrates the purpose of the labor agreement. It should not apply in a situation where a city, the public-entity party to the CBA, placed legislation before the voters that unilaterally affected the terms and conditions of employment already agreed upon in the CBA." The dissent also found "it relevant that but for city council placing the charter amendment on the ballot, the voters could not have approved the charter amendment. *Id.* The case thus set a "dangerous precedent by allowing the city to circumvent the rights of the union and to frustrate the purpose of Ohio's collective-bargaining law by allowing a public employer to agree to certain terms and conditions of employment with a union and then shortly thereafter pass legislation that conflicts with those terms." *Id.* at 581–82.

Who has the more convincing argument in *Queen Lodge*? What sort of political acts or advocacy by employers should violate the duty to bargain in good faith? Should some analogous restrictions apply to union political activity, or is there a distinction?

Compare a later decision by another Ohio appellate court, *City of Akron v. SERB*, 195 LRRM (BNA) 2582 (Oh.App. 2013). In this case, the court upheld the state agency's finding that a city employer failed to bargain in good faith with its police union based on the following facts. The city had refused to negotiate layoffs with the union. Instead, the city maintained that layoffs could only be addressed by amending the city's civil service rules. Further, the city stated it would only propose new civil service rules on layoffs if the union withdrew its proposal on this issue from the ongoing contract negotiations. The city then proposed amending the relevant civil service rules without giving any notice to union, and the city's proposed amendment incorporated part, but not all, of the union's contract proposal on the topic. The Ohio SERB found that even though the city subjectively believed it was acting in good faith, the objective standard of good faith bargaining was not met, especially due to the unilateral submission to the civil service commission. The trial and appellate courts agreed with SERB, holding that although adopting new civil service rules that affect employment for bargaining unit members is not by itself a failure to bargain in good faith, the manner in which a city does so is part of the totality of the circumstances that must be considered in determining whether there was good faith bargaining. Is this decision consistent with *Queen Lodge No. 69*? Are the facts sufficiently different to justify a different result?

For a related issue in California, see *Boling v. Public Employees Rel. Bd.*, 5 Cal. 5th 898 (2018). In *Boling*, San Diego's mayor sponsored a citizens' initiative to eliminate pensions for new municipal employees, then rebuffed union demands to bargain over the measure. The relevant agency held that San Diego was obliged to bargain with the union before it could place this initiative on the ballot. An appellate court reversed, holding, among other things, that the initiative was not a *de facto* governing-body-sponsored ballot proposal, and that the mayor's support of the initiative could not be imputed to the city council. Reversing the appellate court, the California Supreme Court held that this matter had to be negotiated. The court held that the appellate court had given insufficient deference to the state agency, and that it had read the statutory obligation to bargain too narrowly.

Problem 9.1

The city of Springfield's Labor Relations Department mailed the Springfield Firefighters Union a copy of a collective bargaining agreement that it had agreed to with the Springfield Police Union. The city attached a cover letter proposing to the Firefighters Union that it agree to the same terms as the Police Union recently had. The Firefighters Union then made counter-proposals, but the city refused to make any counter-proposals itself or engage in any further discussions unless the Firefighters Union altered its wage proposal. The Firefighters Union has now filed a ULP charge claiming that the employer has failed to bargain in good faith; the employer replies that it is merely engaged in hard bargaining.

How should the state labor board rule?

C. Related Practical and Theoretical Issues

In the private sector, the NLRB sometimes assesses the quality of the parties' "faith" by considering both bargaining behavior and evidence extrinsic to the bargaining process pursuant to a "totality of the circumstances" standard. *See Regency Serv. Carts, Inc.*, 345 N.L.R.B. 671 (2005). Recall that in *Pleasantview Nursing Home, Inc. v. NLRB, supra*, an employer representative's statement during bargaining that a particular topic was non-negotiable did not amount to a ULP, even when combined with firm adherence to bargaining positions. Yet, in *NLRB v. Hardesty Co.*, 308 F.3d 859 (8th Cir. 2002), the court of appeals upheld the Board's conclusion that the employer's bargaining behavior and supervisors' statements away from the bargaining table gave evidence that the employer had committed a ULP. After reaching agreement on a number of issues and negotiating "smoothly for several months," the employer withdrew some of its initial proposals and introduced regressive proposals on other issues. The court of appeals suggested that "[o]f itself, such hard-bargaining might not amount to a §8(a)(5) violation, especially if the Company provided compelling explanations for its proposals. However, in this case, the Board found that the explanation for Hardesty's bargaining positions . . . was provided by the Company's away-from-the-table behavior. . . ." *Id.* at 866. This behavior consisted of statements by supervisors that "[t]he Union would be there one year" and "within a year the whole thing would be over with and they'd probably have a new vote," among others. One supervisor told an employee that "it would be to the Company's benefit not to enter into a contract with the Union. The main reason being that it would cost them money and that they would and could wait until all the Union supporters were gone and then they'd have everything their own way." *Id.*; *see also, e.g., NLRB v. Overnite Transp. Co.*, 938 F.2d 815 (7th Cir. 1991) (upholding Board's conclusion that combination of employer representative's statements and refusal to change from its initial bargaining position evidenced a lack of good faith in bargaining).

By contrast, in *ConAgra, Inc. v. NLRB*, 117 F.3d 1435 (D.C. Cir. 1997), the employer sent its parent company a strike contingency plan while also making arrangements to improve security and hire replacement workers—all while bargaining with the union. The Board held that the employer engaged in surface bargaining. The District of Columbia Circuit disagreed, even though the employer also held firmly to its bargaining proposals, including reduced wages and benefits significantly below existing rates. The combination of the employer's bargaining positions, which the court observed would not have reduced wages and benefits below the levels provided by some of the employer's competitors, and contingency plans for a strike were not sufficient evidence of a failure to bargain in good faith.

What role does deference to the Board play in court rulings on allegations of bad-faith bargaining? In *Eastern Maine Medical Center*, the First Circuit suggested that deference to the Board is an essential bulwark against improper intervention in the substance of the collective bargaining agreement:

> There is indeed a tension created by asking the Board to judge the reasonableness of the bargainers, but not to supervise the substance of their bargaining. The major resource making this tension tolerable is the agency's accumulated institutional experience in making precisely those sorts of

judgments. We thus do not lightly disregard the Board's informed judgment in the especially delicate task of judging whether, in context, a strategy of bargaining is more likely calculated to obstruct agreement than to bring about the best compromise possible. 658 F.2d at 10.

Similarly, in the public sector, the Oregon Court in *Ass'n of Oregon Corrections Employees, supra* and the Ohio Court in *SERB v. Queen City Lodge No. 69, supra,* both stressed the importance of deferring to the state agency in good faith bargaining decisions. Is this approach correct? Is deference to a labor board a sufficient safeguard against the government essentially writing or re-writing collective bargaining agreements, or does it open the door to greater intervention in the substance of collective bargaining by the board?

Stewart Schwab introduced Coase's Theorem into the analysis of collective bargaining in **Collective Bargaining and the Coase Theorem**, 72 CORNELL L. REV. 245, 268–69 (1987).[*] Coase's Theorem, simply stated, posits that if parties bargain in the absence of transaction costs, they will negotiate an efficient agreement regardless of which party might hold the initial legal entitlement to the subject under negotiation. *See* RONALD COASE, THE FIRM, THE MARKET, AND THE LAW 13–14 (1988). Coase defined "transaction costs" as those costs necessary "to discover who it is one wishes to deal with, to inform people that one wishes to deal and on what terms, to conduct negotiations leading up to a bargain, to draw up the contract, to undertake the inspection needed to make sure that the terms of the contract are being observed, and so on." Ronald Coase, *The Problem of Social Cost,* 3 J.L. & ECON. 1, 15 (1960). "Strategic behavior"—for example, lying, bluffing, and information withholding for the purpose of claiming more than the party's share of the benefits of the contract—is also considered a transaction cost. *See* Harris, *supra* at 108–09.

Schwab argued that collective bargaining is closer to the unrealizable ideal of zero transaction costs than many other kinds of negotiations:

> The largest impediment to reaching an efficient agreement . . . is coordinating the desires of multiple parties. . . . In a typical labor negotiation, only two parties bargain. Thus, the most substantial transaction cost is absent when a union and a company bargain.
>
> Other features of labor negotiations reinforce the proposition that transaction costs are low in collective bargaining. . . . [First, o]nce the parties are assembled, the marginal cost of discussing an additional item is small. Second, in many cases the parties have established a stable, long-term relationship. . . . The parties may value long-term cooperation more highly than any individual contract term. Third, the representatives of the union and the company are typically experienced, skilled negotiators, able to recognize and react swiftly to cues that agreement or compromise is possible. Schwab, *supra*, at 267–68.

---

[*] Copyright 1987. Reprinted by permission.

Yet, he also acknowledged that collective bargaining may be more susceptible to strategic behavior:

> In a bilateral monopoly, no clear price exists, enabling a party through threats or lies to capture for itself most of the gains from trade. To gain a larger share, one party may threaten destructive behavior. As long as the other side recognizes the threat, however, the parties can negotiate based on the fear of destructive behavior without anyone having to carry out the threat. Thus, bluffs and threats by themselves do not cause inefficiency. Only when strategic behavior actually prevents trade will it prevent efficient contracts. *Id.* at 268–69.

Schwab's analysis suggests two questions that are worth considering throughout this chapter and the next. First, assuming you are persuaded by Coase's Theorem, do the Board's and the courts' interpretations of the duty to bargain in good faith help to reduce transaction costs and thereby increase the likelihood that unions and employers will negotiate efficient contracts? For example, *A-1 King Size Sandwich* might be justified in that it reduces the strategic behavior of surface bargaining. Second, assuming you are persuaded by Schwab's argument that collective bargaining is characterized by low transaction costs, are some of the Boards' and the courts' decisions allocating legal entitlements to one party or the other unnecessary?

Notes

1. Most of the cases above involve employers or unions bargaining hard about a collection of proposals. What if the hard bargaining is focused on a single issue? In *Duffy Tool & Stamping, LLC v. NLRB*, 233 F.3d 995 (7th Cir. 2000), the court of appeals upheld the Board's conclusion that the employer had committed a ULP by declaring an impasse when it could not reach agreement with the union about a "no fault" absenteeism policy and unilaterally implemented the policy, even though the parties were not deadlocked on other mandatory subjects of bargaining. However, in *E.I. DuPont de Nemours & Co. v. NLRB*, 489 F.3d 1310 (D.C. Cir. 2007), the court of appeals upheld the Board's conclusion that the employer did not commit a ULP by separating subcontracting from other issues in bargaining where there was a history of bargaining separately over subcontracting issues and the contract contained an "evergreen" clause giving continuing effect to the balance of contract provisions while bargaining continued. *See also NLRB v. Tomco Commc's, Inc.*, 567 F.2d 871 (9th Cir. 1978) (holding that one issue may loom so large in the negotiations that impasse on that issue "may fairly be said to cripple the prospects of any agreement").

2. The Board, with the support of the courts of appeals, has held that the process of collective bargaining is not a mandatory subject of bargaining. Accordingly, either party's insistence on the presence of a court reporter to create a transcript of bargaining sessions constitutes a failure to bargain in good faith. *See, e.g., Bartlett-Collins Co.*, 237 N.L.R.B. 770 (1978); *Latrobe Steel Co. v. NLRB*, 630 F.2d 171 (3d Cir. 1980); *see also NLRB v. Pennsylvania Telephone Guild*, 799 F.2d 84 (3rd Cir. 1986) (applying *Bartlett-Collins* and *Latrobe Steel* to a union's demand for an audio

recording of grievance meetings). Also, neither party may refuse to engage in face-to-face meetings with the other party and require, instead, that negotiations be conducted through a mediator. *Success Village Apartments, Inc.*, 347 N.L.R.B. 1065 (2006) (holding that mediation is a permissive subject of bargaining, so a party may not insist on bargaining through a mediator).

Problem 9.2

Is there a legally relevant difference between the following two scenarios?

Scenario #1: At the first negotiating session, the union presents its contract proposals, including a union security clause which would require all new employees to pay required dues within thirty days after commencing their employment. Union security clauses are mandatory subjects of bargaining. At the next bargaining session, in response to the union bargaining committee chair's inquiry about the union security clause, the employer's chief negotiator says: "We have studied this problem carefully, and our minds are made up. You guys know all the arguments on both sides and so do I. Let's not waste time repeating them. We won't grant any form of union-security clause, and every time you start talking about it we intend to leave the room." Negotiations continue but, as promised, the employer's negotiators walk out of the room every time the union security clause is proposed.

Scenario #2: The union presents its contract proposals which, again, include the union security clause discussed above. At the second negotiating session, the union bargaining committee chair asks about the union security clause. The employer's chief negotiator responds: "We have studied this problem carefully. We reject your proposal. We are not going to accept it, and every time you raise it the answer is going to be the same: NO!" Negotiations continue but, as promised, the employer's negotiators answer "No" to the union security clause every time it is proposed.

If these two scenarios would produce different legal conclusions, does that difference reduce the duty to bargain in good faith to a challenge for talented wordsmiths to craft the right words for utterance at the bargaining table? Or is it a set of legal rules that actually change collective bargaining behavior in a productive way?

D. The Public-Sector Duty to Meet and Confer

The Missouri Statute, V.A.M.S. § 105.520 provides: "Whenever such proposals are presented by the exclusive bargaining representative to a public body, the public body or its designated representative or representatives shall meet, confer and discuss such proposals relative to salaries and other conditions of employment of the employees of the public body with the labor organization which is the exclusive bargaining representative of its employees in a unit appropriate. Upon the completion of discussions, the results shall be reduced to writing and be presented to the appropriate administrative, legislative or other governing body in the form of an ordinance, resolution, bill or other form required for adoption, modification or rejection."

In *Sumpter v. City of Moberly*, 645 S.W.2d 359, 363 (Mo. 1982), the court explained the obligation under this statute as follows: "The public employer is not required to agree but is required only to 'meet, confer and discuss' . . . The act provides only a procedure for communication between the organization selected by public employees and their employer without requiring adoption of any agreement reached." Quoting *Curators of the University of Missouri v. Public Service Employees Local No. 45*, 520 S.W.2d 54 (Mo. banc 1975), the *Sumpter* decision continued:

> When [the public employees' designated] representative submits proposals and grievances relative to salaries and other conditions of employment, the public body or its designated representative must acknowledge such proposals and grievances and must discuss them with the bargaining representative. Generally, the public body will designate a representative to meet with the representative of the employees. In this event, the public body's representative acts essentially as a hearer and a receptor of the employees' petitions and remonstrances. His duty is to discuss them with the bargaining representative, and to fully apprise himself of the nature and extent of the proposals and grievances presented. The representative of the public body must then transmit to it, in written form, the proposals and grievances and the substance of the discussions. The public body must then give them its consideration 'in the form of an ordinance, resolution, bill or other form required for adoption, modification or rejection." 645 S.W.2d at 362.

What policy reasons support "meet and confer" rules? When should courts find that something less than the traditional duty to bargain in good faith exists?

City and Borough of Sitka v. Int'l Broth. of Elec. Workers, Local Union 1547

Supreme Court of Alaska
653 P.2d 332 (Alaska 1982)

COMPTON, J.

[The court first held that a city ordinance exempting the city from the general state public sector law, the Alaska Public Employment Relations Act, was valid] . . .

III. Sitka Charter

The second issue is whether the creation of an employees' negotiating committee satisfies the mandate set forth in Sitka Charter section 3.05 of "recognizing employee organizations." The personnel policy ordinance defines the structure of the negotiating committee, but also affords municipal employees the opportunity to elect a department representative. Sitka argues that by enacting the personnel policy ordinance, it fulfilled its Charter obligation. In contrast, the IBEW argues that the Charter requires Sitka to recognize the IBEW as bargaining agent for the municipality's electrical department. In our view, the dispositive question centers on the intentions of the framers of the Sitka Charter in using the word "recognizing". . . .

The legislative history surrounding the adoption of Sitka Charter section 3.05 is quite sparse. . . . When discussing the matter, the Charter Commission addressed the relationship between "benefit bargaining" and a provision in the administrative code that apparently required the City to recognize an employee organization:

> Shuler: You don't have a bargain agreement, unless you have a signed agreement with someone.
>
> Wright: Not necessarily.
>
> (Voice): Are you thinking of bargaining rights?
>
> Wright: Yes.
>
> Fager: Our administrative code doesn't say, except just to say recognize an organization, it doesn't say anything about benefit bargaining.
>
> Grussendorf: *That's all you have to do, just recognize the existence of the organization.* Transcript of Sitka Charter Commission (July 15, 1977) (emphasis added).

Although the colloquy quoted above was not directly in reference to the meaning of Charter section 3.05, it offers a valuable insight into the probable intent of the Charter Commission. We therefore reject the IBEW's contention that the phrase "recognizing employee organizations" should be interpreted to require Sitka to engage in collective bargaining with respect to the terms and conditions of employment of municipal employees. "Collective bargaining" is a term of art in labor law that harbors the concomitant duty to bargain in good faith.[12] We recognized in *Kenai Peninsula Borough School District v. Kenai Peninsula Education Association*, 572 P.2d 416 (Alaska 1977), that the good faith standard of collective bargaining may affect the substantive position of the bargaining parties. We stated:

> While the good faith standard of collective bargaining does not compel either party to make concessions, intransigent positions, adopted in an effort to avoid any agreement, are disfavored. Thus a legal determination that a matter is subject to good faith collective bargaining may narrow the policy-making powers of an employer by curtailing any absolute directives on his part.

572 P.2d at 418–19 (footnote omitted). This consequence raises particularly sensitive concerns when collective bargaining in the public sector is at issue because the public employer who is obligated to engage in good faith bargaining relinquishes some of the essential attributes of sovereignty. . . .

Mindful of the nature of collective bargaining in the public sector and of the serious implications of the duty to bargain in good faith, the decision to engage in collective bargaining should not be implied from language that is unclear. It is only when a legislative enactment expressly and unambiguously announces a decision to

---

12. *See* AS 23.40.250(1).

undertake collective bargaining that a court should find that a government entity has bound itself to such a course of dealing. The language employed by the Charter Commission is not so clear and explicit that this court will interpret the phrase to mandate collective bargaining. Instead, the less stringent obligation to "meet and confer" is applicable to discussions between Sitka and recognized employee organizations.[13]

[The court concluded that the City had nonetheless violated the city charter's requirement that it "recognize" the union because it had not allowed the employees to choose their own representatives.]

Notes

1. *Moberly* went so far as to hold that signed agreements between unions and employers made pursuant to the Missouri statute were not actually binding on employers. This part of *Moberly* was reversed by the Missouri Supreme Court in *Independence-Nat. Educ. Ass'n v. Independence School Dist.*, 223 S.W.3d 131 (Mo. 2007). Contracts formed pursuant to the "meet and confer" provisions of the Missouri statute are now binding on both parties. *Independence-Nat. Educ. Ass'n* did not require, however, the traditional duty to bargain in good faith. Yet the court referred to the process under the Missouri statute as "collective bargaining." Perhaps signaling a shift away from this approach, however, *American Federation of Teachers v. Ledbetter*, 387 S.W.3d 360 (Mo. 2012) held that the right to bargain collectively in the Missouri state Constitution did include an obligation to bargain in good faith. *Ledbetter* explicitly held, however, that the "good faith" required in bargaining would be defined by Missouri state law, not federal law. 387 S.W.3d 360, 367–68.

Further, lower courts in Missouri have allowed employers to create "collective" bargaining rules that are employer friendly. For example, one court upheld a system that required secret ballot votes to certify a union, barred a city from paying officers for time spent in collective bargaining, restricted economic terms of labor agreements to one-year terms, and allowed the city to modify the economic terms of agreement in the event of a budget shortfall. *West Central Missouri Region Lodge #50, FOP v. City of Grandview*, 460 S.W.3d 425 (Mo. App. 2015). *See also St. Louis Police Leadership Org. v. City of St. Louis*, 484 S.W.3d 882 (Mo. App. 2016) (approving decertification process that had no provisions for union challenges).

2. Some jurisdictions use the term "meet and confer" in their statutes, but essentially require "bargaining in good faith" as understood under the NLRA. *See, e.g., City of Phoenix Relations Bd. ex rel. AFSCME Local 2384*, 699 P.2d 1323 (Ariz. App. 1985). A few jurisdictions are somewhere in between. In *Kansas Bd. of Regents v.*

---

13. A "meet and confer," or "meet and discuss," obligation imposes only the duty to meet at reasonable times and to discuss recommendations or proposals submitted by the employee organization. We have previously recognized the value of an obligation to meet and confer with recognized employee organizations. *See Kenai Peninsula Borough School Dist. v. Kenai Peninsula Educ. Ass'n*, 572 P.2d at 423.

Pittsburg State University Chapt. Of Kansas National Educ. Ass'n, 233 Kan. 801, 804 (Kan. 1983), the court described the Kansas Act, K.S.A. 75-4321, *et seq.*, as "a hybrid" containing some characteristics of pure "meet and confer" acts with other characteristics of "collective bargaining." "It imposes upon both employer and employee representatives the obligation to meet, confer and negotiate in good faith with affirmative willingness to resolve grievances and disputes, and to endeavor to reach agreement on conditions of employment."

3. Minnesota has a statute which requires public employers to "meet and confer" with public employees who are "professionals" under the statute. Employers must engage in official exchanges of views with unions of professional employees on policy questions relating to employment but outside the scope of mandatory bargaining. But there is no duty to bargain in good faith to impasse. MINN. STAT. ANN. §§ 179.63, 179.65, 179.73. *See Minnesota State Bd. for Community Colleges v. Knight*, 465 U.S. 271 (1984) (upholding the constitutionality of this statute).

4. What actual benefits might unions or employers expect to get from a true "meet and confer" rule that conveys no traditional collective bargaining rights? From a union's perspective, is such a provision better than nothing? From an employer's perspective, what, if anything, positive could it gain from such a process?

III. Information Disclosure and "Good Faith"

Most labor negotiations are characterized by "bilateral asymmetric information." Employers have information that unions and their members do not, and unions and their members have information that employers do not. For example, employers know their costs of production, access to capital markets and credit, industry practices, product market projections, and their own plans regarding human capital issues, among other things. Unions and their members have superior information about workers' professional and personal preferences, but also, in some cases, about how well supervisors, disciplinary processes, and even production systems function. *Cf.* Harris, *supra*, at 1217. All of this information may be relevant to resolving the important workplace issues that are addressed in collective bargaining.

Since the parties do not have the same information at the outset, their expectations about how they should craft their agreement will frequently conflict. Bargaining parties' initial expectations are principally a function of the information on which they are based—that is, the knowledge they bring with them to the bargaining table or, in the case of mature bargaining relationships, acquired over time. Even mature bargaining partners are inevitably confronted with changing circumstances, goals, and priorities over a contract's term. So, even bargaining partners acting with subjective good faith face a substantial challenge. Successful negotiations may well hinge, in part, on how successfully the parties exchange information and, in turn, adjust their initial expectations so that they can move toward some agreeable middle ground.

A. In the Private Sector

NLRB v. Truitt Mfg. Co.
Supreme Court of the United States
351 U.S. 149 (1956)

BLACK, J.

. . . .

The question presented by this case is whether the [NLRB] may find that an employer has not bargained in good faith where the employer claims it cannot afford to pay higher wages but refuses requests to produce information substantiating its claim.

The dispute here arose when a union representing certain of respondent's employees asked for a wage increase of 10 cents per hour. The company answered that it could not afford to pay such an increase, it was undercapitalized, had never paid dividends, and that an increase of more than 2½ cents per hour would put it out of business. The union asked the company to produce some evidence substantiating these statements, requesting permission to have a certified public accountant examine the company's books, financial data, etc. This request being denied, the union asked that the company submit "full and complete information with respect to its financial standing and profits," insisting that such information was pertinent and essential for the employees to determine whether or not they should continue to press their demand for a wage increase. A union official testified before the trial examiner that "[W]e were wanting anything relating to the Company's position, any records or what have you, books, accounting sheets, cost expenditures, what not, anything to back the Company's position that they were unable to give any more money." The company refused all the requests, relying solely on the statement that "the information . . . is not pertinent to this discussion and the company declines to give you such information; You have no legal right to such."

On the basis of these facts the [NLRB] found that the company had "failed to bargain in good faith with respect to wages in violation of Section 8(a)(5) of the Act." The Board ordered the company to supply the union with such information as would "substantiate the Respondent's position of its economic inability to pay the requested wage increase." The Court of Appeals refused to enforce the Board's order. . . .

We think that in determining whether the obligation of good-faith bargaining has been met the Board has a right to consider an employer's refusal to give information about its financial status. While Congress did not compel agreement between employers and bargaining representatives, it did require collective bargaining in the hope that agreements would result. Section 204(a)(1) of the [Taft-Hartley] Act admonishes both employers and employees to "exert every reasonable effort to make and maintain agreements concerning rates of pay, hours, and working conditions. . . ."

In their effort to reach an agreement here both the union and the company treated the company's ability to pay increased wages as highly relevant. The ability of an employer to increase wages without injury to his business is a commonly considered factor in wage negotiations. Claims for increased wages have sometimes been abandoned because of an employer's unsatisfactory business condition; employees have even voted to accept wage decreases because of such conditions.

Good-faith bargaining necessarily requires that claims made by either bargainer should be honest claims. This is true about an asserted inability to pay an increase in wages. If such an argument is important enough to present in the give and take of bargaining, it is important enough to require some sort of proof of its accuracy. And it would certainly not be farfetched for a trier of fact to reach the conclusion that bargaining lacks good faith when an employer mechanically repeats a claim of inability to pay without making the slightest effort to substantiate the claim. Such has been the holding of the Labor Board since shortly after the passage of the Wagner Act. . . . This was the position of the Board when the Taft-Hartley Act was passed in 1947 and has been its position ever since. We agree with the Board that a refusal to attempt to substantiate a claim of inability to pay increased wages may support a finding of a failure to bargain in good faith.

The Board concluded that under the facts and circumstances of this case the respondent was guilty of an unfair labor practice in failing to bargain in good faith. We see no reason to disturb the findings of the Board. We do not hold, however, that in every case in which economic inability is raised as an argument against increased wages it automatically follows that the employees are entitled to substantiating evidence. Each case must turn upon its particular facts. The inquiry must always be whether or not under the circumstances of the particular case the statutory obligation to bargain in good faith has been met. Since we conclude that there is support in the record for the conclusion of the Board here that respondent did not bargain in good faith, it was error for the Court of Appeals to set aside the Board's order and deny enforcement. Reversed.

———————

The Supreme Court has suggested that the obligation to disclose requested information should be defined by a "discovery-type" standard of potential relevance to the union's ability to negotiate effectively and properly perform its other duties. *See NLRB v. Acme Industrial Co.*, 385 U.S. 432 (1967); *see also U.S. Testing Co., Inc. v. NLRB*, 160 F.3d 14 (D.C. Cir. 1998). The District of Columbia Circuit has described this as a "low" burden. *See Country Ford Trucks, Inc. v. NLRB*, 229 F.3d 1184 (D.C. Cir. 2000). Certain kinds of information—wages, benefits, hours, and working conditions included—are so fundamental that they are considered presumptively relevant. *Id.*; *Sunset Station Hotel Casino*, 367 N.L.R.B. No. 62, 2019 WL 156541, at *2 (Jan. 7, 2019), The union bears the burden of proving the relevance of other kinds of information. *See, e.g., Sara Lee Bakery Group, Inc. v. NLRB*, 514 F.3d 422 (5th Cir. 2008) (union did not carry its burden with respect to a request for information about employer's contracting costs).

When the union requests presumptively relevant information, the employer bears the burden of proving irrelevance or some countervailing interest that justifies a good-faith refusal to provide the information. *See Sunset Station Hotel Casino*, 2019 WL 156541, at *2 (finding employer violated § 8(a)(5) where employer stated no basis for rebutting presumption). The union bears the burden of proving relevance when seeking other information. *See NP Palace LLC*, 368 N.L.R.B. No. 148, 2019 WL 7020748, at *4 (Dec. 16, 2019) (holding that nonunit employees' job descriptions, unit employees' Social Security numbers, and customer complaints about unit employees' job performance were not presumptively relevant). When a union seeks disclosure of information that is not ordinarily considered relevant, but which the union asserts became relevant because of the particular circumstances in the workplace, the union will be required to make a heightened showing of specific relevance before disclosure will be required. *See San Diego Newspaper Guild, Local No. 95 v. NLRB*, 548 F.2d 863 (9th Cir. 1977). *See also Tenneco Automotive, Inc.*, 357 N.L.R.B. 953, 954 (2011) (union's request for information regarding employer's basis for installing cameras was relevant at the time requested because it was close to when those incidents occurred), *enforced in relevant part*, 716 F.3d 640, 648 (D.C. Cir. 2013).

Courts interpreting the NLRA have been careful to qualify the parties' obligation as requiring disclosure only "in the absence of countervailing interests." *See, e.g., Crowley Marine Services, Inc. v. NLRB*, 234 F.3d 1295 (D.C. Cir. 2000). Thus, further limits may be imposed on the disclosure of admittedly relevant information when countervailing interests arise, as the next case demonstrates.

Detroit Edison v. NLRB

Supreme Court of the United States
440 U.S. 301 (1979)

STEWART, J.

The duty to bargain collectively, imposed upon an employer by § 8(a)(5) of the [NLRA], includes a duty to provide relevant information needed by a labor union for the proper performance of its duties as the employees' bargaining representative. *NLRB v. Truitt Mfg. Co., supra.* In this case an employer was brought before the [NLRB] to answer a complaint that it had violated this statutory duty when it refused to disclose certain information about employee aptitude tests requested by a union in order to prepare for arbitration of a grievance. The employer supplied the union with much of the information requested, but refused to disclose three items. . . . The Board, concluding that all the items requested were relevant to the grievance and would be useful to the union in processing it, ordered the employer to turn over all of the materials directly to the union, subject to certain restrictions on the union's use of the information. A divided Court of Appeals for the Sixth Circuit ordered enforcement of the Board's order without modification.

We granted certiorari to consider an important question of federal labor law. . . .

[The Utility Workers Union of America, Local 223, represented certain of the Company's operating and maintenance employees in Monroe, Michigan. According to the collective bargaining agreement, promotions within a given unit were to be based on seniority "whenever reasonable qualifications and abilities of the employees being considered are not significantly different." Management decisions to bypass employees with greater seniority were subject to a grievance procedure. The Company used several validated aptitude tests to screen applicants for the job classification of "Instrument Man B." The Company expressly committed that each applicant's test score would remain confidential.]

The present dispute had its beginnings in 1971 when the Company invited bids from employees to fill six Instrument Man B openings at the Monroe plant. Ten Monroe unit employees applied. None received a score [on the aptitude tests] designated as "acceptable," and all were on that basis rejected. The jobs were eventually filled by applicants from outside the Monroe plant bargaining unit.

The Union filed a grievance on behalf of the Monroe applicants, claiming that the new testing procedure was unfair and that the Company had bypassed senior employees in violation of the collective-bargaining agreement. The grievance was rejected by the Company at all levels, and the Union took it to arbitration. In preparation for the arbitration, the Union requested the Company to turn over various materials related to the Instrument Man B testing program. The Company furnished the Union with copies of test-validation studies performed by its industrial psychologists and with a report by an outside consultant on the Company's entire testing program. It refused, however, to release the actual test battery, the applicants' test papers, and their scores, maintaining that complete confidentiality of these materials was necessary in order to insure the future integrity of the tests and to protect the privacy interests of the examinees.

The Union then filed with the Board the unfair labor practice charge involved in this case. The charge alleged that the information withheld by the Company was relevant and necessary to the arbitration of the grievance, "including the ascertainment of promotion criteria, the veracity of the scoring and grading of the examination and the testing procedures, and the job relatedness of the test(s) to the Instrument Man B classification." . . .

The Board, and the Court of Appeals for the Sixth Circuit in its decision enforcing the Board's order, ordered the Company to turn over all the material directly to the Union. They concluded that the Union should be able to determine for itself whether it needed a psychologist to interpret the test battery and answer sheets. Both recognized the Company's interest in maintaining the security of the tests, but both reasoned that appropriate restrictions on the Union's use of the materials would protect this interest.[9] Neither was receptive to the Company's claim that

9. The Board, although it ordered the Company to supply the tests and answer sheets directly to the Union, incorporated by reference the Administrative Law Judge's restrictions on the Union's

employee privacy and the professional obligations of the Company's industrial psychologists should outweigh the Union request for the employee-linked scores.

II

. . . .

Two issues . . . are presented on this record. The first concerns the Board's choice of a remedy for the Company's failure to disclose copies of the test battery and answer sheets. The second, and related, question concerns the propriety of the Board's conclusion that the Company committed an unfair labor practice when it refused to disclose, without a written consent from the individual employees, the test scores linked with the employee names.

A

We turn first to the question whether the Board abused its remedial discretion when it ordered the Company to deliver directly to the Union the copies of the test battery and answer sheets. The Company's position, stripped of the argument that it had no duty at all to disclose these materials, is as follows: It urges that disclosure directly to the Union would carry with it a substantial risk that the test questions would be disseminated. Since it spent considerable time and money validating the Instrument Man B tests and since its tests depend for reliability upon the Examinee's lack of advance preparation, it contends that the harm of dissemination would not be trivial. The future validity of the tests is tied to secrecy, and disclosure to employees would not only threaten the Company's investment but would also leave the Company with no valid means of measuring employee aptitude. The Company also maintains that its interest in preserving the security of its tests is consistent with the federal policy favoring the use of validated, standardized, and nondiscriminatory employee selection procedures reflected in the Civil Rights Act of 1964. . . .

A union's bare assertion that it needs information to process a grievance does not automatically oblige the employer to supply all the information in the manner requested. The duty to supply information under §8(a)(5) turns upon "the circumstances of the particular case," *NLRB v. Truitt Mfg. Co., supra*, and much the same may be said for the type of disclosure that will satisfy that duty. Throughout this proceeding, the reasonableness of the Company's concern for test secrecy has been essentially conceded. The finding by the Board that this concern did not outweigh the Union's interest in exploring the fairness of the Company's criteria for promotion did not carry with it any suggestion that the concern itself was not legitimate

---

use of the materials. Under those restrictions, the Union was given the right "to use the tests and the information contained therein to the extent necessary to process and arbitrate the grievances, but not to copy the tests, or otherwise use them for the purpose of disclosing the tests or the questions to employees who have in the past, or who may in the future take these tests, or to anyone (other than the arbitrator) who may advise the employees of the contents of the tests."

After the conclusion of the arbitration, the Union was required to return "all copies of the battery of tests" to the Company. . . .

and substantial.[13] Indeed, on this record—which has established the Company's freedom under the collective contract to use aptitude tests as a criterion for promotion, the empirical validity of the tests, and the relationship between secrecy and test validity—the strength of the Company's concern has been abundantly demonstrated. The Board has cited no principle of national labor policy to warrant a remedy that would unnecessarily disserve this interest, and we are unable to identify one.

It is obvious that the remedy selected by the Board does not adequately protect the security of the tests. The restrictions barring the Union from taking any action that might cause the tests to fall into the hands of employees who have taken or are likely to take them are only as effective as the sanctions available to enforce them. In this instance, there is substantial doubt whether the Union would be subject to a contempt citation were it to ignore the restrictions. . . . Moreover, the Union clearly would not be accountable in either contempt or unfair labor practice proceedings for the most realistic vice inherent in the Board's remedy—the danger of inadvertent leaks.

We are mindful that the Board is granted broad discretion in devising remedies to undo the effects of violations of the Act, and of the principle that in the area of federal labor law "the relation of remedy to policy is peculiarly a matter for administrative competence." Nonetheless, the rule of deference to the Board's choice of remedy does not constitute a blank check for arbitrary action. The role that Congress in § 10(e) has entrusted to the courts in reviewing the Board's petitions for enforcement of its orders is not that of passive conduit. *See Fibreboard Corp. v. NLRB, infra.* The Board in this case having identified no justification for a remedy granting such scant protection to the Company's undisputed and important interests in test secrecy, we hold that the Board abused its discretion in ordering the Company to turn over the test battery and answer sheets directly to the Union.

B

The dispute over Union access to the actual scores received by named employees is in a somewhat different procedural posture, since the Company did on this issue preserve its objections to the basic finding that it had violated its duty under § 8(a)(5) when it refused disclosure.

We may accept for the sake of this discussion the finding that the employee scores were of potential relevance to the Union's grievance, as well as the position of the Board that the federal statutory duty to disclose relevant information cannot be defeated by the ethical standards of a private group [i.e., the industrial

---

13. The Board limited discussion of its reasons for eliminating the intermediary requirement to the statement that "it is reasonable to assume that, having requested the papers, the Union intends effectively to utilize them." Consequently, it said, it "would not condition the Union's access to the information on the retention of a psychologist but rather would have [the Company] submit the information directly to the Union and let the Union decide whether the assistance or expertise of a psychologist is required."

psychologists]. Nevertheless we agree with the Company that its willingness to disclose these scores only upon receipt of consents from the examinees satisfied its statutory obligations under §8(a)(5).

The Board's position appears to rest on the proposition that union interests in arguably relevant information must always predominate over all other interests, however legitimate. But such an absolute rule has never been established, and we decline to adopt such a rule here. There are situations in which an employer's conditional offer to disclose may be warranted. This we believe is one.

The sensitivity of any human being to disclosure of information that may be taken to bear on his or her basic competence is sufficiently well known to be an appropriate subject of judicial notice. There is nothing in this record to suggest that the Company promised the examinees that their scores would remain confidential in order to further parochial concerns or to frustrate subsequent Union attempts to process employee grievances. And it has not been suggested at any point in this proceeding that the Company's unilateral promise of confidentiality was in itself violative of the terms of the collective-bargaining agreement. Indeed, the Company presented evidence that disclosure of individual scores had in the past resulted in the harassment of some lower scoring examinees who had, as a result, left the Company.

Under these circumstances, any possible impairment of the function of the Union in processing the grievances of employees is more than justified by the interests served in conditioning the disclosure of the test scores upon the consent of the very employees whose grievance is being processed. The burden on the Union in this instance is minimal. The Company's interest in preserving employee confidence in the testing program is well founded.

In light of the sensitive nature of testing information, the minimal burden that compliance with the Company's offer would have placed on the Union, and the total absence of evidence that the Company had fabricated concern for employee confidentiality only to frustrate the Union in the discharge of its responsibilities, we are unable to sustain the Board in its conclusion that the Company, in resisting an unconsented-to disclosure of individual test results, violated the statutory obligation to bargain in good faith. See *NLRB v. Truitt Mfg. Co., supra.* Accordingly, we hold that the order requiring the Company unconditionally to disclose the employee scores to the Union was erroneous. . . .

Notes

1. Are *Truitt* and *Detroit Edison* about employers' subjective intent, or are they more concerned with perfecting the bargaining process by forcing the parties to disclose relevant information? Do these decisions serve the Coasean goal of reducing transaction costs in collective bargaining, as discussed above? Do §§8(d), 8(a)(5), and 8(b)(3) grant authority to the Board and the courts to perfect the bargaining process by reducing transaction costs?

2. As a general matter, the courts of appeals have held that there is no particular verbal or written formulation that triggers an employer's obligation to disclose financial information as required by *Truitt*. However, the Board drew a distinction in *Nielsen Lithographing Co.*, 305 N.L.R.B. 697, 700–01 (1991), between an employer's claim of "competitive disadvantage," which generally does not trigger a duty to disclose, and a claim of an "inability to pay," which gives rise to the disclosure obligation. This distinction, which has been adopted by most courts of appeals, is drawn between an employer that "cannot pay" and an employer that "will not pay." *See Facet Enterprises, Inc. v. NLRB*, 907 F.2d 963, 980 (10th Cir. 1990); *see also ConAgra, Inc. v. NLRB*, 117 F.3d 1435, 1438–42 (D.C. Cir. 1997); *Torrington Extend-A-Care Employee Ass'n v. NLRB*, 17 F.3d 580, 588–90 (2d Cir. 1994); *United Steelworkers of Am., Local Union 14534 v. NLRB*, 983 F.2d 240, 244–45 (D.C. Cir. 1993); *Graphic Commc'ns Int'l Union, Local 508 O-K-I, AFL-CIO v. NLRB*, 977 F.2d 1168, 1171 (7th Cir. 1992). *See generally International Chemical Workers Union Council of the United Food and Commercial Workers Int'l v. NLRB*, 467 F.3d 742, 749–50 (9th Cir. 2006) (noting the change in law, but refusing to change the 9th Circuit's rule which does not recognize the distinction put forward by the Board). The District of Columbia Circuit has held that an employer's assertion that it is losing money does not constitute a claim of an inability to pay. *Lakeland Bus Line, Inc. v. NLRB*, 347 F.3d 955 (D.C. Cir. 2003).

Is this a legitimate distinction? How might a clever labor lawyer have advised the employer's negotiator in *Truitt* to describe the company's economic position to avoid committing a ULP?

3. Unions may also be required to disclose certain relevant information during bargaining in order to demonstrate good faith. *See Local 13, Detroit Newspaper Printing & Graphic Commc's Union v. NLRB*, 598 F.2d 267 (D.C. Cir. 1979).

4. An employer's assertion of countervailing interests does not obviate its obligation to disclose relevant information. Rather, the employer bears the burden of seeking to accommodate the union's request for relevant information while appropriately protecting the countervailing interests—for example, by redacting portions of requested documents to protect workers' privacy, placing strict limitations on the use of the information, or releasing information to a neutral third-party for review and analysis. *See Norris, Dover Resources Co. v. NLRB*, 417 F.3d 1161 (10th Cir. 2005) (enforcing NLRB order that employer produce requested "doctor slips" with confidential information redacted); *Roger J. Au & Son v. NLRB*, 538 F.2d 80 (3d Cir. 1976) (statements of charging parties and potential witnesses obtained by NLRB during investigation of a charge against employer were exempt from disclosure); *Pa. Power Co.*, 301 N.L.R.B. 1104 (1991) (employer must furnish the union with a summary of the information it relied on to require drug tests, but need not reveal the identity of the informants). As the D.C. Circuit explained, "[t]he rationale for this placement of the burden derives from the interest in allowing the parties to work out through an informal process how their corresponding duties and responsibilities can be met. In other words, the onus is on the employer because it is in the better position to

propose how best it can respond to a union request for information. The union need not propose the precise alternative to providing the information unedited." *U.S. Testing Co., Inc. v. NLRB, supra*, 160 F.3d at 21.

Problem 9.3

The United Power and Electric Workers Union represents a unit of Atlantic Gas & Electric Company's employees and has a collective bargaining agreement with the employer. In February 2012, the union sent a letter to AG&E's director of labor relations stating that it was "investigating a class action grievance about maintenance work not being performed in the power-generation plant that can impact employee safety." The Union requested: (1) the most recent "Overdue Repairs Report" and "Backlogged Work Orders Report" (BWOR) for all work units in the plant; and (2) a list or copies of all work orders that had been closed, deleted, or removed from the BWOR without all work having been completed by members of the union. AG&E responded by letter in late February requesting that the union provide all "specific employee safety concerns as they relate to the requested reports." In a series of exchanges spanning some four months, the union continued to request the information it sought in the February letter and AG&E continued to adhere to its position.

In an August 2012 letter, the union stated that it had filed a formal safety complaint with the state's Public Utilities Commission (PUC) concerning incomplete work orders that posed a safety threat to the union's members. The Union again requested all of the reports it had been requesting since February 2012 so that it could "intelligently represent the members of the union before the PUC."

You are AG&E's labor counsel. The director of labor relations brings the August 2012 letter from the union to you and asks your opinion about whether AG&E will commit a ULP if it does not disclose the requested information. What is your best advice?

B. In the Public Sector

Public-sector jurisdictions also consider the duty to provide information to be part of the duty to bargain in good faith, and the scope of the duty is usually the same as under the NLRA. For example, *California Faculty Ass'n v. Trustees of the California State University*, 28 Pub. Emp. Rptr. for Cal. ¶ 75 (Cal. PERC 2004) noted that "the failure to provide necessary and relevant information is a *per se* violation of the duty to bargain in good faith." In that case, the employer violated its duty by delaying its response to the union's request for "Weighted Teaching Unit" information (indicating how the amount of workload credit individual teachers had earned was calculated). However, the Commission dismissed a charge based on a separate request for faculty merit increase information because the union had refused to pay for the cost of obtaining the information. Also, in the public sector, as in the private sector, the obligation to disclose is based in statutory language and not dependent on a labor contract. *Id.*; *Town of Evans*, 37 PERB ¶ 3016 (NY PERB 2004).

As in the private sector, this right is not necessarily limited to documents the employer creates and maintains. *Worcester School Committee and Educ. Ass'n of Worcester*, 43 Mass. Labor Comm. 218 (2017), found that the employer had violated the union's right to information by denying access to an environmental expert the union had designated to conduct testing for polychlorinated biphenyl (PCB) in the schools' exterior calking. The agency explained that the union's request was relevant and necessary to its bargaining obligations regarding health and safety, noting that an Environmental Protection Agency regulation required removing building materials with PCB levels greater than 50 parts per million. Also, evidence suggested than in recent years, five teachers had been diagnosed with cancer and an additional two had died of cancer. The Commission ordered the employer to allow access to the relevant buildings "at reasonable times, with reasonable notice, and in a reasonable manner."

In a public-sector case, the Minnesota Supreme Court held that a union challenging the validity of a civil service exam had a legal right to information including the questions and answer key to the exam. Unlike *Detroit Edison*, however, this case did not involve matching the names of individual employees to specific tests or scores. The Minnesota court also rejected an argument by the employer that the union had no right to this information because the decision to administer the exam was not an issue that the union had a right to negotiate. While agreeing that this decision itself was not negotiable, the court explained that the separate question of whether the exam was fair was negotiable. *Int'l Union of Operating Eng'rs Local 49 v. City of Minneapolis*, 305 Minn. 364, 233 N.W.2d 748 (1975). For more on the principle that a union may have the right to negotiate over the effects of a decision even though it does not have a right to negotiate over the decision itself, see Chapter 10.

Some public-sector jurisdictions have special privacy rules that can limit the type of information unions have a right to get. This is a significant issue in the federal sector. In *Dept. of Defense v. FLRA*, 510 U.S. 487 (1994), unions had requested the home addresses of members of their respective bargaining units, information that is routinely provided in the private sector (*see* the discussion of *Excelsior Underwear* in Chapter 3). The Supreme Court held, in the federal sector, part of the Freedom of Information Act, 5 U.S.C. § 552a(b)(2) (FOIA), shielded this information from union requests. That section provides: "No agency shall disclose any record which is contained in a system of records by any means of communication to any person, or to another agency, except pursuant to a written request by, or with the prior written consent of, the individual to whom the record pertains" unless disclosure of the record would be required under other portions of the FOIA. The Court considered FOIA's Exemption 6, which provides that FOIA's disclosure requirements do not apply to "personnel and medical files and similar files the disclosure of which would constitute a clearly unwarranted invasion of personal privacy." The Court concluded that releasing this information to the union *would* constitute such a clearly unwarranted invasion of personal privacy. 510 U.S. 487, 494–98. In contrast, "[t]he relevant public interest supporting disclosure in this case is negligible, at best. Disclosure of the addresses might allow the unions to communicate more effectively with employees, but it would not appreciably further 'the citizens' right to be informed about what their government is up to.'" *Id.* at 497. The Court added that "[n]owhere . . . does the Labor Statute amend FOIA's disclosure requirements or grant information requesters under the Labor Statute special status under FOIA." *Id.*at 499.

The Michigan Supreme Court, in a split decision with the majority citing *Dept. of Defense*, held that the home addresses and telephone numbers of the employees of a state university are not subject to disclosure under the Michigan Freedom of Information Act. *Michigan Fed'n of Teachers v. Univ. of Michigan*, 481 Mich. 657 (2008).

Most public-sector jurisdictions, however, follow the private-sector approach. For example, *Morris County v. Morris Council No. 6*, 30 NJPER 93 (N.J. Sup.Ct., App. Div. 2004) upheld two decisions by the state agency, PERC, which had found that an employer violated the New Jersey statute by refusing to disclose employee home addresses to two unions. The employer had relied on a state executive order barring it from disclosing employee personnel records. But the court agreed with PERC that the New Jersey Employer-Employee Relations Act (N.J.S.A.34:13A-1) governed, and that under that statute employers must provide unions with information unions request that is needed to fulfill their statutory obligation to represent bargaining unit members. The decision relied heavily on private-sector precedent, and it distinguished *Dept. of Defense v. FLRA, supra*, because of "the absence of a New Jersey statute that expressly protects the kind of information requested by the union. Moreover, the issue before us deals only with the provision of information to the unions. Our reasoning does not depend on statutes that relate to the general public's access to information, and our conclusion in this case does not compel such access."

California Sch. Emp. Ass'n v. Bakersfield City Sch. Dist., 22 PERC ¶ 29089 (Cal. PERB 1998), also followed the private-sector rule, rejecting a defense based on the state's Public Records Act. The California Supreme Court later reaffirmed that public employers must give unions the home addresses and phone numbers of all members of union bargaining units, including those who have not joined the union. In *County of Los Angeles v. Los Angeles County Employee Relations Commission*, 301 P.3d 1102 (Cal. 2013), Los Angeles County had claimed that constitutional privacy protections barred the release of this data, but the court held that the union had a legitimate business need for it that outweighed the county's interest. Similar to *Morris County*, the court noted that unions owe "a duty of fair representation to all employees in the bargaining unit it represents, including employees who are not union members." *Id.* at 1118. Further, "there is no evidence SEIU has ever engaged in harassment of a nonmember." *Id.* at 1119.

Public-sector decisions also balance the needs and interests of the parties in information request cases involving identifying individual employees. In *County of Erie v. State of New York*, 37 PERB ¶ 7008 (N.Y. App. Div. 2004), the court upheld the labor agency's ruling that a union had a right to information the employer had developed during its investigation into a sexual harassment complaint, including the identity of the alleged victim. The union's need for the information in order to decide whether or not to grieve the matter and possibly prepare for grievance proceedings outweighed the employer's interest in maintaining victim confidentiality. *See also Timberlane Regional Educ. Ass'n v. Crompton*, 114 N.H. 315 (1974) (school board ordered to provide teachers' union with names and addresses of all employees, including substitute teachers employed during a strike, for various purposes, including allowing the union to review the credentials of the substitutes). *But cf. Los Rios Community College Dist.*, 12 PERC ¶ 19083, (Cal. PERB 1988) (upholding employer's refusal to give the union the social security numbers of non-unit employees).

In some instances, unions can take advantage of state analogs to FOIA. In *State ex rel. Quolke v. Strongsville City School District Board of Education*, 142 Oh. St. 3d 509 (2015), the Ohio Supreme Court held that, under the Ohio Public Records Act (OH. REV. CODE149.43), a teachers' union had the right to unredacted public records containing the names and identification numbers of all teachers employed as temporary replacements during a teachers' strike. The employer had refused to supply the information, citing some harassment and intimidation of replacements that took place during the strike and claiming that this information would violate the privacy rights of the replacements. The court, however, found little or no evidence of any remaining threats to the replacements' privacy or safety since the strike had ended, and no applicable exception to the Public Records Act.

IV. The Use of Economic Weapons During Bargaining

A. In the Private Sector

NLRB v. Insurance Agents' Int'l Union

Supreme Court of the United States
361 U.S. 477 (1960)

BRENNAN, J.

This case presents an important issue of the scope of the [NLRB's] authority under § 8(b)(3) of the [NLRA], which provides that "It shall be an unfair labor practice for a labor organization or its agents . . . to refuse to bargain collectively with an employer, provided it is the representative of his employees. . . ." The precise question is whether the Board may find that a union, which confers with an employer with the desire of reaching agreement on contract terms, has nevertheless refused to bargain collectively, thus violating that provision, solely and simply because during the negotiations it seeks to put economic pressure on the employer to yield to its bargaining demands by sponsoring on-the-job conduct designed to interfere with the carrying on of the employer's business.

Since 1949 the respondent Insurance Agents' International Union and the Prudential Insurance Company of America have negotiated collective bargaining agreements covering district agents employed by Prudential in 35 States and the District of Columbia. . . .

In January 1956 Prudential and the union began the negotiation of a new contract to replace an agreement expiring in the following March. Bargaining was carried on continuously for six months before the terms of the new contract were agreed upon on July 17, 1956. It is not questioned that, if it stood alone, the record of negotiations would establish that the union conferred in good faith for the purpose and with the desire of reaching agreement with Prudential on a contract.

However, in April 1956, Prudential filed a § 8(b)(3) charge of refusal to bargain collectively against the union. The charge was based upon actions of the union and its members outside the conference room, occurring after the old contract expired in March. The union had announced in February that if agreement on the terms of the new contract was not reached when the old contract expired, the union members would then participate in a "Work Without a Contract" program—which meant that they would engage in certain planned, concerted on-the-job activities designed to harass the company.

A complaint of violation of § 8(b)(3) issued on the charge and hearings began before the bargaining was concluded. It was developed in the evidence that the union's harassing tactics involved activities by the member agents such as these: refusal for a time to solicit new business, and refusal (after the writing of new business was resumed) to comply with the company's reporting procedures; refusal to participate in the company's "May Policyholders' Month Campaign"; reporting late at district offices the days the agents were scheduled to attend them, and refusing to perform customary duties at the offices, instead engaging there in "sit-in-mornings," "doing what comes naturally" and leaving at noon as a group; absenting themselves from special business conferences arranged by the company; picketing and distributing leaflets outside the various offices of the company on specified days and hours as directed by the union; distributing leaflets each day to policyholders and others and soliciting policyholders' signatures on petitions directed to the company; and presenting the signed policyholders' petitions to the company at its home office while simultaneously engaging in mass demonstrations there.

The hearing examiner filed a report recommending that the complaint be dismissed. . . . However, the Board on review . . . rejected the trial examiner's recommendation, and entered a cease-and-desist order. The Court of Appeals for the District of Columbia Circuit . . . set aside the Board's order. We granted the Board's petition for certiorari to review the important question presented.

The hearing examiner found that there was nothing in the record, apart from the mentioned activities of the union during the negotiations, that could be relied upon to support an inference that the union had not fulfilled its statutory duty; in fact nothing else was relied upon by the Board's General Counsel in prosecuting the complaint. The hearing examiner's analysis of the congressional design in enacting the statutory duty to bargain led him to conclude that the Board was not authorized to find that such economically harassing activities constituted a §8(b)(3) violation. The Board's opinion answers flatly "We do not agree" and proceeds to say "... the Respondent's reliance upon harassing tactics during the course of negotiations for the avowed purpose of compelling the Company to capitulate to its terms is the antithesis of reasoned discussion it was duty-bound to follow. Indeed, it clearly revealed an unwillingness to submit its demands to the consideration of the bargaining table where argument, persuasion, and the free interchange of views could take place. In such circumstances, the fact that the Respondent continued to confer with the Company and was desirous of concluding an agreement does not alone establish that it fulfilled its obligation to bargain in good faith. ..." Thus the Board's view is that irrespective of the union's good faith in conferring with the employer at the bargaining table for the purpose and with the desire of reaching agreement on contract terms, its tactics during the course of the negotiations constituted per se a violation of §8(b)(3). Accordingly, as is said in the Board's brief, "The issue here ... comes down to whether the Board is authorized under the Act to hold that such tactics, which the Act does not specifically forbid but Section 7 does not protect, support a finding of a failure to bargain in good faith as required by Section 8(b)(3)."

First.... [T]he nature of the duty to bargain in good faith ... imposed upon employers by §8(5) of the original Act was not sweepingly conceived. The Chairman of the Senate Committee declared: "When the employees have chosen their organization, when they have selected their representatives, all the bill proposes to do is to escort them to the door of their employer and say, 'Here they are, the legal representatives of your employees. What happens behind those doors is not inquired into, and the bill does not seek to inquire into it.'"

The limitation implied by the last sentence has not been in practice maintained—practically, it could hardly have been—but the underlying purpose of the remark has remained the most basic purpose of the statutory provision. That purpose is the making effective of the duty of management to extend recognition to the union; the duty of management to bargain in good faith is essentially a corollary of its duty to recognize the union.... [T]he requirement of collective bargaining, although so premised, necessarily led beyond the door of, and into, the conference room.... Collective bargaining, then, is not simply an occasion for purely formal meetings between management and labor, while each maintains an attitude of "take it or leave it"; it presupposes a desire to reach ultimate agreement, to enter into a collective bargaining contract. This was the sort of recognition that Congress, in the Wagner Act, wanted extended to labor unions; recognition as the bargaining agent of the employees in a process that looked to the ordering of the parties' industrial relationship through the formation of a contract.

But at the same time, Congress was generally not concerned with the substantive terms on which the parties contracted. Obviously there is tension between the principle that the parties need not contract on any specific terms and a practical enforcement of the principle that they are bound to deal with each other in a serious attempt to resolve differences and reach a common ground. And in fact criticism of the Board's application of the "good-faith" test arose from the belief that it was forcing employers to yield to union demands if they were to avoid a successful charge of unfair labor practice. Thus, in 1947 in Congress the fear was expressed that the Board had "gone very far, in the guise of determining whether or not employers had bargained in good faith, in setting itself up as the judge of what concessions an employer must make and of the proposals and counterproposals that he may or may not make." H.R.Rep.No. 245, 80th Cong., 1st Sess., p. 19. Since the Board was not viewed by Congress as an agency which should exercise its powers to arbitrate the parties' substantive solutions of the issues in their bargaining, a check on this apprehended trend was provided by writing the good-faith test of bargaining into §8(d) of the Act. . . .

Second. At the same time as it was statutorily defining the duty to bargain collectively, Congress, by adding §8(b)(3) of the Act through the Taft-Hartley amendments, imposed that duty on labor organizations. Unions obviously are formed for the very purpose of bargaining collectively; but the legislative history makes it plain that Congress was wary of the position of some unions, and wanted to ensure that they would approach the bargaining table with the same attitude of willingness to reach an agreement as had been enjoined on management earlier. It intended to prevent employee representatives from putting forth the same "take it or leave it" attitude that had been condemned in management. 93 Cong.Rec. 4135, 4363, 5005.

Third. It is apparent from the legislative history of the whole Act that the policy of Congress is to impose a mutual duty upon the parties to confer in good faith with a desire to reach agreement, in the belief that such an approach from both sides of the table promotes the over-all design of achieving industrial peace. *See National Labor Relations Board v. Jones & Laughlin Steel Corp., supra.* Discussion conducted under that standard of good faith may narrow the issues, making the real demands of the parties clearer to each other, and perhaps to themselves, and may encourage an attitude of settlement through give and take. The mainstream of cases before the Board and in the courts reviewing its orders, under the provisions fixing the duty to bargain collectively, is concerned with insuring that the parties approach the bargaining table with this attitude. But apart from this essential standard of conduct, Congress intended that the parties should have wide latitude in their negotiations, unrestricted by any governmental power to regulate the substantive solution of their differences.

We believe that the Board's approach in this case—unless it can be defended, in terms of §8(b)(3), as resting on some unique character of the union tactics involved here—must be taken as proceeding from an erroneous view of collective bargaining. It must be realized that collective bargaining, under a system where the Government does not attempt to control the results of negotiations, cannot be equated with an academic collective search for truth—or even with what might be thought to be the ideal of one. The parties—even granting the modification of views that may come from a realization of economic interdependence—still proceed from contrary and to an extent antagonistic viewpoints and concepts of self-interest. The system has not reached the ideal of the philosophic notion that perfect understanding among people would lead to perfect agreement among them on values. The presence of economic weapons in reserve, and their actual exercise on occasion by the parties, is part and parcel of the system that the Wagner and Taft-Hartley Acts have recognized. Abstract logical analysis might find inconsistency between the command of the statute to negotiate toward an agreement in good faith and the legitimacy of the use of economic weapons, frequently having the most serious effect upon individual workers and productive enterprises, to induce one party to come to the terms desired by the other. But the truth of the matter is that at the present statutory stage of our national labor relations policy, the two factors—necessity for good-faith bargaining between parties, and the availability of economic pressure devices to each to make the other party incline to agree on one's terms—exist side by side. . . .

For similar reasons, we think the Board's approach involves an intrusion into the substantive aspects of the bargaining process—again, unless there is some specific warrant for its condemnation of the precise tactics involved here. The scope of § 8(b)(3) and the limitations on Board power which were the design of § 8(d) are exceeded, we hold, by inferring a lack of good faith not from any deficiencies of the union's performance at the bargaining table by reason of its attempted use of economic pressure, but solely and simply because tactics designed to exert economic pressure were employed during the course of the good-faith negotiations. Thus the Board in the guise of determining good or bad faith in negotiations could regulate what economic weapons a party might summon to its aid. And if the Board could regulate the choice of economic weapons that may be used as part of collective bargaining, it would be in a position to exercise considerable influence upon the substantive terms on which the parties contract. As the parties' own devices became more limited, the Government might have to enter even more directly into the negotiation of collective agreements. Our labor policy is not presently erected on a foundation of government control of the results of negotiations. Nor does it contain a charter for the [NLRB] to act at large in equalizing disparities of bargaining power between employer and union.

Fourth. The use of economic pressure, as we have indicated, is of itself not at all inconsistent with the duty of bargaining in good faith. . . . The Board freely (and we think correctly) conceded here that a "total" strike called by the union would not have subjected it to sanctions under § 8(b)(3), at least if it were called after the old contract, with its no-strike clause, had expired. The Board's opinion in the instant case is not so unequivocal as this concession (and therefore perhaps more logical). But in the light of it and the principles we have enunciated, we must evaluate the claim of the Board to power, under § 8(b)(3), to distinguish among various economic pressure tactics and brand the ones at bar inconsistent with good-faith collective bargaining. We conclude its claim is without foundation.

(a) The Board contends that the distinction between a total strike and the conduct at bar is that a total strike is a concerted activity protected against employer interference by §§ 7 and 8(a)(1) of the Act, while the activity at bar is not a protected concerted activity. We may agree arguendo with the Board . . . that the employee conduct here was not a protected concerted activity. On this assumption the employer could have discharged or taken other appropriate disciplinary action against the employees participating in these "slow-down," "sit-in," and arguably unprotected disloyal tactics. *See National Labor Relations Board v. Fansteel Metallurgical Corp., supra.* But surely that a union activity is not protected against disciplinary action does not mean that it constitutes a refusal to bargain in good faith. The reason why the ordinary economic strike is not evidence of a failure to bargain in good faith is not that it constitutes a protected activity but that, as we have developed, there is simply no inconsistency between the application of economic pressure and good-faith collective bargaining. . . .

(b) The Board contends that because an orthodox "total" strike is "traditional" its use must be taken as being consistent with § 8(b)(3); but since the tactics here are not "traditional" or "normal," they need not be so viewed. Further, the Board cites what it conceives to be the public's moral condemnation of the sort of employee tactics involved here. But again we cannot see how these distinctions can be made under a statute which simply enjoins a duty to bargain in good faith. Again, these are relevant arguments when the question is the scope of the concerted activities given affirmative protection by the Act. But as we have developed, the use of economic pressure by the parties to a labor dispute is not a grudging exception to some policy of completely academic discussion enjoined by the Act; it is part and parcel of the process of collective bargaining. On this basis, we fail to see the relevance of whether the practice in question is time-honored or whether its exercise is generally supported by public opinion. It may be that the tactics used here deserve condemnation, but this would not justify attempting to pour that condemnation into a vessel not designed to hold it. The same may be said for the Board's contention that these activities, as opposed to a "normal" strike, are inconsistent with § 8(b)(3) because they offer maximum pressure on the employer at minimum economic cost to the union. One may doubt whether this was so here, but the matter does not turn on that. Surely it cannot be said that the only economic weapons consistent with good-faith bargaining are those which minimize the pressure on the other party or maximize the disadvantage to the party using them. The catalog of union and employer weapons that might thus fall under ban would be most extensive.

Fifth. . . . [W]hen the Board moves in this area, with only § 8(b)(3) for support, it is functioning as an arbiter of the sort of economic weapons the parties can use in seeking to gain acceptance of their bargaining demands. It has sought to introduce some standard of properly "balanced" bargaining power, or some new distinction of justifiable and unjustifiable, proper and "abusive" economic weapons into the collective bargaining duty imposed by the Act. The Board's assertion of power under § 8(b)(3) allows it to sit in judgment upon every economic weapon the parties to a labor contract negotiation employ, judging it on the very general standard of that section, not drafted with reference to specific forms of economic pressure. We have expressed our belief that this amounts to the Board's entrance into the substantive aspects of the bargaining process to an extent Congress has not countenanced.

. . . .

Congress has been rather specific when it has come to outlaw particular economic weapons on the part of unions. *See* § 8(b)(4) of the [NLRA] . . . ; § 8(b)(7). . . . But the activities here involved have never been specifically outlawed by Congress. To be sure, the express prohibitions of the Act are not exclusive—if there were any questions of a stratagem or device to evade the policies of the Act, the Board hardly would be powerless. *Phelps Dodge Corp. v. National Labor Relations Board, supra.* But it is clear to us that the Board needs a more specific charter than § 8(b)(3) before it can add to the Act's prohibitions here.

We recognize without hesitation the primary function and responsibility of the Board to resolve the conflicting interests that Congress has recognized in its labor legislation. Clearly, where the "ultimate problem is the balancing of the conflicting legitimate interests" it must be remembered that "The function of striking that balance to effectuate national labor policy is often a difficult and delicate responsibility, which the Congress committed primarily to the [NLRB], subject to limited judicial review." Certainly a "statute expressive of such large public policy as that on which the [NLRB] is based must be broadly phrased and necessarily carries with it the task of administrative application." *Phelps Dodge Corp. v. National Labor Relations Board, supra.* But recognition of the appropriate sphere of the administrative power here obviously cannot exclude all judicial review of the Board's actions. On the facts of this case we need not attempt a detailed delineation of the respective functions of court and agency in this area. We think the Board's resolution of the issues here amounted not to a resolution of interests which the Act had left to it for case-by-case adjudication, but to a movement into a new area of regulation which Congress had not committed to it. Where Congress has in the statute given the Board a question to answer, the courts will give respect to that answer; but they must be sure the question has been asked. We see no indication here that Congress has put it to the Board to define through its processes what economic sanctions might be permitted negotiating parties in an "ideal" or "balanced" state of collective bargaining. . . . Affirmed.

Separate opinion of Frankfurter, J., joined by Harlan, J. and Whittaker, J.

. . . .

While § 8(b)(3) of course contemplates some play of "economic pressure," it does not follow that the purpose in engaging in tactics designed to exert it is to reach agreement through the bargaining process in the manner which the statute commands, so that the Board is precluded from considering such conduct, in the totality of circumstances, as evidence of the actual state of mind of the actor. Surely to deny this scope for allowable judgment to the Board is to deny it the special function with which it has been entrusted. This Court has in the past declined to pre-empt by broad proscriptions the Board's competence in the first instance to weigh the significance of the raw facts of conduct and to draw from them an informed judgment as to the ultimate fact. It has recognized that the significance of conduct, itself apparently innocent and evidently insufficient to sustain a findings of an unfair labor practice, "may be altered by imponderable subtleties at work which it is not our function to appraise" but which are, first, for the Board's consideration upon all the evidence. Activities in isolation may be wholly innocent, lawful and "protected" by the Act, but that ought not to bar the Board from finding, if the record justifies it, that the isolated parts "are bound together as the parts of a single plan (to frustrate agreement). The plan may make the parts unlawful."

Moreover, conduct designed to exert and exerting "economic pressure" may not have the shelter of § 8(b)(3) even in isolation.... One need not romanticize the community of interest between employers and employees, or be unmindful of the conflict between them, to recognize that utilization of what in one set of circumstances may only signify resort to the traditional weapons of labor may in another and relevant context offend the attitude toward bargaining commanded by the statute. Section 8(b)(3) is not a specific direction, but an expression of a governing viewpoint or policy to which, by the process of specific application, the Board and the courts must give concrete, not doctrinaire content....

[I]t of course does not follow because the Board may find in tactics short of violence evidence that a party means not to bargain in good faith that every such finding must be sustained. Section 8(b)(3) itself, as previously construed by the Board and this Court and as amplified by § 8(d), provides a substantial limitation on the Board's becoming, as the Court fears, merely "an arbiter of the sort of economic weapons the parties can use in seeking to gain acceptance of their bargaining demands." The Board's function in the enforcement of the duty to bargain does not end when it has properly drawn an inference unfavorable to the respondent from particular conduct. It must weigh that inference as part of the totality of inferences which may appropriately be drawn from the entire conduct of the respondent, particularly its conduct at the bargaining table. The state of mind with which the party charged with a refusal to bargain entered into and participated in the bargaining process is the ultimate issue upon which alone the Board must act in each case, and on the sufficiency of the whole record to justify its decision the courts must pass. *National Labor Relations Board v. American National Ins. Co., supra.* . . .

Notes

1. Even though Justice Frankfurter joined the majority in rejecting the Board's conclusion in this case, his analysis of the issue is more deferential to the Board, at least rhetorically, because it seems to encourage giving the Board more leeway to consider the use of economic weapons when adjudicating charges brought under §§ 8(a)(5) and 8(b)(3). Who has the better argument—the majority or Justice Frankfurter? Which argument is most consistent with the reasoning of *Truitt*? Is either argument consistent with the goal of reducing transaction costs to promote Coasean bargaining? Doesn't *Insurance Agents* facilitate strategic behavior in the

form of costly strikes and lockouts? Also, is another way of interpreting *Insurance Agents* to say that the Board and the court generally may not draw an inference of subjective bad faith from the use of economic weapons? Or is subjective bad faith irrelevant to the outcome in *Insurance Agents*?

2. As a general rule, a union's strike or calling for a strike does not terminate the employer's duty to bargain in good faith. *See NLRB v. Powell Elec. Mfg. Co.*, 906 F.2d 1007 (5th Cir. 1990); *Capitol-Husting Co.*, 252 N.L.R.B. 43 (1980), *enf'd* 671 F.2d 237 (9th Cir. 1982). Similarly, a union engaging in unprotected concerted activities does not obviate or modify the employer's duty to bargain in good faith. *See NLRB v. Katz,* 369 U.S. 736, 742, n.7 (1962). There appear to be only two exceptions to these general rules. First, the Board has held that the employer is not subject to a duty to bargain when the union strikes in violation of a no-strike pledge. *See Stamford Taxi, Inc.*, 332 N.L.R.B. 1372 (2000). Second, when employers hire temporary or permanent replacement workers to maintain their operations during the course of a strike or lockout, as discussed in Chapter 11, they are not subject to a duty to bargain with the striking or locked out union regarding the terms on which the replacements are hired or employed. *See Ryan Iron Works, Inc. v. NLRB*, 257 F.3d 1 (1st Cir. 2001) (citing *Serv. Elect. Co.*, 281 N.L.R.B. 633 (1989)). However, an employer may commit a ULP by offering richer employment terms to replacement workers than it has offered at the bargaining table to its unionized workers "if the struck employer is exercising that right in a manner designed to accomplish an illegal objective, i.e., to undermine the bargaining representative, then there would be a basis for finding a violation." *Service Electric Co., supra* at 639, n.11.

3. *Insurance Agents* is a model of purposive statutory interpretation: reading ambiguous text to best serve the Act's purposes. The Board also engaged in purposive statutory interpretation to arrive at the rule ultimately overturned by the Supreme Court. The different results can be explained by disagreements about how best to serve the Act's purposes, purposes the Court and the Board defined similarly. How is it possible to know which approach best serves the Act's purposes? How did the Supreme Court do it in *Insurance Agents*? Does *Insurance Agents* disclose a serious problem with purposive interpretation methodology? Would a textualist methodology produce a more reliable, predictable outcome that is transparent to unions, employers, and the public?

B. In the Public Sector

1. Public Sector Strikes

In the public sector, rules on bargaining in good faith during strikes play out somewhat differently. This is often because public employees in most jurisdictions are not legally allowed to strike (and lockouts by public employers are very rare). Illegal strikes are either ULPs in and of themselves or otherwise sanctionable (*see* Chapter 11), and thus it is often not necessary to reach the "good faith" issue.

Still, the issue comes up in various ways. For example, if a public-sector union engages in an illegal strike, does the employer still have a duty to bargain in good faith? *Saginaw Tp. Bd. of Ed.*, 1970 MERC Lab Op 127 (1970) held that employers still had such a duty, but in 1995 the Michigan Commission reversed itself. The new rule—that employers have no duty to bargain during illegal strikes—was upheld by the court in *Melvindale-Northern Allen Park Fed. of Teachers Local 1051 v. Melvindale-Northern Allen Park Public Schools*, 9 MPER ¶ 27046 (Mich. Ct. App. 1996). *Melvindale-Northern* likely expresses how most jurisdictions would approach this issue. *See, e.g., In the Matter of Town of South Hampton v. New York State PERB*, 37 PERB ¶ 7001 (N.Y. Ct. App. 2004) (quoting approvingly the ALJ's explanation that "as long as an employee organization does not engage in an illegal strike, the duty to negotiate in good faith prohibits an employer from 'unilaterally alter[ing] existing mandatory subjects of negotiations'").

If a state public-sector law makes a strike illegal but not specifically a ULP, is an illegal strike a violation of the duty to bargain in good faith by the union? In *Teamsters State, County & Municipal Workers and Ann Arbor Public Schools*, 16 MPER ¶ 8 (Mich. PERC 2003), the Michigan Commission upheld an ALJ's finding that an illegal strike was *not* necessarily a failure to bargain in good faith. The Commission noted that while the relevant state law made strikes by public employees illegal, it did not make them ULPs. The Commission rejected the employer's argument that it should rely on private sector precedent:

> Charging Party also argues that since there is no directly related PERA provision, the ALJ should have deferred to the [NLRA]. Charging Party points out that Michigan courts have recognized that PERA is patterned after the NLRA and case law interpreting the NLRA has often provided guidance for the interpretation of analogous provisions of PERA. However, PERA and the NLRA are not necessarily analogous in their treatment of strikers. Instead of citing authority for its contention that participation in, or encouragement of, an illegal strike is an unfair labor practice within the meaning of PERA, Charging Party merely asserts '[h]ad the NLRB jurisdiction of this dispute, it would have proceeded to a hearing.' Such assertion is insufficient to make participation in an alleged strike a violation of PERA.

The ALJ recommendation that the Michigan Commission adopted had reasoned as follows:

> . . . the Legislature did not make striking or encouraging a strike an unfair labor practice although it presumably could have easily done so. We have held that a strike may, in the context of other conduct, be evidence of a refusal to bargain in good faith. *Warren Education Association*, 1977 MERC Lab Op 818. Striking prior to utilizing statutory dispute resolution mechanisms, i.e., mediation and fact finding, has been held to be evidence of bad faith bargaining. *Wayne County MEA/NEA*, 1982 MERC Lab Op 1556. . . .

A strike does not constitute a per se failure to bargain in good faith, however. *Detroit Board of Education v. Detroit Federation of Teachers*, 55 Mich. App. 499; *Lamphere School District v. Lamphere Federation of Teachers*, 61 Mich. App. 485 (1976).

As Chapter 11 discusses in detail, most public-sector statutes provide impasse-dispute mechanisms in lieu of the right to strike. It is a ULP to fail to participate in good faith in impasse resolution processes under the statute. *See, e.g.,* California Educational Employees Relations Act §§ 3543.5(e) and 3543.6(d). Perhaps further illustrating the importance of participating in these procedures, some cases have held that a union may invoke a binding impasse resolution process even if the union has failed to bargain in good faith prior to impasse. *See, e.g., City of Manistee v. MERC*, 168 Mich. App. 422, *leave to appeal denied*, 431 Mich. 884 (1988). On the other hand, a party need only do what the statutory mechanisms require. For example, not complying with a non-binding recommendation by a fact-finder is not a failure to bargain in good faith. *Lamphere School Dist.*, 1978 MERC Lab Op 194 (MERC 1978). Do different forms of impasse resolution make the duty to bargain in good faith more or less significant for one side or the other? Consider this question further when reading Chapter 11.

2. The Impact of Public Sector Impasse Procedures

Beyond the fact that most public sector-unions are not allowed to strike, there is another difference in the public sector that creates practical and legal issues in this context. Even where public-sector unions are legally allowed to strike, they almost always must go through a series of impasse resolution procedures first.

Fresno Unified School District v. Fresno Teachers Ass'n, CTA/NEA

California Public Employee Relations Committee
6 PERC ¶ 13110 (Cal. P.E.R.C. 1982)

The Fresno Unified School District (District) excepts to the hearing officer's proposed decision ... finding: (1) that the Fresno Teachers Association, CTA/NEA's (FTA or Association) strike was not a per se violation of EERA subsections 3543.6(b), (c) and (d). . . .

Events Leading to the Strike

In April 1978, the parties began negotiations for a successor agreement to their first collective bargaining contract which was to expire on June 30, 1978. . . .

Bargaining sessions occurred regularly during the spring and fall. . . . By late September, the Association perceived that negotiations were deadlocked on three major issues: class size, contract term, and the no-strike clause. It declared impasse and on September 28 requested that the Public Employment Relations Board (PERB) appoint a mediator. After an investigation, the PERB regional director twice rejected

FTA's request and instructed it to resume bargaining. In November, FTA then abandoned its attempts to engage the impasse procedures. At the unfair practice hearing, the chief negotiator for FTA admitted that one of the reasons he initially sought a PERB declaration of impasse was to avoid a potential damage claim under the collective bargaining agreement in the event of a strike. He also stated that he believed the presence of a mediator might "stimulate some better activity on the part of the District." But, in the face of PERB's action and the District's opposition to impasse, FTA came to believe that the impasse procedures would be used by the District to unnecessarily drag out the negotiating process. As a result, FTA did not further attempt to engage the impasse process and admitted that, if the District had asked the Association to join it in declaring impasse on the eve of the strike, it probably would not have done so.

The strike began on November 20, the first day of Thanksgiving week and lasted until December. . . . Negotiations continued during the strike and, shortly after its termination, a tentative agreement was reached December 3, 1978. . . .

On April 30, 1979, five months after the strike and related events, the District filed an unfair practice charge against the Association alleging that FTA violated subsections 3543.6(a), (b), (c), and (d) by conducting a strike prior to the exhaustion of impasse procedures. . . .

The District claims that the hearing officer erred in refusing to find that a strike before impasse is a per se unfair practice. It argues that public employee strikes are inherently illegal . . . and that a strike is a per se refusal to bargain and to participate in impasse procedures in good faith.

The California Supreme Court in *San Diego Teachers Association v. Superior Court* (1979) 24 Cal.3d 1, specifically rejected the argument that section 3549 of EERA makes strikes illegal.

. . . The Court considered the effect of strikes on the duty to negotiate in good faith and to utilize the statutory impasse procedures.

> [B]y engaging in a strike, the [Association] may have committed at least two of the unfair practices . . . 1) failure to negotiate in good faith . . . and 2) refusal to participate in the impasse procedures. . . .

> The question of negotiation in good faith is resolved by determining whether there was a genuine desire to reach agreement. Under the NLRA, a strike does not, itself, violate the duty to confer in good faith . . . Thus, if the [Association's] strike were held to be legal, it would not constitute a failure to negotiate in good faith as an illegal pressure tactic; however, its happening could support a finding that good faith was lacking.

> . . . [T]he impasse procedures almost certainly were included in the EERA for the purpose of heading off strikes . . . since they assume deferment of a strike at least until their completion, strikes before then can properly be found to be a refusal to participate in the impasse procedures in good faith and, thus, an unfair practice under section 3543.6(d). *Id.* p. 9.

In keeping with the holdings of the Court, PERB adopted, after extensive public testimony, its rule 38100 which states, in pertinent part:

> In recognition of the fact that in some instances work stoppages by public school employees and lockouts by public school employers can be inimical to the public interest and inconsistent with those provisions of the EERA requiring the parties to participate in good faith in the impasse procedure, it is the purpose of this regulation to provide a process by which the Board can respond quickly to injunctive relief requests involving work stoppages or lockouts.

> The EERA imposes a duty on employers and exclusive representatives to participate in good faith in the impasse procedure and treats that duty so seriously that it specifically makes it unlawful for either an employer or an exclusive representative to refuse to do so. The Board considers these provisions [impasse procedures] as strong evidence of legislative intent to head off work stoppages and lockouts until completion of the impasse procedure. . . .

Thus, the effect of the rule, and the *San Diego* decision is to create something similar to a rebuttable presumption that a strike during negotiations or prior to exhaustion of impasse proceedings constitutes an illegal pressure tactic.

In the absence of any sustainable allegation of provocation by the employer, and in light of FTA's admissions that it was seeking to utilize the impasse procedure in part to avoid damage liability, we find evidence of an "illegal pressure tactic" constituting a refusal to negotiate in good faith in violation of subsection 3543.6(c).

However, that portion of the District's charge alleging that FTA violated subsection 3543.5(d) is dismissed. As the Supreme Court indicated, a strike may constitute an unfair practice in two ways: (1) a failure to negotiate in good faith and (2) a refusal to participate in the impasse procedures. FTA did not refuse to participate in impasse procedures. To the contrary, its request for an appointment of a mediator was twice rejected by PERB before the strike occurred.

Notes

1. Filing a notice of intent to strike, without actually striking or refusing to engage in impasse procedures, was held not to be a violation of the duty to bargain in good faith in *City of Ironton v. Council 8, AFSCME*, 24 OPER P 235 (Ohio SERB 2007). *Cf. Chicago Transit Authority v. Ill. Labor Rel. Bd., Local Panel*, 21 PERI ¶ 76 (Ill. Ct. App. 2005) (remanding case to labor board to determine whether a threatened strike would have been legal or illegal, and if the latter, whether it violated the duty to bargain in good faith).

2. In contrast, some state statutes explicitly state that strike threats are a ULP even if the union does not strike. Do such rules violate the First Amendment? In *Commonwealth Employment Relations Bd. v. Boston Teachers Union, Local 66, AFT*, 908 N.E.2d 772 (Mass. App. 2009), the court found that the union had violated the

labor statute by scheduling a strike vote, and it rejected the claim that this was contrary to the First Amendment.

3. An arguably analogous tactic in the public sector is making certain types of appeals to the public during bargaining in order to influence public opinion. For employer acts in this regard, *compare Reno Police Protective Ass'n v. City of Reno*, Item No. 52 (Nev. LGE-MRB 1976) (employer placing misleading newspaper advertisement regarding negotiations violates duty to bargain in good faith) *with Inter-Lakes Educ. Ass'n/NEA-New Hampshire*, 1988–90 PBC ¶ 54,522 (NH PELRB Case No. T-0237, 1989) (employer did not breach its duty to bargain in good faith by buying advertisements publicizing its views about a fact-finder's report).

V. Bargaining, "Impasse," and the Unilateral Imposition of Terms

A. The Private Sector

As Chapter 3 discussed, an employer's unilateral provision of a wage increase, benefit improvement, or other promise of a benefit during the course of an organizing drive would very likely constitute a ULP under §8(a)(1) that would not be saved by §8(c). But does it violate §8(a)(5) if an employer unilaterally changes employees' terms and conditions of employment during the course of negotiations with the employees' union? The next case addresses this question.

NLRB v. Katz
Supreme Court of the United States
369 U.S. 736 (1962)

BRENNAN, J.

Is it a violation of the duty "to bargain collectively" imposed by §8(a)(5) of the [NLRA] for an employer, without first consulting a union with which it is carrying on bona fide contract negotiations, to institute changes regarding matters which are subjects of mandatory bargaining under §8(d) and which are in fact under discussion? The [NLRB] answered the question affirmatively in this case, in a decision which expressly disclaimed any finding that the totality of the respondents' conduct manifested bad faith in the pending negotiations. A divided panel of the Court of Appeals for the Second Circuit denied enforcement of the Board's cease-and-desist order, finding in our decision in *NLRB v. Insurance Agents' Union*, 361 U.S. 477, a broad rule that the statutory duty to bargain cannot be held to be violated, when bargaining is in fact being carried on, without a finding of the respondent's subjective bad faith in negotiating. . . . We find nothing in the Board's decision inconsistent with Insurance Agents and hold that the Court of Appeals erred in refusing to enforce the Board's order.

[The employers are engaged in steel fabricating. The Board certified Local 66 as the collective bargaining representatives of a unit consisting of all technical employees after an election at the company's plant. The Board simultaneously certified the union as representative of similar units at five other companies which, with the company, were members of the Hollow Metal Door & Buck Association. The union sent identical letters and follow-up letters to each of the six companies requesting collective bargaining on an individual or "association wide" basis and proposing subjects for discussion including merit increases, general wage levels and increases, and a sick-leave proposal.]

The first meeting between the company and the union took place on August 30, 1956. On this occasion, as at the ten other conferences held between October 2, 1956, and May 13, 1957, all six companies were in attendance and represented by the same counsel. It is undisputed that the subject of merit increases was raised at the August 30, 1956, meeting although there is an unresolved conflict as to whether an agreement was reached on joint participation by the company and the union in merit reviews, or whether the subject was simply mentioned and put off for discussion at a later date. It is also clear that proposals concerning sick leave were made. Several meetings were held during October and one in November, at which merit raises and sick leave were each discussed on at least two occasions. It appears, however, that little progress was made.

[Further meetings with a mediator in April and May 1957 produced no agreement and no further meetings were held.]

Meanwhile, on April 16, 1957, the union had filed the charge upon which the General Counsel's complaint later issued. As amended and amplified at the hearing and construed by the Board, the complaint's charge of unfair labor practices particularly referred to three acts by the company: unilaterally granting numerous merit increases in October 1956 and January 1957; unilaterally announcing a change in sick-leave policy in March 1957; and unilaterally instituting a new system of automatic wage increases during April 1957. . . .

The [company's] second line of defense was that the Board could not hinge a conclusion that §8(a)(5) had been violated on unilateral actions alone, without making a finding of the employer's subjective bad faith at the bargaining table; and that the unilateral actions were merely evidence relevant to the issue of subjective good faith. This argument prevailed in the Court of Appeals.

. . . The duty "to bargain collectively" enjoined by §8(a)(5) is defined by §8(d) as the duty to "meet . . . and confer in good faith with respect to wages, hours, and other terms and conditions of employment." Clearly, the duty thus defined may be violated without a general failure of subjective good faith; for there is no occasion to consider the issue of good faith if a party has refused even to negotiate *in fact*—"to meet . . . and confer"—about any of the mandatory subjects. A refusal to negotiate in fact as to any subject which is within §8(d), and about which the union seeks to negotiate, violates §8(a)(5) though the employer has every desire to reach agreement with the union upon an over-all collective agreement and earnestly and in all good faith bargains to that end. We hold that an employer's unilateral change in conditions of employment under negotiation is similarly a violation of § 8(a)(5), for it is a circumvention of the duty to negotiate which frustrates the objectives of § 8(a)(5) much as does a flat refusal. . . .

The unilateral actions of the [company] illustrate the policy and practical considerations which support our conclusion.

We consider first the matter of sick leave. A sick-leave plan had been in effect since May 1956, under which employees were allowed ten paid sick-leave days annually and could accumulate half the unused days, or up to five days each year. Changes in the plan were sought and proposals and counterproposals had come up at three bargaining conferences. In March 1957, the company, without first notifying or consulting the union, announced changes in the plan, which reduced from ten to five the number of paid sick-leave days per year, but allowed accumulation of twice the unused days, thus increasing to ten the number of days which might be carried over. This action plainly frustrated the statutory objective of establishing working conditions through bargaining. Some employees might view the change to be a diminution of benefits. Others, more interested in accumulating sick-leave days, might regard the change as an improvement. If one view or the other clearly prevailed among the employees, the unilateral action might well mean that the employer had either uselessly dissipated trading material or aggravated the sick-leave issue. On the other hand, if the employees were more evenly divided on the merits of the company's changes, the union negotiators, beset by conflicting factions, might be led to adopt a protective vagueness on the issue of sick leave, which also would inhibit the useful discussion contemplated by Congress in imposing the specific obligation to bargain collectively.

Other considerations appear from consideration of the [company's] unilateral action in increasing wages. At the April 4, 1957, meeting the employers offered, and the union rejected, a three-year contract with an immediate across-the-board increase of $7.50 per week, to be followed at the end of the first year and again at the end of the second by further increases of $5 for employees earning less than $90 at those times. Shortly thereafter, without having advised or consulted with the union, the company announced a new system of automatic wage increases whereby there would be an increase of $5 every three months up to $74.99 per week; an increase of $5 every six months between $75 and $90 per week; and a merit review every six months for employees earning over $90 per week. It is clear at a glance that the automatic wage increase system which was instituted unilaterally was considerably more generous than that which had shortly theretofore been offered to and rejected by the union. Such action conclusively manifested bad faith in the negotiations, and so would have violated § 8(a)(5) even on the Court of Appeals' interpretation, though no additional evidence of bad faith appeared. An employer is not required to lead with his best offer; he is free to bargain. But even after an impasse is reached he has no license to grant wage increases greater than any he has ever offered the union at the bargaining table, for such action is necessarily inconsistent with a sincere desire to conclude an agreement with the union.[12]

The respondents' third unilateral action related to merit increases, which are also a subject of mandatory bargaining. The matter of merit increases had been raised at three of the conferences during 1956 but no final understanding had been reached. In January 1957, the company, without notice to the union, granted merit increases to 20 employees out of the approximately 50 in the unit, the increases ranging between $2 and $10. This action too must be viewed as tantamount to an outright refusal to negotiate on that subject, and therefore as a violation of §8(a)(5), unless the fact that the January raises were in line with the company's long-standing practice of granting quarterly or semiannual merit reviews—in effect, were a mere continuation of the status quo—differentiates them from the wage increases and the changes in the sick-leave plan. We do not think it does. Whatever might be the case as to so-called "merit raises" which are in fact simply automatic increases to which the employer has already committed himself, the raises here in question were in no sense automatic, but were informed by a large measure of discretion. There simply is no way in such case for a union to know whether or not there has been a substantial departure from past practice, and therefore the union may properly insist that the company negotiate as to the procedures and criteria for determining such increases.

It is apparent from what we have said why we see nothing in *Insurance Agents* contrary to the Board's decision. The union in that case had not in any way whatever foreclosed discussion of any issue, by unilateral actions or otherwise. The conduct complained of consisted of partial-strike tactics designed to put pressure on the employer to come to terms with the union negotiators. We held that Congress had not, in §8(b)(3), the counterpart of §8(a)(5), empowered the Board to pass judgment on the legitimacy of any particular economic weapon used in support of genuine negotiations. But the Board is authorized to order the cessation of behavior which is in effect a refusal to negotiate, or which directly obstructs or inhibits the actual process of discussion, or which reflects a cast of mind against reaching agreement. Unilateral action by an employer without prior discussion with the union does amount to a refusal to negotiate about the affected conditions of employment under negotiation, and must of necessity obstruct bargaining, contrary to the congressional policy. It will often disclose an unwillingness to agree with the union. It will rarely be justified by any reason of substance. It follows that the Board may hold such unilateral action to be an unfair labor practice in violation of §8(a)(5), without also finding the employer guilty of over-all subjective bad faith. While we do not foreclose the possibility that there might be circumstances which the Board

---

12. Of course, there is no resemblance between this situation and one wherein an employer, after notice and consultation, "unilaterally" institutes a wage increase identical with one which the union has rejected as too low. *See National Labor Relations Board v. Bradley Washfountain Co.*, 7 Cir., 192 F.2d 144, 150–152. . . .

could or should accept as excusing or justifying unilateral action, no such case is presented here. . . .

The judgment of the Court of Appeals is reversed and the case is remanded with direction to the court to enforce the Board's order. It is so ordered.

Notes

1. The Board, with court approval, has extended *Katz* to situations where the parties are bargaining over a successor contract. For example, in *Peerless Roofing Co. v. NLRB*, 641 F.2d 734, 735 (9th Cir. 1981), the court endorsed the Board's application of *Katz* where the employer ceased making contributions to union trust funds upon expiration of the CBA. The court based its conclusion on the Board's finding that, during negotiations, the employer never proposed terminating all trust-fund payments. *See also Laborers Health and Welfare Trust Fund v. Advanced Lightweight Concrete Co.*, 484 U.S. 539, 544, n. 6 (1988) (citing *Peerless Roofing* and other cases with approval).

2. Even if an employer implements a proposal and the parties have bargained, the employer could still violate § 8(a)(5) if it makes the unilateral change without bargaining to impasse. *See Litton Fin. Printing Div. v. NLRB*, 501 U.S. 190, 198 (1991).

3. The application of *Katz* to the successor contract situation raises the following question: What happens to the terms of a CBA when the CBA expires, no agreement has been reached, and the parties are not at impasse? Any professional sports fan knows that ball players seem only to strike when the CBA expires. Is this related to the *Katz* rule? It turns out that the answers to these questions depend on the contract term. For example, no-strike clauses expire with the CBA. *See Litton Fin. Printing Div.*, 501 U.S. at 199 (explaining that " in recognition of the statutory right to strike, no-strike clauses are excluded from the unilateral change doctrine, except to the extent other dispute resolution methods survive expiration of the agreement"). That is why ball players wait until the stroke of midnight on the day the CBA expires to strike. The Board similarly concluded that arbitration clauses do not survive contract expiration. *See Hilton-Davis Chem. Co. Div.*, 185 N.L.R.B. 241, 243 (1970) (positing, as the reason behind the rule that arbitration clauses expire with CBA expiration, that because arbitration is a contractual right and obligation, parties cannot be compelled to arbitrate disputes they did not agree to arbitrate). *But see John Wiley & Sons, Inc. v. Livingston*, 376 U.S. 543, 548 (1964) (holding "that, in appropriate circumstances, . . . [a] successor employer may be required to arbitrate with [a] union under the [predecessor's CBA]").

4. In *Bethlehem Steel*, 136 N.L.R.B. 1500 (1962), *remanded on other grounds sub nom. Marine & Shipbuilding Workers v. NLRB*, 320 F.2d 615 (3d Cir. 1963), and its progeny, the Board held that an employer's duty to check off union dues from its employees' wages does not survive contract expiration. However, the Ninth Circuit refused to enforce the Board's *Bethlehem Steel* rule. *See, e.g., Local Joint Exec. Bd. of Las Vegas v. N.L.R.B.*, 657 F.3d 865, 867 (9th Cir. 2011) (concluding that the

Board's rule is "arbitrary and capricious because the Board provides no explanation for the rule it follow[ed] in dismissing the Union's complaint"). In *WKYC-TV, Inc.*, 359 N.L.R.B. 286 (2012), the Board reversed its position to hold that, "like most other terms and conditions of employment, an employer's obligation to check off union dues continues after expiration of a collective-bargaining agreement that establishes such an arrangement." The Board nevertheless dismissed the complaint, refusing to apply the new rule retroactively. In *NLRB v. Noel Canning*, 573 U.S. 513 (2014), the Supreme Court vacated *WKYC-TV, Inc.*, because the Board lacked a three-member quorum when it decided that case. In *Lincoln Lutheran of Racine*, 362 N.L.R.B. 1655 (2015), the Board reasserted its conclusion that an employer's duty to check off union dues from its employees' wages does not survive contract expiration, thereby overruling *Bethlehem Steel* again. In *Valley Hospital Medical Center, Inc.*, the Board returned to the view that

> a dues-checkoff provision properly belongs to the limited category of mandatory bargaining subjects that are exclusively created by the contract and are enforceable through Section 8(a)(5) of the Act only for the duration of the contractual obligation created by the parties. There is no independent statutory obligation to check off and remit dues after expiration of a collective-bargaining agreement containing a checkoff provision, just as no such statutory obligation exists before parties enter into such an agreement. 368 N.L.R.B. No. 139, 2019 WL 6840790, at *1 (Dec. 16, 2019).

5. In *Raytheon Network Centric Systems*, 365 N.L.R.B. No. 161 (2017), the Board narrowed the definition of what counts as a "unilateral change" in the context of negotiating a new contract after an old one has expired. *Raytheon* overturned *E.I. Du Pont de Nemours*, 364 N.L.R.B. No. 113 (2016), which had held that employers could not rely on a past practice of making discretionary changes under a management rights clause to justify a failure to bargain over additional discretionary changes after a contract expired. *Raytheon* held that the employer did not violate §8(a)(5) by unilaterally modifying medical benefits after a contract expired because it had previously made similar unilateral modifications while previous contracts were in effect. Thus, the employer was not changing the status quo. The majority argued this reversal returned the law to a long-understood, commonsense understanding of what constitutes a "change." The dissent argued that allowing employers to unilaterally change terms of employment during successor contract negotiations over those very terms is impermissible as a policy choice and frustrates the process of collective bargaining. Both the majority and dissent insisted that their positions represented the correct interpretation of *Katz*.

6. As discussed in the next section, at impasse, the employer is privileged to implement its last, best final offer. *See Dish Network Corp. v. NLRB*, 953 F.3d 370 (5th Cir. 2020) (explaining that union's rejection of "last, best, and final offer'" made after years of "good-faith, hard bargaining" is a "tell-tale sign of impasse") (internal quotation marks and citation omitted); *cf. FirstEnergy Generation, LLC v. NLRB*, 929 F.3d 321 (6th Cir. 2019) (enforcing Board's order finding that employer

violated § 8(a)(5) when it failed to implement "wage increases and shift differentials set forth in its Second Comprehensive Offer because they were 'inextricably intertwined' with, and a quid pro quo for, the Company's proposal to eliminate retiree health benefits").

B. Determining Whether There Is an Impasse in the Private Sector

Because the right to implement a final offer exists only at impasse in the private sector, some cases raise the issue of whether an impasse actually existed at the time of the implementation. When presented with a ULP charge claiming a unilateral implementation before impasse, the Board investigates whether a genuine impasse had been reached. *See TruServ Corp. v. NLRB*, 254 F.3d 1105 (D.C. Cir. 2003). For example, as noted above, impasse on a single issue would not justify the unilateral imposition of terms in most cases and, as a result, the employer will have committed a ULP. *See Duffy Tool and Stamping LLC v. NLRB, supra.*

The Board considers five factors when assessing whether impasse — essentially, the futility of further bargaining — has been reached: (1) the bargaining history, (2) the good faith of the parties in negotiations, (3) the length of negotiations, (4) the importance of the issues over which there is disagreement, and (5) the contemporaneous understanding of the parties as to the state of negotiations. *See Taft Broadcasting Co.*, 163 N.L.R.B. 475, 482–83 (1967), *enf'd sub nom., AFTRA v. NLRB*, 395 F.2d 622 (D.C. Cir. 1968).

The following case considers what terms a party may unilaterally implement if a genuine impasse has been reached; or, perhaps more precisely, whether there are terms that cannot be unilaterally implemented.

McClatchy Newspapers, Inc. v. NLRB

United States Court of Appeals for the District of Columbia Circuit
131 F.3d 1026 (D.C. Cir. 1997)

SILBERMAN, J.

This dispute encompasses two cases, one involving McClatchy's Sacramento newspaper and the other its Modesto newspaper. In both cases, the [NLRB] found that McClatchy committed an unfair labor practice by unilaterally implementing a discretionary merit pay proposal, even though McClatchy had bargained to impasse over the proposal with the union. . . . McClatchy petitions for review of the orders, and the Board cross-petitions for enforcement. We enforce the Board's Sacramento order, and partially enforce the Board's Modesto order.

I.

At the Sacramento Bee, the Northern California Newspaper Guild, Local 52 represents editorial, advertising, and telephone switchboard employees. McClatchy's most recent collective bargaining agreement with the union, which expired in 1986, set pay through a combination of wage scales and discretionary merit raises. The agreement defined 28 job classifications, each setting a minimum salary that automatically increased with each year of experience. Once an employee reached the maximum salary for his or her classification, raises were based solely on merit, as determined by the company. McClatchy retained full discretion over the timing and amount of these merit raises, and its decisions were excluded from the contractual grievance and arbitration procedure. Within 10 days of performing a merit evaluation, McClatchy would notify the union of the result, and the union then could make nonbinding comments and participate in the appeals process at the employee's request.

When the 1986 agreement expired, McClatchy and the union each proposed a new wage system. From the outset, their proposals were diametrically opposed: McClatchy wanted to move to a system based entirely on its determination of merit; the union wanted to eliminate the merit system altogether. McClatchy's final offer proposed to grandfather current employees earning less than their classification's maximum, but this plan only superficially preserved the old wage scales. Ninety percent of the employees were already at the top salary step in their class, so the offer kept most raises in McClatchy's complete discretion. And, since the 1986 scales were out of step with the cost of living, salaries for the remaining 10% would effectively be determined by the publisher's discretion as well.

The parties bargained in good faith, but ultimately deadlocked over wage terms for the new agreement. Following impasse, McClatchy asserted that it was implementing its final offer and began granting increases to employees without consulting the union. Under the terms of McClatchy's proposal—as was true under the 1986 agreement—the union's role was restricted to making nonbinding comments and participating in the appeal process only if asked by the employee. The union filed an unfair labor practice charge against McClatchy, alleging that implementing "merit" increases without the union's consent violated McClatchy's duty to bargain with the union over wages.

Before the Board resolved the union's Sacramento complaint, [McClatchy] reached an impasse with the union over a similar discretionary pay proposal for its Modesto Bee editorial staff. The only difference in the Modesto proposal was that it fixed the timing of merit increases. At the Sacramento Bee, McClatchy could consider employees for increases as frequently or infrequently as it wished, but at the Modesto Bee, increases were tied to the annual review process. As it had in Sacramento, petitioner implemented its final offer after impasse and gave raises to some employees. . . .

The Board considered the Sacramento case first. The General Counsel argued that because McClatchy had a statutory obligation to bargain over "wages, hours, and terms of employment," granting individual raises without consulting the union violated the [NLRA]. McClatchy maintained that it had satisfied that duty by bargaining to impasse over the discretionary pay proposal. Once it had exhausted the bargaining process by reaching impasse, McClatchy asserted, it was privileged to implement its "last, best, and final offer" over the union's objection.

. . . .

[T]he Board rejected McClatchy's defense. In the Board's view, this case was less about impasse than statutory waiver: an employer who proposes unlimited management discretion over wages is really proposing that the union waive its statutory right to be consulted about wage changes. That is fine, the Board reasoned — if the union agrees. But impasse, by definition a lack of agreement, could not substitute for consent. Without a waiver, nothing relieved McClatchy of its obligation to bargain with the union before changing any employee's pay; unilaterally granting merit increases, therefore, was an unfair labor practice.

[The Board petitioned the court of appeals for enforcement of its order. A three-judge panel of the court of appeals remanded the case. Only Judge Silberman viewed the Board's waiver theory as a potentially legitimate interpretation of the Act. Chief Judge Edwards believed that the waiver theory would not work, but suggested instead a limited exception to the impasse doctrine focused on a conclusion that the employer bypassing the union when setting wage rates was "a kind of de-collectivization of bargaining."]

On remand, although it still used some language redolent of its original waiver theory, the Board essentially adopted Chief Judge Edwards' suggestion and fashioned an exception to the implementation after impasse doctrine. The Board explained that although the doctrine "is designed, in part, to allow an employer to exert unilateral economic force . . . [it is legitimate] only as a method for breaking the impasse." In other words, the Board grounded its new "narrow exception" on the impact that implementation would have on the collective bargaining *process*:

> Were we to allow the Respondent to implement its merit wage increase proposal and thereafter expect the parties to resume negotiations for a new collective-bargaining agreement, it is apparent that during the subsequent negotiations the Guild would be unable to bargain knowledgeably and thus have any impact on the present determination of unit employee wage rates. The Guild also would be unable to explain to its represented employees how any intervening changes in wages were formulated, given the Respondent's retention of discretion over all aspects of these increases. Further, the Respondent's implementation of this proposal would not create any fixed, objective status quo as to the level of wage rates, because the Respondent's proposal for a standardless practice of granting raises would allow recurring, unpredictable alterations of wages [sic] rates and would allow the Respondent to initially set and repeatedly change the standards, criteria, and timing of these increases. The frequency, extent, and basis for these wage changes would be governed only by the Respondent's exercise of its discretion.

Echoing Chief Judge Edwards' de-collectivization remark, the decision noted that [McClatchy's] "ongoing ability to exercise its economic force in setting wage increases [without the Guild's participation] . . . would simultaneously disparage the Guild by showing . . . its incapacity to act as the employees' representative in setting terms and conditions of employment." The Board took pains to emphasize that its holding was limited to a case where an employer refused to state any "definable objective procedures and criteria" for determining merit. It decided the Modesto case by the same reasoning. . . .

II.

Although the parties agree the case is one in which petitioner unilaterally implemented the terms of its final offers, it does seem somewhat anomalous to refer to the institution of the new wage regime as an "implementation of terms." Essentially, these wage proposals—particularly the one for the Sacramento Bee—have no terms. Indeed, the Board's opinion expresses the tentative view that under *NLRB v. Katz, supra*, "a wholly discretionary merit wage policy (*i.e.*, without identifiable procedures and criteria) does not itself 'establish' terms and conditions of employment at any point *prior* to the actual exercise of this discretion in setting discrete wage rates for unit employees." In other words, the Board questioned whether the impasse doctrine should even apply to the employer's action. We think there is something to this query, but since it is not the Board's holding, we obviously cannot rely on it in reviewing the Board's decision.

Although petitioner's argument is somewhat diffuse, we detect three lines of attack against the Board's order. The first is that the NLRA—or at least its "settled doctrine"—contemplates that an employer will be able to implement its last offer to the union after impasse; thus, the argument goes, the Board either lacked authority to craft the "narrow exception" applied in this case or was arbitrary and capricious in doing so. Second, petitioner claims that the Board implicitly treats its merit pay proposal as a permissive bargaining subject, despite the Supreme Court's recognition that comparable management discretion clauses are mandatory subjects of bargaining. Finally, the Board is accused of inadequately setting forth the boundaries of the exception it has crafted and insufficiently reconciling its own precedent. . . .

The NLRA is wholly silent on the question whether an employer may implement its final offer after impasse. To be sure, the general language of the Act, including § 8(a)(5) and § 8(d), have been authoritatively interpreted by the Supreme Court, and the Board is not free under *Chevron* to alter any of those interpretations even if they otherwise would be permissible readings of the Act. *See Lechmere, Inc. v. NLRB*, 502 U.S. 527, 536–37 (1992); *Maislin Indus. v. Primary Steel, Inc.*, 497 U.S. 116, 131 (1990). But the Supreme Court, while it has recognized the Board's doctrine, has never held that an employer has the *right* under the statute to implement its final offer, let alone considered whether the Board is entitled to craft exceptions to this supposed right. Indeed, not even the Board has ever held that the NLRA *requires* this rule. . . .

Even if the Board has never before determined that an exception to its doctrine was warranted, however, it is not clear that the statute prevents it from doing so in this case. Petitioner argues that this exception is inconsistent with *NLRB v. Insurance Agents' International Union, AFL-CIO*, 361 U.S. 477 (1960), which forbids the Board to act "as an arbiter of the sort of economic weapons the parties can use in seeking to gain acceptance of their bargaining demands." But the Supreme Court, in *Charles D. Bonanno Linen Service v. NLRB*, 454 U.S. 404 (1982), has also emphasized that the Board has wide latitude to monitor the bargaining process. . . .

Thus it is true, as petitioner stresses, that *Insurance Agents'* prohibited the Board from "act[ing] at large in equalizing disparities of bargaining power between employer and union." *Insurance Agents, supra.* But it is also true, as *Bonanno Linen* makes apparent, that regulating the process of collective bargaining may involve the Board in making determinations that necessarily implicate—if they do not rest directly on—the Board's appraisal of conditions that will affect the parties' bargaining power. Although the line between economic neutrality and authority over process is exceedingly difficult to draw, we think that this case is marginally closer to *Bonanno Linen* than to *Insurance Agents'*. Here, as in *Bonanno Linen*, the Board has denied the employer a particular economic tactic for the sake of preserving the stability of the collective bargaining process.

The post-impasse rule itself regulates process through power. The Board has told us that its rationale for permitting an employer to unilaterally implement its final offer after impasse is that such an action breaks the impasse and therefore encourages future collective bargaining.[4] The theory might well be thought somewhat strained, for it does not explain why the Board decided to handle impasse with this rule instead of another. The Board could have adopted, for example, a rule requiring the status quo to remain in effect until either the union or the employer was willing to resume negotiations. Stagnancy might pressure both the employer and the union to bend. But the rule it did choose—allowing the employer to implement its final offer—moves the process forward by giving one party, the employer, economic leverage. And in this case, where the employer has advanced no substantive criteria for its merit pay proposal, the Board has decided that the economic power it has granted would go too far. Rather than merely pressuring the union, implementation might well irreparably undermine its ability to bargain. Since the union could not know what criteria, if any, petitioner was using to award individual salary increases, it could not bargain against those standards; instead, it faced a discretionary cloud. As the Board put it, "the present case represents a blueprint for how an employer might effectively undermine the bargaining process while at the same time claiming that it was not acting to circumvent its statutory bargaining obligation." We think that it is within the Board's authority to prevent this development. . . .

---

4. We can find, however, no "seminal case" setting forth the Board's rationale underlying the impasse rule. *Cf.* Ellen J. Dannin, *Collective Bargaining Impasse and Implementation of Final Offers: Have We Created a Right Unaccompanied by Fulfillment?* 19 U. Tol. L. Rev. 41, 44 n.7 (1987). . . .

Not only does an employer's implementation of a proposal such as petitioner's deprive the union of "purchase" in pursuing future negotiations, the Board also concluded that by excluding the union from the process by which individual rates of pay are set [McClatchy] "simultaneously disparag[ed] the Guild by showing . . . its incapacity to act as the employees' representative in setting terms and conditions of employment." It knew no specifics about the merit raises, therefore it had no information to relay. In that regard, the Board echoed concerns expressed in Chief Judge Edwards' prior concurring opinion that petitioner's implementation of its proposal could be seen as seeking de-collectivization of bargaining. The Board concluded that [McClatchy's] action was "so *inherently* destructive of the fundamental principles of collective bargaining that it could not be sanctioned as part of a doctrine created to break impasse and restore active collective bargaining."

. . . .

Nevertheless, petitioner contends that the Board's logic is inconsistent with *NLRB v. American National Insurance*, 343 U.S. 395 (1952), which held that a clause giving an employer discretion over "management functions" such as promotions, discipline and work scheduling is a mandatory subject of bargaining—*i.e.*, one on which an employer is entitled to insist to the point of impasse. The Court there said that the Board is not entitled to "sit in judgment upon the substantive terms of collective bargaining agreements," and petitioner asserts that the Board is doing just that in this case. The Board, petitioner argues, has really based its entire reasoning on its judgment about the substance of petitioner's pay proposal.

It seems to us that petitioner may well overread *American National Insurance*. The Court there dealt with a management functions clause that was traditional in the insurance industry. Can one imagine employees' pay—in *any* industry— being described as a subject of a *management functions* clause? And the Court held only that "[a]ny fears the Board may entertain that use of management functions clauses will lead to *evasion* of an employer's duty to bargain collectively as to "rates of pay, wages, hours, and conditions of employment" do not justify condemning all bargaining for management functions clauses concerning *any* "condition of employment'. . . ." We rather doubt that *American National Insurance* means that no employer proposal could be condemned as a *per se* indication of bad faith bargaining. Suppose, for instance, an employer proposed that all working conditions, including wages and hours, were to be determined in accordance with the employer's total discretion. The offered agreement would have just three clauses: (1) union recognition, (2) the employer's discretion over all terms, and (3) a no-strike clause. That would seem to be the paradigm management functions clause "evading" the employer's collective bargaining duty.

In any event, the Board did not hold, as it did in *American National Insurance*, that petitioner's insistence on its pay proposal was a permissive subject of bargaining; petitioner was therefore entitled to insist on it to impasse. Petitioner claims, however, that by declaring its "implementation" after impasse illegal the Board has done indirectly what it could not do directly. If an employer cannot implement its proposal then the union has a permanent "veto," *see Colorado-Ute Elec. Ass'n v. NLRB*, 939 F.2d 1392, 1404 (10th Cir.1991), which, it is argued, is simply another way for the Board to treat an employer's insistence on the proposal as illegal. Petitioner's argument has a good deal of force, but it does not quite carry the day. As the Board's counsel pointed out, the two steps of bargaining to impasse and implementing after impasse are not practically equivalent and therefore can be judged according to different standards. If a party can force an impasse over a subject, its authority to do so gives it significant leverage over all other matters. That ability is not lost—at least not totally—by the Board's holding that the same proposal may not be unilaterally implemented after impasse.

. . . .

[T]he Board's decision does not prevent an employer from implementing a merit pay proposal post-impasse-so long as the proposal defines "merit" with objective criteria. . . .

Finally, petitioner argues that the Board has not explained adequately why it is making an exception for a proposal that affords an employer complete discretion over the grounds for and timing of wage increases. Petitioner asks, why are wages to be thought different than hours or other working conditions the statute also treats as mandatory subjects of bargaining? The Board explained that wages are "a key term and condition of employment and a primary basis of negotiations." That proposition, drawn perforce from the Board's expertise, seems hard to challenge in a reviewing court. The Board also thought its conclusion that wages were of "paramount importance" was supported by the wording of § 8(d), which lists wages first before hours and working conditions as subjects for collective bargaining. It does seem that the order—particularly when one considers that wages are, after all, a working condition and are nonetheless separately mentioned—is a legitimate point, if only a make-weight.

. . . .

We think the Board is free to draw on its expertise to determine that wages are typically of paramount importance in collective bargaining and to suggest that wages, unlike scheduling or a host of other decisions generally thought closely tied to management operations, are expected to be set bilaterally in a collective bargaining relationship. . . .

Notes

1. An early section of *Katz* seems to suggest a per se rule that "an employer's unilateral change in conditions of employment under negotiation is similarly a violation of § 8(a)(5)." However, near the end of its decision, the *Katz* Court qualified its holding: "Unilateral action by an employer without prior discussion with the union does amount to a refusal to negotiate about the affected conditions of employment under negotiation, and must of necessity obstruct bargaining, contrary to the congressional policy. . . ." Thus, the Court opens the door to unilateral employer action *after*

discussion with the union. In fact, *Katz*'s footnote 12 specifically distinguishes the two scenarios. *McClatchy Newspapers* follows one path leading from that open door.

2. Unions are subject to the same obligation not to effect unilateral changes in employees' terms and conditions of employment during the course of bargaining. *See Teamsters Local 955*, 325 N.L.R.B. 605 (1998) (Gould, concurring).

3. *McClatchy Newspapers* implicates three questions that would be answered separately in any analysis of a §8(a)(5) charge: (1) whether the employer's declaration of impasse was legitimate, (2) whether the employer may unilaterally impose a term with respect to a mandatory subject of bargaining (like wages), and (3) whether the particular term imposed constitutes a failure to bargain in good faith. *McClatchy Newspapers* directly analyzed question (3), but also indirectly addressed question (2) by leaving untouched the "rule" that employers may declare a bargaining impasse and unilaterally impose proposals reasonably included in the proposals it had made during negotiations. *See Taft Broadcasting Co.*, 163 N.L.R.B. 475 (1967), *supra*. However, *McClatchy Newspapers* raised serious doubts about the source of and justification for this Board position and suggests that the Board could reasonably adopt a different approach.

4. Assessing the legitimacy of one party's declaration of impasse in the private sector—typically, a declaration made by the employer—requires a ULP proceeding that inevitably stalls negotiations, potentially for an extended period of time. Does this rule improve the bargaining process? What incentives does it create for the union and the employer? Does it facilitate Coasean collective bargaining by reducing transaction costs, including strategic behavior, or is the declaration of impasse itself strategic behavior that increases the costs of bargaining? Rather than the impasse-and-implementation model, NLRA law could have used the model under the Railway Labor Act (RLA). Under the RLA, the National Mediation Board must declare an impasse before either party may unilaterally impose terms. 45 U.S.C. §155.

5. Ellen Dannin and Terry Wagar have argued that the NLRA's impasse-and-implementation rule significantly contributes to the continuing decline in the union density rate:

> Indeed, the doctrine of implementation upon impasse offers almost no downside for the employer. Demanding deep concessions and demanding unilateral control over working conditions not only get you to an impasse, but once there, the employer is in a position to impose the very terms it wants. If the union strikes, the employer may permanently replace the strikers, and eventually the replacements will vote the union out, or the union will walk away. All through bargaining, an employer can use the threat of replacement to force the union to agree to its terms, because the union does not dare strike. The employer can threaten this or remind the union of the law, but it does not even need to mention it; the union will know it is in a very weak position.

It does not even matter if the workers strike or not; if they stay on the job, the employer can implement its final offer and enter an uneasy situation with increasing employee dissatisfaction with the union because it cannot improve their working conditions. In the end, this may lead to de-unionization. Ellen Dannin & Terry Wagar, *Lawless Law? The Subversion of the National Labor Relations Act*, 34 Loy. L.A. L. Rev. 197, 202–203 (2000).[*]

See also Ellen J. Dannin, *Collective Bargaining Impasse and Implementation of Final Offers: Have We Created a Right Unaccompanied by Fulfillment?* 19 U. Tol. L. Rev. 41 (1987) (cited in *McClatchy Newspapers*). Dannin and Wagar built on earlier work by Paul Weiler that also attributed a portion of the decline in union density to unions' inability to gain first contracts, in part because of the impasse-and-implementation rule. *See* Paul Weiler, *Striking New Balance: Freedom of Contract and the Prospects for Union Representation*, 98 Har. L. Rev. 351 (1984).

Relatedly, "the doctrine that an employer is entitled to institute its last offer after impasse is an ancient one in labor law. Its stated purpose is to accelerate negotiations. . . . . But it should be obvious that it presents an employer — at least one negotiating in good faith — with a powerful weapon. Therefore, typically a Union will seek to frustrate its use by attempting to avoid an impasse." *Mike-Sell's Potato Chip Co. v. NLRB*, 807 F.3d 318, 323 (D.C. Cir. 2015) (citing *McClatchy Newspapers, supra*).

Do the existing rules governing good-faith bargaining and impasse protect against the scenario Dannin and Wagar describe? Is there a way to modify the existing rule to provide the requisite protections? Or is the only effective response, as Weiler argued, a re-balancing of the parties' economic weapons, including assuring that unions have a more effective strike weapon as a check on employers' ability to declare impasse and implement? *Supra.* at 404–05.

6. Despite the skepticism of two members of the original *McClatchy Newspaper* panel about the Board's waiver theory given the circumstances of that case, the general rule is that a union may waive its right to bargain over mandatory subjects. The waiver must be clear and unequivocal. *See Ciba-Geigy Pharm. Div. v. NLRB*, 722 F.2d 1120, 1127 (3d Cir. 1983); *Leeds & Northrup Co. v. NLRB*, 391 F.2d 874 (3d Cir. 1968). For example, a union's strike does not constitute a waiver. *NLRB v. J. H. Bonck Co.*, 424 F.2d 634 (5th Cir. 1970); *see NLRB v. J. H. Bonck Co.*, 424 F.2d 634 (5th Cir. 1970); *Alsey Refractories Company*, 215 N.L.R.B. 785, 787 (1974). In two related cases, the Board recently applied its clear-and-unmistakable doctrine to find that a union had waived its right to bargain over certain benefits because of acquiescence. *See E.I. Du Pont de Nemours & Co.*, 368 N.L.R.B. No. 48 (Sep. 4, 2019) (*DuPont II*) (finding that union clearly and unmistakably waived its right to bargain over the company's dental plan and retirement medical benefits and therefore that the company did not violate § 8(a)(5) when it unilaterally implemented changes to

---

those benefits in 2013); *E.I. DuPont de Nemours & Co.*, 367 N.L.R.B. No. 145, slip op. at 3 (Jun. 21, 2019) (*DuPont I*) (same but changes implemented in 2006).

7. If the parties have not bargained to impasse, employers generally may not cut or raise workers' wages during negotiations absent some economic exigency. *See Prime Healthcare Services — Encino LLC v. NLRB*, 890 F.3d 286 (D.C. Cir. 2018) (upholding Board's finding that anniversary step increases survive contract expiration and therefore that employer violates §8(a)(5) when it unilaterally terminates those increases upon contract expiration); *Pleasantview Nursing Home, Inc. v. NLRB, supra* (collecting cases). To establish an economic exigency, the employer bears a "heavy burden" of proving a "compelling business justification." *See id.* at 755; *Master Window Cleaning, Inc.*, 302 N.L.R.B. 373 (1991) (requiring "extraordinary circumstances"). But what if the employer long ago planned a wage increase that is scheduled to occur during the course of collective bargaining? Dictum in *Katz* suggests that such an automatic (i.e., non-discretionary) wage increase would not constitute a ULP. Absent an impasse, could the employer withhold that increase to unit members, or is it obligated to provide it to maintain the status quo? The answer depends upon whether the employer has given the union notice and an opportunity to bargain. *Compare Daily News of Los Angeles v. NLRB*, 73 F.3d 406 (D.C. Cir. 1996) (employer committed a ULP by unilaterally suspending annual merit wage increase reviews without bargaining with the union) *with TXU Electric Company*, 343 N.L.R.B. 1404 (2004) (employer did not commit a ULP by unilaterally suspending annual salary plan adjustments after giving notice to the union and the union declined to bargain over the suspension).

C. The Public Sector and Public Sector Impasse Procedures

Public-sector jurisdictions routinely use the NLRA rule from *Katz* regarding unilateral implementation and impasse. *See, e.g., Detroit Transp. Corp. and Teamsters Local 214*, 20 MPER ¶ 112 (MERC 2007) (for mandatory subjects of bargaining, the parties must bargain and neither side can take unilateral action absent impasse, citing *Katz*); *Union of American Physicians & Dentists v. State of California*, 30 PERC ¶ 142 (Cal. PERB ALJ 2006) (well-established that a pre-impasse unilateral change in a mandatory condition violates the duty to confer in good faith, citing *Katz*); *Rockford Educ. Ass'n and Rockford School Dist. 205*, 21 PERI ¶ 179 (Ill. ELRB ALJ 2005) (employer's unilateral change in a mandatory subject, without giving the union the opportunity to bargain to agreement or impasse is a ULP, citing *Katz*).

In a relatively high-profile example of this doctrine, *Teachers v. School District of Philadelphia*, 109 A.3d. 298 (Pa. Commw. 2015) enjoined the Philadelphia School District and a School Reform Commission (Commission) from unilaterally changing economic and other conditions of employment covered in an expired contract without first bargaining to impasse. Defendants argued that they had the right to make these changes under state statutes giving the Commission certain powers regarding financially distressed school districts. The court, however, found that these statutes did not create the authority to cancel labor contracts or to unilaterally impose terms of employment where, as here, the applicable public-sector labor statute law required bargaining over such terms. This rule also applies to more mundane matters. The Washington Public Employment Relations Commission held that an employer committed a ULP when it unilaterally discontinued its practice of providing free coffee to correctional employees. This was a mandatory topic of negotiation because it involved working conditions. *King Cnty. Corr. Guild v. King Cnty.*, WPERC Case No. 26573-U-14 (May 26, 2016).

But the public sector features some significant variations. For example, where statutory impasse resolution procedures exist, when does an "impasse" arise?

Moreno Valley Unified School District v. Public Employment Relations Board

California Court of Appeals
142 Cal. App. 3d 191, 191 Cal. Rptr. 60 (Cal. App. 1983)

Morris, J.

This case presents an important issue concerning the authority of California's Public Employment Relations Board (. . . PERB, or the Board). Specifically, whether the Board's determination that a public employer's unilateral implementation of changes in employment conditions during the pendency of the statutory impasse procedure constitutes a per se unfair labor practice is a reasonable interpretation of the Educational Employment Relations Act (EERA). . . .

The first collective bargaining agreement between the Moreno Valley Unified School District (District) and the Moreno Valley Educators Association (Association), representing about 320 certificated employees, was due to expire on August 31, 1978. Negotiations for a new agreement began on March 23, 1978. The parties met on 16 separate occasions through September 15, but were unable to reach agreement on most issues. The school year began on September 11. Four days later the parties mutually agreed they were at an impasse, and requested that the Board appoint a mediator pursuant to the statutory impasse procedure. (*Gov. Code, § 3548 et seq.*) The Board appointed a mediator on September 20. Nevertheless, on or shortly after September 15, the District unilaterally implemented the terms of its "last best offer."

Mediation proceeded in accordance with the statutory impasse procedure. On October 2, 1978, the Association filed an unfair labor practice charge against the District. . . .

. . . [The PERB hearing officer concluded] that it was a per se unfair practice for a public employer to implement unilateral changes in terms and conditions of employment subject to the scope of representation prior to the exhaustion of the statutory impasse procedures; this practice was held to violate section 3543.5, subdivisions (a), (b), (c) and (e) [specifying various ULPs, including to "refuse or fail to meet and negotiate in good faith"].

... [T]he Board adopted the hearing officer's statement of facts, and partially adopted his reasoning and conclusions of law. "[Following] a declaration of impasse, a unilateral change regarding a subject within the scope of negotiations prior to exhaustion of the impasse procedure is, absent a valid affirmative defense, *per se* an unfair practice," the Board stated. (*Moreno Valley Educators Assn. v. Moreno Valley Unified School Dist.* (1982) P.E.R.B. Dec. No. 206, p. 5.) ...

. . . .

[T]o the extent the language and provisions of the [NLRA] ... parallel those of the Educational Employment Relations Act, cases construing the former are persuasive in interpreting the latter. . . .

The District argued ... that "since a strike or work stoppage after impasse but before completing post-impasse procedures does not constitute a *per se* unfair practice, it therefore follows that implementation of a last best offer after impasse does not constitute a *per se* unfair practice." The thrust of this argument is that it is unfair to treat "employee self help" (in the form of strikes) by a totality-of-conduct test[3] while condemning "employer self-help" (in the form of unilateral changes in employment conditions) as per se unlawful. This argument inverts the reasoning of the hearing officer in this case, who found that because employee organizations could not use "self-help" during impasse, neither should employers be allowed to do so.

Both the District's argument and, as PERB recognized, the hearing officer's rationale, are premised on a flawed equation of employee strikes with unilateral changes in employment conditions made by employers. It is manifest that a unilateral change in employment conditions is not the same thing as a strike, at any stage of an employment dispute. The management equivalent of a strike is a lockout. . . .

Strikes and unilateral changes in employment conditions have very different consequences for the labor dispute resolution process. A strike, like a lockout, has the necessary result that neither labor nor management achieves its goals. A lockout or strike is designed to exert economic pressure on the other party to resolve disputed issues. In sharp contrast, a unilateral imposition of terms by an employer signals an end to the mutual dispute resolution process regarding those terms. The

---

3. The Board explained the distinction between the totality of conduct and per se tests in *Stockton Teachers Assn. CTA/NEA v. Stockton Unified School Dist.* (1980) P.E.R.B. Decision No. 143, page 22:

"The standard generally applied to determine whether good faith bargaining has occurred has been called the 'totality of conduct' test. This test looks to the entire course of negotiations to determine whether the employer has negotiated with the requisite subjective intention of reaching an agreement. There are certain acts, however, which have such a potential to frustrate negotiations and to undermine the exclusivity of the bargaining agent that they are held unlawful without any determination of subjective bad faith on the part of the employer. The latter violations are considered *per se* violations. An outright refusal to bargain or a unilateral change in the terms and conditions of employment are two examples of *per se* violations of the duty to negotiate. . . ."

employer loses incentive to participate in the dispute resolution process, because it has imposed terms it has deemed satisfactory.

The District's [next] argument is that the Board "failed to distinguish between pre-impasse bargaining and statutory impasse procedures." Under the [NLRA], the District stresses, unilateral employer action on subjects of negotiations taken before impasse is reached is per se unfair, while unilateral action after impasse is not. *See Labor Board v. Katz* (1962) 369 U.S. 736.

However, this argument assumes a correspondence between federal law and the EERA which does not exist. Unlike the EERA, the NLRA has no statutory impasse procedure, failure to participate in which is explicitly made an unlawful labor practice.

EERA's impasse procedure is set forth at Government Code sections 3548 through 3548.8. The sections provide that either the employer or the employee organization may declare that an impasse exists; if PERB determines that is the case, it must appoint a mediator, who must meet with the parties in an effort to resolve the differences. Should the mediator not effect a settlement within 15 days of his appointment, PERB must appoint a factfinding panel on request of either party; the factfinding panel must conduct its operations according to statutory guidelines. Under certain circumstances, binding arbitration may occur. Government Code sections 3543.5, subdivision (e) and 3543.6, subdivision (d) explicitly make it unlawful for a public school employer or an employee organization, respectively, to refuse to participate in good faith in the statutory impasse procedure.

Recognizing that federal law differed significantly in having no statutorily prescribed impasse procedures, the Board in this case rejected the District's analogy to federal law, reasoning as follows: "The assumption of unilateral control over the employment relationship prior to exhaustion of the impasse procedures frustrates the EERA's purpose of achieving mutual agreement in exactly the same ways that such conduct frustrates that purpose when it occurs at an earlier point. . . . The impasse procedures of EERA contemplate a continuation of the bilateral negotiations process. Mediation remains fundamentally a bargaining process, albeit with the assistance of a neutral third party." (*Moreno Valley Educators Assn. v. Moreno Valley Unified School Dist., supra,* PERB Dec. No. 206, pp. 4–5.)

The Board's conclusion that impasse under the EERA is, unlike NLRA impasse,[6] a continuation of mutual dispute resolution efforts and not a signal that economic pressure tactics may begin, is a reasonable interpretation of the statutory scheme. . . .

---

6. The Supreme Court has recently clarified that under the NLRA, impasse is "a temporary deadlock or hiatus in negotiations 'which in almost all cases is eventually broken, through either a change of mind or the application of economic force.'" ("*Charles D. Bonanno Linen Service v. NLRB* (1982), 454 U.S. 404, 412. (1982). The high court accepted the NLRB's view that, during NLRA impasse, "bargaining is temporarily replaced by economic warfare." *Id.* at p. 412, fn. 8. . . .

"For the reasons set forth in *San Mateo County Community College District*, we find that following a declaration of impasse, a unilateral change regarding a subject within the scope of negotiations prior to exhaustion of the impasse procedure is, absent a valid affirmative defense, *per se* an unfair practice," the Board stated. (*Moreno Valley Educators Assn. v. Moreno Valley Unified School Dist., supra*, PERB Dec. No. 206, at p. 5.) The Board's *San Mateo* decision set forth four reasons why unilateral changes in employment conditions by an employer prior to statutory impasse warranted *per se* treatment:

"One reason unilateral changes are disfavored is their destabilizing and disorienting impact on employer-employee affairs. *Fibreboard Paper Products Corp. v. NLRB* (1964) 379 U.S. 203, 211.... An employer's single-handed assumption of power over employment relations can spark strikes or other disruptions at the work place. Similarly, negotiating prospects may also be damaged as employers seek to negotiate from a position of advantage, forcing employees to talk the employer back to terms previously agreed to. This one-sided edge to the employer surely delays, and may even totally frustrate, the process of arriving at a contract.

"A second reason to prohibit unilateral changes of employment conditions is to protect employer-employee freedom of choice in selecting an exclusive representative. Employer unilateral actions derogate the representative's negotiating power and ability to perform as an effective representative in the eyes of employees....

"Third, the rule against unilateral changes promotes negotiating equality consistent with the statutory design. EERA compels negotiations with an exclusive representative, gives employee organizations negotiating rights prior to final budget-making by management, establishes public notice procedures to prevent behind-closed-doors decision-making, and, provides for neutral third party mediation and factfinding when impasse has occurred.... [An] employer's unilateral act prior to negotiations inherently tips the negotiating balance so carefully structured by the various provisions of the EERA. In short, the bilateral duty to negotiate is negated by the assertion of power by one party through unilateral action on negotiable matters.

"Finally, when carried out in the context of declining revenues, an employer's unilateral actions may also unfairly shift community and political pressure to employees and their organizations, and at the same time reduce the employer's accountability to the public. This type of potential competition is unique to the public sector...." (*San Mateo Community College Dist., supra*, at pp. 14–16.)

Since "impasse" under EERA's statutory scheme denotes a continuation of the labor management dispute resolution process, while "impasse" under federal law indicates a halt to that process, we think the Board reasonably determined that the considerations warranting per se treatment of unilateral changes at the negotiation stage also warranted per se treatment of such changes prior to the exhaustion of the statutory impasse procedure.

Thus, the Board reasonably interpreted the statute in finding a per se violation of the statutory duty of employers to participate in good faith in the impasse procedure. . . .

Notes

1. *Moreno* states the common public-sector rule that, where impasse resolution procedures exist, employers cannot unilaterally implement their proposals unless and until the parties have exhausted their obligations under those procedures. This means, among other things, that where the final step of a statutory process is mandatory, binding arbitration that decides the issues at impasse, the employer may never have an "impasse" defense to a charge that it has unilaterally implemented a change in a mandatory subject of bargaining. *See, e.g., Green County*, 7 NPER 51-16028, Dec. No. 20308-B (Wisc. Emp. Rel. Comm., 1984), and *id.* note 16 (collecting cases).

2. This approach can also mean that "impasse," for the purpose of this rule in the public sector, can arise at different points for different types of employees under one state law. For example, *Alaska Public Emp. Ass'n v. State of Alaska*, 776 P.2d 1030 (Alaska 1989) explained that under the Alaska statute, employees are divided into three classes. "Class I" employees may never strike. "Class II" employees have a limited right to strike: after an impasse in negotiations, they must submit to mediation, and if mediation fails, Class II employees may strike as long as the public's health, safety or welfare is not endangered (if it is, the strike can be enjoined and the parties go to arbitration). "Class III" employees may legally strike after an impasse in negotiations, without such limitations. 776 P.2d 1030, 1030. The court cited NLRA precedent and held as follows. "[T]he state may implement unilateral contract changes when negotiations reach an impasse. For Class II employees, an impasse is reached when the parties have reached a good faith impasse and the mediation process has been exhausted. For Class III employees, an impasse is reached when negotiations are deadlocked." *Id.* at 1033.

3. In Ohio, a regulation provides the rule. O.A.C. §4117-09-02(E) requires that the terms of a collective bargaining agreement be maintained until one of three conditions is met: "until 60 days after a party gives notice; until the expiration of the CBA; or until the statutory dispute resolution procedures are exhausted, whichever occurs later." *See SERB v. Cincinnati Metro. Housing Auth.*, 23 OPER ¶ 354 (Oh. SERB 2006).

4. Pennsylvania uses an unusual variation. For employees who are allowed to strike, even if the parties are at impasse, the employer cannot implement unilaterally so long as the union does not strike. In *Philadelphia Housing Auth. v. Penn. Labor Rel. Bd.*, 620 A.2d 594, 600 (Pa. 1993) explained:

> It would not serve the legislature's declared goal of promoting orderly and
> constructive relationships between public employers and their employees

through good faith collective bargaining to allow a public employer to implement its final offer when the employees have not disrupted the continuation of public service by striking. Unilateral action by an employer during a period of no contract while employees continue to work serves to polarize the process and would encourage strikes by employees who otherwise may wish to continue working under the terms of the expired agreement while negotiations continue.

On the other hand, *Central Dauphin Educ. Ass'n v. Central Dauphin Sch. Dist.*, 792 A.2d 691 (Pa. Commw. Ct. 2001) suggests that this reasoning does not apply to employees who have a significantly limited or no right to strike. Why might a court make this distinction? Are there good arguments to the contrary?

D. Impasse and "Status Quo" in the Public Sector

In the public sector, while the basic definition of "impasse" is the same as in the private sector, "impasses" exist at various levels: after the parties have failed to reach an agreement in their initial negotiations, but also after various impasse resolution procedures have been tried. These procedures will be discussed further in Chapter 11.

The public sector sometimes differs from the private on a related issue: if employers must maintain the status quo on mandatory topics until the parties have bargained to agreement or impasse, what exactly is meant by "status quo," especially when an old contract has expired?

Pennsylvania State Park Officers Ass'n v. Pennsylvania Labor Relations Bd.

Commonwealth Court of Pennsylvania
854 A.2d 674 (Pa. Commw. Ct. 2004)

LEAVITT, J.

[The union filed a ULP charge claiming that the Commonwealth had violated the PLRA by unilaterally ceasing longevity wage increases during the interest arbitration process. The Secretary of the Board declined to issue a ULP complaint]. The Secretary reasoned as follows:

> The status quo following contract expiration does not include the continuation of periodic wage adjustments. . . .

> . . . The Board affirmed the Secretary's decision not to issue a complaint and dismissed Complainants' exceptions. This appeal followed. . . .

Complainants' primary argument is that the Commonwealth, by refusing to pay longevity wage increases post contract expiration, unlawfully altered the *status quo*. In Complainants' view, this was an unfair labor practice under Section 6(1)(a) and (e) of the PLRA, *43 P.S. § 211.6(1)(a) and (e)*.

. . . [T]here is no dispute that the officers' compensation structure is a mandatory subject of bargaining. . . . Thus, any unilateral change by the Commonwealth with respect to the officers' compensation would be an unfair labor practice. . . .

As aptly observed by the Board, however, the distinct legal issue in the present case is *how to define the status quo.* The Board found that it means freezing wages at the moment the collective bargaining agreements expired. Complainants, on the other hand, argue that maintaining the *status quo* means increasing their members' wages according to the automatic wage escalators, as provided in the expired agreements.

In addressing this legal issue, the Board found *Fairview School District v. Unemployment Compensation Board of Review*, 499 Pa. 539 (1982) to be controlling. In *Fairview*, a collective bargaining agreement between the teachers' union and the school district expired on August 26, 1979, and a successor contract was not in place when the teachers reported for work on September 5, 1979. The teachers received their regularly scheduled bi-weekly paychecks on September 7, 1979, which were computed on the basis of the prior school year's salary matrix set forth in the expired agreement. The checks did not include any step-up in pay based on an additional year of service beyond the 1978–1979 school year covered by the expired contract.

The union filed a grievance, alleging that the district had violated the extended collective bargaining agreement by failing to step-up the teachers' salaries based on an additional year of service. A work stoppage commenced on September 14, 1979, and continued until October 22, 1979. . . .

[Regarding claims for unemployment benefits, the Pennsylvania Supreme Court] had to determine which side, union or management, first refused to continue operations under the *status quo* after the contract had expired. For purposes of its analysis, the Court defined the *status quo* as "the last actual, peaceable and lawful noncontested status which preceded the controversy." The Court concluded that the district did not violate the *status quo* by refusing to pay stepped-up salary increases after the collective bargaining agreement expired, reasoning as follows:

> The underlying rationale for the status quo requirement is that during the interim period between contracts, the employer may continue operations and the employee may continue working, while the parties are free to negotiate on an equal basis in good faith. Maintenance of the status quo is merely another way of stating that the parties must continue the existing relationship in effect at the expiration of the old contract. *To require the School District to pay stepped up salary increases beyond the specified years contained in the expired contract changes the existing relationship in the context of the terms and conditions subject to the very negotiations sought to be fostered.*
>
> We therefore hold that the School District's refusal to pay stepped up salaries did not constitute a disruption of the status quo. 499 Pa. at 546–547 (emphasis added). . . .

Echoing the *Fairview* court's rationale, the Board argues that the Commonwealth was not obligated to pay longevity wage increases to Complainants' members since wages were one of the matters under negotiation.

Complainants argue that *Fairview* is distinguishable because that case concerned "stepped-up" salary increases whereas the present controversy concerns discrete longevity wage increases that the Commonwealth contemplated having to make regardless of the outcome of arbitration. In our view this is a distinction without a difference. Both schemes provide financial rewards based upon an employee's length of service, and in this case the incentives were part of the overall salary structure that was a mandatory subject of bargaining between the parties. . . .

We also disagree with Complainants' suggestion that the definition of "*status quo*" should vary according to the context in which a controversy arises. Our Supreme Court has established that the *status quo* is always the "last actual, peaceable and lawful non-contested status which preceded [a] controversy." *Fairview*, 499 Pa. at 544. It is a theoretical level playing field on which the parties begin negotiations for a successor agreement. It matters not whether the underlying controversy involves a labor dispute or eligibility for unemployment benefits. In our view, it would only lead to confusion to define the *status quo* differently from one situation to the next.

In sum, we agree with the Board that *Fairview* is not only controlling here but reflective of sound labor policy. Recognizing that the issue of contractual wage increases during a *status quo* period was one of first impression, the *Fairview* court cited two cases from other jurisdictions as persuasive. One of those cases, *Board of Cooperative Educational Services of Rockland County v. New York State Public Employment Relations Board*, 41 N.Y.2d 753 (N.Y. 1977), is particularly instructive to our analysis.

In *Rockland County*, a labor dispute arose between the Board of Cooperative Educational Services, a public employer, and the union representing its instructional employees. The employer refused to pay step increments to returning unit employees, opting instead to maintain salaries at the rate in effect at the expiration of the former collective bargaining agreement. The New York State Public Employment Relations Board ordered the employer to negotiate in good faith, cease and desist from refusing to pay the increments and make retroactive payments to affected employees. The Court of Appeals reversed, holding that "it is not a violation of a public employer's duty to negotiate in good faith to discontinue during the negotiations for a new agreement the payment of automatic annual salary increments, however long standing the practice of paying such increments may have been." *Id.* at 1175.

The Court of Appeals began its analysis by recognizing that there are fundamental distinctions between public and private employers. It acknowledged the benefits inherent in the concept of longevity wage increases; employees receive a financial reward for their commitment to the employer and the employer benefits by retaining experienced personnel and expending less time and resources on training. The *Rockland County* court concluded, however, that requiring public employers to pay longevity wage increments following expiration of a collective bargaining agree-ment is "fraught with problems, equitable and economic in nature." *Id.* at 1177. For instance, public employers conduct their operations using public money and so face unique budgetary pressures. As the Court eloquently observed,

> in thriving periods the increment of the past may not squeeze the public purse, nor may it on the other hand be even fair to employees, but in times of escalating costs and diminishing tax bases, many public employers sim-ply may not be able in good faith to continue to pay automatic increments to their employees. *Id.*

The same concerns hold true for the Commonwealth in this case, which faced its own budgetary crisis during the summer of 2003 when the present controversy devel-oped. Although the longevity wage increases may have been economically feasible for the Commonwealth when it executed the now-expired collective bargaining agree-ments, that presumption is certainly subject to change from one budgetary cycle to the next. It would be unfair to compel the Commonwealth, or any governmental entity, to maintain financial commitments in perpetuity in the face of a shrinking tax base, declining population or any other unforeseen adverse circumstance.

The New York Court of Appeals also flatly rejected the union's argument that pay-ment of the increments preserves the existing relationship between the parties until different conditions are established through collective bargaining. In the Court's view, this argument was based on the erroneous assumption that it is the "exist-ing relationship" which is being preserved when, in reality, forcing an employer to pay incremental wage increases not only changes the relationship established by the parties but gives a bargaining advantage to the union by making negotiation of that point more difficult. Similarly, requiring the Commonwealth to make longev-ity payments essentially removes that issue from the bargaining process and forces the Commonwealth to come to the table already burdened with a wage scheme that may no longer be economically viable. The effect would be to threaten the tenuous balance in bargaining power between public employers and their employees.

One final observation by the *Rockland County* court regarding the *status quo* issue is worth repeating here:

> To say that the status quo must be maintained during negotiations is one thing; to say that the status quo includes a change and means automatic increases in salary is another. *The matter of increments can be negotiated and, if it is agreed that such increments can and should be paid, provision can be made for payment retroactively. Id.* (emphasis added).

This analysis is equally applicable to the situation before us, where nothing in the expired collective bargaining agreements indicated an intention to extend the sched-uled wage increases beyond June 30, 2003.[16] Going forward, whenever Complainants

---

16. The absence of such an agreement between the employer and the union was a dispositive factor in the other foreign case cited by our Supreme Court in: *M.S.A.D. No. 43 Teachers' Asso. v.*

and the Commonwealth negotiate wage terms, they must necessarily decide whether to abolish the longevity wage scheme altogether or, if it is continued in the successor agreement, whether to compensate affected officers retroactively. The parties are quite capable of anticipating the present scenario and can negotiate an appropriate course of action to follow during "gap" periods between contracts. . . .

We agree with the Board that the Commonwealth did not commit an unfair practice under Section 6(1)(a) or (e) of the PLRA by discontinuing the longevity wage increases provided for in the expired agreements. The policy reasons articulated by the Court in *Fairview* are equally compelling here and comport with Act 111's goal of fostering collective bargaining. . . .

Notes

1. This case adopts (without using the term) the "static status quo" model, as opposed to the "dynamic status quo" model used under the NLRA and in most public-sector jurisdictions. The static status quo rule requires, or at least permits, public employers "to pay only those wages in effect when the agreement expired, unless the agreement provides otherwise," while under the dynamic status quo, the employer generally must "pay wages according to the wage plan of the expired agreement, including any scheduled step increases." Steven Scott, *The Status Quo Doctrine: An Application to Salary Step Increases for Teachers*, Note, 83 Cornell L. Rev. 194, 216 (1997).

2. The majority rule in the public sector is the dynamic status quo rule. *See Bd. of Trustees of the Univ. of Maine Sys. v. Associated Colt Staff*, 659 A.2d 842, 847 & n. 1 (1995) (Judge Wathen dissenting and citing cases using the dynamic rule from Illinois, Michigan, California, Wisconsin, Indiana, and Florida). The New York legislature codified the dynamic status quo rule, formerly known in that state as the *Triborough* doctrine (*see Triborough Bridge and Tunnel Auth.*, 5 P.E.R.B. 3037 (1972)), except that the statute, Civil Service Law § 209-1.1(e), applies to all contract terms, whereas the prior case law applied only to contract terms on mandatory subjects of bargaining.

3. In contrast, the majority in *Bd. of Trustees of the Univ. of Maine Sys.* reversed the Maine Labor Board's use of the dynamic rule and reinstated the static rule,

---

M.S.A.D. No. 43 Bd. of Directors, 432 A.2d 395 (Me. 1981). In that case, the public employer paid newly hired teachers by applying the salary schedule set forth in the expired collective bargaining agreement. The employer paid returning teachers the same salary that they received in the prior school year, as though the agreement had expired. The Supreme Judicial Court of Maine affirmed an order of the Maine Labor Relations Board that employer cease this practice. Quoting the Board, the Supreme Judicial Court noted that "[the employer] . . . acted properly in paying the returning teachers at the same step which the teachers occupied during the 1977–78 school year. In *Easton Teachers Association v. Easton School Committee*, M.L.R.B. No. 79-14 at 7 (1979), we held that during the interim period between expiration of a contract and execution of a successor contract, 'the status quo should be maintained as if the existing conditions were frozen rather than to give effect to a built-in wage escalator.'" *Id.* at 397 (citing *Rockland County* decision for support).

which Maine had previously used. As in *Pa. State Park Officers State Park Officers Ass'n*, the court in *Bd. of Trustees of the Univ. of Maine Sys.* stressed the importance of protecting the public fisc. "The static status quo rule is consistent with the Legislature's clearly expressed intent to protect municipal and state agency budgets from increases in wages imposed without agreement by the governing body [while the] dynamic status quo rule . . . obligates the University to pay substantial increases in wages not approved by its trustees." 659 A.2d 842, 845–46. The dissent responded to these concerns as follows. "Unquestionably, there are significant fiscal implications involved when a public employer is required to continue a past practice set forth in an expired wage provisions . . . while bargaining for a new contract. There is a meaningful legal difference, however, between compelling an agreement and preserving the status quo while the parties are bargaining." Maine reaffirmed its adherence to the static status quo in *City of Augusta v. Maine Labor Relations Board*, 70 A.3d 268 (Me. 2013).

4. For further thoughts on the merits of these two approaches, see Scott, *The Status Quo Doctrine, supra.* Is there a stronger case for the static status quo rule in the public sector? Private employers have legitimate financial concerns, and they can and do go through difficult financial periods as well. Should the law be more solicitous of public-sector employers in this regard? Keep in mind that, given the various impasse dispute mechanisms in the public sector, it can take significantly longer to get to and through impasse and thus to get a new contract in the public sector than in the private. On the other hand, can you think of ways in which public-sector unions in a static status quo jurisdiction could obtain the same practical result as if they were operating under the dynamic status quo rule?

5. New Jersey is unusual in that it uses both rules: the dynamic status quo rule for most public employees, but the static status quo rule for teachers. For an explanation of how this came about, and a court's rejection of the state labor agency's attempt to change from dynamic to static for non-teaching employees, see *In re County of Atlantic and PBA Local 243*, 445 N.J. Super. 1 (N.J. App. 2016), *aff'd*, 230 N.J. 237 (2017).

VI. Duty to Bargain During the Contract's Term

A. In the Private Sector

As noted in the Introduction to this chapter, Congress originally implied a duty to bargain in good faith in § 8(5) of the Wagner Act because the right to form unions and bargain collectively "is a mere delusion" if not accompanied by a duty to negotiate "in a bona fide effort to arrive at a collective bargaining agreement." *NLRB v. American Nat'l Ins. Co.*, 343 U.S. 395, 403 n.10 (1952) (citing S. Rep. No. 573, 74th Cong., 1st Sess. 12 (1935)).

Yet, when the Taft-Hartley Act codified the duty to bargain in good faith, Congress did not expressly limit the duty's application to the initial bargaining that precedes a collective bargaining agreement. Section 8(d) applies the duty to "confer in good faith" equally to "the negotiation of an agreement, *or any question arising thereunder*" (emphasis added). It also holds that:

> [T]he duties so imposed shall not be construed as requiring either party to discuss or agree to any modification of the terms and conditions contained in a contract for a fixed period, if such modification is to become effective before such terms and condition can be reopened under the provisions of the contract. Pub. L. No. 101, 80th Cong., 1st Sess. (June 23, 1947).

Finally, §8(d) establishes a set of impasse procedures "where there is in effect a collective-bargaining contract" that will be discussed in the next chapter. In sum, the duty to bargain in good faith continues after the collective bargaining agreement becomes effective.

The continuation of the duty to bargain during the life of the contract means that the jurisdiction of the Board, in its role as the enforcer of the duty to bargain in good faith, may overlap with contractual dispute resolution mechanisms (e.g., arbitration). For example, if a union refuses to negotiate with an employer over wage concessions pursuant to a clause allowing either party to "reopen" the contract's economic provisions, has the union committed a ULP under §8(b)(3), opened itself to a grievance under the contract that will be resolved by an arbitrator, or both? Who should decide? The Board's "deferral doctrine," addressed in Chapter 13, answers these questions in favor of the arbitrator, at least in the first instance.

Other questions arise from this overlapping jurisdiction. What is the Board's role in enforcing the duty to bargain in good faith and what is the scope of that duty during the term of a collective bargaining agreement? How does the statutory duty to bargain in good faith interact with a contractual obligation to bargain over particular subjects or one party's purported waiver of a duty to bargain? The next case and the notes following it address these questions.

The Jacobs Mfg. Co.

National Labor Relations Board
94 N.L.R.B. 1214 (1951)

In July 1948, the Respondent and the Union executed a 2-year bargaining contract which, by its terms, could be reopened 1 year after its execution date for discussion of "wage rates." In July 1949 the Union invoked the reopening clause of the 1948 contract, and thereafter gave the Respondent written notice of its "wage demands." In addition to a request for a wage increase, these demands included a request that the Respondent undertake the entire cost of an existing group insurance program, and another request for the establishment of a pension plan for the Respondent's employees. When the parties met thereafter to consider the Union's demands, the Respondent refused to discuss the Union's pension and insurance requests on the ground that they were not appropriate items of discussion under the reopening clause of the 1948 contract.

The group insurance program to which the Union alluded in its demands was established by the Respondent before 1948. It was underwritten by an insurance company, and provided life, accident, health, surgical, and hospital protection. All the Respondent's employees were eligible to participate in the program, and the employees shared its costs with the Respondent. When the 1948 contract was being negotiated, the Respondent and the Union had discussed changes in this *insurance program*, and had agreed to increase certain of the benefits as well as the costs. However, neither the changes thereby effected, nor the insurance program itself, was mentioned in the 1948 contract.

As indicated by the Union's request, there was no pension plan for the Respondent's employees in existence in 1949. The subject of *pensions*, moreover, had not been discussed during the 1948 negotiations; and, like insurance, that subject is not mentioned in the 1948 contract.

a. For the reasons stated below, *Chairman Herzog* and *Members Houston* and *Styles* agree with the Trial Examiner's conclusion that the Respondent violated Section 8(a)(5) of the Act by refusing to discuss the matter of *pensions* with the Union.

[The majority agreed with the trial examiner that the Respondent had not, as it asserted, expressed its willingness to discuss pensions and insurance at a meeting separate from the meeting called for a discussion of wage rates.]

We are satisfied . . . that the 1948 contract did not in itself impose on the Respondent any obligation to discuss pensions or insurance. The reopening clause of that contract refers to *wage rates*, and thus its intention appears to have been narrowly limited to matters directly related to the amount and manner of compensation for work. For that reason, a requirement to discuss pensions or insurance cannot be predicated on the language of the contract.

On the other hand, a majority of the Board believes that, regardless of the character of the reopening clause, the Act itself imposed upon the Respondent the duty to discuss *pensions* with the Union during the period in question.

It is now established as a principle of law that the matter of pensions is a subject which falls within the area where the statute requires bargaining. And, as noted above, the 1948 contract between the Respondent and the Union was silent with respect to the subject of pensions; indeed, the matter had never been raised or discussed by the parties. The issue raised, therefore, is whether the Respondent was absolved of the obligation to discuss pensions because of the limitation contained in Section 8(d) of the amended Act dealing with the duty to discuss or agree to the modification of an existing bargaining contract. . . .

The crucial point at issue here, as in the earlier cases, is the construction to be given the phrase "terms and conditions *contained in* a contract." . . . Section 8(d) does not itself license a party to a bargaining contract to refuse, during the life of the contract, to discuss a bargainable subject unless it has been made a part of the agreement itself. Applied here, . . . [this] construction of Section 8(d) means that the Respondent was obligated to discuss the Union's pension demand. . . .

By making mandatory the discussion of bargainable subjects not already covered by a contract, the parties to the contract are encouraged to arrive at joint decisions with respect to bargainable matters, that, at least to the party requesting discussion, appear at the time to be of some importance. The Act's policy of "encouraging the practice and procedure of collective bargaining" is consequently furthered. A different construction of Section 8(d) in the circumstances—one that would permit a party to a bargaining contract to avoid discussion when it was sought on subject matters not contained in the contract—would serve, at its best, only to dissipate whatever the good will that had been engendered by the previous bargaining negotiations that led to the execution of a bargaining contract; at its worst, it could bring about the industrial strife and the production interruptions that the policy of the Act also seeks to avert.

The significance of this point cannot be overemphasized. It goes to the heart of our disagreement with our dissenting colleague, *Member Reynolds*. His dissent stresses the need for "contract stability," and asserts that the furtherance of sound collective bargaining requires that the collective bargaining agreement be viewed as fixing, for the term of the contract, all aspects of the employer-employee relationship, and as absolving either party of the obligation to discuss, during that term, even those matters which had never been raised, or discussed in the past. We could hardly take issue with the virtue of "contract stability," at least in the abstract, and we would certainly agree that everyone is better off when, in negotiating an agreement, the parties have been able to foresee what all the future problems may be, to discuss those problems, and either to embody a resolution of them in the contract, or to provide that they may not be raised again during the contract. But we are here concerned with the kind of case in which, for one reason or another, this has *not* been done, and the question is what best effectuates the policies of the Act in *such* a case. . . .

The construction of Section 8(d) adopted by the Board . . . serves also to simplify, and thus to speed, the bargaining process. It eliminates the pressure upon the parties at the time when a contract is being negotiated to raise those subjects that may not then be of controlling importance, but which might in the future assume a more significant status. It also assures to both unions and employers that, if future conditions require some agreement as to matters about which the parties have not sought, or have not been able to obtain agreement, then some discussion of those matters will be forthcoming when necessary.

We cannot believe that Congress was unaware of the foregoing considerations when it amended the Act by inserting Section 8(d), or that it sought, by the provision in question, to freeze the bargaining relationship by eliminating any mandatory discussion that might lead to the addition of new subject matter to an existing contract. What Section 8(d) does do is to reject the pronouncements contained in some pre-1947 Board and court decisions . . . to the effect that the duty to bargain continues even as to those matters upon which the parties have reached agreement and which are set forth in the terms of a written contract. But we believe it does no more. Those bargainable issues which have never been discussed by the parties, and which are in no way treated in the contract, remain matters which both the union and the employer are obliged to discuss at any time.

. . . .

[I]f the parties originally desire to avoid later discussion with respect to matters not specifically covered in the terms of an executed contract, they need only so specify in the terms of the contract itself. Nothing in our construction of Section 8(d) precludes such an agreement, entered into in good faith, from foreclosing future discussion of matters not contained in the agreement.

b. *Chairman Herzog* . . . believes that — unlike the pensions issue — the Respondent was under no obligation to bargain concerning the *group insurance program.*

However, *Members Houston* and *Styles* — a minority of the Board on this issue — are of the further opinion that the considerations discussed above leading to the conclusion that the Respondent was obligated to discuss the matter of pensions, also impel the conclusion that the Respondent was obligated to discuss the Union's group insurance demand. Like pensions, the matter of group insurance benefits is a subject which has been held to be within the area of compulsory bargaining; and like pensions, the Respondent's group insurance program was not mentioned in the terms of the 1948 contract. *Members Houston* and *Styles* therefore believe that so far as the controlling facts are concerned, the ultimate issues presented by the Union's pension and group insurance demands are identical. . . .

Members Houston and *Styles* believe, moreover, that the view adopted by *Chairman Herzog* on the insurance issue is subject to the same basic criticism as is the view of *Member Reynolds* — it exalts "contract stability" over industrial peace; it eliminates mandatory collective bargaining on subjects about which one of the parties *now* wants discussion, and concerning which it may well be willing to take economic action if discussion is denied, solely because the matter has once been discussed in a manner which may warrant an inference that the failure to mention that subject in the contract was part of the bargain. *Members Houston* and *Styles* are constrained to reject the view of *Chairman Herzog* for the further reason that it would establish a rule which is administratively unworkable, and would inject dangerous uncertainty into the process of collective bargaining. Apart from the extremely difficult problems of proof . . . which would constantly confront the Board in cases of this type, the parties to collective bargaining negotiations would always be faced with this question after a subject has been *discussed* — "Have we really *negotiated*, or are we under an obligation to discuss the subject further if asked to?" To this query, the [Board's] rule gives a clear and concise answer: "You are obligated to discuss any bargainable subject upon request unless you have reduced your agreement on that subject to writing or unless you have agreed in writing not to bargain about it during the term of the contract." *Members Houston* and *Styles* would apply that rule without deviation.

[Chairman Herzog's opinion concurring in part and dissenting in part, Member Reynolds's opinion concurring in part and dissenting in part, and Member Murdock's dissenting opinion are omitted.]

Notes

1. In subsequent cases, the Board clarified its splintered decision in *Jacobs Manufacturing* and held that the applicability of the duty to bargain over mandatory subjects not addressed in the collective bargaining agreement should be analyzed using a waiver standard. *See NLRB v. Henry Vogt Mach. Co.*, 718 F.2d 802 (6th Cir. 1983). In this context, "to meet the 'clear and unmistakable' standard, the contract language must be specific, or it must be shown that the matter claimed to have been waived was fully discussed by the parties and that the party alleged to have waived its rights consciously yielded its interest in the matter." *Allison Corp.*, 330 N.L.R.B. 1363, 1365 (2000).

2. Contractual "zipper clauses" are sometimes offered as evidence of waiver. In essence, a zipper clause waives both parties' right to bargain collectively with respect to subjects that are covered by the contract, subjects that are not covered by the contract, or both. See *A-1 King Size Sandwich, supra*, for an example of a zipper clause. The Supreme Court has said that courts and the Board should "not infer from a general contractual provision that the parties intended to waive a statutorily protected right unless the undertaking is 'explicitly stated.'" *Metro. Edison Co. v. NLRB*, 460 U.S. 693, 708 (1983).

Thus, "general zipper clauses"—clauses that do not specify particular subjects to which the waiver applies—waive only the duty to bargain over new subjects that might be added to the agreement. The Board has said that a zipper clause is a "shield" from a refusal to bargain ULP charge, but it cannot be used as a "sword" to unilaterally modify the contract without bargaining. *See Michigan Bell Tel.*, 306 N.L.R.B. 281, 282 (1992). Thus, general clauses would not abrogate an employer's duty to bargain over the unilateral imposition of a particular term without first bargaining with the union. For example, in *Johnson-Bateman Co.*, 295 N.L.R.B. 180 (1989), the Board found that the union had not waived its right to bargain over mandatory employee drug and alcohol testing when it agreed to a general zipper clause or a broad management rights clause; therefore, the employer's unilateral imposition of the testing policy was a ULP.

3. Since the duty to bargain continues during the life of the collective bargaining agreement, the same issues associated with impasse-and-implementation seen in *NLRB v. Katz* and *McClatchy Newspapers* can arise. Of course, "modification" of a collective bargaining contract, even if unilateral and mid-term, is a ULP only when it changes a mandatory term rather than a permissive term. *See Allied Chem. & Alkali Workers of America v. Pittsburgh Plate Glass Co.*, 404 U.S. 157 (1971). However, unlike for bargaining over an initial contract, the Taft-Hartley Act created procedures governing negotiations over mid-term modifications. Section 8(d)(4) limits both parties' (but more likely employers', as a practical matter) ability to unilaterally modify an existing collective bargaining agreement. Modification or termination of a contract is permitted only if the party seeking that step continues the contract in full force without a strike or lock-out for sixty days after providing

notice to the other party or the contract's expiration date. *See NLRB v. Lion Oil Co.,* 352 U.S. 282 (1957) (interpreting §8(d)(4)). This provision introduces the perhaps surprising question of what constitutes a "modification."

———————

In *Milwaukee Spring Div. of Illinois Coil Spring Co.,* 265 N.L.R.B. 206 (1982) ("*Milwaukee Spring I*"), the Board held that the company violated §8(a)(5) by transferring its assembly operations from its unionized Milwaukee Spring facility to its non-union McHenry Spring facility during the term of a collective bargaining agreement and without the union's agreement. The move, which the company justified by pointing to higher labor costs, resulted in layoffs for unit employees. In **Milwaukee Spring Division of Illinois Coil Spring Co.,** 268 N.L.R.B. 601 (1984) ("*Milwaukee Spring II*"), the Board reconsidered and reversed its original decision.

The parties' collective bargaining agreement provided that the company "recognizes the Union as the sole and exclusive collective bargaining agent for all production and maintenance employees in the Company's plant at Milwaukee, Wisconsin." However, the agreement did not contain a "work preservation" clause providing protection of the jobs held by employees in the unionized plant. During the term of the agreement, the employer asked the union to forgo a scheduled wage increase and to grant other contract concessions, including relocating its assembly operations to the nonunionized McHenry facility. The union rejected the proposed reduction in wages and benefits. Thereafter, the company's negotiators submitted a document entitled "Terms Upon Which Milwaukee Assembly Operations Will Be Retained in Milwaukee" to the union. The union rejected these proposals for alternatives to relocation and declined to bargain further over the company's decision to transfer its assembly operations. The company then announced its decision to relocate the Milwaukee assembly operations to the McHenry facility. The parties stipulated that the employer had bargained with the union over the decision to relocate the assembly operations.

The Board held that §8(d)'s impasse procedures governing mid-term contract modifications did not apply to the company's decision. The rules would be relevant only if the Board could

> identify a specific term "contained in" the contract that the Company's decision to relocate modified. In *Milwaukee Spring I,* the Board never specified the contract term that was modified by [the Company's] decision to relocate the assembly operations. The Board's failure to do so is not surprising, for we have searched the contract in vain for a provision requiring bargaining unit work to remain in Milwaukee.

> *Milwaukee Spring I* suggests, however, that the Board may have concluded that [the Company's] relocation decision, because it was motivated by a desire to obtain relief from the Milwaukee contract's labor costs, modified that contract's wage and benefits provisions. We believe this reasoning is flawed. While it is true that the Company proposed modifying the wage

and benefits provisions of the contract, the Union rejected the proposals. Following its failure to obtain the Union's consent, [the Company], in accord with Section 8(d), abandoned the proposals to modify the contract's wage and benefits provisions. Instead, [the Company] decided to transfer the assembly operations to a different plant where different workers (who were not subject to the contract) would perform the work. In short, [the Company] did not disturb the wages and benefits at its Milwaukee facility, and consequently did not violate Section 8(d) by modifying, without the Union's consent, the wage and benefits provisions contained in the contract.

Nor do we find that [the Company's] relocation decision modified the contract's recognition clause....

Language recognizing the Union as the bargaining agent "for all production and maintenance employees in the Company's plant at Milwaukee, Wisconsin," does not state that the functions that the unit performs must remain in Milwaukee. No doubt parties could draft such a clause; indeed, work-preservation clauses are commonplace. It is not for the Board, however, to create an implied work-preservation clause in every American labor agreement based on wage and benefits or recognition provisions, and we expressly decline to do so. 268 N.L.R.B. 601, 602.

The Board then found that "no other term contained in the contract restricts [the Company's] decision-making regarding relocation." *Id.* As a result, the Board concluded that the Company's decision "to relocate did not modify the collective-bargaining agreement in violation of §8(d). In view of the parties' stipulation that [the Company] satisfied its obligation to bargain over the decision, we also conclude that the [Company] did not violate Section 8(a)(5)." *Id.* at 603–04.

The Board's conclusion necessitated overruling several earlier decisions on which it had relied in *Milwaukee Spring I.* The Board offered this rationale:

[The earlier decisions] discourage truthful midterm bargaining over decisions to transfer unit work. Under those decisions, an employer contemplating a plant relocation for several reasons, one of which is labor costs, would be likely to admit only the reasons unrelated to labor costs in order to avoid granting the union veto power over the decision. The union, unaware that labor costs were a factor in the employer's decision, would be unlikely to volunteer wage or other appropriate concessions. Even if the union offered to consider wage concessions, the employer might hesitate to discuss such suggestions for fear that bargaining with the union over the union's proposals would be used as evidence that labor costs had motivated the relocation decision.

We believe our holding today avoids this dilemma and will encourage the realistic and meaningful collective bargaining that the Act contemplates. Under our decision, an employer does not risk giving a union veto power over its decision regarding relocation and should therefore be willing to disclose all factors affecting its decision. Consequently, the union will be in a better position to evaluate whether to make concessions. Because both parties will no longer have an incentive to refrain from frank bargaining, the likelihood that they will be able to resolve their differences is greatly enhanced. *Id.* at 605.

Member Zimmerman dissented on the grounds that Congress must have

> intended the Act to prohibit such midterm relocations where the employer's relocation decision was motivated solely or predominantly by a desire to avoid terms of a collective-bargaining agreement.
>
> . . . .
>
> It is well settled, and my colleagues agree, that an employer acts in derogation of its bargaining obligations under Section 8(d), and thereby violates Section 8(a)(5), when it makes any midterm change in the contractual wage rate even though the employer's action is compelled by economic necessity or the employer has offered to bargain with the union over the change and the union has refused. Obviously then, my colleagues and I would agree that had [the Company] . . . decided to reduce the wages paid to the assembly employees while continuing to perform the assembly work at Milwaukee, [that] decision would violate Section 8(a)(5). [The Company's] decision to relocate the assembly work to McHenry would achieve the same result, albeit indirectly: its employees would continue to perform assembly work but at reduced wage rates. The issue then is whether the fact that Respondent decided to relocate the work takes Respondent's decision outside the proscriptions of Section 8(d), or . . . whether the Act allows Respondent "to achieve by indirection that which [it could not] achieve by direct means under Section 8(d) of the Act." . . .
>
> I find that Respondent's midterm relocation decision was proscribed under Section 8(d) of the Act. Such decision, admittedly motivated solely to avoid the contractual wage rates, was simply an attempt to modify the wage rate provisions in the contract, albeit indirectly. [The Company] voluntarily obligated itself to pay a certain amount of wages to employees performing assembly work during the term of the contract, and it cannot avoid this obligation merely by unilaterally relocating the work to another of its facilities, just as it could not by unilaterally reducing the wage rate. . . .
>
> In my view the determinative factor in deciding whether an employer's midterm relocation decision is proscribed under Section 8(d) is the employer's motive. Where, as here, the decision is controlled by a desire to avoid a contractual term with regard to a mandatory subject of bargaining, such as wages, then the decision is violative under Sections 8(d) and 8(a)(5), and the employer may not implement the decision during the term of the contract without the union's consent. But where the decision is motivated by reasons unrelated to contract avoidance, then the employer may

unilaterally implement its decision after bargaining to impasse with the union.

My colleagues claim that this approach encourages employers to deny that a relocation decision is motivated by a desire to reduce labor costs. I disagree. An employer considering relocation to reduce labor costs has substantial incentive to tell the union why it needs relief and how much relief it needs: relocation will usually involve the transfer of equipment and management personnel, as well as the training of new employees to perform the relocated work. An employer who can avoid these kinds of disruption to production by bargaining with the union for contract concessions will likely do so. . . . . *Id.* at 609–12.

Notes

1. Who has the better argument in *Jacobs Manufacturing*? In *Milwaukee Spring II*? What incentives do the rules eventually adopted by the Board — a waiver standard for subjects discussed during negotiations along with impasse-and-implementation — create for the parties? Does it strengthen the collective bargaining process, or does it encourage strategic behavior? For an economic analysis of these rules, see Keith N. Hylton, *An Economic Theory of the Duty to Bargain*, 83 Geo. L.J. 19 (1994).

2. *Milwaukee Spring II* is relevant only to mandatory subjects of bargaining. As Chapter 10 explains, the parties are not subject to a duty to bargain over permissive subjects. Thus, if a permissive subject is not addressed in the collective bargaining agreement, there is no restraint on the employer's unilateral action. On the other hand, if the permissive subject is addressed in the collective bargaining agreement, there is no duty to bargain and § 8(d)(4)'s provisions do not apply, but the party instituting a unilateral change may be subject to a breach of contract claim brought under § 301. *See Pittsburgh Plate Glass*, supra.

3. Unions are subject to the same obligations under § 8(d) that *Jacobs Manufacturing* and its progeny apply to employers. Although it may seem unlikely or impractical, unions can, in some circumstances, unilaterally alter certain terms of a collective bargaining agreement. For example, a union might require its members to reduce the number of hours they work below the contractually mandated minimum. *See New York Dist. Council No. 9 v. NLRB*, 453 F.2d 783, 787 (2d Cir. 1971), *cert. den.* 408 U.S. 930 (1972).

4. Stewart Schwab used the *Milwaukee Spring* decisions as illustrations of his argument based on Coase's Theorem that collective bargaining rules cannot increase overall economic efficiency or "industrial peace":

> The Coase Theorem . . . predicts that, in the absence of transaction costs, Milwaukee I or II cannot affect job security or the mobility of capital during the contract term. Instead, the parties' preferences determine the contract terms. Recall that, in justifying Milwaukee I, the Board proclaimed that the result promoted industrial peace by fostering contract stability. If

contract stability means that the company should not be able to transfer work during the contract term, the Coase Theorem demonstrates that the Board's decision is irrelevant. Regardless of the Board's holding, the company will stay only if the union values a stay clause more than the company values mobility. . . . Some commentators support Milwaukee II by arguing that it ensures capital mobility and the free flow of commerce, a goal expressed in section 1 of the NLRA. Rubbish, says the Coase Theorem. Again, only the preferences of the parties, not the rule of law, determine whether the company may leave during the contract term. The law simply cannot affect the efficiency of contracts. Schwab, *Collective Bargaining and the Coase Theorem, supra*, at 260–01.

However, Schwab acknowledged that *Milwaukee Spring II* could have the effect of enhancing employers' bargaining strength which would, in the long run, result in less favorable results for unions and the employees they represent. *Id.* at 262–65. Does Schwab's law-and-economics analysis therefore reach the same conclusion advanced by Dannin and Wagar, and Paul Weiler, as discussed above?

B. Mid-Term Bargaining in the Public Sector

In the public sector, rules for mid-term bargaining and zipper clauses are generally the same as under the NLRA. *See, e.g., SEIU Local 73 and Illinois Secretary of State*, 24 PERI ¶ 22 (Ill. LBSP 2008) (mid-term bargaining over mandatory subjects is required if the subjects were neither fully bargained during the course of negotiating the collective bargaining agreement nor the subject of a clause in a collective bargaining agreement, and were not waived by a clear zipper clause); *Teamsters Local 764 v. Snyder County*, 36 PPER ¶ 96 (Pa. LRB 2005) (discussing mid-term bargaining obligations and a zipper clause).

Some variations exist. In ***SERB v. Toledo Dist. Bd. Of Ed.***, 18 OPER ¶ 1645 (OH SERB 2001), the Ohio Board cited a number of public sector jurisdictions that had adopted the rule that "a party cannot modify the existing collective bargaining agreement without negotiation by and agreement of both parties." Such a flat, *per se* rule was, however "too restrictive" in that the "parties must be able to respond to emergency situations that arise during the term of the collective bargaining agreement, especially in situations where they cannot reach agreement after engaging in good-faith negotiations." SERB thus re-stated the rule with two exceptions: "a party cannot modify an existing collective bargaining agreement without the negotiation by and agreement of both parties unless immediate action is required due to (1) exigent circumstances that were unforeseen at the time of negotiations or (2) legislative action taken by a higher-level legislative body after the agreement became effective that requires a change to conform to the statute." For an example of (2), see *SERB v. Queen Lodge No. 69*, 174 Oh. App. 3d 570, *supra*.

As to (1), neither *Toledo Dist. Bd. of Ed.* nor subsequent cases have defined what "exigent circumstances" means. In times of economic difficulties, employers may be tempted to invoke this exception. What should count as "exigent circumstances" such that a public employer can unilaterally modify a collective bargaining agreement? In *Toledo Police Command Officers' Association v. SERB*, 32 OPER ¶ 41 (Oh. App. 2014), an Ohio appellate court upheld a lower court's reversal of SERB's finding of exigent circumstances. The appellate court stressed that exigent circumstances must be *unforeseen* at the time the contract was made. Thus, even though the city was facing significant budget deficits and generally difficult economic circumstances in March 2010 when it unilaterally modified the relevant labor contract, it should have foreseen and indeed did foresee these circumstances when it entered into the contract in August 2009. As of this writing, no Ohio case has, in the end, found unforeseen exigent circumstances. The COVID-19 crisis may raise an opportunity for a public employer to make a successful argument, however. What should the rules and criteria be in this area? *See* Steven Steel, *Fix It or Nix It: Exigent Circumstances in the Public Sector Labor Law Context*, 48 U. TOLEDO L. REV. 387 (2017).

Some other states have similar rules, and some are in statutes, not case law. For example, in 2015, Nevada amended its statute to allow public employers to reopen union contracts if a "fiscal emergency" exists. S.B.168. The bill defines what constitutes a "fiscal emergency": *e.g.*, if the revenue received by the local government employer (from all recurring sources) declined by 5 percent or more from the previous fiscal year. S.B. 168, § 1-4-(a). In Florida, the state Supreme Court interpreted a statute permitting modification of labor contracts in cases of "financial urgency" to require that the employer show that the funds were not available from any other possible reasonable source, and that the parties had completed impasse resolution proceedings and failed to ratify an agreement. The court added that a "financial urgency" is a dire financial condition requiring immediate attention and demanding prompt and decisive action, but not necessarily a financial emergency or bankruptcy. *Headley v. City of Miami*, 215 So. 3d 1 (Fla. 2017).

Note that whatever a state statute provides (or may be interpreted to provide), a unilateral change in a collective bargaining agreement by a public employer might violate the Contract Clause of the U.S. Constitution. Serious financial distress, however, may be a defense to a Contract Clause violation. For a good discussion of this issue, see Stephen Befort, *Unilateral Alteration of Public Sector Collective Bargaining Agreements and the Contract Clause*, 59 BUFF. L. REV.1 (2011).

Toledo Dist. Bd. of Ed. also explained that in Ohio, statutory impasse procedures are not used for mid-term bargaining; rather, the parties are encouraged to specify their own procedures for such bargaining in their contracts. In the absence of such procedures, the employer may implement its last best offer at impasse. Contrast *Teamsters Local 764 v. Snyder County, supra*, in which the Pennsylvania Board rejected the employer's argument that the statutory impasse procedure did not apply to mid-term bargaining. The Pennsylvania Board reasoned that the impasse procedures were the statutory *quid pro quo* for the bar on strikes over mandatory subjects, that this principle applied to mid-term negotiations, and that therefore employers could not implement mid-term proposals on mandatory subjects without agreement or completing statutory impasse procedures. While the latter rule is more common in the public sector, is there something about mid-term bargaining that arguably makes statutory impasse procedures less appropriate?

The issue of mid-term bargaining has been contentious in federal employment. In *National Federation of Federal Employees v. Dept. of Interior*, 526 U.S. 86 (1999), the U.S. Supreme Court resolved a circuit split and held that the federal-sector labor statute, 5 U.S.C. §7101, *et seq.*, delegated to the Federal Labor Relations Authority (FLRA) the power to determine whether and when mid-term bargaining could be required. On remand, the FLRA re-stated its original position: "agencies are obligated to bargain during the term of a collective bargaining agreement on negotiable union proposals concerning matters that are not 'contained in or covered by' the term agreement, unless the union has waived its right to bargain about the subject matter involved." *U.S. Dep't of the Interior & U.S. Geological Survey, Reston, VA*, 56 F.L.R.A. 45, 50 (2000). Later, the FLRA took the position that at least some contract clauses requiring mid-term bargaining and some related types of zipper clauses were permissive, rather than mandatory, subjects of bargaining. The D.C. Circuit remanded an FLRA decision so holding for further consideration and support in *National Treasury Employees Union v. FLRA*, 399 F.3d 334 (D.C. Cir. 2005). On remand, the FLRA held that a proposal for mid-term bargaining was mandatory. *National Treasury Employees Union and United Customs Service*, 64 F.L.R.A. 156 (2009).

Chapter 10

Subjects Included in the Duty to Bargain Collectively

I. Introduction

Even before the Taft-Hartley Act added § 8(d), the Wagner Act specified that certain subjects were expected to be part of any negotiation between unions and employers. Section 9(a) states that worker representatives designated or selected by a majority of employees "shall be the exclusive representatives of all the employees . . . for the purposes of collective bargaining in respect to rates of pay, wages, hours of employment, or other conditions of employment." Section 8(d) echoed this litany when it defined "bargain collectively" to mean to "confer in good faith with respect to wages, hours, and other terms and condition of employment." In short, Congress required employers and unions in the private sector to bargain in good faith regarding these "statutory" or "mandatory" subjects. The preceding chapter described the content of the duty to bargain.

Nonetheless, §§ 8(d) and 9(a) left substantial questions for the Board and courts to answer. Which topics are included within the definition of "wages, hours, and terms and conditions of employment" and, particularly, the seemingly open-ended "terms and conditions of employment"? How would the Board determine which subjects should be included and excluded? In particular, must employers bargain with their employees' representatives over capital allocation decisions—for example, plant closings, plant relocations and subcontracting—that would undeniably affect workers' employment status and/or job security? If not, why not, given the broad statutory language? If so, would that mean that the duty to bargain in good faith makes employees *de facto* co-managers of the business with respect to these types of decisions?

Further, if the parties are not obliged to negotiate over a topic (if it is not a "mandatory subject of bargaining") what obligations, if any, do they have? This is critical, because courts have held that the duty to bargain in good faith, as described in Chapter 9, applies only to mandatory topics. As to other issues, must the parties bargain over them, or may they merely discuss or entirely ignore them? The Act is silent on this question and, therefore, the Board and the courts must decide. Their decisions set the bargaining table for unions and the employers.

If possible, § 10(c) offers even less guidance regarding what remedies are available to enforce the parties' duty to bargain in good faith. The Board is authorized to take "affirmative action." How should the Board exercise this authority to remedy failures to bargain without requiring the parties to "agree" or "concede," as § 8(d) proscribes, or seizing control over the substance of the collective-bargaining agreement, as the previous chapter explained would be anathema?

There are substantial differences between private-sector labor law and public-sector labor law, and among different public-sector laws in different jurisdictions, regarding subjects of bargaining. Public-sector labor laws often, but not always, use the same general structure found in the law of private-sector collective bargaining: distinguishing mandatory subjects from permissive and illegal subjects. But the lists of subjects in those categories often differ, and the scope of bargaining in the public sector is almost always narrower than under the NLRA. In some jurisdictions, the differences are quite stark. For example, as discussed below, most federal employee unions are not permitted to bargain over compensation.

The majority of jurisdictions permitting public-sector collective bargaining do treat as mandatory many of the topics that are mandatory under the NLRA. Still, concerns that certain matters of public policy should be under democratic control and related concepts of inherent governmental functions have prompted decision-makers to restrict the ability of public-sector unions to negotiate over certain issues. These restrictions come from various sources: labor board rulings, court decisions, and explicit statutory language.

II. Categories of Bargaining Subjects in the Private Sector

A. "Mandatory," "Permissive" and "Illegal" Subjects in the Private Sector

NLRB v. Wooster Division of Borg-Warner Corp.

Supreme Court of the United States
356 U.S. 342 (1958)

BURTON, J.

In these cases an employer insisted that its collective-bargaining contract with certain of its employees include: (1) a "ballot" clause calling for a prestrike secret vote of those employees (union and nonunion) as to the employer's last offer, and (2) a "recognition" clause which excluded, as a party to the contract, the International Union which had been certified by the [NLRB] as the employees' exclusive bargaining agent, and substituted for it the agent's uncertified local affiliate. The Board held that the employer's insistence upon either of such clauses amounted to a refusal to bargain, in violation of § 8(a)(5) of the [NLRA], as amended. The issue turns on whether either of these clauses comes within the scope of mandatory collective bargaining as defined in § 8(d) of the Act. For the reasons hereafter stated, we agree with the Board that neither clause comes within that definition. Therefore, we sustain the Board's order directing the employer to cease insisting upon either clause as a condition precedent to accepting any collective-bargaining contract.

Late in 1952, the International Union, United Automobile, Aircraft and Agricultural Implement Workers of America, CIO (here called International) was certified by the Board to the Wooster (Ohio) Division of the Borg-Warner Corporation (here called the company) as the elected representative of an appropriate unit of the company's employees. Shortly thereafter, International chartered Local No. 1239, UAW-CIO (here called the Local). Together the unions presented the company with a comprehensive collective-bargaining agreement. In the "recognition" clause, the unions described themselves as both the "International Union, United Automobile, Aircraft and Agricultural Implement Workers of America and its Local Union No. 1239, U.A.W.-C.I.O. . . . ."

The company submitted a counterproposal which recognized as the sole representative of the employees "Local Union 1239, affiliated with the International Union, United Automobile, Aircraft and Agricultural Implement Workers of America (UAW-CIO)." The unions' negotiators objected because such a clause disregarded the Board's certification of International as the employees' representative. The negotiators declared that the employees would accept no agreement which excluded International as a party.

The company's counterproposal also contained the "ballot" clause. . . . In summary, this clause provided that, as to all nonarbitrable issues (which eventually included modification, amendment or termination of the contract), there would be a 30-day negotiation period after which, before the union could strike, there would have to be a secret ballot taken among all employees in the unit (union and nonunion) on the company's last offer. In the event a majority of the employees rejected the company's last offer, the company would have an opportunity, within 72 hours, of making a new proposal and having a vote on it prior to any strike. The unions' negotiators announced they would not accept this clause "under any conditions."

From the time that the company first proposed these clauses, the employees' representatives thus made it clear that each was wholly unacceptable. The company's representatives made it equally clear that no agreement would be entered into by it unless the agreement contained both clauses. In view of this impasse, there was little further discussion of the clauses, although the parties continued to bargain as to other matters. The company submitted a "package" proposal covering economic issues but made the offer contingent upon the satisfactory settlement of "all other issues. . . ." The "package" included both of the controversial clauses. On March 15, 1953, the unions rejected that proposal and the membership voted to strike on March 20 unless a settlement were reached by then. None was reached and the unions struck. Negotiations, nevertheless, continued. On April 21, the unions asked the company whether the latter would withdraw its demand for the "ballot" and "recognition" clauses if the unions accepted all other pending requirements of the company. The company declined and again insisted upon acceptance of its "package," including both clauses. Finally, on May 5, the Local, upon the recommendation of International, gave in and entered into an agreement containing both controversial clauses.

In the meantime, International had filed charges with the Board claiming that the company, by the above conduct, was guilty of an unfair labor practice within the meaning of § 8(a)(5) of the Act. The trial examiner found no bad faith on either side. However, he found that the company had made it a condition precedent to its acceptance of any agreement that the agreement include both the "ballot" and the "recognition" clauses. For that reason, he recommended that the company be found guilty of a per se unfair labor practice in violation of § 8(a)(5). He reasoned that, because each of the controversial clauses was outside of the scope of mandatory bargaining as defined in § 8(d) of the Act, the company's insistence upon them, against the permissible opposition of the unions, amounted to a refusal to bargain as to the mandatory subjects of collective bargaining. The Board, with two members dissenting, adopted the recommendations of the examiner. . . . [T]he Court of Appeals set aside that portion of the order relating to the "ballot" clause, but upheld the Board's order as to the "recognition" clause.

Because of the importance of the issues and because of alleged conflicts among the Courts of Appeals, we granted the Board's petition for certiorari. . . .

Read together, [sections 8(a)(5) and 8(d)] establish the obligation of the employer and the representative of its employees to bargain with each other in good faith with respect to "wages, hours, and other terms and conditions of employment. . . ." The duty is limited to those subjects, and within that area neither party is legally obligated to yield. *National Labor Relations Board v. American Insurance Co., supra.* As to other matters, however, each party is free to bargain or not to bargain, and to agree or not to agree.

The company's good faith has met the requirements of the statute as to the subjects of mandatory bargaining. But that good faith does not license the employer to refuse to enter into agreements on the ground that they do not include some proposal which is not a mandatory subject of bargaining. We agree with the Board that such conduct is, in substance, a refusal to bargain about the subjects that are within the scope of mandatory bargaining. This does not mean that bargaining is to be confined to the statutory subjects. Each of the two controversial clauses is lawful in itself. Each would be enforceable if agreed to by the unions. But it does not follow that, because the company may propose these clauses, it can lawfully insist upon them as a condition to any agreement.

Since it is lawful to insist upon matters within the scope of mandatory bargaining and unlawful to insist upon matters without, the issue here is whether either the "ballot" clause or the "recognition" clause is a subject within the phrase "wages, hours, and other terms and conditions of employment" which defines mandatory bargaining. The "ballot" clause is not within that definition. It relates only to the procedure to be followed by the employees among themselves before their representative may call a strike or refuse a final offer. It settles no term or condition of employment—it merely calls for an advisory vote of the employees. It is not a partial "no-strike" clause. A "no-strike" clause prohibits the employees from striking during the life of the contract. It regulates the relations between the employer and the employees. See *National Labor Relations Board v. American Insurance Co., supra.* The "ballot" clause, on the other hand, deals only with relations between the employees and their unions. It substantially modifies the collective-bargaining system provided for in the statute by weakening the independence of the "representative" chosen by the employees. It enables the employer, in effect, to deal with its employees rather than with their statutory representative.

The "recognition" clause likewise does not come within the definition of mandatory bargaining. The statute requires the company to bargain with the certified representative of its employees. It is an evasion of that duty to insist that the certified agent not be a party to the collective-bargaining contract. The Act does not prohibit the voluntary addition of a party, but that does not authorize the employer to exclude the certified representative from the contract. . . .

FRANKFURTER, J. joins this opinion insofar as it holds that insistence by the company on the "recognition" clause, in conflict with the provisions of the Act requiring an employer to bargain with the representative of his employees, constituted an unfair labor practice. He agrees with the views of HARLAN, J. regarding the "ballot" clause. The subject matter of that clause is not so clearly outside the reasonable range of industrial bargaining as to establish a refusal to bargain in good faith, and is not prohibited simply because not deemed to be within the rather vague scope of the obligatory provisions of § 8(d).

HARLAN, J., CLARK, J., and WHITTIKER, J., concurring in part and dissenting in part.

I agree that the company's insistence on the "recognition" clause constituted an unfair labor practice, but reach that conclusion by a different route from that taken by the Court. However, in light of the finding below that the company bargained in "good faith," I dissent from the view that its insistence on the "ballot" clause can support the charge of an unfair labor practice. . . .

Preliminarily, I must state that I am unable to grasp a concept of "bargaining" which enables one to "propose" a particular point, but not to "insist" on it as a condition to agreement. The right to bargain becomes illusory if one is not free to press a proposal in good faith to the point of insistence. Surely adoption of so inherently vague and fluid a standard is apt to inhibit the entire bargaining process because of a party's fear that strenuous argument might shade into forbidden insistence and thereby produce a charge of an unfair labor practice. This watered-down notion of "bargaining" which the Court imports into the Act with reference to matters not within the scope of § 8(d) appears as foreign to the labor field as it would be to the commercial world. To me all of this adds up to saying that the Act limits effective "bargaining" to subjects within the three fields referred to in § 8(d), that is "wages, hours, and other terms and conditions of employment," even though the Court expressly disclaims so holding. . . .

I.

At the start, I question the Court's conclusion that the "ballot" clause does not come within the "other terms and conditions of employment" provision of § 8(d). The phrase is inherently vague and prior to this decision has been accorded by the Board and courts an expansive rather than a grudging interpretation. . . . And since a "no-strike" clause is something about which an employer can concededly bargain to the point of insistence, I find it difficult to understand even under the Court's analysis of this problem why the "ballot" clause should not be considered within the area of bargaining described in § 8(d). It affects the employer-employee relationship in much the same way, in that it may determine the timing of strikes or even whether a strike will occur by requiring a vote to ascertain the employees' sentiment prior to the union's decision.

Nonetheless I shall accept the Court's holding that this clause is not a condition of employment, for even though the union would accordingly not be obliged under § 8(d) to bargain over it, in my view it does not follow that the company was prohibited from insisting on its inclusion in the collective bargaining agreement. In other words, I think the clause was a permissible, even if not an obligatory, subject of good faith bargaining. . . .

It must not be forgotten that the Act requires bargaining, not agreement. . . . Here the employer concededly bargained but simply refused to agree until the union would accept what the Court holds would have been a lawful contract provision. It may be that an employer or union, by adamant insistence in good faith upon a provision which is not a statutory subject under § 8(d), does in fact require the other party to bargain over it. But this effect is traceable to the economic power of the employer or union in the circumstances of a given situation and should not affect our construction of the Act. If one thing is clear, it is that the Board was not viewed by Congress as an agency which should exercise its powers to aid a party to collective bargaining which was in an economically disadvantageous position. . . .

. . . I do not deny that there may be instances where unyielding insistence on a particular item may be a relevant consideration in the over-all picture in determining "good faith," for the demands of a party might in the context of a particular industry be so extreme as to constitute some evidence of an unwillingness to bargain. But no such situation is presented in this instance by the "ballot" clause. "No-strike" clauses, and other provisions analogous to the "ballot" clause limiting the right to strike, are hardly novel to labor agreements. . . .

II.

The company's insistence on the "recognition" clause . . . presents a different problem. In my opinion the company's action in this regard did constitute an unfair labor practice since it contravened specific requirements of the Act.

... The Board under §9(c) is authorized to direct a representation election and certify its results. The employer's duty to bargain with the representatives includes not merely the obligation to confer in good faith, but also "... the execution of a written contract incorporating any agreement reached if requested ..." by the employees' representatives. §8(d). I think it hardly debatable that this language must be read to require the company, if so requested, to sign any agreement reached with the same representative with which it is required to bargain. By conditioning agreement upon a change in signatory from the certified exclusive bargaining representative, the company here in effect violated this duty. ...

———————

Thus arose the modern tripartite division of types of subjects of bargaining: mandatory, permissive, and illegal. When a union and an employer sit down to bargain, they can choose to bargain over and reach agreement on "mandatory" and "permissive" subjects. The distinctions between these categories become relevant if the parties are unable to reach agreement and one party objects to the other's bargaining tactics; if one party takes unilateral action on a topic without bargaining to impasse or agreement; or if, after the agreement has been struck, it becomes necessary to enforce the agreement. In the first two circumstances, the Board investigates and adjudicates ULP disputes. In the last, as Chapter 13 explains, courts determine whether the collective-bargaining agreement has been breached. Note here that illegal provisions are not subject to bargaining because they are not enforceable in court regardless of the parties' agreement. *See, e.g., Eddy Potash, Inc.,* 331 N.L.R.B. 552 (2000) (employer committed ULP by insisting to impasse on 12-hour work days prohibited by statute and lease); *see generally United Paperworkers Int'l Union v. Misco, Inc.,* 484 U.S. 29, 42 (1987) (courts will not enforce agreements to do illegal acts).

Categorizing subjects of bargaining helps the Board and courts determine when they may intervene in collective bargaining. If a subject is "mandatory," both parties are subject to liability for a failure to bargain in good faith over the subject; the parties may "insist" on their position during bargaining over the subject without committing a ULP; the parties may use "economic weapons" in support of their bargaining position on the subject without committing a ULP; the parties must disclose information regarding the subject, if requested, or face liability; either party taking unilateral action regarding the subject absent a bargaining impasse or waiver by the other party is subject to liability; and either party unilaterally modifying the portions of the collective-bargaining agreement dealing with the subject absent the other party's consent is subject to liability. In each of these cases, the door is opened to the Board intervening in bargaining subject to judicial review. Does involving the Board and the courts in certain subjects of bargaining, but not others, strengthen the bargaining process? Does it make the Coasean bargaining described in Chapter 9 more likely or less likely? Or are there other values served by this categorization process?

The system endorsed in *Borg-Warner* was not the only possible interpretation of the Act. The Supreme Court could have read §§8(d) and 9(a) as delegating the task of determining which topics fit within "wages, hours, and other terms and conditions of employment" to the bargaining parties rather than the Board and the courts. As Justice Harlan suggests, the parties' comparative economic power could decide which subjects will be bargained over. Arguably, this approach would have been more consistent with the legislative history of § 8(d). As the Supreme Court described in footnote 14 of *First National Maintenance v. NLRB, infra*, Congress rejected a proposal in the House version of the Taft-Hartley Act to limit the subjects of bargaining to "(i) [w]age rates, hours of employment, and work requirements; (ii) procedures and practices relating to discharge, suspension, lay-off, recall, seniority, and discipline, or to promotion, demotion, transfer and assignment within the bargaining unit; (iii) conditions, procedures, and practices governing safety, sanitation, and protection of health at the place of employment; (iv) vacations and leaves of absence; and (v) administrative and procedural provisions relating to the foregoing subjects." *First National Maintenance v. NLRB*, 452 U.S. 666, 675 (1981) (*citing* H.R. 3020 § 2(11), 80th Cong., 1st Sess. (1947)). The rejection of a specific list of mandatory subjects could be interpreted as evidencing congressional intent to create the greatest flexibility for the parties possible.

For scholarly discussions generally consistent with Justice Harlan's approach, see WILLIAM GOULD, AGENDA FOR REFORM: THE FUTURE OF EMPLOYMENT RELATIONSHIPS AND THE LAW, at 170–73 (1993) and JAMES ATLESON, VALUES AND ASSUMPTIONS IN AMERICAN LABOR LAW, at 115–24 (1983). For early critiques of *Borg-Warner*, see Archibald Cox, *Labor Decisions of the Supreme Court at the October Term, 1957*, 44 VA. L. REV. 1057 (1958) and HARRY WELLINGTON, LABOR AND THE LEGAL PROCESS, at 63–90 (1968).

––––––––––––

The Supreme Court has held that mandatory subjects "include[] only issues that settle an aspect of the relationship between the employer and employees." *Allied Chemical & Alkali Workers of America v. Pittsburgh Plate Glass Co.*, 404 U.S. 157 (1971). Topics affecting non-"employees" (*e.g.*, retirees) are not categorically excluded from mandatory status. They are mandatory if they affect the terms and conditions of employment of "employees." 404 U.S. 157, 178; *see, e.g., Mississippi Power Co. v. NLRB*, 284 F.3d 605, 613–15 (5th Cir. 2002) (changes in benefits for "future retirees" are mandatory subjects). These decisions suggest a very broad scope for mandatory subjects.

Ford Motor Co. (Chicago Stamping Plant) v. NLRB, 441 U.S. 488 (1979), also offered an expansive definition of mandatory subjects. The issue was whether prices for cafeteria and vending machine food and beverages provided to its employees by Ford Motor Company in its Chicago Heights plant were a mandatory subject of bargaining. During the course of a longstanding bargaining relationship, the parties had negotiated about certain aspects of the food services, but Ford had always refused to bargain about the prices of food and beverages served in its in-plant facilities. In 1976, Ford notified the union that prices would rise. The union asked to bargain over the prices (as well as seeking information about the food services).

Ford again refused. The Board held that Ford had violated § 8(a)(5) by refusing to bargain over the food prices and ordered Ford both to bargain and to supply the union with the relevant information requested. The Board based its decision on its long-held position, rejected by several courts of appeals, that prices of in-plant food and beverages are generally mandatory bargaining subjects. The Court of Appeals enforced the Board's order, but focused on the lack of reasonable food alternatives for the employees at the Chicago Heights plant.

The Supreme Court agreed with the result the Court of Appeals reached, but did not limit its decision to the availability of food options for these employees. The Court began with a strong presumption of deference to the Board regarding what constitutes a mandatory subject:

> The Board has consistently held that in-plant food prices are among those terms and conditions of employment defined in § 8(d) and about which the employer and union must bargain under §§ 8(a)(5) and 8(b)(3).... Because it is evident that Congress assigned to the Board the primary task of construing these provisions in the course of adjudicating charges of unfair refusals to bargain and because the "classification of bargaining subjects as 'terms or conditions of employment' is a matter concerning which the Board has special expertise," its judgment as to what is a mandatory bargaining subject is entitled to considerable deference. *Id.* at 494–95.

Thus, courts should uphold a Board determination if "its construction of the statute is reasonably defensible, [and] it should not be rejected merely because the courts might prefer another view of the statute." On the other hand, the Board's determination should be overturned if it had "no reasonable basis in law," was "fundamentally inconsistent with the structure of the Act," or regulated in an area Congress had not delegated to it. *Id.* at 498.

The Court concluded that the Board had acted well within its regulatory authority and interpreted the Act reasonably. But the Court also justified the Board's longstanding view that in-plant food prices are a mandatory subject and, in the process, offered something like a test for determining what is a mandatory subject of bargaining:

> It is not suggested by [Ford] that an employee should work a full 8-hour shift without stopping to eat. It reasonably follows that the availability of food during working hours and the conditions under which it is to be consumed are matters of deep concern to workers.... By the same token, where the employer has chosen, apparently in his own interest, to make available a system of in-plant feeding facilities for his employees, the prices at which food is offered and other aspects of this service may reasonably be considered among those subjects about which management and union must bargain. The terms and conditions under which food is available on the job are plainly germane to the "working environment," *Fibreboard Paper Products Corp. v. NLRB, supra,* (STEWART, J., concurring). Furthermore, the

company is not in the business of selling food to its employees, and the establishment of in-plant food prices is not among those "managerial decisions, which lie at the core of entrepreneurial control." *Id.* . . .

Including within § 8(d) the prices of in-plant-supplied food and beverages would also serve the ends of the [NLRA]. "The object of this Act was not to allow governmental regulation of the terms and conditions of employment, but rather to insure that employers and their employees could work together to establish mutually satisfactory conditions. The basic theme of the Act was that through collective bargaining the passions, arguments, and struggles of prior years would be channeled into constructive, open discussions leading, it was hoped, to mutual agreement." *H.K. Porter Co. v. NLRB, infra.* As illustrated by the facts of this case, substantial disputes can arise over the pricing of in-plant-supplied food and beverages. National labor policy contemplates that areas of common dispute between employers and employees be funneled into collective bargaining. The assumption is that this is preferable to allowing recurring disputes to fester outside the negotiation process until strikes or other forms of economic warfare occur. *Id.* at 498–99.

The Court found that the trend of industrial practice, which "is highly relevant in construing the phrase 'terms and conditions of employment,'" supported its conclusion: "many contracts are now being negotiated that contain provisions concerning in-plant food services." *Id.* at 499–500.

Finally, the Court rejected Ford's argument that "in-plant food prices and services are too trivial to qualify as mandatory subjects." *Id.* at 501. While acknowledging the Board's contrary view on this question, the Court also responded that "the bargaining-unit employees in this case considered the matter far from trivial since they pressed an unsuccessful boycott to secure a voice in setting food prices. They evidently felt, and common sense also tells us, that even minor increases in the cost of meals can amount to a substantial sum of money over time." *Id.*

Notes

1. Does *Ford Motor Co.*'s very broad definition of "terms and conditions of employment"—apparently encompassing all "matters of deep concern to workers" and issues that are "plainly germane to the working environment"—place any meaningful limitations on the scope of the mandatory subjects? Is the only effective limitation found in the distinction between issues that are part of the employee-employer relationship and those that are not? *See, e.g., Allied Chemical & Alkali Workers of America v. Pittsburgh Plate Glass Co., supra* (adjustments to employer's contributions to retirees' health insurance are not a mandatory subject of bargaining because retirees are not "employees" under the Act or members of the bargaining unit for which the union was negotiating); *Borg-Warner, supra* (recognition clause is not a mandatory subject of bargaining); *NLRB v. Greensburg Coca-Cola Bottling Co.,* 40 F.3d 669 (3d Cir. 1994) (scope of the bargaining unit is not a mandatory subject

of bargaining); *Star Tribune*, 295 N.L.R.B. 543 (1989) (drug testing of job applicants is not a mandatory subject because applicants are not "employees"). Would the Board and the Court have been better off defining the issue of in-plant prices in *Ford Motor Co.* as a "wages" issue in that higher food prices in the absence of alternatives effects a pay cut for the employees? Would this approach have expanded the definition of "wages" to its breaking point?

2. Chapter 8 discussed voluntary recognition ("card check") agreements between unions and employers in which the employer agrees to recognize the union if it can collect some percentage of authorization cards greater than 50 percent from the employees in one of the employer's units. Is this a mandatory subject? In ***Pall Corp. v. NLRB***, 275 F.3d 116 (D.C. Cir. 2002), the court rejected the Board's categorization of a union proposal requiring the employer to recognize the union if work performed by union members at the employer's first facility were shifted to a second facility. The Board had held that the proposal addressed a mandatory subject. But reading *Pittsburgh Plate Glass, supra*, and *Local 24, Int'l Bhd. of Teamsters v. Oliver*, 358 U.S. 283 (1959) together, the court concluded that it was not sufficient that the transfer of work from the first facility to the second facility would "vitally affect" the bargaining unit members in the first facility. The proposal also had to be a "direct frontal attack" on the work transfer. *Pall Corp., supra*, at 120 (quoting *Oliver*).

The court reasoned that the union's proposal was not a "direct frontal attack" because it neither prohibited the work transfer nor created a disincentive to it by applying the collective-bargaining agreement to the employees in the second facility. *Id.* at 122. In this way, the court distinguished two earlier Board decisions: *Kroger Co.*, 219 N.L.R.B. 388 (1975) (agreement that employees in any acquired stores would become part of the existing bargaining unit was a mandatory subject); and *United Mine Workers*, 231 N.L.R.B. 573 (1977), *enforcement denied*, 639 F.2d 545 (10th Cir. 1980) (employees in any facilities acquired by the employer would be bound by the existing collective-bargaining agreement). *But see Douds v. Int'l Longshoremen's Ass'n*, 241 F.2d 278 (2d Cir. 1957) (union committed a ULP by insisting that collective-bargaining agreement apply to all longshore workers on the east coast of the U.S. rather than only those in the Port of Greater New York and vicinity, even though Board certified union to represent only those workers in the New York port).

3. "Wages" has also evaded easy definition in certain areas. Pay levels and methods of determining pay levels, including whether a worker is paid on a commissioned, salaried or hourly basis, are mandatory subjects. *NLRB v. Pepsi Cola Bottling Co. of Fayetteville, Inc.*, 2001 U.S. App. LEXIS 22594 (4th Cir., Oct. 12, 2001). "Wages" also includes most other forms of compensation like health insurance, pension benefits, vacation pay, profit-sharing plans, and sick pay. "Wages," however, does not include "gratuities." Bonuses that are not linked to seniority or an employee's individual performance, particularly if they are not a longstanding practice, are "gratuities," not "wages," *Exxel/Atmos, Inc. v. NLRB*, 147 F.3d 972, 976–77 (D.C.

Cir. 1998). Bonuses that are tied to other compensation and paid regularly over an extended period of time, if they create a "reasonable expectation," become "wages" and, therefore, a mandatory subject. *Int'l B'hood of Elec. Workers v. NLRB*, 795 F.2d 150, 153 (D.C. Cir. 1986); *NLRB v. Nello Pistoresi & Son, Inc.*, 500 F.2d 399 (9th Cir. 1974); *see generally Radio Television Technical School, Inc. v. NLRB*, 488 F.2d 457 (3d Cir. 1973) (setting forth a five-part test). Unions may also negotiate minimum rates of pay, permitting individual members of the bargaining unit to negotiate individually above that level. Most commonly, this happens in professional sports leagues. In *Wood v. National Basketball Assoc.*, 809 F.2d 954 (2d Cir. 1987), the Second Circuit held that minimum salaries applicable to all players, fringe benefits, minimum aggregate team salaries, and guaranteed revenue sharing were mandatory subjects of bargaining. However, in *Silverman on behalf of NLRB v. Major League Baseball Player Relations Comm.*, 516 F. Supp. 588 (S.D.N.Y. 1981), the district court held that salary levels for individual baseball players above the minimum rate set in the collective-bargaining agreement was a permissive subject because the agreement set only a minimum salary rate and individual players negotiated independently with clubs as to their salary above that rate.

4. Merit pay systems introduce a difficult categorization issue. As a general matter, merit pay increases are mandatory subjects of bargaining. *See, e.g., NLRB v. M.A. Harrison Mfg. Co.*, 682 F.2d 580 (6th Cir. 1982). As discussed in Chapter 9, however, the D.C. Circuit in *McClatchy Newspapers Inc. v. NLRB* upheld the Board's conclusion that an employer could not unilaterally implement a merit pay proposal that vested the employer with unlimited discretion to determine merit pay even though the parties had bargained to impasse. As Note 1 above explained, the general rule is that employers *may* implement terms relating to mandatory subjects after impasse. While the court emphasized the effect of unilateral implementation on the collective-bargaining process, does the D.C. Circuit's decision suggest that discretionary merit pay proposals lacking objective criteria are permissive subjects? The Board has expanded *McClatchy's* application to cases where merit pay systems had some objective criteria, but the courts of appeals have generally rejected these decisions. *See, e.g., Detroit Typographical Union No. 18 v. NLRB*, 216 F.3d 109 (D.C. Cir. 2000); *Edward S. Quirk Co. v. NLRB*, 241 F.3d 41 (1st Cir. 2001).

5. Grievance procedures, arbitration provisions, and subjects related to employee discipline, like polygraph testing and drug and alcohol testing, are all mandatory subjects of bargaining. *Georgia Power Co. v. NLRB*, 427 F.3d 1354 (11th Cir. 2005) (grievance and arbitration procedures); *Colgate-Palmolive Co.*, 323 N.L.R.B. 515 (1997) (polygraph testing and drug and alcohol testing). Similarly, dues checkoff is a mandatory subject, as are union security clauses (discussed in Chapter 14), where those clauses are legal. *See, e.g., Phelps Dodge Specialty Copper Products, Co.*, 337 N.L.R.B. 455 (2002) (employer concedes both these topics are mandatory).

6. Is the recognition clause in *Borg-Warner* "illegal"? The majority states that the Act "requires the company to bargain with the certified representative of its employees. It is an evasion of that duty to insist that the certified agent not be a

party to the collective-bargaining contract." The International was certified by the Board, but the employer refused to recognize it in the collective-bargaining agreement. Did the Court simply ignore this issue to set up the mandatory-permissive distinction, even though it did not fit the actual facts of *Borg-Warner*?

Problem 10.1

National Manufacturing Incorporated (NMI) employs approximately 750 hourly employees and has had a collective-bargaining relationship with the union that represents those employees for 20 years. Jim Johnson is employed in NMI's shipping department. Recently, Johnson was assigned to cleaning duties in NMI's administrative offices. While he was in the second-floor restrooms, he looked up and observed a camera in the air-vent angled toward him. Johnson had never seen any surveillance camera inside the plant prior to that day. He brought it to the attention of three other unit employees, including his union shop steward Bill Williams, who also saw the camera. Williams and Johnson complained to the union's president Willie Wyzard. Wyzard, who also had never before seen any surveillance cameras inside NMI's facility, went to the administrative offices with Williams and Johnson and observed the camera in the air vent. Wyzard immediately called Karen Killingsworth, NMI's Vice-President for Human Resources, to object to the presence of the camera. Wyzard noted in his conversation with Killingsworth that he had attended every negotiating session prior to signing the collective-bargaining agreement between the union and NMI and he had never heard any mention of surveillance cameras. Killingsworth told Wyzard that NMI had reason to believe that theft was in progress and that its general counsel had advised her she could place a camera in the employees' restroom to catch and discipline the perpetrators. Killingsworth also said that, now that the camera had been discovered, it would be immediately taken down. But Killingsworth also told Wyzard that NMI has the absolute right to install internal surveillance cameras whenever it suspects theft of its property. Finally, Killingsworth told Wyzard that all remaining surveillance cameras (around 11 cameras) were in plain view in areas where the thefts were likely to occur. Killingsworth claimed that "the union must have known about these cameras—they are everywhere," and that the union had no reason to complain since all of NMI's employees should know that theft would lead to discipline and/or discharge.

You are the union's counsel. Wyzard seeks your advice about whether the union can force the employer to bargain over the surveillance cameras. What is the best advice you can offer?

B. "The Core of Entrepreneurial Control"

Consider the cases in this section in the context of the deindustrialization in the northeast and midwest (and indeed, in the U.S. as a whole) during in the 1970s and 1980s.

Fibreboard Paper Products Corporation v. NLRB

Supreme Court of the United States
379 U.S. 203 (1964)

WARREN, J.

This case involves the obligation of an employer and the representative of his employees under §§ 8(a)(5), 8(d) and 9(a) of the [NLRA] to "confer in good faith with respect to wages, hours, and other terms and conditions of employment." The primary issue is whether the "contracting out" of work being performed by employees in the bargaining unit is a statutory subject of collective bargaining under those sections.

. . . [The Union] has been the exclusive bargaining representative for a unit of the Company's maintenance employees. In September 1958, the Union and the Company entered the latest of a series of collective bargaining agreements which was to expire on July 31, 1959. The agreement provided for automatic renewal for another year unless one of the contracting parties gave 60 days' notice of a desire to modify or terminate the contract. On May 26, 1959, the Union gave timely notice of its desire to modify the contract and sought to arrange a bargaining session with Company representatives. On June 2, the Company acknowledged receipt of the Union's notice and stated: "We will contact you at a later date regarding a meeting for this purpose." As required by the contract, the Union sent a list of proposed modifications on June 15. Efforts by the Union to schedule a bargaining session met with no success until July 27, four days before the expiration of the contract, when the Company notified the Union of its desire to meet.

The Company, concerned with the high cost of its maintenance operation, had undertaken a study of the possibility of effecting cost savings by engaging an independent contractor to do the maintenance work. At the July 27 meeting, the Company informed the Union that it had determined that substantial savings could be effected by contracting out the work upon expiration of its collective bargaining agreements with the various labor organizations representing its maintenance employees. The Company delivered to the Union representatives a letter which stated in pertinent part: "For some time we have been seriously considering the question of letting out our Emeryville maintenance work to an independent contractor, and have now reached a definite decision to do so effective August 1, 1959. [. . .] In these circumstances, we are sure you will realize that negotiation of a new contract would be pointless. However, if you have any questions, we will be glad to discuss them with you."

After some discussion of the Company's right to enter a contract with a third party to do the work then being performed by employees in the bargaining unit, the meeting concluded with the understanding that the parties would meet again on July 30.

By July 30, the Company had selected Fluor Maintenance, Inc., to do the maintenance work. Fluor had assured the Company that maintenance costs could be curtailed by reducing the work force, decreasing fringe benefits and overtime payments, and by preplanning and scheduling the services to be performed. . . . The contract . . . provided that the Company would pay Fluor the costs of the operation plus a fixed fee of $2,250 per month.

At the July 30 meeting, the Company's representative, in explaining the decision to contract out the maintenance work, remarked that during bargaining negotiations in previous years the Company had endeavored to point out through the use of charts and statistical information "just how expensive and costly our maintenance work was and how it was creating quite a terrific burden upon the Emeryville plant." . . . The Company also distributed a letter stating that "since we will have no employees in the bargaining unit covered by our present Agreement, negotiation of a new or renewed Agreement would appear to us to be pointless." On July 31, the employment of the maintenance employees represented by the Union was terminated and Fluor employees took over. That evening the Union established a picket line at the Company's plant.

[The Union filed unfair labor practice charges against the Company, alleging violations of sections 8(a)(1), 8(a)(3) and 8(a)(5). The Board originally accepted the ALJ's recommendation and dismissed the complaint, but granted petitions for reconsideration. Upon reconsideration, the Board concluded that the Company's motive in contracting out was economic rather than anti-union, but found nonetheless that its failure to bargain violated section 8(a)(5).]

The Board ordered the Company to reinstitute the maintenance operation previously performed by the employees represented by the Union, to reinstate the employees to their former or substantially equivalent positions with back pay computed from the date of the Board's supplemental decision, and to fulfill its statutory obligation to bargain.

On appeal, the Court of Appeals for the District of Columbia Circuit granted the Board's petition for enforcement. Because of the importance of the issues and because of an alleged conflict among the courts of appeals, we granted certiorari. . . .

We agree with the Court of Appeals that, on the facts of this case, the "contracting out" of the work previously performed by members of an existing bargaining unit is a subject about which the [NLRA] requires employers and the representatives of their employees to bargain collectively. . . .

I.

. . . "Read together, [§§ 8(a)(5) and 8(d)] establish the obligation of the employer and the representative of its employees to bargain with each other in good faith with respect to 'wages, hours, and other terms and conditions of employment. . . .' The duty is limited to those subjects, and within that area neither party is legally obligated to yield. *National Labor Relations Board v. American (Nat.) Ins. Co., supra.* As to other matters, however, each party is free to bargain or not to bargain. . . ." *National Labor Relations Board v. Wooster Div. of Borg-Warner Corp., supra.* Because of the limited grant of certiorari, we are concerned here only with whether the subject upon which the employer allegedly refused to bargain—contracting out of plant maintenance work previously performed by employees in the bargaining unit, which the employees were capable of continuing to perform—is covered by the phrase "terms and conditions of employment" within the meaning of § 8(d).

The subject matter of the present dispute is well within the literal meaning of the phrase "terms and conditions of employment." A stipulation with respect to the contracting out of work performed by members of the bargaining unit might appropriately be called a "condition of employment." The words even more plainly cover termination of employment which, as the facts of this case indicate, necessarily results from the contracting out of work performed by members of the established bargaining unit.

The inclusion of "contracting out" within the statutory scope of collective bargaining also seems well designed to effectuate the purposes of the [NLRA]. One of the primary purposes of the Act is to promote the peaceful settlement of industrial disputes by subjecting labor-management controversies to the mediatory influence of negotiation. The Act was framed with an awareness that refusals to confer and negotiate had been one of the most prolific causes of industrial strife. *National Labor Relations Board v. Jones & Laughlin Steel Corp., supra.* To hold, as the Board has done, that contracting out is a mandatory subject of collective bargaining would promote the fundamental purpose of the Act by bringing a problem of vital concern to labor and management within the framework established by Congress as most conducive to industrial peace.

The conclusion that "contracting out" is a statutory subject of collective bargaining is further reinforced by industrial practices in this country. While not determinative, it is appropriate to look to industrial bargaining practices in appraising the propriety of including a particular subject within the scope of mandatory bargaining. *National Labor Relations Board v. American Nat. Ins. Co., supra.* Industrial experience is not only reflective of the interests of labor and management in the subject matter but is also indicative of the amenability of such subjects to the collective bargaining process. Experience illustrates that contracting out in one form or another has been brought, widely and successfully, within the collective bargaining framework. Provisions relating to contracting out exist in numerous collective bargaining agreements, and "(c)ontracting out work is the basis of many grievances; and that type of claim is grist in the mills of the arbitrators." *United Steelworkers of America, etc. v. Warrior & Gulf Nav. Co., infra.* . . .

The facts of the present case illustrate the propriety of submitting the dispute to collective negotiation. The Company's decision to contract out the maintenance work did not alter the Company's basic operation. The maintenance work still had to be performed in the plant. No capital investment was contemplated; the Company merely replaced existing employees with those of an independent contractor to do the same work under similar conditions of employment. Therefore, to require the employer to bargain about the matter would not significantly abridge his freedom to manage the business.

The Company was concerned with the high cost of its maintenance operation. It was induced to contract out the work by assurances from independent contractors that economies could be derived by reducing the work force, decreasing fringe benefits, and eliminating overtime payments. These have long been regarded as matters peculiarly suitable for resolution within the collective bargaining framework, and industrial experience demonstrates that collective negotiation has been highly successful in achieving peaceful accommodation of the conflicting interests. Yet, it is contended that when an employer can effect cost savings in these respects by contracting the work out, there is no need to attempt to achieve similar economies through negotiation with existing employees or to provide them with an opportunity to negotiate a mutually acceptable alternative. The short answer is that, although it is not possible to say whether a satisfactory solution could be reached, national labor policy is founded upon the congressional determination that the chances are good enough to warrant subjecting such issues to the process of collective negotiation.

The appropriateness of the collective bargaining process for resolving such issues was apparently recognized by the Company. In explaining its decision to contract out the maintenance work, the Company pointed out that in the same plant other unions "had joined hands with management in an effort to bring about an economical and efficient operation," but "we had not been able to attain that in our discussions with this particular Local." Accordingly, based on past bargaining experience with this union, the Company unilaterally contracted out the work. While "the Act does not encourage a party to engage in fruitless marathon discussions at the expense of frank statement and support of his position," *National Labor Relations Board v. American Nat. Ins. Co., supra*, it at least demands that the issue be submitted to the mediatory influence of collective negotiations. As the Court of Appeals pointed out, "(i)t is not necessary that it be likely or probable that the union will yield or supply a feasible solution but rather that the union be afforded an opportunity to meet management's legitimate complaints that its maintenance was unduly costly."

We are thus not expanding the scope of mandatory bargaining to hold, as we do now, that the type of "contracting out" involved in this case—the replacement of employees in the existing bargaining unit with those of an independent contractor to do the same work under similar conditions of employment—is a statutory subject of collective bargaining under § 8(d). Our decision need not and does not encompass other forms of "contracting out" or "subcontracting" which arise daily in our complex economy. . . . Affirmed.

Stewart J., Douglas J., and Harlan, J., concurring.

. . . The question posed is whether the particular decision sought to be made unilaterally by the employer in this case is a subject of mandatory collective bargaining within the statutory phrase "terms and conditions of employment." That is all the

Court decides. The Court most assuredly does not decide that every managerial decision which necessarily terminates an individual's employment is subject to the duty to bargain. Nor does the Court decide that subcontracting decisions are as a general matter subject to that duty. The Court holds no more than that this employer's decision to subcontract this work, involving "the replacement of employees in the existing bargaining unit with those of an independent contractor to do the same work under similar conditions of employment," is subject to the duty to bargain collectively. Within the narrow limitations implicit in the specific facts of this case, I agree with the Court's decision. . . .

It is true, as the Court's opinion points out, that industrial experience may be useful in determining the proper scope of the duty to bargain. . . . But data showing that many labor contracts refer to subcontracting or that subcontracting grievances are frequently referred to arbitrators under collective bargaining agreements, while not wholly irrelevant, do not have much real bearing, for such data may indicate no more than that the parties have often considered it mutually advantageous to bargain over these issues on a permissive basis. In any event, the ultimate question is the scope of the duty to bargain defined by the statutory language.

It is important to note that the words of the statute are words of limitation. The [NLRA] does not say that the employer and employees are bound to confer upon any subject which interests either of them; the specification of wages, hours, and other terms and conditions of employment defines a limited category of issues subject to compulsory bargaining. The limiting purpose of the statute's language is made clear by the legislative history of the present Act. As originally passed, the Wagner Act contained no definition of the duty to bargain collectively. In the 1947 revision of the Act, the House bill contained a detailed but limited list of subjects of the duty to bargain, excluding all others. In conference the present language was substituted for the House's detailed specification. While the language thus incorporated in the 1947 legislation as enacted is not so stringent as that contained in the House bill, it nonetheless adopts the same basic approach in seeking to define a limited class of bargainable issues.

The phrase "conditions of employment" is no doubt susceptible of diverse interpretations. At the extreme, the phrase could be construed to apply to any subject which is insisted upon as a prerequisite for continued employment. Such an interpretation, which would in effect place the compulsion of the Board behind any and all bargaining demands, would be contrary to the intent of Congress, as reflected in this legislative history. Yet there are passages in the Court's opinion today which suggest just such an expansive interpretation, for the Court's opinion seems to imply that any issue which may reasonably divide an employer and his employees must be the subject of compulsory collective bargaining.[6]

---

6. The opinion of the Court seems to assume that the only alternative to compulsory collective bargaining is unremitting economic warfare. But to exclude subjects from the ambit of compulsory collective bargaining does not preclude the parties from seeking negotiations about them on

Only a narrower concept of "conditions of employment" will serve the statutory purpose of delineating a limited category of issues which are subject to the duty to bargain collectively. . . . In common parlance, the conditions of a person's employment are most obviously the various physical dimensions of his working environment. What one's hours are to be, what amount of work is expected during those hours, what periods of relief are available, what safety practices are observed, would all seem conditions of one's employment. There are other less tangible but no less important characteristics of a person's employment which might also be deemed "conditions"—most prominently the characteristic involved in this case, the security of one's employment. On one view of the matter, it can be argued that the question whether there is to be a job is not a condition of employment; the question is not one of imposing conditions on employment, but the more fundamental question whether there is to be employment at all. However, it is clear that the Board and the courts have on numerous occasions recognized that union demands for provisions limiting an employer's power to discharge employees are mandatorily bargainable. Thus, freedom from discriminatory discharge, seniority rights, the imposition of a compulsory retirement age, have been recognized as subjects upon which an employer must bargain, although all of these concern the very existence of the employment itself.

While employment security has thus properly been recognized in various circumstances as a condition of employment, it surely does not follow that every decision which may affect job security is a subject of compulsory collective bargaining. Many decisions made by management affect the job security of employees. Decisions concerning the volume and kind of advertising expenditures, product design, the manner of financing, and sales, all may bear upon the security of the workers' jobs. Yet it is hardly conceivable that such decisions so involve "conditions of employment" that they must be negotiated with the employees' bargaining representative.

In many of these areas the impact of a particular management decision upon job security may be extremely indirect and uncertain, and this alone may be sufficient reason to conclude that such decisions are not "with respect to . . . conditions of employment." Yet there are other areas where decisions by management may quite clearly imperil job security, or indeed terminate employment entirely. An enterprise may decide to invest in labor-saving machinery. Another may resolve to liquidate its assets and go out of business. Nothing the Court holds today should be understood as imposing a duty to bargain collectively regarding such managerial decisions, which lie at the core of entrepreneurial control. Decisions concerning the commitment of investment capital and the basic scope of the enterprise are not in themselves primarily about conditions of employment, though the effect of the decision may be necessarily to terminate employment. If, as I think clear, the purpose of § 8(d) is to describe a limited area subject to the duty of collective bargaining, those

---

a permissive basis. And there are limitations upon the use of economic force to compel concession upon subjects which are only permissively bargainable.

management decisions which are fundamental to the basic direction of a corporate enterprise or which impinge only indirectly upon employment security should be excluded from that area.

Applying these concepts to the case at hand, I do not believe that an employer's subcontracting practices are, as a general matter, in themselves conditions of employment. Upon any definition of the statutory terms short of the most expansive, such practices are not conditions—tangible or intangible—of any person's employment. The question remains whether this particular kind of subcontracting decision comes within the employer's duty to bargain. On the facts of this case, I join the Court's judgment, because all that is involved is the substitution of one group of workers for another to perform the same task in the same plant under the ultimate control of the same employer. . . .

This kind of subcontracting falls short of such larger entrepreneurial questions as what shall be produced, how capital shall be invested in fixed assets, or what the basic scope of the enterprise shall be. In my view, the Court's decision in this case has nothing to do with whether any aspects of those larger issues could under any circumstances be considered subjects of compulsory collective bargaining under the present law. . . .

First National Maintenance Corporation v. NLRB

Supreme Court of the United States
452 U.S. 666 (1981)

Blackmun, J.

Must an employer, under its duty to bargain in good faith "with respect to wages, hours, and other terms and conditions of employment," §§ 8(d) and 8(a)(5) of the National Labor Relations Act (Act), as amended, negotiate with the certified representative of its employees over its decision to close a part of its business? In this case, the National Labor Relations Board (Board) imposed such a duty on petitioner with respect to its decision to terminate a contract with a customer, and the United States Court of Appeals, although differing over the appropriate rationale, enforced its order.

I

Petitioner, First National Maintenance Corporation (FNM), is a New York corporation engaged in the business of providing housekeeping, cleaning, maintenance, and related services for commercial customers in the New York City area. It supplies each of its customers, at the customer's premises, contracted-for labor force and supervision in return for reimbursement of its labor costs (gross salaries, FICA and FUTA taxes, and insurance) and payment of a set fee. It contracts for and hires personnel separately for each customer, and it does not transfer employees between locations.

During the spring of 1977, petitioner was performing maintenance work for the Greenpark Care Center, a nursing home in Brooklyn. Its written agreement dated April 28, 1976, with Greenpark specified that Greenpark "shall furnish all tools, equipment [*sic*], materials, and supplies, and would pay petitioner weekly "the sum of five hundred dollars plus the gross weekly payroll and fringe benefits." Its weekly fee, however, had been reduced to $250 effective November 1, 1976. . . . Petitioner employed approximately 35 workers in its Greenpark operation.

Petitioner's business relationship with Greenpark, seemingly, was not very remunerative or smooth. In March 1977, Greenpark gave petitioner the 30 days' written notice of cancellation specified by the contract, because of "lack of efficiency." This cancellation did not become effective, for FNM's work continued after the expiration of that 30-day period. Petitioner, however, became aware that it was losing money at Greenpark. On June 30, by telephone, it asked that its weekly fee be restored at the $500 figure and, on July 6, it informed Greenpark in writing that it would discontinue its operations there on August 1 unless the increase were granted. By telegram on July 25, petitioner gave final notice of termination.

While FNM was experiencing these difficulties, District 1199, National Union of Hospital and Health Care Employees, Retail, Wholesale and Department Store Union, AFL-CIO (union), was conducting an organization campaign among petitioner's Greenpark employees. On March 31, 1977, at a Board-conducted election, a majority of the employees selected the union as their bargaining agent. On July 12, the union's vice president, Edward Wecker, wrote petitioner, notifying it of the certification and of the union's right to bargain, and stating: "We look forward to meeting with you or your representative for that purpose. Please advise when it will be convenient." Petitioner neither responded nor sought to consult with the union.

On July 28, petitioner notified its Greenpark employees that they would be discharged three days later. Wecker immediately telephoned petitioner's secretary-treasurer, Leonard Marsh, to request a delay for the purpose of bargaining. Marsh refused the offer to bargain and told Wecker that the termination of the Greenpark operation was purely a matter of money, and final, and that the 30 days' notice provision of the Greenpark contract made staying on beyond August 1 prohibitively expensive. . . . With nothing but perfunctory further discussion, petitioner on July 31 discontinued its Greenpark operation and discharged the employees.

[The union filed a ULP charge against FNM alleging violations of §§ 8(a)(1) and 8(a)(5). The Board upheld the ALJ's findings that the employer had committed ULPs. The Board required FNM, if it agreed to resume its Greenpark operations, to offer the terminated employees reinstatement to their former jobs or substantial equivalents. If agreement was not reached, FNM was ordered to offer the employees equivalent positions at its other operations.]

The United States Court of Appeals for the Second Circuit, with one judge dissenting in part, enforced the Board's order, although it adopted an analysis different from that espoused by the Board. The Court of Appeals reasoned that no *per se* rule could be formulated to govern an employer's decision to close part of its business. Rather, the court said, § 8(d) creates a *presumption* in favor of mandatory bargaining over such a decision, a presumption that is rebuttable "by showing that the purposes of the statute would not be furthered by imposition of a duty to bargain," for example, by demonstrating that "bargaining over the decision would be futile," or that the decision was due to "emergency financial circumstances," or that the "custom of the industry, shown by the absence of such an obligation from typical collective bargaining agreements, is not to bargain over such decisions." ...

II

A fundamental aim of the [Act] is the establishment and maintenance of industrial peace to preserve the flow of interstate commerce. *NLRB v. Jones & Laughlin Steel Corp., supra.* Central to achievement of this purpose is the promotion of collective bargaining as a method of defusing and channeling conflict between labor and management. § 1 of the Act, as amended. Congress ensured that collective bargaining would go forward by creating the Board and giving it the power to condemn as unfair labor practices certain conduct by unions and employers that it deemed deleterious to the process, including the refusal "to bargain collectively." §§ 3 and 8.

Although parties are free to bargain about any legal subject, Congress has limited the mandate or duty to bargain to matters of "wages, hours, and other terms and conditions of employment." A unilateral change as to a subject within this category violates the statutory duty to bargain and is subject to the Board's remedial order. *NLRB v. Katz, supra.* Conversely, both employer and union may bargain to impasse over these matters and use the economic weapons at their disposal to attempt to secure their respective aims. *NLRB v. American National Ins. Co., supra.* Congress deliberately left the words "wages, hours, and other terms and conditions of employment" without further definition, for it did not intend to deprive the Board of the power further to define those terms in light of specific industrial practices.

Nonetheless, in establishing what issues must be submitted to the process of bargaining, Congress had no expectation that the elected union representative would become an equal partner in the running of the business enterprise in which the union's members are employed. Despite the deliberate open-endedness of the statutory language, there is an undeniable limit to the subjects about which bargaining must take place:

> Section 8(a) of the Act, of course, does not immutably fix a list of subjects for mandatory bargaining. ... But it does establish a limitation against which proposed topics must be measured. In general terms, the limitation includes only issues that settle an aspect of the relationship between the employer and the employees. *Chemical & Alkali Workers v. Pittsburgh Plate Glass Co., supra.*

Some management decisions, such as choice of advertising and promotion, product type and design, and financing arrangements, have only an indirect and attenuated impact on the employment relationship. See *Fibreboard, supra* (Stewart, J., concurring). Other management decisions, such as the order of succession of layoffs and recalls, production quotas, and work rules, are almost exclusively "an aspect of the relationship" between employer and employee. *Chemical Workers, supra.* The present case concerns a third type of management decision, one that had a direct impact on employment, since jobs were inexorably eliminated by the termination, but had as its focus only the economic profitability of the contract with Greenpark, a concern under these facts wholly apart from the employment relationship. This decision, involving a change in the scope and direction of the enterprise, is akin to the decision whether to be in business at all, "not in [itself] primarily about conditions of employment, though the effect of the decision may be necessarily to terminate employment." *Fibreboard, supra* (Stewart, J., concurring). Cf. *Textile Workers v. Darlington Co., supra* ("an employer has the absolute right to terminate his entire business for any reason he pleases"). At the same time, this decision touches on a matter of central and pressing concern to the union and its member employees: the possibility of continued employment and the retention of the employees' very jobs.

Petitioner contends it had no duty to bargain about its decision to terminate its operations at Greenpark. This contention requires that we determine whether the decision itself should be considered part of petitioner's retained freedom to manage its affairs unrelated to employment.[15] The aim of labeling a matter a mandatory subject of bargaining, rather than simply permitting, but not requiring, bargaining, is to "promote the fundamental purpose of the Act by bringing a problem of vital concern to labor and management within the framework established by Congress as most conducive to industrial peace," *Fibreboard, supra.* The concept of mandatory bargaining is premised on the belief that collective discussions backed by the parties' economic weapons will result in decisions that are better for both management and labor and for society as a whole. *Ford Motor Co., supra*; *Borg-Warner, supra.* This will be true, however, only if the subject proposed for discussion is amenable to resolution through the bargaining process. Management must be free from the constraints of the bargaining process to the extent essential for the running of a profitable business. It also must have some degree of certainty beforehand as to when it may proceed to reach decisions without fear of later evaluations labeling its conduct an unfair labor practice. Congress did not explicitly state what issues of mutual concern to union and management it intended to exclude from mandatory bargaining. Nonetheless, in view of an employer's need for unencumbered decision-making, bargaining over management decisions that have a substantial impact on the continued availability of employment should be required only if the benefit, for labor-management relations and the collective-bargaining process, outweighs the burden placed on the conduct of the business.

---

15. There is no doubt that petitioner was under a duty to bargain about the results or effects of its decision to stop the work at Greenpark, or that it violated that duty. Petitioner consented to enforcement of the Board's order concerning bargaining over the effects of the closing and has reached agreement with the union on severance pay.

The Court in *Fibreboard* implicitly engaged in this analysis with regard to a decision to subcontract for maintenance work previously done by unit employees. Holding the employer's decision a subject of mandatory bargaining, the Court relied not only on the "literal meaning" of the statutory words, but also reasoned:

> The Company's decision to contract out the maintenance work did not alter the Company's basic operation. The maintenance work still had to be performed in the plant. No capital investment was contemplated; the Company merely replaced existing employees with those of an independent contractor to do the same work under similar conditions of employment. Therefore, to require the employer to bargain about the matter would not significantly abridge his freedom to manage the business.

The Court also emphasized that a desire to reduce labor costs, which it considered a matter "peculiarly suitable for resolution within the collective bargaining framework," was at the base of the employer's decision to subcontract....

The prevalence of bargaining over "contracting out" as a matter of industrial practice generally was taken as further proof of the "amenability of such subjects to the collective bargaining process."

With this approach in mind, we turn to the specific issue at hand: an economically motivated decision to shut down part of a business.

III

Both union and management regard control of the decision to shut down an operation with the utmost seriousness. As has been noted, however, the Act is not intended to serve either party's individual interest, but to foster in a neutral manner a system in which the conflict between these interests may be resolved. It seems particularly important, therefore, to consider whether requiring bargaining over this sort of decision will advance the neutral purposes of the Act.

A union's interest in participating in the decision to close a particular facility or part of an employer's operations springs from its legitimate concern over job security. The Court has observed: "The words of [§ 8(d)] . . . plainly cover termination of employment which . . . necessarily results" from closing an operation. *Fibreboard, supra.* The union's practical purpose in participating, however, will be largely uniform: it will seek to delay or halt the closing. No doubt it will be impelled, in seeking these ends, to offer concessions, information, and alternatives that might be helpful to management or forestall or prevent the termination of jobs. It is unlikely, however, that requiring bargaining over the decision itself, as well as its effects, will augment this flow of information and suggestions. There is no dispute that the union must be given a significant opportunity to bargain about these matters of job security as part of the "effects" bargaining mandated by § 8(a)(5). And, under § 8(a)(5), bargaining over the effects of a decision must be conducted in a meaningful manner and at a meaningful time, and the Board may impose sanctions to insure its adequacy. A union, by pursuing such bargaining rights, may achieve valuable concessions from an employer engaged in a partial closing. It also may secure in contract negotiations provisions implementing rights to notice, information, and fair bargaining. . . .

Management's interest in whether it should discuss a decision of this kind is much more complex and varies with the particular circumstances. If labor costs are an important factor in a failing operation and the decision to close, management will have an incentive to confer voluntarily with the union to seek concessions that may make continuing the business profitable. At other times, management may have great need for speed, flexibility, and secrecy in meeting business opportunities and exigencies. It may face significant tax or securities consequences that hinge on confidentiality, the timing of a plant closing, or a reorganization of the corporate structure. The publicity incident to the normal process of bargaining may injure the possibility of a successful transition or increase the economic damage to the business. The employer also may have no feasible alternative to the closing, and even good-faith bargaining over it may both be futile and cause the employer additional loss.

There is an important difference, also, between permitted bargaining and mandated bargaining. Labeling this type of decision mandatory could afford a union a powerful tool for achieving delay, a power that might be used to thwart management's intentions in a manner unrelated to any feasible solution the union might propose. . . .

While evidence of current labor practice is only an indication of what is feasible through collective bargaining, and not a binding guide, see *Chemical Workers, supra*, that evidence supports the apparent imbalance weighing against mandatory bargaining. We note that provisions giving unions a right to participate in the decisionmaking process concerning alteration of the scope of an enterprise appear to be relatively rare. Provisions concerning notice and "effects" bargaining are more prevalent. . . .

We conclude that the harm likely to be done to an employer's need to operate freely in deciding whether to shut down part of its business purely for economic reasons outweighs the incremental benefit that might be gained through the union's participation in making the decision,[22] and we hold that the decision itself is *not* part of § 8(d)'s "terms and conditions," over which Congress has mandated bargaining. . . .

The judgment of the Court of Appeals, accordingly, is reversed, and the case is remanded to that court for further proceedings consistent with this opinion.

Brennan, J. and Marshall, J., dissenting.

. . . As this Court has noted, the words "terms and conditions of employment" plainly cover termination of employment resulting from a management decision to close an operation. *Fibreboard Paper Products Corp. v. NLRB, supra.* As the Court today admits, the decision to close an operation "touches on a matter of central and pressing concern to the union and its member employees." Moreover, as the Court today further concedes, Congress deliberately left the words "terms and conditions

---

22. In this opinion we of course intimate no view as to other types of management decisions, such as plant relocations, sales, other kinds of subcontracting, automation, etc., which are to be considered on their particular facts. . . .

of employment" indefinite, so that the NLRB would be able to give content to those terms in light of changing industrial conditions. In the exercise of its congressionally delegated authority and accumulated expertise, the Board has determined that an employer's decision to close part of its operations affects the "terms and conditions of employment" within the meaning of the Act, and is thus a mandatory subject for collective bargaining. Nonetheless, the Court today declines to defer to the Board's decision on this sensitive question of industrial relations, and on the basis of pure speculation reverses the judgment of the Board and of the Court of Appeals. I respectfully dissent.

The Court bases its decision on a balancing test. It states that "bargaining over management decisions that have a substantial impact on the continued availability of employment should be required only if the benefit, for labor-management relations and the collective-bargaining process, outweighs the burden placed on the conduct of the business." I cannot agree with this test, because it takes into account only the interests of *management*; it fails to consider the legitimate employment interests of the workers and their union. . . . This one-sided approach hardly serves "to foster in a neutral manner" a system for resolution of these serious, two-sided controversies.

Even if the Court's statement of the test were accurate, I could not join in its application, which is based solely on speculation. Apparently, the Court concludes that the benefit to labor-management relations and the collective-bargaining process from negotiation over partial closings is minimal, but it provides no evidence to that effect. The Court acknowledges that the union might be able to offer concessions, information, and alternatives that might obviate or forestall the closing, but it then asserts that "[i]t is unlikely, however, that requiring bargaining over the decision . . . will augment this flow of information and suggestions." Recent experience, however, suggests the contrary. Most conspicuous, perhaps, were the negotiations between Chrysler Corporation and the United Auto Workers, which led to significant adjustments in compensation and benefits, contributing to Chrysler's ability to remain afloat. Even where labor costs are not the direct cause of a company's financial difficulties, employee concessions can often enable the company to continue in operation—if the employees have the opportunity to offer such concessions.*

The Court further presumes that management's need for "speed, flexibility, and secrecy" in making partial closing decisions would be frustrated by a requirement to bargain. In some cases the Court might be correct. In others, however, the decision will be made openly and deliberately, and considerations of "speed, flexibility, and secrecy" will be inapposite. Indeed, in view of management's admitted duty to bargain

---

* Indeed, in this case, the Court of Appeals found: "On the record, . . . there is sufficient reason to believe that, given the opportunity, the union might have made concessions, by accepting reduction in wages or benefits (take-backs) or a reduction in the work force, which would in part or in whole have enabled Greenpark to give FNM an increased management fee. At least, if FNM had bargained over its decision to close, that possibility would have been tested, and management would still have been free to close the Greenpark operation if bargaining did not produce a solution."

over the effects of a closing, it is difficult to understand why additional bargaining over the closing itself would necessarily unduly delay or publicize the decision.

I am not in a position to judge whether mandatory bargaining over partial closings *in all cases* is consistent with our national labor policy, and neither is the Court. The primary responsibility to determine the scope of the statutory duty to bargain has been entrusted to the NLRB, which should not be reversed by the courts merely because they might prefer another view of the statute. . . .

––––––––––

First National Maintenance created a quandary for the Board and courts of appeals. It did not overturn *Fibreboard*; however, it relied heavily on the concurrence in *Fibreboard* rather than the majority decision in that case. And, of course, the two decisions reached arguably inconsistent results. Confusion prevailed for some time as the Board and the courts attempted to sort out how and whether to reconcile *First National Maintenance* and *Fibreboard*. In *Whitehead Bros. Co.*, 263 N.L.R.B. 895 (1982), and *Bob's Big Boy Family Restaurants*, 264 N.L.R.B. 1369 (1982), the Board respectively characterized the closing of an in-house trucking operation and a shrimp processing division as "subcontracting" and required the employers to bargain over those decisions. In *Otis Elevator Co.*, 269 N.L.R.B. 891 (1984) ("*Otis II*"), the Board concluded that the employer's decision to consolidate and relocate certain operations was not a mandatory subject by focusing almost exclusively on whether the decision was motivated by labor costs. In *Arrow Automotive, Inc.*, 284 N.L.R.B. 487 (1987), the Board followed its own rule from *Otis II* and held that labor costs were the "major reason" for a decision to close a plant and consolidate work; therefore, the employer committed a ULP by failing to bargain before implementing the decision. But the Fourth Circuit reversed the Board's decision, rejected the *Otis II* approach to reconciling *Fibreboard* and *First National Maintenance*, and chastised the Board for giving insufficient respect to *First National Maintenance*. The Board then reentered the fray, seeking to clarify this area.

United Food & Commercial Workers, Local 150-A v. NLRB (Dubuque Packing)

U.S. Court of Appeals for the District of Columbia
1 F.3d 24 (1993)

Buckley, J.

Dubuque Packing Company petitions for review of [an NLRB] order holding that it committed unfair labor practices by breaching its duty to bargain with its union regarding the relocation of its "hog kill and cut" operations. We hold that the new standard adopted by the Board for evaluating such claims is an acceptable reading of the [NLRA] and Supreme Court precedents; that the Board's finding that Dubuque owed a duty to bargain was supported by substantial evidence; and that the Board properly applied its new test retroactively to the facts of this case. Hence, we deny Dubuque's petition and enforce the Board's remedial order. . . .

I. Background

A. Facts and Procedural History

... Beginning about 1977, the Dubuque Packing Company, a processor and packager of beef and pork, began losing money at its Dubuque, Iowa, home plant. In 1978, Dubuque won an agreement from the plant's workers, who were represented by the United Food and Commercial Workers International Union ("UFCW"), requiring the workers to produce at higher rates in return for a one-time cash payment. In August 1980, Dubuque extracted concessions worth approximately $5 million per annum in return for a pledge that it would not ask for further concessions before the September 1, 1982, expiration of the union contract then in effect. In March 1981, however, it again requested concessions, this time in the form of additional productivity increases in its hog kill department.

On March 30, 1981, the events at issue here began to unfold. On that date, Dubuque gave six-months' notice, as required by its labor contract, of its intention to close its hog kill and cut operations at Dubuque. Various maneuvers between the company and the UFCW ensued, culminating in the union's rejection of a wage freeze aimed at keeping the Dubuque hog kill and cut operation open. The following day, June 10, 1981, the company announced that it was considering relocating—rather than closing—its hog kill and cut department, and that it was also considering relocating up to 900 Dubuque plant pork processing jobs. The UFCW responded by requesting detailed financial information from Dubuque, which the company refused to provide. Dubuque then advised its employees in writing that they could save their jobs by approving its wage freeze proposal. On June 28, 1981, the wage freeze was resubmitted to the workers for a vote, accompanied by the union leadership's recommendation that it be rejected until Dubuque opened its books. The workers voted overwhelmingly with their union and against the company. Three days later, Dubuque informed the union that its decision to close the hog kill and cut department was "irrevocable."

Over the next few months, Dubuque and the UFCW continued to negotiate over Dubuque's proposed relocation of its pork processing operations. On October 1, 1981, Dubuque opened a hog kill and cut operation at its newly acquired Rochelle, Illinois, plant and, two days later, eliminated approximately 530 hog kill and cut jobs at the Dubuque plant. On October 19, 1981, an agreement was signed granting wage concessions for the remaining workers at the Dubuque plant in return for the company's agreement to keep the 900 pork processing jobs in Dubuque and to extend the current labor agreement. By early 1982, however, the company's hope of obtaining new financing had collapsed, taking with it Dubuque's prospects for remaining in business at Dubuque and Rochelle. Both plants were closed and sold on October 15, 1982.

On June 26, 1981, and August 7, 1981, the UFCW filed unfair labor practice complaints with the Board. It claimed that Dubuque had refused to bargain in good faith as to both the consummated relocation and the proposed one, objecting especially to the company's alleged duplicity and its refusal to disclose financial data. On June 17,

1985, an administrative law judge ("ALJ") rendered a decision on these complaints. The ALJ suggested that Dubuque's conduct may indeed have fallen below the standards of good-faith bargaining, but he nevertheless held that Dubuque committed no unfair labor practice because it was under no duty to negotiate over its decision to relocate. Over two years later, the NLRB summarily affirmed the ALJ, adopting his findings and opinion.

On review of the Board's decision, we remanded the case, declaring that the Board's opinion had been inadequately explained. At the time, the NLRB had no single standard for determining whether companies were bound to bargain with their unions over plant relocations. . . . [W]e held that, given the confusion of the law, we could not trace the Board's reasoning to ensure that its action was not arbitrary. We strongly advised, but did not demand, that a single majority rule be adopted by the Board.

On remand, the Board unanimously approved a new test. . . . It applied its new test to the relocation of the Dubuque hog kill and cut operation and found that a duty to bargain had existed and had been breached. As a remedy, it ordered Dubuque to pay back wages to all employees terminated as a result of the relocation, from the date of their termination to October 15, 1982, the date operations ceased at Dubuque and Rochelle. The Board, however, declined to apply its new test to the threatened relocation of Dubuque's pork processing operations, finding that issue to be beyond the scope of this court's remand instructions. . . .

B. Legal Framework

The critical question in this litigation is whether Dubuque's relocation of its hog kill and cut operation constitutes a mandatory subject of bargaining under the [NLRA]. Although parties to collective bargaining agreements are free to bargain about any legal subject, Congress has imposed on employers and unions "a mandate or duty" to bargain about certain issues. *First National Maintenance Corp. v. NLRB, supra.* Any "unilateral change as to a subject within this category violates the statutory duty to bargain and is subject to the Board's remedial order." *Id.*

. . . The narrow issue in this case is whether a plant relocation such as the one executed by Dubuque constitutes a "term[ ] [or] condition[ ] of employment" under section 8(d) of Act; if it does, then Dubuque's failure to bargain in good faith over the relocation constitutes an unfair labor practice under section 8(a)(5). The two critical Supreme Court decisions interpreting "terms and conditions of employment" for these purposes are *First National Maintenance Corp. v. NLRB, supra*, which held that an employer's decision to close a part of its business is not a mandatory subject of bargaining, and *Fibreboard Paper Products Corp. v. NLRB, supra*, which held that the replacement of union labor with subcontracted workers is.

II. Discussion

. . . 1. The Legality of the Board's New Test

Dubuque claims the Board erred in finding that its relocation involved a "term[] [or] condition[] of employment" subject to mandatory bargaining under the NLRA.

In particular, it argues that the Board's new test represents an impermissible reading of the Supreme Court's decision in *First National Maintenance*. In reviewing such claims, we will respect the Board's "policy choices," so long as "its interpretation of what the Act requires is reasonable, in light of the purposes of the Act and the controlling precedent of the Supreme Court." . . .

In these proceedings, the Board set out to enunciate a new legal test "guided by the principles set forth in *First National Maintenance*." It adopted the following standard for determining whether "a decision to relocate [bargaining] unit work" is a mandatory subject of bargaining:

> Initially, the burden is on the [NLRB] General Counsel to establish that the employer's decision involved a relocation of unit work unaccompanied by a basic change in the nature of the employer's operation. If the General Counsel successfully carries his burden in this regard, he will have established prima facie that the employer's relocation decision is a mandatory subject of bargaining. At this juncture, the employer may produce evidence rebutting the prima facie case by establishing that the work performed at the new location varies significantly from the work performed at the former plant, establishing that the work performed at the former plant is to be discontinued entirely and not moved to the new location, or establishing that the employer's decision involves a change in the scope and direction of the enterprise. Alternatively, the employer may proffer a defense to show by a preponderance of the evidence: (1) that labor costs (direct and/or indirect) were not a factor in the decision, or (2) that even if labor costs were a factor in the decision, the union could not have offered labor cost concessions that could have changed the employer's decision to relocate.

. . . The only question facing us . . . is whether the Board could properly find a duty to bargain where all the elements included in its test have been proved.

The Board's test involves three distinct layers of analysis. First, the test recognizes a category of decisions lying "at the core of entrepreneurial control," *Fibreboard, supra* (Stewart, J., concurring), in which employers may unilaterally take action. Specifically, the test exempts from the duty to bargain relocations involving (1) "a basic change in the nature of the employer's operation," (2) "a change in the scope and direction of the enterprise," (3) situations in which "the work performed at the new location varies significantly from the work performed at the former plant," or (4) situations in which "the work performed at the former plant is to be discontinued entirely and not moved to the new location."

This language would appear broad enough to cover key entrepreneurial decisions such as setting the scale (e.g., the quantity of product produced) and scope (e.g., the type of product produced) of the employer's operations, and determining the basic method of production. Moreover, as to these issues, the Board's test requires an analysis based on the objective differences between the employer's old and new operations. It asks whether various types of "basic change," "change," "vari[ance]," or "discontinu[ance]" were involved in the relocation. Where such objective differences appear, an entrepreneurial decision is deemed to have been taken, and the employer is permitted to relocate without negotiating.

The second layer of the Board's analysis is a subjective one. . . . Under this heading, the relevant question is whether "labor costs (direct and/or indirect) were . . . a factor" in the employer's relocation decision. As illustrated by the Board, this analysis will distinguish relocations motivated by labor costs from those motivated by other perceived advantages of the new location.

The third layer includes a futility provision. As we shall see below, the Board permits an employer to relocate without negotiating where its union either would not or could not offer sufficient concessions to change its decision. Also, the Board has pledged to consider circumstances such as the need to implement a relocation "expeditiously" in determining whether bargaining over a relocation has reached "a bona fide impasse" that is, the point at which a party may act unilaterally.

. . . Dubuque argues that relocation decisions must be exempt from the duty to bargain because they involve the reallocation of capital, observing that allocations of capital are "core managerial decisions."

We pause to emphasize that our analysis of the Board's test is premised on our resolution of an important ambiguity in the Board's statement of its second affirmative defense. As stated by the Board, that defense requires an employer to establish that "the union *could not* have offered labor cost concessions that *could* have changed the employer's decision to relocate." On its face, this language might be read as an impossibility exception—a provision allowing an employer to eschew negotiations only if its union could not possibly have changed the relocation decision no matter how accommodating the union might have been at the bargaining table. . . .

Despite this evidence, we think this defense was intended to cover situations in which bargaining would be futile, as well as ones in which it would be impossible for the union to persuade the employer to rescind its relocation decision. . . .

Viewing the Board's test through the lens of this interpretation, we find it sufficiently protective of an employer's prerogative to manage its business. Under *First National Maintenance*, employers may be required to negotiate management decisions where "the benefit, for labor-management relations and the collective-bargaining process, outweighs the burden placed on the conduct of the business." The Board's test exempts from the duty to negotiate relocations that, viewed objectively, are entrepreneurial in nature. It exempts decisions that, viewed subjectively, were motivated by something other than labor costs. And it explicitly excuses employers from attempting to negotiate when doing so would be futile or impossible. What is left are relocations that leave the firm occupying much the same entrepreneurial position as previously, that were taken because of the cost of labor, and that offer a realistic hope for a negotiated settlement. The Board's determination that bargaining over such decisions promises benefits outweighing the "burden[s] placed on the conduct of [an employer's] business" was in no way unreasonable. . . .

2. The Application of the Board's Test to Dubuque

. . . Dubuque objects . . . to the Board's finding that its relocation did not constitute a change in the scope and direction of its business. . . .

. . . The ALJ stated that Dubuque . . . used the Rochelle facility to substantially replace the Dubuque facility. As production in Rochelle increased, there was a corresponding reduction at Dubuque until the hog kill and cut processing departments and related operations there were completely phased out. Larry J. Tangeman, general plant superintendent at Dubuque, became superintendent of the Rochelle facility and about 13 members of Dubuque management also were transferred to Rochelle, as was certain production equipment. The purposes of the Rochelle plant, to slaughter hogs, dress carcasses, and to process pork into hams, bacon, and sausage, were the same as at the Dubuque plant.

. . . Viewed as a whole, the record offers substantial support for the Board's position.

Dubuque's second contention is that because "the record . . . is very clear that the union 'would not' offer labor concessions," bargaining would have been futile; hence it was not required.

. . . While we agree that our precedent, like the Board's test, relieves employers from any duty to bargain in the face of a union's adamantine intransigence, that principle has no bearing here. As counsel for the UFCW pointed out at oral argument, the UFCW "could, would, and did" accept concessions—in 1978, in August 1980, and again in October 1981—all in a vain attempt to keep the Dubuque facility open. Indeed, the vote that led to Dubuque's "irrevocable" decision to relocate was not a vote to categorically refuse Dubuque's overtures, but a vote to insist on financial disclosure as a prelude to bargaining. The Board's finding that good-faith bargaining between Dubuque and the UFCW might not have been futile was substantially supported by the record. . . .

III. Conclusion

For the foregoing reasons, we deny Dubuque's petition for review, enforce the Board's remedial order against Dubuque, grant the UFCW's petition for review, and remand to the Board the issue of Dubuque's duty to bargain over its proposed pork processing relocation.

Notes

1. Chief Justice Warren explicitly limited his decision in *Fibreboard* to the facts of that case and left open the possibility that other "subcontracting" or "contracting out" decisions might not be mandatory subjects of bargaining. See the discussion of *Dorsey Trailers, infra,* note 4. Can *First National Maintenance* be read in the same way? Do the particularized facts of that case suggest that other partial closure decisions could be mandatory subjects? *Cf. Parma Industries, Inc.,* 292 N.L.R.B. 90 (1988) (applying *Otis II*'s labor costs analysis to find that employer committed a ULP by failing to bargain over a plant closure).

2. Neither the text of §§ 8(d) and 9(a) nor the legislative history of these sections, as discussed above, offered any guidance for the decisions in *Fibreboard* and *First National Maintenance.* The Act is silent on the question of employers' "right to manage" their businesses profitably. As Michael Harper has argued, a common justification for Justice Blackmun's decision in *First National Maintenance*—promoting "economic efficiency" by assuring that employers can make profitable capital allocation decisions—also lends little support to the decision:

> According to the conventionally accepted economic model, allocating capital to those uses which will reap the greatest return will ensure production of the maximum aggregate resources for society. The economic efficiency argument, however, proves too much. The allocation of funds to compensate or benefit employees, whether through wages, pensions, the purchase of safety equipment, or the maintenance of a relatively inefficient plant, diverts capital that the employer could have invested elsewhere. Any concerted employee pressure that extracts more compensation than an employer would decide to give absent collective bargaining reduces the amount of funding available for capital investment below the presumably 'efficient' market level. Moreover, the fundamental policy of the Labor Act is to facilitate employees' efforts to extract as much compensation from their employer as their concerted economic power permits. The Act must intend to sacrifice any 'economic efficiency' that accrues from unencumbered employer decisions if it is to achieve its goal of balancing the generally superordinate position of employers in the labor market. Michael Harper, *Leveling the Road from* Borg-Warner *to* First National Maintenance: *The Scope of Mandatory Bargaining*, 68 VA. L. REV. 1447, 1458 (1982).

So, did the *First National Maintenance* court have the authority to exclude from the scope of "other terms and conditions of employment" partial closures and analogous decisions that would result in unionized employees losing their jobs? Is there a principled distinction drawn in *First National Maintenance* that finds support in the statute's text (a textualist's question) or its purpose (a purposivist's question)? Harper offers an alternative principle that might support the result in *First National Maintenance*: "This principle rests on a social policy allowing consumers, and only consumers, to influence management's product market decisions. This principle would exclude from compulsory bargaining *all decisions to determine what products are created and sold, in what quantities, for which markets, and at what prices.*" Harper, *Leveling the Road*, at 1463–64 (emphasis in original). Does this principle find any support in the statute's text or purposes?

3. *First National Maintenance* expressly requires employers that have closed parts of their businesses to engage in "effects bargaining": "There is no dispute that the union must be given a significant opportunity to bargain about . . . matters of job security as part of the 'effects' bargaining mandated by § 8(a)(5). And, under § 8(a) (5), bargaining over the effects of a decision must be conducted in a meaningful manner and at a meaningful time, and the Board may impose sanctions to insure

its adequacy." Do unions have any economic weapons they can deploy effectively to influence the results of effects bargaining after a partial closure or similar capital allocation decision by the employer? What incentives does the employer have to reach agreement with the union or to make concessions in effects bargaining?

4. When should the *Dubuque Packing* burden-shifting framework apply? In *Torrington Industries, Inc.*, 307 N.L.R.B. 809 (1992), the Board did not apply it because the case involved a subcontracting decision that the Board considered factually similar to *Fibreboard*—that is, the employer replaced unionized employees with non-union employees to perform the same work. The Board reasoned, therefore, that *Fibreboard* governed. *See also Rock-Tenn v. NLRB*, 101 F.3d 1441 (D.C. Cir. 1996) (same); *Geiger Ready-Mix Co. v. NLRB*, 87 F.3d 1363 (D.C. Cir. 1996) (declining to apply *Dubuque Packing* and applying a different framework to hold that a double-breasted employer's decision to transfer work from its union facility to its non-union facility was a mandatory subject). The Third Circuit has harshly criticized the *Torrington* approach and expressed its preference for an exploration of employers' motivations using the *Dubuque Packing* framework. *Furniture Rentors of America, Inc. v. NLRB*, 36 F.3d 1240 (3d Cir. 1994). In *Dorsey Trailers, Inc. v. NLRB*, 134 F.3d 125 (3d Cir. 1998), however, the Third Circuit rejected the Board's conclusion that an employer was obligated to bargain in good faith over a decision which the court characterized as "subcontracting." While the court distinguished *Fibreboard*, it did not apply the *Dubuque Packing* framework. Similarly, in a different case bearing the same name, *Dorsey Trailers, Inc. v. NLRB*, 233 F.3d 831 (4th Cir. 2000) the Fourth Circuit refused to apply *Dubuque Packing* when analyzing an employer's relocation decision and, instead, based its conclusion that the decision was not a mandatory subject of bargaining on a broad application of *First National Maintenance*.

Yet, in *Regal Cinemas, Inc. v. NLRB*, 317 F.3d 300 (D.C. Cir. 2003), even though the Board followed *Torrington* and *Fibreboard* rather than *Dubuque Packing*, the D.C. Circuit upheld the Board's conclusion that the movie theater chain had committed a ULP by failing to bargain with its unions over converting to "manager-operated" theaters that resulted in union projectionists being laid off. The court agreed with the Board that a transfer of work from unionized employees to managers was sufficiently analogous to the subcontracting in *Fibreboard* to justify applying that precedent rather than *Dubuque Packing*. So, when should the Board and courts apply *Dubuque Packing* and when should they follow either *Fibreboard* or *First National Maintenance*? Is its applicability limited to relocation decisions that are strictly analogous to the facts of *Dubuque Packing*?

5. Not surprisingly, an employer's decision to hire replacement workers during a strike is not a mandatory subject of bargaining. *American Cyanamid Co. v. NLRB*, 592 F.2d 356 (7th Cir. 1979); *Hawaii Meat Co. v. NLRB*, 321 F.2d 397 (9th Cir. 1963). However, a decision to subcontract work permanently during the course of a legal lockout or strike is a mandatory subject. *Int'l Paper Co. v. NLRB*, 115 F.3d 1045 (D.C. Cir. 1997); *Land Air Delivery, Inc. v. NLRB*, 862 F.2d 354 (D.C. Cir. 1988). What reasons might justify this distinction?

6. The Worker Adjustment Retraining and Notification Act (WARN), 29 U.S.C. §§ 2101–2108, requires employers with 100 or more employees to notify their employees (or the employees' union, if they have one) at least 60 days in advance of any "mass layoff" or facility closure that will result in 50 or more employees losing their jobs within a 30-day period. A "mass layoff" is defined as a reduction in force of either 500 employees at a single site or 50 employees if that is at least 33 percent of the workforce. The employer need not give advance notice if (1) the employer is "actively seeking" capital or business that would keep the facility open or postpone its closure and providing notice would preclude getting the capital or business, or (2) the layoff or facility closure was the result of business circumstances that were not "reasonably foreseeable." The effects of strikes, lockouts, and the hiring of permanent striker replacements do not trigger the WARN Act's provisions. The WARN Act creates a private right of action that allows individual employees or a union to bring a claim to federal court. How does the WARN Act affect bargaining over plant closures, relocations, layoffs, and other capital allocations decisions? Does it strengthen unions' position when bargaining over effects?

Problem 10.2

In January 2020, Advanced Widget Technologies (AWT) acquired Federated Widgets, Inc. An analysis of Federated provided to AWT's chief executive officer by an outside management consulting firm reported that Federated's technology was outdated, resulting in product designs that were too expensive and not competitive in the worldwide widget market. Federated's share of that market had been declining steadily. The analysis suggested that part of the problem was that Federated's technology activities were scattered throughout North America and work performed in one location was being duplicated elsewhere. In particular, Federated had a research and development division in its Omaha, Nebraska facility, but performed similar work at its engineering center in Lincoln, Nebraska. AWT had its major research and development center in Tuscaloosa, Alabama employing approximately 1,000 employees working on substantially more sophisticated widget engineering, research, and development than anything performed in Omaha or Lincoln. Based on its review of Federated's problems, AWT decided to terminate research and development operations in Omaha and Lincoln and consolidate them at significantly enhanced, more technologically sophisticated Tuscaloosa facility.

Beginning in March 2020, AWT invested between $2 and $3.5 million in expanding and upgrading the technology in its Tuscaloosa facility. In May 2020, AWT's chief executive officer informed all of the Omaha and Lincoln employees of AWT's plans: a high-tech, re-tooled research and development center in Tuscaloosa housing all of the company's research, development, and product engineering operations. In July 2020, AWT closed its Omaha and Lincoln research and development divisions, transferred those operations to Tuscaloosa, and relocated approximately 30 employees from Omaha to Tuscaloosa.

Throughout 2020, AWT refused to bargain with the United Widgetmakers Union, which represents the research and development division employees in the Omaha and Lincoln facilities. You are counsel to the union. The president of the union would like to stop the transfer of research and development work from Nebraska to Alabama by forcing AWT to bargain over its decisions. Would you advise the union's president that an unfair labor practice filed with the Board is likely to succeed?

III. Scope of Bargaining in the Public Sector

A. Introduction: Policy Considerations in the Public Sector

By the end of the 1980s, 27 public-sector labor statutes in 21 states used statutory language identical or substantively identical to the NLRA's language on bargaining over wages, hours, and other terms and conditions of employment. B.V.H. Schneider, *Public Sector Labor Legislation — An Evolutionary Analysis, in* Benjamin Aaron, Joyce Najita, & James Stern, Public Sector Bargaining 216 (2d ed. 1990). Through today, a majority of the states that permit public employees to bargain collectively use this model. Yet "scope of bargaining" issues can be quite contentious in the public sector, and it is one of the areas in which public-sector labor laws can and do differ from each other and from the NLRA most dramatically. Why is that so?

Clyde Summers, *Bargaining in the Government's Business: Principles and Politics*
18 U. Tol. L. Rev. 265 (1987)[*]

Public employee bargaining chronically suffers from cognitive dissonance. There is repeated acknowledgment that collective bargaining in the public sector is different from collective bargaining in the private sector. At the same time, the statutes enacted for public sector bargaining, and the administrative rules and decisions announced under those statutes are modeled on the statutory rules and decisions of the private sector. Often the same paragraph or even the same sentence affirms both of these perspectives with equal confidence and no overt recognition of the dissonance. This dissonance confuses our discussion and obscures our understanding of many of the problems in public employee bargaining. . . .

From the union perspective, the public and private sectors have much in common. Both sectors involve the same kind of work; jobs in the public sector are matched by jobs in the private sector — truck drivers, building maintenance, typists, record keepers, teachers, guards, safety personnel, and firefighters. The employees' goals are the same — wages, medical insurance, pensions, holidays, working

---

conditions, job security, and protection against arbitrary supervision. Workers in both sectors seek to protect these interests by the same means — collective representation and collective agreements which secure those rights and make them enforceable through a reasonably prompt and reliable procedure.

From the public employer's side, the perspective is quite different because bargaining is framed by legal and political considerations. Pension benefits may be statutorily defined, public services may be legally required, and personnel matters may be governed by civil service rules. More importantly, employer representatives at the bargaining table have limited authority to make binding agreements because wage increases or benefits are dependent on the budget, which is dependent on taxes, and these are matters for the legislative body, not the negotiators.

The crucial difference is that in the public sector the collective agreement is not a private decision, but a governmental decision; it is not so much a contract as a legislative act. Labor costs may be seventy percent of a city's budget. Bargaining on wages and other economic items, therefore, inevitably involves the level of taxes and the level of services. An agreement to increase wages requires either an increase in taxes or a decrease in services. Negotiated holidays close city services for the day. Other contractual provisions may affect the kind or quality of public services provided.

In the public sector the ultimate employer is not the mayor or the council but the voters. They are the ones who pay the taxes and receive the services. They are the ones to whom those who make the collective agreement are answerable. From the employer's side, the collective agreement is not an economic decision but a political decision; it shapes policy choices which rightfully belong to the voters to be made through the political processes. Collective bargaining in the public sector is properly and inevitably political; to try to make it otherwise denies democratic principles. . . .

It may be helpful to compare how certain decisions are made with and without collective bargaining. Consider, for example, the question of whether the salaries of teachers should be raised. In the absence of bargaining, individual teachers or teacher organizations will try to persuade the superintendent by petition, discussion or otherwise to provide for an increase in the next school budget. When the budget comes before a public hearing, the teachers, perhaps reinforced by parents or the PTA, will argue for the fairness and need for an increase. Taxpayers, individualized and organized, will argue against the increases and protest the level of taxes the budget will require. The school board or finance committee will retire to executive session and reach a decision. Consider a second question of class size. The process will be much the same, with perhaps more vigorous advocacy by the PTA, but less vigorous advocacy by the taxpayers who may not recognize the relation to taxes. Consider third the question of the teacher's authority to discipline students. Here the teachers will not speak with one voice; some will ask for authority to paddle, and some will ask that paddling be prohibited. The parents will also be divided, and the PTA's may be paralyzed. In both cases, the school board will listen, go into executive session and decide.

Collective bargaining significantly changes the political process. The union, as an exclusive bargaining representative, formulates its demands, and on each of these issues, proceeds to negotiate with the school board's representative behind closed doors. The board is required to respond by giving reasons for its positions, meeting arguments with arguments, and having those arguments examined. Parent organizations and taxpayer organizations are not present. Individual teachers with different views are not present. When an agreement is reached, it is then presented as part of a package decision including many other issues. The taxpayer, the parents and the dissenting teachers do not know the background information, the competing considerations, or the compromises which led to the decision. They have no active voice until the next election when they may vote to change the composition of the school board.

It becomes immediately evident that collective bargaining gives the teachers' collective representative a much more effective voice in the decision-making. The union has more direct access in the decision-making than the taxpayers, the parents or any other voters, and they purport to represent the viewpoint of all teachers although many may disagree. The union is able to deal with public decision-makers behind closed doors without other interests being heard, and to arrive at agreements which are politically difficult, if not legally impossible to change.

Giving employees and their collective representatives this special role in government decision-making is a significant departure from our traditional political processes. This is the discomfort of our cognitive dissonance; how do we reconcile this process with our democratic principles? I do not raise this question to argue against public employee bargaining. On the contrary, my purpose is to try to understand more exactly why we have public employee bargaining. With that understanding we may better shape the structure and scope of the system. . . .

The first, and for me, compelling reason for public employee bargaining is that our political system has a built-in bias which requires it. The ultimate public employer is the electorate, the taxpayer and the users of public service. Much like other employers they want from their employees high production and low labor costs. In political terms, they want more public service with lower taxes. With labor costs making up seventy percent or more of the public employer's budget, the political pressure of the whole electorate — taxpayers and service users — is to hold down wages and other economic benefits. No matter how well organized public employees are and what strategic positions they occupy, they are massively outnumbered in votes. The voter is not as compelled by self-interest as a private employer confronting non-union competition, but may be more resistant to wage demands than an employer whose competitors are also unionized and subject to standardized wage terms. Public employees are always at risk that the political demands for low taxes and more service will be placated at their expense.

The collective bargaining process which gives public employees more direct access and ability to persuade the political decision-makers helps offset this built-in political disadvantage. The public employees' greater voice in the process, however, scarcely compensates for their greater stake in the decision, for it is their livelihood or standard of living which is at issue, as against a one or two mill tax increase for the taxpayer.

The second reason for collective bargaining is that many matters of primary importance to employers are of little or no importance to the voter. For example, voters have no knowledge and little concern with seniority rules, job bidding, individual discharges, grievance procedures or arbitration. These are problems between the employees and the managing bureaucracy, with as much or more danger of favoritism, arbitrariness or oppressive treatment than in the private sector. Collective bargaining is needed to protect against arbitrary authority, and is especially appropriate because of voter indifference. . . .

Public sector bargaining, in defining subjects of bargaining, originally borrowed from private sector bargaining, with legislation and courts copying directly the language and logic of the National Labor Relations Act. Experience has demonstrated that such aping of the private sector was monkey business in the public sector. Many states have now legislatively or judicially attempted more restrictive, elaborate, and often incomprehensible standards. Clear and precise definitions are not possible, but we can obtain some guidance if we start with the special character of the animal with which we are dealing. . . .

Public officials in refusing to bargain commonly borrow language from the private sector, claiming 'management prerogatives.' This is most often a misnomer. The basic principle is that certain public decisions belong to the public and cannot be removed from the normal political processes. Therefore, these decisions cannot be submitted to a collective bargaining process which restricts the public's participation.

Notes

1. In other parts of the article excerpted above, Summers discusses whether the following topics should be mandatory subjects of bargaining or not:

(1) compensation, including wages, pensions, medical benefits, and severance pay;

(2) protection against unjust discharge;

(3) seniority rules which protect against arbitrary treatment;

(4) demands for safety equipment;

(5) authority of teachers to use corporal punishment;

(6) creation of a police review board to investigate charges of police abuse;

(7) content of school curriculum and choice of text books;

(8) reducing the size of the police force and the number of police on each shift; and

(9) limiting class size in public schools to 25 students.

Summers argues that under his approach, it is clear which of these should be mandatory topics and which should not. In your opinion, either using his approach or one you believe might be better, which should be mandatory and which should not? Is the answer always clear?

2. Reread the final paragraph in the Summers' excerpt. Can you make an argument based on his approach that the category of *permissive* subjects should not exist in the public sector, *i.e.*, that there should only be mandatory subjects and illegal subjects (topics employers and unions may not enter into binding agreements over, even if both sides are willing to do so)? As shown below, almost all public-sector jurisdictions use all three of the categories that developed under the NLRA (mandatory, permissive, and illegal). The "mandatory" category, however, tends to be smaller in the public sector. Also consider, as you go through this section, which topics that are not mandatory you think should be permissive and which you think should be illegal.

Problem 10.3

Public employees in the city of Gotham are covered by a general state public-sector labor law which uses language on the scope of bargaining substantively identical to that in the NLRA: employers and unions must bargain in good faith over "wages, hours, and other terms and conditions of employment." The statute adds, however, that "matters of inherent management rights" are not mandatory topics.

A long-standing practice exists in Gotham that police officers ride with a partner, *i.e.*, in groups of two per car. Recently, though, a crime wave has hit the city. This has caused increased and significant harm to people and property, a public outcry, and negative publicity for city officials. The Gotham police chief, seeking to combat this crime wave, has just increased the number of police cars on patrol by ordering that officers must now ride only one per car. The Gotham Police Officers' Union has filed a ULP charge, claiming a unilateral change in a mandatory subject of bargaining: staffing. The union also argues that this change implicates employee safety, in that it is more dangerous for police officers to confront criminals alone than with a partner.

(a) How would this type of case be decided under the NLRA?

(b) Should the public sector use the same rule for this type of case? Why or why not?

(c) In deciding what the rule in the public sector should be for cases such as this, would it be better to have specific statutory language governing this (and perhaps other) particular subjects of bargaining, or would it be better to use broad statutory language which agencies and courts would then interpret?

———————

While the scope of bargaining is generally more restricted in the public sector than in the private, there is considerable diversity. In some public-sector jurisdictions, most, if not all, topics that are mandatory under the NLRA are mandatory; on the other extreme, some jurisdictions severely limit what unions can negotiate.

Restrictions on the scope of bargaining arise from three main sources. First, in jurisdictions with statutes that use the NLRA's language, agencies and courts have found some topics not to be mandatory, even if they are mandatory under the NLRA, because of policy concerns specific to government employment. Second, some state statutes specifically list which topics are and are not mandatory. Finally, public-sector employment is governed by myriad legal rules separate from labor laws, including but not limited to civil service rules, public pension systems, tenure laws, regulations governing police oversight and discipline, and constitutional law. In some significant areas, collective bargaining cannot alter the "default" terms of employment these laws set; in others, bargaining can.

B. Public-Sector Statutes with Broad Language Similar to the NLRA

Again, many state laws provide that unions and employers have a duty to bargain over "wages, hours, and other terms and conditions of employment." Typically, though, these statutes also contain language stating that certain "management rights" are not negotiable or at least not mandatory, and they use broad, often quite unspecific language to describe management rights. How should labor boards and courts apply such language?

1. Balancing Tests

In re State Employment Relations Board v. Youngstown City School District Board of Education

Ohio State Employment Relations Board
12 Ohio Pub. Employee Rep. ¶ 1543 (1995)

[The issue was whether the Youngstown City School District Board of Education committed a ULP by unilaterally implementing a mandatory subject of bargaining, specifically, an Early Retirement Incentive Plan (ERIP) without bargaining with the Youngstown Education Association, OEA/NEA (YEA).] . . .

A. Balancing Test Is Announced

O.R.C. § 4117.08(A) provides:

> All matters pertaining to wages, hours, or terms and other conditions of employment and the continuation, modification, or deletion of an existing provision of a collective bargaining agreement are subject to collective bargaining between the public employer and the exclusive representative, except as otherwise specified in this section. . . .

At the same time, O.R.C. § 4117.08(C) provides in part:

> Unless a public employer agrees otherwise in a collective bargaining agreement, nothing in Chapter 4117 . . . impairs the right and responsibility of each public employer to:

(1) Determine matters of inherent managerial policy which include, but are not limited to areas of discretion or policy such as the functions and programs of the public employer, standards of services, its overall budget, utilization of technology and organizational structure;

(2) Direct, supervise, evaluate, or hire employees;

(3) Maintain and improve the efficiency and effectiveness of governmental operations;

(4) Determine the overall methods, process, means, or personnel by which governmental operations are to be conducted:

(5) Suspend, discipline, demote, or discharge for just cause, or lay off, transfer, assign, schedule, promote, or retain employees;

(6) Determine the adequacy of the work force;

(7) Determine the overall mission of the employer as a unit of government;

(8) Effectively manage the work force;

(9) Take actions to carry out the mission of the public employer as a governmental unit.

The employer is not required to bargain on subjects reserved to the management and direction of the governmental unit except as affect wages, hours, terms and conditions of employment, and the continuation, modification, or deletion of an existing provision of a collective bargaining agreement.

Divisions (A) and (C) of this section spell out facially contradictory statements regarding a public employer's bargaining obligations and its right to make management decisions. . . . If these categories in divisions (A) and (C) were mutually exclusive of each other, there would be no conflict. However, labor agencies and courts alike, when confronted with specific cases, have concluded that almost any managerial policy will have some effect on conditions of employment. . . .

Divisions (A) and (C) of . . . § 4117.08, when read together, illustrate an effort by the legislature to somehow balance the needs of public employers to make management decisions against the right of public employees to bargain about their working conditions. In establishing what issues must be submitted to the process of collective bargaining, the legislature had no expectation that the elected exclusive representative would become an equal partner in the running of the business enterprise in which the employee organization's members are employed. *See, e.g., First National Maintenance Corp. v. NLRB*, 452 U.S. 666 (1981). The statute's aim is not realized by requiring bargaining over every management decision that affects employee working conditions.

The aim of the statute is better realized by adopting a standard, in the form of a balancing test, to identify those subjects about which public employers must bargain in Ohio. This standard must balance the right of employers to run the public business with the right of their employees to engage in collective bargaining. . . .

Pursuant to . . . § 4117.08, a public employer is required to bargain with an exclusive representative on all matters relating to wages, hours, or terms and other conditions of employment. The Ohio Supreme Court recognized "mandatory," "permissive" and "illegal" subjects of bargaining under this section. . . . Illegal subjects of bargaining are those described in O.R.C. 4117.08(B). Mandatory subjects are those which . . . § 4117.08(A) requires the parties to bargain over in good faith. A "permissive" subject of collective bargaining is one whose inclusion in the agreement is not prohibited by law, but which is not one of the mandatory subjects of bargaining listed in . . . § 4117.08(A). While parties to a collective bargaining relationship are required to bargain over mandatory subjects, they are not required to do so with regard to permissive subjects.

. . . Accordingly, in this matter and henceforth, if a given subject is alleged to affect and is determined to have a material influence upon wages, hours, or terms and other conditions of employment and involves the exercise of inherent management discretion, the following factors must be balanced to determine whether it is a mandatory or permissive subject of bargaining:

1) The extent to which the subject is logically and reasonably related to wages, hours, terms and conditions of employment;

2) The extent to which the employer's obligation to negotiate may significantly abridge its freedom to exercise those managerial prerogatives set forth in and anticipated by O.R.C. 4117.08(C), including an examination of the type of employer involved and whether inherent discretion on the subject matter at issue is necessary to achieve the employer's essential mission and its obligations to the general public; and

3) The extent to which the mediatory influence of collective bargaining and, when necessary, any impasse resolution mechanisms available to the parties are the appropriate means of resolving conflicts over the subject matter.

Those management decisions which are found, on balance, to be permissive subjects, can be implemented without bargaining the decision unless a contract provision would conflict with it. . . .

B. Balancing Tests Are Well-Accepted Tools for Resolving Conflicting Rights

The construction of a balancing test to determine whether certain subjects are mandatory or permissive is a generally accepted principle of labor law, utilized and approved by reviewing courts in other public sector jurisdictions such as California, Pennsylvania and Illinois and by the NLRB with U.S. Supreme Court approval in *First National Maintenance Corp. v. NLRB*, supra.

The three-prong balancing test developed by the California Public Employment Relations Board ("PERB") is nearly identical to the test adopted herein. PERB's test finds a subject to be 'negotiable, even though not specifically enumerated if it (1) is logically and reasonably related to hours, wages or an enumerated term and condition of employment, (2) the subject is of such concern to both management and employees that conflict is likely to occur and the mediatory influence of collective negotiations is the appropriate means of resolving the conflict; and (3) the employer's obligation to negotiate would not significantly abridge his freedom to exercise those managerial prerogatives (including matters of fundamental policy) essential to the achievement of the District's mission.' ... This test was approved by the California Supreme Court in *San Mateo City School Dist. v. PERB*, 33 Cal.3d 850 (1983).

The Pennsylvania Supreme Court has also approved a balancing test in *Penn. Labor Relations Bd. v. State College Area School Dist*, 90 L.R.R.M. 2081 (1975). ... "It is the duty of the Board ... to determine whether the impact of the issue on the interest of the employe (sic) in wages, hours and terms and conditions of employment outweighs its probable effect on the basic policy of the system as a whole." *Id.* at 2085.

... In *Central City Education Assn. v. Ill. Educational Labor Relations Bd.*, 599 N.E.2d 892 (1992), the Supreme Court of Illinois reconciled statutory language requiring public employers 'to bargain collectively with regard to policy matters directly affecting wages, hours and terms and conditions of employment as well as the impact thereon upon request by employee representatives,' but not requiring them to 'bargain over matters of inherent managerial policy,' through the use of a three-part balancing test. If the Illinois Board determines the matter concerns 'wages, hours and terms and conditions of employment' (part one) and it is also one of 'inherent managerial policy' (part two), the Board must determine which interests are greater (part three). *Id.* at 899. ...

D. Balancing Test Is Not Always Necessary

... [T]his three-part balancing test is not necessary or appropriate in every situation. Only those subjects that both have a material influence upon wages, hours or terms and other conditions of employment and involve the exercise of inherent managerial discretion are subject to the three-part balancing test. The balancing test analysis is not necessary when the subject matter at issue is an inherently managerial prerogative not affecting wages, hours or terms and conditions of employment; pertains only to wages, hours, or terms and conditions of employment; or is preempted by legislation.

For example, in a case involving the tape recording of a pre-disciplinary hearing by an employer, SERB held that because the taping itself did not affect wages, hours, terms and other conditions of employment, it was unnecessary to apply a balancing test to determine whether taping is a mandatory or permissive subject of bargaining. In a case involving the unilateral changing of hours and benefits of a bargaining unit position by the employer, again SERB did not rely on a balancing test to reach the conclusion that hours and benefits are mandatory subjects of bargaining and, therefore, a unilateral change without bargaining constituted a violation of ... § 4117.11(A) (1) and (5). ... In both cases, since it was readily apparent the subject matters at issue were not a mixture of inherently managerial prerogatives and wages, hours, terms and other conditions, application of a balancing test was unnecessary. ...

F. Bargaining the Decision to Implement the ERIP Was Required

... In the present case, the Employer asserts the 1993 ERIP was developed primarily to reduce administrative staff and, subsequently, was applied to this bargaining unit by operation of law, not by design. Thus, given the Employer's assertion, analysis under the three-part balancing test is necessary.

Under the first part of the test set forth above, it was clearly established that retirement or pension benefits are logically and reasonably related to wages, hours, terms and other conditions of employment. This is a position held in the private sector and a substantial number of public sector labor jurisdictions that have considered the matter. ERIPs directly affect the wages, hours, terms and conditions of employment of those individuals potentially participating in the plan.

Analysis of the facts under the second part of the balancing test is problematic. While the Respondent could argue that an ERIP is a necessary element to assist it in implementing its determination of 'the adequacy of the work force' pursuant to ... § 4117.08(C) (6), or that an ERIP effects its right to 'layoff, transfer, assign, schedule, promote, or retain employees' pursuant to ... § 4117.08(C) (5), an ERIP basically just speeds up the natural process of staff reductions through attrition. Accordingly, while the weight of the YEA's interest in the first part is relatively strong, the weight to be given the Employer's concern under the second part is relatively weak in this instance. The Employer has failed to establish an overriding management objective that would justify the unilateral action under the second part.

Finally, the third part of the balancing test requires an examination of the extent to which the collective bargaining process is an appropriate method to resolve the conflict over the instant subject matter. We conclude that it is to a great extent. The parties do not assert that the bargaining process is an inappropriate or cumbersome means for developing and negotiating an ERIP. The bargaining history of these parties has demonstrated that bargaining over an ERIP has not significantly abridged the Employer's freedom to manage the School District using the inherent discretion to make the decisions essential to its mission and its obligations to the general public. This is evidenced by the several previous collective bargaining agreements between the parties that contained negotiated ERIPS. A compelling reason for a union to cooperate in negotiations over an ERIP is that the alternative is often layoffs of the least senior employees ... Again, the parties' history with respect to bargaining over ERIPs demonstrates that addressing the subject through these channels has proven successful in resolving their conflicts.

Thus, analysis under the three-part balancing test clearly indicates that the 1993 ERIP constituted a mandatory subject of bargaining. Therefore, the Board of Education's unilateral implementation, without bargaining the decision to implement an ERIP with the YEA, was in violation of O.R.C. § 4117.11(A) (1) and (5).

———————

As *Youngstown* indicates, many public-sector jurisdictions have adopted a "balancing test" or other formulation which, at least primarily, weighs and compares the interest of the employees in wages, hours, and working conditions against the employer's interest in its inherent managerial authority. *See, also, e.g., Connecticut State Employees Ass'n and State of Connecticut*, Conn. State Bd. of Labor Relations, Dec. No. 4096 (2005) (balance "the directness and the depth of the item's impingement on conditions of employment" against "the extent of the employer's need for unilateral action without negotiation in order to serve or preserve an important policy decision committed to by law to the employer's discretion"); *Appeal of the State of New Hampshire (New Hampshire Public Employee Labor Relations Board)*, 138 N.H. 716, 722 (1994) (first, the subject must not be reserved to the exclusive managerial authority of the public employer by statute or other external law; second, the proposal "must primarily affect the terms and conditions of employment, rather than matters of broad managerial policy"; and third, if the proposal were adopted, it would not "interfere with public control of governmental functions" contrary to statutory law).

In these jurisdictions, many of the topics that are mandatory in the private sector have been found mandatory under the public-sector law: wages, hours of work, and a broad range of conditions, including but not limited to discipline and discharge rules, grievance and arbitration machinery, and health and safety rules.

Some issues, however, raise concerns about inherent governmental authority sufficiently serious that they are often or always found to be non-mandatory topics. Sometimes this seems to depend on the topic involved, and sometimes it seems to depend on the type of employee and government service involved.

Further complicating matters is the fact that, as in the private sector, public-sector rules typically provide that even if a substantive decision by management is not a mandatory topic of bargaining, the *effects* of that decision on employees may still be a mandatory topic.

2. Balancing Tests, Inherent Governmental Authority, and "Effects" Bargaining

Claremont Police Officers Ass'n v. City of Claremont

Supreme Court of California
39 Cal. 4th 623, 47 Cal. Rptr. 3d 69, 139 P.3d 532 (2006)

CHIN, J.

In this case, we consider a provision of the Meyers-Milias-Brown Act (MMBA) (Gov.Code, § 3500 et seq.), which governs labor-management relations at the local government level. Section 3505 mutually obligates a public employer and an employee organization to meet and confer in good faith about a matter within the "scope of representation" concerning, among other things, "wages, hours, and other terms and conditions of employment" (§ 3504). A fundamental managerial or policy decision, however, is outside the scope of representation (§ 3504), and is excepted from section 3505's meet-and-confer requirement. . . .

I. Factual and Procedural Background

Plaintiff Claremont Police Officers Association (Association) is an employee organization representing public employees of defendant City of Claremont (City), including police officers. . . . In February 2002, the police commission adopted [a subcommittee's] recommendation that the Department implement a "Vehicle Stop Data Collection Study" (Study), which is at issue in this case. This Study required officers on all vehicle stops to complete a preprinted scantron form called a "Vehicle Stop Data Form" (Form). The Form included questions regarding the "driver's perceived race/ethnicity," and the "officers' prior knowledge of driver's race/ethnicity." On average, the Form takes two minutes to complete, and an officer may complete between four and six Forms for each 12-hour shift. Each Form is traceable to the individual officer making the stop. The Study was to last 15 months, commencing July 1, 2002.

. . . [T]he Association requested that the City meet and confer regarding the Study because it asserted "the implementation of policy and procedures in regards to this area falls under California Government Code section 3504." . . . [T]he City gave written notice disagreeing that the Study fell within the scope of representation under section 3504. On June 27, 2002, the Department informed officers it would implement the Study effective July 1, 2002. On July 11, 2002, the Association filed a petition for writ of mandate to compel the City and the Department not to implement the Study until they meet and confer in good faith under the MMBA.

On August 22, 2002, the superior court denied the petition. . . . [T]he court concluded, among other things, that the Study did not substantially affect the terms and conditions of the Association members' employment, and that "given the de minimis impact upon workload, and the predominantly policy directed objectives of the Study, . . . the Study falls primarily within management prerogatives under § 3504, and is not a matter within the scope of representation requiring compliance with the meet and confer provisions of the MMBA."

The Court of Appeal reversed. While it concluded the City's decision to take measures to combat the practice of racial profiling and the public perception that it occurs is "a fundamental policy decision that directly affects the police department's mission to protect and to serve the public," the Court of Appeal held that "the decision precisely *how to implement* that fundamental policy, however, involves several variables affecting law enforcement officers and is not itself a fundamental policy decision." The Court of Appeal explained that "the vehicle stop policy significantly affects officers' working conditions, particularly their job security and freedom from disciplinary action, their prospects for promotion, and the officers' relations with the public. Racial profiling is illegal. An officer could be accused of racial profiling and subjected to disciplinary action, denial of promotion, or other adverse action based in part on the information collected under the new policy. For this reason, the manner that the information is collected and the accuracy of the data and data analysis are matters of great concern to the association's members." . . .

II. Discussion

A. Background of the MMBA

[The MMBA] . . . obligates employers to bargain with employee representatives about matters that fall within the 'scope of representation.' (§§ 3504.5, 3505. . . .)

1. "Scope of representation"

Section 3504 defines "scope of representation" to include "all matters relating to employment conditions and employer-employee relations, including, but not limited to, *wages, hours, and other terms and conditions of employment*, except, however, that the scope of representation shall not include consideration of the *merits, necessity, or organization* of any service or activity provided by law or executive order." (Italics added.) The definition of "scope of representation" and its exception are "arguably vague" and "overlapping." *Building Material & Construction Teamsters' Union v. Farrell* (1986) 41 Cal.3d 651, 660 (*Building Material*) '[W]ages, hours and working conditions,' which, broadly read could encompass practically any conceivable bargaining proposal; and 'merits, necessity or organization of any service' which, expansively interpreted, could swallow the whole provision for collective negotiation and relegate determination of all labor issues to the city's discretion." *Fire Fighters Union v. City of Vallejo* (1974), 12 Cal.3d at p. 615 (*Fire Fighters Union*).

Courts have interpreted "wages, hours, and other terms and conditions of employment," which phrase is not statutorily defined, to include the transfer of bargaining-unit work to nonunit employees; mandatory drug testing of employees; work shift changes; and the adoption of a disciplinary rule prohibiting use of city facilities for personal use. Notwithstanding section 3504's broad language, to require an employer to bargain, its action or policy must have "a significant and adverse effect on the wages, hours, or working conditions of the bargaining-unit employees." (*Building Material, supra*).

2. "Merits, necessity or organization"

Even if an employer's action or policy has a significant and adverse effect on the bargaining unit's wages, hours, and working conditions, the employer may be excepted from bargaining requirements under the "merits, necessity, or organization" language of section 3504. This exclusionary language, which was added in 1968, was intended to "forestall any expansion of the language of 'wages, hours and working conditions' to include more general managerial policy decisions." "Federal and California decisions both recognize the right of employers to make unconstrained decisions when fundamental management or policy choices are involved." (*Building Material, supra*, ["To require public officials to meet and confer with their employees regarding fundamental policy decisions such as those here presented, would place an intolerable burden upon fair and efficient administration of state and local government"]; see also *First National Maintenance Corp. v. NLRB* (1981). . . .

Such fundamental managerial or policy decisions include changing the policy regarding a police officer's use of deadly force (*San Jose Peace Officer's Assn. v. City of San Jose* (1978) 78 Cal. App. 3d 935 (*San Jose Peace Officer's Assn.*)), permitting a member of the citizen's police review commission to attend police department hearings regarding citizen complaints and sending a department member to review commission meetings and, in the context of private labor relations, closing a plant for economic reasons *(N.L.R.B. v. Royal Plating & Polishing Co.* (3d Cir.1965) 350 F.2d 191, 196 (Royal Plating)).

B. Distinction Between an Employer's Fundamental Decision and the Implementation and Effects of That Decision

Both parties agree that the City's decision to take measures against racial profiling, specifically its decision to implement the Study as a necessary first step, is a fundamental managerial or policy decision. . . . The Legislature has made clear that the practice of racial profiling "presents a great danger to the fundamental principles of a democratic society. It is abhorrent and cannot be tolerated." (Pen.Code, § 13519.4, subd. (d) (1).) The City's decision to implement the Study was made in hopes to "improve relations between the police and the community and establish the Claremont Police Department as an open and progressive agency committed to being at the forefront of the best professional practices in law enforcement." (See *Building Material, supra,* [matters relating to "the betterment of police-community relations . . . are of obvious importance, and directly affect the quality and nature of public services"]; *see also San Jose Peace Officer's Assn., supra* ["the use of force policy is as closely akin to a managerial decision as any decision can be in running a police department"].) Thus, the Association concedes that the City "may have the right to unilaterally decide to implement a racial profiling study."

However, the Association maintains that the Study's implementation and effects involve many factors that are distinct from the City's fundamental decision to adopt the Study. These factors include, on the one hand, determining the methodology used in collecting the data, and on the other, determining the effects or use of the Study's data, i.e., whether the data would be used only for study purposes, whether results based on the analyzed data or results regarding individual officers would be made public, whether and under what circumstances the results could be used against officers (including imposing discipline or denying promotions), and what the implications are for officers' privacy and the potential for self-incrimination. The Association concludes that meeting and conferring on the Study's implementation and effects will not directly interfere with the City's right to exercise its managerial prerogative. The Association contends that although *Building Material* is distinguishable, it "completely recognizes this 'dichotomy.'"

The City, however, counters that the Court of Appeal misinterpreted section 3504 and calls this dichotomy "unprecedented." It maintains that a public employer's fundamental decision and the implementation of that decision "are integral to the nature of the public agency and are thus, *equally excluded* from the bargaining process under Section 3504." The City's amicus curiae, League of California Cities (League), argues that drawing an implementation distinction is both "artificial and unworkable" because "[i]t is pointless to adopt a policy if it cannot be implemented." . . . Another amicus curiae, Metropolitan Water District of Southern California, adds that "the policy and its implementation cannot be severed and analyzed separately. Rather, the former is interwoven with the latter, such that a decision to compel negotiation of the implementation would inevitably compel negotiation of the policy decision itself."

At the outset, we agree with the Association that there is a long-standing distinction under the [NLRA] between an employer's unilateral management decision and the *effects* of that decision (29 U.S.C. § 158(d)), the latter of which are subject to mandatory bargaining. (*First National Maintenance, supra; Kirkwood Fabricators, Inc. v. N.L.R.B.* (8th Cir.1988) 862 F.2d 1303, 1306 ["Requiring effects bargaining maintains an appropriate balance between an employer's right to close its business and an employee's need for some protection from arbitrary action"].) In other words, although "an employer has the right unilaterally to decide that a layoff is necessary, he must bargain about such matters as the timing of the layoffs and the number and identity of employees affected." (*Los Angeles County Civil Service Com. v. Superior Court* (1978) 23 Cal.3d 55, 64, [discussing cases under the NLRA]). . . .

We agree with the City, however, that the issue before us is whether it was compelled to meet and confer with the Association before it required officers on their vehicle stops to fill out the Forms as part of the Study. Based on the limited record before us, there is no evidence regarding what effects would result from implementing the Study; for instance, whether the data collected and later analyzed will result in discipline if an officer is found to have engaged in racial profiling, or whether the City will publicize the Study's raw data. It is also not clear from the record what exact methodology the City has adopted to analyze the collected data to determine any racial profiling. Nor can we say that racial profiling studies have been so historically associated with employee discipline that their implementation invariably raises disciplinary issues. . . . Thus, we do not decide the issue whether the City was required to meet and confer with the Association over any effects resulting from the City's decision to implement the Study. (*See Fibreboard Corp. v. NLRB* (1964) . . . (conc. opn. of Stewart, J.) [an "extremely indirect and uncertain" impact on job security may alone suffice to conclude such decisions do not concern conditions of employment].)

We disagree with the City's amici curiae that drawing a distinction between an employer's fundamental managerial or policy decision and the implementation of that decision, as a general matter, would be impossible or impractical. The reality is that "practically every managerial decision has some impact on wages, hours, or other conditions of employment." Indeed, section 3504 of the MMBA codifies the unavoidable overlap between an employer's policymaking discretion and an employer's action impacting employees' wages, hours, and working conditions. As we shall explain in greater detail below, while drawing a distinction may sometimes be difficult, the alternative—which would risk sheltering any and all actions that flow from an employer's fundamental decision from the duty to meet and confer—is contrary to established case law. Although *Building Material* did not specifically decide the issue, our decision, as the City acknowledges, expressly contemplates that the implementation of an employer's fundamental decision ("action . . . taken pursuant to a fundamental managerial or policy decision"), is a separate consideration for purposes of section 3505's meet-and-confer requirement.

Instead, we turn our focus to the City's implementation of the Study, requiring officers to fill out the Forms in order to collect data on possible racial profiling.

C. The Applicable Test

Emphasizing that the Court of Appeal erroneously created an "automatic presumption that a meet and confer is required if implementation of a fundamental decision significantly affects the terms and conditions of employment," the City urges that our decision in *Building Material, supra*, requires us to perform a balancing test that also considers the employer's need for unencumbered decisionmaking. If the balance weighs in favor of the employer, there is no need to bargain even if the employer's action has a significant and adverse impact on the employees' working conditions. The Association counters that *Building Material's* balancing test would apply only to the fundamental decision itself and not to its implementation or its effects.

In *Building Material*, . . . we concluded that the city was required to meet and confer with the Union because the city's transfer of duties to a non-bargaining unit had a significant and adverse effect on the bargaining unit's wages, hours, and working conditions. We rejected the city's assertion that its action was exempted as a fundamental policy decision because it concerned the effective operation of local government. The "decision to reorganize certain work duties was hardly 'fundamental.' It had little, if any, effect on public services. Rather, it primarily impacted the wages, hours, and working conditions of the employees in question and thus was a proper subject for mandatory collective bargaining. Indeed, defendants' claim to the contrary is in conflict with the statutory framework of the MMBA: "any issue involving wages, for example, would affect the cost of government services, but such matters are specifically included in the scope of representation as defined in section 3504."

Going on to explain that an employer's fundamental decision may have a significant and adverse effect on the bargaining unit's wages, hours, or working conditions, we considered whether "an action . . . taken pursuant to a fundamental managerial or policy decision" may be within the scope of representation and thus subject to a duty to meet and confer. (*Building Material, supra*). As relevant here, such an action would encompass an employer's steps to implement the details of the fundamental decision. Under that circumstance, a balancing test would apply: "If an action is taken pursuant to a fundamental managerial or policy decision, it is within the scope of representation only if the employer's need for unencumbered decisionmaking in managing its operations is outweighed by the benefit to employer-employee relations of bargaining about the action in question." (*Building Material, supra*, citing *First National Maintenance, supra*.)

The high court applied a similar balancing test in *First National Maintenance, supra*. While recognizing an employer's "freedom to manage its affairs unrelated to employment," the high court balanced the competing interests to determine whether mandatory bargaining was required when a fundamental management decision directly impacted employment. . . .

The balancing test under *Building Material* . . . properly considers the competing interests while furthering the MMBA's neutral purpose to "promote communication between public employers and employees and to improve personnel management. (§ 3500)". . . . We conclude it applies to determine whether management must meet and confer with a recognized employee organization when the implementation of a fundamental managerial or policy decision significantly and adversely affects a bargaining unit's wages, hours, or working conditions.

In view of the vast range of management decisions and to give guidance on whether a particular matter is subject to a duty to meet and confer (§ 3505) under *Building Material, supra*, we find instructive the high court's observation that "[t]he concept of mandatory bargaining is premised on the belief that collective discussions backed by the parties' economic weapons will result in decisions that are better for both management and labor and for society as a whole. This will be true, however, only if the subject proposed for discussion is amenable to resolution through the bargaining process." (*First National Maintenance, supra*.) To that end, when balancing competing interests a court may also consider whether "the transactional cost of the bargaining process outweighs its value." (*Social Services Union v. Board of Supervisors* (1978) 82 Cal. App. 3d 498, 505 [discussing NLRA].) We believe this "transactional cost" factor is not only consistent with the *Building Material* balancing test, but its application also helps to ensure that a duty to meet and confer is invoked only when it will serve its purpose.

In summary, we apply a three-part inquiry. First, we ask whether the management action has "a significant and adverse effect on the wages, hours, or working conditions of the bargaining-unit employees." If not, there is no duty to meet and confer. Second, we ask whether the significant and adverse effect arises from the implementation of a fundamental managerial or policy decision. If not, then, as in *Building Material*, the meet-and-confer requirement applies. Third, if both factors are present—if an action taken to implement a fundamental managerial or policy decision has a significant and adverse effect on the wages, hours, or working conditions of the employees-we apply a balancing test. The action "is within the scope of representation only if the employer's need for unencumbered decisionmaking in managing its operations is outweighed by the benefit to employer-employee relations of bargaining about the action in question." In balancing the interests to determine whether parties must meet and confer over a certain matter a court may also consider whether the "transactional cost of the bargaining process outweighs its value." . . . .

D. Application to the Present Case

Applying the test under *Building Material*, we conclude that the implementation of the Study did not have a significant and adverse effect on the officers' working conditions. The record reflects that "[i]n those cases resulting in citation or arrest, the Study requires slightly more information to be collected by the officer than required in completing the citation or arrest report." Based on "undisputed evidence," the superior court determined that officers may complete a Form in about two minutes and may complete between four and six such Forms in a 12-hour shift. The superior court concluded that the impact on the officers' working conditions was de minimis. We agree and conclude the City was not required to meet and confer (§ 3505) with the Association before implementing the Study. Because there was no significant and adverse effect, we need not balance the City's need for unencumbered decisionmaking — in this case, its policymaking prerogative to eliminate the practice and perception of racial profiling and to determine the best means for doing so-against the benefit to employer-employee relations from bargaining about the subject.

In conclusion, we emphasize the narrowness of our holding. In determining that the City was not required to meet and confer with the Association before implementing the Study, we do not decide whether such a duty would exist should issues regarding officer discipline, privacy rights, and other potential effects arise after the City implements the Study. Based on the record, that question is not before us. . . .

Moreno, J., concurring

I agree with the majority's narrow holding. . . .

That having been said, it is no doubt true that the study results may potentially be used to discipline police officers or may have other adverse employment consequences for them, because racial profiling is a serious form of police misconduct. In my view, the use of the study as an additional basis for discipline would give rise to a duty on the City's part to meet and confer with the Association. The City's adoption of a new basis for disciplining police officers goes to the heart of officers' employment security, and is therefore one of the critical "terms and conditions of employment" at the core of Government Code section 3504. Although the City plainly has the authority and responsibility to discipline officers who persistently engage in racial profiling, its unfettered right to do so does not outweigh the Association's interest in ensuring, through negotiations with the City, that any such discipline follows due process and that the study results have been accurately and fairly analyzed.

Notes

1. Youngstown cites *First National Maintenance* as persuasive (or at least analogous) authority for scope of bargaining cases in the public sector, and *City of Claremont* relies heavily on private-sector precedent. Summers, *supra*, argues that the

concerns about inherent employer authority in the public and private sector are quite distinct. In your opinion, to what extent are the private-sector cases on management rights helpful in crafting rules for the public sector?

2. Consider the critique of *Claremont's* rule by the *amici* for the employer along with the concurrence. Recall that even if only "effects" or "impact" bargaining over a decision is mandatory, such bargaining typically must take place before an employer may implement its decision. Does "effects" bargaining raise different issues in the public sector than in the private sector?

3. *Youngstown* balances employee and employer interests, and then adds a third prong which assesses the extent to which the "mediatory influence" of collective bargaining and impasse procedures are an "appropriate means" to resolve the conflict. Similarly, the *Claremont* test looks at the "benefit to employer-employee relations of bargaining about the action in question," including whether the "transactional cost of the bargaining process outweighs its value." What, exactly, do these final steps add to the analysis? What should this factor mean, in practice?

In *SERB v. Kent State University*, 23 Ohio Pub. Emp. Rep. ¶ 73 (2004), the Ohio SERB adopted an ALJ's order holding that the distribution of licensing and royalty income from faculty inventions was a permissive, not mandatory, subject. The ALJ found that under the first prong, the employees had an interest, but not a great one (because "the invention by the faculty member is only the beginning of a lengthy process . . . which may or may not lead, several years later, to the receipt of patent income"). Under the second prong, the employer interest was relatively strong (since some university programs were highly dependent on patent income, and the University needed to have flexibility to devote patent income to areas of greatest need). *Id.*

The ALJ then held that the third prong favored a finding that the topic was permissive.

> The participatory governance structure in place at the University, including the University Patent and Copyright Board and the Faculty Senate, provides ample opportunity for the parties to discuss and address areas of concern regarding the Guidelines, while allowing the University to exercise the managerial discretion necessary to further its research mission. While the AAUP asserts that collective bargaining is necessary to address issues such as notification to faculty members when their inventions are licensed, the University already has agreed to notify faculty inventors, on an ongoing basis, when their inventions are licensed, and to inform faculty recipients of income distributions that an accounting of such income is available upon written request. The mediatory influence of collective bargaining is not necessary to resolve conflicts over this subject matter. *Id.*

Under this approach, if a public university in Ohio does not use the particular "participatory governance structure" in place at Kent State, would this topic be mandatory at that University?

4. In contrast, *Chicago Park Dist. v. Illinois Lab. Rel. Bd.*, 354 Ill. App. 3d 595 (2004) held that a reduction in work hours available was a mandatory topic, using the three-part balancing test from *Central City Educ. Ass'n* that was cited in *Youngstown*. The court explained that this issue clearly had an impact on employees, but also that the employer had shown the reduction was driven by financial constraints, implicating concerns about its overall budget and standards of service it could provide. The court then held that "the benefits of bargaining an economically-motivated reduction in hours could be substantial": the union "may offer concessions in other areas to achieve the financial savings which the employer seeks or identify employees who wish to work reduced hours." Employees "may be able to identify cost-saving measures of which the employer is unaware." 354 Ill. App. 3d 595, 602–04.

5. Some jurisdictions differ in how they describe the legal rules that determine whether a topic is mandatory. For example, the Delaware Board insists that it does not "balance" the interests but "rather looks to determine where the greater interest lies" using the following test: "compare the direct impact on the individual teacher in wages, salaries, hours, grievance procedures and working conditions as opposed to its probable effect on the operation of the school system as a whole. If the probable effect on the school system as a whole clearly outweighs the direct impact on the interest of the teachers" it is not mandatory; otherwise it is. *Red Clay Consolidated Sch. Dist. v. Red Clay Ed. Ass'n*, DS/ULP No. 06-06-524 (Del. Pub. Employment Rel. Bd. 2007). Is this substantively the same as the balancing tests in the cases discussed above? *Red Clay* added that its test "on its face favors a finding of negotiability." *Id.* If this is a different test, is it better?

3. Recurring Topics Implicating Inherent Governmental Authority: Public Safety Staffing, School Issues, and Subcontracting

In some instances, the issue of whether a topic involves inherent government authority seems to depend in part on the type of employee involved. Many such cases involve either public safety workers or school teachers. In other cases, the bargaining topic itself arguably has different implications in the public sector than in the private: for example, certain proposals regarding staffing or subcontracting. Complicating this further, as discussed earlier, even if a substantive decision is not mandatory, bargaining over the effects of the decision typically is.

As to public safety officers, some cases, like *Claremont*, involve important matters of government policy. For example, *Claremont* cites *San Jose Peace Officer's Assn. v. City of San Jose*, 78 Cal. App. 3d 935, 947 (1978). *San Jose Police Officer's* held that a city policy adding limits on when police officers could use deadly force was not a mandatory subject. It rejected the union's argument that the policy raised important concerns about employee safety. In *Matter of Sergeants Benevolent Ass'n of the City of New York, Inc. v. City of New York*, 6 N.Y.S.3d 474 (2015), the court upheld the labor board's ruling that it was not a ULP for a police department to unilaterally implement a policy requiring alcohol testing for police officers when their discharge of a firearm had resulted in an injury or death. The court held that the board had rationally found that this matter was within the Police Commissioner's disciplinary authority, and thus it was not a mandatory subject. On the other hand, *International B'hood of Teamsters Local 700 v. Illinois Labor Rel. Bd.*, 73 N.E.3d 108 (Ill. 2017), held that a sheriff's department order stating that its employees may not associate with gang members was a mandatory subject of bargaining.

Some cases involve topics that would almost certainly be mandatory in the private sector. For example, **Oak Park Public Safety Officers Ass'n v. City of Oak Park**, 277 Mich. App. 317 (2007) held that the following proposals, which the union titled "safety/staffing," were not mandatory:

> To the extent the City of Oak Park continues to operate a public safety department, providing joint fire and police protection, the City shall maintain on duty, at all times, assigned to the operations division . . . a safety/ staffing level of seven public safety officers, of which a minimum of five . . . shall be fire certified, in addition to possessing law enforcement certification. A minimum of five fire certified public safety officers shall be deployed for a structural fire, including one fire certified public safety officer to operate fire apparatus including pumping equipment, and no less than four fire certified public safety officers to suppress the structural fire, of which no less than two fire certified public safety officers shall be required to physically enter the hazardous area of a structural fire, with two fire certified safety officers outside the hazardous area available for assistance, rescue and operation of additional fire equipment and apparatus. When a fire incident arises, a minimum of two public safety officers shall be deployed as primary and back-up to perform law enforcement responsibilities. . . . 277 Mich. App. 317, 319–20.

Under the Michigan statute, mandatory subjects include "wages, hours, and other terms and conditions of employment." MICH. COMP. LAWS § 423.215(1). Still, the court agreed with MERC, the state agency, that to be mandatory, the "impact of a staffing decision on working conditions, including safety, must be proven to be significant. . . . To adopt the union's position would be tantamount to requiring that most, if not all, minimum staffing proposals—particularly with regard to [public safety officers] . . . —be subject to mandatory bargaining, given that a reduction in the number of these employees will arguably have some—albeit minimal—impact on safety. Such a conclusion would have the effect of invading the city's prerogative to determine the size and scope of its business, including the services it will provide." 277 Mich. App. at 329–30.

The Michigan Supreme Court, citing *Oak Park* approvingly, later explained that a staffing proposal must be "'inextricably intertwined with safety' to be a mandatory subject of bargaining." *Detroit Fire Fighters Ass'n v. City of Detroit*, 482 Mich. 18, 22–23 (2008). *See also City of South Milwaukee Firefighters' Protective Ass'n, Local 1633 IAFF v. City of South Milwaukee*, Dec. No. 32059 (Wisc. Emp. Rel. Comm., Mar. 27, 2007) (proper legal test for a proposal that would have reduced the number of firefighters on a shift from seven to six involved considering a "variety of factors" evaluating the change on firefighter safety and then balancing that against the "municipal employer's service level choices"). In contrast, *City of Allentown v. IAFF Local 302*, 157 A.3d 899 (Pa. 2017), held that under Pennsylvania law, the number of firefighters on duty per shift was a mandatory subject of bargaining, not a matter of inherent management prerogative.

Public safety employers sometimes prevail in negotiability determinations concerning staffing and even hours of work by convincing the tribunal that protecting the public is a significant factor in their decision. *City of Patterson and PBA Local 1*, 32 NJPER ¶ 13 (PERC 2006) rejected a police union's claim that implementing a redistricting plan which reduced the numbers of police squads and changed the work schedules of a number of officers was a mandatory topic because work schedules were mandatory topics. The employer argued its actions "were non-negotiable governmental policy determinations in response to public safety concerns regarding an upward trend in violent crimes." The agency, in ruling for the employer, explained that "[p]olice work schedules are generally mandatorily negotiable unless the employer demonstrates a particularized need to preserve or change a work schedule to support or implement a governmental policy determination." Specifically, an employer may legally "unilaterally change work schedules where it has demonstrated a need to improve supervision, enforce discipline, train rank-and-file officers, and align a unit's schedule with the time services are most needed." Here, the justifications of responding to a rise in violent crime, the need to deploy officers more effectively, and the goal of increasing command accountability made the topic non-mandatory.

City of Everett v. Int'l Ass'n of Firefighters, Case No. 127504-U-5 (Wash. Pub. Empt' Rel. Comm'n, Oct. 3, 2017), *aff'd, City of Everett v. Public Employee Relations Committee*, 11 Wash. App. 2d 1 (2019), used a balancing test and determined that staffing for firefighters was a mandatory subject. The agency noted, however, that in this area, whether a proposal was mandatory or permissive would depend on the facts of individual cases. It explained that its balancing test "does not provide parties with certainty about what topics are mandatory . . . [but] it does effectuate the appropriate balance." If you find this troublingly unclear, consider the alternative of specific statutory lists of negotiable and non-negotiable topics when you read subsection C, *infra*. In affirming, the court noted that substantial evidence supported PERC's finding that the increase in the number of calls responded to during each shift directly impacted firefighters' safety, to support determination that union's proposal was a mandatory subject.

Further, it is generally true that even when "manpower issues are not mandatory subjects of bargaining . . . there is a duty to bargain over the impact of manpower decisions to the extent that they related to workload and safety." *City of Sault Ste. Marie v. Fraternal Order of Police Labor Council*, 163 Mich. App. 350 (1987). For example, *Philadelphia Fire Fighters' Union, Local 22, IAFF v. City of Philadelphia*, 37

Penn. Pub. Emp. Rep. ¶ 67 (Commw. Ct. 2006) held that while the substantive decision to reorganize the fire department was not a mandatory subject, the city had a duty to engage in effects bargaining after the implementation of the plan because of its impact on terms and conditions of employment. What might those mandatory effects be?

Problem 10.4

Suppose, in response to layoffs in a fire department, a union made the following proposal:

> The City has increased the safety risks to employees and has required employees to perform additional labor, without additional compensation, as a result of a decrease in minimum manning from 28 firefighters to 22 firefighters per shift. The City has not decreased the amount of equipment in operation, with the result that fewer employees are now required to perform the duties than prior to the staffing reductions. Thus, firefighters will be paid at the rate of time-and-a-half when fewer than four firefighters are assigned to a piece of equipment.

The City argues that the proposal is non-mandatory because staffing level of firefighters is a managerial prerogative and the proposal interferes with its right to exercise that prerogative.

Assume that the relevant statute uses the type of general language found in the cases above, but that the relevant labor board generally holds that staffing levels of firefighters is a non-mandatory subject. Should this proposal be held to be a mandatory topic?

Cases involving public schools, notably class size and the school year, also raise issues of inherent government policy. *Racine Ed. Ass'n v. Racine Unified School District*, Dec. No. 27972-C (Wis. Emp. Rel. Comm. 1996) held that the employer's decision to adopt a year-round education program was not a mandatory subject. The then-applicable statute required employers to bargain over "wages, hours, and conditions of employment," but stated that employers "shall not be required to bargain on subjects reserved to management and direction of the governmental unit" except for effects bargaining. *Id.*

The Wisconsin Commission held that the employer's decision was based on educational policy judgments that learning opportunities would improve, so it had a direct, substantial relationship to educational policy. While it also had a direct, substantial impact on the timing of employee vacations, and thus on hours and conditions, the educational policy concerns predominated. The Commission stressed that this did not alter prior holdings that in-service days, convention days, holidays, pay days, and when snow days were made up were all mandatory topics. *Id.* The Wisconsin Appeals Court affirmed. *Racine Educ. Ass'n v. WERC*, 571 N.W.2d 887 (Wis. Ct. App. 1997).

Jurisdictions are split over the more common issue of starting and ending dates for the school year. For example, *Clark County Sch. Dist. v Local Government Employee Management Rel. Bd.*, 90 Nev. 442 (1974) held that the school calendar is a mandatory subject because selection of the days a teacher must work in a given school year is significantly related to the teacher's working conditions and the amount of work that the teacher is expected to perform for a fixed compensation. It rejected the argument that negotiability of the calendar would interfere with managerial prerogatives. In contrast, *Eastbrook Community Schools Corp. v. Indiana Education Employment Rel. Bd.*, 446 N.E.2d 1007 (Ind. Ct. App.), *reh'g denied*, 450 N.E.2d 1006 (Ind. Ct. App. 1983) held that changes in the school calendar were not mandatory. The formulation of the calendar was within the school board's exclusive managerial prerogative; also, the decision affected only the scheduling of days, not total number of days, on which teachers had to teach.

Class size has been litigated repeatedly, and jurisdictions are divided. *See* Martin Malin & Charles Kerchner, *Charter Schools and Collective Bargaining: Compatible Marriage or Illegitimate Relationship?*, 30 Harv. J.L. & Pub. Pol'y 885, 915 (2007). A significant number of cases have held that it is not a mandatory subject because, while it does affect conditions for teachers, it is a matter of education policy. *See, e.g., Hillsborough Classroom Teachers Ass'n, Inc. v. School Bd. of Hillsborough County*, 423 So. 2d 969 (Fla. Dist. Ct. App. 1982); *Kenai Peninsula Dist. v. Kenai Peninsula Educ. Ass'n*, 572 P.2d 416 (Alaska 1977); *Beloit Educ. Ass'n v. WERC*, 73 Wis. 2d 43 (1976); *City of Biddeford v. Biddeford Teachers Ass'n*, 304 A.2d 387 (Me. 1973).

For example, **West Irondequoit Bd. of Educ.**, 4 PERB ¶ 3070 (N.Y. 1971), *aff'd sub nom. Matter of West Irondequoit Teachers' Ass'n v. Helsby*, 35 N.Y.2d 46 (1974) held that class size was a permissive topic. The union argued that class size was a condition of employment in part because excess class size could affect a teacher's emotional or mental well-being. 35 N.Y.2d 46, 49. But the state board ruled that the issue went to the manner and means by which education service is rendered, a nondelegable duty of the employer. "[B]asic decisions as to public policy should not be made in the isolation of the negotiation table, but rather . . . by those having the direct and sole responsibility therefor, and whose actions . . . are subject to review in the electoral process." 4 PERB ¶ 3070.

If that is true, does it mean that class size should be an *illegal* subject of bargaining, rather than a permissive one? Yet *West Irondequoit* affirmed the labor board's holding which clarified that "this decision does not prohibit negotiations on class size." Indeed "consulting" with teachers' unions "should be encouraged so as to take advantage of the teacher's professional expertise." *Id.* Soon thereafter, the court in *Bd. of Educ. v Greenburgh Teachers Fed.*, 381 N.Y.S.2d 517 (1976) held that class size was permissive and that the parties could enter into binding contract terms on the issue. But, under the logic of *West Irondequoit*, why should the parties even be allowed to agree to decide the subject in the "isolation of the negotiation table"? Consider further the issue of permissive topics in the public sector generally when reading *Local 195, IFPTE, AFL CIO v. State of New Jersey*, 88 N.J. 393 (1982), *infra*.

On the other hand, class size is a mandatory subject in a number of jurisdictions. *See, e.g., Oroville Union High Sch. Dist. v. Oroville Secondary Teacher's Ass'n*, 26 PERC ¶ 33083 (Cal. PERB ALJ 2002); *Decatur Bd. of Educ. Dist. No. 61 v. IELRB*, 180 Ill. App. 3d 770 (1989); *West Hartford Educ. Ass'n v. DeCourcy*, 162 Conn. 566 (1972). *West Hartford* explained that "policy questions are involved in these matters but that cannot be decisive." Citing private-sector precedent broadly defining "conditions of employment," the court concluded that "class size and teacher load chiefly define the amount of work expected of a teacher, a traditional indicator of whether an item is a 'condition of employment.'" 162 Conn. 566, 585–86. *Clark County School Dist. v. Local Gov. Emp. Management Rel. Bd.*, 90 Nev. 442 (1974) held that class size was mandatory because it is significantly related to wages, hours, and working conditions. Student density affects teacher workload, including required hours of preparation and post-class evaluation; it affects teacher control of classes and discipline problems; it affects teaching and communication techniques; and it affects the total amount of work required. The court rejected the argument that negotiability of class size would impermissibly interfere with the management prerogatives. Is this the better view?

Also, *West Irondequoit* seemed to indicate that while class size is not mandatory, teaching load is. "At first look, class size and teaching load may seem the same, but as we see them, they are not. The first represents a determination by the public employer as to an educational policy made in light of its resources and other needs of its constituency" while "the number of teaching periods" was "clearly mandatory." 4 PERB ¶ 3070. Is this a sensible distinction? See *New Providence Bd. of Educ. v. New Providence Educ. Ass'n*, 9 NJPER 14038 (Pub. Emp. Rel. Comm. 1982) (class size was not a mandatory subject, and a clause that established workload in terms of class size was "primarily directed at class size limitation rather than mandatory negotiable offsets for workload increases").

Some decisions on other issues involving teachers have stressed policies favoring bargaining. Relying heavily on private-sector precedent, *Bonner Sch. Dist. No. 14 v. Bonner Educ. Ass'n*, 341 Mont. 97 (2007) held that teacher transfers and reassignments were mandatory subjects. The court cited *Fibreboard* for the idea that "refusals to confer and negotiate had been one of the most prolific causes of industrial strife" before modern labor law. 341 Mont. 97, 106. Bargaining thus promoted the purpose of the Montana statute: to "remove certain recognized sources of strife and unrest" and "arrive at friendly adjustment of all disputes between public employers and their employees." 341 Mont. at 109. *Bonner* also noted that bargaining did not require the employer to agree to union proposals. In sum, "bargaining provides a process that places little actual burden on the employer but can do so much to 'defuse and channel conflict between labor and management.' *First National Maintenance.*" *Id.* Similarly, *Mars Area Educational Support Personnel Ass'n v. Mars Area Sch. Dist.*, 32 PPER ¶ 32023 (PA LRB Hearing Examiner 2000) held that the employer's proposal to change the length of the school year (from 188 to 205 days for certain employees) was a mandatory subject. *Eastern Westmoreland Career and Tech. Ctr. Ed. Ass'n v. Eastern Westmoreland Career and Tech. Ctr.*, 37 PPER ¶ 5 (PA LRB Hearing Examiner 2006) held that the decision to rescind a flexible work schedule under which teachers could choose whether to come in at 7:00 a.m. or 7:30 a.m. was a mandatory topic. This was because the change had a significant impact on the teachers' interests in hours and working conditions, but no demonstrable effect on the district's basic policy of educating students. Also, applying a standard "balancing test," the New Hampshire agency held that a school system moving from a "block" schedule to an "A/B" schedule for classes was a mandatory subject of bargaining, rejecting the employer's argument that this should be a matter of educational policy reserved to management. *Sugar River Educ. Ass'n v. Claremont School Dist.*, Dec. No. 2016-176, Case No. E-0188-2 (N.H. PERB, July 29, 2016).

Concerns about inherent government powers also arise when public employers propose to contract out public services. In a majority of jurisdictions, subcontracting is at least usually a mandatory subject of bargaining. For example, in ***Rialto Police Benefit Ass'n v. City of Rialto***, 66 Cal. Rptr. 3d 714 (Ct. App. 2007), the court, following the test articulated in *Claremont, supra*, held that the city of Rialto's decision to change the provider of its police services from the Rialto Police Department to the San Bernadino County Sheriff's Department was a mandatory topic. Relying heavily on private-sector precedent, the court held that this decision was more analogous to *Fibreboard* than to *First National Maintenance*, and, as such, as in *Fibreboard*, the decision to subcontract was a mandatory subject. *See also Interurban Transit Partnership*, 17 MPER ¶ 40 (Mich. Emp. Rel. Comm. 2004) (subcontracting "on demand" transportation system that formerly had been performed by bargaining unit members was a mandatory subject).

Some jurisdictions, however, view subcontracting as a matter of inherent governmental right. *See, e.g., Amalgamated Transit Union Local 1593 v. Hillsborough Area Regional Transit Auth.*, 742 So. 2d 380 (Fla. Dist. Ct. App. 1999) (upholding labor board's decision that public-sector subcontracting is not a mandatory subject). The court briefly explained:

> Appellant relies on the private sector model found in *Fibreboard* . . . We distinguish the instant case from *Fibreboard* on the basis that private sector employers are quite different from public sector employers. The Florida Supreme Court has recognized that there are critical distinctions between private and public sector bargaining. *State v. Florida Police Benevolent Assoc., Inc.*, 613 So.2d 415 (Fla.1992). We, therefore, agree with PERC's interpretation of section 447.209, Florida Statutes, that the right to subcontract is a management prerogative which is not a subject of mandatory collective bargaining. 742 So. 2d at 381.

Consider also the following decision.

Local 195, IFPTE, AFL-CIO v. State of New Jersey

Supreme Court of New Jersey
88 N.J. 393, 443 A.2d 187 (1982)

PASHMAN, J.

[The State and Local 195 were bargaining over a new contract, and they filed a joint petition for a scope of negotiations determination with the Public Employment Relations Commission (PERC) over clauses which limited contracting and subcontracting.]

. . . In deciding that subcontracting was a negotiable issue, PERC relied on its earlier cases, arguing that subcontracting must be mandatorily subject to negotiation since a decision to subcontract would effectively terminate the employment relationship vis-a-vis the employees in a negotiations unit and would have a "cataclysmic effect on wages, hours, and working conditions. . . ."

[The Appellate Division] divided on the negotiability of subcontracting. The majority reversed PERC and held that the determination to subcontract work is an inherent managerial prerogative. Judge Morgan dissented, arguing that the majority had failed to consider the interests of public employees in reaching its decision. Applying a balancing test, Judge Morgan would have found subcontracting to be a mandatorily negotiable issue.

Scope of Negotiability

. . . The parameters of collective negotiations about such proposals were established in 1968 by the New Jersey Employer-Employee Relations Act, N.J.S.A. 34:13A-1 to -21, and later by judicial decisions.

The central issue in a scope of negotiations determination is whether or not a particular subject matter is negotiable. This depends on careful consideration of the legitimate interests of the public employer and the public employees. The process of balancing those competing interests is constrained by the policy goals underlying relevant statutes and by the Constitution.

The Legislature has recognized that, like private employees, public employees have a legitimate interest in engaging in collective negotiations about issues that affect "terms and conditions of employment." N.J.S.A. 34:13A-5.3. However, the scope of negotiations in the public sector is more limited than in the private sector.[7] This is so because the employer in the public sector is government, which has special responsibilities to the public not shared by private employers.[8] What distinguishes

---

7. For example, there are generally no permissive subjects of negotiation in New Jersey public employment.

8. Thus, we have consistently held that federal precedents concerning the scope of collective bargaining in the private sector are of little value in determining the permissible scope of negotiability in the public sphere. For this reason, the United States Supreme Court decision holding

the State from private employers is the unique responsibility to make and implement public policy.

Matters of public policy are properly decided, not by negotiation and arbitration, but by the political process. This involves the panoply of democratic institutions and practices, including public debate, lobbying, voting, legislation and administration. We have stated that

> "the very foundation of representative democracy would be endangered if decisions on significant matters of governmental policy were left to the process of collective negotiations . . . Our democratic system demands that governmental bodies retain their accountability to the citizenry." *Ridgefield Park Ed. Ass'n v. Ridgefield Park Bd. of Ed.*, 78 N.J. 144, 163 (1978).

We have therefore divided subjects of public employment negotiation into two categories: "mandatorily negotiable terms and conditions of employment and non-negotiable matters of governmental policy." *Id.* at 162, 393 A.2d 278.

The role of the courts in a scope-of-negotiations case is to determine, in light of the competing interests of the State and its employees, whether an issue is appropriately decided by the political process or by collective negotiations. In making this sensitive determination, the mere invocation of abstract categories like "terms and conditions of employment" and "managerial prerogatives" is not helpful. To determine whether a subject is negotiable, the Court must balance the competing interests by considering the extent to which collective negotiations will impair the determination of governmental policy.

Our opinions on public employment have established a three-part test for scope-of-negotiations determinations. First, a subject is negotiable only if it "intimately and directly affect(s) the work and welfare of public employees. . . ." The prime examples of subjects that fall within this category are rates of pay and working hours. Any subject which does not satisfy this part of the test is not negotiable.

Second, an item is not negotiable if it has been preempted by statute or regulation. If the Legislature establishes a specific term or condition of employment that leaves no room for discretionary action, then negotiation on that term is fully preempted. If the statute sets a minimum or maximum term or condition, then negotiation may be confined within the parameters established by these limits. . . .

Third, a topic that affects the work and welfare of public employees is negotiable only if it is a matter "on which negotiated agreement would not significantly interfere with the exercise of inherent management prerogatives pertaining to the determination of governmental policy." This principle rests on the assumption that most decisions of the public employer affect the work and welfare of public employees to some extent and that negotiation will always impinge to some extent on the

---

subcontracting to be a negotiable subject in the context of a private employer is not persuasive authority in this case. See *Fibreboard Paper Products Corp. v. NLRB*, 379 U.S. 203 (1964).

determination of governmental policy. The requirement that the interference be "significant" is designed to effect a balance between the interests of public employees and the requirements of democratic decision making. . . .

To summarize, a subject is negotiable between public employers and employees when (1) the item intimately and directly affects the work and welfare of public employees; (2) the subject has not been fully or partially preempted by statute or regulation; and (3) a negotiated agreement would not significantly interfere with the determination of governmental policy. To decide whether a negotiated agreement would significantly interfere with the determination of governmental policy, it is necessary to balance the interests of the public employees and the public employer. When the dominant concern is the government's managerial prerogative to determine policy, a subject may not be included in collective negotiations even though it may intimately affect employees' working conditions.

. . . The contract provision in Local 195 states:

> The State agrees to meet with the Union to discuss all incidences of contracting or subcontracting whenever it becomes apparent that a layoff or job displacement will result. (Article XXXIV).

[This] would require negotiation or discussion only if subcontracting might result in layoffs or displacement. "Nothing more directly and intimately affects a worker than the fact of whether or not he (or she) has a job." The clause clearly meets the requirements of the first part of the test for negotiability.

[The Court then held that no statute pre-empted the ability of the employer to subcontract.]

Finally, we consider whether negotiation on the substantive decision to contract or subcontract would significantly interfere with the determination of governmental policy. The issue of subcontracting does not merely concern the proper technical means for implementing social and political goals. The choice of how policies are implemented, and by whom, can be as important a feature of governmental choice as the selection of ultimate goals. See *North Bergen Bd. of Ed. v. No. Bergen Fed'n of Teachers*, 141 N.J.Super. 97 (App.Div.1976) ("the board's right to select (the best qualified) candidates from within or without the system involves major educational policy and as such must be considered a managerial prerogative"). It is a matter of general public concern whether governmental services are provided by government employees or by contractual arrangements with private organizations. This type of policy determination does not necessarily concern solely fiscal considerations. It requires basic judgments about how the work or services should be provided to best satisfy the concerns and responsibilities of government. Deciding whether or not to contract out a given government service may implicate important tradeoffs.

Allowing such decisions to be subject to mandatory negotiation would significantly impair the ability of public employers to resort to subcontracting. We have previously held that decisions to reduce the work force for economy or efficiency are non-negotiable subjects. The decision to contract out work or to subcontract is similarly an area where managerial interests are dominant. This is highlighted by the fact that allowing subcontracting to be negotiable may open the road to grievance arbitration. Imposing a legal duty on the state to negotiate all proposed instances of subcontracting would transfer the locus of the decision from the political process to the negotiating table, to arbitrators, and ultimately to the courts. The result of such a course would significantly interfere with the determination of governmental policy and would be inimical to the democratic process.

We therefore hold that to the extent the contractual provision at issue . . . includes negotiation on the ultimate substantive decision to subcontract, it is a non-negotiable matter of managerial prerogative. We recognize that our ruling on subcontracting is at odds with decisions in other jurisdictions. . . . These decisions rest on the assumption that subcontracting "does not represent a choice among alternative social or political goals or values." As we have stated, we do not agree that the decision to contract out work necessarily concerns merely the technical means of implementing policy. The decision can be an important policy choice in its own right.

These out-of-state decisions also emphasize the wisdom of pursuing discussion between public employers and employees. . . . We fully agree that such discussions are valuable and should be fostered. They would undoubtedly promote labor peace and harmony, a major goal of the New Jersey Employer-Employee Relations Act. N.J.S.A. 34:13A-2. Moreover, they may even result in greater efficiency or economy. If a public employer is considering subcontracting as a means to achieve these goals, employees may be motivated to suggest changes in working conditions that could accomplish the same or better results.

For these reasons, we fully expect that discussion between public employers and employees will be undertaken by the State. It is clearly in the interest of the State to do so. . . . We do not mean to stifle discussion. We encourage it. State officials would be derelict in their public responsibilities if they did not pursue such discussions.

To this end, we hold that a public employment contract may include a provision reciting an agreement by the State to discuss decisions to contract or subcontract whenever it becomes apparent that a layoff or job displacement will result, if the proposed subcontracting is based on solely fiscal considerations. In such situations, the public would clearly benefit from suggestions by public employees directed toward improving economy or efficiency. While the public employees have no right to negotiate on the ultimate decision to subcontract, they may have a procedural right to present their position on the economic issue. Thus, for example, they could seek to show the employer that the employees are willing to perform the same job at a price competitive with the private replacements.

Discussion of subcontracting which is contemplated for purely fiscal reasons does not implicate governmental policy to the extent that it would if the decision were based on non-fiscal reasons. Replacing public employees with private employees solely to save money does entail a choice about the level of government spending, a matter of great public concern. However, discussion about such a replacement would not significantly interfere with the determination of public goals. In fact, as we have explained, such discussions would be in the public interest, since employees could demonstrate that they would do the same work more efficiently than a private contractor.

In Local 195, the contract provision would be acceptable if it limited discussion to occasions of subcontracting or contracting likely to result in job layoffs only when the subcontracting is done solely for fiscal or economic reasons. However, as written, the provision is overly broad. Placing a legal duty on the State to discuss subcontracting when proposed for broader policy purposes would place too great a burden on the determination of governmental policy. Only when the contracting out is proposed for purely economic reasons does the employee interest in discussion of alternative solutions become dominant.

. . . To the extent the provisions impose a duty on the State to negotiate procedural aspects of the subcontracting decision as they affect employees, the clauses are negotiable. For example, negotiation could occur on the issue of adequate notice to employees that they are going to be laid off. We have held that, although substantive policy decisions may be non-negotiable matters, procedural aspects of the decision are negotiable. Negotiation about the procedures for laying off employees will not significantly interfere with the underlying policy determination. They are therefore negotiable terms and conditions of employment.

We emphasize that our holding today does not grant the public employer limitless freedom to subcontract for any reason. The State could not subcontract in bad faith for the sole purpose of laying off public employees or substituting private workers for public workers. State action must be rationally related to a legitimate governmental purpose. Our decision today does not leave public employees vulnerable to arbitrary or capricious substitutions of private workers for public employees. . . .

———————

Notes

1. Again, this case represents the minority view on subcontracting. Is it appropriate to have different rules on this issue in the public sector than in the private? Should the decision to privatize public services be negotiable? Not surprisingly, it is not in New Jersey. *See Matawan-Aberdeen Regional Bd. of Educ. and SEIU, Local 74,* 29 NJPER ¶ 173 (PERC 2003).

2. If this is the better approach to subcontracting, is it best that this rule be created by courts and boards, or the legislature? As shown *infra,* legislatures can and sometimes do specify in statutes that certain topics are or are not mandatory subjects of bargaining.

3. *Local 195* reiterates that there are no permissive subjects under this New Jersey statute. A topic is either appropriate for negotiation and therefore mandatory, or it is not appropriate for negotiation and therefore illegal. **Ridgefield Park Educ. Ass'n**

v. Ridgefield Park Bd. of Educ., 78 N.J. 144, 163 (1978) established this dichotomy. It relied in part on an arguably slight difference between the language in NLRA referring to "collective bargaining" and the term "collective negotiations" in the New Jersey statute. "It is crystal clear that in using the term 'collective negotiations' the Legislature intended to recognize inherent limitations on the bargaining power of public employer and employee." 78 N.J. 144, 159. Is that really so clear?

More substantively, the *Ridgefield* court explained:

> We are hesitant to find the existence of a permissive category of negotiable matters in public employment labor relations . . . because such a classification might create serious problems in our democratic system. These potential difficulties should be carefully considered by the Legislature before taking any action expressly to authorize permissive negotiability with respect to all public employees. . . . We deem it appropriate for this Court to comment on these difficult questions concerning the permissibility of delegating governmental powers to private groups or of entrusting the formulation of governmental policy to an arena where the democratic voice of the electorate cannot be heard. . . .

> A private employer may bargain away as much or as little of its managerial control as it likes. However, the very foundation of representative democracy would be endangered if decisions on significant matters of governmental policy were left to the process of collective negotiation, where citizen participation is precluded. This Court would be most reluctant to sanction collective agreement on matters which are essentially managerial in nature, because the true managers are the people. Our democratic system demands that governmental bodies retain their accountability to the citizenry.

> Our concern is with the very function of government. Both state and federal doctrines of substantive due process prohibit delegations of governmental policy-making power to private groups where a serious potential for self- serving action is created thereby. . . . To be constitutionally sustainable, a delegation must be narrowly limited, reasonable, and surrounded with stringent safeguards to protect against the possibility of arbitrary or self-serving action detrimental to third parties or the public good generally. 78 N.J. 144, 162–64.

See also Montgomery City Educ. Ass'n v. Bd. of Educ., 534 A.2d 980 (Md. 1987) (no "permissive" category under the Maryland act covering teachers).

This is a distinctly minority approach. Even in New Jersey, a separate public-sector labor statute governing police and firefighters explicitly provides for permissive topics. *Ridgefield*, 78 N.J. at 158, *citing* L. 1977, C. 85, N.J. Stat. Ann. §§ 34:13A-14 to 21.

Consider, though, whether this approach is better for the public sector than the NLRA model. If a matter is best left to democratic control through "citizen participation," why should an individual public employer even be *allowed* to settle the matter through negotiations with a union? Consider also how, exactly, certain issues are or could be settled by "citizen participation," and how, specifically, collective bargaining reduces "accountability to the citizenry" (if it does at all), especially in the context of a subject that is merely permissive.

4. To what extent, if any, do the final paragraphs of *Local 195* undercut the purpose of *Ridgefield* approach, in that they: (a) permit negotiations over subcontracting if the motivation is purely economic; (b) permit negotiations over effects of any subcontracting; and (c) encourage "discussions" over the issue even where negotiations are barred?

Problem 10.5

Refer to the facts of Problem 10.1 and modify them as follows. First, the employer is a police department. Second, employer representative Killingsworth argues that the employer need not negotiate the decision to install the video surveillance cameras because the employer has a management right to monitor access to a police department building for security reasons.

Assume the relevant statute has general language on the scope of bargaining and uses a "balancing test" as described in cases above. First, should the analysis and result be the same as in Problem 10.1? Second, if you believe the substance of this decision should not be negotiable, what types of permissible "effects" bargaining might the union wish to engage in? *See Nebraska Association of Public Employees Local 61, AFSCME v. State of Nebraska, Dept. of Correctional Services,* Case No. 1448 (Oct. 26, 2018) (requiring police body cams is a mandatory topic given that footage could be used in disciplinary hearings); *Matter of Belleville Educ. Ass'n,* 455 N.J.Super. 387 (N.J. App. July 16, 2018) (using audio and video recording devices in schools to help respond to student shooting incidents was mandatory due to potential use in discipline and privacy issues).

C. Statutory Language Providing Specific Lists of Topics

Some states address negotiability issues by putting specific lists of topics in the text of their statutes. For example, Michigan's law generally provides that public-sector unions and employers must bargain over "wages, hours and other . . . conditions of employment." But in the mid-1990s, it was amended to restrict the scope of bargaining for public school employers. The statute now lists subjects that these employers and unions of their employees may not negotiate, including but not limited to: the starting day of the school year; the amount of pupil contact time required; whether to contract with a third party for noninstructional support services (including the impact of such contracts); who will be the policyholder of an employee group insurance benefit; the use of experimental or pilot programs; and any compensation or additional work intended to reimburse an employee for any monetary penalty imposed under the law. MICH. COMP. LAWS § 423.215. § 15(1),

(3). As noted in Chapter 1, in 2011, Michigan added more statutory restrictions to the scope of bargaining for public schools. Among other things, under the revised § 423.15, school employees may not negotiate over decisions regarding teacher placement, or the impact of such decisions; personnel decisions involving a staffing or program reduction or any other personnel determination resulting in the elimination of a position, or the impact of those decisions; a school's performance evaluation system, including classroom observations, or the impact of those systems; or decisions concerning the performance-based compensation of an individual employee, or the impact of those decisions.

Oregon also has special rules for public schools, in Or. Rev. Stat. § 243.650(7)(e):

> For school district bargaining, "employment relations" excludes class size, the school or educational calendar, standards of performance or criteria for evaluation of teachers, the school curriculum, reasonable dress, grooming and at-work personal conduct requirements respecting smoking, gum chewing and similar matters of personal conduct, the standards and procedures for student discipline, the time between student classes, . . . requirements for expressing milk under ORS 653.077, and any other subject proposed that is permissive under paragraphs (b), (c) and (d) of this subsection.

In the mid-1990s, Wisconsin and Illinois also limited the scope of negotiability for public schools, and some other states narrowed the scope of bargaining for wider groups of public employees. *See* Malin & Kerchner, *supra*, 918–21. Why impose specific limitations on public schools only? As to the part of the Michigan statute forbidding reimbursements for monetary penalties, incurred under the labor statute, consider its purpose after reading Chapter 11's discussion of penalties for illegal strikes by government employees.

Some state statutes have specific lists of negotiable and/or non-negotiable items for all covered public employees. For example, Iowa Code § 20.9 requires unions and employers:

> [T]o negotiate in good faith with respect to wages, hours, vacations, insurance, holidays, leaves of absence, shift differentials, overtime compensation, supplemental pay, seniority, transfer procedures, job classifications, health and safety matters, evaluation procedures, procedures for staff reduction, in-service training and other matters mutually agreed upon. Negotiations shall also include terms authorizing dues checkoff for members of the employee organization and grievance procedures for resolving any questions arising under the agreement, which shall be embodied in a written agreement and signed by the parties.

All retirement systems shall be excluded from the scope of negotiations.

What are the practical consequences of such specific statutory language?

Black Hawk County and Public Professional & Maintenance Employees, Local 2003

Iowa Public Relations Board
Case No. 7218 (2006)

... We apply a two-step analysis in determining whether a proposal is a mandatory subject under Iowa Code section 20.9. First, the proposal must come within the meaning of a section 20.9 mandatory bargaining subject. Second, the proposal must not be illegal under any other provision of law.

In determining whether a proposal "comes within" the meaning of a section 20.9 mandatory bargaining subject, we look only at the subject matter and not the merits of the proposal. The mandatory subjects listed in section 20.9 are construed narrowly and restrictively. We must determine whether the proposal at issue, on its face, fits within a definitionally fixed section 20.9 mandatory bargaining subject. In order to make that determination, we do not merely look for the topical word listed in section 20.9. Rather, we look to what the proposal, if incorporated through arbitration into the collective bargaining agreement, would bind an employer to do. The answer to this inquiry reveals the subject, scope or "predominant characteristic" of the proposal. If the proposal's predominant characteristic is a section 20.9 mandatory topic, and the proposal is not illegal, it is mandatory. If not, the proposal is, at best, permissive.

The proposals at issue are as follows . . . :

Proposal 2: (only the underlined sentences are at issue)

ARTICLE 5. GRIEVANCE PROCEDURE AND ARBITRATION

The parties agree that an orderly and expeditious resolution of grievances is desirable. <u>The Employer will follow a progressive discipline procedure based on the seriousness of the offense.</u> All matters of dispute that may arise between the Employer and an employee or employees regarding the violation, application, or interpretation of the expressed provisions of this Agreement shall be adjusted in accordance with the following procedure: . . .

Step 3: If the department head's answer in Step 2 fails to resolve the grievance, the Union and/or the aggrieved employee may refer the grievance to the Human Resources Director within three (3) working days of the receipt of the Step 2 answer. <u>The Human Resources Director may designate a representative for the bargaining unit to conduct hearings on grievances which do not involve termination or loss of pay issues.</u> Following a meeting with the aggrieved employee and/or the Union, the Human Resources Director shall answer the grievance in writing within seven (7) working days. . . .

RULING: The predominant characteristic of the first underlined sentence is employee discipline. Discipline is not within any section 20.9 topic, and the sentence is thus a permissive subject of bargaining. *See, e.g., Des Moines County*, 00 PERB 6197.

In *Black Hawk County*, 06 PERB 7012, the County argued that the presence of the word "termination" in a sentence identical to the second underlined sentence above rendered it permissive because matters involving discipline and discharge are permissive topics of bargaining. We found, however, that the predominant characteristic of the sentence was not discipline, but rather the procedure to be followed in processing certain non-disciplinary grievances. We ruled the sentence to be mandatory under the section 20.9 topic "grievance procedures," and found that it was not rendered permissive by the mere presence of the word "termination." *Id.*

The County now argues that the second underlined sentence is permissive because it limits the County's ability to designate representatives for grievances that involve termination. We do not think the sentence has that effect. Instead, it is the final sentence of the "step 3" provision, which is not at issue, which prescribes the management representative who shall answer at that stage of the process (*i.e.*, the language which "limits" the County). Rather than limiting the County, the sentence at issue provides it with the procedural option of designating an alternative representative to answer certain types of grievances at step 3.

But even if the second sentence at issue did "limit" the County's ability to designate a third-step decision maker, we do not think such would render it permissive. Provisions concerning other steps in the procedure which specify that the grievance shall be answered by certain employer representatives (such as appear in these parties' existing agreement) clearly have the effect of "limiting" the employer's ability to designate a different representative. Such provisions are not permissive, however, because their predominant characteristic is nonetheless the procedure to be followed at that step of the grievance process. The predominant characteristic of the second underlined sentence is the procedure for the processing of certain types of grievances, and it is mandatorily negotiable under the section 20.9 topic "grievance procedures." . . . .

Proposal 4:

ARTICLE 7. SENIORITY

. . . An employee shall lose his seniority, and the employment relationship shall be broken and terminated as follows: . . . Employee is discharged for proper cause.

RULING: This proposal is a mandatory subject of bargaining under the Iowa Code section 20.9 topic "seniority." . . .

Proposal 9:

ARTICLE 14. HOURS OF WORK AND OVERTIME

. . . Section 4, Shift Defined: The first shift shall be any shift commencing between 7:00 a.m. and 2:59 p.m. The second shift shall be any shift commencing between 3:00 p.m. and 10:59 p.m. The third shift shall be any shift commencing on or after 11:00 p.m. Flex-time may vary the above time if agreed to by the department head and the employee. The flex-time will not cause any increase or loss of wages or benefits. <u>The employee's (sic) work schedule will be posted by the Employer two (2) weeks in advance.</u>

RULING: In *Black Hawk County*, 06 PERB 7012, the Board determined that the starting and quitting times for employees on each work shift is a mandatory subject of bargaining under the section 20.9 topic "hours," but that the assignment of employees to particular shifts is not included within that or any other section 20.9 topic. We also found permissive a requirement that the employer post employees' work schedules three weeks in advance and notify employees and the Union at least three days in advance of any schedule changes.

The proposal at issue here does not establish starting and quitting times for employees on each shift. On its face, the proposal simply labels each shift as "first," "second" or "third" on the basis of when it commences. The proposal does not specify when any of the three shifts actually begins or ends (*i.e.,* the starting and quitting times). Since the first three sentences of the proposal do not establish hours of work, the flex time language which refers to those sentences also does not relate to hours. While the Union may have intended this proposal to establish the starting and quitting times of each shift, we must read proposals literally as they come before us, and may not rewrite the parties' proposals.

Although we determined in *Black Hawk County*, 06 PERB 7012, that a proposal requiring advance notification to employees of their work schedule and schedule changes was a permissive bargaining topic, upon further consideration we are convinced that ruling was in error and that we should overrule it and find the last sentence of the proposal above (in bold) to be a mandatory subject of bargaining under the section 20.9 topic "hours."

In Case No. 7012, some of the language at issue in the "hours" article dealt with the matter of shift assignment. When we reached the issue concerning advance posting of employee's work schedule, we made an assumption, which may have been incorrect, that the term "work schedule" referred to employee shift assignments. We stated that "assuming the reference to 'work schedule' means a shift assignment," the language dealing with notification of the work schedule and schedule changes was permissive. We note, however, that regardless of what the parties may have intended, in making negotiability determinations we are to give words their ordinary and commonly understood meaning. We think the ordinary and commonly understood meaning of the term "work schedule" is the days and hours (*i.e.,* starting and quitting times) an employee is expected to work.

We think that the matter of when an employee is to be notified of his or her scheduled hours of work is a fundamental aspect of the section 20.9 topic "hours" and thus encompassed within it, just as the timing of wage payments is a fundamental aspect of the topic "wages," properly encompassed within the meaning of that section 20.9 topic.

We remain convinced that proposals specifying which shift an employee will be assigned to are not mandatorily negotiable, as their predominant characteristics are assignment and staffing—not the section 20.9 topic "hours." However, there is no question that a shift assignment has an impact on an employee's hours of work. Thus, while the matter of shift assignment is permissive, we think that the predominant characteristic of a proposal requiring notification to the employee of his or her hours of work, whether stated in terms of a "work schedule" or a "shift assignment," is within the section 20.9 topic "hours," and a mandatory subject of bargaining.

The proposal above is a permissive topic of bargaining except for its final sentence, which is mandatory. . . .

Proposal 11:

ARTICLE 19 JOB CLASSIFICATIONS AND STRAIGHT-TIME HOURLY WAGE RATES

Section 2, Job Classification: Whenever an employee's job responsibilities have been significantly and unavoidably changed or increased, the Union and/or the employee's department head may request a reclassification to a higher or different job classification. The Union and/or the department head must submit a written request to the County's Human Resources Department to audit and review the job. The written request must explain the significant change in job responsibilities and why the change(s) is unavoidable. The review request will be submitted to the Classification Audit Committee. The Board of Supervisors shall approve or deny the reclassification request. The Union shall be provided with written notice of all reclassification approvals or denials in the bargaining unit. The Union may grieve an approval or denial by the Board by submitting a request for arbitration to the Board within seven (7) working days from receipt of the written notification.

Section 3, Classification Audit Committee (also known as CAC):

A. *Members:* The Committee shall be comprised of three (3) union bargaining team members and/or union officers, one (1) Human Resources representative, one (1) elected official or their designated representative and one (1) appointed department head or their designated representative. The remaining committee members will designate an alternate if the audit concerns that member's department.

B. *Purpose:* The purpose of the committee is to address and make consensus recommendation using Interest Based Bargaining (IBB) principles regarding job classifications using the point-factor system. The committee's scope addresses newly-elected job classifications by the Board, department-wide reviews of existing classifications, or requests by either the Union or Department Head under the current bargaining agreement that an employee's job classification be changed. A CAC audit recommendation may include creation of a new job classification.

The Interest Based Bargaining Committee will meet with department heads, supervisors and employees to explain the existing point-factor system, review existing factor points for Unit 1 classifications, and explain the purpose of CAC.

CAC will make a written report to the Board of Supervisors and Union regarding their activities in the past 3-year period and make any recommendations on system-wide changes or problems.

C *Audit Review:* Request for all new job classifications shall be reviewed by the CAC, who will make recommendations to the Board of Supervisors. The Board of Supervisors decision whether to create a new job classification is final, with wages to be negotiated with the Union.

RULING: This proposal is a permissive subject of bargaining. Although "job classifications" is listed as a mandatory topic in Iowa Code section 20.9, this is not a proposal to establish or change job classifications. It is, rather, a proposal which establishes procedures for requesting the reclassification of existing jobs and for reaching consensus recommendations on job classifications, utilizing a joint labor-management committee.

Had the legislature chosen to list "procedures for job classification" or similar language as a section 20.9 topic, much of section 2 of this proposal might well be viewed as mandatorily negotiable, since its predominant characteristic is procedures to address reclassification requests. The legislature, however, chose instead to mandate bargaining only on the narrower topic of "job classifications," and the procedures for reclassification in section 2 of the proposal are not within the scope of that section 20.9 topic. As to section 3 of the proposal, it is well settled that proposals to establish and operate labor-management committees to study and make recommendations concerning mandatory topics are not mandatory subjects of bargaining.

Notes

1. Apart from the specifics of the Iowa statute and this case, what are the advantages and disadvantages generally of legislatures putting detailed lists of what is and is not negotiable in the text of statutes, as opposed to using broad statutory language, which boards and courts will then interpret?

In *Waterloo Educ. Ass'n v. Iowa Public Employment Relations Bd.*, 740 N.W.2d 418 (Iowa 2007), the Iowa Supreme Court compared the Iowa statute favorably with the "balancing test" approach. It characterized the latter as inevitably featuring "a conflict between the expansive concepts of employee rights and traditional public employer prerogatives. These are two highly territorial pikes at large in the legal pond of collective bargaining, each with the capacity of devouring the other." 740 N.W.2d 418, 423. Further, "it is impossible to objectively measure or quantify the weight of employer and employee interests. . . . No court has been able to successfully advance a convincing formula for determining how many employee rights apples it takes to equal an employer rights orange." 740 N.W.2d at 423.

One possible advantage to statutes with specific lists is that both unions and employers will understand more clearly what is and is not negotiable, and there will be less litigation over negotiability issues. But does *Black Hawk County* cast some doubt on this? Iowa has used this approach for decades. This 2006 case involved a total of 17 litigated proposals; the union and employer each prevailed on some issues; and the Iowa Board reversed itself on one topic. Did the statutory language clearly compel the results in this case? Also, in *Waterloo Educ. Ass'n, supra*, the Iowa Supreme Court found a union proposal mandatory that both the state board and the lower court had held to be permissive. 740 N.W.2d at 419.

2. Are statutes that limit the scope of negotiability for teachers but not other government employees good policy? One result in Michigan is that subcontracting work is permissive for school employees, *Detroit Public Schools and Int'l Ass'n of Machinists and Aerospace Workers*, 17 MPER ¶ 14 (Mich. Emp. Rel. Comm. 2004), while it is generally mandatory for other public employees in Michigan law (*see, e.g., Interurban Transit Partnership, supra*).

3. As Chapter 1 noted, Iowa amended its statute in 2017 to, among other things, radically restrict the scope of bargaining for bargaining units comprised of less than 30 percent public safety employees. The "laundry list" approach still applies to other bargaining units, however.

D. Restrictions on the Scope of Bargaining from External Law

Public employment is governed by a wide variety of legal rules apart from collective-bargaining laws. Many of these, notably pension, tenure, and civil service laws, significantly predate labor laws, and at least most were passed to further important public interests in government and public employment. For example, civil service laws arose, beginning in the late 19th century, with the goal of ensuring that public employees would be hired, fired, promoted, and otherwise evaluated according to their merit, rather than their loyalty to a particular politician or political machine. *See* Joseph Slater, *Homeland Security vs. Workers' Rights? What the Federal Government Should Learn from History and Experience, and Why*, 6 U.Pa. J. Lab. & Emp. L. 295, 351–53 (2004).

Conflicts, or potential conflicts, arise not infrequently between rules and terms of employment which external laws set and rules and terms of employment for which unions wish to bargain. For example, civil service laws often provide both substantive rights (*e.g.*, in hiring, promotions, discipline and discharge) and procedural mechanisms (*e.g.*, a Civil Service Commission or similar administrative tribunal to enforce such rights). Most public employees in union bargaining units are covered by such civil service rules. To what extent can unions and employers negotiate subjects that are at least to some extent covered by such laws?

In some jurisdictions, the labor law itself explains how potential conflicts with other laws should be resolved. For example, the Ohio public-sector labor statute first provides that certain traditionally important civil service rules cannot legally be altered by bargaining. "The conduct and grading of civil service examinations, the rating of candidates, the establishment of eligible lists from the examinations, and the original appointments from the eligible lists are not appropriate subjects for collective bargaining." Ohio Rev. Code. § 4117.08(B).

Section 4117.10(A) of the Ohio statute then specifies which other laws trump collectively bargained rules, which other laws provide minimums that collectively bargained rules can go beyond, and thus which terms set by other laws may be superseded by collective bargaining agreements. State statutes pertaining to, *e.g.*, civil rights, unemployment compensation, workers' compensation, and retirement prevail over any provisions in labor contracts. State statutes regarding compensation and leaves of absence for public employees set the floor but not the ceiling for collectively bargained contracts. Labor contract rules take precedence over statutory rules entirely in areas not listed in this section (which is set out in full in the Documentary Supplement). How does this language work in practice?

Null v. Ohio Department of Mental Retardation & Developmental Disabilities

Court of Appeals for the State of Ohio
137 Ohio App. 3d 152, 738 N.E.2d 105 (2000)

Bryant, J.

[Plaintiff Anne Null alleged that defendant, her employer, had violated the Ohio Minimum Fair Wage Standards Act, Ohio Rev. Code § 4111.01, in denying her overtime compensation for certain activities. Defendant argued that pursuant to the state labor law, Ohio Rev. Code § 4117.10(A), the agreement to arbitrate in the collective bargaining agreement covering plaintiff barred her claims under the Chapter 4111 (the Wage Standards Act). The trial court agreed that § 4117.10(A) controlled her claim, and thus the trial court had no jurisdiction over her claim under Chapter 4111.]

. . . [W]e are asked to determine which prevails in determining jurisdiction over plaintiff's claim under R.C. 4111.03: the collective bargaining agreement and its binding arbitration clause, or R.C. Chapter 4111 pursued through an action in the common pleas court.

R.C. 4117.10(A) establishes the relationship between the provisions of a collective bargaining agreement and state laws. It provides:

> "An agreement between a public employer and an exclusive representative entered into pursuant to this chapter governs the wages, hours, and terms and conditions of public employment covered by the agreement. If the agreement provides for a final and binding arbitration of grievances, public employers, employees, and employee organizations are subject solely to that grievance procedure and the state personnel board of review or civil service commissions have no jurisdiction to receive and determine any appeals relating to matters that were the subject of a final and binding grievance

procedure. Where no agreement exists or where an agreement makes no specification about a matter, the public employer and public employees are subject to all applicable state or local laws or ordinances pertaining to the wages, hours, and terms and conditions of employment for public employees. . . . [T]his chapter prevails over any and all other conflicting laws, resolutions, provisions, present or future, except as otherwise specified in this chapter or as otherwise specified by the general assembly."

Pursuant to R.C. 4117.10(A) when no state or local law addresses a matter addressed in a collective bargaining agreement, no conflict exists between the agreement and the law, and the agreement governs the parties as to that matter. Conversely, when a collective bargaining agreement does not address a matter but a state or local law does, again no conflict arises: pursuant to R.C. 4117.10(A) state or local law generally would apply to a public employer and its public employees regarding "wages, hours and terms and conditions" of employment. When, however, a state or local law pertaining to a specific exception listed in R.C. 4117.10(A) conflicts with a provision in a collective bargaining agreement addressing the same matter, the law prevails and the provision of the collective bargaining agreement is unenforceable. If the conflict does not pertain to one of the specific exceptions listed in R.C. 4117.10(A), then the collective bargaining agreement prevails.

Here Article 24 [of the CBA] is not silent on the issue of overtime compensation, but rather states: "Employees shall receive compensatory time or overtime pay for authorized work performed in excess of forty (40) hours per week." R.C. 4111.03 also addresses overtime compensation and provides: "An employer shall pay an employee for overtime at a wage rate of one and one-half times the employee's wage rate for hours worked in excess of forty hours in one workweek, in the manner and methods provided in and subject to the exemptions of section 7 and section 13 of the Fair Labor Standards Act of 1938 . . . [FLSA].

The provision of the collective bargaining agreement thus not only addresses but conflicts with the terms of R.C. 4111.03. While R.C. 4111.03 requires an employer to provide for overtime compensation in the manner prescribed by the FLSA, the collective bargaining agreement does not. Although the agreement requires the additional hours to be "authorized," R.C. 4111.03 does not specifically require authorization. While R.C. 4111.03(A) requires overtime compensation for "hours worked" in excess of forty, the collective bargaining agreement requires overtime compensation for "hours in active pay status" greater than forty. Given the conflict, the bargaining agreement prevails unless one of the exceptions in R.C. 4117.10(A) applies. Because R.C. 4117.10(A) does not list R.C. 4111.03 or the matter of overtime compensation as an exception, the collective bargaining agreement with its arbitration provision prevails. . . .

R.C. 4117.10(A) further states that if the labor agreement provides for final and binding arbitration, then employers, employees, and labor unions are subject solely to that grievance procedure as set forth in the labor contract. Section 7.07(F) of the collective bargaining agreement at issue provides for final and binding arbitration.

Accordingly, the trial court properly concluded it lacked jurisdiction over plaintiff's claims under R.C. 4111.03.

———————

Note that this case involved a conflict between a *state* wage and hour law (which used definitions from the federal FLSA) and the state collective-bargaining law. Provisions in labor contracts made pursuant to state public-sector laws cannot waive rights under *federal* law, such as the FLSA. Sometimes, though, unions seek to exempt provisions in collective bargaining agreements from state and local minimum wage laws. For an example from the private sector, *see* http://www.latimes .com/local/lanow/la-me-ln-los-angeles-minimum-wage-unions-20150526-story .html. Why would unions do that?

Patrolmen's Benevolent Ass'n of City of New York, Inc. v. New York State Public Emp. Rel. Bd.

Court of Appeals of New York State
6 N.Y.3d 563, 815 N.Y.S.2d 1, 848 N.E.2d 448 (2006)

SMITH, J.

[This decision joined the appeal of two cases which raised essentially the same issue.] The Patrolmen's Benevolent Association of the City of New York (N.Y.CPBA) seeks to annul a decision by the Public Employment Relations Board (PERB) that the City need not bargain with the NYCPBA over five subjects, even though those subjects had been dealt with in an expired collective bargaining agreement. The expired agreement had provided: (1) that police officers being questioned in a departmental investigation would have up to four hours to confer with counsel; (2) that certain guidelines for interrogation of police officers would remain unchanged; (3) that a "joint subcommittee" would "develop procedures" to assure the timely resolution of disciplinary charges; (4) that a pilot program would be established to refer disciplinary matters to an agency outside the police department; and (5) that employees charged but not found guilty could petition to have the records of disciplinary proceedings expunged. PERB found that all these provisions concerned "prohibited subjects of bargaining."

[The] Supreme Court upheld PERB's decision on the ground that the New York City Charter and Administrative Code . . . required that the discipline of New York City police officers be left to the discretion of the Police Commissioner. The Appellate Division affirmed, as do we. . . .

We confront, not for the first time, a tension between the "strong and sweeping policy of the State to support collective bargaining under the Taylor Law" (*Matter of Cohoes City School Dist. v. Cohoes Teachers Assn.*, 40 N.Y.2d 774, 778 [1976]) and a competing policy—here, the policy favoring strong disciplinary authority for those in charge of police forces. We have held that the policy of the Taylor Law prevails, and collective bargaining is required, where no legislation specifically commits police discipline to the discretion of local officials (*Matter of Auburn Police*

Local 195, Council 82, Am. Fedn. of State, County & Mun. Empls., AFL-CIO v. Helsby, 46 N.Y.2d 1034, [1979]. . . . Since *Auburn* was decided, however, the First, Second and Third departments of the Appellate Division have held that, where such legislation is in force, the policy favoring control over the police prevails, and collective bargaining over disciplinary matters is prohibited. We decide today that these Appellate Division holdings were correct.

The Taylor Law (Civil Service Law art. 14) requires collective bargaining over all "terms and conditions of employment" . . . Civil Service Law § 204[2]).

We have often stressed the importance of this policy, and have made clear that "the presumption . . . that all terms and conditions of employment are subject to mandatory bargaining" cannot easily be overcome. . . .

On the other hand, we have held that some subjects are excluded from collective bargaining as a matter of policy, even where no statute explicitly says so. Thus, we have held that local boards of education may not surrender, in collective bargaining agreements, their ultimate responsibility for deciding on teacher tenure (*Cohoes*), or their right to inspect teachers' personnel files (*Board of Educ., Great Neck Union Free School Dist. v. Areman*, 41 N.Y.2d 527 [1977]). We have held that a police department may not be required to bargain over the imposition of certain requirements on officers receiving benefits following injuries in the line of duty and that a city may not surrender, in collective bargaining, its statutory right to choose among police officers seeking promotion. And we have held that public policy bars enforcement of a provision in a collective bargaining agreement that would limit the power of the New York City Department of Investigation to interrogate city employees in a criminal investigation.

In none of these cases did a statute exclude a subject from collective bargaining in so many words. In each case, however, we found a public policy strong enough to warrant such an exclusion. As we explained in *Cohoes*, the scope of collective bargaining may be limited by "'plain and clear, rather than express, prohibitions in the statute or decisional law'" or "in some instances[,] by '[p]ublic policy . . . whether explicit or implicit in statute or decisional law, or in neither.'"

Is there a public policy strong enough to justify excluding police discipline from collective bargaining? It might be thought this question could be answered yes or no, but the relevant statutes and case law are not so simple. In general, the procedures for disciplining public employees, including police officers, are governed by Civil Service Law §§ 75 and 76, which provide for a hearing and an appeal. In *Auburn*, a case involving police discipline, the Appellate Division rejected the argument that these statutes should be interpreted to prohibit collective bargaining agreements "that would supplement, modify or replace" their provisions, and we adopted the Appellate Division's opinion. Thus, where Civil Service Law §§ 75 and 76 apply, police discipline may be the subject of collective bargaining.

But Civil Service Law § 76(4) says that sections 75 and 76 shall not "be construed to repeal or modify" preexisting laws, and among the laws thus grandfathered are several that, in contrast to sections 75 and 76, provide expressly for the control of police discipline by local officials in certain communities. Such laws are applicable in the City of New York. . . .

Section 434(a) of the New York City Charter provides: "The [police] commissioner shall have cognizance and control of the government, administration, disposition *and discipline* of the department, and of the police force of the department" (emphasis added). New York City Administrative Code § 14-115(a) provides that, in cases of police misconduct: "The commissioner shall have power, in his or her discretion, . . . to punish the offending party." Though these two provisions are now New York City legislation, both were originally enacted as state statutes; the Charter provision was adopted by the State Legislature in 1897 . . . and the Code provision in 1873. . . . Thus, they reflect the policy of the State that police discipline in New York City is subject to the Commissioner's authority. . . .

Appellate Division cases—one of which we have referred to favorably—have consistently held that legislation of this kind overcomes the presumption in favor of collective bargaining where police discipline is concerned. . . .

[The NYCPBA argues] that this line of Appellate Division cases is wrong. In this they are supported by PERB, which, although it is bound by and has followed the Appellate Division decisions, now urges us to reject them. This is not a case, however, in which we defer to PERB's judgment. The primary issue here is not the application of the Taylor Law to particular facts, an area in which PERB is entitled to deference. . . . *Matter of West Irondequoit Teachers Assn. v. Helsby*, . . . but the relative weight to be given to competing policies, including those reflected in the New York City Charter [and] the New York City Administrative Code . . . legislation not within PERB's area of expertise. We think the Appellate Division decisions evaluated these policies correctly.

While the Taylor Law policy favoring collective bargaining is a strong one, so is the policy favoring the authority of public officials over the police. As long ago as 1888, we emphasized the quasi-military nature of a police force, and said that "a question pertaining solely to the general government and discipline of the force . . . must, from the nature of things, rest wholly in the discretion of the commissioners" (*People ex rel. Masterson v. French*, 110 N.Y. 494, 499 [1888]). This sweeping statement must be qualified today; as *Auburn* demonstrates, the need for authority over police officers will sometimes yield to the claims of collective bargaining. But the public interest in preserving official authority over the police remains powerful. It was the basis for our holding, only last June, that the statutory right of a police commissioner to select "an officer to fill a position important to the safety of the community" may not be surrendered in a collective bargaining agreement. . . .

The New York City Charter and Administrative Code . . . state the policy favoring management authority over police disciplinary matters in clear terms. In New York City, the police commissioner "shall have cognizance and control of the . . . discipline of the department" (N.Y. City Charter § 434[a]) and "shall have power, in his or her discretion[,] . . . to punish [an] offending party" (Administrative Code of City of N.Y. § 14-115[a]). . . . These legislative commands are to be obeyed even where the result is to limit the scope of collective bargaining. The issue is not, as the unions argue, whether these enactments were intended by their authors to create an exception to the Taylor Law; obviously they were not, since they were passed decades before the Taylor Law existed. The issue is whether these enactments express a policy so important that the policy favoring collective bargaining should give way, and we conclude that they do. . . .

_____

Notes

1. For a different result on an issue similar to that in *Patrolmen's Benevolent Ass'n*, see *City of Taylorville and Policemen's Benevolent Labor Comm.*, 21 PERI ¶ 222 (Ill. Lab. Rel. Bd. Gen. Counsel 2005) (a state law governing police discipline did not preempt collective bargaining on the topic, because the law exempted certain employers and unions that had negotiated discipline policies prior to the enactment of the law).

2. Civil service rules have probably been the single biggest source of litigation involving claims that external laws restrict or prevent union bargaining. Some challenges have been quite broad. For example, *Pacific Legal Foundation v. Brown*, 29 Cal. 3d 168 (1981) rejected a claim that California's State Employer Employee Relations Act (SEERA), which grants collective-bargaining rights to state employees, impermissibly conflicted with the general "merit principles" of civil service employment in the state constitution. The court held that SEERA did not conflict with the state constitution by reserving ultimate salary decisions for state civil service employees to the Governor and legislature rather than the State Personnel Board. Also, the court upheld provisions of the SEERA granting the state Public Employment Relations Board initial jurisdiction to investigate and adjudicate ULPs, even though the state constitution gave authority to the State Personnel Board to review disciplinary actions against civil service employees. The court explained that the constitutional provisions still left the legislature with a relatively free hand to create laws relating to personnel administration for the best interests of state, and thus SEERA's collective-bargaining process did not on its face conflict with the constitutional principles establishing the merit system.

3. Although the era of such broad challenges may be over, litigation over specific or alleged conflicts between labor laws and civil service laws continues. For example, *Abel v. City of Pittsburgh*, 890 A.2d 1 (Pa. Commw. Ct. 2005) involved a challenge to a union contract provision that required the city to lay off employees by job title and individual department in reverse order of seniority within three separate seniority units. The challenge was based on a provision in the state's Civil Service Act stating that the last employee appointed should be the first to be laid off, regardless of job title or classification. *Abel* held that despite this rule, under the state labor law, seniority and layoff were proper terms of collective bargaining. While the Civil

Service Act established a procedure for layoffs, it did not expressly bar the city from making any other agreements as to layoffs with employees represented by a union.

4. On the other hand, *Connecticut State Employees Ass'n and State of Connecticut*, Dec. No. 4096 (Conn. State Bd. Lab. Rel. 2005) held nonnegotiable a union proposal that would have required the employer to retain and make available for inspection a description of the process for ranking and evaluating candidates who completed a civil service merit exam. Section 5-272(d) of the state labor statute expressly exempted "the establishment, conduct and grading of merit examinations, the rating of candidates and the establishment of lists from such examinations" from the collective-bargaining process. "No matter what spin the Union attempts to place on its proposal, it is clear that this is an attempt to obtain information about a subject over which the Union cannot demand bargaining."

5. Often, unionized public employees are covered both by a just cause discharge clause in a contract that can be enforced through arbitration, and a similar rule in a civil service law that can be enforced through a civil service commission hearing. Should the employee be allowed to pursue both claims? If not, which one should govern? States vary both as to whether their statute explicitly addresses this issue and as to how they resolve the question. *See* Ann Hodges, *The Interplay of Civil Service Law and Collective Bargaining Law in Public Sector Employee Discipline Cases*, 32 B.C. L. Rev. 95 (1990).

6. State education statutes may also trump collective-bargaining laws, on matters ranging from the status of probationary employees to standards for teacher tenure. *See, e.g., Baumgartner v. Perry Public Schools*, 202 L.R.R.M. (BNA) 3525 (Mich. App. 2015) (Amendments to state School Code in 2011 removed the issue of teacher layoffs from the jurisdiction of both the Michigan Public Employment Relations Commission and the State Tenure Commission and gave full authority over the matter to local school boards); *Bd. of Educ. of the Round Valley Unified Sch. District v. Round Valley Teachers Ass'n*, 20 PERC ¶ 27076 (Cal. 1996) (union and school employer cannot legally agree to grant probationary teachers who were not rehired greater procedural protections than they were entitled to under the state Education Code); *Matter of Cohoes City Sch. Dist. v. Cohoes Teachers Ass'n*, 40 N.Y.2d 774 (1976) (while the state Education Law does not expressly bar the subject of tenure decisions from collective bargaining, such a conclusion is "inescapably implicit" in provisions of the statute); *Ass'n of N.J. State College Faculties, Inc. v. Dungan*, 64 N.J. 338 (1974) (new, more stringent requirements for tenure are not negotiable, as New Jersey's Education Law gives the Board of Higher Education the right to set education policy).

7. As is discussed further in Chapter 11, Section III-B-3-c-(ii), in almost all jurisdictions, at least most issues regarding public employee pensions, including pension benefit formulas, are set by statute and are not legal subjects of bargaining.

8. A wide variety of statutes can appear in this sort of litigation. *See, e.g., Dept. of Corrections and Dept. of Public Welfare v. Pa. State Corrections Officers Ass'n*,

932 A.2d 359 (Pa. Commw. Ct. 2007) (Administrative Code provision stating that the Commonwealth will not provide an attorney to defend a present or former official or employee in a criminal case is a binding regulation, and a public employer and union are not allowed to agree to the contrary).

E. Constitutional Restrictions

Public employers are subject to some constitutional restrictions in their dealings with their employees. As Chapter 1 noted, public employees have a First Amendment right to join and support unions. A variety of other constitutional provisions apply to public employees. These protections are independent of labor laws, but, relevant here, they can affect the scope of negotiability.

For example, public employers are constrained by Fourth Amendment limits when searching the offices of their employees and when instituting drug tests. *O'Connor v. Ortega*, 480 U.S. 709 (1987) held that searches by public employers must be judged by a standard of "reasonableness under all the circumstances," and that both the inception and scope of the intrusion must be reasonable. *National Treasury Employees Union v. Von Raab*, 489 U.S. 656 (1989) held that under the Fourth Amendment, only employees in "safety sensitive" jobs could be drug tested without reasonable individualized suspicion of drug use. Thus, it is unconstitutional to subject employees who are *not* "safety sensitive" to random drug tests as a condition of employment. Which employees are "safety sensitive"? Most commonly, police (*e.g., Carroll v. City of Westminster*, 233 F.3d 208 (4th Cir. 2000)), firefighters (*e.g., Aguilera v. City of East Chicago, Fire Civil Service Comm.*, 768 N.E.2d 978 (Ind. Ct. App. 2002)), and those who operate public transportation (*e.g., Southwest Ohio Regional Trans. Auth. v. Amal. Trans. Union, Local 627*, 91 Ohio St. 3d 108 (2001)). Also, the Sixth Circuit has held that public school teachers are public safety employees (because of their responsibility for children). *Knox County Educ. Assoc. v. Knox County Bd. of Educ.*, 158 F.3d 361 (6th Cir. 1998).

These rules are distinct from rules on scope of negotiability. The rule that randomly drug testing public safety workers does not violate the Constitution does not determine whether or not such testing is a mandatory topic of bargaining. For drug testing that does not violate the Constitution, some cases hold that any testing of any current employees (as opposed to applicants), is a mandatory subject. *See, e.g., County of Cook v. Licensed Practical Nurses Ass'n of Ill., Div. I*, 284 Ill. App. 3d 145 (1996) (citing NLRA precedent and holding that suspicionless drug testing of licensed practical nurses at a county jail was a mandatory topic); *Holliday v. City of Modesto*, 229 Cal. App. 3d 528 (1991) (citing NLRA precedent and holding that a drug test was a mandatory topic even though individual suspicion of drug use existed).

But some jurisdictions seem to have adopted the distinctions made under Fourth Amendment jurisprudence for the purposes of negotiability determinations. For example, *In re Canton*, 11 OPER 1433 (Ohio SERB 1994) held that drug testing was a mandatory topic if employees were not in safety sensitive positions. *Fraternal Order of Police, Miami Lodge 20 v. City of Miami*, 609 So. 2d 31 (Fla. 1992) held that compulsory drug testing of specific officers who have been identified as having allegedly committed drug offenses was not mandatory.

Other variations exist, some involving special circumstances. *Law Enforcement Labor Services, Inc. v. Sherburne County*, 695 N.W.2d 630 (Minn. Ct. App. 2005) held that random testing of safety-sensitive employees in a police department was not a mandatory subject, at least in part because a state statute, the Workplace Testing Act (MINN. STAT. § 181.951, subd. 1), authorized employers to "request or require" drug and alcohol testing. *Sherburne* also noted that it did not violate the Fourth Amendment to do such testing in this case because the relevant employees were safety sensitive. *Illinois Depts. of Central Management Services & Corrections* (Ill. State Lab. Rel. Bd. 1988), *aff'd sub nom. AFSCME v. ISLRB*, 190 Ill. App. 3d 259 (1989), held drug testing of prison guards was not mandatory under the particular facts in that case. The employer had a strong interest in protecting the health and safety of employees and inmates; there was evidence that bargaining unit employees were selling and using drugs; the testing was done only on the basis of reasonable suspicion; and the employees had a diminished expectation of privacy (the employer already did dog-sniffs, pat-downs, and strip searches of employees). In both of these cases, the employer had to bargain over the effects of the testing, *e.g.*, discipline that would result from it.

Could drug testing that is otherwise barred by the Constitution ever be a legal topic of negotiation? *In the Matter of Buffalo Police Benev. Ass'n v. City of Buffalo*, 20 NYPER 3048 (PERB 1987) held that while the employer could not insist on bargaining over a random drug testing plan that was unconstitutional, the topic was permissively negotiable. A "waiver" of the constitutional right could be accomplished through consent, and "the bargaining agent may act in the place of the individual employees to grant or withhold consent." *Id.* Is that a good approach?

Also, as shown above, some states distinguish among groups of public employees with regard to the scope of bargaining. Do such distinctions, *per se*, violate equal protection rules? In **Central State University v. American Association of University Professors, Central State University Chapter**, 526 U.S. 124 (1999), the Supreme Court answered no.

In *Central State*, the state of Ohio, ostensibly to address the decline in the amount of time public university professors devoted to teaching as opposed to researching, enacted OHIO REV. CODE § 3345.45 (1993). This section required public universities in Ohio to develop standards for instructional workloads for faculty "in keeping with the universities' missions and with special emphasis on the undergraduate learning experience." The law also specified that "policies adopted under this section are not appropriate subjects for collective bargaining." 526 U.S. at 125.

The Ohio Supreme Court held that this violated both the Equal Protection Clause of the federal constitution, and analogous language in the Ohio Constitution, because the collective-bargaining exemption bore no rational relationship to the State's interest in correcting the imbalance between research and teaching at its public universities. The Ohio court held that "there is not a shred of evidence in the entire record which links collective bargaining with the decline in teaching over the last decade, or in any way purports to establish that collective bargaining contributed in the slightest to the lost faculty time devoted to undergraduate teaching." 526 U.S. at 127.

The U.S. Supreme Court disagreed, noting that "a classification neither involving fundamental rights nor proceedings along suspect lines . . . cannot run afoul of the Equal Protection Clause if there is a rational relationship between disparity of treatment and some legitimate governmental purpose." Here, the "legislature could quite reasonably have concluded that the policy animating the law would have been undercut and likely varied if it were subject to collective bargaining." 526 U.S. at 127–28.

Justice Stevens began his dissent, "While surveying the flood of law reviews that cross my desk, I have sometimes wondered whether law professors have any time to spend teaching their students about the law." 526 U.S. at 130. Still, he noted that "everyone agrees, there is no evidence that collective bargaining has had any effect on the increased emphasis on research over teaching that gave rise to the enactment of § 3345.45." 526 U.S. at 131. Noting that all other public employees in Ohio could bargain over workload, Justice Stevens found no "rational basis for discriminating against faculty members by depriving them of bargaining assistance that is available to all other public employees in the State of Ohio." 526 U.S. at 133.

Justice Stevens also would have left the matter to the Ohio Supreme Court, especially given that the Court had decided that the law violated the Ohio Constitution. On remand, the Ohio Supreme Court reversed itself regarding the claim under the Ohio Constitution, holding that the analogous clause in the Ohio Constitution should be "construed and analyzed identically" as the federal Equal Protection Clause. So, the same rational basis test applied, and the union's claim failed under this test. The State did not have to provide any actual evidence linking bargaining with a decline in teaching time. *Am. Ass'n of Univ. Professors, Cent. State Univ. Chap. v. Cent. State*, 87 Oh. St. 3d 55 (1999).

As this casebook shows, states often treat different types of public employees differently under state labor laws. This is generally not considered to be an Equal Protection violation. But even after *Central State*, could some distinctions fail the rational basis test? Chapter 1 summarizes the radical changes that Wisconsin Act 10 made in the state's public-sector law in 2011. These changes applied to all government employees *except* certain public safety employees. Is there a rational basis for this distinction? Suppose the evidence showed that the main reason for the distinction was that the exempted unions disproportionately supported the political party in power in Wisconsin when Act 10 was passed, and other unions disproportionately supported the main opposition party. Would that create any constitutional problems?

As noted in Chapter 1, ***Wisconsin Educ. Ass'n Council v. Walker***, 824 F. Supp. 2d 856 (W.D. Wis. 2012), while generally upholding the principle that public-sector labor laws may provide different rights for different types of public workers, also struck down two provisions of Act 10. The court held that distinguishing between these two groups of employees with regard to these provisions violated the Equal Protection Clause, mixed with a concern for the First Amendment. One of the provisions the court struck down made dues-checkoff provisions an illegal subject of bargaining for employees not designated as public safety employees. The court explained that the State:

> [H]as not articulated, and the court is now satisfied cannot articulate, a rational basis for picking and choosing from among public unions, those (1) that must annually obtain an absolute majority of its voluntary members to remain in existence or (2) that are entitled to voluntary, assistance with fundraising by automatic deduction, at least not a rational basis that does not offend the First Amendment. So long as the State of Wisconsin continues to afford ordinary certification and dues deductions to mandatory public safety unions with sweeping bargaining rights, there is no rational basis to deny those rights to voluntary general unions with severely restricted bargaining rights. 824 F. Supp. 2d 856, 860.

As also noted in Chapter 1, however, the Seventh Circuit reversed this decision in *Wisconsin Educ. Ass'n Council v. Walker*, 705 F.3d 640 (7th Cir. 2013). Which court was more convincing? Also, even if any distinctions a public-sector labor law could make by creating different rules for different types of employees could survive rational basis scrutiny, what types of distinctions *should* such laws make for different types of employees? What are the best arguments for and against the distinctions you have seen in this chapter?

F. Note on the Federal Sector

Scope of negotiability rules are notoriously complex for employees and employers in the federal government. The Federal Service Labor-Management Relations Statute (FSLMRS) governs most, but not all eligible Federal employees (the U.S. Postal Service is the largest exception). The FSLMRS provides that covered employees have the right to bargain collectively with respect to "conditions of employment." 5 U.S.C. § 7102. "Conditions of employment" is defined broadly to include "personnel policies, practices, and matters . . . affecting working conditions," 5 U.S.C. § 7103(a)(14).

However, the FSLMRS exempts many matters from the duty to bargain. First, many important subjects, including wages and benefits, are not negotiable because they are set by external statute and/or regulation. *See* 5 U.S.C. § 7103(a)(14)(C) (exempting from the scope of bargaining matters covered by federal statute). Second, 5 U.S.C. § 7106(a)(2) limits negotiability by listing a significant set of management rights. These include:

(A) to hire, assign, direct, layoff, and retain employees in the agency, or to suspend, remove, reduce in grade or pay, or take other disciplinary action against such employees;

(B) to assign work, to make determinations with respect to contracting out, and to determine the personnel by which agency operations shall be conducted; . . . [or]

(D) to take whatever actions may be necessary to carry out the agency mission during emergencies.

Also, §7106(b)(1) lists topics over which bargaining may take place "at the election of the agency," including decisions concerning "the technology, methods, and means of performing work."

Thus, the federal sector has perhaps the most limited scope of negotiability of all public-sector bargaining laws. So, what *is* mandatory in the federal sector? Aside from various topics not barred by the above rules, federal unions have a right to negotiate the "impact and implementation" of management decisions that have more than a *de minimis* adverse effect on bargaining unit members' conditions of employment (what is often called "effects" bargaining in other sectors). Unions may also negotiate "procedures" and "appropriate arrangements" under §7106(b)(2) and (3) for the exercise of management rights. This can be significant. For example, while management has the right to "remove" employees, "just cause" discipline clauses enforceable through negotiated grievance and arbitration procedures are mandatory topics.

This has led to an arguably not entirely coherent body of cases deciding whether certain union proposals go primarily to the substantive exercise of a management right, or whether they are an attempt to bargain a procedure or appropriate arrangement for employees. The following excerpt is an example of such a case.

National Treasury Employees Union v. FLRA

U.S. Court of Appeals, District of Columbia Circuit
404 F.3d 454 (2005)

Sᴇɴᴛᴇʟʟᴇ, C.J.

National Treasury Employees Union ("NTEU" or "the Union") petitions for review of a decision of the Federal Labor Relations Authority ("FLRA" or "the Authority"), wherein the Authority held that the United States Customs Service ("Customs" or "the Service") is not required to negotiate over a Union proposal concerning the storage of handguns. Although the Authority correctly ruled that the proposal came within the exemption of negotiability for "internal security practices" created by 5 U.S.C. §7106(a)(1), the Authority erred in failing to follow its own precedent in determining whether the bargaining proposal constituted an "appropriate arrangement" subjecting it to bargainability under 5 U.S.C. §7106(b)(3). Therefore, for the reasons more fully set out below, we grant the petition for review.

I. Background

Petitioner Union represents Customs Service employees who, as a condition of their employment as law enforcement officers, are required to carry firearms. Customs employees have carried firearms as a part of their duties for many years, and over the years Customs has promulgated a number of internal security practices relating to the use and storage of those firearms. In 1986, Customs Directive No. 45-07 (Feb. 10, 1986) required that "[e]ach Customs officer carrying a firearm in the performance of official duties is responsible for the safe storage, operation, general care and maintenance of the firearm." In 1996, Customs issued a "Firearms and Use of Force Handbook," that again emphasized the individual employee's responsibility for securing his firearm: "Employees are expected to exercise good judgment in providing adequate security to all Service-issued and Service-authorized, personally-owned firearms." Finally, in 2000, Customs issued two policy statements on the subject of firearms. On March 3, 2000, the Acting Assistant Commissioner of Customs, Office of Field Operations, issued a memorandum authorizing customs agents, at their election, to carry their firearms twenty-four hours a day. Prior to that time, Customs had directed employees to store their firearms overnight in the Customs facilities "where appropriate security is available," or to "go directly home from work" in order to secure their firearms at home. Under the new twenty-four-hour carry policy, the agency in effect decreased the burden on employees by removing the requirement of travel directly to and from home and work and giving them greater freedom of movement, subject to such restraints as avoiding the consumption of alcohol while carrying firearms.

On December 28, 2000, the Under Secretary of Treasury for Enforcement issued a memorandum on the subject "Implementation of Treasury Firearm Safety and Security Policy," which detailed safety and security responsibilities required of firearms-carrying personnel. Among other things, the memorandum required that the firearm be placed in a secure locked container in a government office, or, if stored in a residence, that the employee install a safety lock device and guard against theft or unauthorized use of the firearm.

In response to the December 28, 2000 memorandum, the Union introduced a proposal that would have required Customs to provide secure on-site overnight firearms storage:

> Customs will ensure that either a lockbox or other secure and locked container such as a safe, file cabinet, or desk is available at all government offices where armed employees work or are assigned. Routine overnight storage of a firearm in a government office is permitted.

NTEU v. U.S. Dep't of the Treasury, U.S. Customs Service, 59 F.L.R.A. 749 (2004). Customs declared the proposal nonnegotiable. The Union filed a petition for review with the Authority. The Authority held that the proposal interfered with Customs's right to determine its "internal security practices" under 5 U.S.C. § 7106(a)(1) and also that the proposal did not constitute a "procedure" or an "appropriate arrangement" under 5 U.S.C. §§ 7106(b)(2) & (3). Together, these holdings constitute the Authority's ruling that the proposal is nonnegotiable. The Union petitioned us for review.

II. Analysis

The Federal Service Labor Management Relations statute, 5 U.S.C. §§ 7101–7135 ("the statute"), governs relations between federal agency employers and federal employees. The statute imposes a general duty upon the parties to bargain in good faith, 5 U.S.C. § 7117, subject to specified statutory exceptions. The Authority ruled that the proposal before it came within one of those exceptions. Specifically, the Authority relied upon the "management rights" section of the statute, which protects the authority of management officials and agencies, *inter alia*, "to determine the . . . internal security practices of the agency." 5 U.S.C. § 7106(a)(1). However, the management rights section limits that protection by providing that "[n]othing in this section shall preclude any agency and any labor organization from negotiating . . . procedures which management officials of the agency will observe in exercising any authority under this section; or . . . appropriate arrangements for employees adversely affected by the exercise of any authority under this section by such management officials." 5 U.S.C. § 7106(b)(2) & (3). The Authority went on to rule that the proposal before it did not constitute a "procedure" exempting the proposal from the management rights negotiability preclusion under § 7106(b)(2), or an "appropriate arrangement" exempting the proposal under § 7106(b)(3).

We review decisions of the Authority under the Administrative Procedure Act ("APA"), and will set such a decision aside when it is "arbitrary, capricious, an abuse of discretion, or otherwise not in accordance with law. . . .

First, the Authority concluded that the Service had established a link between its objective of securing its operations and its policy or practices, and that the proposal conflicted with its policy or practices. Therefore, the Authority held that the proposal affected management's right to determine its internal security practices under § 7106(a)(1). . . .

Second, the Authority concluded that the proposal required adoption of security measures to ensure a specific level of security. Therefore, the Authority held that the proposal was not a negotiable procedure under Section 7106(b)(2). . . .

With respect to Sections 7106(a)(1) and 7106(b)(2), the Authority's decision quite clearly was not arbitrary or capricious. Storage of firearms at Service facilities certainly implicates management's right to determine its internal security practices. 5 U.S.C. § 7106(a)(1). Likewise, because the proposal would directly interfere with management's right to determine its internal security practices by forcing the Agency to commit to a change in its current security practices, the proposal is simply not a negotiable procedure. 5 U.S.C. § 7106(b)(2). . . .

However, the Authority and the court still are left with the question of whether the proposal constituted a negotiable "appropriate arrangement" under § 7106(b)(3). The Authority's conclusion on that subject is not so unassailable as the first two. Authority precedent established nearly twenty years ago holds that:

> In this and future cases where the Authority addresses a management allegation that a union proposal of appropriate arrangements is nonnegotiable because it conflicts with management rights described in section 7106(a) or (b)(1), the Authority will consider whether such an arrangement is appropriate for negotiation within the meaning of section 7106(b)(3) or, whether it is inappropriate *because it excessively interferes with the exercise of management's rights.*

Nat'l Assoc. of Gov't Employees, Local R14-87 v. Kansas Army Nat'l Guard, 21 F.L.R.A. 24, 31 (1986) ("*KANG*") (emphasis added). More specifically, the *KANG* test asks first what "the nature and extent of the impact experienced by adversely affected employees . . . is." 21 F.L.R.A. at 32. Otherwise put, the Authority determines "what conditions of employment are affected and to what degree." *Id.* If the effect is there so as to raise the opportunity of an appropriate arrangement, the Authority then asks "what is the precise limitation imposed by the proposed arrangement on management's exercise of its reserved discretion or to what extent is managerial judgment preserved?" *Id.* In the present context, to apply the *KANG* test the Authority had to ascertain how the agency exercised its right to determine its internal security practices so that the Authority could then determine whether the proposal "excessively interfere[d]" with the agency's exercise of its right. In the decision before us, the Authority did not follow its own precedent established in *KANG*. *See, e.g., Association of Civilian Technicians v. FLRA*, 370 F.3d 1214, 1221 (D.C.Cir.2004) (vacating an Authority decision and directing application of the *KANG* test on rehearing).

It is well established that, despite the narrow scope of court review of FLRA decisions, any agency's "unexplained departure from prior agency determinations" is inherently arbitrary and capricious in violation of APA. . . . The Authority's failure to follow its own well-established precedent without explanation is the very essence of arbitrariness. Therefore, we must set aside its determination that the proposal did not constitute an appropriate arrangement and return the question to the Authority for further proceedings consistent with this opinion and Authority precedent.

Under *KANG*, the Authority must conduct a so-called "excessively interferes with" inquiry "by weighing the practical needs of the employees and managers." 21 F.L.R.A. at 31–32. It did not do so on the present record. The Authority's path to error was set when it erroneously found that "the agency has exercised its right to determine its internal security by having employees who are trained and qualified to carry firearms maintain possession and access to their weapons when off duty." 59 F.L.R.A. at 754. That finding was crucial to the Authority's conclusion that the proposal "would operate so as to completely preclude the agency from exercising that right." In fact, the record did not support the Authority's description of the agency's security policy. On the record, the agency apparently, in many locations, permitted on-site storage of firearms of off-duty officers, and, indeed, provided facilities for such storage. We are not suggesting that the Authority must rule that the agency must make such arrangements in all locations, but only that the Authority must consider the evidence in the record before it, conduct the balanced inquiry required by the *KANG* line of precedent, and then reach its conclusion as to whether the proposal "excessively interferes" with the agency's internal security practices.

On the record before it and this Court, the Authority has not established that the proposal would "negate and nullify" the agency's right to implement the practice it followed at the time the Union made the proposal. The most the proposal would require is the institution at other facilities of a method of carrying out agency internal security policies already in place at some locations. Whether this constitutes an appropriate arrangement is a question for the Authority to answer in the first instance, but it must do so on findings based on the record before it, and by a process consistent with its own precedent.

III. Conclusion

For the reasons set forth above, we hold that the petition for review is allowed. The Authority's order is vacated and remanded for further proceedings consistent with this opinion.

––––––––––

Notes

1. On remand, what arguments should counsel for the agency make? What arguments should counsel for the union make? What facts would help show "excessive interference" in the exercise of the management right, and what facts would help show no excessive interference?

2. Despite the many restrictions on what is negotiable in the federal sector, collective-bargaining agreements between unions and federal agencies are often quite lengthy. Can you imagine some of the topics these agreements might cover?

3. Also, despite the restrictive negotiability rules, a relatively large number of federal employees are in union bargaining units. In 2014, 22.9 percent of federal employees covered by the FSLMRS were covered by union collective bargaining agreements. This figure excludes employees of the U.S. Postal Service, who may legally bargain over compensation and other issues pursuant to NLRA rules. The union density rate of those covered by the FSLMRS was, however, far below the 2014 union density rate within the Postal Service (68.2 percent), and the rates in state government (32.8 percent) and local government (45.5 percent). Samuel Estreicher, *The Paradox of Federal Sector Labor Relations: Voluntary Unionism Without Collective Bargaining Over Wages and Employee Benefits*, New York University Public Law & Legal Theory Research Paper Series Working Paper No. 15–40 (Sept. 2015), 3.

4. After the attacks on 9/11, the Bush administration moved to reduce further the collective-bargaining rights of many federal employees, notably those in the Transportation Safety Administration (TSA), the Department of Homeland Security (DHS), and the Department of Defense. For the background to this, see Slater, *Homeland Security vs. Workers' Rights?, supra.* The Bush administration insisted that the statute authorizing the DHS should allow the DHS to create a more

"flexible" personnel system outside of and more limited than existing federal rules on collective bargaining. Democrats preserved the basic right for DHS employees to bargain collectively, which set the stage for litigation. 5 U.S.C. § 9701(a), § 9701(b)(1)–(4).

The DHS then set up a very restrictive system. Among other things, it allowed the DHS to void, unilaterally, any provision of any union contract it had agreed to. The union representing DHS workers sued, claiming this was not "collective bargaining" as the statute required. In *National Treasury Employees Union v. Chertoff*, 452 F.3d 839 (D.C. Cir. 2006), the court agreed with the union. "Collective bargaining" is a "term of art," and it could not mean, *inter alia*, a system in which one side was not bound by collectively bargained and signed contracts. 452 F.3d 839, 857–60.

The issue has remained highly contentious. In 2007, the Senate approved a broad bill that would have given collective-bargaining rights to TSA workers, but that language was stripped from the bill after President Bush threatened a veto. President Obama's first nominee to head the TSA, Erroll Southers, withdrew his name from consideration at least in significant part due to Republican opposition to collective-bargaining rights for TSA employees. Ultimately, John Pistole was named TSA head. In 2011, Director Pistole issued a Memorandum granting limited bargaining rights to TSA employees (even more limited than the general federal sector statute). John Pistole, *Determination: Transportation Security Officers and Collective Bargaining*, Feb. 4, 2011, *available at* https://federalnewsnetwork.com/wp-content/uploads/296/08/TSA-determination.pdf. The American Federation of Government Employees then successfully won a certification election for TSA agents.

IV. Remedies for Failing to Bargain in Good Faith

A. Remedies in the Private Sector

1. Initial Contract Terms

H.K. Porter Company v. NLRB
Supreme Court of the United States
397 U.S. 99 (1970)

BLACK, J.

After an election respondent United Steelworkers Union was, on October 5, 1961, certified by the [NLRB] as the bargaining agent for certain employees at the Danville, Virginia, plant of the petitioner, H.K. Porter Co. Thereafter negotiations commenced for a collective-bargaining agreement. Since that time the controversy has seesawed between the Board, the Court of Appeals for the District of Columbia Circuit, and this Court. This delay of over eight years is not because the case is exceedingly complex, but appears to have occurred chiefly because of the skill of the company's negotiators in taking advantage of every opportunity for delay in an act more noticeable for its generality than for its precise prescriptions. The entire lengthy dispute mainly revolves around the union's desire to have the company agree to "check off" the dues owed to the union by its members, that is, to deduct those dues periodically from the company's wage payments to the employees. The record shows, as the Board found, that the company's objection to a checkoff was not due to any general principle or policy against making deductions from employees' wages. The company does deduct charges for things like insurance, taxes, and contributions to charities, and at some other plants it has a checkoff arrangement for union dues. The evidence shows, and the court below found, that the company's objection was not because of inconvenience, but solely on the ground that the company was "not going to aid and comfort the union." Efforts by the union to obtain some kind of compromise on the checkoff request were all met with the same staccato response to the effect that the collection of union dues was the "union's business" and the company was not going to provide any assistance. Based on this and other evidence the Board found, and the Court of Appeals approved the finding, that the refusal of the company to bargain about the checkoff was not made in good faith, but was done solely to frustrate the making of any collective-bargaining agreement. In May 1966, the Court of Appeals upheld the Board's order requiring the company to cease and desist from refusing to bargain in good faith and directing it to engage in further collective bargaining, if requested by the union to do so, over the checkoff.

In the course of that opinion, the Court of Appeals intimated that the Board conceivably might have required petitioner to agree to a checkoff provision as a remedy for the prior bad-faith bargaining, although the order enforced at that time did not contain any such provision. [After further litigation] the Board issued a supplemental order requiring the petitioner to "[g]rant to the Union a contract clause providing for the checkoff of union dues." The Court of Appeals affirmed this order. We granted certiorari to consider whether the Board in these circumstances has the power to remedy the unfair labor practice by requiring the company to agree to check off the dues of the workers. For reasons to be stated we hold that while the Board does have power under the [NLRA], 61 Stat. 136, as amended, to require employers and employees to negotiate, it is without power to compel a company or a union to agree to any substantive contractual provision of a collective-bargaining agreement. . . .

The object of [the NLRA] was not to allow governmental regulation of the terms and conditions of employment, but rather to ensure that employers and their employees could work together to establish mutually satisfactory conditions. The basic theme of the Act was that through collective bargaining the passions, arguments, and struggles of prior years would be channeled into constructive, open discussions leading, it was hoped, to mutual agreement. But it was recognized from the beginning that agreement might in some cases be impossible, and it was never intended that the Government would in such cases step in, become a party to the negotiations and impose its own views of a desirable settlement. . . .

In discussing the effect of [adding § 8(d) in 1947] this Court said it is "clear that the Board may not, either directly or indirectly, compel concessions or otherwise sit in judgment upon the substantive terms of collective bargaining agreements." *NLRB v. American Nat. Ins. Co.*, 343 U.S. 395 (1952). Later this Court affirmed that view stating that "it remains clear that § 8(d) was an attempt by Congress to prevent the Board from controlling the settling of the terms of collective bargaining agreements." *NLRB v. Insurance Agents' Inter. Union*, 361 U.S. 477, 487 (1960). The parties to the instant case are agreed that this is the first time in the 35-year history of the Act that the Board has ordered either an employer or a union to agree to a substantive term of a collective-bargaining agreement.

Recognizing the fundamental principle "that the [NLRA] is grounded on the premise of freedom of contract," the Court of Appeals in this case concluded that nevertheless in the circumstances presented here the Board could properly compel the employer to agree to a proposed checkoff clause. The Board had found that the refusal was based on a desire to frustrate agreement and not on any legitimate business reason. On the basis of that finding the Court of Appeals approved the further finding that the employer had not bargained in good faith, and the validity of that finding is not now before us. Where the record thus revealed repeated refusals by the employer to bargain in good faith on this issue, the Court of Appeals concluded that ordering agreement to the checkoff clause "may be the only means of assuring the Board, and the court, that (the employer) no longer harbors an illegal intent."

In reaching this conclusion the Court of Appeals held that § 8(d) did not forbid the Board from compelling agreement. That court felt that "[s]ection 8(d) defines collective bargaining and relates to a determination of whether a . . . violation has occurred and not to the scope of the remedy which may be necessary to cure violations which have already occurred." We may agree with the Court of Appeals that as a matter of strict, literal interpretation that section refers only to deciding when a violation has occurred, but we do not agree that that observation justifies the conclusion that the remedial powers of the Board are not also limited by the same considerations that led Congress to enact § 8(d). It is implicit in the entire structure of the Act that the Board acts to oversee and referee the process of collective bargaining, leaving the results of the contest to the bargaining strengths of the parties. It would be anomalous indeed to hold that while § 8(d) prohibits the Board from relying on a refusal to agree as the sole evidence of bad-faith bargaining, the Act permits the Board to compel agreement in that same dispute. The Board's remedial powers under § 10 of the Act are broad, but they are limited to carrying out the policies of the Act itself. One of these fundamental policies is freedom of contract. While the parties' freedom of contract is not absolute under the Act, allowing the Board to compel agreement when the parties themselves are unable to agree would violate the fundamental premise on which the Act is based-private bargaining under governmental supervision of the procedure alone, without any official compulsion over the actual terms of the contract. . . .

In reaching its decision the Court of Appeals relied extensively on the equally important policy of the Act that workers' rights to collective bargaining are to be secured. In this case the court apparently felt that the employer was trying effectively to destroy the union by refusing to agree to what the union may have considered its most important demand. Perhaps the court, fearing that the parties might resort to economic combat, was also trying to maintain the industrial peace that the Act is designed to further. But the Act as presently drawn does not contemplate that unions will always be secure and able to achieve agreement even when their economic position is weak, or that strikes and lockouts will never result from a bargaining impasse. It cannot be said that the Act forbids an employer or a union to rely ultimately on its economic strength to try to secure what it cannot obtain through bargaining. It may well be true, as the Court of Appeals felt, that the present remedial powers of the Board are insufficiently broad to cope with important labor problems. But it is the job of Congress, not the Board or the courts, to decide when and if it is necessary to allow governmental review of proposals for collective-bargaining agreements and compulsory submission to one side's demands. The present Act does not envision such a process.

The judgment is reversed and the case is remanded to the Court of Appeals for further action consistent with this opinion.

Douglas, J. and Stewart, J., concurring in part and dissenting in part.

The Court correctly describes the general design and main thrust of the Act. . . .

Yet the Board has the power, where one party does not bargain in good faith, "to take such affirmative action . . . as will effectuate the policies" of the Act. § 10(c) of the Act.

Here the employer did not refuse the checkoff for any business reason, whether cost, inconvenience, or what not. Nor did the employer refuse the checkoff as a factor in its bargaining strategy, hoping that delay and denial might bring it in exchange favorable terms and conditions. Its reason was a resolve to avoid reaching any agreement with the union.

In those narrow and specialized circumstances, I see no answer to the power of the Board in its discretion to impose the checkoff as "affirmative action" necessary to remedy the flagrant refusal of the employer to bargain in good faith. . . .

———————

Notes

1. After *H.K. Porter*, what remedy could the Board permissibly order after finding a violation of § 8(a)(5)?

2. The litigation in this case, from initial charge to Supreme Court decision, took eight years. Which side benefits from this sort of delay? Does that provide any insight as to why the employer here spent so much money in litigation ostensibly to avoid agreeing to dues check-off, a matter which has little or no direct effect on

the employer? Some employer consultants advise companies to "stall or prolong the bargaining process, almost indefinitely." John Logan, *Consultants, Lawyers, and the "Union Free" Movement in the USA Since the 1970s*, 33 INDUS. REL. J. 197, 209 (2002).

3. Recall the materials on remedies in Chapter 6 as well as the materials in this chapter. Why does the court choose to read the language of § 10(c) — granting the Board the power "to take such affirmative action . . . as will effectuate the policies' of the Act" — so narrowly? What are the concerns with reading it more broadly?

Ex-Cell-O Corporation

National Labor Relations Board
185 N.L.R.B. 107 (1970)

[The United Automobile Workers (UAW) won a certification election. The company filed objections to the election, which the Board ultimately rejected. The employer then refused to bargain with the UAW, as a means to gain court review of the Board's ruling on its objections to the election. The Trial Examiner found a § 8(a)(5) violation and recommended that, in addition to a cease-and-desist order, the company be ordered to make its employees whole for any monetary losses suffered because of the employer's violation.]

It is not disputed that Respondent refused to bargain with the Union, and we hereby affirm the Trial Examiner's conclusion that Respondent thereby violated Section 8(a)(1) and (5) . . . . The compensatory remedy which he recommends, however, raises important issues concerning the Board's powers and duties to fashion appropriate remedies in its efforts to effectuate the policies of the [NLRA].

It is argued that such a remedy exceeds the Board's general statutory powers. In addition, it is contended that it cannot be granted because the amount of employee loss, if any, is so speculative that an order to make employees whole would amount to the imposition of a penalty. And the position is advanced that the adoption of this remedy would amount to the writing of a contract for the parties, which is prohibited by Section 8(d).

We have given most serious consideration to the Trial Examiner's recommended financial reparations Order, and are in complete agreement with his finding that current remedies of the Board designed to cure violations of Section 8(a)(5) are inadequate. A mere affirmative order that an employer bargain upon request does not eradicate the effects of an unlawful delay of 2 or more years in the fulfillment of a statutory bargaining obligation. It does not put the employees in the position of bargaining strength they would have enjoyed if their employer had immediately recognized and bargained with their chosen representative. It does not dissolve the inevitable employee frustration or protect the Union from the loss of employee support attributable to such delay. The inadequacy of the remedy is all the more egregious where, as in the recent *NLRB v. Tiidee Products, Inc.*, case, [426 F.2d 1243 (C.A.D.C.),] the court found that the employer had raised "frivolous" issues in order to postpone or avoid its lawful obligation to bargain. We have weighed these considerations most carefully. For the reasons stated below, however, we have reluctantly concluded that we cannot approve Trial Examiner's Recommended Order that Respondent compensate its employees for monetary losses incurred as a consequence of Respondent's determination to refuse to bargain until it had tested in court the validity of the Board's certification.

Section 10(c) of the Act directs the Board to order a person found to have committed an unfair labor practice to cease and desist and "to take such affirmative action including reinstatement of employees with or without back pay, as will effectuate the policies of this Act." This authority, as our colleagues note with full documentation, is extremely broad and was so intended by Congress. It is not so broad, however, as to permit the punishment of a particular respondent or a class of respondents. Nor is the statutory direction to the Board so compelling that the Board is without discretion in exercising the full sweep of its power, for it would defeat the purposes of the Act if the Board imposed an otherwise proper remedy that resulted in irreparable harm to a particular respondent and hampered rather than promoted meaningful collective bargaining. Moreover, as the Supreme Court recently emphasized, the Board's grant of power does not extend to compelling agreement. (*H.K. Porter Co., Inc., v. N.L.R.B.*, 397 U.S. 99.) It is with respect to these three limitations upon the Board's power to remedy a violation of Section 8(a)(5) that we examine the UAW's requested remedy in this case.

The Trial Examiner concluded that the proposed remedy was not punitive, that it merely made the employees partially whole for losses occasioned by the Respondent's refusal to bargain, and was much less harsh than a backpay order for discharged employees, which might require the Respondent to pay wages to these employees as well as their replacements. Viewed solely in the context of an assumption of employee monetary losses resulting directly from the Respondent's violation of Section 8(a)(5), as finally determined in court, the Trial Examiner's conclusion appears reasonable. There are, however, other factors in this case which provide counterweights to that rationale. In the first place, there is no contention that this Respondent acted in a manner flagrantly in defiance of the statutory policy. On the contrary, the record indicates that this Respondent responsibly fulfills its legally established collective-bargaining obligations. It is clear that Respondent merely sought judicial affirmance of the Board's decision that the election of October 22, 1964, should not be set aside on the Respondent's objections. In the past, whenever an employer has sought court intervention in a representation proceeding the Board has argued forcefully that court intervention would be premature, that the employer had an unquestioned right under the statute to seek court review of any Board order before its bargaining obligation became final. Should this procedural right in 8(a)(5) cases be tempered by a large monetary liability in the event the employer's position in the representation case is ultimately found to be without merit? Of course, an employer or a union which engages in conduct later found in violation of the Act, does so at the peril of ultimate conviction and responsibility for a make-whole remedy. But the validity of a particular Board election tried in an unfair labor practice case is not, in our opinion, an issue on the same plane as the discharge of employees for union activity or other conduct in flagrant disregard of employee rights. There are wrongdoers and wrongdoers. Where the wrong in refusing to bargain is, at most, a debatable question, though ultimately found a wrong, the imposition of a large financial obligation on such a respondent may come close to a form of punishment for having elected to pursue a representation question beyond the Board and to the courts. . . .

In *Tiidee Products* the court suggested that the Board need not follow a uniform policy in the application of a compensatory remedy in 8(a)(5) cases. Indeed, the court noted that such uniformity in this area of the law would be unfair when applied "to unlike cases." The court was of the opinion that the remedy was proper where the employer had engaged in a "manifestly unjustifiable refusal to bargain" and where its position was "palpably without merit." . . . *Tiidee Products* distinguished those cases in which the employer's failure to bargain rested on a "debatable question." With due respect for the opinion of the Court of Appeals for the District of Columbia, we cannot agree that the application of a compensatory remedy in 8(a)(5) cases can be fashioned on the subjective determination that the position of one respondent is "debatable" while that of another is "frivolous." What is debatable to the Board may appear frivolous to a court, and vice versa. Thus, the debatability of the employer's position in an 8(a)(5) case would itself become a matter of intense litigation. . . .

It is argued that the instant case is distinguishable from *H.K. Porter* in that here the requested remedy merely would require an employer to compensate employees for losses they incurred as a consequence of their employer's *failure to agree* to a contract he *would* have agreed to *if* he had bargained in good faith. In our view, the distinction is more illusory than real. The remedy in *H.K. Porter* operates prospectively to bind an employer to a specific contractual term. The remedy in the instant case operates retroactively to impose financial liability upon an employer flowing from a *presumed* contractual agreement. The Board infers that the latter contract, though it never existed and does not and need not exist, was *denied* existence by the employer because of his refusal to bargain. In either case the employer has not agreed to the contractual provision for which he must accept full responsibility *as though he had agreed to it*. Our colleagues contend that a compensatory remedy is not the "writing of a contract" because it does not "specify new or continuing terms of employment and does not prohibit changes in existing terms and conditions." But there is no basis for such a remedy unless the Board finds, as a matter of fact, that a contract would have resulted from bargaining. The fact that the contract, so to speak, is "written in the air" does not diminish its financial impact upon the recalcitrant employer who, willy-nilly, is forced to accede to terms never mutually established by the parties. Despite the admonition of the Supreme Court that Section 8(d) was intended to mean what it says, i.e., that the obligation to bargain "does not compel either party to agree to a proposal or require the making of a concession," one of the parties under this remedy is forced by the Government to submit to the other side's demands. It does not help to argue that the remedy could not be applied unless there was substantial evidence that the employer would have yielded to these demands during bargaining negotiations. Who is to say in a specific case how much an employer is prepared to give and how much a union is willing to take? Who is to say that a favorable contract would, in any event, result from the negotiations? And it is only the employer of such good will as to whom the Board might conclude that he, at least, would have given his employees a fair increase, who can be made subject to a financial reparations order; should such an employer be singled out for the imposition of such an order? To answer these questions the Board would be required to engage in the most general, if not entirely speculative, inferences to reach the conclusion that employees were deprived of specific benefits as a consequence of their employer's refusal to bargain.

Much as we appreciate the need for more adequate remedies in 8(a)(5) cases, we believe that, as the law now stands, the proposed remedy is a matter for Congress, not the Board. In our opinion, however, substantial relief may be obtained immediately through procedural reform, giving the highest possible priority to 8(a)(5) cases combined with full resort to the injunctive relief provisions of Section 10(j) and (e) of the Act. . . .

Members MCCULLOCH and BROWN, dissenting in part:

[W]e part company with our colleagues on the majority in that we would grant the compensatory remedy recommended by the Trial Examiner. . . . Unlike our colleagues, we believe that the Board has the statutory authority to direct such relief and that it would effectuate the policies of the Act to do so in this case.

Section 10(c) . . . directs the Board to remedy unfair labor practices by ordering the persons committing them to cease and desist from their unlawful conduct "and to take such affirmative action including reinstatement of employees with or without back pay, as will effectuate the policies of this Act. . . ." The phrase "affirmative action" is nowhere qualified in the statute, except that such action must "effectuate the policies of this Act," and indicates the intent of Congress to vest the Board with remedial powers coextensive with the underlying policies of the law which is to be enforced. . . .

The declared policy of the Act is to promote the peaceful settlement of disputes by encouraging collective bargaining and by protecting employee rights. To accomplish this purpose, Board remedies for violations of the Act should, on one hand, have the effect of preventing the party in violation from so acting in the future, and from enjoying any advantage he may have gained by his unlawful practices. But they must also presently dissipate the effects of violations on employee rights in order that the employees so injured receive what they should not have been denied. . . .

Deprivation of an employee's statutory rights is often accompanied by serious financial injury to him. Where this is so, an order which only guarantees the exercise of his rights in the future often falls far short of expunging the effects of the unlawful conduct involved. Therefore, one of the Board's most effective and well-established affirmative remedies for unlawful conduct is an order to make employees financially whole for losses resulting from violations of the Act. . . . The most familiar of these is the backpay order used to remedy the effect of employee discharges found to be in violation of Section 8(a)(3). . . .

The Board has already recognized in certain refusal-to-bargain situations that the usual bargaining order is not sufficient to expunge the effects of an employer's unlawful and protracted denial of its employees' right to bargain. . . . In a number of situations the Board has ordered the employer who unlawfully refused to bargain to compensate its employees for their resultant financial losses. Thus, some employers unlawfully refuse to sign after an agreement. The Board has in these cases ordered the employer to execute the agreement previously reached and, according to its terms, to make whole the employees for the monetary losses suffered because of the unlawful delay in its effectuation.

Similarly, in *American Fire Apparatus Co.*, [160 NLRB 1318, *enfd.* 380 F.2d 1005 (C.A. 8),] the employer violated Section 8(a)(5) by unilaterally discontinuing payment of Christmas bonuses, and the Board concluded that only by requiring the bonuses to be paid could the violation be fully remedied. . . .

And in *Fibreboard Paper Products Corp.*, the employer unilaterally contracted out its maintenance operations in violation of Section 8(a)(5). The Board concluded that an order to bargain about this decision could not, by itself, adequately remedy the effects of the violation. It further ordered the employer to reinstate the employees and to make them whole for any loss of earnings suffered on account of the unlawful conduct. The Supreme Court upheld the compensatory remedy, and stated that "There has been no showing that the Board's order restoring the *status quo ante* to insure meaningful bargaining is not well designed to promote the policies of the Act." . . .

The present remedies for unlawful refusals to bargain often fall short, as in the present case, of adequately protecting the employees' right to bargain. Recent court decisions, congressional investigations, and scholarly studies have concluded that, in the present remedial framework, justice delayed is often justice denied. . . .

The present case is but another example of a situation where a bargaining order by itself is not really adequate to remedy the effects of an unlawful refusal to bargain. The Union herein requested recognition on August 3, 1964, and proved that it represented a majority of employees 2-1/2 months later in a Board-conducted election. Nonetheless, since October 1965 the employer, by unlawfully refusing to bargain with the Union, has deprived its employees of their legal right to collective bargaining through their certified bargaining representative. While a bargaining order at this time, operating prospectively, may insure the exercise of that right in the future, it clearly does not repair the injury to the employees here, caused by the Respondent's denial of their rights during the past 5 years.

In these refusal-to-bargain cases there is at least a legal injury. Potential employee losses incurred by an employer's refusal to bargain in violation of the Act are not limited to financial matters such as wages. Thus, it is often the case that the most important employee gains arrived at through collective bargaining involve such benefits as seniority, improved physical facilities, a better grievance procedure, or a right to arbitration. Therefore, even the remedy we would direct herein is not complete, limited as it is to only some of the monetary losses which may be measured or estimated. The employees would not be made whole for all the losses incurred through the employer's unfair labor practice. But, where the legal injury is accompanied by financial loss, the employees should be compensated for it. . . .

This type of compensatory remedy is in no way forbidden by Section 8(d). It would be designed to compensate employees for injuries incurred by them by virtue of the unfair labor practices and would not require the employer to accept the measure of compensation as a term of any contract which might result from subsequent collective bargaining. The remedy contemplated in no way "writes a contract" between the employer and the union, for it would not specify new or continuing terms of employment and would not prohibit changes in existing terms and conditions. All of these would be left to the outcome of bargaining, the commencement of which would terminate Respondent's liability.

Furthermore, this compensatory remedy is not a punitive measure. It would be designed to do no more than reimburse the employees for the loss occasioned by the deprivation of their right to be represented by their collective-bargaining agent during the period of the violation. The amount to be awarded would be only that which would reasonably reflect and be measured by the loss caused by the unlawful denial of the opportunity for collective bargaining. Thus, employees would be compensated for the injury suffered as a result of their employer's unlawful refusal to bargain, and the employer would thereby be prohibited from enjoying the fruits of its forbidden conduct to the end, as embodied in the Act, that collective bargaining be encouraged and the rights of injured employees be protected . . . [I]t is well established that, where the defendant's wrongful act prevents exact determination of the amount of damage, he cannot plead such uncertainty in order to deny relief to the injured person, but rather must bear the risk of the uncertainty which was created by his own wrong. The Board is often faced with the task of determining the precise amount of a make-whole order where the criteria are less than ideal, and has successfully resolved the questions presented.

. . . It is well established that the rule which precludes recovery of "uncertain damages" refers to uncertainty as to the fact of injury, rather than to the amount. Where, as here, the employer has deprived its employees of a statutory right, there is by definition a legal injury suffered by them, and any uncertainty concerns only the amount of the accompanying reimbursable financial loss. . . .

A showing at the compliance stage by the General Counsel or Charging Party by acceptable and demonstrable means that the employees could have reasonably expected to gain a certain amount of compensation by bargaining would establish a *prima facie* loss, and the Respondent would then be afforded an opportunity to rebut such a showing. This might be accomplished, for example, by adducing evidence to show that a contract would probably not have been reached, or that there would have been less or no increase in compensation as a result of any contract which might have been signed.

... [T]here are many methods for determining the measurable financial gain which the employees might reasonably have expected to achieve, had the Respondent fulfilled its statutory obligation to bargain collectively. The criteria which prove valid in each case must be determined by what is pertinent to the facts. ... [i]f the particular employer and union involved have contracts covering other plants of the employer, possibly in the same or a relevant area, the terms of such agreements may serve to show what the employees could probably have obtained by bargaining. The parties could also make comparisons with compensation patterns achieved through collective bargaining by other employees in the same geographic area and industry. ...

In the instant case, as noted above, a *prima facie* showing of loss can readily be made out by measuring the wage and benefit increments that were negotiated for employees at Respondent's other organized plants against those given employees in this bargaining unit during the period of Respondent's unlawful refusal to bargain. Granted that the task of determining loss may be more difficult in other cases where no similar basis for comparison exists, this is not reason enough for the Board to shirk its statutory responsibilities and no reason at all for it to do so in a case such as this where that difficulty is not present.

———————

Notes

1. Who is more convincing, the majority or the dissent?

2. Does it matter that in this case, as the dissent points out, the employer had multiple, similar facilities, and it had entered into collective-bargaining agreements with unions at those other facilities?

3. On appeal of the *Ex-Cello-O* decision, the D.C. Circuit insisted that distinctions between "frivolous" and "fairly debatable" employer objections to elections could and should be made. But it also concluded that in the *Ex-Cell-O* case itself, the employer's objections were "fairly debatable." The court then enforced the Board's order that the employer bargain with the union. This order came over six years after the certification election. *International Union, UAW v. NLRB*, 449 F.2d 1046 (D.C. Cir. 1971).

4. Still, little seems to remain of the *Tiidee* concept that compensatory damages may be ordered where the employer's objections were "frivolous." For the end of that litigation, see *Int'l Union of Electrical Workers v. NLRB*, 502 F.2d 349 (D.C. Cir. 1974).

For example, in *Fieldcrest Cannon, Inc. v. NLRB*, 97 F.3d 65 (4th Cir. 1996), the court upheld findings of more than 100 ULPs against the employer, many of them quite serious. It also upheld remedies including a new election, rescinding various employer rules, increased access for the union (including an order allowing a union representative to give a 30-minute speech to employees during working time), and ordering that the company publish notices of its violation of the NLRA not only at the worksite but also in local newspapers. The Board had also ordered a one percent pay increase, on the grounds that the employer had given a 5.5 percent raise to its non-union employees, but only a 4.5 percent raise to union employees. The court refused to enforce that remedy. 97 F.3d 65, 68, 74.

5. Thus, for a ULP based on a party's refusal to bargain over forming contract terms, the standard remedy is an order to cease refusing to bargain and on request, bargain in good faith. If the employer continues to refuse to bargain in good faith, the Board may seek court enforcement, and if the employer still refuses, the court ultimately could order contempt sanctions. While this likely means that employers such as H.K. Porter will ultimately have to agree to dues check-off clauses, consider the effect of many years of litigation on contract negotiations and support for the union. Recall here the rules on presumptions of majority support in the context of decertification elections, discussed in Chapter 7.

6. It has been estimated that less than half of newly certified unions achieve a contract within one year after bargaining begins, and 37 percent of unions in first-contract situations still do not have a contract after two years. Ross Eisenbrey, *Employers Can Stall First Union Contracts for Years*, ECONOMIC POLICY INSTITUTE, May 20, 2009, *available at* https://www.epi.org/publication/snapshot-20090520/. To what extent do you think this could be attributable to inadequate remedies for employer failure to bargain in good faith? Can you think of any solutions to this problem beyond the type of remedies these cases have rejected?

7. What about attorneys' fees? In *Unbelievable, Inc. v. NLRB*, 118 F.3d 795 (D.C. Cir. 1997), the Board had found an § 8(a)(5) violation due to the employer's "unresponsive, aggressive, and flagrantly disrespectful" bargaining. The Board's remedy included attorneys' fees both for the NLRB and the union, because the employer's frivolous defenses wasted the resources of the union and the NLRB. The D.C. Circuit reversed the award of litigation expenses, concluding that § 10(c) was not sufficient to authorize deviation from the normal rule that each side must pay its own expenses.

8. On the other hand, in *Fallbrook Hosp. Corp.*, 360 N.L.R.B. 644 (2014), the Board, in a 2–1 decision, ordered the employer to reimburse the union for its expenses during six months of unproductive bargaining. Also, the Board unanimously ruled that the employer's bad-faith bargaining justified an extension of the "certification year" of the union (in which the union enjoys an irrebuttable presumption of majority status, see Chapter 7). In this case, the ALJ had found multiple violations. Among other things, the hospital had: simply stopped responding to union requests for bargaining; refused to bargain about the discharge of two employees; refused to submit contract proposals or counter proposals for long periods of time; made various false claims about why they were not negotiating; and left two of the bargaining sessions

they did attend literally within a few minutes. The employer had also filed a lawsuit against the union claiming that the union had waived its right to file ULP charges, but a court dismissed that suit. The majority ordered bargaining expenses, concluding that the employer's actions "infected the core of the bargaining process to such an extent that its effects cannot be eliminated by the mere application of our traditional remedy of an affirmative bargaining order."

In enforcing the Board's order in this case, the D.C. Circuit stated that "[t]he Board's discretion in fashioning remedies under the Act is extremely broad and subject to very limited judicial review. . . . This means that the court has no business second-guessing the Board's judgments regarding remedies for unfair labor practices." *Fallbrook Hosp. Corp. v. NLRB*, 785 F.3d 729, 738 (D.C. Cir. 2015).

9. *Fallbrook Hospital Corp.* was not the first time the Board has extended the period of time in which a union has an irrebuttable presumption of majority support. *See, e.g., Virginia Mason Medical Center v. NLRB*, 558 F.3d 891 (9th Cir. 2009) (enforcing the Board's extension of the certification year). However, such extensions are not granted in all cases finding § 8(a)(5) violations. *See, e.g., Spurlino Materials, LLC*, 353 N.L.R.B. 1198 (2009) (extension improper; employer had not completely refused to bargain, and no evidence the unilateral changes had affected the parties' negotiations).

10. If an employer and union reach a tentative agreement on a package of proposals, but the employer then withdraws its agreement in a manner that violates § 8(a) (5), the Board may order the employer to implement the proposals. *TNT USA, Inc. v. NLRB*, 208 F.3d 362 (2000). How is this situation distinguishable from that in *Ex-Cell-O*?

2. Remedies for Other Types of Bad-Faith Bargaining

If an employer has made a unilateral change in a mandatory subject of bargaining without bargaining to impasse, the standard remedy is to order both that the employer bargain in good faith and, usually, to restore the status quo ante and make employees whole for any benefits they were denied because of the unilateral change. So, for example, if an employer unilaterally reduces wages from $15 an hour to $12 an hour without agreement or bargaining to impasse, the Board would order that the employer restore the wage rate to $15 and compensate the employees for the period in which the employer had illegally underpaid them. This principle is not limited to wages. For example, in *Regal Cinemas, Inc. v. NLRB*, 317 F.3d 300 (D.C. Cir. 2003), the remedy for bad faith bargaining was that the employer rehire a group of projectionists it had terminated when it converted to "manager operated" theaters unilaterally, without bargaining. *Accord Pan American Grain Co. v. NLRB*, 558 F.3d 22 (1st Cir. 2009) (enforcing reinstatement and back pay as a remedy for layoffs done without bargaining in violation of § 8(a)(5)).

Some cases, however, raise difficult issues as to whether the status quo can or should be restored; if not, such a remedy will not be appropriate. In *Naperville*

Ready Mix, Inc. v. NLRB, 242 F.3d 744 (7th Cir. 2001), the Board found that a trucking company had unilaterally shifted some of its hauling business to subcontractors in violation of § 8(a)(5), and it ordered that the company restore the operations and rehire bargaining unit members. The Seventh Circuit enforced this order. But when another company violated § 8(a)(5) by subcontracting its trucking operations, leading the Board to order the company to restore those operations to bargaining unit employees, the Fifth Circuit refused to enforce that part of the order. *NLRB v. American Mfg. Co.*, 351 F.2d 74 (5th Cir. 1965). The court found no evidence that "coerced investment" by the employer in a fleet of trucks and related equipment was necessary to effectuate the policies of Act. 351 F.2d 74, 81.

Should there be a flat rule as to what remedy is appropriate in such situations? If so, what should the rule be? Or should the remedy depend on certain facts in the case? If so, which facts?

B. Remedies in the Public Sector

In almost all instances, public-sector law tracks private-sector law in this area. Still, the public-sector context can occasionally create a unique issue.

Seattle v. Public Employment Relations Commission

Washington Supreme Court
118 Wash. 2d 621, 826 P.2d 158 (1992)

ANDERSON, J.

The question raised by this appeal is whether the Public Employment Relations Commission (PERC) has authority to order "interest" arbitration as part of an unfair labor practice remedy. We hold that, in limited circumstances, it does.

The PERC order challenged in this action requires the employer, Municipality of Metropolitan Seattle (Metro), to participate in interest arbitration if collective bargaining between Metro and the International Federation of Professional and Technical Engineers, Local 17, AFL-CIO (Local 17) does not result in a collective bargaining agreement. . . .

This case concerns five employees who, until April 1984, worked as clerical employees for the City of Seattle's commuter pool. The city employees were represented by their exclusive bargaining agent, Local 17. In 1982 or 1983, Metro, a public transit authority serving the greater Seattle area, began negotiating with the City of Seattle for a transfer of the City's commuter pool program to Metro. The plan involved the transfer of approximately 29 employees, including the five clerical employees who were members of Local 17. The statute authorizing such transfers places certain obligations, including the duty to collectively bargain with existing unions, upon any metropolitan corporation which acquires an existing transportation system.

The five commuter pool employees were transferred to Metro in early April 1984. In the years from the date of that transfer to the present time, Metro has refused to recognize Local 17 as the appropriate bargaining unit for the transferred employees. During those years, Metro has also refused to bargain with the union, despite court and PERC orders to do so. . . .

Local 17's complaint alleged a refusal to bargain on the part of Metro. Although the hearing on the unfair labor practice complaint was held in early November 1986, the decision was not issued until January 1988. The delay was due to PERC's decision to hold the matter in abeyance until a decision was reached by the King County Superior Court in Metro's unit clarification action. In the unfair labor practice case, Metro argued that it had changed its operations to such an extent that the commuter pool which was transferred from the City was no longer intact and thus no longer existed as a separate bargaining unit. The PERC hearing examiner found this argument to be "frivolous" in light of settled law requiring that the "effects" of such significant changes in working conditions must be bargained before being implemented. The hearing examiner noted that during the pendency of the action, and after the previous unit clarification petition had been dismissed, Metro had filed yet another petition with PERC asking that its bargaining obligations toward Local 17 be terminated. The hearing examiner found:

> METRO has attempted at every turn to evade its bargaining obligations. It is evident that METRO has not given up the fight, and that it is still not prepared to fulfill its bargaining obligations towards Local 17. . . . METRO will likely continue to put up one defense after another in an ongoing attempt to defeat having a bargaining relationship with Local 17. . . . METRO has asserted, and continues to assert, inherently frivolous defenses in an ongoing effort to subvert and avoid its bargaining obligations towards Local 17.

The hearing examiner then crafted the order which is now before us on Metro's challenge. The order requires Metro to restore the status quo with respect to the five commuter pool employees and to make those employees whole. Based on a finding of bad faith on the part of Metro, it requires Metro to pay the union's reasonable attorneys' fees and costs. It orders Metro to post notices with respect to the unfair labor practice and orders that Metro [bargain in good faith] and, if no agreement is reached through bilateral negotiations within sixty (60) days after Local 17 has requested to bargain, either party may request the Public Employment Commission Relations [sic] to provide the services of a mediator to assist the parties. If no agreement is reached by using the mediation process, and the Executive Director, on the request of either of the parties and the recommendation of the assigned mediator, concludes that the parties are at impasse following a reasonable period of negotiations, shall submit the remaining issues to interest arbitration using the procedures of 41.56.450, et seq., and the standards for . . . firefighters. The decision of the neutral arbitration panel shall be final and binding upon both the parties. . . .

On appeal, Metro challenged the PERC order on the grounds that (1) PERC did not have the authority to order Metro to return its employees to the status quo that existed in August 1984 (6 months before the unfair labor practice complaint was filed) and (2) PERC did not have authority to order interest arbitration as an unfair labor practice remedy. The Court of Appeals affirmed the order requiring restoration of the status quo but reversed that portion of the order directing interest arbitration in the event of bargaining impasse.

PERC and Local 17 petitioned this court for review of the interest arbitration issue; we [conclude that] PERC does have the authority, in limited and extraordinary circumstances, to order interest arbitration as part of an unfair labor practice remedy. Such a remedy must be cautiously and sparingly used, however, and used only in those cases where there is a clear history of bad faith refusal to bargain and where there is a very strong likelihood that such refusal will continue despite PERC's order to bargain in good faith.

This case presents a conflict between the need to preserve the integrity of the collective bargaining process on the one hand, and, on the other, the genuine need to remedy flagrant abuses of that process in situations where employees are unable, through legal means or by use of traditional economic weapons, to remedy the situation themselves. The Public Employees' Collective Bargaining Act, Rcw 41.56, was enacted in 1967, in order to promote the continued improvement of the relationship between public employers and their employees. . . . The Act requires public employers, including municipal corporations such as Metro, to participate in collective bargaining with the exclusive bargaining representatives of its employees. . . .

Employers have traditionally not been compelled to agree or to accept the terms of a collective bargaining contract to which they do not agree. Resolution of bargaining impasses has thus depended on the economic pressures that the employer and employees could bring to bear upon one another. Where those economic pressures can be limited or prohibited or where their usefulness is questionable, other—more peaceful—methods of resolving contract impasses may be advantageous. While interest arbitration is generally a voluntary process both this court and the Legislature have given limited approval to the use of compulsory interest arbitration to resolve collective bargaining impasses in the public employment arena. RCW 41.56.450 requires interest arbitration between law enforcement and firefighter unions and their employers when contract negotiations and mediation have failed to produce a contract. In *Green River Comm'ty College v. Higher Educ. Personnel Bd.*, 95 Wash.2d 108, 622 P.2d 826 (1980), *modified on reconsideration*, 95 Wash.2d 962, 633 P.2d 1324 (1981), this court approved a regulation promulgated by the Higher Education Personnel Board (HEP Board) that permitted either a college or its employee union to submit unresolved collective bargaining issues to the HEP Board for compulsory resolution through interest arbitration. Heretofore we have not determined whether PERC has the power to order interest arbitration as a remedy for an unfair labor practice.

An agency has only those powers which are expressly granted or which are necessarily implied from statutory grants of authority. . . . In addition to other duties, PERC is empowered and directed to prevent any unfair labor practice and to issue appropriate remedial orders. RCW 41.56.160.

When interpreting the Public Employees' Collective Bargaining Act, we will liberally construe the Act in order to accomplish its purpose. The purpose of the Act "is to provide public employees with the right to join and be represented by labor organizations of their own choosing, and to provide for a uniform basis for implementing that right." With that purpose in mind, we interpret the statutory phrase "appropriate remedial orders" to be those necessary to effectuate the purposes of the collective bargaining statute and to make PERC's lawful orders effective. The authority granted PERC by the remedial provision of the statute has been interpreted to be broad enough to authorize an award of attorney fees when such an award "is necessary to make the order effective and if the defense to the unfair labor practice is frivolous or meritless."

In *State ex rel. Wash. Fed'n of State Employees v. Board of Trustees*, 93 Wash.2d 60 (1980), this court stated that the HEP Board's determination as to remedies under the Public Employees' Collective Bargaining Act should be accorded considerable judicial deference, and noted that the "relation of remedy to policy is peculiarly a matter of administrative competence." PERC's expertise in resolving labor disputes also has been judicially recognized and accorded deference. . . .

PERC thus has authority to issue appropriate orders that it, in its expertise, believes are consistent with the purposes of the Act, and that are necessary to make its orders effective unless such orders are otherwise unlawful.

. . . Metro argues that because the Legislature did not include transit workers within the interest arbitration provisions of the statute, it intended that those workers not participate in interest arbitration. . . . Many of the arguments here presented by Metro were considered in *Green River*, where this court rejected those arguments and ruled that the HEP Board, through its regulatory powers, could require all public colleges and their employees to participate in interest arbitration, if collective bargaining and contract mediation failed. This court found such a regulation to be consistent with the intent and purpose of the law governing collective bargaining between public colleges and their employees.

The *Green River* court distinguished significant federal precedent that is now relied on by Metro. In *Green River*, this court declined to follow *H.K. Porter Co. v. NLRB*, 397 U.S. 99 (1970). . . .

This court, in distinguishing *H.K. Porter Co.*, stated that reliance on NLRA precedents in the present context is inappropriate. The NLRA regulates labor relations only in the private sector. The Act specifically guarantees employees the right to strike. Private sector bargaining and public sector bargaining are radically different, as both parties agree. *Green River* supports the union's and PERC's position that interest arbitration need not be specifically permitted or required by statute in order for it to be lawful.

Metro also argues that compelled interest arbitration is contrary to traditional collective bargaining principles and to the philosophy behind collective bargaining. When faced with a situation such as that which exists here, there is little that a union can legally do to enforce the collective bargaining rights of its members. For 7 years Metro has been involved in litigation over the representation rights of these five employees. Court orders and financial sanctions have had no effect on Metro. The employer's delays and legal maneuvering have, in fact, resulted in a prolonged period in which the employees have not had an opportunity to negotiate the terms and conditions of their employment. During this time Metro accomplished the disbursement of the employees represented by Local 17 so that the bargaining unit became unidentifiable. This disbursement of employees throughout other bargaining units was the reason for PERC's order requiring a return to the status quo. The conflict here thus arises because the employer in this case has been able to use the law to avoid its clear obligation to collectively bargain with the union and now, when ordered to participate in interest arbitration, claims that such an order is violative of the philosophy behind collective bargaining. In this case PERC specifically found that the remedy of interest arbitration, upon impasse, was necessary to make its order to bargain effective. In the very limited circumstances presented by the facts of this case, such an order is not contrary to collective bargaining principles. Instead, it serves as an impetus to successfully negotiate an agreement. . . .

Notes

1. As the court noted, this case arose in a state which provided for mandatory, binding interest arbitration for some public employees but not for others. Would this remedy be less appropriate in a state that did not provide such a procedure for any public employees?

2. This case seems to rely in part on the finding that the employer's defenses were frivolous. Is this, essentially, adopting the reasoning of *Tiidee Products*? If so, is that a good approach?

3. What other possible solutions existed? Could or should the court itself have simply ordered a substantive remedy? What are the advantages and disadvantages to that? Could the court have remanded the case to the state agency and ordered it to craft a substantive remedy? Does it matter whether a court, a state agency or an interest arbitrator orders a certain substantive result?

Chapter 11

Economic Weapons and Impasse Resolution

I. Introduction

As Chapter 10 explained, in the private sector, the law does not require either party to make concessions or reach agreement as part of their duty to bargain in good faith. This limit on government intervention is meant to ensure that the substance of collective-bargaining agreements remains the domain of the parties. Union and employer use of economic weapons to influence each other's bargaining positions, and Board and court regulation of those weapons, is therefore an organic and critical part of the collective-bargaining process.

In that process, strikes — employees collectively withholding their labor from their employer — may be the quintessential concerted activity. This chapter begins with a study of strikes and the law regulating and protecting them. It examines the right to strike in the private sector, limits on the exercise of that right and related conduct, and legal rules regarding various employer responses to strikes. Perhaps the most important and controversial employer response is permanently replacing striking workers with other workers. This chapter describes when that is and is not permitted. It also considers employers' economic weapons in the collective-bargaining process, particularly employers' analog to strikes: lockouts.

In contrast, public employees can strike in only a minority of states. More commonly, bargaining impasses in the public sector are resolved using a range of alternative techniques. These include mediation, fact-finding, and interest arbitration. State laws vary considerably as to how these techniques are used (*e.g.*, which processes are used, whether a given process is mandatory or voluntary, what factors interest arbitrators must consider in making their decisions, and whether the final step of the process is binding or merely advisory). This chapter examines public-sector strikes, alternative impasse resolution systems, and judicial review of those systems. As you study these materials, consider: which system offers the better means of achieving the goals of collective bargaining? Also, is there a difference between the private and public sectors which necessitates different means of resolving disputes in collective bargaining?

II. Strikes, Lockouts, and Employer Responses to Employee Concerted Activities in the Private Sector

A. Strikes in the Collective Bargaining Process

Section 1 of the NLRA defines a strike as a "form of industrial strife or unrest" that disrupts commerce. Section 1 adds that one reason to protect the right to bargain collectively is that it "promotes the flow of commerce by removing certain recognized sources of industrial strife and unrest"; it is "the policy of the United States to eliminate the causes of certain substantial obstructions to the free flow of commerce and to mitigate and eliminate these obstructions . . . by encouraging the practice and procedure of collective bargaining." Further, §7 protects workers engaging in "concerted activities," which certainly includes strikes. Most directly, §13 states that the NLRA should not be interpreted "either to interfere with or impede or diminish in any way the right to strike, or to affect limitations or qualifications on that right."

How can the Act condemn strikes as a form of strife and unrest that harms commerce but then lend statutory protection to strikes? *NLRB v. Insurance Agents Int'l Union*, 361 U.S. 477, 488–89 (1960) indicated that strikes are a necessary, if paradoxical, part of collective bargaining. "It must be realized that collective bargaining . . . cannot be equated with an academic collective search for truth. . . . The presence of economic weapons in reserve, and their actual exercise on occasion by the parties, is part and parcel of the system that the Wagner and Taft-Hartley Acts have recognized."

In theory, strikes are unions' most powerful economic weapon in support of their bargaining demands. By collectively walking off the job, workers seek to impose substantial costs on their employers for failing to agree to their unions' demands. In the private sector, a struck employer might be forced to stop operating, surrender production and/or sales for days or months, perhaps lose relationships with suppliers and customers and, ultimately, sacrifice product market share. Employers that continue operating by sending managers and supervisors to the front line or hiring temporary workers to replace strikers bear the added costs of recruiting and training these replacements, perhaps at higher wages, and an inability to manage their businesses normally. Striking workers also bear significant costs, including the wages lost during the strike, the emotional uncertainty of living in an unsettled environment without a predictable outcome, and in many strikes, the risk of losing their job to a permanent replacement worker.

If a strike yields better compensation or terms of employment than the strikers otherwise would have won at the bargaining table, the workers' benefits might exceed their costs. Also, the struck employer benefits if the strike fails and workers are forced to accept a contract that is substantially more favorable to the employer. Thus, strikes and lockouts are a high-stakes game. It is also possible that neither party will be better off than they would have been in the absence of a strike or lockout. So, why do strikes happen? The following summarizes an economic explanation.

Kenneth Dau-Schmidt & Arthur Traynor, *Regulating Unions and Collective Bargaining*

in Kenneth Dau-Schmidt, Seth Harris & Orly Lobel, Labor and Employment Law and Economics (2008)

... Strikes are a very curious phenomenon in the context of the traditional neo-classical economic model of perfect information, individual preferences and competitive markets. Why would two rational parties engage in such costly behavior to arrive at a bargain that is necessarily inferior to the one they could have negotiated before the strike dissipated some of the joint benefits of production? At the very least, one would expect two cooperative parties to forgo the strike, adopt the contract they would have obtained after the work stoppage, and split the profits gained by continuing production. Economists have generally explained strikes as the result of imperfect information or strategic behavior.

(1). Imperfect information

Traditionally, economists explain strikes as the result of imperfect information. According to this view, strikes occur when both sides believe that they will gain more in concessions than they will suffer in costs from a strike. Since this cannot be true for both sides to the conflict, one or both must be mistaken due to imperfect information. In these models, unions undertake strikes either to adjust unrealistic expectations among rank-and-file workers as to the wage increase that is possible or to sort out low-wage from high-wage employers. Employers may also gain information about employee organization and resolve from a strike. Hicks opined that the strike weapon "grow(s) rusty if unused" and union leaders would have to occasionally undertake a strike just to maintain their bargaining power with the employer by demonstrating that their members were up to a confrontation. Thus, in these models strikes are merely the cheapest way to educate the workers or union leadership as to the optimal wage that can be extracted from the employer or the cheapest way to educate the employer on the resolve of the workers.

The primary implication of these models of strikes for public policy is that regulation can reduce the number of strikes by promoting a reliable exchange of information between the parties. This could be done through a number of means including requiring public filings on revenue and costs by employers, requiring exchanges of information as part of "good faith" bargaining, prohibiting lying in negotiations and encouraging mediation or factfinding in disputes to encourage exchanges of relevant information. . . . If the disclosure of information minimizes the chances of a strike, one might think that employers would voluntarily adopt this strategy. . . . However, . . . each side might gain at the expense of the other by not bluffing about their true preferences and cost structures to obtain a better settlement. It may also be that an employer may not want to make its entire cost structure publicly known and available to credit markets and competitors for fear that this will raise its costs in borrowing money or sacrifice some competitive advantage. Nevertheless, if minimizing industrial strife is a driving purpose of labor law, accurate disclosure of relevant cost and profit information may be more important than the value to either side in non-disclosure that facilitates bluffing the other to accept a worse bargain.

(2). Strategic behavior

Even if there were perfect information, strategic behavior in which one side tries to benefit at the expense of the other can lead to strikes. This can be seen by considering a simple bargaining game in which the union and employer have to decide how to divide a rent. There are two negotiating strategies each side must choose between, cooperation or intransigence. If both sides are cooperative, we assume they just split the rent. However, either side might do better by being intransigent. We assume that intransigence in bargaining is a positional externality in that, if only one side is intransigent, they will do better in bargaining relative to the other side. If both sides are intransigent, however, their efforts cancel each other and their strategic behavior serves only to waste a portion of the cooperative surplus in a strike or lockout.

Imagine an array of all possible divisions of a $10 rent between the employees and employer, from $10 for the employees and none for the employer, to $5 for each, to none for the employees and $10 for the employer. If both sides bargain cooperatively, they split the surplus and each party receives $5. Consistent with the assumption that one side can benefit if it is intransigent while the other is cooperative, the ultimate bargain when the union is intransigent but the employer is cooperative would yield $8 for the union and $2 for the employer. When the employer is intransigent but the union is cooperative, the results are reversed. Finally, if both sides are intransigent, the result is a costly strike that consumes a portion of the cooperative surplus and the ultimate bargain is struck at $3 for each party—off the line of optimal results.

Although very simple, this example demonstrates the potential for conflicts in industrial relations to escalate into costly affairs if the parties act only according to their own individual best interests. The parties' choice as to whether to bargain cooperatively or intransigently displays a classic divergence of individual and collective interests. . . . Based on individual incentives, the dominant strategy for each party is to be intransigent since regardless of the strategy the other side adopts, each party will do better individually by being intransigent. Regardless of the strategy the employer chooses to adopt, the employees do better if the union is intransigent. Similarly, regardless of which strategy the union adopts, the employer does better individually by being intransigent. However, if both parties follow this individually rational strategy and are intransigent, the result is a strike that wastes a portion of the cooperative surplus ($4) and each party gets just $3. The parties can improve on this result by instead acting on their collective interest in cooperation and just dividing the available rent at $5 each. . . .

———————

B. Protected and Unprotected Activity in the Strike Context

1. Activity Unprotected by § 7

Despite the language of § 7 and § 13, not all "strikes" are protected concerted activity under the NLRA. Perhaps the most notorious example is the "sit-down strike" of the late 1930s, a tactic which helped to spark the newly emerging industrial union movement. In 1937, a group of ninety-five employees occupied the key buildings of their employer, Fansteel Metallurgical Corporation, to protest its refusal to bargain with their chosen union representative and its support of a company union. Co-workers supported the sit-down strikers with food and other supplies as the occupation stretched over days. After defying a state court injunction ordering them to vacate the buildings, the strikers were eventually evicted by sheriff's deputies. The strikers were charged and punished for criminal contempt. Fansteel fired them.

In *National Labor Relations Board v. Fansteel Metallurgical Corp.*, 306 U.S. 240 (1939), the Court held that the sit-down strikes were not protected activities, even though they protested the employer's ULPs:

> reprehensible as was th[e] conduct of [Fansteel], there is no ground for saying that it made [Fansteel] an outlaw or deprived it of its legal rights to the possession and protection of its property. The employees had the right to strike but they had no license to commit acts of violence or to seize their employer's plant. . . . To justify such conduct because of the existence of a labor dispute or of an unfair labor practice would be to put a premium on resort to force instead of legal remedies and to subvert the principles of law and order which lie at the foundations of society. 306 U.S. 240, 253.

Thus, Fansteel did not commit a ULP by discharging the strikers. *See also Peck, Inc.*, 226 N.L.R.B. 1174 (1976) (employee sit-in protest unprotected).

Subsequent courts have observed that, notwithstanding *Fansteel*, not all sit-down strikes are unprotected. *See, e.g., NLRB v. Am. Mfg. Co.*, 106 F.2d 61 (2d Cir. 1939) (temporary work stoppage induced by employer's ULPs was protected where the employees "were not claiming to hold the premises in defiance of the right of possession of the owner"); *NLRB v. Serv-Air, Inc.*, 401 F.2d 363 (10th Cir. 1968) (employees' refusal to return to work until employer discussed various grievances was protected, since "in the absence of an established grievance procedure a spontaneous work stoppage to present a grievance was a protected activity"). Do these cases suggest that the line between protected and unprotected sit-down strikes turns on the employees' intent to "claim[] . . . hold of the premises in defiance of the owner's right of possession"? *See NLRB v. Pepsi-Cola Bottling Co.*, 449 F.2d 824, 829 (5th Cir. 1971).

Generally, § 7 does not protect strikes that feature significant unlawful conduct. For example, *Southern S.S. Co. v. NLRB*, 316 U.S. 31, 38–49 (1942) held that the Board had erred in finding that § 7 protected from discharge seamen who engaged in a work stoppage aboard a ship away from its home port where such conduct constituted mutiny in violation of federal criminal law. The Board has since applied *Southern S.S. Co.* to hold that § 7 did not protect fish processors who, as seamen, could not lawfully engage in a work stoppage, *Phoenix Processor Ltd.*, 348 N.L.R.B. 28 (2006), *enforced sub nom. Cornelio v. NLRB*, 276 Fed. Appx. 608 (9th Cir. 2008), but that § 7 did protect seamen who engaged in a work stoppage aboard a tugboat docked primarily at the home dock where there was no evidence that the seamen had disobeyed their captain's order, *Pantex Towing Corp.*, 258 N.L.R.B. 837, 841–43 (1981).

Also, violence and destruction of property are not protected. As *Fansteel, supra,* explained:

> This was not the exercise of "the right to strike" to which the Act referred . . . It was an illegal seizure of the buildings in order to prevent their use by the employer in a lawful manner and thus by acts of force and violence to compel the employer to submit. . . . There is not a line in the statute to warrant the conclusion that it is any part of the policies of the Act to encourage employees to resort to force and violence in defiance of the law of the land. On the contrary, the purpose of the Act is to promote peaceful settlements of disputes by providing legal remedies for the invasion of the employees' rights. . . . The affirmative action that is authorized is to make these remedies effective in the redress of the employees' rights, to assure them self-organization and freedom in representation, not to license them to commit tortious acts or to protect them from the appropriate consequences of unlawful conduct. We are of the opinion that to provide for the reinstatement or reemployment of employees guilty of the acts which the Board finds to have been committed in this instance would not only not effectuate any policy of the Act but would directly tend to make abortive its plan for peaceable procedure. 306 U.S. at 256–57.

Similarly, "strike misconduct"—including but not limited to violence—is generally not protected concerted activity. The Board has defined "strike misconduct" to be activity which "under the circumstances existing . . . may reasonably tend to coerce or intimidate employees in the exercise of rights protected under the Act." *Clear Pine Mouldings*, 268 N.L.R.B. 1044, 1046 (1984), *enforced*, 765 F.2d 148 (9th Cir. 1985); *Detroit Newspapers*, 340 N.L.R.B. 1019 (2003). An employer may discharge or refuse to reinstate a returning economic striker who has engaged in serious strike misconduct. *Union de Tronquistas de Puerto Rico, Local 901*, 202 N.L.R.B. 399 (1973).

Strike-related conduct need not violate state or other laws to lose protection under § 7. In *NLRB v. Insurance Agents*, 361 U.S. 477 at 492, the Supreme Court accepted *arguendo* the Board's contention that a union's partial strike was not a protected concerted activity. In *Elk Lumber Co.*, 91 N.L.R.B. 333, 337 (1950), the Board held unprotected the conduct of five car loaders engaged in a work slowdown in response to its employer's unilateral change in rates of pay. The Board explained that the employer had discharged the carloaders not for engaging in concerted activity but for unsatisfactory productivity. In *Yale University*, 330 N.L.R.B. 246 (1999), the Board reiterated its view that § 7 does not protect a "partial strike." Graduate teaching assistants (who were "employees" under the law at the time, *see* Chapter 3) either teaching their own classes or assisting faculty in teaching classes had refused to submit their students' final grades to the university until repeated threats from faculty members and university administrators changed their minds. A majority of the Board held that withholding grades while performing other job-related duties—that is, "both working and striking"—constituted a partial strike which lies outside the protection of § 7. *See also Swope Ridge Geriatric Center*, 350 N.L.R.B. 64 (2007) (recurring weekend strike activity was an unprotected intermittent strike).

The courts, in somewhat similar situations, have held that such conduct is just cause for discharge. For example, *C. G. Conn, Ltd. v. NLRB*, 108 F.2d 390, 398 (7th Cir. 1939) held an employer was justified in discharging employees who refused to work overtime, explaining:

> We are awar[e] of no law or logic that gives the employee the right to work upon terms prescribed solely by him. That is plainly what was sought to be done in this instance. It is not a situation in which employees ceased work in protest against conditions imposed by the employer, but one in which the employees sought and intended to work upon their own notion of the terms which should prevail. If they had a right to fix the hours of their employment, it would follow that a similar right existed by which they could prescribe all conditions and regulations affecting their employment.

See also N.L.R.B. v. Montgomery Ward & Co., 157 F.2d 486 (8th Cir. 1946) (unprotected slowdown where employees at one of the employer's plants refused to process orders from another plant where a strike was in progress). Again, the consequence of finding such behavior unprotected is that the employer may legally discharge the employee for that behavior, and indeed the court upheld such discharges in *Montgomery Ward*.

Why should the law refuse to protect "partial strikes" in which workers may intermittently leave work, return to work, and leave work again, or perform only some of their duties, when it protects strikes in which workers leave work entirely and do not return until the strike ends? Is the distinction that partial strikes are more disruptive of employers' operations? Is the Board balancing employees' right to strike with employers' need to manage their businesses? In light of Chapter 10's discussion of *NLRB v. Insurance Agents* and related cases, is it appropriate for the Board to engage in this kind of balancing of economic weapons? Or is the Board requiring employees to accept a sacrifice equivalent to the disruptions their strike inflicts on the employer's business—leaving their jobs and abandoning their paychecks—rather than "both working and striking"? If so, is that consistent with NLRA § 13? For a recent decision reiterating that "intermittent" strikes are unprotected by the Act, see *Walmart Stores, Inc.*, 368 N.L.R.B. No. 24 (2019).

Some concerted activity may receive only limited protection. Consider the "sympathy strike": a refusal by workers who are not in a striking bargaining unit to cross the picket lines of another striking union. This is generally protected concerted activity. *Indianapolis Power & Light v. NLRB*, 898 F.2d 524 (7th Cir. 1990). However, at least one court of appeals has suggested that the scope of this "right to sympathy strike" must be balanced against an employer's business justification in taking reasonable steps to deal with the honoring of the picket line, "and that what is reasonable depends on the totality of the circumstances in each case." *Business Services by Manpower Inc. v. NLRB*, 784 F.2d 442 (2d Cir. 1986) (discussing the history of the rule governing workers who honor "stranger" picket lines). Is this kind of balancing appropriate? Is it consistent with the language and purpose of the statute?

Picketing and handbilling are normally legal, but at some point they lose protection. Peaceful picketing outside the employer's premises is an ordinary and perhaps necessary part of most strikes, so it is usually protected. *See, e.g., Electrical Workers (IUE) Local 761 v. NLRB*, 366 U.S. 667, 681 (1961). Still, there are exceptions: "employees who engage in violence, mass picketing, unfair labor practices, contract violations, or other improper conduct, or who force the employer to violate the law, do not have any immunity under the act." *Complete Auto Transit, Inc. v. Reis*, 451 U.S. 401, 415 n.16 (1981). "Mass picketing" has been defined as picketing "which absolutely prevents all the office force from going into the office of a plant." *NLRB v. Allis-Chalmers Mfg. Co.*, 388 U.S. 175, 189 n.25 (1967). Picketers may not trespass on or block access to the employer's property; in other words, state property and criminal laws apply to strike-related picketing at the struck employer. Chapter 12 discusses §8(b)(4)'s rules governing picketing away from the employer's premises (*e.g.*, picketing customer or supplier companies of the primary employer).

Also, strikes are unprotected activity if they do not comply with the procedures of NLRA §8(d), which contains certain notice requirements and requires a "cooling off" period. For example, §8(d)(3) requires a union to file a notice with the Federal Mediation and Conciliation Service (FMCS) 30 days before striking, and §8(d)(4) requires the parties to continue the terms of an existing contract without strikes or lockouts for 60 days after notice to the FMCS or until the contract expires (whichever occurs later). Section 8(g) requires unions in the health care industry to provide notice to the employer and the FMCS 10 days before any strike or picketing. While these provisions are purely procedural (unlike impasse rules in the public sector, discussed *infra*, they do not involve the substance of contracts), failure of a union covered by the NLRA to comply with these provisions makes a strike illegal. *See, e.g., Int'l Alliance of Theatrical and Stage Employees v. NLRB*, 334 F.3d 27, 30 (D.C. Cir. 2003). Failure by the employer to comply with these notice requirements means it cannot lawfully unilaterally implement its final proposals after impasse. *American Water Works Company, Inc.*, 361 N.L.R.B. 64 (2014).

Finally, §7 generally does not protect strikes in violation of no-strike clauses in collective bargaining agreements. As Chapter 13 discusses in more detail, most union contracts contain "no-strike, no-lockout" clauses in which the parties agree that, for the term of the contract, they will not use these economic weapons (and will instead use the contract's grievance-arbitration process). Strikes in violation of a no-strike clause are typically unprotected activity. "The Act does not prohibit an effective discharge for repudiation by the employee of his agreement, any more than it prohibits such discharge for a tort committed against the employer." *NLRB v. Sands Mfg. Co.*, 306 U.S. 332, 344 (1939).

2. No-Strike Clauses and Unfair Labor Practice Strikes

One exception to this general rule exists: certain strikes protesting the employer's unfair labor practices. This will not be the only distinction labor law makes between "economic strikes"—those undertaken to pressure an employer to accept the union's bargaining proposals—and "unfair labor practice" strikes—strikes to protest employer ULPs.

In ***Mastro Plastics Corp. v. National Labor Relations Board***, 350 U.S. 270, 278 (1956), the Supreme Court began its analysis by distinguishing between economic strikes and ULP strikes:

> [P]etitioners' unfair labor practices provide adequate ground for the orderly strike that occurred here. Under those circumstances, the striking employees do not lose their status and are entitled to reinstatement with back pay, even if replacements for them have been made. Failure of the Board to enjoin petitioners' illegal conduct or failure of the Board to sustain the right to strike against that conduct would seriously undermine the primary objectives of the Labor Act.

The Court recognized that the right to engage in a ULP strike can be waived, among other ways, through contractual "no-strike" provisions. However, the Court upheld the Board and appellate court's narrow interpretation of the relevant contract's broad no-strike clause, which required the union "to refrain from engaging in any strike or work stoppage during the term." The Court found that the union's ULP strike did not violate the "no strike" provision:

> Petitioners argue that the words "any strike" leave no room for interpretation and necessarily include all strikes, even those against unlawful practices destructive of the foundation on which collective bargaining must rest. We disagree. We believe that the contract, taken as a whole, deals solely with the economic relationship between the employers and their employees. It is a typical collective-bargaining contract dealing with terms of employment and the normal operations of the plant. . . . Its strike and lockout clauses are natural adjuncts of an operating policy aimed at avoiding interruptions of production prompted by efforts to change existing economic relationships. . . .
>
> To adopt petitioners' all-inclusive interpretation of the clause is quite a different matter. That interpretation would eliminate, for the whole year, the employees' right to strike, even if petitioners, by coercion, ousted the

employees' lawful bargaining representative and, by threats of discharge, caused the employees to sign membership cards in a new union. Whatever may be said of the legality of such a waiver when explicitly stated, there is no adequate basis for implying its existence without a more compelling expression of it than appears in . . . this contract. . . . 350 U.S. at 281–83.

Finally, the Court rejected the argument that ULP strikes undertaken within the 60-day waiting period contained in § 8(d)(4) deprived the strikers of their status as "employees" under the Act. The Court concluded that § 8(d) was inapposite because ULP strikes do not seek to terminate or modify the contract; rather, as the Court explained, they are "designed instead to protest the unfair labor practices of petitioners." *Id.* at 286.

Thus, without a contractual waiver or a statutory bar to the ULP strike, the strike was legal, and the strikers protected as "employees" under the Act.

Notes

1. The most important distinction between economic strikers and ULP strikers is that ULP strikers are entitled to reinstatement to their jobs with back pay, even if they have been replaced during the course of the strike by their employer. *NLRB v. Int'l Van Lines*, 409 U.S. 48 (1972) (citing *Mastro Plastics*). This distinction does not appear in the NLRA. See subsection C *infra*, for more details on this distinction and rules on striker replacements.

2. Subsequent decisions have clarified the rule of *Mastro Plastics* regarding contractual "no-strike" provisions. While a union may waive its members' right to engage in a ULP strike, no waiver will be found if the employer commits "serious" ULPs or has materially breached a fundamental contractual obligation to its employees. *NLRB v. Northeast Oklahoma City Mfg.*, 631 F.2d 669 (10th Cir. 1980); *Arlan's Department Store*, 133 N.L.R.B. 802 (1961). *Compare Dow Chemical Co. v. NLRB*, 636 F.2d 1352 (3d Cir. 1980) *with Isla Verde Hotel Corp. v. NLRB*, 702 F.2d 268 (1st Cir. 1983).

3. *Mastro Plastics* offers a clear statement of the purposive statutory interpretation methodology which the Court uses to reach its decision: "If the above words are read in complete isolation from their context in the Act, such an interpretation is possible. However, '[i]n expounding a statute, we must not be guided by a single sentence or member of a sentence, but look to the provisions of the whole law, and to its object and policy.'" 350 U.S. at 285. Would a textualist have reached the same decision? What provisions of the statute might a textualist have focused on?

4. May an employer refuse to reinstate an unfair labor practice striker who has engaged in strike misconduct? *NLRB v. Thayer Co.*, 213 F.2d 748 (1st Cir.), *cert. denied*, 348 U.S. 883 (1954), held that the Board should balance the seriousness of the ULP striker's misconduct with the severity of the employer's ULPs to determine whether reinstatement of the striker should be required. The Board's subsequent

decision in *Clear Pine Mouldings, supra*, raised doubts about the continuing vitality of the *Thayer* balancing test. *See Tube Craft, Inc.*, 287 N.L.R.B. 491 (1987) (applying *Clear Pine Mouldings*). However, the Sixth Circuit has held that the "*Thayer* doctrine" remains effective even after those subsequent Board decisions. *M.P.C. Plating, Inc. v. NLRB*, 953 F.2d 1018 (6th Cir. 1992).

3. Liability of Unions and Employees for Illegal Strikes

As discussed above, if a union strike is unprotected, an employer may discipline or discharge the employees involved without running afoul of the NLRA. What about lawsuits for damages for an illegal primary strike? (Chapter 12 discusses damages for secondary labor activity.) Could an employer sue the union or its members for money damages?

In *Atkinson v. Sinclair Refining*, 370 U.S. 238 (1962), the Supreme Court considered an employer's claim for damages against unions (local and international) and individual union members for a strike that violated a no-strike clause. The Court permitted the claim of damages against the unions. However, *Atkinson* held that individual officers and members of a union are not liable for the damages caused by an illegal strike. The Court relied on the language of § 301(b) of the Taft-Hartley Act, which provides, in relevant part, that "Any money judgment against a labor organization . . . shall be enforceable only against the organization as an entity . . . and shall not be enforceable against any individual member or his assets" (for more on § 301, *see* Chapter 13). *Atkinson* explained that this language was intended to avoid the result of the *Danbury Hatters* case which permitted treble damages against individual union members (*see* Chapter 1).

In *Complete Auto Transit, Inc. v. Reis*, 451 U.S. 401 (1981), the Court extended this protection of individual strikers to those who took part in "wildcat" strikes (work stoppages the union did not authorize). Since the union was not responsible for this strike, it could not be held liable for damages either. The Court noted that § 301(b) only explicitly bars money judgments against unions from being enforced against individual union members. Here, there was no money judgment against the union. Still, the Court reasoned that "the legislative history of § 301 clearly reveals Congress' intent to shield individual employees from liability for damages . . . whether or not the union participated in or authorized the illegality." 451 U.S. 401, 407.

This means that in cases involving wildcat strikes, the question of whether the union is responsible has significant practical importance. This is complicated by the fact that unions typically are structured with locals affiliated with regional bodies and national and international bodies. Even if a local is responsible for a strike, the other bodies might not be and thus would not be liable for damages. *See Carbon Fuel Co. v. United Mine Workers*, 444 U.S. 212 (1979). What factors should be used to determine whether a local, regional body, or even international union is in fact responsible for an illegal strike such that it should be liable for damages? In addition to *Carbon Fuel, see Consolidation Coal Co. v. Local 1261*, 725 F.2d 1258 (10th Cir. 1984).

Is it unfair that an employer may not receive damages for an illegal wildcat strike if the union did not authorize, encourage, or prolong it? Two dissenters in *Complete Auto Transit* thought so. Recall, though, that the employer is permitted to fire employees engaged in any sort of unprotected strike.

Compare this regime to the rather elaborate array of sanctions for illegal strikes in the public sector, discussed in § III-A-4 of this Chapter, *infra*.

C. Employer Use of Economic Weapons

1. Replacing Striking Workers

a. Permanent Replacements of Economic Strikers

NLRB v. Mackay Radio & Telegraph Co.
Supreme Court of the United States
304 U.S. 333 (1938)

Roberts, J.

The Circuit Court of Appeals refused to decree enforcement of an [NLRB] order. . . .

The respondent, a California corporation, is engaged in the transmission and receipt of telegraph, radio, cable, and other messages between points in California and points in other States and foreign countries. It maintains an office in San Francisco for the transaction of its business wherein it employs upwards of sixty supervisors, operators and clerks, many of whom are members of Local No. 3 of the American Radio Telegraphists Association, a national labor organization. . . . At midnight Friday, October 4, 1935, all the men there employed went on strike. The respondent, in order to maintain service, brought employes from its Los Angeles office and others from the New York and Chicago offices of the parent company to fill the strikers' places.

Although none of the San Francisco strikers returned to work Saturday, Sunday, or Monday, the strike proved unsuccessful in other parts of the country and, by Monday evening, October 7th, a number of the men became convinced that it would fail and that they had better return to work before their places were filled with new employes. One of them telephoned the respondent's traffic supervisor Monday evening to inquire whether the men might return. He was told that the respondent would take them back. . . . Before leaving the company's office for this purpose, the supervisor consulted with his superior, who told him that . . . the company had promised eleven men brought to San Francisco they might remain if they so desired, the supervisor would have to handle the return of the striking employes in such fashion as not to displace any of the new men who desired to continue in San Francisco. . . . [E]leven strikers . . . would have to file applications for reinstatement, which applications would be subject to the approval of an executive of the company in New York. . . . Then or shortly thereafter, six of the eleven in question took their places and resumed their work without challenge. It turned out that only five of the new men brought to San Francisco desired to stay.

Five strikers who were prominent in the activities of the union and in connection with the strike . . . reported at the office at various times between Tuesday and Thursday. Each of them was told that he would have to fill out an application for employment; that the roll of employes was complete, and that his application would be considered in connection with any vacancy that might thereafter occur. These men not having been reinstated in the course of three weeks, the secretary of Local No. 3 presented a charge to the [NLRB] that the respondent had violated §8(1) and (3) of the [NLRA]. Thereupon the Board filed a complaint charging that . . . by such discharge respondent had interfered with, restrained, and coerced the employes in the exercise of their rights guaranteed by §7 of the [NLRA] and so had been guilty of an unfair labor practice within the meaning of §8(1) of the Act. The complaint further alleged that the discharge of these men was a discrimination in respect of their hire and tenure of employment and a discouragement of membership in Local No. 3, and thus an unfair labor practice within the meaning of §8(3) of the Act. . . . [The Board found that the respondent had violated §§8(1) and (3) and ordered the five strikers fully reinstated with back pay, among other remedies. The Court of Appeals reversed.]

. . . There is no evidence and no finding that the respondent was guilty of any unfair labor practice in connection with the negotiations in New York. On the contrary, it affirmatively appears that the respondent was negotiating with the authorized representatives of the union. Nor was it an unfair labor practice to replace the striking employes with others in an effort to carry on the business. Although §13 provides, "Nothing in this Act shall be construed so as to interfere with or impede or diminish in any way the right to strike," it does not follow that an employer, guilty of no act denounced by the statute, has lost the right to protect and continue his business by supplying places left vacant by strikers. And he is not bound to discharge those hired to fill the places of strikers, upon the election of the latter to resume their employment, in order to create places for them. The assurance by respondent to those who accepted employment during the strike that if they so desired their places might be permanent was not an unfair labor practice nor was it such to reinstate only so many of the strikers as there were vacant places to be filled. But the claim put forward is that the unfair labor practice indulged by the respondent was discrimination in reinstating striking employes by keeping out certain of them for the sole reason that they had been active in the union. As we have said, the strikers retained, under the Act, the status of employes. Any such discrimination in putting them back to work is, therefore, prohibited by §8.

. . . The Board's findings as to discrimination are supported by evidence. . . . There was evidence, which the Board credited, that several of the five men in question were told that their union activities made them undesirable to their employer. . . . The Board found, and we cannot say that its finding is unsupported, that, in taking back six of the eleven men and excluding five who were active union men, the respondent's officials discriminated against the latter on account of their union activities and that the excuse given that they did not apply until after the quota was full was an afterthought and not the true reason for the discrimination against them.

As we have said, the respondent was not bound to displace men hired to take the strikers' places in order to provide positions for them. It might have refused reinstatement on the ground of skill or ability, but the Board found that it did not do so. It might have resorted to any one of a number of methods of determining which of its striking employes would have to wait because five men had taken permanent positions during the strike, but it is found that the preparation and use of the list, and the action taken by respondent, were with the purpose to discriminate against those most active in the union. There is evidence to support these findings. . . .

The judgment of the Circuit Court of Appeals is reversed. . . .

Notes

1. This case established that hiring "permanent replacements" for certain types of strikers does not violate the NLRA, a rule that has come to be enormously important in labor relations. Yet, was it necessary to decide that issue in this case? The holding in *Mackay* (on which the Board and union prevailed) was that the employer violated § 8(a)(3) by discriminating in reinstating certain strikers and not others because of their relative lack of support for a strike. For an argument that the rule on permanent replacements was *dicta* (and erroneous at that), see Note, *Replacement of Workers During Strikes*, 75 YALE L.J.630, 631–32 (1966). For an argument that this rule was consistent with at least some labor board precedent, but that it gives employers an unfair advantage, see Julius Getman & Thomas Kolher, *The Story of NLRB v. Mackay Radio & Telegraph Co.: The High Cost of Solidarity, in* LABOR LAW STORIES 13–53 (Laura Cooper & Catherine Fisk eds., 2005).

2. Is this rule the best interpretation of the NLRA? When *Mackay* was decided, no part of the Act referred in any way to an employer's right to replace strikers. Further, again, § 13 provides in relevant part that "[n]othing in this Act, except as specifically provided for herein, shall be construed so as to either interfere with or impede or diminish, in any way, the right to strike." Moreover, why is permanently replacing a striker not "discrimination in regard to hire or tenure of employment" in violation of § 8(a)(3)? Given this, on what was the *Mackay* rule based?

3. Beyond what the NLRA says, is this a good rule as a matter of policy? Most other industrialized democracies bar permanently replacing strikers. *See, e.g.,* Peter Cramton, Morley Gunderson & Joseph Tracy, *Impacts of Strike Replacement Bans in Canada*, 50 LAB. L.J. 173 (1999) (Canadian federal labor law and the law of several Canadian provinces ban permanent replacements).

4. Notably, although this rule was established in 1938, employers did not start using the tactic of permanent replacements regularly and consistently until the 1980s. Why might that be?

5. In 1992, the Senate failed by three votes to overcome a Republican-led filibuster against the Workplace Fairness Act, S. 55, which would have barred permanently replacing strikers (it would have allowed temporary replacements). A compromise proposal that was also defeated would have allowed an employer to use permanent replacements if it had previously offered to settle the contract impasse by binding interest arbitration. Similarly, if a union struck without offering to settle via interest arbitration, its members could be permanently replaced. *See* 138 Cong. Rec. S8056–8089. Would either of these proposals have been an improvement over current law? Why or why not? Consider the compromise alternative when you review the materials on binding impasse arbitration in the public sector in Section III, *infra*.

In 1995, President Clinton issued Executive Order No. 12,954, which authorized the Secretary of Labor to terminate federal contracts and bar future contracts with companies that had permanently replaced economic strikers. However, *Chamber of Commerce of the U.S. v. Reich*, 74 F.3d 1322 (D.C. Cir. 1996) struck down this Order, essentially holding that it was preempted by the NLRA. *See* Chapter 16 for more on preemption.

6. An employer cannot simply fire economic strikers, *see, e.g., NLRB v. Browning-Ferris Indus.*, 700 F.2d 385 (7th Cir. 1983), and being permanently replaced is not exactly like being fired. First, a striker must actually be replaced to lose a right to reinstatement. Second, permanently replaced strikers have a limited right to reinstatement. Specifically, they must be reinstated if a vacancy becomes available, the striker has made an unconditional offer to return to work, and the striker has not "abandoned" employment with the original employer for substantially equivalent employment. *Laidlaw Corp.*, 171 N.L.R.B. 1366 (1968), *enforced*, 414 F.2d 99 (7th Cir. 1969). There is no time limit on an employer's obligation to reinstate economic strikers. *Brooks Research & Mfg., Inc.*, 202 N.L.R.B. 634 (1973). The Supreme Court has held that if and when a job for which a former striker is qualified becomes available, the striker is entitled to an offer of reinstatement unless the employer can show legitimate and substantial business justifications for denying reinstatement. *NLRB v. Fleetwood Trailer Co.*, 389 U.S. 375 (1967). An employer may require unreinstated strikers to indicate, every so often, their continued interest in reinstatement. *Aqua-Chem, Inc.*, 288 N.L.R.B. 1108 (1988), *enforced*, 910 F.2d 1487 (7th Cir. 1990).

Still, in many cases, permanent replacement has the same practical effect as being fired.

7. The Taft-Harley Act added a reference to permanently replaced economic strikers, stating that, even if permanently replaced, the strikers had a right to vote in any representation elections at the struck company that took place within a year of the beginning of the strike. Section 9(c)(3).

8. Suppose an employer hires replacement workers, tells them they will have permanent positions, and then later, as part of a strike settlement, takes back the

striking union workers (who were economic strikers) and discharges the replacements. What result if the replacements sue on breach of contract and misrepresentation claims? *See Belknap v. Hale*, 463 U.S. 491 (1983).

b. Distinguishing "Unfair Labor Practice Strikers"

The *Mackay Radio* rule applies to "economic strikers," as opposed to "unfair labor practice strikers." Do you see the language in *Mackay Radio* that sets the stage for this distinction?

It is well-established that "ULP strikers" are entitled to reinstatement to their former positions if and when they make an unconditional offer to return to work. *See, e.g., NLRB v. Int'l Van Lines*, 409 U.S. 48, 50–51 (1972); *Pennant Foods Co.*, 347 N.L.R.B. 460 (2006). Once again, the text of the NLRA does not contain this rule. Is it better to give greater reinstatement rights to workers who are striking over the employer's ULPs than to strikers who are striking over wages, hours, or working conditions? Why or why not? And if not, what rights should both types of strikers have?

This distinction means, in practical terms, that often in a strike situation, both sides will maneuver to try to get the strike classified either as an economic strike (the employer's goal) or a ULP strike (the union's goal). Two rules complicate this inquiry. First, to classify a strike as an "ULP," the employer's ULPs need not have been the sole or "but for" cause of the strike. Rather, they need only to have been a significant contributing factor; *i.e.*, the employees' decisions regarding whether to strike must have been motivated in part by the ULP. *See, e.g., Teamsters Local 515 v. NLRB*, 906 F.2d 719 (D.C. Cir. 1990); *Northern Wire Corp. v. NLRB*, 887 F.2d 1313 (7th Cir. 1989); *Post Tension of Nev., Inc.*, 352 N.L.R.B. 1153 (2008).

Second, a strike that begins as an economic strike can be "converted" into an ULP strike by the employer's acts during the strike, specifically when the employer commits an intervening ULP that causes the strike to last longer because of protests over the employer's illegal behavior. *See, e.g., Citizens Publ'g & Printing Co. v. NLRB*, 263 F.3d 224 (3d Cir. 2001) (false statement that economic strikers had been replaced converted strike to a ULP strike); *Gen. Indus. Employees Union, Local 42 v. NLRB*, 951 F.2d 1308 (D.C. Cir. 1991). *NLRB v. Champ Corp.*, 933 F.2d 688 (9th Cir. 1990). But there must be evidence that the employer's ULPs actually prolonged the strike. *See, e.g., NLRB v. Harding Glass Co.*, 80 F.3d 7 (1st Cir. 1996) (no evidence employer's ULP motivated or prolonged strike). By the same logic, could a ULP strike be converted into an economic strike?

This can be a high-stakes game. For example, in **Detroit Newspaper Agency**, 327 N.L.R.B. 871 (1999), the Board addressed the following issue. Given that a strike (in and of itself) does not nullify the existence of a union bargaining unit (*see* Chapter 7's discussion of *NLRB v. Curtin Matheson*), does §8(a)(5) require an employer to negotiate over the initial terms and conditions of employment of striker replacements? First, what is the better answer to this question? The

Board split 3–2. *See also Service Electric Co. v. Int'l B'hood of Electrical Workers,* 281 N.L.R.B. 633 (1986).

Second, the holding in *Detroit Newspaper Agency* helped determine whether a large group of strikers were "ULP strikers" entitled to reinstatement or "economic strikers" who were not. This consequence was almost certainly more significant than the substantive issue in the case—whether or not the Board would issue the standard remedy for failure to bargain (*see* Chapter 9).

2. Other Economic Weapons and "Inherently Destructive" Acts

NLRB v. Erie Resistor Corp.

Supreme Court of the United States
373 U.S. 221 (1963)

WHITE, J.

The question before us is whether an employer commits an unfair labor practice under §8(a) of the [NLRA] when he extends a 20-year seniority credit to strike replacements and strikers who leave the strike and return to work. . . .

Erie Resistor Corporation and Local 613 of the International Union of Electrical, Radio and Machine Workers were bound by a collective bargaining agreement which was due to expire on March 31, 1959. In January 1959, both parties met to negotiate new terms but, after extensive bargaining, they were unable to reach agreement. Upon expiration of the contract, the union, in support of its contract demands, called a strike which was joined by all of the 478 employees in the unit.

The company, under intense competition and subject to insistent demands from its customers to maintain deliveries, decided to continue production operations. Transferring clerks, engineers and other nonunit employees to production jobs, the company managed to keep production at about 15% to 30% of normal during the month of April. On May 3, however, the company notified the union members that it intended to begin hiring replacements and that strikers would retain their jobs until replaced. . . .

Replacements were told that they would not be laid off or discharged at the end of the strike. To implement that assurance, particularly in view of the 450 employees already laid off on March 31, the company notified the union that it intended to accord the replacements some form of super-seniority. At regular bargaining sessions between the company and union, the union made it clear that, in its view, no matter what form the super-seniority plan might take, it would necessarily work an illegal discrimination against the strikers. As negotiations advanced on other issues, it became evident that super-seniority was fast becoming the focal point of disagreement. On May 28, the company informed the union that it had decided to award 20 years' additional seniority both to replacements and to strikers who returned to work, which would be available only for credit against future layoffs and which could not be used for other employee benefits based on years of service. The strikers, at a union meeting the next day, unanimously resolved to continue striking now in protest against the proposed plan as well.

The company made its first official announcement of the super-seniority plan on June 10, and by June 14, 34 new employees, 47 employees recalled from layoff status and 23 returning strikers had accepted production jobs. The union, now under great pressure, offered to give up some of its contract demands if the company would abandon super-seniority or go to arbitration on the question, but the company refused. In the following week, 64 strikers returned to work and 21 replacements took jobs, bringing the total to 102 replacements and recalled workers and 87 returned strikers. When the number of returning strikers went up to 125 during the following week, the union capitulated. . . .

Following the strike's termination, the company reinstated those strikers whose jobs had not been filled (all but 129 were returned to their jobs). At about the same time, the union received some 173 resignations from membership. By September of 1959, the production unit work force had reached a high of 442 employees, but by May of 1960, the work force had gradually slipped back to 240. Many employees laid off during this cutback period were reinstated strikers whose seniority was insufficient to retain their jobs as a consequence of the company's super-seniority policy.

The union filed a charge with the [NLRB] alleging that awarding super-seniority during the course of the strike constituted an unfair labor practice and that the subsequent layoff of the recalled strikers pursuant to such a plan was unlawful. . . . [T]he Board [denied] "that specific evidence of Respondent's discriminatory motivation is required to establish the alleged violations of the Act". . . . Moreover, in the Board's judgment, the employer's insistence that its overriding purpose in granting super-seniority was to keep its plant open and that business necessity justified its conduct was unacceptable since "to excuse such conduct would greatly diminish, if not destroy, the right to strike guaranteed by the Act, and would run directly counter to the guarantees of Sections 8 (a)(1) and (3) that employees shall not be discriminated against for engaging in protected concerted activities." . . .

The Court of Appeals rejected as unsupportable the rationale of the Board that a preferential seniority policy is illegal however motivated. . . . It consequently denied the Board's petition for enforcement and remanded the case for further findings.

We think the Court of Appeals erred in holding that, in the absence of a finding of specific illegal intent, a legitimate business purpose is always a defense to an unfair labor practice charge. Cases in this Court dealing with unfair labor practices have recognized the relevance and importance of showing the employer's intent or motive to discriminate or to interfere with union rights. But specific evidence of such subjective intent is "not an indispensable element of proof of violation." *Radio Officers v. Labor Board*, 347 U.S. 17, 44. "Some conduct may by its very nature contain the implications of the required intent; the natural foreseeable consequences of certain action may warrant the inference. . . . The existence of discrimination may at times be inferred by the Board, for 'it is permissible to draw on experience in factual inquiries.'" *Teamsters Local v. Labor Board*, 365 U.S. 667, 675.

Though the intent necessary for an unfair labor practice may be shown in different ways, proving it in one manner may have far different weight and far different consequences than proving it in another. When specific evidence of a subjective intent to discriminate or to encourage or discourage union membership is shown, and found, many otherwise innocent or ambiguous actions which are normally incident to the conduct of a business may, without more, be converted into unfair labor practices. Such proof itself is normally sufficient to destroy the employer's claim of a legitimate business purpose, if one is made, and provides strong support to a finding that there is interference with union rights or that union membership will be discouraged. Conduct which on its face appears to serve legitimate business ends in these cases is wholly impeached by the showing of an intent to encroach upon protected rights. The employer's claim of legitimacy is totally dispelled.

The outcome may well be the same when intent is founded upon the inherently discriminatory or destructive nature of the conduct itself. The employer in such cases must be held to intend the very consequences which foreseeably and inescapably flow from his actions and if he fails to explain away, to justify or to characterize his actions as something different than they appear on their face, an unfair labor practice charge is made out. *Radio Officers v. Labor Board, supra.* But, as often happens, the employer may counter by claiming that his actions were taken in the pursuit of legitimate business ends and that his dominant purpose was not to discriminate or to invade union rights but to accomplish business objectives acceptable under the Act. Nevertheless, his conduct *does* speak for itself—it *is* discriminatory and it *does* discourage union membership and whatever the claimed overriding justification may be, it carries with it unavoidable consequences which the employer not only foresaw but which he must have intended. As is not uncommon in human experience, such situations present a complex of motives and preferring one motive to another is in reality the far more delicate task . . . of weighing the interests of employees in concerted activity against the interest of the employer in operating his business in a particular manner and of balancing in the light of the Act and its policy the intended consequences upon employee rights against the business ends to be served by the employer's conduct.

The Board made a detailed assessment of super-seniority and, to its experienced eye, such a plan had the following characteristics:

(1) Super-seniority affects the tenure of all strikers whereas permanent replacement, proper under *Mackay*, affects only those who are, in actuality, replaced. It is one thing to say that a striker is subject to loss of his job at the strike's end but quite another to hold that in addition to the threat of replacement, all strikers will at best return to their jobs with seniority inferior to that of the replacements and of those who left the strike.

(2) A super-seniority award necessarily operates to the detriment of those who participated in the strike as compared to nonstrikers.

(3) Super-seniority made available to striking bargaining unit employees as well as to new employees is in effect offering individual benefits to the strikers to induce them to abandon the strike.

(4) Extending the benefits of super-seniority to striking bargaining unit employees as well as to new replacements deals a crippling blow to the strike effort. At one stroke, those with low seniority have the opportunity to obtain the job security which ordinarily only long years of service can bring, while conversely, the accumulated seniority of older employees is seriously diluted. This combination of threat and promise could be expected to undermine the strikers' mutual interest and place the entire strike effort in jeopardy. The history of this strike and its virtual collapse following the announcement of the plan emphasize the grave repercussions of super-seniority.

(5) Super-seniority renders future bargaining difficult, if not impossible, for the collective bargaining representative. Unlike the replacement granted in *Mackay* which ceases to be an issue once the strike is over, the plan here creates a cleavage in the plant continuing long after the strike is ended. Employees are henceforth divided into two camps: those who stayed with the union and those who returned before the end of the strike and thereby gained extra seniority. This breach is re-emphasized with each subsequent layoff and stands as an ever-present reminder of the dangers connected with striking and with union activities in general.

In the light of this analysis, super-seniority by its very terms operates to discriminate between strikers and nonstrikers, both during and after a strike, and its destructive impact upon the strike and union activity cannot be doubted. The origin of the plan, as respondent insists, may have been to keep production going and it may have been necessary to offer super-seniority to attract replacements and induce union members to leave the strike. But if this is true, accomplishment of respondent's business purpose inexorably was contingent upon attracting sufficient replacements and strikers by offering preferential inducements to those who worked as opposed to those who struck. . . .

The Court of Appeals and respondent rely upon *Mackay* as precluding the result reached by the Board but we are not persuaded. Under the decision in that case an employer may operate his plant during a strike and at its conclusion need not discharge those who worked during the strike in order to make way for returning strikers. It may be, as the Court of Appeals said, that "such a replacement policy is obviously discriminatory and may tend to discourage union membership." But *Mackay* did not deal with super-seniority, with its effects upon all strikers, whether replaced or not, or with its powerful impact upon a strike itself. Because the employer's interest must be deemed to outweigh the damage to concerted activities caused by permanently replacing strikers does not mean it also outweighs the far greater encroachment resulting from super-seniority in addition to permanent replacement. . . .

Consequently, because the Board's judgment was that the claimed business purpose would not outweigh the necessary harm to employee rights—a judgment which we sustain—it could properly put aside evidence of respondent's motive and decline to find whether the conduct was or was not prompted by the claimed business purpose. Reversed and remanded.

Notes

1. Can this case be reconciled with *Mackay Radio*? Why does it violate §8(a)(3) to give strikebreakers super-seniority—which disadvantages reinstated strikers in certain contexts—but not violate §8(a)(3) to replace strikers permanently, which seems to be a greater harm to the worker? "It is as though the law permits killing but not wounding." Julius Getman, Betrand Pogrebin, and David Gregory, Labor Management Relations and The Law 166 (2d ed. 1999). Or is there a plausible distinction? What does the *Erie Resistor* Court say to this issue?

2. After *Mackay Radio* and *Erie Resistor*, should strikers who cross the picket line and return to work be treated as permanent replacements such that they can "replace" workers who remained on strike? *Trans World Airlines, Inc. v. Indep. Fed. of Flight Attendants*, 489 U.S. 426 (1989) held that they could. "We see no reason why those employees who chose not to gamble on the success of the strike should suffer the consequences when the gamble proves unsuccessful." 489 U.S. 426, 438. Still, the Court distinguished, rather than overruled, *Erie Resistor.* On what basis could such a distinction be made? The Court found it significant that in *Trans World Airlines*, any striker who did not cross the picket line and was reinstated only after the strike ended would be reinstated with full seniority. Under the factors in *Erie Resistor*, why might that matter?

3. Generally, §8(a)(3) requires proof that the employer intended to discriminate. *Erie Resistor* and some cases following it create an exception to this rule for acts by the employer that are "inherently destructive" of §7 rights. Consider the scope of that rule in the following materials.

———

The next major case in this area was **American Ship Building Co. v. NLRB**, 380 U.S. 300 (1965). This case involved a "lock out," essentially the flip side of the strike coin. In a lockout, the employer closes its facilities or otherwise denies workers the opportunity to work (and therefore, to earn money). As with strikes, a key issue for lockouts is often timing: when the employer can best withstand a cessation of operations. This is especially true for employers in industries where the amount of work can vary significantly at different points in the year.

Some early cases had held that an "offensive" lockout could violate §8(a)(3). An offensive lockout was one that the employer initiated without a reasonable belief that a strike was imminent, simply to pressure employees during the bargaining process. In *American Ship Building*, the employer operated four shipyards in a highly seasonal business: most work was done in the winter when the freezing of the Great Lakes made shipping impossible. Bargaining between the employer and its union reached impasse in August of one year, and in that month the employer essentially locked out most or all of its employees. The Board applied its rule that "absent special circumstances, an employer may not during bargaining negotiations either threaten to lock out or lock out his employes in aid of his bargaining position." Such conduct presumptively violated §8(a)(1) and (a)(3). 380 U.S. 300, 306.

The Court held that such a lockout did not violate §8(a)(1). It was "inaccurate to say that the employer's intention was to destroy or frustrate the process of collective bargaining. What can be said is that [he] intended to resist the demands made of [him] in the negotiations and to secure modification of these demands. We cannot see that this intention is in any way inconsistent with the employees' rights to bargain collectively." *Id.* at 309.

The Court then turned to the §8(a)(3) issue.

> It has long been established that a finding of violation under this section will normally turn on the employer's motivation. . . . [W]e have consistently construed the section to leave unscathed a wide range of employer actions taken to serve legitimate business interests in some significant fashion, even though the act committed may tend to discourage union membership. See, e.g., *National Labor Relations Board v. Mackay Radio & Telegraph Co.* . . . .

> This is not to deny that there are some practices which are inherently so prejudicial to union interests and so devoid of significant economic justification that no specific evidence of intent to discourage union membership or other antiunion animus is required. In some cases, it may be that the employer's conduct carries with it an inference of unlawful intention so compelling that it is justifiable to disbelieve the employer's protestations of innocent purpose . . . *National Labor Relations Board v. Erie Resistor Corp.* Thus where many have broken a shop rule, but only union leaders have been discharged, the Board need not listen too long to the plea that shop discipline was simply being enforced. . . .

> But this lockout does not fall into that category of cases arising under §8(a)(3) in which the Board may truncate its inquiry into employer motivation. As this case well shows, use of the lockout does not carry with it any necessary implication that the employer acted to discourage union membership or otherwise discriminate against union members as such. The purpose and effect of the lockout were only to bring pressure upon the union to modify its demands. Similarly, it does not appear that the natural tendency of the lockout is severely to discourage union membership while serving no significant employer interest. . . . There is no claim that the employer locked out only union members, or locked out any employee simply because he was a union member; nor is it alleged that the employer

conditioned rehiring upon resignation from the union. It is true that the employees suffered economic disadvantage because of their union's insistence on demands unacceptable to the employer, but this is also true of many steps which an employer may take during a bargaining conflict. . . . [T]here is nothing in the Act which gives employees the right to insist on their contract demands, free from the sort of economic disadvantage which frequently attends bargaining disputes. Therefore, we conclude that where the intention proven is merely to bring about a settlement of a labor dispute on favorable terms, no violation of § 8(a)(3) is shown. *Id.* at 311–13.

Notes

1. In what type of § 8(a)(3) cases does the Board not need to prove anti-union motivation, and what is the reason anti-union motivation is not necessary? Is it because the acts are so destructive to § 7 rights? Because the employer lacks any legitimate motivation for the acts? Because we can infer from the previous two factors that anti-union motivation must be the "real" reason for the acts?

2. Just as unions may legally strike before a bargaining impasse (*NLRB v. Insurance Agents Int'l Union, see* Chapter 9), employers may (assuming a legitimate economic motive) legally institute a lockout before a bargaining impasse. *Lane v. NLRB*, 418 F.2d 1208 (D.C. Cir. 1969).

3. An employer may use temporary replacements during a legal lockout. *Harter Equipment, Inc.*, 280 N.L.R.B. 597 (1986), *enforced sub nom. Local 825 Int'l Union of Operating Engineers v. NLRB*, 829 F.2d 458 (3d Cir. 1987). Could an employer permanently replace workers it has locked out? The Board has held no, but courts have largely dodged the issue. *See Johns-Manville Products Corp. v. NLRB*, 557 F.2d 1126 (5th Cir. 1977) (Board holds permanently replacing locked-out workers is a *per se* violation of the NLRA, but court finds there actually was a strike, so permanent replacement was legal); *NLRB v. Ancor Concepts, Inc.*, 166 F.3d 55 (2d Cir. 1999) (Board reaffirms its rule, but court finds the employer did not actually hire permanent replacements). The D.C. Circuit has observed that permanently replacing locked out workers "might too easily become a device for union busting." *Int'l B'hood of Boilermakers v. NLRB*, 858 F.2d 756, 769 (D.C. Cir. 1988).

Can you think of any distinctions between an employer permanently replacing economic strikers and an employer permanently replacing employees the employer has locked out that suggest the legal rule should be different for the two situations?

4. What if, instead of using permanent replacements, an employer permanently subcontracts bargaining unit work during a lawful lockout? Is that inherently destructive of § 7 rights? Is it a violation of § 8(a)(3)? The Board and the D.C. Circuit came to different conclusions in *Int'l Paper Co. v. NLRB*, 115 F.3d 1045 (D.C. Cir. 1997). How would you argue the different sides of this issue? Should these cases turn on certain facts (*e.g.*, timing, motivation, economic constraints, or etc.)? If so, what specific types of facts?

5. If an employer did attempt to permanently subcontract work during a strike or lockout, would it have a duty to bargain over that decision under §8(a)(5)? Would certain facts matter to this determination? *See Land-Air Delivery Inc. v. NLRB*, 862 F.2d 354 (D.C. Cir. 1988).

6. Are these cases better analyzed as §8(a)(1) cases, §8(a)(3) cases, or both? In other words, what (if anything) does or should §8(a)(1) add? Recall that, generally, §8(a)(1) does not require proving that the employer acted out of anti-union animus. *See, e.g., Republic Aviation*, discussed in Chapter 3.

NLRB v. Great Dane Trailers, Inc.
Supreme Court of the United States
388 U.S. 26 (1967)

WARREN, C.J.

The issue here is whether, in the absence of proof of an antiunion motivation, an employer may be held to have violated §§8(a)(3) and (1) . . . when it refused to pay striking employees vacation benefits accrued under a terminated collective bargaining agreement while it announced an intention to pay such benefits to striker replacements, returning strikers, and nonstrikers who had been at work on a certain date during the strike.

The respondent company and the union entered into a collective bargaining agreement which was effective by its terms until March 31, 1963. The agreement contained a commitment by the company to pay vacation benefits to employees who met certain enumerated qualifications. In essence, the company agreed to pay specified vacation benefits to employees who, during the preceding year, had worked at least 1,525 hours. It was also provided that, in the case of a 'lay-off, termination or quitting,' employees who had served more than 60 days during the year would be entitled to pro rata shares of their vacation benefits. Benefits were to be paid on the Friday nearest July 1 of each year.

The agreement was temporarily extended beyond its termination date, but on April 30, 1963, the union gave the required 15 days' notice of intention to strike over issues which remained unsettled at the bargaining table. Accordingly, on May 16, 1963, approximately 350 of the company's 400 employees commenced a strike which lasted until December 26, 1963. The company continued to operate during the strike, using nonstrikers, persons hired as replacements for strikers, and some original strikers who had later abandoned the strike and returned to work. On July 12, 1963, a number of the strikers demanded their accrued vacation pay from the company. The company rejected this demand, basing its response on the assertion that all contractual obligations had been terminated by the strike and, therefore, none of the company's employees had a right to vacation pay. Shortly thereafter, however, the company announced that it would grant vacation pay—in the amounts and subject to the conditions set out in the expired agreement—to all employees who had reported for work on July 1, 1963. The company denied that these payments were founded on the agreement and stated that they merely reflected a new 'policy' which had been unilaterally adopted.

The refusal to pay vacation benefits to strikers, coupled with the payments to nonstrikers, formed the bases of an unfair labor practice complaint filed with the Board while the strike was still in progress. [The Board upheld the ALJ's finding that the company had violated §§ 8(a)(3) and (1) and the proposed remedy which included paying the accrued vacation benefits to strikers.]

. . . [T]he Court of Appeals held that, although discrimination between striking and nonstriking employees had been proved, the Board's conclusion that the company had committed an unfair labor practice was not well-founded inasmuch as there had been no affirmative showing of an unlawful motivation to discourage union membership or to interfere with the exercise of protected rights. Despite the fact that the company itself had not introduced evidence of a legitimate business purpose underlying its discriminatory action, the Court of Appeals speculated that it might have been motivated by a desire '(1) to reduce expenses; (2) to encourage longer tenure among present employees; or (3) to discourage early leaves immediately before vacation periods.' Believing that the possibility of the existence of such motives was sufficient to overcome the inference of an improper motive which flowed from the conduct itself, the court denied enforcement of the order. We granted certiorari to determine whether the treatment of the motivation issue by the Court of Appeals was consistent with recent decisions of this Court. . . .

The unfair labor practice charged here is grounded primarily in § 8(a)(3) which requires specifically that the Board find a discrimination and a resulting discouragement of union membership. *American Ship Building Co. v. National Labor Relations Board*, 380 U.S. 300, 311 (1965). There is little question but that the result of the company's refusal to pay vacation benefits to strikers was discrimination in its simplest form. . . . Some employees who met the conditions specified in the expired collective bargaining agreement were paid accrued vacation benefits in the amounts set forth in that agreement, while other employees who also met the conditions but who had engaged in protected concerted activity were denied such benefits. Similarly, there can be no doubt but that the discrimination was capable of discouraging membership in a labor organization within the meaning of the statute. Discouraging membership in a labor organization 'includes discouraging participation in concerted activities . . . such as a legitimate strike.' *National Labor Relations Board v. Erie Resistor Corp.*, 373 U.S. 221 (1963). The act of paying accrued benefits to one group of employees while announcing the extinction of the same benefits for another group of employees who are distinguishable only by their participation in protected concerted activity surely may have a discouraging effect on either present or future concerted activity.

But inquiry under § 8(a)(3) does not usually stop at this point. The statutory language 'discrimination . . . to . . . discourage' means that the finding of a violation normally turns on whether the discriminatory conduct was motivated by an anti-union purpose. . . . It was upon the motivation element that the Court of Appeals based its decision not to grant enforcement, and it is to that element which we now turn. In three recent opinions we considered employer motivation in the context of asserted § 8(a)(3) violations. *American Ship Building Co. v. National Labor Relations Board, supra; National Labor Relations Board v. Brown*, 380 U.S. 278 (1965); and *National Labor Relations Board v. Erie Resistor Corp., supra*. We noted in *Erie Resistor, supra*, 373 U.S. at 227, that proof of an antiunion motivation may make unlawful certain employer conduct which would in other circumstances be lawful. Some conduct, however, is so 'inherently destructive of employee interests' that it may be deemed proscribed without need for proof of an underlying improper motive. . . . That is, some conduct carries with it 'unavoidable consequences which the employer not only foresaw but which he must have intended' and thus bears 'its own indicia of intent.' . . . If the conduct in question falls within this 'inherently destructive' category, the employer has the burden of explaining away, justifying or characterizing 'his actions as something different than they appear on their face,' and if he fails, 'an unfair labor practice charge is made out.' And even if the employer does come forward with counter explanations for his conduct in this situation, the Board may nevertheless draw an inference of improper motive from the conduct itself and exercise its duty to strike the proper balance between the asserted business justifications and the invasion of employee rights in light of the Act and its policy. On the other hand, when 'the resulting harm to employee rights is . . . comparatively slight, and a substantial and legitimate business end is served, the employers' conduct is prima facie lawful,' and an affirmative showing of improper motivation must be made. . . .

From this review of our recent decisions, several principles of controlling importance here can be distilled. First, if it can reasonably be concluded that the employer's discriminatory conduct was 'inherently destructive' of important employee rights, no proof of an antiunion motivation is needed and the Board can find an unfair labor practice even if the employer introduces evidence that the conduct was motivated by business considerations. Second, if the adverse effect of the discriminatory conduct on employee rights is 'comparatively slight,' an antiunion motivation must be proved to sustain the charge if the employer has come forward with evidence of legitimate and substantial business justifications for the conduct. Thus, in either situation, once it has been proved that the employer engaged in discriminatory conduct which could have adversely affected employee rights to some extent, the burden is upon the employer to establish that he was motivated by legitimate objectives since proof of motivation is most accessible to him.

Applying the principles to this case then, it is not necessary for us to decide the degree to which the challenged conduct might have affected employee rights. As the Court of Appeals correctly noted, the company came forward with no evidence of legitimate motives for its discriminatory conduct. The company simply did not meet the burden of proof, and the Court of Appeals misconstrued the function of judicial review when it proceeded nonetheless to speculate upon what might have motivated the company. Since discriminatory conduct carrying a potential for adverse effect upon employee rights was proved and no evidence of a proper motivation appeared in the record, the Board's conclusions were supported by substantial evidence . . . and should have been sustained.

The judgment of the Court of Appeals is reversed and the case is remanded with directions to enforce the Board's order. It is so ordered.

[Dissent of HARLAN, J., joined by STEWART, J., omitted]

Notes

1. Under this test, what sort of evidence would Great Dane have needed to avoid violating §8(a)(3)? More generally, is this a useful and workable framework for deciding these cases in a predictable manner?

2. For example, analyze the act of an employer permanently replacing economic strikers — as *Mackay Radio* still allows — under the *Great Dane* framework. What answer do you get?

3. Does this case reaffirm that in some §8(a)(3) cases (those involving "inherently destructive" activity), the Board need not prove anti-union animus? Consider that issue in the following case and the materials following it.

Local 15, IBEW v. NLRB
Court of Appeals for the Seventh Circuit
429 F.3d 651 (2005)

FLAUM, C.J.

Petitioner Local 15, International Brotherhood of Electrical Workers, AFL-CIO ("Union") petitions this Court for review of an order of the National Labor Relations Board ("NLRB" or "Board") finding that the Intervenor, Midwest Generation, EME, LLC ("Midwest"), did not violate sections 8(a)(1) and (3) of the National Labor Relations Act ("NLRA"). Because substantial evidence did not support the Board's decision, we reverse the holding and remand to the Board to determine whether Midwest's unfair labor practices render the current collective bargaining agreement void. . . .

The only issue for resolution submitted to the Board, and therefore the only issue for this Court to review, was stipulated to by the parties:

> Whether the Company violated Sections 8(a)(1) and (3) . . . by locking out and/or refusing to reinstate those employees who were on strike at the time of the union's unconditional offer to return to work, while not locking out and/or reinstating those individuals employed by the Company who, prior to the union's unconditional offer to return to work, had ceased participating in the strike by making an offer to return to work, and had either returned to work or scheduled a return to work at the Company?

. . . The first question in the *Great Dane* framework is whether the employer's conduct is "inherently destructive of important employee rights." Actions that harm the collective bargaining process, interfere with employees' right to strike, or are taken against employees based upon union status are "inherently destructive." To be "inherently destructive," the effect on the collective bargaining process must be more than temporary; it must instead establish a barrier to future collective bargaining. If an action by an employer is inherently destructive of important rights, no proof of an anti-union motivation is needed. *Great Dane*, 388 U.S. at 34.

A harmful action by an employer that is not inherently destructive is classified as "comparatively slight." These two categories, "inherently destructive" harm and "comparatively slight" harm, make up the two prongs of the *Great Dane* framework. Under the first prong of the *Great Dane* test ("inherently destructive"), an employer's actions are submitted to a stringent test. Such actions are permissible only if after balancing business justifications against employee rights, the business justification is found to be superior. Under the second prong of the *Great Dane* test, ("comparatively slight"), an employer's actions are more likely to be justified. "[A] finding of comparatively slight harm calls for a threshold test of business justification, rather than a balancing of interests." *Int'l Bhd. of Boilermakers v. NLRB*, 858 F.2d 756, 762 n. 2 (D.C.Cir.1988). If an individual employer's actions cannot be justified under the comparatively slight harm standard, which requires a legitimate and substantial business justification, they clearly cannot be justified under the "inherently destructive" standard.

Under either prong, once it has been established that the employer's conduct negatively affects protected section 7 rights, the key question for the Board, informed by *Great Dane*, is whether the employer can state a business justification for its actions. If an employer can show no legitimate and substantial business justification, the lockout is presumptively an unfair labor practice under either prong of the *Great Dane* analysis.

Thus, the question of whether a "legitimate and substantial" business justification exists is a threshold question, properly asked prior to any decision as to whether an action is "comparatively slight" or "inherently destructive" under *Great Dane*. If a legitimate and substantial business justification is found for an employer's action, the question of whether the harm caused was "inherently destructive" or "comparatively slight" is then examined and the *Great Dane* analysis proceeds.

... The issue then is whether Midwest has shown that its lockout had any business justification that was neither frivolous nor based upon an impermissible violation of section 7 rights.

The Board's majority opinion advanced two arguments in support of its finding that Midwest instituted the partial lockout for the valid purpose of "bringing economic pressure to bear in support of its legitimate bargaining position." *Midwest Generation*, 343 N.L.R.B. 69 (2004). First, the Board stated that partial lockouts are legal "when justified by operational needs and without regard to union membership status." ... Second, the Board concluded that locking out only those participating in the strike on August 31 was a lawful means of pressuring holdouts to abandon their bargaining position.

The dissent responded to these justifications for the partial lockout, noting:

> Notwithstanding the complete lack of supporting argument and evidence, the majority sua sponte proclaims that the Respondent's operational needs justified the partial lockout. The majority's concoction of a post hoc operational rationalization for the partial lockout does not and cannot fulfill the Respondent's obligation to proffer a legitimate and substantial business justification.

1. Operational needs did not justify the partial lockout.

Prior to the Board's decision, Midwest offered no proof that its operational needs justified the partial lockout. Indeed, the record indicates that Midwest's operational needs were being "successfully maintained . . . through the efforts of supervisory personnel, contractors, and some temporary replacement employees." In raising the operational needs justification sua sponte, the Board cited two cases, *Bali Blinds Midwest*, 292 N.L.R.B. 243, 246–47 (1988) and *Laclede Gas Co.*, 187 N.L.R.B. 243, 243–44 (1970). These cases are not analogous to the factual situation faced by Midwest. Rather, these cases illustrate the extreme business exigencies necessary to justify a partial lockout based upon operational needs.

In *Bali Blinds Midwest*, the employer's partial lockout was justified because it ensured that repeated work stoppages, which were legitimately feared, would not delay production and result in a loss of customers. In *Laclede Gas Co.*, the Board found that the need to ensure continuing business operations and avoid public hazards justified the employer's disregard of normal seniority practices during a lockout. ("[T]he temporary shutdown of the construction crew's operations was actually necessitated by the exigencies of the business operation[.] . . . [O]perating on the basis of daily contract extensions was difficult, unproductive, and potentially dangerous to the public[.] . . . [The lockout] was motivated by a desire to eliminate those operations which negotiations had rendered tentative and to protect the [employer] from overextending itself at a critical moment, all of which were essentially defensive purposes[.]"). There has been no comparable allegation of exigent circumstances in the instant case.

In its brief, Midwest attempts to support the Board's operational needs justification by citing additional cases in which partial lockouts were permitted. Among those cases is *General Portland, Inc.*, 283 N.L.R.B. 826 (1987). Unlike the factual situation faced by Midwest, *General Portland* illustrates an extreme situation in which operational needs justify a partial lockout. General Portland allowed employees to continue to manage enormous kilns that operate at 2700 degrees Fahrenheit and take between twelve hours and three days to shut down completely. Crossovers continually staffed these kilns in an effort to prevent "explosions, injury, and damage." *Id.* at 827. In contrast, the record is silent as to any necessity that would sanction the use of a partial lockout by Midwest.

The facts of this case further belie the operational needs justification. First, Midwest's own claims demonstrate that it successfully maintained operations throughout the strike without the use of crossover employees or non-strikers. Midwest does not argue that the lockout was based upon operational needs, but rather states its intent "to pressure [the employees] to abandon [their] demands." Second, the last six crossover employees did not even start work until after the August 31 unconditional offer to return to work, which demonstrates that these employees were unnecessary for continued operation. Third, early in the strike Midwest was able to maintain operations with only eight of the approximately 1,150 employees who were members of the bargaining unit. The claim that these eight employees and/or the last six crossovers, together representing less than 2% of the total bargaining unit, were so vital to the maintenance of business operations that it was necessary for Midwest to violate employees' section 7 rights stretches the bounds of credulity.

Every indication in the stipulated facts is that the crossovers and non-strikers were unnecessary to the continuation of business operations. Midwest and the majority opinion of the Board charge the dissent with advocating for a standard of "indispensab[ility] to continued operations in order to be retained" during a partial lockout. The dissent, however, never employs the word "indispensable." The dissent accurately notes that the "Respondent does not even argue that it needed the non-strikers and crossovers to maintain operations during the lockout." *Midwest Generation*, 343 N.L.R.B. 69, 74 (2004) (Walsh, dissenting).

In any event, a standard less demanding than "indispensable" cannot provide employers with carte blanche to lock out employees of their choosing without regard to seniority or any other criteria. Such an approach would allow employers acting under the guise of maintaining business operations to engage in exactly the type of action Midwest undertook: punishing those who stood with the Union and rewarding those who crossed picket lines.

Demanding more than Midwest's labeling of its conduct as "necessary for business operations" does not establish strike-hiring practices that are difficult for employers to comply with. Instead, it merely avoids creating a "business operations" exception with no limiting principle, which would sanction discriminatory conduct by an employer where the employer chooses to announce its position as "necessary for business operations" without evidence supporting such a need. Simply put, to justify a partial lockout on the basis of operational need, an employer must provide a reasonable basis for finding some employees necessary to continue operations and others unnecessary.

2. The partial lockout was not justified as a lawful means of economically pressuring holdouts.

Throughout the course of this litigation, Midwest contended that it allowed the non-strikers and crossovers to return to work because they "had removed themselves from the Union's economic action," making it unnecessary to pressure them into abandoning the Union's bargaining position. This allegation rests on the proposition that "working for a struck employer may, without more, be equated with abandonment of the Union's bargaining demands." *Midwest Generation*, 343 N.L.R.B. 69, 74 (Walsh, dissenting) (2004). This assumption is fatally flawed. There can be several reasons why an employee might choose to cross a picket line. Abandonment of the Union's bargaining demands is merely one possible explanation, standing alongside individual financial motivations, personal relationships with employers, indifference, an attempt to impress management, etc. Midwest has failed to offer any direct correlation between employees' non-participation in a strike and lack of support for the Union's demands. . . .

Midwest argues that an employee who has returned to work no longer demonstrates a commitment to the Union's position. Therefore, no economic pressure against such an employee is required. What Midwest fails to note is that at the time of the lockout, all employees had offered to return to work.

There is no evidence in the record indicating why individual employees chose not to participate in the strike. It is unclear and unknown whether non-strikers and crossovers voted for or against Midwest's collective bargaining agreement proposals. . . .

Midwest relies upon a common sense notion that employees who cross a picket line have abandoned the Union's position. While this is not an unreasonable conclusion, it is not supported by any evidence beyond mere conjecture.

The Board also justified the use of a partial lockout on the basis that "there is nothing in the law that requires an employer to use maximum economic pressure." While this statement is a truism, it does not address the relevant question before the Board. The burden remains upon the employer to prove that it had a legitimate and substantial basis for its actions. In this case, the Board appears to find sufficient any reason presented by Midwest without evidence of a "legitimate and substantial" basis for distinguishing between those employees it locked out and those it did not.

While we find no foundation for the assumption that those employees who crossed the picket line were not supporters of the Union's position, assuming arguendo that Midwest could irrefutably prove that crossovers and non-strikers had abandoned the Union's bargaining position, it still could not discriminate on this basis.

Both the NLRB and the Fifth Circuit have found that an employer "may not discriminate against certain employees merely because it anticipates that they will honor a picket line or otherwise engage in protected activity." *National Fabricators v. NLRB*, 903 F.2d 396, 400 (5th Cir.1990). An employer's discriminatory lockout on the basis of a protected activity is unlawful even when it is supportive of an employer's bargaining position.

> Lockouts are not all protected. . . . The *American Ship Building* rule does not give the employer license to pick and choose among its employees and suspend those whose protected picket line activities are most damaging to it. The mere selection of such an employee from among all those in the unit

for suspension is per se discriminatory. *Thrift Drug Co.*, 204 N.L.R.B. 41, 43 (1973).

The Board in this case appears to launch a new approach with no discernable parameters. If employers were free to exercise economic penalties selectively against those employees whom they believe economic coercion would be most effective, an employer could take discriminatory actions that have traditionally been barred. Under the Board's analysis, an employer could choose to lock out only union leaders or only employees it believes voted against a proposed contract. This type of discrimination cannot be a legitimate and substantial business justification for a partial lockout.

... In the context of collective bargaining negotiations, nearly all employer actions are attempts to win an economic battle. Merely because retribution against strikers may be effective does not make such actions legitimate and substantial. The fact that employers have acted with the "best judgment as to the interests of their business ... has not been deemed an absolute defense to an unfair labor practice charge." *NLRB v. Erie Resistor Corp.*, 373 U.S. 221, 229 n. 8 (1963).

Based on the record presented in this appeal, there is no line that can be drawn between those employees that agreed to return to work before August 31 and those employees who agreed to return to their positions after August 31. As of the time of the lockout, every employee had made an unconditional offer to return to work. Without a valid basis for distinction between those locked out and those allowed to work, Midwest's claim of a legitimate and substantial business justification fails.

3. Midwest displayed anti-union animus.

If Midwest's claim of no anti-union animus were to have any basis, it necessarily would contradict its earlier claim of a legitimate and substantial business justification. Either employees were locked out in a completely blind fashion, thereby offering no legitimate and substantial business justification, or they were chosen on the basis of their Union activities and therefore the action was based upon invalid anti-union motivations.

By acting only against those who had exercised their section 7 right to strike, Midwest appears to have demonstrated an anti-union animus. The *only* distinction between the two groups of employees at the time of the lockout was their participation in Union activities. Discriminating in a way that has a natural tendency to discourage participation in concerted union activities is a violation of section 8(a) (3)....

A partial lockout is a significant measure that requires a justification beyond economic effectiveness. The fact that employees could avoid partial lockouts by agreeing to employer demands would in effect validate all partial lockouts. Undoubtedly, this would render ineffective the requirement of a legitimate and substantial business justification for discriminatory employer action and would be in derogation of nearly four decades of employee protection. *See NLRB v. Great Dane Trailers, Inc.*, 388 U.S. 26 (1967); *see also* 29 U.S.C. §§ 157, 158(a)(1), (3).

III. Conclusion

For the reasons set forth above, we REVERSE the findings of the Board and REMAND to the Board with instructions to find that the partial lockout was an unfair labor practice. We also REMAND to the Board to consider whether this unfair labor practice coerced the Union and its members into ratifying Midwest's contract offer, thereby voiding the collective bargaining agreement.

Notes

1. What made the employer's actions in this case illegal? In future cases involving a partial lockout, what factors would you examine to determine whether it was legal or not?

2. Was the rationale for this result that the employer's act was inherently destructive and lacked a substantial business motivation—and therefore, a finding of anti-union motivation was not necessary? Or was it that the employer was in fact motivated by anti-union animus? Or was it that, whether the employer's act was inherently destructive or not, the employer lacked sufficient justification?

Consider *Contractors' Labor Pool v. NLRB*, 323 F.3d 1051 (D.C. Cir. 2003). In that case, the employer challenged the Board's holding that the employer's policy of refusing to hire applicants whose recent wages were 30 percent higher or lower than its starting wages violated § 8(a)(3). The employer claimed that not hiring those who had previously made significantly higher wages helped it retain employees. The Board found that the policy was inherently destructive to § 7 rights because it tended to discriminate against employees who had previously held unionized (and therefore better-paying) jobs. This raised the issue of whether a "disparate impact" theory of discrimination was available under the NLRA as it is under Title VII of the Civil Rights Act (essentially, employer policies that may lack specific intent to discriminate, but still have a significant adverse impact on a protected group without a sufficient business-related justification). The court thought not, and it added some interesting thoughts on the relationship between "inherently destructive" activity and anti-union animus under § 8(a)(3). The court explained that, contrary to the Board's interpretation of *Great Dane Trailers*, the case had to be resolved in the employer's favor once the Board had found no evidence of anti-union animus.

> The keystone of the Board's decision is its reliance on a discrete quotation from *Great Dane*:
>
>> First, if it can reasonably be concluded that the employer's discriminatory conduct was "inherently destructive" of important employee rights, *no proof* of an *antiunion motivation is needed* and the Board can find an unfair labor practice even if the employer introduces evidence that the conduct was motivated by business considerations.
>
> *Great Dane Trailers*, 388 U.S. at 34 (emphasis added). Drawing on this language the Board concluded it was free to hold that petitioner violated § 8(a)(3) even if it also found that petitioner's motive was blameless. The Board

analogized its new legal rationale to "the disparate impact theory long applied in cases prosecuted under Title VII of the Civil Rights Act of 1964." Petitioner argues, and we agree, that the Board over reads the quotation from *Great Dane*, particularly in light of Supreme Court cases upon which *Great Dane* relied as well as cases that followed *Great Dane* and interpreted it. . . .

[*Great Dane*] pointed out that some conduct carries with it "unavoidable consequences which the employer not only foresaw but which he must have intended and thus bears its own indicia of intent." *Id*. at 33 (quoting *N.L.R.B. v. Erie Resistor Corp.* . . .)

That articulation makes clear that certain employer practices permit the Board to draw what is often referred to as "secondary inferences," of a discriminatory motive without any other evidence. To be sure, the quote upon which the Board relies, if read alone, could support the notion that, given certain conduct, an employer's motive is not relevant. . . . However, the wording upon which the Board relies is in the paragraph immediately following the Court's discussion of its prior cases and its quote from *Erie Resistor*. . . . It seems rather plain to us, therefore, that the Court did not mean to deviate from its past line of cases when it said, "no proof of an antiunion motivation is needed." *Id*. It obviously meant no *further* proof of antiunion motivation, because if the employer's conduct was inherently destructive of union rights the Board could legitimately draw the inference that the employer had the proscribed motivation. If there were any doubt as to the Court's meaning in *Great Dane*—which we do not harbor—some years later in *Metropolitan Edison*, the Court described *Great Dane* as holding that "[s]ome conduct is so inherently destructive of employee interests that it carries with it *a strong inference of impermissible motive*." *Metropolitan Edison*, 460 U.S. at 701 (emphasis added). 323 F.3d 1051, 1058–59.

Is this reading of *Great Dane* and *Erie Resistor* correct? If you were litigating a case involving allegedly inherently destructive activities in the D.C. Circuit after *Contractors' Labor Pool*, what, exactly, would the Board need to prove a §8(a)(3) violation? What would an employer need to convince the court not to enforce a Board order finding such a violation?

The court concluded that there was not a sufficient factual record to determine whether the policy in *Contractors' Labor Pool* was "inherently destructive." What facts, regarding this type of hiring policy, could be relevant to this determination?

3. Was *Contractors' Labor Pool* convincing in holding that the NLRA should not incorporate a "disparate impact" theory of discrimination? The D.C. Circuit reasoned that "Title VII is broader than §8(a)(3)." 323 F.3d at 1059. Yet when the Supreme Court approved this theory for Title VII cases in *Griggs v. Duke Power Co.*, 401 U.S. 424 (1971), the statutory language in Title VII did not specifically describe a disparate theory approach. Rather, using language quite analogous to that in

§ 8(a)(3), Title VII made it an "unlawful employment practice for an employer" to "discriminate" against an employee "because of such individual's race, color, religion, sex or national origin." 42 U.S.C. § 2000e-2. Apart from comparing statutory language, would adopting a "disparate impact" theory under the NLRA be good policy?

4. *Contractors' Labor Pool* cited *Metropolitan Edison Co. v. NLRB*, 460 U.S. 693 (1983). *Metropolitan Edison* held that an employer disciplining union officers more severely than other employees who engaged in an illegal strike was inherently destructive of § 7 rights and a ULP. In that case, the union officials had not acted as leaders of the illegal strike, and the Court saw no business justification for treating them differently.

5. *Local 15, IBEW* reasoned that the fact that an employee had returned to work was, by itself, insufficient proof that the employee had abandoned the union's position. Is that convincing? Recall the holding in *NLRB v. Curtin Matheson*, discussed in Chapter 7.

III. Impasse Resolution in the Public Sector

Impasse resolution rules are one of the most important parts of public-sector labor law. First, they have great practical significance because they are the processes used to determine substantive contract terms. Second, they are quite different from private-sector rules, and they also vary significantly among jurisdictions. Third, rules in this area reflect fundamental policy choices.

As Chapter 1 explained, policymakers in the U.S. have a long history of antipathy toward strikes by government employees. In the "pre-collective bargaining" era that lasted up to the 1960s, courts routinely cited fears of strikes in upholding bars on public workers merely organizing unions. Even after unions began winning collective-bargaining rights, strikes remained highly controversial and infrequently allowed. None of the early public-sector labor statutes passed in the 1960s permitted strikes. B.V.H. Schneider, *Public-Sector Labor Legislation—An Evolutionary Analysis, in* Public Sector Bargaining 196–98 (Benjamin Aaron, Joyce Najita & James Stern eds., 2d ed. 1988).

By the year 2007, while around three-quarters of the states allowed at least some of their public employees to bargain collectively, only 13 allowed any public workers the right to strike under any circumstances, and after Act 10 abolished the limited right to strike in Wisconsin in 2011, that number was reduced to 12. Richard Kearney & Patrice Mareschal, Labor Relations in the Public Sector 245–46 (5th ed. 2014). Police officers and firefighters are not allowed to strike in any jurisdiction. Significantly, even the minority of states that permit some public-sector workers to strike usually allow such strikes only after unions and employers have completed mandatory alternative impasse resolution procedures, typically mediation and/or fact-finding.

The majority of laws that allow public-sector collective-bargaining bar strikes and instead use alternative forms of impasse resolution. These laws typically provide for mediation, fact-finding, and/or interest arbitration procedures. Different states use different variations and combinations of these procedures.

The issues in public-sector impasse resolution are, therefore, as follows. First, which employees, if any, are allowed or should be allowed, to strike? Second, especially where strikes are illegal, what actions by workers count as "strikes"? Third, if a union strikes illegally, what should the remedies be, and who should be able to sue? Fourth, in jurisdictions where public employees have the right to bargain collectively but no right to strike, how are bargaining impasses resolved, and what are the advantages and disadvantages of various alternative impasse dispute mechanisms? Fifth, where strikes are legal, to what extent should public-sector rules on strikes differ from those in the private sector?

The discussion of these issues is divided into three general sections. The first covers illegal strikes, policy and law. The second focuses on the alternative impasse resolution procedures used in the public sector — fact-finding, mediation, and interest arbitration — and the variations in these processes that states have adopted. The third covers legal strikes, policy and law.

A. Illegal Strikes

1. Policy Arguments for Banning Strikes in the Public Sector

Michael Gottesman, *Wellington's Labors*

45 N.Y.L. Sch. L. Rev. 77 (2001)[*]

. . . Given today's predominance of public sector unionism, I want to recall briefly the book Harry [Wellington] co-authored with Ralph Winter in 1971, The Unions and the Cities. They saw that public employment was the emerging growth area for unionization. In the decade before their book, the number of public employees in America had increased more than 50%, and the number represented by unions had grown exponentially to nearly two million. As this rise coincided with the start of the decline in private sector unionism, public sector employees had risen in that decade from 5% to 11% of America's unionized workers. . . .

The Unions and the Cities was prompted by what Wellington and Winter saw as troubling signs in the public sector: politicians' capitulations, in the face of strike threats, to what they (the authors) thought were extravagant union demands. States and cities were then considering what set of legal rules and institutions would regulate public sector collective bargaining, and the authors feared that they would unthinkingly adopt those that had long prevailed in the private sector. Their book

---

undertook to show that differences in the public sector justified radically different legal rules and institutions.

The Wellington-Winter thesis was rooted in public choice theory, although it wasn't called that then. . . .

A. Should Public Employees Be Allowed to Strike?

. . . Wellington and Winter urged that strikes in public employment be banned, and their argument for that position diverged radically from that of others who then opposed public sector strikes. The usual argument advanced for banning such strikes was that public employees perform vital services that can't be interrupted. But as Wellington and Winter showed, that argument is ultimately unpersuasive, and if that was all that could be advanced in opposition, the union's quest for a right to strike was likely to carry the day. They recognized that some public employees do indeed perform services so vital that the public cannot afford their interruption: police and fire are the paradigmatic examples. But the case cannot be made that a strike by most other categories of public workers—park employees, tax collectors, or even teachers—would be more harmful to society than lawful strikes in some parts of the private sector (e.g., transportation and basic manufacturing industries).

Wellington and Winter opposed public sector strikes for quite a different reason. Public employees, in their quest for higher wages, are competing against other citizens with other claims on what is ultimately a limited public fisc. If, alone among the citizen claimants, public employees can rely not only on their lobbying power (the weapon enjoyed by all claimants) but also their capacity to disrupt public services, they will enjoy an inflated arsenal that will give primacy to their demands over competing claimants, and the end result may be a socially-undesirable allocation of public resources. This is especially so, Wellington and Winter argued, because public officials will be more likely to surrender to unreasonable union demands backed by strike threats than will their private sector counterparts. Public officials are motivated by electoral concerns, not the bottom line. If satisfying worker's immediate demands and thus avoiding strikes keeps the public happy in the short run, elected officials are unlikely to stand fast against union demands and unleash a strike that disrupts public services and may rebound to their political disadvantage. They will instead take the short-term expedient route: yield to the union's extravagant demands, and visit the ultimate public price for that surrender—reduced expenditures on other government services, or increased taxes—in later omnibus bills where the causal role of the earlier surrender will be undetectable. . . .

Their methodology throughout was built upon their central premise, reiterated provocatively in their postscript:

> [T]he principal issue in public employee unionism is the distribution of political power among those groups pressing claims on government. . . . [It] would seem that every responsible union leader must be committed to the proposition that what's good for public employees is good for the cities, counties, and states of the nation. Our rejection of that proposition has

served as the major normative premise of this book. We believe that in the cities, counties, and states there are other claimants with needs at least as pressing as those of the public employees. Such claimants can never have the power the unions will win if we mindlessly import into the public sector all the collective bargaining practices developed in the private sector. Make no mistake about it, government is not just another industry.

At this gathering celebrating Harry, I will refrain from propounding my reactions to the book's proposals. Let me just say that I read them with interest, although, of course, I didn't agree with them.

But, in the end, we can all be pleased. The law has developed much as Wellington and Winter proposed. Yet, despite these departures from the private sector legal rules, public sector unionism has prospered beyond anything ever achieved in the private sector. Most states forbid strikes by public employees, and the rest impose limits on the right to strike that minimize the prospects of its exercise. . . .

It is quite possible that public sector unionism has thrived precisely because the right to strike is denied. The past two decades have shown that the private sector right to strike is a paper tiger, if employers are prepared to hire permanent replacements for the strikers. The prospect of job loss through striking, and the absence of any other mechanism for inducing an employer's submission to a collective bargaining agreement, have rendered unionization futile in most parts of the private sector. But the denial of a strike right in the public sector is usually accompanied by the creation of some dispute-resolution mechanism for settling the parties' differences: mediation, arbitration, or the like. Even where these do not exist, an organized constituency's lobbying power has proved sufficient to give public employees enhanced leverage in competition with the more diffuse, and more diffusely represented interests of the larger citizenry.

Notes

1. Wellington and Winter believed that if public workers were allowed to strike, government officials would give in to union demands because strikes would burden the public and thus undermine the officials' chances for reelection. Is it fair to assume this will always, or even usually, be the case? Public-sector strikes are often unpopular. Thus, the incentives for politicians often may not be what Wellington and Winter feared. *See* Craig Olson, *Dispute Resolution in the Public Sector, in* AARON, NAJITA & STERN, PUBLIC SECTOR BARGAINING 162 (2d ed. 1988).

2. Other traditional objections to strike rights in the public sector include claims that such strikes threaten the provision of vital government services (some of which are essentially monopolies), undermine government sovereignty, give employees excessive bargaining power, and also that public employers often lack the ability to change conditions of work set by the legislature. *See, e.g.,* Schneider, *supra*, 202; Kurt Hanslowe & John Acierno, *The Law and Theory of Strikes by Government Employees,* 67 CORNELL L. REV. 1055, 1060–66 (1982). Many of these arguments are discussed

in *County Sanitation District No. 2 of Los Angeles County v. Los Angeles County Employees Ass'n, Local 660*, 38 Cal. 3d 564 (1985), *infra*.

3. The specter of the Boston police strike (*see* Chapter 1) continues to play a role as well. *See, e.g.,* Norma Riccuci, Katherine Naff et al., Personnel Management In Government: Politics and Process 477 (6th ed. 2007), arguing that although "many years have elapsed" between the Boston police strike and the present, "the basic problems involved are essentially the same and remain without substantial resolution." Is that convincing? Do most public-sector strikes today raise the same issues and problems as the Boston police strike of 1919?

4. A few public-sector strikes have been portrayed in a more positive light. Notably, Martin Luther King, Jr.'s tragic assassination took place when he was in Memphis to support a strike by local sanitation workers: an illegal public-sector strike. Joseph McCartin, *"Fire the Hell Out of Them": Sanitation Workers' Struggles and the Normalization of the Striker Replacement Strategy in the 1970s*, 2 Labor: Studies In The Working Class History of the Americas 67 (2005) places this event in the history of public- and private-sector labor relations.

5. Policy debates usually focus on whether any public workers should be allowed to strike, *i.e.*, the extent to which private-sector rules should be imported into the public sector. But Professor Gottesman raises a different and provocative question. Has the most common approach in the public sector—banning strikes and instead using alternative impasse resolution procedures—actually *helped* public-sector unions, or otherwise been a successful model for labor relations generally? If so, should policy makers consider importing some impasse dispute mechanisms from the public sector into the private sector? Consider these questions as you go through this section.

2. Bars on Illegal Strikes

a. Public-Sector Strikes Under Common Law

The traditional and still clear majority rule is that public-sector strikes are illegal under common law and thus are illegal unless a statute specifically authorizes them. *Anchorage Educ. Ass'n v. Anchorage Sch. Dist.*, 648 P.2d 993 (Alaska 1982) cited cases from fourteen states as authority for the proposition that, "[b]y 1972, not one of the jurisdictions which had considered the question of strikes by public employees had found such strikes to be legal in the absence of express statutory permission. . . . Against this background, we cannot say that the absence of legislative action implies permission to strike. Rather, it is more reasonable to assume that the legislature intended that in its silence, the generally held rule would be followed." 648 P.2d 993, 995–96.

The issue in *Anchorage* involved teachers, who, somewhat oddly, were omitted from the Alaska statute's rules on who could and could not legally strike. The court explained:

> Since the legislature has neither expressly given the teachers the right to strike nor explicitly prohibited work stoppages, we must address whether

there is a right to strike derived from the common law. . . . Our reasons for following the majority rule are not founded on the traditional fear of strikes as illegal conspiracies . . . but rather on a recognition of the special role that teachers fill in society and our acknowledgment of the functional limitations of this court when attempting to make social policy decisions.

Resolution of this controversy involves a delicate balancing of the citizens' need for a timely school year and of the teachers' need for an effective tool to influence their working conditions. . . . While a teachers' strike would not directly affect the public's safety as would a police officers' strike, nonetheless teachers can be considered indispensable to the daily functioning of society during the scheduled academic year. . . . Either refusing teachers the right to strike or finding such a right in Alaska common law would be an action by this court tipping the social balance in this state's labor relations. This social balance is more properly set by the legislature. . . . Thus, as a matter of common law in the area of labor relations, we will defer to what we believe the legislature intended by its silence.

The second reason for our decision is a realization of our functional limitations. If we found a right to strike, we would be allowing teachers to strike without the attendant mutual employee/employer obligations . . . which have contributed to the fairness of strikes. It is beyond our power to create a system of legislation and regulations to ensure a fair setting for strikes.

Three years after this case, however, the California Supreme Court pioneered an alternative approach to this issue.

County Sanitation Dist. No. 2 of Los Angeles County v. Los Angeles County Employees Ass'n Local 660, Service Employees International Union, AFL-CIO

Supreme Court of California
38 Cal. 3d 564, 214 Cal. Rptr. 424, 699 P.2d 835 (1985)

BROUSSARD, J.

Defendants appeal from a judgment awarding plaintiff sanitation district damages and prejudgment interest in connection with defendant union's involvement in a labor strike against plaintiff. The case squarely presents issues of great import to public sector labor-management relations, namely whether all strikes by public employees are illegal and, if so, whether the striking union is liable in tort for compensatory damages. After careful review of a long line of case law and policy arguments, we conclude that the common law prohibition against all public employee strikes is no longer supportable. . . .

I. Statement of the Case.

Defendant union (Local 660 or the union) is a labor organization affiliated with the Service Employees International Union, AFL-CIO, and has been the certified bargaining representative of the blue collar employees of the Los Angeles Sanitation District since 1973. Plaintiff is one of 27 sanitation districts within Los Angeles County and is charged with providing, operating and maintaining sewage transport and treatment facilities and landfill disposal sites throughout the county. The District employs some 500 workers who are directly or indirectly responsible for the operation and maintenance of its facilities and who are members of, or represented by, Local 660. Since 1973, the District and Local 660 have bargained concerning wages, hours and working conditions pursuant to the Meyers-Milias-Brown Act (MMBA). (Gov.Code, §§ 3500–3511.) Each year these negotiations have resulted in a binding labor contract or memorandum of understanding (MOU). . . .

On July 5, 1976, approximately 75 percent of the District's employees went out on strike after negotiations between the District and the union for a new wage and benefit agreement reached an impasse and failed to produce a new MOU. The District promptly filed a complaint for injunctive relief and damages and was granted a temporary restraining order. The strike continued for approximately 11 days, during which time the District was able to maintain its facilities and operations through the efforts of management personnel and certain union members who chose not to strike. On July 16, the employees voted to accept a tentative agreement on a new MOU, the terms of which were identical to the District's offer prior to the strike.

The District then proceeded with the instant action for tort damages. The trial court found the strike to be unlawful and in violation of the public policy of the State of California and thus awarded the District $246,904 in compensatory damages, prejudgment interest in the amount of $87,615.22 and costs of $874.65.

II. The Traditional Prohibition Against Public Employee Strikes.

Common law decisions in other jurisdictions at one time held that no employee, whether public or private, had a right to strike in concert with fellow workers. In fact, such collective action was generally viewed as a conspiracy and held subject to both civil and criminal sanctions. Over the course of the 20th century, however, courts and legislatures gradually acted to change these laws as they applied to private sector employees; today, the right to strike is generally accepted as indispensable to the system of collective bargaining and negotiation, which characterizes labor-management relations in the private sector. . . .

By contrast, American law continues to regard public sector strikes in a substantially different manner. A strike by employees of the United States government may still be treated as a crime and strikes by state and local employees have been explicitly allowed by courts or statute in only 11 states.[8]

. . . [T]his court has repeatedly stated that the legality of strikes by public employees in California has remained an open question. . . .

---

8. . . . Interestingly, the United States is virtually alone among Western industrial nations in upholding a general prohibition of public employee strikes. Most European countries have permitted them, with certain limitations, for quite some time as has Canada. . . .

. . . [T]he Legislature has also chosen to reserve judgment on the general legality of strikes in the public sector. . . . With the exception of firefighters (Lab.Code, § 1962), no statutory prohibition against strikes by public employees in this state exists. The MMBA, the statute under which the present controversy arose, does not directly address the question of strikes.

The MMBA sets forth the rights of municipal and county employees in California. . . . [State employees, transit authority employees, and education employees are covered by separate statutes.] The MMBA protects the right of such employees "to form, join, and participate in the activities of employee organizations . . . for the purpose of representation on all matters of employer-employee relations." It also requires public employers to "meet and confer" in good faith with employee representatives on all issues within the scope of representation. As explained in its preamble, one of the MMBA's main purposes is to improve communications between public employees and their employers by providing a reasonable method for resolving disputes. A further stated purpose is to promote improved personnel relations by "providing a uniform basis for recognizing the right of public employees to join organizations of their own choice."

On its face, the MMBA neither denies nor grants local employees the right to strike. This omission is noteworthy since the Legislature has not hesitated to expressly prohibit strikes for certain classes of public employees. For example, the above-noted prohibition against strikes by firefighters was enacted nine years before the passage of the MMBA and remains in effect today. Moreover, the MMBA includes firefighters within its provisions. Thus, the absence of any such limitation on other public employees covered by the MMBA at the very least implies a lack of legislative intent to use the MMBA to enact a general strike prohibition. . . .

In sum, the MMBA establishes a system of rights and protections for public employees which closely mirrors those enjoyed by workers in the private sector. The Legislature, however, intentionally avoided the inclusion of any provision which could be construed as either a blanket grant or prohibition of a right to strike, thus leaving the issue shrouded in ambiguity. In the absence of clear legislative directive on this crucial matter, it becomes the task of the judiciary to determine whether, under the law, strikes by public employees should be viewed as a prohibited tort.

III. The Common Law Prohibition Against Public Employee Strikes.

. . . [T]he Court of Appeal and various lower courts in this and other jurisdictions have repeatedly stated that, absent a specific statutory grant, all strikes by public employees are per se illegal. A variety of policy rationales and legal justifications have traditionally been advanced in support of this common law "rule". . . . The various justifications for the common law prohibition can be summarized into four basic arguments. First—the traditional justification—that a strike by public employees is tantamount to a denial of governmental authority/sovereignty. Second, the terms of public employment are not subject to bilateral collective bargaining, as in the private sector, because they are set by the legislative body through unilateral lawmaking. Third, since legislative bodies are responsible for public employment decision making, granting public employees the right to strike would afford them excessive bargaining leverage, resulting in a distortion of the political process and an improper delegation of legislative authority. Finally, public employees provide essential public services which, if interrupted by strikes, would threaten the public welfare.

Our determination of the legality of strikes by public employees necessarily involves an analysis of the reasoning and current viability of each of these arguments. The first of these justifications, the sovereignty argument, asserts that government is the embodiment of the people, and hence those entrusted to carry out its function may not impede it. This argument was particularly popular in the first half of the 20th century. . . .

The sovereignty concept, however, has often been criticized in recent years as a vague and outdated theory based on the assumption that "the King can do no wrong." As Judge Harry T. Edwards has cogently observed, "the application of the strict sovereignty notion—that governmental power can never be opposed by employee organizations—is clearly a vestige from another era, an era of unexpanded government. . . . With the rapid growth of the government, both in sheer size as well as in terms of assuming services not traditionally associated with the 'sovereign,' government employees understandably no longer feel constrained by a notion that 'The King can do no wrong.' The distraught cries by public unions of disparate treatment merely reflect the fact that, for all intents and purposes, public employees occupy essentially the same position vis a vis the employer as their private counterparts." Edwards, *The Developing Labor Relations Law in the Public Sector* (1972) 10 Duq.L.Rev. 357, 359–360. . . .

In recent years, courts have rejected the very same concept of sovereignty as a justification for governmental immunity from tort liability. . . . Similarly, the use of this archaic concept to justify a per se prohibition against public employee strikes is inconsistent with modern social reality and should be hereafter laid to rest.

The second basic argument underlying the common law prohibition of public employee strikes holds that since the terms of public employment are fixed by the Legislature, public employers are virtually powerless to respond to strike pressure, or alternatively that allowing such strikes would result in "government by contract" instead of "government by law." . . . This justification may have had some merit before the California Legislature gave extensive bargaining rights to public employees. However, at present, most terms and conditions of public employment are arrived at through collective bargaining under such statutes as the MMBA. . . .

The overall framework of the MMBA represents a nearly exact parallel to the private sector system of collective bargaining—a system which sets forth the guidelines for labor-management relations in the private sphere and which protects the right of private employees to strike. By enacting these significant and parallel protections for public employees through the MMBA, the Legislature effectively removed many of the underpinnings of the common law per se ban against public employee strikes. . . .

The [next argument] draws upon the different roles of market forces in the private and public spheres. This rationale suggests that because government services are essential and demand is generally inelastic, public employees would wield excessive bargaining power if allowed to strike. Proponents of this argument assume that economic constraints are not present to any meaningful degree in the public sector. Consequently, in the absence of such constraints, public employers will be forced to make abnormally large concessions to workers, which in turn will distort our political process by forcing either higher taxes or a redistribution of resources between government services.

There are, however, several fundamental problems with this "distortion of the political process" argument. For one, as will be discussed more fully below, a key assumption underlying the argument — that all government services are essential — is factually unsupportable. Modern governments engage in an enormous number and variety of functions, which clearly vary as to their degree of essentiality. As such, the absence of an unavoidable nexus between most public services and essentiality necessarily undercuts the notion that public officials will be forced to settle strikes quickly and at any cost. The recent case of the air-traffic controllers' strike is yet another example that governments have the ability to hold firm against a strike for a considerable period, even in the face of substantial inconvenience.

Other factors also serve to temper the potential bargaining power of striking public employees and thus enable public officials to resist excessive demands: First, wages lost due to strikes are as important to public employees as they are to private employees. Second, the public's concern over increasing tax rates will serve to prevent the decision-making process from being dominated by political instead of economic considerations. A third and related economic constraint arises in such areas as water, sewage and, in some instances, sanitation services, where explicit prices are charged. Even if representatives of groups other than employees and the employer do not formally enter the bargaining process, both union and local government representatives are aware of the economic implications of bargaining which leads to higher prices which are clearly visible to the public. A fourth economic constraint on public employees exists in those services where subcontracting to the private sector is a realistic alternative. For example, Warren, Michigan resolved a bargaining impasse with an American Federation of State, County and Municipal Employees (AFSCME) local by subcontracting its entire sanitation service; Santa Monica, California, ended a strike of city employees by threatening to subcontract its sanitation operations. . . . If this subcontract option is preserved, wages in the public sector clearly need not exceed the rate at which subcontracting becomes a realistic alternative.

The proponents of a flat ban on public employee strikes not only ignore such factors as the availability of subcontracting, but also fail to adequately consider public sentiment towards most strikes and assume that the public will push blindly for an early resolution at any cost. In fact, public sentiment toward a strike often limits the pressure felt by political leaders, thereby reducing the strike's effectiveness. A Pennsylvania Governor's Commission Report stressed just such public sentiment as an important reason to *grant* a limited right to strike: "[T]he limitations on the right to strike which we propose . . . will appeal to the general public as so much fairer than a general ban on strikes that the public will be less likely to tolerate strikes beyond these boundaries. Strikes can only be effective so long as they have public support. *In short, we look upon the limited and carefully defined right to strike as a safety valve that will in fact prevent strikes.* (Italics in original.)

In sum, there is little, if any empirical evidence which demonstrates that governments generally capitulate to unreasonable demands by public employers in order to resolve strikes. The result of the strike in the instant case clearly suggests the opposite. During the 11-day strike, negotiations resumed, and the parties subsequently reached an agreement on a new MOU, the terms of which were *precisely the same* as the District's last offer prior to the commencement of the strike. Such results certainly do not illustrate a situation where public employees wielded excessive bargaining power and thereby caused a distortion of our political process.

The fourth and final justification for the common law prohibition is that interruption of government services is unacceptable because they are essential. As noted above, in our contemporary industrial society the presumption of essentiality of most government services is questionable at best. In addition, we tolerate strikes by private employees in many of the same areas in which government is engaged, such as transportation, health, education, and utilities; in many employment fields, public and private activity largely overlap. . . .

We of course recognize that there are certain "essential" public services, the disruption of which would seriously threaten the public health or safety. In fact, defendant union itself concedes that the law should still act to render illegal any strikes in truly essential services which would constitute a genuine threat to the public welfare. Therefore, to the extent that the "excessive bargaining power" and "interruption of essential services" arguments still have merit, specific health and safety limitations on the right to strike should suffice to answer the concerns underlying those arguments. . . .

At least 10 states have granted most of their public employees a right to strike; and the policy rationale behind this statutory recognition further undercuts several of the basic premises relied upon by strike-ban advocates. As the aforementioned Pennsylvania Governor's Commission Report concluded: "The collective bargaining process will be strengthened if this qualified right to strike is recognized. It will be some curb on the possible intransigence of an employer; and the limitations on the right to strike will serve notice on the employee that there are limits to the hardships that he can impose." . . .

It is unrealistic to assume that disputes among public employees and their employers will not occur; in fact, strikes by public employees are relatively frequent events in California. For example, 46 strikes occurred during 1981–1983, which actually marks a significant decline when compared to the number during the 5 previous years. Although the circumstances behind each individual strike may vary somewhat, commentators repeatedly note that much of the reason for their occurrence lies in the fact that without the right to strike, or at least a credible strike threat, public employees have little negotiating strength. This, in turn, produces frustrations which exacerbate labor-management conflicts and often provoke "illegal" strikes. . . .

In the absence of some means of equalizing the parties' respective bargaining positions, such as a credible strike threat, both sides are less likely to bargain in good faith; this in turn leads to unsatisfactory and acrimonious labor relations and ironically to more and longer strikes. Equally as important, the possibility of a strike often provides the best impetus for parties to reach an agreement at the bargaining table, because *both* parties lose if a strike actually comes to pass. Thus by providing a clear incentive for resolving disputes, a credible strike threat may serve to avert, rather than to encourage, work stoppages. . . .

A final policy consideration in our analysis addresses a more philosophical issue — the perception that the right to strike, in the public sector as well as in the private sector, represents a basic civil liberty. The widespread acceptance of that perception leads logically to the conclusion that the right to strike, as an important symbol of a free society, should not be denied unless such a strike would substantially injure paramount interests of the larger community.

Plaintiff's argument that only the Legislature can reject the common law doctrine prohibiting public employee strikes flies squarely in the face of both logic and past precedent. Legislative silence is not the equivalent of positive legislation and does not preclude judicial reevaluation of common law doctrine. If the courts have created a bad rule or an outmoded one, the courts can change it.

. . . For the reasons stated above, we conclude that the common law prohibition against public sector strikes should not be recognized in this state. Consequently, strikes by public sector employees in this state as such are neither illegal nor tortious under California common law. We must immediately caution, however, that the right of public employees to strike is by no means unlimited. Prudence and concern for the general public welfare require certain restrictions.

The Legislature has already prohibited strikes by firefighters under any circumstance. It may conclude that other categories of public employees perform such essential services that a strike would invariably result in imminent danger to public health and safety, and must therefore be prohibited. . . .

[W]e believe the following standard may properly guide courts in the resolution of future disputes in this area: strikes by public employees are not unlawful at common law unless or until it is clearly demonstrated that such a strike creates a substantial and imminent threat to the health or safety of the public. This standard allows exceptions in certain essential areas of public employment (e.g., the prohibition against firefighters and law enforcement personnel) and also requires the courts to determine on a case-by-case basis whether the public interest overrides the basic right to strike.

Although we recognize that this balancing process may impose an additional burden on the judiciary, it is neither a novel nor unmanageable task. Indeed, an examination of the strike in the instant case affords a good example of how this new standard should be applied. The 11-day strike did not involve public employees, such as firefighters or law enforcement personnel, whose absence from their duties would clearly endanger the public health and safety. Moreover, there was no showing by the District that the health and safety of the public was at any time imminently threatened. That is not to say that had the strike continued indefinitely, or had the availability of replacement personnel been insufficient to maintain a reasonable sanitation system, there could not have been at some point a clear showing of a substantial threat to the public health and welfare. However, such was not the case here, and the legality of the strike would have been upheld under our newly adopted standard. . . .

Defendant union has also urged this court to find that a per se prohibition of all public employee strikes violates the California Constitution's guarantees of freedom of association, free speech, and equal protection. They do not contend that such a constitutional infringement is present when a court exercises its equitable authority to enjoin a strike based on a showing that the strike represents a substantial and imminent danger to the public health or safety. Instead, the union argues that in the absence of such a showing, per se prohibition is constitutionally unsupportable. . . .

As the union contends, however, the right to unionize means little unless it is accorded some degree of protection regarding its principal aim—effective collective bargaining. For such bargaining to be meaningful, employee groups must maintain the ability to apply pressure or at least threaten its application. A creditable right to strike is one means of doing so. As yet, however, the right to strike has not been accorded full constitutional protection, the prevailing view being that "[t]he right to strike, because of its more serious impact upon the public interest, is more vulnerable to regulation than the right to organize and select representatives for lawful purposes of collective bargaining which this Court has characterized as a "fundamental right. . . .'"

. . . We are not persuaded that the personal freedoms guaranteed by the United States and California Constitutions confer an *absolute right* to strike, but the arguments above may merit consideration at some future date. . . .

Since we have already concluded that the traditional per se prohibition against public employee strikes can no longer be upheld on common law grounds, we do not find it necessary to reach the issue in constitutional terms. . . .

We conclude that it is not unlawful for public employees to engage in a concerted work stoppage for the purpose of improving their wages or conditions of employment, unless it has been determined that the work stoppage poses an imminent threat to public health or safety. Since the trial court's judgment for damage in this case was predicated upon an erroneous determination that defendants' strike was unlawful, the judgment for damages cannot be sustained.

The judgment is reversed.

[Concurrence by KAUS, J., joined by REYNOSO, J., and Concurrence by GRODIN, J. omitted].

BIRD, C.J., concurring.

. . . The majority opinion suggests that the right to strike may have constitutional dimensions. I write separately to elaborate on this point. . . . If the right to strike does indeed differentiate this country from those that are not free, then it must be given substance and enforced.

The constitutional right to strike rests on a number of bedrock principles: (1) the basic personal liberty to pursue happiness and economic security through productive labor (U.S. Const., 5th and 14th Amends.; Cal. Const., art. I, §§ 1, 7, subd. (a)); (2) the absolute prohibition against involuntary servitude (U.S. Const., 13th Amend.; Cal. Const., art. I, § 6); and (3) the fundamental freedoms of association and expression (U.S. Const., 1st Amend.; Cal. Const., art. I, §§ 2, subd. (a), 3).

It is beyond dispute that the individual's freedom to withhold personal service is basic to the constitutional concept of "liberty." Without this freedom, working people would be at the total mercy of their employers, unable either to bargain effectively or to extricate themselves from an intolerable situation. Such a condition would make a mockery of the fundamental right to pursue life, liberty and happiness by engaging in the common occupations of the community. . . .

Justice Brandeis once declared, in a case involving a peaceful, concerted refusal to work: "If, on the undisputed facts of this case, refusal to work can be enjoined, Congress [has] created . . . an instrument for imposing restraints upon labor which reminds of involuntary servitude." (*Bedford Co. v. Stone Cutters Assn.* 274 U.S. 37, 65, (1927) (dis. opn. of Brandeis, J., joined by Holmes, J.).

. . . The close connection between the right to strike and the prohibition against involuntary servitude derives from the purposes of the 13th Amendment. That amendment guarantees the freedom to terminate employment not for its own sake, but in order to "prohibit[ ] that control by which the personal service of one man is disposed of or coerced for another's benefit which is the essence of involuntary servitude." (*Bailey v. Alabama* (1911) 219 U.S. 219.)

Accordingly, the amendment is concerned not merely with the formal right to quit, but also with the *practical ability of working people to protect their interests in the workplace:* . . . . "When the master can compel and the laborer cannot escape the obligation to go on, there is no power below to redress and no incentive above to relieve a harsh overlordship or unwholesome conditions of work." (*Pollock v. Williams* (1944) 322 U.S. 4.)

As courts and commentators universally acknowledge, the group right to strike has replaced the individual right to "change employers" as the principal defense of working people against oppressive conditions. . . . To withdraw the right to strike is to deprive the worker of his or her only effective bargaining power.

Working people enjoy the constitutional right to form and join unions. . . . Without a constitutionally protected right to strike, the use of these freedoms would be "little more than an exercise in sterile ritualism." (*School Committee v. Westerly Teachers Ass'n* (1973) 111 R.I. 96 (dis. opn. of Roberts, C.J.); see also *United Federation of Postal Clerks v. Blount* (D.D.C.1971) 325 F.Supp. 879, 885 (conc. opn. of Wright, J.). . . .

Accordingly, a restraint on the right to strike should be upheld under the California Constitution only if it serves a compelling state interest by the least restrictive means. . . .

It remains only to determine whether the common law's flat prohibition on public employee strikes is necessary to serve a compelling state interest. The majority have convincingly refuted the traditional justifications for that ban. . . .

LUCAS, J, dissenting.

. . . In my view, public employees in this state neither have the right to strike, nor should they have that right. In any event, in light of the difficulty in fashioning proper exceptions to the basic "no strike" rule, and the dangers to public health and safety arising from even a *temporary* cessation of governmental services, the courts should defer to the Legislature, a body far better equipped to create such exceptions.

The majority paints a glowing picture of the public strike weapon as a means of "enhanc[ing] labor-management relations," "equalizing the parties' respective bargaining positions," assuring "good faith" collective bargaining, and "providing a clear incentive for resolving disputes." Indeed, so enamored is the majority with the concept of the public strike that it elevates this heretofore *illegal* device to a "basic civil liberty." Though wholly unnecessary to its opinion, the majority in dictum even suggests that public employees may have a *constitutional* right to strike which cannot be legislatively abridged absent some "substantial or compelling justification."

Thus, in the face of an unbroken string of Court of Appeal cases commencing nearly 35 years ago which hold that public strikes are illegal, we suddenly announce our finding that public strikes are not only lawful in most cases, but indeed they may constitute a panacea for many of the social and economic ills which have long beset the public sector. One may wonder, as I do, why we kept that revelation a secret for all these years. . . .

Despite the majority's encomiums, the fact remains that public strikes may devastate a city within a matter of days, or even hours, depending on the circumstances. For this reason, among many others, the courts of this state (and the vast majority of courts in other states and the federal government) have declared *all* public strikes illegal. . . .

The common law rule [that public sector strikes are illegal] has been adopted or confirmed statutorily by 20 states and the federal government. . . .

The decision to allow public employee strikes requires a delicate and complex balancing process best undertaken by the Legislature, which may formulate a comprehensive regulatory scheme designed to avoid the disruption and chaos which invariably follow a cessation or interruption of governmental services. The majority's own proposal, to withhold the strike weapon only where "truly essential" services are involved and a "substantial and imminent threat" is posed will afford little guidance to our trial courts who must, on a "case-by-case" basis decide such issues. Nor will representatives of labor or management be able to predict with any confidence or certainty whether a particular strike is a lawful one or, being lawful at its inception, will become unlawful by reason of its adverse effects upon the public health and safety. In short, the majority's broad holding will prove as unworkable as it is unwise.

Of the few states that permit strikes by public employees, virtually all do so by comprehensive statutory provisions. Some of the statutory schemes begin by creating classifications of employees, distinguishing, for example, workers whose services are deemed essential (e.g., police, firefighters), those whose services may be interrupted for short periods of time (e.g., teachers), and those whose services may be omitted for an extended time (e.g., municipal golf course attendants). These schemes typically define various prerequisites to the exercise of the right to strike for those categories of workers permitted that option. The prerequisites include a period of mandatory mediation as well as advance notice to the employer. In addition, some statutory schemes lay out the ground rules for binding arbitration.

In contrast, the majority's new California rule is hopelessly undefined and unstructured. In addition to the breadth of the majority's "truly essential" standard, the statutes presently provide no systematic classification of employees according to the nature of their work and the degree to which the public can tolerate work stoppages. Only firefighters are expressly prohibited from striking and giving recognition to picket lines. (Lab.Code, § 1962.) Moreover, the four principal statutory schemes regulating other public employees establish widely differing approaches to labor relations for different types and levels of employees. (Compare Gov.Code, §§ 35003510 [Meyers-Milias-Brown Act, covering local government employees]; 3512–3524 [State Employer-Employee Relations Act, covering state employees]; 3540–3549.3 [Ed. Employment Relations Act, covering public school employees]; 3560–3599 [governing employment in higher education].) Thus, these statutes produce inconsistent results when, as here, the right to strike is given recognition almost across the board. . . .

Notes

1. This case prompted some harsh criticism. The court "not only intruded upon determinations best left to the legislature, but also unnecessarily reconsidered a decision the legislature had already made." G. Murray Snow, County Sanitation District No. 2 v. Los Angeles County Employees Ass'n, Local 660: *A Study in Judicial Legislation*, 1986 BYU L. REV. 206. The court "obliterated any conceptual distinction between private sector and public sector impasse resolution" and improperly bypassed citizen input in so doing. Raymond Hogler, *The Common Law of Public Employee Strikes: A New Rule in California*, 37 LAB. L.J. 94, 102–03 (1986).

Do you agree? Notably, the California legislature did not respond to this case by passing an explicit no-strike provision covering these employees. Schneider, *supra*, 204–05.

2. *County Sanitation District* remains a minority rule, but some other courts have held that some strikes by public employees are legal even where no statute explicitly permits them. *See, e.g., State of Montana v. Public Employees Craft Council of Mont.*, 529 P.2d 785 (Mont. 1974) (strike permitted under the general "right to engage in concerted activities" language of the statute). *Local 1494, IAFF v. City of Coeur d' Alene*, 99 Idaho 630 (1978) held that while the Idaho statute expressly barred strikes by firefighters during the term of a labor contract, firefighters had a "residual" right to strike after a contract had expired and before a new one was formed. In *Davis v. Henry*, 555 So. 2d 457 (La. 1990), the Louisiana Supreme Court held that public employees have the right to strike, except for strikes which clearly endanger the public health and safety. The court found the majority common law rule inapplicable because Louisiana is not a common law state. 555 So. 2d 457, 463.

3. On the other hand, a year after *County Sanitation District*, the Massachusetts Supreme Court reaffirmed the traditional approach in *Boston Hous. Auth. v. LRC*, 398 Mass. 715 (1986). The court applied a general ban on public employee strikes in the state to public housing workers, even though such workers were covered by a separate labor law which did not contain an explicit ban on strikes. The court explained that, "[t]raditionally, public employees have been denied the right to strike"; "[t]he rationale for such policy is that public employees provide essential services and serve the public purpose"; and "[s]trikes by public employees are contrary to the public welfare and could under certain conditions paralyze segments of society." 398 Mass. 715, 719–20.

4. Justice Bird argued that strike bans may violate the Thirteenth Amendment. For further thoughts along those lines, *see* the discussion in Chapter 4. So far, no court has accepted this idea, but it did appear in Judge J. Skelly Wright's concurrence in **United Federation of Postal Clerks v. Blount**, 325 F. Supp. 879 (D.D.C. 879), *aff'd*, 404 U.S. 802 (1971). *Blount* rejected a constitutional challenge to the bar on strikes by federal employees. It noted that no case had found a constitutional right for public or private employees to strike, and, for public workers, there was "no compelling reason to imply the existence" of a constitutional right to strike from

the right to associate. 325 F. Supp. 879, 882–83. Judge Wright concurred with the result, but with some caveats:

> It is by no means clear to me that the right to strike is not fundamental. The right to strike seems intimately related to the right to form labor organizations, a right which the majority recognizes as fundamental and which, more importantly, is generally thought to be constitutionally protected. . . . [T]he inherent purpose of a labor organization is to bring the workers' interests to bear on management, the right to strike is, historically and practically, an important means of effectuating that purpose. A union that never strikes, or which can make no credible threat to strike, may wither away in ineffectiveness. That fact is not irrelevant to the constitutional calculations. Indeed, in several decisions, the Supreme Court has held that the First Amendment right of association is at least concerned with essential organizational activities which give the particular association life and promote its fundamental purposes. . . . I do not suggest that the right to strike is co-equal with the right to form labor organizations. . . . But I do believe that the right to strike is, at least, within constitutional concern and should not be discriminatorily abridged without substantial or 'compelling' justification." 325 F. Supp. 879, 885.

b. Statutory Prohibitions

Statutory bans on public-sector strikes arose well before any public workers had the right to bargain collectively. As Chapter 1 noted, the Boston police strike of 1919 prompted a number of such bans. In 1946, a nationwide strike wave included some strikes by public workers; in response, in 1947, eight states passed laws barring strikes by government employees and the Taft-Hartley Act banned strikes by federal workers. Schneider, *supra*, 193.

By the early 21st century, 38 states had passed no-strike laws for public workers, and a majority of public-sector collective-bargaining statutes barred strikes. Schneider, *supra*, 202. For example, here is part of the Michigan statute, MICH. COMP. LAWS § 423.202.

> Sec. 2. A public employee shall not strike and a public school employer shall not institute a lockout. A public school employer does not violate this section if there is a total or partial cessation of the public school employer's operations in response to a strike held in violation of this section.

3. *What Is a Strike?*

Even where public-sector strikes are illegal, some public employees have tried to use similar job actions to further their goals. These actions are often generically called the "blue flu," based on a police tactic of calling in sick in large numbers as part of a concerted labor campaign. How should the law handle such actions?

In re City of Youngstown and Fraternal Order of Police, Lodge #28

Ohio State Employment Relations Board
SERB 87-002 (1987)

Day, Chair:

On the 27th day of January 1987, the Administration of the Youngstown Police Department (YPD) received 16 notices of illness from the 17 police officers on "C" turn and 12 from 16 on "B" turn. The following day three notices were received from "C" turn and two from "B" turn. Various reasons were alleged for the incapacities of the officers involved.

II

The union claims that the organization had nothing whatever to do with the individual employee actions; that it did nothing to instigate them or to steer any concert of action that is arguably present. In fact, there is nothing in the stipulations of the parties or the evidence that implicates the union. If either the Fraternal Order of Police (FOP) or its Lodge #28 (Lodge) is responsible for the rash of sick notices, the proofs are not here.

III

Whoever or whatever triggered the traumatic and/or viral epidemic which engulfed the YPD, only the naive would attribute it to coincidence. Even a modicum of street sense will recognize the events in this case for what they are. They are symptoms of blue-flu—a euphemism for a badly camouflaged job action. The State Employment Relations Board (SERB) will not characterize as aleatory the conjunction of group trauma and collective contagion which has settled so selectively on the officers of the YPD.

SERB finds the coordination of individual disasters here to be a strike of safety forces without union sanction or instigation. Under Chapter 4117 of the Ohio Revised Code, the job actions are unauthorized and, therefore, illegal. . . .

However, it may still be unconstitutional to discipline employees for merely advocating, rather than participating in, a strike.

Notes

1. This tactic has a long history, and agencies and courts are appropriately suspicious, given certain facts. *In re Forestville Transportation Ass'n*, 4 PERB ¶ 8020 (N.Y. PERB 1971) explained:

> What must now be determined is whether or not the instant sick call constituted a concerted work stoppage or was in actuality the mere coincidence of a large number of employees becoming "emotionally upset" at the same

time and for the same duration. In this connection, the testimony has indicated that normal absenteeism due to sickness was no more than two drivers per day. This alone raises serious doubt as to the probability that 12 employees could, independently of each other, get sick or upset at the same time. Additionally, the fact that all employees apparently "recovered" at the same moment increases this doubt.

Similarly, in *Airhart v. New Orleans Fire Dept.*, 807 So. 2d 1043, 1045–46 (La. Ct. App. 2002), a large group of firefighters testified that they really were sick on a certain day. The court rejected these claims, relying in part on the testimony of an industrial psychologist who prepared a statistical analysis demonstrating the improbability of 119 out of 161 employees actually being sick on the same day. Also, for this group of firefighters, average daily attendance over the previous six months had been 97.2 percent, but on the day in question it was only 26 percent.

2. Because of this tactic, many public-sector statutes prohibit not just strikes, but also other concerted "job actions." *See, e.g.*, the New Hampshire law, N.H. Rev. Stat. § 273-A:13, which prohibits "strikes and other forms of job action by public employees."

3. Not every organized campaign to avoid any sort of work is an illegal strike. In *Appeal of City of Manchester*, 144 N.H. 320 (1999), the union encouraged its members not to volunteer for certain overtime details. The court held this was not an illegal strike, partly because the city retained the power to order officers to work overtime, and the union did not attempt to impede that process.

4. Pickets in support of illegal strikes may not be illegal in and of themselves. For example, *Wayne State University and UAW Local 2071*, 4 MPER ¶ 22082 (MERC 1991), held that using criminal trespass statutes to have picketers arrested for carrying union strike signs during an illegal strike was an unlawful interference with the employees' protected rights. The mere fact that the work stoppage was illegal did not render attendant sign carrying and picket activity per se illegal since sign carrying and picketing did not fall within the statutory definition of "strike." Conversely, not all pickets in support of legal strikes are lawful. *See, e.g., Harrison Hills Teachers' Ass'n v. State Emp. Rel. Bd.*, 56 N.E.3d 986 (Oh. App. 2016) (rejecting a constitutional challenge to a provision making it a ULP for a union to induce or encourage any individual in connection with a labor dispute to picket any place of private employment of any public official).

5. Courts have found illegal strikes where unions employed tactics other than calling in sick. *Bd. of Education v. Shanker*, 283 N.Y.S.2d 432 (Sup. Ct.), *aff'd w/out opinion*, 286 N.Y.S.2d 453 (App. Div. 1967) raised the interesting question of whether a threat to quit *en masse* constituted a strike. Obviously, an individual teacher can quit in response to what that teacher considers to be unsatisfactory terms of employment. In *Shanker*, a sizeable group of teachers signed petitions stating they would resign if a satisfactory contract agreement was not reached

with their union. The court held this was an illegal strike, reasoning that the purpose of the petitions was not truly to quit work but rather to compel the employer to agree to union demands. As a result of this case, Albert Shanker, the president of the union, was sentenced to jail for 15 days and the union was fined $150,000 dollars.

Was that a good result? What if the teachers had actually resigned? What if many of them genuinely planned to resign absent a satisfactory contract? What if fewer teachers made a similar gesture? *Board of Education v. N.J. Educ. Ass'n*, 53 N.J. 29 (1968) also held that a mass resignation was illegal. That court stated, "although the right of an individual to resign or refuse public employment is undeniable, yet two or more may not agree to follow a common course to the end that an agency of government shall be unable to function." 53 N.J. 29, 38. "Two or more" may not agree to quit together? Does this raise Thirteenth Amendment concerns?

6. Also, some cases have held that union "work to rule" campaigns violate no-strike laws. *Local 252, TWU v. N.Y. State Public Employment Relations Board*, 58 N.Y.2d 354 (1983), found an illegal job action when bus drivers engaged in a concerted refusal to drive buses which violated the requirements of the state Vehicle and Traffic Law in ways that did not pose imminent dangers to people or property.

7. Consider whether these facts, as reported in a news story from 2005, constitute a strike.

> BERKELEY, Calif.—Berkeley students aren't getting written homework assignments because teachers are refusing to grade work on their own time after two years with no pay raise.
>
> So far, a black history event had to be canceled and parents had to staff a middle-school science fair because teachers are sticking strictly to the hours they're contracted to work.
>
> Teachers say they don't want to stop volunteering their time. "It's hard," said high school math teacher Judith Bodenhauser. "I have stacks of papers I haven't graded. Parents want to talk to me; I don't call them back."
>
> The action was organized by the Berkeley Federation of Teachers, which wants a cost-of-living increase next year.
>
> District Superintendent Michele Lawrence said she sympathizes with teachers but said there isn't money for raises.
>
> The union declared an impasse in negotiations last June and has not had a contract for two years.

County Sanitation District, supra, created a general test to apply to individual sets of facts. Under that test, could a "blue flu" action be legal where a traditional strike would not be?

City of Santa Ana v. Santa Ana Police Benevolent Association et al.

Court of Appeal of California
207 Cal. App. 3d 1568, 255 Cal. Rptr. 688 (1989)

SILLS, J.

May police officers engage in a "sick-out" (blue flu) during labor negotiations? *No.*

The Santa Ana Police Benevolent Association (PBA), a non-profit association of sworn and non-sworn public safety employees of the Santa Ana Police Department and the City of Santa Ana were engaged in a "meet and confer" bargaining process for a new memorandum of understanding when their old one expired. An agreement had not been reached, when, on July 9, 1987, 16 of the 18 officers on the graveyard shift telephoned that they were sick. These absences required 24 evening shift officers to remain on duty and work overtime for several hours each. Later that same day, 41 evening shift officers called in sick. On the following morning, 83 day shift officers claimed to be ill; and the entire graveyard shift remained on duty so that normal police operations could continue. At this point, the city obtained a temporary restraining order enjoining the PBA members from striking or "being absent from work claiming illness when not ill." The PBA complied with the order and there were no further work slowdowns. Later in the month, the court issued a preliminary injunction prohibiting the officers from "striking or calling or inducing a strike or work stoppage, including a work slowdown, or being absent from work claiming illness when not ill in the nature of a strike."

II

The parties agree that all police functions were adequately staffed during the July 9 and 10 sick-out by using other officers working overtime or extra shifts. And, it appears the PBA and city recently reached an accord on a new memorandum of understanding. Nevertheless, the issues raised in this appeal are "of continuing public interest and likely to recur in circumstances where, as here, there is insufficient time to afford full appellate review. Thus, it is appropriate to resolve the matter."

The PBA frames the issue in this appeal as "whether or not it is proper, under state law, for a court to enjoin a public safety employee organization from engaging in a 'sick-out' which is organized in a manner calculated to avoid an imminent threat to public health or safety." The city maintains that pretextual illnesses of officers involved in labor negotiations create unreasonable overtime demands on officers who do report for duty, thus seriously impairing the efficiency of the police department.

Regardless of the precautions taken to maximize officer and public safety under these circumstances, the city insists officers cannot work as effectively when they are burdened with extra shift duty.

The law on this subject has undergone a relatively recent change. Courts of Appeal traditionally held sick-outs by public employees to be per se illegal and the proper objects of injunctive, and in some cases tort, relief. . . .

In 1985, however, a plurality of the California Supreme Court . . . rejected this analysis in *County Sanitation Dist. No. 2*. . . . The three-justice plurality then directed trial courts to consider public employee strike cases on an individual basis. . . .

In the context of the instant case, it seems clear that work slowdowns or stoppages by police officers tread dangerous waters. Contrary to the position taken in the city's brief, strikes by law enforcement officers are not specifically and unequivocally exempted from the court's decision in *Sanitation District*. The court did, however, allude to strikes by law enforcement as ones which would be restrained under the new test. References to law enforcement as being an area for continued application of the common law rules appear throughout the opinion. . . .

The police argue that the particular activity sought to be enjoined must be analyzed in terms of whether a threat to public safety is present. We do not read *Sanitation District* as reaching this conclusion. Repeated references to strikes by police officers as ones which would still be prohibited lead us to conclude that police work stoppages are still per se illegal. On reflection, application of such a test to police functions would be an impossible task for the trier of fact. On most days, a work slowdown or stoppage by the police will not pose a threat to the public health or safety. On good days, there are no murders, no gridlock, and no chemical spills. A work slowdown by the graveyard shift on a quiet night might never be noticed. How wonderful hindsight. Appellate courts can look back months or years and conclude that a police strike did or did not imperil public safety. Unfortunately, trial judges asked to enjoin police strikes are not blessed with clairvoyant powers—they cannot foresee an earthquake, a madman's shooting spree or a riot. If a disaster occurs during a police slowdown or strike, the inevitable investigation which will follow will undoubtedly point to the absent dispatcher or tardy patrol car as a cause. In the words of Milton, "They also serve who only stand and wait."

When a city is required to use the service of every officer who has already worked the night shift to meet the demands of the day shift, the obvious threat to public safety hardly merits discussion. The association presents the issue in their brief by asking: "May police officers lawfully engage in a short-term sick-out during labor negotiations if the concerted job action is conducted in such a manner as to allow for adequate staffing?" This framing of the issue begs the question. To argue that using officers who have already worked a shift constitutes adequate staffing is hokum. In addition, attempting to characterize the sick-out as "short-term" finds no support in the record: The "sick-out" turned out to be short-term only because it was terminated by court order. . . .

4. Remedies and Penalties for Illegal Strikes

What remedies and penalties are available for illegal strikes? Consider actions against the union and against individual strikers. Also, who should be able to bring the actions and collect penalties: the employer, the state labor agency, or private parties affected by the strike? And should it matter if the employer provoked an illegal strike by committing ULPs during negotiations?

Some statutes provide specific remedies for illegal strikes; in others, remedies and penalties come under the general remedial powers of the labor board. While remedies vary among jurisdictions, typically, they provide that individual strikers may be discharged, fined, and some limitations placed on their future public employment; and that unions may be fined, decertified, or lose the right to dues checkoff and/or dues deductions for a specified period. A few jurisdictions, including the federal sector, make illegal strikes a criminal offense. Courts also have the authority to enjoin illegal strikes and issue contempt sanctions for violations of such injunctions.

a. Remedies Against Individual Strikers

Perhaps most famously, New York's Taylor Act mandates, among other things, fines equal to twice the strikers' daily rate of pay for each day on strike. N.Y. Civ. Serv. Law § 210. While considered fairly harsh, this provision is not unique. Ohio, which permits many public employees to strike if they comply with statutory requirements, has a similar sanction for illegal strikes. Ohio Rev. Code § 4117.23(B) provides that if a strike is illegal, the public employer:

(1) May remove or suspend those employees who one day after notification by the public employer of the board decision that a strike is not authorized continue to engage in the nonauthorized strike; and

(2) If the employee is appointed or reappointed, employed, or reemployed, as a public employee, within the same appointing authority, may impose the following conditions:

(a) The employee's compensation shall in no event exceed that received by him immediately prior to the time of the violation.

(b) The employee's compensation is not increased until after the expiration of one year from the appointment or reappointment, employment, or reemployment.

(3) Shall deduct from each striking employee's wages, if the board also determines that the public employer did not provoke the strike, the equivalent of two days' wages for each day the employee remains on strike commencing one day after receiving the notice called for in division (B)(1) of this section.

Note that under subsection (3), the two-day pay penalty in Ohio can be avoided if the public employer provoked the strike. What is the purpose of that rule? Is it good policy? Note also the requirement that, before disciplining or fining an employee, the state agency must first find that an illegal strike has occurred and the employer must notify the employee of that decision. What is the purpose of that rule? Is it good policy?

Employers usually have broad discretion in determining discipline for illegal strikers. In *Hortonville Jt. Sch. Dist. v. Hortonville Educ. Ass'n*, 426 U.S. 482 (1976), some teachers in Wisconsin admitted they had struck illegally but claimed their employer, the local school board, had violated their due process rights in firing them. The teachers argued that the board's ULPs had provoked the strike, that this was a mitigating factor, and further that the school board members in charge of the discharge hearing were unconstitutionally biased because they were judging their own behavior. The U.S. Supreme Court rejected these arguments, holding that state law vested broad policymaking powers in the board to govern the schools, including the power to employ and dismiss teachers. Also, showing that the board was involved in the events leading up to the discipline was not enough to "overcome the presumption of honesty and integrity in policymakers with decision-making power." 426 U.S. 482, 497. The Court stressed that in this case, it was undisputed that the teachers had engaged in an illegal strike.

What if an employee misses a day of work during an illegal strike, but this particular employee had not intended to strike? Typically, employees can rebut the presumption that they were illegally striking if they can prove they truly were, *e.g.*, sick or on vacation. *See, e.g., City of Pittsburgh v. Fraternal Ass'n of Professional Paramedics*, 592 A.2d 786 (Pa. Commw. Ct. 1991) (employees on vacation at the time of the strike were not illegal strikers).

If an employee is disciplined for merely advocating an illegal strike, does that violate the First Amendment? Courts are split. *Compare Brown v. Department of Transp., F.A.A.*, 735 F.2d 543 (Fed. Cir. 1984) (supervisor who did not participate in an illegal strike could be fired for urging traffic controllers to "stay together" during PATCO strike), *and Commonwealth Emp. Rel. Bd. v. Boston Teachers Union, Local 66, AFT*, 908 N.E.2d 772 (Mass. App. Ct. 2009) (rejecting First Amendment challenge to finding that union violated a law barring inducing, encouraging, or condoning a strike by scheduling a strike vote), *with Tygrett v. Barry*, 627 F.2d 1279 (D.C. Cir. 1980) (probationary police officer improperly fired for advocating a "blue flu" action).

Problem 11.1

Consider the practical issues. Employers typically have the legal power to discharge illegal strikers, but they do not always exercise that option. For example, in the spring of 2018, teachers engaged in state-wide walkouts in West Virginia, Oklahoma, Tennessee, Arizona, and Colorado. These strikes were generally successful, despite the fact that all of these states not only made such strikes illegal but also did not even grant collective bargaining rights to teachers. Thus, the teachers all could have been fired, but they were not. Joseph Slater, *The Teachers' Strikes of 2018 in Historical Perspective*, 20 Marq. Benefits & Soc. Welfare L. Rev. 191, 192 (2019). What factors might inhibit public employers from firing certain employees who struck illegally? What factors would make it more or less likely that the employer would fire illegal strikers?

b. Remedies Against Unions

Unions may also be sanctioned for illegal strikes, although, as with "wildcat" strikes in the private sector discussed in Section II of this chapter, it must be shown that the union condoned or encouraged the strike. In some cases, boards and courts have found that union officials were not responsible for an illegal strike and therefore the union could not be sanctioned. *See, e.g., In re City of Youngstown and Fraternal Order of Police, Lodge #28, supra; Ann Arbor Public Schools and Teamsters State, County, and Municipal Workers Local 214*, 15 MPER ¶ 33037 (MERC 2002).

(i.) Injunctions

Often, the most urgent goal of an employer faced with an illegal strike is simply to end the strike. The legal remedy that accomplishes this is an injunction. Injunctions are, however, an extraordinary remedy and have a special history in labor law generally. *See* Chapter 1. What factors should courts consider in determining whether to enjoin an illegal public-sector strike?

Feaster v. Vance

District of Columbia Court of Appeals
832 A.2d 1277 (2003)

Glickman, J.

The Superintendent of the District of Columbia Public Schools ("DCPS") and the District of Columbia filed suit in Superior Court against appellants, two Teamsters Union locals and their presidents, to enjoin an unlawful strike by school employees. After holding an evidentiary hearing, the court entered a preliminary injunction against the threatened strike. This appeal followed. Appellants contend that the Superior Court lacked jurisdiction to grant injunctive relief, either because the Public Employee Relations Board had exclusive jurisdiction over the complaint in its entirety or because the federal Norris-LaGuardia Act barred the Superior Court from issuing an injunction against a labor strike. Alternatively, appellants contend that the court abused its discretion in granting injunctive relief. They argue that a strike by DCPS employees is not an unlawful strike "against the District." Appellants further argue that an injunction was unwarranted because the threatened strike would not have caused irreparable injury and because the DCPS had failed to bargain in good faith and hence had "unclean hands."

We reject appellants' contentions. We hold that the looming school employee strike was prohibited by law, the Superior Court had jurisdiction to enjoin the strike at the behest of the Superintendent of Schools and the District of Columbia, and the court did not abuse its discretion in granting preliminary injunctive relief.

I.

Teamsters Local 639 and Teamsters Local 730 are the Board-certified exclusive bargaining agents for food service workers, bus drivers, bus attendants, custodians, and engineers employed by the District of Columbia Public Schools. These workers provide services to some 70,000 public school children in the District. The two Teamsters locals bargain jointly with the DCPS and are covered by the same collective bargaining agreement. The Teamsters' chief labor negotiator and spokesperson, appellant Phillip A. Feaster, is Local 639's President.

In 1996 the Teamsters and DCPS commenced negotiations over a collective bargaining agreement for the years 1996 to 1999. The parties negotiated intermittently without success. After a lengthy hiatus, the Teamsters and DCPS agreed to resume active negotiations after school opened in September 1999. The central dispute in the negotiations at that time was over the issue of economic "parity" between the Teamsters and two other DCPS bargaining units, which were known as Compensation Units I and II. Under the rubric of parity, the Teamsters demanded the same bonuses and pay raises for their employees that the employees in Compensation Units I and II had received in their separate labor negotiations. The DCPS did not agree to the Teamsters' demands.

By December 1999 there was talk of a strike over the parity issue. . . . [O]n January 14, Feaster told the Superintendent that there would be "a serious disruption to the school system" unless the DCPS agreed to the Teamsters' demands. Two days later, the members of the two Teamsters locals convened and voted by 470 to 4 in favor of a strike. . . . On January 19 the Superintendent told Feaster that the DCPS was making progress on the question of a bonus but that there were no funds available for wage increases. Feaster responded that the strike would be deferred but there would be a "serious work stoppage" on Monday, January 24, if an agreement was not reached by then.

On January 21, the Superintendent of Schools and the District of Columbia filed their complaint in Superior Court to enjoin the Teamsters from engaging in an unlawful strike. The court issued an agreed-upon temporary restraining order that same day. . . . While the temporary restraining order was in effect, Teamsters officials distributed to parents at a Public Schools Enrollment Fair a leaflet that outlined the Union's grievances and predicted that the Superintendent of Schools "will cause major chaos in the school system by forcing workers to strike."

. . . On April 12, Judge Zeldon . . . issued an order enjoining the Teamsters from "in any manner, calling, continuing, encouraging, aiding or otherwise participating in any strike or other job action, including, without limitation, any work stoppage, slow down, sick-out or 'work to the rule' action or any other job action . . . or otherwise interfering with or affecting the functioning of the District of Columbia Public Schools." . . .

Judge Zeldon began her analysis of the issues by determining that the plaintiffs had shown a substantial likelihood of success on the merits because a strike by DCPS employees would violate the prohibition against strikes by District government employees set forth in D.C. Code § 1-617.05, as well as a Board of Education regulation and the Teamsters' contractual obligations. Judge Zeldon rejected the Teamsters' argument that the Superior Court was divested of jurisdiction by virtue of the fact that a public employee strike would be an unfair labor practice within the primary jurisdiction of the Public Employee Relations Board. The plaintiffs were not required to go to the Board to enforce the prohibition in D.C. Code § 1-617.05, Judge Zeldon reasoned, "because [that statutory provision] is independent from the unfair labor practice provisions over which [the Board] has jurisdiction." Judge Zeldon also rejected the argument that injunctive relief against the Teamsters' strike was barred by the Norris-LaGuardia Act. The general prohibition against labor injunctions contained in that Act, Judge Zeldon held, does not apply to injunctions against strikes by public employees. On the merits of the request for a preliminary injunction, Judge Zeldon found — in addition to the requisite likelihood of success on the merits — that a strike would result in irreparable harm by causing a substantial disruption in the education of children in the public schools. The judge further found that more harm would result from denying the injunction than granting it and that the public interest would be served by granting the injunction. Finally, Judge Zeldon rejected the Teamsters' contention that the DCPS should be denied injunctive relief because of "unclean hands." The judge noted that the Teamsters had not charged the DCPS with failure to bargain in good faith by filing an unfair labor practice charge with the Public Employee Relations Board.

The Teamsters appealed the preliminary injunction order to this court. . . .

We address first appellants' jurisdictional challenges. . . .

A.

In 1978 the Council of the District of Columbia enacted the Comprehensive Merit Personnel Act ("CMPA"), D.C. Code §§ 1-601.01 et seq. . . . The CMPA contains two separate provisions prohibiting strikes by District government employees. One of those provisions, D.C. Code § 1-617.05, declares that "it shall be unlawful for any District government employee or labor organization to participate in, authorize, or ratify a strike against the District." . . . D.C. Code § 1-617.04 (b)(4), makes it one of a number of specifically prohibited unfair labor practices for District government employees to engage in a strike or for their union to condone a strike.

The CMPA commits the responsibility to resolve allegations of unfair labor practices to the Public Employee Relations Board. . . .

[P]laintiffs ordinarily must exhaust their administrative remedies with the Board before they may seek relief on arguable unfair labor practice claims in Superior Court. . . .

[A]ppellants argue that since a strike by D.C. government employees is an unfair labor practice, the PERB is vested with primary jurisdiction over the complaint in this case and the Superior Court was without jurisdiction to proceed on it. Judge Zeldon rejected that argument on the ground that the Superintendent of Schools and the District of Columbia invoked a prohibition against strikes in the CMPA that is independent of the statutory unfair labor practice provisions.

We agree with Judge Zeldon. Under D.C. Code § 11-921(a), the Superior Court is a court of general jurisdiction "with the power to adjudicate any civil action at law or in equity involving local law." . . . "Unless a contrary legislative intent clearly appears," . . . the Superior Court has jurisdiction over a claim that employees of the District government are violating or about to violate D.C. law by going on strike. Unlike in the case of other unfair labor practices, such a "contrary legislative intent" does not "clearly appear" with respect to the subject of public employee strikes. The Council has not manifested its intent to commit complaints about such strikes exclusively to the PERB for initial resolution. Rather, by enacting D.C. Code § 1-617.05 as an independent statutory prohibition, the Council manifested its intent to enable the District government to go directly to Superior Court to enjoin strikes by public employees.

It is indeed noteworthy that the CMPA contains not one but two provisions prohibiting strikes by government employees, only one of which bans them as unfair labor practices. The second provision, a categorical declaration that such strikes are unlawful, is outside the unfair labor practice framework and makes no reference to enforcement through the PERB. Other unfair labor practices do not receive such redoubled statutory attention. We are loath to construe the second provision as mere surplusage. . . . The statute provides no criminal penalty. Nor (unlike comparable statutes in other jurisdictions) does § 1-617.05 specify non-criminal penalties such as payroll deductions. If § 1-617.05 does not furnish a basis on which the D.C. government may apply directly to the Superior Court for relief against an unlawful strike by its employees, it is difficult to see what purpose § 1-617.05 serves.

On the other hand, the availability of a direct action in Superior Court to enjoin an unlawful public employee strike as an alternative or supplement to an unfair labor practice complaint in the PERB furthers the public policy embodied in the CMPA and is not duplicative. When an illegal strike by government employees that may threaten serious harm to the public is imminent or already under way, time may be of the essence in effectuating the statutory policy. Relief may be delayed if the District government can proceed against the strike only by way of an unfair labor practice complaint before the Board, for the Board must first investigate and decide the merits of the complaint, then decide upon a remedial order, and then apply to the Superior Court to enforce its order if the strikers are recalcitrant. . . . Moreover, the issue before the Superior Court in an action for injunctive relief is comparatively narrow—the court is not called upon in such an action to intrude on the Board's area of labor relations expertise and usurp the Board's discretionary authority to choose among a range of other available remedies, such as decertification of the bargaining unit or compelling the parties to bargain in good faith. . . .

We hold that the CMPA does not deprive the Superior Court of jurisdiction over a complaint by the District of Columbia for injunctive relief against an unlawful strike by government employees.

B.

The Norris-LaGuardia Act broadly prohibits "courts of the United States" from issuing injunctions in labor disputes:

> No court of the United States, as herein defined, shall have jurisdiction to issue any restraining order or temporary or permanent injunction in a case involving or growing out of a labor dispute, except in a strict conformity with the provisions of this Act; nor shall any such restraining order or temporary or permanent injunction be issued contrary to the public policy declared in this Act. 29 U.S.C. § 101; see also 29 U.S.C. § 104 (a) (specifically barring injunctive relief against strikes in labor disputes).

. . . The Norris-LaGuardia Act is not quite as broad as it appears on its face, however. In *United States v. United Mine Workers*, 330 U.S. 258, 276–82 (1947), the Supreme Court held that the Act was not intended to restrict the right of a sovereign government to secure injunctive relief in a labor dispute with its own employees. The holding of *Mine Workers* applies whether the sovereign in question is the United States (as in that case) or another sovereign body, such as an individual State. . . .

In the context of public employee labor relations and the Norris-LaGuardia Act, the District of Columbia government is akin to a sovereign State. . . . The District of Columbia government is . . . both the *de jure* and the *de facto* sovereign with respect to local public employee labor relations in the District. Under the authority of *Mine Workers*, we conclude that the Norris-LaGuardia Act therefore does not preclude the District of Columbia government from applying to its courts to enjoin an unlawful strike by its employees.

C.

In exercising its discretion to grant or deny preliminary injunctive relief, a trial court must consider four criteria:

> . . . whether the moving party has clearly demonstrated (1) that there is a substantial likelihood he [or she] will prevail on the merits; (2) that he [or she] is in danger of suffering irreparable harm during the pendency of the action; (3) that more harm will result to him [or her] from the denial of the injunction than will result to the defendant from its grant; and, in appropriate cases, that the public interest will not be disserved by the issuance of the requested order. . . .

[A]ppellants raise three discrete issues.

First, attacking the finding of a likelihood of success on the merits, appellants argue that a strike against the District of Columbia Board of Education is not a prohibited strike "against the District" within the meaning of D.C. Code § 1-617.05. Appellants premise this argument on the status of the Board of Education as an independent agency of government, for which the CMPA created a "separate personnel management system." The argument is fallacious, however. Although the

Board of Education is an independent agency, the Board is still, as the CMPA states, one of the "subdivisions of the District government." . . .

Appellants' remaining contentions do not merit extended discussion. Judge Zeldon's factual findings . . . amply support her determination of irreparable injury. Those findings confirm the Teamsters' own prediction that a strike would cause "major chaos in the school system." As for appellants' claim that the DCPS had "unclean hands" because it had not bargained in good faith, the "unclean hands" doctrine is inapplicable here. *See International Tours & Travel, Inc. v. Khalil*, 491 A.2d 1149, 1155 (D.C. 1985) ("The equitable doctrine of unclean hands only applies where there is misconduct by the plaintiff *in the same transaction* that is the subject of his claim.") (emphasis added). If the DCPS failed to bargain with the Teamsters in good faith, that fact would justify an unfair labor practice complaint before the PERB. It would not justify a strike in violation of law. The DCPS's alleged failure to bargain in good faith does not undermine Judge Zeldon's determinations that the threatened strike would be illegal, that it would cause irreparable injury, and that the balance of harms and the public interest weighed in favor of preventing the strike. We see no reason to disturb Judge Zeldon's ruling.

Notes

1. In some earlier cases, courts refused to issue injunctions if the employer had provoked the strike (typically by failing to bargain in good faith) using the traditional equitable defense of "unclean hands." *See, e.g., School Dist. No. 351 Oneida County v. Oneida Educ. Ass'n*, 98 Idaho 486 (1977); *School Dist. for City of Holland v. Holland Educ. Ass'n*, 380 Mich. 314 (1968). A few other courts denied injunctions because irreparable harm was not shown. *See, e.g., Wilson v. Pulaski Ass'n of Classroom Teachers*, 330 Ark. 298 (1997). These are now distinctly minority approaches. For an example of the majority approach, see *Anchorage Education Ass'n v. Anchorage School Dist.*, 648 P.2d 993 (Alaska 1982) (illegality of a strike itself is sufficient harm to justify injunctive relief).

Michigan law on this subject contains an interesting wrinkle. A 1994 amendment to the state statute overruled the *Holland* case and essentially presumed irreparable harm in all teacher strikes. The amendment stated that courts will grant injunctions if public school employees have illegally struck, "without regard to the existence of other remedies, demonstration of irreparable harm, or other factors." MICH. COMP. LAWS § 423.202a(10). A state Circuit Court then held that this irrebuttable presumption of irreparable harm was unconstitutional, because "the issuance of injunctions against strikes without regard to traditional equity factors . . . violates the doctrine of separation of powers by invading the province of the judiciary." Quoted in *Michigan State AFL-CIO v. MERC*, 212 Mich. App. 472, 478 (1995). The appellate court in this case did not address that specific holding, however, because it was not appealed, 212 Mich. App. 472, 478 n.1, and thus the issue remains somewhat in doubt.

2. Is the majority rule on both these issues convincing? If an employer provokes a strike by refusing to bargain in good faith, why shouldn't the "unclean hands"

doctrine bar the employer from the equitable relief of an injunction? Is *Feaster* really saying that a strike is not part of the "same transaction" as the bargaining that led to the strike? Is there a better defense of the same result? Also, should courts automatically assume that all illegal public-sector strikes will cause "irreparable harm"? Why or why not? Is the fact that some states permit some public employees to strike relevant to that question?

3. The Ohio statute, as noted above, provides that if employer ULPs provoked a strike, illegal strikers are not subject to the normal fines of two days' pay for each day on strike. Ohio Rev. Code § 4117.23(B). Yet Ohio follows the majority rule that employer ULPs in provoking a strike are not a defense to an injunction for at least many illegal strikes. Ohio Rev. Code § 4117.23 provides that in strikes by public safety and other personnel not permitted to strike in Ohio, employer ULPs are "not a defense" to injunction proceedings. What rationale supports this distinction?

4. *Feaster* held that a claim alleging an illegal strike could be brought directly to court without an agency adjudicating the matter first. This is the majority approach. *But see San Jose v. Operating Engineers Local 3*, 49 Cal. 4th 597 (2010), holding that in at least most cases where an employer sought an injunction against a threatened illegal strike, the employer must first seek relief from the state agency, PERB, before asking a court for injunctive relief. This "applied to PERB the same rule of jurisdiction that the United States Supreme Court had adopted with respect to the [NLRB]." 49 Cal. 4th 597, 604.

(ii.) Contempt

What if a union strikes or continues to strike in violation of an injunction? The most common remedy is to find the union in contempt and fine the union. Contempt in more serious situations can also be criminal. A transit workers' strike in New York City in many ways creates a serious situation. Criminal cases, however, raise legal issues beyond those raised in civil cases.

New York City Transit Authority v. Transport Workers Union of America

New York Supreme Court, Appellate Division
35 A.D.3d 73, 822 N.Y.S.2d 579 (2006)

Miller, J.

Shortly before Christmas 2005, the members of various transportation workers' unions went on strike in the City of New York, in violation of a previously-issued injunction. As is relevant to this appeal, as a result of that violation, following a bench trial, the appellant, Local 100 of Transport Workers Union of America, AFL-CIO (hereinafter Local 100), subsequently was adjudged in contempt, and fined at the rate of $1 million per day. Among the issues presented for our review is the question of whether Local 100 had a Sixth and Fourteenth Amendment right to a jury trial on the question of its contempt. We conclude that none of Local 100's arguments has merit, and accordingly affirm the order and judgment on appeal.

I.

. . . Prior to the expiration of the CBA in mid-December 2005, with no successor agreement yet in place, officers and members of Local 100 made statements to the press and engaged in activities indicating that they planned to strike if a new CBA was not in place effective December 16, 2005. On December 10, 2005, Local 100 conducted a mass meeting of its members. The members present voted unanimously to authorize Local 100's Executive Board to call a strike in the event no agreement was reached on a new CBA by the time the existing one expired.

On December 12, 2005, the plaintiffs commenced this action pursuant to article 14 of the Civil Service Law . . . otherwise known as the Taylor Law (Civil Service Law §§ 200–212). Among other things, the plaintiffs sought an injunction to prevent Local 100 and its members from striking. . . . The court heard the parties' arguments, and then issued the requested preliminary injunction.

. . . Despite the preliminary injunction, at 3:01 A.M. on December 20, 2005, Local 100 went on strike. Most of the plaintiffs' hourly-paid employees complied with the call for a strike, and thereby shut down the plaintiffs' mass transit facilities.

Accordingly, by order to show cause dated December 20, 2005, the plaintiffs moved, inter alia, pursuant to Judiciary Law §§ 750 and 751 to adjudge Local 100 guilty of criminal contempt for the willful violation of the December 13, 2005, preliminary injunction by engaging in the strike. As a sanction against Local 100 for that alleged violation, the plaintiffs sought a $1 million fine for the violation of the preliminary injunction on December 20, 2005, with successive doubling of that fine for each day it continued on strike. . . .

Local 100 submitted a pre-hearing memorandum of law in which it argued, inter alia, that . . . it had a Sixth Amendment right to a jury trial on the issue of contempt. Local 100 further claimed that the plaintiffs provoked the strike, and that the proposed fines were excessive.

. . . [A]fter hearing argument on the issue, the court denied the application of Local 100 for a jury trial on the contempt issue. . . .

Among other things, to demonstrate the impact of the strike upon the City and its residents, the plaintiffs submitted the affirmation of Joseph F. Bruno, Commissioner of the New York City Office of Emergency Management, which the court received in evidence. Bruno stated, inter alia, that in the last 39 years, the City had experienced two extended transit strikes, both of which caused complete disruption to life in the City, which is "heavily dependent on . . . public bus and subway service." He alleged that during each day of a strike, the City would lose between approximately $8 million and $12 million in tax revenue . . . and that businesses would suffer losses of between $440 million and $660 million per day. Bruno referred to the 11-day 1980 transit strike in support of his position. For example, during that strike, businesses in the City suffered losses of about $1.1 billion. In addition, the City lost $1 million per day in sales tax revenue and $500,000 in income tax revenue for each day of the strike. Thus, the loss in sales and income tax revenues to the City amounted to approximately $16.5 million for the 11-day strike. Direct monetary losses to the City (e.g., overtime costs for police, fire, and transportation personnel) were about $3.1 million per day. Bruno alleged that in 2005, the cost for additional police activity alone would be more than $10 million per day. Additional costs to the New York City Department of Transportation were alleged to be $142,000 per day, and costs for staffing and operating the City's Emergency Operations Center would exceed $70,000 per day.

Furthermore, Bruno stated that a strike would affect the health and safety of New Yorkers. For example, increased traffic volume would slow the response time of emergency vehicles, thus putting lives at risk. During the 1980 strike, traffic flow into Manhattan increased by 26%, and there was a "sharp decrease" in the number of people who visited clinics and emergency rooms operated by the New York City Health and Hospitals Corporation.

Education of the City's children also would be affected. Almost 500,000 children attending schools in the City rely on public transportation to travel to and from school, and might not be able to get there in the event of a strike. Bruno alleged that based on the experience of the 1980 strike, tens of thousands of students would not attend school in the event of a transit strike.

Bruno further alleged that the damages caused by the 1980 transit strike would "pale in comparison" to a strike in 2005, since the public had come to depend more on public transportation in the intervening years. . . . Furthermore, in 1980, the strike took place in April. A strike taking place during the 2005 Christmas holiday season would have a "devastating" effect on a number of industries in the City which relied on business during the holiday period, such as the retail and tourism industries.

The plaintiffs submitted evidence regarding the assets of Local 100, in the form of a Department of Labor financial statement, which showed that for the 2004 calendar year, the local had over $3.6 million in net assets. Also submitted was a news report, dated December 2, 2005, stating that the local had received an offer of $60 million for the building housing its headquarters, located on the Upper West Side of Manhattan. . . .

[Local 100, through testimony of its general counsel, Walter Meginniss, argued that the MTA had not bargained in good faith various ways, notably by insisting on reducing pension benefits in the negotiations despite the fact that pension benefits were not a legal subject of bargaining.]

. . . Following the hearing, the Supreme Court issued an order and judgment which granted that branch of the plaintiffs' motion which was to adjudge Local 100 in contempt for disobeying the December 13, 2005, injunction. As for punishment, the court fined the Local the sum of $1 million per day for its disobedience, for as long as it remained on strike, beginning December 20, 2005.

Local 100 remained on strike until about 3:00 P.M. on December 22, 2005. The court . . . set the total fine to be paid by Local 100 at the sum of $2.5 million. . . . The Supreme Court specifically recognized that Local 100 ordered its members back to work at or about midday on December 22, 2005, rather than waiting until 11:59 P.M. Thus, the total fine was arrived at by multiplying the per diem fine of $1 million by two for the first two full days of the strike, and prorating the third day to credit the local for calling off the strike at or about mid-day.

II.

We reject the argument of Local 100 that it was denied its Sixth and Fourteenth Amendment rights to a jury trial in connection with the contempt hearing.

A.

Enacted in 1967 to succeed the Condon-Wadlin Act, the. . . . Taylor Law prohibits strikes against public employers by unions representing public employees. . . .

[T]he Court of Appeals [has] held that neither public employees nor their unions are entitled, as a matter of right, to a jury trial in a criminal contempt proceeding brought against them for violation of an anti-strike injunction entered under the Taylor Law (see *Rankin v Shanker*, 23 N.Y.2d 111). The Court reviewed the statute and its history, and concluded that there was no legislative intent to grant such a right. There was "at least one vital reason" why trial by jury was not, in the view of the Court of Appeals, desirable in the context of determining sanctions for the violation of an anti-strike injunction entered against public employees or their representative unions. "Prompt determinations," said the Court, "unencumbered by the long, drawn-out procedures involved in jury trials, are needed in criminal contempt proceedings under the Taylor Law in order to deter the continuance of paralyzing public strikes by visiting speedy punishment on the offenders." In addition to rejecting the appellants' state-law argument in favor of the right to a jury trial, the *Rankin* Court rejected various federal law contentions, including the appellants' argument that the Sixth and Fourteenth Amendments of the United States Constitution required that they be tried by a jury. Reviewing federal precedents, . . . the Court of Appeals concluded that the right to a jury trial was confined to "serious" crimes, as opposed to "petty offenses." Punishment imposed for criminal contempts may be incarceration or a fine. The Court in *Rankin* noted that, for purposes of federal law, the Supreme Court had concluded that a sentence of imprisonment of six months is short enough to be petty. Under federal law, it is now clear that any offense for which a sentence of more than six months may be imposed requires a jury trial (see *United Mine Workers of America v Bagwell*, 512 US 821, 826). . . .

Rankin, which concerned a teachers' strike, involved a fine on the subject union of $10,000 per day (or 1/52 of the union's total annual membership dues, whichever was less), and the Court found that it was not serious as a matter of law, adopting the then-prevailing federal, bright-line rule that the serious/petty distinction was only relevant where a prison sentence was at issue. . . . A fine, "even though sizeable in amount, furnishes no valid criterion for the [appellants'] claim that the contempt charged against them constitutes a serious crime."

In light of *Rankin*, Local 100 does not contend that the Taylor Law accorded it the right to a jury trial. Nor does it argue that the New York State Constitution did so. It limits its argument to the Sixth and Fourteenth Amendments of the United States Constitution, and relies on *United Mine Workers of America v Bagwell* decided 26 years after *Rankin*. . . . *Bagwell* held that the imposition of serious criminal contempt fines, without an accompanying prison term, constitutionally requires a jury trial if demanded. Thus, in light of *Bagwell*, we must update *Rankin* to the extent of determining whether, as applied to the facts of this Taylor Law case, the Sixth and Fourteenth Amendments of the United States Constitution required a trial by jury of the contempt issue.

B.

We note that the Sixth Amendment right to a jury trial in a contempt proceeding arises only in criminal, as opposed to civil, contempt cases. . . . As is clear from a reading of *Bagwell*, drawing the distinction between the two types of contempt is not always straightforward, and even where one may conclude that the contempt at issue is criminal, the jury-trial right attaches only in the case of "serious" crimes. . . . Although the plaintiffs moved in the Supreme Court to impose a sanction for Local 100's alleged "criminal" contempt . . . [i]t is the substance of the proceeding and the character of the relief that is critical and controlling. . . .

Bagwell involved the violation by a union of an injunction in the coal mining industry, and the issue presented was whether $52 million in fines levied against the petitioner unions were "coercive" civil, as opposed to criminal, fines.

. . . [*Bagwell* involved seven] contempt hearings, which were not held before a jury, as a result of which the unions were found in contempt for over 400 separate violations of the injunction. The court imposed more than $64 million in fines on the unions about $12 million of which was to be paid to the companies. The remaining $52 million was to be paid to the Commonwealth of Virginia. . . .

. . . [T]he Supreme Court of Virginia ultimately rejected the contention that the $52 million fine, payable to the Commonwealth, was criminal in nature, and thus could not be imposed without the protections normally accorded in a criminal trial. . . .

The United States Supreme Court reversed. The Supreme Court initially reviewed some general principles, which we review as well. . . .

A contempt sanction is viewed as civil if it is "remedial," and for the benefit of the complainant, but is criminal if its purpose is punitive, and to "vindicate the authority of the court". . . . Coercive penalties designed to modify the contemnor's behavior, generally speaking, are civil in nature, while penalties meant to punish the contemnor for past acts of disobedience are criminal.

Contempt sanctions may involve imprisonment or fines. The sanction of imprisonment is not necessarily criminal. For example, imprisonment for a fixed term, during which the contemnor may "purge" the contempt and obtain early release by committing an affirmative act, is a coercive, civil penalty. A fixed sentence of imprisonment is viewed as criminal if imposed retrospectively for a completed act of disobedience, and where the contemnor cannot shorten or avoid prison through later compliance. . . .

Making the distinction between civil and criminal contempts is not a mere formalistic exercise. If the contempt is characterized as criminal, then greater procedural protections apply, such as, among other things, the right to have the contempt proved beyond a reasonable doubt, and the right to the assistance of counsel.

Once it is determined that a contempt sanction is criminal, however, the Sixth Amendment right to a jury trial does not automatically attach. An additional inquiry must be made, and that is whether the offense is "serious" or "petty"—if the latter, the right to a jury trial is not applicable. Where the criminal contempt sanction is imprisonment, the serious/petty distinction is triggered at imprisonment of six months; the right to a jury trial attaches only where the term is more than six months. Where the criminal contempt sanction is a fine, there is no bright-line rule governing the distinction.

. . . *Bagwell* concluded that the $52 million fine was criminal in nature, for several reasons. The Court observed that neither the parties nor any court had suggested that the fines there involved were compensatory. . . . Also of relevance was the fact that the injunction the unions violated was, in effect, a "detailed code of conduct" the court had imposed. The unions' contumacy, according to the Court, did not involve "simple, affirmative" acts. Rather, the state court "levied contempt fines for widespread, ongoing, out-of-court violations of a complex injunction". . . . The contumacy lasted months, and evidently "spanned a substantial portion" of the Commonwealth of Virginia. . . . In addition, the fine imposed—$52 million—was . . . "unquestionably . . . serious." Each of the foregoing factors combined to mandate "disinterested factfinding and evenhanded adjudication"—that is, a trial by jury.

We now turn to the application of *Bagwell* to the facts of this case.

C.

. . . In light of the fact that the relevant branch of the plaintiffs' motion sought an "immediate" fine of $1 million for the December 20, 2005, violation of the anti-strike injunction, which had already occurred prior to making of the motion and the Supreme Court's ruling thereon, and then a doubling of the fine for each day the local's disobedience persisted, we conclude that the fines imposed in this case had both a retrospective, criminal component as well as a prospective, civil component. Part of the fines imposed were designed to punish Local 100 for violation of the preliminary injunction that occurred prior to the contempt adjudication, and the remaining part was designed to compel the local to end the strike and get the transit system up and running.

The latter portion was, in our view, civil in nature. It could have been avoided had the local directed its members back to work once the Supreme Court issued its judgment. . . . We conclude that this portion of the fine was in the nature of a coercive, per diem sanction meant to compel Local 100 to alter its conduct to comply with the December 13, 2005, order. We also note that unlike the situation in *Bagwell*, the December 13, 2005, order was basically a "no-strike" injunction. As such, while it certainly was meant to direct Local 100's members back to work, it was not in any way akin to the "detailed code of conduct" imposed by the Virginia court in *Bagwell* which the contempt hearing was designed to "police." . . .

Thus, under the circumstances of this case, there was no Sixth Amendment right to a jury trial in connection with the prospective portion of the Supreme Court's sanction. There was such a right in connection with the retrospective portion only if the fine involved was "serious."

Of course, our characterization raises the question of precisely what part of the total fines ultimately imposed pertains to Local 100's pre-judgment conduct, and what part to the post-judgment conduct. . . . [E]ven assuming the criminal contempt fine was the full per diem amount of $1 million, given Local 100's financial circumstances and its ability to spread the fine over an extremely large membership, it was not "serious" within the meaning of the jury trial contempt case law. . . . We see no reason why Local 100 may not satisfy the criminal portion of the contempt fine imposed upon it by spreading the cost over its membership, which would require each member of Local 100 to pay about $30. . . . We further note that Local 100 has substantial assets, put at about $3.6 million on its calendar year 2004 Department of Labor financial statement—and that does not include the valuable West End Avenue real estate which its counsel conceded the local indirectly owns. . . . We conclude that the foregoing is not a "serious" penalty that requires a jury trial before it may be imposed. . . .

III.

We disagree with Local 100's contention that it was entitled to have a jury consider the issue of the MTA's alleged "extreme provocation." Local 100 argues that the MTA's insistence that the local agree to changes in the pension system was improper, as pension changes are a prohibited subject of collective bargaining. . . . As such, the local further contends that the MTA's proposal demonstrated a failure to bargain in good faith, constituted "extreme provocation," and should have been considered by a jury in mitigation of the fines imposed. Even if we assume that the MTA's pension proposal for new hires constituted "extreme provocation"—a proposition with which we do not agree—we note that, as Meginniss conceded at the hearing, it does not constitute a legal defense to a motion to hold a public-employee association in contempt for violating the no-strike provisions of a preliminary injunction order. Nor is it a basis for mitigation of the contempt fines. As further discussed below, under Judiciary Law § 751(2)(a), "extreme provocation" is a discretionary factor to be considered in the fixing of the contempt fine. . . .

In addition, the fines imposed were not excessive. Judiciary Law § 751(2)(a) authorizes the court, in a case growing out of a strike held in violation of Civil Service Law § 210, to punish a public-employee union that willfully disobeys a mandate of the court with, inter alia, "a fine fixed in the discretion of the court." Such a fine may include a fine for "each day that such contempt persists." In fixing the amount of the fine, the court is directed to consider all the facts and circumstances directly related to the contempt, including, but not limited to: (1) the extent of the willful defiance of or a resistance to the court's mandate, (2) the impact of the strike on the public health, safety, and welfare of the community, and (3) the ability of the employee organization to pay the fine imposed. . . . In addition, the court is has the discretion to consider, as additional factors, whether either the union or the employer refused to submit to mediation and, if alleged by the union, whether the employer "engaged in such acts of extreme provocation as to detract from the responsibility of the employee organization for the strike."

In the instant dispute, the Supreme Court stated on the record that it had considered the statutory factors "very carefully." Based upon our independent review of the record, we conclude that the court providently exercised its discretion in connection with the amount of the fines imposed. . . . Moreover, the determination made by the Supreme Court was in line with the fines imposed upon similarly-situated public employee unions held to have violated similar court mandates (see . . . *Burns Jackson Miller Summit & Spitzer v Lindner*, 88 AD.2d 50, 55 aff'd 59 NY2d 314. . . .)

In particular, we note that in the context of the 11-day April 1980 transit strike, Local 100 was fined $750,000 (see *Burns Jackson Miller Summit & Spitzer, supra* at 55). We are not persuaded that 25 years later, the fine imposed here for a 2 1/2-day strike just prior to the holiday season of 2005 was, under the circumstances, in any way excessive. . . .

Notes

1. For more details on the 2005 TWU strike, see RICCUCI, NAFF, ET AL., *supra*, 473–75; Erin Russ, *Strike Three—You're Out! Revamping the New York State Taylor Law in Response to Three Transport Workers' Strikes*, 9 CARDOZO J. CONFLICT RESOL. 163 (2007).

2. Individuals may be liable in contempt as well. For example, a related proceeding, *New York City Transit Authority v. Transport Workers Union of America*, 39 NYPER ¶ 7510 (N.Y. Sup. Ct. Apr. 19, 2006), held the following about TWU officials involved in the 2005 strike:

> Finally, the court turns to plaintiffs' application . . . for an order holding certain individual officers of Local 100, specifically Roger Toussaint, President of Local 100, Ed Wall, Secretary-Treasurer of Local 100, and Darlyne

Lawson, Recording Secretary of Local 100, to be in contempt of the court's December 13, 2005 order.

In proceedings before the court on April 10, 2006, Mr. Toussaint, Mr. Watt, and Ms. Lawson, through counsel, conceded and otherwise did not contest the fact that they acted in willful defiance of the court's December 13, 2005 preliminary injunction order. Consequently, the only issue before the court is the appropriate penalty for this contempt.

Judiciary Law § 751(1) states in relevant part that "punishment for a contempt . . . may be by fine, not exceeding one thousand dollars, or by imprisonment, not exceeding thirty days . . . or both, in the discretion of the court." Where individual officers of a union willfully disobey a court's order precluding them from striking in violation of the Taylor Law, both fines and incarceration may be appropriate punishments. . . . In fact, incarceration may be warranted even when the legal officer for the government entity involved in the case does not seek such a sanction. . . . Given the circumstances of this case, and in particular, the individuals' willful disobedience of the court's preliminary injunction order, the following penalties are hereby imposed with respect to: (1) Mr. Toussaint, a fine of $1,000.00 . . . and 10 days incarceration; (2) Mr. Watt, a fine of $500.00; and (3) Ms. Lawson, a fine of $500.00.

(iii.) Dues Forfeitures

MTA Bus Company v. Transport Workers Union of America

New York Supreme Court
12 Misc. 3d 943, 820 N.Y.S.2d 479 (2006)

. . . Plaintiff moves for an order, pursuant to § 34 of Chapter 929 of the Laws of 1986 (hereafter, § 34) and Civil Service Law § 210(3), imposing forfeiture of the dues deduction right of Local 100. In support of this motion, plaintiff points out that Civil Service Law § 210(3)(f) specifically requires that, where PERB determines that an employee organization has violated Civil Service Law § 210(1), PERB "shall order the forfeiture of the [employee organization's dues collection rights] for such period of time as the board shall determine, or in the discretion of [PERB], for an indefinite period of time subject to restoration upon application." Plaintiff further argues that, in enacting § 34, the Legislature specifically transferred the responsibility and jurisdiction for enforcing Civil Service Law § 210(3) from PERB to the court. . . .

With respect to the duration of the dues forfeiture, plaintiff maintains that the court should order an indefinite forfeiture, which should only be terminated after Local 100 demonstrates a sufficient period of good faith compliance with the mandates of the Taylor Law. In the alternative, plaintiff avers that the court should order a forfeiture for a definite period of time. . . . Finally, plaintiff suggests that, since the court has already determined that Local 100 violated Civil Service Law § 210(1), and evidence has already been presented (at the December 20, 2005 contempt hearing) regarding the impact of the strike, the extent of the union's defiance and the financial resources of Local 100, no new hearing is necessary prior to the imposition of the forfeiture sanction. . . .

In further opposition to plaintiff's motion for the imposition of a dues forfeiture sanction, Local 100 argues that even if MTA Bus is entitled to this relief, the court must conduct a hearing prior to determining the duration of this forfeiture penalty. In this regard, Local 100 notes that Civil Service Law § 210(3)(d) specifically requires that a hearing be conducted before the court determines the duration of the forfeiture. In addition, Local 100 avers that the previous contempt hearings are insufficient to satisfy the hearing requirement set forth in Civil Service Law § 210(3)(d) since Local 100's financial resources (which the court must consider in setting the duration of the forfeiture) have changed since the December 2005 contempt hearings. Furthermore, Local 100 maintains that there are mitigating factors, including provocation on the part of plaintiff, which the court should consider prior to determining the duration of the forfeiture. . . .

[T]he court agrees with Local 100 that, prior to setting the duration of any dues forfeiture, hearings must be conducted wherein the court must consider the extent of Local 100's willful defiance of Civil Service Law § 210(1), the impact of the strike on the public health, safety, and welfare of the community, as well as the financial resources of Local 100. . . . Moreover, while it is true that the court conducted similar hearings in connection with the December 2005 contempt proceedings, this does not obviate the need for a new hearing on the matter since the financial condition of Local 100 may have changed in the ensuing months and new evidence should be certainly available regarding the actual impact of the strike upon the community welfare. However, since the factors which the court must weigh in the contempt and dues check-off proceedings are nearly identical, the court will consider the evidence and record accumulated in the December 20, 2005 contempt proceeding in reaching a determination regarding the appropriate duration of the forfeiture of Local 100's dues check-off rights.

On April 7, 10, 11, 12, and 17, 2006, the court conducted hearings in order to determine whether the imposition of a forfeiture sanction against Local 100 was warranted, and if so, what the appropriate duration of such a sanction should be. . . . [T]he court has determined that, pursuant to Civil Service Law § 210(3) and § 34, such a sanction is not only warranted, but in fact, required by law.

Turning to the issue of the appropriate duration of the forfeiture sanction, the court initially notes that, under Civil Service Law § 210(3)(f), in making a determination in this regard, the court must consider the extent of Local 100's willful defiance of Civil Service Law § 210(1), the impact of the strike on the public health, safety, and welfare of the community, and the financial resources of the employee organization. In addition, the court may consider any other factors that it considers relevant including whether the public employer (i.e., the plaintiffs) engaged in "acts of extreme provocation as to detract from the responsibility of [Local 100] for the strike."

Accordingly, at the April 2006 hearings, as well as the December 20, 2005 contempt hearing, evidence in the form of sworn witness testimony, affidavits, reports, and letters were presented to the court regarding the above stated required factors and the court has given due consideration to such evidence. Moreover, the court has considered Local 100's conduct with respect to prior contract negotiations including an 11 day transit strike in 1980 as well as conduct which necessitated the issuance of preliminary injunctions in 1999 and 2002 (see Matter of Webutuck Teachers Assn., 13 PERB ¶ 3041 [1980] wherein PERB noted that it generally imposed a more severe penalty for a second violation of the Taylor Law . . .). In addition, evidence regarding Local 100's efforts to mitigate the effect of the strike, by safeguarding transit facilities and equipment and by ensuring that all bus and train operators finished their appointed runs prior to walking off the job was presented to the court, and the court has considered this factor in determining the appropriate duration of the forfeiture sanction.

Finally, during the course of the hearings, Local 100 called numerous witnesses and presented various documentary evidence in an effort to establish that the plaintiff engaged in acts of "extreme provocation" during the course of the contract negotiations leading up to the strike. Although not required to do so, the court was prepared to consider this factor in determining the duration of the dues forfeiture sanction. However, none of the plaintiff's actions which came to light during the course of the hearings qualify as such extreme provocation. . . . Indeed, much of what occurred merely amounted to the type of routine posturing and strategic ploys that are typical in employment contract negotiations, particularly between parties (such as plaintiff and Local 100) which have an acrimonious history. Furthermore, even Local 100's more legitimate complaints, such as plaintiff's insistence that Local 100 place the issue of pensions on the bargaining table, do not qualify as extreme provocation. In this regard, Local 100 could and should have resolved this matter by appealing to PERB rather than engaging in an unlawful and crippling transit strike during the holiday season.

Accordingly, having conducted the hearing, and after considering all the mandatory factors set forth in Civil Service Law § 210(3)(f), as well as all other relevant and mitigating factors, the court hereby imposes upon Local 100 an indefinite term of forfeiture commencing 30 days after entry of this order, unless Local 100 makes an application within said 30-day period with respect to the commencement date of the forfeiture sanction. Local 100 may seek reinstatement of its dues check-off right no earlier than three months after implementation of the forfeiture sanction. At that time, Local 100 may appear before this court, and upon a showing of good faith compliance with the mandates of the Taylor Law, and submission of an affirmation that it no longer asserts the right to strike . . . apply for reinstatement of its right to have the employers automatically deduct membership dues from the paychecks of union members.

Notes

1. How long should dues forfeitures last? It depends in part on the extent of the union's bad behavior. *In the Matter of City of New Rochelle and Uniformed Fire Fighters Ass'n, Inc., Local 273 of the IAFF*, 35 NYPER ¶ 3005 (PERB 2002) reasoned as follows:

> [W]e find the Association violated § 210.1 of the Act in that it engaged in a strike as charged. We further find that the public inconvenience was limited to the financial impact of calling in additional firefighters on overtime; that the parties are now attempting to repair their damaged labor relationship; and that, as there is no evidence that the Association has previously engaged in any strike activity, a suspension of the dues and agency shop fee deductions of six (6) months is a reasonable one and will effectuate the policies of the Act.

2. The employer's behavior is also relevant. *In the Matter of Buffalo Teachers Federation*, 16 NYPER ¶ 3018 (PERB 1983) held that in light of the employer school district's acts of "extreme provocation" during the negotiations that preceded a teachers' strike, the union's dues deduction and agency shop fee privileges should be suspended only for a definite period of six months, rather than for indefinite period of not less than 18 months. Eighteen months would have been the usual penalty assessed against a union that, as here, had engaged in a previous illegal strike. What counts as "extreme provocation"? In *Buffalo Teachers Federation*, the employer violated its duty to bargain in good faith in a number of ways. Given that, was *MTA Bus Company* right to hold that it was not extreme provocation for the employer to insist that the union negotiate over an illegal topic of bargaining?

3. Is forfeiture of dues deduction an appropriate penalty? Who really gets hurt? *United Federation of Teachers, Local 2, NYSUT, AFT*, 15 NYPER ¶ 3091 (PERB 1982) reduced the duration of a dues forfeiture penalty because the union had lost so much income it was no longer able to represent its members effectively. The union had lost 30 percent of its normal income, and thus had to reduce services to bargaining unit members, including temporarily closing its borough offices through which it provided various representation services, and laying off staff members. Is this different from weighing a union's finances to determine the amount of a fine?

4. Perhaps the most famous example of penalties for an illegal public-sector strike occurred in 1981 when the Professional Air Traffic Controllers Union (PATCO) struck in violation of the federal sector labor law. First, President Reagan fired all the strikers (the harshest available penalty). Then, after the strike, the FLRA decertified PATCO. *See PATCO v. FLRA*, 685 F.2d 547 (D.C. Cir. 1982). Additionally, the Office of Personnel Management, pursuant to a directive from President Reagan, declared that all PATCO strikers were barred indefinitely from employment with the Federal Aviation Administration (FAA). The FAA also inserted into its contracts with private employers a clause barring those companies from employing any former PATCO striker. These policies remained in place until 1993 when President Clinton

repealed them. *See Clarry v. United States*, 85 F.3d 1041 (2d Cir. 1996) (upholding the FAA's actions). A number of PATCO's leaders were prosecuted criminally.

The reaction to the PATCO strike was widely interpreted as "sending a signal" to the private sector and ushering in a new era of aggressive anti-union tactics. *See, e.g.,* JOSEPH MCCARTIN, COLLISION COURSE: RONALD REAGAN, THE AIR TRAFFIC CONTROLLERS, AND THE STRIKE THAT CHANGED AMERICA (2011).

5. Before the PATCO strike, perhaps the most significant modern public-sector strike was the postal workers strike of 1970, which involved around 200,000 postal workers. President Nixon declared a national emergency, sending 27,500 National Guard members to sort and deliver mail in New York City. Soon after the strike, the Postal Reorganization Act was passed. This law, among other things, permitted postal workers to bargain about wages, which previously had been set by law. But it remains illegal for these workers to strike. RICCUCI, NAFF, ET AL., *supra*, 478–79.

c. Private Suits

Burns Jackson Miller Summit & Spitzer v. Lindner

New York Court of Appeals
59 N.Y.2d 314, 464 N.Y.S.2d 712, 451 N.E.2d 459 (1983)

MEYER, J.

. . . This appeal involves separate action[s] by two New York City law firms to recover damages resulting from the April, 1980 transit strike. The first, begun in Queens County by Burns Jackson Miller Summit & Spitzer ("Burns Jackson"), is a class action against the Transport Workers Union of America, AFL-CIO (TWU), the Amalgamated Transit Union, AFL-CIO (ATU), Local 100 of TWU, Locals 726 and 1056 of ATU and their respective officers. It alleges that the strike was intentional and in violation of both section 210 of the Civil Service Law and of a preliminary injunction issued March 31, 1980 by the Supreme Court and seeks damages of $50,000,000 per day for each day of the strike. The complaint sets forth two causes of action: prima facie tort and public nuisance.

The second action, begun in New York County by Jackson, Lewis, Schnitzler and Krupman ("Jackson, Lewis"), likewise alleges an intentional strike in violation of the statute and preliminary injunction. It was, however, brought only against the TWU and its Local 100, and officers of both, sought but $25,000 in damages, and did not ask class action status. It declared on six causes of action: for violation of the Taylor Law, prima facie tort, intentional interference with plaintiff's business, willful injury, conspiracy and breach of plaintiff's rights as third-party beneficiary of the contract between defendant unions and the New York City Transit Authority (NYCTA) and the Manhattan and Bronx Surface Transit Operating Authority (MABSTOA).

. . . [The Appellate Division] in an extensive opinion, modified the order appealed from to dismiss both complaints in their entirety. . . . We conclude (1) that the Taylor Law was neither intended to proscribe private damage actions by persons caused injury by a strike by public employees nor to establish a new private right of action for such damages, and (2) that the complaints fail to state a cause of action for (a) prima facie tort, (b) public nuisance, (c) intentional interference with business, or (d) breach of plaintiffs' rights as third-party beneficiary of defendants' contracts with NYCTA or MABSTOA. We, therefore, affirm.

The effect of the Taylor Law, whether as preemptive of previously permissible private damage actions or as initiating a new form of private action for damages resulting from a strike in violation of its provisions, turns on what the Legislature intended. The general rule is and long has been that "when the common law gives a remedy, and another remedy is provided by statute, the latter is cumulative, unless made exclusive by the statute". . . .

Absent explicit legislative direction, however, it is for the courts to determine, in light of those provisions, particularly those relating to sanctions and enforcement, and their legislative history, and of existing common-law and statutory remedies, with which legislative familiarity is presumed, what the Legislature intended. . . . Whether a private cause of action was intended will turn in the first instance on whether the plaintiff is "one of the class for whose especial benefit the statute was enacted." . . . But the inquiry does not, as plaintiffs suggest, end there, for to do so would consider but one of the factors involved in the Legislature's determination. Important also are what indications there are in the statute or its legislative history of an intent to create (or conversely to deny) such a remedy and, most importantly, the consistency of doing so with the purposes underlying the legislative scheme.

Analysis begins, of course, with the statute itself. It contains no explicit statement as to either exclusivity or intent to create a private cause of action. Examination of the history and genesis of the Taylor Law leads us to conclude, however, that it is cumulative, not exclusive, and was not intended to establish a new cause of action.

New York's first statutory proscription against strikes by public employees was the Condon-Wadlin Act, passed in 1947 as a result of a strike by public school teachers in Buffalo. . . . It punished violation by automatic termination, and imposed severe restrictions on re-employment, precluding salary increases for a re-employed striker for three years and requiring that the re-employed person be treated as probationary for five years. . . . [T]he harshness of its penalties resulted in their being enforced but twice over a period of 20 years . . . and in widespread criticism and agitation for revision. . . .

On January 15, 1966, prompted by a massive strike of New York City transit workers which began January 1, 1966, Governor Rockefeller appointed a Committee on Public Employee Relations, chaired by Professor George W. Taylor. The committee was charged "to make legislative proposals for protecting the public against the disruption of vital public services by illegal strikes, while at the same time protecting the rights of public employees". . . .

The Taylor Law, . . . effective September 1, 1967 . . . continued the prohibition against public employee strikes (§ 210) but replaced Condon-Wadlin's harsh penalties with provisions for injunction without limitation on the fine for violation . . . and for discipline of individual strikers under section 75 of the Civil Service Law. It subjected the employee organization, however, only to forfeiture of dues checkoff for a period limited to 18 months . . .

Nevertheless, a number of changes were made in the act in 1969. . . . Striking employees became subject not only to disciplinary action but also to a one-year probationary period and the deduction of two days' pay for each day of violation was reinstated. . . . The imposition of penalties against employees and employee organizations was made mandatory. . . .

The same act made clear, however, the Legislature's intent to protect employee organizations from destruction, even though they may have participated in an illegal strike. Thus, although the 18-month limitation on forfeiture of the union's dues deduction privilege was removed, both that provision . . . and section 751 . . . (dealing with the fines imposable for criminal contempt) were amended to make the union's ability to pay a factor in the determination of the penalty to be assessed.

Against that background, for a number of reasons, legislative intent to provide a private remedy cannot be discerned. Although Jackson, Lewis is "one of the class for whose especial benefit the statute was enacted" and a right of action in a member of the class may be implied when clearly in furtherance of the legislative purpose . . . the provisions of the present statute and the history of their enactment strongly suggest that a private action based upon the statute was not intended. True such an action would be a powerful deterrent to public employee strikes, but it would also, as the claim for damages in the Burns Jackson complaint suggests, impose a crushing burden on the unions and each of the employees participating in the strike, who could be held jointly and severally liable with the union for the damages resulting from violation. . . . It would do so, moreover, notwithstanding that the penalties of the Condon-Wadlin Act were repealed "precisely because that was a statute punitive rather than constructive in nature" . . . notwithstanding the "unusually elaborate enforcement provisions, conferring authority to sue for this purpose both on government officials and private citizens" which strongly suggest that the Legislature "provided precisely the remedies it considered appropriate" and notwithstanding the 1966 decision in *Jamur Prods. Corp. v. Quill*, 273 N.Y.S.2d 348, which had held that a private cause of action could not be implied from the Condon-Wadlin Act.

Implication of a private action is, moreover, inconsistent with the purposes of the Taylor Law. Its primary purposes, as both Taylor Committee reports emphasize, was to defuse the tensions in public employer-employee relations by reducing the penalties and increasing reliance on negotiation and the newly created Public Employment Relations Board as a vehicle toward labor peace. . . . A private action, which would impose per se liability without any of the limitations applicable to the common-law forms of action hereafter considered, would inevitably upset the delicate balance established after 20 years of legislative pondering. As the Washington Supreme Court has noted, "the schemes created by statute for collective bargaining and dispute resolution must be allowed to function as intended, without the added coercive power of the courts being thrown into the balance on one side or the other" (*Burke & Thomas v. International Organization of Masters, Mates & Pilots*, 92 Wash.2d 762, 772; accord *Lamphere Schools v. Lamphere Federation of Teachers*, 400 Mich. 104). Having explicitly directed that in assessing penalties PERB and the courts consider the union's ability to pay and refused to enact a decertification provision, the Legislature must be deemed to have negated the unlimited liability, not only to third parties but to public employers as well, and the consequent demise of public employee unions, that would result from recognition of a new statutory cause of action.

That no new per se action was contemplated by the Legislature does not, however, require us to conclude that the traditional, though more limited, forms of action are no longer available to redress injury resulting from violation of the statute. The penalties imposable by PERB and the courts for such a violation provide some solace, but no recompense, for those injured by acts which not only violate the statute but also constitute a breach of duty, independent of the statute, which common-law remedies made compensable. Although it is within the competence of the Legislature to abolish common-law causes of action . . . there is no express provision to that effect in the statute. . . . It is one thing to conclude that limitation of penalties payable to the public treasury and denial of a decertification sanction are inconsistent with the imposition of a new strict liability cause of action, and quite another to conclude that persons damaged by action tortious before public strikes were declared illegal should be denied the recompense to which they would be otherwise entitled in the interest of labor peace. . . .

The conclusion that the statute is not exclusive requires that we consider the common-law causes of action asserted in the two complaints, the allegations of which are for purposes of such consideration deemed true. . . .

The cause of action common to the two complaints is that in prima facie tort. The elements of such a cause of action as stated in prior New York cases are (1) intentional infliction of harm, (2) resulting in special damages, (3) without excuse or justification, and (4) by an act or series of acts that would otherwise be lawful. . . . Plaintiff suggests, however, that it is anomalous to deny a cause of action on the ground that the injury-causing act was *un*lawful. . . .

We need not now decide whether an unlawful act can be the predicate for prima facie tort, for there is no recovery in prima facie tort unless malevolence is the sole motive for defendant's otherwise lawful act or, in Justice Holmes' characteristically colorful language, unless defendant acts from "disinterested malevolence" . . . by which is meant "that the genesis which will make a lawful act unlawful must be a malicious one unmixed with any other and exclusively directed to injury and damage of another". . . .

Here the prima facie tort causes of action cannot stand because, although they allege intentional and malicious action, they do not allege that defendants' sole motivation was "disinterested malevolence."

The Burns Jackson complaint alleges in its second cause of action that the strike engaged in by defendants "caused widespread economic dislocation and damage and substantial interference with the public health, safety, comfort and convenience within the New York City metropolitan area, thereby creating a nuisance." Although the allegation of substantial interference with the common rights of the public at large is a sufficient predicate for a private action based on public nuisance . . . and additional expense in the performance of a specific contract can constitute the "private and peculiar injury" required for a private action . . . it is, nevertheless, true that the harm suffered must be "of a different kind from that suffered by other persons exercising the same public right" and that "invasions of rights common to all of the public should be left to be remedied by action by public officials" (Restatements, Torts 2d, § 821C, Comment *b*; . . . .)

The damages here alleged are for additional out-of-pocket expenses resulting from defendants' conduct and for loss of business profits. Such damages, though differing as to the nature of the expense or the particular contract from which greater profit was expected, were, as the Appellate Division noted, suffered by every person, firm and corporation conducting his or its business or profession in the City of New York. Indeed, the class as envisioned by plaintiff's complaint consists of "professional and business entities conducted for profit . . . that rely on the public transportation system serving the City of New York to enable them to practice their profession and to operate their businesses and that have been damaged as a consequence of the defendants' disruption of the service provided by that system."

When the injury claimed to be peculiar is of the same kind suffered by all who are affected, when it "is common to the entire community" . . . or, as Prosser put it . . . "it becomes so general and widespread as to affect a whole community," the injury is not peculiar and the action cannot be maintained. The economic loss which results from a transit strike is not recoverable in a private action for public nuisance because the class includes all members of the public who are affected by the strike. . . .

The two remaining causes of action may be dealt with more summarily. Jackson, Lewis' brief devotes but a two-sentence footnote to its third cause of action for intentional interference with business. The complaint alleges that defendants "intentionally and maliciously interfered with the business of the plaintiff" to plaintiff's special damage in that the productivity of partners and employees was reduced and extra expense incurred. What is apparently sought to be pleaded, therefore, is a claim within section 766A of the Restatement of Torts, Second, for causing plaintiff's performance of its contracts with its clients to be more expensive or burdensome.

No New York case recognizing such a cause of action has been cited or has been found by us. We need not, however, now decide whether such a cause of action should be recognized by us in other situations. The interference here alleged was but an incidental result of defendants' conduct and, although that conduct was in violation of the Taylor Law, we conclude that as a matter of policy we should not recognize a common-law cause of action for such incidental interference when the Legislature has, in establishing an otherwise comprehensive labor plan for the governance of public employer-employee relations, failed to do so. . . .

The Jackson, Lewis contract cause of action alleges that contracts existed between defendant unions and NYCTA and MABSTOA up to and including March 31, 1980, that they continued by operation of law until negotiation of successor agreements ended, that between April 1 and April 11, 1980, defendants and their members engaged in a strike against NYCTA and MABSTOA in violation of the contracts, that plaintiff is a third-party beneficiary of the contracts and that plaintiff was damaged by their breach.

A third party may be the beneficiary of a public as well as a private contract. . . . He may recover, however, only by establishing (1) the existence of a valid and binding contract between other parties, (2) that the contract was intended for his benefit and (3) that the benefit to him is sufficiently immediate, rather than incidental, to indicate the assumption by the contracting parties of a duty to compensate him if the benefit is lost. . . .

Existence of a valid and binding contract is, thus, a *sine qua non*. . . . Here, however, the complaint itself states that the contracts expired on March 31, 1980. . . . The contracts having expired before the strike, any rights of plaintiff as a third-party beneficiary of them expired with it.

. . . Further reason why Jackson, Lewis' contract cause of action cannot succeed is that plaintiff is but an incidental beneficiary of the collective bargaining agreement . . . the "intention to assume an obligation of indefinite extension to every member of the public . . . [being] the more improbable when we recall the crushing burden that the obligation would impose". . . .

Notes

1. This case represents the majority rule. For example, *White v. Int'l Ass'n of Firefighters, Local 42*, 738 S.W.2d 933 (Mo. Ct. App. 1987), held that a suit by private plaintiffs who had suffered property damage from a fire during an illegal firefighter's strike did not state a valid claim. *White* sounded a recurring theme in the majority approach: the state legislature had balanced the proper amounts of penalties in the labor statute, and allowing private suits would disturb the balance and interfere with public employer-employee relations and labor peace. *White* also explained that numerous private civil actions could inhibit effective firefighting, as the potential liability of individual firefighters would discourage people joining the profession. Further, strikes could be prolonged, as unions would insist on indemnifications from tort actions as a condition of settling the matter. Also, the private parties were not members of a class for whose especial benefit the public-sector law was enacted.

For a similar holding, *see Jackson v. Chicago Firefighters Union, Local No. 2*, 160 Ill. App. 3d 975 (1987).

2. For the minority approach, see *Boyle v. Anderson Firefighters Ass'n Local 1262*, 497 N.E.2d 1073 (Ind. Ct. App. 1986). *Boyle* held that because a firefighter's strike was illegal, the strikers owed a duty to property owners (i) not to strike or (ii) to fight fires. Therefore, the strikers could be held individually liable for damages proximately caused by their breach of that duty.

3. Whether the struck *employer* can recover in tort against illegally striking unions is a different issue. For example, *White, supra*, distinguished *State v. Kansas City Firefighters Local 42*, 672 S.W.2d 99 (Mo. Ct. App. 1984), which had held that a public employer could bring a valid tort suit against a union for damages it incurred because of an illegal strike. The employer *was* a member of the class for whose especial benefit the public-sector law was passed. *See also Coons by Coons v. Kaiser*, 567 N.E.2d 851 (Ind. Ct. App. 1991) (only a public employer could sue teachers for illegally striking, and thus an individual student could not sue the teachers for deprivation of education or emotional distress); *Franklin Township Bd. of Educ. v. Quakertown Educ. Ass'n*, 643 A.2d 34 (N.J. Super. Ct. App. Div. 1994) (allowing a tort suit by the employer against striking teachers). What sort of damages might an employer be able to recover in such a suit?

4. Some jurisdictions hold that employers cannot sue the union in tort either. Again, the theory is that the legislature balanced the interests when it determined the penalties and remedies available under the labor statute and allowing additional damages would disturb that balance. *See, e.g., City and County of San Francisco v. United Ass'n of Journeyman and Apprentices of the Plumbing and Pipefitting Industry of the United States and Canada, Local 38*, 42 Cal. 3d 810 (1986).

5. What are the best arguments for and against allowing private parties to sue in tort? For allowing the employer to sue in tort?

B. Alternative Impasse Resolution Procedures

1. Overview and Mediation

The aversion of U.S. policy-makers to public-sector strikes has led to the creation of alternative processes for dealing with bargaining impasses. These typically involve mediation, fact-finding, and/or interest arbitration. In many jurisdictions, some or all of these procedures are mandatory when the parties are at impasse, and in many jurisdictions (although not all) interest arbitration results in a labor contract that is binding on the parties. Even jurisdictions that permit some public employees to strike often require them to go through mediation and/or fact-finding before striking. These alternate forms of impasse resolution are central to public-sector labor law.

Mediation involves a third party, with no power to impose a contract, meeting with the parties to try to work out a voluntary agreement. Mediators are sometimes private parties simply chosen by the parties, but more often, state agencies or the Federal Mediation and Conciliation Service (FMCS) supplies them. As of 2012, 36 states used mediation for at least some public-sector impasses. In many jurisdictions, either party may invoke mediation; in some, both must request it; and in some, the state labor agency can trigger mediation on its own initiative. Mediation is usually inexpensive, and it may help inform the parties about the strengths and weaknesses of the positions of each side. But there is no finality or ability to impose a settlement. Also, it is often unsuccessful where major issues such as pay are at stake, or where at least one of the parties is under pressure not to compromise. KEARNEY & MARESCHAL, *supra*, at 269–76. For a discussion of some mediation techniques, see Harold Newman, *Mediation and Fact-Finding, in* LABOR-MANAGEMENT RELATIONS IN THE PUBLIC SECTOR: REDEFINING COLLECTIVE BARGAINING 180–86 (John Bonner ed., 1999).

2. Fact-Finding

As of 2012, 28 states use fact-finding for at least some public-sector impasses. Fact-finding uses an outside, neutral party, who typically conducts an investigation, often including a hearing with formal presentations from both sides. Fact-finders usually issue reports, which often include non-binding recommendations. Also, fact-finder reports are often used as evidence in interest arbitrations. Fact-finding can give one or both sides a more realistic assessment of their position or at least their chances of prevailing at arbitration. Also, making fact-finder reports public (which typically can happen at some point in the process) can bring additional pressure on one or both sides to be more reasonable. On the other hand, fact-finding also lacks finality, and some argue that the availability of fact-finding "chills" the bargaining process by allowing the parties a way to put off tough decisions. KEARNEY & MARESCHAL *supra*, at 268–71, 277–80; Newman, *supra*, at 189.

The following is an example of a Fact-Finder's report. It demonstrates the types of issues and reasoning common to such reports.

Mattituck-Cutchogue Free School District and Mattituck-Cutchogue Teachers Association

PERB Case. No. M2015-135 (Thomas J. Linden, Nov. 17, 2016).

. . . DISTRICT AND BARGAINING UNIT PROFILE

The Mattituck-Cutchogue Union Free School District (hereinafter, "District") is a small suburban public school district located in the Town of Southold, Suffolk County, New York. . . . There are approximately 240 full and part time employees and 1197 students. According to the District's brief, there are 132 teachers represented by the Mattituck-Cutchogue Teachers Association (hereinafter, "Union") . . . . The budgeted expenditures for the 2014–15 fiscal year were approximately $39.6 million. . . .

The Issues

Salary

Health Insurance Contribution

Salary

District Position on Salary

The District first points to the mandated tax levy cap instituted in 2011, which took effect on January 1, 2012, two and a half years prior to the expiration date of the current CBA. This tax cap establishes a limit on the annual growth of property taxes levied by local governments and school districts to two percent or the rate of inflation, whichever is less. The only way this tax cap can be "pierced" or overridden, is by a super majority vote of 60% or more, of District residents.

The District further points out that the allowable tax cap number for the 2016/2017 school year is .46%, and that the projected tax cap for the 2017/2018 school year will also be less than 1%. The District states "that potential has a significant impact on the District's ability to provide employees with contractual increases, inclusive of contractual increment, that exceed the tax cap." The District believes it has consistently maintained throughout the negotiating process, that it has a "legitimate, compelling need to propose salary increases that are mindful of the constraints imposed by the tax cap."

The District contends that "of additional significance is the fact that the District has experienced stagnant state aid over the past ten (10) years." The District points out that during the 2007/2008 school year, state aid constituted 7.83% of the District's budget and that nine years later, during the 2016/2017 school year, projected state aid will likely constitute 6.3% of the budget. Those numbers, the District argues, "clearly demonstrate that revenues from state aid are not keeping up with corresponding increases to the budget." With the foregoing in mind, the District made the following financial proposal to the Union at the fact finding/mediation session on September 28, 2016:

2014/2015	increment only
2015/2016	increment only
2016/2017	increment only
2017/2018	½ increment plus .5%
2018/2019	½ increment plus .5%
2019/2020	increment, plus $1,000 cash for frozen members
2020/2021	increment, plus .25%

This proposal was rejected by the Union, which then made a proposal of its own which was, in turn, rejected by the District. The District submits that the last proposal of the Union, as communicated to the mediator, is not reasonable in light of the cost of increment and the limitations imposed by the tax cap. It believes that the confluence of rising costs due to the inflationary nature of the salary schedule and the increases in health insurance premium amounts, provide additional stressors to the already high cost of doing business.

Union Position on Salary

The Union believes that throughout the process it has offered many different proposals, all of which fell on deaf ears and, without any financial justification, the District has insisted on the Union taking a pay cut or reduction from its current financial position in order to reach a settlement. The Union further contends that the District has never demonstrated financial difficulty in paying current salaries and, in fact, their financial position is very strong as evidenced by the budget analysis done by NYSUT and the Independent Audit Report of the New York State Comptroller dated January 2014. The Union believes NYSUT's budget analysis is extremely compelling in that the District has historically overestimated its expenditures by an annual average of $1,310,342 or 3.4% of the budget and underestimated its revenues on average by .7% each year for the past three years. This has resulted in an annual average operating surplus each year of $1,547,626 or 3.9% of the budget. . . .

The Union contends that there are at least seven Suffolk County districts that have recently negotiated contracts providing more in the way of salary increases than those offered in the District's proposal. None of these, except one, contain provisions which cut increments in half or eliminate them. . . . The Union argues that these and many other districts have negotiated fair contracts that consider the full financial position of their districts and "not just alleging that the annual TAX CAP is the only factor to consider." . . .

Fact Finder Discussion of Salary

In the years following the great recession of 2008, all forms of government have gone through an unprecedented financial downturn that has also affected every citizen. In addition to this, and perhaps because of it, there has been a top down revision and reassessment of property taxes that was initiated by a change in philosophy of the Governor's Office and the Legislature, to wit, the hard statutory tax cap legislation. This has placed a tremendous burden on both school districts and union members within those districts to reign in salaries, decelerate step increases, and reduce health insurance coverage and/or increase contribution rates. This has led to a diminishment in the ability of school boards to raise expenditures on a year by year basis and has produced tremendous pressure at the bargaining table.

. . . The fact finder . . . must make a recommendation that recognizes economic realities and, at the same time, does not penalize the District for its obvious showing of fiscal responsibility. . . .

While the Union has not agreed to any disentitlement to increments, it has shown that it is willing to accept and maintain a responsible position that recognizes the financial constraints faced by the District. The District believes that by just paying increments, with no percentage across the board salary increases, it will spend all revenue raised, up to the salary cap. It is also significant, from the Union side, that for the first three years after the expiration date of the agreement, all members except those frozen on step or at top step received increments only. Were the Union to accept the District's salary proposal with the attendant proposed increase in health insurance premium contribution amounts, it would indeed be accepting a pay decrease. It is also fair to note that currently, all unit members frozen between or at top step, are participating in what could be characterized as a "soft freeze."

In its brief, the District points to increments, as components of salary, as the largest impediment to providing anything like the salary increases sought by the Union. . . .

This aligns closely with the fact finder's salary recommendation which keeps full increments throughout the seven years with percentage increases for frozen step members in the last four years and across the board increases for non frozen or non top step members during the last three years of the agreement. . . .

Addressing the ability to pay issue, it seems clear that the District's financial situation is quite adequate to fund the last proposal of the Union. With that in mind it is the fact finder's recommendation that the District accept the Union's last proposal with two additions. The reason for these additions will be discussed during the health insurance (rate of contribution) phase of this report. The recommendation on salary is as follows:

2014/15	Increment Only
2015/16	Increment Only
2016/17	Increment Only
2017/18	Increment Plus 1% Top/Frozen Step, plus .5% all others
2018/19	Increment Plus 1% Top/Frozen Step, plus .5% all others
2019/2020	Increment Plus 1% Top/Frozen Step, plus .5% all others
2020/2021	Increment Plus 1% Top/Frozen Step, plus .5% all others

District and Union Positions on Health Insurance Contribution Rate

Presently, all unit members, those with individual and family coverage, pay 15% toward the cost of health insurance premiums with the District paying the lion's share of 85%. The District has proposed that employees increase their contribution rate by 5% over the life of the agreement, going from 15% to 20%. The Union has never made a proposal in this area.

Fact Finder Discussion of Health Insurance Contribution Rate

A review of health care costs going back many years shows us that costs have never trended downward. In addition, health care costs and premium costs have increased dramatically in the recent past. These increases have exceeded previous projections and actuarial assumptions, and employee contribution rates have been slowly trending upward. Contribution rates have increased across all public sector bargaining units including police units, the last bastion of fully paid programs that were previously immune to such increases. Tremendous pressure on employers has resulted in a substantial cost shifting to employees who are now participating more and more in the form of incremental percentage increases in contribution rates.

With this in mind it is the fact finder's recommendation that unit members increase their contribution rate to 18%, decreasing the District's contribution rate to 82%. This would be accomplished over the last three years of the agreement by increasing the employee contribution rate by one per cent each year starting with the 2018/2019 year. Because salary and health insurance are inextricably linked, this increase would be concurrent with the .5% salary increase recommended for each of the last three years of the agreement. . . .

Notes

1. Unlike many public-sector statutes, the New York statute does not specify what criteria fact-finders should use in formulating their decisions. What seemed to be important to the fact-finder in the case above? Why did the union present evidence about pay in other school districts? As is discussed in detail below, most public-sector statutes provide that fact-finders should use the same criteria as interest arbitrators use. Some fact-finding decisions in New York explicitly use the factors the New York statute requires interest arbitrators to use. *See, e.g., Town of Tonawanda and Tonawanda Salaried Workers' Ass'n*, Findings of Facts and Recommendations, Case No. M2016-137 (Lise Gelentner, Dec. 29, 2017).

2. A number of states require that fact-finder reports be made public at some point. For example, the Ohio statute also provides that the fact-finder's report is private, unless and until the parties reject the fact-finder's recommendations and move on to further stages in the impasse resolution process. At that point, the fact-finder's decision is publicized. OHIO REV. CODE §4117.14(C)(6)(a). How would such a rule affect your strategy?

3. In deciding whether to accept or reject a fact-finder's recommendations, should the duty to bargain in good faith require the parties to meet and discuss the recommendations of the fact-finder? The California PERB has rejected that theory: the employer need only consider the fact-finder's report in good faith and, as relevant in that case, the union's offer to accept it. *Charter Oak Educators Association, CTA/NEA v. Charter Oak Unified School District*, 15 P.E.R. Cal. ¶ 22067 (PERB 1991). Is that a good rule?

4. If you are troubled that the fact-finder did not give sufficiently detailed rationales for his recommendations, bear in mind that the recommendations are not binding, and if the parties do not voluntarily accept the recommendations, in many states (including New York), the parties may proceed to interest arbitration. In arbitration, parties can again press their positions, and while the fact-finder's report is usually evidence, it is not binding on the interest arbitrator. The decisions of interest arbitrators are usually more detailed than those of fact-finders.

5. How much deference should interest arbitrators give to the facts and recommendations in fact-finders' reports? Most arbitrators give great deference. *City of Painesville, Ohio v. IAFF Local 434*, 2017-MED-1346 (Conciliator Bernardini). *But cf. City of Broadview Heights, Ohio v. IAFF Local 3646*, 2017-MED-09-1139 (Conciliator Klein) (arbitrators are not required to "rubber stamp" a fact-finder's conclusions because positions and facts can change between the fact-finding hearing and the arbitration). Consider this issue when reading the next section.

3. Interest Arbitration

As of 2012, 27 states use interest arbitration as the final step in at least some public-sector impasse resolutions. KEARNEY & MARESCHAL, *supra*, at 269–70. In this system a neutral arbitrator (or a board of neutrals) holds a hearing, evaluates evidence, follows sometimes quite specific legal criteria, and makes a decision that in most jurisdictions is binding as to what the terms of the collective-bargaining agreement will be. The arbitrator may be selected by the parties or appointed by the state agency. In states using a "tripartite" structure, each party selects an arbitrator, and either the two selected arbitrators or the state agency picks the third. *Id.* at 280–85. A typical interest arbitration hearing involves some witness testimony (for substantive and political reasons), but most of the evidence is usually documentary, *e.g.*, showing the terms and conditions of comparable employees. Significant variations exist within this type of process, however.

a. Policy and Definitions

Arvid Anderson & Loren Krause, *Interest Arbitration: The Alternative to the Strike*
56 FORDHAM L. REV. 153 (1987)[*]

The right to bargain collectively has been so connected with the right to strike in this country that legitimate questions arise as to whether genuine collective bargaining can occur without the right to strike. The thesis of this Article is that an alternative to the right to strike exists and that that alternative is final and binding interest arbitration. . . .

Interest arbitration is a process in which the terms and conditions of the employment contract are established by a final and binding decision of the arbitration panel. It differs from grievance arbitration, which involves the interpretation of the employment contract to determine whether the conditions of employment have been breached. Thus, interest arbitration essentially is a legislative process, while grievance arbitration essentially is a judicial process. . . .

It is our view that either the right to strike or interest arbitration is needed to make collective bargaining work. The success of collective bargaining requires only

---

one of these alternatives. . . . In those states that have adopted interest arbitration, illegal strikes are virtually nonexistent.

Undeniably, in some cases the strike weapon can be extremely effective in obtaining bargaining rights for employees as well as in achieving contract gains. Unfortunately, however, a strike can result in the self-immolation of those employees without the power to strike effectively. Moreover, even states that have sanctioned the right to strike for some public employees have not done so for police, firefighters and other categories of employees who have the power to threaten seriously the health and safety of the community if they strike. We submit that interest arbitration enables all employees to achieve favorable employment contract terms by offering an alternative to the strike that similarly stimulates bargaining. . . .

A. Types of Interest Arbitration Procedures: State Laws

. . . Some state statutes provide for conventional arbitration, which gives the arbitrator the discretion to decide the issues in dispute based upon the parties' evidence and arguments as measured against the relevant statutory criteria. Other state statutes utilize final offer arbitration, which requires that the arbitrator pick either the employer's or the employee organization's final offer on the issues in dispute. In some instances the statutes include provisions that permit the parties to agree voluntarily on the type of interest arbitration procedure to be used.

Some statutes adopt a combination of conventional arbitration and final offer arbitration, treating economic and non-economic issues differently. Michigan's police and firefighters statute, for example, provides for final offer arbitration on an issue-by-issue basis on economic issues and for conventional arbitration on non-economic issues. . . . New Jersey's law embodies yet another variation, requiring the arbitrator to choose either the employer's or the union's last offer as a total economic package, but allowing the arbitrator to resolve non-economic issues on a final offer, issue-by-issue basis. . . .

Each of the above noted procedures has strengths and weaknesses. . . . Our preference is for conventional arbitration, because it gives the arbitrator the greatest latitude in deciding the issues in dispute.

B. Statutory Standards

Virtually all interest arbitration statutes either expressly or implicitly provide standards to guide the arbitrator's evaluation of the evidence and arguments presented. They do so by requiring the arbitrator to focus on particular facts in reaching his decision. Statutory standards that arbitrators must address usually include 'the lawful authority of the employer,' 'the interests and welfare of the public,' the comparability of the wages, hours and working conditions of similarly situated employees, and the cost of living. In addition, arbitrators may be required to consider the peculiarities of a particular trade or profession, past agreements of the parties, the ability of the employer to finance economic adjustments, and the effect of an award on the standard of services provided.

The type of interest arbitration procedure mandated by the statute, or agreed to by the parties, will have an impact on the arbitrator's application of the statutory criteria and the rationale for his decisions. When, for example, the statute requires arbitrators to use final offer arbitration, arbitrators exercise much more limited discretion than they do when the statute or agreement provides for conventional arbitration of both economic and non-economic issues. Indeed, in a final offer, total package scheme, the arbitrators must choose one or the other offer regardless of their views on the merits of individual economic and non-economic issues.

The most significant statutory standard for arbitration in the public sector is comparability. Because the profit motive is absent in the public sector, and therefore the full range of market forces generally governing the value of jobs is lacking, comparability provides an acceptable substitute measure of job worth. Comparability establishes the market value of public sector labor by analyzing, among other things, the effects of inflation and cost of living increases on compensation of comparable employees. The arbitrators therefore must answer the question of with which employers and employees the comparison should be made.

Typically, the statute requires a comparison of the overall compensation of the employees involved in the dispute with the overall compensation of comparable employees performing similar work in both private and public employment in a particular community or like communities. . . . But what constitutes 'like work' and what is a 'comparable employee'? Exact public sector and private sector parallels often exist. For example, a comparison of the compensation of private hospital employees with their public counterparts seems appropriate. The same is true of many other occupations. But, the comparison fails when applied to, for example, police and firefighters with private employees.

The general term 'interest and welfare of the public,' included in a number of state laws, is subject to different interpretations because it is not self-defining. In New York City, for example, the term 'interest and welfare of the public' requires consideration of the employer's 'ability to pay,' a separate criterion in most statutes. . . .

Bargaining patterns assume particular importance in the public sector, where the employer is required to bargain with a number of different labor organizations. The economic settlements for uniformed employees, for example, influence settlements for non-uniformed employees and vice versa. The wages paid by the state also may be relevant in determining the wages that should be paid by a county or a city for persons performing similar work, such as law enforcement or clerical duties. In addition, historic parity relationships may exist, particularly among uniformed forces, police officers and firefighters. Such patterns are considered under the general standard of interest and welfare of the public.

The criterion of the interest and welfare of the public determines, in part, the priority to be given to the wages and economic benefits of public sector employees. Obviously, the decision to increase wages and improve economic benefits will affect the overall allocation of the employer's resources. Should more money be spent to raise the salaries of the existing workforce, to increase the number of workers, or for capital improvements and increased services? . . .

The employer's ability to pay constitutes another major factor in collective bargaining negotiations and interest arbitration. Indeed, the economic circumstances of a given jurisdiction may make it the decisive factor in negotiations or in arbitration. . . .

In addition to explicit statutory standards, a number of jurisdictions use a catch-all standard that refers to '[s]uch other factors . . . which are normally or traditionally taken into consideration in the determination of wages, hours and conditions of employment.' A provision like this enables the arbitrator to choose those criteria that he deems most important in a particular case as long as he discusses the other statutory factors that were also considered in the opinion. . . .

Notes

1. As this excerpt notes, interest arbitration should be distinguished from grievance arbitration (which Chapter 13 discusses). Quoting a leading treatise, the Delaware Public Employee Relations Board explained the different purposes of the two types of arbitrations.

> Arbitration of contract terms differs radically from arbitration of grievances. The latter calls for a judicial determination of existing contract rights; the former calls for a determination, upon consideration of policy, fairness and expediency, of what the contract rights ought to be. In submitting this case to arbitration, the parties have merely extended their negotiations—they have left it to [the arbitrator] to determine what they should, by negotiation, have agreed upon. *Delaware State Troopers Ass'n and State of Delaware, Dept. of Safety and Homeland Security, Div. of Police*, BIA 08-02-612 (Delaware Pub. Empl. Rel. Bd., June 1, 2009) at 4252, *quoting* ELKOURI & ELKOURI, HOW ARBITRATION WORKS (6th ed. 2003), 1358.

2. Similarly, *City of Taylor and The Command Officers' Ass'n of Michigan*, MERC Case No. D06C0326 (Jan. 30, 2008) stated that the role of interest arbitration is "to effect the settlement the parties would have reached if negotiations had continued when the parties are confronted with the realities of the situation," *i.e.*, "to try to replicate the settlement the parties themselves would have reached had their negotiations been successful." *Id.* at 5.

3. Are these statements about the purpose of interest arbitration helpful? The existence of impasse likely means the parties had a different view of what they "should have" agreed on and what a "successful" outcome would be. Also, how could one determine what settlement the parties "would have" reached without considering the incentives a given impasse resolution mechanism puts on the parties during negotiation? Further, as the article discusses and as is described in detail below, state statutes providing for interest arbitration (including the statutes governing the *Delaware State Troopers* and *City of Taylor* cases) generally list a series

of criteria which interest arbitrators must consider in making their decisions. Will decisions based on statutory factors always be consistent with what the parties would or should have done?

b. Variations: Conventional, Final Offer Issue-by-Issue, and Final Offer Total Package Arbitration

As the Anderson and Krause excerpt notes, there are three basic models of interest arbitration: conventional; final offer total package; and final offer issue-by-issue. In conventional arbitration, the arbitrator can pick between the party's proposals, create compromises, or even go beyond the party's proposals. In final offer total package arbitration, the arbitrator may only choose the final set of proposals from the union or the final set of proposals from the employer, as a package. In final offer issue-by-issue arbitration, the arbitrator must choose final proposals from one side or the other, but the arbitrator can choose final proposals on some issues from one side and final proposals on other issues from the other side. Different states use different models. For examples, see Charles Rehmus, "Interest Arbitration" in Bonner, Ed., *supra*, 206–07.

Also, some states use different models for different types of employees, or "mix and match" models (*e.g.*, final offer arbitration for economic issues but not for others). Other variations exist. In Ohio (for employees not allowed to strike), the default is final offer issue-by-issue arbitration, but the parties can mutually choose other alternatives, including but not limited to conventional arbitration and final offer total package arbitration. Ohio Rev. Code § 4117.14(C)(1), (D)(1), and (G)(7).

The following is a relatively straightforward interest arbitration case that nonetheless raises some important issues about the process.

City of Helena Montana and IAFF, Local 448, Helena, Montana

Decision and Award of Arbitrator
BOPA CASE # 5-2010 (407-2010) (Apr. 19, 2010)

Jeffrey Jacobs, Arbitrator

Preliminary Statement

The parties were unable to resolve certain issues concerning the terms of the collective bargaining agreement and requested mediation from the Montana Board of Personnel Appeals, BOPA. The City of Helena and the International Association of Firefighters, Local #448 which represents the bargaining unit employees of the City of Helena Fire Department entered into a collective bargaining agreement for a three-year period commencing July 1, 2007, and will terminate on June 30, 2010. . . . For the third year of the Agreement, the parties agreed as follows: "Effective July 1, 2009 (FY10), monthly wages will increase by CPI-U, US City Average, December 2008. . . . The Union has the option to reopen wage negotiations under Section 12 only, relating to the wage adjustment for FY10."

The Union reopened the contact with respect to that provision and sought wage adjustments above the 0.1% from the CPI adjustment. Two mediation sessions were held with mediators from the BOPA and the parties negotiated in good faith but were unable to resolve the wage issue herein.

. . . The matter has been submitted on a final offer — total package basis. . . .

Statutory Authority

Montana Statutes Section 39-34-103(5) sets forth the required circumstances as follows:

"(5) In arriving at a determination, the arbitrator shall consider any relevant circumstances, including:

(a) comparison of hours, wages, and conditions of employment of the employees involved with employees performing similar services and with other services generally;

(b) the interests and welfare of the public and the financial ability of the public employer to pay;

(c) appropriate cost-of-living indices;

(d) any other factors traditionally considered in the determination of hours, wages, and conditions of employment."

Union's Position

. . . The Union's position results in varying percentages of increases for different positions but results in an overall increase of some 3.89% . . . . The Battalion Chiefs/Fire Marshals would receive approximately 5.3%, Captains 3.9%, Lieutenants 3.1%, Firefighter II's 3.1%, Firefighter I's 2.0%, Confirmed Firefighter 0.80 % and Probationary Firefighter 0.45%. It should be noted that there are currently no Confirmed Firefighters on staff. . . .

In support of this position the Union made the following contentions: . . .

3. . . . that wages paid to Helena firefighters should be comparable to wages paid in the other Montana "first class" cities, of Billings, Bozeman, Butte, Great Falls, Kalispell and Missoula. While there were some cities that did not have the same classifications and not all of the other cities have all of the same classifications as Helena, the parties were able to agree on the specific job titles from those other cities that are comparable to the different job classifications in Helena. . . .

5. The Union noted that the schedules are somewhat complicated and include a so-called "Kelly Day," which is an unpaid day off every 6th day. The parties agree that the bargaining unit employees work 2,434.93 hours per year. The Union pointed out that the Firefighters in other comparable cities work varying numbers of hours, some work more and some fewer. Billings' firefighters work 2272, Bozeman's, 2756, Butte's 2112, Great Falls and Missoula's both work 2184 and Kalispell's work 2682.

6. The Union asserted most strenuously that the bargaining unit employees are hourly employees under both Section 207(k) of the Fair Labor Standards Act . . . and the parties' labor agreement. The mere fact that they are paid on what appears to be a monthly basis does not make them salaried. The wage structure is set up to equalize the pay for the firefighter due to their irregular schedule. . . .

7. Accordingly, the Union argued that the focus when comparing Helena firefighters' wages to other comparable jurisdiction must be their hourly wage, not, as the City suggests, their monthly wage. . . . [T]he other cities do not require the same number of hours as in Helena and their wages are vastly different as well. It thus makes no sense to compare monthly wages because of this disparity in the wages and number of hours.

8. The Union further argued that the history of negotiations for collective bargaining agreements between these parties shows that they have traditionally focused on hourly wages and not monthly salary or the like. . . .

9. The Union argued that the City is now seeking to suddenly change the focus to monthly wages without any justification or rational basis. The Union asserted that because these employees are non-exempt the law requires that the hourly comparisons be used.

10. The Union asserted that the appropriate methodology for determining the appropriate wage for the firefighters is thus to reduce their pay to an hourly rate. In short, the Union calculated the hourly wage paid to Helena bargaining unit firefighters and compared that to the average hourly wage paid to firefighters in comparable positions in comparable cities. The Union then noted that it determined the hourly wage for each rank in the bargaining unit and the hourly wage for each comparable position in the comparable cities and then averaged the hourly wage paid to employees in the comparable positions. The Union's position is thus based on the pay increases for each rank equal to the amount needed to bring that rank to the average hourly wage paid to firefighters in comparable positions in comparable cities.

11. The Union's position . . . with respect to hourly wages as compared to the average wages of the comparable cities is as follows: (note that the position set forth above was for the monthly salary but these figures are the extensions of those to hourly wage figures):

Rank	Helena Existing Pay Per Hour	Statewide Average Per Hour/Union Offer
Battalion Chief	$27.84	$29.40
Captain	$24.11	$25.09
Lieutenant	$22.16	$22.87
Firefighter II	$20.57	$21.21
Firefighter I	$19.66	$20.06
Confirmed FF	$19.02	$19.18
Probationary FF	$17.75	$18.59

12. The Union contends that even though there was agreement on the wage figures for literally all but one of the ranks in each of the comparable cities, the parties did not agree on the base wages for Bozeman. The Union argued that it was not appropriate to reduce the Bozeman wages by 4% due to the holiday pay structure there. The Union argued that the true measure of the Bozeman wages should thus include the additional 4% whether one uses an average or the median. The Union pointed out that until 1992 the Bozeman firefighters received no holiday pay but that Bozeman ended this practice and increased the base monthly wage by 4%. Thus, in reality, the Bozeman employees actually get holiday pay and the 4% should be included.

13. The Union asserted that the City should not use a median to calculate the appropriate comparable wage. Instead the Union asserted, the appropriate measure should be [a mean] average. The Union noted that the parties have agreed to most of the wage rates (with the exception of the Bozeman wage rates set forth herein) and argued that using the median results in a skewed result when compared to the comparison cities. An average keeps Helena firefighters where they have traditionally been when compared to the comparison cities whereas a median does not.

14. Moreover, the City included the City of Helena in the list for determining the median. It is not appropriate to include Helena on that list of comparables since it is at that point comparing itself to itself. Thus, not only is the City using the incorrect method, i.e. a median as compared to an average, it is not even applying the correct methodology for using the median. Accordingly, the City's number are skewed. . . .

16. The Union asserted that the most important [statutory] criteria is "the interest and welfare of the public is not served by a salary and benefit package for Helena firefighters that is substandard." The Union asserted that the parties agreed that the interest and welfare of the public is served best if Helena firefighters' wages are comparable to the wages paid in other first class Montana cities. . . .

17. The Union took issue with the assertion by the City that it does not have the money to pay for the Union's requested increases. The Union pointed out the tautological reasoning of the assertion that the City "did not have this budgeted" and notes that if that were the determining criterion all a public employer would have to do is to set its own internal budget for what it offered and leave it at that—this would be the equivalent to simply disregarding the language of the statute cited above.

18. The Union further asserted that the City is in reasonably healthy financial shape and that there would be no untoward consequences if the Union's proposal were ordered. It would be only $60,657.32 more than the City's offer. (The Union noted that the total cost of the Union's offer over the 2009 pay rates was $67,732.52 but that the City must have the ability to pay for its own offer so the best measure is to look at the difference between the two offers to determine the true "additional cost" of the Union's proposal.)

19. The Union asserted that even this modest actual additional cost on a budget of more than $1.742 million is not by any means an unreasonable request. Moreover, the Chief testified that at worst he would simply leave [a currently vacant fire suppression] position unfilled for a short time to make up the additional cost to the City of the Union's request. There would be no "parade of horribles" that would occur either financially nor to public safety. Finally, the City did not raise this issue until the hearing and did not raise it at the mediation nor at any time prior to the hearing. Thus the City's argument in this regard should be viewed with considerable skepticism at best and should be rejected as without sufficient evidentiary support at the very least.

20. The essence then of the Union's argument is that the parties have agreed to most of the facts necessary to determine this issue and have agreed that the wages should be comparable to wages paid in Montana's other first class cities. The Union further argues that the law is firmly established that firefighters are hourly employees and that the hourly wages of the comparable cities should be used to determine this issue. Here, the Union asserted that if one uses the average of those hourly rates, the arbitrator should conclude that the Union's is the more reasonable of the offers and award its position in this matter as set forth above.

City's Position

The City's position is for a 0.1% increase in wages for the bargaining unit members in 2010. This results in a wage structure as follows:

POSITION	FY 10 salary
Battalion Chief—Suppression	$5,650.28
Fire Marshal—Prevention	$5,650.28
Captain	$4,892.28
Lieutenant	$4,495.69
Firefighter II	$4,174.34
Firefighter I	$3,988.85
Confirmed Firefighter	$3,860.11
Probationary Firefighter	$3,602.59

In support of this position the City made the following contentions:

1. . . . [T]he wage provisions of the current agreement call for an adjustment pursuant to Section 12 as follows: "Effective July 1, 2009 (FY10), monthly wages will increase by CPI-U, US City Average, December 2008. An adjustment approved by the commission for any positive wage adjustment will be given." The City notes that this was done and a 0.1% increase was granted. The City asserted that this was all that was justified given the circumstances in place now.

2. The City further asserted that it conducted a wage study that showed the relative wages of the various positions within the Fire Department. This showed the Captains' pay was low so the City adjusted the wages for the Captains' position by

$73.70/month. The City further asserted that the remainder of the positions were either at or slightly above market and were thus not adjusted.

3. The City asserted that basic methodology for the wage survey was to compare the annual salaries paid by the City against the median of annual salaries paid by comparable jurisdictions, i.e. Bozeman, Great Falls, Billings, Kalispell, Missoula and Butte. The City agreed that the above referenced jurisdictions were the appropriate comparables to use to determine the wages for the Helena bargaining unit.

4. The City's methodology was to use monthly salaries and find the median, which included the City's wages for each position. The City asserted that using the median is the most appropriate measure since it maintains the relative position that Helena has been in over time when compared to the comparison jurisdictions. The City noted that when one compares the hours worked in the various comparison cities, it become obvious that an hourly number is not accurate since several of the cities require far fewer hours than Helena does. . . . [U]sing hourly figures . . . the [mean] average becomes overly weighed because of the lower hours of the largest three cities.

5. The . . . issue here is whether the arbitrator should accept the City's methodology of using the median based upon monthly wages or the Local's proposal to use the [mean] average hourly wage that excludes the City's wages in the calculation. The City asserted that its methodology is more appropriate here since it maintains the same relative position as Helena has had with respect to the comparison jurisdictions in the past.

6. The City compared the populations of the various comparison cities and noted that Helena's is 6th out of the seven cities yet its wages rank far higher than that. . . . The City noted that . . . even if the monthly salary is constant for all six of the comparable cities, the City's monthly salary is higher than either the median or the average.

7. The City argued that the holiday pay for the Bozeman employees should be backed out given the history of that unit going back to 1992 when the Bozeman employees were given a 4% increase for their holiday pay. Helena fire fighters are given a specific holiday pay benefit as a part of their contract and are thus getting that "on top of" regular wages. Thus, it is appropriate to alter the figures from Bozeman. The City agreed with all of the Union's wage figures for the other cities. . . .

9. The City asserted that a monthly figure is a far more accurate measure than hourly figures. The City insisted that the employees like the predictability of a monthly figure since they work irregular schedules, especially given the Kelly Days. Further, the Fire Marshal and Deputy Fire Marshal work 2080 hours per years, as opposed to the 2434.93 worked by the other employees. Thus, using a monthly figure for comparison purposes is a far more accurate and sensible measure.

10. The City also noted that its position maintains the relative position with respect to the external comparison cities. . . . Further, the City noted that the other cities' labor contracts were in virtually all cases negotiated for FY 2010 as a part of

the multi year contract. Again, in virtually all cases, those agreements run from July 1, 2008 through June 30, 2010. . . . These contracts were negotiated before the sudden and radical change in the nation's and Montana's economy, which occurred in the fall of 2008. Thus, the assumptions under which those agreements were negotiated have changed and would likely not be negotiated in that same way today. The economy of 2010 is frankly not the same as the economy of 2008 before the "crash."

11. The City also pointed to internal comparisons as well and argued that only two of the five collective bargaining units in the City received any increases at all. Police and Support Services Division received a pay increase for 2010 of 2% during the second year of a three-year contract and that was based on the salary survey. Here the Union is seeking an overall increase of nearly 4% which is simply not justifiable under any measure — internal or external. . . .

13. . . . [T]here is a finite amount of money available and that fire fighting services while important, do not somehow trump or take precedence over police or other public services provided. Thus, any increase in wages for the fire unit must come from somewhere and, not surprisingly, it will have to come from other services. The City cannot create additional revenue for itself. . . . [U]nder Montana Law it has only a very limited ability to increase taxes. . . .

14. Moreover, the voters in Helena denied permission to increase funding for the fire Department in the 2008 election. . . . Funding is a problem and even though the City could make the adjustment by keeping the vacant position open for a longer time this could result in decreased services and response times. Moreover, future increases in funding are unlikely to come any time soon.

15. . . . [T]here was no evidence that the working conditions or job duties and requirements have changed nor was there any reason to justify the increase sought by the Union. Further, there was no evidence of any change in any of the comparison jurisdictions that somehow made their work different from what those positions have been required to do over time either. Thus, the Union has not met its burden of showing why a nearly 4% increase is justified in today's economy.

16. The City asserted that the ultimate goal is equality of treatment of these employees with respect to other Helena employees. Fairness in pay between the City's employees will be achieved best by awarding its position. The Union's position will achieve only the elevation of these employees over their peers within the City and in comparison to their peers in other Montana jurisdictions.

Memorandum and Discussion

This is a total offer final package arbitration. The arbitrator must therefore select either the City's or the Union's total package. This limitation makes it difficult on occasion to select between positions as there are many times when one party's position is reasonable and justifiable in one respect while in some others another party's position may well also have considerable merit. When that is the case, as here, there is a temptation to find a figure somewhere in the middle of the two respective positions that reflects the relative merits of both parties' arguments.

With this type of interest arbitration however that option does not exist. The arbitrator must therefore select the most reasonable and justifiable position as a total package. . . . [A] total offer final package arbitration of this nature removes any power to modify or fine tune either side's position or to fashion an award that reflects the best of both arguments or conforms to the most appropriate evidence brought forth by either side. For better or worse, the arbitrator must select the least unreasonable option. . . .

The parties agreed on the comparison cities to be used. These were Billings, Missoula, Kalispell, Butte, Great Falls and Bozeman. They agreed for the most part on the wage figures in those cities and on the comparable positions to which the Helena positions should be compared.

There was one exception to the agreement on the wage figures for Bozeman based on the question of holiday pay. The City argued that the wage figures should be reduced by some 4% because of holiday pay. There was very little evidence adduced at the hearing as to why the city reduced the Bozeman wages for comparison purposes here other than the somewhat bald assertion that the Bozeman firefighters holiday pay is somehow different than Helena's and therefore the 4% Bozeman firefighters receive should be "backed out" for purposes of wage comparisons. The Union on the other hand asserted that until 1992 Bozeman firefighters did not receive holiday pay and were instead paid a separate check once per year to cover the holidays. After that they apparently received holidays off but if they worked the holiday they received a day's pay for it, in effect receiving double time for it. This is apparently the same benefit granted to Helena firefighters as well. On this record the Union's position with regard to the 4% has merit. Thus, for purposes of wage comparison the Union's figures for Bozeman were used.

There was then a major disagreement on whether hourly wages should be used or monthly figures. The City argued that a monthly figure should be used since the wage figures are listed as monthly salary figures in the collective bargaining agreement. The City also pointed out the fact that the so-called Kelly Days can sometimes affect the monthly wages if hourly figures are used so the parties have agreed to place monthly figures in the agreement.

The Union on the other hand argued that firefighters are by law hourly employees; they are not exempt under the FLSA and are entitled to overtime based on an hourly wage. The fact that there are monthly figures placed in the agreement is more for convenience of both parties and so the employees can count on a regular paycheck that is unaffected by the vagaries of the sometimes unusual and irregular schedule of firefighters.

On this record the Union's assertions had greater merit. Firefighters are indeed hourly employees even though their wages are listed in the contact as monthly figures. They are certainly not "salaried" in the sense that their wages are considered monthly. This too was reflected in [an earlier interest arbitration award] which, while not controlling here on the ultimate question of the appropriate wage, did set forth certain findings whose logic carried over to this matter. There was no evidence that the parties have changed the understandings that were in place at the time of that earlier award sufficient to change these employees status. Thus, an hourly figure should be used to determine the appropriate wage.

The City argued in this regard that the population figures in these various cities should have an impact on this discussion. There was little merit to this position. A city's population may be an interesting comparison but it is not a governing factor here. Population may well be a measure of *how many* employees may be needed to provide coverage for the services required by that City but does little to provide guidance on the question of the appropriate wage to be paid. That frankly may depend on the number of hours required to be worked, as discussed herein, but the number of hours required does not appear to correlate well to the size of the city.[4]

Next there was a disagreement between the parties as to whether the median of the comparison cities should be used or the [mean] average should be used. . . .

However, the parties were in apparent agreement that the Helena firefighters' pay should be maintained at a relative level when compared to those other jurisdictions, at least when using an external comparability standard.

The Union argued that the prior award by Arbitrator Axon used hourly figures and used [a mean] average in order to maintain the position Helena has with respect to the other jurisdictions. Several distinguishing factors appear in that award however. First, the parties' approach to the case was somewhat different in that the comparisons for the wages were the top Firefighter hourly base wages. The parties did not break down each individual category, i.e. Battalion Chef, Captain, Lieutenant, Firefighter I and II, Provisional and Confirmed Firefighter, as they did here. It was thus far easier to arrive at an average in that case.

Clearly, Arbitrator Axon used average hourly figures. . . . What was also apparent was the crux of the decision to keep Helena where it was with respect to its ranking as compared to the comparison jurisdictions. . . . Here that same general consideration is at work as well.

. . . [T]he parties were both using fairly complex mathematical calculations to support their positions. The City applied a somewhat complicated and frankly mathematically confusing formula that compared the median salary to the population of those cities. As noted above however the population is not a good measure of salary. (Certainly, size of a city might affect the actual cost of living there and other quality of life factors but those were not strictly at issue here nor was there any evidence of how those factors played into this consideration).

---

4. As an example, the largest city in Montana is Billings with slightly over 100,000 people yet it requires 2272 hours of its employees as compared to the 2343.93 in Helena. Helena has a population of approximately 28,000 people. On the other hand, Kalispell has a slightly smaller population than Helena, with some 20,300 people, yet it requires 2756 hours of its employees. . . . Thus, there was no real correlation between population and the number of hours worked. . . .

Several factors were at work in making the determination of whether to use average figures as the Union suggests or median salary as the City suggests. First, the City's methodology of using Helena as a part of the median was inappropriate and resulted in a skewed figure for the median—the Union is correct—one should not compare oneself to oneself in determining a median. Thus the City's figures were incorrect in that regard. The Union's calculations, while not perfect, were a better measure of how Helena's wages compare to the comparison jurisdictions and were used. Second . . . the hourly figure is the better measure of the pay for firefighters and an average of those figures would result in the better measure of how Helena's wages compare to other jurisdictions.

Finally, a review of the wages paid for 2010 in the other jurisdiction shows that indeed they were granted increases in the range of approximately 4%. Some were lower but the Union's proposal is for a 3.89% increase overall and that certainly was far closer to the wage increases granted for 2010 in the comparison jurisdictions than the City's 0.1%. These factors weighed heavily in this decision.

It should also be noted that the bulk of the comparison jurisdictions had multi-year contracts with the 2010 wages already set in those contracts. The City argued that it is likely given the economic realities of the present time that those same wage increases might not be granted if those jurisdictions were negotiating anew for their 2010 wage rates. That is speculative at best even though there was frankly some intuitive logic to that argument. On this record however, the arbitrator was faced with the evidence of what the jurisdictions actually settled for and cannot ascribe or divine what might have happened under different facts. Obviously, this is a factor that the parties might well want to consider in the bargaining for future contracts but for now we are faced with the facts we have.

Certainly too, there is some danger in a case where the comparison jurisdictions have already set wage increases for 2010, that Helena's will eventually fall too far behind if the City's proposal is awarded and that is a major concern.

Other factors were considered as well. Not the least of them was the fact that internally, most of the other employee groups were not given any increase at all. The Police and Support Services Division received 2% increases during the second year of a three-year contract and those were apparently based on the salary survey. . . . There was some evidence to suggest that these units were slightly underpaid when compared to the market and so they, like the Fire Captains, were granted a salary increase based on the salary survey done by the City. . . . This certainly was a factor that mitigated in favor of the City.[5]

---

5. . . . [I]nternal consistency is certainly a factor to consider in interest arbitrations generally. If there had been jurisdiction to award something other than the final offer of one or the other of the parties, this figure would have been given very strong consideration in order to arrive at a figure that was both appropriate internally and externally. As noted however, there was no such option.

There was considerable discussion and disagreement about the City's ability to pay. The City argued that its ability to raise additional revenue is severely hampered by State law and economic reality. Moreover, the voters rejected a referendum recently that would have added revenue to the fire department. The City argued that they have already budgeted for their increase only and cannot now go back and change that figure.

There was some evidence to suggest that the financial straits of the City are not completely bad. And that the City is relatively healthy financially. There was insufficient evidence to suggest that the City was unable to pay for the increases or that it faces any sort of economic crisis or anything of the sort. The City is growing, even compared to the rest of Montana. . . . Thus, the increases sought by the Union, even though clearly larger than the City's proposal, will not result in a diminution of services or response times for the Fire Department.

Further, the argument that the City has already budgeted for this is somewhat tautological. If an employer can avoid a wage increase simply by failing or refusing to budget for it the notion of collective bargaining and interest arbitrations would be severely undermined. The question is, as always, not whether the City can pay for the increases or whether it has budgeted for it but rather whether the factors mandated by the statute make the increase appropriate or not.

Here the Union demonstrated that the City has the ability to pay for the increase and that it will result in an increase in cost of approximately $67,732 over the City's proposal. Further, there was some evidence that the Department will simply leave open the now vacant position that is already open for a period of time to "make-up" the difference in the cost of the Union's proposal. The position has been vacant for some time without apparent difficulty (at least no such evidence was adduced on this record) so the cost to the City will be manageable and not unreasonable. . . .

[I]n discussing the criteria to be applied here, the Union correctly pointed out that "the statute does not require that these criteria be applied with anything approaching objective certainty and the statute does not define the weight to be given to each of the criteria."

The statute Montana Statute, 39-34-103(5) provides as follows:

"(5) In arriving at a determination, the arbitrator shall consider any relevant circumstances, including: . . ."

Thus the main guidepost is simply that the arbitrator "shall consider any relevant circumstances." The statute goes on to provide a list of things the arbitrator might consider but the list is not exclusive.

Here many of the matters on the list were considered. There was certainly a comparison of the hours, wages and conditions of employment with employees performing similar services. This was the comparison to other Montana jurisdictions as discussed above. As noted, a comparison of the average hourly wages was considered the most appropriate comparison for purposes of comparing these wages.

There was also a review of the other terms of employment, such as the holiday pay issue in Bozeman. The parties did not provide evidence of the other terms and conditions of employment in those jurisdictions and presumably were concerned only with the wages for those comparison cities and not how the Helena bargaining unit employees' terms may have compared to the other cities.

There was also a comparison of the wages to the other employees generally. As noted above, internal consistency is a factor to be considered, and one that is "traditionally used in the determination of wages, hours and conditions of employment." However, while fringe benefits and other terms of employment are best compared internally, wages are compared both to internal and external sets of employees. Here a factor that weighed heavily was the amount of the increases for 2010 given to the external jurisdiction employees. Certainly, as noted herein, if there had been jurisdiction to determine a different number, the 2% granted to the Police and Social Service employees within the City of Helena might well have changed the result here. On balance though, the fact that most other external jurisdictions were granted approximately 4% makes the Union's position reasonable.

Consumer Price Index, CPI, considerations were also considered. While the CPI was somewhat lower than what the Union is seeking, the Union's request is so not so unreasonable as to trump the other considerations here. The CPI-U was shown to be 2.72% for 2010. . . .

The City was shown to have the ability to pay for the increase. While "can" should never be equated with "should" there was here a showing that the increase can and perhaps already has been absorbed by the Department in the vacancy that currently exists. Had there been a showing of a detriment to public safety or that there would be some other dire consequence either financially or on the operation of the Department by granting the Union's request the result might again have been different. On this record no such showing was made. Finally, the City made what was essentially an equitable plea and asserted that fundamental fairness and one's "gut" sense should govern here as well. While there is some pull to that argument, especially given the economic circumstances around the nation and the state of Montana, this is neither a statutory criterion nor is it one that is traditionally used to determine appropriate awards either in arbitration or in negotiations. Interest arbitrators . . . should rule based on evidence and logic, argument and well-established rules of process and negotiations—they should in short rule with their heads rather than with their hearts and this case provides a good example of how that well reasoned admonition manifests itself. While there was some cogency to the claim that at this point in history even a small increase should be regarded as something of great benefit, the evidence and assertions demonstrated by a preponderance of the evidence that the Union's position was more justified than the City's on this record.

Accordingly, taking into consideration the factors listed by the statute and those traditionally used in the determination of interest matters it is determined that the Union's proposal is awarded.

Notes

1. Even though only one issue was at impasse, and even though the parties agreed on a number of important matters, this decision still had to resolve a number of disputed points, ranging from methodology to policy. Interest arbitration decisions, which usually involve multiple issues, are often fairly long and quite fact-dependent. For example, *Snohomish County v. Snohomish County Corrections Officers Guild*, Case No. 12771-1-15 (Arb. Cavanagh, 2017), an interest arbitration case from Washington state, featured fifteen separate contract issues (the union mostly prevailed on wages and health insurance, the employer on the remaining thirteen). *Illinois Dept. of State Police and Illinois Troopers Lodge #41, F.O.P.*, Case No. S-MA-15-347 (Arb. Nielsen, 2016), involved *twenty-five* issues. These are also among the most important cases that practitioners handle, given that the results of the case set contract terms.

2. The arbitrator was obliged to use final offer total package in this case. Even though there was only one issue in this case, the arbitrator still seemed to wish that he could award a compromise, not just the final offer of one party or another, on the issue. Thus, the arbitrator was implicitly critiquing final offer issue-by-issue arbitration as well; he seemed to prefer conventional arbitration. What are the best arguments in favor of conventional arbitration as opposed to final offer arbitration? What are the potential drawbacks of conventional arbitration, as opposed to a final offer model?

3. A traditional argument against conventional arbitration is that it discourages realistic, hard bargaining because the parties expect the arbitrator to "split the baby"; thus, both sides have an incentive to cling to relatively extreme proposals. *See, e.g.,* Frederic Champlin & Mario Bognanno, *"Chilling" Under Arbitration and Mixed Strike-Arbitration Regimes*, 6 J. Lab. Res. 375 (1985); James Chelius & Marian Extejt, *The Narcotic Effect of Impasse-Resolution Procedures*, 38 Indus. & Lab. Rel. Rev. 629 (1985). Some studies conclude, however, that arbitrators do not simply split the difference in the most conventional interest arbitrations. *See, e.g.,* Henry Farber, *Splitting-the-Difference in Interest Arbitration*, 35 Indus. & Lab. Rel. Rev. 70 (1981).

4. The fact that most final offer total package cases involve more than one issue creates another potential problem. Both parties may make a very reasonable offer on one issue, but an unreasonable offer on another, and the arbitrator must accept the reasonable with the unreasonable as a package. For example, in a Wisconsin case, Arbitrator Amedeo Greco wrote:

> How to balance these two proposals is a difficult task because adopting either Final Offer will result in a very undesirable consequence. . . . [B]y requiring new hires to pay 5% towards their health insurance just like the Firefighters, a desired result is reached, but at the cost of requiring new hires to take an unjustified pay cut which is a bad result. Alternatively, adopting the Association's Final Offer will result in not changing the wage schedule which is a good result under the facts of this case, but at the cost

of retaining the *status quo* on health insurance which is a bad result. The case thus boils down to whether the City's justified health insurance proposal is outweighed by the City's unjustified wage schedule proposal. *City of Cudahy Professional Police Ass'n Local 235 and City of Cudahy*, Case 102, No. 63721 MIA-2603, Decision No. 31376-A (June 5, 2006).

5. If you were an arbitrator in a "total package" case and each side had made some good proposals and some bad ones, how would you decide which "package" to choose? Count up the number of superior proposals by each side? Have some calculus that gave extra weight, one way or another, to proposals that were exceptionally good or exceptionally bad? Isn't it likely that some types of issues—for example, wages, or other issues that involve more money—will "count" more heavily than other issues in influencing the arbitrator as to which total package to choose? What does that mean, practically, for the parties? Also, is this an advantage or disadvantage to the total package model? If it is a disadvantage, does it outweigh the advantages of this model?

6. Final offer issue-by issue arbitration avoids the problems described in the previous note. But can you think of some advantages total package arbitration might have over issue-by-issue? Consider the incentives for the parties at the bargaining table under each system.

Also, issue-by-issue arbitration can spawn litigation over whether proposals on closely related topics should be considered separate issues or a single issue. *City of Cambridge, OH v. FOP Ohio Labor Council*, 2018-MED-0648, 0649, 0650 (Arbitrator Lavelle, Aug. 9, 2019), was an extreme example of this. The City argued that each Article of the contract contained one issue, period. The Union argued that each disputed provision within each article was a separate issue. Thus, the City contended that Article 27 of the contract was one issue, while the Union contended that Article 27 contained 15 separate issues. The Arbitrator ruled for the union on this matter.

7. In "final offer" systems, statutes vary as to the time by which the parties must make a final offer, from, *e.g.*, five days before the arbitration hearing to "at or before the conclusion of the arbitration hearing." Rehmus, *supra*, 207. What might be the advantages and disadvantages to these different rules?

8. In any event, using binding arbitration to resolve impasses significantly lowers the probability of strikes. Rehmus, *supra*, 202; Olson, *Dispute Resolution in the Public Sector, in* Aaron, Najita & Stern, *supra*, 165; Kearney & Mareschal, *supra*, at 285 (collecting sources). *See also* Thomas Kochan, David Lipsky, Mary Newhart & Alan Benson, *The Long Haul Effects of Interest Arbitration: The Case of New York State's Taylor Law*, 63 Indus. & Lab. Rel. Rev. 565, 569 (2010) (study of effect of mandatory, binding arbitration on police and fire employees shows that as to the "primary purpose . . . to avoid work stoppages by essential public service employees, the arbitration statute has clearly met its objectives: no police or firefighter unit has engaged in a strike" in the 30 years the study covers).

c. Statutory Criteria Arbitrators Must Consider

Montana's statute is typical in setting out specific factors that arbitrators must consider in making interest arbitration awards. As shown later in this chapter, courts will reverse interest arbitration awards for not sufficiently complying with statutory criteria. Some statutes use only broad language, *e.g.,* "equity" and "the public interest." But more often, the criteria are fairly detailed, *e.g.,* not just listing the employer's "ability to pay," but also specifying which types of comparable employees, cost of living numbers, and financial data from the employer the arbitrator should consider. KEARNEY & MARESCHAL, *supra*, at 283–85. Many statutes use similar, or even identical, criteria. For example, the criteria in the Michigan statute covering public safety employees set out in *White Lake Township and Police Officers Labor Council*, MERC Case No. D06 G-1698 (Sept. 11, 2008), *infra*, are the same as the criteria in the Illinois statute. *See* MICH. COMP. LAWS § 423.239; 5 ILL. COMP. STAT.315/14(h).

Some statutes specifically instruct arbitrators to give certain criteria the most weight. For example, Oregon's statute states that the "first priority" is the "interest and welfare of the public." The Oregon statute also gives relatively specific guidance on "comparables."

> Arbitrators shall base their findings and opinions on these criteria giving first priority to paragraph (a) of this subsection and secondary priority to paragraphs (b) to (h) of this subsection as follows:
>
> (a) The interest and welfare of the public.
>
> (b) The reasonable financial ability of the unit of government to meet the costs of the proposed contract giving due consideration and weight to the other services, provided by, and other priorities of, the unit of government as determined by the governing body. A reasonable operating reserve against future contingencies, which does not include funds in contemplation of settlement of the labor dispute, shall not be considered as available toward a settlement.
>
> (c) The ability of the unit of government to attract and retain qualified personnel at the wage and benefit levels provided.
>
> (d) The overall compensation presently received by the employees, including direct wage compensation, vacations, holidays and other paid excused time, pensions, insurance, benefits, and all other direct or indirect monetary benefits received.
>
> (e) Comparison of the overall compensation of other employees performing similar services with the same or other employees in comparable communities. As used in this paragraph, "comparable" is limited to communities of the same or nearest population range within Oregon. Notwithstanding the provisions of this paragraph, the following additional definitions of "comparable" apply in the situations described as follows:

(A) For any city with a population of more than 325,000, "comparable" includes comparison to out-of-state cities of the same or similar size;

(B) For counties with a population of more than 400,000, "comparable" includes comparison to out-of-state counties of the same or similar size; and

(C) For the State of Oregon, "comparable" includes comparison to other states.

(f) The CPI-All Cities Index, commonly known as the cost of living.

(g) The stipulations of the parties.

(h) Such other factors, consistent with paragraphs (a) to (g) of this subsection as are traditionally taken into consideration in the determination of wages, hours, and other terms and conditions of employment. However, the arbitrator shall not use such other factors, if in the judgment of the arbitrator, the factors in paragraphs (a) to (g) of this subsection provide sufficient evidence for an award. Or. Rev. Stat. § 243.746.

If you were an arbitrator or advocate in Oregon, what would you take "the interest and welfare of the public" to refer to? Presumably, it would be things other than the factors listed in subsections (b) to (h). But what else that could be relevant and significant to an arbitrator's decision is not included in those factors?

Advocates should present their cases with the statutory criteria in mind. *City of Helena, supra*, explained that "[h]ad there been a showing of a detriment to public safety or that there would be some other dire consequence either financially or on the operation of the Department by granting the Union's request the result might again have been different." What evidence could an employer use in a case involving the wages of public safety officers to help show any of those things?

(i.) "Comparables"

As *City of Helena* illustrates, in most interest arbitration decisions, "comparables" are a very important factor. There are two types of "comparables": external and internal. External comparables are employees of other public employers who do work that is the same or very similar to the work of the employees in the arbitration for similar public employers. For example, police in mid-sized city A could be external comparables to police in mid-sized city B in the same state. Even when the parties agree about which cities and employees are comparable, they may still disagree on how exactly to do the comparisons (*e.g.*, in *City of Helena*, mean as opposed to median averages, and hourly as opposed to monthly wages). "Internal" comparables involve other employees of the same public employer. This issue is often labeled "internal consistency." See footnote 4 in *City of Helena*. For example, in a police arbitration, arbitrators can look to wages, hours, and working conditions of firefighters in the same city, or employees of the police department who are not in the police officers' bargaining unit.

Some decisions give more importance to external comparables, while some give more importance to internal comparables. *Compare Hennepin County of Paramedics and Hennepin County Medical Center*, BMS No. 17PNO203 (Arb. Befort, 2017) (focusing on internal comparables), *with Capital City Labor Program Supervisory Division and Ingham County*, MERC Case No. L15H0958 (Arb. Stratton, 2016) (rejecting internal comparables, because the relevant employees "are not responsible for what the County does with respect to other employee groups"). Should one type of "comparable" generally be more important than the other, or should it depend on the facts of the particular case? If the latter, what facts should matter?

What if interest arbitrators traditionally relied heavily on internal comparables for a certain issue between the parties, but then the collective bargaining rights of the comparable employees, but not the employees in the union at issue, were revoked by a statutory amendment? In *City of Dubuque and Dubuque Policeman's Protective Association* (Arb. Perry, June 21, 2018), the city argued that internal comparables—other city employees—had recently increased their payments toward health insurance premiums to 15%, while payments for the police employees at issue in the arbitration remained at 10%. While granting that these numbers were correct and that arbitrators had traditionally given great weight to internal comparables on this issue with these parties, the arbitrator also noted that most of the other city employees had recently lost their collective bargaining rights when the Iowa Public Employment Relations Act was amended. The arbitrator awarded the union's position of remaining at 10%.

Because comparables are such a significant factor, many interest arbitrations spend a good deal of time on the issue of which other employers and employees are proper comparisons. Where statutory language does not resolve the issue completely (which it rarely does), how should arbitrators decide which other public employers are comparable? Consider the discussion from the following case.

White Lake Township and Police Officers Labor Council
Mich. Emp. Rel. Comm. Case No. D06 G-1698 (Sept. 11, 2008)

Arbitration Panel: WILLIAM LONG (Chair); HOWARD SHIFMAN (Employer Delegate); JOHN VIVIANA (Union Delegate).

Introduction

[The parties agreed to submit two issues for arbitration.] Both of those issue are economic issues. They involve proposed revisions to: Article 16—Pension; Article 17—Insurance.

... [T]he panel was guided by Section 8 of Act 312. Section 8 provides that "as to each economic issue, the arbitration panel shall adopt the last offer of settlement, which in the opinion of the arbitration panel, more nearly complies with the applicable factors prescribed in Section 9."

The applicable factors to be considered as set forth in Section 9 are as follows.

(a) The lawful authority of the employer.

(b) Stipulations of the parties.

(c) The interests and welfare of the public and the financial ability of the unit of government to meet these costs.

(d) Comparison of the wages, hours and conditions of employment of the employees involved in the arbitration proceeding with the wages, hours and conditions of employment of other employees performing similar services and with other employees generally:

    (i) In public employment in comparable communities.

    (ii) In private employment in comparable communities.

(e) The average consumer prices for goods and services, commonly known as the cost of living.

(f) The overall compensation presently received by the employees, including direct wage compensation, vacations, holidays and other excused time, insurance and pensions, medical and hospitalization benefits, the continuity and stability of employment, and all other benefits received.

(g) Changes in any of the foregoing circumstances during the pendency of the arbitration proceedings.

(h) Such other factors, not confined to the foregoing, which are normally or traditionally taken into consideration in the determination of wages, hours and conditions of employment through voluntary collective bargaining, mediation, factfinding, arbitration or otherwise between the parties, in the public service or in private employment.

... Comparables Proposed by the Parties

Both parties agreed that the communities of Brownstown Township, Van Buren Township, and the Village of Milford/Milford Township are comparable communities. In addition, the Union proposed that Chesterfield Township be considered as a community comparable to White Lake Township.

... Act 312 and the rules governing the Act do not prescribe specific factors the panel must consider when determining comparability. Generally, factors commonly considered include size of the community to be served, form of government, SEV ["State Equalized Value," a measure of property tax assessment] and taxing authority, tax effort and other economic factors, scope of duties, the location of the comparable communities as they relate to the local labor market and population demographics. ...

Union Position

The Union urged the panel to recognize the stipulated communities and the Union's proposed community of Chesterfield Township as comparable to White Lake Township. The Union points out that Chesterfield Township, like the three communities that the parties have stipulated to as comparable, has a population

956 · 11 · ECONOMIC WEAPONS AND IMPASSE RESOLUTION

and taxable value that falls within 50% of that of White Lake Township. The Union also says that Chesterfield Township is within Macomb County which is in the tri-county region and therefore geographically situated similar to the other comparable communities. In its closing brief the Union says Macomb, Oakland and Wayne Counties form a unique financial system within the State of Michigan and the exclusion of Chesterfield Township, which is the only proposed comparable within Macomb County, would ignore the combined strengths of these counties together. The Union says including Chesterfield Township as a comparable will provide the panel with a better representation of the wages and benefits of employees performing similar services within those comparable communities.

Employer Position

The Employer opposes inclusion of Chesterfield Township as one of the comparable communities. The Employer points out that the 2006 taxable value of Chesterfield Township is over 1/3 more than that of White Lake Township. The Employer also notes . . . that additionally, Chesterfield Township compared to White Lake Township has 46 police officers compared to 25 in White Lake Township; double the mills to fund police protection; and less need to rely on general funds to support the police department. . . .

Discussion and Findings

. . . The parties in this case have agreed on use of three of the four proposed external comparable communities. The question left for the panel is whether Chesterfield Township is a comparable community to White Lake Township, as the union proposes or not comparable, as the Employer argues. A review of the evidence presented reveals the following: 1) Brownstown and Van Buren Townships population estimates for 2006 and taxable values for 2007 are relatively comparable to that of White Lake Township. 2) The two communities that have a greater percentage difference in these factors with that of White Lake Township are Milford Village/Township and Chesterfield Township. 3) A review of population comparables reveals Chesterfield Township's 2006 estimated population is 48% greater than that of White Lake Township. However, Milford Township's 2006 estimated population, a comparage both parties agreed to, is 54% less than that of White Lake Township. So the Chesterfield township comparable population is not outside the range of at least one of the agreed upon comparables. 4) A review of the 2007 taxable value of the proposed comparables also shows the communities of Milford Village/Township and Chesterfield Township to be of a higher percentage difference than the other two comparable communities agreed upon by the parties. The 2007 taxable value for Milford Village/Township is 26% less and the Chesterfield Township 2007 taxable value 46% more than that of White Lake Township. The question is what is a reasonable range for comparison purposes? There is no set standard, and in this case at least both of these higher percentage differences are within 50% of that of White Lake Township. The panel would also note that the percentage difference in taxable value between Chesterfield Township and White Lake Township actually dropped from 47% in 2006 to 46% in 2007.

The Union argued that Chesterfield Township should be included because it is the only proposed comparable within Macomb County and there is a unique financial link between Wayne, Oakland and Macomb counties that should be recognized. There was little evidence presented to support this unique financial link argument. On the other hand, it is noted that two of the three comparable communities the parties agreed to, Brownstown and Van Buren, are within Wayne County and the third, Milford Village/Township, is within Oakland. As noted above, location of the comparable communities is often considered in the context of their relationship to a local or similar type labor market and population demographics. Again, little evidence was presented on this factor but the panel does note that the geographic proximity of White Lake Township to Chesterfield Township in Macomb County is not much different than the proximity of White Lake Township to Brownstown Township in Wayne County. . . .

. . . [T]he panel will note that its decision on external comparable communities in this proceeding is based on only the limited evidence provided and this panel is of the opinion it should not be considered as a precedent in future arbitrations.

Based on the limited evidence in this proceeding the panel finds that . . . there is not a significant difference between the comparables agreed upon, taken as a whole, and those factors inclusive of Chesterfield Township. Therefore in the panel's opinion, it is not unreasonable to include Chesterfield Township as one of the Comparable communities for this proceeding. . . .

Notes

1. *White Lake Township* clearly implies that evidence beyond the types it discusses could be relevant to determining whether two cities are "comparable." What other types of evidence can you think of that could be relevant and persuasive? *City of Helena* mentions hours worked by certain employees. Can you think of other, job-specific factors?

2. What is the basic purpose of using comparables in interest arbitrations, as at least most statutes require? Is it just some notion of "fairness"? Is "what similar employers pay" the best way to determine what the market wage (or its equivalent) is for a given job in government employment?

At least one other important concern is involved. *City of Helena* warned of "some danger" if comparable jurisdictions had significant wage increases for similar employees in 2010 and Helena did not. Helena's wages "will eventually fall too far behind if the City's proposal is awarded and that is a major concern." The potential danger is not abstract unfairness to Helena's employees. Rather, it is that Helena would be unable to recruit and retain good employees if nearby, comparable cities were paying noticeably higher wages for basically the same jobs.

3. For that reason, some arbitrators stress geographic proximity as an important factor in determining comparability. "It may be interesting in the abstract to know what police officers make in Cheney; but what a Kelso officer could make by driving

to Centralia or Battle Ground is much more personal data." *Fircrest Police Officers Guild and City of Fircrest, WA*, PERC Case No. 21294-1-07-500 (July 15, 2008) (Arbitrator Amedeo Greco).

4. Other statutes and arbitration decisions get at the retention issue in other ways. The Oregon statute, *supra*, § 243.746(c), specifically lists the "ability of the unit of government to attract and retain qualified personnel at the wage and benefit levels provided" as a factor. A decision on the pay of New York City police officers discussed retention as part of the "Interest and Welfare of the Public" criteria. *The City of New York and Patrolmen's Benevolent Ass'n of the City of New York, Inc.*, Case No. IA 2006-24; M 2006-093 (May 22, 2008, Arb. Panel Chair Susan McKenzie).

5. Debates over comparables can be complicated. Oregon's statute, *supra*, gives comparatively specific guidance on how comparables should be determined (mainly, cities in Oregon within specified population ranges). Still, the decision in *City of Roseburg, Oregon and Int'l Ass'n of Firefighters, Local 1110*, Case No. IA-09-06 (May 22, 2007) devoted 28 pages solely to the issue of which cities are comparable to Roseburg, Oregon regarding firefighters. Some small Oregon cities the size of Roseburg were part of larger "fire districts," but Roseburg was not. The cities in larger fire districts had greater resources for their fire departments. Under the language of the Oregon statute—which again, is more detailed than most on this issue—could such cities be "comparables"? Arbitrator Michael Cavanaugh ultimately decided that they could be.

6. The Michigan statute in *White Lake Township* provides for a tripartite arbitration panel: a neutral chair, an employer delegate, and an employee delegate. Note that the employer's delegate dissented from the part of the award (favoring the union) holding that Chesterfield was an appropriate comparable. The employer's delegate also dissented from part of the awards (not excerpted above) holding in favor of the union on a retiree insurance issue. The union's delegate was in the majority on those two issues, but dissented from the holding (not excerpted above) in favor of the employer on a pension issue.

This type of result is not uncommon in the tripartite model: union delegates generally vote for the union's position and employer delegates generally vote for the employer's position. Thus, the neutral is the tie-breaker and ultimate decision-maker. What might be the advantages or disadvantages of this system compared to using a single, neutral arbitrator?

(ii.) The Employer's Ability to Pay (and Hard Economic Times)

City of Helena discusses the severe recession that began in December 2007 and was still ongoing in 2010 when that decision was issued. Most statutes require arbitrators to consider the employer's ability to pay, and in interest arbitrations, employers rarely maintain they are affluent. But the recession made this a central factor in interest arbitrations across the country. The economic downturn the COVID-19 pandemic caused will undoubtedly create similar issues.

City of Helena decided that comparables were, under the facts of that case, more significant than the economic crisis. That was not the majority approach on this issue. The following case, which dealt directly and at length with the recession, is more typical.

State of Illinois, Dept. of Central Management Services and Int'l B'hood of Teamsters Local 726

Case Nos.: S-MA-08-262, Arb. Ref. 08.208 (Jan. 27, 2009)

Edward Benn, Arbitrator

. . . a. The Present Economic Climate

At the time the disputed issues in this case were heard on August 5 and September 5, 2008 and as subsequently briefed by the parties, the Union focused on comparability arguments while the [Employer, Illinois State Police, "ISP"] focused on the statutory factors found in Section 14(h) of the Act, but mainly sought to counter the Union's comparability arguments.

That was then. This is now. During the pendency of the arbitration proceedings . . . the economy went into free-fall after the second day of hearing.

First, on the initial day of hearing on August 5, 2008, the Dow Jones Industrial Average ("DJI") was at 11,616.14. On the second day of hearing on September 5, 2008, the DJI was at 11,221. . . . On January 26, 2009—the trading day before the issuance of this award—the DJI stood at 8116, still 30% down from the commencement of these proceedings. . . .

Second, contemporaneous with the dramatic fall in the stock market and since the close of the hearing on September 5, 2008, credit markets have frozen up, companies have gone out of business or cut back operations, massive layoffs have occurred and government bailouts of staggering proportions have been announced in an effort to get the economy moving. . . .

As bad as the national unemployment rate is, the State's unemployment picture is worse. . . . These are the worst unemployment rates in Illinois since June 1993. . . .

At the time the AFSCME-State contract was negotiated, compelling reasons justifying [a 15.25% wage increase over four years] were common sense realizations concerning the cost-of-living as it existed in August 2008 when that contract was finalized. For example, . . . when the predecessor July 1, 2004—June 30, 2008 AFSCME-State contract expired, the average price of a gallon of regular gasoline rose from $1.92 to $4.20 over the life of that contract. . . . When this proceeding began in early August 2008, the average cost of a gallon of regular gasoline was $4.02; which then dropped to $3.91 in early September 2008; hit a low of $1.65 in early December 2008; and, as of January 26, 2009 was at $1.95. Therefore, during the pendency of these proceedings, with respect to the price of gasoline, the exact *opposite* experience existed from that which occurred during the four year period of the predecessor AFSCME-State contract—*i.e.*, during that contract, the cost of gasoline more than doubled, while during the pendency of these proceedings, the cost of gasoline fell by approximately 50%.

. . . "[T]he economy" and fluctuations in gasoline prices are not specific statutory factors found in Section 14(h) of the Act. However, "[t]he average consumer prices for goods and services, commonly known as the cost of living" is a specific factor — Section 14(h)(5). The economy and gasoline prices just discussed are reflected in cost-of-living numbers. . . .

[P]rior to August 2008 and going back to December 2007 . . . the CPI was increasing — a factor that would be favorable to the Union . . . However, . . . commencing in August 2008, the changes in the CPI began to fall and went to zero or slipped into the negative range — a factor not favorable to the Union because costs of goods began to decrease. . . .

In short, during the pendency of these proceedings, the economy simply tanked. . . .

b. Selection Of The Offers

For the Union, the above described economic events could not have come at a worse time in its efforts to increase the rank differential for the Master Sergeants. As the Union methodically laid out its position in the proceedings before me on why a higher rank differential than that offered by the ISP should be imposed through this process, the economic rug was pulled out from under it. And, Section 14(h) of the Act addresses such a situation. Section 14(h)(7) provides that interest arbitrators consider "[c]hanges in any of the foregoing circumstances during the pendency of the arbitration proceedings." Given the crash of the economy described above which occurred while this case was being presented, to say that "[c]hanges . . . during the pendency of the arbitration proceedings" occurred in this case would be an understatement. . . .

While the rank differential percentage change in the ISP offer may seem low (going from 6.95% in effect January 1, 2008 to 7.5% at the end of the Agreement), when coupled with the 15.25% increase given to the Sergeants upon which the rank differential is then applied and then considering increases in the step lane movements due to longevity, the *actual* wage increases for the Master Sergeants under the ISP's offer are quite significant — both in real dollars and percentages.

. . . [T]he ISP's rank differential offer is by no stretch of the imagination regressive. On the contrary, the ISP's offer will result in significant monetary and percentage increases for the Master Sergeants. In the economic climate now facing the parties, those kinds of significant increases must be given great weight. Given the significant increases resulting from the ISP's offer, the Union's offer, which, in real dollars shows very significant increases, simply cannot be justified in this economy or under the statutory factors found in Section 14(h) of the Act.

When weighed against the above, the Union's arguments concerning comparability do not change the result. The short answer to the Union's reliance upon the jurisdictions it selected for comparison purposes is that even assuming those jurisdictions are valid comparables, those contracts were not negotiated under the economic circumstances that have existed since these proceedings began in August 2008. But in any event, on balance, given the extraordinary circumstances which presented in this case since August 2008, the comparability factor in Section 14(h)(4) must yield to the other factors cited above.

The ISP's offer on rank differential is therefore selected.

c. Caveats

For the parties and interest arbitrators trying to formulate contracts, these are remarkably difficult times. . . . The difficulty from my end as an interest arbitrator is that in these uncertain and volatile times, Section 14(g) of the Act ties my hands. This is final offer interest arbitration and I do not have the authority to impose an economic term different from the ones offered by the parties. . . .

Perhaps a cautious and practical way to approach negotiations and interest arbitrations in these uncertain and changing times is for parties to negotiate reopeners on economic items or to tie reopeners to triggers in the out years of agreements— *i.e.*, if changes in the cost-of-living or insurance costs occur, the parties have the option to reopen agreed upon provisions mid-term during the period of a contract. With negotiated reopeners, the parties can then assess the situation as the economy changes rather than project years out into the future with fixed obligations having no idea what the economic conditions will be. For now, final offer interest arbitration does not serve the parties well. . . .

Notes

1. Most arbitrators gave more weight to the recession's effect on the employer's ability to pay than to favorable comparables data for unions or other factors. "[T]his Arbitrator took the position that in the current tough economic times the State's ability to pay trumps all of the other statutory factors." *State of Washington and SEIU Local 775 NW*, Supplemental Interest Award (Arbitrator Timothy Williams, Sept. 29, 2009). Similarly Arbitrator Mario Bognanno explained:

> Minnesota's general economic conditions have deteriorated sharply since CY 2007. For this reason, the wage and insurance terms that the instant parties might have voluntarily negotiated under the prevailing economic and fiscal regime most likely would have been different from those that were negotiated by comparable external bargaining units during better times—2007. Accordingly, the Arbitrator is not inclined to rely on the "dated" negotiated settlements of comparable external bargaining units— a conclusion that is strongly attenuated by the Employer's increasingly strained ability-to-pay. *The Metropolitan Council, Metro Transit Police Dept. and Law Enforcement Labor Services, Inc., Local 203—Police Administration & Command Employees*, BMS Case No. 08-PN-1141 (Feb. 27, 2009).

2. In *State of Illinois, Department of Central Management*, Arbitrator Benn suggests some ways the parties could conduct future negotiations (*e.g.*, agreeing to "reopeners") because, in the arbitrator's view, final offer arbitration (in this case issue-by-issue) does not provide sufficient flexibility. Are his suggestions good ones? Are they appropriate for him to make?

3. According to Arbitrator Benn, the union in *Department of Central Management* still wound up with a decent raise, even though he rejected its proposals. Other public-sector unions fared worse in the recession. In a Minnesota case, Arbitrator John Miller noted that, "the vast majority of cities in the Employer's comparison group are proposing 0% [wage increases] for 2010. . . . Some cities and counties are settling at 0%." *City of West St. Paul, Minnesota and Law Enforcement Labor Services, Inc., Local No 72 (Police Officer Unit)*, BMS Case. No. 09-PN-1062 (Jan. 19, 2010). For an award that actually cut salaries and benefits, see *IAFF Local 1908 and Clark County, Nevada* (Case No. 3243, Jan 19, 2011) (Arbitrator Norman Brand).

4. Beyond interest arbitration awards, many public employers, including those with unionized employees, have imposed involuntary furloughs and staffing cuts. Legal challenges to furloughs have largely been unsuccessful. *See, e.g., Fraternal Order of Police Lodge No. 89 v. Prince George's County, MD*, 608 F.3d 183 (4th Cir. 2010) (rejecting a Contract Clause challenge to involuntary furloughs).

5. A more dramatic strategy involves a municipal employer declaring bankruptcy and thus voiding its obligations in collective-bargaining agreements. *In re Vallejo*, 432 B.R. 262 (E.D. Cal. 2010) rejected a union's legal challenge to this process.

In December 2013, the city of Detroit, Michigan entered into Chapter 9 bankruptcy, putting both the terms of CBAs and pensions of current and past city employees at significant risk. Pursuant to a settlement, Detroit emerged from bankruptcy in December 2014. An estimated 20,000 retirees had their pension payments reduced, but the cuts were not as severe as some had feared. The state and a group of philanthropic organizations entered into a "Grand Bargain," contributing more than $800 million to the city's pensions. Before that, in April 2014, the city and fourteen unions had reached a tentative agreement on "major aspects" of CBAs covering approximately 3,500 city employees. *In re City of Detroit*, 524 B.R. 147 (Bankr. E.D. Mich. 2014); Nora Macaluso, "Detroit Emerges from Bankruptcy Protection; Governor Ends Receivership," 28 LRW (BNA) (Dec. 17, 2014).

Also, in August 2013, a federal judge granted the city of San Bernardino, California Chapter 9 bankruptcy protection. *In re City of San Bernardino*, 499 B.R. 776 (Bankr. C.D. Cal. 2013) (summary judgment orally granted 8/28/13). Among other things, this permitted the city to reject CBAs through the bankruptcy process. *See San Bernardino City Prof'l Firefighters Local 891 v. City of San Bernardino*, 530 B.R. 474 (C.D. Cal. 2015) (affirming order of bankruptcy court granting city's motion to reject a labor contract with a firefighters' union, where the city made reasonable efforts to make voluntary modifications to contract, and the contract was a financial burden).

6. More broadly, the recession prompted political attacks on public employees and their unions that led to the 2011 laws restricting public-sector union rights discussed in Chapter 1.

> Spurred by state budget crunches and an angry public mood, Republican and some Democratic leaders are focusing with increasing intensity on public workers and the unions that represent them, casting them as overpaid obstacles to good government and demanding cuts in their often-generous benefits. . . . "We have a new privileged class in America," said Indiana Gov. Mitch Daniels, who rescinded state workers' collective bargaining power on his first day in office in 2006. "We used to think of government workers as underpaid public servants. Now they are better paid than the people who pay their salaries." Ben Smith & Maggie Haberman, *Pols Turn on Labor Unions*, POLITICO, June 6, 2010, *available at* http://www.politico.com/news/stories/0610/38183.html. For more on this, *see* Joseph Slater, *Public-Sector Labor in the Age of Obama*, 87 IND. L.J. 189, 192–93 (2012).[*]

7. The claim that public employees are overpaid relative to private-sector employees has been hotly contested, and in fact, the majority of studies on the issue have concluded that public employees are actually paid somewhat less than comparable private-sector employees as a whole. *See* Joseph Slater & Elijah Welenc, *Are Public-Sector Employees "Overpaid" Relative to Private-Sector Employees? An Overview of the Studies*, 52 WASHBURN L.J. 533 (2013); David Lewin, Thomas Kochan *et al.*, *Getting It Right: Empirical Evidence and Policy Implications from Research on Public-Sector Unionism and Collective Bargaining* 11–12 (Emp't Policy Research Network, Labor and Emp't Relations Ass'n Working Paper Series 2011), *available at* http://ssrn.com/abstract=1792942.

For example, one study in 2010 concluded:

> Wages and salaries of state and local employees are lower than those for private sector workers with comparable earnings determinants (e.g., education). State employees typically earn 11 percent less; local workers earn 12 percent less. . . . Over the last 20 years, the earnings for state and local employees have generally declined relative to comparable private sector employees. . . . Benefits (e.g., pensions) comprise a greater share of employee compensation in the public sector. . . . [Including benefits] State and local employees have lower total compensation than their private sector counterparts. On average, total compensation is 6.8 percent lower for state employees and 7.4 percent lower for local workers, compared with comparable private sector employees. Keith Bender & John Heywood, Out of Balance? Comparing Public and Private Compensation over 20 Years (National Institute on Retirement Security 2010), *available at* http://www

---

[*] Copyright 2010. Reprinted by permission.

.nirsonline.org/storage/nirs/documents/final_out_of_balance_report_
april_2010.pdf.*

Similarly, an analysis published in 2012 found that

> state and local public employees are not overpaid. Comparisons control-
> ling for education, experience, hours of work, gender, race, ethnicity, and
> disability reveal no significant overpayment. Instead, the data reveal that
> on a per-hour basis, public employees are slightly undercompensated when
> compared to similar private-sector employees. . . . [F]ull-time state and
> local employees are, on average, undercompensated by 5.6%. The public
> employee compensation penalty is smaller for local government employees
> (4.1%) than state government workers (8.3%). Jeffrey Keefe, *State and Local
> Public Employees: Are They Overcompensated?* 27 A.B.A.J. Lab. & Emp. L.
> 239 (2012).

Still, some studies have found a "public sector pay premium." *See, e.g.,* Maury
Gittleman & Brooks Pierce, *Compensation for State and Local Government Workers,* 26 J. Econ. Persp. 217 (2011); Jason Richwine & Andrew Biggs, *Public-Sector
Compensation: Correcting the Economic Policy Institute, Again,* Heritage Foundation (Mar. 31, 2011), *available at* http://www.heritage.org/research/reports/2011/03
/public-sector-compensation-correcting-the-economic-policy-institute-again.

Almost all pay studies agree on some findings. First, at the very bottom of the
pay scale (*e.g.,* janitors), public workers have slightly higher compensation than
their private-sector analogs, while at the upper end of the scales (*e.g.,* lawyers and
other professionals), public workers are paid less than comparable private-sector
employees. Second, almost all studies agree that in terms of take-home pay, public
workers receive less than private-sector workers. And most studies agree that public
workers generally receive more generous health and pension benefits than comparable private-sector workers. When combining pay and benefits, again, a majority of
studies still find a "public-sector penalty," but others do not.

Most of the disagreements are about employees in the middle of the pay scale.
Important methodological differences in the studies include how to calculate the
value (and current cost) of future benefits, how to compare certain types or ranges
of jobs across sectors, and whether to assign monetary value to "job security" for
government employees (and if so, how much). Further, controlling for employer
size seems to matter: studies that do not use such controls are more likely to find a
public-sector premium than studies that do. *See* Slater & Welenc, *supra.* Complicating matters, while some public-sector jobs have private-sector analogs (*e.g.,* janitors and lawyers), some large and important categories of public employees, notably
police and fire, do not.

8. Part of the problem was that declines in the stock market contributed to significant underfunding in a number of public-sector pension plans. That put an

---

* Copyright 2010. Reprinted by permission.

additional strain on already-weakened public budgets. Smith & Haberman, *Pols Turn on Labor Unions, supra,* noted:

> A recent study from the Pew Center on the States found that states are short $1 trillion toward the $3.35 trillion in pension, health care and other retirement benefits states have promised their current and retired workers, the product of a combination of political decisions and the recent recession.
>
> But the immediate cause of the new spotlight on public sector unions is the collapse in tax revenues that came with the 2008 Wall Street crash, something that union leaders bitterly note is not their fault.

9. In this regard, it is important to understand that pension formulas and benefits for public workers are almost always set by statute and are not subject to bargaining by unions. *See* Gerald McEntee, *Don't Blame Public Pensions Opposing View*, U.S.A. TODAY, Jan. 17, 2011, at 6A, *available at* http://www.usatoday.com/printedition /news/20110118/editorial18_st1.art.htm (public employee pension systems "predated public employee bargaining rights, and few plans are subject to the bargaining process today"). *See, e.g.*, OHIO REV. CODE Ch. 145 (statute setting pension rules and benefits for public employees); OHIO REV. CODE §4117.10 (provisions of laws pertaining to, *inter alia*, retirement of public employees prevail over any provisions in a union contract); recall from the discussion in Transport Workers Union cases, *supra*, that the parties were not permitted to bargain over pension benefits.

10. Interest arbitrators had to deal with hard economic times before the recession that began in December 2007. For example, more than two years before that crash, in a case involving police in Ohio, Arbitrator Robert Stein explained:

> These are uncertain times for Ohio public employers. Financial uncertainty continues to loom in northeastern Ohio, punctuated by periodic announcements of companies downsizing or moving their operations out of Ohio. Ohio is not the only state affected by these corporate downsizing moves; however, its past dependence upon manufacturing has left it particularly vulnerable. There continues to be a marked movement of manufacturing jobs out of the country and reluctance by companies remaining to restore manufacturing jobs even when the economy turns more favorable. During this same period the federal government is reducing aid to the states and, in turn, the states are reducing aid to municipalities and other local government entities.
>
> As with all business, there is a bottom line to watch, and the business of public government is no exception. . . .
>
> Approximately one-half of the service department employees were laid off in 2004, and further reductions have been made by attrition. In 2004 the safety bargaining units made significant sacrifices by accepting a freeze on wage increases. Again, I can appreciate the bargaining units' frustration with the current economic condition of the City. Yet they and the City have no choice but to take the necessary steps to preserve city services and bring

about economic stability. . . . *Fraternal Order of Police, OLC, Inc. and City of Eastlake*, SERB Case No. 04-MED-10-1014,1015-16 MAD (Feb. 1, 2006).

How should arbitrators handle cases in times and regions of the country where the economy is doing poorly? Should that factor "trump" all other factors? How should advocates on each side prepare and argue their cases in such conditions?

11. In *City of South Bay, Florida v. IAM Lodge #166*, SM 2014-030 (Special Magistrate Brady, 2014), all parties agreed that the employer's significant budget deficit had been caused by the employer's financial mismanagement, including significant fraud by the employer's agents in the recent past. Still, the fact-finder, noting that the city truly was experiencing financial hardship, recommended the city's proposals. What are the arguments for and against that approach?

12. A few states have specified that some different rules should apply in interest arbitration for cities that are "financially distressed." It is unclear how much of a difference such rules have made so far. *See Walker v. Read*, 91 N.Y.S.3d 807 (Sup. Ct. App. Div. 2019) (interest arbitration award granting a 2% wage increase to firefighters upheld over employer challenge, despite the fact that the employer (Plattsburgh, NY) was a "fiscally eligible municipality" under a state law that required arbitrators to give a weight of 70% to such an employer's ability to pay, because the arbitration panel complied with that mandate); *Fraternal Order of Police Fort Pitt Lodge No. 1. v. City of Pittsburgh*, 203 A.3d 965 (Pa. 2019) (interest arbitration award involving a city under a recovery plan pursuant to the state Municipal Financial Recovery Act upheld over a union challenge, as award did not deviate from the plan).

d. The Significance of Precedent

Interest arbitrators often take seriously past arbitration decisions involving the same or similar employees and past arbitral interpretations of statutory language. As to statutory language, in *City of Roseburg, Oregon, supra*, Arbitrator Cavanaugh explained, "I believe it promotes stability in public employee bargaining for an arbitrator to follow the decisions of prior arbitrators, and a party asking for a deviation from established interpretations of the law carries a heavy burden. That is so, in my view, even if I might have decided the issue differently as a matter of first impression. Not that slavish devotion to precedent is required. If I were convinced that my fellow arbitrators had utterly misread the statute, I might be willing to strike out on my own in a different direction now."

Arbitrators also follow precedent when a substantive issue was decided in an earlier interest arbitration. For example, *In City of Alton, IL and IAFF Local 1255*, Ill. Lab. Rel. Bd. No. S-MA-006 (Arbitrator John Fletcher, 2007), the union asked for an expansion of a residency requirement despite having lost on that same issue in a 2005 arbitration with a different arbitrator. The arbitrator rejected this, stressing the importance of precedent.

> [T]he Union's case, though once again passionately articulated, is a trip down memory lane. While this was not automatically fatal . . . the Union

was nevertheless subject to a higher burden of proof in light of Arbitrator Meyers' conclusions a mere two years ago. . . . Arbitrator Meyers' award should be given deference equal to that of a negotiated *status quo.* . . . [P]utting the parties back to ground zero . . . would be tantamount to rendering the entire purpose of interest arbitration useless. . . . [It] would promote a practice of "arbitrator shopping" until the party petitioning for departure from the *status quo* was finally satisfied with the outcome, after which the "loser" could do the same. Clearly, this practice was never contemplated under the Act, given the final and binding nature of arbitration and statutory guidance as to how the arbitrator should reasonably (if not always absolutely perfectly) discern what the "natural extension of the bargaining process" should produce.

Indeed, most interest arbitration awards are closely linked to previous contracts between the parties. Barring changes in the law or significant changes in circumstances, arbitrators often require a significant *quid pro quo* for any substantial departure from previous contracts. This has prompted one commentator to suggest that the process "could probably be accomplished more inexpensively by averaging the parties' final offers and adding on some noise using a computer's random number generator." D.E. Bloom, *Arbitrator Behavior in Public Sector Wage Disputes, in* Richard Freeman and Casey Ichniowski, eds., When Public Sector Workers Unionize 123 (1988). If true, does that call into question the significance of legal rules setting guidelines for interest arbitrations? Or does it show that these rules are working?

Problem 11.2

In response to a police department ordering the use of body cams, a police union made the following bargaining proposal about the effects of this order: officers and their union should have unlimited access to their video footage to assist officers in writing reports, and in preparing for testimony in legal proceedings. The employer's proposal was to give the Chief of Police discretion to determine whether officers should have access to video footage in instances of officer-involved shootings, in-custody deaths, or incidents where officers are alleged to have engaged in criminal activity or serious misconduct. At the interest arbitration, assuming typical statutory criteria, what do you think the best arguments for each side are? Also, had you been the arbitrator, how would you have ruled? *See City of Ithaca, NY v. Ithaca Police Benevolent Ass'n*, PERB Case No. 1A 2016-024 (Arbitrator Gorman) (adopting the union's proposal on this issue).

Problem 11.3

The Employee Free Choice Act would have required parties covered by the NLRA to engage in binding interest arbitration if they could not reach agreement on a first contract within a specified amount of time. Unlike public-sector statutes, however, EFCA did not contain any criteria for interest arbitrators to use in crafting their decisions. Nor did it explain whether the arbitrator should use the conventional model or some form of final offer model.

First, based on your understanding of how interest arbitration works in the public sector, what are the pros and cons of this section of EFCA, which would have applied this process in certain circumstances in the private sector?

Second, if amendments to the NLRA requiring binding interest arbitration in some situations are ever enacted, would it be better to include specific criteria interest arbitrators should consider? If so, what should those criteria be? The same as public-sector statutes commonly use? Should any factors be deleted (*e.g.,* "the public interest")? Should any factors be added? If "comparables" are a factor, should the statute explain how to determine which employers and employees in the private sector are "comparable"? If so, how?

4. Impasse Procedures Without Mandatory, Binding Arbitration

The principle behind mandatory, binding interest arbitration is that is it the *quid pro quo* for being denied the right to strike. *See, e.g., Snyder County Prison Bd. and County of Snyder v. Pa. Lab. Rel. Bd. and Teamsters Local 764*, 912 A.2d 356, 367 (Pa. Commw. Ct. 2006) ("Because of the need to have prison guards on duty, the legislature has denied prison guards the right to strike. . . . The *quid pro quo* for such an arrangement is the provision of mandatory mediation and interest arbitration"; the legislature intended "to balance the bargaining positions of public employers and public employees who are not permitted to strike").

In a minority of jurisdictions, however, interest arbitrators issue opinions that are merely advisory rather than binding. The obvious criticism is that this sort of arbitration gives unions no more than a fact-finder's recommendations: the employer may still implement what it wants to implement. In other jurisdictions, both parties must agree to use a binding process. Also, a minority of states (*e.g.,* Florida) which authorize collective bargaining but prohibit strikes simply have no step after mediation or factfinding. *See* KEARNEY & MARESCHAL, *supra*, at 269, 281. What are the best arguments in favor of any of these systems? In a jurisdiction where interest arbitration is only advisory, what could a union do, practically, if an employer decided not to implement the arbitrator's recommendations?

Some states have binding, mandatory arbitration for some public employees, but not others. For example, Michigan uses binding arbitration for certain public safety workers, but not for other public employees. *Compare* MICH. COMP. LAWS §§ 423.231–33 (compulsory and binding arbitration for police and fire), *and* MICH. COMP. LAWS §§ 423.271–87 (same for state police troopers and sergeants), *with* MICH. COMP. LAWS §§ 423.207–207(a) (mediation is the final step for all other public employees, and if mediation fails, the employer can implement its final offer). In 2011, Wisconsin Act 10 took away the right to binding interest arbitration (and a limited right to strike) from most public employees, but kept binding interest arbitration for certain public safety unions. Are there principled reasons to make these distinctions?

Constitutional objections to binding interest arbitration also exist. As Chapter 1 explained, before the 1960s, courts routinely held that grievance arbitration and collective bargaining in the public sector violated constitutional non-delegation rules by improperly transferring inherent government power to private parties such as arbitrators. Most jurisdictions have abandoned that approach. By the mid-1980s, courts in 14 states had rejected claims that mandatory binding arbitration rules violated the non-delegation doctrine, and in only three states had courts held that mandatory binding arbitration was unconstitutional. *See* Schneider, *supra*, 208 and nn.69–70 (collecting cases). By the 1990s, 16 states had rejected non-delegation claims. KEARNEY & MARESCHAL, *supra*, at 287. Among other grounds, courts held that a public employer's rights are protected by its statutory right to appeal any arbitration award. *See, e.g., Office of Administration v. Pa. Lab. Rel. Bd.*, 528 Pa. 472, 479 (1991). But five states had upheld such challenges: South Dakota, Colorado, Utah, Nebraska, and Maryland. KEARNEY & MARESCHAL, *supra*, at 287. In some cases, courts struck down statutes because they failed to provide enough criteria for arbitrators to base awards. Rehmus, *supra*, 198.

While the clear majority of cases considering the issue have found that mandatory arbitration systems are constitutional, the issue can sometimes still be an obstacle to interest arbitration.

County of Riverside v. Superior Court

Supreme Court of California
30 Cal. 4th 278, 132 Cal. Rptr. 2d 713, 66 P.3d 718 (2003)

CHIN, J.

The Legislature recently enacted Senate Bill No. 402, which requires counties and other local agencies to submit, under certain circumstances, to binding arbitration of economic issues that arise during negotiations with unions representing firefighters or law enforcement officers. We must determine whether this legislation violates either or both of two provisions of article XI of the California Constitution. Section 1, subdivision (b), states that a county's "governing body shall provide for the . . . compensation . . . of employees." Section 11, subdivision (a), forbids the Legislature to "delegate to a private person or body power to . . . interfere with county or municipal corporation . . . money . . . or perform municipal functions."

We conclude . . . that Senate Bill 402 violates both constitutional provisions. It deprives the county of its authority to provide for the compensation of its employees (Section 1, subd. (b)) and delegates to a private body the power to interfere with county financial affairs and to perform a municipal function (Section 11, subd. (a)). . . .

I. Facts and Procedural History

Riverside County (the County) and the Riverside Sheriff's Association (Sheriff's Association) engaged in negotiations over compensation for employees of the probation department. In May 2001, they reached an impasse. The Sheriff's Association requested that the dispute be submitted to binding arbitration pursuant to Code of Civil Procedure Section 1299 et seq. The County refused, claiming that those provisions violate the California Constitution. The Sheriff's Association filed an action in the superior court to compel arbitration. The court ordered arbitration. It found the binding arbitration law constitutional, explaining, "The matters at issue, to wit, the possible disruption of law enforcement and firefighter services, are not matters of purely local concern but rather are of statewide concern. This statewide concern authorizes the Legislature to act and supports the constitutionality of this legislation."

. . . The Court of Appeal . . . found that Senate Bill 402 violates both Section 1, subdivision (b), and Section 11, subdivision (a). . . .

II. Discussion

A. Background

Senate Bill 402, entitled "Arbitration of Firefighter and Law Enforcement Officer Labor Disputes," added Section 1299 et seq. to the Code of Civil Procedure. The Court of Appeal opinion describes the bill: "Senate Bill 402 empowers unions representing public safety employees to declare an impasse in labor negotiations and require a local agency to submit unresolved economic issues to binding arbitration. Each party chooses an arbitrator, who together choose the third arbitrator. . . ."

The County argues that the Legislature's compelling it to enter into binding arbitration of compensation issues violates Section 1, subdivision (b), and Section 11, subdivision (a). At the outset, we emphasize that the issue is not whether a county may voluntarily submit compensation issues to arbitration, i.e., whether the county may delegate its own authority, but whether the Legislature may compel a county to submit to arbitration involuntarily. The issue involves the division of authority between the state and the county, not what the county may itself do. . . .

B. Section 1, subdivision (b)

Section 1, subdivision (b), provides as relevant: "The governing body [of each county] shall provide for the number, compensation, tenure, and appointment of employees." The County argues that Senate Bill 402 violates this provision by compelling it to submit to binding arbitration of compensation issues. We agree. The constitutional language is quite clear and quite specific: the county, not the state, not someone else, shall provide for the compensation of its employees. Although the language does not expressly limit the power of the Legislature, it does so by "necessary implication." An express grant of authority to the county necessarily implies the Legislature does not have that authority. But Senate Bill 402 compels the county to enter into mandatory arbitration with unions representing its employees, with the potential result that the arbitration panel determines employee compensation. Senate Bill 402 permits the union to change the county's governing board from the body that sets compensation for its employees to just another party in arbitration. It thereby deprives the county of authority Section 1, subdivision (b), specifically gives to counties. . . .

The Sheriff's Association argues that Senate Bill 402 is valid because it involves a matter of "statewide concern." It cites the legislative findings in support of the bill, including that "strikes taken by firefighters and law enforcement officers against public employers are a matter of statewide concern," and that the "dispute resolution procedures" the bill establishes "provide the appropriate method for resolving public sector labor disputes that could otherwise lead to strikes by firefighters or law enforcement officers." These findings are entitled to great weight. But they are not controlling. A court may not simply abdicate to the Legislature, especially when the issue involves the division of power between local government and that same Legislature. The judicial branch, not the legislative, is the final arbiter of this question. . . .

The Sheriff's Association cites two cases that permitted the Legislature to regulate relations between local governmental entities and their employees. In *Baggett v. Gates*, 32 Cal.3d 128 (1982), we held that the Public Safety Officers' Procedural Bill of Rights Act, which, as its name suggests, provides procedural protections to public safety officers, applies to chartered cities despite the home rule provisions of the current Section 5, subdivision (b). . . . [W]e said that "general laws seeking to accomplish an objective of statewide concern"—in that case, creating uniform fair labor practices—"may prevail over conflicting local regulations even if they impinge to a limited extent upon some phase of local control." We found that "the maintenance of stable employment relations between police officers and their employers is a matter of statewide concern." . . .

We agree that Legislature may regulate as to matters of statewide concern even if the regulation impinges "to a limited extent" on powers the Constitution specifically reserves to counties (Section 1) or charter cities (Section 5). However, regulating labor relations is one thing; depriving the county entirely of its authority to set employee salaries is quite another.

In *Sonoma County Organization of Public Employees v. County of Sonoma*, 32 Cal.3d 128 (1982), we noted that Section 5 expressly gives charter cities authority over their employees' compensation. Because of this constitutional mandate, as well as prior authority, we held that "the determination of the wages paid to employees of charter cities as well as charter counties is a matter of local rather than statewide concern." Accordingly, we found unconstitutional Government Code Section 16280, which prohibited the distribution of certain state funds to local public agencies that granted their employees cost-of-living increases, despite a legislative declaration that the statute was a matter of statewide concern. For similar reasons, and despite a similar legislative declaration, we later invalidated legislation requiring the University of California to pay its employees at least prevailing wages. *San Francisco Labor Council v. Regents of University of California*, 26 Cal.3d 785 (1979).

. . . In *Baggett v. Gates*, we distinguished those two cases by noting that the Public Safety Officers' Procedural Bill of Rights Act, which was limited to providing procedural safeguards, "impinges only minimally on the specific directives of Section 5, subdivision (b)." Especially pertinent here, we stressed "that the Act does not interfere with the setting of peace officers' compensation." By contrast, Senate Bill 402 does not minimally impinge on a specific constitutional directive; it contravenes that directive entirely. Section 1, subdivision (b), specifically directs that counties have authority over the compensation of their employees; Senate Bill 402 takes that authority away from counties. . . .

For these reasons, we agree with the Court of Appeal: "Senate Bill 402 removes from local jurisdictions, at the option of public safety unions, the authority to set the compensation of public safety employees that is expressly given to them by Section 1, subdivision (b). This clearly violates Section 1, subdivision (b)."

C. Section 11, subdivision (a)

Section 11, subdivision (a), provides: "The Legislature may not delegate to a private person or body power to make, control, appropriate, supervise, or interfere with county or municipal corporation improvements, money, or property, or to levy taxes or assessments, or perform municipal functions." The county argues that in enacting Senate Bill 402, the Legislature has impermissibly delegated to a private body—the arbitration panel—the power to interfere with county money (by potentially requiring the county to pay higher salaries than it chooses) and to perform municipal functions (determining compensation for county employees). Again, we agree. This constitutional provision expressly denies the Legislature the power to act in this way. . . .

As with Section 1, subdivision (b), the Sheriff's Association argues that the Legislature's power to regulate labor relations as to matters of statewide concern permits it to delegate this regulatory authority to an arbitration panel. The argument fails for the same reasons: Senate Bill 402 does not just permit the arbitration panel to impinge minimally on the county's authority; it empowers the panel actually to set employee salaries. The Sheriff's Association also argues that binding arbitration is a "quid pro quo for the lack of a right to strike." This may (or may not) provide a policy argument in favor of binding arbitration, but it provides no reason to disregard a clear constitutional mandate. . . .

The Sheriff's Association argues that the arbitration panel is a public, not private, body within the meaning of Section 11, subdivision (a). We disagree. The statute requires the two parties to select a "person" to be a member of the panel. These two then select "an impartial person with experience in labor and management dispute resolution to act as chairperson of the arbitration panel." . . . Nothing in the statute requires the arbitrators to be public officials; indeed, the statute appears to contemplate, and the parties assume, they will be private persons.

The Sheriff's Association agrees that the members of the arbitration panel may be private persons, but it argues that empowering them to render binding arbitration decisions makes them a public body. . . . [I]f delegating to private persons the power to do a public act makes them a public body for purposes of Section 11, subdivision (a), then "the constitutional provision would never be violated." . . . The act of delegation does not change a private body into a public body and thereby validate the very delegation the Section prohibits. The Legislature has, indeed, delegated authority to a private body. . . .

Notes

1. After this decision, the California legislature amended the interest arbitration statute such that the employer's governing body could, by unanimous vote, reject the arbitration award. Does that fix the delegation problem? *County of Sonoma v. Superior Court*, 173 Cal. App. 4th 322 (2009), held it did not. Why not? Is there any possible legislative amendment that would permit binding interest arbitration for these employees but not run afoul of the provisions of the California Constitution on which *County of Riverside* relied?

2. This decision remains the minority approach. It is based on specific language in the California Constitution, and this far has not ushered in a revival of holdings that mandatory, binding arbitration violates constitutional non-delegation principles.

5. Judicial Review of Interest Arbitration Decisions

Public-sector statutes generally permit the parties to appeal the decisions of interest arbitrators to court. What types of errors should be grounds for overturning an award? What should the standard of review be? Often, the issue is whether the arbitrator has properly considered the criteria that the state statute requires interest arbitrators to use.

In re Buffalo Professional Firefighters Ass'n, Inc., Local 282, IAFF (Masiello)

New York Appellate Division
50 A.D.3d 106, 850 N.Y.S.2d 744 (2008)

LUNN, J.

In this appeal we are asked to decide whether Supreme Court properly vacated a compulsory public interest arbitration award on the ground that the arbitration panel, in making its award, exceeded its authority by failing to set forth the basis for its findings with the requisite specificity.

The collective bargaining agreement between petitioner, the Union representing City of Buffalo Firefighters, and the City of Buffalo (respondent) expired on June 30, 2002. Despite the efforts of the parties to negotiate a new collective bargaining agreement, several issues remained unresolved, resulting in the filing of a joint Declaration of Impasse on September 30, 2003. Mediation did not result in a new collective bargaining agreement, however, and petitioner thus sought compulsory public interest arbitration pursuant to Civil Service Law § 209(4)(c), resulting in the selection of a three-member arbitration panel pursuant to that statute.

Hearings were held over a six-day period in November 2004 and January 2005, during which both petitioner and respondent called witnesses and made presentations in support of their respective positions. Additionally, the Buffalo Fiscal Stability Authority (BFSA), which had been established pursuant to the New York Public Authorities Law to oversee respondent's fiscal activities and to balance respondent's budget, also presented evidence during the course of the arbitration hearings. The most contentious issue concerned wage increases. Petitioner sought wage increases of 3.4% for each of the two years that were the subject of the compulsory arbitration as well as a retroactive increase of $5,000 in base wages or salaries, effective July 1, 2002. Respondent, supported by the BFSA, proposed no increase to base wages or salaries for the two years that were the subject of the compulsory arbitration.

On July 18, 2005, the arbitration panel issued its award. The award was signed by the chairperson and the arbitrator representing respondent, who also issued a concurring opinion. The arbitrator representing petitioner issued a dissenting opinion. The award granted petitioner's members a general wage increase of 2.1% in the first year and 3.4% in the second year, but did not award the retroactive $5,000 increase in base wages or salaries. In arriving at its award, the panel majority noted that the evidence presented by the parties "was considered against the criteria set forth in [section 209(4)] of the Civil Service Law, including, but not limited to a comparison of wages, hours and conditions of employment, of other employees performing similar services or requiring similar skills under similar working conditions; the interest and welfare of the public and the financial ability of the public employer to pay; the peculiarities in regard to other professions such as hazards, educational qualifications, training and skills; and the terms of collective agreements negotiated between the parties in the past providing for compensation and fringe benefits" (see § 209[4][c][v][a] — [d]). With respect to petitioner's wage increase proposal, the panel majority found three of the statutory factors, namely, parity with the police, respondent's ability to pay, and the nature of the duties undertaken by firefighters, to be "key components" of its analysis. Specifically, with respect to parity and ability to pay, the panel majority determined that, in light of respondent's fiscal condition, "an essential question in this proceeding is whether there should be a deviation from the long historical practice of parity." The panel majority detailed the record evidence before it, which resulted in the structural imbalance between respondent's revenues and expenditures and created an "unprecedented" fiscal crisis that in turn led to the State Legislature's passage of the Buffalo Stability Authority Act. Citing the "genuine limitation" of respondent with respect to its ability to pay that was not in existence when the previous interest arbitration awards were issued, the panel majority was "constrained to break the pattern of parity to some extent." In arriving at its conclusion, the panel majority noted "the professionalism required of members of the Union and the extremely dangerous work they face each day," and the panel majority further noted that "[t]he public depends as much on the Union members as it does on their counterparts in the [Police Benevolent Association] for protection of life, limb and property." Finally, the panel majority also determined that "strict parity cannot be followed" here because the wage increases achieved by the police union occurred as a result of that union's other substantial concessions to respondent, which concessions were not offered by petitioner. . . .

On October 5, 2005, petitioner commenced this proceeding pursuant to CPLR 7511 seeking to vacate the arbitration award on the grounds that the panel majority failed to provide a specific basis for its findings and thereby exceeded its authority. The court granted the petition and vacated the award. Resolution of the issue of remittal to an appropriate arbitration panel was to be considered by the court at a future date. In vacating the award, the court found that the arbitration panel did not follow the requirements of Civil Service Law § 209(4)(c)(v) because it focused on only three "considerations," gave "scant discussion" to certain statutory factors, and failed to address the statutory factors in their entirety. We conclude that the court erred in vacating the arbitration panel's award with respect to wage increases and that the order therefore should be modified accordingly.

Civil Service Law § 209(4)(c)(v) provides in relevant part that, in determining the matters in dispute, compulsory public interest arbitration panels "shall specify the basis for its findings," taking into consideration four factors that are then set out in detail, in addition to any other relevant factors. The four factors are as follows: a comparison of the wages, hours, and conditions of employment of the employees involved in the arbitration proceeding with those of other employees performing similar services and other employees generally in comparable communities; the public welfare and the ability of the public employer to pay; a comparison of peculiarities of the employment at issue with other employment, including hazards of employment, physical qualifications, educational qualifications, mental qualifications, and job training and skills; and the terms of past collective bargaining agreements (see § 209[4][c][v][a] — [d]). The Second Department has interpreted the statute as requiring an arbitration panel to discuss separately each of the statutory factors for each of its awards in order to avoid vacatur of the award (see *City of Yonkers v Mutual Aid Assn. of Paid Fire Dept. of City of Yonkers, Local 628, Intl. Assn. of Fire Fighters*, 80 AD2d 597). We cannot agree with that interpretation, nor do we continue to adhere to our decision in *Matter of Buffalo Police Benevolent Assn. v City of Buffalo* (82 AD2d 635) to the extent that it may be deemed to endorse that interpretation.

The specificity requirement in the decision of the Second Department and, as noted, to some extent this Department's decision in *Buffalo Police Benevolent Assn.*, was largely derived from the Governor's Approval Memorandum to the 1977 amendment to the statute. The 1977 amendment deleted an arbitration panel's consideration of the statutory factors only "so far as it deems them applicable" and substituted the requirement that the panel shall "specify the basis for its findings" after taking into consideration the four statutory factors (L 1977, ch 216, at 280). The Governor's Approval Memorandum stated that the amendment was intended "to make it clear that arbitrators must make findings with respect to each statutory criterion which the parties put in issue, that each such finding must have an evidentiary basis in the record, and that the arbitrators must specify in their final determination what weight was given to each finding and why" (Governor's Mem approving

L 1977, ch 216, 1977 NY Legis Ann, at 129). The Court of Appeals, however, has since made it clear that such statements of legislative intent must be viewed with caution because they "suffer from the same infirmities as those made during floor debates by legislators" (*Majewski v Broadalbin-Perth Cent. School Dist.*, 91 NY2d 577. As noted by the Court in *Majewski*, statements of legislators in floor debates are not helpful to courts in ascertaining legislative intent, and statements contained in a governor's memorandum are "[o]n the same footing" (*id.*).

Where the language of a statute is clear and unambiguous, the court must discern the legislative intent from the language of the statute, and the court "should construe [the statute] so as to give effect to the plain meaning of the words used". . . . In this case, the language of the statute is clear and unambiguous and plainly does not require discussion of each of the statutory factors or those factors put in issue by the parties. The statute simply requires, as it expressly states, that the panel consider the statutory factors and "specify the basis for its findings". . . . Certainly, the Legislature could have chosen language that would require public arbitration panels to make express findings with respect to each of the statutory factors, or even each factor put in issue by the parties, but it did not. Thus, the Legislature has not required arbitration panels to engage in unnecessary discussion in their awards of factors not raised by the parties or thought to be relevant by either the parties or the panel. Judicial review of public arbitration awards otherwise would devolve into mere mechanical checklists, despite the fact that an award may appear on its face to be reasonable and to have a rational basis.

Reviewing the arbitration award at issue with respect to wage increases, we conclude that the record establishes that the panel majority properly considered all of the statutory factors and set forth, with the requisite specificity, the basis for its findings in making its award. . . . The panel majority expressly stated more than once that it considered the evidence in light of the four statutory factors, and it quoted those required factors from the statute. The panel majority then set forth the basis for its finding with respect to wage increases by identifying the factors it considered to be most important in making its wage award and the evidentiary basis in the record for the weight ultimately given to these factors. Further, the factors on which the panel majority focused were those factors emphasized by the parties as being most important to the dispute. In sum, the panel majority did not exceed its authority or imperfectly execute it with respect to its wage increase award. . . .

GORSKI, J., joined by GREEN, J., dissenting

. . . As the majority correctly notes, Civil Service Law § 209(4)(c)(v), the statute at issue herein, is clear and unambiguous. It provides that "the public arbitration panel shall make a just and reasonable determination *of the matters in dispute.* In arriving at such determination, the panel shall specify the basis for its findings, taking into consideration, in addition to any other relevant factors, the following:

> a. comparison of the wages, hours and conditions of employment of the employees involved in the arbitration proceeding with the wages, hours,

and conditions of employment of other employees performing similar services or requiring similar skills under similar working conditions and with other employees generally in public and private employment in comparable communities.

b. the interests and welfare of the public and the financial ability of the public employer to pay;

c. comparison of peculiarities in regard to other trades or professions, including specifically, (1) hazards of employment; (2) physical qualifications; (3) educational qualifications; (4) mental qualifications; [and] (5) job training and skills;

d. the terms of collective agreements negotiated between the parties in the past providing for compensation and fringe benefits, including, but not limited to, the provisions for salary, insurance and retirement benefits, medical and hospital benefits, paid time off and job security" (emphasis added).

In our view, the plain language of the statute *requires* an arbitration panel to do more than merely parrot that language by reporting in a conclusory fashion that it took into consideration the four enumerated factors. Indeed, the Legislature carefully crafted the language of the statute by stating that "the panel *shall* make a just and reasonable determination of the matters in dispute," thus rendering mandatory the arbitration panel's consideration of the four enumerated factors, and compliance with the statute is lacking in the absence of specific discussion of those factors. . . . We therefore are unable to discern the basis for the statement of the majority that the statute "plainly does not require discussion of each of the statutory factors or those factors put in issue by the parties."

The Legislature, with the approval of the Governor, enacted significant changes in the language of Civil Service Law § 209 shortly after the Court of Appeals decided *Caso v. Coffey* (41 NY2d 153) and *Matter of City of Buffalo v. Rinaldo* (41 NY2d 764), which essentially stood for the proposition that, if there was any rational basis for the panel's award, it could be sustained. The Governor's Approval Memorandum stated:

"These changes impart to the Courts the wisdom of the Legislature that judicial review must be strengthened so that it operates as an effective safeguard against arbitral abuses. *This bill is intended to narrow the expansive authority accorded to arbitrators by the Court of Appeals in City of Buffalo v. Rinaldo and to make it clear that arbitrators must make findings with respect to each statutory criterion which the parties put in issue, that each such finding must have an evidentiary basis in the record, and that the arbitrators must specify in their final determination what weight was given to each finding and why*". . . . [emphasis added].

In *Matter of Buffalo Police Benevolent Assn. v City of Buffalo* (82 AD2d 635), this Court held that, pursuant to the subject statute, an arbitration panel "must specifically exhibit that it took into consideration, in addition to other relevant factors," the factors set forth in Civil Service Law §209(4)(c)(v). Unlike the majority, we do not believe that the legal principles expressed in that decision should be disavowed. As we stated therein, citing to the Legislative history of the statute, "[t]he specificity requirement is intended to tighten the procedures in compulsory arbitration, to facilitate meaningful judicial review of arbitration determinations and to insure that an arbitrator's work was rational and not arbitrary or capricious" (*id.*). Moreover, in a proceeding pursuant to CPLR article 75, the courts have both the power and the duty to ensure that an arbitration panel has not acted in excess of the authority given by statute or "in disregard of the standard prescribed by the [L]egislature". . . . Compliance with the statutory mandate of specificity, therefore, is necessary to permit the prescribed degree of review by the courts and to encourage confidence in the arbitration procedure. We conclude that the failure of an arbitration panel to provide an adequate specification concerning the basis of its findings with respect to each of the factors enumerated in the statute requires vacatur of the award with respect to the issue of wage increases. . . .

We further disagree with the majority that specific discussion of the factors enumerated in the statute requires arbitration panels "to engage in unnecessary discussion," particularly where, as here, one of those factors is put in issue by a party. Here, petitioner specifically requested that the arbitration panel undertake a comparison of the firefighters' wages with the wages of Rochester firefighters, a statutory factor that mandates consideration, yet the panel majority failed to address that issue in its award. Indeed, the only issue discussed at any length by the panel majority was parity with the City of Buffalo police. There was scant discussion, except in conclusory fashion, of the peculiarities of the work of petitioner's members, pursuant to the statutory factor set forth in section 209(4)(c)(v)(c). Thus, in our view, the award with respect to the issue of wage increases is not in compliance with the statute, and the record does not reflect, as the majority asserts, "that the panel majority properly considered *all* of the statutory factors and set forth, with the requisite specificity, the basis for its findings in making its award" (emphasis added). . . .

Notes

1. What are the pros and cons of requiring interest arbitrators to discuss each factor in a statute specifically in each interest arbitration case? More broadly, what are the pros and cons of greater or lesser judicial deference to the decisions of interest arbitrators?

2. To the extent that finality in arbitration decisions is an argument for judicial deference, note that (perhaps ironically), the decision in this case was later vacated by a higher court (the New York Court of Appeals). This was not because of the issue the Appellate Division discussed above. Rather, it was because (in a portion of the decision not excerpted above), the Appellate Division had vacated a part of the original arbitration award that had considered a proposal the city made on health care issues. The Appellate Division held that the city had, in effect, agreed to

withdraw that proposal, so the arbitrator should not have considered it. On appeal, the New York Court of Appeals agreed with the Appellate Decision that the arbitrator should not have considered the health care proposal. However, the Court of Appeals continued:

> the Appellate Division erred in vacating only the health insurance portion of the arbitration award. The arbitration panel did not consider the issue of wages in isolation. Indeed, the arbitration panel explained that it was rejecting the City's wage proposal, but that it would generate savings for the City on the health insurance portion of the arbitration award. As the parties agree, the separate portions of the arbitration award were so interdependent, no part thereof could be vacated without affecting the merits of the remainder of the award. *Arbitration between Buffalo Professional Firefighters Ass'n, Inc., Local 282, IAFF and Masiello*, 918 N.E.2d 887, 888 (N.Y. 2009).

3. As Chapter 13 discusses, courts are usually extremely deferential to arbitrators in *grievance* arbitrations. Is there a reason to have a different standard of deference for the decisions of interest arbitrators? *Hillsdale PBA Local 207 v. Borough of Hillsdale*, 137 N.J. 71 (1994) explained that the general standard of review for interest arbitrations is whether the award is supported by substantial credible evidence in the record as a whole. That decision further explained that this standard is more stringent than for other types of arbitration because such arbitration is statutorily mandated, public funds are at stake, and it affects the public in many ways (in that case, the cost and adequacy of police and fire protection). 137 N.J. 71, 82.

4. Courts will also vacate an interest arbitration award if it violates other statutory requirements. Arbitrators cannot issue awards on matters not properly before them (*e.g.*, issues not raised properly in the process or illegal topics of bargaining). Arbitrators must also follow rules designating the type of arbitration to be used. For example, in *McFaul v. UAW Region 2*, 130 Ohio App. 3d 111 (1998), the court vacated an arbitration award because the arbitrator "split the baby" instead of choosing a final offer, as the default process in Ohio's statute requires. The union's final offer was a five percent raise; the employer offered three percent; and the arbitrator ordered 4.2 percent. Further, courts can vacate arbitration awards obtained by fraud, bribery, or other improper means, typically pursuant to statutes governing arbitrations generally (not just interest arbitrations).

C. Legal Strikes

1. The Policy of Allowing Strikes in the Public Sector

In 1967, a scholar of public-sector labor relations wrote that no legislature had allowed public employees to strike, "and public opinion seems to indicate that such a development is not likely in the foreseeable future." Schneider, *supra*, 199 (quoting Andrew Thompson). Yet in 1970, both Pennsylvania and Hawaii passed statutes granting limited rights to strike. In Pennsylvania, a commission had recommended the change in a 1968 report. The Governor's Commission to Revise the Public Employee Law of Pennsylvania stated that:

> Twenty years of experience [under a no-strike law] has taught us that such a policy is unreasonable and unenforceable. . . . It is based upon a philosophy that one may not strike against the sovereign. But today's sovereign is engaged not only in government but in a great variety of other activities. The consequence of a strike by a policeman are very different from those of a gardener in a public park. . . . The collective bargaining process will be strengthened if this qualified right to strike is recognized. It will be some curb on the possible intransigence of an employer; and the limitations on the right to strike will serve notice on the employee that there are limits to the hardships that he can impose. . . . We can look upon the limited and carefully defined right to strike as a safety valve that will in fact prevent strikes. *Quoted in* Schneider, *supra*, 199.

In addition to the Pennsylvania law of 1970, public employees were also given limited strike rights by statute in the following states: Vermont (1967, municipal employees only); Montana (1969, nurses only); Hawaii (1970); Oregon (1973); Alaska (1974); Minnesota (1975); Wisconsin (1977, municipal employees and teachers only); Illinois (1983); and Ohio (1983). The Wisconsin right was eliminated in 2011 by Wisconsin Act 10.

All these statutes bar strikes if they create a threat to public health, safety, and/or welfare, and in most cases, the employees must engage in some alternative impasse procedures before striking. Schneider, *supra*, 201 & n.38; Kearney & Mareschal, *supra*, at 245–46. Most states that allow any public employees to strike allow most public employees to strike, but police, firefighters, and other public safety workers generally cannot strike. Riccuci, Naff, et al., *supra*, at 509.

The article excerpt below explains some of the rationales for permitting strikes.

Kurt Hanslowe & John Acierno, *The Law and Theory of Strikes by Government Employees*
67 Cornell L. Rev. 1055 (1982)[*]

. . . A Tentative Case for the Right to Strike Against the Government

In the face of the rather overwhelming position to the contrary, constructing a case in support of a right to strike by public employees poses a formidable challenge. One must remember, however, that the legitimation of private sector unionism evolved against strong opposition. . . .

Just as the private sector union was said to interfere with the "natural laws" of the market, public sector unions are today said to interfere with "normal" political processes through economic coercion. The private sector union was said to be a law

---

[*] Copyright 1982. Reprinted by permission.

unto itself. Public sector unions are said to usurp from the government parts of the latter's law-making authority.

Despite early admonitions against private sector unionism, legislatures eventually enacted statutes securing the rights of organization and collective bargaining, and the courts upheld their constitutionality. Similar protections have been extended to public sector bargaining, except that the protected behavior generally excludes the right to strike. A number of considerations, however, call into question the continuing practicality of excluding public strikes: the experience of jurisdictions that permit public strikes; the demonstrated market restraints on and inessentiality of many government services; and the legitimacy of using economic influence in the political arena.

A. Statutory Recognition of a Public Employee's Right to Strike

Arguments that public strikes are incompatible with democratic process and the Constitution lose some vitality in the face of the significant number of jurisdictions that recognize a right to strike in the public sector. Eight states have granted some of their public employees a right to strike. . . . Thus, the public sector strike has begun to achieve some degree of legitimacy, despite the strong opposition of critics. . . .

B. Market Restraints and Nonessential Services in the Public Sector

. . . In rebuttal to the arguments of Wellington and Winter and the Taylor Committee, Burton and Krider maintain that economic constraints in the public sector limit the effectiveness of the public sector strike weapon, and thus should enable public officials to resist excessive demands:

> First, wages lost due to strikes are as important to public employees as they are to employees in the private sector. Second, the public's concern over increasing tax rates may prevent the decision-making process from being dominated by political instead of economic considerations. . . . A third and related economic constraint arises from such services as water, sewage, and, in some instances, sanitation, where explicit prices are charged. Even if representatives of groups other than employees and the employer do not enter the bargaining process, both union and local government are aware of the economic implications of bargaining which leads to higher prices which are clearly visible to the public. A fourth economic constraint on employees exists in those services where subcontracting to the private sector is a realistic alternative. [John Burton and Charles Krider, *The Role and Consequences of Strikes by Public Employees*, 79 YALE L.J. 418, 425 (1970).]

The assumption that services rendered by public employees are essential underlies the "lack of market constraints" argument. Former Secretary of Labor Willard Wirtz asserted that "[e]very governmental function is essential in the broadest term. If it weren't the government shouldn't be doing it." Under a stringent test of essentiality, the Wirtz formula would require a reduction of activities in proportions so drastic as to give pause even to the most devoted conservative. Perhaps in a market economy organized along classical lines, in which the government did nothing but maintain the peace and enforce contracts, the Wirtz statement would be defensible. In our complex contemporary industrial state, however, it is unrealistic. Public services vary as to essentiality; many privately-operated services are more essential than public ones. In many categories of employment, among the largest of which is education, public and private activity substantially overlap.

Recently, the Supreme Court implicitly departed from its traditional equation of public ownership of an industry with the essentiality of that industry. In *United Transportation Union v. Long Island Railroad*, [455 U.S. 678 (1982)] the Court held that employees of a formerly-private railroad recently acquired by a governmental entity retained their limited right to strike under the Railway Labor Act. The Court found that the public acquisition did not change the character of the service provided by the railroad, and that the supremacy clause required continued application of federal labor law. . . .

Under *United Transportation Union*, the public railroad employees continued to enjoy a right to strike notwithstanding their public employment status. Although its basis in the supremacy clause limits its effect on labor law, the case provides insight into the Court's changing view of the essentiality of public services. . . . The Court implicitly held that the railroad became no more essential after its public acquisition than it was when privately operated. The case thus represents a significant departure from the Court's earlier holding that a service becomes essential when it comes under government control.

The absence of an unavoidable nexus between public services and essentiality undercuts the argument that public officials will be compelled to settle strikes quickly and at any cost. Burton and Krider maintain that because the essentiality of every public service varies, public officials will not necessarily be pressured to settle every strike. The pressure to settle will depend on the essentiality of the service. The case of the air-traffic controllers' strike surely demonstrates governmental ability to hold the line firmly against a strike for a considerable period, even in the face of substantial inconvenience. Indeed, rather paradoxically, the government's resourcefulness and resolve manifested in the air-controller case tends to undercut the claim that the essentiality of the particular public service involved necessitates the imposition of the absolute strike ban in the first place!

The proponents of the public strike ban also fail to consider public sentiment toward a given strike. They assume that the public will push blindly for the resolution of all strikes at all costs. Public sentiment toward a strike, however, may limit the pressure felt by political leaders, and thereby reduce the strike's effect. . . .

The [Pennsylvania Governor's] Commission thus believed that a limited right to strike would actually relieve political pressures on public officials to settle quickly those strikes that remain illegal. Thus, "public officials are, to some degree, able to accept long strikes. The ability of governments to so choose indicates that political pressures generated by strikes are not so strong as to undesirably distort the entire decision-making process of government."

C. Public Sector Bargaining as an Economic Process

The strike-ban argument distinguishes between political and economic forms of influence. This dominant view of the American democratic process deems political pressure legitimate and economic pressure heretical. Burton and Krider respond that economic pressure is as legitimate as political influence, and that there are no fundamental differences between them. Indeed, economic influence is actually a form of political influence: both seek to influence executive and legislative policies, and to distinguish between them is misplaced.

Viewing public sector bargaining as essentially an economic process limits its political dimensions, either by blurring the line between the private (economic) and the public (political) sector, or by equating the two. Ironically, by subjecting democratic legal processes to an orthodox economic analysis, the Burton and Krider approach produces the unorthodox advocacy of public sector strikes. Furthermore, as the market economy deviates from its pure, classical model and increasingly becomes a mixed and pluralistic one, the case for public strikes strengthens. Once the functional line between public and private enterprise becomes blurred, a corresponding blurring occurs between political and economic activity, rendering the absolute prohibition of all public sector strikes difficult to defend. . . .

Ironically, the conservative argument that public sector bargaining and striking is undemocratic (because government activity is *ex definitione* in the public interest) closely parallels the socialist view that striking by workers is antisocial—indeed revisionist and reactionary—conduct in a system operated for the benefit of all. . . .

The traditional American ban against public sector strikes fails to recognize the artificial distinctions drawn between the public and the private sectors, and between economic and political tactics. Because the traditional arguments advanced to justify the public strike prohibition ignore the realities of current public sector employment, some adjustment of American legal treatment of public strikes is in order. Courts and legislatures should consider at least limited protection for public sector strikes.

Notes

1. Are the arguments above convincing? To the extent they are, which public employees should be allowed to strike?

2. This article was written about a decade after a handful of states first gave the right to strike to some public employees. Thus, it does not have the benefit of the additional decades of experience with legal public-sector strikes since then. Reconsider the arguments as you go through the materials in the rest of this section, including but not limited to the evidence in subsection 5, *infra*, that legalizing public-sector strikes may actually reduce the total number of strikes.

2. Statutes

Statutes granting strike rights to public workers differ in some ways, but they have some similarities. First, again, police and firefighters generally cannot strike anywhere. Second, even workers who are legally allowed to strike typically lose that right if and when their strike threatens public health, safety, or welfare. Also, statutes usually provide various procedures unions (and employers) must go through before unions can legally strike. Such procedures vary by state, and even within states, can vary by type of employee. Below are two examples.

a. Ohio

In Ohio, while certain public employees cannot legally strike (notably although not exclusively police, fire, and corrections workers) most public employees are entitled to strike. Before such employees can strike, however, they must go through a series of steps. The Ohio statute sets out a "default" procedure the parties must use at impasse, although it also permits the parties to pick alternate procedures, if both sides agree. OHIO REV. CODE § 4117.14(C).

Under the default procedures, first, if, 50 days before the contract's expiration date the parties are unable to reach an agreement, either party may request the state labor board, SERB, to intervene. If an impasse exists or 45 days before an existing contract expires, then SERB will appoint a mediator to assist the parties. § 4117.14(C)(2). Any time after the appointment of the mediator, either party may request a fact-finding panel. § 4117.14(C)(3).

Within 15 days after a request for a fact-finding panel, SERB must appoint such a panel. The panel may have no more than three members, and the parties select the members in accordance with SERB rules. *Id.* Each party must specify in writing the unresolved issues and its position on each issue to the fact-finding panel. The panel gathers facts and makes recommendations as to all the unresolved issues. § 14(C)(3)(a). Section 14(C)(4)(e) requires fact-finders to consider a list of factors contained in § 4177.14(G)(7)(a) to (f); these are also the factors arbitrators must consider in making interest arbitration decisions for employees not allowed to strike (a fairly standard list). Also, the fact-finding panel's recommendations may only be shared with the parties at this point. § 14(C)(4)(e).

No later than seven days after the findings and recommendations are sent to the parties, the parties must each decide whether to accept or reject the recommendations. § 14(C)(6)(a). Notably, rejection requires a super-majority vote: a three-fifths vote of the legislative body or by three-fifths of the union bargaining unit (the statute specifies three-fifths of the entire bargaining unit, not merely of those voting). If neither rejects the recommendations, the recommendations shall be deemed agreed upon. But if one or both sides reject the recommendations, SERB "shall publicize the findings of fact and recommendations of the fact-finding panel." *Id.*

If the parties are unable to reach agreement within seven days after the publication of findings and recommendations from the fact-finding panel or the contract has expired, then public employees who are allowed to strike may legally strike, but even then only after giving 10 days' notice. § 14(D). Also, courts retain the power to enjoin otherwise legal strikes if and when it "creates clear and present danger to the health or safety of the public." § 4117.16.

Thus, although most public-sector unions can strike in Ohio, they must go through many more procedures before they can exercise that right than private-sector unions do. What are the purposes of all these rules in general? Specifically, what is the purpose of requiring a super-majority vote to reject a fact-finder's recommendations? What is the purpose of keeping the recommendations private unless and until they are rejected? What is the purpose of the 10-day notice? Assuming a statute will grant strike rights to some public employees, is the Ohio statute a good model? Should there be more procedures? Fewer? Different ones?

b. Alaska

Alaska uses a different model, dividing public employees into three groups. The first group cannot legally strike (mostly, but not exclusively, police, fire, and correctional workers). ALASKA STAT. § 23.40.200(b). The second group of employees includes public utility, snow removal, sanitation, and educational institution employees other than employees of a school district. ALASKA STAT. § 23.40.200(c). These employees perform services that "may be interrupted for a limited period but not for an indefinite period of time." ALASKA STAT. § 23.40.200(a)(2). They can legally strike following an impasse, a secret ballot vote authorizing a strike, and after exhausting mediation. But the strike is only permitted "for a limited time. The limit is determined by the interests of the health, safety, or welfare of the public." If the strike threatens the health, safety, or welfare of the public, courts are authorized to enjoin it. ALASKA STAT. § 23.40.200(c). The final group consists of all other types of public employees covered by the statute. These employees may strike legally after a secret ballot vote. ALASKA STAT. § 23.40.200(d). The only caveat is that employees of municipal school districts and state boarding schools must go to advisory arbitration before voting to strike, may not strike until they have given 72 hours' notice, and cannot begin a strike until after a day of school with students in attendance has passed. ALASKA STAT. § 23.40.200(g).

Both groups of public employees in Alaska that are allowed to strike can strike without going through as many procedures as public employees in Ohio, and a significant number of public employees in Alaska can strike without going through any procedures beyond a secret ballot vote. Is this a better approach than that taken in Ohio? Also, Alaska divides up employees entitled to strike into two categories, one with more limitations on the right than the other. Is this a better approach than the Ohio model of treating all employees with the right to strike the same way?

3. Partial Strikes

Public-sector jurisdictions that allow strikes follow the private-sector rule that "partial" strikes (in which employees perform some but not all of their job tasks) are illegal. *East Cleveland Educ. Ass'n v. SERB*, 12 OPER ¶ 1219 (Ct. Com. Pl. 1995), explained:

> The remedy for the aggrieved employee is to be either on strike or not on strike, not a combination of both. He must either face the potential

consequences of a strike or remain on the job until some agreement is accomplished. To accomplish their end, employees must give up their salaries and benefits in whole and not in part. Total chaos is the only foreseeable result of working these intermittent hours, chaos which will result in harm to the public.

4. Enjoining Otherwise Legal Strikes That Threaten Public Health, Safety, or Welfare

Statutes that permit strikes by public workers usually have caveats barring (and providing for injunctions against) otherwise legal strikes that threaten public health, safety, and/or welfare.

Masloff v. Port Authority of Allegheny County

Supreme Court of Pennsylvania
531 Pa. 416, 613 A.2d 1186 (1992)

ZAPPALA, J.

Amalgamated Transit Union Local 85 (Local 85) and its President, Larry L. Klos, appeal from the adjudication and decree entered on April 10, 1992, by Judge Silvestri of the Commonwealth Court permanently enjoining the work stoppage by the Union and directing the authorized representatives of Local 85 and the Port Authority of Allegheny County (PAT) to engage in court-supervised negotiations until an agreement was reached.

Local 85 is the certified collective bargaining representative for approximately 2,700 individuals employed by PAT. Local 85 and PAT were parties to a collective bargaining agreement that expired by its terms on November 30, 1991. The parties' negotiations for a successor agreement were initiated in October, 1991, but were unsuccessful.

On March 16, 1992, the members of Local 85 went on strike. On March 31, 1992, Sophie Masloff, individually and as the mayor of the City of Pittsburgh, and the City of Pittsburgh filed a Complaint in Equity against PAT and Local 85 in the Court of Common Pleas of Allegheny County seeking, *inter alia*, injunctive relief enjoining the strike. The City also filed an Application for Extraordinary Relief with this Court requesting that we assume plenary jurisdiction of this matter. . . . On April 1, 1992, we entered an order assuming jurisdiction of this matter. . . .

Hearings were held by Judge Silvestri on April 7–9, 1992, during which the City introduced testimony of various witnesses to demonstrate that the strike created a clear and present danger and a threat to the health, safety, and welfare of its citizens. Judge Silvestri concluded that the City had presented sufficient evidence of the far-reaching effect that the strike had upon commercial, academic, medical and social institutions and that the evidence submitted by PAT was neither of the quantity nor quality sufficient to rebut the overwhelming evidence presented by the City.[2] Based upon the evidence, Judge Silvestri determined that a permanent injunction enjoining Local 85 from continuing the work stoppage was necessary to ensure the safety of the citizens and to prevent the immediate and irreparable harm that would result from a denial of the requested relief. An adjudication and decree was entered on April 10, 1992, enjoining the work stoppage, establishing a schedule for the representatives of Local 85 and PAT to engage in court-supervised negotiations, and directing the parties and participants to refrain from making any public statements without prior court approval.

. . . Section 3 of the Port Authority Act . . . establishes the revised collective bargaining procedures governing PAT and its employees. . . . In the case of any labor dispute where collective bargaining does not result in an agreement, the dispute may be submitted to final and binding interest arbitration only with the written consent of both parties. . . .

When the parties have agreed to submit the labor dispute to binding arbitration, all contract provisions remain the status quo during the period of arbitration. No lock-outs, strikes, or other interference with or interruption of transit operations are permitted during the arbitration period. 55 P.S. § 563.2(f).

Within forty-five days of the termination date of the collective bargaining agreement, either party may make a written request for the appointment of a neutral factfinder by the Pennsylvania Labor Relations Board (PLRB). When factfinding has not been requested by either party prior to the expiration of the term of the collective bargaining agreement, both parties must immediately make a written request that the PLRB appoint a neutral factfinder. Collective bargaining may continue during the factfinding process. 55 P.S. § 563.2(g).

Within forty-five days of the appointment, the factfinder must submit findings of facts and recommendations to the PLRB and both parties. 55 P.S. § 563.2(I). The parties are required to notify the PLRB and each other whether or not the recommendations of the factfinder are accepted. The findings and recommendations are publicized if they are rejected. 55 P.S. § 563.2(j).

Once the recommendations have been rejected and PAT and the employees' representative have refused to mutually agree to final and binding interest arbitration, the employees shall have the right to strike in regard to that dispute. No strike is permitted, however, until the completion of a thirty-day "cooling-off" period, beginning immediately after the termination of the collective bargaining agreement. 55 P.S.§ 563.2(l). When the employees have exercised their right to strike, the Port Authority Act provides:

> . . . such strike shall not be prohibited unless or until such a strike creates a clear and present danger or threat to the health, safety or welfare of the

---

2. Local 85 did not present any evidence during the hearings.

public: Provided that such strike shall not be prohibited on the grounds that it creates a clear and present danger or threat to the health, safety or welfare of the public unless the court's order granting relief further mandates that both parties submit the labor dispute to final and binding interest arbitration by a board of arbitration under the provisions of this Section. No party, other than the authority, shall have any standing to seek any relief in any court of this Commonwealth under this Subsection. 55 P.S. § 563.2(k).

. . . Local 85 contends that the City failed to establish the existence of a clear and present danger to the public that would justify the issuance of an injunction. The case law definition of "clear and present danger" which has been employed in the context of labor disputes by public employees under the Public Employee Relations Act, 43 P.S. § 1101.101 et seq. is applicable in this instance. In *Armstrong Education Association v. Armstrong School District*, 5 Pa.Cmwlth. 378, 383 (1972), the Commonwealth Court utilized the following definition:

> The "clear" in that epigram is not limited to a threat indubitably etched in every microscopic detail. It includes that which is not speculative but real, not imagined but actual. The "present" in the epigram is not restricted to the climatically imminent. It includes that which exists as contrasted with that which does not yet exist and that which has ceased to exist.

The ordinary inconveniences resulting from a strike will not suffice to establish a clear and present danger to the health, safety, or welfare of the public. The concept of "clear and present danger" will encompass the consideration of the effects which are ordinarily incidental to a strike, however, when such matters accumulate to such an extent, have continued for so long, or are aggravated by unexpected developments that the public's health, safety, or welfare is endangered.

In his adjudication and decree, Judge Silvestri addressed the testimony that was introduced by the City, stating:

> During the parade of thirty (30) witnesses presented by the City, testimony was elicited about the impact of the mass transit strike upon families, individuals, and businesses. Blind, epileptic, professional, student, and blue-collar witnesses testified about the effect of the lack of public transportation upon their lives. While the lack of such transportation is a matter of inconvenience for some, it is devastating to others. Renal, cancer and psychiatric patients are often unable to get to appropriate medical facilities for treatment. Emergency medical services are delayed in attempts to reach citizens in need. Citizens are endangering their safety by walking along public roads to get to work because other modes of transportation are unavailable. Residents have been forced to find alternate living accommodations with friends or family because of the inaccessibility to work, school or day care. From the testimony presented, the City has demonstrated the far-reaching effect the strike has had upon commercial, academic, medical and social institutions.

Local 85 argues that the evidence was insufficient because it reflected what one would ordinarily expect to occur in the event of a cessation of virtually all public transportation in a metropolitan area. The City's evidence did not simply establish the disruption of the witnesses' daily routines, however. The evidence established, *inter alia*, that public services, such as ambulance, fire, and police services, were severely hampered by the increased traffic congestion resulting from the strike. To the extent that Local 85's argument suggests that the adverse effect on and threat to essential public services such as fire and police protection and emergency medical services are the ordinary and anticipated consequences of a transit strike, we are unpersuaded. We conclude that reasonable grounds existed for the equitable relief ordered by Judge Silvestri. . . .

Larsen, J., dissenting:

. . . I strongly disagree . . . with the majority's conclusion that reasonable grounds existed for the equitable relief ordered by the Chancellor in this case. . . .

All of the consequences of the strike described by the Chancellor in his adjudication are precisely the kinds of inconveniences, disruptions and hardships which are incident to and normally expected when a transit strike occurs in a major metropolitan area. For example, it is reasonable to expect that persons who rely on public transportation to go to work or school will walk along public roads to get to work or school during a mass transit strike. Also, it is a normal expectation that business will decline at retail stores which depend upon customers who use public transportation. None of the consequences described by the witnesses in this case can be said to be unexpected or unanticipated by the Legislature when it enacted legislation permitting the Union to strike. The courts and the legislature of this Commonwealth have recognized that certain inconveniences, disruptions and hardships are inherent in any strike and such inherent inconveniences, disruptions and hardships do not constitute a clear and present danger or threat to the health, safety or welfare of the public. *Armstrong School District v. Armstrong Education Ass'n*, 291 A.2d 120 (1972).

> . . . In this light, the determination of whether or not a strike presents a clear and present danger to the health, safety or welfare of the public must, therefore, require the court to find that the danger or threat is real or actual and that a strong likelihood exists that it will occur. *Additionally, it seems to us that the 'danger' or 'threat' concerned must not be one which is normally incident to a strike by public employees. By enacting [legislation] which authorizes such strikes, the legislature may be understood to have indicated its willingness to accept certain inconveniences for such are inevitable, but it obviously intended to draw the line at those which pose a danger to the public health, safety or welfare.* (Emphasis supplied). 291 A.2d 123–24.

. . . The majority herein, in reaching to uphold the Chancellor's injunction, does not rely only upon the inconveniences and disruptions of the public's normal daily routines as being sufficient to constitute a clear and present danger to the health, safety or welfare of the public, but combines the evidence of the daily inconveniences and disruptions with an unsupported declaration that ambulance, fire and police services and protection were severely hampered in concluding that there was a clear and present danger which justified an injunction. The majority states:

> The City's evidence did not simply establish the disruption of the witnesses' daily routines, however. The evidence established, *inter alia*, that public services, such as ambulance, fire and police services, were severely hampered by the increased traffic congestion resulting from the strike. To the extent that Local 85's argument suggests that the adverse effect on and threat to essential public services such as fire and police protection and emergency medical services are the ordinary and anticipated consequences of a transit strike, we are unpersuaded.

I must respectfully disagree with the majority's characterization of the evidence and the argument of the Union. There was scant evidence of disruption of the City's ability to provide adequate fire protection, police protection and emergency medical services because of the strike. As the Union points out in its brief, no testimony was offered by the City pertaining to the City's ability or inability to provide adequate fire and police protection as a result of the strike. The only evidence offered by the City which directly pertained to the City's ability to provide emergency medical services was the testimony of Robert Kennedy, Chief of the Bureau of Emergency Medical Services for the City of Pittsburgh Department of Public Safety. Chief Kennedy testified that peak demand for emergency medical services is from 2:00 p.m. to 10:00 p.m. Monday through Saturday. Mr. Kennedy testified that his Bureau did experience some difficulty in moving units to respond to calls. He testified anecdotally to a report of a unit on the North Side of Pittsburgh dispatched to the South Side of Pittsburgh in response to a call at approximately 3:30 p.m. on March 30. Due to the volume of traffic at that time, the unit was unable to cross either the West End bridge or the Fort Duquesne bridge, even with its warning devices, and could not complete the call. He testified as to "having some problem entering downtown [Pittsburgh] from the east due to congestion on Liberty Avenue;" "we are very often forced now to go long distances down Liberty Avenue into town opposing traffic." Chief Kennedy stated that paramedics have reported to him that they were finding difficulty on secondary roads because of the presence of more traffic than usual on those roads. The traffic conditions and delays described by Chief Kennedy are not dissimilar to that which is encountered during busy traffic hours when traffic on a major thoroughfare (such as the Parkway East or Parkway West in Pittsburgh) is limited because of the resurfacing and/or repairs of such thoroughfare. The City offered no other evidence of its inability to provide adequate fire and police protection and emergency medical services. . . .

The disruptions of routine daily activities such as, traveling to and from employment, school, meetings, business appointments, personal appointments, medical appointments, social functions, etc. are indeed significant and often painful inconveniences to the public, particularly for the young and the elderly. These disruptions and inconveniences are inherent in the very nature of any mass transit strike in a metropolitan area. The majority, by elevating these disruptions and inconveniences to a clear and present danger or threat to the health, safety or welfare of the public renders the right to strike granted transit workers by the Port Authority Act illusory. I cannot conceive of a strike by transit employees which did not impact the public in the various ways described by the witnesses in this case. Surely, the disruptive effect of a mass transit strike upon the public is rightfully a matter for concern. In enacting the Port Authority Act, 55 P.S. 551, *et seq.*, however, the General Assembly weighed the competing interests which would be affected by legislation permitting Port Authority employees to strike and enacted legislation in favor of allowing such strikes. The majority's opinion in this case which makes it inevitable that all strikes by Port Authority employees will be enjoined upon petition renders the Legislature's action useless. . . .

Under the majority's holding today that the inconveniences and hardships resulting from the transit strike constitute a clear and present danger to the health, safety and welfare of the public, and its construction of . . . the Port Authority Act, the Port Authority Transit employees are left naked. They are effectively deprived of the right to strike . . . Now, there is no incentive for the Port Authority to bargain in good faith to avert a strike. The majority's opinion encourages the Port Authority to hold fast to its bargaining position, whether it be reasonable or unreasonable, and wait until the transit workers call for a work stoppage and go out on strike. As soon as a strike impacts upon the public with the inconveniences, delays and hardships that are inherent in such a work stoppage, the Port Authority is further encouraged to do nothing and wait for political pressure to build and cause a third party in interest, such as the City of Pittsburgh, to seek an injunction. . . . It is beyond all possibility that the Legislature intended such a result. . . .

Notes

1. Who is more convincing, the majority or the dissent? More broadly, under the rule that otherwise legal strikes can be enjoined if they threaten the public health, safety or welfare, what sorts of facts should be enough to meet this test? What sorts of facts (showing some "ordinary inconveniences" or even harm) should not be enough to meet this test?

2. As footnote two indicates, the union did not put on any evidence in this case. Why not? Consider: what types of evidence could a union use to try to show that a specific strike did *not* threaten the public health, safety, or welfare?

3. After enjoining the strike, the *Masloff* court ordered the parties to negotiate under court supervision. This approach is not uncommon. *See also Carroll v. Ringgold Educ. Ass'n*, 545 Pa. 192 (1996).

4. Suppose an otherwise legal teachers' strike threatens a loss of state subsidies to affected schools because it will cause a failure to comply with a state requirement of providing 180 days of instruction. Should a court enjoin the strike for creating a

"clear and present danger to the public"? *See Jersey Shore Educ. Ass'n. v. Jersey Shore Area School Dist.*, 548 A.2d 1202 (Pa. 1988).

5. Legal Strikes and Their Alternatives

What are the actual effects of statutes making some strikes by some public employees legal? Do such laws necessarily mean there will be more strikes by public employees? Consider the following, which also compares alternatives to strikes.

Martin Malin, *Public Employees' Right to Strike: Law and Experience*
26 U. Mich. J.L. Reform 313 (1993)[*]

... Experience shows that unions are not benefitting inordinately from an excessively powerful strike weapon. For example, a study of teacher strikes found that, generally, "strike use affects salary changes but not salary levels." This finding led to the conclusion that teacher strikes generally are defensive in nature. Another study found that noneducation local government employees tended to strike when their salaries were above average, but that their strikes tended to last longer than other groups of public employees, thereby indicating strong employer resistance. A significant number of public employee strikes end without any agreement at all.

Moreover, the union wage effect—the impact that unions have on wage increases—is less in the public sector than it is in the private sector. There is also reason to believe that the union wage effect in the public sector results more from the availability of interest arbitration than from the strike weapon. In Canada, for example, where the right to strike is more prevalent in the public sector, unions achieve greater wage increases through interest arbitration than through threatened and actual strikes. Perhaps this is because public officials find interest arbitration more politically expedient than operating under a strike threat. An employer that loses in arbitration can avoid accountability by blaming the arbitrator. Despite this advantage, many public employers prefer to take the heat of a strike rather than to operate under interest arbitration. This preference suggests that they do not believe that political pressure will cause them to cave in to excessive union demands. ...

B. Fact-Finding and Strike Prohibitions

... Experience with fact-finding has demonstrated that it functions poorly as an impasse-resolution device. The absence of finality greatly reduces the risk of proceeding to fact-finding. Consequently, it is common for parties not to engage in much meaningful bargaining prior to the fact-finding hearing.

Unions do not refrain from striking merely because the strike is illegal. Prohibitions on public employee strikes also raise the potential costs of striking to unions and employees. The increased costs often lead the union to reduce its final prestrike

---

offer below what it would have been had the strike been legal. If the increased costs bring the union's offer from a point above the maximum level that the employer finds acceptable to a point below it, the strike prohibition will have prevented a strike.

Strike prohibitions, however, also affect employer calculations. Each side's final offer is affected directly not only by its estimate of its own strike costs, but also by its estimate of its opponent's strike costs. Recognizing this, parties frequently misrepresent their strike costs as lower than what they actually are. Opposing parties, recognizing the probability of such misrepresentations, often discount the information they receive from the other side.

In jurisdictions where strikes are illegal, employers will value the union's strike costs higher than if the strikes were legal and will reduce their final offers accordingly. Thus, the strike prohibition may reduce the employer's final offer to the same extent that it reduced the union's final offer, leaving the parties as far apart as they would have been had strikes been legal. When this happens, the strike prohibition has not narrowed the differences between the parties' positions and does not reduce the likelihood of a strike.

The combination of misrepresentations of strike costs and discounting the other side's representations may lead employers to overvalue the strike prohibition's effect on the union's strike costs. Under these circumstances, because the employer will reduce its final offer to a greater extent than the union, the strike prohibition will have the ironic effect of exacerbating the parties' differences and increasing the probability of a strike.

Most studies of the effect of legal policy on strike activity compare aggregate strike data by state, categorizing the states by legal policy. Their results are inconsistent. The most comprehensive study of the impact of legal policy on public sector strike activity covered experiences in seven states during the 1970s. The study found that the differences in the probabilities of strikes occurring in Pennsylvania, where they were legal, and Ohio and Illinois, where they were illegal at the time, were insignificant.

The one state where a strike prohibition appeared to deter strikes significantly was New York. New York's Taylor Law provides for several strike penalties, including suspension of the union's dues checkoff and a penalty of two days' pay for each day an employee is on strike. The employer collects the two-for-one penalties, which are imposed in the overwhelming majority of strikes. The two-for-one penalty appears to be the most significant sanction in the New York law. It not only raises the union's and employees' strike costs substantially, but it lowers the employer's strike costs as well through the receipt of the funds that the penalty generates. This strike deterrence is achieved, however, at substantial cost to the bargaining process. The impact on the parties' strike costs creates a situation in which the union's bargaining power is eroded sufficiently that it has no choice but to concede to the employer because of the union's strong need to avoid a strike. . . .

C. Interest Arbitration

. . . [T]he key issue is whether adjudication is a preferable method for setting terms and conditions of employment in the public sector. As the following analysis demonstrates, it is not.

Arbitrators are inherently conservative as adjudicators. Arbitrators are called upon to write the contract for the parties because the parties' negotiation process has broken down. The arbitrator's function in these circumstances is to devise a contract that the parties likely would have reached had the process not broken down. To do this, arbitrators rely primarily on two factors: what the parties have done in the past and what other parties have done recently. . . .

Arbitrators are strongly inclined against changing the status quo. They typically award across-the-board percentage pay increases rather than tinker with existing pay structures. A party seeking to change perceived inequities in existing pay structures stands very little chance of doing so in arbitration. . . .

In negotiations under the threat of a strike, a party perceiving a problem with an existing contract term may demand change, but must assess the importance of the change to its constituency. If the issue seems very important, the party can make it a strike issue. If the issue is not as important to the other side, there may well be a concession. Yet if the other side also views it as a strike issue, the parties will be forced to seek compromises that take into account the needs of both parties' constituencies.

In negotiations under interest arbitration, however, the importance of the proposed changes to the parties' constituencies plays a much weaker role in the ultimate result of the process. The dominant factor is the strength of their adjudication arguments. Invariably, the proponent of change will have the weaker argument from the arbitrator's perspective, and the party resisting change will have little incentive to compromise. Thus, arbitration stifles creativity and problem solving in bargaining. Although arbitration is a real strike substitute, it is an artificial method of setting terms and conditions of employment. . . .

The Effect of Legalizing Public Employee Strikes in Illinois and Ohio

In 1984, public employees in Illinois and Ohio obtained the right to strike. One could expect that such action would lead to an increase in public sector strikes in those jurisdictions for several reasons. First, it seems intuitive that legalizing an activity that was previously illegal would tend to encourage that activity. Second, the strike legalization accompanied each state's first comprehensive public employee collective bargaining act. Thus, along with the right to strike came procedures to compel employer recognition of and negotiation with unions representing their workers. By increasing the number of units engaged in collective bargaining, such legislation increased the opportunities for strikes. Third, the experience in states other than Illinois and Ohio suggests that, at least initially, increased strike activity may accompany the legalization of public employee strikes. Contrary to this expectation, however, strike activity actually has declined in both states since legalization.

Ohio's legislation of public employee strikes took effect on April 1, 1984. Over the eight years beginning April 1, 1984, through April 30, 1992, there have been 110 strikes in Ohio. Seven of the strikes were unauthorized, presumably because the union failed to comply with the statutory procedures. In three of the seven cases, the union apparently corrected its errors and struck shortly thereafter. . . .

[A table listed the number of strikes in the years preceding the enactment of the Ohio law by various employees. This table included the number of strikes by employees who were not in law enforcement or fire protection, *i.e.*, the number of strikes by employees whom the Ohio law would later give the right to strike. The number of strikes per year by such employees were as follows: 1974-39; 1975-47; 1976-38; 1977-54, 1978-57; 1979-51.]

Comparing these data . . . it is apparent that there have been far fewer strikes in Ohio since they were legalized. . . .

Studies and data from the [Ohio SERB] suggest that many potential strikes are headed off in the prestrike procedures. . . .

Under the Ohio impasse procedures, there have been far fewer strikes than occurred prior to the statute. This has been accomplished through a combination of procedural prodding to reach an agreement and the imposition of fact-finding "agreements" by making rejections difficult. The Ohio experience raises the question: Is such strict control of the strike weapon necessary to avoid public employee strikes? This question leads to an examination of the relatively laissez-faire approach to economic weapons found in Illinois.

Strikes outside of education are almost nonexistent in the Illinois public sector. They typically occur less than once per year. . . . [F]rom 1974 through 1979, [noneducational] employees averaged 9.67 strikes per year, a considerably higher frequency than has occurred since strikes were legalized.

During the first year of the IELRA [covering educational employees], 776 K-12 school districts engaged in teacher bargaining, representing a fifty-three percent increase over the pre-Act years. The increase does not include the nonteaching staff and higher education units. During the nine years preceding the statute, K-12 teacher strikes averaged 24.56 per year. The incidence of thirty-five strikes experienced in 1984–85 is roughly comparable, given the increase in bargaining. Since the first year of the IELRA, strike activity has dropped dramatically, hitting a low of six in the 1987–88 and 1988–89 school years, even though the number of bargaining units increased substantially.

Thus, the experiences in Ohio and Illinois run counter to the expectation that enactment of comprehensive public sector bargaining laws containing a right to strike would increase the incidence of strikes. Despite an increase in bargaining activity in the first eight years under the Ohio statute, strikes averaged 13.75 per year, compared with an average of 55.71 strikes per year from 1974 to 1980. In the first eight years of the Illinois statute, strikes averaged 15.75 throughout public education, despite an increase in bargaining, compared to an average of 24.56 strikes per year among K-12 teachers prior to the IELRA.

Of course, the enactment of the new legislation was not the only factor which might have influenced the changes in strike activity over the years in Ohio and Illinois. Two economic factors which merit attention are the unemployment rate and the inflation rate. Studies in the private sector generally agree that strikes decline as the unemployment rate increases. Intuition suggests a similar result in the public sector. As unemployment increases, employees lower their expectations for a new collective bargaining agreement. Higher levels of unemployment also reduce the availability of temporary work while on strike and increase the availability of striker replacements. Studies in the public sector, however, have reached inconsistent results regarding the relationship between unemployment rates and strikes, although most find a relationship similar to that in the private sector.

As the inflation rate increases, employees' expectations in collective bargaining probably increase as they try to regain losses in real wage levels. Therefore, it is not surprising that studies generally find that the incidence of public sector strikes is positively correlated with inflation. . . .

To further evaluate the experiences in Ohio and Illinois with legalizing public employee strikes, we ran single and multivariate regression analyses of the data. . . . Each regression showed a very strong correlation between the change in the law in Ohio and the decrease in the number of strikes.

Regression analyses of the experience with strikes in Illinois public education yielded considerably weaker results. . . .

Several caveats apply to the data from both states. First, the data in both states do not take into account the increase in bargaining activity that followed the enactment of the statutes. To this extent, the data underestimate the effects of the statutes on decreasing strike frequency.

Second, the data do not take into account other factors that may affect strike frequency. Chief among these omitted factors is the employer's fiscal climate. Experienced negotiators generally agree that tight fiscal constraints often lead to more strikes. Another factor not captured by the data is the relative experience of the negotiators.

Third, the pre-Act data in both states are not completely comparable to the post-Act data. The pre-Act Ohio data may include some strikes by employees who now have the right to go to interest arbitration, such as nurses and employees of the state schools for the blind and deaf and the state retirement system. . . .

Finally, the data may overestimate the effect of legalizing public employee strikes on decreasing strike frequency because the data do not distinguish between strikes over bargaining impasses and strikes over recognition. In addition to legalizing strikes, the Illinois and Ohio statutes provide procedures whereby a union may force recognition by petitioning for and winning a representation election conducted by the labor board. There is strong evidence that by reducing the union's need to resort to self-help to force recognition, comprehensive public employee collective bargaining statutes reduce strikes over recognition as well as strikes over the parties' first collective bargaining agreement. . . .

It is not likely, however, that this accounts for most of the reduction. . . .

Reasonable theoretical grounds exist for believing that legalizing strikes may reduce the number of strikes overall. Artificial strike prohibitions distort the communication value of the union's strike threat. While at the bargaining table, unions threatening an illegal strike usually maintain that they are fully prepared to deal with the consequences of the strike's illegality. Employers may excessively discount such representations, thereby underestimating the settlement that the union is willing to accept. A lawful and credible strike threat is a great incentive for peaceful settlement. Eliminating artificial strike prohibitions may promote more realistic bargaining.

The data presented in this Article, however, do not firmly support a conclusion that the legalization of public employee strikes in Illinois and Ohio caused their frequency to decrease. On the other hand, there is no evidence that legalization caused strikes to increase in frequency. All of the evidence is to the contrary.

Notes

1. If the goal is to prevent strikes in the public sector, the worst alternative may be to have no statute authorizing collective bargaining. One study found the following:

> Our results suggest that "no legislation" is the worst form of collective-bargaining legislation. Strike costs, as measured by the incidence and length of strikes, are greatest in the absence of legislation requiring employers to bargain. Requiring employers to bargain in good faith and permitting strikes does not significantly increase either the incidence or severity of strikes. One possible explanation for these results is that, while strikes are more costly when they are illegal, both workers and employers face more uncertainty when there is no explicit legal framework governing negotiations. This uncertainty leads to more frequent strikes. Janet Currie & Sheena McConnell, *The Impact of Collective-Bargaining Legislation on Disputes in the U.S. Public Sector: No Legislation May Be the Worst Legislation*, 37 J.L. & Econ. 519, 520–21 (1994).

The wave of teachers' strikes in the spring of 2018, discussed above in Problem 11.1, arguably supports this thesis. Again, these strikes took place in states that not only make such strikes illegal but also do not grant collective bargaining rights to teachers. What lessons should unions, public employers, and policy-makers take from these strikes?

2. It is hard to gauge the number of public-sector strikes, as the main source of such information, the Department of Labor's Bureau of Labor Standards, stopped collecting detailed data about strikes after the 1980s. According to data from

1982–85, public-sector workers accounted for 11 percent of all major strikes (those affecting 1,000 workers or more) in that period, even though during that period public-sector union members were one third of total union membership. Daniel Mitchell, *Collective Bargaining and Compensation in the Public Sector*, in AARON, NAJITA & STERN, *supra*, at 154–55.

Still, some state boards collect strike data, and at least in Ohio, the effect Professor Malin described continued in following decades. From 1993–99, there were only fifty public-sector strikes in Ohio. From 2000–10, there were only forty-three such strikes. *See* Joseph Slater, *The Rise and Fall of SB-5: The Rejection of an Anti-Union Law in Historical and Political Context*, 43 U. TOL. L. REV. 473, 481 (2012).

3. As Professor Malin suggests, there is some evidence that some public-sector managers prefer strikes to binding arbitration. *See also* Mitchell, *supra*, at 155. Why might that be? What about the other side? If you were a union leader in a state in which binding arbitration settled impasses, would you favor an amendment to the law permitting (most) public-sector workers to strike?

Unions traditionally have preferred strike rights over other mechanisms to resolve bargaining impasses. However, in May 2015, public-sector unions in Illinois, frustrated by negotiations with Illinois Governor Bruce Rauner (R), supported a bill (S.B. 1229) that would have substituted binding interest arbitration for strike rights for state employees. The bill passed both houses of the state legislature, but the governor vetoed it. The state Senate then voted to override the veto, but the state House did not. Unions backed essentially identical legislation in the summer of 2016, with events playing out the same way (the state House ultimately failed to override the Governor's veto). Why might these unions have preferred interest arbitration to the right to strike, why might the governor feel otherwise, and what (if anything) does this say about Wellington and Winter's arguments about public-sector strikes?

4. Do strikes have other advantages over alternative forms of impasse resolution? A study of public-sector strikes in the U.S. and Canada concluded that bans on strikes "diminish such positive effects of the right to strike as eliciting information, adjusting expectations, and providing catharsis." Robert Hebdon, *Behaviour Determinants of Public Sector Illegal Strikes, Cases from Canada and the U.S.*, 53 RELATIONS INDUSTRIELLES/INDUSTRIAL RELATIONS 667, 669 (1998).

5. What are the effects of teachers' strikes on students? A study of Pennsylvania schools found no statistical relationship between the incidence of teachers' strikes or their duration and school district-level student performance on 46 different state school assessment tests. Harris Zwerling, *Pennsylvania Teachers' Strikes and Academic Performance*, 32 J. OF COLLECTIVE NEGOTIATIONS 151 (2008). Similar studies (*e.g.*, on teachers' strikes in Ohio, using data from 1984–90) came to the same conclusion. *Id.* at 152. Also, when teachers strike, officials often reschedule any school days missed because of the strike. In the 1970s, in about two-thirds of 305 total teacher strikes, students received the mandated 180 days of instruction even though the mean strike duration was almost 13 days. Olson, *Dispute Resolution in the Public*

Sector, supra, 161. Is this data significant in deciding whether public school teachers should have the right to strike?

D. Permanent Replacement of Strikers

While permanent replacement of strikers is an extremely important issue in the private sector, it has little to no importance in the public sector. First, strikes are often illegal, and public employers generally may simply discharge illegal strikers. For how that tactic developed, see McCartin, *Fire the Hell Out of Them, supra.*

For legal strikes, while public employers are allowed to use temporary replacement workers, only a very few decisions have even hinted that public employers could use permanent replacements. In *SERB v. Central Ohio Transit Authority*, 6 Ohio Pub. Emp. Rep. ¶ 6060 (PERB 1988), a public labor board hearing officer noted the lack of precedent on permanent replacements in the public sector and labeled the issue "a very difficult one." While he decided that in theory, employers could legally use permanent replacements, there is no reported case in which an Ohio public employer actually used such replacements, and the authors of this casebook have not found any case in which a public employer used permanent replacements for legal public-sector strikers. *See* Joseph Slater, *The "American Rule" That Swallows the Exceptions*, 11 EMP. RTS. & EMP. POL'Y J. 53, 86 (2007).

Some cases at least imply that legal public-sector strikers could not be permanently replaced. A California labor board case explained that while private-sector employers could hire permanent replacements for economic strikers, "the public sector employer does not have the economic pressure devices available" to respond to strikes. *Fremont Unified School Dist. v. Fremont Unified Dist. Teachers Ass'n*, 14 Pub. Employee Rep. for California ¶ 21107 (PERB 1990). More recently, *California Nurses Ass'n v. Regents of the University of California*, 34 Pub. Employee Rep. for Cal. ¶ 41 (PERB 2010) also stated that public employers did not have the "economic weapons" available to private employers, specifically listing striker replacements as one such weapon. The decision added: "Moreover, it is rarely feasible for a public employer to hire permanent replacements for striking workers, particularly when the bargaining unit, like the one in this case, is geographically extensive and includes many employees with highly specialized skills." *Id.*

Another factor may be at play as well. Many and probably most members of union bargaining units in the public sector are covered by civil service laws which allow discipline and discharge only for "just cause." Assuming it would be fair to categorize permanent replacement as something akin to discipline or discharge—and it is often, in effect, essentially the same as discharge—it might be difficult to argue successfully that participation in a legal strike is "just cause."

As in the private sector, though, public employees who engage in a legal strike will lose reinstatement rights if they engage in sufficiently serious misconduct during the strike. *See Hinesburg Sch. Dist. v. Vermont NEA*, 147 Vt. 558 (1986) (acknowledging the rule, but upholding the labor board's finding of no such misconduct).

E. Conclusion

Problem 11.4

If you were writing a public-sector labor statute, how would you design the impasse resolution portions, and why?

Problem 11.5

Recall the suggestion by Gottesman, *supra*, that public-sector unions have *benefitted* from strike bans and the alternatives that arose in their place. Note that in the mid-1980s, the AFL-CIO seemed willing to consider alternatives from the public sector for private-sector workers, proposing, among other things, "a bargaining approach based on solving problems through arbitration or mediation rather than through ultimate recourse to economic weapons." Mitchell, *supra*,159, *quoting* AFL-CIO, THE CHANGING SITUATION OF WORKERS AND THEIR UNIONS 18 (1985). Also, EFCA would have required interest arbitration in certain situations involving first contracts.

Should policy makers consider adopting for the private sector any aspects of the mediation, fact-finding, and interest arbitration models used in the public sector? If so, which procedures, in what situations, and why? If not, given the problems with the right to strike in the private sector described in the first part of this chapter, why not?

Chapter 12

Legal Constraints on Concerted Activity: Secondary Boycotts, Picketing, and Handbilling, and Recognitional Picketing

I. Introduction

This chapter discusses lawful and unlawful union activity under §§ 8(b)(4) and 8(b)(7). Section 8(b)(4) makes it unlawful for unions to engage in some forms of secondary concerted activity. But the statutory definition of secondary activity is difficult to parse, especially because it must be reconciled with the First Amendment. Section I of this chapter distinguishes between primary and secondary activity. Section II explores the constitutional limitations of § 8(b)(4). Sections III and IV further deconstruct the language of § 8(b)(4) to determine what constitutes unlawful secondary boycotts, picketing, and handbilling. Section V examines § 8(b)(7) and the extent to which picketing for union recognition is lawful. These issues are not significant in the public sector (as you review these materials, consider why that is), so there are no materials devoted to the public sector in this chapter.

II. Overview: Distinctions Between Primary and Secondary Concerted Activity

When reading the following excerpt from Professor Lesnick's article, think about how you would distinguish between primary and secondary concerted activity.

Howard Lesnick, *The Gravamen of the Secondary Boycott*
62 COLUM. L. REV. 1363 (1962)*

"The gravamen of a secondary boycott," Judge Learned Hand has told us, "is that its sanctions bear, not upon the employer who alone is a party to the dispute, but upon some third party who has no concern in it. Its aim is to compel him to stop business with the employer in the hope that this will induce the employer to give in to his employees' demands." [*IBEW v. NLRB*, 181 F.2d 34, 37 (2d Cir. 1950).] That is the Law, from the pen of one of its major prophets; what follows is an attempt at commentary.

Federal regulation of secondary pressure is embodied in §8(b)(4)-(B), a section aptly described as "surely one of the most labyrinthine provisions ever included in a federal labor statute." [Aaron, *The Labor-Management Reporting and Disclosure Act of 1959* (pt. 2), 73 HARV. L. REV. 1086, 1113 (1960)]. The text of the statute condemns refusals to perform any services, or the inducement of such refusals, when an object thereof is forcing one employer to cease doing business with another. Although the focus of congressional attention was on the secondary strike—"a strike against employer A for the purpose of forcing that employer to cease doing business with employer B . . . (with whom the union has a dispute)"—the language reaches picketing, which is typically calculated to "induce or encourage" such a strike, as well. While the act does not use the term, it has been more or less generally recognized since its passage that boycott action must be "secondary" in character to fall within the bar of §8(b)(4), and since 1959 this limitation has been explicit in the proviso declaring §8(b)(4)(B) inapplicable to "any primary strike or primary picketing." The content of the dichotomy thus made relevant, between primary and secondary picketing—"unquestionably the area of greatest difficulty and importance in the administration of the statute" [Koretz, *Federal Regulation of Secondary Strikes and Boycotts-Another Chapter*, 59 COLUM. L. REV. 125, 129 (1959)]—is the subject of this article.

The setting of the problem can be no more succinctly provided than by borrowing the words of Professor, now Solicitor General, Archibald Cox:

> Historically, a boycott is a refusal to have dealings with an offending person. To induce customers not to buy from an offending grocery store is to organize a primary boycott. To persuade grocery stores not to buy [boycotted] products is also a primary boycott. In each case the only economic pressure is leveled at the offending person—in terms of labor cases, at the employer involved in the labor dispute.

The element of "secondary activity" is introduced when there is a refusal to have dealings with one who has dealings with the offending person. For example, there is a secondary boycott when housewives refuse to buy at any grocery store which

---

deals with Swift & Co. For members of the Plumbers Union to refuse to work for any contractor who buys pipe from the United States Pipe Co. is, strictly speaking, a secondary strike but is called a secondary boycott and is, of course, the only kind of secondary activity which was prohibited under the Taft-Hartley Act [prior to the 1959 amendments]. Thus, there are two employers in every secondary boycott resulting from a labor dispute.

Picketing at the scene of a labor dispute often requires the drawing of fine distinctions between primary and secondary activities. NLRA § 8(b)(4)(A) obviously makes it unlawful for the Teamsters Union to induce the employees of the ABC Express Co. to refuse to transport furniture delivered at the ABC terminal by the Modern Furniture Co., some of whose employees are on strike, for one of the Teamsters Union's objectives would be to force the express company to cease doing business with the furniture company. Suppose, however, a second case, where the furniture company telephones the express company to pick up the furniture at the factory, but the strikers dissuade the express company's drivers from entering. The refusal to cross the picket line, not the strike, applies the economic pressure. The words of § 8(b)(4)(A) are equally as applicable as in the first case. . . . [Cox, *The Landrum-Griffin Amendments to the National Labor Relations Act*, 44 MINN. L. REV. 257, 271 (1959)].

Whether the act bars the conduct described in the prototype case put by Cox, or in more complex variations of it, is a problem that the Board and courts . . . have struggled with for . . . years. Time, however, has not yielded a growing agreement on an approach to the problem. Through the many shifts of emphasis and approach manifested by the precedents, perhaps the most stable element has been discord; whatever the result, one can ordinarily expect Board decisions in this field to be divided. . . .

Problem 12.1

A union, seeking to represent employees of a mill, strikes. Truck drivers attempt to enter the mill's premises to deliver goods to the mill for processing. A union representative asks truck drivers not to cross the picket line, and the drivers choose not to make delivery. What result? In *NLRB v International Rice Milling Co.*, 341 U.S. 665 (1951), the Court held that the union did not violate § 8(b)(4). This was true even though there was an impact on secondary employers (in this example, the trucking company and presumably the company whose goods were on board the truck). Consider why that Court would hold that way.

III. The Constitutional Framework for Distinguishing Among Different Types of Concerted Activities

Now that you have a sense of the distinction between primary and secondary activity, re-read § 8(b)(4). The next section will focus on deconstructing the statutory language, so for now, simply notice that a Proviso protects union "publicity, other than picketing" regarding labor disputes, as long as certain conditions are met. Likewise, §8(b)(7), discussed at the end of this chapter, singles out picketing for regulation. This section discusses the extent of First Amendment protection for union secondary picketing as compared to other forms of expression. You read the materials, consider whether the distinction is justified. As you do so, you may want to revisit the discussion in Chapter 4.II.A concerning protections for picketing in other contexts.

As Chapter 1 describes, before Congress enacted the NLRA, courts used common law doctrines to enjoin picketing—especially when directed at secondary businesses—under a variety of legal theories. Congress twice passed laws—the Clayton Act and the Norris-LaGuardia Act—to remove from federal courts the jurisdiction to enjoin labor picketing. The tide seemed to turn in *Thornhill v. Alabama*, 310 U.S. 88 (1940), discussed in Chapter 4, when the Court declared unconstitutional a state statute criminalizing picketing. The following year, in *AFL v. Swing*, 312 U.S. 321 (1941), the Court declared unconstitutional a state injunction against union picketing grounded in a state policy barring picketing appeals to neutral third parties. *Swing* marks the height of constitutional protection of labor picketing. Shortly thereafter, the Court began to view picketing as "more than free speech."

In a series of cases between 1942 and 1957, the Court cut back on its "broad pronouncements" made in *Thornhill* and *Swing*. In *Teamsters, Local 695 v. Vogt, Inc.*, 354 U.S. 284, 289 (1957), discussed in Chapter 4, the Court decreed:

> [P]icketing, even though "peaceful," involved more than just communication of ideas and could not be immune from all state regulation. "Picketing by an organized group is more than free speech, since it involves patrol of a particular locality an since the very presence of a picket line may include action of one kind or another, quire irrespective of the nature of the ideas which are being disseminated." *Vogt*, 354 U.S. at 289 (quoting *Bakery Drivers Local v. Wohl*, 315 U.S. 769, 776 (1942) and citing *Carpenters Union v. Ritter's Café*, 315 U.S. 722, 725–28 (1942)).

The Court continued:

> The implied reassessments of the broad language of the *Thornhill* case were finally generalized in a series of cases sustaining injunctions against peaceful picketing, even when arising in the course of a labor controversy, when such picketing was counter to valid state policy in a domain open to state regulation. The decisive reconsideration came in *Giboney v. Empire Storage & Ice Co.*, 336 U.S. 490 (1949). A union, seeking to organize peddlers, picketed a wholesale dealer to induce it to refrain from selling to non-union peddlers. The state courts, finding that such an agreement would constitute a conspiracy in restraint of trade in violation of the state antitrust laws, enjoined the picketing. This Court affirmed unanimously. . . .
>
> The Court . . . concluded that it was "clear that appellants were doing more than exercising a right of free speech or press. . . . They were exercising

their economic power together with that of their allies to compel Empire to abide by union rather than by state regulation of trade." *Id.* at 503. *Vogt*, 354 U.S. at 291–92 (quoting *Giboney*).

The Court reaffirmed its view of labor picketing in *NLRB v. Retail Stores, Local 1001*, 447 U.S. 607 (1980), where it affirmed the constitutionality of the NLRA's ban on secondary picketing. In the context of declaring § 8(b)(4) constitutional, Justice Stevens characterized labor picketing as follows:

> The statutory ban in this case affects only that aspect of the union's efforts to communicate its views that *calls for an automatic response to a signal, rather than a reasoned response to an idea.* And the restriction on picketing is limited in geographical scope to sites of neutrals in the labor dispute. Because I believe that such restrictions on conduct are sufficiently justified by the purpose to avoid embroiling neutrals in a third party's labor dispute. I agree that the statute is consistent with the First Amendment. *Id.* at 619 (Stevens, J., concurring) (emphasis added).

As discussed in Chapter 4, the Court's most recent pronouncements on picketing have come outside of the labor context, and they have been quite protective of picketers' First Amendment rights. Presumably, the same standards should apply in the labor context; yet, the Supreme Court has not overturned its earlier cases that seem to allow greater regulation of labor picketing under the First Amendment. One way that the NLRB and the circuit courts sometimes attempt to reconcile these competing demands is to construe narrowly the definition of "picketing." *See Sheet Metal Workers' Intern. Ass'n, Local 15 v. NLRB*, 491 F.3d 429, 432 (D.C. Cir. 2007):

> [T]he Union staged a "mock funeral" outside the Hospital and distributed leaflets headed "Going to Brandon Hospital Should Not Be a Grave Decision"; the leaflets detailed several malpractice suits against the Hospital — the implication being the alleged malpractice was linked to the Hospital's use of non-union labor. The "mock funeral" comprised one person in a "Grim Reaper" costume carrying a "plastic sickle" and four other people, dressed in street clothes, carrying a prop coffin and occasionally handing out leaflets.

The Board concluded that the Union's conduct constituted unlawful secondary picketing. The court rejected the Board's holding, finding that the mock funeral was not even picketing but "a combination of street theater and handbilling." Although not central to its holding, the court observed that the Union's conduct was consistent with *Madsen* and *Hill*. *Id.* at 437.

Recently, a union argued that it was unconstitutional to apply § 8(b)(4) to secondary picketing of government offices, relying on the recent Supreme Court decision in *Reed v. Town of Gilbert*, 153 S. Ct. 2218 (2015) (holding that strict scrutiny applied to ordinance imposing different restrictions on signs intended for different purposes, and striking down sign ordinance). The Ninth Circuit rejected the challenge, writing that "a plain reading of § 8(b)(4)(ii)(B) reflects that the statute regulates conduct rather than content." *NLRB v. Int'l Ass'n of Bridge, Structural, Ornamental & Reinforcing Ironworkers Union, Local 433*, 891 F.3d 1182, 1187 (9th Cir. 2018).

In contrast with picketing, as the case excerpted below shows, the courts have given handbilling robust constitutional protection. This case also deals with the publicity proviso, which will be discussed in greater detail later in this chapter.

Edward J. Debartolo Corp. v. Florida Gulf Coast Building & Construction Trades Council

Supreme Court of the United States
485 U.S. 568, 108 S. Ct. 1392, 99 L. Ed. 2d 645 (1988)

WHITE, J.

This case centers around the union's peaceful handbilling of the businesses operating in a shopping mall in Tampa, Florida, owned by petitioner, the Edward J. DeBartolo Corporation (DeBartolo). The union's primary labor dispute was with H.J. High Construction Company (High) over alleged substandard wages and fringe benefits. High was retained by the H.J. Wilson Company (Wilson) to construct a department store in the mall, and neither DeBartolo nor any of the other 85 or so mall tenants had any contractual right to influence the selection of contractors.

The union, however, sought to obtain their influence upon Wilson and High by distributing handbills asking mall customers not to shop at any of the stores in the mall "until the Mall's owner publicly promises that all construction at the Mall will be done using contractors who pay their employees fair wages and fringe benefits." [1]

---

1. The Handbill read:

"PLEASE *DON'T SHOP AT EAST LAKE SQUARE MALL* PLEASE

"The FLA. GULF COAST BUILDING TRADES COUNCIL, AFL-CIO, is requesting that you do not shop at the stores in the East Lake Square Mall because of The Mall ownership's contribution to substandard wages.

"The Wilson's Department Store under construction on these premises is being built by contractors who pay substandard wages and fringe benefits. In the past, the Mall's owner, The Edward J. DeBartolo Corporation, has supported labor and our local economy by insuring that the Mall and its stores be built by contractors who pay fair wages and fringe benefits. Now, however, and for no apparent reason, the Mall owners have taken a giant step backwards by permitting our standards to be torn down. The payment of substandard wages not only diminishes the working person's ability to purchase with earned, rather than borrowed, dollars, but it also undercuts the wage standard of the entire community. Since low construction wages at this time of inflation means decreased purchasing power, do the owners of East Lake Mall intend to compensate for the decreased purchasing power of workers of the community by encouraging the stores in East Lake Mall to cut their prices and lower their profits?

"CUT-RATE WAGES ARE NOT FAIR UNLESS MERCHANDISE PRICES ARE ALSO CUT-RATE.

"We ask for your support in our protest against substandard wages. Please do not patronize the stores in the East Lake Square Mall until the Mall's owner publicly promises that all construction at the Mall will be done using contractors who pay their employees fair wages and fringe benefits.

The handbills' message was that "[t]he payment of substandard wages not only diminishes the working person's ability to purchase with earned, rather than borrowed, dollars, but it also undercuts the wage standard of the entire community." The handbills made clear that the union was seeking only a consumer boycott against the other mall tenants, not a secondary strike by their employees. At all four entrances to the mall for about three weeks in December 1979, the union peacefully distributed the handbills without any accompanying picketing or patrolling.

DeBartolo . . . filed a complaint with the NLRB (Board), charging the union with engaging in ULPs under § 8(b)(4). The Board's General Counsel issued a complaint, but the Board eventually dismissed it, concluding that the handbilling was protected by the publicity proviso of § 8(b)(4). The [Fourth Circuit] affirmed the Board . . . but this Court reversed in *Edward J. DeBartolo Corp. v. NLRB*, 463 U.S. 147 (1983). There, we concluded that the handbilling did not fall within the proviso's limited scope of exempting "publicity intended to inform the public that the primary employer's product is 'distributed by' the secondary employer" because DeBartolo and the other tenants, as opposed to Wilson, did not distribute products of High. *Id.* at 155–57. Since there had not been a determination below whether the union's handbilling fell within the prohibition of § 8(b)(4), and, if so, whether it was protected by the First Amendment, we remanded the case.

On remand, the Board held that the union's handbilling was proscribed by § 8(b)(4)(ii)(B). It stated that under its prior cases "handbilling and other activity urging a consumer boycott constituted coercion." The Board reasoned that "[a]ppealing to the public not to patronize secondary employers is an attempt to inflict economic harm on the secondary employers by causing them to lose business," and "such appeals constitute 'economic retaliation' and are therefore a form of coercion." It viewed the object of the handbilling as attempting "to force the mall tenants to cease doing business with DeBartolo in order to force DeBartolo and/or Wilson's not to do business with High."

The [Eleventh Circuit] denied enforcement of the Board's order. Because there would be serious doubts about whether § 8(b)(4) could constitutionally ban peaceful handbilling not involving nonspeech elements, such as patrolling, the court applied our decision in *NLRB v. Catholic Bishop of Chicago*, 440 U.S. 490, (1979), to determine if there was a clear congressional intent to proscribe such handbilling. [Finding that there was not, t]he court went on to construe the section as not prohibiting consumer publicity; DeBartolo petitioned for certiorari. Because this case presents important questions of federal constitutional and labor law, we granted the petition . . . and now affirm.

"IF YOU MUST ENTER THE MALL TO DO BUSINESS, please express to the store managers your concern over substandard wages and your support of our efforts.
"We are appealing only to the public-the consumer. We are not seeking to induce any person to cease work or to refuse to make deliveries."

The Board . . . has construed § 8(b)(4) . . . to cover handbilling at a mall entrance urging potential customers not to trade with any retailers in the mall, in order to exert pressure on the proprietor of the mall to influence a particular mall tenant not to do business with a nonunion construction contractor. That statutory interpretation by the Board would normally be entitled to deference unless that construction [was] clearly contrary to the intent of Congress. *Chevron U.S.A. Inc. v. Natural Resources Defense Council, Inc.*, 467 U.S. 837, 842–843, and n. 9 (1984).

Another rule of statutory construction, however, is pertinent here: where an otherwise acceptable construction of a statute would raise serious constitutional problems, the Court will construe the statute to avoid such problems unless such construction is plainly contrary to the intent of Congress. *Catholic Bishop*, 440 U.S. at 499–501, 504. . . . As was stated in *Hooper v. California*, 155 U.S. 648, 657 (1895), ". . . every reasonable construction must be resorted to, in order to save a statute from unconstitutionality." . . . The courts will therefore not lightly assume that Congress intended to infringe constitutionally protected liberties or usurp power constitutionally forbidden it.

We agree with the Court of Appeals and [unions] that this case calls for the invocation of the *Catholic Bishop* rule, for the Board's construction of the statute, as applied in this case, poses serious questions of the validity of § 8(b)(4) under the First Amendment. The handbills involved here truthfully revealed the existence of a labor dispute and urged potential customers of the mall to follow a wholly legal course of action, namely, not to patronize the retailers doing business in the mall. The handbilling was peaceful. No picketing or patrolling was involved. On its face, this was expressive activity arguing that substandard wages should be opposed by abstaining from shopping in a mall where such wages were paid. Had the union simply been leafleting the public generally, including those entering every shopping mall in town, pursuant to an annual educational effort against substandard pay, there is little doubt that legislative proscription of such leaflets would pose a substantial issue of validity under the First Amendment. The same may well be true in this case, although here the handbills called attention to a specific situation in the mall allegedly involving the payment of unacceptably low wages by a construction contractor.

That a labor union is the leafletter and that a labor dispute was involved does not foreclose this analysis. We do not suggest that communications by labor unions are never of the commercial speech variety and thereby entitled to a lesser degree of constitutional protection. The handbills involved here, however, do not appear to be typical commercial speech such as advertising the price of a product or arguing its merits, for they pressed the benefits of unionism to the community and the dangers of inadequate wages to the economy and the standard of living of the populace. Of course, commercial speech itself is protected by the First Amendment, *Virginia Pharmacy Bd. v. Virginia Citizens Consumer Council, Inc.*, 425 U.S. 748, 762 (1976), and however these handbills are to be classified, the Court of Appeals was plainly correct in holding that the Board's construction would require deciding serious constitutional issues. . . .

The Board was urged to construe the statute in light of the asserted constitutional considerations, but thought that it was constrained by its own prior authority and cases in the Courts of Appeals, as well as by the express language of the Act, to hold that §8(b)(4) must be construed to forbid the handbilling involved here. Even if this construction of the Act were thought to be a permissible one, we are quite sure that in light of the traditional rule followed in *Catholic Bishop*, we must independently inquire whether there is another interpretation, not raising these serious constitutional concerns, that may fairly be ascribed to §8(b)(4)(ii)(B). This the Court has done in several cases.

In *NLRB v. Drivers*, 362 U.S. 274, 284 (1960), for example, the Court rejected the Board's interpretation of the phrase "restrain or coerce" to include peaceful recognitional picketing and stated:

> "In the sensitive area of peaceful picketing Congress has dealt explicitly with isolated evils which experience has established flow from such picketing. Therefore, unless there is the clearest indication in the legislative history of §8(b)(1)(A) supporting the Board's claim of power under that section, we cannot sustain the Board's order here. We now turn to an examination of the legislative history."

That examination of the legislative history failed to yield the requisite "clearest indication." Similarly, in *NLRB v. Fruit Packers*, 377 U.S. 58, 63 (1964) (*Tree Fruits*), we disagreed with the Board's determination that §8(b)(4)(ii)(B) prohibited all consumer picketing at a secondary establishment, no matter the economic consequences of that picketing, because our examination of the legislative history led us to "conclude that it does not reflect with the requisite clarity a congressional plan to proscribe all peaceful consumer picketing at secondary sites, and, particularly, any concern with peaceful picketing when it is limited, as here, to persuading" customers not to purchase a specific product of the secondary establishment. We once more looked for the "isolated evils" that Congress had focused on because "[b]oth the congressional policy and our adherence to this principle of interpretation reflect concern that a broad ban against peaceful picketing might collide with the guarantees of the First Amendment." *Id.* at 62–63; *see id.* at 67, 71. Because there was not the required "clearest indication in the legislative history," we rejected the Board's interpretation that limited expressive activities. Again, in *Catholic Bishop*, we independently determined whether the Board's jurisdiction extended to parochial schools in the face of a substantial First Amendment challenge, although the Board itself had previously considered the First Amendment challenge and presumably interpreted the statute cognizable of those limits. 440 U.S. at 497–499.

We follow this course here and conclude, as did the Court of Appeals, that the section is open to a construction that obviates deciding whether a congressional prohibition of handbilling on the facts of this case would violate the First Amendment.

The case turns on whether handbilling such as involved here must be held to "threaten, coerce, or restrain any person" to cease doing business with another, within the meaning of §8(b)(4)(ii)(B). We note first that "induc[ing] or encourag[ing]" employees of the secondary employer to strike is proscribed by §8(b)(4)(i). But more than mere persuasion is necessary to prove a violation of §8(b)(4)(ii)(B): that section requires a showing of threats, coercion, or restraints. Those words, we have said, are "nonspecific, indeed vague," and should be interpreted with "caution" and not given a "broad sweep," *Drivers*, 362 U.S. at 290; and in applying §8(b)(1)(A) they were not to be construed to reach peaceful recognitional picketing. Neither is there any necessity to construe such language to reach the handbills involved in this case. There is no suggestion that the leaflets had any coercive effect on customers of the mall. There was no violence, picketing, or patrolling and only an attempt to persuade customers not to shop in the mall.

The Board nevertheless found that the handbilling "coerced" mall tenants and explained in a footnote that "[a]ppealing to the public not to patronize secondary employers is an attempt to inflict economic harm on the secondary employers by causing them to lose business. As the case law makes clear, such appeals constitute 'economic retaliation' and are therefore a form of coercion." Our decision in *Tree Fruits*, however, makes untenable the notion that *any* kind of handbilling, picketing, or other appeals to a secondary employer to cease doing business with the employer involved in the labor dispute is "coercion" within the meaning of §8(b)(4)(ii)(B) if it has some economic impact on the neutral. In that case, the union picketed a secondary employer, a retailer, asking the public not to buy a product produced by the primary employer. We held that the impact of this picketing was not coercion within the meaning of §8(b)(4) even though, if the appeal succeeded, the retailer would lose revenue.

NLRB v. Retail Store Employees, 447 U.S. 607 (1980) (*Safeco*), in turn, held that consumer picketing urging a general boycott of a secondary employer aimed at causing him to sever relations with the union's real antagonist was coercive and forbidden by §8(b)(4). It is urged that *Safeco* rules this case because the union sought a general boycott of all tenants in the mall. But "picketing is qualitatively 'different from other modes of communication,'" *Babbitt v. Farm Workers*, 442 U.S. 289, 311, n. 17 (1979) (quoting *Hughes v. Superior Court*, 339 U.S. 460, 465 (1950)), and *Safeco* noted that the picketing there actually threatened the neutral with ruin or substantial loss. As Justice STEVENS pointed out in his concurrence in *Safeco*, 447 U.S., at 619, picketing is "a mixture of conduct and communication" and the conduct element "often provides the most persuasive deterrent to third persons about to enter a business establishment." Handbills containing the same message, he observed, are "much less effective than labor picketing" because they "depend entirely on the persuasive force of the idea." *Ibid.* Similarly, the Court stated in *Hughes v. Superior Court*, 339 U.S. at 465:

> "Publication in a newspaper, or by distribution of circulars, may convey the same information or make the same charge as do those patrolling a picket line. But the very purpose of a picket line is to exert influences, and it produces consequences, different from other modes of communication."

In *Tree Fruits*, we could not discern with the "requisite clarity" that Congress intended to proscribe all peaceful consumer picketing at secondary sites. There is even less reason to find in the language of § 8(b)(4)(ii)(B), standing alone, any clear indication that handbilling, without picketing, "coerces" secondary employers. The loss of customers because they read a handbill urging them not to patronize a business, and not because they are intimidated by a line of picketers, is the result of mere persuasion, and the neutral who reacts is doing no more than what its customers honestly want it to do.

Of course, as we have explained in the text, the post-1959 decisions of the Board construing § 8(b)(4)(ii)(B) to reach nonpicketing publicity do not foreclose our independent inquiry into the meaning of that section.

It is nevertheless argued that the second proviso to § 8(b)(4) makes clear that that section, as amended in 1959, was intended to proscribe nonpicketing appeals such as handbilling urging a consumer boycott of a neutral employer.

By its terms, the proviso protects nonpicketing communications directed at customers of a distributor of goods produced by an employer with whom the union has a labor dispute. Because handbilling and other consumer appeals not involving such a distributor are not within the proviso, the argument goes, those appeals must be considered coercive within the meaning of § 8(b)(4)(ii)(B). Otherwise, it is said, the proviso is meaningless, for if handbilling and like communications are never coercive and within the reach of the section, there would have been no need whatsoever for the proviso.

This approach treats the proviso as establishing an exception to a prohibition that would otherwise reach the conduct excepted. But this proviso has a different ring to it. It states that § 8(b)(4) "shall not be construed" to forbid certain described nonpicketing publicity. That language need not be read as an exception. It may indicate only that without the proviso, the particular nonpicketing communication the proviso protects might have been considered to be coercive, even if other forms of publicity would not be. Section 8(b)(4), with its proviso, may thus be read as not covering nonpicketing publicity, including appeals to customers of a retailer as they approach the store, urging a complete boycott of the retailer because he handles products produced by nonunion shops.

The Board's reading of § 8(b)(4) would make [a ULP] out of any kind of publicity or communication to the public urging a consumer boycott of employers other than those the proviso specifically deals with. On the facts of this case, newspaper, radio, and television appeals not to patronize the mall would be prohibited; and it would be [a ULP] for unions in their own meetings to urge their members not to shop in the mall. Nor could a union's handbills simply urge not shopping at a department store because it is using a nonunion contractor, although the union could safely ask the store's customers not to buy there because it is selling mattresses not carrying the union label. It is difficult, to say the least, to fathom why Congress would consider appeals urging a boycott of a distributor of a nonunion product to be more deserving of protection than nonpicketing persuasion of customers of other neutral employers such as that involved in this case.

Neither do we find any clear indication in the relevant legislative history that Congress intended §8(b)(4)(ii)(B) to proscribe peaceful handbilling, unaccompanied by picketing, urging a consumer boycott of a neutral employer. That section was one of several amendments to the NLRA enacted in 1959 and aimed at closing what were thought to be loopholes in the protections to which secondary employers were entitled. We recounted the legislative history in *Tree Fruits* and *NLRB v. Servette, Inc.*, 377 U.S. 46 (1964), and the Court of Appeals carefully reexamined it in this case and found "no affirmative intention of Congress clearly expressed to prohibit nonpicketing labor publicity." . . . [W]e agree with that conclusion. . . . [T]he judgment of the Court of Appeals is [affirmed].

Notes

1. Courts have consistently distinguished between picketing and handbilling. In *Edward J. Debartolo Corp., supra*, the Court makes this distinction when it finds that the NLRA's legislative history fails to show a "clear indication . . . that Congress intended §8(b)(4)(ii)(B) to proscribe peaceful handbilling, *unaccompanied by picketing*." This statement naturally leaves us with the question, what is the difference between picketing and handbilling and is this distinction defensible? Indeed, courts have permitted greater regulation of labor picketing than other forms of speech. Here are some of the conventional arguments given for that view:

a. *Labor picketing is inherently coercive because it calls for an automatic rather than reasoned response to a signal.* According to Justice Stevens, one difference between picketing and handbilling is that handbilling is much closer to pure speech than picketing: "no doubt the principal reason why handbills containing the same message are so much less effective than labor picketing is that the former depend entirely on the persuasive force of the idea." *NLRB v. Retail Stores Employee U., Local 1001*, 447 U.S. 607, 619 (1980).

Justice Frankfurter made similar observations decades earlier:

> Publication in a newspaper, or by distribution of circulars, may convey the same information or make the same charge as do those patrolling a picket line. But the very purpose of a picket line is to exert influences, and it produces consequences, different from other modes of communication. The loyalties and responses evoked and exacted by picket lines are unlike those flowing from appeals by printed word. *Hughes v. Superior Court*, 339 U.S. 460, 465 (1950) (cited with approval in *Hudgens v. NLRB*, 424 U.S. 507, 533 (1976)).

b. *Picketing is not pure speech; it is speech plus conduct.* At other times, the Court has suggested that picketing is a mixture of speech and conduct, and that the conduct involved in picketing may be regulated without violating the First Amendment. *Bldg. Serv. Emps. Int'l Union, Local 262 v. Gazzam*, 339 U.S. 532, 536–37 (1950) (picketing is "more than speech and establishes a locus in quo that has far more potential for inducing action or nonaction than the message the pickets convey"); *see also Bakery Drivers v. Wohl*, 315 U.S. 769, 776–77 (1942) (Douglas, J., concurring) ("[p]icketing by an organized group is more than free speech, since it involves patrol of a particular locality and since the very presence of a picket line may induce action of one kind or another, quite irrespective of the nature of the ideas which are being disseminated. Hence, those aspects of picketing make it the subject of restrictive regulation."). The Court has at times drawn the same distinction in the civil rights context. *Shuttlesworth v. City of Birmingham, Ala.*, 394 U.S. 147 (1969) (the First Amendment does not "afford the same kind of freedom to those who would communicate ideas by conduct such as patrolling, marching, and picketing on streets and highways, as these amendments afford to those who communicate ideas by pure speech.") (quoting *Cox v. Louisiana*, 379 U.S. 536, 555 (1965)). Given this precedent, do you think that the courts are more concerned with the actual picket signs themselves or the patrolling that accompanies picketing?

c. *Labor picketing is commercial or economic speech.* In *Carey v. Brown*, the Court struck down a statute that prohibited picketing at private residences, but provided an exception for labor picketing. 447 U.S. 455 (1980). In holding that Chicago had not offered a sufficient justification for the statute (or its content-discriminatory approach to labor picketing), the Court contrasted labor picketing from "picketing on issues of broader social concern." *Id.* at 465. Similarly, in holding that commercial speech is protected by the First Amendment, the Court stated that "[t]he interests of the contestants in a labor dispute are primarily economic." *VA State Bd. of Pharmacy v. VA Citizens Consumer Council*, 425 U.S. 748, 762 (1976). However, the Court has rejected a per se rule that labor speech always falls into the commercial speech category. *See Edward J. Debartolo Corp.*, 485 U.S. at 576.

d. *Congress has struck an appropriate balance between workers' and employers' interests in regulating picketing under the NLRA.* In *NAACP v. Claiborne Hardware Co.*, 458 U.S. 886 (1982), the Court held that the First Amendment precluded the imposition of tort liability on the NAACP for damages associated with a secondary boycott. The NAACP had called for (and enforced through informal coercion) a boycott of white merchants in order to pressure Claiborne County government to agree to desegregate public institutions, including schools. Justice Blackmun, concurring in part, wrote: "Secondary boycotts and picketing by labor unions may be prohibited, as part of 'Congress' striking of the delicate balance between union freedom of expression and the ability of neutral employers, employees, and consumers to remain free from coerced participation in industrial strife.'" *Id.* at 192 (quoting *NLRB v. Retail Store Employees*, 447 U.S. 607, 617–18 (1980)). As one court has pointed out, the Court's observation "leaves open the question what constitutes 'coerced participation' in a labor dispute and, of course, does nothing to suggest coercion may be defined so broadly as to crimp the free speech guarantee of the First Amendment." *Sheet Metal Workers' Int'l Ass'n, Local 15 v. NLRB*, 491 F.3d 429, 437 (D.C. Cir. 2007).

Problem 12.2

A union handbills a construction site, informing the public that one of the non-union subcontractors was not observing area standards. In tiny print, the handbills stated that the union was not asking any person to cease work or stop deliveries. What result? *See Iron Workers Local 386*, 325 N.L.R.B. 748 (1998) (no violation), *rev'd sub nom. Warshawsky & Co. v. N.L.R.B.*, 182 F.3d 948 (D.C. Cir. 1999).

* * *

Is "bannering" handbilling or picketing? Protected or unprotected? In recent years, unions have displayed large stationary banners announcing the labor dispute at a secondary employer's business to elicit "shame on" the secondary employers and to persuade customers not to patronize these employers. In the cases, the Board has found that such conduct does not violate §8(b)(4)(ii)(B), where, for example, "[t]he banners were held stationary on a public sidewalk or right-of-way, no one patrolled or carried picket signs, and no one interfered with persons seeking to enter or exit from any workplace or business." *Carpenters Local 1506 (Eliason & Knuth of Arizona, Inc.)*, 355 N.L.R.B. 797 (2010). How does the First Amendment play into this? Consider the following case.

Carpenters Local 1506 (Eliason & Knuth of Arizona, Inc.)
The National Labor Relations Board
355 N.L.R.B. 797 (2010)

[T]he Union has been involved in primary labor disputes with four employers engaged in construction: [E&K, Delta, Enterprise, and Hardrock]. The Union asserts that those companies (the primary employers or primaries) do not pay their employees wages and benefits that accord with area standards. In furtherance of its labor disputes with the primary employers, the Union engaged in peaceful protest activities at three locations. . . . The stipulation does not indicate whether the Union also had labor disputes with . . . the companies operating at the sites of the union activities and to which the primaries were providing services regarding the treatment of their employees or with . . . the general contractors who directly retained the primaries to perform work for the secondaries. For purposes of this opinion, therefore, we assume that no such disputes existed. These companies (the secondary employers or "secondaries") had no collective-bargaining relationship with the Union, and the Union was not seeking to organize their employees. . . .

At each of those locations . . . the Union placed and maintained a banner on a public sidewalk or public right-of-way outside of the secondary employer's facility, facing away from the facility such that the banner's message could be seen by passing motorists. The banners were held parallel to the sidewalk at the edge of the street so they in no way blocked the sidewalks. The banners were 3 or 4 feet high and from 15 to 20 feet long and . . . read: "SHAME ON [secondary employer]" in large letters, flanked on either side by "Labor Dispute" in smaller letters. [Another] banner read, "DON'T EAT 'RA' SUSHI." The banners were placed between 15 and 1,050 feet from the nearest entrance to the secondaries' establishments. At each location, several union representatives (normally two or three) held the banner in place. The parties stipulated that the number of union representatives accompanying the banner (a maximum of four) was limited to the number needed to hold it up with staggered breaks. The parties also stipulated that at all material times the banners were held stationary.

In addition to displaying the banners at those locations, the union representatives offered flyers to interested members of the public. The handbills explained the nature of the labor dispute referred to on the banners. . . . The parties stipulated that the union representatives did not chant, yell, march, or engage in any "similar conduct." . . . [T]he representatives did not block persons seeking to enter or exit any of the secondaries' facilities. . . . [T]he representatives "did no more than hold up the banner and give flyers to any interested member of the public" and, apart from the unresolved question of whether the display of a banner is confrontational, "did not engage in any other activity that is considered confrontational within the context of this matter." . . .

The General Counsel and Charging Parties argue that the Union's banner displays violated § 8(b)(4)(ii)(B) because they constituted coercive conduct that had an object of forcing the neutral employers to cease doing business with the primary employers. . . .

The Union argues that the secondary boycott provisions of § 8(b)(4) are not intended to reach the display of a stationary banner. Relying on the Supreme Court's decision in *DeBartolo*, the Union argues that the Court has instructed the Board to avoid, if possible, construing § 8(b)(4)'s statutory language, "threaten, coerce, or restrain," in a manner that would raise serious questions under the First Amendment. The Union argues that although picketing has been found to constitute unlawful coercive conduct under § 8(b)(4), the banner displays here did not constitute picketing, because there was no patrolling or confrontational conduct. To the contrary, the Union argues that the banner displays were peaceful at all times and should be considered a form of pure "speech" similar to handbilling, which the Court in *DeBartolo* found lawful. Accordingly, the Union argues that the complaint should be dismissed. . . .

In answering the question before us, we turn first to the text of the Act. [F]or conduct to violate § 8(b)(4)(ii)(B), the conduct must "threaten, coerce, or restrain." There is no contention that the Respondent threatened the secondary employers or anyone else. Nor is there any contention that the Respondent coerced or restrained the secondaries as those words are ordinarily understood, i.e., through violence, intimidation, blocking ingress and egress, or similar direct disruption of the secondaries' business. A reading of the statutory words "coerce" or "restrain" to require "more than mere persuasion" of consumers is compelled by the Supreme Court's holding in *DeBartolo*. 485 U.S. at 578. Here, however, there is nothing more. . . .

The General Counsel argues that the display of the stationary banners is equivalent to conduct that the Board has found to constitute unlawful picketing. We disagree. The Act does not define "picketing," and the legislative history does not suggest that Congress understood the term to encompass the mere display of a stationary banner. Further, we must evaluate the sweep of the suggestion in the legislative history that Congress intended to bar picketing in light of both the express statutory terms that bar only actions that "threaten, coerce, or restrain" and . . . the protections of the First Amendment. Under our jurisprudence, categorizing peaceful, expressive activity at a purely secondary site as picketing renders it unlawful without any showing of actual threats, coercion or restraint, unless it falls into the narrow exception for consumer product picketing defined in *Tree Fruits.* Moreover, the consequences of categorizing peaceful expressive activity as proscribed picketing are severe. The activity is stripped of protection and employees participating in it can be fired. . . . The activity becomes an unfair labor practice and the Board is required, upon a finding of "reasonable cause" to believe such activity has occurred, to go into federal district court and seek a prior restraint against the continuation of the activity. *See* 29 U.S.C. § 160(l). And, finally, a labor organization engaged in such activity is subject to suit in Federal court where damages can be awarded. *See* 29 U.S.C. § 187. For each of these reasons, we must take care not to define the category of proscribed picketing more broadly than clearly intended by Congress.

The Supreme Court has made clear that "picketing is qualitatively 'different from other modes of communication.'" *Babbit v. Farm Workers,* 442 U.S. 289, 311 fn. 17 (1979) (quoting *Hughes v. Superior Court,* 339 U.S. 460, 465 (1950). Thus, expressive activity that bears some resemblance to picketing should not be classified as picketing unless it is qualitatively different from other nonproscribed means of expression and the qualitative differences suggest that the activity's impact owes more to intimidation than persuasion. Precisely for this reason, the term picketing has developed a core meaning in the labor context. The Board and courts have made clear that picketing generally involves persons carrying picket signs and patrolling back and forth before an entrance to a business or worksite . . . *see also NLRB v. Retail Store Union, Local 1001,* 447 U.S. 607 (1980) (*"Safeco"*) (Justice Stevens, concurring) (picketing "involves patrol of a particular locality") (quoting *Bakery Drivers v. Wohl,* 315 U.S. 769, 776–777 (1942) (Justice Douglas, concurring)); *Overstreet v. Carpenters Local 1506,* 409 F.3d 1199, 1213 (9th Cir. 2005) ("Classically, picketers *walk* in a line and, in so doing, create a symbolic barrier.") (Emphasis supplied.)

The core conduct that renders picketing coercive under § 8(b)(4)(ii)(B) is not simply the holding of signs (in contrast to the distribution of handbills), but the combination of carrying of picket signs and persistent patrolling of the picketers back and forth in front of an entrance to a work site, creating a physical or, at least, a symbolic confrontation between the picketers and those entering the worksite. This element of confrontation has long been central to our conception of picketing for purposes of the Act's prohibitions. *See also Sheet Metal Workers' Local 15 v. NLRB,* 491 F.3d 429, 438 (D.C. Cir. 2007) ("mock funeral" procession outside a hospital did not constitute picketing, because the participants did not "physically or verbally interfere with or confront Hospital patrons" or create a "symbolic barrier"). To fall within the prohibition of § 8(b)(4)(ii)(B), picketing must entail an element of confrontation.

The banner displays here did not constitute such proscribed picketing because they did not create a confrontation. Banners are not picket signs. Furthermore, the union representatives held the banners stationary, without any form of patrolling. Nor did the union representatives hold the banner in front of any entrance to a secondary site in a manner such that anyone entering the site had to pass between the union representatives. The banners were located at a sufficient distance from the entrances so that anyone wishing to enter or exit the sites could to do so without confronting the banner holders in any way. Nor can it be said that the Union "posted" the individuals holding the banners at the "approach" to a secondary's place of business in a manner that could have been perceived as threatening to those entering the sites. The message side of the banner was directed at passing vehicular traffic, rather than at persons entering or leaving the secondaries' premises, and the union representatives faced in the same direction. There is no evidence that the banner holders kept any form of lists of employees or others entering the site or even interacted with passersby, other than to offer a handbill—an [indisputably] noncoercive act. Thus, members of the public and employees wishing to enter the secondaries' sites did not confront any actual or symbolic barrier and, "[j]ust as members of the public [and employees] can 'avert [their] eyes' from billboards or movie screen visible from a public street, they could ignore the [union representatives] and the union's banners." *Overstreet*, 409 F.3d at 1214. Like the mock funeral at issue in *Sheet Metal Workers*, the display of stationary banners here "was not the functional equivalent of picketing as a means of persuasion because it had none of the coercive character of picketing." *Sheet Metal* Workers, supra at 438. In short, the holding of stationary banners lacked the confrontational aspect necessary to a finding of picketing proscribed as coercion or restraint within the meaning of § 8(b)(4)(ii)(B). . . .

The Board has found non-picketing conduct to be coercive only when the conduct directly caused, or could reasonably be expected to directly cause, disruption of the secondary's operations. Blocking ingress or egress is one obvious example of such coercive conduct. In a variety of other instances, the Board and the courts have recognized that disruptive, non-picketing activity directed against secondaries can constitute coercion. For example, a union that engaged in otherwise lawful area-standards publicity violated § 8(b)(4)(ii)(B) by broadcasting its message at extremely high volume through loudspeakers facing a condominium building that had hired the primary employer as a subcontractor. *Carpenters (Society Hill Towers Owners' Assn.)*, 335 N.L.R.B. 814, 820–823 (2001), *enforced*, 50 Fed. Appx. 88 (3d Cir. 2002) (unpub.). The common link among all of these cases is that the union's conduct was or threatened to be the direct cause of disruption to the secondary's operations. There was no such disruption or threatened disruption here.

The banner holders did not move, shout, impede access, or otherwise interfere with the secondary's operations. In sum, we find that the peaceful, stationary holding of banners announcing a "labor dispute" fell far short of "threatening, coercing, or restraining" the secondary employers.

Notes

1. Some union protests involve not a banner, but instead a large inflatable rat, affectionately known in union circles as "Scabby." (There are also variations on Scabby, including large inflatable cockroaches, skunks, "fat cats," and pigs.) These balloons are much more conspicuous than a banner — they are usually at least one story tall — so they can draw more public attention to labor disputes. Thus, secondary employers who discover an inflatable rat outside their doors may argue that the rat qualifies as an unlawful secondary picket. On the other hand, like banners, the inflatable rats are stationary — they are generally staked to the ground to prevent them from falling over.

Scabby the Rat has been in use for years, but it was uncertain whether rat balloons constituted picketing until recently. *See, e.g., Laborers E. Region Org. Fund,* 346 N.L.R.B. 1251 (2006) (declining to decide whether use of rat constitutes picketing). That changed in *Sheet Metal Workers Int'l Ass'n, Local 15 & Galencare, Inc.,* 356 N.L.R.B. 1290 (2011), wherein the Board relied on *Eliason & Knuth* to hold that displaying an inflatable rat at a hospital entrance in connection with a protest against a building contractor did not violate § 8(b)(4). The Board found that the rat display, like the stationary banner in *Eliason,* "entailed no element of confrontation" because it was "stationary and located at sufficient distances from the vehicle and building entrances to the hospital that visitors were not confronted by an actual or symbolic barrier as they arrived at, or departed from, the hospital." *Id.* at 1292. Keep in mind the Board's caveat that the inflatable rat was far enough from the building entrance to avoid forcing confrontations with customers or staff — another set of facts involving a rat placed directly in an employer's doorway would likely have a different result.

In a case presenting a somewhat different question, the Sixth Circuit wrote that "[i]n our view, there is no question that the use of a rat balloon to publicize a labor protest is constitutionally protected expression within the parameters of the First Amendment, especially given the symbol's close nexus to the Union's message." *Tucker v. City of Fairfield, OH,* 398 F.3d 457, 462 (6th Cir. 2005). Applying strict scrutiny, the Sixth Circuit enjoined the application to Scabby of a municipal ordinance banning structures in public rights-of-way. The court found that "the balloon has not been shown to cause any danger that could justify a restriction" on its use. *Id.* at 463. Moreover, the court held that "the application of the City's ordinance prohibiting the Union's use of the balloon, and the consequential adverse effect on Union organizational efforts, are sufficient to constitute irreparable harm." *Id.* at 464.

Recently, the office of NLRB's General Counsel has argued in several cases that the Board should reverse its recent precedent holding that the use of large banners or inflatable rats is neither equivalent to picketing nor coercive. So far, these arguments have not met with success, either before Administrative Law Judges (who are bound by the Board's precedent in *Eliason & Knuth* and *Sheet Metal Workers*), or district courts. *See King v. Construction & General Building Laborers' Local 79*, Case No. 1:19-cv-03496, 2019 WL 2743839 (E.D.N.Y. July 1, 2019); *IUOE Local 150*, Case 25-CC-228342, 2019 WL 3073999 (NLRB Div. of Judges, July 15, 2019); *IBEW, Local 98 (Shree Sai Siddhi Spruce)*, Case 04-CC-223346, 2019 WL 2296952 (NLRB Div. of Judges, May 28, 2019). *See also* NLRB Office of the General Counsel, Advice Memorandum, Case 13-CC-225655 (Dec. 20, 2018).

2. Unions may also stage theatrical events, like mock funerals, to draw attention to labor disputes. When these events are staged in front of a secondary employer, should they be held to constitute unlawful picketing? In 2009, the Board found to be unlawful secondary picketing a "mock funeral procession"—complete with a casket and Grim Reaper—which was held at a hospital in connection with a dispute with a building contractor. *Sheet Metal Workers' Int'l Ass'n, Local 15 & Galencare, Inc.*, 346 N.L.R.B. 199 (2006). The Board relied on the fact that the mock funeral involved "patrolling." *Id.* at 200 (Member Liebman, concurring in part). However, the D.C. Circuit reversed the Board, holding as a matter of constitutional avoidance that the mock funeral was not picketing, but rather "a combination of street theater and handbilling." *Sheet Metal Workers' Int'l Ass'n v. NLRB*, 491 F.3d 429, 437 (D.C. Cir. 2007); *cf. Kentov v. Sheet Metal Workers' Int'l Ass'n*, 418 F.3d 1259, 1265 (11th Cir. 2005) (holding that there was reason to believe mock funeral was equivalent to secondary picketing and patrolling because it "could reasonably be expected to discourage persons from approaching the hospital").

IV. Hallmark Violations: Secondary Boycotts, Picketing, and Handbilling

A. Deconstructing the Statutory Language

The Court has repeatedly observed that the literal language of §8(b)(4) is both overly broad and overly narrow. In other words, it is poorly drafted. Accordingly, this is one of the few areas of labor law where courts have routinely given less weight to the NLRA's statutory language and more weight to divining which types of secondary activity Congress intended to make unlawful. (At this point, carefully review the statutory language provided in your statutory supplement.)

The section below deconstructs the statutory language into three parts: (I) unlawful means; (II) unlawful objects; and (III) provisos. This deconstruction demonstrates that §8(b)(4) makes it a ULP for a union to use unlawful means (i, ii) to engage one of four unlawful objects (A–D), subject to several provisos.

A simplified outline of the deconstructed statutory language might look like the following:

Section 8(b)(4) makes it an unfair labor practice for a union to—

I. Use unlawful means (i) or (ii)

> (i) to engage in, or to induce or encourage an employee to engage in, a strike or to refuse to handle or work on any materials or to perform any services; or

> (ii) to threaten, coerce, or restrain an employer.

II. To obtain unlawful object (A), (B), (C), or (D)

> (A) Forcing any employer to enter into a hot cargo agreement;

> (B) [**Hallmark violations**] forcing or requiring any person to cease dealing in the products of another employer, or to cease doing business with another employer, or forcing any other employer to recognize or bargain with an uncertified union;

> (C) Forcing any employer to recognize or bargain with a particular union if another union has been certified as the representative of its employees;

> (D) [**Jurisdictional disputes**] forcing an employer to assign particular work to employees in Union A rather than to employees in Union B.

III. Subject to the Provisos

> (1) Primary picketing or other primary activity proviso

> (2) Sympathy strike proviso

> (3) Publicity proviso

Simplifying the language even further might look like this:

Section 8(b)(4) makes it an unfair labor practice for a union to—

I. Unlawful means

> (i) against employees of a neutral employer; or

> (ii) against neutral employers.

II. Unlawful objects

> (A) Forcing any employer to enter into a hot cargo agreement;

> (B) Forcing any individual to engage in one of the hallmark violations;

> (C) Forcing any employer to recognize a union;

> (D) Jurisdictional disputes.

III. Provisos

> (1) Primary picketing or other primary activity proviso

> (2) Sympathy strike proviso

> (3) Publicity proviso

The following sections present Board and court constructions of the statutory language. In reading these cases, try to remember that Congress added § 8(b) in 1947 and then amended it in 1959. Accordingly, hallmark violations that would now be violations of § 8(b)(4)(B) were, in earlier times, § 8(b)(4)(A) violations.

B. Unlawful Means: Finding the Neutral Employer

1. Ally Doctrine: Defining the Neutral Employer

As discussed in the case excerpted below, the Ally Doctrine is a line of cases developed by the Board, with court approval, for determining when a nominally neutral employer becomes a permissible union target because of its involvement with the primary employer. If an employer loses its status as an unconcerned neutral during a labor dispute, then a union's concerted activity directed at the "ally" is not unlawful under § 8(b)(4).

Boich Mining Company v. NLRB

United States Court of Appeals for the Sixth Circuit
955 F.2d 431 (1992)

Timbers, J.

Appellant Boich Mining Company petitions for review of the decision and order of the NLRB affirming a finding made by an administrative law judge that Boich and the Aloe Coal Company (Aloe) are allies within the meaning of §§ 8(b)(4)(i) and (ii)(B). . . .

The sole issue . . . is whether the [Board's] finding . . . is supported by substantial evidence. Since we agree with Boich that the Board misapplied the standard for determining whether Boich is a neutral employer worthy of protection under § 8(b) (4)(i) and (ii)(B), we grant the petition for review, reverse the Board's dismissal of the complaint and remand the case to the Board with instructions to reinstate the complaint, to find that the United Mine Workers violated §§ 8(b)(4)(i) and (ii)(B) by striking and picketing Boich, and to provide an appropriate remedy.

I. . . . Boich is an Ohio corporation which operates a surface coal mine in Bloomingdale, Ohio. Aloe is a Pennsylvania corporation which operates a surface coal mine near Imperial, Pennsylvania, approximately thirty one miles from Boich's surface mine. Both corporations are wholly owned subsidiaries of Aloe Holding Company . . . , a Pennsylvania corporation owned and operated by six individuals.

The UMW, its District 6 and its Local No. 7449 . . . represent the production and maintenance employees at Boich for the purposes of collective bargaining. The UMW also represents the production and maintenance employees at Aloe. Prior to 1988, both Boich and Aloe operated under collective bargaining agreements with their union employees. In 1988, Boich and its union employees agreed to a subsequent collective bargaining agreement which currently is in effect. On July 11, 1989,

Aloe's employees, unable to agree to a subsequent collective bargaining agreement with Aloe, went on strike.

On August 3, 1989, the UMW called upon the employees of Boich to strike in support of the striking workers at Aloe. Boich asserted that this second strike was to prevent Boich from continuing its regular business with Aloe. . . . Boich filed [a ULP] charge against UMW, alleging that the strike violated §§ 8(b)(4)(i) and (ii) (B) . . . because it constituted a . . . strike against a neutral employer.

[A]fter a full hearing, [the ALJ] rendered a decision and order finding that Boich and Aloe were a single or allied employer and that the UMW strike against Boich was a permissible extension of the original strike on Aloe. Pursuant to the finding that Boich was not a neutral employer, the ALJ dismissed Boich's complaint. [T]he Board affirmed . . . rel[ying] on evidence of common ownership and interrelation of operations. . . . Boich appealed to this court.

II. . . . Section 8(b)(4) . . . makes it unlawful for a labor organization to picket or otherwise pressure an employer with whom it has no dispute. . . . The purpose of this statutory provision is to preserve the rights of employees to strike against their employers with whom they have a legitimate dispute, while protecting other neutral or secondary employers from becoming enmeshed in the dispute because they happen to conduct business with the employer being struck. . . . As a result, "the provision makes it unlawful to resort to a secondary boycott to injure the business of a third person who is 'wholly unconcerned' or 'not involved in any way' in the dispute between an employer and his employees." *Teamsters Local 50 (E.J. Dougherty Oil)*, 269 N.L.R.B. 170, 174 (1984) [(citation omitted)].

The Board, however, has held consistently that an otherwise neutral employer may lose this protection if that employer becomes . . . "allied" with the primary employer. Under this "ally doctrine", a neutral employer may be stripped of its neutral status (1) if it performs "struck work" for the employer, i.e. work that it otherwise would not perform absent a strike, or (2) if the two employers become so closely entwined as to function essentially as a single entity. . . . In both instances, the union bears the burden of establishing that the two employers are allies. . . .

The Board and the courts have enunciated four criteria to determine whether two employers should be treated as a single entity: (1) common ownership; (2) common management; (3) centralized control of labor relations; and (4) interrelationship of operations. . . . While not all factors need be present and no single factor bears overwhelming importance in the analysis, the Board has established a hierarchy among these factors:

> "Of 'paramount significance is the nature of day-to-day operations and of labor policies in the entities in question.' . . . [I]t is active rather than potential control which is significant. . . . [E]ven in the absence of common ownership, the Board will find separate but related employers not to be neutrals if they jointly control the labor relations of a group of employees."

. . . In short, the analysis of whether two companies should be considered allied depends on the practical, day-to-day operations of the companies, and the issue will be decided on a case-by-case evaluation of the factual relationship between the two entities.

Applying these considerations to the relationship between Boich and Aloe, we hold that the union's efforts to ally the two coal companies constitute a violation of §§ 8(b)(4)(i) and (ii)(B).

It is true that both Boich and Aloe are wholly owned subsidiaries of Aloe Holding Company. It is not unusual, however, to find that two companies are not allied simply because they are under common ownership. *E.g.*, *United Food & Commercial Workers Int'l Union, Local No. 1439*, 271 N.L.R.B. 754, 756 (1984) ("Common ownership and potential control of the day-to-day activities of corporate divisions is inherent in every corporate division relationship, and certainly is not a factor to be accorded weight.").

This is particularly true where the management operations of the subsidiaries are kept separate intentionally. [Here], Boich and Aloe each has a separate management, under a different company president and vice-president. Boich's president, Abe Bryan, was responsible for his company's operations, including hiring, firing, day-to-day labor relations, safety and all personnel and grievance matters. Aloe's vice-president, Grant MacSwain, had similar responsibilities at Aloe. At each company, labor relations are entirely separate. Each company's operations are completely separate: Aloe and Boich maintain separate offices, payroll systems, bank accounts, financial and accounting operations. There is no interchange of either employees or supervisors. The two companies do not sell coal to the same principal customers. Boich's coal is normally hauled by trucking companies completely unrelated to Aloe Holding. Based on these factors, both the ALJ and the Board agreed that Boich appeared to be a neutral party.

In evaluating the interrelatedness of operations, the last of the four factors stated above, however, the Board held that Boich could not be considered a neutral party. Boich purchased several pieces of equipment from Aloe, in what the Board termed "arm's length transactions." The Board also held that Boich and Aloe participated in a coal washing and blending process. Taken as a whole, the Board concluded that the evidence established that the two companies were interrelated. We disagree with the Board's conclusion that, based on this evidence, Boich and Aloe are allies.

In the washing and blending process, a certain amount of Boich's coal regularly is sent to the Aloe facility, where it is washed and blended with Aloe coal before it is shipped to customers. In this process, some of the Boich coal is washed to remove dirt and debris. The Boich coal then is blended with the Aloe coal to produce a mixture that is lower in sulfer content than Boich coal, and lower in ash content than Aloe coal. The parties agreed at oral argument that the ultimate product is a blend of coal distinctly different from that produced independently by either company.

At the end of the washing process, each company takes a proportionate share of the final product based on the amount of coal contributed. The amount of Boich's coal used in this process is approximately 8% of its total output. The amount of Aloe's coal used is approximately 5–6%.

Contrary to the Board decision, we hold that the new product created through this washing and blending process is not only a relatively small amount but also is based on a typical arms-length business transaction. Arms-length transactions are rarely present in a single employer situation. . . . [Here], Boich and Aloe agreed to produce a certain type of blended coal. This type of transaction is not enough to ally the two companies.

We hold that the Board's decision affirming the ALJ's finding that Boich was not a neutral employer because of its participation in the washing and blending operation with Aloe is not supported by substantial evidence.

. . . To summarize . . . Boich and Aloe maintain clearly separate management and control over labor relations. While they are both wholly owned subsidiaries of the same holding company, this in and of itself is not enough to establish that the two companies are so closely entwined as to be treated as a single entity. Their shared participation in a coal washing and blending process does not involve a large amount of coal; rather, it is a relatively minor arms-length business transaction for both companies. Taking these factors as a whole, Boich is a neutral employer under §§ 8(b)(4)(i) and (ii)(B) . . . .

Notes

1. As the Court in *Boich Mining* explained, the Board has developed two types of ally doctrines. Accordingly,

> a neutral employer may be stripped of its neutral status (1) if it performs "struck work" for the employer, i.e. work that it otherwise would not perform absent a strike, or (2) if the two employers become so closely entwined as to function essentially as a single entity. . . . In both instances, the union bears the burden of establishing that the two employers are allies under the Act.

The decision above is part of a line of cases dealing with the common ownership and control ally doctrine. In these cases, the Board, with court approval, has found that an employer can lose its neutral status where there is "(1) common ownership; (2) common management; (3) centralized control of labor relations; and (4) interrelationship of operations." Not all factors need to be present.

2. Does a neutral employer lose its neutral status merely because there is common ownership between it and the primary? No, not necessarily. As *Boich* recognized, common ownership does not necessarily make a neutral employer an ally and common ownership is not necessary where "separate but related employers . . . jointly control the labor relations of a group of employees." *See, e.g., J.G. Roy & Sons v. NLRB*, 251 F.2d 771 (1st Cir. 1958) (finding that the fact that the

same five brothers owned both companies and were officers in and on the board of directors of both companies did not necessarily make the two companies allies); *Packinghouse Employees Local 616*, 203 N.L.R.B. 645 (1973) (union may not lawfully picket parent company of primary company, even though the primary company is a wholly owned subsidiary of parent company, where there are no common personnel, no common facilities, and no common checking or banking accounts; the companies do not participate in joint purchases; and they have no joint financial ventures).

3. Suppose Company O owns Company P and Company N. Company P and its union are in the midst of bargaining over a successor contract. To place economic pressure on Company P, the union strikes. Under what circumstances may the union also picket Company N or Company O? Should it make a difference whether Company N has some control over Company P's bargaining positions? In *AFTRA v. NLRB*, 462 F.2d 887 (D.C. Cir. 1992), the union, which had a labor dispute with WBAL-TV, picketed the Baltimore News American. Both were owned by the Hearst Corporation. The court ruled that the Baltimore News American was a neutral entitled to the protections afforded under §8(b)(4) even though Hearst owned both companies, because the two divisions operated autonomously.

4. The "ally doctrine" means that an employer may also lose its neutral status if it performs "struck work." In *Douds v. Metropolitan Fed'n of Architects*, 75 F. Supp. 672 (S.D.N.Y. 1948), a primary employer substantially increased the work it had contracted out to a "neutral/secondary" employer. The union picketed the "neutral/secondary" employer. The court, as part of a §10(l) injunction proceeding to halt the union's picketing, held that the two employers were not "doing business" within the meaning of §8(b). It concluded that the employer—by doing the primary employer's work—was no longer a neutral employer, but an ally of the primary employer, and therefore legally subject to the union's economic pressures.

5. Consider whether the ally doctrine applies where:

a. The primary employer merely announces to its customers that another employer is available to meet its customers' needs and the customers take advantage of this self-help? *See United Marine Div., NMY*, 131 N.L.R.B. 693 (1961) (no). In such cases, is the "neutral" employer more of an ally of the primary employer or more of a competitor who is harming the primary employer?

b. The primary employer arranges with a neutral employer to render comparable services for the primary employer's customers? In *Blackhawk Engraving Co. v. NLRB*, 540 F.2d 1296 (7th Cir. 1976), the Board applied the ally doctrine, distinguishing between customer self-help, which would not draw the neutral into the primary dispute, and an "illicit arrangement," which would. In *NLRB v. Business Machine, Local 459 (Royal Typewriter Co.)*, 228 F.2d 553 (2d Cir. 1955), the court also applied the ally doctrine in a similar situation, even though there was no formal agreement between the primary and the "neutral/

secondary," because the secondary knew that the work would have been done by the primary in the absence of the strike.

c. The "neutral/secondary" merely continues to perform work for the primary that it performed prior to the strike? *See NLRB. v. Wine Workers Local 1,* 178 F.2d 584 (2d Cir. 1949) (no).

2. Ambulatory Situs Picketing

Sometimes a union can lawfully picket at the site of a neutral employer where the primary situs (location) of the dispute is on the grounds of the neutral employer. This typically arises in two situations, where the situs is ambulatory or when the situs is shared by several employers, such as at a construction site.

Sailors' Union of the Pacific (Moore Dry Dock)
The National Labor Relations Board
92 N.L.R.B. 547 (1950)

[The key facts of *Moore Dry Dock* are as follows: In 1949, a company called Kaiser Gypsum entered a contract with a Panamanian shipping company, Samsoc, to carry gypsum between the Mexico and the US aboard a ship called the *Phopho*. Previously, Kaiser had engaged a shipping company that employed unionized shipping crews who were paid at a significantly higher rate. Therefore, the union whose members were going to lose Kaiser's work wrote to Samsoc to inquire about representing the crew of the *Phopho*. When Samsoc refused, the union began picketing the *Phopho*. However, the *Phopho* was then undergoing a retrofit process undertaken by a third company—Moore—and was located in Moore's shipyard. Therefore, the picketing took place in front of the Moore shipyard, although the picket signs made clear that the labor dispute was with the *Phopho*, and not Moore. After picketing began, Moore employees refused to continue work on the *Phopho*, though they did not stop work on their other assignments, and area unions that operated hiring halls refused to send workers to do work on the *Phopho*, though they continued to send workers for other jobs at Moore.]

... Section 8(b)(4)(A) [now §8(b)(4)(B)] is aimed at secondary boycotts and secondary strike activities. It was not intended to proscribe primary action by a union having a legitimate labor dispute with an employer. Picketing at the premises of a primary employer is traditionally recognized as primary action even though it is "necessarily designed to induce and encourage third persons to cease doing business with the picketed employer." As we said in 1949,

[Section 8(b)(4)(A)] ... was intended only to outlaw certain *secondary* boycotts, whereby unions sought to enlarge the economic battleground beyond the premises of the primary Employer. When picketing is wholly at the premises of the employer with whom the union is engaged in a labor dispute, it cannot be called "secondary" even though, as is virtually always the case, an object of the picketing is to dissuade all persons from entering such premises for business reasons. . . .

Hence, if Samsoc, the owner of the S. S. *Phopho*, had had a dock of its own in California to which the *Phopho* had been tied up while undergoing conversion by Moore Dry Dock employees, picketing by the Respondent at the dock site would unquestionably have constituted *primary* action, even though the Respondent might have expected that the picketing would be more effective in persuading Moore employees not to work on the ship than to persuade the seamen aboard the *Phopho* to quit that vessel. The difficulty in the present case arises therefore, not because of any difference in picketing objectives, but from the fact that the *Phopho* was not tied up at its own dock, but at that of Moore, while the picketing was going on in front of the Moore premises.

In the usual case, the *situs* of a labor dispute is the premises of the primary employer. Picketing of the premises is also picketing of the *situs*. . . . But in some cases the *situs* of the dispute may not be limited to a fixed location; it may be ambulatory. Thus in [*Teamsters Local 807 (Schultz Refrigerated Service, Inc.*), 87 N.L.R.B. 502 (1949)], a majority of the Board held that the truck upon which a truck driver worked was the *situs* of a labor dispute between him and the owner of the truck. Similarly, we hold in the present case that, as the *Phopho* was the place of employment of the seamen, it was the *situs* of the dispute between Samsoc and the Respondent over working conditions aboard that vessel.

When the *situs* is ambulatory, it may come to rest temporarily at the premises of another employer. The perplexing question is: Does the right to picket follow the *situs* while it is stationed at the premises of a secondary employer, when the only way to picket that *situs* is in front of the secondary employer's premises? Admittedly, no easy answer is possible. Essentially the problem is one of balancing the right of a union to picket at the site of its dispute as against the right of a secondary employer to be free from picketing in a controversy in which it is not directly involved.

When a secondary employer is harboring the *situs* of a dispute between a union and a primary employer, the right of neither the union to picket nor of the secondary employer to be free from picketing can be absolute. The enmeshing of premises and *situs* qualifies both rights. In the kind of situation that exists in this case, we believe that picketing of the premises of a secondary employer is primary if it meets the following conditions: (a) The picketing is strictly limited to times when the *situs* of dispute is located on the secondary employer's premises; (b) at the time of the picketing the primary employer is engaged in its normal business at the *situs*; (c) the picketing is limited to places reasonably close to the location of the *situs;* and (d) the picketing discloses clearly that the dispute is with the primary employer. All these conditions were met in the present case.

(a) During the entire period of the picketing the *Phopho* was tied up at a dock in the Moore shipyard.

(b) Under its contract with Samsoc, Moore agreed to permit the former to put a crew on board the *Phopho* for training purposes during the last 2 weeks before the vessel's delivery to Samsoc. At the time the picketing started on February 17, 1950, 90 percent of the conversion job had been completed, practically the entire crew had been hired, the ship's oil bunkers had been filled, and other stores were shortly to be put aboard. The various members of the crew commenced work as soon as they reported aboard the *Phopho*. Those in the deck department did painting and cleaning up; those in the steward's department, cooking and cleaning up; and those in the engine department, oiling and cleaning up. The crew [was] thus getting the ship ready for sea. They were on board to serve the purposes of Samsoc, the *Phopho*'s owners, and not Moore. The normal business of a ship does not only begin with its departure on a scheduled voyage. The multitudinous steps of preparation, including hiring and training a crew and putting stores aboard, are as much a part of the normal business of a ship as the voyage itself. We find, therefore, that during the entire period of the picketing, the *Phopho* was engaged in its normal business.

(c) Before placing its pickets outside the entrance to the Moore shipyard, the Respondent Union asked, but was refused, permission to place its pickets at the dock where the *Phopho* was tied up. The Respondent therefore posted its pickets at the yard entrance which, as the parties stipulated, was as close to the *Phopho* as they could get under the circumstances.

(d) Finally, by its picketing and other conduct the Respondent was scrupulously careful to indicate that its dispute was solely with the primary employer, the owners of the *Phopho*. Thus the signs carried by the pickets said only that the *Phopho* was unfair to the Respondent. The *Phopho* and not Moore was declared "hot." Similarly, in asking cooperation of other unions, the Respondent clearly revealed that its dispute was with the *Phopho*. Finally, Moore's own witnesses admitted that no attempt was made to interfere with other work in progress in the Moore yard.

We believe that our dissenting colleagues' expressions of alarm are based on a misunderstanding of our decision. We are not holding . . . that a union which has a dispute with a shipowner over working conditions of seamen aboard a ship may lawfully picket the premises of an independent shipyard to which the shipowner has delivered his vessel for overhaul and repair. We are only holding that, if a shipyard permits the owner of a vessel to use its dock for the purpose of readying the ship for its regular voyage by hiring and training a crew and putting stores aboard ship, a union representing seamen may then, within the careful limitations laid down in this decision, lawfully picket in front of the shipyard premises to advertise its dispute with the shipowner.

It is true . . . that the *Phopho* was delivered to the Moore yard for conversion into a bulk gypsum carrier. But Moore in its contract agreed that "During the last two weeks, . . . [the *Phopho*'s] Owner shall have the right to put a crew on board the vessel for training purposes, provided, however, that such crew shall not interfere in any way with the work of conversion." Samsoc (the *Phopho*'s owner) availed itself of this contract privilege. When it did, Moore and Samsoc were simultaneously engaged in their separate businesses in the Moore yard.

The dissent finds it "logically" difficult to believe in this duality. We find no such difficulty. Nor did Moore, apparently, when it included the above clause in its contract. Indeed, from a practical standpoint, there was a strong reason why Samsoc should ready the ship for sea while the conversion work was still going on. A laid-up ship does not earn money. By completing training and preparation for sea while the ship was still undergoing conversion, the lay-up time was reduced, with a consequent money saving to owner Samsoc.

Under the circumstances of this case, we therefore find that the picketing practice followed by the Respondent was primary and not secondary and therefore did not violate § 8(b)(4)(A)....

We agree with the Trial Examiner that the Respondent's other activities, its "hot" letters and appeals for cooperation to Moore employees and other unions, invited action only at the *situs* of dispute. Therefore under the holding in the *Pure Oil* case, they must be considered as primary action. Accordingly, we shall dismiss the complaint in its entirety.

Notes

1. "Common situs picketing at [a dock], a construction site [or any other common situs] violates the Act's ban on secondary boycotts unless it is conducted in conformity with the criteria established in Moore Dry Dock Co." *Lawhon Constr. Co. v. Carpet Decorators, Local 1179*, 394 F. Supp. 520, 523 (W.D. Mo. 1973). The Supreme Court approved of, without applying, the *Moore Dry Dock* factors in *Local 761, IUE v. NLRB*, 366 U.S. 667, 673, 676–77 (1961).

2. The *Moore Dry Dock* test can be succinctly stated:

> [P]icketing of the premises of a secondary employer is primary if it meets the following conditions: (a) The picketing is strictly limited to times when the *situs* of dispute is located on the secondary employer's premises; (b) at the time of the picketing the primary employer is engaged in its normal business at the *situs*; (c) the picketing is limited to places reasonably close to the location of the *situs;* and (d) the picketing discloses clearly that the dispute is with the primary employer. 92 N.L.R.B. 547, 549.

Neither the Board nor the courts have applied these factors rigidly. In *Linbeck Construction Corp. v. NLRB*, 550 F.2d 311 (5th Cir. 1977), for example, the union picketed the secondary situs (to protest a non-union subcontractor's practices) during the daytime, technically at times during which the primary employer was not engaged in its "normal [construction] business." In that case, the Board applied a more flexible standard:

> If the primary can come and go on the site without giving the Union adequate notice when it will be present, one should not conclude that the primary is

not engaged in his normal course of business merely because he is absent; otherwise, the primary could forever play a "hide-and-seek" game with the Union. . . . Likewise, the Board has not allowed the employers on a site to benefit from the Union's breach of this Moore Dry Dock requirement when these parties have given the Union false and misleading information as to when the primary's employees will be on the job. *Linbeck*, 550 F.2d at 319.

In applying that standard, the Court, upholding the Board, concluded:

Luckie [non-union subcontractor] informed the Union that it would be engaged in operations on the site only during weeknights and weekends. Instead, deliveries of supplies integral to its operation were made during the day a time when it was supposed to be absent. Even if we accepted Linbeck's [the general contractor's] argument that legal ownership of materials is dispositive, we note that it never made the Union privy to the change in its own internal accounting system and operations whereby it, instead of Luckie, took title to the materials and began receiving the goods instead of having Luckie employees sign for them. Witnessing the delivery of crushed stone that it knew was intended for Luckie's use, the Union was predictably misled by this maneuver as to Luckie's presence at the site during the day.

3. Early evidence suggests that the Trump Board plans to apply the *Moore Dry Dock* guidelines strictly. In *Preferred Building Services, Inc.*, 366 N.L.R.B. No. 159 (Aug. 28, 2018), the Board held that union picketing outside an office building constituted unlawful secondary conduct, and that therefore the employer's decision to fire the employees in retaliation for their participation in the picketing did not violate the NLRA. The picketing involved janitorial employees whose employer was hired by the office building's management company. While the picket signs themselves named the picketers' employer, the Board held that picketers' conduct did not meet the *Moore Dry Dock* criteria because their leaflets requested that a building tenant "ensure that 'their' janitors obtain better working conditions." In the Board's view, "the picketers led the public to believe that [the tenant] — who was not involved in the dispute — was their employer." Then, the Board added that even if the pickets satisfied *Moore Dry Dock*, their conduct was unlawful because "the picketing was intended to 'seriously disrupt' the business relationship between" the janitors' employer and the building management company.

4. "[I]f a union notifies neutral employers at a common situs that it intends to picket the primary employer, the union 'has an affirmative obligation to qualify its threat by clearly indicating that the picketing would conform to *Moore Dry Dock* standards or otherwise be in uniformity with Board law.'" *IBEW Local Union 357*, 367 N.L.R.B. No. 61 (2018). Why would the Board adopt this rule? Is it required by the NLRA?

Problem 12.3

An insurance company develops a tract of land that it owns. The insurance company serves as the general contractor of the development project and hires labor represented by a union. It also hires a neutral subcontractor. The union becomes involved in a labor dispute with the insurance company. The union strikes against the company and pickets the entire work site, characterizing the entire development project as "unfair." The employees of the subcontractor walk off the job. Would you apply the *Moore Dry Dock* criteria to this situation? If so, what result? *See Carpenters Local 55 (Prof'l & Business Men's Life Ins. Co.)*, 108 N.L.R.B. 363 (1954).

3. Common Situs Picketing and Reserve Gates

The *Moore Dry Dock* criteria were widely applied in the trucking industry, where striking unions often demonstrated at the pickup and delivery sites. The *Moore Dry Dock* criteria soon became prevalent in so-called reserve gate cases—picketing at the common entrance/exit to the primary situs, where the employees of secondary employers may come and go. The Supreme Court addressed the lawfulness of picketing under these circumstances in the following case:

Local 761, IBEW v. NLRB (General Electric Company)

Supreme Court of the United States
366 U.S. 667, 81 S. Ct. 1285, 6 L. Ed. 2d 592 (1961)

FRANKFURTER, J.

. . . General Electric Corporation operates a plant outside of Louisville, Kentucky, where it manufactures washers, dryers, and other electrical household appliances. The square-shaped, thousand-acre, unfenced plant is known as Appliance Park. A large drainage ditch makes ingress and egress impossible except over five roadways across culverts, designated as gates.

Since 1954, General Electric sought to confine the employees of independent contractors . . . who work on the premises of the Park, to the use of Gate 3-A and confine its use to them. The undisputed reason for doing so was to insulate General Electric employees from the frequent labor disputes in which the contractors were involved. Gate 3-A is 550 feet away from the nearest entrance available for General Electric employees, suppliers, and deliverymen. Although anyone can pass the gate without challenge, the roadway leads to a guardhouse where identification must be presented. Vehicle stickers of various shapes and colors enable a guard to check on sight whether a vehicle is authorized to use Gate 3-A. Since January 1958, a prominent sign has been posted at the gate which states: 'Gate 3-A For Employees Of Contractors Only—G.E. Employees Use Other Gates.' On rare occasions . . . a General Electric employee was allowed to pass the guardhouse, but such occurrence was in violation of company instructions. There was no proof of any unauthorized attempts to pass the gate during the strike in question.

The independent contractors are utilized for a great variety of tasks on the Appliance Park premises. Some do construction work on new buildings; some install and repair ventilating and heating equipment; some engage in retooling and rearranging operations necessary to the manufacture of new models; others do "general maintenance work." These services are contracted to outside employers either because the company's employees lack the necessary skill or manpower, or because the work can be done more economically by independent contractors. The latter reason determined the contracting of maintenance work for which the Central Maintenance department of the company bid competitively with the contractors. While some of the work done by these contractors had on occasion been previously performed by Central Maintenance, the findings do not disclose the number of employees of independent contractors who were performing these routine maintenance services, as compared with those who were doing specialized work of a capital-improvement nature.

The Union [International Union of Electrical, Radio and Machine Workers, Local 761], petitioner here, is the certified bargaining representative for the production and maintenance workers who constitute approximately 7,600 of the 10, 500 employees of General Electric at Appliance Park. On July 27, 1958, the Union called a strike because of 24 unsettled grievances with the company. Picketing occurred at all the gates, including Gate 3-A, and continued until August 9 when an injunction was issued by a Federal District Court. The signs carried by the pickets at all gates read: "Local 761 On Strike G.E. Unfair." Because of the picketing, almost all of the employees of independent contractors refused to enter the company premises.

Neither the legality of the strike or of the picketing at any of the gates except 3-A nor the peaceful nature of the picketing is in dispute. The sole claim is that the picketing before the gate exclusively used by employees of independent contractors was conduct proscribed by § 8(b)(4)(A).

The Trial Examiner recommended that the Board dismiss the complaint. He concluded that the limitations on picketing which the Board had prescribed in so-called "common situs" cases were not applicable to the situation before him, in that the picketing at Gate 3-A represented traditional primary action which necessarily had a secondary effect of inconveniencing those who did business with the struck employer. He reasoned that if a primary employer could limit the area of picketing around his own premises by constructing a separate gate for employees of independent contractors, such a device could also be used to isolate employees of his suppliers and customers, and that such action could not relevantly be distinguished from oral appeals made to secondary employees not to cross a picket line where only a single gate existed.

The Board rejected the Trial Examiner's conclusion. . . . It held that, since only the employees of the independent contractors were allowed to use Gate 3-A, the Union's object in picketing there was "to enmesh these employees of the neutral employers in its dispute with the Company," thereby constituting a violation of § 8(b)(4)(A) because the independent employees were encouraged to engage in a concerted refusal to work "with an object of forcing the independent contractors to cease doing business with the Company."

The [D.C. Circuit enforced] the Board's order.

I.

Section 8(b)(4)(A) ... could not be literally construed; otherwise it would ban most strikes historically considered to be lawful, so-called primary activity. "While §8(b)(4) does not expressly mention 'primary' or 'secondary' disputes, strikes or boycotts, that section often is referred to in the Act's legislative history as one of the Act's 'secondary boycott sections.'" *NLRB v. Denver Building & Const. Trades Council*, 341 U.S. 675, 686. "Congress did not seek by §8(b)(4), to interfere with the ordinary strike. . . ." *NLRB v. Int'l Rice Milling Co.*, 341 U.S. 665, 672. The impact of the section was directed toward what is known as the secondary boycott whose "sanctions bear, not upon the employer who alone is a party to the dispute, but upon some third party who has no concern in it." *IBEW, Local 501 v. NLRB*, 181 F.2d 34, 37 (2d Cir.). Thus the section "left a striking labor organization free to use persuasion, including picketing, not only on the primary employer and his employees but on numerous others. Among these were secondary employers who were customers or suppliers of the primary employer and persons dealing with them . . . and even employees of secondary employers so long as the labor organization did not . . . 'induce or encourage the employees of any employer to engage, in a strike or a concerted refusal in the course of their employment' . . . ." *NLRB v. Local 294, Teamsters*, 284 F.2d 887, 889 (2d Cir.).

But not all so-called secondary boycotts were outlawed in §8(b)(4)(A). "The section does not speak generally of secondary boycotts. It describes and condemns specific union conduct directed to specific objectives. . . . Employees must be induced . . . to engage in a strike or concerted refusal; an object must be to force or require their employer or another person to cease doing business with a third person. Thus, much that might argumentatively be found to fall within the broad and somewhat vague concept of secondary boycott is not in terms prohibited." *Local 1976, Carpenters v. NLRB*, 357 U.S. 93, 98.

Important as is the distinction between legitimate "primary activity" and banned "secondary activity," it does not present a glaringly bright line. The objectives of any picketing include a desire to influence others from withholding from the employer their services or trade. *See Moore Dry Dock*, 92 N.L.R.B. 547. "(I)ntended or not, sought for or not, aimed for or not, employees of neutral employers do take action sympathetic with strikers and do put pressure on their own employers." *Seafarers Int'l U. v. NLRB*, 265 F.2d 585, 590. "It is clear that, when a union pickets an employer with whom it has a dispute, it hopes, even if it does not intend, that all persons will honor the picket line and that hope encompasses the employees of neutral employers who may in the course of their employment (deliverymen and the like) have to enter the premises." *Id.* at 591. "Almost all picketing, even at the situs of the primary employer and surely at that of the secondary, hopes to achieve the forbidden objective, whatever other motives there may be and however small the chances of success." *Local 294*, 284 F.2d at 890. But picketing which induces secondary employees to respect a picket line is not the equivalent of picketing which has an object of inducing those employees to engage in concerted conduct against their employer in order to force him to refuse to deal with the struck employer. *NLRB v. International Rice Milling Co., supra.*

However difficult the drawing of lines more nice than obvious, the statute compels the task. Accordingly, the Board and the courts have attempted to devise reasonable criteria drawing heavily upon the means to which a union resorts in promoting its cause. . . . "(I)n the absence of admissions by the union of an illegal intent, the nature of acts performed shows the intent." *Seafarers Int'l U.,* 265 F.2d at 591. . . .

II.

The early decisions of the Board following the Taft-Hartley amendments involved activity which took place around the secondary employer's premises. . . .

. . . [T]he Board eliminated picketing which took place around the situs of the primary employer—regardless of the special circumstances involved—from being held invalid secondary activity under §8(b)(4)(A) (now §8(b)(4)(B)).

However, the impact of the new situations made the Board conscious of the complexity of the problem. . . . This became clear in the "common situs" cases—situations where two employers were performing separate tasks on common premises. [*Moore Dry Dock*] laid out the Board's new standards in this area. . . . These tests were widely accepted by reviewing federal courts. . . . As is too often the way of law or, at least, of adjudications, soon the Dry Dock tests were mechanically applied so that a violation of one of the standards was taken to be presumptive of illegal activity. For example, failure of picket signs clearly to designate the employer against whom the strike was directed was held to be violative of §8(b)(4)(A). . . .

In *Local 55 (PBM),* 108 N.L.R.B. 363, the Board for the first time applied the Dry Dock test, although the picketing occurred at premises owned by the primary employer. There, an insurance company owned a tract of land that it was developing, and also served as the general contractor. A neutral subcontractor was also doing work at the site. The union, engaged in a strike against the insurance company, picketed the entire premises, characterizing the entire job as unfair, and the employees of the subcontractor walked off. The [Tenth Circuit] enforced the Board's order which found the picketing to be illegal on the ground that the picket signs did not measure up to the Dry Dock standard that they clearly disclose that the picketing was directed against the struck employer only. . . .

The Board's application of the *Dry Dock* standards to picketing at the premises of the struck employer was made more explicit in *Retail Fruit & Vegetable Clerks (Crystal Palace Market),* 116 N.L.R.B. 856. The owner of a large common market operated some of the shops within, and leased out others to independent sellers. The union, although given permission to picket the owner's individual stands, chose to picket outside the entire market. The Board held that this action was violative of §8(b)(4)(A) in that the union did not attempt to minimize the effect of its picketing, as required in a common-situs case, on the operations of the neutral employers utilizing the market. "We believe . . . that the foregoing principles should apply to all common situs picketing, including cases where, as here, the picketed premises are owned by the primary employer." 116 N.L.R.B. at 859. . . . "In such cases, we adhere to the rule established by the Board . . . that more latitude be given to picketing at such separate primary premises that at premises occupied in part (or entirely) by secondary employers." 116 N.L.R.B. at 860, n. 10.

In rejecting the ownership test in situations where two employers were performing work upon a common site, the Board was naturally guided by this Court's opinion in *Rice Milling*, in which we indicated that the location of the picketing at the primary employer's premises was "not necessarily conclusive" of its legality. 341 U.S. at 671. Where the work done by the secondary employees is unrelated to the normal operations of the primary employer, it is difficult to perceive how the pressure of picketing the entire situs is any less on the neutral employer merely because the picketing takes place at property owned by the struck employer. The application of the *Dry Dock* tests to limit the picketing effects to the employees of the employer against whom the dispute is directed carries out the "dual congressional objectives of preserving the right of labor organizations to bring pressure to bear on offending employers in primary labor disputes and of shielding unoffending employers and others from pressures in controversies not their own." *NLRB v. Denver Building & Const. Trades Council*, 341 U.S. at 692.

III.

From this necessary survey of the course of the Board's treatment of our problem, the precise nature of the issue before us emerges. With due regard to the relation between the Board's function and the scope of judicial review of its rulings, the question is whether the Board may apply the *Dry Dock* criteria so as to make unlawful picketing at a gate utilized exclusively by employees of independent contractors who work on the struck employer's premises. The effect of such a holding would not bar the union from picketing at all gates used by the employees, suppliers, and customers of the struck employer. Of course an employer may not, by removing all his employees from the situs of the strike, bar the union from publicizing its cause. . . . The basis of the Board's decision in this case would not remotely have that effect, nor any such tendency for the future.

The Union claims that, if the Board's ruling is upheld, employers will be free to erect separate gates for deliveries, customers, and replacement workers which will be immunized from picketing. This fear is baseless. The key to the problem is found in the type of work that is being performed by those who use the separate gate. It is significant that the Board has since applied its rationale, first stated in the present case, only to situations where the independent workers were performing tasks unconnected to the normal operations of the struck employer-usually construction work on his buildings. In such situations, the indicated limitations on picketing activity respect the balance of competing interests that

Congress has required the Board to enforce. On the other hand, if a separate gate were devised for regular plant deliveries, the barring of picketing at that location would make a clear invasion on traditional primary activity of appealing to neutral employees whose tasks aid the employer's everyday operations. The 1959 Amendments to the NLRA, which removed the word "concerted" from the boycott provisions, included a proviso that "nothing contained in this clause (B) shall be construed to make unlawful, where not otherwise unlawful, any primary strike or primary picketing." . . . The proviso was directed against the fear that the removal of "concerted" from the statute might be interpreted so that "the picketing at the factory violates § 8(b)(4)(A) because the pickets induce the truck drivers employed by the trucker not to perform their usual services where an object is to compel the trucking firm not to do business with the . . . manufacturer during the strike." . . .

In a case similar to the one now before us, the [Second Circuit] sustained the Board in its application of § 8(b)(4)(A) to a separate gate situation. "There must be a separate gate marked and set apart from other gates; the work done by the men who use the gate must be unrelated to the normal operations of the employer and the work must be of a kind that would not, if done when the plant were engaged in its regular operations, necessitate curtailing those operations." *Steelworkers v. NLRB*, 289 F.2d 591, 595 (2d Cir.). These seem to us controlling considerations.

IV.

The foregoing course of reasoning would require that the judgment below sustaining the Board's order be affirmed but for one consideration, even though this consideration may turn out not to affect the result. The legal path by which the Board and the Court of Appeals reached their decisions did not take into account that if Gate 3-A was in fact used by employees of independent contractors who performed conventional maintenance work necessary to the normal operations of General Electric, the use of the gate would have been a mingled one outside the bar of § 8(b)(4)(A). In short, such mixed use of this portion of the struck employer's premises would not bar picketing rights of the striking employees. While the record shows some such mingled use, it sheds no light on its extent. It may well turn out to be that the instances of these maintenance tasks were so insubstantial as to be treated by the Board as de minimis. We cannot here guess at the quantitative aspect of this problem. It calls for Board determination. For determination of the questions thus raised, the case must be remanded by the Court of Appeals to the Board. . . . Reversed.

Notes

1. On remand, the Board concluded that the work of independent contractors who were using Gate 3-A—*e.g.*, installing shower rooms, repairing roads, constructing a sound room, and enlarging the ventilating system—was "necessarily related to GE's normal operations" and therefore that the picketing was primary. *Local 761, I.U.E.*, 138 N.L.R.B. 342 (1962) (supplemental decision).

2. Why are the *Moore Dry Dock* criteria—developed in the case of ambulatory situses—applied to reserve gates cases? What do the two situations have in common?

Problem 12.4

General Contractor, G, employs subcontractor S. Union is involved in a labor dispute with S regarding wages and working conditions. G anticipates the dispute and establishes a reserved gate system at the site—neutral employers are to use the west gate and S is to use the east gate. Another contractor L sends an employee to do some work at the site, entering via the neutral gate. However, employee tells L that he refuses to do work at the site while picketing is going on at the east gate because it is "a matter of his conscience." L suspends employee. The Union files ULP charges against L for violating CBA section permitting its employees to refuse to cross picket lines. L then files §8(b)(4) charges against the Union for attempting to enforce a picket line at a neutral gate. *See NLRB v. International Union of Elevator Constructors*, 902 F.2d 1297 (8th Cir. 1990).

Problem 12.5

Consider whether, in the following situations, the purportedly neutral employer is eligible for a neutral reserve gate because it is doing work that is unrelated to the normal operations of the primary employer and that would not require curtailing the normal operations of the primary employer:

a. A construction company (the purported neutral) is building an addition on a struck TV studio, which continues to operate in its original space during construction. *See Elec. Workers IBEW Local 76*, 268 N.L.R.B. 230 (1983).

b. A company specializing in the installation of automated "stock retrieval" systems (the struck employer) builds such a system at its own facility, then ships it to a neutral aerospace manufacturing facility and installs and assembles it. *See, IBEW Local 332*, 241 N.L.R.B. 674 (1979).

Problem 12.6

A construction contractor hires a subcontractor, Hoff, to install an electrical system at a large building project. Upon learning that Hoff pays its employees less than the prevailing wage, a union begins picketing at the work site. The contractor quickly sets up and labels a reserve gate for Hoff's use, and bans Hoff from using the other gate at the project. However, once a week, a third-party carrier delivers purchased construction materials for Hoff's use via the neutral gate. The union begins picketing the neutral gate, which Hoff alleges to be a violation of §8(b)(4). What result? *See J.E. Hoff Elec. Co. v. NLRB*, 642 F.2d 1266 (D.C. Cir. 1980).

Consider whether the analysis would change in a situation where a neutral employer happens to use the gate reserved for the struck employer; would that conduct affect the validity of the neutral gate?

C. Unlawful Object: Forcing a Neutral Employer to Cease Doing Business with Another Employer

1. *Forcing a General Contractor to Fire a Non-Union Subcontractor*

NLRB v. Denver Bldg. & Const. Trades Council

The Supreme Court of the United States
341 U.S. 675, 71 S. Ct. 943, 95 L. Ed. 1284 (1951)

Burton, J.

The principal question here is whether a labor organization committed [a ULP], within the meaning of §8(b)(4)(A) [now §8(b)(4)(B)], by engaging in a strike, an object of which was to force the general contractor on a construction project to terminate its contract with a certain subcontractor on that project. . . . [W]e hold that such [a ULP] was committed.

. . . Doose & Lintner was the general contractor for the construction of a commercial building. . . . It awarded a subcontract for electrical work on the building . . . to Gould & Preisner, a firm which for 20 years had employed nonunion workmen on construction work in that city. The latter's employees proved to be the only nonunion workmen on the project. Those of the general contractor and of the other subcontractors were members of unions affiliated with the respondent Denver Building and Construction Trades Council (here called the Council). In November a representative of one of those unions told Gould that he did not see how the job could progress with Gould's nonunion men on it. Gould insisted that they would complete the electrical work unless bodily put off. The representative replied that the situation would be difficult for both Gould & Preisner and Doose & Lintner.

January 8, 1948, the Council's Board of Business Agents instructed the Council's representative "to place a picket on the job stating that the job was unfair" to it. In keeping with the Council's practice, each affiliate was notified of that decision. That notice was a signal in the nature of an order to the members of the affiliated unions to leave the job and remain away until otherwise ordered. Representatives of the Council and each of the respondent unions visited the project and reminded the contractor that Gould & Preisner employed nonunion workmen and said that union men could not work on the job with nonunion men. They further advised that if Gould & Preisner's men did work on the job, the Council and its affiliates would put a picket on it to notify their members that nonunion men were working on it and that the job was unfair. All parties stood their ground.

January 9, the Council posted a picket at the project carrying a placard stating "This Job Unfair to Denver Building and Construction Trades Council." He was paid by the Council and his picketing continued from January 9 through January 22. During that time the only persons who reported for work were the nonunion electricians of Gould & Preisner. January 22, before Gould & Preisner had completed its subcontract, the general contractor notified it to get off the job so that Doose & Lintner could continue with the project. January 23, the Council removed its picket and shortly thereafter the union employees resumed work on the project. Gould & Preisner protested this treatment but its workmen were denied entrance to the job.

On charges filed by Gould & Preisner, the [General Counsel] issued the complaint . . . against the Council and the . . . unions. It alleged that they had engaged in a strike or had caused strike action to be taken on the project by employees of the general contractor and of other subcontractors, an object of which was to force the general contractor to cease doing business with Gould & Preisner on that project.

. . . [After a hearing, the Board] ordered respondents to cease and desist from engaging in the activities charged. Respondents petitioned . . . the [D.C.] Circuit for [review]. . . . That court . . . unanimously set aside the [Board's] order . . . and said: "Convinced that the action in the circumstances of this case is primary and not secondary we are obliged to refuse to enforce the order based on § 8(b)(4) (A)." . . . The Board claimed a conflict between that conclusion and the reasoning of the . . . Second Circuit . . . and of that for the Sixth Circuit . . . We granted certiorari in each case. . . .

III. The Secondary Boycott.

We now reach the merits. They require a study of the objectives of the strike and a determination whether the strike came within the definition of [a ULP] stated in § 8(b)(4)(A). . . .

While § 8(b)(4) does not expressly mention "primary" or "secondary" disputes, strikes or boycotts, that section often is referred to in the Act's legislative history as one of the Act's "secondary boycott sections." The other is § 303, 29 U.S.C. § 187, which uses the same language in defining the basis for private actions for damages caused by these proscribed activities. . . .

A. We must first determine whether the strike in this case had a proscribed object. . . .

[By way of background], there was a longstanding labor dispute between the Council and Gould & Preisner due to the latter's practice of employing nonunion workmen on construction jobs in Denver. The respondent labor organizations contend that they engaged in a primary dispute with Doose & Lintner alone, and that they sought simply to force Doose & Lintner to make the project an all-union job. If there had been no contract between Doose & Lintner and Gould & Preisner there might be substance in their contention that the dispute involved no boycott. If, for example, Doose & Lintner had been doing all the electrical work on this project through its own nonunion employees, it could have replaced them with union men and thus disposed of the dispute. However, the existence of the Gould & Preisner

1040 12 · LEGAL CONSTRAINTS ON CONCERTED ACTIVITY

subcontract presented a materially different situation. The nonunion employees were employees of Gould & Preisner. The only way that respondents could attain their purpose was to force Gould & Preisner itself off the job. This, in turn, could be done only through Doose & Lintner's termination of Gould & Preisner's subcontract. The result is that the Council's strike, in order to attain its ultimate purpose, must have included among its objects that of forcing Doose & Lintner to terminate that subcontract. On that point, the Board adopted the following finding: "That an object, if not the only object, of what transpired with respect to ... Doose & Lintner was to force or require them to cease doing business with Gould & Preisner seems scarcely open to question, in view of all of the facts. And it is clear at least as to Doose & Lintner, that that purpose was achieved." (Emphasis supplied.) 82 N.L.R.B. at 1212.

We accept this crucial finding. It was an object of the strike to force the contractor to terminate Gould & Preisner's subcontract.

B. We hold also that a strike with such an object was [a ULP] within the meaning of § 8(b)(4)(A).

It is not necessary to find that the sole object of the strike was that of forcing the contractor to terminate the subcontractor's contract. This is emphasized in the legislative history of the section. . . .

We agree with the Board also in its conclusion that the fact that the contractor and subcontractor were engaged on the some construction project, and that the contractor had some supervision over the subcontractor's work, did not eliminate the status of each as an independent contractor or make the employees of one the employees of the other. The business relationship between independent contractors is too well established in the law to be overridden without clear language doing so. The Board found that the relationship between Doose & Lintner and Gould & Preisner was one of "doing business" and we find no adequate reason for upsetting that conclusion. . . .

For these reasons we conclude that the conduct of respondents [violated] § 8(b)(4)(A). The judgment of the Court of Appeals accordingly is reversed and the case is remanded to it for procedure not inconsistent with this opinion. . . .

Note

The Board characterizes Doose & Lintner (the general contractor) as the neutral employer and Gould & Preiser (the non-union subcontractor) as the primary employer. Does this characterization make a difference to the case's outcome? Hint: What result in *Denver Building & Construction Trades Council* if the *Moore Dry Dock* criteria or *General Electric*'s reserve gate analysis is applied?

2. Requesting Managers to Make Lawful Managerial Decisions or to Boycott Other Employers' Products Under § 8(b)(4)(i)(B)

NLRB v. Servette, Inc.

Supreme Court of the United States
377 U.S. 46, 84 S. Ct. 1098, 12 L. Ed. 2d 121 (1964)

Brennan, J.

Respondent Servette, Inc., is a wholesale distributor of specialty merchandise stocked by retail food chains in Los Angeles, California. In 1960, during a strike which Local 848 of the Wholesale Delivery Drivers and Salesmen's Union was conducting against Servette, the Local's representatives sought to support the strike by asking managers of supermarkets of the food chains to discontinue handling merchandise supplied by Servette. In most instances the representatives warned that handbills asking the public not to buy named items distributed by Servette would be passed out in front of stores which refused to cooperate, and in a few cases handbills were in fact passed out.[2] A complaint was issued on charges by Servette that this conduct violated . . . [§ 8(b)(4)(i) and (ii)] . . . .

The NLRB dismissed the complaint. The Board adopted the finding of the Trial Examiner that "the managers of McDaniels Markets were authorized to decide as they best could whether to continue doing business with Servette in the face of threatened or actual handbilling. This, a policy decision, was one for them to make. The evidence is persuasive that the same authority was vested in the managers of Kory." . . . The Board held that on these facts the Local's efforts to enlist the cooperation of the supermarket managers did not constitute inducement of an "individual" within the meaning of that term in subsection (i); the Board held further that the handbilling, even if constituting conduct which "threaten(s), coerce(s), or restrain(s) any person" under subsection (ii), was protected by the [publicity] proviso to amended § 8(b)(4). . . . The Court of Appeals set aside the Board's

---

2. The handbill was as follows:
"To the Patrons of This Store
"Wholesale Delivery Drivers & Salesmen's Local No. 848 urgently requests that you do not buy the following products distributed by Servette, Inc.:
"Brach's Candy.
"Servette Candy
"Good Season Salad Dressing
"Old London Products
"The Servette Company which distributes these product refuses to negotiate with the Union that represents its drivers. The Company is attempting to force the drivers to sign individual 'Yellow Dog' contracts.
"These contracts will destroy the wages and working conditions that the drivers now enjoy, and will set them back 20 years in their struggle for decent wages and working conditions.
"The drivers of Servette appreciate your cooperation in this fight."

order, holding that the term "individual" in subsection (i) was to be read literally, thus including the supermarket managers, and that the distributed products were not "produced" by Servette within the meaning of the proviso, thus rendering its protection unavailable. We granted certiorari. . . . We reverse the judgment of the Court of Appeals.

The Court of Appeals correctly read the term "individual" in subsection (i) as including the supermarket managers, but it erred in holding that the Local's attempts to enlist the aid of the managers constituted inducement of the managers in violation of the subsection. The 1959 statute amended § 8(b)(4)(A) . . . , which made it unlawful to induce or encourage "the employees of any employer" to strike or engage in a "concerted" refusal to work. We defined the central thrust of that statute to be to forbid "a union to induce employees to strike against or to refuse to handle goods for their employer when an object is to force him or another person to cease doing business with some third party." *Local 1976, Carpenters v. NLRB,* 357 U.S. 93, 98. In the instant case, however, the Local, in asking the managers not to handle Servette items, was not attempting to induce or encourage them to cease performing their managerial duties in order to force their employers to cease doing business with Servette. Rather, the managers were asked to make a managerial decision which the Board found was within their authority to make. Such an appeal would not have been a violation of § 8(b)(4)(A) before 1959, and we think that the legislative history of the 1959 amendments makes it clear that the amendments were not meant to render such an appeal [a ULP].

The 1959 amendments were designed to close certain loopholes in the application of § 8(b)(4)(A) which had been exposed in Board and court decisions. . . . To close these loopholes, subsection (i) substituted the phrase "any individual employed by any person" for "the employees of any employer," and deleted the word "concerted." The first change was designed to make the provision applicable to refusals by employees who were not technically "employees" within the statutory definitions, and the second change was intended to make clear that inducement directed to only one individual was proscribed. But these changes did not expand the type of conduct which § 8(b)(4)(A) condemned, that is, union pressures calculated to induce the employees of a secondary employer to withhold their services in order to force their employer to cease dealing with the primary employer.

Moreover, the division of § 8(b)(4) into subsections (i) and (ii) by the 1959 amendments has direct relevance to the issue presented by this case. It had been held that § 8(b)(4)(A) did not reach threats of labor trouble made to the secondary employer himself. Congress decided that such conduct should be made unlawful, but only when it amounted to conduct which "threaten(s), coerce(s) or restrain(s) any person"; hence the addition of subsection (ii). The careful creation of separate standards differentiating the treatment of appeals to the employees of the secondary employer not to perform their employment services, from appeals for other ends which are attended by threats, coercion or restraint, argues conclusively against the interpretation of subsection (i) as reaching the Local's appeals to the supermarket managers in this case. If subsection (i), in addition to prohibiting inducement of employees to withhold employment services, also reaches an appeal that the managers exercise their delegated authority by making a business judgment to cease dealing with the primary employer, subsection (ii) would be almost superfluous. Harmony between (i) and (ii) is best achieved by construing subsection (i) to prohibit inducement of the managers to withhold their services from their employer, and subsection (ii) to condemn an attempt to induce the exercise of discretion only if the inducement would "threaten, coerce, or restrain" that exercise.

Finally, the warnings that handbills would be distributed in front of noncooperating stores are not prohibited as "threats" within subsection (ii). The statutory protection for the distribution of handbills would be undermined if a threat to engage in protected conduct were not itself protected. . . . Reversed.

Notes

1. The *Servette* Court noted (n.4) that the Board's doctrine, articulated in *Carolina Lumber Co.*, 130 N.L.R.B. 1438, 1443 (1961) — construing the NLRA as distinguishing between "low level" supervisors and "high level" supervisors and holding that inducement of "low level" supervisors is lawful while inducement of "high level" supervisors is permissible — is incorrect: "We hold today that this is not the distinction drawn by the statute; rather, the question of the applicability of subsection (i) turns upon whether the union's appeal is to cease performing employment services, or is an appeal for the exercise of managerial discretion."

2. The longest-running strike in American history took place at Chicago's Congress Plaza hotel between 2003 and 2013. Midway through the strike, the union began asking neutral businesses planning meetings or events at the hotel to go elsewhere. These requests came in many forms (including, in one colorful instance, via cow pie), but they did not involve picketing. The hotel filed suit against the union, alleging that the union's activities nonetheless coerced the neutral businesses, amounting to § 8(b)(4) violations. The district court granted summary judgment, but the Seventh Circuit reversed in part, holding that some of the union's activities, if proven at trial, qualified as "coercive, as in the sense of a boycott or picket," rather than "persuasive, as in the case of handbilling outside an establishment." *520 South Michigan Ave. Assocs. v. Unite Here Local 1*, 760 F.3d 708, 720 (7th Cir. 2014).

The United States Court of Appeals for the Seventh Circuit stated that a union violates § 8(b)(4) when its "conduct amounts to harassment or involves repeated trespass or both." *Id.* at 722. Then, the Court reversed the grant of summary judgment as to the union's conduct at three neutral businesses based on the following factual allegations. At the first business, the union: 1) "snuck into [locked] offices unobserved and dropped literature"; 2) threatened to attend the business's event at Congress Plaza "in order to disrupt it"; and 3) threatened to confront affiliates of the neutral business at home or work. *Id.* at 728–29. At the second, union representatives: 1) made several "unwanted appearances," eventually resulting in a call to the police; and 2) walked past security and shouted "shame on you" at the company president; in addition, the business reasonably believed the union would attempt to occupy busses running to its trade show at the Congress Plaza and otherwise disrupt the show. *Id.* at 730–31. Finally, as to the third business, a group of union delegates followed the decision-maker from store to store, with as many as ten union delegates approaching him at once. *Id.* at 732. In reconciling this holding with *Servette*, the court stated:

> Finally, we think that *Servette* gives the Union ample breathing room to express its views by permitting delegates to approach and talk to decision-makers of neutral businesses, even if they are initially uninvited. But once that decision-maker says that she is not interested, and that the Union delegates are no longer welcome, the Union's free speech interests start to wane, and the property and privacy rights of the neutral target become dispositive. Certainly, when the police are called to haul the delegates away, it should be clear that the Union's attempts to persuade have been rebuffed.

Some of the union's actions, if ultimately proven to have taken place, may have violated laws other than § 8(b)(4), such as local trespass laws. But others seem to turn on finer lines — for example, the union's activity with respect to the third business took place in public and was described as "polite," so it was only a matter of degree that caused it to rise to the level of "coercion" in the Court's view. Could the outcome in this case — a remand for an expensive trial with the possibility of financial liability at the end — chill legitimate protest? What might you advise a union client about how it can avoid liability while attempting to persuade neutral businesses not to do business with a struck primary? What might you advise a primary employer about how to respond to aggressive union attempts to persuade neutrals to take their business elsewhere?

3. Consumer Boycotts Under § 8(b)(4)(ii)(B)

NLRB v. Fruit and Vegetable Packers, Local 760 (Tree Fruits)

Supreme Court of the United States
377 U.S. 58, 84 S. Ct. 1063, 12 L. Ed. 2d 129 (1964)

BRENNAN, J.

Under § 8(b)(4)(ii)(B) . . . , it is [a ULP] for a union "to threaten, coerce, or restrain any person," with the object of "forcing or requiring any person to cease using, selling, handling, transporting, or otherwise dealing in the products of any other producer . . . or to cease doing business with any other person. . . ." A proviso excepts, however, "publicity, other than picketing, for the purpose of truthfully advising the public . . . that a product or products are produced by an employer with whom the labor organization has a primary dispute and are distributed by another employer, as long as such publicity does not have an effect of inducing any individual employed by any person other than the primary employer in the course of his employment to refuse to pick up, deliver, or transport any goods, or not to perform any services, at the establishment of the employer engaged in such distribution." (Italics supplied.) The question in this case is whether the respondent unions violated this section when they limited their secondary picketing of retail stores to an appeal to the customers of the stores not to buy the products of certain firms against which one of the respondents was on strike.

Respondent Local 760 called a strike against fruit packers and warehousemen doing business in Yakima, Washington. The struck firms sold Washington State apples to the Safeway chain of retail stores in and about Seattle, Washington. Local 760, aided by respondent Joint Council, instituted a consumer boycott against the apples in support of the strike. They placed pickets who walked back and forth before the customers' entrances of 46 Safeway stores in Seattle. The pickets—two at each of 45 stores and three at the 46th store—wore placards and distributed hand-bills which appealed to Safeway customers, and to the public generally, to refrain from buying Washington State apples, which were only one of numerous food products sold in the stores.[3]

Before the pickets appeared at any store, a letter was delivered to the store manager informing him that the picketing was only an appeal to his customers not to buy Washington State apples, and that the pickets were being expressly instructed "to patrol peacefully in front of the consumer entrances of the store, to stay away from the delivery entrances and not to interfere with the work of your employees, or with deliveries to or pickups from your store." A copy of written instructions to the pickets—which included the explicit statement that "you are also forbidden to request that the customers not patronize the store"—was enclosed with the letter. Since it was desired to assure Safeway employees that they were not to cease work, and to avoid any interference with pickups or deliveries, the pickets appeared after the stores opened for business and departed before the stores closed. At all times

---

3. The placard worn by each picket stated: "To the Consumer: Non-Union Washington State apples are being sold at this store. Please do not purchase such apples. Thank you. Teamsters Local 760, Yakima, Washington."

A typical handbill read:

"DON'T BUY WASHINGTON STATE APPLES

THE 1960 CROP OF WASHINGTON STATE APPLES IS BEING PACKED BY NON-UNION FIRMS

Included in this non-union operation are twenty-six firms in the Yakima Valley with which there is a labor dispute. These firms are charged with being

UNFAIR

by their employees who, with their union, are on strike and have been replaced by non-union strikebreaking workers employed under substandard wage scales and working conditions.

In justice to these striking union workers who are attempting to protect their living standards and their right to engage in good-faith collective bargaining, we request that you

DON'T BUY WASHINGTON STATE APPLES

TEAMSTERS UNION LOCAL 760 YAKIMA, WASHINGTON

This is not a strike against any store or market.

P.S.—PACIFIC FRUIT & PRODUCE CO. is the only firm packing Washington State Apples under a union contract.)"

during the picketing, the store employees continued to work, and no deliveries or pickups were obstructed. Washington State apples were handled in normal course by both Safeway employees and the employees of other employers involved. Ingress and egress by customers and others was not interfered with in any manner.

A complaint issued on charges that this conduct violated § 8(b)(4) as amended. . . . The Board held [on stipulated facts] . . . that "by literal wording of the proviso (to § 8(b)(4)) as well as through the interpretive gloss placed thereon by its drafters, consumer picketing in front of a secondary establishment is prohibited." . . . [The D.C. Circuit] set aside the Board's order and remanded. The court rejected the Board's construction and held that the statutory requirement of a showing that respondents' conduct would "threaten, coerce, or restrain" Safeway could only be satisfied by affirmative proof that a substantial economic impact on Safeway had occurred, or was likely to occur as a result of the conduct. Under the remand the Board was left "free to reopen the record to receive evidence upon the issue whether Safeway was in fact threatened, coerced, or restrained." . . . We granted certiorari. . . .

The Board's reading of the statute—that the legislative history and the phrase "other than picketing" in the proviso reveal a congressional purpose to outlaw all picketing directed at customers at a secondary site—necessarily rested on the finding that Congress determined that such picketing always threatens, coerces or restrains the secondary employer. We therefore have a special responsibility to examine the legislative history for confirmation that Congress made that determination. Both the congressional policy and our adherence to this principle of interpretation reflect concern that a broad ban against peaceful picketing might collide with the guarantees of the First Amendment.

We have examined the legislative history of the amendments to § 8(b)(4), and conclude that it does not reflect with the requisite clarity a congressional plan to proscribe all peaceful consumer picketing at secondary sites, and, particularly, any concern with peaceful picketing when it is limited, as here, to persuading Safeway customers not to buy Washington State apples when they traded in the Safeway stores. All that the legislative history shows in the way of an "isolated evil" believed to require proscription of peaceful consumer picketing at secondary sites was its use to persuade the customers of the secondary employer to cease trading with him in order to force him to cease dealing with, or to put pressure upon, the primary employer. This narrow focus reflects the difference between such conduct and peaceful picketing at the secondary site directed only at the struck product. In the latter case, the union's appeal to the public is confined to its dispute with the primary employer, since the public is not asked to withhold its patronage from the secondary employer, but only to boycott the primary employer's goods. On the other hand, a union appeal to the public at the secondary site not to trade at all with the secondary employer goes beyond the goods of the primary employer, and seeks the public's assistance in forcing the secondary employer to cooperate with the union in its primary dispute. This is not to say that this distinction was expressly alluded to in the debates. It is to say, however, that the consumer picketing carried on in this case is not attended by the abuses at which the statute was directed.

The story of the 1959 amendments, which we have detailed at greater length in our opinion filed today in *NLRB v. Servette, Inc.*, 377 U.S. 46.

Peaceful consumer picketing to shut off all trade with the secondary employer unless he aids the union in its dispute with the primary employer, is poles apart from such picketing which only persuades his customers not to buy the struck product. The proviso indicates no more than that the Senate conferees' constitutional doubts led Congress to authorize publicity other than picketing which persuades the customers of a secondary employer to stop all trading with him, but not such publicity which has the effect of cutting off his deliveries or inducing his employees to cease work. On the other hand, picketing which persuades the customers of a secondary employer to stop all trading with him was also to be barred.

In sum, the legislative history does not support the Board's finding that Congress meant to prohibit all consumer picketing at a secondary site, having determined that such picketing necessarily threatened, coerced or restrained the secondary employer. Rather, the history shows that Congress was following its usual practice of legislating against peaceful picketing only to curb "isolated evils."

This distinction is opposed as "unrealistic" because, it is urged, all picketing automatically provokes the public to stay away from the picketed establishment. The public will, it is said, neither read the signs and handbills, nor note the explicit injunction that "This is not a strike against any store or market." Be that as it may, our holding today simply takes note of the fact that Congress has never adopted a broad condemnation of peaceful picketing, such as that urged upon us by petitioners, and an intention to do so is not revealed with that "clearest indication in the legislative history," which we require.

We come then to the question whether the picketing in this case, confined as it was to persuading customers to cease buying the product of the primary employer, falls within the area of secondary consumer picketing which Congress did clearly indicate its intention to prohibit under §8(b)(4)(ii). We hold that it did not fall within that area, and therefore did not "threaten, coerce, or restrain" Safeway. While any diminution in Safeway's purchases of apples due to a drop in consumer demand might be said to be a result which causes respondents' picketing to fall literally within the statutory prohibition, "it is a familiar rule that a thing may be within the letter of the statute and yet not within the statute, because not within its spirit nor within the intention of its makers." *Holy Trinity Church v. United States*, 143 U.S. 457, 459. When consumer picketing is employed only to persuade customers not to buy the struck product, the union's appeal is closely confined to the primary dispute. The site of the appeal is expanded to include the premises of the secondary employer, but if the appeal succeeds, the secondary employer's purchases from the struck firms are decreased only because the public has diminished its purchases of the struck product. On the other hand, when consumer picketing is employed to persuade customers not to trade at all with the secondary employer, the latter stops buying the struck product, not because of a falling demand, but in response to pressure designed to inflict injury on his business generally. In such case, the union does more than merely follow the struck product; it creates a separate dispute with the secondary employer.

We disagree therefore with the Court of Appeals that the test of "to threaten, coerce, or restrain" for the purposes of this case is whether Safeway suffered or was likely to suffer economic loss. A violation of § 8(b)(4)(ii)(B) would not be established, merely because respondents' picketing was effective to reduce Safeway's sales of Washington State apples, even if this led or might lead Safeway to drop the item as a poor seller.

The judgment of the Court of Appeals is vacated and the case is remanded with direction to enter judgment setting aside the Board's order.

Notes

1. Justice Black drafted a concurring opinion in *Tree Fruits*, concluding that "Congress, in passing [§ 8(b)(4)(ii)(b)], intended to forbid the striking employees of one business to picket the premises of a neutral business where the purpose of the picketing is to persuade customers of the neutral business not to buy goods supplied by the struck employer." As a consequence, he determined that the statutory provision was unconstitutional, because "the section is aimed at outlawing free discussion of one side of a certain kind of labor dispute and cannot be sustained as a permissible regulation of patrolling." 377 U.S. at 78.

In contrast, Justices Harlan and Stewart dissented. They interpreted the statute in the same way as Justice Black, writing that they were "unable to discern in § 8(b)(4)(ii)(B) or in its legislative history any basis for the Court's subtle narrowing of these statutory provisions." *Id.* at 81. However, they found no constitutional problem with this interpretation because, in their view, Congress was free to determine that "the social consequences of the 'non-communicative' aspect of picketing may certainly be thought desirable in the case of 'primary' picketing and undesirable in the case of 'secondary' picketing." *Id.* at 94.

2. In order to qualify for the *Tree Fruits* exception, the union bears the "burden of identifying the struck products at the secondary situs." *Atlanta Typographical Union No. 48 (Times-Journal, Inc.)*, 180 N.L.R.B . 1014 (1970). Thus, a union representing newspaper employees had to do more than simply ask the public not to by "products advertised by" neutral employers in the struck newspaper, because it would be too hard for consumers to know which products were covered by the "do not buy" request. *See also Soft Drink Workers Union Local 812 v. NLRB*, 657 F.2d 1252 (D.C. Cir. 1980) (*Tree Fruits* exception did not apply to picketing that requested consumers to buy locally made sodas, but did not identify which sodas were locally made).

3. In "*Tree Fruits*," the Court held that picketing that advocates a boycott of a portion of the secondary employer's business is not unlawful under § 8(b)(4)(ii)(B). By contrast, in *NLRB v. Retail Store Employees, Local 1001*, 447 U.S. 607 (1980) (*Safeco*

Title Insurance Co.), the Court held picketing that advocates a boycott of a truly substantial portion of secondary employer's business to be unlawful under § 8(b)(4)(ii)(B). In *Safeco*, the union picketed local title companies, 90 percent of whose business was selling Safeco policies. In that case, the Court held that, notwithstanding *Tree Fruits*, the union's conduct was unlawful because of the effect that it had on the neutral company's business. Where the struck product has a substantial impact on the neutral party's business, the consumer is essentially asking the public to cease doing business with the neutral party, a violation of § 8(b)(4)(ii)(B). As the Court explained:

> As long as secondary picketing only discourages consumption of a struck product, incidental injury to the neutral is a natural consequence of an effective primary boycott. . . . But the Union's secondary appeal against the central product sold by the title companies in this case is "reasonably calculated to induce customers not to patronize the neutral parties at all." The resulting injury to their businesses is distinctly different from the injury that the Court considered in *Tree Fruits*. Product picketing that reasonably can be expected to threaten neutral parties with ruin or substantial loss simply does not square with the language or the purpose of § 8(b)(4)(ii)(B). 447 U.S. 607, 614–15.

Is this distinction workable? What constitutes "ruin or substantial loss"? In *United Paperworkers Int'l Union (Duro Paper Bag Mfg. Co.)*, 236 N.L.R.B. No. 183 (1978), the Board held that a union was covered by the *Tree Fruits* exception when it asked grocery store customers to refrain from using paper bags, which were made by the struck employer. During the picketing, the store was able to give some customers boxes, and some customers brought their own bags, but other customers left the store without buying anything for want of a way to get their groceries home. However, the Sixth Circuit denied enforcement, holding that "[w]e are also unable to find evidence in the record that any other meaningful alternatives to paper bags exist." *Kroger Co. v. N.L.R.B.*, 647 F.2d 634 (6th Cir. 1980).

4. These cases often also involve the issue of whether or not the union's conduct is protected by the "publicity proviso" to § 8(b)(4). Keep this in mind as you read the following section, which discusses this proviso.

5. A union in a labor dispute with a bread manufacturer pickets a restaurant. The pickets state: "TO THE CONSUMER BRAND X BREAD SOLD HERE." In *American Bread Co. v. NLRB*, 411 F.2d 147 (6th Cir. 1969), the court upheld the Board's decision finding that the union violated § 8(b)(4)(ii)(B), explaining that: Because the bread was part of almost every meal sold by the restaurant, it "had become so integrated into the food served that to cease purchasing the [bread] would almost amount to customers stopping all trade with the secondary employer.'" *Id.* at 154. This case illustrates the "merged product rule."

6. A construction union involved in a labor dispute with a subcontractor who does the carpentry work for a new housing development engages in area standards

picketing at housing developer's sales office. What result where the union is directing the picketing at the subcontractor? In *K & K Const. Co., Inc. v. NLRB*, 592 F.2d 1228 (3d Cir. 1979), the court, applying the merged product rule, reversed the Board, holding that the union violated § 8(b)(4)(ii)(B). The court reasoned as follows:

> *Tree Fruits* created an exception to § 8(b)(4), one whose limitations must be defined in a variety of circumstances. In that case the secondary employer stocked many items and the easily identifiable struck product was sold in essentially the same form as when obtained from the primary. Quite a different problem is presented when the primary's product or service is merged with the secondary's and the union cannot limit its public appeal for a boycott without enmeshing the neutral in its dispute. Since the consumer cannot separate the struck product from that of the secondary, picketing in those circumstances is tantamount to urging the prospective purchaser not to deal with the secondary employer. At its extreme, if the sole output of the secondary contains the product of the primary, the prospective purchaser may of necessity cease patronizing the secondary altogether. 592 F.2d at 1232.

Here, the construction work done by the subcontractor merged with the finished houses; therefore, picketing the housing sales office violated § 8(b)(4)(ii)(B).

7. A union has a primary dispute with a newspaper publisher which distributes its newspaper for free, relying on advertisements for revenue. Can the union lawfully picket a secondary employer who advertises in that paper asking consumers to boycott the advertised products? *Honolulu Typographical Union No. 37 v. NLRB*, 401 F.2d 952 (D.C. Cir. 1968) presented such a circumstance. There, those who advertised in the free newspaper were predominantly restaurants. The union picketed the restaurants asking consumers not to patronize these restaurants because of their dispute with the newspaper. The court upheld the Board's finding that such picketed violated § 8(b)(4)(ii)(B). The court explained:

> [T]he Board's interpretation of *Tree Fruits* gives broader immunity to those secondary sellers who happen to be retailing struck primary products that are so merged into the seller's total business as to be indistinguishable there from. The short answer, however, is that the law makes distinctions in terms of the tradition and economic realities of Union pressure, even though this may result in differences not easily subject to logical delineation between the scope and kinds of picketing available to unions in different labor circumstances. 401 F.2d 952, 955–56.

D. Provisos

1. Primary Picketing/Primary Activity Proviso

Soon after its passage, labor advocates noticed that the literal text of § 8(b)(4)(ii) (B) was written so broadly as to cover activity that Congress never intended to make illegal. This dispute over the breadth of §8(b)(4)(ii)(B) came to a head in *NLRB v. International Rice Milling*, 341 U.S. 665 (1951), where union picketers who were lawfully picketing their primary employer were charged with a §8(b)(4)(ii)(B) violation because those picketers had discouraged truckers employed by a secondary employer from crossing the picket line to make a delivery to the primary employer. *Id.* at 669–70. The Court held that "the pickets' request to a driver of a single truck to discontinue a pending trip to a picketed mill" does not constitute unlawful "inducement" or "encouragement." *Id.* at 671. To ensure that future courts would not limit the holding of *International Rice Milling* to the circumstances presented in that case, Congress amended the NLRA to provide that "nothing contained in [clause (B)] shall be construed to make unlawful" any otherwise-lawful primary strike or primary picketing.

2. Sympathy Strike Proviso

Section 8(b)(4)'s sympathy strike proviso dictates that:

> nothing contained in [§8(b)] shall be construed to make unlawful a refusal by any person to enter upon the premises of any employer (other than his own employer), if the employees of such employer are engaged in a strike ratified or approved by a representative of such employees whom such employer is required to recognize under this Act.

The Board's and courts' construction of this proviso is checkered, confusing, and at times incoherent. The Board's most recent construction of the proviso seems to protect an employee's narrow right "to honor another union's picket line." *Torrington Construction Co.*, 235 N.L.R.B. 1540, 1541 (1978), *overruled in part on other grounds by Chambersburg County Market*, 293 N.L.R.B. 654 (1989). Accordingly, an employer may not discharge these so-called sympathy strikers so long as the primary strike is a lawful strike. However, an employer may permanently replace such sympathy strikers because they are essentially economic strikers. *Butterworth-Manning-Ashmore Mortuary*, 270 N.L.R.B. 1014 (1984). Finally, the right to honor a picket line may be waived in a collective bargaining agreement, although the waiver must be "clear and unmistakeable." *Gary-Hobart Water Corp. & Int'l Union of Dist. 50, Allied & Tech. Workers*, 210 N.L.R.B. 742, 744 (1974).

3. Publicity Proviso

A third proviso states that §8(b)(4) does not prohibit "publicity, other than picketing, for the purpose of truthfully advising the public, including consumers and members of a labor organization, that a product or products are produced by an employer with whom the labor organization has a primary dispute and are distributed by another employer," as long as the publicity does not cause anyone not employed by the primary employer to stop work. The Court's holding in *DeBartolo II* makes this proviso largely irrelevant. Do you see why?

V. Other Unlawful Objects

A. Hot Cargo Agreements and Work Preservation Under §§ 8(e) and 8(b)(4)(ii)(A), (B)

Section 8(e) essentially makes it a ULP for a union and an employer to enter into an agreement that compels the employer to refrain from handling non-union products. These so-called "hot cargo agreements" are "unenforceable and void." Section 8(b)(4)(ii)(A) makes it a ULP for a union to coerce an employer "to enter into" a § 8(e) agreement. Section 8(b)(4)(ii)(B) makes it a ULP for a union to attempt to enforce a § 8(e) agreement against an employer. But recall that unions generally are allowed to negotiate a wide variety of work rules, including those specifying which employees are and are not allowed to do certain types of work. The following case provides important guidelines as to what contract terms do and do not violate § 8(e) agreement.

National Woodwork Manufacturers Association v. NLRB

The Supreme Court of the United States
386 U.S. 612, 87 S. Ct. 1250, 18 L. Ed. 2d 357 (1967)

BRENNAN, J.

. . . Frouge Corporation . . . was the general contractor on a housing project in Philadelphia. Frouge had a collective bargaining agreement with the Carpenters' International Union under which Frouge agreed to be bound by the rules and regulations agreed upon by local unions with contractors in areas in which Frouge had jobs. Frouge was therefore subject to the provisions of a collective bargaining agreement between the Union and an organization of Philadelphia contractors, the General Building Contractors Association, Inc. A sentence in a provision of that agreement entitled Rule 17 provides that ". . . No member of this District Council will handle . . . any doors . . . which have been fitted prior to being furnished on the job. . . ."[2]

Frouge's Philadelphia project called for 3,600 doors. Customarily, before the doors could be hung on such projects, "blank" or "blind" doors would be mortised

---

2. The full text of Rule 17 is as follows:

"No employee shall work on any job on which cabinet work, fixtures, millwork, sash, doors, trim or other detailed millwork is used unless the same is Union-made and bears the Union Label of the United Brotherhood of Carpenters and Joiners of America. No member of this District Council will handle material coming from a mill where cutting out and fitting has been done for butts, locks, letter plates, or hardware of any description, nor any doors or transoms which have been fitted prior to being furnished on job, including base, chair, rail, picture molding, which has been previously fitted. This section to exempt partition work furnished in sections."

The NLRB determined that the first sentence violated § 8(e) . . . and the Union did not seek judicial review of that determination.

for the knob, routed for the hinges, and beveled to make them fit between jambs. These are tasks traditionally performed in the Philadelphia area by the carpenters employed on the jobsite. However, precut and prefitted doors ready to hang may be purchased from door manufacturers. Although Frouge's contract and job specifications did not call for premachined doors, and "blank" or "blind" doors could have been ordered, Frouge contracted for the purchase of premachined doors from a Pennsylvania door manufacturer which is a member of the National Woodwork Manufacturers Association. . . . The Union ordered its carpenter members not to hang the doors when they arrived at the jobsite. Frouge thereupon withdrew the prefabricated doors and substituted "blank" doors which were fitted and cut by its carpenters on the jobsite.

The National Woodwork Manufacturers Associations and another filed charges with the NLRB against the Union alleging that by including the "will not handle" sentence of Rule 17 in the collective bargaining agreement the Union committed the [ULP] under §8(e) of entering into an "agreement . . . whereby (the) employer . . . agrees to case or refrain from handling . . . any of the products of any other employer . . . ," and alleging further that in enforcing the sentence against Frouge, the Union committed the [ULP] under §8(b)(4)(B) of "forcing or requiring any person to cease using . . . the products of any other . . . manufacturer. . . ." The NLRB dismissed the charges. . . . The Board [concluded] that the "will not handle" sentence in Rule 17 was language used by the parties to protect and preserve cutting out and fitting as unit work to be performed by the jobsite carpenters. The Board also [concluded] that both the sentence of Rule 17 itself and its maintenance against Frouge were therefore "primary" activity outside the prohibitions of §§8(e) and 8(b)(4)(B). The following statement of the Trial Examiner was adopted by the Board:

> "I . . . find that the tasks of cutting out and fitting millwork, including doors, has, at least customarily, been performed by the carpenters employed on the jobsite. . . . [Rule 17] guards against encroachments on the cutting out and fitting work of the contract unit employees who have performed that work in the past. Its purpose is plainly to regulate the relations between the general contractor and his own employees and to protect a legitimate economic interest of the employees by preserving their unit work. Merely because it incidentally also affects other parties is no basis for invalidating this provision.
>
> "I find that . . . (the provision) is a lawful work-protection or work-preservation provision and that Respondents have not violated §8(e) . . . by entering into agreements containing this provision and by thereafter maintaining and enforcing this provision.'" . . .

The [Seventh Circuit] reversed the Board . . . , held that the "will not handle" agreement violated §8(e) . . . , and remanded to the Board. . . . In the court's view, the sentence was designed to effect a product boycott . . . , and Congress meant, in enacting §8(e) and §8(b)(4)(B), to prohibit such agreements and conduct forcing employers to enter into them.

The Court of Appeals sustained, however, the dismissal of the §8(b)(4)(B) charge. The court agreed with the Board that the Union's conduct as to Frouge involved only a primary dispute with it, and held that the conduct was therefore not prohibited by that section but expressly protected by the proviso "(t)hat nothing contained in this clause (B) shall be construed to make unlawful, where not otherwise unlawful, any primary strike or primary picketing. . . ."

We granted certiorari [and reverse the Seventh Circuit and uphold the Board].

I.

. . . Even on the doubtful premise that the words of §8(e) unambiguously embrace the sentence of Rule 17, this does not end inquiry into Congress' purpose in enacting the section. It is a "familiar rule, that a thing may be within the letter of the statute and yet not within the statute, because not within its spirit nor within the intention of its makers." *Holy Trinity Church v. United States*, 143 U.S. 457, 459. . . .

Strongly held opposing views have invariably marked controversy over labor's use of the boycott to further its aims by involving an employer in disputes not his own. But congressional action to deal with such conduct has stopped short of proscribing identical activity having the object of pressuring the employer for agreements regulating relations between him and his own employees. That Congress meant §§8(e) and 8(b)(4)(B) to prohibit only "secondary" objectives clearly appears from an examination of the history of congressional action on the subject. . . .

II.

. . . The Landrum-Griffin Act amendments in 1959 were adopted only to close various loopholes in the application of §8(b)(4)(A) which had been exposed in Board and court decisions. . . . "[T]hese changes did not expand the type of conduct which §8(b)(4)(A) condemned, that is, union pressures calculated to induce the employees of a secondary employer to withhold their services in order to force their employer to cease dealing with the primary employer." *NLRB v. Servette, Inc.*, 377 U.S. 46, 52–53.

Section 8(e) simply closed still another loophole. In Local 1976, *United Bhd. of Carpenters, etc., v. NLRB (Sand Door)*, 357 U.S. 93, the Court held that it was no defense to [a ULP] charge under §8(b)(4)(A) that the struck employer had agreed, in a contract with the union, not to handle nonunion material. However, the Court emphasized that the mere execution of such a contract provision (known as a "hot cargo" clause because of its prevalence in Teamsters Union contracts), or its voluntary observance by the employer, was not unlawful under §8(b)(4)(A). Section 8(e) was designed to plug this gap in the legislation by making the "hot cargo" clause itself unlawful. The *Sand Door* decision was believed by Congress not only to create the possibility of damage actions against employers for breaches of "hot cargo" clauses, but also to create a situation in which such clauses might be employed to exert subtle pressures upon employers to engage in "voluntary" boycotts. . . .

This loophole-closing measure likewise did not expand the type of conduct which §8(b)(4)(A) condemned. Although the language of §8(e) is sweeping, it closely tracks that of §8(b)(4)(A), and just as the latter and its successor §8(b)(4)(B) did not reach employees' activity to pressure their employer to preserve for themselves work traditionally done by them, §8(e) does not prohibit agreements made and maintained for that purpose.

The legislative history of §8(e) confirms this conclusion. . . .

Moreover, our decision in [*Fibreboard Paper Prods. Corp. v. NLRB*, 379 U.S. 203, 210–11 (1964)], implicitly recognizes the legitimacy of work preservation clauses like that involved here. Indeed, in the circumstances presented in *Fibreboard*, we held that bargaining on the subject was made mandatory by §8(a)(5) . . . , concerning as it does "terms and conditions of employment," §8(d). *Fibreboard* involved an alleged refusal to bargain with respect to the contracting-out of plant maintenance work previously performed by employees in the bargaining unit. The Court recognized that the "termination of employment which . . . necessarily results from the contracting out of work performed by members of the established bargaining unit," is "a problem of vital concern to labor and management. . . ." It would therefore be incongruous to interpret §8(e) to invalidate clauses over which the parties may be mandated to bargain and which have been successfully incorporated through collective bargaining in many of this Nation's major labor agreements.

Finally, important parts of the historic accommodation by Congress of the powers of labor and management are §§7 and 13. . . . The former section assures to labor "the right . . . to bargain collectively through representatives of their own choosing, and to engage in other concerted activities for the purpose of collective bargaining or other mutual aid or protection. . . ." Section 13 preserves the right to strike, of which the boycott is a form, except as specifically provided in the Act. In the absence of clear indicia of congressional intent to the contrary, these provisions caution against reading statutory prohibitions as embracing employee activities to pressure their own employers into improving the employees' wages, hours, and working conditions. . . .

III.

. . . The determination whether the "will not handle" sentence of Rule 17 and its enforcement violated §8(e) and §8(b)(4)(B) cannot be made without an inquiry into whether, under all the surrounding circumstances, the Union's objective was preservation of work for Frouge's employees, or whether the agreements and boycott were tactically calculated to satisfy union objectives elsewhere. Were the latter the case, Frouge, the boycotting employer, would be a neutral bystander, and the agreement or boycott would, within the intent of Congress, become secondary. There need not be an actual dispute with the boycotted employer, here the door manufacturer, for the activity to fall within this category, so long as the tactical object of the agreement and its maintenance is that employer, or benefits to other than the boycotting employees or other employees of the primary employer thus making the agreement or boycott secondary in its aim. The touchstone is whether the agreement or its maintenance is addressed to the labor relations of the contracting employer vis-à-vis his own employees. This will not always be a simple test to apply. But "(h)owever difficult the drawing of lines more nice than obvious, the statute compels the task." . . .

That the "will not handle" provision was not [a ULP] in these cases is clear. The finding of the Trial Examiner, adopted by the Board, was that the objective of the sentence was preservation of work traditionally performed by the jobsite carpenters. This finding is supported by substantial evidence, and therefore the Union's making of the "will not handle" agreement was not a violation of § 8(e).

Similarly, the Union's maintenance of the provision was not a violation of § 8(b) (4)(B). The Union refused to hang prefabricated doors whether or not they bore a union label, and even refused to install prefabricated doors manufactured off the jobsite by members of the Union. This and other substantial evidence supported the finding that the conduct of the Union on the Frouge jobsite related solely to preservation of the traditional tasks of the jobsite carpenters. . . .

Notes

1. In *National Woodwork Manufacturers Association*, above, the Court held that work preservation clauses are not unlawful under § 8(e). In so holding, the Court rejected what the dissent considered to be the more literal position—that work preservation clauses are, in fact, an agreement not to handle certain products. In so holding, the majority relied on Congress's intent to make unlawful only those agreements with an unlawful secondary objective. Work preservation clauses are primary and therefore lawful because they are intended to benefit the unionized employees by preserving bargaining unit work. Indeed, the union had no labor dispute with door manufacturer. This case instructs us that it is unlawful for an employer to promise not to purchase non-union or hot goods, whereas it is lawful for an employer to promise not to purchase goods that bargaining unit employees have traditionally made.

Are either of the following clauses unlawful?

a. An agreement not to punish employees who refuse to deliver goods to another company engaged in a primary labor dispute: In *Truck Drivers Local 413 v. NLRB*, 334 F.2d 539 (D.C. Cir. 1964), the union and its employer entered into an agreement that immunized the bargaining unit employees from discipline for refusing to cross a picket line. The Court held that this agreement was not unlawful under § 8(e) because that section concerns itself only with secondary activity, whereas a refusal to cross a picket line is itself protected concerted activity and therefore within the § 8(b)(4) proviso protecting primary activity. *But see Drivers Local 695 v. NLRB*, 361 F.2d 547 (D.C. Cir. 1966) (holding, among other things, that an agreement to immunize employees from discipline for refusing to cross a secondary picket line is unlawful).

b. An agreement that employees who refuse to enter a neutral gate at a construction site will not be punished: In *NLRB v. Int'l U. of Elevator Constructors*, 902 F.2d 1297 (8th Cir. 1990), an employee refused to enter a neutral gate at a construction site and report for work with his employer, because another subcontractor was being picketed at a reserve gate. When the union filed a grievance based on the employer's suspension of the employee, the employer filed §8(b)(4)(ii)(A) and §8(e) charges against the union. The Court, agreeing with the Board, concluded that the union's attempt to defend the grievance on these grounds was based on a construction of its collective-bargaining agreement that would violate §8(e), and therefore that the union had violated §8(b)(4)(ii)(A) by attempting to enforce a contractual picket line clause protecting from discipline employees who refuse to enter a neutral gate.

2. In *Houston Insulation Contractors Association v. NLRB*, 386 U.S. 664 (1967), decided the same day as *National Woodwork*, the Court held that a local union could refuse to handle goods covered by a work-preservation agreement between a company and another local union where the employees of both local unions were working for the same company that was in violation of that lawful work-preservation clause.

3. The employer "advanced several reasons, grounded in economic and technological factors, why 'will not handle' clauses should be invalid in all circumstances." The *National Woodwork* Court concluded that:

> [t]hose arguments are addressed to the wrong branch of government. It may be "that the time has come for a re-evaluation of the basic content of collective bargaining as contemplated by the federal legislation. But that is for Congress. Congress has demonstrated its capacity to adjust the Nation's labor legislation to what, in its legislative judgment, constitutes the statutory pattern appropriate to the developing state of labor relations in the country. Major revisions of the basic statute were enacted in 1947 and 1959. To be sure then, Congress might be of opinion that greater stress should be put on ... eliminating more and more economic weapons from the ... (Union's) grasp. ... But Congress' policy has not yet moved to this point. ..." (citation omitted). 386 U.S. 612, 644.

Congress has not substantially amended the NLRA since 1959. What can a party do when Congress becomes unresponsive to the needs of the various parties affected by the law? Does the Court have a role to play in such cases?

4. What if the union's purpose in negotiating a clause in its collective-bargaining agreement is not to preserve work traditionally done by its bargaining unit members but to acquire new work? In one line of cases, the Board, with court approval, has found such clauses lawful to the extent that the union is seeking new work that is functionally similar to which its members had previously done or work that is "fairly claimable." According to the Board, "fairly claimable work is work that is identical to or very similar to that already performed by the bargaining unit and

that bargaining unit members have the necessary skill and are otherwise able to perform." *Newspaper and Mail Deliverers' Union*, 298 N.L.R.B. 564 (1990).

5. In *Meat & Highway Drivers, Local Union No. 710 v. NLRB*, 335 F.2d 709 (D.C. Cir. 1964), the court held that collective-bargaining agreement clauses limiting subcontracting to companies with union *standards* of pay, do not violate § 8(e), but limiting subcontracting to companies that are *actually unionized* does violate § 8(e). However, as the next note explains, this limitation does not apply to the construction and garment industries.

6. Section 8(e) excludes two industries from its prohibition on hot cargo agreements: the garment industry and the construction industry.

a. Under the garment industry proviso it is lawful to enter into an agreement to subcontract work only to union shops and also for a union to use economic pressure to obtain such an agreement. Congress's purpose in allowing this exception was "aimed at eradicating the scandalous sweatshop culture existing in the garment and apparel industries when § 8(e) was passed." *R.M. Perlman, Inc. v. N.Y. Coat Workers, Local 89-22-1*, 33 F.3d 145 (2d Cir. 1994). The garment industry proviso creates an exemption from § 8(b)(4) and § 8(e) for employers "in the relation of a jobber, manufacturer, contractor, or subcontractor working on the goods or premises of the jobber or manufacturer or performing parts of an integrated process of production in the apparel and clothing industry."

b. Section 8(e) also expressly exempts agreements "relating to the contracting or subcontracting of work to be done at the site of the construction." As demonstrated in the construction industry cases described above, the construction industry proviso is limited. It does not cover construction employer agreements to refuse to handle non-union goods; such an agreement would violate § 8(e) and economic pressure to obtain such a clause would violate § 8(b)(4)(ii)(A). What result if a union and its employer agree to use prefabricated doors and windows only if those doors and windows were prepared by union labor? Is this an agreement related to the subcontracting or work or is it a refusal to handle non-union goods? According to the Board in *Ohio Valley Carpenters Dist. Council*, 136 N.L.R.B. 977 (1962), the provision was unlawful because the work was being performed away from the jobsite.

7. It is important to note that Congress has created additional remedies for § 8(b)(4) violations. First, under § 10(l) of the NLRA, the Regional Director is *required* to seek injunctive relief where he or she has "reasonable cause to believe such charge [under §§ 8(b)(4)(ii)(A)–(C), 8(e) or 8(b)(7)] is true." This provision differs from § 10(j), which simply *permits* the Regional Director to seek an injunction for all other ULPs. Second, § 303 of the Taft-Hartley Act authorizes persons (including primary or secondary employers as well as neutral parties) "injured in his business or property by reason of any violation" of § 8(b)(4) to recover tort-style damages in federal district court. Can you think of possible justifications for the distinction in remedies? Do you think those justifications are convincing?

B. Jurisdictional disputes

Section 8(b)(4)(D) makes it an ULP for a union to use economic pressure or coercion to force an employer to assign work to one bargaining unit over another. When a § 8(b)(4)(D) charge is filed and there is reasonable cause to believe that a violation has been committed, the Board must hold what is called a § 10(k) hearing at which the Board must "decide which union or group of employees is entitled to the disputed work. . . . Whether the § 8(b)(4)(D) charge will be sustained or dismissed is thus dependent on the outcome of the § 10(k) proceeding." *NLRB v. Plasterers' Local Union No. 79*, 404 U.S. 116 (1971). Sections 8(b)(4)(D) and 10(k) establish administrative procedures for protecting employers from becoming trapped between the competing claims of rival unions, both of whom demand the right to perform the same work. The purpose of the § 10(k) hearing is to identify "the real nature and origin of the [parties'] dispute." *Teamsters Local 578 (USCP-Wesco, Inc.)*, 280 N.L.R.B. 818, 820 (1986), *aff'd*, 827 F.2d 581 (9th Cir. 1987).

To determine who is entitled to the work at issue in a jurisdictional dispute, the Board undertakes a flexible consideration of a number of factors. They include "the skills and work involved, certifications by the Board, company and industry practice, agreements between unions and between employers and unions, awards of arbitrators, joint boards, and the AFL-CIO, in the same or related cases, the assignment made by the employer, and the efficient operation of the employer's business." *Machinists Lodge 1743 (J.A. Jones Constr. Co.)*, 135 N.L.R.B. 1402 (1962). However, this list is only illustrative of the types of factors the Board will consider; it has also considered additional factors such as employees' refusal to work if the jobs are assigned to one unit or the other, or potential job losses. *Typographical Union No. 2 (Philadelphia) (Philadelphia Inquirer)*, 142 N.L.R.B. 36 (1963).

There is no jurisdictional dispute where an employer's unilateral actions have precipitated the dispute, typically by depriving one group of employees of work that it traditionally performed under a collective-bargaining agreement and reassigning that work to another group of employees that previously had no claim to the work. In such cases, the matter is appropriately viewed as a contractual work-preservation dispute between the employer and the employee group that had traditionally performed the work under a collective-bargaining agreement until the employer decided to reassign it. *See, e.g., Machinists Local 1414 v. NLRB*, 2007 U.S. App. LEXIS 25612 (9th Cir. Oct. 30, 2007) (upholding the Board's finding that employer caused the dispute when it reassigned work traditionally done by the International Longshore and Warehouse Union and therefore that neither the employer nor the ILWU could avail itself of the 10(k) process).

C. Featherbedding

Featherbedding is a practice of adopting various types of make-work rules such as excessive staffing. Section 8(b)(6) outlaws "featherbedding" by making it a ULP for a union "to cause or attempt to cause an employer to pay or deliver or agree to pay or deliver any money or other thing of value, in the nature of an exaction, for services which are not performed or not to be performed." In *NLRB v. Gamble Enterprises, Inc.*, 345 U.S. 117 (1953), the Supreme Court, agreeing with the Board, narrowly construed § 8(b)(6). The Court held that a union's insistence that a theater employ local musicians in exchange for the union's consent to the theater's interest in having traveling band performances was not unlawful featherbedding. Rather, it was a lawful attempt to preserve work for local musicians. In short, it does not violate § 8(b)(6) for a clause in the CBA to require work that the employer does not need done, or even work that is obviously of no use, such as creating something then immediately destroying it. *See American Newspaper Publishers Association v. NLRB*, 345 U.S. 100 (1953) (clause providing for the setting of type and then the destruction of the type does not violate § 8(b)(6)).

Section 8(b)(6) violations are rare. But the Board found one in *Metallic Lathers Union of NY*, 207 N.L.R.B. 631 (1973). In that case, the lathers' union asked an employer to hire one of the union's members, John Duffy. The employer initially refused, but changed its mind in response to union picketing. Upon being hired, Duffy refused to perform most jobs in the plant because those jobs were under the jurisdiction of the Teamsters union. When assigned to do office work, Duffy alternatively performed so poorly that he was told to stop work, or refused to do assigned tasks. When reassigned a second time to make deliveries, Duffy would work for 3–4 hours per day, and spend the rest of the 8-hour day on personal activities. Finally, Duffy was assigned to paint building facilities, but he refused this assignment too. The employer fired Duffy after about three months, and the union re-commenced picketing. The Board agreed with an ALJ that the union's demand that the employer hire Duffy was not a "bona fide offer of competent performance of relevant services."

VI. Protests Seeking Union Recognition: Section 8(b)(7)

Section 8(b)(7) regulates picketing to force an employer to recognize, or to force employees to select, a union (a.k.a. recognitional or organizational picketing). Like § 8(b)(4), § 8(b)(7) is difficult to decipher; it prohibits picketing, and even threatening to participate in picketing, which has a recognitional or organizational purpose, in the circumstances stated in subsections (A), (B), or (C), and subject to the two provisos to subsection (C). Picketing is recognitional for purposes of § 8(b)(7) so long as one of its purposes is recognitional, even if the picketing also has other objectives. Section 8(b)(7) does not, however, proscribe other types of picketing such as economic or area-standards picketing so long as it does not have a recognitional objective.

International Hod Carriers Building & Common Laborers Union, Local 840 (Blinne Construction Co.)

The National Labor Relations Board
135 N.L.R.B. 1153 (1962)

Supplemental Decision and Order

[T]he Board . . . issued a Decision and Order . . . finding that Respondent Union had [violated] § 8(b)(7)(C). . . . Thereafter, . . . Respondent Union filed with the Board a motion for reconsideration and for dismissal of the complaint. . . .

I.

. . . The Decision and Order in the instant case is one of several issued on February 20, 1961, and immediately thereafter, dealing with § 8(b)(7)(C) . . . , which became effective on November 13, 1959, pursuant to the Landrum-Griffin amendments. § 8(b)(7)(C) is one of three interrelated subsections comprising § 8(b)(7). . . .

As indicated by its text, the thrust of § 8(b)(7) is to deal with recognition and organization picketing, a matter not dealt with directly in the Taft-Hartley Act except to the limited extent provided in § 8(b)(4)(C) of that Act. Congress concluded that legislation was needed in this area and, in the words of the Supreme Court, [*NLRB v. Drivers, Chauffeurs and Helpers Local U. No. 639*, 362 U.S. at 291] went beyond the Taft-Hartley Act to legislate a comprehensive code governing organizational strikes and picketing. . . . While proscribing peaceful organizational strikes in many situations, it also established safeguards against the Board's interference with legitimate picketing activity. . . .

Even a cursory examination of the legislative history of the provisions here in issue reveals that, like the so-called "secondary boycott" provisions of the Taft-Hartley Act, § 8(b)(7) was also "to a marked degree, the result of conflict and compromise between strong contending forces and deeply held views on the role of organized labor in the free economic life of the Nation and the appropriate balance to be struck between the uncontrolled power of management and labor to further their respective interests." *Local 1976, United Brotherhood of Carpenters and Joiners of America (Sand Door & Plywood Co.) v. NLRB*, 357 U.S. 93, 99–100. . . .

II.

. . . Before proceeding to determine the application of § 8(b)(7)(C) to the facts of the instant case, it is essential to note the interplay of the several subsections of § 8(b)(7), of which subparagraph (C) is only a constituent part.

The section as a whole, as is apparent from its opening phrases, prescribes limitations only on picketing for an object of "recognition" or "bargaining" (both of which terms will hereinafter be subsumed under the single term "recognition") or for an object of organization. Picketing for other objects is not proscribed by this section. Moreover, not all picketing for recognition or organization is proscribed. A "currently certified" union may picket for recognition or organization of employees for whom it is certified. And even a union which is not certified is barred from recognition or organization picketing only in three general areas. The first area, defined in subparagraph (A) of § 8(b)(7), relates to situations where another union has been lawfully recognized and a question concerning representation cannot appropriately be raised. The second area, defined in subparagraph (B), relates to situations where, within the preceding 12 months, a "valid election" has been held.

The intent of subparagraphs (A) and (B) is fairly clear. Congress concluded that where a union has been lawfully recognized and a question concerning representation cannot appropriately be raised, or where the employees within the preceding 12 months have made known their views concerning representation, both the employer and employees are entitled to immunity from recognition or organization picketing for prescribed periods.

Congress did not stop there, however. Deeply concerned with other abuses, most particularly "blackmail" picketing, Congress concluded that it would be salutary to impose even further limitations on picketing for recognition or organization. Accordingly, subparagraph (C) provides that even where such picketing is not barred by the provisions of (A) or (B) so that picketing for recognition or organization would otherwise be permissible, such picketing is limited to a reasonable period not to exceed 30 days unless a representation petition is filed prior to the expiration of that period. Absent the filing of such a timely petition, continuation of the picketing beyond the reasonable period becomes [a ULP]. On the other hand, the filing of a timely petition stays the limitation and picketing may continue pending the processing of the petition. Even here, however, Congress by the addition of the first proviso to subparagraph (C) made it possible to foreshorten the period of permissible picketing by directing the holding of an expedited election pursuant to the representation petition.

The expedited election procedure is applicable, of course, only in a § 8(b)(7)(C) proceeding, i.e., where an 8(b)(7)(C) [ULP] charge has been filed. Congress rejected efforts to amend the provisions of § 9(c) ... so as to dispense generally with preelection hearings. Thus, in the absence of an 8(b)(7)(C) [ULP] charge, a union will not be enabled to obtain an expedited election by the mere device of engaging in recognition or organization picketing and filing a representation petition. And on the other hand, a picketing union which files a representation petition pursuant to the mandate of § 8(b)(7)(C) and to avoid its sanctions will not be propelled into an expedited election, which it may not desire, merely because it has filed such a petition. In both the above situations, the normal representation procedures are applicable; the showing of a substantial interest will be required, and the preelection hearing directed in § 9(c)(1) will be held.

This, in our considered judgment, puts the expedited election procedure prescribed in the first proviso to subparagraph C in its proper and intended focus. That procedure was devised to shield aggrieved employers and employees from the adverse effects of prolonged recognition or organization picketing. Absent such a grievance, it was not designed either to benefit or to handicap picketing activity. ...

Subparagraphs (B) and (C) serve different purposes. But it is especially significant to note their interrelationship. Congress was particularly concerned, even where picketing for recognition or organization was otherwise permissible, that the question concerning representation which gave rise to the picketing be resolved as quickly as possible. It was for this reason that it provided for the filing of a petition pursuant to which the Board could direct an expedited election in which the employees could freely indicate their desires as to representation. If, in the free exercise of their choice, they designate the picketing union as their bargaining representative, that union will be certified and it will by the express terms of § 8(b)(7) be exonerated from the strictures of that section. If, conversely, the employees reject the picketing union, that union will be barred from picketing for 12 months thereafter under the provisions of subparagraph (B).

The scheme which Congress thus devised represents what that legislative body deemed a practical accommodation between the right of a union to engage in legitimate picketing for recognition or organization and abuse of that right. One caveat must be noted in that regard. The congressional scheme is, perforce, based on the premise that the election to be conducted under the first proviso to subparagraph (C) represents the free and uncoerced choice of the employee electorate. Absent such a free and uncoerced choice, the underlying question concerning representation is not resolved and, more particularly, subparagraph (B) which turns on the holding of a "valid election" does not become operative.

There remains to be considered only the second proviso to subparagraph (C). In sum, that proviso removes the time limitation imposed upon, and preserves the legality of, recognition or organization picketing falling within the ambit of subparagraph (C), where that picketing merely advises the public that an employer does not employ members of, or have a contract with, a union unless an effect of such picketing is to halt pickups or deliveries, or the performance of services. Needless to add, picketing which meets the requirements of the proviso also renders the expedited election procedure inapplicable.

Except for the final clause in § 8(b)(7) which provides that nothing in that section shall be construed to permit any act otherwise proscribed under § 8(b) . . . , the foregoing sums up the limitations imposed upon recognition or organization picketing by the Landrum-Griffin amendments. However, at the risk of laboring the obvious, it is important to note that structurally, as well as grammatically, subparagraphs (A), (B), and (C) are subordinate to and controlled by the opening phrases of § 8(b)(7). In other words, the thrust of all the § 8(b)(7) provisions is only upon picketing for an object of recognition or organization, and not upon picketing for other objects. Similarly, both structurally and grammatically, the two provisos in subparagraph (C) appertain only to the situation defined in the principal clause of that subparagraph.

III.

. . . Having outlined, in concededly broad strokes, the statutory framework of § 8(b)(7) and particularly subparagraph (C) thereof, we may appropriately turn to a consideration of the instant case which presents issues going to the heart of that legislation.

The relevant facts may be briefly stated. On February 2, 1960, all three common laborers employed by Blinne at the Fort Leonard Wood jobsite signed cards designating the Union to represent them for purposes of collective bargaining. The next day the Union demanded that Blinne recognize the Union as the bargaining agent for the three laborers. Blinne not only refused recognition but told the Union it would transfer one of the laborers, Wann, in order to destroy the Union's majority. Blinne carried out this threat and transferred Wann 5 days later, on February 8. Following this refusal to recognize the Union and the transfer of Wann the Union started picketing at Fort Wood. The picketing, which began on February 8, immediately following the transfer of Wann, had three announced objectives: (1) recognition of the Union; (2) payment of the Davis-Bacon scale of wages; and (3) protest against Blinne's [ULPs] in refusing to recognize the Union and in threatening to transfer and transferring Wann.

The picketing continued, with interruptions due to bad weather, until at least March 11, 1960, a period of more than 30 days from the date the picketing commenced. The picketing was peaceful, only one picket was on duty, and the picket sign he carried read "C. A. Blinne Construction Company, unfair." The three laborers on the job (one was the replacement for Wann) struck when the picketing started.

The Union, of course, was not the certified bargaining representative of the employees. Moreover, no representation petition was filed during the more than 30 days in which picketing was taking place. On March 1, however, about 3 weeks after the picketing commenced and well within the statutory 30-day period, the Union filed [ULP] charges against Blinne, alleging violations of §8(a)(1), (2), (3), and (5). On March 22, the Regional Director dismissed the 8(a)(2) and (5) charges, whereupon the Union forthwith filed a representation petition under §9(c). . . . Subsequently, on April 20, the Regional Director approved a unilateral settlement agreement with Blinne with respect to the §8(a)(1) and (3) charges which had not been dismissed. In the settlement agreement, Blinne neither admitted nor denied that it had committed [ULPs].

General Counsel argues that a violation of §8(b)(7)(C) has occurred within the literal terms of that provision because (1) the Union's picketing was concededly for an object of obtaining recognition; (2) the Union was not currently certified as the representative of the employees involved; and (3) no petition for representation was filed within 30 days of the commencement of the picketing. Inasmuch as the Union made no contention that its recognition picketing was "informational" within the meaning of the second proviso to subparagraph (C) or that it otherwise comported with the strictures of that proviso, General Counsel contends that a finding of [ULP] is required.

Respondent Union, for its part, points to the manifest inequity of such a finding and argues that Congress could not have intended so incongruous a result. In essence, its position is that it was entitled to recognition because it represented all the employees in the appropriate unit, that Blinne by a series of [ULPs] deprived the Union and the employees it sought to represent of fundamental rights guaranteed by the Act, and that the impact of a finding adverse to the Union would be to punish the innocent and reward the wrongdoer. More specifically, Respondent argues that § 8(b)(7)(C) was not intended to apply to picketing by a majority union and that, in any event, Blinne's [ULPs] exonerated it from the statutory requirement of filing a timely representation petition. . . .

IV.

A. The contention that § 8 (b)(7)(C) does not proscribe picketing for recognition or organization by a majority union. . . .

Respondent, urging the self-evident proposition that a statute should be read as a whole, argues that § 8(b)(7)(C) was not designed to prohibit picketing for recognition by a union enjoying majority status in an appropriate unit. Such picketing is for a lawful purpose inasmuch as §§ 8(a)(5) and 9(a) . . . specifically impose upon an employer the duty to recognize and bargain with a union which enjoys that status. Accordingly, Respondent contends, absent express language requiring such a result, § 8(b)(7)(C) should not be read in derogation of the duty so imposed.

There is grave doubt that the argument here made is apposite in this case. But, assuming its relevance, we find it to be without merit. To be sure, the legislative history is replete with references that Congress in framing the 1959 amendments was primarily concerned with "blackmail" picketing where the picketing union represented none or few of the employees whose allegiance it sought. Legislative references susceptible to an interpretation that Congress was concerned with the evils of majority picketing are sparse. Yet it cannot be gainsaid that § 8(b)(7) by its explicit language exempts only "currently certified" unions from its proscriptions. Cautious as we should be to avoid a mechanical reading of statutory terms in involved legislative enactments, it is difficult to avoid giving the quoted words, essentially words of art, their natural construction. Moreover, such a construction is consonant with the underlying statutory scheme which is to resolve disputed issues of majority status, whenever possible, by the machinery of a Board election. Absent [ULPs] or preelection misconduct warranting the setting aside of the election, majority unions will presumably not be prejudiced by such resolution. On the other hand, the admitted difficulties of determining majority status without such an election are obviated by this construction.

Congress was presumably aware of these considerations. In any event, there would seem to be here no valid considerations requiring that Congress be assumed to have intended a broader exemption than the one it actually afforded.

B. The contention that employer ULPs are a defense to a charge of a § 8 (b)(7)(C) violation.

. . . We turn now to the second issue, namely, whether employer ULPs are a defense to an 8(b)(7)(C) violation. . . . [T]he Union argues that Blinne was engaged in ULPs within the meaning of §8(a)(1) and (3) . . . ; that it filed appropriate ULP charges against Blinne within a reasonable period of time after the commencement of the picketing; that it filed a representation petition as soon as the 8(a)(2) and (5) allegations of the charges were dismissed; that the 8(a)(1) and (3) allegations were in effect sustained and a settlement agreement was subsequently entered into with the approval of the Board; and that, therefore, this sequence of events should satisfy the requirements of §8(b)(7)(C).

The majority of the Board in the original Decision and Order rejected this argument. Pointing out that the representation petition was concededly filed more than 30 days after the commencement of the picketing, the majority concluded that the clear terms of §8(b)(4)(C) had been violated.

The majority also addressed itself specifically to the Union's contention that §8(b)(7)(C) could not have been intended by Congress to apply where an employer ULP had occurred. Its opinion alludes to the fact that the then Senator, now President, Kennedy had proposed statutory language to the effect that any employer ULP would be a defense to a charge of an 8(b)(7) violation both with respect to an application to the courts for a temporary restraining order and with respect to the ULP proceeding itself. The majority noted that the Congress did not adopt this proposal but instead limited itself merely to the insertion of a proviso in §10(1) prohibiting the application for a restraining order under §8(b)(7)(C) if there was reason to believe that a §8(a)(2) violation existed. Accordingly, the majority concluded that Congress had specifically rejected the very contention which Respondent urged. . . .

Congress was unwilling to write an exemption into §8(b)(7)(C) dispensing with the necessity for filing a representation petition wherever employer ULPs were alleged. The fact that the bill as ultimately enacted by the Congress did not contain the amendment to §10(1) which the Senate had adopted in S. 1555 . . . cogently establishes that this reluctance was not due to oversight. On the other hand, it strains credulity to believe that Congress proposed to make the rights of union and employees turn upon the results of an election which, because of the existence of unremedied ULPs, is unlikely to reflect the true wishes of the employees.

We do not find ourselves impaled on the horns of this dilemma. Upon careful reappraisal of the statutory scheme we are satisfied that Congress meant to require, and did require, in an 8(b)(7)(C) situation, that a representation petition be filed within a reasonable period, not to exceed 30 days. By this device machinery can quickly be set in motion to resolve by a free and fair election the underlying question concerning representation out of which the picketing arises. This is the normal situation, and the situation which the statute is basically designed to serve.

There is legitimate concern, however, with the abnormal situation, that is, the situation where because of unremedied ULPs a free and fair election cannot be held. We believe Congress anticipated this contingency also. Thus, we find no mandate in the legislative scheme to compel the holding of an election pursuant to a representation petition where, because of unremedied ULPs or for other valid reason, a free and uncoerced election cannot be held. On the contrary, the interrelated provisions of subparagraphs (B) and (C), by their respective references to a "valid election" and to a "certif[ication of] results" presuppose that Congress contemplated only a fair and free election. Only after such an election could the Board certify the results and only after such an election could the salutary provisions of subparagraph (B) become operative.

In our view, therefore, Congress intended that, except to the limited extent set forth in the first proviso, the Board in 8(b)(7)(C) cases follow the tried and familiar procedures it typically follows in representation cases where ULP charges are filed. That procedure, as already set forth, is to hold the representation case in abeyance and refrain from holding an election pending the resolution of the ULP charges. Thus, the fears that the statutory requirement for filing a timely petition will compel a union which has been the victim of ULPs to undergo a coerced election are groundless. No action will be taken on that petition while ULP charges are pending, and until a valid election is held pursuant to that petition, the union's right to picket under the statutory scheme is unimpaired.

On the other side of the coin, it may safely be assumed that groundless ULP charges in this area, because of the statutory priority accorded §8(b)(7) violations, will be quickly dismissed. Following such dismissal an election can be directed forthwith upon the subsisting petition, thereby effectuating the congressional purpose. Moreover, the fact that a timely petition is on file will protect the innocent union, which through a mistake of fact or law has filed a groundless ULP charge, from a finding of an 8(b)(7)(C) violation. Thus, the policy of the entire Act is effectuated and all rights guaranteed by its several provisions are appropriately safeguarded. *See Mastro Plastics Corp.* v. *NLRB*, 350 U.S. 270, 285.

The facts of the instant case may be utilized to demonstrate the practical operation of the legislative scheme. Here the union had filed ULP charges alleging violations by the employer of §8(a)(1), (2), (3), and (5). . . . General Counsel found the allegations of 8(a)(2) and (5) violations groundless. Hence had these allegations stood alone and had a timely petition been on file, an election could have been directed forthwith and the underlying question concerning representation out of which the picketing arose could have been resolved pursuant to the statutory scheme. The failure to file a timely petition frustrated that scheme.

On the other hand, the §8(a)(1) and (3) charges were found meritorious. Under these circumstances, and again consistent with uniform practice, no election would have been directed notwithstanding the currency of a timely petition; the petition would be held in abeyance pending a satisfactory resolution of the ULP charges. The aggrieved union's right to picket would not be abated in the interim and the sole prejudice to the employer would be the delay engendered by its own ULPs. The absence of a timely petition, however, precludes disposition of the underlying question concerning representation which thus remains unresolved even after the §8(a)(1) and (3) charges are satisfactorily disposed of. Accordingly, to condone the refusal to file a timely petition in such situations would be to condone the flouting of a legislative judgment. Moreover, and most important, to impose a lesser requirement would fly in the face of the public interest which prompted that judgment. . . .

Because we read § 8(b)(7)(C) as requiring in the instant case the filing of a timely petition and because such a petition was admittedly not filed until more than 30 days after the commencement of the picketing, we find that Respondent violated § 8(b)(7)(C). . . . As previously noted, it is undisputed that "an object" of the picketing was for recognition. It affords Respondent no comfort that its picketing was also in protest against the discriminatory transfer of an employee and against payment of wages at a rate lower than that prescribed by law. Had Respondent confined its picketing to these objectives rather than, as it did, include a demand for recognition, we believe none of the provisions of § 8(b)(7) would be applicable. Under the circumstances here, however, § 8(b)(7)(C) is applicable. . . .

Notes

1. Review subsections (A), (B), and (C) of § 8(b)(7), focusing on what these statutory terms prohibit. What are the purposes of these bans?

   a. Section 8(b)(7)(A) bans recognitional picketing when the employer has lawfully recognized another union. The ban on recognitional picketing recognizes that no question concerning representation (QCR) can be appropriately raised where another union has an irrebuttable presumption of majority status.

   b. Section 8(b)(7)(B) similarly bans recognitional picketing where a valid Board election has been held within the preceding twelve months. As with § 8(b)(7)(A), this ban recognizes, among other things, that no QCR can be raised where the certification-year bar is in place.

   c. Section 8(b)(7)(C) regulates recognitional picketing that is not otherwise banned by § 8(b)(7)(A) or § 8(b)(7)(B). It provides that such picketing is permissible up to a maximum of thirty days unless a representation election petition is filed. Where such an election petition has been filed, recognitional picketing may continue pending the election outcome.

2. Section 8(b)(7)(C) contains two provisos. Proviso one allows for expedited elections so long as all the pertinent procedures are followed. The necessity of these procedures is the subject of the excerpted case, *International Hod Carriers, Local 840 (Blinne Construction Co.)*, 135 N.L.R.B. 1153 (1962), where the Board analyzed the effect of employer ULPs on a union's § 8(b)(7)(C) obligation to file an election petition to trigger the expedited election. Why are these procedures so important?

Proviso two immunizes informational picketing from the bans described in subsections (A) and (B) where the picketing is for the purpose of truthfully advising the public that the picketed "employer does not employ members of, or have a contract with a labor organization" so long as the picketing does not interfere with deliveries to the targeted employer.

3. Would §8(b)(7)(C) prohibit picketing:

a. to compel an employer to comply with a collective-bargaining agreement? *Bldg. & Constr. Trades Council*, 146 N.L.R.B. 1086 (1964).

b. to protest an employee's discharge? *Local 259, Int'l U., United Automobile, Aircraft & Agricultural Implement Workers of Am.*, 133 N.L.R.B. 1468 (1961).

c. to protest the employer's use of "scabs" and unfair treatment, where the union's lawyer indicated to the employer that "picketing would cease if the Employer hired employees directly or entered into an agreement with a delivery service whose employees were represented by" the union? *Newspaper & Mail Deliverers (Macromedia Pub.)*, 289 NLRB 537 (1988).

4. Would an employee-striker who picketed in violation of §8(b)(7) be entitled to reinstatement? *See, e.g., Motor Freight Drivers Local 707 (Claremont Polychem. Corp.)*, 196 N.L.R.B. 613, 614 (1972) (no).

Chapter 13

Grievance Arbitration

I. Introduction

Grievance arbitration is a continuation of the collective-bargaining process: interpreting and enforcing the rules in the negotiated contract that bargaining produced. It is a vitally important part of the day-to-day practice of labor law in the private and public sectors.

Section II of this chapter consists of secondary materials describing the nature of grievance-arbitration and how the arbitrator's role differs from the role of a judge. Section III contains the "Steelworkers Trilogy," the Supreme Court decisions which have greatly limited the role of courts in disturbing arbitrators' interpretations of collective-bargaining agreements. Section IV discusses courts' limited authority to overturn private-sector arbitration awards because they are purportedly contrary to public policy. In contrast, some public-sector jurisdictions give courts broader authority to set aside arbitral awards for this reason. Section V describes the limited circumstances under which courts may issue injunctions to protect, but not block, arbitration. Section VI examines arbitration's preemption of employees' state employment law claims. Section VII explores some special issues in the public sector.

II. Grievance Arbitration

A. Overview of the Grievance-Arbitration Process

Disputes over the rights and obligations arising under a collective-bargaining agreement (CBA) are typically disputes over contract language. In general, arbitrators are the main source of authority in such disputes, leaving only a limited role for courts and an even more limited role for the NLRB.

CBAs typically contain grievance-arbitration clauses, which establish the procedures that aggrieved workers (grievants), union representatives, and management officials must follow to resolve disputes arising under the CBA. Those clauses can be written to encompass any dispute arising under the CBA, or more narrowly tailored to exclude certain topics.

Grievance and arbitration proceedings are much more informal than judicial proceedings. The typical grievance-arbitration clause requires the grievant, union representatives, and management officials to follow several grievance steps prior to arbitration. The grievance steps are internal, and typically involve one or more meetings with the grievant's supervisor or a management representative with authority to settle the dispute. These internal grievance steps typically have built-in appeals at each level.

To illustrate, a grievance-arbitration clause might look something like this:

Grievances must proceed along the following steps:

Step One: The grievant or the Union shall present the grievance to the immediate supervisor, in writing, within ten (10) business days following the date on which the aggrieved party or the Union representative had knowledge of the facts giving rise to the grievance. A management representative shall answer the grievance in writing within ten business days following the date on which the grievance was presented.

Step Two: Absent resolution of the grievance at *Step One*, the grievant or the Union, within ten (10) business days of the Step One answer, may present the grievance in writing to the Manager of the shop for which the employee is working. A management representative shall answer the grievance in writing within ten business days following the date on which the grievance was presented.

Step Three: Absent resolution of the grievance at *Step Two*, the grievant or the Union, within ten (10) business days of the Step Two answer, may present the grievance in writing to the Vice President of Human Resources. A management representative shall answer the grievance in writing within twenty business days following the date on which the grievance was presented.

In addition to the time limits and other procedural requirements in the grievance clause, the steps may also provide for ways in which management and union representatives might meet to discuss the grievance. Such meetings give an opportunity for grievants to air their side of the story verbally and allow for flexible resolution of workplace disputes. Following these mandatory steps is known as "exhausting contractual grievance remedies."

The grievance-arbitration clause will also typically establish the procedure for referring a grievance to binding arbitration. An arbitration clause might look something like this:

If a grievance is not resolved at the final step of the grievance procedures as set forth in this Agreement, the Union may refer the grievance to arbitration by giving written notice to the Vice President of Human Resources within twenty (20) business days following receipt of the *Step Three* final grievance decision.

The arbitration clause read together with the grievance clause makes clear that the grievant must exhaust remedies before electing to go to arbitration. But the clause does not compel the union to take all grievances to arbitration.

The grievance-arbitration clause may also detail how an arbitrator is selected. In some industries, master agreements provide permanent arbitrators appointed for a fixed term. More commonly, an arbitrator is selected from lists provided by the Federal Mediation and Conciliation Service (FMCS) or American Arbitration Association (AAA). The agreement may specify that such arbitrators be members of the National Academy of Arbitrators.

B. Arbitration Issues

The FMCS tracks the types of issues that its arbitrators hear in settling contractual disputes. According to its 2018 Annual Report, those issues included disputes over discharge and discipline, seniority, wage increases, overtime pay, healthcare and retirement benefits, flex-time, whistleblower complaints, subcontracting, jurisdictional disputes, supervision, job posting, evaluation or classification, and arbitrability. 2018 FMCS ANNUAL REPORT, *available at* https://www.fmcs.gov/wp-content/uploads/2019/08/2018-FMCS-Annual-Report.pdf. The following sections explore some of those issues.

1. Just Cause

"Few things are more significant to employees than limitations on their employer's power to discipline or discharge them." Roger Abrams & Dennis Nolan, *Toward a Theory of "Just Cause" in Employee Discipline Cases*, 1985 DUKE L.J. 594, 594 (1985). According to the FMCS's 2008 Annual Report, 38.6 percent of all cases brought to an FMCS arbitrator that year concerned discipline and discharge questions, making that the largest category of disputes brought. *See* 61 FMCS 8–9. A typical CBA limits the employer's power to discipline or discharge its workers by requiring employers to use "just cause" when exercising those powers. Because "[j]ust cause is hardly an obvious concept," its meaning is often in part subject to an arbitrator's discretion. Abrams & Nolan, *supra*, at 595–96 (concluding that most arbitration awards can be understood as consistent with the authors' theory of just cause).

Roger I. Abrams & Dennis R. Nolan, *Toward a Theory of "Just Cause" in Employee Discipline Cases*

1985 DUKE L.J. 594 (1985)[*]

. . .

II. The Fundamental Understanding

. . . This fundamental understanding of the employment relationship can be easily summarized: both parties realize that the employer must pay the agreed wages and benefits and that the employee must do "satisfactory" work. "Satisfactory"

---

work, in this context, has four elements: (1) regular attendance, (2) obedience to reasonable work rules, (3) a reasonable quantity and quality of work, and (4) avoidance of any conduct that would interfere with the employer's ability to operate the business successfully. . . .

A collective agreement incorporates the fundamental understanding, but also provides it with sufficient detail that it properly can be termed a bargain. The result is likely to be more balanced than the fundamental understanding itself. For example, the agreement may carefully define the quantity and type of work required, and it almost certainly will spell out in some detail the benefits employees are to receive.

For the employees, the most important effect of the collective agreement is the correction of what they perceive to be the major flaw of the fundamental understanding—the insecurity of the relationship. . . . Because the fundamental understanding is limited to the exchange of money for work done, either side may terminate the relationship at will. . . . This usually presents little problem for employers, but for employees with continuing obligations and limited alternatives it can be devastating. Thus, the main addition to the fundamental understanding that unions seek in collective agreements is job security. Occasionally unions achieve this by negotiating an explicit guarantee of work. . . . More frequently, the agreements provide partial job security by instituting a seniority system. . . . More frequently still, the agreement protects job security by limiting the employer's power to discipline and discharge. . . .

It is impractical for negotiators to spell out every possible offense that would allow an employer to discharge or discipline an employee. In fact, negotiators seldom attempt to include such a comprehensive list in the agreement. Instead they agree that discipline may be imposed only for "just cause" or some similar term. . . . Thus, the fundamental understanding, as amended in the collective bargaining agreement, can be stated as follows: employees will provide "satisfactory" work, in return for which the employer will pay the agreed wages and benefits, and will continue the employment relationship unless there is just cause to terminate it.

Just cause is obviously not a precise concept. It cannot be applied to a particular dispute by an employer or an arbitrator without analysis and the exercise of judgment. . . . There will never be a simple definition of "just cause," nor even a consensus on its application to specific cases, but this does not mean the phrase is devoid of meaning. On the contrary, it is possible to make sense of the term and to give it substance. This can be done by viewing the just cause standard as an amended form of the fundamental understanding. Just cause, in other words, embodies the idea that the employee is entitled to continued employment, provided he attends work regularly, obeys work rules, performs at some reasonable level of quality and quantity, and refrains from interfering with his employer's business by his activities on or off the job. An employee's failure to meet these obligations will justify discipline. . . .

The nature and severity of the employee's offense, among other things, will determine what form of discipline is appropriate. A small departure from "satisfactory" work may result in a verbal or written warning. . . . A more serious or repeated offense may produce a suspension without pay. . . . In an extreme case, the employer may be justified in discharging an employee. . . . The employee may protest the discipline through the contractual grievance procedure. If the parties fail to resolve the grievance, the union may take the case to an impartial arbitrator for final and binding resolution. The question for the arbitrator is whether the employee's conduct constituted a sufficiently serious breach of his obligation under the fundamental understanding to warrant the discipline imposed. . . .

III. Management's Interests

Why would management discipline an employee? Whim or prejudice explain some disciplinary decisions . . . but such cases are rare. The profit motive alone discourages arbitrary discipline. . . .

Most discipline is imposed for more rational purposes. There are at least three possible motivations for employee discipline: (1) rehabilitation, (2) deterrence, which may be either specific or general, and (3) protection of profitability. . . .

The just cause standard precludes one common objective for discipline — retribution. Management may not discipline an employee merely to punish him for his transgressions. Indeed, it has no economic interest in doing so. Individual managers may desire retribution, but a business entity has no legitimate interest beyond productivity and profitability

All of the legitimate management interests in discipline are consistent with the fundamental understanding. Rehabilitation and specific deterrence are aimed at improving the transgressing employee's work. General deterrence serves to reinforce the work rules which all employees must observe if the business is to prosper. Finally, protection of profitability justifies prohibition of conduct that harms the employer's business relations.

IV. The Union's Interests

What does a union seek in a discharge or discipline case? A cynic might argue that the union's goal is unqualified job security. Like the extreme management ideal of unlimited discretion, such a union goal cannot be considered legitimate; nor does it reflect true union interests. A union cannot reasonably expect management to carry on its employment rolls someone who has breached the fundamental understanding. A union may certainly question the extent to which a particular instance of employee conduct may harm productivity, but it must acknowledge that an employee's failure to meet his obligations works to the detriment of other employees as well as the employer. In the short run, an unsatisfactory employee simply makes the jobs of co-workers more difficult. In the long run, continued tolerance of substandard performance will endanger the employer's competitive position, and that, in turn, will threaten the wages and even the jobs of the rest of the workforce. The economic welfare of workers and management is interdependent.

The union's real interest in disciplinary matters is fairness. A union pursues this interest in a variety of ways. First, it seeks fairness in disciplinary procedures. For example, employees must have actual or constructive notice as to their work obligations. . . . A union also seeks fairness in the administration of discipline. Disciplinary measures must be based on facts; management must ascertain what actually occurred before it imposes discipline. . . . Management must also give the employee an opportunity to explain and must allow him union representation during the investigation, if he so requests. . . . Finally, discipline should be imposed in gradually increasing degrees. . . . These concerns for procedural fairness might be termed "industrial due process."

A union will also seek procedural fairness in the arbitration process, particularly in the allocation of the burden of proving just cause. A disciplinary grievance, like other grievances, alleges that the employer breached the collective bargaining agreement. Although the burden of proof usually rests with the party asserting the breach, the union will seek to shift the burden of proof to management when the case involves discipline. The fundamental understanding, as amended by the collective agreement, provides for continued employment *unless* there is just cause for discipline. Management, in the union's view, thus bears the burden of demonstrating just cause. . . . It has singled out an individual employee for disciplinary action or termination, it knows why it took the action, and for that reason it should bear the burden of explaining why discipline is justified.

The second way in which a union seeks "fairness" in discipline is through consistent treatment of similar cases. For example, if one employee is not punished for certain conduct, co-workers who engage in the same conduct should be treated in the same manner. Like cases should be treated alike. . . . In a disciplinary situation, a union seeks what might be termed "industrial equal protection."

Finally, a union seeks "fairness" for the disciplined individual by compelling management to consider mitigating factors. . . . Perhaps the most important of these is the employee's work record. . . . For any given offense, an employee with a long record of excellent work and no prior discipline should be treated more leniently than a junior employee with a history of unsatisfactory work and several prior offenses. . . . Other mitigating factors may be tied to the particular offense. If two employees have been fighting, the aggressor deserves more severe discipline than the victim. . . . In appropriate cases, an employee's attitude, demeanor, and other personal factors might warrant mitigation of the penalty. . . .

Thus both management and union interests in discipline are consistent with the fundamental understanding. The next question is whether the interests are consistent with each other. If so, a theory of just cause premised on the fundamental understanding can be developed and applied, without sacrificing the objectives of either party.

V. The Congruence of Management and Union Interests

. . . In order to establish just cause for disciplinary action, management must first show that its interests were significantly affected by the employee's conduct. For instance, when an employee has been discharged for violating a work rule, management may show that the employee's prior conduct demonstrates he is unlikely to fulfill the obligations of his job in the future. . . . Alternatively, management may show that even though the employee is unlikely to repeat the wrongful conduct, it is important to deter other employees from such conduct and that discharge is the only effective form of deterrence. Either of these two explanations would establish a prima facie showing of just cause. In order to rebut this showing of just cause, a union must prove that management failed to give the employee industrial due process or industrial equal protection, or failed to consider mitigating factors. For example, the union may show that management took disciplinary action without adequate investigation, or singled out the employee for discipline when others had been excused for the same conduct, or ignored mitigating circumstances such as illness or provocation.

Union and management interests are fundamentally congruent, though it may not seem so to the parties. Management's objective of productive efficiency is served by industrial due process. For example, it is in the employer's interest to give employees adequate notice of their obligations. If a company wants employees to meet their performance obligations, it must, at the very least, let them know what those obligations are. Similarly, management's objective of productive efficiency is served by investigating the facts of a case before imposing discipline. A wrongful accusation undermines the integrity of the disciplinary system, creates resentment, and, in a discharge case, deprives management of a satisfactory employee, while imposing on it the costs of obtaining and training a replacement. Just as employees must know that when they fulfill their obligations they will not be disciplined, employees must also know that when they fail, they will be disciplined—but proportionately and equally. Thus, management benefits by responding to the union's interest in industrial due process. . . .

Management's desire for efficiency is also congruent with the union's interest in individualized treatment of employees through consideration of mitigating circumstances. This congruency, however, is not obvious. The consideration of mitigating circumstances does not detract from management's interest in productive efficiency. For example, consider the employee fired for poor attendance. Though his recent attendance violates standards, his long and productive work record may indicate that he is capable of performing the essential responsibilities of his job in the future and that his wrongful conduct was atypical. In such a case, management's interest in productive efficiency might actually be furthered by retention of the employee combined with efforts to cure the problem. On the other hand, consider the employee who is fired for striking his supervisor, a "mortal sin" in the workplace. In such a case, a long and satisfactory work record should not mitigate his discharge. The broken rule is so important that firing even a senior employee can be justified as a necessary deterrent for other workers.

VI. A Theory of Just Cause

. . . From this congruence, a theory of just cause can be derived, a theory which accommodates the parties' needs and reflects their mutual understanding.

A. Just cause for discipline exists only when an employee has failed to meet his obligations under the fundamental understanding of the employment relationship. The employee's general obligation is to provide satisfactory work. Satisfactory work has four components:

1. Regular attendance.

2. Obedience to reasonable work rules.

3. A reasonable quality and quantity of work.

4. Avoidance of conduct, either at or away from work, which would interfere with the employer's ability to carry on the business effectively.

B. For there to be just cause, the discipline must further one or more of management's three legitimate interests:

1. Rehabilitation of a potentially satisfactory employee.

2. Deterrence of similar conduct, either by the disciplined employee or by other employees.

3. Protection of the employer's ability to operate the business successfully.

C. The concept of just cause includes certain employee protections that reflect the union's interest in guaranteeing "fairness" in disciplinary situations.

1. The employee is entitled to *industrial due process.* This includes:

   a. actual or constructive notice of expected standards of conduct and penalties for wrongful conduct;

   b. a decision based on facts, determined after an investigation that provides the employee an opportunity to state his case, with union assistance if he desires it;

   c. the imposition of discipline in gradually increasing degrees, except in cases involving the most extreme breaches of the fundamental understanding. In particular, discharge may be imposed only when less severe penalties will not protect legitimate management interests, for one of the following reasons: (1) the employee's past record shows that the unsatisfactory conduct will continue, (2) the most stringent form of discipline is needed to protect the system of work rules, or (3) continued employment would inevitably interfere with the successful operation of the business; and

   d. proof by management that just cause exists.

2. The employee is entitled to *industrial equal protection,* which requires like treatment of like cases.

3. The employee is entitled to *individualized treatment.* Distinctive facts in the employee's record or regarding the reason for discipline must be given appropriate weight.

Notes

1. Just-cause discipline and discharge grievances and arbitrations are a significant part of the practice of labor law on the union and employer sides. Do you agree that both sides have congruent interests in just-cause rules? Might certain types of cases be exceptions for the union? Might certain types of cases be exceptions for employers?

2. While many CBAs simply require "just cause" for all discipline or discharge, many have more specific rules. For example, some specifically state that certain offenses either may or must be cause for discharge (*e.g.*, a clause stating that illegal drug use or sleeping on the job "shall be cause for discharge"). Some require progressive discipline (discipline short of discharge) for certain types of offenses, or as a default rule for discipline generally. If you were representing an employer, what types of specific rules might you want to craft? If you were representing a union?

3. One option in discipline (or in an arbitral award) is the "last chance" agreement. In these cases generally, the employer has discharged the employee for a serious offense, and the employee admits to the offense (or the arbitrator finds the offense occurred as charged). The employer then agrees to rescind the discharge on the condition that if the employee repeats the offense, the employee and union waive the right to contest the discharge. In what types of cases might such agreements be used in a way that serves the interests of both sides?

Problem 13.1

Honey Soit makes keys for MalDePense, Inc. Soit is a long-time employee with a good work record and no previous discipline. The CBA that covers Soit has a standard just cause clause for discipline and discharge, including the following two clauses: (1) "Possession of, or being under the influence of drugs, will result in immediate disciplinary action, up to and including discharge"; and (2) "Punishment is a last resort to be used only when all other corrective action has failed. Seriousness of the offense and the employee's past record will be considered in determining discipline." In addition to the CBA language, the employer has posted signs stating that drug use is strictly forbidden at MalDePense.

Soit was caught twice, on consecutive days, smoking marijuana in a company break room. While there was no evidence that she was too impaired to do her job, she did initially deny that she committed both infractions.

The employer discharged Soit, the union grieved, and the case is now at arbitration. What would you argue if you represented the employer? If you represented the union? Also, are there any additional facts you would like to know? *See Mallinckrodt, Inc.* 83-2 CCH Arb. ¶ 8358 (Arb. Seidman 1983).

2. Seniority

Unions typically attempt to negotiate clauses that make seniority a significant factor in a variety of contexts, including but not limited to layoffs, recalls, promotions, and choice of work assignments. For example, a typical clause provides that in promotion decisions, when all other factors are at least roughly equal, the promotion will go to the more senior employee.

In re Stroh Die Casting Company and International Association of Machinists

FMCS Case No. 09/60928 February 4, 2010

DITCHER, ARBITRATOR

The parties agreed upon the following issue: Did the Employer violate the agreement when it laid off Union Committeemen in the Tool Room Department prior to Journeymen Tool and Die Makers? If so, what is the appropriate remedy?

Stroh Die Casting, hereinafter referred to as the Employer, operated a die casting business in Milwaukee, Wisconsin. District 10 of the Machinists Union, hereinafter referred to as the Union has represented the employees at the facility. . . . The Parties had a Collective Bargaining Agreement that ran from February 19, 2005-February 19, 2008. . . .

A successor Agreement was then negotiated by the Parties. It took effect on April 19, 2009. That was the Agreement in effect when the Grievances arose.

The Employer in February of 2009 determined that it needed to lay off a substantial number of its employees. . . . Article IV, Section 2(b) of the Agreement addressed layoffs. It states:

(b) Reduction in Force Procedure

4. Layoffs shall be made by job classification within the department. An employee so laid off may bump an employee in a department with less seniority if the employee had the obvious ability to perform the work without training and trial if the "bump" is to a higher-rated job classification.

One of the Departments affected by the layoffs was the Tool Room. There are two classifications in the Tool Room, Journeymen Tool and Die Makers and Tool Room Machinists & Die Repairmen. There were prior to the layoffs four Journeymen Tool and Die Makers and three Machinists. All three Machinists were laid off on April 27, 2009. These layoffs included the two Grievants. The four Journeymen were retained for a short period of time. . . .

Article IX is entitled "Union Matters." Under Section 1 of that Article the Union s permitted to have up to "four (4) committee members." Section 1 then states:

. . . Shop committee persons of the union, not to exceed four (4) in number, shall head the seniority list in their respective departments during their respective terms in office, and when their terms expire and they are succeeded by others, they will again be placed in their regular position on the seniority list. . . .

The two Grievants were both committeemen at the time they were laid off. The Union filed a grievance alleging that their layoffs violated Article IX, Section 1.

There are really two issues before the Arbitrator. First it must be determined whether the layoff of the Grievants violated Article IX. To answer that question the interplay between Articles IV and IX must be discussed. If it is determined Article IX was violated, then the next question is whether there were any damages as a result of the violation. . . .

Article IV sets forth generally the procedures to be followed when there is a layoff. Layoffs are by seniority by job classification within a department. Section 2(c) 4 of the Article lists the Departments. The Tool Room is listed as one of those departments. There are two classifications in the Tool Room. Thus, pursuant to Article IV the junior person in a classification is laid off. The Employer would be free to layoff all of the employees in one classification without any layoffs in the other. It could layoff all of the Machinists and retain all of the Journeymen. That would be true of all Departments. Interestingly, the prior agreement listed a separate procedure for the Tool Room. A formula was established as to how many in each classification could be laid off as more and more layoffs occurred. That provision was eliminated in the present agreement. This meant the general procedure set forth in Section 2(b) applied to them as well.

If Article IV were the only Article impacted here then the layoffs of the Grievants would unquestionably be in accordance with the provisions of the Agreement. Of course, it is not that simple. Grievants were Committeemen and a separate Article addresses their rights. Grievants as Committeemen are granted super-seniority. Many Agreements have such a provision. It gives superior rights to those employees who are acting on behalf of their fellow employees. Under the Super-seniority provision in this Agreement, the Stewards or Committeemen "head the seniority list in their respective departments." That meant for the seven employees that worked in the Tool Room prior to the layoffs, Grievants were one and two on the seniority list. There are no exceptions listed in the Section. Article IV does mention that employees who seek to bump other employees must "have the ability to perform the work," but this limitation is not in Article IX and there is no bumping involved here. It is the right to retain the position that is issue not the right to bump and Article IX gave that right to the Grievants.

The Arbitrator can find nothing in the Agreement that would allow the Employer to by-pass the Grievants super-seniority and lay them off. Whether they could do the remaining work or not is not an issue in Article IX. It says clearly they are at the top of the seniority list in their Department, not just their classification but the whole Department. Contrary to the assertion of the Employer, the Department did not cease operating following the Grievants layoffs. The Tool Room continued. It may very well be the character of the room changed as the scope of work changed, but it was still the Tool Room. As such, Grievants were at the top of the seniority list. The Arbitrator, therefore, finds the Employer violated the Agreement when it laid off the Grievants before it laid off the Journeymen.

The Employer has argued if it were required to keep the Grievants in lieu of the Journeymen it would simply have closed the Tool Room and farmed out the work. The Grievants maintained they could and did do the work that remained. The Arbitrator has no way of knowing if that is so or not. However, it is clear they were not given the chance to prove or disprove their claim. . . .

The Employer next argues Grievants failed to mitigate their damages by refusing to exercise their bumping rights. The Employer asserts that even if they had less seniority than other employees they still could bump using their super-seniority. The Unions counters by arguing the employees lose their super-seniority when going to another Department. . . .

Grievants' layoff rights under the Agreement were violated. Mitigation for back pay purposes generally is raised in cases involving discharge for alleged cause. This was not such a case. Nevertheless certain principles still apply as to when it is required and when it is not. As the Union noted the question of when an employee must mitigate is addressed in Elkouri and Elkouri. The Sixth Edition at p. 1227 provides: "Furthermore, the employee may not be required to accept unsuitable or lower rated work during the pendency of the appeal."

The Employer observed in its argument one of the reasons the Grievants did not want to bump to another job was it paid less. It did not believe this was a valid reason to decline the opportunity. In actuality, it is. The jobs in the Department into which they could bump are lower in pay. In addition, the character of the work was arguably "unsuitable" as it was totally different from the work they did. Grievants indicated they would be uncomfortable doing the type of work they would have been required to do if they bumped. That is a valid concern. The Arbitrator finds Grievants were not required to bump into a lower rated position and were not guilty of failing to mitigate their damages. . . . The Grievance is sustained.

Notes

1. Are the interests of the employer and the union "congruent" in a case like this? What about in other cases in which more senior employees are given preferences?

2. This case involved rules that give extra seniority preference to union stewards, but unions generally try to negotiate rules that give preferences to more senior employees regardless of whether that gives union officials any advantages. Given that unions represent more senior and less senior employees, why do unions do that?

3. Past Practice

Rules for interpreting CBAs under the NLRA can diverge from rules for interpreting other types of contracts under general contract law. One of the most important distinctive features of interpreting labor contracts is the use of past practice.

Richard Mittenthal, *Past Practice and the Administration of Collective Bargaining Agreements*
59 Mich. L. Rev. 1017 (1961)[*]

. . . In [*United Steel Workers of America v. Warrior & Gulf Navigation Co.*, 363 U.S. 574, 581–82 (1960)], Justice Douglas of the United States Supreme Court recently stated that "the labor arbitrator's source of law is not confined to the express provisions of the contract, as the industrial common law—the past practices of the industry and the shop—is equally a part of the collective bargaining agreement although not expressed in it." . . . The purpose of this paper is to examine in depth one of the more important standards upon which . . . many of our decisions are based—past practice. Custom and practice profoundly influence every area of human activity. . . . It is hardly surprising, therefore, to find that past practice in an industrial plant plays a significant role in the administration of the collective agreement.

Past practice is one of the most useful and hence one of the most commonly used aids in resolving grievance disputes. It can help the arbitrator in a variety of ways in interpreting the agreement. It may be used to clarify what is ambiguous, to give substance to what is general, and perhaps even to modify or amend what is seemingly unambiguous. It may also, apart from any basis in the agreement, be used to establish a separate, enforceable condition of employment.

The Nature of a Practice

. . . Although the conception of what constitutes a practice differs from one employer to another and from one union to another, there are certain characteristics which typify most practices. . . . For example, in the steel industry, Sylvester Garrett [Chairman, Board of Arbitration, U.S. Steel-Steelworkers] has lucidly defined a practice in these words:

> A custom or practice is not something which arises simply because a given course of conduct has been pursued by Management or the employees on one or more occasions. A custom or a practice is a usage evolved by men as a normal reaction to a recurring type situation. It must be shown to be the *accepted* course of conduct characteristically repeated in response to the given set of underlying circumstances. This is not to say that the course of conduct must be *accepted* in the sense of both parties having agreed to it, but rather that it must be *accepted* in the sense of being regarded by the men involved as the *normal* and *proper* response to the underlying circumstances presented.

In short, something qualifies as a practice if it is shown to be the understood and accepted way of doing things over an extended period of time. What qualities must a course of conduct have before it can legitimately be regarded as a practice?

---

[*] Copyright 1961. Reprinted by permission.

First, there should be *clarity* and *consistency*. A course of conduct which is vague and ambiguous or which has been contradicted as often as it has been followed can hardly qualify as a practice. But where those in the plant invariably respond in the same way to a particular set of conditions, their conduct may very well ripen into a practice.

Second, there should be *longevity* and *repetition*. A period of time has to elapse during which a consistent pattern of behavior emerges. Hence, one or two isolated instances of a certain conduct do not establish a practice. . . .

Third, there should be *acceptability*. The employees and the supervisors alike must have knowledge of the particular conduct and must regard it as the correct and customary means of handling a situation. Such acceptability may frequently be implied from long acquiescence in a known course of conduct. . . .

And, finally, the significance to be attributed to a practice may possibly be affected by whether or not it is supported by *mutuality*. Some practices are the product, either in their inception or in their application, of a joint understanding; others develop from choices made by the employer in the exercise of its managerial discretion without any intention of a future commitment.

Functions of Past Practice

Clarifying Ambiguous Language

The danger of ambiguity arises not only from the English language . . . but also from the nature of the collective bargaining agreement. The agreement is a means of governing "complex, many-sided relations between large numbers of people in a going concern for very substantial periods of time." . . . It is seldom written with the kind of precision and detail which characterize other legal instruments. Although it covers a great variety of subjects, many of which are quite complicated, it must be simply written so that its terms can be understood by the employees and their supervisors. . . . Issues are often settled by a general formula because the negotiators recognize they could not possibly foresee or provide for the many contingencies which are bound to occur during the life of the agreement. . . .

These characteristics inevitably cause portions of the agreement to be expressed in ambiguous and general terms. With the passage of time, however, this language may be given a clear and practical construction, either through managerial action which is acquiesced in by the employees (or, conceivably, employee action which is acquiesced in by management) or through the resolution of disputes on a case-by-case basis. This accumulation of plant experience results in the development of practices and procedures of varying degrees of consistency and force. . . .

Implementing General Contract Language

Practice is also a means of implementing general contract language. In areas which cannot be made specific, the parties are often satisfied to state a general rule and to allow the precise meaning of the rule to develop through the day-to-day administration of the agreement.

For instance, the right to discipline and discharge is usually conditioned upon the existence of "just cause." Similarly, the right to deviate from a contract requirement may be conditioned upon the existence of "circumstances beyond the employer's control." . . .

But, in time, this kind of general language does tend to become more concrete. As the parties respond to the many different situations confronting them—approving certain principles and procedures, disputing others, and resolving their disputes in the grievance procedure—they find mutually acceptable ways of doing things which serve to guide them in future cases. Instead of rearguing every matter without regard to their earlier experiences, acceptable principles and procedures are applied again and again. . . .

Suppose, for example, that tardiness of less than five minutes has always been overlooked but that after it becomes extremely widespread, management disciplines a few employees without any advance notice of its change in policy. In view of this long toleration of tardiness, it is doubtful that there would be "just cause" for discipline. Plant practice thus injects something tangible into the "just cause" provision, giving employees a clear notion of what is acceptable and unacceptable in plant behavior. Of course, once the men are notified that tardiness will no longer be ignored the employer would be free to take reasonable disciplinary action. . . .

Duration and Termination of a Practice

Once the parties become bound by a practice, they may wonder how long it will be binding and how it can be terminated. . . .

It is a well-settled principle that where past practice has established a meaning for language that is subsequently used in an agreement, the language will be presumed to have the meaning given it by practice. Thus, this kind of practice can only be terminated by mutual agreement, that is, by the parties rewriting the ambiguous provision to supersede the practice, by eliminating the provision entirely, etc. . . .

Notes

1. Past practice is often used to establish the meaning of ambiguous contract provisions or even to establish certain rules on subjects where the CBA is silent. Arbitrators should not, however, use past practice to glean rules that are contrary to the explicit language of a CBA. *See* FRANK ELKOURI & EDNA ELKOURI, HOW ARBITRATION WORKS 651–54 (5th ed. 1997).

2. Based on this article, what types of past practices by an employer should be enforceable as incorporated into a CBA where the CBA is silent on the matter? A ten-year tradition of having two employees work a machine at all times? A three-year tradition of giving employees a turkey on Thanksgiving? A general practice that being late less than an hour, for a first offense, merits no more than a verbal warning as discipline? What factors matter most?

3. The issue of whether past practice provides a certain right can arise in at least two distinct ways. First, during an arbitration, to help define an ambiguous term in a CBA. For example, the parties might dispute what specifically "just cause" means in a case both sides believe the union had a right to arbitrate. Second, grievances in which the union argues that past practice creates a right in an area where the specific language of the CBA is silent. In this type of case, the employer may dispute that the union has a right to arbitrate the case at all and may refuse to arbitrate. This second situation is discussed further, *infra*.

III. Court Intervention in Private-Sector Grievance-Arbitration

A. General Rules Under § 301

Disputes over the rights and obligations arising under a CBA can jeopardize industrial peace and cause obstructions to commerce. To minimize this problem, Congress included § 301 in the Taft-Hartley amendments to the NLRA. Section 301 of the Taft-Hartley Act provides:

(a) Suits for violation of contracts between an employer and a labor organization representing employees in an industry affecting commerce as defined in this chapter, or between any such labor organizations, may be brought in any district court of the United States having jurisdiction of the parties, without respect to the amount in controversy or without regard to the citizenship of the parties.

(b) Any labor organization which represents employees in an industry affecting commerce as defined in this chapter and any employer whose activities affect commerce as defined in this chapter shall be bound by the acts of its agents. Any such labor organization may sue or be sued as an entity and in behalf of the employees whom it represents in the courts of the United States. Any money judgment against a labor organization in a district court of the United States shall be enforceable only against the organization as an entity and against its assets, and shall not be enforceable against any individual member or his assets.

Prior to § 301, unions did not have legal status under federal law and were not legal entities, with the capacity to sue or be sued, in most state fora. Section 301, as interpreted by the Supreme Court in the following case and in the Steelworkers Trilogy, *infra*, cured these problems by granting legal status to unions, conferring subject-matter jurisdiction on federal courts to hear disputes arising under collective-bargaining agreements, and solving the question of what law should be applied in these cases. The final sentence of § 301(b) was designed to avoid the problem of union members being personally liable for a union's unlawful acts: recall

Loewe v. Lawlor, 208 U.S. 274 (1908) (the "Danbury Hatters Case"), discussed in Chapter 1.

Textile Workers Union of America v. Lincoln Mills of Alabama

Supreme Court of the United States

353 U.S. 448 (1957)

Douglas, J.

Petitioner-union [and Respondent-employer] entered into a collective bargaining agreement in 1953 . . . to run . . . year to year . . . unless terminated on specified notices. The agreement provided that there would be no strikes or work stoppages and that grievances would be handled pursuant to a specified procedure. The last step in the grievance procedure—a step that could be taken by either party—was arbitration.

This controversy involves several grievances that concern work loads and work assignments. The grievances were processed through the various steps in the grievance procedure and were finally denied by the employer. The union requested arbitration, and the employer refused. Thereupon the union brought this suit in the District Court to compel arbitration.

The District Court concluded that it had jurisdiction and ordered the employer to comply with the grievance arbitration provisions of the collective bargaining agreement. The Court of Appeals reversed by a divided vote. . . .

There has been considerable litigation involving § 301 and courts have construed it differently. There is one view that § 301(a) merely gives federal district courts jurisdiction in controversies that involve labor organizations in industries affecting commerce, without regard to diversity of citizenship or the amount in controversy. Under that view § 301(a) would not be the source of substantive law; it would neither supply federal law to resolve these controversies nor turn the federal judges to state law for answers to the questions. Other courts . . . hold that § 301(a) is more than jurisdictional—that it authorizes federal courts to fashion a body of federal law for the enforcement of these collective bargaining agreements and includes within that federal law specific performance of promises to arbitrate grievances under collective bargaining agreements. . . . That is our construction of § 301(a), which means that the agreement to arbitrate grievance disputes, contained in this collective bargaining agreement, should be specifically enforced.

From the face of the Act it is apparent that § 301(a) and § 301(b) supplement one another. Section 301(b) makes it possible for a labor organization, representing employees in an industry affecting commerce, to sue and be sued as an entity in the federal courts. Section 301(b) in other words provides the procedural remedy lacking at common law. Section 301(a) certainly does something more than that. Plainly, it supplies the basis upon which the federal district courts may take jurisdiction and apply the procedural rule of §301(b). The question is whether §301(a) is more than jurisdictional.

The legislative history of §301 is somewhat cloudy and confusing. But there are a few shafts of light that illuminate our problem.

The bills, as they passed the House and the Senate, contained provisions which would have made the failure to abide by an agreement to arbitrate an unfair labor practice. . . . This feature of the law was dropped in Conference. As the Conference Report stated, "Once parties have made a collective bargaining contract, the enforcement of that contract should be left to the usual processes of the law and not to the [NLRB]." . . .

Both the Senate and the House took pains to provide for "the usual processes of the law" by provisions which were the substantial equivalent of §301(a) in its present form. Both the Senate Report and the House Report indicate a primary concern that unions as well as employees should be bound to collective bargaining contracts. But there was also a broader concern—a concern with a procedure for making such agreements enforceable in the courts by either party.

. . . Congress was also interested in promoting collective bargaining that ended with agreements not to strike. The Senate Report states:

> "If unions can break agreements with relative impunity, then such agreements do not tend to stabilize industrial relations. The execution of an agreement does not by itself promote industrial peace. The chief advantage which an employer can reasonably expect from a collective labor agreement is assurance of uninterrupted operation during the term of the agreement. Without some effective method of assuring freedom from economic warfare for the term of the agreement, there is little reason why an employer would desire to sign such a contract.

> "Consequently, to encourage the making of agreements and to promote industrial peace through faithful performance by the parties, collective agreements affecting interstate commerce should be enforceable in the Federal courts. Our amendment would provide for suits by unions as legal entities and against unions as legal entities in the Federal courts in disputes affecting commerce."

Thus collective bargaining contracts were made "equally binding and enforceable on both parties." . . . [T]he Senate Report . . . summed up the philosophy of §301 as follows: "Statutory recognition of the collective agreement as a valid, binding, and enforceable contract is a logical and necessary step. It will promote a higher degree of responsibility upon the parties to such agreements, and will thereby promote industrial peace."

Plainly the agreement to arbitrate grievance disputes is the quid pro quo for an agreement not to strike. Viewed in this light, the legislation does more than confer jurisdiction in the federal courts over labor organizations. It expresses a federal policy that federal courts should enforce these agreements on behalf of or against labor organizations and that industrial peace can be best obtained only in that way. . . .

The question then is, what is the substantive law to be applied in suits under § 301(a)? We conclude that the substantive law to apply in suits under § 301(a) is federal law, which the courts must fashion from the policy of our national labor laws. . . . The Labor Management Relations Act expressly furnishes some substantive law. It points out what the parties may or may not do in certain situations. Other problems will lie in the penumbra of express statutory mandates. Some will lack express statutory sanction but will be solved by looking at the policy of the legislation and fashioning a remedy that will effectuate that policy. The range of judicial inventiveness will be determined by the nature of the problem. . . . Federal interpretation of the federal law will govern, not state law. . . . But state law, if compatible with the purpose of § 301, may be resorted to in order to find the rule that will best effectuate the federal policy. . . . Any state law applied, however, will be absorbed as federal law and will not be an independent source of private rights.

It is not uncommon for federal courts to fashion federal law where federal rights are concerned. . . . Congress has indicated by § 301(a) the purpose to follow that course here. There is no constitutional difficulty. . . .

The question remains whether jurisdiction to compel arbitration of grievance disputes is withdrawn by the Norris-LaGuardia Act. . . . Section 7 of that Act prescribes stiff procedural requirements for issuing an injunction in a labor dispute. The kinds of acts which had given rise to abuse of the power to enjoin are listed in § 4. The failure to arbitrate was not a part and parcel of the abuses against which the Act was aimed. Section 8 of the Norris-LaGuardia Act does, indeed, indicate a congressional policy toward settlement of labor disputes by arbitration, for it denies injunctive relief to any person who has failed to make "every reasonable effort" to settle the dispute by negotiation, mediation, or "voluntary arbitration." Though a literal reading might bring the dispute within the terms of the Act . . . we see no justification in policy for restricting § 301(a) to damage suits, leaving specific performance of a contract to arbitrate grievance disputes to the inapposite procedural requirements of that Act. . . . The congressional policy in favor of the enforcement of agreements to arbitrate grievance disputes being clear, there is no reason to submit them to the requirements of § 7 of the Norris-LaGuardia Act. . . .

[The concurring opinion of BURTON, J., joined by HARLAN, J. and the dissenting opinion of FRANKFURTER, J., are omitted.]

Notes

1. In *Dowd Box Co. v. Courtney*, 368 U.S. 502 (1962), the Supreme Court further held that federal court jurisdiction over § 301 actions was concurrent with state court jurisdiction and therefore that § 301 actions could be brought in either federal or state court.

2. In *Smith v. Evening News Association*, 371 U.S. 195, 197 (1962), the Court explained that the "authority of the Board to deal with an ULP which also violates a collective bargaining contract is not displaced by § 301, but it is not exclusive and does not destroy the jurisdiction of the courts in suits under § 301." The court noted that concurrent jurisdiction of the Board and courts might very well raise "serious problems," but courts would "face those cases when they arise." *Id.* at 197–98. What fact patterns could lead to allegations of both ULPs and violations of a CBA? What problems might arise from concurrent jurisdiction of the Board and courts?

3. Since § 301 actions are typically breach of contract actions which would normally be governed by state law, courts had to decide what substantive law to apply. Ultimately, the Supreme Court in *Lincoln Mills* concluded that § 301 authorized federal courts to fashion a body of federal law to enforce those agreements, including the authority to order a party to arbitrate grievances. Several years later, in *Local 174, Teamsters v. Lucas Flour Co.*, 369 U.S. 95, 102 (1962), the Court held that state courts, exercising concurrent jurisdiction under § 301(a), must apply federal law. What policies do these rules promote?

What types of policies should federal law under § 301 promote? Consider the following, the first case of the "Steelworkers Trilogy."

United Steelworkers of America v. American Mfg. Co.

Supreme Court of the United States
363 U.S. 564 (1960)

DOUGLAS, J.

This suit was brought by petitioner union in the District Court to compel arbitration of a "grievance" that petitioner, acting for one Sparks, a union member, had filed with the respondent, Sparks' employer. The employer defended on the ground (1) that Sparks is estopped from making his claim because he had a few days previously settled a workmen's compensation claim against the company on the basis that he was permanently partially disabled, (2) that Sparks is not physically able to do the work, and (3) that this type of dispute is not arbitrable under the collective bargaining agreement in question.

The agreement provided that during its term there would be "no strike," unless the employer refused to abide by a decision of the arbitrator. The agreement sets out a detailed grievance procedure with a provision for arbitration (regarded as the standard form) of all disputes between the parties "as to the meaning, interpretation and application of the provisions of this agreement." [The agreement also gives the arbitrator the power to "interpret this agreement and apply it to the particular case under consideration" but not the authority to add to, subtract from, or modify the terms of the agreement."]

The agreement reserves to the management power to suspend or discharge any employee "for cause." It also contains a provision that the employer will employ and promote employees on the principle of seniority "where ability and efficiency are equal." Sparks left his work due to an injury and while off work brought an action for compensation benefits. The case was settled, Sparks' physician expressing the opinion that the injury had made him 25% "permanently partially disabled." That was on September 9. Two weeks later the union filed a grievance which charged that Sparks was entitled to return to his job by virtue of the seniority provision of the collective bargaining agreement. Respondent refused to arbitrate and this action was brought. The District Court held that Sparks, having accepted the settlement on the basis of permanent partial disability, was estopped to claim any seniority or employment rights and granted the motion for summary judgment. The Court of Appeals affirmed for different reasons. After reviewing the evidence it held that the grievance is "a frivolous, patently baseless one, not subject to arbitration under the collective bargaining agreement." . . .

Section 203(d) of the Labor Management Relations Act states, "Final adjustment by a method agreed upon by the parties is hereby declared to be the desirable method for settlement of grievance disputes arising over the application or interpretation of an existing collective-bargaining agreement. . . ." That policy can be effectuated only if the means chosen by the parties for settlement of their differences under a collective bargaining agreement is given full play.

A state decision [*International Ass'n of Machinists v. Cutler-Hammer, Inc.*, 271 App. Div. 917, aff'd 297 N.Y. 519] that held to the contrary announced a principle that could only have a crippling effect on grievance arbitration. . . . [That case] held that "If the meaning of the provision of the contract sought to be arbitrated is beyond dispute, there cannot be anything to arbitrate and the contract cannot be said to provide for arbitration." . . . The lower courts in the instant case had a like preoccupation with ordinary contract law. The collective agreement requires arbitration of claims that courts might be unwilling to entertain. In the context of the plant or industry the grievance may assume proportions of which judges are ignorant. Yet, the agreement is to submit all grievances to arbitration, not merely those that a court may deem to be meritorious. There is no exception in the "no strike" clause and none therefore should be read into the grievance clause, since one is the quid pro quo for the other. The question is not whether in the mind of the court there is equity in the claim. Arbitration is a stabilizing influence only as it serves as a vehicle for handling any and all disputes that arise under the agreement.

The collective agreement calls for the submission of grievances in the categories which it describes, irrespective of whether a court may deem them to be meritorious. In our role of developing a meaningful body of law to govern the interpretation and enforcement of collective bargaining agreements, we think special heed should be given to the context in which collective bargaining agreements are negotiated and the purpose which they are intended to serve. See *Lewis v. Benedict Coal Corp.*, 361 U.S. 459, 468. The function of the court is very limited when the parties have agreed to submit all questions of contract interpretation to the arbitrator. It is confined to ascertaining whether the party seeking arbitration is making a claim which on its face is governed by the contract. Whether the moving party is right or wrong is a question of contract interpretation for the arbitrator. In these circumstances the moving party should not be deprived of the arbitrator's judgment, when it was his judgment and all that it connotes that was bargained for.

The courts, therefore, have no business weighing the merits of the grievance, considering whether there is equity in a particular claim, or determining whether there is particular language in the written instrument which will support the claim. The agreement is to submit all grievances to arbitration, not merely those which the court will deem meritorious. The processing of even frivolous claims may have therapeutic values of which those who are not a part of the plant environment may be quite unaware.

The union claimed in this case that the company had violated a specific provision of the contract. The company took the position that it had not violated that clause. There was, therefore, a dispute between the parties as to "the meaning, interpretation and application" of the collective bargaining agreement. Arbitration should have been ordered. When the judiciary undertakes to determine the merits of a grievance under the guise of interpreting the grievance procedure of collective bargaining agreements, it usurps a function which under that regime is entrusted to the arbitration tribunal. . . . Reversed.

Notes

1. This case established the rule that employers must arbitrate properly brought grievances that allege violations of the CBA, even if substantively, the allegation clearly lacks merit. Thus, if union member Jane kills a co-worker in cold blood, an employer may not refuse to arbitrate the union's claim that this act did not constitute just cause for discharge, if the union wishes to bring such a case. Why does the Supreme Court think this is good policy? What types of incentives and disincentives do unions have in deciding whether or not to arbitrate grievances that are obviously weak on the merits?

2. The Court, 363 U.S. at 568 n.6, quoted from a law review article:

> "The typical arbitration clause is written in words which cover, without limitation, all disputes concerning the interpretation or application of a collective bargaining agreement. Its words do not restrict its scope to meritorious disputes or two-sided disputes, still less are they limited to disputes which a judge will consider two-sided. . . . What one man considers frivolous another may find meritorious, and it is common knowledge in industrial relations circles that grievance arbitration often serves as a safety valve for troublesome complaints. Under these circumstances it seems proper to read the typical arbitration clause as a promise to arbitrate every claim, meritorious or frivolous, which the complainant bases upon the contract. The objection that equity will not order a party to do a useless act is outweighed by the cathartic value of arbitrating even a frivolous grievance and by the dangers of excessive judicial intervention." Archibald Cox, *Current Problems in the Law of Grievance Arbitration*, 30 ROCKY MTN. L. REV. 247, 261 (1958).

What is the point of this passage?

3. The Supreme Court has determined that an arbitrator decides whether a dispute comes within the meaning of the CBA. The following cases examine the scope of the arbitrator's jurisdiction. Consider the following questions. As among the Board, courts, and arbitrators, who deserves the most deference in interpreting CBAs? When there are conflicting views, whose interpretation should govern? Does the answer to the latter question depend on the context in which the question of contract interpretation arose?

United Steelworkers of America v. Warrior & Gulf Navigation Co.

Supreme Court of the United States
363 U.S. 574 (1960)

DOUGLAS, J.

Respondent transports steel and steel products by barge and maintains a terminal at Chickasaw, Alabama, where it performs maintenance and repair work on its barges. The employees at that terminal constitute a bargaining unit covered by a collective bargaining agreement negotiated by petitioner union. Respondent between 1956 and 1958 laid off some employees, reducing the bargaining unit from 42 to 23 men. This reduction was due in part to respondent contracting maintenance work, previously done by its employees, to other companies. The latter used respondent's supervisors to lay out the work and hired some of the laid-off employees of respondent (at reduced wages). Some were in fact assigned to work on respondent's barges. A number of employees signed a grievance which petitioner presented to respondent, the grievance reading:

> "We are hereby protesting the Company's actions, of arbitrarily and unreasonably contracting out work to other concerns, that could and previously has been performed by Company employees.

> "This practice becomes unreasonable, unjust and discriminatory in lieu (sic) of the fact that at present there are a number of employees that have been laid off for about 1 and 1/2 years or more for allegedly lack of work.

> "Confronted with these facts we charge that the Company is in violation of the contract by inducing a partial lock-out, of a number of the employees who would otherwise be working were it not for this unfair practice."

The collective agreement had both a "no strike" and a "no lockout" provision. It also had a grievance procedure which provided in relevant part as follows:

> "Issues which conflict with any Federal statute in its application as established by Court procedure or matters which are strictly a function of management shall not be subject to arbitration under this section.

> "Should differences arise between the Company and the Union or its members employed by the Company as to the meaning and application of

the provisions of this Agreement, or should any local trouble of any kind arise, there shall be no suspension of work on account of such differences but an earnest effort shall be made to settle such differences immediately in the . . . manner [set forth in the agreement]."

Settlement of this grievance was not had and respondent refused arbitration. This suit was then commenced by the union to compel it [under § 301(a)].

The District Court granted respondent's motion to dismiss the complaint. . . . It held . . . that the agreement did not "confide in an arbitrator the right to review the defendant's business judgment in contracting out work." . . . It further held that "the contracting out of repair and maintenance work, as well as construction work, is strictly a function of management not limited in any respect by the labor agreement involved here." . . . The Court of Appeals affirmed by a divided vote, . . . the majority holding that the collective agreement had withdrawn from the grievance procedure "matters which are strictly a function of management" and that contracting out fell in that exception. . . .

We held in [*Lincoln Mills*] that a grievance arbitration provision in a collective agreement could be enforced by reason of § 301(a) . . . and that the policy to be applied in enforcing this type of arbitration was that reflected in our national labor laws. . . . The present federal policy is to promote industrial stabilization through the collective bargaining agreement [§ 8(d)]. A major factor in achieving industrial peace is the inclusion of a provision for arbitration of grievances in the collective bargaining agreement.

Thus the run of arbitration cases, illustrated by *Wilko v. Swam*, 346 U.S. 427, becomes irrelevant to our problem. There the choice is between the adjudication of cases or controversies in courts with established procedures or even special statutory safeguards on the one hand and the settlement of them in the more informal arbitration tribunal on the other. In the commercial case, arbitration is the substitute for litigation. Here arbitration is the substitute for industrial strife. Since arbitration of labor disputes has quite different functions from arbitration under an ordinary commercial agreement, the hostility evinced by courts toward arbitration of commercial agreements has no place here. For arbitration of labor disputes under collective bargaining agreements is part and parcel of the collective bargaining process itself.

The collective bargaining agreement states the rights and duties of the parties. It is more than a contract; it is a generalized code to govern a myriad of cases which the draftsmen cannot wholly anticipate. . . . The collective agreement covers the whole employment relationship. It calls into being a new common law-the common law of a particular industry or of a particular plant. . . .

A collective bargaining agreement is an effort to erect a system of industrial self-government. When most parties enter into contractual relationship they do so voluntarily, in the sense that there is no real compulsion to deal with one another, as opposed to dealing with other parties. This is not true of the labor agreement.

The choice is generally not between entering or refusing to enter into a relationship, for that in all probability pre-exists the negotiations. Rather it is between having that relationship governed by an agreed-upon rule of law or leaving each and every matter subject to a temporary resolution dependent solely upon the relative strength, at any given moment, of the contending forces. The mature labor agreement may attempt to regulate all aspects of the complicated relationship, from the most crucial to the most minute over an extended period of time. Because of the compulsion to reach agreement and the breadth of the matters covered, as well as the need for a fairly concise and readable instrument, the product of negotiations (the written document) is, in the words of the late Dean Shulman, "a compilation of diverse provisions: some provide objective criteria almost automatically applicable; some provide more or less specific standards which require reason and judgment in their application; and some do little more than leave problems to future consideration with an expression of hope and good faith." . . . Gaps may be left to be filled in by reference to the practices of the particular industry and of the various shops covered by the agreement. Many of the specific practices which underlie the agreement may be unknown, except in hazy form, even to the negotiators. Courts and arbitration in the context of most commercial contracts are resorted to because there has been a breakdown in the working relationship of the parties; such resort is the unwanted exception. But the grievance machinery under a collective bargaining agreement is at the very heart of the system of industrial self-government. Arbitration is the means of solving the unforeseeable by molding a system of private law for all the problems which may arise and to provide for their solution in a way which will generally accord with the variant needs and desires of the parties. The processing of disputes through the grievance machinery is actually a vehicle by which meaning and content are given to the collective bargaining agreement.

Apart from matters that the parties specifically exclude, all of the questions on which the parties disagree must therefore come within the scope of the grievance and arbitration provisions of the collective agreement. The grievance procedure is, in other words, a part of the continuous collective bargaining process. It, rather than a strike, is the terminal point of a disagreement. . . .

The labor arbitrator performs functions which are not normal to the courts; the considerations which help him fashion judgments may indeed by foreign to the competence of courts. . . . The labor arbitrator's source of law is not confined to the express provisions of the contract, as the industrial common law — the practices of the industry and the shop — is equally a part of the collective bargaining agreement although not expressed in it. The labor arbitrator is usually chosen because of the parties' confidence in his knowledge of the common law of the shop and their trust in his personal judgment to bring to bear considerations which are not expressed in the contract as criteria for judgment. The parties expect that his judgment of a particular grievance will reflect not only what the contract says but, insofar as the collective bargaining agreement permits, such factors as the effect upon productivity of a particular result, its consequence to the morale of the shop, his judgment whether tensions will be heightened or diminished. For the parties' objective in using the arbitration process is primarily to further their common goal of uninterrupted production under the agreement, to make the agreement serve their specialized needs. The ablest judge cannot be expected to bring the same experience and competence to bear upon the determination of a grievance, because he cannot be similarly informed.

The Congress, however, has by §301 of the Labor Management Relations Act, assigned the courts the duty of determining whether the reluctant party has breached his promise to arbitrate. For arbitration is a matter of contract and a party cannot be required to submit to arbitration any dispute which he has not agreed so to submit. Yet, to be consistent with congressional policy in favor of settlement of disputes by the parties through the machinery of arbitration, the judicial inquiry under §301 must be strictly confined to the question whether the reluctant party did agree to arbitrate the grievance or did agree to give the arbitrator power to make the award he made. An order to arbitrate the particular grievance should not be denied unless it may be said with positive assurance that the arbitration clause is not susceptible of an interpretation that covers the asserted dispute. Doubts should be resolved in favor of coverage.

We do not agree with the lower courts that contracting-out grievances were necessarily excepted from the grievance procedure of this agreement. To be sure, the agreement provides that "matters which are strictly a function of management shall not be subject to arbitration." But it goes on to say that if "differences" arise or if "any local trouble of any kind" arises, the grievance procedure shall be applicable.

Collective bargaining agreements regulate or restrict the exercise of management functions; they do not oust management from the performance of them. Management hires and fires, pays and promotes, supervises and plans. All these are part of its function, and absent a collective bargaining agreement, it may be exercised freely except as limited by public law and by the willingness of employees to work under the particular, unilaterally imposed conditions. A collective bargaining agreement may treat only with certain specific practices, leaving the rest to management but subject to the possibility of work stoppages. When, however, an absolute no-strike clause is included in the agreement, then in a very real sense everything that management does is subject to the agreement, for either management is prohibited or limited in the action it takes, or if not, it is protected from interference by strikes. This comprehensive reach of the collective bargaining agreement does not mean, however, that the language, "strictly a function of management," has no meaning.

"Strictly a function of management" might be thought to refer to any practice of management in which, under particular circumstances prescribed by the agreement, it is permitted to indulge. But if courts, in order to determine arbitrability, were allowed to determine what is permitted and what is not, the arbitration clause would be swallowed up by the exception. Every grievance in a sense involves a claim that management has violated some provision of the agreement.

Accordingly, "strictly a function of management" must be interpreted as referring only to that over which the contract gives management complete control and unfettered discretion. Respondent claims that the contracting out of work falls within this category. Contracting out work is the basis of many grievances; and that type of claim is grist in the mills of the arbitrators. A specific collective bargaining agreement may exclude contracting out from the grievance procedure. Or a written collateral agreement may make clear that contracting out was not a matter for arbitration. In such a case a grievance based solely on contracting out would not be arbitrable. Here, however, there is no such provision. Nor is there any showing that the parties designed the phrase "strictly a function of management" to encompass any and all forms of contracting out. In the absence of any express provision excluding a particular grievance from arbitration, we think only the most forceful evidence of a purpose to exclude the claim from arbitration can prevail, particularly where, as here, the exclusion clause is vague and the arbitration clause quite broad. Since any attempt by a court to infer such a purpose necessarily comprehends the merits, the court should view with suspicion an attempt to persuade it to become entangled in the construction of the substantive provisions of a labor agreement, even through the back door of interpreting the arbitration clause, when the alternative is to utilize the services of an arbitrator.

The grievance alleged that the contracting out was a violation of the collective bargaining agreement. There was, therefore, a dispute "as to the meaning and application of the provisions of this Agreement" which the parties had agreed would be determined by arbitration.

The judiciary sits in these cases to bring into operation an arbitral process which substitutes a regime of peaceful settlement for the older regime of industrial conflict. Whether contracting out in the present case violated the agreement is the question. It is a question for the arbiter, not for the courts. . . . Reversed.

Notes

1. Courts have repeatedly held that a grievance-arbitration clause is the *quid pro quo* for a no-strike clause. Courts have gone so far as to hold that even in the absence of a no-strike clause, the inclusion of a grievance-arbitration process for resolving disputes waives the employees' right to strike absent clear contractual language to the contrary. *Local 174, Teamsters v. Lucas Flour Co.*, 369 U.S. 95 (1962). What values does this principle favor? What are the arguments for and against this approach?

2. The Court attempted to flesh out the arbitrator's function by quoting the following passage: "A proper conception of the arbitrator's function is basic. He is not a public tribunal imposed upon the parties by superior authority which the parties are obliged to accept. He has no general charter to administer justice for a community which transcends the parties. He is rather part of a system of self-government created by and confined to the parties." 363 U.S. 574, 581, *quoting* Harry Shulman, *Reason, Contract, and Law in Labor Relations*, 68 Harv. L. Rev. 999, 1016 (1955).

How does this conception of the arbitrator's function differ from a court's function? Consider, when reviewing materials concerning the public sector, whether this point is equally valid in that context, and if not, what the legal consequences of that difference should be.

3. Courts decide substantive arbitrability—whether the subject matter of the dispute is arbitrable—unless the parties agree to empower the arbitrator to decide that issue. In contrast, arbitrators (not courts) decide questions of procedural arbitrability—whether the grievant has followed the correct procedures in the CBA's grievance and arbitration clauses, *e.g.*, meeting contractual timelines. *John Wiley & Sons v. Livingston*, 376 U.S. 543, 557–58 (1964). *See, e.g., Operating Engineers Local 150 v. Flair Builders*, 406 U.S. 487 (1972) (arbitrator, not court, must resolve an employer's claim that laches barred the union's arbitration request). Will clear lines between court and the arbitral jurisdiction always exist in this regard?

4. Courts continue to find grievances arbitrable based on very broad interpretations of CBA language. For example, *IBEW, Local 21 v. Ill. Bell Tel. Co.*, 491 F.3d 685 (7th Cir. 2007), held that a grievance over a new performance evaluation system was arbitrable based on the recognition clause in the CBA, which stated that "The Company recognizes the Union as the exclusive bargaining agent for [the] employees of the Company." First, how could the court have come to that result? Second, recall that holding that a grievance is *arbitrable* is an entirely separate question from whether the grievance, even if arbitrable, is *meritorious*.

In the final case of the trilogy, the Supreme Court considered the effect of an expired CBA and, more broadly, judicial review of labor arbitration awards.

United Steelworkers of America v. Enterprise Wheel & Car Corp.

Supreme Court of the United States
363 U.S. 593 (1960)

Douglas, J.

Petitioner union and respondent during the period relevant here had a collective bargaining agreement which provided that any differences "as to the meaning and application" of the agreement should be submitted to arbitration and that the arbitrator's decision "shall be final and binding on the parties." Special provisions were included concerning the suspension and discharge of employees. The agreement stated:

> "Should it be determined by the Company or by an arbitrator in accordance with the grievance procedure that the employee has been suspended unjustly or discharged in violation of the provisions of this Agreement, the Company shall reinstate the employee and pay full compensation at the employee's regular rate of pay for the time lost."

The agreement also provided:

". . . It is understood and agreed that neither party will institute civil suits or legal proceedings against the other for alleged violation of any of the provisions of this labor contract; instead all disputes will be settled in the manner outlined in this Article III-Adjustment of Grievances."

A group of employees left their jobs in protest against the discharge of one employee. A union official advised them at once to return to work. An official of respondent at their request gave them permission and then rescinded it. The next day they were told they did not have a job any more "until this thing was settled one way or the other."

A grievance was filed; and when respondent finally refused to arbitrate, this suit was brought for specific enforcement of the arbitration provisions of the agreement. The District Court ordered arbitration. The arbitrator found that the discharge of the men was not justified, though their conduct, he said, was improper. In his view the facts warranted at most a suspension of the men for 10 days each. After their discharge and before the arbitration award the collective bargaining agreement had expired. The union, however, continued to represent the workers at the plant. The arbitrator rejected the contention that expiration of the agreement barred reinstatement of the employees. He held that the provision of the agreement above quoted imposed an unconditional obligation on the employer. He awarded reinstatement with back pay, minus pay for a 10-day suspension and such sums as these employees received from other employment.

Respondent refused to comply with the award. Petitioner moved the District Court for enforcement. The District Court directed respondent to comply. . . . The Court of Appeals, while agreeing that the District Court had jurisdiction to enforce an arbitration award under a collective bargaining agreement, held that the failure of the award to specify the amounts to be deducted from the back pay rendered the award unenforceable. That defect, it agreed, could be remedied by requiring the parties to complete the arbitration. It went on to hold, however, that an award for back pay subsequent to the date of termination of the collective bargaining agreement could not be enforced. It also held that the requirement for reinstatement of the discharged employees was likewise unenforceable because the collective bargaining agreement had expired. . . .

The refusal of courts to review the merits of an arbitration award is the proper approach to arbitration under collective bargaining agreements. The federal policy of settling labor disputes by arbitration would be undermined if courts had the final say on the merits of the awards. As we stated in [*Warrior & Gulf Navigation Co.*], the arbitrators under these collective agreements are indispensable agencies in a continuous collective bargaining process. They sit to settle disputes at the plant level—disputes that require for their solution knowledge of the custom and practices of a particular factory or of a particular industry as reflected in particular agreements.

When an arbitrator is commissioned to interpret and apply the collective bargaining agreement, he is to bring his informed judgment to bear in order to reach a fair solution of a problem. This is especially true when it comes to formulating remedies. There the need is for flexibility in meeting a wide variety of situations. The draftsmen may never have thought of what specific remedy should be awarded to meet a particular contingency. Nevertheless, an arbitrator is confined to interpretation and application of the collective bargaining agreement; he does not sit to dispense his own brand of industrial justice. He may of course look for guidance from many sources, yet his award is legitimate only so long as it draws its essence from the collective bargaining agreement. When the arbitrator's words manifest an infidelity to this obligation, courts have no choice but to refuse enforcement of the award.

The opinion of the arbitrator in this case, as it bears upon the award of back pay beyond the date of the agreement's expiration and reinstatement, is ambiguous. It may be read as based solely upon the arbitrator's view of the requirements of enacted legislation, which would mean that he exceeded the scope of the submission. Or it may be read as embodying a construction of the agreement itself, perhaps with the arbitrator looking to "the law" for help in determining the sense of the agreement. A mere ambiguity in the opinion accompanying an award, which permits the inference that the arbitrator may have exceeded his authority, is not a reason for refusing to enforce the award. Arbitrators have no obligation to the court to give their reasons for an award. To require opinions free of ambiguity may lead arbitrators to play it safe by writing no supporting opinions. This would be undesirable for a well-reasoned opinion tends to engender confidence in the integrity of the process and aids in clarifying the underlying agreement. Moreover, we see no reason to assume that this arbitrator has abused the trust the parties confided in him and has not stayed within the areas marked out for his consideration. It is not apparent that he went beyond the submission. The Court of Appeals' opinion refusing to enforce the reinstatement and partial back pay portions of the award was not based upon any finding that the arbitrator did not premise his award on his construction of the contract. It merely disagreed with the arbitrator's construction of it.

The collective bargaining agreement could have provided that if any of the employees were wrongfully discharged, the remedy would be reinstatement and back pay up to the date they were returned to work. Respondent's major argument seems to be that by applying correct principles of law to the interpretation of the collective bargaining agreement it can be determined that the agreement did not so provide, and that therefore the arbitrator's decision was not based upon the contract. The acceptance of this view would require courts, even under the standard arbitration clause, to review the merits of every construction of the contract. This plenary review by a court of the merits would make meaningless the provisions that the arbitrator's decision is final, for in reality it would almost never be final. This underlines the fundamental error which we have alluded to in [*American Manufacturing Co.*]. As we there emphasized, the question of interpretation of the collective bargaining agreement is a question for the arbitrator. It is the arbitrator's construction which was bargained for; and so far as the arbitrator's decision concerns construction of the contract, the courts have no business overruling him because their interpretation of the contract is different from his.

We agree with the Court of Appeals that the judgment of the District Court should be modified so that the amounts due the employees may be definitely determined by arbitration. In all other respects we think the judgment of the District Court should be affirmed. Accordingly, we reverse the judgment of the Court of Appeals, except for that modification, and remand the case to the District Court for proceedings in conformity with this opinion. It is so ordered.

Notes

1. To illustrate the importance of arbitrators, the Court, 363 U.S. 593, 596 n.2, quoted the following passage (from Walker, *Life in the Automatic Factory*, 36 Harv. Bus. Rev. 111, 117 (1958)):

> "Persons unfamiliar with mills and factories—farmers or professors, for example—often remark upon visiting them that they seem like another world. This is particularly true if, as in the steel industry, both tradition and technology have strongly and uniquely molded the ways men think and act when at work. The newly hired employee, the 'green hand,' is gradually initiated into what amounts to a miniature society. There he finds himself in a strange environment that assaults his senses with unusual sounds and smells and often with different 'weather conditions' such as sudden drafts of heat, cold, or humidity. He discovers that the society of which he only gradually becomes a part has of course a formal government of its own— the rules which management and the union have laid down—but that it also differs from or parallels the world outside in social classes, folklore, ritual, and traditions."

How is the arbitrator's role different from the judge's? Does this passage illustrate why arbitrators, rather than courts, should have the final say on contract interpretation?

2. The Court also coined the oft-quoted phrase that an arbitrator "does not sit to dispense his own brand of industrial justice." How does the Court's observation square with its earlier observation that arbitrators are in a better position than courts to interpret contracts because of the industrial expertise they develop by working with particular parties in specific industries?

3. The Court carved out a narrow role for itself, explaining that the arbitration "award is legitimate only so long as it draws its essence from the collective bargaining agreement. When the arbitrator's words manifest an infidelity to this obligation, courts have no choice but to refuse enforcement of the award." To what extent does the arbitrator's expertise and experience with an industry help or hinder it in this obligation?

4. In *Major League Baseball Players Ass'n v. Garvey*, 532 U.S. 504 (2001), an arbitrator rejected the grievance of former professional baseball player Steve Garvey. Garvey had claimed that the failure of the San Diego Padres to offer him a contract was a product of collusion among team owners. The union had submitted as evidence a letter written by a former Padres executive admitting to the collusion, but the arbitrator held the letter unreliable because it was inconsistent with the executive's statements years earlier. The Ninth Circuit found the arbitrator's decision "inexplicable," and directed the trial court to enter judgment for Garvey. The Supreme Court summarily reversed, on the grounds that courts should not overturn arbitration decisions because they disagreed with the arbitrator's credibility determinations.

5. Given this extremely deferential standard of review, when may a court properly overturn the decision of an arbitrator? *Michigan Family Resources v. SEIU Local 517M*, 475 F.3d 746, 753–54 (6th Cir. 2007) (*en banc*), gave this general explanation:

> The [Supreme] Court's repeated insistence that the federal courts must tolerate "serious" arbitral errors suggests that judicial consideration of the merits of a dispute is the rare exception, not the rule. At the same time, we cannot ignore the specter that an arbitration decision could be so "ignor[ant]" of the contract's "plain language" . . . as to make implausible any contention that the arbitrator was construing the contract. An interpretation of a contract thus could be "so untethered to" the terms of the agreement . . . that it would cast doubt on whether the arbitrator indeed was engaged in interpretation. Such an exception of course is reserved for the rare case. For in most cases, it will suffice to enforce the award that the arbitrator appeared to be engaged in interpretation, and if there is doubt we will presume that the arbitrator was doing just that. . . .
>
> This view of the "arguably construing" inquiry no doubt will permit only the most egregious awards to be vacated. But it is a view that respects the parties' decision to hire their own judge to resolve their disputes, a view that respects the finality clause in most arbitration agreements . . . and a view whose imperfections can be remedied by selecting better arbitrators.

6. Still, if an arbitrator's award is directly contrary to explicit, unambiguous contract language, courts will overturn the result. *See, e.g., Beaird Indus. v. Local 2297, UAW*, 404 F.3d 942 (5th Cir. 2005) (arbitrator's award contrary to language in CBA that unambiguously allowed the employer complete discretion in subcontracting).

One of the most famous grievances of recent history is the now infamous Deflategate controversy, in which the National Football League (NFL) alleged that officials of the New England Patriots underinflated footballs used in the 2014 American Football Conference (AFC) Championship Game, played on January 18, 2015, between the Patriots and the Indianapolis Colts. By way of background, a few days after the game, the NFL initiated a formal investigation led by NFL Executive Vice President and General Counsel Jeff Pash and New York attorney Theodore V. Wells of Paul, Weiss, Rifkind, Wharton, & Garrison LLP. On May 6, 2015, the

Pash/Wells Report was released to the public. That Report concluded, among other things, that (1) it was "'more probable than not that New England Patriots personnel participated in violations of the Playing Rules and were involved in a deliberate effort to circumvent the rules;'" (2) "Patriots employees Jim McNally . . . the Officials Locker Room attendant, and John Jastremski . . . a Patriots equipment assistant in charge of footballs, "'participated in a deliberate effort to release air from Patriots game balls after the balls were examined by the referee [on January 18, 2015];'" (3) "'it is more probable than not that [Patriots Quarterback Tom] Brady was at least generally aware of the inappropriate activities of McNally and Jastremski involving the release of air from Patriots game balls;'" and (4) "'it is unlikely that an equipment assistant and a locker room attendant would deflate game balls without Brady's knowledge and approval.'" *See NFL Mgmt. Council v. NFLPA*, quoting Wells Report at pp.2, 17, 19. Based on these findings, McNally and Jastremski were indefinitely suspended. By letter dated May 11, 2015, NFL Executive Vice President Troy Vincent imposed a four-game suspension on Brady for his role in using the under-inflated balls. By letter dated May 11, 2015, to Patriots owner Robert K. Kraft, the Patriots were fined $1,000,000 and forfeiture of the first-round pick in the 2016 NFL draft and fourth-round pick in the 2017 NFL draft.

Shortly thereafter, Brady through the Players Association appealed his four-game suspension to arbitration. Under CBA Art. 46, §2(a), NFL Commissioner Roger Goodell designated himself as arbitrator of this appeal. The Players Association filed several motions including (1) a motion for Commissioner Goodell to recuse himself on grounds of bias; (2) a motion for several investigatory documents; and (3) a motion to compel Pash's and Wells's testimony. Goodell denied all motions, except the motion to compel Well's testimony. After an arbitral hearing, Goodell upheld the suspension, based in part on Brady's destruction of his cell phone during the investigation, which Goodell characterized as "willful destruction of potentially relevant evidence."

In *National Football League Management Council v. National Football League Players Association*, 2015 U.S. Dist. LEXIS 117662 (S.D.N.Y. Sept. 3, 2015), the district court vacated the arbitrator's award. The court based its decision on the following reasons. First, it found that Brady had no notice that he could receive a four-game suspension for general knowledge of deflated balls. Relatedly, the court rejected the arbitrator's analogy to suspensions for anabolic steroid use. Second, the arbitrator's denial to give Brady the opportunity to examine Pash as a witness was "fundamentally unfair" and in violation of 9 U.S.C. §10(a)(2), which allows a district court to vacate an arbitral decision where the arbitrator engages in misconduct by refusing to hear pertinent evidence. Third, the arbitrator's decision to deny Brady access to investigatory files was "fundamentally unfair," in violation of 9 U.S.C. §10(a)(2), and prejudiced Brady. The court did not reach the question of bias. The NFL appealed the case to the Second Circuit.

In *NFL Mgmt. Council v. NFLPA*, 820 F.3d 527, 541 (2d Cir. 2016), the Second Circuit reversed the district court's decision and reinstated the arbitral award.

The majority held that Goodell did not exceed his authority as an appellate arbitrator by upholding the suspension on new grounds, namely, Brady's destruction of his cell phone, because "[n]othing in Article 46 [of the Collective Bargaining Agreement (CBA)] limits the authority of the arbitrator to examine or reassess the factual basis for a suspension." The court added that although Commissioner Goodell upheld the suspension on new grounds, he "did not increase the punishment as a consequence of the destruction of the cell phone—the four game suspension was not increased. Rather, the cell phone destruction merely provided further support for the Commissioner's determination that Brady had failed to cooperate, and served as the basis for an adverse inference as to his participation in the scheme to deflate footballs." The court denied the Patriots' and Brady's petition for rehearing en banc. Anne Marie Lofaso, *Deflategate: What's the Steelworkers Trilogy Got to Do with It?* 6 BERKELEY J. ENTERTAINMENT & SPORTS LAW 48, 56 (2017).

Which court's analysis is more persuasive? Which court's review of the arbitrator's award conforms more to the principles of judicial review of arbitrator's awards outlined in the cases above?

In *Nolde Brothers, Inc. v. Bakery Workers*, 430 U.S. 243 (1977), the Supreme Court held that employees' claims for severance pay arose under the CBA and thus were arbitrable even though the claims arose after the CBA expired. In **Litton Financial Printing Div. v. NLRB**, 501 U.S. 190 (1991), the Court narrowed this rule somewhat and held that a case must be arbitrated after a CBA expires only if the dispute arose before expiration or involved a "vested right." *Litton* involved layoffs which occurred well after the CBA had expired. The Board held that Litton had improperly refused to process the layoff grievances, but the Court disagreed, finding that the contract provision did not confer a vested right.

> The contractual right at issue, that "in case of layoffs, lengths of continuous service will be the determining factor if other things such as aptitude and ability are equal" . . . involves a residual element of seniority. Seniority provisions, the Union argues, "create a form of earned advantage, accumulated over time, that can be understood as a special form of deferred compensation for time already worked." . . . Leaving aside the question whether a provision requiring all layoffs to proceed in inverse order of seniority would support an analogy to the severance pay at issue in *Nolde Brothers*, which was viewed as a form of deferred compensation, the layoff provision here cannot be so construed, and cannot be said to create a right that vested or accrued during the term of the Agreement or a contractual obligation that carries over after expiration.
>
> The order of layoffs under the Agreement was to be determined primarily with reference to "other factors such as aptitude and ability." Only where all such factors were equal was the employer required to look to seniority. Here, any arbitration proceeding would of necessity focus upon whether aptitude and ability—and any unenumerated "other factors"—were equal

long after the Agreement had expired, as of the date of the decision to lay off employees and in light of Litton's decision to close down its cold type printing operation.

The important point is that factors such as aptitude and ability do not remain constant, but change over time. They cannot be said to vest or accrue or be understood as a form of deferred compensation. Specific aptitudes and abilities can either improve or atrophy. And the importance of any particular skill in this equation varies with the requirements of the employer's business at any given time. Aptitude and ability cannot be measured on some universal scale, but only by matching an employee to the requirements of an employer's business at that time. We cannot infer an intent on the part of the contracting parties to freeze any particular order of layoff or vest any contractual right as of the Agreement's expiration. 501 U.S. 190, 209–10.

Per *Litton*, the obligation to maintain employment conditions at the expiration of a collective-bargaining contract is statutory, not contractual. *NLRB v. Katz*, 369 U.S. 736 (1962); *UAW Local 33 v. R.E. Dietz Co.*, 996 F. 2d 592, 597 (2d Cir. 1993). But *Litton* also held that arbitration clauses are excluded from the bar on unilateral changes under *Katz* and its progeny.

In addition to severance pay and other forms of deferred compensation, a classic example of a "vested right" case is when an employer disciplines an employee for alleged misconduct during the time the CBA was in effect, but the discipline and/ or the arbitration of the discipline came after the CBA expired. *See, e.g., Operating Engineers Local 3 v. Newmont Mining Corp.*, 476 F.3d 690 (9th Cir. 2007).

Suppose a CBA provision arguably guaranteed an employee a job for the rest of his life, the contract expires, and the employee is then discharged. Is the case arbitrable? *See Washington Mailers Union Local M-29 v. Washington Post*, 699 F. Supp. 2d 130 (D.D.C. 2010).

Litton also held that the Board has authority to resolve questions of contract interpretation in exercising its authority to remedy ULPs. *See also NLRB v. C & C Plywood Corp.*, 385 U.S. 421 (1967). But *Litton* further noted that courts need not be deferential to Board interpretations of CBA language. Based on the § 301 cases above, what argument would support that position? *See Litton*, 501 U.S. 190, 202–03; *Local Jt. Exec. Bd. of Las Vegas v. NLRB*, 540 F.3d 1072, 1078 (9th Cir. 2008). Is this position consistent with the principle that reviewing courts must defer to the Board's reasonable interpretation of ambiguous statutory language under *Chevron*? With the principle that courts defer to the Board because of its expertise in labor relations?

B. Judicial Intervention in Grievance Arbitration in Defense of Public Policy

A distinct subset of cases involving judicial review of arbitration decisions focuses on whether courts should reverse the decision because it violates an important public policy. Clearly, an arbitration decision could not require the parties to violate the NLRA or other applicable laws (*e.g.*, an order upholding a closed shop or pay rates below what state or federal laws require). But beyond that, when, if ever, should courts reverse arbitration awards on public policy grounds?

The Supreme Court has addressed this question three times, thereby creating a very narrow public-policy exception in the private sector. In *W.R. Grace & Co. v. Rubber Workers*, 461 U.S. 757, 764, 766 (1983), the Court held that it would not vacate an arbitration award — reinstating and awarding back pay to two men laid off in violation of the CBA's seniority provisions — "[u]nless the arbitral decision [failed] to 'dra[w] its essence from the collective bargaining agreement,'" or unless the contract, as interpreted by the arbitrator "violates some explicit public policy" that is "well defined and dominant" and is "ascertained 'by reference to ... laws and legal precedents and not from general considerations of supposed public interests.'" The Court so held notwithstanding the fact that the company had violated the CBA in good faith: to comply with an EEOC conciliation agreement, settling race and sex discrimination claims against it.

In *United Paperworkers Int'l Union v. Misco, Inc.*, 484 U.S. 29, 32–33 (1987), the Court again refused to vacate an arbitration award reinstating an employee. *Misco* involved an employee discharged for allegedly violating a rule barring the possession or use of controlled substances on company property. The company argued the discharge was for just cause in part because police found the employee — whose job required him to operate "a slitter-rewinder machine, which uses sharp blades to cut rolling coils of paper" — in the back seat of a co-worker's car parked in the company's parking lot with a lit marijuana cigarette in the front seat ashtray. The Court rejected the lower court's reasoning that the arbitral award violated a public policy against people under the influence of drugs operating dangerous machinery. 484 U.S. at 35. Applying the standard in *W.R. Grace*, the Court explained that its role was to determine "whether the [arbitral] award created any explicit conflict with other 'laws and legal precedents," rather than assessing 'general considerations of supposed public interests.'" *Id.* at 43. The Court left open the question of whether "a court may refuse to enforce an award on public policy grounds only when the award itself violates a statute, regulation, or other manifestation of positive law, or compels conduct by the employer that would violate such a law." *Id.* at 45 n.12.

The following case is the third case in this series.

Eastern Associated Coal Corp. v. United Mine Workers, Dist. 17

Supreme Court of the United States
531 U.S. 57 (2000)

BREYER, J.

A labor arbitrator ordered an employer to reinstate an employee truck driver who had twice tested positive for marijuana. The question before us is whether considerations of public policy require courts to refuse to enforce that arbitration award.

We conclude that they do not. The courts may enforce the award. And the employer must reinstate, rather than discharge, the employee.

I

Petitioner, Eastern Associated Coal Corp., and respondent, United Mine Workers of America, are parties to a collective-bargaining agreement with arbitration provisions. The agreement specifies that, in arbitration, in order to discharge an employee, Eastern must prove it has "just cause." Otherwise the arbitrator will order the employee reinstated. The arbitrator's decision is final. . . .

James Smith worked for Eastern as a member of a road crew, a job that required him to drive heavy trucklike vehicles on public highways. As a truck driver, Smith was subject to Department of Transportation (DOT) regulations requiring random drug testing of workers engaged in "safety-sensitive" tasks. 49 CFR §§ 382.301, 382.305 (1999).

In March 1996, Smith tested positive for marijuana. Eastern sought to discharge Smith. The union went to arbitration, and the arbitrator concluded that Smith's positive drug test did not amount to "just cause" for discharge. Instead the arbitrator ordered Smith's reinstatement, provided that Smith (1) accept a suspension of 30 days without pay, (2) participate in a substance-abuse program, and (3) undergo drug tests at the discretion of Eastern (or an approved substance-abuse professional) for the next five years.

Between April 1996 and January 1997, Smith passed four random drug tests. But in July 1997 he again tested positive for marijuana. Eastern again sought to discharge Smith. The union again went to arbitration, and the arbitrator again concluded that Smith's use of marijuana did not amount to "just cause" for discharge, in light of two mitigating circumstances. First, Smith had been a good employee for 17 years. . . . And, second, Smith had made a credible and "very personal appeal under oath . . . concerning a personal/family problem which caused this one time lapse in drug usage." . . .

The arbitrator ordered Smith's reinstatement provided that Smith (1) accept a new suspension without pay, this time for slightly more than three months; (2) reimburse Eastern and the union for the costs of both arbitration proceedings; (3) continue to participate in a substance-abuse program; (4) continue to undergo random drug testing; and (5) provide Eastern with a signed, undated letter of resignation, to take effect if Smith again tested positive within the next five years. . . .

Eastern brought suit in federal court seeking to have the arbitrator's award vacated, arguing that the award contravened a public policy against the operation of dangerous machinery by workers who test positive for drugs. . . . The District Court, while recognizing a strong regulation-based public policy against drug use by workers who perform safety-sensitive functions, held that Smith's conditional reinstatement did not violate that policy. . . . And it ordered the award's enforcement. . . .

The Court of Appeals for the Fourth Circuit affirmed on the reasoning of the District Court. . . . We granted certiorari in light of disagreement among the Circuits. . . .

II

Eastern claims that considerations of public policy make the arbitration award unenforceable. In considering this claim, we must assume that the collective-bargaining agreement itself calls for Smith's reinstatement. That is because both employer and union have granted to the arbitrator the authority to interpret the meaning of their contract's language, including such words as "just cause." See *Steelworkers v. Enterprise Wheel & Car Corp.*, 363 U.S. 593, 599 (1960). They have "bargained for" the "arbitrator's construction" of their agreement. . . . And courts will set aside the arbitrator's interpretation of what their agreement means only in rare instances. . . . Of course, an arbitrator's award "must draw its essence from the contract and cannot simply reflect the arbitrator's own notions of industrial justice." *Paperworkers v. Misco, Inc.*, 484 U.S. 29, 38 (1987). "But as long as [an honest] arbitrator is even arguably construing or applying the contract and acting within the scope of his authority," the fact that "a court is convinced he committed serious error does not suffice to overturn his decision." . . . [S]ee . . . *Enterprise Wheel*, 363 U.S. at 596 (the "proper" judicial approach to a labor arbitration award is to "refus[e] . . . to review the merits"). Eastern does not claim here that the arbitrator acted outside the scope of his contractually delegated authority. Hence we must treat the arbitrator's award as if it represented an agreement between Eastern and the union as to the proper meaning of the contract's words "just cause." . . .

We must then decide whether a contractual reinstatement requirement would fall within the legal exception that makes unenforceable "a collective-bargaining agreement that is contrary to public policy." . . . The Court has made clear that any such public policy must be "explicit," "well defined," and "dominant." . . . It must be "ascertained 'by reference to the laws and legal precedents and not from general considerations of supposed public interests.'" . . . And, of course, the question to be answered is not whether Smith's drug use itself violates public policy, but whether the agreement to reinstate him does so. To put the question more specifically, does a contractual agreement to reinstate Smith with specified conditions . . . run contrary to an explicit, well-defined, and dominant public policy, as ascertained by reference to positive law and not from general considerations of supposed public interests? . . .

III

Eastern initially argues that the District Court erred by asking, not whether the award is "contrary to" public policy "as ascertained by reference" to positive law, but whether the award "violates" positive law, a standard Eastern says is too narrow. We believe, however, that the District Court correctly articulated the standard set out in *W.R. Grace* and *Misco* . . . and applied that standard to reach the right result.

We agree, in principle, that courts' authority to invoke the public policy exception is not limited solely to instances where the arbitration award itself violates positive law. Nevertheless, the public policy exception is narrow and must satisfy the principles set forth in *W.R. Grace* and *Misco*. Moreover, in a case like the one before us, where two political branches have created a detailed regulatory regime in a specific field, courts should approach with particular caution pleas to divine further public policy in that area.

Eastern asserts that a public policy against reinstatement of workers who use drugs can be discerned from an examination of that regulatory regime, which consists of the Omnibus Transportation Employee Testing Act of 1991 and DOT's implementing regulations. The Testing Act embodies a congressional finding that "the greatest efforts must be expended to eliminate the . . . use of illegal drugs, whether on or off duty, by those individuals who are involved in [certain safety-sensitive positions, including] the operation of . . . trucks." . . . The Act adds that "increased testing" is the "most effective deterrent" to "use of illegal drugs." § 2(5). It requires the Secretary of Transportation to promulgate regulations requiring "testing of operators of commercial motor vehicles for the use of a controlled substance." 49 U.S.C. § 31306(b)(1)(A). It mandates suspension of those operators who have driven a commercial motor vehicle while under the influence of drugs. 49 U.S.C. § 31310(b)(1)(A) (requiring suspension of at least one year for a first offense); § 31310(c)(2) (requiring suspension of at least 10 years for a second offense). And DOT's implementing regulations set forth sanctions applicable to those who test positive for illegal drugs. 49 CFR § 382.605 (1999).

In Eastern's view, these provisions embody a strong public policy against drug use by transportation workers in safety-sensitive positions and in favor of random drug testing in order to detect that use. Eastern argues that reinstatement of a driver who has twice failed random drug tests would undermine that policy — to the point where a judge must set aside an employer-union agreement requiring reinstatement.

Eastern's argument, however, loses much of its force when one considers further provisions of the Act that make clear that the Act's remedial aims are complex. The Act says that "rehabilitation is a critical component of any testing program," § 2(7), . . . that rehabilitation "should be made available to individuals, as appropriate," . . . and that DOT must promulgate regulations for "rehabilitation programs," 49 U.S.C. § 31306(e). The DOT regulations specifically state that a driver who has tested positive for drugs cannot return to a safety-sensitive position until (1) the driver has been evaluated by a "substance abuse professional" to determine if treatment is needed, 49 CFR § 382.605(b) (1999); (2) the substance-abuse professional has certified that the driver has followed any rehabilitation program prescribed, § 382.605(c)(2)(i); and (3) the driver has passed a return-to-duty drug test, § 382.605(c)(1). In addition, (4) the driver must be subject to at least six random drug tests during the first year after returning to the job. § 382.605(c)(2)(ii). Neither the Act nor the regulations forbid an employer to reinstate in a safety-sensitive position an employee who fails a random drug test once or twice. The congressional and regulatory directives require only that the above-stated prerequisites to reinstatement be met.

Moreover, when promulgating these regulations, DOT decided not to require employers either to provide rehabilitation or to "hold a job open for a driver" who has tested positive, on the basis that such decisions "should be left to management/

driver negotiation." 59 Fed.Reg. 7502 (1994). That determination reflects basic background labor law principles, which caution against interference with labor-management agreements about appropriate employee discipline. . . .

The award before us is not contrary to these several policies, taken together. The award does not condone Smith's conduct or ignore the risk to public safety that drug use by truck drivers may pose. Rather, the award punishes Smith by suspending him for three months, thereby depriving him of nearly $9,000 in lost wages . . . ; it requires him to pay the arbitration costs of both sides; it insists upon further substance-abuse treatment and testing; and it makes clear (by requiring Smith to provide a signed letter of resignation) that one more failed test means discharge.

The award violates no specific provision of any law or regulation. It is consistent with DOT rules requiring completion of substance-abuse treatment before returning to work, see 49 CFR § 382.605(c)(2)(i) (1999), for it does not preclude Eastern from assigning Smith to a non-safety-sensitive position until Smith completes the prescribed treatment program. It is consistent with the Testing Act's 1-year and 10-year driving license suspension requirements, for those requirements apply only to drivers who, unlike Smith, actually operated vehicles under the influence of drugs. See 49 U.S.C. §§ 31310(b), (c). The award is also consistent with the Act's rehabilitative concerns, for it requires substance-abuse treatment and testing before Smith can return to work.

The fact that Smith is a recidivist—that he has failed drug tests twice—is not sufficient to tip the balance in Eastern's favor. The award punishes Smith more severely for his second lapse. And that more severe punishment, which included a 90-day suspension, would have satisfied even a "recidivist" rule that DOT once proposed but did not adopt—a rule that would have punished two failed drug tests, not with discharge, but with a driving suspension of 60 days. . . . Neither Congress nor the Secretary has seen fit to mandate the discharge of a worker who twice tests positive for drugs. We hesitate to infer a public policy in this area that goes beyond the careful and detailed scheme Congress and the Secretary have created.

We recognize that reasonable people can differ as to whether reinstatement or discharge is the more appropriate remedy here. But both employer and union have agreed to entrust this remedial decision to an arbitrator. We cannot find in the Act, the regulations, or any other law or legal precedent an "explicit," "well defined," "dominant" public policy to which the arbitrator's decision "runs contrary." *Misco*, 484 U.S. at 43; *W.R. Grace*, 461 U.S. at 766. We conclude that the lower courts correctly rejected Eastern's public policy claim. . . .

SCALIA, J., with whom THOMAS, J. joins, concurring.

. . . I agree that no public policy prevents the reinstatement of James Smith. . . . I do not endorse, however, the Court's statement that "[w]e agree, in principle, that courts' authority to invoke the public policy exception is not limited solely to instances where the arbitration award itself violates positive law." . . . There is not a single decision, since this Court washed its hands of general common-lawmaking authority, *see Erie R. Co. v. Tompkins*, 304 U.S. 64 (1938), in which we have refused to enforce on "public policy" grounds an agreement that did not violate, or provide for the violation of, some positive law. . . .

It is hard to imagine how an arbitration award could violate a public policy, identified [as the majority defines it] without conflicting with positive law. If such an award could ever exist, it would surely be so rare that the benefit of preserving the courts' ability to deal with it is far outweighed by the confusion and uncertainty . . . that the Court's Delphic "agree[ment] in principle" will engender. . . ."

Notes

1. Is Justice Scalia correct? Can you imagine an arbitration decision that would violate public policy under the majority's standard that would not involve a violation of positive law? And even if you can, is it correct that these cases would be so rare as to not be worth the potential uncertainty the majority's standard creates?

2. It seems to defy common sense that the Supreme Court would repeatedly reverse lower court decisions that refuse to reinstate drug and alcohol abusers to safety-sensitive positions. When the question is framed that way, it does defy common sense. But the question is not whether a court, de novo, could affirm and employer's discharge of an employee for abusing drugs and alcohol at the workplace. After determining the threshold question—whether the arbitral award draws its essence from the collective-bargaining agreement—court review is limited to whether "'the contract as interpreted by [the arbitrator] violates some explicit public policy.'" *Cont'l Airlines, Inc. v. Air Line Pilots Ass'n, Int'l*, 555 F.3d 399, 415 (5th Cir. 2009) (citing *W.R. Grace & Co. v. Rubber Workers*, 461 U.S. 757, 764, 766 (1983), *supra*). In answering that question, reviewing courts will consider whether the arbitral award is in conflict with positive law that establishes a sufficiently "explicit," "defined," and "dominant" public policy. *Id.* at 418.

Accordingly, it is important to understand in these cases that the "violation of public policy" that could justify reversing an arbitrator's decision is not the employee's behavior but the arbitration decision itself. The question is not, for example, whether an employee's drug use violates public policy, but rather whether an arbitration decision reinstating the employee to a job does.

Misco, supra, illustrates this point. There, the company discharged Isaiah Cooper after Cooper truthfully told his employer that he had been arrested for marijuana possession in his home. The company lost the arbitration on grounds that it did not meet its burden of proving just cause. In particular, the arbitrator found that, for the following two reasons, the employer, which claimed it had fired Cooper for using marijuana on company property, could not rely on evidence (a) that the police had arrested Cooper after finding him sitting in the backseat of another person's car (parked on the company's lot) with a lighted marijuana cigarette in the front-seat ashtray or (b) that a police search of his car on the company's lot revealed marijuana gleanings and a plastic scale case. First, the arbitrator found that the company had not proven that Cooper was smoking marijuana in his friend's car. At most, it had proven that the police found Cooper in the back of a car with a burning marijuana cigarette in the front of the car, which had just been occupied by two of his friends. Second, the company could not rely on the police search because it only learned of that search after the discharge. *See United Paperworkers Int'l Union, AFL-CIO v. Misco, Inc.*, 484 U.S. 29, 33 (1987). The arbitrator ordered the company to reinstate Cooper with backpay and seniority. The company convinced a district court and a court of appeals to reverse the arbitral decision on grounds that ordering an employee who smokes marijuana to return to work to operate dangerous machinery was contrary to public policy.

The Supreme Court reversed the lower-court decisions on grounds that the arbitral award itself — to reinstate an employee whose termination was without just cause — does not itself violate public policy. The Court rejected the employer's argument that the arbitrator's factual findings were incorrect in light of the overwhelming circumstantial evidence (Cooper was found in a car with a burning marijuana cigarette) and the after-acquired evidence (police search of Cooper's car uncovered marijuana gleanings). The Court held that, absent dishonesty or fraud, "improvident, even silly, factfinding . . . is hardly a sufficient basis for disregarding" an arbitrator's factual findings. *Id.* at 39. The Court added that the company could not rely on after-acquired evidence to support its public-policy argument.

Many courts have since relied on the Court's "improvident, even silly, factfinding" language to prevent a lower court from vacating an arbitrator's award on grounds that the court simply disagreed with the arbitrator's fact-finding. For example, and as discussed above, in *Major League Baseball Players Ass'n v. Garvey*, the Ninth Circuit characterized an arbitrator's refusal to credit evidence of contractual language as "at worst 'irrational' and at best 'bizarre.'" 532 U.S. 504, 510 (2001). The Supreme Court, applying this standard specifically in the context of a contract dispute between First Basemen Steve Garvey and Major League Baseball, reversed the Ninth Circuit and reinstated the arbitral award. *See, e.g., DBM Technologies, Inc. v. Local 227, United Food & Commercial Workers Int'l Union*, 257 F.3d 651, 659 (6th Cir. 2001) (refusing to reverse arbitrator's fact-finding where there is no dishonesty alleged); *Ario v. Underwriting Members of Syndicate 53 at Lloyds for 1998 Year of Account*, 618 F.3d 277, 296 (3d Cir. 2010), *as amended* (Dec. 7, 2010) (same).

3. Should the rules in this area be different in the public sector? *See* Section VI, *infra*.

IV. Judicial Intervention in Defense of Grievance Arbitration

This section examines the circumstances under which courts can enjoin strikes, notwithstanding the anti-injunction provisions of the Norris-LaGuardia Act. As Chapter 1 explained, Congress passed Norris-LaGuardia in response to judicial repression of labor unions through unwarranted and excessive use of injunctive powers. Section 1 of this Act states that "[n]o court of the United States . . . shall have jurisdiction to issue any restraining order or temporary or permanent injunction in a case involving or growing out of a labor dispute," except as provided by the Act itself. 29 U.S.C. § 101. It further prohibits the issuance of such orders or injunctions that are "contrary to the public policy declared [therein]." *Id.* But § 4 of this Act, 29 U.S.C. § 104, gives specific, narrow exceptions to the ban on injunctions.

In deciding whether to enjoin strikes over matters subject to a bargained-for grievance-arbitration procedure, courts sought to balance the right to strike, the contractual arbitration obligation, the underlying policy of industrial peace served by grievance-arbitration, and the policies underlying the Norris-LaGuardia Act. The Supreme Court ultimately held unlawful a union strike in support of a discharged employee, where the CBA's arbitration clause prohibited "suspension of work" during an arbitration but did not otherwise prohibit midterm strikes. *Local 174, Teamsters v. Lucas Flour Co.*, 369 U.S. 95 (1962). In particular, the Court held that the strike in support of the discharged worker violated an implied no-strike obligation.

The following case discusses the circumstances under which the Norris-LaGuardia Act permits enjoining a strike over an employer's refusal to arbitrate an arbitrable grievance.

Boys Markets, Inc. v. Retail Clerk's Union, Local 770

Supreme Court of the United States
398 U.S. 235 (1970)

BRENNAN, J.

. . . [W]e re-examine the holding of *Sinclair Refining Co. v. Atkinson*, 370 U.S. 195 (1962), that the anti-injunction provisions of the Norris-LaGuardia Act preclude a federal district court from enjoining a strike in breach of a no-strike obligation under a collective-bargaining agreement, even though that agreement contains provisions, enforceable under § 301(a) . . . , for binding arbitration of the grievance dispute concerning which the strike was called. The . . . Ninth Circuit, considering itself bound by *Sinclair* reversed the grant by the District Court . . . of petitioner's prayer for injunctive relief. . . . Having concluded that *Sinclair* was erroneously decided and that subsequent events have undermined its continuing validity, we overrule that decision and reverse the judgment of the Court of Appeals.

I

In February 1969, . . . petitioner and respondent were parties to a collective-bargaining agreement which provided, inter alia, that all controversies concerning its interpretation or application should be resolved by adjustment and arbitration procedures set forth therein and that, during the life of the contract, there should be "no cessation or stoppage of work, lock-out, picketing or boycotts. . . ." The dispute arose when petitioner's frozen foods supervisor and certain members of his crew who were not members of the bargaining unit began to rearrange merchandise in the frozen food cases of one of petitioner's supermarkets. A union representative insisted that the food cases be stripped of all merchandise and be restocked by union personnel. When petitioner did not accede to the union's demand, a strike was called and the union began to picket petitioner's establishment. Thereupon petitioner demanded that the union cease the work stoppage and picketing and sought to invoke the grievance and arbitration procedures specified in the contract.

The following day, since the strike had not been terminated, petitioner filed a complaint in California Superior Court seeking a temporary restraining order, a preliminary and permanent injunction, and specific performance of the contractual arbitration provision. The state court issued a temporary restraining order forbidding continuation of the strike and also an order to show cause why a preliminary injunction should not be granted. Shortly thereafter, the union removed the case to the Federal District Court and there made a motion to quash the state court's temporary restraining order. In opposition, petitioner moved for an order compelling arbitration and enjoining continuation of the strike. Concluding that the dispute was subject to arbitration under the collective-bargaining agreement and that the strike was in violation of the contract, the District Court ordered the parties to arbitrate the underlying dispute and simultaneously enjoined the strike, all picketing in the vicinity of petitioner's supermarket, and any attempts by the union to induce the employees to strike or to refuse to perform their services.

II

. . . We do not agree that the doctrine of stare decisis bars a re-examination of *Sinclair* in the circumstances of this case. We fully recognize that important policy considerations militate in favor of continuity and predictability in the law. Nevertheless, . . . "[S]tare decisis is a principle of policy and not a mechanical formula of adherence to the latest decision, however recent and questionable, when such adherence involves collision with a prior doctrine more embracing in its scope, intrinsically sounder, and verified by experience." *Helvering v. Hallock*, 309 U.S. 106, 119 (1940). . . . It is precisely because *Sinclair* stands as a significant departure from our otherwise consistent emphasis upon the congressional policy to promote the peaceful settlement of labor disputes through arbitration and our efforts to accommodate and harmonize this policy with those underlying the anti-injunction provisions of the Norris-LaGuardia Act that we believe *Sinclair* should be reconsidered. Furthermore, in light of developments subsequent to *Sinclair*, in particular our decision in *Avco Corp. v. Aero Lodge 735*, 390 U.S. 557 (1968), it has become clear that the *Sinclair* decision does not further but rather frustrates realization of an important goal of our national labor policy. . . .

III

. . . *Lincoln Mills* held generally that "the substantive law to apply in suits under § 301(a) is federal law, which the courts must fashion from the policy of our national labor laws," . . . and more specifically that a union can obtain specific performance of an employer's promise to arbitrate grievances. We rejected the contention that the anti-injunction proscriptions of the Norris-LaGuardia Act prohibited this type of relief, noting that a refusal to arbitrate was not "part and parcel of the abuses against which the Act was aimed," . . . and that the Act itself manifests a policy determination that arbitration should be encouraged. . . .

Serious questions remained, however, concerning the role that state courts were to play in suits involving collective-bargaining agreements. Confronted with some of these problems in *Charles Dowd Box Co. v. Courtney*, 368 U.S. 502 (1962), we held that Congress clearly intended not to disturb the pre-existing jurisdiction of the state courts over suits for violations of collective-bargaining agreements. . . .

Subsequent to the decision in *Sinclair*, we held in *Avco Corp. v. Aero Lodge 735* . . . that § 301(a) suits initially brought in state courts may be removed to the designated federal forum under the federal question removal jurisdiction delineated in 28 U.S.C. § 1441. In so holding, however, the Court expressly left open the questions whether state courts are bound by the anti-injunction proscriptions of the Norris-LaGuardia Act and whether federal courts, after removal of a § 301(a) action, are required to dissolve any injunctive relief previously granted by the state courts. . . .

The decision in *Avco*, viewed in the context of *Lincoln Mills* and its progeny, has produced an anomalous situation which, in our view, makes urgent the reconsideration of *Sinclair*. The principal practical effect of *Avco* and *Sinclair* taken together is nothing less than to oust state courts of jurisdiction in § 301(a) suits where injunctive relief is sought for breach of a no-strike obligation. Union defendants can, as a matter of course, obtain removal to a federal court, and there is obviously a compelling incentive for them to do so in order to gain the advantage of the strictures upon injunctive relief which *Sinclair* imposes on federal courts. The sanctioning of this practice, however, is wholly inconsistent with our conclusion in *Dowd Box* that the congressional purpose embodied in § 301(a) was to supplement, and not to encroach upon, the pre-existing jurisdiction of the state courts. It is ironic indeed that the very provision that Congress clearly intended to provide additional remedies for breach of collective-bargaining agreements has been employed to displace previously existing state remedies. We are not at liberty thus to depart from the clearly expressed congressional policy to the contrary.

On the other hand, to the extent that widely disparate remedies theoretically remain available in state, as opposed to federal, courts, the federal policy of labor law uniformity elaborated in *Lucas Flour Co.*, is seriously offended. This policy, of course, could hardly require, as a practical matter, that labor law be administered identically in all courts, for undoubtedly a certain diversity exists among the state and federal systems in matters of procedural and remedial detail, a fact that Congress evidently took into account in deciding not to disturb the traditional jurisdiction of the States. The injunction, however, is so important a remedial device, particularly in the arbitration context, that its availability or non-availability in various courts will not only produce rampant forum shopping and maneuvering from one court to another but will also greatly frustrate any relative uniformity in the enforcement of arbitration agreements.

Furthermore, the existing scheme, with the injunction remedy technically available in the state courts but rendered inefficacious by the removal device, assigns to removal proceedings a totally unintended function. . . .

It is undoubtedly true that each of the foregoing objections to *Sinclair-Avco* could be remedied either by overruling *Sinclair* or by extending that decision to the States. While some commentators have suggested that the solution to the present unsatisfactory situation does lie in the extension of the *Sinclair* prohibition to state court proceedings, we agree with Chief Justice Traynor of the California Supreme Court that "whether or not Congress could deprive state courts of the power to give such (injunctive) remedies when enforcing collective bargaining agreements, it has not attempted to do so either in the Norris-LaGuardia Act or section 301." *McCarroll v. Los Angeles County Dist. Council of Carpenters*, 49 Cal.2d 45, 63 (1957), *cert. denied*, 355 U.S. 932 (1958). . . .

An additional reason for not resolving the existing dilemma by extending *Sinclair* to the States is the devastating implications for the enforceability of arbitration agreements and their accompanying no-strike obligations if equitable remedies were not available. As we have previously indicated [in *Lincoln Mills*], a no-strike obligation, express or implied, is the quid pro quo for an undertaking by the employer to submit grievance disputes to the process of arbitration. Any incentive for employers to enter into such an arrangement is necessarily dissipated if the principal and most expeditious method by which the no-strike obligation can be enforced is eliminated. While it is of course true, as respondent contends, that other avenues of redress, such as an action for damages, would remain open to an aggrieved employer, an award of damages after a dispute has been settled is no substitute for an immediate halt to an illegal strike. Furthermore, an action for damages prosecuted during or after a labor dispute would only tend to aggravate industrial strife and delay an early resolution of the difficulties between employer and union.

. . . [B]ecause *Sinclair*, in the aftermath of *Avco*, casts serious doubt upon the effective enforcement of a vital element of stable labor-management relations — arbitration agreements with their attendant no-strike obligations — we conclude that Sinclair does not make a viable contribution to federal labor policy.

IV

We have also determined that the dissenting opinion in *Sinclair* states the correct principles concerning the accommodation necessary between the seemingly absolute terms of the Norris-LaGuardia Act and the policy considerations underlying § 301(a). . . . Although we need not repeat all that was there said, a few points should be emphasized at this time.

The literal terms of § 4 of the Norris-LaGuardia Act must be accommodated to the subsequently enacted provisions of § 301(a) of the Labor Management Relations Act and the purposes of arbitration. Statutory interpretation requires more than concentration upon isolated words; rather, consideration must be given to the total corpus of pertinent law and the policies that inspired ostensibly inconsistent provisions. . . .

The Norris-LaGuardia Act was responsive to a situation totally different from that which exists today. In the early part of this century, the federal courts generally were regarded as allies of management in its attempt to prevent the organization and strengthening of labor unions; and in this industrial struggle the injunction became a potent weapon that was wielded against the activities of labor groups. . . . The result was a large number of sweeping decrees, often issued ex parte, drawn on an ad hoc basis without regard to any systematic elaboration of national labor policy. *See Milk Wagon Drivers' Union, etc. v. Lake Valley Co.*, 311 U.S. 91, 102 (1940).

In 1932 Congress attempted to bring some order out of the industrial chaos that had developed and to correct the abuses that had resulted from the interjection of the federal judiciary into union-management disputes on the behalf of management. See declaration of public policy, Norris-LaGuardia Act, § 2. . . . Congress, therefore, determined initially to limit severely the power of the federal courts to issue injunctions "in any case involving or growing out of any labor dispute. . . ." § 4 . . . Even as initially enacted, however, the prohibition against federal injunctions was by no means absolute. See Norris-LaGuardia Act, §§ 7, 8, 9. . . .

As labor organizations grew in strength and developed toward maturity, congressional emphasis shifted from protection of the nascent labor movement to the encouragement of collective bargaining and to administrative techniques for the peaceful resolution of industrial disputes. This shift in emphasis was accomplished, however, without extensive revision of many of the older enactments, including the anti-injunction section of the Norris-LaGuardia Act. Thus it became the task of the courts to accommodate, to reconcile the older statutes with the more recent ones.

A leading example of this accommodation process is *Brotherhood of Railroad Trainmen v. Chicago River & Ind. R. Co.*, 353 U.S. 30 (1957). There we were confronted with a peaceful strike which violated the statutory duty to arbitrate imposed by the Railway Labor Act. The Court concluded that a strike in violation of a statutory arbitration duty was not the type of situation to which the Norris-LaGuardia Act was responsive, that an important federal policy was involved in the peaceful settlement of disputes through the statutorily mandated arbitration procedure, that this important policy was imperiled if equitable remedies were not available to implement it, and hence that Norris-LaGuardia's policy of nonintervention by the federal courts should yield to the overriding interest in the successful implementation of the arbitration process.

The principles elaborated in *Chicago River* are equally applicable to the present case. To be sure, *Chicago River* involved arbitration procedures established by statute. However, we have frequently noted, in such cases as *Lincoln Mills*, the *Steelworkers Trilogy*, and *Lucas Flour*, the importance that Congress has attached generally to the voluntary settlement of labor disputes without resort to self-help and more particularly to arbitration as a means to this end. Indeed, it has been stated that *Lincoln Mills*, in its exposition of § 301(a), "went a long way towards making arbitration the central institution in the administration of collective bargaining contracts."

The *Sinclair* decision, however, seriously undermined the effectiveness of the arbitration technique as a method peacefully to resolve industrial disputes without resort to strikes, lockouts, and similar devices. Clearly employers will be wary of assuming obligations to arbitrate specifically enforceable against them when no similarly efficacious remedy is available to enforce the concomitant undertaking of the union to refrain from striking. On the other hand, the central purpose of the Norris-LaGuardia Act to foster the growth and viability of labor organizations is hardly retarded—if anything, this goal is advanced—by a remedial device that merely enforces the obligation that the union freely undertook under a specifically enforceable agreement to submit disputes to arbitration. We conclude, therefore, that the unavailability of equitable relief in the arbitration context presents a serious impediment to the congressional policy favoring the voluntary establishment of a mechanism for the peaceful resolution of labor disputes, that the core purpose of the Norris-LaGuardia Act is not sacrificed by the limited use of equitable remedies to further this important policy, and consequently that the Norris-LaGuardia Act does not bar the granting of injunctive relief in the circumstances of the instant case.

V

Our holding . . . is a narrow one. We do not undermine the vitality of the Norris-LaGuardia Act. We deal only with the situation in which a collective-bargaining contract contains a mandatory grievance adjustment or arbitration procedure. Nor does it follow from what we have said that injunctive relief is appropriate as a matter of course in every case of a strike over an arbitrable grievance. The dissenting opinion in *Sinclair* suggested the following principles for the guidance of the district courts in determining whether to grant injunctive relief-principles that we now adopt:

> "A District Court entertaining an action under § 301 may not grant injunctive relief against concerted activity unless and until it decides that the case is one in which an injunction would be appropriate despite the Norris-LaGuardia Act. When a strike is sought to be enjoined because it is over a grievance which both parties are contractually bound to arbitrate, the District Court may issue no injunctive order until it first holds that the contract does have that effect; and the employer should be ordered to arbitrate, as a condition of his obtaining an injunction against the strike. Beyond this, the District Court must, of course, consider whether issuance of an injunction would be warranted under ordinary principles of equity— whether breaches are occurring and will continue, or have been threatened and will be committed; whether they have caused or will cause irreparable injury to the employer; and whether the employer will suffer more from the denial of an injunction than will the union from its issuance." 370 U.S. at 228. (Emphasis in original.)

In the present case there is no dispute that the grievance in question was subject to adjustment and arbitration under the collective-bargaining agreement and that the petitioner was ready to proceed with arbitration at the time an injunction against the strike was sought and obtained. The District Court also concluded that, by reason of respondent's violations of its no-strike obligation, petitioner "has suffered irreparable injury and will continue to suffer irreparable injury." Since we now overrule *Sinclair*, the holding of the Court of Appeals in reliance on *Sinclair* must be reversed. . . .

Notes

1. The Court stressed that its holding was "narrow." In emphasizing that point, the Court adopted the *Sinclair* dissent's guidelines for when a court may enjoin a strike.

   a. First, a strike must be over an arbitral dispute (as defined in the Steelworkers Trilogy, see *Gateway Coal Co. v. Mine Workers District 4, Local 6330*, 414 U.S. 368 (1974)). When would that not be the case? *Buffalo Forge Co. v. United Steelworkers of America*, 428 U.S. 397, 407–08 (1976) affirmed a lower court's refusal to enjoin a sympathy strike on this basis. *Boys Markets* did not control because the labor dispute—a strike in support of a fellow union—was not caused by an issue the employer could arbitrate with the union it sought to enjoin. Thus, the anti-injunction provisions of the Norris-LaGuardia Act applied.

   b. Second, the court must order the employer to arbitrate as a condition of obtaining injunctive relief against the strike. *See Teamsters Local 807 v. Bohack Corp.*, 541 F.2d 312 (2d Cir. 1976) (setting aside *Boys Market* injunction where district court failed to order arbitration of the underlying contract dispute).

   c. Third, the strike must be in breach of the relevant CBA, although an express no-strike clause is not necessary to meet this condition. *Teamsters v. Lucas Flour Co.*, 369 U.S. 95 (1962).

   d. Fourth, the district court must evaluate whether injunctive relief is warranted in light of ordinary principles of equity. This includes determining whether the alleged contractual breach would cause irreparable injury to the employer and whether the employer would suffer more from the denial of an injunction than the union would from its issuance.

2. Unions can sometimes use a related doctrine, called a "reverse *Boys Markets* injunction." In such cases, instead of following the normal "work then grieve" rule usually applicable when a union believes an employer is about to violate a CBA provision, the union files for an injunction that would require the employer to arbitrate a proposed action before the employer takes the action. Unions should be granted such injunctions to preserve the status quo pending arbitration if: "(1) the underlying dispute is subject to mandatory arbitration; and (2) the injunction is necessary to prevent the arbitration process from becoming a 'hollow formality' or

'meaningless ritual.'" *Aeronautical Indus. Dist. Lodge 91, IAM v. United Technologies Corp.*, 230 F.3d 569, 581 (2d Cir. 2000). The latter requirement means that if the employer goes through with the proposed action, it could not effectively be undone or remedied later: *e.g.*, proposing to sell a division of the company in a manner that violates the CBA. *Local Lodge No. 1266, IAM v. Panoramic Corp.*, 668 F.2d 276 (7th Cir. 1981). Traditional equity factors (including the union showing a likelihood of prevailing on the merits in the arbitration) apply.

V. Grievance Arbitration and Federal Statutory Claims

As Chapter 16 explains, the NLRA preempts certain state law claims, *e.g.*, common law contract claims based on the CBA. But what if an employee has very similar or identical rights under a federal statute and under a CBA?

A. Arbitration and Labor Law Violations

1. Concurrent Jurisdiction of Arbitrators and Labor Boards

Just as arbitrators lack authority to enforce the NLRA, the NLRB lacks authority to adjudicate disputes arising under a CBA. But sometimes an employer's act violates both the terms of a CBA and some part of NLRA § 8. Can you think of some plausible examples? These cases raise jurisdictional questions between arbitrators and labor boards.

The Supreme Court has generally permitted concurrent jurisdiction between arbitrators and the NLRB in such cases. The Court developed this policy in the context of three cases. First, in *Carey v. Westinghouse Elec. Corp.*, 375 U.S. 261 (1964), the Court examined whether an arbitrator could decide a dispute over a topic the Board normally handles, a jurisdictional dispute between two unions. Under § 8(b)(4)(D), it is a ULP for a union to strike to force an employer to assign work to a particular group of employees rather than to another. The Board is empowered through § 10(k) to hear and resolve such disputes. *See* Chapter 12. In *Carey*, the employer refused to arbitrate a grievance filed by one union alleging that the employer had assigned work to members of another union in violation of the CBA. The employer claimed that because this dispute involved defining the scope of a bargaining unit, it was a representational matter over which the Board has exclusive authority. The Court held that the arbitrator had jurisdiction over the grievance and compelled arbitration. A suit to enforce contractual remedies was thus proper, "even though an alternative remedy before the Board is available, which, if invoked by the employer, will protect him." 375 U.S. 268.

In *NLRB v. C & C Plywood Corp.*, 385 U.S. 421 (1967), the Court held that the Board had jurisdiction to construe a CBA to determine whether an employer violated § 8(a)(5) by unilaterally changing the terms of the CBA. The Court rejected the lower court's rationale, that the Board lacked jurisdiction because the lawfulness of the employer's conduct did "'not turn entirely upon the provisions of the Act, but arguably upon a good-faith dispute as to the correct meaning of the provisions of the collective bargaining agreement.'" 385 U.S. 421, 425. The Board "has done no more than merely enforce a statutory right." 385 U.S. at 428.

In *NLRB v. Acme Industrial Co.*, 385 U.S. 432 (1967), the Court held that the employer violated §8(a)(5) by refusing to furnish relevant information the union had requested. The Court rejected the employer's claim that, before finding a §8(a)(5) violation, the NLRB should have waited for an arbitrator to determine relevance because the CBA contained an arbitration clause. But *Acme Industrial* raised an important policy question for the Board: under what circumstances should the Board defer to an arbitrator, even if it is not compelled to wait for an arbitrator to decide a question of contract interpretation?

2. The Arbitral Deferral Doctrine

The Board has developed a doctrine to guide it in determining when it is appropriate to defer to an arbitration award in deciding the merits of the underlying ULP. Using what are called the *Spielberg/Olin* standards, the Board considers the following four factors: (1) Were the arbitration proceedings fair and regular? (2) Did all parties agree to be bound? (3) Has the arbitrator "considered" the ULP issue, in that the contractual issue is "factually parallel" to the ULP issue and the arbitrator was presented generally with the facts relevant to resolving the ULP charge? And, (4) is the resulting decision not "clearly repugnant" to the NLRA? *Olin Corp.*, 268 N.L.R.B. 573, 573–74 (1984) (clarifying *Spielberg Mfg. Co.*, 112 N.L.R.B. 1080 (1955)).

The Board has reconsidered its *Olin/Spielberg* standard for post-arbitration deferral. In *Babcock & Wilcox Construction Inc.*, 361 N.L.R.B. 1127 (2014), the Board adopted a new standard for post-arbitral deferral based on its conclusion that the *Olin/Spielberg* standard did "not adequately protect employees' exercise of their rights under Section 7" insofar as that standard

> amount[ed] to a conclusive presumption that the arbitrator "adequately considered" the statutory issue if the arbitrator was merely presented with facts relevant to both an alleged contract violation and an alleged unfair labor practice. The presumption is theoretically rebuttable, but, as indicated above, the burden is on the party opposing deferral to show that the conditions for deferral are not met. In many, if not most arbitral proceedings, the parties do not file written briefs; there is no transcript of proceedings; and decisions often are summarily stated. In such situations, it is virtually impossible to prove that the statutory issue was not considered.

The Board thereby modified its standard as follows:

> If the arbitration procedures appear to have been fair and regular, and if the parties agreed to be bound, the Board will defer to an arbitral decision

if the party urging deferral shows that: (1) the arbitrator was explicitly authorized to decide the unfair labor practice issue; (2) the arbitrator was presented with and considered the statutory issue, or was prevented from doing so by the party opposing deferral; and (3) Board law reasonably permits the award. This modified framework is intended to rectify the deficiencies in the current deferral standard in a way that provides greater protection of employees' statutory rights while, at the same time, furthering the policy of peaceful resolution of labor disputes through collective bargaining. Thus, . . . this approach will enable us to determine whether the arbitrator has actually resolved the unfair labor practice issue in a manner consistent with the Act, without placing an undue burden on unions, employers, arbitrators, or the arbitration system itself. 361 N.L.R.B. 1127, slip op. at *6–*7.

The Board explained that the proponent of deferral bore the burden of showing that these deferral standards have been met. *Id.* at *8.

The Board noted that its modified postarbitral deferral standard evoked two additional changes in Board doctrine. First, the Board modified its prearbitral deferral standard under *Collyer Insulated Wire*, 192 N.L.R.B. 837 (1971), and *United Technologies Corp.*, 268 N.L.R.B. 557 (1984), holding that it would "no longer defer unfair labor practice allegations to the arbitral process unless the parties have explicitly authorized the arbitrator to decide the unfair labor practice issue, either in the collective-bargaining agreement or by agreement of the parties in a particular case." 361 N.L.R.B. 1127, slip op. at *17–*18. Second, the Board modified its standard for determining whether to defer to grievance-arbitration settlement agreements to be in line with its postarbitral deferral standard. In particular, the Board held that it will "apply the same deferral principles to prearbitral settlement agreements as to arbitral awards (*i.e.*, as the Board has done under the current standard) . . . . Thus, it must be shown that the parties intended to settle the unfair labor practice issue; that they addressed it in the settlement agreement; and that Board law reasonably permits the settlement agreement." *Id.* at *18.

On December 23, 2019, in *United Parcel Service, Inc.*, 369 N.L.R.B. No. 1 (2019), the Board overruled *Babcock & Wilcox* and returned to its traditional standard for post-arbitral deferral set forth in *Spielberg* and *Olin*. The Board will once again defer to the arbitrator's decision where (1) the arbitral proceedings appear to have been fair and regular, (2) all parties have agreed to be bound, (3) the arbitrator considered the unfair labor practice issue, and (4) the arbitrator's decision is not clearly repugnant to the Act. In *United Parcel Service*, the Board also restored the policies for pre-arbitral deferral established in *United Technologies Corp.*, 268 N.L.R.B. 557 (1984), and for deferral to pre-arbitral settlement agreements set forth in *Alpha Beta Co.*, 273 N.L.R.B. 1546 (1985).

Notwithstanding the *Spielberg/Olin* standards, the Board will not defer to arbitration in several specific instances. First, under *Collyer Insulated Wire*, 192 N.L.R.B. 837 (1971), the Board will not defer if the employer's action constitutes a unilateral alteration of the scope of the unit, because the Board does not defer to the parties' grievance-arbitration procedure when the dispute raises issues as to unit scope, composition, and representation of employees. *See, e.g., Paper Mfrs. Co.*, 274 N.L.R.B. 491, 494–96 (1985), *enforced*, 786 F.2d 163 (3d Cir. 1986) (deferral to an arbitration award unwarranted because accretion issues have been traditionally reserved for the Board). Second, the Board will not defer disputes over information requests where the requested information is "inextricably related to the matter on which deferral is sought." *See, e.g., Mt. Sinai Hospital*, 331 N.L.R.B. 895, 896 (2000) (information inextricably related to transfer of unit work issue). Instead, the Board will process those allegations as §8(a)(5) violations. This is because Board enforcement of the duty to furnish information relevant to the disposition of grievances is an essential means of assuring that arbitration awards will be supported by substantial evidence. Third, the Board will not defer to arbitral awards that are repugnant to the policies underlying the NLRA. *See Mobil Oil Exploration & Producing*, 325 N.L.R.B. 176, 177, 179 (1997), *enforced*, 200 F.3d 230 (5th Cir. 1999) (arbitrator's award was repugnant to the Act because employer's asserted just cause for discipline was based on protected concerted conduct).

Finally, the Board also will not defer to arbitration where one party is seeking an "illegal objective." The Board extends to arbitration proceedings the principle that a state court lawsuit may be enjoined if it has "an objective that is illegal under federal law." *Bill Johnson's Restaurant v. NLRB*, 461 U.S. 731, 737 n.5 (1983). A union's grievance seeks an "illegal objective" if the outcome sought by the union would itself violate the NLRA. *See, e.g., Elevator Constructors Local 3 (Long Elevator)*, 289 N.L.R.B. 1095, 1095 (1988), *enforced*, 902 F.2d 1297 (8th Cir. 1990) (union's construction of contract clause would violate §8(e)). Why would the Board have such a policy? Assuming such a case goes to arbitration and the arbitrator construes the case in a manner unlawful under the NLRA, what would the losing party's recourse be under the Steelworkers Trilogy?

Moreover, with respect to how cases will be handled where deferral under *Dubo Manufacturing Corp.*, 142 N.L.R.B. 431 (1963), is raised, *i.e.*, where the unfair labor practice issue is being processed through the grievance-arbitration machinery and there is a reasonable chance that use of that machinery will resolve the dispute or put it to rest, General Counsel Robb recently issued a memo instructing:

> [T]he General Counsel wishes to reaffirm the role of *Dubo* in the administration of the Act, and to clarify the circumstances and procedures applicable to *Dubo* deferrals. Accordingly . . . Regions should continue to defer under *Dubo* Section 8(a)(1) and (3) cases meeting the standards for deferral set forth herein, and should otherwise consider *Dubo* deferral in any Section 8(a)(1), (3) and (5) and Section 8(b)1(A) and (3) case where the allegations of the charge fall within its scope and the Charging Party or individual grievant has previously filed a grievance in a contractual process leading to binding arbitration. Memorandum GC 19-03, *Deferral under Dubo Manufacturing Company*, dated Dec. 28, 2018.

B. Arbitration of Other Types of Federal Statutory Claims

Suppose an employee alleges conduct that violates both a CBA and a federal statute that is not the NLRA; *e.g.*, a claim that the employee's pay violates both the CBA and the Fair Labor Standards Act (FLSA), or that the employer had discriminated on the basis of race in a way that violates both Title VII and a CBA clause barring race discrimination. The Supreme Court has decided several cases in this area, but some aspects of the issue remain unclear.

The first case the Court decided, *Alexander v. Gardner-Denver Co.*, 415 U.S. 36 (1974), involved a race discrimination claim. The union arbitrated the claim under a CBA and lost. The employee, Alexander, then brought a Title VII lawsuit in court. The employer argued (and the Tenth Circuit agreed) that the arbitration decision barred the lawsuit. Reversing the Tenth Circuit, the Supreme Court held that the two claims were independent of each other; therefore, the Title VII claim could go forward despite the loss in arbitration. Further, the Court noted that the union, rather than the individual employee, typically controlled whether a grievance would go to arbitration. Finally, the court stressed that arbitration was not an appropriate means to vindicate statutory rights. *See also Barrentine v. Arkansas-Best Freight System*, 450 U.S. 728 (1981) (allowing a court suit under the FLSA to go forward, even though no grievance had been filed under the CBA on the issue).

In the following decades, however, an increasing number of non-unionized employers began to use agreements that required individual employees to arbitrate statutory employment law claims (and barred bringing such claims in court). Courts generally approved this practice. In *Gilmer v. Interstate/Johnson Lane Corp.*, 500 U.S. 20 (1991), the Supreme Court held that an employee not in a union bargaining unit who had signed such an agreement could be compelled to arbitrate a claim under the Age Discrimination in Employment Act (ADEA). *Gilmer* criticized *Gardner-Denver's* "mistrust of the arbitral process." 500 U.S. 20, 34 n.5.

This raised the question of whether language in a CBA could ever bind members of a union bargaining unit to arbitrate federal statutory claims under their CBA. In *Wright v. Universal Maritime Serv. Corp.*, 525 U.S. 70 (1998), the Supreme Court left open the question of whether a "clear and unmistakable waiver" of a judicial forum for federal statutory claims in a CBA could have that effect. The Court did not decide the issue because it held that the CBA in *Wright* did not contain such a waiver.

The Court took up the issue again in *14 Penn Plaza LLC v. Pyett*, 556 U.S. 247 (2009). In *Pyett*, the relevant CBA language provided:

> 30. NO DISCRIMINATION "There shall be no discrimination against any present or future employee by reason of race, creed, color, age, disability, national origin, sex, union membership, or any other characteristic protected by law, including, but not limited to, claims made pursuant to Title VII of the Civil Rights Act, the Americans with Disabilities Act, the Age Discrimination in Employment Act, the New York State Human Rights

Law, the New York City Human Rights Code, . . . or any other similar laws, rules, or regulations. All such claims shall be subject to the grievance and arbitration procedure (Articles V and VI) as the sole and exclusive remedy for violations. Arbitrators shall apply appropriate law in rendering decisions based upon claims of discrimination." 556 U.S. 247, 252.

Employees covered by this contract grieved a work assignment. After the union lost the arbitration, the employees brought suit in court claiming the assignments violated the ADEA. The lower courts allowed the suits to go forward, relying on *Gardner-Denver*, although the Second Circuit noted tensions between that case and *Gilmer* and *Wright*. 556 U.S. 247, 253–54.

In a 5–4 decision, the Supreme Court reversed. It explained that "[p]arties generally favor arbitration precisely because of the economics of dispute resolution." 556 U.S. at 257. Further,

> The *Gilmer* Court's interpretation of the ADEA fully applies in the collective-bargaining context. Nothing in the law suggests a distinction between the status of arbitration agreements signed by an individual employee and those agreed to by a union representative. This Court has required only that an agreement to arbitrate statutory antidiscrimination claims be "explicitly stated" in the collective-bargaining agreement. *Wright*, 525 U.S. at 80. The CBA under review here meets that obligation. 556 U.S. at 258–59.

As to *Gardner-Denver's* questioning of the competence of arbitrators to decide federal statutory claims,

> These misconceptions have been corrected. For example, the Court has "recognized that arbitral tribunals are readily capable of handling the factual and legal complexities of antitrust claims, notwithstanding the absence of judicial instruction and supervision" and that "there is no reason to assume at the outset that arbitrators will not follow the law." . . . An arbitrator's capacity to resolve complex questions of fact and law extends with equal force to discrimination claims brought under the ADEA. Moreover, the recognition that arbitration procedures are more streamlined than federal litigation is not a basis for finding the forum somehow inadequate; the relative informality of arbitration is one of the chief reasons that parties select arbitration. . . . In any event, "[i]t is unlikely . . . that age discrimination claims require more extensive discovery than other claims that we have found to be arbitrable, such as RICO and antitrust claims." 556 U.S. at 268–69.

The *Pyett* majority then addressed *Gardner-Denver's* point regarding the union's exclusive control over the arbitration process. It noted the concern that the "union's interests and those of the individual employee are not always identical or even compatible. As a result, the union may present the employee's grievance less vigorously, or make different strategic choices, than would the employee." *Pyett*, 556 U.S. at 269–70, citing *Gardner-Denver*, 415 U.S. at 58.

The *Pyett* majority then explained:

> We cannot rely on this judicial policy concern as a source of authority for introducing a qualification into the ADEA that is not found in its text. Absent a constitutional barrier, "it is not for us to substitute our view of . . . policy for the legislation which has been passed by Congress." . . . Congress is fully equipped "to identify any category of claims as to which agreements to arbitrate will be held unenforceable." . . . Until Congress amends the ADEA to meet the conflict-of-interest concern identified in the *Gardner-Denver* dicta, and seized on by respondents here, there is "no reason to color the lens through which the arbitration clause is read" simply because of an alleged conflict of interest between a union and its members. . . .
>
> The conflict-of-interest argument also proves too much. Labor unions certainly balance the economic interests of some employees against the needs of the larger work force as they negotiate collective-bargain agreements and implement them on a daily basis. But this attribute of organized labor does not justify singling out an arbitration provision for disfavored treatment. This "principle of majority rule" to which respondents object is in fact the central premise of the NLRA. *Emporium Capwell Co. v. Western Addition Community Organization*, 420 U.S. 50, 62 (1975). . . . Respondents' argument that they were deprived of the right to pursue their ADEA claims in federal court by a labor union with a conflict of interest is therefore unsustainable; it amounts to a collateral attack on the NLRA.
>
> In any event, Congress has accounted for this conflict of interest in several ways. As indicated above, the NLRA has been interpreted to impose a "duty of fair representation" on labor unions, which a union breaches "when its conduct toward a member of the bargaining unit is arbitrary, discriminatory, or in bad faith." . . . Thus, a union is subject to liability under the NLRA if it illegally discriminates against older workers in either the formation or governance of the collective-bargaining agreement, such as by deciding not to pursue a grievance on behalf of one of its members for discriminatory reasons. . . . In addition, a union is subject to liability under the ADEA if the union itself discriminates against its members on the basis of age. See 29 U.S.C. § 623(d). . . . 556 U.S. at 270–72.

Then, however, the majority added a potentially hugely significant caveat:

> Respondents also argue that the CBA operates as a substantive waiver of their ADEA rights because it not only precludes a federal lawsuit, but also allows the Union to block arbitration of these claims. Petitioners contest this characterization of the CBA, and offer record evidence suggesting that the Union has allowed respondents to continue with the arbitration even though the Union has declined to participate. But not only does this question require resolution of contested factual allegations, it was not fully

briefed to this or any court and is not fairly encompassed within the question presented. Thus, although a substantive waiver of federally protected civil rights will not be upheld, see *Mitsubishi Motors Corp.*, 473 U.S., at 637, and n. 19; *Gilmer*, 500 U.S., at 29, we are not positioned to resolve in the first instance whether the CBA allows the Union to prevent respondents from "effectively vindicating" their "federal statutory rights in the arbitral forum," *Green Tree Financial Corp.-Ala. v. Randolph*, 531 U.S. 79 (2000). Resolution of this question at this juncture would be particularly inappropriate in light of our hesitation to invalidate arbitration agreements on the basis of speculation. 556 U.S. at 273–74.

This language appears to leave open the possibility that the *Pyett* rule allowing a CBA to waive a judicial forum for federal statutory rights does not apply in cases where the union controls access to arbitration. Notably, CBAs almost always give unions control over whether or not to arbitrate a grievance (*see* Chapter 14).

The dissent (Justice Souter, joined by Justices Stevens, Ginsburg, and Breyer), faulted the majority for slighting the reasons *Gardner-Denver* relied on in holding that a clause in a CBA cannot waive the right to go to court on a statutory claim. According to the dissent, the fact that the CBA in *Gardner-Denver* did not explicitly mention statutory claims was only one of many reasons for its holding. "One need only read *Gardner-Denver* itself to know that it was not at all so narrowly reasoned." 556 U.S. at 282. As to the majority's suggestion that an individual employee could have a duty of fair representation (DFR) suit against a union which did not arbitrate a discrimination claim, the dissent noted that a union could decline to process a grievance that would be the basis of a valid discrimination claim for a variety of reasons without violating its DFR. *Id.* at 284 n.4 (consider this point again when you read Chapter 14). The dissent also noted the significant caveat above, concluding:

> On one level, the majority opinion may have little effect, for it explicitly reserves the question whether a CBA's waiver of a judicial forum is enforceable when the union controls access to and presentation of employees' claims in arbitration . . . which "is usually the case". . . . But as a treatment of precedent in statutory interpretation, the majority's opinion cannot be reconciled with the *Gardner-Denver* Court's own view of its holding, repeated over the years and generally understood. . . . *Id.* at 285–86.

Notes

1. The majority opinion in *Pyett* posits that the substantive right at issue in that case was the right to a workplace free of age discrimination, not the right to litigate the age discrimination claim in a federal court. The majority explained that earlier decisions deriding the efficacy and fairness of arbitration in resolving federal claims have been since repudiated, and that arbitration is a perfectly acceptable, if not more efficient, forum for addressing grievances related to employment discrimination. Is this rationale persuasive?

2. The dissent posits that the majority's opinion is "impossible to square with our conclusion in *Gardner-Denver* that 'Title VII . . . stands on plainly different ground' from 'statutory rights related to collective activity': 'it concerns not majoritarian processes, but an individual's right to equal employment opportunities.'" *Id.* at 282. Is Title VII different in this regard, *e.g.*, such that Title VII claims should be treated differently than, say, FLSA claims in this area?

3. After *Pyett*, several district court decisions have refused to find a waiver where the union had control of the arbitration process. *See De Souza Silva v. Pioneer Janitorial Services*, 777 F. Supp. 2d 198 (D. Mass. 2011), *citing, e.g., Morris v. Temco Serv. Indus. Inc.*, No. 09 Civ. 6194(WHP) (S.D.N.Y. Aug. 12, 2010). Is this the correct result (and should the Supreme Court so rule if it returns to this issue)?

4. *Pyett* is properly seen as one step in the inexorable judicial expansion of the Federal Arbitration Act (FAA), 9 U.S.C. 1 *et seq.*, away from that statute's origins in the resolution of commercial disputes and into the labor and employment law arena.

The FAA, enacted in 1925, was intended to provide for the enforcement of commercial arbitration agreements. The insinuation of the FAA into employment law came much later and began in earnest with *Gilmer*. In *Gilmer*, the Court stated the question presented was "whether a claim under the Age Discrimination in Employment Act of 1967 (ADEA), 81 Stat. 602, as amended, 29 U.S.C. §621 et seq., can be subjected to compulsory arbitration pursuant to an arbitration agreement in a securities registration application." *Id.* at 23. The Fourth Circuit had held the ADEA claim subject to mandatory arbitration, and the Supreme Court affirmed.

In reaching its conclusion, the Court noted that §1 of the FAA contains an exemption providing that "nothing herein contained shall apply to contracts of employment of seamen, railroad employees, or any other class of workers engaged in foreign or interstate commerce," and that several *amici* had argued that this exemption excluded from the FAA's coverage *all* "contracts of employment." Justice White, writing for the majority, disregarded the amici's contention, as it had not been raised below, was not addressed by the courts below, and was not among the questions presented in the petition for certiorari. Also, the arbitration provision was not contained in Gilmer's contract of employment, but rather in Gilmer's securities registration application. The Court held that §1's exclusionary clause did not apply to the arbitration agreement at issue and Justice White concluded: "Thus, we leave for another day the issue raised by amicus curiae." *Gilmer*, at 25, fn. 2.

Justice Stevens, writing for himself and Justice Marshall in dissent, noted: "When the FAA was passed in 1925, I doubt that any legislator who voted for it expected it to apply to statutory claims, to form contracts between parties of unequal bargaining power, or to the arbitration of disputes arising out of the employment relationship." *Gilmer*, at 42 (Stevens, J., dissenting). He further argued that, despite the failure to raise the issue below, the Court should have decided it, as the parties had addressed the question in their briefs and at oral argument, and "resolution of the question is so clearly antecedent to disposition of this case." *Id.* at 36–37. On the merits, he was persuaded that the FAA was intended to exclude arbitration agreements between employees and employers.

The "another day" presaged by Justice White came nine years later in *Circuit City Stores, Inc. v. Adams*, 532 U.S. 105 (2001), where, in an opinion written by Justice Kennedy, the court ruled, again 5–4, that the Section 1 FAA exemption for contracts of employment of seamen, railroad employees, or any other class of workers engaged in foreign or interstate commerce only applied to transportation workers.

VI. Grievance Arbitration in the Public Sector

A. The Steelworkers Trilogy in the Public Sector

The rules of the Steelworkers Trilogy are generally accepted in the public sector. *See, e.g., United Teachers of Los Angeles v. Los Angeles Unified School Dist.*, 54 Cal. 4th 504, 514–15 (2012); *State System of Higher Ed. (Cheyney University) v. State College and University Professional Ass'n*, 560 Pa. 135, 143–50 (1999); *State Employment Relations Bd. v. Franklin County Sheriff*, 7 OPER ¶ 7986 (OH SERB Hearing Officer Sept. 26, 1990). While these rules are usually imported by court decision, after the New Jersey Supreme Court refused to adopt the presumption in favor of arbitrability in public-sector cases (in *Camden Bd. of Ed. v. Alexander*, 181 N.J. 187 (2004)), the New Jersey legislature passed a statute applicable to the public sector that provided as follows. "In interpreting the meaning and extent of a provision of a collective negotiation agreement providing for grievance arbitration, a court or agency shall be bound by a presumption in favor of arbitration. Doubts as to the scope of an arbitration clause shall be resolved in favor of requiring arbitration." N.J. STAT. ANN.§ 34:13A-5.3; *see Board of Ed. of Borough of Alpha, Warren County v. Alpha Ed. Ass'n*, 190 N.J. 34, 47–48 (2006).

But some concerns and variations exist. As shown above, the private-sector rules give significant power to arbitrators—typically a private party—over matters that potentially concern the public. A few public-sector cases cite the old non-delegation doctrine (*see* Chapters 1 and 10) in holding that certain issues are not arbitrable in the public sector. More commonly, the issue arises because the question of whether a topic is negotiable—and therefore whether a CBA provision on the topic is arbitrable—is often a harder problem in the public sector (*see* Chapter 10). Finally, some courts use the "public policy" exception to enforcing arbitration decisions more readily in the public sector than in the private. *See generally* Ann Hodges, *The Steelworkers Trilogy in the Public Sector*, 66 CHI.-KENT L. REV. 631 (1990).

Consider the following case, holding a grievance non-arbitrable.

City of New York v. Uniformed Fire Officers Ass'n, Local 854, IAFF

New York Court of Appeals
95 N.Y.2d 273, 716 N.Y.S.2d 353, 739 N.E.2d 719 (2000)

WESLEY, J.

The issue we must address today is whether public policy bars arbitration of this dispute over whether the employee rights provisions of a collective bargaining agreement (CBA) can be invoked to limit or restrict the procedures of criminal investigations commenced by the New York City Department of Investigation (DOI). We conclude that it does.

In February 1996, DOI subpoenaed several firefighters as part of criminal investigations it was conducting. One investigation concerned an attempt by a firefighter to obtain higher pension benefits by fraudulently claiming that he sustained a disabling injury in the line of duty. The scheme involved one firefighter calling in a false alarm to afford the injured firefighter the opportunity to claim that his injury occurred in responding to the alarm. Among those firefighters interviewed were members of appellant Union, Uniformed Fire Officers Association, Local 854 (UFOA).

The applicable citywide CBA contains provisions for individual employee rights under Article XVII and arbitration of grievances under Articles XVIII and XXI. Article XVII relates to interrogations, interviews, trials and hearings. Those afforded by Article XVII include the requirement that the employee be given written notice of an interview, interrogation, trial or hearing. The employee must be informed of the subject matter of the proceeding and must be informed if he or she is being considered a suspect or a non-suspect. Any questioning of an employee is to be of reasonable duration and the interrogator is prohibited from using offensive or profane language, from threatening the employee for failure to answer questions and from promising anything to the employee if that employee does answer questions. Where an employee is "a suspect in a departmental investigation or trial" the employee must be advised of the right to refuse to answer questions, that the answers may not be used against him or her in criminal proceedings so long as they are truthful and that the failure to answer renders the employee subject to dismissal. The employee must also be advised of the right to counsel and of the right to union representation. If the employee invokes the right to counsel and/or union representation, the matter must be adjourned for two working days.

Article XVII further imposes restrictions on the scope of any questioning concerning personal behavior outside of work except with respect to matters related to official business, extra-departmental employment, conflict of interest, injuries or illness, residency, performance as a volunteer firefighter or loss or improper use of departmental property. Non-suspect employees are required to cooperate and their statements may not be used against them. Finally, where the City fails to comply with the provisions of Article XVII, any questions put to an employee shall be withdrawn and the refusal to answer any such questions shall not be prejudicial to the employee.

During one of the February 1996 DOI interviews, a fire officer's union representative was excluded over objections of the union counsel. At another interview, the union counsel questioned the adequacy of the notice under Article XVII. The Union thereafter filed a request for arbitration of the grievance, claiming that the City was violating Article XVII by the failure of its agency, DOI, to abide by Article XVII. The City challenged the arbitrability of the request before appellant New York City Board of Collective Bargaining (BCB). The BCB issued a determination finding the dispute to be arbitrable.

The City thereafter commenced this special proceeding pursuant to CPLR articles 75 and 78 in Supreme Court, seeking to annul the BCB's determination and to enjoin arbitration of the dispute. According to the City, it never agreed to arbitrate the procedures employed by the DOI in conducting its criminal investigations; the CBA cannot, as a matter of public policy, supplant or impair those procedures; and the grievances are not arbitrable because to do so would violate public policy.

The Supreme Court set aside the BCB's determination and enjoined arbitration, stating that "the core function of ensuring governmental integrity is a public policy sufficiently strong as to preclude referral of this dispute to arbitration." . . . The Appellate Division unanimously affirmed, holding that public policy, as reflected in the New York City Charter and in decisional law, prohibits any interference with DOI's authority to question public employees in the course of an investigation. . . . We now affirm.

Determining arbitrability requires a two-pronged inquiry. . . . First, a court must decide whether "arbitration claims with respect to the particular subject matter of the dispute [are] authorized," i.e., that the claims are "lawfully fit for arbitration." . . . Second, the court must ascertain whether the authority to arbitrate was in fact exercised and the parties consented by the terms of their particular agreement to refer disputes in this specific area to arbitration. . . .

Under the first prong, the subject matter of the dispute controls the analysis. . . . The court must determine "that there is nothing in statute, decisional law or public policy which would preclude the municipality and its employee or group of employees from referring the dispute to arbitration." . . . If there is some statute, decisional law or public policy that prohibits arbitration of the subject matter of dispute," then the answer to the first inquiry is no, and the claim is not arbitrable regardless of the answer to the second question." . . . We have recognized limited instances where arbitration is prohibited on public policy grounds alone. See, e.g., *Matter of Blackburne (Governor's Off. of Empl. Relations)*, 87 N.Y.2d 660 (1996) (termination of an employee who violated the Hatch Act); *Honeoye Falls-Lima Cent. School Dist. v. Honeoye Falls-Lima Educ. Assn.*, 49 N.Y.2d 732 (1980) (school district's ability to layoff those with the least seniority to maintain academic standards); . . . *Matter of Cohoes City School Dist. v. Cohoes Teachers Assn.,* 40 N.Y.2d 774 (1976) (school board's ability to terminate probationary teachers and make tenure decisions).

The public policy at stake here is DOI's ability to conduct criminal investigations. We have recognized that "[p]ublic policy, whether derived from, and whether explicit or implicit in statute or decisional law, or in neither, may . . . restrict the freedom to arbitrate." *Matter of Susquehanna Val. Cent. School Dist. [Susquehanna Val. Teachers' Assn.],* 37 N.Y.2d 614 (1975). From our review of the statutory and decisional law concerning the DOI, its purpose and its powers, we conclude that a strong public policy enjoins the arbitration of the grievance here.

The Legislature has recognized the importance of allowing a city to conduct investigations into its internal affairs. General City Law § 20(21) empowers every city in the State to "investigate and inquire into all matters of concern to the city or its inhabitants, and to require and enforce by subpoena the attendance of witnesses at such investigations." DOI is the entity charged by the City of New York with the critical responsibility of investigating possible criminal conduct and conflicts affecting City agencies or City employees (N.Y. City Charter § 803). The power to investigate matters pertaining to corrupt or other criminal activity, conflicts of interest, gross mismanagement or abuse of authority within the City, is firmly vested with DOI. . . . To effectuate this mandate, DOI is authorized "to compel the attendance of witnesses, to administer oaths and to examine such persons as [it] may deem necessary." (N.Y. Charter § 805(a). . . .)

It is evident from the Charter that DOI enjoys full latitude in conducting its investigations; Section 1128(a) of the City Charter prohibits any person from preventing, interfering with, obstructing or hindering in any way, an investigation conducted pursuant to the Charter and renders any attempt to do so cause for suspension or removal from office or employment. Moreover, Section 1128(b) of the Charter mandates full cooperation with the Commissioner of the DOI.

The courts have also recognized the important role DOI plays in facilitating the honest workings of the City of New York. As Chief Judge Cardozo noted in sustaining the broad investigatory powers of the Commissioner of Accounts (the predecessor to the Commissioner of the DOI), "[t]he powers devolved by the charter upon the Commissioner of Accounts are of great importance for the efficient administration of the huge machinery of government in the City of New York. . . ." *Matter of Edge Ho Holding Corp,* 256 N.Y. 374 (1931).

The City (and its residents) has a significant interest in ensuring that the inner workings of the machinery of public service are honest and free of corruption. We conclude that this public policy restricts the freedom to arbitrate under the circumstances presented here. . . . To allow an arbitrator to grant a city employee or a union the ability to restrict the DOI's investigatory procedures by invoking the employee rights provisions of a CBA would amount to an impermissible delegation of the broad authority of the City to investigate its internal affairs. . . . It is DOI, and not an arbitrator, that is the entity mandated by law to control all aspects of the criminal investigation; permitting an arbitrator, who may not have any background information on the nature or complexity of the DOI investigation or the severity of the offense, to dictate the procedures over who should be present at a DOI interview or to direct that notice be given to an employee concerning the subject matter of the DOI investigation would only hinder the DOI's role as a fact investigator and would contravene the City Charter's prohibition against interference with an investigation. N.Y. City Charter § 1128[a]. Moreover, subjecting DOI inquiries to the arbitration process would introduce elements that could compromise criminal investigations.

We further reject the contention of the Union and our dissenting colleague that the courts below acted too quickly in staying the arbitration in that an arbitrator could fashion an award to determine the dispute in a manner that would not offend public policy considerations.

We have recognized that judicial intervention to stay arbitration on public policy grounds is not without restrictions. . . . For example, we have noted that although a school district's statutory authority in certain areas of school operation may not be bargained away or otherwise delegated, the violations of the procedural and substantive aspects of those reserved powers must nevertheless be treated separately. . . . While a Board of Education may not surrender its ultimate responsibility for making tenure decisions or restrict its exclusive right to terminate probationary teacher appointments, the courts may not nullify the bargained-for procedural steps preliminary to the board's final action to grant or withhold tenure. . . .

Thus, in [*Matter of Port Washington Union Free School Dist. v. Port Washington Teachers Assn.*, 45 N.Y.2d 411 (1978)] we acknowledged that situations may exist in which although public policy would be violated by granting the remedy requested by one or more of the parties, it may still be premature for a court to intercede because the arbitrator may be able to fashion a remedy not in violation of public policy. . . . We have also recognized other situations in which no remedy could be granted without violating public policy. See *Matter of Blackburne [Governor's Off. of Empl. Relations]*, 87 N.Y.2d 660 (1996). In *Blackburne*, an employee, who had violated the Federal Hatch Act, claimed that he was terminated in violation of the procedural guarantees found in the CBA. This Court held that the arbitrator could not mandate compliance with the CBA's procedural guarantees concerning employee termination without subjecting the State to loss of Federal funds for the Hatch Act violation. To allow the arbitrator to make such a decision constituted an impermissible delegation of the State's sovereign authority. . . .

In this case, the procedural protections afforded a City employee under Article XVII of the CBA cannot be separated from their impact on a DOI criminal investigation. The granting of any relief under the procedural protections of the CBA would not only impinge on DOI's ability to conduct a criminal investigation, but would add another layer of process, decision-making and potential conflict. Thus, to the extent that public policy considerations preclude arbitration here, the courts below did not act precipitously and arbitration must be permanently stayed. . . .

KAYE, C.J., dissenting.

In a freely-negotiated collective bargaining agreement (CBA), the City of New York agreed to give fire officers certain procedural rights—including notice, representation by counsel and a union representative, and use immunity—when interrogated by their "Employer." . . .

Several longstanding policies of this State weigh against granting the City's petition to stay arbitration at this early stage.

First, the public policy exception to arbitrability is very narrow. "[J]udicial intervention to stay arbitration on public policy grounds is exceptional and itself limited to circumstances specifically identified or rooted in statute or case law." *Matter of New York City Dept. of Sanitation v. MacDonald*, 87 N.Y.2d 650 (1996). By and large, this Court has "overwhelmingly rejected contentions by public employers that particular issues fall outside the scope of permissible grievance arbitration." *Matter of Board of Educ. [Watertown Educ. Assoc.]*, 93 N.Y.2d 132 (1999) (collecting cases). As this Court recently reaffirmed, public policy bars arbitration only where "strong and well-defined policy considerations embodied in constitutional, statutory or common law prohibit a particular matter from being decided or certain relief from being granted by an arbitrator." *Matter of New York State Correctional Officers & Police Benevolent Assn. v. State of New York*, 94 N.Y.2d 321 (1999).

Further, a petition to stay arbitration is an extreme remedy that will be granted only if there is no possibility that the arbitrator could fashion any relief consistent with public policy. . . .

As an initial matter, the arbitrator could very well issue a ruling that would moot the City's public policy argument. As the Majority acknowledges, the City's argument rests on the assertion that the collective bargaining agreement impedes "DOI's ability to conduct criminal investigations." We do not yet know, however, whether the CBA applies to criminal investigations, or, for that matter, to any investigation conducted by DOI. Indeed, the Individual Rights provisions of the CBA make repeated references to interrogations by the "Employer," and to "Departmental" investigations and trials. Arguably, these provisions apply only to internal Fire Department investigations—not to DOI investigations or serious criminal investigations. Were the arbitrator to make such a finding, the CBA would not violate public policy. Alternatively, the arbitrator could find that some of the CBA provisions apply to DOI investigations but not others. . . .

A stay would also be particularly inappropriate here because there appear to be lingering factual questions that are not made clear by the record. Significantly, contrary to the Majority, it is not clear whether DOI in this case was conducting a criminal investigation of the fire officers. The City asserts that it was; the Union, however, insists that this was merely a disciplinary investigation.

Finally, there is no concern that arbitration would delay a criminal investigation in the case at hand. The investigation has already been completed; the Union has not sought to stay interrogations or any investigative proceedings. Rather, the

Union is seeking a post-deprivation remedy for alleged violations that occurred in the past. . . .

Notes

1. On what grounds does the majority find that this matter is not arbitrable: (1) that the rights in the CBA conflict with an overriding city-wide rule; (2) general concerns of public policy; or (3) the non-delegation doctrine? To the extent it is (1), does that mean the contract clause itself (in whole or in part) was not a legal topic of bargaining? To the extent it is (2), compare that with the private-sector rules on refusing to enforce arbitration awards on the grounds of public policy in the private sector, discussed *supra*, and analogous cases in the public sector, discussed *infra*. To the extent it is (3), what, if anything, is the concept of "non-delegability" adding here? Is it anything beyond (1) and (2)?

2. Some court decisions in public-sector cases say they are applying rules from the Steelworkers Trilogy, yet they at least arguably allow a greater role for courts than do private-sector cases. For example, *Classified Employees Ass'n v. Matanuska-Susitna Borough Sch. Dist.*, 204 P.3d 347 (Alaska 2009), citing private-sector precedent, held that a grievance over contracting out custodial work was non-arbitrable because the CBA did not bar such acts. The dissent insisted that under private-sector precedent the arbitrator should have been allowed to interpret the CBA to determine whether it barred the employer's act. In *County of Allegheny v. Allegheny County Prison Employees Indep. Union*, 476 Pa. 27 (1977), the majority also claimed it was following the Steelworkers Trilogy when it overturned an arbitration award that found a binding past practice regarding meal time conditions for prison guards. The dissent argued the majority was not truly applying the "essence of the contract" test.

Courts also vacate some arbitral decisions in the public sector under the traditional, narrow Steelworkers Trilogy test. *See, e.g., City of Chicago v. Fraternal Order of Police*, 2020 IL 124831 (Ill., June 18, 2020) (enforcing CBA rule requiring destruction of all disciplinary and investigatory records after five years violates public policy because rule conflicts with express provisions of a statute, the Local Records Act); *Lake City Fire & Rescue Ass'n, Local 2288 IAFF v. City of Lake City*, 240 So. 3d 128 (Fla. App. 2018) (arbitrator exceeded his authority in reducing penalty where CBA specified that arbitrator couldn't rule on extent of discipline, only on whether employee did what he was accused of); *Civil Service Employees Local 1000 v. Bd. of Trustees of Mount Vernon Pub. Library*, 75 N.Y.S.3d 840 (N.Y. Sup. Ct., 2018) (arbitrator exceeded his authority by ordering a provision on pay parity removed from the CBA, when only issue before arbitrator was whether the employer had violated that provision).

3. Do the rationales in the Steelworkers Trilogy apply equally in the public sector? One rationale is that courts should use a strong presumption in favor of arbitrability because arbitration is the quid pro quo for giving up the right to strike. In the public sector, as Chapter 11 shows, most jurisdictions do not permit employees to

strike. Does that mean that the presumption of arbitrability should be weaker or stronger in the public sector? In either case, should there be different presumptions for employees who can strike and for those who cannot?

4. A second rationale in the Trilogy is that there is value in arbitrating even frivolous grievances. Is that equally true in the public sector? Consider the costs and who is paying. If this is not equally true, how should courts adjust the rules for the public sector?

B. The Public Policy Exception

In the public sector, some courts have been more willing to use the public policy exception to vacate arbitration awards. For example, in *AFSCME v. Department of Central Management Services*, 173 Ill. 2d 299 (1996), Vera Dubose, a Child Welfare Specialist with the Illinois Department of Children and Family Services (DCFS), was fired because although she had filed a progress report stating that she had seen three children she was assigned to supervise and they were "doing fine," it was later discovered that the three children had died in a fire at their home a month before the report. The union claimed the DCFS had failed to impose discipline in a timely manner. The CBA required that discipline "shall be imposed as soon as possible after the Employer is aware of the event or action giving rise to the discipline and has a reasonable period of time to investigate the matter," and in any event not more than 45 days after the predisciplinary meeting. Dubose submitted her report in February 1990; the employer learned it was false in August 1990. An investigator's report, submitted in December 1990, noted that Dubose had failed to submit case plans for the family for the prior three years. The predisciplinary hearing was not conducted until June 24, 1991, and the predisciplinary report was not issued until September 2, 1991. 173 Ill. 2d 299, 300–03.

The arbitrator sustained the grievance and reinstated Dubose, holding that the agency's discipline was untimely. The Illinois Supreme Court, however, set aside the award, holding that it was contrary to public policy. The "State's interest in its children's welfare and protection must override AFSCME's concerns for timeliness." 173 Ill. 2d at 317. According to the court, the arbitrator

> [failed to make] *any* determination that the welfare of the minors in the DCFS system will not be compromised by such a reinstatement. Rather, he avoided discussion of the charges against DuBose. He did not take any precautionary steps to ensure the misconduct at issue here will not be repeated, and he neither considered nor respected the pertinent public policy concerns that arose from them. Thus, the remedy in this case violates public policy in that it totally ignores any legitimate public policy concerns. 173 Ill. 2d at 317–18.

Further, "[e]ven if the arbitrator had considered issues of public policy, we may not abdicate to him our responsibility to protect the public interest at stake. . . . DCFS, in agreeing to a time provision that does not allow for exigent disciplinary circumstances, has compromised its ability to discharge its duties as expressed by the General Assembly." *Id.* at 318.

One judge dissented: "I recognize that there exists a general public policy favoring the diligent protection of minors. . . . However, there exists no policy that mandates the discharge of every DCFS employee that files a false report, regardless of the circumstances." *Id.* at 345.

Who was right? It is unlikely that a court in an analogous case in the private sector would have overturned the arbitrator's award. Also, suppose an employer fired an employee because it believed she had filed a false report similar to that in this case, but later evidence showed that the employee had actually not filed such a report. Suppose further that the union grieved the matter, but because the union missed a deadline in the grievance procedure, the right to arbitrate was lost. Should a court intervene to reverse that result? Is there a distinction?

More broadly, on one hand, the "public policy" argument often seems stronger in cases involving public employees. And the employees in these cases are often not particularly sympathetic. On the other hand, does the public have an interest in the finality (at least in most cases) of grievance-arbitration? Might the prospect of courts reversing more arbitration awards encourage more appeals of such awards, at some cost to the public fisc?

Some courts hew more closely to the private-sector approach. In ***Shamokin Area Sch. Dist. v. AFSCME Dist. Council 86***, 20 A.3d 579 (Pa. Commw. Ct. 2011), a school employee called the school superintendent to complain about his supervisor. The employee then failed to hang up his phone before yelling to a co-worker about the supervisor, "I wish I could punch him right in the . . . mouth. I'm just gonna pay somebody. I can't do it so I'm just gonna pay somebody. I'll say here's a hundred dollars. Put a . . . dusting on him." 20 A.3d 579, 580 n.1. The employer fired the employee, but an arbitrator reduced the penalty. The employer appealed, claiming this award violated public policy. The lower court agreed with the employer, but the appellate court reversed and upheld the arbitration award.

> We recognize that there is a distinct public policy of protecting students from violence on school property, which is derived from the Pennsylvania school code. . . . [T]he public policy protecting students from violence is a well-defined and established policy. We also recognize that the District has a zero tolerance policy for violence in schools, and that the District has a direct responsibility for the safety of its pupils. . . . Further, we note that Weaver was, in fact, on school property when he indirectly threatened the safety of his supervisor.

> Contrary to the trial court's determination that Weaver's actions violated the public policy against violence in schools, however, we conclude that Weaver's conduct did not trigger the public policy against violence in schools because it did not implicate the public concern of protection *of students* from violence. . . . Although his statements were highly inappropriate,

they constituted nothing more than a rant about a supervisor, which was not directed immediately toward that supervisor. Weaver's conduct did not rise to the level of violating the public policy of protecting students from violence on school property, in part because the statements were made in an isolated garage away from the students. . . .

[T]he appropriate test is not whether Weaver's actions violated public policy, but whether the Arbitrator's award violates public policy. Here, the Arbitrator made a finding that Weaver's discharge for making a threatening statement was without just cause because "the District denied him his proper due process." Further, the Arbitrator found that Weaver's "treatment was palpably disparate, and for that reason, without just cause." The arbitration award was not based on findings regarding the implication of student safety. In fact, the Arbitrator made absolutely no findings regarding whether Weaver's conduct implicated student safety. Again, the award was based on the denial of due process and disparate treatment, not student safety.

We, therefore, hold that within the context of this case, reinstating a groundskeeper, who vented about a supervisor by screaming in a garage which was isolated from students, conditioned upon a one-year probation and a required anger management program, does not violate the public policy of protecting students from violence on school property. While we recognize that reinstating a school district employee who had actually struck a student, bullied a student, or threatened violence upon a student on school grounds, could very well trigger the established public policy of protecting students from violence on school property, this is not such a case. 20 A.3d 579, 582–83.

Also, in *City of Lynn v. Thompson*, 435 Mass. 54 (2001), an arbitrator found no just cause for discharging a police officer after he broke the arm of a mentally ill woman. The two lower courts held that the award should be vacated on public policy grounds, but the state Supreme Court reversed. "It may be distasteful to keep such an officer on the force, but it does not violate public policy." 435 Mass. 54, 64. How would you argue for or against this result? What facts could be relevant in those arguments? What if the officer had been accused of using excessive force in earlier incidents? What if an arbitrator had exonerated the officer from the previous charges?

Cuyahoga Metropolitan Housing Auth. v. Fraternal Order of Police, Ohio Labor Council, 108 N.E.3d 1220 (Ohio App. 2018), rejected an argument that an arbitrator reducing a discharge to a suspension violated public policy. In this case, a City Housing Authority had fired a police officer for his improper conduct while investigating a suspected drug transaction (including use of excessive force) and for being dishonest during the employer's investigation of the incident. The court held that the arbitrator's award of a sixteen-month, unpaid suspension drew its essence from the contract, and the majority stated that no law barred reinstatement of a police officer who had made dishonest statements during an investigation. A dissent argued that Ohio had a well-defined and dominant public policy favoring an honest police force made up of officers who command the public trust, and that reinstating a police officer who committed acts of dishonesty in his official capacity violated that policy.

Similarly using the narrower approach found in the private sector, the Alaska Supreme Court, in a 3–2 decision, partly upheld an arbitrator's decision to reinstate with back pay a police officer who had consensual sex with a victim of domestic violence he met while responding to an incident at her home. The employer argued that this violated public policy because it conflicted with the Police Standards Council's decision to revoke officer's police certification, and because the conduct was morally repugnant. The lower court upheld the back pay award, although it reasoned it could not uphold the reinstatement because the employee now lacked proper certification. The Alaska Supreme Court affirmed, stating that the arbitrator's decision did not violate explicit, well-defined and dominant public policy. This was because, among other things, Alaska law and regulations containing the policy of aiding domestic violence victims did not indicate that such a reinstatement would violate public policy. Further, the state could use progressive discipline and was not required to fire police officers for engaging in consensual sexual misconduct. Also, the revocation of the certificate came after the discharge and was a reaction to the discharge. *State v. Public Safety Employees Ass'n*, 323 P.3d 670 (Alaska 2014).

The majority stressed that "the relevant inquiry is whether the arbitrator's *decision* to reinstate the employee violates public policy, not whether an employee's *conduct* does, *so statutes or regulations that merely prohibit the conduct are insufficient to support the public policy exception*." 323 P.3d 670, 677 (emphasis in original). The dissent argued that "a contractual arbitration remedy requiring that a state trooper be reinstated after his commander has, *with very good reason*, lost confidence in the trooper's judgment, moral character, and effectiveness as a law enforcement officer violates Alaska public policy." 323 P.3d, 686–87 (emphasis in original). Further, while "the public policy exception to the enforcement of arbitration awards is sparingly applied. . . . the court today requires an unrealistic degree of precision from the codes of acceptable conduct that other branches of government are entitled to expect their employees to follow." *Id.* at 687. Which opinion is more convincing?

In contrast, *City of Chicago v. Fraternal Order of Police*, 2019 IL App. (1st) 172907, (Ill. App. 2019), held that an arbitrator erred in ordering the City of Chicago to destroy records of alleged police misconduct that were more than five years old, even though the relevant CBA required the destruction of such records. Using the private-sector test, the court held that state and local law established a well-defined public policy favoring the proper retention of important public records for access by the public. Further, the U.S. Department of Justice (which had opened an investigation into the department's use of force policies in 2015) had concluded that this CBA provision could deprive the DOJ of important information needed to monitor historical patterns of police misconduct.

Consider *Amalgamated Transit Union, Local 1300 v. Maryland Transit Admin.*, 244 Md. App. 1 (Md. App. 2019). In this case, Wilson, a Maryland Transit Administration (MTA) bus driver, stabbed Rosebrough, a retired bus driver and Wilson's estranged stepfather. The MTA fired Wilson. The arbitrator overturned the discharge and reinstated Wilson without pay, explaining that the MTA had not followed the CBA's progressive discipline rules because it refused to consider the mitigating circumstances of his "respectable work and disciplinary records." 244 Md. App. 1, 8. The trial court vacated the order to reinstate on the grounds that it violated public policy, and the appellate court affirmed, even though it stressed that "[t]he scope of judicial review of arbitral awards is 'very narrowly limited.'" *Id.* at 12. While endorsing the private-sector standards for the public-policy exception, the appellate court relied heavily on the fact that Sec. 11-105 of the Maryland State Code provided that unjustified intentional conduct that "seriously injures another person" or "seriously threatens the safety of the workplace" is a cause for "automatic termination of employment" of state employees. 244 Md. App. 1, 21. Absent such explicit language in a state statute on which to base a public policy objection, would a court using private-sector rules in this area vacate this arbitration award?

Problem 13.2

Thomas, an employee of a city public agency, was accused of sexually harassing a co-worker, Stephanie, through numerous sexually explicit comments and inappropriate touching over the course of a year. Thomas denied most of the allegations, and attributed others to good-natured "horseplay" that took place at the worksite. The employer investigated, found Stephanie credible and Thomas not credible, and it discharged Thomas. Thomas's union arbitrated the discharge. While the arbitrator found that Thomas's behavior was "lewd, lascivious and extraordinarily perverse," the arbitrator also found that after a supervisor had given a warning to Thomas about his behavior, Thomas engaged in no further inappropriate behavior. Given this, the arbitrator ruled that the employer did not have just cause to terminate Thomas's employment, and the arbitrator ordered Thomas reinstated.

The employer is now arguing before a court that this arbitration award should be vacated because it violates public policy. What are the employer's strongest arguments that the award should be vacated? What are the union's strongest arguments on behalf of the employee that the award should not be vacated? How should the court rule, and why? Also, should the court treat a case like this differently than it would had the case arisen in the private sector? Why or why not? *See Philadelphia Housing Auth. v. American Federation of State, County and Municipal Employees Council 33*, 617 Pa. 69 (2012); *New York Transit Auth. v. Phillips*, 75 N.Y.S.3d 133 (N.Y. Sup. Ct. App. Div. 2018).

C. Arbitration, Civil Service, and Other Laws

Public-sector CBAs may provide substantive rights and procedures that overlap with rights and procedures under other laws, *e.g.*, civil service and tenure laws.

Sometimes, civil service laws provide that they are the exclusive remedy for certain employer actions; in such cases, arbitration under a CBA is barred. *See, e.g., Kucera v. Baldazo*, 745 N.W.2d 481 (Iowa 2008) (deputy sheriff may not arbitrate discharge under CBA because civil service process was exclusive). In other jurisdictions, employees may challenge discipline both in an arbitration under a CBA and in a civil service hearing. *See, e.g., Civil Service Comm. v. City of Kelso*, 137 Wash. 2d 166 (1999).

In such a jurisdiction, what could or should an employer do if the two fora produce conflicting results? *See id.* (suggesting the parties negotiate an agreement requiring employees to choose one forum or the other). Some laws require the employee to choose one forum. *See* FLA. STAT. ANN. §447.401 (1999) (for certain cases, employees can use the civil service appeal procedure, the ULP procedure, or a grievance procedure, but cannot use more than one of these procedures). *See generally* Ann Hodges, *The Interplay of Civil Service Law and Collective Bargaining Law in Public Sector Employee Discipline Cases*, 32 B.C. L. REV. 95 (1990).

Other laws governing public employment may give employees or employers rights regarding discipline and discharge that may trump or at least go beyond rules in a CBA.

L'Anse Creuse Public Schools and Michigan Educ. Ass'n, NEA Local 1

125 Lab. Arb. (BNA) 527 (2008)

DANIEL, ARB.

The grievant is a tenured teacher employed by the district since 1999. She holds an elementary teacher certification as well as certification for grades 6 through 8 in math and Spanish. Her past record has been good and her evaluations quite satisfactory.

During the summer of 2005, the grievant was asked to take an engaged couple and their friends in her boat to the "Jobbie Nooner" instead of having separate bachelor and bachelorette parties. This party occasion of Jobbie Nooner has been notorious for many years and is held in Lake St. Clair around Gull Island, which is not far from the L'Anse Creuse community. This gathering of party boaters attracts as many as 1000 watercraft and upwards of 5000 people. It is a very rowdy occasion with widespread public consumption of alcohol, often to high levels of intoxication, public nudity, and public sexual activity. The boats are arranged in such a fashion as to create a space known as the "gauntlet" where attendees walk around and observe the various activities which are going on.

The grievant and the rest of her group were walking in this area when they came upon a boat where two mannequins, one "male" and one "female" had been specially rigged with tubing running from the neck of the mannequin down through the torso and out the genitalia. In the case of the male mannequin this simulated a male penis. Bystanders were invited to perform fellatio and cunnilingus on the mannequins and in return receive a shot of liquor down the tube. The grievant's group decided to participate and the grievant obtained her "shot" by performing the necessary act. While it was obvious that the mannequins were exactly that, they were dressed in bathing attire and the torsos from very close range were not discernible as not human.

While the grievant was in the process of getting her "shot," pictures were being taken. The grievant testified that she was totally unaware that her picture was taken, though from the subsequent photos introduced in evidence it would appear the camera was at a range of only several feet. Without the grievant's knowledge or permission these photographs were placed on a 2007 website and available for public viewing by anyone who happened upon that website.

Shortly after the start of school in early September, 2007, a parent notified the grievant that her daughter had heard rumors regarding the website photographs. Rumors and descriptions were widely circulated among students and came to the attention of teaching colleagues and parents. Finally the grievant, though unable to find the website, decided to notify the principal of Central Middle School of the situation and how it had come about, explaining that she was simply "taking a shot." She did not advise the principal of the circumstances. . . . She contended that what she did off school property and off school time was "not anybody's business," and expressed no regret or remorse for her conduct.

Rumors and information about the matter became widespread among the student body at Central immediately after the start of school in 2007. . . .

The school district conducted an investigation and determined that it would not return the grievant to active duty and would file tenure charges which were adopted October 15, 2007. The grievant was put on a suspension which is provided for under the terms of the Teacher's Tenure Act, requiring that in such instance "the teacher's salary shall continue during the suspension." . . . The grievance which was subsequently filed contended that the suspension or paid administrative leave pending tenure proceedings did not comply with teacher rights under the collective bargaining agreement and constituted disciplinary action subject to the grievance and arbitration process. The employer's response was that the grievant had not been disciplined but rather suspended in accordance with the Tenure Act and that the employer possessed the right to act in that fashion and did so properly. . . .

Teacher Tenure Act Article IV, Section 3

> Sec. 3. (1) On the filing of charges in accordance with this Article, the controlling board may suspend the accused teacher from active performance of duty until 1 of the following occurs: . . . (b) A preliminary decision and order discharging or demoting the teacher is issued by the administrative law judge under section 4(5)(i) of this article. . . .

. . . This is not the ordinary case as contemplated by the contract of some obvious or clear misconduct of the teacher in the course of employment. Here the grievant was involved in an acknowledged adult activity of a salacious nature, however it did not directly involve either the school or her capacity to teach. For this reason the arbitrator must find that the employer would not have had just cause for terminating her employment or otherwise disciplining her.

But the employer contends that this is not discipline but that it has acted simply because the result of the grievant's outside activity has carried over into the school community and has caused great disruption and widespread disrespect for the teacher. It is its contention that under the circumstances it cannot cause students to be taught by the grievant until the matter of her continued employment is resolved. It views its actions, then, as protective as opposed to disciplinary. In this respect the arbitrator agrees. Even though it was not the grievant's fault that the information became widely disseminated, nevertheless, her actions did create the potential for such public knowledge.

The Tenure Act specifically recognizes that there may be circumstances under which a teacher may or should be removed from teaching duties while the issue of termination of employment is considered by the Tenure Commission. Certain safe guards and protections are provided that the individual teacher not lose compensation during the period of such a suspension. Obviously under the Tenure Act the fact of being suspended is not regarded as conclusive or even relevant to the issue of misconduct or any basis for discharge. In other words the Tenure Act regards the suspension of a teacher, under such circumstances, as necessary for the continued operation of the educational process.

This case presents the single issue of whether the board acted within its authority in suspending the grievant. Although the board has certain management rights to suspend, such did not pertain to this particular situation. Here, the board has exercised a right which is authorized by the Teacher Tenure Act and has done so in an appropriate and proper manner. Exercising rights under the Teacher Tenure Act cannot constitute a violation of the collective bargaining agreement nor can it be regarded as disciplinary, since the Tenure Act itself does not so regard it. In no respect has the employer asserted that its actions were disciplinary, and in fact it has complied in every respect to protect the grievant economically during this period of time.

Because it is been found that such does not constitute disciplinary action, but rather the exercise of a legally provided right, it must be found that there is no basis for grievance in this matter and therefore it is dismissed.

Notes

1. One of the (perhaps many) lessons of this case is that various statutes governing public employees can provide rules that may be enforced no matter what the CBA says. But also note the arbitrator's claim that this conduct would not have justified discharge—or any other discipline—under the CBA's general "just cause" provision. Do you agree? If not, what discipline would have been appropriate under a "just cause" standard?

2. Suppose, in the absence of the Teacher Tenure Act, the school district had discharged the teacher. Further, suppose that an arbitrator had then overturned the discharge and ordered the employee reinstated (because of her prior good record, the fact that her actions were away from the school, and/or because the teacher did not realize that pictures of her acts would be made public). The employer then appeals to court, arguing that this award violates public policy. How should the court rule, and why?

3. To complete the story, in litigation before the State Tenure Commission ("Commission"), while an ALJ within the Commission upheld Land's discharge, the full Commission reversed that decision. A court then upheld the Commission's decision that Land should not have been fired. *Land v. L'Anse Creuse Public School Board of Education*, 2010 Mich. App. LEXIS 999 (Mich. Ct. App. May 27, 2010).

Chapter 14

Individual Workers and Their Unions

I. Introduction

This chapter discusses two important aspects of the relationship between individual employees and the unions that represent them: the duty of fair representation and union security clauses. First, because the law makes unions the "exclusive representative" of all employees in a bargaining unit, including those who oppose the union, labor laws in both the public and private sectors give individuals in a bargaining unit a cause of action against their union if it breaches its "duty of fair representation" (DFR) by bargaining or administering a contract in bad faith, or in a hostile, discriminatory, or arbitrary manner. Note that the courts' role in DFR cases opens the door to judicial involvement in the substance of collective bargaining and grievance and arbitration handling. Accordingly, DFR law balances the rights of workers to fair representation with the law's hostility to intervention in the substantive relationship between unions and employers. Note also that employers are frequently joined in these cases (for reasons described below), in what are known as "hybrid DFR/§ 301" claims. Public-sector jurisdictions have almost all adopted DFR rules similar or identical to private-sector rules.

Second, this chapter discusses a contract term commonly found in private-sector collective-bargaining agreements: the union security clause. In essence, union security clauses require employees whom the union is obligated to represent to pay at least some portion of union dues as a condition of employment. This chapter addresses several topics related to union security agreements, including the definition of union "membership," what activities unions can and cannot "charge" objecting members of the bargaining unit for, and procedures for implementing these clauses consistent with the rights of individual employees. It will also discuss the right-to-work provision of the NLRA under which (unlike other NLRA topics) states can choose a different rule than the default rule. Specifically, states can choose to make all union security clauses illegal.

In the public sector, before the Supreme Court's 2018 decision in *Janus v. AFSCME*, *infra*, most jurisdictions either allowed union security clauses using the same procedural and substantive laws as in the private sector, or adopted the right-to-work rule. Then *Janus* held that union security clauses in the public sector violate the First Amendment.

II. Exclusive Representation and the Duty of Fair Representation

A. The Emergence of the Duty of Fair Representation

Although the duty of fair representation is a very important doctrine, it does not appear in the text of the NLRA. Instead, the DFR is a creation of courts and the NLRB. The policy justification is fairly straightforward: it is a necessary corollary to the statutory mandate of exclusive representation. If an employee is represented by a union, that employee cannot deal individually with the employer over wages, hours, and conditions of work (or, more precisely, can only do so with the approval of the union). In short, the union should have an obligation to treat the employees it represents fairly, and with a minimum level of competence.

The power of the exclusivity principle was evident early on. For example, in *J.I. Case Co. v. NLRB*, 321 U.S. 332 (1944), the Supreme Court held that a union CBA trumped contracts that the employer had entered into with individual employees. The Court explained that the union was in the best position to accommodate conflicting interests of bargaining-unit members, and even employees who could make more favorable deals would have to defer to the union's position. The principle of exclusive representation has been a central feature of U.S. labor law ever since. *See, e.g., Emporium Capwell v. Western Addition Community Organization*, 420 U.S. 50 (1975) (referring to the "long and consistent adherence to the principle of exclusive representation").

In 1944, in *Steele v. Louisville & Nashville R. Co.*, 323 U.S. 192 (1944), the Court, in an RLA case, inferred a duty of fair representation from the exclusive representative status.

> Section 2, Second, requiring carriers to bargain with the representative so chosen, operates to exclude any other from representing a craft. The minority members of a craft are thus deprived by the statute of the right, which they would otherwise possess, to choose a representative of their own, and its members cannot bargain individually on behalf of themselves as to matters which are properly the subject of collective bargaining. . . .
>
> . . . We hold that the language of the Act to which we have referred, read in the light of the purposes of the Act, expresses the aim of Congress to impose on the bargaining representative of a craft or class of employees the duty to exercise fairly the power conferred upon it on behalf of all those for whom it acts, without hostile discrimination against them.
>
> This does not mean that the statutory representative of a craft is barred from making contracts which may have unfavorable effects on some of the members of the craft represented. Variations in the terms of the contract based on differences relevant to the authorized purposes of the contract in conditions to which they are to be applied, such as differences in seniority, the type of work performed, the competence and skill with which it is

performed, are within the scope of the bargaining representation of a craft, all of whose members are not identical in their interest or merit. 323 U.S. 192, 202–03.

Tunstall v. Locomotive Firemen, 323 U.S. 210 (1944), a companion case to *Steele*, found a right to be represented without discrimination under the RLA. Indeed, a significant percentage of the early DFR cases, including *Steele*, involved unions discriminating against black bargaining-unit members. Recall that these early cases were decided before the passage of Title VII, which, among other things, bars certain forms of race discrimination by unions.

Completing the trio of 1944 cases, *Wallace Corp. v. NLRB*, 323 U.S. 248, 255 (1944), held that unions under the NLRA must represent employees "fairly and impartially." A few years later, in *Ford Motor Co. v. Huffman*, 345 U.S. 330, 337 (1953), another NLRA case, the Court held that unions' "statutory obligation to represent all members of an appropriate unit requires them to make an honest effort to serve the interests of all of those members without hostility to any." In *Humphrey v. Moore*, 375 U.S. 335 (1964), also involving the NLRA, the Court cited RLA precedent and reaffirmed that the "undoubted broad authority of the union as exclusive bargaining agent in the negotiation and administration of a collective bargaining contract is accompanied by a responsibility of equal scope, the responsibility and duty of fair representation." 375 U.S. 335, 342.

Because the duty is considered a necessary corollary to exclusive representation, unions have a duty to fairly represent members of the bargaining unit who are not members of the union (Section IV of this chapter describes how this situation arises). *See, e.g., Smith v. Sheet Metal Workers Local 25*, 500 F.2d 741 (5th Cir. 1974).

B. Breach of the Duty as an Unfair Labor Practice

The cases discussed above did not describe the exact form the DFR action would take. Again, the NLRA does not list a "duty of fair representation" in §8 (or elsewhere). So, are DFR actions ULPs, and if so, must those alleging a DFR violation file their claim with the NLRB initially? Notably, the RLA has no enforcing agency equivalent to the NLRB, and the early DFR cases under the RLA allowed suits directly in federal court. This subsection traces the historical development of the relationship of the DFR to ULPs under the NLRA.

In *NLRB v. Miranda Fuel Co.*, 140 N.L.R.B. 181 (1962), *enforcement denied*, 326 F.2d 172 (2d Cir. 1963), the Board held that it is a violation of the DFR and a ULP for a union to improperly induce an employer to discipline an employee for reasons other than that the employee was not a union member. Sections 8(a)(3) and 8(b)(2) explicitly cover unions inducing employers to discipline employees for not being union members. *Miranda Fuel* extended this to union inducements motivated by other invidious or capricious reasons, finding that §7 gave employees an implied right to be free from such conduct. While the Second Circuit denied enforcement, that decision contained no majority opinion as to whether the DFR violation was also a ULP.

A divided Board further expanded this approach in *Independent Metal Workers Local 1 (Hughes Tool Co.)*, 147 N.L.R.B. 1573 (1964). The union in that case had discriminated against a black employee, refusing to process his grievance because of his race. A three-member majority found that the union's discriminatory conduct violated §§ 8(b)(1), (2), and (3): in short, the DFR violation was also a ULP. The dissent agreed on the § 8(b)(1) violation (the local was segregated, and thus the refusal could be seen as improper discrimination on the basis of union membership in a manner that 8(b)(1)(A) prohibits). But the dissent disagreed that race discrimination *qua* race discrimination was a ULP. The dissent noted, among other things, that the Taft-Hartley Act, which created union ULPs, was signed into law three years after *Steele*, and yet Congress did not make race discrimination by unions a ULP.

Still, the NLRB has consistently taken the position that a DFR violation is, in fact, a union ULP, and courts have accepted this position. While the Supreme Court in *DelCostello v. Int'l B'hood of Teamsters*, 462 U.S. 151 (1983), formally reserved the question, it also seemed to support the logic underlying the position that DFR claims are ULPs. The specific holding in *DelCostello* was that the statute of limitations for DFR claims should be one hundred eighty days — the same as that which NLRA § 10(b) sets for ULP claims. The Court rejected the argument that it should borrow from the analogous state statute of limitations, explaining that in most cases this would be too short. Instead, it chose as the best analogy the six-month period of § 10(b):

> The NLRB has consistently held that all breaches of a union's duty of fair representation *are* in fact unfair labor practices. *E.g., Miranda Fuel Co.* . . . We have twice declined to decide the correctness of the Board's position, and we need not address that question today. Even if not all breaches of the duty are unfair labor practices, however, the family resemblance is undeniable, and indeed there is substantial overlap. Many fair representation claims . . . include allegations of discrimination based on membership status or dissident views, which would be unfair labor practices under § 8(b)(1) or (2). Aside from these clear cases, duty-of-fair-representation claims are allegations of unfair, arbitrary, or discriminatory treatment of workers by unions — as are virtually all unfair labor practice charges made by workers against unions. . . . Similarly, it may be the case that alleged violations by an employer of a collective-bargaining agreement will also amount to unfair labor practices. 462 U.S. 151, 170.

As is shown below, however, there are some important procedural differences between DFR cases and other ULP cases.

C. The Creation of Modern DFR Law: Jurisdiction, Parties, Standards, and Damages

Vaca v. Sipes was the first major Supreme Court case to explore the DFR in detail. *Vaca* touched on a number of central issues in DFR law. First, should the NLRB have exclusive jurisdiction initially, as with other ULP cases? Second, what type of union conduct creates a DFR violation? Third, how could employers be joined? After all, employers frequently committed bad acts contributing to a DFR plaintiff's harm (*e.g.*, by violating an employee's rights under a CBA, which a union then improperly fails to grieve). Fourth, if both the employer and union contributed to the employee's harm, how should damages be apportioned?

Vaca v. Sipes

Supreme Court of the United States
386 U.S. 171 (1967)

WHITE, J.

On February 13, 1962, Benjamin Owens filed this class action against petitioners, as officers and representatives of the National Brotherhood of Packinghouse Workers and of its Kansas City Local No. 12 (the Union), in the Circuit Court of Jackson County, Missouri. Owens, a Union member, alleged that he had been discharged from his employment at Swift & Company's (Swift) Kansas City Meat Packing Plant in violation of the collective bargaining agreement then in force between Swift and the Union, and that the Union had "arbitrarily, capriciously and without just or reasonable reason or cause" refused to take his grievance with Swift to arbitration under the fifth step of the bargaining agreement's grievance procedures. . . .

Petitioners' answer included the defense that the Missouri courts lacked jurisdiction because the gravamen of Owens' suit was "arguably and basically" an unfair labor practice under §8(b) of the National Labor Relations Act (N.L.R.A.) . . . within the exclusive jurisdiction of the [NLRB]. After a jury trial, a verdict was returned awarding Owens $7,000 compensatory and $3,300 punitive damages. The trial judge set aside the verdict and entered judgment for petitioners on the ground that the NLRB had exclusive jurisdiction over this controversy, and the Kansas City Court of Appeals affirmed. The Supreme Court of Missouri reversed and directed reinstatement of the jury's verdict. . . . We granted certiorari to consider whether exclusive jurisdiction lies with the NLRB and, if not, whether the finding of Union liability and the relief afforded Owens are consistent with governing principles of federal labor law. . . . Although we conclude that state courts have jurisdiction in this type of case, we hold that federal law governs, that the governing federal standards were not applied here, and that the judgment of the Supreme Court of Missouri must accordingly be reversed.

I.

In mid-1959, Owens, a long-time high blood pressure patient, became sick and entered a hospital on sick leave from his employment with Swift. After a long rest during which his weight and blood pressure were reduced, Owens was certified by his family physician as fit to resume his heavy work in the packing plant. However, Swift's company doctor examined Owens upon his return and concluded that his blood pressure was too high to permit reinstatement. After securing a second authorization from another outside doctor, Owens returned to the plant, and a nurse permitted him to resume work on January 6, 1960. However, on January 8, when the doctor discovered Owens' return, he was permanently discharged on the ground of poor health. . . .

II.

Petitioners challenge the jurisdiction of the Missouri courts on the ground that the alleged conduct of the Union was arguably an unfair labor practice and within the exclusive jurisdiction of the NLRB. Petitioners rely on *Miranda Fuel Co.*, 140 N.L.R.B. 181 (1962) . . . where a sharply divided Board held for the first time that a union's breach of its statutory duty of fair representation violates N.L.R.A. §8(b), as amended. . . . For the reasons which follow, we reject this argument.

It is now well established that, as the exclusive bargaining representative of the employees in Owens' bargaining unit, the Union had a statutory duty fairly to represent all of those employees, both in its collective bargaining with Swift, see *Ford Motor Co. v. Huffman*, 345 U.S. 330 (1953) . . . and in its enforcement of the resulting collective bargaining agreement, see *Humphrey v. Moore*, 375 U.S. 335 (1964). . . . Under this doctrine, the exclusive agent's statutory authority to represent all members of a designated unit includes a statutory obligation to serve the interests of all members without hostility or discrimination toward any, to exercise its discretion with complete good faith and honesty, and to avoid arbitrary conduct. . . . It is obvious that Owens' complaint alleged a breach by the Union of a duty grounded in federal statutes, and that federal law therefore governs his cause of action. . . .

Although N.L.R.A. §8(b) was enacted in 1947, the NLRB did not until *Miranda Fuel* interpret a breach of a union's duty of fair representation as an unfair labor practice. . . . In *Miranda Fuel*, the Board's majority held that N.L.R.A. §7 gives employees "the right to be free from unfair or irrelevant or invidious treatment by their exclusive bargaining agent in matters affecting their employment," and "that Section 8(b)(1)(A) of the Act accordingly prohibits labor organizations, when acting in a statutory representative capacity, from taking action against any employee upon considerations or classifications which are irrelevant, invidious, or unfair." . . . The Board also held that an employer who "participates" in such arbitrary union conduct violates §8(a)(1), and that the employer and the union may violate §§8(a) (3) and 8(b)(2), respectively, "when, for arbitrary or irrelevant reasons or upon the basis of an unfair classification, the union attempts to cause or does cause an employer to derogate the employment status of an employee." . . .

[P]etitioners argue that Owens' state court action was based upon Union conduct that is arguably proscribed by N.L.R.A. §8(b), was potentially enforceable by the NLRB, and was therefore pre-empted under the *Garmon* line of decisions. . . .

This pre-emption doctrine, however, has never been rigidly applied to cases where it could not fairly be inferred that Congress intended exclusive jurisdiction to lie with the NLRB. Congress itself has carved out exceptions to the Board's exclusive jurisdiction: Section 303 of the Labor Management Relations Act . . . expressly permits anyone injured by a violation of N.L.R.A. §8(b)(4) to recover damages in a federal court even though such unfair labor practices are also remediable by the Board; §301 of that Act . . . permits suits for breach of a collective bargaining agreement regardless of whether the particular breach is also an unfair labor practice within the jurisdiction of the Board. . . .

A primary justification for the pre-emption doctrine—the need to avoid conflicting rules of substantive law in the labor relations area and the desirability of leaving the development of such rules to the administrative agency created by Congress for that purpose—is not applicable to cases involving alleged breaches of the union's duty of fair representation. The doctrine was judicially developed in *Steele* and its progeny, and suits alleging breach of the duty remained judicially cognizable long after the NLRB was given unfair labor practice jurisdiction over union activities by the L.M.R.A. Moreover, when the Board declared in *Miranda Fuel* that a union's breach of its duty of fair representation would henceforth be treated as an unfair labor practice, the Board adopted and applied the doctrine as it had been developed by the federal courts. . . . Finally, as the dissenting Board members in *Miranda Fuel* have pointed out, fair representation duty suits often require review of the substantive positions taken and policies pursued by a union in its negotiation of a collective bargaining agreement and in its handling of the grievance machinery; as these matters are not normally within the Board's unfair labor practice jurisdiction, it can be doubted whether the Board brings substantially greater expertise to bear on these problems than do the courts, which have been engaged in this type of review since the *Steele* decision. . . .

There are also some intensely practical considerations which foreclose pre-emption of judicial cognizance of fair representation duty suits, considerations which emerge from the intricate relationship between the duty of fair representation and the enforcement of collective bargaining contracts. For the fact is that the question of whether a union has breached its duty of fair representation will in many cases be a critical issue in a suit under L.M.R.A. §301 charging an employer with a breach of contract. To illustrate, let us assume a collective bargaining agreement that limits discharges to those for good cause and that contains no grievance, arbitration or other provisions purporting to restrict access to the courts. If an employee is discharged without cause, either the union or the employee may sue the employer under L.M.R.A. §301. Under this section, courts have jurisdiction over suits to enforce collective bargaining agreements even though the conduct of the employer which is challenged as a breach of contract is also arguably an unfair labor practice within the jurisdiction of the NLRB. . . .

[I]f the wrongfully discharged employee himself resorts to the courts before the grievance procedures have been fully exhausted, the employer may well defend on the ground that the exclusive remedies provided by such a contract have not been exhausted. Since the employee's claim is based upon breach of the collective bargaining agreement, he is bound by terms of that agreement which govern the manner in which contractual rights may be enforced. For this reason, it is settled that the employee must at least attempt to exhaust exclusive grievance and arbitration procedures established by the bargaining agreement. . . . However, because these contractual remedies have been devised and are often controlled by the union and the employer, they may well prove unsatisfactory or unworkable for the individual grievant. The problem then is to determine under what circumstances the individual employee may obtain judicial review of his breach-of-contract claim despite his failure to secure relief through the contractual remedial procedures. . . .

We think that another situation when the employee may seek judicial enforcement of his contractual rights arises, if, as is true here, the union has sole power under the contract to invoke the higher stages of the grievance procedure, and if, as is alleged here, the employee-plaintiff has been prevented from exhausting his contractual remedies by the union's wrongful refusal to process the grievance. It is true that the employer in such a situation may have done nothing to prevent exhaustion of the exclusive contractual remedies to which he agreed in the collective bargaining agreement. But the employer has committed a wrongful discharge in breach of that agreement, a breach which could be remedied through the grievance process to the employee-plaintiff's benefit were it not for the union's breach of its statutory duty of fair representation to the employee. To leave the employee remediless in such circumstances would, in our opinion, be a great injustice. We cannot believe that Congress, in conferring upon employers and unions the power to establish exclusive grievance procedures, intended to confer upon unions such unlimited discretion to deprive injured employees of all remedies for breach of contract. Nor do we think that Congress intended to shield employers from the natural consequences of their breaches of bargaining agreements by wrongful union conduct in the enforcement of such agreements. . . .

For these reasons, we think the wrongfully discharged employee may bring an action against his employer in the face of a defense based upon the failure to exhaust contractual remedies, provided the employee can prove that the union as bargaining agent breached its duty of fair representation in its handling of the employee's grievance. We may assume for present purposes that such a breach of duty by the union is an unfair labor practice, as the NLRB and the Fifth Circuit have held. The employee's suit against the employer, however, remains a § 301 suit, and the jurisdiction of the courts is no more destroyed by the fact that the employee, as part and parcel of his § 301 action, finds it necessary to prove an unfair labor practice by the union, than it is by the fact that the suit may involve an unfair labor practice by the employer himself. The court is free to determine whether the employee is barred by the actions of his union representative, and, if not, to proceed with the case. And if, to facilitate his case, the employee joins the union as a defendant, the situation is not substantially changed. The action is still a § 301 suit, and the jurisdiction of the courts is not pre-empted under the *Garmon* principle. . . . And, insofar as adjudication of the union's breach of duty is concerned, the result should be no different if the employee, as Owens did here, sues the employer and the union in separate actions. There would be very little to commend a rule which would permit the Missouri courts to adjudicate the Union's conduct in an action against Swift but not in an action against the Union itself.

For the above reasons, it is obvious that the courts will be compelled to pass upon whether there has been a breach of the duty of fair representation in the context of many § 301 breach-of-contract actions. If a breach of duty by the union and a breach of contract by the employer are proven, the court must fashion an appropriate remedy. Presumably, in at least some cases, the union's breach of duty will have enhanced or contributed to the employee's injury. What possible sense could there be in a rule which would permit a court that has litigated the fault of employer and union to fashion a remedy only with respect to the employer? Under such a rule, either the employer would be compelled by the court to pay for the union's wrong—slight deterrence, indeed, to future union misconduct—or the injured employee would be forced to go to two tribunals to repair a single injury. Moreover, the Board would be compelled in many cases either to remedy injuries arising out of a breach of contract, a task which Congress has not assigned to it, or to leave the individual employee without remedy for the union's wrong.[12] Given the strong reasons for not pre-empting duty of fair representation suits in general, and the fact that the courts in many § 301 suits must adjudicate whether the union has breached its duty, we conclude that the courts may also fashion remedies for such a breach of duty.

It follows from the above that the Missouri courts had jurisdiction in this case. . . .

Petitioners contend . . . that Owens failed to prove that the Union breached its duty of fair representation in its handling of Owens' grievance. Petitioners also argue that the Supreme Court of Missouri, in rejecting this contention, applied a standard that is inconsistent with governing principles of federal law with respect to the Union's duty to an individual employee in its processing of grievances under the collective bargaining agreement with Swift. We agree with both contentions. . . .

Quite obviously, the question which the Missouri Supreme Court thought dispositive of the issue of liability was whether the evidence supported Owens' assertion that he had been wrongfully discharged by Swift, regardless of the Union's good faith in reaching a contrary conclusion. . . .

A breach of the statutory duty of fair representation occurs only when a union's conduct toward a member of the collective bargaining unit is arbitrary, discriminatory,

---

12. Assuming for the moment that Swift breached the collective bargaining agreement in discharging Owens and that the Union breached its duty in handling Owens' grievance, this case illustrates the difficulties that would result from a rule pre-empting the courts from remedying the Union's breach of duty. If Swift did not "'participate'" in the Union's unfair labor practice, the Board would have no jurisdiction to remedy Swift's breach of contract. Yet a court might be equally unable to give Owens full relief in a § 301 suit against Swift. Should the court award damages against Swift for Owens' full loss, even if it concludes that part of that loss was caused by the Union's breach of duty? Or should it award Owens only partial recovery hoping that the Board will make him whole? These remedy problems are difficult enough when one tribunal has all parties before it; they are impossible if two independent tribunals, with different procedures, time limitations, and remedial powers, must participate.

or in bad faith. *See Humphrey v. Moore, supra; Ford Motor Co. v. Huffman, supra.* . . . Some have suggested that every individual employee should have the right to have his grievance taken to arbitration. Others have urged that the union be given substantial discretion (if the collective bargaining agreement so provides) to decide whether a grievance should be taken to arbitration, subject only to the duty to refrain from patently wrongful conduct such as racial discrimination or personal hostility.

Though we accept the proposition that a union may not arbitrarily ignore a meritorious grievance or process it in perfunctory fashion, we do not agree that the individual employee has an absolute right to have his grievance taken to arbitration regardless of the provisions of the applicable collective bargaining agreement. . . . In providing for a grievance and arbitration procedure which gives the union discretion to supervise the grievance machinery and to invoke arbitration, the employer and the union contemplate that each will endeavor in good faith to settle grievances short of arbitration. Through this settlement process, frivolous grievances are ended prior to the most costly and time-consuming step in the grievance procedures. Moreover, both sides are assured that similar complaints will be treated consistently. . . . And finally, the settlement process furthers the interest of the union as statutory agent and as coauthor of the bargaining agreement in representing the employees in enforcement of that agreement. . . .

If the individual employee could compel arbitration of his grievance regardless of its merit, the settlement machinery provided by the contract would be substantially undermined, thus destroying the employer's confidence in the union's authority and returning the individual grievant to the vagaries of independent and unsystematic negotiation. Moreover, under such a rule, a significantly greater number of grievances would proceed to arbitration. This would greatly increase the cost of the grievance machinery and could so overburden the arbitration process as to prevent it from functioning successfully. . . . Nor do we see substantial danger to the interests of the individual employee if his statutory agent is given the contractual power honestly and in good faith to settle grievances short of arbitration. For these reasons, we conclude that a union does not breach its duty of fair representation . . . merely because it settled the grievance short of arbitration. . . .

For these same reasons, the standard applied here by the Missouri Supreme Court cannot be sustained. For if a union's decision that a particular grievance lacks sufficient merit to justify arbitration would constitute a breach of the duty of fair representation because a judge or jury later found the grievance meritorious, the union's incentive to settle such grievances short of arbitration would be seriously reduced. The dampening effect on the entire grievance procedure of this reduction of the union's freedom to settle claims in good faith would surely be substantial. Since the union's statutory duty of fair representation protects the individual employee from arbitrary abuses of the settlement device by providing him with recourse against both employer (in a § 301 suit) and union, this severe limitation on the power to settle grievances is neither necessary nor desirable. Therefore, we conclude that the Supreme Court of Missouri erred in upholding the verdict in this case solely on the ground that the evidence supported Owens' claim that he had been wrongfully discharged.

Applying the proper standard of union liability to the facts of this case, we cannot uphold the jury's award, for we conclude that as a matter of federal law the evidence does not support a verdict that the Union breached its duty of fair representation. As we have stated, Owens could not have established a breach of that duty merely by convincing the jury that he was in fact fit for work in 1960; he must also have proved arbitrary or bad-faith conduct on the part of the Union in processing his grievance. The evidence revealed that the Union diligently supervised the grievance into the fourth step of the bargaining agreement's procedure, with the Union's business representative serving as Owens' advocate throughout these steps. When Swift refused to reinstate Owens on the basis of his medical reports indicating reduced blood pressure, the Union sent him to another doctor of his own choice, at Union expense, in an attempt to amass persuasive medical evidence of Owens' fitness for work. When this examination proved unfavorable, the Union concluded that it could not establish a wrongful discharge. It then encouraged Swift to find light work for Owens at the plant. When this effort failed, the Union determined that arbitration would be fruitless and suggested to Owens that he accept Swift's offer to send him to a heart association for rehabilitation. At this point, Owens' grievance was suspended in the fourth step in the hope that he might be rehabilitated.

In administering the grievance and arbitration machinery as statutory agent of the employees, a union must, in good faith and in a nonarbitrary manner, make decisions as to the merits of particular grievances. . . . In a case such as this, when Owens supplied the Union with medical evidence supporting his position, the Union might well have breached its duty had it ignored Owens' complaint or had it processed the grievance in a perfunctory manner. . . . But here the Union processed the grievance into the fourth step, attempted to gather sufficient evidence to prove Owens' case, attempted to secure for Owens less vigorous work at the plant, and joined in the employer's efforts to have Owens rehabilitated. Only when these efforts all proved unsuccessful did the Union conclude both that arbitration would be fruitless and that the grievance should be dismissed. There was no evidence that any Union officer was personally hostile to Owens or that the Union acted at any time other than in good faith. Having concluded that the individual employee has no absolute right to have his grievance arbitrated under the collective bargaining agreement at issue, and that a breach of the duty of fair representation is not established merely by proof that the underlying grievance was meritorious, we must conclude that that duty was not breached here.

[The Court then held that the judgment below was improper in that it awarded damages against the union only, and not also against the employer. Even if the union had violated its DFR, plaintiff's damages would also have been attributable to the employer's violation of the labor contract (discharge without just cause). The Court speculated as to appropriate remedies. Simply ordering the union and employer to arbitrate a case such as this would likely be insufficient, because arbitrators in just cause discharge cases typically lack the power to order damages against the union. Thus, the Court held that courts should be able to apportion damages, according to the damage caused by the fault of each party. Here, the Court indicated, even had the union violated its DFR, most or all of plaintiff's damages would have been attributable to his wrongful discharge.]

FORTAS, J., with whom THE CHIEF JUSTICE and HARLAN, J. join, concurring.

In my view, a complaint by an employee that the union has breached its duty of fair representation is subject to the exclusive jurisdiction of the NLRB. It is a charge of unfair labor practice. . . . There is no basis for failure to apply the pre-emption principle in the present case. . . . The relationship between the union and the individual employee with respect to the processing of claims to employment rights under the collective bargaining agreement is fundamental to the design and operation of federal labor law. It is not "merely peripheral," as the Court's opinion states. It "presents difficult problems of definition of status, problems which we have held are precisely 'of a kind most wisely entrusted initially to the agency charged with the day-to-day administration of the Act as a whole.'" . . .

As the Court in effect acknowledges, we are concerned with the subtleties of a union's statutory duty faithfully to represent employees in the unit, including those who may not be members of the union. The Court—regrettably, in my opinion—ventures to state judgments as to the metes and bounds of the reciprocal duties involved in the relationship between the union and the employee. In my opinion, this is precisely and especially the kind of judgment that Congress intended to entrust to the Board and which is well within the pre-emption doctrine that this Court has prudently stated. . . .

BLACK, J., dissenting.

The Court today opens slightly the courthouse door to an employee's incidental claim against his union for breach of its duty of fair representation, only to shut it in his face when he seeks direct judicial relief for his underlying and more valuable breach-of-contract claim against his employer. This result follows from the Court's announcement in this case, involving an employee's suit against his union, of a new rule to govern an employee's suit against his employer. The rule is that before an employee can sue his employer under § 301 of the L.M.R.A. for a simple breach of his employment contract, the employee must prove not only that he attempted to exhaust his contractual remedies, but that his attempt to exhaust them was frustrated by "arbitrary, discriminatory, or . . . bad faith" conduct on the part of his union. With this new rule and its result I cannot agree.

The Court recognizes as it must, that the jury in this case found at least that Benjamin Owens was fit for work, that his grievance against Swift was meritorious, and that Swift breached the collective bargaining agreement when it wrongfully discharged him. The Court also notes in passing that Owens has a separate action for breach of contract pending against Swift in the state courts. And in Part IV of its opinion, the Court vigorously insists that "there is no reason to exempt the employer from contractual damages which he would otherwise have had to pay," that the "employee should have no difficulty recovering these damages from the employer" for his "unrelated breach of contract," and that "the employee (is) assured of direct recovery from the employer." But this reassurance in Part IV gives no comfort to Owens, for Part IV is based on the assumption that the union breached its duty to Owens, an assumption which, in Part III of its opinion, the Court finds unsupported by the facts of this case. What this all means, though the Court does not expressly say it, is that Owens will be no more successful in his pending breach-of-contract action against Swift than he is here in his suit against the union. For the Court makes it clear "that the question of whether a union has breached its duty of fair representation will . . . be a critical issue in a suit under L.M.R.A. § 301," that "the wrongfully discharged employee may bring an action against his employer" only if he "can prove that the union . . . breached its duty of fair representation in its handling of the employee's grievance," and "that the employee, as part and parcel of his § 301 action, finds it necessary to prove an unfair labor practice by the union." Thus, when Owens attempts to proceed with his pending breach-of-contract action against Swift, Swift will undoubtedly secure its prompt dismissal by pointing to the Court's conclusion here that the union has not breached its duty of fair representation. Thus, Owens, who now has obtained a judicial determination that he was wrongfully discharged, is left remediless, and Swift, having breached its contract, is allowed to hide behind, and is shielded by, the union's conduct. I simply fail to see how it should make one iota of difference, as far as the "unrelated breach of contract" by Swift is concerned, whether the union's conduct is wrongful or rightful. . . .

Certainly, nothing in *Republic Steel Corp. v. Maddox* supports this new rule. . . . [T]he Court there held that the employee "must attempt use of the contract grievance procedure," . . . and "must afford the union the opportunity to act on his behalf," . . . I dissented on the firm belief that an employee should be free to litigate his own lawsuit with his own lawyer in a court before a jury, rather than being forced to entrust his claim to a union which even if it did agree to press it, would be required to submit it to arbitration. . . . Here, of course, Benjamin Owens did not "completely sidestep available grievance procedures in favor of a lawsuit." . . . [H]e not only gave the union a chance to act on his behalf, but in every way possible tried to convince it that his claim was meritorious and should be carried through the fifth step to arbitration. In short, he did everything the Court's opinion in Maddox said he should do, and yet now the Court says so much is not enough. . . .

If the Court here were satisfied with merely holding that in this situation the employee could not recover damages from the union unless the union breached its duty of fair representation, then it would be one thing to say that the union did not do so in making a good-faith decision not to take the employee's grievance to arbitration. But if, as the Court goes on to hold, the employee cannot sue his employer for breach of contract unless his failure to exhaust contractual remedies is due to the union's breach of its duty of fair representation, then I am quite unwilling to say that the union's refusal to exhaust such remedies — however non-arbitrary — does not amount to a breach of its duty. Either the employee should be able to sue his employer for breach of contract after having attempted to exhaust his contractual remedies, or the union should have an absolute duty to exhaust contractual remedies on his behalf. The merits of an employee's grievance would thus be determined by either a jury or an arbitrator. Under today's decision it will never be determined by either. . . .

The Court suggests three reasons for giving the union this almost unlimited discretion to deprive injured employees of all remedies for breach of contract. The first is that "frivolous grievances" will be ended prior to time-consuming and costly arbitration. But here no one, not even the union, suggests that Benjamin Owens' grievance was frivolous. The union decided not to take it to arbitration simply because the union doubted the chance of success. Even if this was a good-faith doubt, I think the union had the duty to present this contested, but serious, claim to the arbitrator whose very function is to decide such claims on the basis of what he believes to be right. Second, the Court says that allowing the union to settle grievances prior to arbitration will assure consistent treatment of "major problem areas in the interpretation of the collective bargaining contract." But can it be argued that whether Owens was "fit to work" presents a major problem in the interpretation of the collective bargaining agreement? The problem here was one of interpreting medical reports, not a collective bargaining agreement, and of evaluating other evidence of Owens' physical condition. I doubt whether consistency is either possible or desirable in determining whether a particular employee is able to perform a particular job. Finally, the Court suggests that its decision "furthers the interest of the union as statutory agent." I think this is the real reason for today's decision which entirely overlooks the interests of the injured employee, the only one who has anything to lose. . . . I simply fail to see how the union's legitimate role as statutory agent is undermined by requiring it to prosecute all serious grievances to a conclusion or by allowing the injured employee to sue his employer after he has given the union a chance to act on his behalf. . . .

Today's decision, while giving the worker an ephemeral right to sue his union for breach of its duty of fair representation, creates insurmountable obstacles to block his far more valuable right to sue his employer for breach of the collective bargaining agreement.

The various issues *Vaca* raised are discussed in the subsections below.

1. Going Directly to Court: How DFR Procedures Differ from Other ULP Cases

Vaca held that, because the NLRA does not preempt DFR claims, plaintiffs in DFR cases do not need to file first with the NLRB but instead may go directly to court. For more on "*Garmon* preemption," see Chapter 16. Are the reasons the majority gives for that result persuasive? Justice Fortas, writing for two other justices, disagreed with the majority's rationale that the NLRB lacks special expertise in the subjects that form the basis of DFR cases: contract negotiations and grievance/arbitration handling. Is the majority convincing that judges will be as good as the NLRB in evaluating union conduct in these areas?

The *Vaca* majority gave another reason why DFR plaintiffs should be allowed to go directly to court: in many DFR cases, plaintiffs will allege CBA breaches by their employers. Indeed, *Vaca* itself exemplifies one of the most common types of DFR claim: the employer disciplined or discharged a bargaining-unit member in violation of the CBA, and the union failed to prosecute the grievance. In this situation, *Vaca* reasoned, a plaintiff should be allowed to sue the employer to enforce the CBA under § 301. Suits under § 301 may begin in court and, *Vaca* explained, it would be inefficient at best to require plaintiff to bring a DFR suit before the NLRB (which would not have jurisdiction over the § 301 claim) and a separate suit against the employer in court under § 301. Thus, plaintiffs should be allowed to sue both in a combined action in federal court.

There is force to this logic. But what about DFR cases that do not involve the employer?

Breininger v. Sheet Metal Workers International Association Local Union No. 6

Supreme Court of the United States
493 U.S. 67 (1989)

BRENNAN, J.

[One issue in this case is] whether the National Labor Relations Board (NLRB or Board) has exclusive jurisdiction over a union member's claims that his union . . . breached its duty of fair representation . . . by discriminating against him in job referrals made by the union hiring hall. . . . The . . . Sixth Circuit held that petitioner's suit fell within the exclusive jurisdiction of the Board. . . . We reverse the Court of Appeals' decision. . . .

I

Petitioner Lynn L. Breininger was at all relevant times a member of respondent, Local Union No. 6 of the Sheet Metal Workers International Association. Pursuant to a multi-employer collective-bargaining agreement, respondent operates a hiring hall through which it refers both members and nonmembers of the union for construction work. Respondent maintains an out-of-work list of individuals who wish to be referred to jobs. When an employer contacts respondent for workers, he may request certain persons by name. If he does not, the union begins at the top of the list and attempts to telephone in order each worker listed until it has satisfied the employer's request. . . .

Petitioner's first amended complaint contained two counts. First, he asserted a violation of the duty of fair representation, contending that respondent, "in its representation of [petitioner], has acted arbitrarily, discriminatorily, and/or in bad faith and/or without reason or cause." . . . Second, petitioner alleged that his union, "in making job referrals, . . . has favored a faction of members . . . who have been known to support . . . the present business manager," as "part of widespread, improper discipline for political opposition. . . .

The District Court held that it lacked jurisdiction to entertain petitioner's suit because "discrimination in hiring hall referrals constitutes an unfair labor practice," and "[t]he NLRB has exclusive jurisdiction over discrimination in hiring hall referrals." . . .

The Court of Appeals affirmed. . . . With respect to the fair representation claim, the court noted that "[c]ircuit courts have consistently held that . . . fair representation claims must be brought before the Board" and that "if the employee fails to affirmatively allege that his *employer* breached the collective bargaining agreement, which [petitioner] failed to do in the case at bar, he cannot prevail." (emphasis in original). . . .

II

A.

We have long recognized that a labor organization has a statutory duty of fair representation under the [NLRA] "to serve the interests of all members without hostility or discrimination toward any, to exercise its discretion with complete good faith and honesty, and to avoid arbitrary conduct." . . . In *Miranda Fuel Co.* . . . the NLRB determined that violations of the duty of fair representation might also be unfair labor practices under § 8(b) of the NLRA. . . . While petitioner alleged a breach of the duty of fair representation, his claim might relate to conduct that under *Miranda Fuel* also constitutes an unfair labor practice. And, as a general matter, neither state nor federal courts possess jurisdiction over claims based on activity that is "arguably" subject to §§ 7 or 8 of the NLRA. . . .

Nevertheless, the District Court was not deprived of jurisdiction. In *Vaca v. Sipes*, we held that *Garmon's* pre-emption rule does not extend to suits alleging a breach of the duty of fair representation. . . .

We decline to create an exception to the *Vaca* rule for fair representation complaints arising out of the operation of union hiring halls. . . . As an initial matter, we have never suggested that the *Vaca* rule contains exceptions based on the subject matter of the fair representation claim presented, the relative expertise of the NLRB in the particular area of labor law involved, or any other factor. We are unwilling to begin the process of carving out exceptions now, especially since we see no limiting principle to such an approach. Most fair representation cases require great sensitivity to the tradeoffs between the interests of the bargaining unit as a whole and the rights of individuals. Furthermore, we have never indicated that NLRB "experience" or "expertise" deprives a court of jurisdiction over a fair representation claim. . . . Adopting a rule that NLRB expertise bars federal jurisdiction would remove an unacceptably large number of fair representation claims from federal courts. . . .

The Court of Appeals below also held that if an employee fails to allege that his *employer* breached the collective-bargaining agreement, then he cannot prevail in a fair representation suit against his *union*. This is a misstatement of existing law. In *Vaca*, we identified an "intensely practical consideratio[n]," of having the same entity adjudicate a joint claim against both the employer and the union when a wrongfully discharged employee who has not obtained relief through any exclusive grievance and arbitration procedures provided in the collective-bargaining agreement brings a breach-of-contract action against the employer pursuant to § 301(a). . . .

Our reasoning in *Vaca* in no way implies, however, that a fair representation action *requires* a concomitant claim against an employer for breach of contract. Indeed, the earliest fair representation suits involved claims against unions for breach of the duty in *negotiating* a collective-bargaining agreement, a context in which no breach-of-contract action against an employer is possible. *Ford Motor Co. v. Huffman*, . . . ; *Steele v. Louisville & Nashville R. Co.*, ... Even after a collective-bargaining agreement has been signed, we have never required a fair representation plaintiff to allege that his *employer* breached the agreement in order to prevail. . . .

In the hiring hall context, the Board may bring a claim alleging a violation of § 8(b)(1)(A) against the union, and a parallel suit against the employer under § 8(a)(3), without implicating the duty of fair representation at all. Or, as in the instant case, an employee may bring a claim solely against the union based on its wrongful refusal to refer him for work. While in *Vaca* an allegation that the union had breached its duty of fair representation was a necessary component of the § 301 claim against the employer, the converse is not true here: a suit against the union need not be accompanied by an allegation that an employer breached the contract, since whatever the employer's liability, the employee would still retain a legal claim against the union. . . .

Federal courts have jurisdiction to hear fair representation suits whether or not they are accompanied by claims against employers.

Notes

1. In any type of DFR case, plaintiffs have the option of either filing a ULP complaint with the NLRB or going to court. If you were representing a plaintiff in a DFR case, which forum would you prefer and why? What if you were representing a union? Would it matter what type of DFR case it was?

2. When considering your responses to the questions in note 1, be aware that the Supreme Court has held that in DFR actions in which plaintiffs seek backpay (in practice, the vast majority of DFR cases), there is a right to a jury trial. *Teamsters Local 391 v. Terry*, 494 U.S. 558 (1990). Thus, individual employees can get their case before a jury when claiming their union violated the NLRA, while union claims of employer violations of the NLRA are heard only by the NLRB and federal appeals courts.

3. Does *Breininger* simply implement *Vaca*'s logic? Further, would it really be bad policy to require plaintiffs in DFR cases that do not involve a claim against the employer to file initially with the NLRB, as all other ULP claimants are required to do? There is a significant category of DFR cases that do not involve §301 claims against employers: claims involving union conduct in contract negotiations. Does that matter?

4. Is a DFR violation really best understood as a type of ULP? If not, what is it?

5. The Supreme Court further expanded the reach of §301 suits in *Wooddell v. Int'l B'hood of Electrical Workers Local 71*, 502 U.S. 93 (1991). In *Wooddell*, plaintiff claimed that a local union's refusal to refer him from its hiring hall was discrimination that violated the constitution of the local's parent union. The Supreme Court allowed this claim to go forward under §301 in federal court, as it involved a labor contract: the parent union's constitution.

2. "Hybrid DFR/§301" Cases: Parties and Necessary Claims

The types of claims *Vaca* discussed—those involving a DFR claim against the union for failing to handle a grievance fairly and a §301 claim against the employer for violating the CBA—are commonly called "hybrid DFR/§301 claims." In such cases, plaintiffs sue both the employer and the union. Thus, this is one of the rare occasions in which the union attorney and management attorney are on the same side of a case, which can be an interesting experience for both.

More specifically, under *Vaca* and its progeny, a plaintiff's claim against the union is a necessary part of the claim against the employer. Again, these cases are an exception to the general rule that when a member of a union bargaining unit alleges a violation of a CBA, the employee's remedy is *not* a suit under §301 (or any other type of contract suit). Rather, the employee must normally pursue the matter under the grievance and arbitration clause of the CBA. But, the overwhelming majority of labor contracts allow only the union, and not the individual employee, to decide whether or not to take a case to arbitration. And *Vaca* was clear that the union need not take every grievance to arbitration. This means that the *only* situation in which an employee can sue the employer in court for a violation of a CBA is if the employee can show that the union violated its DFR in handling his grievance or arbitration. In the language of *Vaca*, the employee must show that his attempts to exhaust his contractual remedies were stymied by the union's DFR violation.

In other words, as Judge Easterbrook colorfully explained: "Federal labor law ensures that disputes of this kind are resolved by the affected parties over the bargaining table, or by arbitrators knowledgeable about the business, rather than in court. That's why a hybrid contract/DFR suit does not get to first base unless the worker shows that the union has abandoned him to the wolves." *Pease v. Production Workers of Chicago and Vicinity Local 707*, 386 F.3d 819, 823 (7th Cir. 2004). Put more prosaically, "[w]ithout sufficient evidence that Local 327 breached its duty of fair representation, Garrison's hybrid §301 action must fail. Accordingly, we need not address Cassens's alleged breach of the collective bargaining agreement." *Garrison v. Cassens Transport Co.*, 334 F.3d 528 (6th Cir. 2003).

This, in turn, means that if the union has reasonably decided not to arbitrate a case (or has arbitrated and lost), the employee has no legal recourse against either employer or union regarding what the employee may strongly feel was discipline or discharge in violation of the labor contract. What are the pros and cons of this rule? Also, what would alternatives look like? Justice Black, dissenting in *Vaca, supra*, objected to this result, and suggested the following alternatives. "Either the employee should be able to sue his employer for breach of contract after having attempted to exhaust his contractual remedies, or the union should have an absolute duty to exhaust contractual remedies on his behalf." What would be the pros and cons of those alternatives?

A related rule is that in a hybrid DFR/§301 claim, even if an employee can successfully prove that the union violated its DFR, the employee will still recover nothing unless the employee can prove that the employer actually violated the contract. So, for example, if a union refuses to handle a discharge grievance for reasons that violate the DFR, the employee will still recover nothing unless the employee can show that the employer violated a just cause discipline/discharge rule in the contract. What rationale supports that rule? *See Vencl v. International Union of Operating Engineers, Local 18*, 137 F.3d 420, 424 (6th Cir. 1998).

Clayton v. International Union, United Automobile Workers, 451 U.S. 679 (1981) added another wrinkle to the requirement that the employee exhaust his contractual remedies before bringing a hybrid DFR/§301 suit in court. Generally, this exhaustion requirement means that the employee must attempt to get the union to handle his or her grievance or arbitration (or handle it fairly) under the labor contract's grievance and arbitration rules. *Clayton* raised the issue of whether an employee can be required to exhaust a union's internal appeal procedures as well.

In *Clayton*, the UAW's constitution provided that a union-represented employee "who feels aggrieved by any action, decision, or penalty imposed upon him" by the union must, before starting a legal action, seek relief from the membership of the local. The employee could further appeal to the UAW's International Executive Board, and eventually to either the union's Constitutional Appeals Committee or a Public Review Board composed of "impartial persons" who are not members or employees of the union. 451 U.S. 679, 683–84.

The Supreme Court held (5–4) that employees were not required to exhaust internal union procedures where union officials were sufficiently hostile to the employee that the employee could not receive a fair hearing, or where (as was the case in *Clayton*), the procedures could not reactivate the employee's grievance or award him the full relief sought against the employer, or where exhaustion would unreasonably delay the employee's opportunity to go to court. 451 U.S. at 690. Thus, the employee in *Clayton* was not required to exhaust internal union procedures.

But *Clayton* indicated that in some circumstances, an employee could be required to exhaust internal union remedies before filing a DFR claim.

> Where internal appeals procedures can result in either complete relief to an aggrieved employee or reactivation of his grievance, exhaustion would advance the national labor policy of encouraging private resolution of contractual disputes. *Id.* at 692.

Since *Clayton*, courts have required an employee to exhaust an internal union appeals process before bringing a court suit where the court found that the process and facts of the case fit the *Clayton* criteria for requiring such exhaustion. *See, e.g., Bell v. DaimlerChrysler Corp.*, 547 F.3d 796 (7th Cir. 2008).

3. Nature of the Duty in Bargaining and Contract Administration

For reasons discussed above, much rides on whether or not the union actually breached its DFR, and thus on the specific requirements of the duty. What, precisely, should the union's duty be? When should courts defer to the judgment of unions and their leaders about bargaining strategy and grievance handling, and when should courts find that the union's representation is so "unfair" that an employee has a valid claim against the union? On one hand, a union member in the minority on a given issue can seem quite powerless: unions negotiate contracts, and while members typically vote on whether or not to ratify a contract, an individual or a handful of dissenting members can be outvoted. And as noted above, unions, not individual employees, generally control whether a given contract grievance goes to arbitration. On the other hand, it is inevitable that bargaining units will be composed of employees who have some different interests as to certain contract terms: those in different job categories, with more or less seniority, more or less skill, and more or less interest in a variety of potential benefits and rules. Also, while we would normally think it unfair for a union to refuse to arbitrate what appears to be a strong case for a bad reason, it would probably not be good policy to obligate unions and employers to arbitrate every case that an employee wants arbitrated (*e.g.,* cases which are sure losers, given the facts and CBA language). Further, in close cases, who should decide whether a given grievance is worth arbitrating: the union or judges? Fundamentally, when should courts step in?

The Supreme Court early on took note of the DFR's complexity. As far back as *Ford Motor Co. v. Huffman, supra,* in 1953, the Court observed:

> Inevitably differences arise in the manner and degree to which the terms of any negotiated agreement affect individual employees and classes of employees. The mere existence of such differences does not make them invalid. The complete satisfaction of all who are represented is hardly to be expected. A wide range of reasonableness must be allowed a statutory bargaining representative in serving the unit it represents, subject always to complete good faith and honesty of purpose in the exercise of its discretion. 345 U.S. at 338.

Vaca spoke of a DFR violation if the union's conduct was "arbitrary, discriminatory, or in bad faith." 386 U.S. at 190. Further, the union cannot engage in "patently wrongful conduct such as racial discrimination or personal hostility." *Id.* Also, the union may not "arbitrarily ignore a meritorious grievance or process it in perfunctory fashion." *Id.* at 191. In *Electrical Workers (IBEW) v. Foust*, 442 U.S. 42, 47 (1979), the Supreme Court explained that under the DFR doctrine, "a union must represent fairly the interest of all bargaining-unit members during the negotiation, administration, and enforcement of collective-bargaining agreements."

After *Vaca*, some courts developed somewhat different standards for cases involving contract *administration* (grievance and arbitration handling) as opposed to contract *negotiation* (see the discussion in the following case, *Air Line Pilots v. O'Neil*). What might be the rationale for this distinction? Consider reasons for the federal policy of avoiding imposing substantive contract terms. Courts also varied on other aspects of DFR rules. Some required intentional bad behavior to prove a DFR violation. *See, e.g., Olsen v. United Parcel Service*, 892 F.2d 1290 (7th Cir. 1990) (not even gross negligence is sufficient). Others allowed DFR claims based on mere negligence. *See, e.g., Dutrisac v. Caterpillar Tractor Co.*, 749 F.2d 1270 (9th Cir. 1983). Most circuits fell somewhere in between.

In 1990, the Supreme Court rejected the "ordinary negligence" standard, explaining that "mere negligence, even in the enforcement of a collective-bargaining agreement, would not state a claim for breach of the duty of fair representation." *United Steelworkers of America. v. Rawson*, 495 U.S. 362, 372–73 (1990). In *Rawson*, the Court rejected a DFR claim based on the allegation that the union had been negligent in performing certain safety duties for which it was responsible under its CBA (ninety-one miners had been killed in an underground fire allegedly caused in part by the union's negligence). The year after *Rawson*, the Court further standardized the rules.

Air Line Pilots Association, International v. O'Neil

Supreme Court of the United States
499 U.S. 65 (1991)

STEVENS, J.

We granted certiorari to clarify the standard that governs a claim that a union has breached its duty of fair representation in its negotiation of a back-to-work agreement terminating a strike. We hold that the rule announced in *Vaca v. Sipes*, 386 U.S. 171 (1967) — that a union breaches its duty of fair representation if its actions are either "arbitrary, discriminatory, or in bad faith" — applies to all union activity, including contract negotiation. We further hold that a union's actions are arbitrary only if, in light of the factual and legal landscape at the time of the union's actions, the union's behavior is so far outside a "wide range of reasonableness," *Ford Motor Co. v. Huffman*, 345 U.S. 330, 338 (1953), as to be irrational.

I

This case arose out of a bitter confrontation between Continental Airlines, Inc. (Continental), and the union representing its pilots, the Air Line Pilots Association, International (ALPA). On September 24, 1983, Continental filed a petition for reorganization under Chapter 11 of the Bankruptcy Code. Immediately thereafter, with the approval of the Bankruptcy Court, Continental repudiated its collective-bargaining agreement with ALPA and unilaterally reduced its pilots' salaries and benefits by more than half. ALPA responded by calling a strike that lasted for over two years.

Of the approximately 2,000 pilots employed by Continental, all but about 200 supported the strike. By the time the strike ended, about 400 strikers had "crossed over" and been accepted for reemployment in order of reapplication. . . . By August 1985, there were 1,600 working pilots and only 1,000 strikers.

The strike was acrimonious, punctuated by incidents of violence and the filing of a variety of lawsuits, charges, and countercharges. In August 1985, Continental notified ALPA that it was withdrawing recognition of ALPA as the collective-bargaining agent for its pilots. ALPA responded with a federal lawsuit alleging that Continental was unlawfully refusing to continue negotiations for a new collective-bargaining agreement. In this adversary context, on September 9, 1985, Continental posted its "Supplementary Base Vacancy Bid 1985-5" (85-5 bid) — an act that precipitated not only an end to the strike, but also the litigation that is now before us.

For many years Continental had used a "system bid" procedure for assigning pilots to new positions. Bids were typically posted well in advance in order to allow time for necessary training without interfering with current service. When a group of vacancies was posted, any pilot could submit a bid specifying his or her preferred position (captain, first officer, or second officer), base of operations, and aircraft type. In the past, vacant positions had been awarded on the basis of seniority, determined by the date the pilot first flew for Continental. The 85-5 bid covered an unusually large number of anticipated vacancies — 441 future captain and first officer positions and an undetermined number of second officer vacancies. Pilots were given nine days — until September 18, 1985 — to submit their bids.

Fearing that this bid might effectively lock the striking pilots out of jobs for the indefinite future, ALPA authorized the strikers to submit bids. Several hundred did so, as did several hundred working pilots. Although Continental initially accepted bids from both groups, it soon became concerned about the bona fides of the striking pilots' offers to return to work at a future date. It therefore challenged the strikers' bids in court and announced that all of the 85-5 bid positions had been awarded to working pilots.

. . . . ALPA's negotiating committee and Continental reached an agreement, which was entered as an order by the Bankruptcy Court on October 31, 1985. The agreement provided for an end to the strike, the disposition of all pending litigation, and reallocation of the positions covered by the 85-5 bid.

The agreement offered the striking pilots three options. Under the first, pilots who settled all outstanding claims [in bankruptcy proceedings] with Continental were eligible to participate in the allocation of the 85-5 bid positions. Under the second option, pilots who elected not to return to work received severance pay of $4,000 per year of service (or $2,000 if they had been furloughed before the strike began). Under the third option, striking pilots retained their individual claims against Continental and were eligible to return to work only after all the first option pilots had been reinstated.

Pilots who chose the first option were thus entitled to some of the 85-5 bid positions that, according to Continental, had previously been awarded to working pilots. The first 100 captain positions were allocated to working pilots and the next 70 captain positions were awarded, in order of seniority, to returning strikers who chose option one. Thereafter, striking and nonstriking pilots were eligible for captain positions on a 1-to-1 ratio. The initial base and aircraft type for a returning striker was assigned by Continental, but the assignments for working pilots were determined by their bids. After the initial assignment, future changes in bases and equipment were determined by seniority, and striking pilots who were in active service when the strike began received seniority credit for the period of the strike.

II

[Respondents alleged that the union breached its DFR in negotiating and accepting the settlement. The District Court granted the union's motion for summary judgement.]

In his oral explanation of his ruling, the District Judge opined that "the agreement that was achieved looks atrocious in retrospect, but it is not a breach of fiduciary duty badly to settle the strike."

The Court of Appeals reversed. It first rejected ALPA's argument that a union cannot breach its duty of fair representation without intentional misconduct. The court held that the duty includes "'three distinct'" components. . . . A union breaches the duty if its conduct is "'arbitrary, discriminatory, or in bad faith.'" . . .

[T]he Court of Appeals concluded that a jury could find that ALPA acted arbitrarily because the jury could find that the settlement "left the striking pilots worse off in a number of respects than complete surrender to [Continental]." That conclusion rested on the court's opinion that the evidence suggested that, if ALPA had simply surrendered and made an unconditional offer to return to work, the strikers would have been entitled to complete priority on all the positions covered by the 85-5 bid. . . . In addition, the Court of Appeals ruled that the evidence raised a genuine issue of material fact whether the favored treatment of working pilots in the allocation of 85-5 bid positions constituted discrimination against those pilots who had chosen to strike. . . .

We granted certiorari to review the Court of Appeals' statement of the standard governing an alleged breach of a union's duty of fair representation and the court's application of the standard in this case.

III

ALPA's central argument is that the duty of fair representation requires only that a union act in good faith and treat its members equally and in a nondiscriminatory fashion. The duty, the union argues, does not impose any obligation to provide *adequate* representation. The District Court found that there was no evidence that ALPA acted other than in good faith and without discrimination. Because of its view of the limited scope of the duty, ALPA contends that the District Court's finding, which the Court of Appeals did not question, is sufficient to support summary judgment.

The union maintains, not without some merit, that its view that courts are not authorized to review the rationality of good-faith, nondiscriminatory union decisions is consonant with federal labor policy. The Government has generally regulated only "the *process* of collective bargaining," *H.K. Porter Co. v. NLRB*, 397 U.S. 99, 102 (1970) (emphasis added), but relied on private negotiation between the parties to establish "their own charter for the ordering of industrial relations".... As we stated in *NLRB v. Insurance Agents*, 361 U.S. 477 (1960), Congress "intended that the parties should have wide latitude in their negotiations, unrestricted by any governmental power to regulate the substantive solution of their differences."...

There is, however, a critical difference between governmental modification of the terms of a private agreement and an examination of those terms in search for evidence that a union did not fairly and adequately represent its constituency. Our decisions have long recognized that the need for such an examination proceeds directly from the union's statutory role as exclusive bargaining agent....

The duty of fair representation is thus akin to the duty owed by other fiduciaries to their beneficiaries. For example, some Members of the Court have analogized the duty a union owes to the employees it represents to the duty a trustee owes to trust beneficiaries.... Others have likened the relationship between union and employee to that between attorney and client. The fair representation duty also parallels the responsibilities of corporate officers and directors toward shareholders. Just as these fiduciaries owe their beneficiaries a duty of care as well as a duty of loyalty, a union owes employees a duty to represent them adequately as well as honestly and in good faith....

ALPA suggests that a union need owe no enforceable duty of adequate representation because employees are protected from inadequate representation by the union political process. ALPA argues, as has the Seventh Circuit, that employees "do not need ... protection against representation that is inept but not invidious" because if a "union does an incompetent job ... its members can vote in new officers who will do a better job or they can vote in another union."... In *Steele*, the case in which we first recognized the duty of fair representation, we also analogized a union's role to that of a legislature.... Even legislatures, however, are subject to *some* judicial review.

ALPA relies heavily on language in *Ford Motor Co. v. Huffman*, 345 U.S. 330 (1953), which, according to the union, suggests that no review of the substantive terms of a settlement between labor and management is permissible. In particular, ALPA stresses our comment in the case that "[a] wide range of reasonableness must be allowed a statutory bargaining representative in serving the unit it represents, subject always to complete good faith and honesty of purpose in the exercise of its discretion." 345 U.S. 330 at 338. Unlike ALPA, we do not read this passage to limit review of a union's actions to "good faith and honesty of purpose," but rather to recognize that a union's conduct must also be within "[a] wide range of reasonableness."

Although there is admittedly some variation in the way in which our opinions have described the unions' duty of fair representation, we have repeatedly identified three components of the duty, including a prohibition against "arbitrary" conduct. . . .

The union correctly points out, however, that virtually all of those cases can be distinguished because they involved contract administration or enforcement rather than contract negotiation. ALPA argues that the policy against substantive review of contract terms applies directly only in the negotiation area. Although this is a possible basis for distinction, none of our opinions has suggested that the duty is governed by a double standard. Indeed, we have repeatedly noted that the *Vaca v. Sipes* standard applies to "challenges leveled not only at a union's contract administration and enforcement efforts but at its negotiation activities as well." *Communications Workers v. Beck*, 487 U.S. 735 (1988) . . . . We have also held that the duty applies in other instances in which a union is acting in its representative role, such as when the union operates a hiring hall. *See Breininger v. Sheet Metal Workers*, 493 U.S. 67, 87–89 (1989).

We doubt, moreover, that a bright line could be drawn between contract administration and contract negotiation. Industrial grievances may precipitate settlement negotiations leading to contract amendments, and some strikes and strike settlement agreements may focus entirely on questions of contract interpretation. . . . Finally, some union activities subject to the duty of fair representation fall into neither category. *See Breininger.* . . .

We are, therefore, satisfied that the Court of Appeals correctly concluded that the tripartite standard announced in *Vaca v. Sipes* applies to a union in its negotiating capacity. We are persuaded, however, that the Court of Appeals' further refinement of the arbitrariness component of the standard authorizes more judicial review of the substance of negotiated agreements than is consistent with national labor policy.

As we acknowledged above, Congress did not intend judicial review of a union's performance to permit the court to substitute its own view of the proper bargain for that reached by the union. Rather, Congress envisioned the relationship between the courts and labor unions as similar to that between the courts and the legislature. Any substantive examination of a union's performance, therefore, must be highly deferential, recognizing the wide latitude that negotiators need for the effective performance of their bargaining responsibilities. *Cf. Day-Brite Lighting, Inc.*

v. Missouri, 342 U.S. 421, 423 (1952) (court does "not sit as a superlegislature to weigh the wisdom of legislation nor to decide whether the policy which it expresses offends the public welfare"). . . . For that reason, the final product of the bargaining process may constitute evidence of a breach of duty only if it can be fairly characterized as so far outside a "wide range of reasonableness," *Ford Motor Co. v. Huffman*, 345 U.S., at 338, that it is wholly "irrational" or "arbitrary."

The approach of the Court of Appeals is particularly flawed because it fails to take into account either the strong policy favoring the peaceful settlement of labor disputes . . . or the importance of evaluating the rationality of a union's decision in light of both the facts and the legal climate that confronted the negotiators at the time the decision was made. . . .

IV

The Court of Appeals placed great stress on the fact that the deal struck by ALPA was worse than the result the union would have obtained by unilateral termination of the strike. Indeed, the court held that a jury finding that the settlement was worse than surrender could alone support a judgment that the union had acted arbitrarily and irrationally. This holding unduly constrains the "wide range of reasonableness" within which unions may act without breaching their fair representation duty.

For purposes of decision, we may assume that the Court of Appeals was correct in its conclusion that, if ALPA had simply surrendered and voluntarily terminated the strike, the striking pilots would have been entitled to reemployment in the order of seniority. Moreover, we may assume that Continental would have responded to such action by rescinding its assignment of all of the 85-5 bid positions to working pilots. After all, it did rescind about half of those assignments pursuant to the terms of the settlement. Thus, we assume that the union made a bad settlement—one that was even worse than a unilateral termination of the strike.

Nevertheless, the settlement was by no means irrational. A settlement is not irrational simply because it turns out *in retrospect* to have been a bad settlement. Viewed in light of the legal landscape at the time of the settlement, ALPA's decision to settle rather than give up was certainly not illogical. At the time of the settlement, Continental had notified the union that all of the 85-5 bid positions had been awarded to working pilots and was maintaining that none of the strikers had any claim on any of those jobs. . . .

Given the background of determined resistance by Continental at all stages of this strike, it would certainly have been rational for ALPA to recognize the possibility that an attempted voluntary return to work would merely precipitate litigation over the right to the 85-5 bid positions. Because such a return would not have disposed of any of the individual claims of the pilots who ultimately elected option one or option two of the settlement, there was certainly a realistic possibility that Continental would not abandon its bargaining position without a complete settlement.

At the very least, the settlement produced certain and prompt access to a share of the new jobs and avoided the costs and risks associated with major litigation.

Moreover, since almost a third of the striking pilots chose the lump-sum severance payment rather than reinstatement . . . the settlement was presumably more advantageous than a surrender to a significant number of striking pilots. In labor disputes, as in other kinds of litigation, even a bad settlement may be more advantageous in the long run than a good lawsuit. In all events, the resolution of the dispute over the 85-5 bid vacancies was well within the "wide range of reasonableness" . . . that a union is allowed in its bargaining.

The suggestion that the "discrimination" between striking and working pilots represented a breach of the duty of fair representation also fails. If we are correct in our conclusion that it was rational for ALPA to accept a compromise between the claims of the two groups of pilots to the 85-5 bid positions, some form of allocation was inevitable. A rational compromise on the initial allocation of the positions was not invidious "discrimination" of the kind prohibited by the duty of fair representation. Unlike the grant of "super-seniority" to the crossover and replacement workers in *NLRB v. Erie Resistor Corp.*, 373 U.S. 221 (1963), this agreement preserved the seniority of the striking pilots after their initial reinstatement. In *Erie*, the grant of extra seniority enabled the replacement workers to keep their jobs while more senior strikers lost theirs during a layoff subsequent to the strike. . . . The agreement here only provided the order and mechanism for the reintegration of the returning strikers but did not permanently alter the seniority system. This case therefore more closely resembles our decision in *Trans World Airlines, Inc. v. Flight Attendants*, 489 U.S. 426 (1989), in which we held that an airline's refusal, after a strike, to displace cross-over workers with more senior strikers was not unlawful discrimination.

The judgment of the Court of Appeals is reversed, and the case is remanded for further proceedings consistent with this opinion.

Notes

1. *O'Neil* clarified the law in two ways. First, the same standard applies to cases involving contract negotiation (including strike settlements) and contract administration (grievance/arbitration handling). Second, the union violates its DFR if it acts in a way that is "arbitrary, discriminatory, or in bad faith," with "arbitrary" defined as "outside a wide range of reasonableness." The Court rejected the two extremes that some circuit courts had adopted (mere negligence can suffice, and intentional bad conduct is required). *See Ooley v. Household Manufacturing, Schwitzer Division*, 961 F.2d 1293 (7th Cir. 1992) (acknowledging *O'Neil* was inconsistent with the court's prior rule requiring intentional misconduct); *Hansen v. Qwest Communications*, 564 F.3d 919 (8th Cir. 2009) (failing to tell grievant that the ADR procedure the union suggested had an eighteen-month back-pay cap was at most negligent and therefore not a DFR violation).

Still, does this case, decided forty-seven years after the first DFR cases, and after a number of other Supreme Court decisions on the topic, give you a clear notion of exactly what type of conduct by unions would (or would not) violate the DFR in an arguably close case?

2. In *O'Neil*, the Supreme Court agreed with the district court's observation: "the agreement that was achieved looks atrocious in retrospect, but it is not a breach of fiduciary duty badly to settle the strike." Why not?

3. After *O'Neil*, what facts are likely to lead to a finding that the union violated its DFR?

a. Bad faith or intentional misconduct, *e.g.*, lying regarding a significant subject in a way that prejudices the plaintiff. For example, in *Beck v. Food & Commercial Workers Local 99*, 506 F.3d 874 (9th Cir. 2007), the court held that a union's unexplained failure to file a grievance after it had promised plaintiff it would do so was a DFR violation. *See also Lewis v. Tuscan Dairy Farms*, 25 F.3d 1138 (2d Cir. 1994) (union president's intentional misrepresentation to a plant's employees about how seniority would be handled if the plant were purchased was a DFR violation).

b. Discrimination for personal or other invidious reasons. Many labor contracts "discriminate" among employees based on factors that do *not* raise DFR issues: *e.g.*, skill, seniority, training, or education. Discrimination because of race (or sex, or other category not relevant to the workplace) is a DFR violation. In modern times, a smaller proportion of DFR cases involve such claims (both because Title VII, where applicable, provides better remedies, and because societal progress since the 1940s and 1950s has led to more labor unions becoming more institutionally favorable to civil rights). Discriminating against an individual because he was, *e.g.*, a political rival within the union or supported a different union is also typically a DFR violation. *See, e.g., Ramey v. District 141, IAM*, 378 F.3d 269 (2d Cir. 2004) (discrimination against a group of employees because they previously had supported another union was a DFR violation).

However, the Ninth Circuit explained that a union did not violate its DFR by removing members of a competing union from their positions as shop stewards: "A union's selecting stewards from whom it might expect undivided loyalty—that is, from members of an affiliated union, rather than an unaffiliated union—is not unreasonable discrimination and does not, without more, breach the duty of fair representation." *United Bhd. of Carpenters and Joiners of Am. v. Metal Trades Dep't*, 770 F.3d 846 (9th Cir. 2014).

4. What if a union steward misses a contractual deadline for filing a grievance or arbitration request, thus extinguishing the claim? Suppose the steward did not act out of an impermissible motivation, but rather simply forgot about a deadline, misunderstood the deadline rules, or did not request arbitration properly before the deadline. In *Vencl v. Int'l Union of Operating Engineers Local 18*, 137 F.3d 420 (6th Cir. 1998), the union notified the employer orally that it wished to arbitrate a grievance, but the CBA required a written request. There was no allegation that this was anything other than a mistake by the union. The Sixth Circuit found a DFR violation: "A union acts arbitrarily by failing to take a basic and required step. Timely filing is both basic and required." 137 F.3d 420, 426. *See also Beavers v. United*

Paperworkers Int'l Union, Local 1741, 72 F.3d 97 (8th Cir. 1995) (unexplained late filing of a grievance may violate the DFR). What if there is an established past practice between the union and the employer to grant extensions of deadlines? *See Ruzicka v. General Motors Corp.*, 707 F.2d 259 (6th Cir. 1983).

A conceptual tension exists in these cases. *Vaca* held that a union cannot process a grievance in a "perfunctory" manner, but *O'Neil* held that mere negligence does not constitute a DFR. Is simply forgetting or not understanding a time deadline, without more, improper "perfunctory" handling (in which case it is a DFR), or mere negligence (in which case it is not a DFR)? Should courts look closely at the specific facts in such cases? If so, what facts? *See Beavers, supra.*

In 2018, the NLRB's General Counsel issued a memo giving his view of the line between arbitrary conduct by unions and "mere negligence." The memo stated that "[i]n cases where a union asserts a mere negligence defense based on its having lost track, misplaced or otherwise forgotten about a grievance . . . the union should be required to show the existence of established, reasonable procedures or systems in place to track grievances." The memo went on to state that "a union's failure to communicate decisions related to a grievance or to respond to inquiries for information or documents by the charging party . . . constitutes more than mere negligence . . . unless there is a reasonable excuse or meaningful explanation." Office of the General Counsel, Memorandum GC 19-01(Oct. 24, 2018), https://apps.nlrb.gov/link/document.aspx/09031d4582992b84.

5. Many DFR claims involve a union refusing to take an employee's grievance to arbitration. Again, as *Vaca* and other cases make clear, a union is not obligated to arbitrate every grievance. For example, it does not violate the DFR if the union refuses to arbitrate because it has investigated a grievance case and made a good faith determination that the case is weak, *see, e.g., Williams v. Sea-Land Corp.*, 844 F.2d 17 (1st Cir. 1988), or if the costs of the arbitration would greatly outweigh the benefits of even a successful result. *See, e.g., Hamilton v. Consolidated Freightways*, 612 F.2d 343 (8th Cir. 1979) (union's general policy of deferring grievances about warning letters until more serious discipline was instituted did not violate the DFR).

So, what exactly must the union do when a bargaining-unit member wants to arbitrate a grievance? One court explained that a union "may refuse to process a grievance or handle the grievance in a particular manner for a multitude of reasons, but it may not do so without reason." *Griffin v. Auto Workers*, 469 F.2d 181, 183 (4th Cir. 1972). If you were a union official, what exactly should you do (and what should you consider) when deciding whether to arbitrate a grievance? If you are representing a plaintiff in a DFR case in which a union has refused to arbitrate a grievance, but without intentional bad acts, what type of "arbitrary" behavior by the union would provide the factual basis for a successful DFR suit? As to the latter, see *Cruz v. Electrical Workers (IBEW) Local 3*, 34 F.3d 1148 (2d Cir. 1994) (union breached DFR when it failed to investigate complaints that employer had violated seniority system, where union possessed information about employees' relative seniority).

6. Grievances that involve conflicting claims or conflicting interests between two or more bargaining-unit members present tricky issues for unions. Suppose a contract requires severe discipline if an employee starts a fight, and lesser or no discipline if an employee in a fight was merely acting defensively. Suppose further the employer issued severe discipline to two bargaining-unit members who were found fighting, and both employees told the union the other employee started the fight. Or suppose the employer disciplined a bargaining-unit member for sexually harassing another bargaining-unit member, and the alleged harasser denies the allegation and wants the union to represent him in the grievance-arbitration process. Or suppose a CBA provides (as many do) that for promotions, if all other qualifications are relatively equal, the employer will promote the employee with the most seniority. Two employees bid for a promotion. One claims she has better job skills, the other claims his skills are equal to hers but he has more seniority. The employer promotes one, and the other wants to grieve and arbitrate this decision.

In all these examples, the union has a duty to fairly represent both bargaining-unit members. Based on the rules discussed above, what should the DFR rule require or allow unions to do in this type of situation? Should the union be allowed to represent both members, even to the extent it would require presenting conflicting claims? Should the union be *required* to do that? Should the union be *forbidden* to make conflicting claims? Or, should the union, at least in some of these cases, be allowed to pick one employee to represent, but not the other? If so, based on what criteria? *See Smith v. Hussmann Refrigerator Co.*, 619 F.2d 1229 (8th Cir. 1980).

7. It is simpler to have one standard for contract negotiation and contract administration. But did defendant ALPA (relying on some circuit court opinions prior to *O'Neil*) make a plausible argument that courts should be more deferential to unions in contract negotiation, given the general NLRA policy that the Board and courts should not interfere with substantive contract terms?

Consider the following. When two companies merge and the employees come together in one bargaining unit, there are various ways to merge the seniority lists of the predecessor companies. "Dovetailing" merges the seniority lists such that all employees get full seniority credit in the new company for all the time served in the predecessor companies. "Endtailing" favors the employees of one of the predecessor companies (sometimes by simply placing all those from one predecessor ahead of all those from another). *Truck Drivers Local 568 v. NLRB (Red Ball Motor Freight, Inc.)*, 379 F.2d 137 (D.C. Cir. 1967) found a DFR violation where the union refused to consider dovetailing and instead proposed endtailing where its motive was to win a representation election in a new combined unit by favoring the larger group. But more recent cases have allowed unions more discretion, and endtailing itself is not necessarily a DFR violation. *See, e.g., Ackley v. Local Union 337, UAW*, 948 F.2d 267 (6th Cir. 1991).

8. As noted above, unions generally have a duty to fairly represent members of the bargaining unit who are not union members. For example, unions cannot make union membership or lack thereof a factor in deciding whether to take a grievance

to arbitration. This is true even though a nonmember may be paying less in dues than members, or in a right-to-work jurisdiction, no dues at all (*see* Section IV, *infra*), and the union is obligated to pay the costs of the arbitration. *See Abilene Sheet Metal v. NLRB*, 619 F.2d 332 (5th Cir. 1980) (refusing to represent grievant because of his previous nonunion employment and nonmember status was a DFR violation); *United Teachers of Dade v. School District of Miami-Dade Co.*, 38 FPER ¶ 86 (Fl. App. Ct. 3d Dist. Sept. 7, 2011) (ULP for union to have a policy, in a public-sector right-to-work jurisdiction, of not representing teachers who did not pay dues in performance evaluation meetings). Nor can unions intentionally discriminate against non-members in contract negotiations.

But unions can make some distinctions in limited areas. While unions must consider the views and interests of nonmembers in contract negotiations, it is not a DFR violation to exclude nonmembers from a contract ratification vote. *Branch 6000, Nat'l Association of Letter Carriers*, 232 N.L.R.B. 263 (1977), *enforced*, 595 F.2d 808 (D.C. Cir. 1979). Also, it is not a DFR violation to exclude nonmembers from a vote to affiliate with another union. *NLRB v. Financial Institution Employees of America, Local 1182*, 475 U.S. 192 (1986). But beyond these narrow exceptions, unions have the same duty of fair representation toward members of their bargaining unit who are not union members as to those who are. Consider the implications of this further in the discussion of agency fee rules in Section IV, *infra*.

9. When a union takes a case to arbitration, it need not provide a lawyer or "lawyer-quality" representation, and failing to raise certain arguments through negligence or poor judgment does not, without more, breach the DFR. *See, e.g., Cannon v. Consolidated Freightways Corp.*, 524 F.2d 290 (7th Cir. 1975). But at some point, grossly negligent or arbitrary handling of an arbitration is a DFR violation. What if a union takes an employee's grievance to arbitration, handles the arbitration so badly that it violates its DFR, and this poor handling results in the employer winning the case? Can the employer rely on arbitrator's decision? Or does the union's DFR allow further legal action by the employee? The following case addresses this issue.

Hines v. Anchor Motor Freight, Inc.

Supreme Court of the United States
424 U.S. 554 (1976)

Wʜɪᴛᴇ, J.

The issue here is whether a suit against an employer by employees asserting breach of a collective-bargaining contract was properly dismissed where the accompanying complaint against the union for breach of duty of fair representation has withstood the union's motion for summary judgment and remains to be tried.

Petitioners who were formerly employed as truck drivers by respondent Anchor Motor Freight, Inc. (Anchor), were discharged on June 5, 1967. The applicable collective-bargaining contract forbade discharges without just cause. The company charged dishonesty. The practice at Anchor was to reimburse drivers for money spent for lodging while the drivers were on the road overnight. Anchor's assertion was that petitioners had sought reimbursement for motel expenses in excess of the actual charges sustained by them. At a meeting between the company and the union, Local 377, International Brotherhood of Teamsters (Union), which was also attended by petitioners, Anchor presented motel receipts previously submitted by petitioners which were in excess of the charges shown on the motel's registration cards; a notarized statement of the motel clerk asserting the accuracy of the registration cards; and an affidavit of the motel owner affirming that the registration cards were accurate and that inflated receipts had been furnished petitioners. The Union claimed petitioners were innocent and opposed the discharges. It was then agreed that the matter would be presented to the joint arbitration committee for the area . . . [Petitioners'] suggestion that the motel be investigated was answered by the Union representatives' assurances that "there was nothing to worry about" and that they need not hire their own attorney.

A hearing before the joint area committee was held on July 26, 1967. Anchor presented its case. Both the Union and petitioners were afforded an opportunity to present their case and to be heard. Petitioners denied their dishonesty, but neither they nor the Union presented any other evidence contradicting the documents presented by the company. The committee sustained the discharges. . . .

There were later indications that the motel clerk was in fact the culprit; and the present suit was filed in June 1969, against Anchor, the Union, and its International. The complaint alleged that the charges of dishonesty made against petitioners by Anchor were false . . . and that the discharges had been in breach of contract. It was also asserted that the falsity of the charges could have been discovered with a minimum of investigation, that the Union had made no effort to ascertain the truth of the charges, and that the Union had violated its duty of fair representation by arbitrarily and in bad faith depriving petitioners of their employment and permitting their discharge without sufficient proof.

The Union denied the charges and relied on the decision of the joint area committee. Anchor asserted that petitioners had been properly discharged for just cause. It also defended on the ground that petitioners, diligently and in good faith represented by the Union, had unsuccessfully resorted to the grievance and arbitration machinery provided by the contract and that the adverse decision of the joint arbitration committee was binding upon the Union and petitioners under the [contract]. . . . Discovery followed, including a deposition of the motel clerk revealing that he had falsified the records and that it was he who had pocketed the difference between the sums shown on the receipts and the registration cards.

III

Even though under *Vaca* the employer may not insist on exhaustion of grievance procedures when the union has breached its representation duty, it is urged that when the procedures have been followed and a decision favorable to the employer announced, the employer must be protected from relitigation by the express contractual provision declaring a decision to be final and binding. We disagree. The union's breach of duty relieves the employee of an express or implied requirement that disputes be settled through contractual grievance procedures; if it seriously undermines the integrity of the arbitral process the union's breach also removes the bar of the finality provisions of the contract. . . .

Anchor would have it that petitioners are foreclosed from judicial relief unless some blameworthy conduct on its part disentitles it to rely on the finality rule. But it was Anchor that originated the discharges for dishonesty. If those charges were in error, Anchor has surely played its part in precipitating this dispute. Of course, both courts below held there were no facts suggesting that Anchor either knowingly or negligently relied on false evidence. . . .

Nevertheless there remains the question whether the contractual protection against relitigating an arbitral decision binds employees who assert that the process has fundamentally malfunctioned by reason of the bad-faith performance of the union, their statutorily imposed collective-bargaining agent.

As is the case where there has been a failure to exhaust . . . we cannot believe that Congress intended to foreclose the employee from his § 301 remedy otherwise available against the employer if the contractual processes have been seriously flawed by the union's breach of its duty to represent employees honestly and in good faith and without invidious discrimination or arbitrary conduct. . . .

Petitioners are not entitled to relitigate their discharge merely because they offer newly discovered evidence that the charges against them were false and that in fact they were fired without cause. The grievance processes cannot be expected to be error-free. The finality provision has sufficient force to surmount occasional instances of mistake. But it is quite another matter to suggest that erroneous arbitration decisions must stand even though the employee's representation by the Union has been dishonest, in bad faith, or discriminatory; for in that event error and injustice of the grossest sort would multiply. The contractual system would then cease to qualify as an adequate mechanism to secure individual redress for damaging failure of the employer to abide by the contract. Congress has put its blessing on private dispute settlement arrangements provided in collective agreements, but it was anticipated, we are sure, that the contractual machinery would operate within some minimum levels of integrity. In our view, enforcement of the finality provision where the arbitrator has erred is conditioned upon the union's having satisfied its statutory duty fairly to represent the employee in connection with the arbitration proceedings. Wrongfully discharged employees would be left without jobs and without a fair opportunity to secure an adequate remedy. . . .

Petitioners, if they prove an erroneous discharge and the Union's breach of duty tainting the decision of the joint committee, are entitled to an appropriate remedy against the employer as well as the Union. . . .

Notes

1. *Hines* did not reach the question of whether the union actually violated its DFR. Based on the facts described in the excerpt above, do you think it did? Why or why not?

2. A dissent by two justices in *Hines* (omitted above) argued that the decision undermined the finality of arbitration. It also showed some sympathy to the employer, "which concededly acted in good faith throughout these proceedings" but now "is to be subjected to a damage suit because of the Union's alleged misconduct." 424 U.S. at 576. Are these good criticisms of the result in *Hines*? What is the argument that the employer is not, in fact, such a sympathetic party here?

4. Remedies for a Breach of the Duty of Fair Representation

Hines is a good segue to the final issue in *Vaca*: remedies and damages. *Vaca* explained that in a standard hybrid DFR/§ 301 claim, damages should be apportioned between the employer (whose contract violation caused harm) and the union (whose DFR violation prevented the harm from being remedied in a timely fashion). But how should that apportionment be calculated?

Bowen v. United States Postal Service

Supreme Court of the United States
459 U.S. 212 (1983)

POWELL, J.

The issue is whether a union may be held primarily liable for that part of a wrongfully discharged employee's damages caused by his union's breach of its duty of fair representation.

I

On February 21, 1976, following an altercation with another employee, petitioner Charles V. Bowen was suspended without pay from his position with the United States Postal Service. Bowen was a member of the American Postal Workers Union, AFL-CIO, the recognized collective bargaining agent for Service employees. After Bowen was formally terminated on March 30, 1976, he filed a grievance with the Union as provided by the collective-bargaining agreement. When the Union declined to take his grievance to arbitration, he sued the Service and the Union in the United States District Court for the Western District of Virginia, seeking damages and injunctive relief.

Bowen's complaint charged that the Service had violated the collective bargaining agreement by dismissing him without "just cause" and that the Union had breached its duty of fair representation. His evidence at trial indicated that the responsible Union officer, at each step of the grievance process, had recommended pursuing the grievance but that the national office, for no apparent reason, had refused to take the matter to arbitration.

Upon return of a special verdict in favor of Bowen and against both defendants, the District Court entered judgment, holding that the Service had discharged Bowen without just cause and that the Union had handled his "apparently meritorious grievance . . . in an arbitrary and perfunctory manner. . . ." In so doing, both the Union and the Service acted "in reckless and callous disregard of [Bowen's] rights." The court found that Bowen could not have proceeded independently of the Union and that if the Union had arbitrated Bowen's grievance, he would have been reinstated.

The court ordered that Bowen be reimbursed $52,954 for lost benefits and wages. Although noting that "there is authority suggesting that only the employer is liable for damages in the form of back pay," it observed that "this is a case in which both defendants, by their illegal acts, are liable to plaintiff. . . . The problem in this case is not one of liability but rather one of apportionment. . . ." The jury had found that the Union was responsible for $30,000 of Bowen's damages. The court approved that apportionment, ordering the Service to pay the remaining $22,954.[6]

II

In *Vaca v. Sipes* . . . the Court held that an employee such as Bowen, who proves that his employer violated the labor agreement and his union breached its duty of fair representation, may be entitled to recover damages from both the union and the employer. The Court explained that the award must be apportioned according to fault:

> "The governing principle, then, is to apportion liability between the employer and the union according to the damage caused by the fault of each. Thus, damages attributable solely to the employer's breach of contract should not be charged to the union, but increases if any in those damages caused by the union's refusal to process the grievance should not be charged to the employer." *Id.* . . .

Although *Vaca*'s governing principle is well established, its application has caused some uncertainty. The Union argues that the Court of Appeals correctly determined that it cannot be charged with any damages resulting from a wrongful discharge. *Vaca*'s "governing principle," according to the Union, requires that the employer be solely liable for such damages. The Union views itself as liable only for Bowen's litigation expenses resulting from its breach of duty. It finds support for this view in *Vaca*'s recognition that a union's breach of its duty of fair representation does not absolve an employer of all the consequences of a breach of the collective-bargaining contract. . . . The Union contends that its unrelated breach of

---

6. The District Court found as a fact that if Bowen's grievance had been arbitrated he would have been reinstated by August, 1977. Lost wages after that date were deemed the fault of the Union: "While the [Service] set this case in motion with its discharge, the [Union's] acts, upon which [Bowen] reasonably relied, delayed the reinstatement of [Bowen] and it is a proper apportionment to assign fault to the [Union] for approximately two-thirds of the period [Bowen] was unemployed up to the time of trial."

the duty of fair representation does not make it liable for any part of the discharged employee's damages; its default merely lifts the bar to the employee's suit on the contract against his employer.

The difficulty with this argument is that it treats the relationship between the employer and employee, created by the collective-bargaining agreement, as if it were a simple contract of hire governed by traditional common law principles. This reading of *Vaca* fails to recognize that a collective-bargaining agreement is much more than traditional common law employment terminable at will. Rather, it is an agreement creating relationships and interests under the federal common law of labor policy.

A

. . . The interests thus identified in *Vaca* provide a measure of its principle for apportioning damages. Of paramount importance is the right of the employee, who has been injured by both the employer's and the union's breach, to be made whole. In determining the degree to which the employer or the union should bear the employee's damages, the Court held that the employer should not be shielded from the "natural consequences" of its breach by wrongful union conduct. The Court noted, however, that the employer may have done nothing to prevent exhaustion. Were it not for the union's failure to represent the employee fairly, the employer's breach "could [have been] remedied through the grievance process to the employee-plaintiff's benefit." The fault that justifies dropping the bar to the employee's suit for damages also requires the union to bear some responsibility for increases in the employee's damages resulting from its breach. To hold otherwise would make the employer alone liable for the consequences of the union's breach of duty. . . .

It is true that the employer discharged the employee wrongfully and remains liable for the employee's backpay. . . . The union's breach of its duty of fair representation, however, caused the grievance procedure to malfunction resulting in an increase in the employee's damages. Even though both the employer and the union have caused the damage suffered by the employee, the union is responsible for the increase in damages and, as between the two wrongdoers, should bear its portion of the damages.[12]

Vaca's governing principle reflects this allocation of responsibility. As the Court stated, "damages attributable *solely* to the employer's breach of contract should not be charged to the union, but *increases* if any in those damages caused by the union's refusal to process the grievance should not be charged to the employer." 386 U.S., at 197–198 (emphasis added). The Union's position here would require us to read out of the *Vaca* articulation of the relevant principle the words emphasized above. . . .

---

12. Although the union remains primarily responsible for the portion of the damages resulting from its default, *Vaca* made clear that the union's breach does not absolve the employer of liability. Thus if the petitioner in this case does not collect the damages apportioned against the Union, the Service remains secondarily liable for the full loss of backpay.

B

... Although each party participates in the grievance procedure, the union plays a pivotal role in the process since it assumes the responsibility of determining whether to press an employee's claims. The employer, for its part, must rely on the union's decision not to pursue an employee's grievance. ...

When the union, as the exclusive agent of the employee, waives arbitration or fails to seek review of an adverse decision, the employer should be in substantially the same position as if the employee had had the right to act on his own behalf and had done so. . . . [15]

The principle announced in *Vaca* reflects this allocation of responsibilities in the grievance procedure—a procedure that contemplates that both employer and union will perform their respective obligations. In the absence of damages apportionment where the default of both parties contributes to the employee's injury, incentives to comply with the grievance procedure will be diminished. Indeed, imposing total liability solely on the employer could well affect the willingness of employers to agree to arbitration clauses as they are customarily written.

Nor will requiring the union to pay damages impose a burden on the union inconsistent with national labor policy. It will provide an additional incentive for the union to process its members' claims where warranted. . . . This is wholly consistent with a union's interest. It is a duty owed to its members as well as consistent with the union's commitment to the employer under the arbitration clause. . . . [16]

IV

In this case, the findings of the District Court, accepted by the Court of Appeals, establish that the damages sustained by petitioner were caused initially by the Service's unlawful discharge and increased by the Union's breach of its duty of fair representation. Accordingly, apportionment of the damages was required by *Vaca*. We reverse the judgment of the Court of Appeals and remand for entry of judgment

---

15. Under the dissent's analysis, the employer may not rely on the union's decision not to pursue a grievance. Rather it can prevent continued liability only by reinstating the discharged employee. . . . This leaves the employer with a dubious option: it must either reinstate the employee promptly or leave itself exposed to open-ended liability. If this were the rule, the very purpose of the grievance procedure would be defeated. It is precisely to provide the exclusive means of resolving this kind of dispute that the parties agree to such a procedure and national labor policy strongly encourages its use. . . .

16. Requiring the union to pay its share of the damages is consistent with the interests recognized in *International Brotherhood of Electrical Workers v. Foust*, 442 U.S. 42 (1979). In *Foust*, we found that a union was not liable for punitive damages. The interest in deterring future breaches by the union was outweighed by the debilitating impact that "unpredictable and potentially substantial" awards of punitive damages would have on the union treasury and the union's exercise of discretion in deciding what claims to pursue. . . . An award of compensatory damages, however, normally will be limited and finite. Moreover, the union's exercise of discretion is shielded by the standard necessary to prove a breach of the duty of fair representation. Thus, the threat that was present in *Foust* is absent here.

allocating damages against both the Service and the Union consistent with this opinion.[19]

WHITE, J., with whom MARSHALL, J., BLACKMUN, J., and REHNQUIST, J. join, concurring in part and dissenting in part.

The Court holds that an employer who wrongfully discharges an employee protected by a collective bargaining agreement with an arbitration clause is only responsible for backpay that accrues prior to the hypothetical date upon which an arbitrator would have issued an award had the employee's union taken the matter to arbitration. All backpay damages that accrue after this time are the sole responsibility of the union, even where, as here, the union is in no way responsible for the employer's decision to terminate the employee. This rationale . . . does not give due regard to our prior precedents, to equitable principles, or to the national labor policy. I therefore respectfully dissent. For the following reasons, I believe that the employer should be primarily liable for all backpay. . . .

Vaca made clear that, with respect to an *employer*, the only consequence of a union's breach of a fair-representation duty to an *employee* is that it provides the employee with the means of defeating the employer's "defense based upon the failure to exhaust contractual remedies" in a § 301 suit. The Court explicitly stated that the union's violation of its statutory duty in no way "exempt[ed] the employer from contractual damages which he would otherwise have had to pay" . . . and that the employer could not "hide behind the union's wrongful failure to act." . . .

In *Hines v. Anchor Motor Freight, Inc.*, 424 U.S. 554 (1976), we reiterated that a union's breach of duty to an employee does not shield an employer from damages that it would otherwise owe . . . even though the employer was in no way responsible for the alleged union malfeasance. . . .

Thus, under our previous holdings, as far as the employer is concerned, a union's breach of a fair-representation duty does no more than remove the procedural exhaustion-of-remedies bar to a § 301 suit by an aggrieved employee. The union's breach does not affect the employer's potential liability, including backpay liability, if the employee prevails in the § 301 judicial proceedings by showing that the employer had breached its contract in discharging him. . . .

What, then, is the proper measure of the union's damages in a hybrid § 301/ breach-of-duty suit? We considered this question in *Czosek v. O'Mara*, 397 U.S. 25 (1970), and concluded that, under the *Vaca* rule, the union is liable in damages to the extent that its misconduct "add[s] to the difficulty and expense of collecting

---

19. We need not decide whether the District Court's instructions on apportionment of damages were proper. The Union objected to the instructions only on the ground that no back wages at all could be assessed against it. It did not object to the manner of apportionment if such damages were to be assessed. Nor is it necessary in this case to consider whether there were degrees of fault, as both the Service and the Union were found to have acted in "reckless and callous disregard of [Bowen's] rights."

from the employer." *Czosek* reassured unions that they would not be forced to pay damages "for which the employer is wholly *or partly* responsible." *Id.* at 28–29 (emphasis added).

It is true that, under the *Vaca-Czosek* rule, the union may sometimes only have *de minimis* liability, and we unanimously acknowledged this fact in *Electrical Workers v. Foust,* . . . "The damages a union will have to pay in a typical unfair representation suit are minimal; under *Vaca*'s apportionment formula, the bulk of the award will be paid by the employer, the perpetrator of the wrongful discharge, in a parallel § 301 action." . . . The *Foust* majority nevertheless reaffirmed *Vaca* and, moreover, further insulated unions from liability by holding that punitive damages could not be assessed in an action for breach of the duty of fair representation. In reaching these conclusions, the Court relied on the policy of affording individual employees redress for injuries caused by union misconduct without compromising the collective interests of union members in protecting limited union funds. As in *Vaca*, considerations of deterrence were deemed insufficient to risk endangering union "financial stability." . . . [6]

II

. . . It cannot be denied that, contrary to *Vaca* and its progeny, under the Court's new rule, the "bulk of the award" for backpay in a hybrid § 301/breach-of-duty suit will have to be borne by the union, not the employer. In the present case, for example, the jury, which was instructed in accordance with the Court's new test, assessed $30,000 in compensatory damages against the union, and only $17,000 against the employer. The union should well consider itself fortunate that this dispute proceeded to trial less than three years after the cessation of petitioner Bowen's employment. Most of the cases of this nature that have been reviewed by this Court have taken the better part of a decade to run their course. Because the hypothetical arbitration date will usually be less than one year after the discharge . . . it is readily apparent that, under the Court's rule, in many cases the union will be subject to large liability, far greater than that of the employer, the extent of which will not be in any way related to the union's comparative culpability. Nor will the union have any readily apparent way to limit its constantly increasing liability.

Bowen and the Postal Service argue that the employer is not the "cause" of an employee's lost earnings after the date on which an arbitral decision would have reinstated or otherwise compensated the employee. In the "but for" sense, of course, this is patently false, as the Court concedes. But for the employer's breach of contract, there would be no occasion for *anyone* to reimburse the plaintiff for lost wages accumulated either before or after a hypothetical arbitration. . . . The union's

---

6. Even though *Foust* requires that punitive damages not be assessed against a union, the *Vaca* rule nevertheless provides for a credible deterrent against wrongful union conduct. Attorney's fees and other litigation expenses have been assessed as damages against unions, because such damages measure the extent by which the union's breach of duty adds to the difficulty and expense of collecting from the employer. . . .

failure to arbitrate does not make the discharge and the refusal to reinstate any less wrongful. . . .

It bears re-emphasizing that both before and after the hypothetical arbitration date, the union did not in any way prevent the employer from reinstating Bowen, and that the employer could reinstate him. Under these circumstances, it is bizarre to hold, as the Court does, that the relatively impotent union is *exclusively* liable for the bulk of the backpay. . . . The employer's wrongful conduct clearly was the generating cause of Bowen's loss, and only the employer had the continuing ability to right the wrong and limit liability by reinstating Bowen. The employer has the sole duty to pay wages, and it should be responsible for all back wages to which Bowen is entitled. . . .

[S]ince the practical consequence of today's holding is that unions will take many unmeritorious grievances to arbitration simply to avoid exposure to the new breach-of-duty liability, the Court's rule actually impairs the ability of the grievance machinery to provide for orderly dispute resolution. . . .

Accordingly, I would affirm the Court of Appeals' judgment that the union was not liable for backpay damages, but I would reverse the remainder of the judgment and remand the case with instructions that the District Court be directed to enter judgment against the Postal Service for the entire amount of Bowen's backpay loss.

Notes

1. Who is more convincing, the majority or the dissent? What incentives does each opinion create for employers and unions in hybrid § 301/DFR cases?

2. As the dissent explains, *Foust* held that punitive damages are not available against unions in DFR cases. Given that violating the DFR usually requires some fairly bad, often intentionally bad, behavior by the union, is that a good rule? Is *Foust's* rationale for that rule (partially summarized in the dissent) convincing? Consider, in answering this question, what types of damages are available (and not available) in other labor law and ULP claims.

III. The DFR in the Public Sector

Duty of fair representation rules in the public sector are generally quite similar—and often identical—to private-sector DFR rules. A few differences exist. Unlike the private sector, in some public-sector jurisdictions, DFR rules are written into the statute. *See, e.g.,* Ohio Rev. Code § 4117.11(B)(6) (it is a union ULP to "[f]ail to fairly represent all public employees in a bargaining unit"). But in other jurisdictions, as in the private sector, courts have simply held that the DFR is a necessary corollary to exclusive representation. *See, e.g., Belanger v. Matteson,* 346 A.2d 124 (R.I. 1975) (finding a DFR in under Rhode Island law despite no explicit statutory mention, relying on private-sector precedents).

In both situations, the substantive standards for DFR violations in the public sector are nearly always the same as in the private sector after *O'Neil. See, e.g., State ex rel. Hall v. State Employment Relations Board*, 912 N.E.2d 1120 (Ohio 2009) *Belanger, supra*. Deviations are rare, although Illinois — by statute — requires intentional bad behavior by the union. *See* 115 Ill. Comp. Stat. §5/14(b)(1) (Educational Labor Relations Act); 5 Ill. Comp. Stat. §315/10(b) (Public Labor Relations Act).

States differ somewhat as to procedures. A number of states follow the private-sector model and permit plaintiffs to bring DFR claims either to the labor board or directly to court. *See, e.g., Farber v. City of Paterson*, 440 F.3d 131 (3d Cir. 2006); *Demings v. Ecorse*, 377 N.W.2d 275 (Mich. 1985). But in some states, plaintiffs must bring DFR claims with the state agency initially; they cannot go directly to court. *City of Mesquite v. Eighth Judicial District Court of Nevada, Clark County*, 445 P.3d 1244 (Nev. 2019). What about the practical problems with this approach that *Vaca* described? In such jurisdictions, the labor board is generally empowered to grant relief against the employer as well. *See, e.g., Piteau v. Board of Education of Hartford*, 15 A.3d 1067 (Conn. 2011); *Brown v. Maine State Employees Association*, 690 A.2d 956 (Me. 1997); *Karahalios v. Nat'l Fed. of Federal Employees*, 489 U.S. 527 (1989) (federal sector). Third, in some states, plaintiffs must bring DFR claims to court; they cannot bring them to the labor board. *See, e.g., Ziccardi v. Commonwealth of Pennsylvania*, 456 A.2d 979 (Pa. 1982).

A few other variations exist. For example, contrary to the private-sector rule from *Foust*, New Mexico allows punitive damages in certain DFR claims. *See Akins v. United Steel Workers of America, Local 187*, 148 N.M. 442 (2010). Also, unlike the private-sector rule, Alaska permits an employee to sue the employer for breach of a CBA if the union declines to arbitrate the employee's case, even if the union's actions in handling the matter did not violate its DFR. Are any of these alternative rules used in the public sector better than the NLRA rules? Why or why not?

A more substantive variation some states have recently adopted in response to *Janus* is discussed *infra*.

IV. Union Security Clauses

This section covers "union security clauses," a generic term for CBA provisions that obligate members of a union bargaining unit to pay at least some dues to the union that represents them as a condition of employment. This topic is similar to the DFR issue discussed above in two significant ways. First, although union security clause cases may appear to be primarily complaints that individual employees have about their union, these cases can also involve employers (employers are signatories to CBAs as well as unions). Second, the rules for the public and private sectors were almost always the same, until the 2018 decision in *Janus v. AFSCME, infra*. The latter was true even though courts based the private-sector rules on statutory language and based the public-sector rules on the First Amendment.

A. Union Security Issues Before the 1960s

Unions rely on numbers to present a strong collective front to employers. Unions also need dues to fund representational activities. Thus, unions have long tried to ensure that the workers they represent are dues-paying union members. But not all workers in a bargaining unit necessarily support the union (and perhaps even if they do, not all are enthused about paying dues). So, unions have long sought union security clauses, and some other parties have long opposed such clauses.

As Chapter 1 explained, before the NLRA, unions often pushed for union security agreements called the "closed shop" and the "union shop." In a closed shop, an employer and union agreed that the employer would not hire anyone who was not, at the time of hire, a dues-paying member of the union. In a union shop, the union and employer agreed that anyone the employer hired into a position represented by the union would have to join the union after being hired, as a condition of employment. Meanwhile, employers pushed for what was called the "open shop" — refusing to agree to any sort of union security clause. Sometimes employers and unions would enter into what is called a "maintenance of membership" clause: an employee was not obligated to pay dues, but if the employee voluntarily agreed to pay dues at the beginning of the term of a collective-bargaining agreement, the employee would be obligated, as a condition of employment, to pay dues through the end of the term of the contract.

Today, both the closed shop and union shop are illegal in the private sector. Under the NLRA, in about half of states — the so-called right-to-work states — unions may not require represented employees to pay dues as a condition of employment. Further, in 2018, the Supreme Court held that this rule was constitutionally required in all public-sector employment.

In states that are not right-to-work jurisdictions, the most that is allowed in the private sector is what is called the "agency shop" or "fair share" agreement: a clause that requires employees to pay for activities related to collective bargaining. Further, while such a union security clause can legally require payment of at least a significant portion of union dues, a union security clause cannot require an employee represented by a union to be or become a member of the union. Hence, instead of referring to those represented by a union as "union members," especially in this context, it is necessary to use the slightly more cumbersome but more accurate term, "bargaining-unit members."

How did the law develop this way? The original Wagner Act in 1935 did not contain any restrictions on union security arrangements, and thus it permitted unions and employers to agree to the closed shop, union shop, maintenance of membership, or open shop (and, at least in theory, other variations). But in 1947, the Taft-Hartley Act changed the law of union security clauses in two important ways. First, Taft-Hartley added § 14(b) to the NLRA: the right-to-work option for states. Second, Taft-Hartley amended § 8(a)(3) to make the closed shop illegal everywhere.

The Creation of the Right-to-Work State: Section 14(b) allows individual states to adopt right-to-work rules under which any form of union security clause in a CBA is illegal. In other words, only the "open shop" is allowed. Notably, this is the only part of the NLRA that permits a state to choose to vary a rule. Currently, twenty-seven states are right-to-work states: Alabama, Arizona, Arkansas, Florida, Georgia, Idaho, Indiana, Iowa, Kansas, Kentucky, Louisiana, Michigan, Mississippi, Nebraska, Nevada, North Carolina, North Dakota, Oklahoma, South Carolina, South Dakota, Tennessee, Texas, Utah, Virginia, West Virginia, Wisconsin, and Wyoming. Almost all these states became right-to-work states no later than the 1950s. This list is split between jurisdictions that adopted their right to work laws in the decade or so after Taft-Hartley was enacted, and those that adopted their laws more recently. The list of more recent adopters contains: Oklahoma (2001), Indiana (2012), Michigan (2012), Wisconsin (2015), West Virginia (2016), and Kentucky (2017).

The preceding list includes only states, and no municipalities. But municipalities have also begun to enact right-to-work ordinances, raising the question of whether those ordinances are preempted by the NLRA. The main textual argument in favor of preemption is that NLRA § 14(b) says the Act does not preempt "State or Territorial" right-to-work laws. But municipalities are neither states nor territories, so their right-to-work laws are preempted by § 8(a)(3), which permits the negotiation of union security agreements. Further, proponents of this view argue that Congress generally intended to preempt the entire field of regulation of union security clauses, and as a result, it accords with probable congressional intent to read § 14(b) narrowly. A district court in Illinois accepted this view in *Int'l Union of Operating Eng'rs, Local 399 v. Village of Lincolnshire*, 228 F. Supp. 3d 824 (N.D. Ill. 2017). The Seventh Circuit affirmed, and the defendants filed a cert petition. While that petition was pending, Illinois passed a law barring municipal right-to-work laws. As a result, the Supreme Court vacated the Seventh Circuit's judgment and directed that that case be dismissed as moot. *Vill. of. Lincolnshire v. Int'l Union of Operating Eng'rs Local 399*, 139 S. Ct. 2692 (2019). Conversely, the Sixth Circuit held that local right-to-work laws are permitted under § 14(b) in *United Auto., Aerospace, & Agric. Implement Workers of Am. Local 3047 v. Hardin Cty.*, 842 F.3d 407 (6th Cir. 2016). In *Hardin County*, the court reasoned that § 14(b)'s use of the word "state" includes political subdivisions of the state, relying in part on the text of the statute, and in part on cases suggesting that statutes should be construed in a manner that preserves the traditional ability of states to delegate lawmaking authority to their subdivisions.

The new round of right-to-work legislation has sparked new interest in legal challenges aimed at limiting the impact of these laws. For example, in 2012, Indiana enacted HB 1001, a right-to-work law. In 2014, the Supreme Court of Indiana rejected a challenge to this law, reversing a lower court holding that the law violated Article 1, Section 21 of the Indiana Constitution. That provision bars a "person's particular service" from being demanded "without just compensation." *Zoeller v. Sweeney*, 19 N.E.3d 749 (Ind. 2014). The lower court had reasoned that unions must represent members of bargaining units who do not pay dues (*see* Chapter 14 above, discussing DFR). A separate challenge to this law filed in federal court argued that the NLRA preempted the law and also that it violated the Takings and Equal Protection clauses. *Sweeney v. Pence*, 767 F.3d 654 (7th Cir. 2014). The argument regarding preemption focused on § 14(b) of the NLRA, which permits the application of state laws that prohibit unions and employers from "requiring membership in a labor organization as a condition of employment." Indiana's law, the challengers reasoned, went beyond § 14(b)'s safe harbor because it prohibited unions and employers from requiring employees to pay their unions *any* amount of money, even if less than membership dues. The Seventh Circuit rejected this argument in a 2–1 decision, in part because many decades-old right-to-work laws that were similar to Indiana's had not been disapproved by the Supreme Court. In dissent, Judge Wood argued that the law worked an unconstitutional taking by requiring unions to represent non-paying non-members.

Are right-to-work laws good policy? They clearly hurt unions. Fewer bargaining-unit members pay dues in right-to-work jurisdictions. Unions complain that the rule creates a classic "free rider" problem. Recall from the discussion above that unions have a duty of fair representation to bargaining-unit members who do not pay dues, a duty that is in almost all ways identical to the duty the union has toward full dues-paying members. For example, if a bargaining-unit member who has never paid dues wishes to arbitrate his discharge, the union cannot consider his lack of dues payment in deciding whether to arbitrate the case — even though the union's lawyer handling the arbitration will typically be paid from the union dues of those who pay. Nor can the union discriminate in contract terms on the basis of who does and does not pay dues. So, the argument continues, a non-dues paying member of the bargaining unit gets — without paying anything for it — a contract which likely includes higher compensation than the employee would otherwise have received, a just-cause discharge provision (which the employee would almost certainly not have without the union), and quite possibly the right to a free union lawyer to represent him in the arbitration. All funded by those employees who pay dues. This is "free riding."

On the other hand, proponents of right-to-work rules argue that if unions do a good job, more members of their bargaining units will be more willing to pay dues voluntarily. Right-to-work rules do not ban payment of dues; rather, they make it illegal to make any dues payments a condition of employment. Thus, proponents of these rules argue, right-to-work rules will create incentives for better union representation. Further, union opponents are free riders only because of the exclusive representation rule. They would, at least often, prefer not to be represented by a union at all.

Which arguments do you find most convincing, and why? Remember that the DFR includes the duty to represent non-members in grievance proceedings. Should the Board overrule its existing rule, which does not allow unions to charge grievance-processing fees to nonmembers? *See Int'l Ass'n of Machinists & Aerospace Workers, Local Union No. 697 (The H.O. Canfield Rubber Co. of VA, Inc.)*, 223 N.L.R.B. 832 (1976) (holding that union violated DFR by charging non-paying non-member in right-to-work state for cost of processing grievance, where union did not charge members for grievance representation). If it does change that rule, should the union be permitted to charge the actual cost of processing the grievance, an amount equal to the agency fee that could have been charged in a non-right-to-work state, or some other amount?

The Development of the Agency Shop: As stated above, Taft-Hartley amended § 8(a)(3) to make the closed shop illegal everywhere. This language will come up again later, so it is worth quoting here. Section 8(a)(3) makes it an employer ULP to engage in:

> discrimination in regard to hire or tenure of employment or any term or condition of employment to encourage or discourage membership in any labor organization: *Provided*, That nothing in this subchapter, or in any other statute of the United States, shall preclude an employer from making an agreement with a labor organization ... to require as a condition of employment membership therein on or after the thirtieth day following the beginning of such employment or the effective date of such agreement, whichever is the later. .... *Provided further*, That no employer shall justify any discrimination against an employee for nonmembership in a labor organization (A) if he has reasonable grounds for believing that such membership was not available to the employee on the same terms and conditions generally applicable to other members, or (B) if he has reasonable grounds for believing that membership was denied or terminated for reasons other than the failure of the employee to tender the periodic dues and the initiation fees uniformly required as a condition of acquiring or retaining membership.

This would appear to make the *union* shop legal. The language after the first "*provided*" allows employers to require union membership as a condition of employment beginning thirty days (or later) after employment begins. Not surprisingly, unions require full dues as a condition of membership, so this language, for a time, allowed union security clauses to require membership and full dues. The language after the "*provided further*" clause seemed to underscore this. It seemed designed to bar application of a union shop clause to an employee if the employee had been denied union membership for some reason "other than the failure to tender the periodic dues and initiation fees uniformly required" of all members. So, for example, if a union "blackballed" an employee for some improper motive (*e.g.*, race discrimination, or discrimination on political or personal grounds) the employer could not be compelled to fire the employee pursuant to the union security clause.

Also relevant here is the parallel language of § 8(b)(2), which makes it a union ULP:

> to cause or attempt to cause an employer to discriminate against an employee in violation of subsection (a)(3) of this section or to discriminate against an employee with respect to whom membership in such organization has been denied or terminated on some ground other than his failure to tender the periodic dues and the initiation fees uniformly required as a condition of acquiring or retaining membership.

Thus, unions cannot attempt (through a union security clause) to make an employer discriminate against a bargaining-unit member because union member- ship was denied, *if* the reason membership was denied was "some ground other than" failure to pay regular dues and fees. Also, Taft-Hartley added § 8(b)(5), which bars unions from requiring employees covered by union security clauses to pay "excessive or discriminatory" initiation fees.

The next statutory change regarding union security clauses came in 1959, when the Landrum-Griffin Act added § 8(f) to the NLRA. Section 8(f) permits "pre-hire" contracts in the construction industry, which may apply after seven days, instead of after thirty days. As with other special rules for the construction industry, this rule is premised on the fact that in the construction trades, employment is often for a short term, and employees work for a variety of different employers.

Thus, by the end of the 1950s, it appeared that in a state that had not chosen the right-to-work option, a union and employer could legally negotiate a union secu- rity clause requiring that, after an employee had been employed for thirty days, the employee was obligated to become a union member and pay full union dues, as a condition of employment.

But that is not the law today. The relevant statutory language has not changed. What happened?

B. Membership "Whittled Down to Its Financial Core"

NLRB v. General Motors Corp., 373 U.S. 734 (1963), made an early conceptual step toward modern union security law under the NLRA. In *General Motors*, the employer had refused to bargain about a union security proposal that would have required what was called an "agency shop." This form of agency shop required employees to pay full dues and fees as a condition of employment along the lines of § 8(a)(3), but did not require the bargaining-unit members to formally become union members.

General Motors upheld the agency fee clause as legal, rejecting a claim that the union shop was the *only* type of union security clause § 8(a)(3) permitted.

> When Congress enacted the Taft-Hartley Act, it added the following to the language of the original proviso to § 8(3). . . .
>
> These additions were intended to accomplish twin purposes. On the one hand, the most serious abuses of compulsory unionism were eliminated by abolishing the closed shop. On the other hand, Congress recognized that in the absence of a union-security provision "many employees sharing the benefits of what unions are able to accomplish by collective bargaining will refuse to pay their share of the cost." S.Rep.No.105, 80th Cong., 1st Sess., p. 6. . . . Consequently, under the new law "employers would still be permit- ted to enter into agreements requiring all the employees in a given bargain- ing unit to become members 30 days after being hired," but "expulsion from a union cannot be a ground of compulsory discharge if the worker is not

delinquent in paying his initiation fee or dues." S.Rep.No.105, p. 7.... As far as the federal law was concerned, all employees could be required to pay their way. The bill "abolishes the closed shop but permits voluntary agreements for requiring such forms of compulsory membership as the union shop or maintenance of membership...." S.Rep.No.105, p. 3....

We find nothing in the legislative history of the Act indicating that Congress intended the amended proviso to §8(a)(3) to validate only the union shop and simultaneously to abolish, in addition to the closed shop, all other union-security arrangements permissible under state law. There is much to be said for the Board's view that, if Congress desired in the Wagner Act to permit a closed or union shop and in the Taft-Hartley Act the union shop, then it also intended to preserve the status of less vigorous, less compulsory contracts which demanded less adherence to the union. 373 U.S. at 741.

The *General Motors* decision continued, however, to define what "member" in the NLRA's statutory language actually meant.

[The employer] relies upon the express words of the proviso which allow employment to be conditioned upon "membership": since the union's proposal here does not require actual membership but demands only initiation fees and monthly dues, it is not saved by the proviso. This position, of course, would reject administrative decisions concerning the scope of §8(3) of the Wagner Act.... Moreover, the 1947 amendments not only abolished the closed shop but also made significant alterations in the meaning of "membership" for the purposes of union-security contracts. Under the second proviso to §8(a)(3), the burdens of membership upon which employment may be conditioned are expressly limited to the payment of initiation fees and monthly dues. It is permissible to condition employment upon membership, but membership, insofar as it has significance to employment rights, may in turn be conditioned only upon payment of fees and dues. "Membership" as a condition of employment is whittled down to its financial core. This Court has said as much before in *Radio Officers' Union v. Labor Board*, 347 U.S. 17, 41 [(1954)]:

"This legislative history clearly indicates that Congress intended to prevent utilization of union security agreements for any purpose other than to compel payment of union dues and fees. Thus Congress recognized the validity of unions' concern about 'free riders,' i.e., employees who receive the benefits of union representation but are unwilling to contribute their fair share of financial support to such union, and gave unions the power to contract to meet that problem while withholding from unions the power to cause the discharge of employees for any other reason...."

... If an employee in a union shop unit refuses to respect any union-imposed obligations other than the duty to pay dues and fees, and membership in the union is therefore denied or terminated, the condition of "membership" for § 8(a)(3) purposes is nevertheless satisfied and the employee may not be discharged for nonmembership even though he is not a formal member. 373 U.S. at 742–43.

What does this decision mean for union security clauses that require employees to formally join the union? Also, would a union security clause that required payment of dues but not joining the union be legal in a right-to-work state? *Retail Clerks, Intern. Ass'n Local 1625 v Schermerhorn*, 375 U.S. 96 (1963), held no.

C. The Emergence of Limits on Union Security Clauses Under the RLA

In the seven years before *General Motors*, the Supreme Court was crafting different rules for unions and employers covered by the Railway Labor Act. The two major decisions were *Railway Employees Dept. v. Hanson*, 351 U.S. 225 (1956) and *Int'l Ass'n of Machinists v. Street*, 367 U.S. 740 (1961). Notably, *General Motors*, decided in 1963, did not mention either case. It thus appeared at the time that RLA and NLRA rules were separate. This would later change, however.

International Association of Machinists v. Street
Supreme Court of the United States
367 U.S. 740 (1961)

BRENNAN, J.

A group of labor organizations, appellants here, and the carriers comprising the Southern Railway System, entered into a union-shop agreement pursuant to the authority of § 2, Eleventh of the Railway Labor Act.[1] The agreement requires each of the appellees, employees of the carriers, as a condition of continued employment, to pay the appellant union representing his particular class of craft the dues, initiation fees and assessments uniformly required as a condition of acquiring or retaining union membership. The appellees, in behalf of themselves and of employees

---

1. 64 Stat. 1238, 45 U.S.C. § 152, Eleventh. The section provides:
"Eleventh. . . . any carrier or carriers as defined in this chapter and a labor organization or labor organizations duly designated and authorized to represent employees in accordance with the requirements of this chapter shall be permitted—
"(a) to make agreements, requiring, as a condition of continued employment, that within sixty days following the beginning of such employment, or the effective date of such agreements, whichever is the later, all employees shall become members of the labor organization representing their craft or class: Provided, That no such agreement shall require such condition of employment with respect to employees to whom membership is not available upon the same terms and conditions as are generally applicable to any other member or with respect to employees to whom membership was denied or terminated for any reason other than the failure of the employee to tender the periodic dues, initiation fees, and assessments (not including fines and penalties) uniformly required as a condition of acquiring or retaining membership. . . ."

similarly situated, brought this action in the Superior Court of Bibb County, Georgia, alleging that the money each was thus compelled to pay to hold his job was in substantial part used to finance the campaigns of candidates for federal and state offices whom he opposed, and to promote the propagation of political and economic doctrines, concepts and ideologies with which he disagreed.

I. The Hanson Decision.

We held in *Railway Employes' Dept. v. Hanson*, 351 U.S. 225 (1956) that enactment of the provision of § 2, Eleventh authorizing union-shop agreements between interstate railroads and unions of their employees was a valid exercise by Congress of its powers under the Commerce Clause and did not violate the First Amendment or the Due Process Clause of the Fifth Amendment. It is argued that our disposition of the First Amendment claims in *Hanson* disposes of appellees' constitutional claims in this case adversely to their contentions. We disagree. As appears from its history, that case decided only that § 2, Eleventh, in authorizing collective agreements conditioning employees' continued employment on payment of union dues, initiation fees and assessments, did not on its face impinge upon protected rights of association. . . . We said: 'It is argued that compulsory membership will be used to impair freedom of expression. But that problem is not presented by this record. . . . If the exaction of dues, initiation fees, or assessments is used as a cover for forcing ideological conformity or other action in contravention of the Fifth Amendment, this judgment will not prejudice the decision in that case. For we pass narrowly on § 2, Eleventh of the Railway Labor Act. . . ."

The record in this case is adequate squarely to present the constitutional questions reserved in Hanson. These are questions of the utmost gravity. However, the restraints against unnecessary constitutional decisions counsel against their determination unless we must conclude that Congress, in authorizing a union shop under § 2, Eleventh, also meant that the labor organization receiving an employee's money should be free, despite that employee's objection, to spend his money for political causes which he opposes. Federal statutes are to be so construed as to avoid serious doubt of their constitutionality. 'When the validity of an act of the Congress is drawn in question, and even if a serious doubt of constitutionality is raised, it is a cardinal principle that this Court will first ascertain whether a construction of the statute is fairly possible by which the question may be avoided.' We conclude that such a construction is not only 'fairly possible' but entirely reasonable, and we therefore find it unnecessary to decide the correctness of the constitutional determinations made by the Georgia courts.

II. The Rail Unions and Union Security.

The history of union security in the railway industry is marked first, by a strong and long-standing tradition of voluntary unionism on the part of the standard rail unions; second, by the declaration in 1934 of a congressional policy of complete freedom of choice of employees to join or not to join a union; third, by the modification of the firm legislative policy against compulsion, but only as a specific response to the recognition of the expenses and burdens incurred by the unions in the administration of the complex scheme of the Railway Labor Act. . . .

III. The Safeguarding of Rights of Dissent.

. . . Congress incorporated safeguards in the statute to protect dissenters' interests. Congress became concerned during the hearings and debates that the union shop might be used to abridge freedom of speech and beliefs. . . . [I]t was strenuously protested that the proposal provided no protection for an employee who disagreed with union policies or leadership. It was argued, for example, that 'the right of free speech is at stake. . . . A man could feel that he was no longer able freely to express himself because he could be dismissed on account of criticism of the union. . . .' House Hearings, p. 115. . . . Objections of this kind led the rail unions to propose an addition to the proviso to §2, Eleventh to prevent loss of job for lack of union membership 'with respect to employees to whom membership was denied or terminated for any reason other than the failure of the employee to tender the periodic dues, fees, and assessments uniformly required as a condition of acquiring or retaining membership.' House Hearings, p. 247. Mr. Harrison presented this text and stated, 'It is submitted that this bill with the amendment as suggested in this statement remedies the alleged abuses of compulsory union membership as claimed by the opposing witnesses, yet makes possible the elimination of the 'free rider' and the sharing of the burden of maintenance by all of the beneficiaries of union activity.' House Hearings, p. 253. . . .

A congressional concern over possible impingements on the interests of individual dissenters from union policies is therefore discernible. It is true that opponents of the union shop urged that Congress should not allow it without explicitly regulating the amount of dues which might be exacted or prescribing the uses for which the dues might be expended. We may assume that Congress was also fully conversant with the long history of intensive involvement of the railroad unions in political activities. But it does not follow that §2, Eleventh places no restriction on the use of an employee's money, over his objection, to support political causes he opposes merely because Congress did not enact a comprehensive regulatory scheme governing expenditures. For it is abundantly clear that Congress did not completely abandon the policy of full freedom of choice embodied in the 1934 Act, but rather made inroads on it for the limited purpose of eliminating the problems created by the 'free rider.' That policy survives in §2, Eleventh in the safeguards intended to protect freedom of dissent. Congress was aware of the conflicting interests involved in the question of the union shop and sought to achieve their accommodation. . . .

We respect this congressional purpose when we construe §2, Eleventh as not vesting the unions with unlimited power to spend exacted money. We are not called upon to delineate the precise limits of that power in this case. We have before us only the question whether the power is restricted to the extent of denying the unions the rights, over the employee's objection, to use his money to support political causes which he opposes. Its use to support candidates for public office, and advance political programs, is not a use which helps defray the expenses of the negotiation or administration of collective agreements, or the expenses entailed in the adjustment of grievances and disputes. In other words, it is a use which falls clearly outside the reasons advanced by the unions and accepted by Congress why authority to make unionshop agreements was justified. On the other hand, it is equally clear that it is a use to support activities within the area of dissenters' interests which Congress enacted the proviso to protect. We give § 2, Eleventh the construction which achieves both congressional purposes when we hold, as we do, that § 2, Eleventh is to be construed to deny the unions, over an employee's objection, the power to use his exacted funds to support political causes which he opposes.

Notes

1. *Street* held that while the union shop was generally valid, unions could not, under such a clause, charge dissenters dues that would be spent for political purposes. Is this a good reading of the statutory language? The majority opinion in *Street* argues that it is at least a permissible construction, to which it resorted in order to avoid possible constitutional problems.

2. Would an interpretation permitting private-sector unions to collect union dues from dissenters to pay for political activities violate the First Amendment? An antecedent question is whether a contractual provision, agreed to by two private parties, implicates the First Amendment at all. In *Ry. Emps. Dep't v. Hanson*, 351 U.S. 225 (1956), the Supreme Court held that contracts governed by the RLA involved state action because the RLA preempts state right-to-work laws. As the Court put it, "[i]f private rights are being invaded, it is by force of an agreement made pursuant to federal law which expressly declares that state law is superseded." *Id.* at 232.

Is this holding surprising? Consider that it would not violate the First Amendment if a private employer entered into individual contracts with employees requiring, as a condition of employment, membership in a private club or other organization (some groups would raise issues under anti-discrimination laws, but not the Constitution). Indeed, no precedent holds that a private employer would violate the First Amendment by requiring, as a condition of employment, employees— through contract or otherwise—to join a political party. Some state statutes would bar this, and it would be an unconstitutional condition for most public-sector jobs. But there would be no constitutional claim in the private sector because there is no state action.

3. The majority did not actually hold that it would violate the First Amendment to permit private sector unions to spend mandatory dues on politics—rather, it construed the RLA to avoid having to answer that question. Justice Black, in a dissent omitted above, adopted the contrary interpretation, and concluded that it did violate the First Amendment:

> There can be no doubt that the federally sanctioned union-shop contract here, as it actually works, takes a part of the earnings of some men and turns it over to others, who spend a substantial part of the funds so received in efforts to thwart the political, economic and ideological hopes of those

whose money has been forced from them under authority of law. This injects federal compulsion into the political and ideological processes, a result which I have supposed everyone would agree the First Amendment was particularly intended to prevent. 367 U.S. at 789.

4. On the other hand, Justice Frankfurter, writing for himself and Justice Harlan in another dissent omitted above, while agreeing with Justice Black that the statutory language permitted union shop agreements that charged dissenters for political activities, did not agree that this violated the First Amendment. This dissent first argued that the "statutory provision cannot be meaningfully construed except against the background and presupposition of what is loosely called political activity of American trade unions in general and railroad unions in particular—activity indissolubly relating to the immediate economic and social concerns that are the raison d'etre of unions." 367 U.S. at 800. It continued:

> No one's desire or power to speak his mind is checked or curbed. The individual member may express his views in any public or private forum as freely as he could before the union collected his dues. . . . Congress has not commanded that the railroads shall employ only those workers who are members of authorized unions. Congress has only given leave to a bargaining representative, democratically elected by a majority of workers, to enter into a particular contractual provision arrived at under the give-and-take of duly safeguarded bargaining procedures. . . . When we speak of the Government "acting" in permitting the union shop, the scope and force of what Congress has done must be heeded. There is not a trace of compulsion involved. . . .
>
> In conclusion, then, we are asked by union members who oppose these expenditures to protect their right to free speech—although they are as free to speak as ever—against governmental action which has permitted a union elected by democratic process to bargain for a union shop and to expend the funds thereby collected for purposes which are controlled by internal union choice. To do so would be to mutilate a scheme designed by Congress for the purpose of equitably sharing the cost of securing the benefits of union exertions; it would greatly embarrass if not frustrate conventional labor activities which have become institutionalized through time. 367 U.S. at 806–09, 818.

5. *Street* reaffirmed that the union shop was permitted to the extent it did not require employees to support political causes they objected to. So, after *Street*, if an RLA union spent five percent of its dues money on politics and 95 percent on activities related to collective bargaining, a union security clause could only require an objecting member of the bargaining unit to pay ninety-five percent of her dues.

6. How should this rule be enforced? *Street* suggested, but did not mandate, two possible methods. First, an employee must inform union officials that he objected to his dues being spent on political causes. Then,

[o]ne remedy would be an injunction against expenditure for political causes opposed by each complaining employee of a sum, from those moneys to be spent by the union for political purposes, which is so much of the moneys exacted from him as is the proportion of the union's total expenditures made for such political activities to the union's total budget. . . . A second remedy would be restitution to each individual employee of that portion of his money which the union expended, despite his notification, for the political causes to which he had advised the union he was opposed. 376 U.S. at 774–75.

7. At this time, and for twenty-five years after *Street*, it appeared that this was an RLA rule that did not apply to the NLRA. Fourteen years after *Street*, a parallel development occurred in public-sector labor law.

D. Union Security Clauses in the Public Sector

1. *Phase 1:* Abood v. Detroit Board of Education *and the Chargeable/Non-Chargeable Distinction*

Abood v. Detroit Board of Education

Supreme Court of the United States
431 U.S. 209 (1977)

Stewart, J.

The State of Michigan has enacted legislation authorizing a system for union representation of local governmental employees. A union and a local government employer are specifically permitted to agree to an "agency shop" arrangement, whereby every employee represented by a union even though not a union member must pay to the union, as a condition of employment, a service fee equal in amount to union dues. The issue before us is whether this arrangement violates the constitutional rights of government employees who object to public-sector unions as such or to various union activities financed by the compulsory service fees. . . .

II

A

Consideration of the question whether an agency-shop provision in a collective-bargaining agreement covering governmental employees is, as such, constitutionally valid must begin with two cases in this Court that on their face go far toward resolving the issue. The cases are *Railway Employes' Dept. v. Hanson* . . . and *Machinists v. Street.* . . .

The holding in *Hanson*, as elaborated in *Street*, reflects familiar doctrines in the federal labor laws. The principle of exclusive union representation, which underlies the [NLRA] as well as the Railway Labor Act, is a central element in the congressional structuring of industrial relations. . . . The designation of a single representative avoids the confusion that would result from attempting to enforce two or more agreements specifying different terms and conditions of employment. It prevents inter-union rivalries from creating dissension within the work force and eliminating the advantages to the employee of collectivization. It also frees the employer from the possibility of facing conflicting demands from different unions, and permits the employer and a single union to reach agreements and settlements that are not subject to attack from rival labor organizations. . . .

The designation of a union as exclusive representative carries with it great responsibilities. The tasks of negotiating and administering a collective-bargaining agreement and representing the interests of employees in settling disputes and processing grievances are continuing and difficult ones. They often entail expenditure of much time and money. . . . The services of lawyers, expert negotiators, economists, and a research staff, as well as general administrative personnel, may be required. Moreover, in carrying out these duties, the union is obliged "fairly and equitably to represent all employees . . . , union and nonunion," within the relevant unit. . . . A union-shop arrangement has been thought to distribute fairly the cost of these activities among those who benefit, and it counteracts the incentive that employees might otherwise have to become "free riders" to refuse to contribute to the union while obtaining benefits of union representation that necessarily accrue to all employees. . . .

To compel employees financially to support their collective-bargaining representative has an impact upon their First Amendment interests. An employee may very well have ideological objections to a wide variety of activities undertaken by the union in its role as exclusive representative. His moral or religious views about the desirability of abortion may not square with the union's policy in negotiating a medical benefits plan. One individual might disagree with a union policy of negotiating limits on the right to strike, believing that to be the road to serfdom for the working class, while another might have economic or political objections to unionism itself. An employee might object to the union's wage policy because it violates guidelines designed to limit inflation, or might object to the union's seeking a clause in the collective-bargaining agreement proscribing racial discrimination. The examples could be multiplied. To be required to help finance the union as a collective-bargaining agent might well be thought, therefore, to interfere in some way with an employee's freedom to associate for the advancement of ideas, or to refrain from doing so, as he sees fit. But the judgment clearly made in *Hanson* and *Street* is that such interference as exists is constitutionally justified by the legislative assessment of the important contribution of the union shop to the system of labor relations established by Congress. . . .

B

. . . Michigan has chosen to establish for local government units a regulatory scheme which, although not identical in every respect to the NLRA or the Railway Labor Act is broadly modeled after federal law. . . .

The governmental interests advanced by the agency-shop provision in the Michigan statute are much the same as those promoted by similar provisions in federal labor law. The confusion and conflict that could arise if rival teachers' unions, holding quite different views as to the proper class hours, class sizes, holidays, tenure provisions, and grievance procedures, each sought to obtain the employer's agreement, are no different in kind from the evils that the exclusivity rule in the Railway Labor Act was designed to avoid. . . . The desirability of labor peace is no less important in the public sector, nor is the risk of "free riders" any smaller.

Our province is not to judge the wisdom of Michigan's decision to authorize the agency shop in public employment. Rather, it is to adjudicate the constitutionality of that decision. The same important government interests recognized in the *Hanson* and *Street* cases presumptively support the impingement upon associational freedom created by the agency shop here at issue. Thus, insofar as the service charge is used to finance expenditures by the Union for the purposes of collective bargaining, contract administration, and grievance adjustment, those two decisions of this Court appear to require validation of the agency-shop agreement before us.

While recognizing the apparent precedential weight of the *Hanson* and *Street* cases, the appellants advance two reasons why those decisions should not control decision of the present case. First, the appellants note that it is government employment that is involved here, thus directly implicating constitutional guarantees, in contrast to the private employment that was the subject of the Hanson and Street decisions. Second, the appellants say that in the public sector collective bargaining itself is inherently "political," and that to require them to give financial support to it is to require the "ideological conformity" that the Court expressly found absent in the *Hanson* case. . . . We find neither argument persuasive.

Because it is employment by the State that is here involved, the appellants suggest that this case is governed by a long line of decisions holding that public employment cannot be conditioned upon the surrender of First Amendment rights. But, while the actions of public employers surely constitute "state action," the union shop, as authorized by the Railway Labor Act, also was found to result from governmental action in *Hanson*. The plaintiffs' claims in *Hanson* failed, not because there was no governmental action, but because there was no First Amendment violation. The appellants' reliance on the "unconstitutional conditions" doctrine is therefore misplaced.

The appellants' second argument is that in any event collective bargaining in the public sector is inherently "political" and thus requires a different result under the First and Fourteenth Amendments. This contention rests upon the important and often-noted differences in the nature of collective bargaining in the public and private sectors. . . .

The government officials making decisions as the public "employer" are less likely to act as a cohesive unit than are managers in private industry, in part because different levels of public authority department managers, budgetary officials, and legislative bodies are involved, and in part because each official may respond to a distinctive political constituency. And the ease of negotiating a final agreement with the union may be severely limited by statutory restrictions, by the need for the approval of a higher executive authority or a legislative body, or by the commitment of budgetary decisions of critical importance to others.

Finally, decisionmaking by a public employer is above all a political process. The officials who represent the public employer are ultimately responsible to the electorate, which for this purpose can be viewed as comprising three overlapping classes of voters taxpayers, users of particular government services, and government employees.

The only remaining constitutional inquiry evoked by the appellants' argument, therefore, is whether a public employee has a weightier First Amendment interest than a private employee in not being compelled to contribute to the costs of exclusive union representation. We think he does not.

Public employees are not basically different from private employees; on the whole, they have the same sort of skills, the same needs, and seek the same advantages. "The uniqueness of public employment is not in the employees nor in the work performed; the uniqueness is in the special character of the employer." Summers, *Public Sector Bargaining: Problems of Governmental Decisionmaking*, 44 U. Cin. L. Rev. 669, 670 (1975). . . . The very real differences between exclusive-agent collective bargaining in the public and private sectors are not such as to work any greater infringement upon the First Amendment interests of public employees. A public employee who believes that a union representing him is urging a course that is unwise as a matter of public policy is not barred from expressing his viewpoint. Besides voting in accordance with his convictions, every public employee is largely free to express his views, in public or private orally or in writing.

The differences between public- and private-sector collective bargaining simply do not translate into differences in First Amendment rights. . . . We conclude that the Michigan Court of Appeals was correct in viewing this Court's decisions in *Hanson* and *Street* as controlling in the present case insofar as the service charges are applied to collective-bargaining, contract administration, and grievance-adjustment purposes.

C

Because the Michigan Court of Appeals ruled that state law "sanctions the use of nonunion members' fees for purposes other than collective bargaining" . . . and because the complaints allege that such expenditures were made, this case presents constitutional issues not decided in *Hanson* or *Street*. . . .

Our decisions establish with unmistakable clarity that the freedom of an individual to associate for the purpose of advancing beliefs and ideas is protected by the First and Fourteenth Amendments. . . . The appellants argue that they . . . have been prohibited, not from actively associating, but rather from refusing to associate. They specifically argue that they may constitutionally prevent the Union's spending a part of their required service fees to contribute to political candidates and to express political views unrelated to its duties as exclusive bargaining representative. We have concluded that this argument is a meritorious one.

One of the principles underlying the Court's decision in *Buckley v. Valeo*, 424 U.S. 1, was that contributing to an organization for the purpose of spreading a political message is protected by the First Amendment. . . . [T]he Court reasoned that limitations upon the freedom to contribute "implicate fundamental First Amendment interests". . . .

The fact that the appellants are compelled to make, rather than prohibited from making, contributions for political purposes works no less an infringement of their constitutional rights. For at the heart of the First Amendment is the notion that an individual should be free to believe as he will, and that in a free society one's beliefs should be shaped by his mind and his conscience rather than coerced by the State. . . . "If there is any fixed star in our constitutional constellation, it is that no official, high or petty, can prescribe what shall be orthodox in politics, nationalism, religion, or other matters of opinion or force citizens to confess by word or act their faith therein." *West Virginia Bd. of Ed. v. Barnette*, 319 U.S. 624. . . .

We do not hold that a union cannot constitutionally spend funds for the expression of political views, on behalf of political candidates, or toward the advancement of other ideological causes not germane to its duties as collective-bargaining representative. Rather, the Constitution requires only that such expenditures be financed from charges, dues, or assessments paid by employees who do not object to advancing those ideas and who are not coerced into doing so against their will by the threat of loss of governmental employment.

Notes

1. *Abood* asserts that *Street* found state action sufficient to trigger constitutional concerns about union security agreements in private employment governed by the RLA similar to those in public employment. Is that a correct reading of *Street*?

2. As to what expenses objectors could not lawfully be charged, *Street* focused on political activities; *Abood* used the phrase "ideological expenditures of any sort that are unrelated to collective bargaining." The court would later use the broader term "expenses unrelated to collective bargaining." *See* subsection F-1, *infra*. Consider, as you go through those materials, how that evolution occurred.

3. *Abood* refers to *Madison Sch. Dist. v. Wisconsin Empl't Rel. Comm'n*, 429 U.S. 167 (1976). That case concerned a limit on the exclusive representation principle in the public sector. In *Madison Sch. Dist.*, the state labor board held that a school board committed a ULP by allowing a teacher, who was a member of a union bargaining unit but not designated by the union as a spokesperson, to speak to the school board at a public hearing about a union contract proposal in ongoing negotiations. Perhaps ironically, the proposal was for an agency fee clause. The Supreme Court ultimately held that the First Amendment protected this speech, and thus a state statute could not make such speech the basis for a ULP. This rule is limited to the public sector; can you see why?

4. After *Abood*, there seemed to be similar rules under the RLA and for the public sector, even though the source of the rules was different (a reading of the statutory text of the RLA in *Street*, the First Amendment in *Abood*). But such rules were not yet applied to the NLRA.

2. Phase 2: The Court's Retreat from Abood

Beginning in 2007, several Supreme Court Justices began signaling that they viewed *Abood* as insufficiently protective of objecting workers' interests. These signals first came in cases about what procedures were required or permitted to enforce *Abood*'s chargeable/non-chargeable distinction. First, in *Davenport v. Wash. Educ. Ass'n*, Justice Scalia wrote that "it is undeniably unusual for a government agency to give a private entity the power, in essence, to tax government employees." 551 U.S. 177, 184 (2007) (holding state could require public-sector labor unions to obtain affirmative consent before spending represented nonmembers' fees for election-related purposes).

Next, in ***Knox v. Serv. Emps. Int'l Union, Local 1000***, 567 U.S. 298, 311 (2012), Justice Alito wrote that the *Abood* rule was "something of an anomaly." *Knox* was another case about procedures to protect union objectors. Specifically, the Court held that unions could not require agency-fee payers to "opt out" of the non-chargeable portion of a mid-year dues assessment; instead, the union had to obtain affirmative consent from non-member represented workers before charging them for any portion of the assessment. (*Knox* did not apply to regular dues assessments—only mid-year increases.) This holding was remarkable less for its substance—mid-year dues increases are relatively rare—than because it went beyond the relief requested by the plaintiff-objectors. They had asked the Court to hold only that the union was required to send them notice of the assessment and then give them an opportunity to opt out; the opt-in requirement was the Court's own innovation, arrived at without benefit of briefing.

Two years later, the Court decided ***Harris v. Quinn***, 573 U.S. 616 (2014). Unlike *Davenport* and *Knox*, *Harris* involved the constitutionality of agency fees, rather than procedures that accompany their collection. *Harris* involved a special set of quasi-public-sector employees: home health aides (also called "personal assistants"), whom Illinois law deemed state employees for the sole purpose of collective bargaining. The Court's decision turned on the particular facts regarding their employment—specifically, that the personal assistants were jointly employed by the state and individual private clients. Thus, while the *Harris* Court harshly criticized *Abood*, it did not overrule it.

Harris arose from an Illinois statutory scheme that created a collective bargaining mechanism for home health aides who worked for individual clients, but who were paid by the state. The aides could elect a union that would represent them in bargaining with the state over only those terms and conditions of employment that the state set, but this mechanism would not affect the relationship between aides and the individual customers who hired them and directed their day-to-day tasks.

A group of aides elected the SEIU to represent them in bargaining with Illinois, and the resulting CBA contained an agency fee clause.

The plaintiffs in *Harris* argued that the requirement that they pay fair share fees violated their First Amendment rights. In a 5–4 decision, the Supreme Court agreed. Justice Alito, writing for the majority, also questioned *Abood*'s continuing viability on several grounds.

The majority began by hinting that it was not satisfied with the First Amendment analysis of private-sector agency fee cases. This portion of the decision is similar to the Court's analysis in *Janus*, which is excerpted below. In the end, however, the *Harris* majority chose to distinguish *Abood* rather than overturn it. *Abood* did not cover the employees here, the majority reasoned, because they were not "full-fledged public employees"; rather, they were "partial-public employees," because private customers primarily controlled their work. Further, these "employees" did not enjoy most of the rights other state employees had. Notably, the scope of bargaining for these employees was extremely narrow, and thus the state's interest in collective bargaining (that is balanced against the First Amendment rights of employees) was atypically weak. "*Abood*'s rationale, whatever its strengths and weaknesses, is based on the assumption that the union possesses the full scope of powers and duties generally available under American labor law."

In 2015, the Supreme Court agreed to re-consider *Abood* in *Friedrichs v. California Teachers' Ass'n*, 136 S. Ct. 1083 (2016). After oral argument, commentators widely predicted that the Court would vote to overturn *Abood*. However, after Justice Scalia died, the Court announced that was equally divided in *Friedrichs*, meaning that the lower court decision (which applied *Abood*) was affirmed.

In 2017, Justice Neil Gorsuch was confirmed to the Supreme Court. A few months later, the Supreme Court granted cert. in another case challenging *Abood*.

Janus v. AFSCME, Council 31
Supreme Court of the United States
138 S. Ct. 2448 (2018)

Alito, J.

Under Illinois law, public employees are forced to subsidize a union, even if they choose not to join and strongly object to the positions the union takes in collective bargaining and related activities. We conclude that this arrangement violates the free speech rights of nonmembers by compelling them to subsidize private speech on matters of substantial public concern.

We upheld a similar law in *Abood v. Detroit Bd. of Ed.*, and we recognize the importance of following precedent unless there are strong reasons for not doing so. But there are very strong reasons in this case. Fundamental free speech rights are at stake. *Abood* was poorly reasoned. It has led to practical problems and abuse. It is inconsistent with other First Amendment cases and has been undermined by more recent decisions. Developments since *Abood* was handed down have shed new light on the issue of agency fees, and no reliance interests on the part of public-sector unions are sufficient to justify the perpetuation of the free speech violations that *Abood* has countenanced for the past 41 years. *Abood* is therefore overruled.

I

A

Under the Illinois Public Labor Relations Act (IPLRA), employees of the State and its political subdivisions are permitted to unionize [by electing an exclusive representative].

Once a union is [elected, it is authorized to bargain over issues] such as merit pay, the size of the work force, layoffs, privatization, promotion methods, and non-discrimination policies. . . . Protection of the employees' interests is placed in the hands of the union, and therefore the union is required by law to provide fair representation for all employees in the unit, members and nonmembers alike.

Employees who decline to join the union are not assessed full union dues but must instead pay what is generally called an "agency fee," which amounts to a percentage of the union dues. Under *Abood*, nonmembers may be charged for the portion of union dues attributable to activities that are "germane to [the union's] duties as collective-bargaining representative," but nonmembers may not be required to fund the union's political and ideological projects. In labor-law parlance, the outlays in the first category are known as "chargeable" expenditures, while those in the latter are labeled "nonchargeable."

The IPLRA provides that an agency fee may compensate a union for the costs incurred in "the collective bargaining process, contract administration[,] and pursuing matters affecting wages, hours[,] and conditions of employment." Excluded from the agency-fee calculation are union expenditures "related to the election or support of any candidate for political office."

Applying this standard, a union categorizes its expenditures as chargeable or nonchargeable and thus determines a nonmember's "proportionate share"; this determination is then audited; the amount of the "proportionate share" is certified to the employer; and the employer automatically deducts that amount from the nonmembers' wages.

After the amount of the agency fee is fixed each year, the union must send nonmembers what is known as a *Hudson* notice. This notice is supposed to provide nonmembers with "an adequate explanation of the basis for the [agency] fee." If nonmembers "suspect that a union has improperly put certain expenses in the [chargeable] category," they may challenge that determination.

As illustrated by the record in this case, unions charge nonmembers, not just for the cost of collective bargaining *per se,* but also for many other supposedly connected activities. Here, the nonmembers were told that they had to pay for "[l]obbying," "[s]ocial and recreational activities," "advertising," "[m]ember-ship meetings and conventions," and "litigation," as well as other unspecified "[s]ervices" that "may ultimately inure to the benefit of the members of the local bargaining unit." The total chargeable amount for nonmembers was 78.06% of full union dues.

B

Petitioner Mark Janus is employed by the Illinois Department of Healthcare and Family Services as a child support specialist. The employees in his unit are among the 35,000 public employees in Illinois who are represented by respondent American Federation of State, County, and Municipal Employees, Council 31 (Union). Janus refused to join the Union because he opposes "many of the public policy positions that [it] advocates," including the positions it takes in collective bargaining. Janus believes that the Union's "behavior in bargaining does not appreciate the current fiscal crises in Illinois and does not reflect his best interests or the interests of Illinois citizens." Therefore, if he had the choice, he "would not pay any fees or other-wise subsidize [the Union]." *Ibid.* Under his unit's collective-bargaining agreement, however, he was required to pay an agency fee of $44.58 per month—which would amount to about $535 per year.

III

In *Abood,* the Court upheld the constitutionality of an agency-shop arrangement like the one now before us, but in more recent cases we have recognized that this holding is "something of an anomaly," and that *Abood*'s "analysis is questionable on several grounds[.]"

We first consider whether *Abood*'s holding is consistent with standard First Amendment principles.

A

The First Amendment, made applicable to the States by the Fourteenth Amend-ment, forbids abridgment of the freedom of speech. We have held time and again that freedom of speech "includes both the right to speak freely and the right to refrain from speaking at all." The right to eschew association for expressive pur-poses is likewise protected.

When speech is compelled, however, additional damage is done. In that situa-tion, individuals are coerced into betraying their convictions.

Compelling a person to *subsidize* the speech of other private speakers raises similar First Amendment concerns. We have therefore recognized that a "'signifi-cant impingement on First Amendment rights'" occurs when public employees are required to provide financial support for a union that "takes many positions during collective bargaining that have powerful political and civic consequences." *Knox* (quoting *Ellis v. Railway Clerks*, 466 U.S. 435 (1984)).

[P]etitioner in the present case contends that the Illinois law at issue should be subjected to "strict scrutiny." [W]e again find it unnecessary to decide the issue of strict scrutiny because the Illinois scheme cannot survive under even the more permissive ["exacting scrutiny"] standard applied in *Knox* and *Harris*.

B

In *Abood*, the main defense of the agency-fee arrangement was that it served the State's interest in "labor peace[.]" By "labor peace," the *Abood* Court meant avoidance of the conflict and disruption that it envisioned would occur if the employees in a unit were represented by more than one union.

We assume that "labor peace," in this sense of the term, is a compelling state interest, but *Abood* cited no evidence that the pandemonium it imagined would result if agency fees were not allowed, and it is now clear that *Abood*'s fears were unfounded.

The federal employment experience is illustrative. Under federal law, a union chosen by majority vote is designated as the exclusive representative of all the employees, but federal law does not permit agency fees. Nevertheless, nearly a million federal employees—about 27% of the federal work force—are union members. The situation in the Postal Service is similar. Although permitted to choose an exclusive representative, Postal Service employees are not required to pay an agency fee, and about 400,000 are union members. Likewise, millions of public employees in the 28 States that have laws generally prohibiting agency fees are represented by unions that serve as the exclusive representatives of all the employees. Whatever may have been the case 41 years ago when *Abood* was handed down, it is now undeniable that "labor peace" can readily be achieved "through means significantly less restrictive of associational freedoms" than the assessment of agency fees.

C

In addition to the promotion of "labor peace," *Abood* cited "the risk of 'free riders'" as justification for agency fees.

Petitioner strenuously objects to this free-rider label. He argues that he is not a free rider on a bus headed for a destination that he wishes to reach but is more like a person shanghaied for an unwanted voyage.

Whichever description fits the majority of public employees who would not subsidize a union if given the option, avoiding free riders is not a compelling interest. As we have noted, "free-rider arguments . . . are generally insufficient to overcome First Amendment objections."

Suppose that a particular group lobbies or speaks out on behalf of what it thinks are the needs of senior citizens or veterans or physicians, to take just a few examples. Could the government require that all seniors, veterans, or doctors pay for that service even if they object? It has never been thought that this is permissible.

Those supporting agency fees contend that the situation here is different because unions are statutorily required to "represen[t] the interests of all public employees in the unit," whether or not they are union members. Why might this matter?

We can think of two possible arguments. It might be argued that a State has a compelling interest in requiring the payment of agency fees because (1) unions would otherwise be unwilling to represent nonmembers or (2) it would be fundamentally unfair to require unions to provide fair representation for nonmembers if nonmembers were not required to pay. Neither of these arguments is sound.

First, it is simply not true that unions will refuse to serve as the exclusive representative of all employees in the unit if they are not given agency fees. As noted, unions represent millions of public employees in jurisdictions that do not permit agency fees. No union is ever compelled to seek that designation. On the contrary, designation as exclusive representative is avidly sought. Why is this so?

Even without agency fees, designation as the exclusive representative confers many benefits. As noted, that status gives the union a privileged place in negotiations over wages, benefits, and working conditions. Not only is the union given the exclusive right to speak for all the employees in collective bargaining, but the employer is required by state law to listen to and to bargain in good faith with only that union.

In addition, a union designated as exclusive representative is often granted special privileges, such as obtaining information about employees, and having dues and fees deducted directly from employee wages.

These benefits greatly outweigh any extra burden imposed by the duty of providing fair representation for nonmembers.

What does this mean when it comes to the negotiation of a contract? The union may not negotiate a collective-bargaining agreement that discriminates against nonmembers, but the union's bargaining latitude would be little different if state law simply prohibited public employers from entering into agreements that discriminate in that way. And for that matter, it is questionable whether the Constitution would permit a public-sector employer to adopt a collective-bargaining agreement that discriminates against nonmembers. To the extent that an employer would be barred from acceding to a discriminatory agreement anyway, the union's duty not to ask for one is superfluous.

What about the representation of nonmembers in grievance proceedings? Unions do not undertake this activity solely for the benefit of nonmembers — which is why Illinois law gives a public-sector union the right to send a representative to such proceedings even if the employee declines union representation. Representation of nonmembers furthers the union's interest in keeping control of the administration of the collective-bargaining agreement, since the resolution of one employee's grievance can affect others. And when a union controls the grievance process, it may, as a practical matter, effectively subordinate "the interests of [an] individual employee . . . to the collective interests of all employees in the bargaining unit."

In any event, whatever unwanted burden is imposed by the representation of nonmembers in disciplinary matters can be eliminated "through means significantly less restrictive of associational freedoms" than the imposition of agency fees. Individual nonmembers could be required to pay for that service or could be denied union representation altogether. Thus, agency fees cannot be sustained on the ground that unions would otherwise be unwilling to represent nonmembers.

IV

Implicitly acknowledging the weakness of *Abood*'s own reasoning, proponents of agency fees have come forward with alternative justifications for the decision, and we now address these arguments.

A

The most surprising of these new arguments is the Union respondent's originalist defense of *Abood*. According to this argument, *Abood* was correctly decided because the First Amendment was not originally understood to provide *any* protection for the free speech rights of public employees.

As an initial matter, we doubt that the Union—or its members—actually want us to hold that public employees have "*no* [free speech] rights."

Nor, in any event, does the First Amendment's original meaning support the Union's claim. The Union offers no persuasive founding-era evidence that public employees were understood to lack free speech protections. While it observes that restrictions on federal employees' activities have existed since the First Congress, most of its historical examples involved limitations on public officials' outside business dealings, not on their speech.

B

The principal defense of *Abood* advanced by respondents and the dissent is based on our decision in *Pickering* [*v. Bd. Of Educ.*, 391 U.S. 563 (1968)], which held that a school district violated the First Amendment by firing a teacher for writing a letter critical of the school administration. Under *Pickering* and later cases in the same line, employee speech is largely unprotected if it is part of what the employee is paid to do, see *Garcetti v. Ceballos*, [547 U.S. 410 (2006),] or if it involved a matter of only private concern, see *Connick* [*v. Myers*, 461 U.S. 138 (1983)]. On the other hand, when a public employee speaks as a citizen on a matter of public concern, the employee's speech is protected unless "'the interest of the state, as an employer, in promoting the efficiency of the public services it performs through its employees' outweighs 'the interests of the [employee], as a citizen, in commenting upon matters of public concern.'"

1

As we pointed out in *Harris*, *Abood* was not based on *Pickering*.

2

First, the *Pickering* framework was developed for use in a very different context—in cases that involve "one employee's speech and its impact on that employee's public responsibilities." This case, by contrast, involves a blanket requirement that all employees subsidize speech with which they may not agree. While we have sometimes looked to *Pickering* in considering general rules that affect broad categories of employees, we have acknowledged that the standard *Pickering* analysis requires modification in that situation. A speech-restrictive law with "widespread impact," we have said, "gives rise to far more serious concerns than could any single supervisory decision."

The core collective-bargaining issue of wages and benefits illustrates this point. Suppose that a single employee complains that he or she should have received a 5% raise. This individual complaint would likely constitute a matter of only private concern and would therefore be unprotected under *Pickering*. But a public-sector union's demand for a 5% raise for the many thousands of employees it represents would be another matter entirely. Granting such a raise could have a serious impact on the budget of the government unit in question, and by the same token, denying a raise might have a significant effect on the performance of government services. When a large number of employees speak through their union, the category of speech that is of public concern is greatly enlarged, and the category of speech that is of only private concern is substantially shrunk.

Second, the *Pickering* framework fits much less well where the government compels speech or speech subsidies in support of third parties. *Pickering* is based on the insight that the speech of a public-sector employee may interfere with the effective operation of a government office. When a public employer does not simply restrict potentially disruptive speech but commands that its employees mouth a message on its own behalf, the calculus is very different.

Third, although both *Pickering* and *Abood* divided speech into two categories, the cases' categorization schemes do not line up. Superimposing the *Pickering* scheme on *Abood* would significantly change the *Abood* regime.

V

Even if we were to apply some form of *Pickering,* Illinois' agency-fee arrangement would not survive.

A

Respondents begin by suggesting that union speech in collective-bargaining and grievance proceedings should be treated like the employee speech in *Garcetti, i.e.,* as speech "pursuant to [an employee's] official duties[.]"

This argument distorts collective bargaining and grievance adjustment beyond recognition. When an employee engages in speech that is part of the employee's job duties, the employee's words are really the words of the employer. The employee is effectively the employer's spokesperson. But when a union negotiates with the employer or represents employees in disciplinary proceedings, the union speaks for the *employees,* not the employer. Otherwise, the employer would be negotiating with itself and disputing its own actions. That is not what anybody understands to be happening.

B

Since the union speech paid for by agency fees is not controlled by *Garcetti*, we move on to the next step of the *Pickering* framework and ask whether the speech is on a matter of public or only private concern.

Illinois, like some other States and a number of counties and cities around the country, suffers from severe budget problems.

In addition to affecting how public money is spent, union speech in collective bargaining addresses many other important matters. As the examples offered by respondents' own *amici* show, unions express views on a wide range of subjects — education, child welfare, healthcare, and minority rights, to name a few.

Unions can also speak out in collective bargaining on controversial subjects such as climate change, the Confederacy, sexual orientation and gender identity, evolution, and minority religions. These are sensitive political topics, and they are undoubtedly matters of profound "'value and concern to the public.'"

Even union speech in the handling of grievances may be of substantial public importance and may be directed at the "public square." For instance, the Union respondent in this case recently filed a grievance seeking to compel Illinois to appropriate $75 million to fund a 2% wage increase. In short, the union speech at issue in this case is overwhelmingly of substantial public concern.

C

The only remaining question under *Pickering* is whether the State's proffered interests justify the heavy burden that agency fees inflict on nonmembers' First Amendment interests. We have already addressed the state interests asserted in *Abood* — promoting "labor peace" and avoiding free riders, and we will not repeat that analysis.

In *Harris* and this case, defenders of *Abood* have asserted a different state interest — in the words of the *Harris* dissent, the State's "interest in bargaining with an adequately funded exclusive bargaining agent." This was not "the interest *Abood* recognized and protected," and, in any event, it is insufficient.

VI

For the reasons given above, we conclude that public-sector agency-shop arrangements violate the First Amendment, and *Abood* erred in concluding otherwise. There remains the question whether *stare decisis* nonetheless counsels against overruling *Abood*. It does not.

"*Stare decisis* is the preferred course because it promotes the evenhanded, predictable, and consistent development of legal principles, fosters reliance on judicial decisions, and contributes to the actual and perceived integrity of the judicial process." We will not overturn a past decision unless there are strong grounds for doing so.

The doctrine "is at its weakest when we interpret the Constitution because our interpretation can be altered only by constitutional amendment or by overruling our prior decisions." And *stare decisis* applies with perhaps least force of all to decisions that wrongly denied First Amendment rights: "This Court has not hesitated to overrule decisions offensive to the First Amendment (a fixed star in our constitutional constellation, if there is one)."

Our cases identify factors that should be taken into account in deciding whether to overrule a past decision. Five of these are most important here: the quality of *Abood*'s reasoning, the workability of the rule it established, its consistency with other related decisions, developments since the decision was handed down, and reliance on the decision. After analyzing these factors, we conclude that *stare decisis* does not require us to retain *Abood*.

A

An important factor in determining whether a precedent should be overruled is the quality of its reasoning.

Abood went wrong at the start when it concluded that two prior decisions, *Railway Employes v. Hanson,* and *Machinists v. Street*, "appear[ed] to require validation of the agency-shop agreement before [the Court]." Properly understood, those decisions did no such thing. Both cases involved Congress's "*bare authorization*" of *private-sector* union shops under the Railway Labor Act. *Abood* failed to appreciate that a very different First Amendment question arises when a State *requires* its employees to pay agency fees.

B

Another relevant consideration in the *stare decisis* calculus is the workability of the precedent in question, and that factor also weighs against *Abood*.

1

Abood's line between chargeable and nonchargeable union expenditures has proved to be impossible to draw with precision. We tried to give the line some definition in *Lehnert* [*v. Ferris Faculty Ass'n,* 500 U.S. 507 (1991)]. There, a majority of the Court adopted a three-part test requiring that chargeable expenses (1) be "'germane'" to collective bargaining, (2) be "justified" by the government's labor-peace and free-rider interests, and (3) not add "significantly" to the burden on free speech, but the Court splintered over the application of this test.

2

Objecting employees also face a daunting and expensive task if they wish to challenge union chargeability determinations. While *Hudson* requires a union to provide nonmembers with "sufficient information to gauge the propriety of the union's fee," [*Teachers v. Hudson,* 475 U.S. 292 (1986)], the *Hudson* notice in the present case and in others that have come before us do not begin to permit a nonmember to make such a determination.

In this case, the notice lists categories of expenses and sets out the amount in each category that is said to be attributable to chargeable and nonchargeable expenses. Here are some examples regarding the Union respondent's expenditures:

Category	Total Expense	Chargeable Expense
Salary and Benefits	$14,718,708	$11,803,230
Office Printing, Supplies, and Advertising	$148,272	$127,959
Postage and Freight	$373,509	$268,107
Telephone	$214,820	$192,721
Convention Expense	$268,855	$268,855

How could any nonmember determine whether these numbers are even close to the mark without launching a legal challenge and retaining the services of attorneys and accountants? Indeed, even with such services, it would be a laborious and difficult task to check these figures.

The Union respondent argues that challenging its chargeability determinations is not burdensome because the Union pays for the costs of arbitration, but objectors must still pay for the attorneys and experts needed to mount a serious challenge.

C

Developments since *Abood*, both factual and legal, have also "eroded" the decision's "underpinnings" and left it an outlier among our First Amendment cases.

D

In some cases, reliance provides a strong reason for adhering to established law, and this is the factor that is stressed most strongly by respondents, their *amici*, and the dissent. They contend that collective-bargaining agreements now in effect were negotiated with agency fees in mind and that unions may have given up other benefits in exchange for provisions granting them such fees.

[I]t would be unconscionable to permit free speech rights to be abridged in perpetuity in order to preserve contract provisions that will expire on their own in a few years' time.

This is especially so because public-sector unions have been on notice for years regarding this Court's misgivings about *Abood*. In *Knox*, decided in 2012, we described *Abood* as a First Amendment "anomaly." Two years later in *Harris*, we were asked to overrule *Abood*, and while we found it unnecessary to take that step, we cataloged *Abood*'s many weaknesses. In 2015, we granted a petition for certiorari asking us to review a decision that sustained an agency-fee arrangement under *Abood*. *Friedrichs v. California Teachers Assn.*, 136 S. Ct. 1083 (2016). After exhaustive briefing and argument on the question whether *Abood* should be overruled, we affirmed the decision below by an equally divided vote. During this period of time, any public-sector union seeking an agency-fee provision in a collective-bargaining agreement must have understood that the constitutionality of such a provision was uncertain

VII

For these reasons, States and public-sector unions may no longer extract agency fees from nonconsenting employees. Under Illinois law, if a public-sector collective-bargaining agreement includes an agency-fee provision and the union certifies to the employer the amount of the fee, that amount is automatically deducted from the nonmember's wages. No form of employee consent is required.

This procedure violates the First Amendment and cannot continue. Neither an agency fee nor any other payment to the union may be deducted from a nonmember's wages, nor may any other attempt be made to collect such a payment, unless the employee affirmatively consents to pay. By agreeing to pay, nonmembers are waiving their First Amendment rights, and such a waiver cannot be presumed. Unless employees clearly and affirmatively consent before any money is taken from them, this standard cannot be met.

. . . .

Abood was wrongly decided and is now overruled. . . .

JUSTICE SOTOMAYOR, dissenting.

I join Justice Kagan's dissent in full. Although I joined the majority in *Sorrell v. IMS Health Inc.*, 564 U. S. 552 (2011), I disagree with the way that this Court has since interpreted and applied that opinion. Having seen the troubling development in First Amendment jurisprudence over the years, both in this Court and in lower courts, I agree fully with Justice Kagan that *Sorrell*—in the way it has been read by this Court—has allowed courts to "wiel[d] the First Amendment in . . . an aggressive way" just as the majority does today.

JUSTICE KAGAN, with whom JUSTICES GINSBURG, BREYER, and SOTOMAYOR join, dissenting.

For over 40 years, *Abood v. Detroit Bd. of Ed.*, struck a stable balance between public employees' First Amendment rights and government entities' interests in running their workforces as they thought proper. Under that decision, a government entity could require public employees to pay a fair share of the cost that a union incurs when negotiating on their behalf over terms of employment. But no part of that fair-share payment could go to any of the union's political or ideological activities.

That holding fit comfortably with this Court's general framework for evaluating claims that a condition of public employment violates the First Amendment. The Court's decisions have long made plain that government entities have substantial latitude to regulate their employees' speech—especially about terms of employment—in the interest of operating their workplaces effectively. *Abood* allowed governments to do just that. While protecting public employees' expression about non-workplace matters, the decision enabled a government to advance important managerial interests—by ensuring the presence of an exclusive employee representative to bargain with. Far from an "anomaly," the *Abood* regime was a paradigmatic example of how the government can regulate speech in its capacity as an employer.

Not any longer. Today, the Court succeeds in its 6–year campaign to reverse *Abood*. Its decision will have large-scale consequences. Public employee unions will lose a secure source of financial support. State and local governments that thought fair-share provisions furthered their interests will need to find new ways of managing their workforces. Across the country, the relationships of public employees and employers will alter in both predictable and wholly unexpected ways.

Rarely if ever has the Court overruled a decision — let alone one of this import — with so little regard for the usual principles of *stare decisis*. There are no special justifications for reversing *Abood*. It has proved workable. No recent developments have eroded its underpinnings. And it is deeply entrenched, in both the law and the real world. More than 20 States have statutory schemes built on the decision. Those laws underpin thousands of ongoing contracts involving millions of employees. Reliance interests do not come any stronger than those surrounding *Abood*. And likewise, judicial disruption does not get any greater than what the Court does today. I respectfully dissent.

II

Unlike the majority, I see nothing "questionable" about *Abood*'s analysis. The decision's account of why some government entities have a strong interest in agency fees (now often called fair-share fees) is fundamentally sound. And the balance *Abood* struck between public employers' interests and public employees' expression is right at home in First Amendment doctrine.

A

Abood's reasoning about governmental interests has three connected parts. First, exclusive representation arrangements benefit some government entities because they can facilitate stable labor relations. Second, the government may be unable to avail itself of those benefits unless the single union has a secure source of funding. The various tasks involved in representing employees cost money; if the union doesn't have enough, it can't be an effective employee representative and bargaining partner. And third, agency fees are often needed to ensure such stable funding. That is because without those fees, employees have every incentive to free ride on the union dues paid by others.

[B]asic economic theory shows why a government would think that agency fees are necessary for exclusive representation to work. What ties the two together, as *Abood* recognized, is the likelihood of free-riding when fees are absent. Remember that once a union achieves exclusive-representation status, the law compels it to fairly represent all workers in the bargaining unit, whether or not they join or contribute to the union. Because of that legal duty, the union cannot give special advantages to its own members. And that in turn creates a collective action problem of nightmarish proportions. Everyone — not just those who oppose the union, but also those who back it — has an economic incentive to withhold dues; only altruism or loyalty — as *against* financial self-interest — can explain why an employee would pay the union for its services. And so emerged *Abood*'s rule allowing fair-share agreements: That rule ensured that a union would receive sufficient funds, despite its legally imposed disability, to effectively carry out its duties as exclusive representative of the government's employees.

The majority's fallback argument purports to respond to the distinctive position of unions, but still misses *Abood*'s economic insight. [T]he majority again fails to reckon with how economically rational actors behave — in public as well as private workplaces. Without a fair-share agreement, the class of union non-members spirals upward. Employees (including those who love the union) realize that they can get the same benefits even if they let their memberships expire. And as more and more stop paying dues, those left must take up the financial slack (and anyway, begin to feel like suckers) — so they too quit the union.[1] And when the vicious cycle finally ends, chances are that the union will lack the resources to effectively perform the responsibilities of an exclusive representative — or, in the worst case, to perform them at all. The result is to frustrate the interests of every government entity that thinks a strong exclusive-representation scheme will promote stable labor relations.

B

1

In many cases over many decades, this Court has addressed how the First Amendment applies when the government, acting not as sovereign but as employer, limits its workers' speech. Those decisions have granted substantial latitude to the government, in recognition of its significant interests in managing its workforce so as to best serve the public. *Abood* fit neatly with that caselaw, in both reasoning and result. Indeed, its reversal today creates a significant anomaly — an exception, applying to union fees alone, from the usual rules governing public employees' speech.

"Time and again our cases have recognized that the Government has a much freer hand" in dealing with its employees than with "citizens at large."

In striking the proper balance between employee speech rights and managerial interests, the Court has long applied a test originating in *Pickering*.

Abood coheres with that framework. The point here is not, as the majority suggests, that *Abood* is an overt, one-to-one "application of *Pickering*." *Abood* and *Pickering* raised variants of the same basic issue: the extent of the government's authority to make employment decisions affecting expression. And in both, the Court struck

---

1. The majority relies on statistics from the federal workforce (where agency fees are unlawful) to suggest that public employees do not act in accord with economic logic. But first, many fewer federal employees pay dues than have voted for a union to represent them, indicating that free-riding in fact pervades the federal sector. And second, that sector is not typical of other public workforces. Bargaining in the federal sphere is limited; most notably, it does not extend to wages and benefits. That means union operating expenses are lower than they are elsewhere. And the gap further widens because the federal sector uses large, often national, bargaining units that provide unions with economies of scale. For those reasons, the federal workforce is the wrong place to look for meaningful empirical evidence on the issues here.

the same basic balance, enabling the government to curb speech when—but only when—the regulation was designed to protect its managerial interests.

Abood thus dovetailed with the Court's usual attitude in First Amendment cases toward the regulation of public employees' speech. That attitude is one of respect—even solicitude—for the government's prerogatives as an employer. So long as the government is acting as an employer—rather than exploiting the employment relationship for other ends—it has a wide berth, comparable to that of a private employer. And when the regulated expression concerns the terms and conditions of employment—the very stuff of the employment relationship—the government really cannot lose. There, managerial interests are obvious and strong. And so government employees are . . . just employees, even though they work for the government. Except that today the government does lose, in a first for the law. Now, the government can constitutionally adopt all policies regulating core workplace speech in pursuit of managerial goals—save this single one.

2

Consider an analogy, not involving union fees: Suppose a government entity disciplines a group of (non-unionized) employees for agitating for a better health plan at various inopportune times and places. The better health plan will of course drive up public spending; so according to the majority's analysis, the employees' speech satisfies *Pickering*'s "public concern" test. Or similarly, suppose a public employer penalizes a group of (non-unionized) teachers who protest merit pay in the school cafeteria. Once again, the majority's logic runs, the speech is of "public concern," so the employees have a plausible First Amendment claim. (And indeed, the majority appears to concede as much, by asserting that the results in these hypotheticals should turn on various "factual detail[s]" relevant to the interest balancing that occurs at the *Pickering* test's *second* step.) But in fact, this Court has always understood such cases to end at *Pickering*'s *first* step: If an employee's speech is about, in, and directed to the workplace, she has no "possibility of a First Amendment claim." So take your pick. Either the majority is exposing government entities across the country to increased First Amendment litigation and liability—and thus preventing them from regulating their workforces as private employers could. Or else, when actual cases of this kind come around, we will discover that today's majority has crafted a "unions only" carve-out to our employee-speech law.

III

But the worse part of today's opinion is where the majority subverts all known principles of *stare decisis*. The majority makes plain, in the first 33 pages of its decision, that it believes *Abood* was wrong. But even if that were true (which it is not), it is not enough. "Respecting *stare decisis* means sticking to some wrong decisions." Any departure from settled precedent (so the Court has often stated) demands a "special justification—over and above the belief that the precedent was wrongly decided." And the majority does not have anything close. To the contrary: all that is "special" in this case—especially the massive reliance interests at stake—demands retaining *Abood,* beyond even the normal precedent.

Abood is not just any precedent: It is embedded in the law (not to mention, as I'll later address, in the world) in a way not many decisions are.

Over 20 States have by now enacted statutes authorizing fair-share provisions. To be precise, 22 States, the District of Columbia, and Puerto Rico—plus another two States for police and firefighter unions. Many of those States have multiple statutory provisions, with variations for different categories of public employees. Every one of them will now need to come up with new ways—elaborated in new statutes—to structure relations between government employers and their workers.

Still more, thousands of current contracts covering millions of workers provide for agency fees. Usually, this Court recognizes that "[c]onsiderations in favor of *stare decisis* are at their acme in cases involving property and contract rights."

The majority asserts that no one should care much because the canceled agreements are "of rather short duration" and would "expire on their own in a few years' time." But to begin with, that response ignores the substantial time and effort that state legislatures will have to devote to revamping their statutory schemes. And anyway, it misunderstands the nature of contract negotiations when the parties have a continuing relationship. The parties, in renewing an old collective-bargaining agreement, don't start on an empty page. Instead, various "long-settled" terms—like fair-share provisions—are taken as a given. So the majority's ruling does more than advance by a few years a future renegotiation (though even that would be significant). In most cases, it commands new bargaining over how to replace a term that the parties never expected to change.

The majority, though, offers another reason for not worrying about reliance: The parties, it says, "have been on notice for years regarding this Court's misgivings about *Abood.*" Here, the majority proudly lays claim to its 6-year crusade to ban agency fees.

But that argument reflects a radically wrong understanding of how *stare decisis* operates. Justice Scalia once confronted a similar argument for "disregard[ing] reliance interests" and showed how antithetical it was to rule-of-law principles. He noted first what we always tell lower courts: "If a precedent of this Court has direct application in a case, yet appears to rest on reasons rejected in some other line of decisions, [they] should follow the case which directly controls, leaving to this Court the prerogative of overruling its own decisions." He concluded: "[R]eliance upon a square, unabandoned holding of the Supreme Court is *always* justifiable reliance."

IV

There is no sugarcoating today's opinion. The majority overthrows a decision entrenched in this Nation's law—and in its economic life—for over 40 years. As a result, it prevents the American people, acting through their state and local officials, from making important choices about workplace governance. And it does so by weaponizing the First Amendment, in a way that unleashes judges, now and in the future, to intervene in economic and regulatory policy.

The majority has overruled *Abood* for no exceptional or special reason, but because it never liked the decision. It has overruled *Abood* because it wanted to.

Because, that is, it wanted to pick the winning side in what should be—and until now, has been—an energetic policy debate. Some state and local governments (and the constituents they serve) think that stable unions promote healthy labor relations and thereby improve the provision of services to the public. Other state and local governments (and their constituents) think, to the contrary, that strong unions impose excessive costs and impair those services. Americans have debated the pros and cons for many decades—in large part, by deciding whether to use fair-share arrangements. Yesterday, 22 States were on one side, 28 on the other (ignoring a couple of in-betweeners). Today, that healthy—that democratic—debate ends. The majority has adjudged who should prevail. Indeed, the majority is bursting with pride over what it has accomplished: Now those 22 States, it crows, "can follow the model of the federal government and 28 other States."

And maybe most alarming, the majority has chosen the winners by turning the First Amendment into a sword, and using it against workaday economic and regulatory policy. Today is not the first time the Court has wielded the First Amendment in such an aggressive way. See, *e.g., National Institute of Family and Life Advocates v. Becerra*, 138 S. Ct. 2361 (2018) (invalidating a law requiring medical and counseling facilities to provide relevant information to users); *Sorrell v. IMS Health Inc.* (striking down a law that restricted pharmacies from selling various data). And it threatens not to be the last. Speech is everywhere—a part of every human activity (employment, health care, securities trading, you name it). For that reason, almost all economic and regulatory policy affects or touches speech. So the majority's road runs long. And at every stop are black-robed rulers overriding citizens' choices. The First Amendment was meant for better things. It was meant not to undermine but to protect democratic governance—including over the role of public-sector unions.

Notes

1. Note that Janus contains two holdings. First, that union-represented public sector workers cannot be required to pay dues or fees associated with collective bargaining. Second, that unions must obtain affirmative consent, manifested by "clear and convincing evidence," before they can have fees deducted from non-members' paychecks.

2. **Post-*Janus* Legislation.** Anticipating *Janus'* holding, a number of Democratically controlled states passed or proposed legislation designed to mitigate the case's effects. For example, consider the following two amendments to New York's Taylor Law:

(a) Within thirty days of a public employee first being employed or reemployed by a public employer, or within thirty days of being promoted or transferred to a new bargaining unit, the public employer shall notify the employee organization, if any, that represents that bargaining unit of the employee's name, address, job title, employing agency, department or other operating unit, and work location; and

(b) Within thirty days of providing the notice in paragraph a of this subdivision, a public employer shall allow a duly appointed representative of the employee organization that represents that bargaining unit to meet with such employee for a reasonable amount of time during his or her work time without charge to leave credits, unless otherwise specified within an agreement bargained collectively under article fourteen of the civil service law, provided however that arrangements for such meeting must be scheduled in consultation with a designated representative of the public employer. N.Y. Civ. Serv. Law § 208(4).

Notwithstanding any law, rule or regulation to the contrary, an employee organization's duty of fair representation to a public employee it represents but who is not a member of the employee organization shall be limited to the negotiation or enforcement of the terms of an agreement with the public employer. No provision of this article shall be construed to require an employee organization to provide representation to a non-member (i) during questioning by the employer, (ii) in statutory or administrative proceedings or to enforce statutory regulatory rights, or (iii) in any stage of a grievance, arbitration or other contractual process concerning the evaluation or discipline of a public employee where the non-member is permitted to proceed without the employee organization and be represented by his or her own advocate. Nor shall any provision of this article prohibit an employee organization from providing legal, economic or job related services or benefits beyond those provided in the agreement with a public employer only to its members. N.Y. Civ. Serv. Law § 209-a(2).

Consider why New York adopted these amendments in light of *Janus*. What are the amendments' benefits and drawbacks? The leadership of the four biggest public-sector unions (AFSCME, SEIU, NEA, and AFT) have publicly rejected the idea of abandoning or weakening either the duty of fair representation or the exclusive representation system. *See* Public Policy Priorities for Partner Unions, *available at* https://bit.ly/3i5YB8q. Why do you think that might be? And, considering the *Janus* opinion, do you think there are grounds for a legal challenge against any part of these amendments?

Other states have taken different approaches. For example, New Jersey adopted a bill designed to facilitate opportunities for public unions to communicate with represented workers, which also included this provision: "a. A public employer shall not encourage negotiations unit members to resign or relinquish membership in an exclusive representative employee organization and shall not encourage negotiations unit members to revoke authorization of the deduction of fees to an exclusive representative employee organization.; b. A public employer shall not encourage or discourage an employee from joining, forming or assisting an employee organization." 2018 N.J. A3686.

As you can tell from the New York and New Jersey bills, the dominant state response to *Janus* involves facilitating union access to public employees. *See also* CAL. GOV. CODE § 1556 (giving elected unions access to new-employee orientations); OREGON HB 2016 (allowing union representatives to attend to certain union business during work time; providing opportunities for unions to speak with represented employees; providing unions with access to employee contact information; allowing telephonic or email consent to dues deductions; making it an unfair labor practice for an employer to encourage an employee to resign union membership); Martin H. Malin & Catherine Fisk, *After Janus*, 107 CAL. L. REV. 1821 (2019).

But consider whether states could or should respond in other ways. For example, one law professor has called for states and unions to require that represented workers who decide not to pay an agency fee instead contribute the equivalent amount to a charity. Samuel Estreicher, *How Unions Can Survive a Supreme Court Defeat*, BLOOMBERG OPINION, (March 2, 2018), https://www.bloomberg.com/view/articles /2018-03-02/how-unions-can-survive-a-supreme-court-defeat. Another has suggested that states should reimburse unions directly for their bargaining costs, although the major public sector unions have generally opposed this approach. *See* Aaron Tang, *Life After Janus* (2018), 119 COLUMBIA L. REV. 677 (2019); *see also* 2017 HI HB 923 (legislative proposal to establish a state-funded "public employees' bargaining fund").

3. **Post-*Janus* Litigation.** In light of the Court's opinion in *Janus*, what other aspects of public sector collective bargaining might face First Amendment challenges?

A. The National Right to Work Legal Defense Foundation and similar-minded groups and lawyers filed a number of lawsuits seeking back fees for nonmembers, anticipating that *Janus* would overturn *Abood*. After *Janus* was decided, the number of these lawsuits increased dramatically, and they also began to include suits asserting claims for back dues for members and attacking checkoff authorization provisions. In the litigation on behalf of fee payers seeking the return of fees collected prior to *Janus*, the plaintiffs' theory is that *Janus'* declaration that agency fees are unconstitutional is retroactive, so that making nonmembers pay agency fees violated their First Amendment rights even while *Abood* was in effect. Plaintiffs contend that the unions were acting under color of state law in collecting agency fees, and that § 1983 provides a cause of action to redress violations of constitutional rights by a union acting under color of state law. While the unions have advanced a variety of defenses in these cases, courts have been uniformly hospitable to the defense that the unions were acting in good faith pursuant to state laws that had yet to be ruled invalid and had been approved by a directly on point Supreme Court decision. As of the date this book went to print, none of the plaintiffs in these cases have succeeded in their claims. *See, e.g., Wholean v. CSEA SEIU Local 2001*, 955 F.3d

332 (2d Cir. 2020); *Janus v. AFSCME*, 942 F.3d 352 (7th Cir. 2019); *Danielson v. Inslee*, 945 F.3d 1096 (9th Cir. 2019).

B. Other cases from both before and after *Janus* challenge the concept of exclusive representation for both "partial" and traditional public employees. These cases have fared no better than those discussed in the previous paragraph. The plaintiffs in these cases often focus on a particular passage in *Janus* stating: "It is also not disputed that the State may require that a union serve as exclusive bargaining agent for its employees — itself a significant impingement on associational freedoms that would not be tolerated in other contexts." *Janus*, 138 S. Ct. at 2478. Relying on this *dicta*, plaintiffs have asserted that the mere concept of exclusive representation, even divorced from any obligation to pay the fair share of such representation, violates non-members' First Amendment rights. (However, in another part of *Janus*, the Court observes that other than the ban on agency fees, "[s]tates can keep their labor-relations systems exactly as they are." *Id.* at 2485 n.27.)

So far, the courts considering these claims have uniformly dismissed them. They rely on the Supreme Court's decision (discussed briefly in Chapter 5) in *Minn. St. Bd. for Community Colleges v. Knight*, 465 U.S. 271 (1984), which upheld Minnesota's exclusive meet-and-negotiate statute in the face of a First Amendment challenge. *See, e.g., Mentele v. Inslee*, 916 F.3d 783, 788–89 (9th Cir. 2019)*; Bierman v. Dayton*, 900 F.3d 570 (8th Cir. 2018); *Hill v. Serv. Emps. Int'l Union*, 850 F.3d 861, 866 (7th Cir. 2017); *Jarvis v. Cuomo*, 660 Fed. App'x 72, 74 (2d Cir. 2016); *D'Agostino v. Baker*, 812 F.3d 240, 244 (1st Cir. 2016); *Branch v. Commonwealth Employment Relations Board*, 481 Mass. 810 (2019).

C. Does *Janus* alter the general rule that unions may exclude members of a bargaining unit who are not union members from internal union decision-making, including meetings over bargaining proposals? *Branch v. Commonwealth Employment Relations Board*, 120 N.E.3d 1163 (Mass. 2019) held that a union's internal policy prohibiting nonmembers from participating in the selection of bargaining committees and the development of bargaining proposals neither violates the First Amendment nor breaches a union's duty of fair representation.

D. Finally, some plaintiffs are relying on *Janus* to challenge continued deduction of union fees when an employee asks to stop paying fees despite the fact that they had previously signed a checkoff authorization agreement limiting revocation of the checkoff to certain specified times. These cases tend to turn on the particular facts of the resignation, the language of the checkoff authorization agreement and any collective bargaining language addressing the subject, and the specifics of how the union reacted to the member's attempt to revoke authorization. However, a few generalizations with respect to the legal issues these cases raise are possible.

First, these cases are also brought pursuant to 42 U.S.C. § 1983, thus raising a question of whether there is state action involved in a union's decision to enforce a dues-deduction authorization contained in a membership contract between the union and a public employee. One court that considered the question held that state action was not present. *Belgau v. Inslee*, 359 F. Supp. 3d 1000 (W.D. Wash. 2019) (appeal pending).

Second, there is a question of whether the language in particular checkoff authorizations constitutes consent by the members to waive whatever First Amendment rights they may have. In this regard, the Supreme Court's decision in *Cohen v. Cowles Media Co.*, 501 U.S. 663 (1991), is instructive. In that case, the Supreme Court rejected a claim that the First Amendment prohibited enforcement of a newspaper's promise to keep the identity of a source confidential. The Court concluded: "the First Amendment does not confer . . . a constitutional right to disregard promises that would otherwise be enforced under state law." *Id.* at 672.

4. **Post-*Janus* Bargaining.** In her *Janus* dissent, Justice Kagan observed that "thousands of current contracts covering millions of workers provide for agency fees." How might unions take *Janus* into account when bargaining new contracts with employers?

One answer is that unions might bargain for opportunities to communicate with represented workers, similar to the legislative fixes discussed above. But in one interest arbitration, the union requested and the arbitrator awarded a union the right not to represent non-paying non-members in grievances. Citing *Janus*, the arbitrator wrote that "the *Janus* decision, that overrode decades of precedent, is precisely the type of compelling event that supports modification of existing contractual language," which required the union to represent non-members in grievances. Instead of union representation, non-members may represent themselves in the grievance process. *Clark County v. Clark County Correctional Guild*, Case No. 131479-1-19 (Washington PERC, Nov. 1, 2019) (Arbitrator Richard Ahearn). Consider the benefits and drawbacks of this arrangement for the union, the employer, and the employees.

E. Agency Fee Rules Come to the NLRA

Communications Workers v. Beck

Supreme Court of the United States
487 U.S. 735 (1988)

BRENNAN, J.

Section 8(a)(3) of the National Labor Relations Act of 1935 (NLRA) . . . permits an employer and an exclusive bargaining representative to enter into an agreement requiring all employees in the bargaining unit to pay periodic union dues and initiation fees as a condition of continued employment, whether or not the employees otherwise wish to become union members. Today we must decide whether this provision also permits a union, over the objections of dues-paying nonmember employees, to expend funds so collected on activities unrelated to collective bargaining, contract administration, or grievance adjustment, and, if so, whether such expenditures violate the union's duty of fair representation or the objecting employees' First Amendment rights.

I

In accordance with §9 of the NLRA . . . a majority of the employees of American Telephone and Telegraph Company and several of its subsidiaries selected petitioner Communications Workers of America (CWA) as their exclusive bargaining representative. As such, the union is empowered to bargain collectively with the employer on behalf of all employees in the bargaining unit over wages, hours, and other terms and conditions of employment . . . and it accordingly enjoys "broad authority . . . in the negotiation and administration of [the] collective bargaining contract." *Humphrey v. Moore*. . . . This broad authority, however, is tempered by the union's "statutory obligation to serve the interests of all members without hostility or discrimination toward any," *Vaca v. Sipes*. . . . CWA chartered several local unions, copetitioners in this case, to assist it in discharging these statutory duties. In addition, at least in part to help defray the considerable costs it incurs in performing these tasks, CWA negotiated a union-security clause in the collective-bargaining agreement under which all represented employees, including those who do not wish to become union members, must pay the union "agency fees" in "amounts equal to the periodic dues" paid by union members. . . .

In June 1976, respondents, 20 employees who chose not to become union members, initiated this suit challenging CWA's use of their agency fees for purposes other than collective bargaining, contract administration, or grievance adjustment (hereinafter "collective-bargaining" or "representational" activities). Specifically, respondents alleged that the union's expenditure of their fees on activities such as organizing the employees of other employers, lobbying for labor legislation, and participating in social, charitable, and political events violated petitioners' duty of fair representation, §8(a)(3) of the NLRA, the First Amendment, and various common-law fiduciary duties.

II

Respondents . . . claim that the union failed to represent their interests fairly and without hostility by negotiating and enforcing an agreement that allows the exaction of funds for purposes that do not serve their interests and in some cases are contrary to their personal beliefs. The necessity of deciding the scope of §8(a)(3) arises because *petitioners* seek to defend themselves on the ground that the statute authorizes precisely this type of agreement. . . .

III

Added as part of the Labor Management Relations Act, 1947, or Taft-Hartley Act, §8(a)(3) makes it an unfair labor practice for an employer "by discrimination in regard to hire or tenure of employment . . . to encourage or discourage membership in any labor organization." The section contains two provisos without which all union-security clauses would fall within this otherwise broad condemnation: the first states that nothing in the Act "preclude[s] an employer from making an agreement with a labor organization . . . to require as a condition of employment membership there in "30 days after the employee attains employment, *id.*; the second, limiting the first, provides:

> "[N]o employer shall justify any discrimination against an employee for nonmembership in a labor organization (A) if he has reasonable grounds for believing that such membership was not available to the employee on the same terms and conditions generally applicable to other members, or (B) if he has reasonable grounds for believing that membership was denied or terminated for reasons other than the failure . . . to tender the periodic dues and the initiation fees uniformly required as a condition of acquiring or retaining membership." *Id.*

Taken as a whole, § 8(a)(3) permits an employer and a union[2] to enter into an agreement requiring all employees to become union members as a condition of continued employment, but the "membership" that may be so required has been "whittled down to its financial core." *NLRB v. General Motors Corp.* . . . The statutory question presented in this case, then, is whether this "financial core" includes the obligation to support union activities beyond those germane to collective bargaining, contract administration, and grievance adjustment. We think it does not.

Although we have never before delineated the precise limits § 8(a)(3) places on the negotiation and enforcement of union-security agreements, the question the parties proffer is not an entirely new one. Over a quarter century ago we held that § 2, Eleventh of the RLA does not permit a union, over the objections of nonmembers, to expend compelled agency fees on political causes. *Machinists v. Street,* . . . Because the NLRA and RLA differ in certain crucial respects, we have frequently warned that decisions construing the latter often provide only the roughest of guidance when interpreting the former. See, *e.g., Street, supra.* . . . Our decision in *Street*, however, is far more than merely instructive here: we believe it is controlling, for § 8(a)(3) and § 2, Eleventh are in all material respects identical. Indeed, we have previously described the two provisions as "statutory equivalent[s]," *Ellis v. Railway Clerks*, 466 U.S. 435, 452, n. 13 (1984), and with good reason, because their nearly identical language reflects the fact that in both Congress authorized compulsory unionism only to the extent necessary to ensure that those who enjoy union-negotiated benefits contribute to their cost. Thus, in amending the RLA in 1951, Congress expressly modeled § 2, Eleventh on § 8(a)(3), which it had added to the NLRA only four years earlier, and repeatedly emphasized that it was extending "to railroad labor the same rights and privileges of the union shop that are contained in the Taft-Hartley Act." 96 Cong.Rec. 17055 (1951) (remarks of Rep. Brown). . . . In these circumstances, we think it clear that Congress intended the same language to have the same meaning in both statutes.

---

2. Section 8(b)(2) makes it unlawful for unions "to cause or attempt to cause an employer to discriminate against an employee in violation of subsection (a)(3)"; accordingly, the provisos to § 8(a)(3) also allow unions to seek and enter into union-security agreements.

A

Both the structure and purpose of §8(a)(3) are best understood in light of the statute's historical origins. . . .

The legislative solution embodied in §8(a)(3) allows employers to enter into agreements requiring all the employees in a given bargaining unit to become members 30 days after being hired as long as such membership is available to all workers on a nondiscriminatory basis, but it prohibits the mandatory discharge of an employee who is expelled from the union for any reason other than his or her failure to pay initiation fees or dues. As we have previously observed, Congress carefully tailored this solution to the evils at which it was aimed:

> "Th[e] legislative history clearly indicates that Congress intended to prevent utilization of union security agreements for any purpose other than to compel payment of union dues and fees. Thus Congress recognized the validity of unions' concerns about 'free riders,' *i.e.,* employees who receive the benefits of union representation but are unwilling to contribute their *fair share* of financial support to such union, and gave unions the power to contract to meet *that problem* while withholding from unions the power to cause the discharge of employees for any other reason." *Radio Officers v. NLRB*, 347 U.S. 17, 41 (1954) (emphasis added).

This same concern over the resentment spawned by "free riders" in the railroad industry prompted Congress, four years after the passage of the Taft-Hartley Act, to amend the RLA. . . .

In drafting what was to become §2, Eleventh, Congress did not look to §8(a)(3) merely for guidance. Rather, as Senator Taft argued in support of the legislation, the amendment "inserts in the railway mediation law almost the exact provisions, so far as they fit, of the Taft-Hartley law, so that the conditions regarding the union shop and the check-off are carried into the relations between railroad unions and the railroads." 96 Cong.Rec. 16267 (1950). This was the universal understanding, among both supporters and opponents, of the purpose and effect of the amendment. . . .

In *Street* we concluded "that §2, Eleventh contemplated compulsory unionism to force employees to share the costs of negotiating and administering collective agreements, and the costs of the adjustment and settlement of disputes," but that Congress did not intend "to provide the unions with a means for forcing employees, over their objection, to support political causes which they oppose." . . . Given the parallel purpose, structure, and language of §8(a)(3), we must interpret that provision in the same manner. Like §2, Eleventh, §8(a)(3) permits the collection of "periodic dues and initiation fees uniformly required as a condition of acquiring or retaining membership" in the union, and like its counterpart in the RLA, §8(a)(3) was designed to remedy the inequities posed by "free riders" who would otherwise unfairly profit from the Taft-Hartley Act's abolition of the closed shop. In the face of such statutory congruity, only the most compelling evidence could persuade us that Congress intended the nearly identical language of these two provisions to have different meanings. Petitioners have not proffered such evidence here.

B

(1)

Petitioners claim that the union-security provisions of the RLA and NLRA can and should be read differently in light of the vastly different history of unionism in the industries the two statutes regulate. . . .

We find this argument unpersuasive for several reasons. . . .

Finally, however much union-security practices may have differed between the railway and NLRA-governed industries prior to 1951, it is abundantly clear that Congress itself understood its actions in 1947 and 1951 to have placed these respective industries on an equal footing insofar as compulsory unionism was concerned. Not only did the 1951 proponents of the union shop propose adding to the RLA language nearly identical to that of § 8(a)(3), they repeatedly insisted that the purpose of the amendment was to confer on railway unions precisely the same right to negotiate and enter into union-security agreements that all unions subject to the NLRA enjoyed. . . .

(2)

. . . Petitioners also deem it highly significant that prior to 1947 unions "'rather typically'" used their members' dues for a "'variety of purposes . . . in addition to meeting the . . . costs of collective bargaining *Retail Clerks v. Schermerhorn*, 373 U.S. 746 (1963), and yet Congress, which was presumably well aware of the practice, in no way limited the uses to which unions could put fees collected from nonmembers. This silence, petitioners suggest, should be understood as congressional acquiescence in these practices. The short answer to this argument is that Congress was equally well aware of the same practices by railway unions, see *Street*, 367 U.S., at 767 ("We may assume that Congress was . . . fully conversant with the long history of intensive involvement of the railroad unions in political activities") . . . yet neither in *Street* nor in any of the cases that followed it have we deemed Congress' failure in § 2, Eleventh to prohibit or otherwise regulate such expenditures as an endorsement of fee collections unrelated to collective-bargaining expenses. We see no reason to give greater weight to Congress' silence in the NLRA than we did in the RLA.

(3)

We need not decide whether the exercise of rights permitted, though not compelled, by § 8(a)(3) involves state action. Cf. *Steelworkers v. Sadlowski*, 457 U.S. 102, 121, n. 16 (1982) (union's decision to adopt an internal rule governing its elections does not involve state action); *Steelworkers v. Weber*, 443 U.S. 193, 200 (1979) (negotiation of collective-bargaining agreement's affirmative-action plan does not involve state action). Even assuming that it does not, and that the NLRA and RLA therefore differ in this respect, we do not believe that the absence of any constitutional concerns in this case would warrant reading the nearly identical language of § 8(a)(3) and § 2, Eleventh differently. It is, of course, true that federal statutes are to be construed so as to avoid serious doubts as to their constitutionality, and that when faced with such doubts the Court will first determine whether it is fairly possible to interpret the statute in a manner that renders it constitutionally valid. *Edward J. DeBartolo Corp. v. Florida Gulf Coast Building & Construction Trades Council*, 485 U.S. 568 (1988). In *Street*, we concluded that our interpretation of § 2, Eleventh was "not only 'fairly possible' but entirely reasonable," 367 U.S., at 750, and we have adhered to that interpretation since. We therefore decline to construe the language of § 8(a)(3) differently from that of § 2, Eleventh on the theory that our construction of the latter provision was merely constitutionally expedient. Congress enacted the two provisions for the same purpose, eliminating "free riders," and that purpose dictates our construction of § 8(a)(3) no less than it did that of § 2, Eleventh, regardless of whether the negotiation of union-security agreements under the NLRA partakes of governmental action.

IV

We conclude that § 8(a)(3), like its statutory equivalent, § 2, Eleventh of the RLA, authorizes the exaction of only those fees and dues necessary to "performing the duties of an exclusive representative of the employees in dealing with the employer on labor-management issues." *Ellis*, 466 U.S., at 448. Accordingly, the judgment of the Court of Appeals is *Affirmed*.

BLACKMUN, J., with whom O'CONNOR, J. and SCALIA, J. join, concurring in part and dissenting in part.

I . . . agree that the Court of Appeals had jurisdiction to decide the § 8(a)(3) question raised by respondents' duty-of-fair-representation claim.[1]

My agreement with the majority ends there, however, for I cannot agree with its resolution of the § 8(a)(3) issue. Without the decision in *Machinists v. Street* . . . the Court could not reach the result it does today. Our accepted mode of resolving statutory questions would not lead to a construction of § 8(a)(3) so foreign to that section's express language and legislative history, which show that Congress did not intend to limit either the amount of "agency fees" (or what the majority labels "dues-equivalents") a union may collect under a union-security agreement, or the union's expenditure of such funds. The Court's excessive reliance on *Street* to reach a contrary conclusion is manifested by its unique line of reasoning. No sooner is the language of § 8(a)(3) intoned, than the Court abandons all attempt at construction of *this* statute and leaps to its interpretation over a quarter century ago of another statute enacted by a different Congress, a statute with a distinct history and purpose. . . . I am unwilling to offend our established doctrines of statutory

---

1. Like the majority, I do not reach the First Amendment issue raised below by respondents, and therefore similarly do not address whether a union's exercise of rights pursuant to § 8(a)(3) involves state action.

construction and strain the meaning of the language used by Congress in § 8(a)(3), simply to conform § 8(a)(3)'s construction to the Court's interpretation of similar language in a different later-enacted statute, an interpretation which is itself "not without its difficulties." *Abood v. Detroit Board of Education*, 431 U.S. 209, 232(1977) (characterizing the Court's decision in *Street*). I therefore dissent from Parts III and IV of the Court's opinion.

I

As the Court observes, "we have never before delineated the precise limits § 8(a) (3) places on the negotiation and enforcement of union-security agreements." Unlike the majority, however, I think the issue is an entirely new one. I shall endeavor, therefore, to resolve it in accordance with our well-settled principles of statutory construction.

A

As with any question of statutory interpretation, the starting point is the language of the statute itself. Section 8(a)(3) makes it unlawful for an employer to "discriminat[e] in regard to hire or tenure of employment or any term or condition of employment to encourage or discourage membership in any labor organization." Standing alone, this proscription, and thus § 8(b)(2)'s corollary proscription, effectively would outlaw union-security agreements. The proscription, however, is qualified by two provisos. The first, which appeared initially in § 8(a)(3) of the NLRA as originally enacted in 1935, generally excludes union-security agreements from statutory condemnation by explaining that

> "nothing in [the NLRA] or in any other statute of the United States, shall preclude an employer from making an agreement with a labor organization . . . to require as a condition of employment membership therein . . . if such labor organization is the representative of the employees as provided in section 159(a) of this title. . . ." § 8(a)(3).

The second proviso, incorporated in § 8(a)(3) by the Taft-Hartley Amendments of 1947 circumscribes the first proviso's general exemption by the following limitations:

> "[N]o employer shall justify any discrimination against an employee for nonmembership in a labor organization . . . if he has reasonable grounds for believing that membership was denied or terminated for reasons other than the failure of the employee to tender the periodic dues and the initiation fees uniformly required as a condition of acquiring or retaining membership."

The plain language of these statutory provisions, read together, permits an employer and union to enter into an agreement requiring *all* employees, as a condition of continued employment, to pay uniform periodic dues and initiation fees. The second proviso expressly allows an employer to terminate any "employee," pursuant to a union-security agreement permitted by the first proviso, if the employee fails "to tender the periodic dues and the initiation fees uniformly required as a condition of acquiring or retaining membership" in the union. . . . The term "employee," as statutorily defined, includes any employee, without regard to union membership.

"[W]e assume 'that the legislative purpose is expressed by the ordinary meaning of the words used.' *American Tobacco Co. v. Patterson*, 456 U.S. 63, 68 (1982). . . . The terms "dues" and "fees," as used in the proviso, can refer to nothing other than the regular, periodic dues and initiation fees paid by "voluntary" union members. This was the apparent understanding of the Court in those decisions in which it held that § 8(a)(3) permits union-security agreements. *See NLRB v. General Motors Corp.* (approving a union-security proposal that would have conditioned employment "upon the payment of sums equal to the initiation fee and regular monthly dues paid by the union members"); *Retail Clerks v. Schermerhorn*, 373 U.S. 746 (1963) (upholding agreement requiring nonmembers to pay a "service fee [which] is admittedly the exact equal of membership initiation fees and monthly dues"). It also has been the consistent view of the NLRB, "the agency entrusted by Congress with the authority to administer the NLRA." . . . The provisos do not give any employee, union member or not, the right to pay less than the full amount of regular dues and initiation fees charged to all other bargaining-unit employees.

The Court's conclusion that § 8(a)(3) prohibits petitioners from requiring respondents to pay fees for purposes other than those "germane" to collective bargaining, contract administration, and grievance adjustment simply cannot be derived from the plain language of the statute. In effect, the Court accepts respondents' contention that the words "dues" and "fees," as used in § 8(a)(3), refer not to the periodic amount a union charges its members but to the portion of that amount that the union expends on statutory collective bargaining.[6] Not only is this reading implausible as a matter of simple English usage, but it is also contradicted by the decisions of this Court and of the NLRB interpreting the section. Section 8(a)(3) does not speak of "dues" and "fees" that employees covered by a union-security agreement may be required to tender to their union representative; rather, the section speaks only of "the periodic dues and the initiation fees *uniformly required as a condition of acquiring or retaining membership*" (emphasis added). Thus, the section,

---

6. Under our settled doctrines of statutory construction, were there any ambiguity in the meaning of § 8(a)(3) — which there is not — the Court would be constrained to defer to the interpretation of the NLRB, unless the agency's construction were contrary to the clear intent of Congress. *Chevron U.S.A. Inc. v. National Resources Defense Council, Inc.*, 467 U.S. 837, 842–843, n. 9 (1984). Although the Court apparently finds such ambiguity, it fails to apply this doctrine. By reference to a narrow view of congressional "purpose" gleaned from isolated statements in the legislative history, and in reliance upon this Court's interpretation of another statute, the Court constructs an interpretation that not only finds no support in the statutory language or legislative history of § 8(a)(3), but also contradicts the Board's settled interpretation of the statutory provision. The Court previously has directed: "Where the Board's construction of the Act is reasonable, it should not be rejected 'merely because the courts might prefer another view of the statute.'" *Pattern Makers v. NLRB*, 473 U.S. 95, 114 (1985). . . . Here, the only apparent motivation for holding that the Board's interpretation of § 8(a)(3) is impermissible, is the Court's view of *another* statute.

by its terms, defines "periodic dues" and "initiation fees" as those dues and fees "uniformly required" of all members, not as a portion of full dues. As recognized by this Court, "dues collected from members may be used for a variety of purposes, in addition to meeting the union's costs of collective bargaining. Unions rather typically use their membership dues to do those things which the members authorize the union to do in their interest and on their behalf." *Retail Clerks v. Schermerhorn*, 373 U.S., at 753–754 (internal quotations omitted). By virtue of § 8(a)(3), such dues may be required from *any* employee under a union-security agreement. Nothing in § 8(a)(3) limits, or even addresses, the purposes to which a union may devote the moneys collected pursuant to such an agreement.

B

The Court's attempt to squeeze support from the legislative history for its reading of congressional intent contrary to the plain language of § 8(a)(3) is unavailing. As its own discussion of the relevant legislative materials reveals, there is no indication that the 1947 Congress intended to limit the union's authority to collect from nonmembers the same periodic dues and initiation fees it collects from members. Indeed, on balance, the legislative history reinforces what the statutory language suggests: the provisos neither limit the uses to which agency fees may be put nor require nonmembers to be charged less than the "uniform" dues and initiation fees. . . .

The legislative debates surrounding the adoption of § 8(a)(3) in 1947, show that in crafting the proviso to § 8(a)(3), Congress was attempting "only to 'remedy the most serious abuses of compulsory union membership. . . .'"

Congress' solution was to ban the closed shop and to permit the enforcement of union-shop agreements as long as union membership is available "on the same terms and conditions" to all employees, and mandatory discharge is required only for "nonpayment of regular dues and initiation fees." S.Rep., at 7, 20. Congress was of the view, that, as Senator Taft stated, "[t]he fact that the employee will have to pay dues to the union seems . . . to be much less important. The important thing is that the man will have the job." 93 Cong.Rec. 4886 (1947). . . .

Throughout the hearings and lengthy debate on one of the most hotly contested issues that confronted the 1947 Congress, not once did any Member of Congress suggest that § 8(a)(3) did not leave employers and unions free to adopt and enforce union-security agreements requiring all employees in the bargaining-unit to pay an amount equal to full union dues and standard initiation fees. Nor did anyone suggest that § 8(a)(3) affected a union's expenditure of such funds. . . .

II

. . . The text of § 8(a)(3) of the NLRA is, of course, very much like the text of the later enacted § 2, Eleventh of the RLA. This similarity, however, does not dictate the conclusion that the 1947 Congress intended § 8(a)(3) to have a meaning identical to that which the 1951 Congress intended § 2, Eleventh to have. The Court previously has held that the scope of the RLA is not identical to that of the NLRA and that courts should be wary of drawing parallels between the two statutes. See, e.g., *First National Maintenance Corp. v. NLRB*.... Thus, parallels between § 8(a)(3) and § 2, Eleventh, "like all parallels between the NLRA and the Railway Labor Act, should be drawn with the utmost care and with full awareness of the differences between the statutory schemes." *Chicago & N.W.R. Co. v. Transportation Union*, 402 U.S. 570, 579, n. 11 (1971). Contrary to the majority's conclusion the two provisions were not born of the "same concern[s]"; indeed, they were born of competing concerns. This Court's interpretation of § 2, Eleventh, therefore, provides no support for construing § 8(a)(3) in a fashion inconsistent with its plain language and legislative history.

The purpose advanced for amending the RLA in 1951 to authorize union-security agreements for the first time was "the elimination of the 'free riders.'" 367 U.S., at 76. Given that background, the Court was persuaded that it was possible to conclude that "Congress did not completely abandon the policy of full freedom of choice embodied in the ... Act, but rather made inroads on it for the limited purpose of eliminating the problems created by the 'free rider'" *Id.*, at 767.

The NLRA does not share the RLA's underlying policy, which propelled the Court's interpretation of § 2, Eleventh in *Street*. Indeed, the history of the NLRA points in the opposite direction: the original policy of the Wagner Act was to permit all forms of union-security agreements, and such agreements were commonplace in 1947. Thus, in enacting § 8(a)(3), the 1947 Congress, unlike the 1951 Congress, was not making inroads on a policy of full freedom of choice in order to provide "a specific response," *id.*, at 751 to a particular problem facing unions. Rather, the 1947 amendments to § 8(a)(3) were designed to make an inroad into a preexisting policy of the absolute freedom of private parties under federal law to negotiate union-security agreements. It was a "limited" inroad, responding to carefully defined abuses that Congress concluded had arisen in the union-security agreements permitted by the Wagner Act. The 1947 Congress did not enact § 8(a)(3) for the "same purpose" as did the 1951 Congress in enacting § 2, Eleventh....

In order to overcome this inevitable conclusion, the Court relies on remarks made by a few Members of the Congress in enacting the 1951 amendments to § 2, Eleventh of the RLA, which the Court contends show that the 1951 Congress viewed those amendments as identical to the amendments that had been made to § 8(a)(3) of the NLRA in 1947.... It would "surely come as a surprise" to the legislators who enacted § 8(a)(3) to learn that, in discerning their intent, the Court listens not to their voices, but to those of a later Congress. Unlike the majority, I am unwilling to put the 1951 legislators' words into the 1947 legislators' mouths.

The relevant sources for gleaning the 1947 Congress' intent are the plain language of § 8(a)(3), and, at least to the extent that it might reflect a clear intention contrary to the plain meaning of the statute, the legislative history of § 8(a)(3). Those sources show that the 1947 Congress did not intend § 8(a)(3) to have the same meaning the Court has attributed to § 2, Eleventh of the RLA. I therefore must disagree with the majority's assertion that the Court's decision in *Street* is "controlling" here....

Notes

1. What do you make of the dispute between the majority and the dissent? On one hand, the majority is correct that the statutory language in the relevant NLRA provisions is essentially identical to the RLA language the court interpreted in *Street*. On the other hand, isn't the dissent correct that the court's interpretation is contrary to the clear and express meaning of the NLRA's language, which seems explicitly to allow agreements that require full dues? And that even if the Court found the statutory language ambiguous, it should have deferred to the NLRB's interpretation?

2. In *Beck*, both the majority and the dissent again avoided the issue of whether union security clauses in the private sector involve state action sufficient to trigger constitutional protections. But concerns about the First Amendment obviously affected the statutory interpretation in *Beck* and *Street*. Should the court finally resolve the constitutional issue? If so, how? The majority in *Beck* cited *Steelworkers v. Weber*, noting that it held that an affirmative action clause in a private-sector CBA did not implicate state action. Is there any basis to distinguish a clause requiring affirmative action in employment from an agency fee clause? For an argument that union security clauses in the private sector do not implicate state action sufficient to trigger the First Amendment, see Joseph Slater, *Will Labor Law Prompt Conservative Justices to Adopt a Radical Theory of State Action?* 96 Nebraska L. Rev. 62 (2017).

3. In any event, after *Beck*, it was clear that agency-fee-payer rules were the same, or at least almost the same, under the RLA, the NLRA, and (before *Janus*) in the public sector.

4. Under *Beck* and related precedent, a bargaining-unit member can be a *Beck* objector only if that person is not a union member (thus one sometimes hears the term "nonmember objector"). Again, while a union's DFR generally extends to members of the bargaining-unit who are not members of the union, a few distinctions are allowed. Specifically, nonmembers may be excluded from contract ratification votes (although their interests must be taken into account in negotiations, see the notes following *O'Neil, supra*) and they may be excluded from votes on union officers. Thus, in order to be an agency fee objector, the employee may be required to relinquish those rights. *See Kidwell v. Transportation Communications Int'l Union*, 946 F.2d 283 (4th Cir. 1991). In a recent lawsuit, public-employee plaintiffs argued that requiring them to make this choice between member or objector violated their First Amendment rights; however, the district court dismissed the suit, holding that the relationship between a public employee and his or her union representative does not implicate state action, and therefore cannot violate the First Amendment. *Bain v. Cal. Teachers Ass'n*, In Chambers Order Granting Defendants' Motion to Dismiss, 156 F. Supp. 3d 1142 (C.D. Cal. 2015), *affirmed on other grounds*, 891 F.3d 1206 (9th Cir. 2018). The Massachusetts Supreme Court reached the same conclusion in *Branch v. Commonwealth Employment Relations Board*, 481 Mass. 810 (2019).

5. Why is there so much litigation over agency fees? As the sections above and below demonstrate, the Supreme Court has decided a surprisingly large number of agency fee cases. This is especially notable given that the vast majority of bargaining-unit members covered by union security clauses do not object to how their fees are used, and that for those who do, the percentage of their dues to which they may legally object (and thus the total amount of money involved) is usually quite small. These cases are often funded by the National Right to Work Committee and its Legal Defense and Education Foundation affiliate; these organizations (and certain wings of the Republican Party) also promote ballot initiatives designed to ban or at least greatly limit union security clauses. What are the practical and principled arguments for both sides of these rules as a matter of policy? Consider this further in the sections below that explore how these rules work in practice.

6. One other section of the NLRA may affect dues payments. NLRA § 19, orig-inally added in 1974 and amended in 1980, exempts from union security agree-ments members of bona fide religions which have historically objected to "joining or financially supporting labor organizations." Such individuals may, however, be required to contribute an equal sum to a non-religious charity, and they may be charged the reasonable cost of grievance processing if they invoke the contractual grievance procedure. However, the Sixth Circuit has held that § 19 unconstitution-ally discriminates among religions. *Wilson v. NLRB*, 920 F.2d 1282 (6th Cir. 1990).

7. Critics of *Beck*'s statutory interpretation may have found some bittersweet amusement in the following case. This case also involves the relationship between agency fee rules and DFR rules.

Marquez v. Screen Actors Guild, Inc.

Supreme Court of the United States
525 U.S. 33 (1998)

O'Connor, J.

Section 8(a)(3) of the National Labor Relations Act (NLRA) . . . permits unions and employers to negotiate an agreement that requires union "membership" as a condition of employment for all employees. We have interpreted a proviso to this language to mean that the only "membership" that a union can require is the pay-ment of fees and dues, *NLRB v. General Motors Corp.* . . . and we have held that § 8(a)(3) allows unions to collect and expend funds over the objection of nonmem-bers only to the extent they are used for collective bargaining, contract administra-tion, and grievance adjustment activities, *Communications Workers v. Beck.* . . . In this case, we must determine whether a union breaches its duty of fair representa-tion when it negotiates a union security clause that tracks the language of § 8(a)(3) without explaining, in the agreement, this Court's interpretation of that language. We conclude that it does not. . . .

[Respondent union Screen Actors Guild entered into collective bargaining agreement with respondent employer Lakeside Productions]. This agreement contained a standard union security clause, providing that any performer who worked under the agreement must be "a member of the Union in good standing." Tracking the language of § 8(a)(3), the clause also provided:

> "The foregoing [section], requiring as a condition of employment membership in the Union, shall not apply until on or after the thirtieth day following the beginning of such employment or the effective date of this Agreement, whichever is the later; the Union and the Producers interpret this sentence to mean that membership in the Union cannot be required of any performer by a Producer as a condition of employment until thirty (30) days after his first employment as a performer in the motion picture industry. . . . The Producer shall not be held to have violated this paragraph if it employs a performer who is not a member of the Union in good standing . . . if the Producer has reasonable grounds for believing that membership in the Union was denied to such performer or such performer's membership in the Union was terminated for reasons other than the failure of the performer to tender the periodic dues and the initiation fee uniformly required as a condition of acquiring or retaining membership in the Union. . . ."

[Petitioner Naomi Marquez was prevented from working on a television show produced by Lakeside because, although she had worked in the motion picture industry from more than 30 days, she did not pay union fees prior to the filming of the project.]

Petitioner filed suit against Lakeside and SAG alleging, among other things, that SAG had breached the duty of fair representation. According to petitioner, SAG had breached its duty by negotiating and enforcing a union security clause . . . [that] required union "membership" and the payment of full fees and dues when those terms could not be legally enforced under *General Motors* and *Beck*. . . .

This case presents a narrow question: Does a union breach its duty of fair representation merely by negotiating a union security clause that tracks the language of § 8(a)(3)? . . .

There is no disagreement about the substance of the union's obligations: If a union negotiates a union security clause, it must notify workers that they may satisfy the membership requirement by paying fees to support the union's representational activities, and it must enforce the clause in conformity with this notification. The only question presented by this case is whether a union breaches the duty of fair representation merely by negotiating a union security clause that uses the statutory language without expressly explaining, in the agreement, the refinements introduced by our decisions in *General Motors* and *Beck*. To rephrase the question slightly, petitioner's claim is that even if the union has an exemplary notification procedure and even if the union enforces the union security clause in perfect conformity with federal law, the mere negotiation of a union security clause that tracks the language of the NLRA breaches the duty of fair representation. We hold that it does not. . . .

[A] union breaches the duty of fair representation when its conduct toward a member of the bargaining-unit is arbitrary, discriminatory, or in bad faith. . . . In this case, petitioner does not argue that SAG's negotiation of the union security clause was discriminatory, so we only consider whether SAG's conduct was arbitrary or in bad faith.

Petitioner argues that in *Beck*, we redefined the standard for evaluating when a union's conduct is "arbitrary." Petitioner reads our decision in *Beck* to hold that the union's conduct was arbitrary *merely* because its actions violated the statute. . . . This is an inaccurate reading of our decision in *Beck*. . . . [W]e did not hold that the finding of a mere statutory violation was sufficient to support a conclusion that the union breached its duty. . . .

In [*Air Line Pilots v. O'Neil*] decided three years after *Beck*, we specifically considered the appropriate standard for evaluating conduct under the "arbitrary" prong of the duty of fair representation. We held that under the "arbitrary" prong, a union's actions breach the duty of fair representation . . . [a] union's conduct can be classified as arbitrary only when it is irrational, when it is without a rational basis or explanation.

Under this standard, SAG's negotiation of a union security clause with language derived from the NLRA section authorizing such a clause is far from arbitrary. Petitioner argues that it is irrational to negotiate a clause that cannot be enforced as written. But this clause *can* be enforced as written, because by tracking the statutory language, the clause incorporates all of the refinements that have become associated with that language. When we interpreted § 8(a)(3) in *General Motors* and *Beck*, we held that the section, fairly read, included the rights that we found. To the extent that these interpretations are not obvious, the relevant provisions of § 8(a)(3) have become terms of art; the words and phrasing of the subsection now encompass the rights that we announced in *General Motors* and *Beck*. After we stated that the statutory language incorporates an employee's right not to "join" the union (except by paying fees and dues) and an employee's right to pay for only representational activities, we cannot fault SAG for using this very language to convey these very concepts.

Petitioner also invites us to conclude that the union's conduct in negotiating the union security clause breached the duty of fair representation because it was done in bad faith. She argues that the negotiation of this clause was in bad faith because the union had no reason to use the statutory language except to mislead employees about their rights under *Beck* and *General Motors*. This argument has two components: that the union intended to mislead workers, and that the union had no other purpose but to mislead. Both claims are unpersuasive. . . . According to petitioner, even if the union always informs workers of their rights and even if it enforces the union security clause in conformity with federal law, it is bad faith for a union to use the statutory language in the collective bargaining agreement because such use can only mislead employees. . . .

In sum, on this record, the union's conduct in negotiating a union security clause that traced the statutory language cannot be said to have been either arbitrary or in bad faith. . . .

KENNEDY, J., with whom THOMAS, J. joins, concurring.

. . . As recognized by other courts and by members of the [NLRB], language like this can facilitate deception. See, *e.g.*, *Bloom v. NLRB*, 153 F.3d 844, 850–851 (8th Cir. 1998) ("As Bloom can well attest, when an employee who is approached regarding union membership expresses reluctance, a union frequently will produce or invoke the collective bargaining agreement. . . . The employee, unschooled in semantic legal fictions, cannot possibly discern his rights from a document that has been designed by the union to conceal them. In such a context, 'member' is not a term of 'art,' . . . but one of deception"); *Wegscheid v. Local 2911, Int'l Union, United Automobile, Aerospace and Agricultural Implement Workers*, 117 F.3d 986, 990 (7th Cir. 1997) ("[T]he only realistic explanation for the retention of the statutory language in collective bargaining agreements . . . is to mislead employees about their right not to join the union"); *Monson Trucking, Inc.*, 324 N.L.R.B. 933, 939 (Chairman Gould, concurring) ("[A] collective-bargaining agreement that speaks in terms of 'membership' or 'membership in good standing' without further definition misleads employees into believing that they can be terminated if they do not become formal, full-fledged union members"). As I understand the Court's opinion, there is no basis in our holding today for an inference that inclusion of the statutory language is somehow a defense when a violation of the fair-representation duty has been alleged and facts in addition to the bare language of the contract have been adduced to show the violation. Rather, our holding reflects only the conclusion that the negotiation of a security clause containing such language does not necessarily, or in all circumstances, violate this duty. . . .

Notes

1. Does *Marquez* rely on the notion that "when fairly read" by a reasonable employee, a CBA clause that tracks the statutory language implicitly includes the "refinements introduced by our decisions in *General Motors* and *Beck*"? Or does it rely more on the fact that the union had an obligation to inform bargaining-unit members of their specific rights under *Beck* in other ways?

2. As to the concurrence, what sort of additional facts would be necessary to find a DFR violation in this sort of case?

3. Note also the principle that a statutory violation and a DFR violation are two different issues, and even had the court found the former it would not require finding the latter.

F. Practical Issues in Agency Fee Cases: What Activities Are Chargeable to Objectors and What Procedures Must Unions and Objectors Follow?

Note that in light of *Janus*, the issue of what activities are chargeable in the public sector is now moot. However, as the following cases show, it is difficult to separate the development of this issue in the private sector from its development in the public sector during the decades when *Abood* was good law.

1. What Is Chargeable?

The first practical question in agency fee cases is, what activities are "non-chargeable" to objecting non-members (what activities they may refuse to pay for under a union security clause), and what activities are "chargeable" (what activities they must pay for even if they object to them)? While *Street* listed only political activities as "non-chargeable," later cases expanded the category somewhat. *Beck* held that activities were chargeable if they were "necessary to 'performing the duties of an exclusive representative of the employees in dealing with the employer on labor-management issues.'" Here, *Beck* was quoting a leading case on what is and is not chargeable: *Ellis v. Brotherhood of Railway, Airline and Steamship Clerks*, 466 U.S. 435, 448 (1984).

Ellis also touched on the second practical issue: what procedures unions and objectors should follow in agency fee matters to fulfill *Beck* obligations and rights.

Ellis v. Brotherhood of Railway Clerks

Supreme Court of the United States
466 U.S. 435 (1984)

WHITE, J.

Petitioners are present or former clerical employees of Western who objected to the use of their compelled dues for specified union activities. Respondents . . . concede that the statutory authorization of the union shop does not permit the use of petitioners' contributions for union political or ideological activities . . . and have adopted a rebate program covering such expenditures. The parties disagree about the adequacy of the rebate scheme, and about the legality of burdening objecting employees with six specific union expenses that fall between the extremes identified in *Hanson* and *Street*: the quadrennial Grand Lodge convention, litigation not involving the negotiation of agreements or settlement of grievances, union publications, social activities, death benefits for employees, and general organizing efforts. . . .

As the Court of Appeals pointed out, there is language in this Court's cases to support the validity of a rebate program. *Street* suggested "restitution to each individual employee of that portion of his money which the union expended, despite his notification, for the political causes to which he had advised the union he was opposed." . . . On the other hand, we suggested a more precise advance reduction scheme in *Railway Clerks v. Allen* . . . where we described a "practical decree" comprising a refund of exacted funds in the proportion that union political expenditures bore to total union expenditures and the reduction of future exactions by the same proportion.

Those opinions did not, nor did they purport to, pass upon the statutory or constitutional adequacy of the suggested remedies. Doing so now, we hold that the pure rebate approach is inadequate.

By exacting and using full dues, then refunding months later the portion that it was not allowed to exact in the first place, the union effectively charges the employees for activities that are outside the scope of the statutory authorization. The cost to the employee is, of course, much less than if the money was never returned, but this is a difference of degree only. The harm would be reduced were the union to pay interest on the amount refunded, but respondents did not do so. Even then the union obtains an involuntary loan for purposes to which the employee objects.

The only justification for this union borrowing would be administrative convenience. But there are readily available alternatives, such as advance reduction of dues and/or interest-bearing escrow accounts, that place only the slightest additional burden, if any, on the union. Given the existence of acceptable alternatives, the union cannot be allowed to commit dissenters' funds to improper uses even temporarily. A rebate scheme reduces but does not eliminate the statutory violation. . . .

[W]e turn to the particular expenditures for which petitioners insist they may not be charged.

1. Conventions. Every four years, BRAC holds a national convention at which the members elect officers, establish bargaining goals and priorities, and formulate overall union policy. We have very little trouble in holding that petitioners must help defray the costs of these conventions. Surely if a union is to perform its statutory functions, it must maintain its corporate or associational existence, must elect officers to manage and carry on its affairs, and may consult its members about overall bargaining goals and policy. Conventions such as those at issue here are normal events about which Congress was thoroughly informed and seem to us to be essential to the union's discharge of its duties as bargaining agent. As the Court of Appeals pointed out, convention "activities guide the union's approach to collective bargaining and are directly related to its effectiveness in negotiating labor agreements." In fact, like all national unions, BRAC is required to hold either a referendum or a convention at least every five years for the election of officers. We cannot fault it for choosing to elect its officers at a convention rather than by referendum.

2. Social Activities. Approximately 0.7% of Grand Lodge expenditures go toward purchasing refreshments for union business meetings and occasional social activities. These activities are formally open to nonmember employees. Petitioners insist that these expenditures are entirely unrelated to the union's function as

collective-bargaining representative and therefore could not be charged to them. While these affairs are not central to collective bargaining, they are sufficiently related to it to be charged to all employees. As the Court of Appeals noted, "[t]hese small expenditures are important to the union's members because they bring about harmonious working relationships, promote closer ties among employees, and create a more pleasant environment for union meetings." . . .

3. Publications. The Grand Lodge puts out a monthly magazine, the Railway Clerk/interchange, paid for out of the union treasury. The magazine's contents are varied and include articles about negotiations, contract demands, strikes, unemployment and health benefits, proposed or recently enacted legislation, general news, products the union is boycotting, and recreational and social activities. . . . The Court of Appeals found that the magazine "is the union's primary means of communicating information concerning collective bargaining, contract administration, and employees' rights to employees represented by BRAC." Under the union's rebate policy, objecting employees are not charged for that portion of the magazine devoted to "political causes." The rebate is figured by calculating the number of lines that are devoted to political issues as a proportion of the total number of lines.

The union must have a channel for communicating with the employees, including the objecting ones, about its activities. Congress can be assumed to have known that union funds go toward union publications; it is an accepted and basic union activity. . . . The magazine is important to the union in carrying out its representational obligations and a reasonable way of reporting to its constituents.

Respondents' limitation on the publication costs charged objecting employees is an important one, however. If the union cannot spend dissenters' funds for a particular activity, it has no justification for spending their funds for writing about that activity. By the same token, the Act surely allows it to charge objecting employees for reporting to them about those activities it can charge them for doing.

4. Organizing. The Court of Appeals found that organizing expenses could be charged to objecting employees because organizing efforts are aimed toward a stronger union, which in turn would be more successful at the bargaining table. Despite this attenuated connection with collective bargaining, we think such expenditures are outside Congress' authorization. Several considerations support this conclusion.

First, the notion that § 2, Eleventh would be a tool for the expansion of overall union power appears nowhere in the legislative history. . . . "Nor was any claim seriously advanced that the union shop was necessary to hold or increase union membership." Street, 367 U.S., at 763, n. 13. . . . Thus, organizational efforts were not what Congress aimed to enhance by authorizing the union shop.

Second, where a union shop provision is in place and enforced, all employees in the relevant unit are already organized. By definition, therefore, organizing expenses are spent on employees outside the collective-bargaining unit already represented. Using dues exacted from an objecting employee to recruit members among workers outside the bargaining-unit can afford only the most attenuated benefits to collective bargaining on behalf of the dues payer.

Third, the free-rider rationale does not extend this far. The image of the smug, self-satisfied nonmember, stirring up resentment by enjoying benefits earned through other employees' time and money, is completely out of place when it comes to the union's overall organizing efforts. If one accepts that what is good for the union is good for the employees, a proposition petitioners would strenuously deny, then it may be that employees will ultimately ride for free on the union's organizing efforts outside the bargaining unit. But the free rider Congress had in mind was the employee the union was required to represent and from whom it could not withhold benefits obtained for its members. Nonbargaining unit organizing is not directed at that employee. Organizing money is spent on people who are not union members, and only in the most distant way works to the benefit of those already paying dues. Any free-rider problem here is roughly comparable to that resulting from union contributions to pro-labor political candidates. As we observed in Street, that is a far cry from the free-rider problem with which Congress was concerned.

5. Litigation. The expenses of litigation incident to negotiating and administering the contract or to settling grievances and disputes arising in the bargaining unit are clearly chargeable to petitioners as a normal incident of the duties of the exclusive representative. The same is true of fair representation litigation arising within the unit, of jurisdictional disputes with other unions, and of any other litigation before agencies or in the courts that concerns bargaining-unit employees and is normally conducted by the exclusive representative. The expenses of litigation not having such a connection with the bargaining-unit are not to be charged to objecting employees. Contrary to the view of the Court of Appeals, therefore, unless the Western Airlines bargaining unit is directly concerned, objecting employees need not share the costs of the union's challenge to the legality of the airline industry mutual aid pact; of litigation seeking to protect the rights of airline employees generally during bankruptcy proceedings; or of defending suits alleging violation of the nondiscrimination requirements of Title VII of the Civil Rights Act of 1964. . . .

Notes

1. Is *Ellis* convincing as to each of the five categories of union activities it discusses? Consider especially the category of union organizing, discussed further in subsection 1, *infra*. Is increasing union density unrelated to a local union's ability to negotiate better contracts?

2. *Ellis* held that a pure rebate procedure was unacceptable. It suggested instead "advance reduction of dues and/or interest-bearing escrow accounts." How, specifically, would such a system work? *See* subsection 2, *infra*.

Ellis remains a leading precedent on chargeability for the issues it discusses, but some more recent developments are worth noting.

Despite *Ellis*, the NLRB has found that some expenses relating to organizing are chargeable. In *Meijer, Inc.*, 329 N.L.R.B. 730 (1999), *enforcement denied in part sub nom. Food and Commercial Workers v. NLRB*, 284 F.3d 1099 (9th Cir.), *modified*, 307 F.3d 760 (9th Cir. 2002), the Clinton Board held that expenses for organizing employees in the same competitive market were chargeable, and the Ninth Circuit upheld this ruling. In *Meijer*, the local union involved was in a grocery store in Colorado, and the expenses at issue helped fund organizing campaigns in similar stores in the same geographical region. As to *Ellis* (which had found that organizing expenses were non-chargeable), the Board in *Meijer* made two points. First, it was not bound by RLA precedent in NLRA cases (which is unusual in agency fee cases, and interesting given that *Beck* was decided explicitly on RLA precedent). Second, the Board in *Meijer* relied on specific expert testimony that a greater percentage of unionization in this particular industry had raised wages in the industry, a fact not present in *Ellis*.

The Bush Board then narrowed this rule in ***Teamsters Local 75 (Schreiber Foods)***, 349 N.L.R.B. 77 (2007). *Schreiber Foods* held that for organizing expenses for other employers in the same competitive market to be chargeable, there must be specific evidence showing "a direct, positive relationship between the wage levels of union-represented employees and the level of organization of employees of employers in the same competitive market." 349 N.L.R.B. at 77. With that standard, the Board rejected the ALJ's finding that the expenses were chargeable. In *Schreiber Foods*, an expert testified that general principles of labor economics indicated that organizing other production and maintenance employees in Green Bay, Wisconsin would help the unit of production and maintenance employees in Green Bay at issue, in part because of the local labor market was relatively small. This was not sufficiently specific for the Board. The D.C. Circuit enforced this part of the Board's order in *Pirlott v. NLRB*, 522 F.3d 423 (D.C. Cir. 2008).

In *Schreiber Foods*, member Schaumber concurred but argued that *Meijer* should be overruled entirely. In contrast, member Leibman dissented in part, arguing that *Meijer* controlled the case and that general economic evidence was enough to make the expenses chargeable. It is likely the Board will revisit this issue. What is the best rule for organizing expenses?

After *Ellis*, the Supreme Court's next detailed decision on chargeable expenses was ***Lehnert v. Ferris Faculty Ass'n***, 500 U.S. 507 (1991). While this was a public-sector case, its rules almost certainly apply to the NLRA (albeit not to the public sector post-*Janus*). Most broadly, in *Lehnert*, the Court formulated a three-part test. To be chargeable, activities must: (1) be "germane" to collective-bargaining activity; (2) be justified by the government's vital interest in labor peace and avoiding free riders; and (3) not significantly add to the burdening of free speech. *Id.* at 507

Applying this test, *Lehnert* held that a local teachers' union could charge objectors their share of costs associated with chargeable activities of the union's state and national affiliates, even if those activities were not performed for the direct benefit of the local bargaining unit, if some indication existed that the activities might inure to the benefit of the local. So, the local could charge objectors expenses for the "Teacher's Voice," a publication of the local's state body (the Michigan Education Association), to the extent it contained information on collective bargaining, as well as portions of the publication concerning the teaching profession generally. Also chargeable were "program expenditures" of the local's parent body (the National Education Association), even if spent in states other than Michigan, since they were for the benefit of all NEA members and were not political in nature. The court stressed that the point of affiliation is that the parent union bodies will use their resources (financial, political, and informational) to help locals. Still, not all payments to parent bodies would be chargeable, and the union has the burden to show what proportion is. Intriguingly, the court found that the costs of preparing for a strike were chargeable, even though the strike itself would have been illegal under Michigan law. The Court observed that Michigan law did not prohibit strike *preparation*, and agreed with the Court of Appeals that such preparation was "within the range of reasonable bargaining tools available to a public sector union during contract negotiations." *Id*. at 531. On the other hand, the court held that objectors could not be charged for lobbying, electoral, or other union political activities outside the context of contract ratification or implementation; for a union program designed to secure funds for public education in Michigan; for portions of the Teacher's Voice that covered those efforts; or for public relations efforts designed to enhance the reputation of the teaching profession.

The Supreme Court returned to the topic of expenses of a national parent union in *Locke v. Karass*, 555 U.S. 207 (2009). In *Locke*, another pre-*Janus* public-sector case, the issue was costs of litigation conducted by the national union, which involved bargaining units other than the objectors' local. *Locke* held that such litigation expenses were chargeable if they met the *Lehnert* test for chargeability of national expenses (they relate to chargeable matters and the local may benefit from the litigation). Here, the expenses were chargeable, as there was a reciprocal benefit to the local. The local could receive help with litigation from the national union, thus benefitting from fees paid by employees in other locals.

The *Locke* opinion unanimously held that there was no reason to distinguish national litigation expenses from the other types of parent body and national union expenses it discussed in *Lehnert*. 555 U.S. 207, 208. Again, why are so many of these cases litigated all the way to the Supreme Court?

In *United Nurses and Allied Professionals*, 359 N.L.R.B. No. 42 (2012), the Board held, 3–1, that certain expenses for lobbying could be chargeable, "to the extent they are germane to collective bargaining, contract administration, or grievance adjustment." The majority reasoned that "lobbying, like litigation, is a means rather than an end — a strategic activity that a union undertakes to advance the interests of its members." Further, as with litigation and other funds spent by union bodies outside the local containing the objector, lobbying funds would still be chargeable if they were "reciprocal in nature": where the "contributing local reasonably expects other locals to contribute similarly . . . on behalf of the contributing local. . . ." This case did not define what types of lobbying expenses would and would not be related to collective bargaining, but rather invited briefs on the subject.

In 2019, the Trump Board reversed course, holding in a 2–1 decision that unions cannot charge non-members for any lobbying expenses. *United Nurses and Allied Professionals (Kent Hospital)*, 367 N.L.R.B. No. 94 (Mar. 1, 2019). *Kent Hospital* also held that unions must provide objectors with audit verification letters to support their agency fee calculations.

Following the Board's decision in *Kent Hospital*, the Board's General Counsel issued a memorandum making it easier for represented workers to file complaints with the NLRB about unions' chargeability calculations. Memorandum GC 19-06 (Apr. 29, 2019). The General Counsel wrote "we will no longer require agency fee objectors to explain why a particular expenditure is nonchargeable and to provide evidence or promising leads to support that contention." The GC also emphasized that "the Region should bear in mind that it is the union's burden to establish that the expenses it has charged to nonmember objectors are germane to collective bargaining, contract administration, and grievance handling."

These cases raise interesting questions about the relationship between "politics" and "collective bargaining" in the private sector. First, imagine you were submitting briefs in *United Nurses and Allied Professionals*. What sorts of lobbying activities (if any) should be considered "related to collective bargaining" under the NLRA? Of course, the Court's decisions in *Knox*, *Harris*, and *Janus* involved discussion of the relationship between politics and collective bargaining in the public sector. How did those concerns play into the Court's analysis in those cases? What (if any) are the major differences between unions' political involvement in the public and private sectors?

2. Procedures

None of the cases above provided detailed guidance as to exactly what procedures objectors and unions must or may use to assert their rights or fulfill their obligations under *Beck*. *Marquez* indicated that unions should give bargaining-unit members specific information about *Beck* rights apart from general contract language. *Ellis* explained that unions could not use a rebate procedure, and instead suggested an advance reduction of dues or an escrow account.

The Supreme Court set out general guidelines for procedures in ***Chicago Teachers Union, Local No. 1 v. Hudson***, 475 U.S. 292 (1986). In *Hudson*, a teachers' union had determined that five percent of its dues were nonchargeable. It notified teachers that if they objected to the amount, they could appeal, first to the union's executive committee, then to the union's executive board, and finally to an arbitrator selected by the union president from a list maintained by the Illinois Board of Education. Objections could be made only after the amounts were deducted from their paychecks pursuant to a dues check-off provision. After objecting teachers brought this case, the union modified the procedure to provide that one hundred percent of an objector's dues would be placed into an interest-bearing escrow account pending determinations on objections. The union provided information about the procedure in its publications.

Hudson held that this procedure was inadequate. The Court first held that taking an objector's money, even if providing a future rebate, did not insure against the union using the money for objectionable purposes. Second, the union had not provided nonmembers with adequate information as to the union had calculated chargeability figures and, relatedly, the union had failed to place the burden of proof as to chargeability on the itself. Specifically, the union had only explained why five percent of union expenses were nonchargeable, not why ninety-five percent were chargeable. The Court did, however, signal its approval of an escrow arrangement, and it indicated that putting all one hundred percent of an objector's fees into escrow would not be required in a valid system.

> We need not hold, however, that a 100% escrow is constitutionally required. Such a remedy has the serious defect of depriving the Union of access to some escrowed funds that it is unquestionably entitled to retain. If, for example, the original disclosure by the Union had included a certified public accountant's verified breakdown of expenditures, including some categories that no dissenter could reasonably challenge, there would be no reason to escrow the portion of the nonmember's fees that would be represented by those categories. On the record before us, there is no reason to believe that anything approaching a 100% "cushion" to cover the possibility of mathematical errors would be constitutionally required. Nor can we decide how the proper contribution that might be made by an independent audit, in advance, coupled with adequate notice, might reduce the size of any appropriate escrow. 475 U.S. at 310.

Without offering any further details, the Court concluded:

> We hold today that the constitutional requirements for the Union's collection of agency fees include an adequate explanation of the basis for the fee, a reasonably prompt opportunity to challenge the amount of the fee before an impartial decisionmaker, and an escrow for the amounts reasonably in dispute while such challenges are pending. *Id.*

Following *Hudson*, The NLRB addressed several important procedural issues in **California Saw and Knife Works**, 320 N.L.R.B. 224 (1995), *enforced sub nom. Int'l Ass'n of Machinists v. NLRB*, 133 F.3d 1012 (7th Cir. 1998). First, the Board discussed a challenge to the method by which the union locals of the International Association of Machinists (IAM) informed bargaining-unit members of their rights under *Beck*. The Board explained:

> The General Counsel alleges that the IAM's *Beck* policy violates Section 8(b)(1)(A) of the Act by failing to provide adequate notification to nonmember employees of their right under *Beck* to object to the expenditure

of dues money for activities unrelated to collective bargaining, contract administration, and grievance adjustment.

First, it is alleged that the IAM's publication notice of its *Beck* policy in the annual December issue of the Machinist is unlawful, because the cover of the publication does not specifically alert nonmembers that the IAM's *Beck* policy is contained therein. Second, the General Counsel alleges that the IAM unlawfully fails to issue additional *Beck* notice—apart from publication notice in the Machinist—to two subgroups of nonmember employees: (1) to newly hired nonmember employees at the time they are hired into the bargaining unit; and (2) to newly resigned nonmember employees when they resign their union membership. . . .

We find . . . that if a union seeks to apply a union-security clause to unit employees, it has an obligation under the duty of fair representation to notify them of their *Beck* rights before they become subject to obligations under the clause. We further find, however, that a union does not have an obligation under the duty of fair representation to issue an additional notice of *Beck* rights to new nonmember employees at the time they resign their union membership.

We further find, in this case, that the Union has an obligation under the duty of fair representation to give *Beck* rights notice to (1) newly hired nonmember employees at the time the Union seeks to obligate these newly hired employees to pay dues and (2) currently employed employees at the time they become nonmembers if these currently employed employees have not been sent a copy of the December issue of the Machinist. We find, however, that the Union has otherwise met its obligations under the duty of fair representation by including its *Beck* policy in the December issue of the Machinist, which, as noted above, the Union mails to all unit employees, and that it did not breach its duty of fair representation by failing to note on the cover of the December Machinist that its *Beck* policy was contained therein. 320 N.L.R.B. 224, 231.

Second, the Board upheld in principle a procedure in which all objections must be filed in a thirty-day "window period" that took place once a year. In the instant case, the Board held that a thirty-day period consisting of the month of January was invalid, but invalid solely as to employees who resigned their membership after the January window period, because it compelled the objector to continue to pay full dues even though not a member and therefore was an arbitrary restriction on the right to resign union membership. 320 N.L.R.B. at 236.

Third, the Board invalidated the union's requirement that objections be sent by certified mail, with each objection in an individual envelope, as unnecessarily burdensome. *Id.* at 236–37.

Fourth, the Board held that the union had given objectors sufficient information to determine whether to challenge the dues reduction calculation.

The IAM's *Beck* policy provides that, upon the receipt of an objection, the IAM sends the objector information detailing the percentage reduction in dues based on the previous year's expenses, as well as a summary of the major categories of expenditures, showing how the reduction was calculated. Since 1990, the IAM has further provided objectors with a summary of the District and Local Lodge surveys that comprise the District and Local portion of the dues reduction. The IAM does not, however, provide objectors with the supporting schedules mentioned in the summary of District and Local Lodge surveys, nor the IAM's audit protocol on which it relies to determine chargeability.

Following receipt of the above-described information, the objector has 30 days within which to file a challenge to the IAM's dues-reduction calculations. All charges are thereafter consolidated in a single arbitral proceeding, wherein the IAM bears the burden of justifying its dues-reduction calculations before an arbitrator chosen through the American Arbitration Association's Rules for Impartial Determination of Union Fees.

The General Counsel argues that the information disclosed to objectors is unlawfully insufficient because it does not include the supporting schedules and audit protocol described above. We do not agree. The summary of the surveys of District and Local Lodge expenditures provided to all objectors since 1990 discloses the major categories of union expenditures. The judge correctly observed that courts that have considered the information to be provided objectors in the public sector context require only that the union's major categories of expenditures be disclosed.

We adopt this standard, and find that the IAM's provision of information disclosing the major categories of union expenditures provides sufficient information to enable objectors to determine whether to challenge the dues-reduction calculations, and accordingly satisfies the duty of fair representation. . . .

The information provided to objectors sets forth certain "mixed" categories of expenditures which may include both chargeable or nonchargeable items. It discloses that certain categories of expenses, such as human rights, community services, and special projects, are deemed partially chargeable, but further explanation is not supplied. The judge found that the mixed category information provided to objectors need not be further explained in order to satisfy the requirements of *Beck*.

The General Counsel and the Charging Parties have excepted to this finding. They essentially contend that categories of expenditures contained in the information provided to objectors must be self-evident from their labeling as either representational or nonrepresentational, or otherwise greater disclosure is required.

We agree with the judge that the IAM's policy with respect to mixed categories is neither arbitrary, discriminatory, nor undertaken in bad faith. The judge correctly warned of the potential for unlawful manipulation by a union hiding nonchargeable expenses in such mixed categories. The judge recognized that there is no contention in this proceeding, however, that the mixed categories were unreasonably large so as to suggest that the IAM was attempting to hide nonchargeable expenses in these mixed categories. Absent such an allegation of manipulation, we agree with the judge that the *limited* use of mixed categories does not breach the duty of fair representation where, as here, the union clearly discloses the major categories of expenditures. *Id.* at 239–40.

Fifth, the Board upheld the union's practice of having in-house auditors (as opposed to independent certified auditors) perform the initial audits of local and regional union bodies from which unions calculated their dues-reduction percentages. *Id.* at 240–42. However, the D.C. Circuit later rejected this holding. In *Ferriso v. NLRB*, 125 F.3d 865, 870–71 (1997), that court held that an independent audit was the "minimal guarantee of the trustworthiness" of the union's calculations.

Sixth, the Board declined to require unions to pay the travel costs of objectors who were attending arbitration hearings challenging the union's dues. *Id.* at 242–43.

As to arbitration hearings to resolve agency fee objections, in *Air Line Pilots Ass'n v. Miller*, 523 U.S. 866 (1998) (three years after *California Saw and Knife*), the Supreme Court held that an agency fee procedure could not require objectors to litigate their claims in an arbitration proceeding; objectors had a right to go directly to court with these claims if they wished. "[A]rbitration is a matter of contract and a party cannot be required to submit to arbitration any dispute which he has not agreed so to submit." 523 U.S. 866, 876. Thus, plaintiffs in agency fee suits, like plaintiffs in DFR suits, have the option (relatively unusual in labor law) to go directly to court.

Most recently, in **Knox v. Service Employees Int'l Union, Local 1000**, 132 S. Ct. 2277 (2012), the Supreme Court held that if a union imposes a mid-year dues increase for political purposes, it must send out a new "*Hudson* notice" to non-member objectors allowing them to make objections to the assessment. In addition, the Court held that objectors could not be required to "opt out" of the non-chargeable portions of such an assessment; to be charged, they would have to "opt in." (*Knox* is discussed earlier in this chapter.)

Notes

1. After reading the above section, were you advising a union, how exactly would you design the procedures for *Beck* objections? What information would you recommend the union include in its initial *Beck* notice? *See United Food & Commercial Workers Int'l Union, Local 700*, 361 N.L.R.B. No. 39 (2014) (holding that a union does not violate the DFR by failing to include in the initial *Beck* notice the specific

amount of dues reduction that would follow a union member's decision to resign from the union and object to paying for non-chargeable expenses).

2. In *Hudson*, the monthly dues for teachers were $17.35; for other covered employees fees were $12.15. 475 U.S. 292, 295. Assuming the union was correct that it spent five percent of its dues income on non-chargeable activities, that means that a teacher could legally object to (and thus be refunded) less than 87 cents per month: a total of $10.41 per year. For other employees, the total would be $7.29 per year.

Such figures are not uncommon, and in some cases, the amount is even less. In the more recent *Locke v. Karass, supra*, the total non-chargeable expenses were only $1.34 per month per employee, and the portion of that attributable to national litigation, the only issue in the case, was "considerably less." 555 U.S. 207, 212. Again, why are so many of these cases litigated to the Supreme Court?

3. For unions, the costs of agency-fee payer rules are not so much in the dues they may not collect: unions generally spend the clear majority of their dues income on chargeable activities, and usually only a small minority of bargaining-unit members are objectors. Rather, the high costs for unions typically come in administering the procedures. Consider the time and resources it takes to calculate what percentage of union funds (broken down into a wide variety of categories) are spent on chargeable vs. non-chargeable activities, employ independent auditors, defend agency fee litigation, etc. As just one example, consider the rule that union publications are chargeable in the proportion that they discuss chargeable activities, but not chargeable in the proportion they discuss, say, politics. This means a union must calculate the proportions (count lines) of its publications that discuss different types of topics. Nor can unions avoid most of these expenses by simply avoiding non-chargeable activities. *Hudson* makes it clear that the union bears the burden of proof to show that its chargeable activities were in fact chargeable.

4. Presidents Obama and George W. Bush each issued executive orders mandating that some employers post notices informing employees of certain rights. Perhaps not surprisingly, the rights involved differed with the two presidents. On February 17, 2001, President Bush signed Executive Order 13201, which required certain government contractors to post notices informing employees of their rights under *General Motors* and *Beck*. *UAW-Labor Employment and Training Corp. v. Chao*, 325 F.3d 360 (D.C. Cir. 2003), held that the NLRA did not pre-empt President Bush's Order. President Obama, on January 30, 2009, rescinded this order and substituted Executive Order 13496, which required certain government contractors to post notices informing employees of their rights to join (as well as not join) a union. Note how soon after their inaugurations both these acts were.

Trade groups challenged the Department of Labor rule that resulted from President Obama's executive order, arguing that the posting requirement violated employers' First Amendment rights against compelled speech, the Administrative Procedures Act, and the NLRA. The District Court rejected all of these arguments. *Nat'l Ass'n of Mfrs. v. Perez*, 2015 U.S. Dist. LEXIS 60467 (D.D.C. May 7, 2015).

G. Statutory Developments in the Public Sector

Sometimes jurisdictions change their statutory rules regarding agency fees. Perhaps not surprisingly, such changes can result in Supreme Court litigation.

In *Ysursa v. Pocatello Education Association*, 555 U.S. 353 (2009), the union challenged an amendment to Idaho's right-to-work law, which barred employees from authorizing payroll deductions for a union's political action fund, in addition to union dues.[13] The lower courts upheld the ban as applied to state employees (based on the cost to the state), but struck down the ban for private and local government employees. On appeal, the Supreme Court upheld the limits on local government as well as state government employees.

> The First Amendment prohibits government from "abridging the freedom of speech"; it does not confer an affirmative right to use government payroll mechanisms for the purpose of obtaining funds for expression. Idaho's law does not restrict political speech, but rather declines to promote that speech by allowing public employee checkoffs for political activities. Such a decision is reasonable in light of the State's interest in avoiding the appearance that carrying out the public's business is tainted by partisan political activity. That interest extends to government at the local as well as state level, and nothing in the First Amendment prevents a State from determining that its political subdivisions may not provide payroll deductions for political activities. 555 U.S. at 355.

The wave of state statutes passed in 2011 restricting public-sector collective-bargaining rights included some significant changes in this area. For example, for the unions it applies to, Act 10 in Wisconsin makes it illegal for an employer to agree to dues deduction for employees who wish to pay dues.

Problem 14.1

Even before *Janus*, Nebraska's public-sector statute had an interesting variation. While the statute generally contains right-to-work rules, it adds the following, in Neb. Rev. Stat. §48-838(4):

> Any employee may choose his or her own representative in any grievance or legal action regardless of whether or not an exclusive collective-bargaining agent has been certified. If an employee who is not a member of the labor organization chooses to have legal representation from the labor organization in any grievance or legal action, such employee shall reimburse the labor organization for his or her pro rata share of the actual legal fees and

---

13. Many union contracts contain "dues check-off clauses." These clauses do not independently obligate employees to pay any dues, but rather obligate the employer—for those employees either required to pay dues under a union security clause or voluntarily paying dues in a right-to-work jurisdiction—to automatically deduct the dues payments from the employee's check and forward the payments to the union.

court costs incurred by the labor organization in representing the employee in such grievance or legal action.

What was the likely purpose of this provision? What would you predict would be the practical effect? Is it good policy?

V. A Note on the Labor Management Reporting and Disclosure Act

Because this casebook focuses mainly on labor-management relations, it does not describe the LMRDA in detail. Students should be aware, however, that this 1959 law provides detailed regulation of internal union governance and affirmative rights for union members in union affairs. Title I contains a "bill of rights" for union members *vis-a-vis* their unions. Title II contains reporting and disclosure requirements for unions and their officers (and also for certain employers and "employer persuaders"). Title III regulates "trusteeships" (when unions impose special controls on subordinate union bodies). Title IV covers elections of union officers. Title V imposes fiduciary duties on union officials. Title VI grants investigative power to the Secretary of Labor and bars retaliation against those who exercise rights under the LMRDA.

Thus, for example, Title I gives union members the rights to free speech in union meetings, to run for union office, to approve dues increases through direct votes or delegate conventions, to due process in disciplinary hearings, to a copy of their CBA, and to sue their unions. Title II requires every union to have a constitution and bylaws and to file them with the Department of Labor. It also requires detailed financial disclosure forms. Title III permits trusteeships only for one of four purposes: to correct local corruption or financial malpractice; to assure performance of the CBA or related duties; to restore democratic procedures; or to otherwise carry out "the legitimate objects of such organization." After eighteen months, a trusteeship must end absent proof that its continuation is necessary. Title IV, among other things, requires unions to hold elections for officers at certain intervals (three to five years, depending on the type of labor organization), requires elections to be held by secret ballot, and allows only "reasonable requirements, uniformly imposed" on eligibility to run for union office.

The LMRDA generally does not apply to a union that consists solely of government employees. But it does apply to union members who are employees of the federal government. 5 U.S.C. § 7120. It also applies to national unions that have local affiliates that represent private-sector employees. 29 U.S.C. § 402(i).

Chapter 15

Bargaining Relationships in Transition

I. Introduction

Changes in business ownership raise questions about the new entity's legal obligations under the NLRA, especially if the prior employer (predecessor) had a bargaining relationship and/or a collective bargaining agreement with a union. Specifically, under what circumstances, if any, is the new (successor) employer obliged to recognize the union that represented employees at the predecessor? Under what circumstances, if any, must the successor assume the CBA of the predecessor (including the obligation to arbitrate disputes under that CBA)? And under what circumstances, if any, is the successor liable for ULPs committed by the predecessor?

The Supreme Court attempted to answer these questions in a series of cases discussed below. Notwithstanding this body of precedent, some aspects of the law in this area remain murky. This chapter reviews these cases, examining both the relevant rules and policies undergirding the rules. It will then discuss some special rules governing debtor-employers who allegedly committed ULPs but who have filed a bankruptcy petition. Finally, it will touch on successorship issues when a unionized public employer contracts out work to a private employer. Bankruptcy in the public sector was discussed in Chapter 11, Section III-B-3-c-(ii).

II. Successorship in the Private Sector

To understand successorship, it is necessary to recall the various bars—the certification-year bar, the recognition bar, and the contract bar—that Chapter 7 discussed. Remember that, under the certification-year bar, a union, once certified by the Board after an election, enjoys an irrebuttable presumption of majority status for a year. Once the year expires, the union enjoys only a rebuttable presumption of majority status, unless a contract bar is in place. Under the contract bar, a union enjoys an irrebuttable presumption of majority status during the term of a CBA, up to three years, with limited window periods during which that presumption is rebuttable. As discussed in Chapter 7, where an employer voluntarily recognizes a majority union, the Board recently promulgated a rule reinstating the rule of *Dana Corp.*, 351 N.L.R.B. 434, 434 (2007), revising the recognition bar by creating a decertification window for the first 45 days after recognition. Once the recognition bar or contract bar expires, the union again enjoys only a rebuttable presumption of majority status. These presumptions are the basis of the employer's duty to recognize and bargain with the union.

A. What Is a Successor and What Are Its Legal Obligations Under the NLRA?

In the following case, the Supreme Court examined two questions. First, was the successor employer required to recognize and bargain with the union that existed at the predecessor employer? Second, was the successor employer bound to honor the CBA that the union and the predecessor had executed?

NLRB v. Burns International Security Services, Inc.

Supreme Court of the United States
406 U.S. 272 (1972)

WHITE, J.

The Wackenhut Corp. provided protection services at the Lockheed plant for five years before Burns International Security Services, Inc. took over this task. On Feb. 28, 1967, a few months before the changeover of guard employers, a majority of the Wackenhut guards selected the [United Plant Guard Workers of America (UPG or the union)] as their exclusive bargaining representative in a Board election after Wackenhut and the union had agreed that the Lockheed plant was the appropriate bargaining unit. On March 8, the Regional Director certified the union as the exclusive bargaining representative for these employees, and, on April 29, Wackenhut and the union entered into a three-year collective-bargaining agreement.

Meanwhile, since Wackenhut's one-year service agreement to provide security protection was due to expire on June 30, Lockheed had called for bids from various companies supplying these services, and both Burns and Wackenhut submitted estimates. At a pre-bid conference attended by Burns [on May 15], a representative of Lockheed informed the bidders that Wackenhut's guards were represented by the union, that the union had recently won a Board election and been certified, and that there was . . . a collective-bargaining contract between Wackenhut and the union. Lockheed then accepted Burns' bid, and on May 31 Wackenhut was notified that Burns would assume responsibility for protection services on July 1. Burns chose to retain 27 of the Wackenhut guards, and it brought in 15 of its own guards from other Burns locations. [Burns employed a total of 42 guards.]

During June, when Burns hired the 27 Wackenhut guards, it supplied them with membership cards of the American Federation of Guards (AFG), another union with which Burns had collective-bargaining contracts at other locations, and informed them that they had to become AFG members to work for Burns, that they would not receive uniforms otherwise, and that Burns "could not live with" the existing contract between Wackenhut and the union. On June 29, Burns recognized the AFG on the theory that it had obtained a card majority. On July 12, however, the UPG demanded that Burns recognize it as the bargaining representative of Burns' employees at Lockheed and that Burns honor the collective-bargaining agreement between it and Wackenhut. When Burns refused, the UPG filed unfair labor practice charges. . . .

The Board . . . held that Burns had violated §§ 8(a)(2) and 8(a)(1) . . . by unlawfully recognizing and assisting the AFG, a rival of the UPG; and that it had violated §§ 8(a)(5) and 8(a)(1) by failing to recognize and bargain with the UPG and by refusing to honor the CBA that had been negotiated between Wackenhut and UPG.

Burns did not contest the § 8(a)(2) unlawful assistance finding . . . but sought review of the unit determination and the order to bargain and [to] observe the collective-bargaining contract. The Court of Appeals accepted the Board's unit determination and enforced the Board's order insofar as it related to the [§ 8(a)(2) and the refusal to bargain] findings . . . but held that the Board had exceeded its powers in ordering Burns to honor the contract executed by Wackenhut. . . .

The trial examiner . . . found, inter alia, that Burns "had in its employ a majority of Wackenhut's former employees," and that these employees had already expressed their choice of a bargaining representative in an election held a short time before. Burns was therefore held to have a duty to bargain, which arose when it selected as its work force the employees of the previous employer to perform the same tasks at the same place they had worked in the past.

The Board . . . accepted the trial examiner's findings and conclusions with respect to the duty to bargain, and we see no basis for setting them aside. In an election held but a few months before, the union had been designated bargaining agent for the employees in the unit and a majority of these employees had been hired by Burns for work in the identical unit. It is undisputed that Burns knew all the relevant facts in this regard and was aware of the certification and of the existence of a collective-bargaining contract. In these circumstances, it was not unreasonable for the Board to conclude that the union certified to represent all employees in the unit still represented a majority of the employees and that Burns could not reasonably have entertained a good-faith doubt about that fact. Burns' obligation to bargain with the union over terms and conditions of employment stemmed from its hiring of Wackenhut's employees and from the recent election and Board certification. It has been consistently held that a mere change of employers or of ownership in the employing industry is not such an "unusual circumstance" as to affect the force of the Board's certification within the normal operative period if a majority of employees after the change of ownership or management were employed by the preceding employer. . . .

It goes without saying, of course, that Burns was not entitled to upset what it should have accepted as an established union majority by soliciting representation cards for another union and thereby committing the unfair labor practice of which it was found guilty by the Board. . . .

It would be a wholly different case if the Board had determined that because Burns' operational structure and practices differed from those of Wackenhut, the Lockheed bargaining unit was no longer an appropriate one. . . . But where the bargaining unit remains unchanged and a majority of the employees hired by the new employer are represented by a recently certified bargaining agent there is little basis for faulting the Board's implementation of the express mandates of § 8(a)(5) and § 9(a) by ordering the employer to bargain with the incumbent union. . . .

It does not follow, however, from Burns' duty to bargain that it was bound to observe the substantive terms of the collective-bargaining contract the union had negotiated with Wackenhut and to which Burns had in no way agreed. Section 8(d) of the Act expressly provides that the existence of such bargaining obligation "does not compel either party to agree to a proposal or require the making of a concession." Congress has consistently declined to interfere with free collective bargaining and has preferred that device, or voluntary arbitration, to the imposition of compulsory terms as a means of avoiding or terminating labor disputes. . . .

These considerations . . . underlay the Board's prior decisions, which until now have consistently held that, although successor employers may be bound to recognize and bargain with the union, they are not bound by the substantive provisions of a collective-bargaining contract negotiated by their predecessors but not agreed to or assumed by them. . . . "In none of the previous successorship cases has the Board ever reached that result. The successor has always been held merely to have the duty of bargaining with his predecessor's union."

The Board, however, has now departed from this view and argues that the same policies which mandate a continuity of bargaining obligation also require that successor employers be bound to the terms of a predecessor's collective-bargaining contract. It asserts that the stability of labor relations will be jeopardized and that employees will face uncertainty and a gap in the bargained-for terms and conditions of employment, as well as the possible loss of advantages gained by prior negotiations, unless the new employer is held to have assumed, as a matter of federal labor law, the obligations under the contract entered into by the former employer. Recognizing that under normal contract principles a party would not be bound to a contract in the absence of consent, the Board notes that in *John Wiley & Sons, Inc. v. Livingston*, 376 U.S. 543, 550 (1964), the Court declared that "a collective bargaining agreement is not an ordinary contract" but is, rather, an outline of the common law of a particular plant or industry. The Court held in *Wiley* that although the predecessor employer which had signed a collective-bargaining contract with the union had disappeared by merger with the successor, the union could compel the successor to arbitrate the extent to which the successor was obligated under the collective-bargaining agreement. The Board contends that the same factors that the Court emphasized in *Wiley*, the peaceful settlement of industrial conflicts and "protection (of) the employees (against) a sudden change in the employment relationship," *id.* at 549, require that Burns be treated under the collective-bargaining contract exactly as Wackenhut would have been if it had continued protecting the Lockheed plant.

We do not find *Wiley* controlling in the circumstances here. *Wiley* arose in the context of a § 301 suit to compel arbitration, not in the context of an unfair labor practice proceeding where the Board is expressly limited by the provisions of § 8(d). . . .

Here there was no merger or sale of assets, and there were no dealings whatsoever between Wackenhut and Burns. On the contrary, they were competitors for the same work, each bidding for the service contract at Lockheed. Burns purchased nothing from Wackenhut and became liable for none of its financial obligations. Burns merely hired enough of Wackenhut's employees to require it to bargain with the union as commanded by § 8(a)(5) and § 9(a). But this consideration is a wholly insufficient basis for implying either in fact or in law that Burns had agreed or must be held to have agreed to honor Wackenhut's collective-bargaining contract.

. . . Here, Burns had notice of the existence of the Wackenhut collective-bargaining contract, but it did not consent to be bound by it. The source of its duty to bargain with the union is not the collective-bargaining contract but the fact that it voluntarily took over a bargaining unit that was largely intact and that had been certified within the past year. Nothing in its actions, however, indicated that Burns was assuming the obligations of the contract, and "allowing the Board to compel agreement when the parties themselves are unable to agree would violate the fundamental premise on which the Act is based-private bargaining under governmental supervision of the procedure alone, without any official compulsion over the actual terms of the contract." *H. K. Porter Co. v. NLRB*, 397 U.S. at 108.

. . . [H]olding either the union or the new employer bound to the substantive terms of an old collective-bargaining contract may result in serious inequities. A potential employer may be willing to take over a moribund business only if he can make changes in corporate structure, composition of the labor force, work location, task assignment, and nature of supervision. Saddling such an employer with the terms and conditions of employment contained in the old collective-bargaining contract may make these changes impossible and may discourage and inhibit the transfer of capital. On the other hand, a union may have made concessions to a small or failing employer that it would be unwilling to make to a large or economically successful firm. The congressional policy manifest in the Act is to enable the parties to negotiate for any protection either deems appropriate, but to allow the balance of bargaining advantage to be set by economic power realities. Strife is bound to occur if the concessions that must be honored do not correspond to the relative economic strength of the parties.

The Board's position would also raise new problems, for the successor employer would be circumscribed in exactly the same way as the predecessor under the collective-bargaining contract. It would seemingly follow that employees of the predecessor would be deemed employees of the successor, dischargeable only in accordance with provisions of the contract and subject to the grievance and arbitration provisions thereof. Burns would not have been free to replace Wackenhut's guards with its own except as the contract permitted. Given the continuity of employment relationship, the pre-existing contract's provisions with respect to wages, seniority rights, vacation privileges, pension and retirement fund benefits, job security provisions, work assignments and the like would devolve on the successor. Nor would the union commit a §8(b)(3) unfair labor practice if it refused to bargain for a modification of the agreement effective prior to the expiration date of the agreement. A successor employer might also be deemed to have inherited its predecessor's pre-existing contractual obligations to the union that had accrued under past contracts and that had not been discharged when the business was transferred. "(A) successor may well acquire more liabilities as a result of *Burns* than appear on the face of a contract." Finally, a successor will be bound to observe the contract despite good-faith doubts about the union's majority during the time that the contract is a bar to another representation election.... For the above reasons, the Board itself has expressed doubts as to the general applicability of its *Burns* rule.

In many cases, of course, successor employers will find it advantageous not only to recognize and bargain with the union but also to observe the pre-existing contract rather than to face uncertainty and turmoil. Also, in a variety of circumstances involving a merger, stock acquisition, reorganization, or assets purchase, the Board might properly find as a matter of fact that the successor had assumed the obligations under the old contract.... Such a duty does not, however, ensue as a matter of law from the mere fact that an employer is doing the same work in the same place with the same employees as his predecessor, as the Board had recognized until its decision in the instant case.... We accordingly set aside the Board's finding of a §8(a)(5) unfair labor practice insofar as it rested on a conclusion that Burns was required to but did not honor the collective-bargaining contract executed by Wackenhut.

It therefore follows that the Board's order requiring Burns to "give retroactive effect to all the clauses of said (Wackenhut) contract, and ... make whole its employees for any losses suffered by reason of (Burns') refusal to honor, adopt and enforce said contract" must be set aside. We note that ... the Board's opinion stated that "(t)he obligation to bargain imposed on a successor-employer includes the negative injunction to refrain from unilaterally changing wages and other benefits established by a prior collective-bargaining agreement even though that agreement had expired. In this respect, the successor-employer's obligations are the same as those imposed upon employers generally during the period between collective-bargaining agreements." ... This statement by the Board is consistent with its prior and subsequent cases that hold that whether or not a successor employer is bound by its predecessor's contract, it must not institute terms and conditions of employment different from those provided in its predecessor's contract, at least without first bargaining with the employees' representative....

Although Burns had an obligation to bargain with the union concerning wages and other conditions of employment when the union requested it to do so, this case is not like a §8(a)(5) violation where an employer unilaterally changes a condition of employment without consulting a bargaining representative. It is difficult to understand how Burns could be said to have changed unilaterally any pre-existing term or condition of employment without bargaining when it had no previous relationship whatsoever to the bargaining unit and, prior to July 1, no outstanding terms and conditions of employment from which a change could be inferred. . . .

Although a successor employer is ordinarily free to set initial terms on which it will hire the employees of a predecessor, there will be instances in which it is perfectly clear that the new employer plans to retain all of the employees in the unit and in which it will be appropriate to have him initially consult with the employees' bargaining representative before he fixes terms. In other situations, however, it may not be clear until the successor employer has hired his full complement of employees that he has a duty to bargain with a union, since it will not be evident until then that the bargaining representative represents a majority of the employees in the unit as required by § 9(a) of the Act. Here, for example, Burns' obligation to bargain with the union did not mature until it had selected its force of guards late in June. The Board quite properly found that Burns refused to bargain on July 12 when it rejected the overtures of the union. It is true that the wages it paid when it began protecting the Lockheed plant on July 1 differed from those specified in the Wackenhut collective-bargaining agreement, but there is no evidence that Burns ever unilaterally changed the terms and conditions of employment it had offered to potential employees in June after its obligation to bargain with the union became apparent. If the union had made a request to bargain after Burns had completed its hiring and if Burns had negotiated in good faith and had made offers to the union which the union rejected, Burns could have unilaterally initiated such proposals as the opening terms and conditions of employment on July 1 without committing an unfair labor practice. *Cf. NLRB v. Katz*, 369 U.S. 736, 745, n. 12 (1962). . . . The Board's order requiring Burns to make whole its employees for any losses suffered by reason of Burns' refusal to honor and enforce the contract, cannot therefore be sustained on the ground that Burns unilaterally changed existing terms and conditions of employment, thereby committing an unfair labor practice which required monetary restitution in these circumstances. Affirmed.

Rehnquist, J., joined by The Chief Justice and Brennan, J. and Powell, J., concurring in part and dissenting in part, stated that they would enforce neither the bargaining obligation nor the contract assumption, and that the Board and the Court of Appeals had "stretched [the successorship] concept beyond the limits of its proper application." 406 U.S. 272, 296.

Notes

1. The Court in *Burns* refers to the Board's substantial continuity test. What is that test? What differences matter to the Court in *Burns*? Consider this question again after reading *Fall River Dyeing, infra*, which also discusses this test.

2. What is the Court's rationale for holding that a successor employer is usually not required to assume the predecessor's CBA? Is the rationale persuasive? Compare

this holding to the rule in the European Union's Acquired Rights Directive, which expressly mandates that successor employers must assume such contracts: "The transferor's [predecessor's] rights and obligations arising from a contract of employment or from an employment relationship existing on the date of a transfer shall, by reason of such transfer, be transferred to the transferee [successor]." E.U. Council Directive 2001/23, 2001 O.J. (L 082) 16-20 (EC), art. 3(1). Which rule better protects workers' rights? What are some of countervailing considerations?

3. *When would a successor employer be bound by its predecessor's CBA?* *Burns* explained that "there will be instances in which it is perfectly clear that the new employer plans to retain all of the employees in the unit and in which it will be appropriate to have him initially consult with the employees' bargaining representative before he fixes terms." This has come to be known as the "perfectly clear successor" doctrine. Shortly after *Burns*, the Board adopted a rule restricting the perfectly clear caveat "to circumstances in which the new employer has either actively or, by tacit inference, misled employees into believing they would all be retained without change in their wages, hours or conditions of employment, or at least to circumstances where the new employer . . . has failed to clearly announce its intent to establish a new set of conditions prior to inviting former employees to accept employment." *Spruce Up Corp.*, 209 N.L.R.B. 194, 195 (1974). *See Coastal Intern. Sec. Inc. v. NLRB*, 2009 U.S. App. LEXIS 7575 (5th Cir. Apr. 9, 2009) (affirming Board decision that an employer commits a ULP by unilaterally changing the training-period wage of newly hired employees under the predecessor-employer's CBA without providing opportunity for employees' union to bargain). Reviewing courts have upheld the Board's narrow interpretation of the perfectly clear caveat as reasonable, *see, e.g., S&F Market Street Healthcare LLC v. NLRB*, 570 F.3d 354, 359 (D.C. Cir. 2009); *but see Canteen Corp. v. NLRB*, 103 F.3d 1355, 1362 (7th Cir. 1997) (questioning the vitality of the *Spruce Up* doctrine). Does the *Spruce Up* exception to the *Burns* "perfectly clear" caveat make sense?

In *Creative Vision Resources, L.L.C. v. NLRB*, 882 F.3d 510, 526 (5th Cir. 2018) the court, in agreement with the Board, held that a union bargaining demand is not necessary to trigger bargaining in the case of perfectly clear successors.

4. Distinguish a *Burns* successor—an employer that is obligated to bargain with the employees' representative but not bound to assume the predecessor's CBA—from an "alter ego" under labor law. An alter ego employer must both recognize the union and assume the CBA from the allegedly previous employer.

The Board's alter ego doctrine developed in the context of determining whether one business entity should be legally responsible for another business entity's ULPs. Notably, it is much more lenient than corporate alter ego law, which developed in the context of determining whether the court should pierce the corporate veil to hold a shareholder liable for a corporation's conduct. *Compare Southport Petroleum Co. v. NLRB*, 315 U.S. 100, 106 (1942) (an alter ego is "merely a disguised continuance of the old employer"), *and Howard Johnson Co., Inc. v. Detroit Local Joint Executive Bd.*, 417 U.S. 249, 259 n.5 (1974) (alter ego involves "a mere technical change in the structure or identity of the employing entity, frequently to avoid the effect of the labor laws, without any substantial change in its ownership or management"), *with U.S. v. Bestfoods*, 524 U.S. 51, 61–63 (1998) (discussing corporate alter ego).

Under the labor law alter ego doctrine, the Board determines whether "the two enterprises have 'substantially identical' management, business purpose, operation, equipment, customers, supervision and ownership." *ADF, Inc.*, 355 N.L.R.B. 81, 83 (2010); *see also Trafford Distribution Center v. NLRB*, 478 F.3d 172, 179 (3d Cir. 2007). The Board does not require the presence of each factor to conclude that alter ego status should be applied, but does consider the "most important factor [to be] centralized control of labor relations." *Id.* Does a close family relationship between the owners of the two entities constitute "substantially identical" ownership? *See id.*; *Fallon-Williams, Inc.*, 336 N.L.R.B. 602 (2001) (finding alter-ego status where the two employers had substantially identical management, business purpose, operations, equipment, customers, and supervisors, shared premises and facilities, and where the two employers were husband and wife).

5. Closely related to the alter ego doctrine is the "single employer doctrine," which applies when "two nominally separate entities are actually part of a single integrated enterprise." *Clinton's Ditch Coop. Co. v. NLRB*, 778 F.2d 132, 137 (2d Cir. 1985). The Board applies the single employer test to determine whether one entity is liable for the ULPs of another entity because they are really a single employer. Under the single employer test, the Board considers the following four factors, with no single factor controlling: interrelation of operations, common management, centralized control of labor relations, and common ownership. *Cooper Craft Plumbing, Inc.*, 354 N.L.R.B. 958 (2009).

6. The Board and reviewing courts also determine whether other transactions should be viewed more as if the same corporation is continuing, and less like a successor. If it is the former, the allegedly "new" entity is still obliged to assume the terms of the CBA. For example, the Board, with court approval, has concluded that the "successorship doctrine is simply inapplicable to a stock sale transaction." *Esmark, Inc. v. NLRB*, 887 F.2d 739, 751 (7th Cir. 1989); *see also Holly Farms Corp. v. NLRB*, 48 F.3d 1360, 1365–66 (4th Cir. 1995) (collecting cases); *TKB Int'l Corp.*, 240 N.L.R.B. 1082, 1083 n.4 (1979) (stock transfer "involves no break or hiatus between two legal entities, but is, rather, the continuing existence of a legal entity, albeit under new ownership"). Along these lines, the Board has also determined that a business entity that purchases a "bankrupt company's business and assets to conduct essentially the same operations using essentially the same work force to perform essentially the same jobs," is a perfectly clear successor that must assume the contract. *Grenada Stamping and Assembly, Inc.*, 351 N.L.R.B. 1152 (2007), *enf'd*, 322 Fed. App'x 404 (5th Cir. 2009). Finally, although an "employer that relinquishes and later reacquires ownership of an operation for legitimate business reasons may be free to negotiate a new CBA with the inherited employees," an employer may not "design[] the transactions . . . to evade its obligations under those CBAs." In such cases, reviewing courts will hold that "the [putative] successor is in reality the same

employer and is subject to all the legal and contractual obligations of the [putative] predecessor." *HealthBridge Management, LLC v. NLRB*, 902 F.3d 37, 45–46 (2018) (citing *Howard Johnson Co., Inc. v. Detroit Local Joint Executive Bd.*, 417 U.S. 249, 259 n.5 (1974))

7. What is the difference between holding that a successor employer (often) has the right to unilaterally set initial terms and conditions of employment before bargaining, and the rule that an employer may not unilaterally change terms and conditions of employment under an expired CBA absent bargaining with the union to impasse? In other words, is the Court's successorship rule consistent with *NLRB v. Katz*, 369 U.S. 736 (1962) (*see* Chapter 9)?

8. Under *Burns*, the successor employer is free to hire its own workforce. What prevents the employer from hiring just enough of its predecessor's employees to escape its bargaining obligation? *See Howard Johnson Co., infra*, 417 U.S. 249, 262 & n.8 (1974) (noting, in a successorship context, that an employer violates § 8(a)(3) when it discriminates in hiring employees on the basis of union membership); *Waterbury Hotel Management, LLC v. NLRB*, 314 F.3d 645, 651 (D.C. Cir. 2003) (explaining that § 8(a)(3)'s "prohibition of discriminatory hiring extends to employers that take over another business"). In such circumstances, the Board and reviewing courts determine whether the employer's conduct was motivated by union animus. *See Capital Cleaning Contractors, Inc. v. NLRB*, 147 F.3d 999, 1005 (D.C. Cir. 1998). Should the Board adopt a rule that failure to hire the predecessor's workforce presumptively violates § 8(a)(3)? Or are there sufficient market incentives, *e.g.*, the efficiency of hiring trained employees, making such a presumption unnecessary?

But how does the Board's General Counsel prove union animus in refusal-to-hire cases? In *Adams and Associates, Inc. v. NLRB*, 871 F.3d 358, 371 n. 3 (5th Cir. 2017), the Board relied on the CEO's own statements, written in an email, that he intended to avoid hiring the predecessor's employees to avoid bargaining, which evinced a corporate strategy to avoid successorship. The court rejected the employer's argument that these statements were attorney-client privileged, and therefore inadmissible evidence, even though several people on the email correspondence were attorneys.

9. A successor employer who discriminatorily hired its workforce must instate those employees who were discriminatorily denied jobs and consult with the union that represented the predecessor's employees before setting its initial terms and conditions of employment. *Golden State Bottling Co., Inc. v. NLRB*, 414 U.S. 168 (1973). The Board's precedent formerly was that this obligation arose even if the employer's unlawful discriminatory conduct made it impossible to determine whether the putative successor would have hired enough of the predecessor's employees to be deemed a successor. *Galloway Sch. Lines*, 321 N.L.R.B. 1422 (1996). However, in *Ridgewood Health Care Center*, 367 N.L.R.B. No. 110 (2019), the Board reversed *Galloway School Lines* and its progeny and held that a successor, who discriminatorily fails to hire predecessor employees to avoid its bargaining obligation, may not set initial terms and conditions of employment prior to bargaining with a union only

where that successor discriminatorily refused to hire all or substantially all of the predecessor's employees.

In *Fall River Dyeing & Finishing Corp. v. NLRB*, the Court again wrestled with what, exactly, makes an employer a "successor" and what sort of obligations different types of successors have toward the union at the predecessor.

Fall River Dyeing & Finishing Corp. v. NLRB

Supreme Court of the United States
482 U.S. 27 (1987)

BLACKMUN, J.

. . . We first must decide whether *Burns* is limited to a situation where the union only recently was certified before the transition in employers, or whether that decision also applies where the union is entitled to a presumption of majority support. Our inquiry then proceeds to three questions. . . . First, we must determine whether there is substantial evidence to support the Board's conclusion that petitioner was a "successor" to Sterlingwale, Corp., its business predecessor. Second, we must decide whether the Board's "substantial and representative complement" rule, designed to identify the date when a successor's obligation to bargain with the predecessor's employees' union arises, is consistent with *Burns*, is reasonable, and was applied properly in this case. Finally, we must examine the Board's "continuing demand" principle to the effect that, if a union has presented to a successor a premature demand for bargaining, this demand continues in effect until the successor acquires the "substantial and representative complement" of employees that triggers its obligation to bargain.

For over 30 years before 1982, Sterlingwale operated a textile dyeing and finishing plant in Fall River, Mass. Its business consisted basically of two types of dyeing, called, respectively, "converting" and "commission." Under the converting process, which in 1981 accounted for 60% to 70% of its business . . . Sterlingwale bought unfinished fabrics for its own account, dyed and finished them, and then sold them to apparel manufacturers. . . . In commission dyeing, which accounted for the remainder of its business, Sterlingwale dyed and finished fabrics owned by customers according to their specifications. . . . The financing and marketing aspects of converting and commission dyeing are different. Converting requires capital to purchase fabrics and a sales force to promote the finished products. . . . The production process, however, is the same for both converting and commission dyeing. . . .

In the late 1970's the textile-dyeing business, including Sterlingwale's, began to suffer from adverse economic conditions and foreign competition. After 1979, business at Sterlingwale took a serious turn for the worse because of the loss of its export market . . . and the company reduced the number of its employees. . . . Finally, in February 1982, Sterlingwale laid off all its production employees, primarily because it no longer had the capital to continue the converting business. . . . It retained a skeleton crew of workers and supervisors to ship out the goods remaining on order and to maintain the corporation's building and machinery. . . . In the months following the layoff, Leonard Ansin, Sterlingwale's president, liquidated the inventory of the corporation and, at the same time, looked for a business partner with whom he could "resurrect the business." . . . Ansin felt that he owed it to the community and to the employees to keep Sterlingwale in operation. . . .

For almost as long as Sterlingwale had been in existence, its production and maintenance employees had been represented by the United Textile Workers of America, AFL-CIO, Local 292 (Union). . . . The most recent collective-bargaining agreement before Sterlingwale's demise had been negotiated in 1978 and was due to expire in 1981. By an agreement dated October 1980, however, in response to the financial difficulties suffered by Sterlingwale, the Union agreed to amend the 1978 agreement to extend its expiration date by one year, until April 1, 1982, without any wage increase and with an agreement to improve labor productivity. . . .

In late summer 1982, however, Sterlingwale finally went out of business. It made an assignment for the benefit of its creditors [who were primarily Ansin's mother, who held a first mortgage on most of Sterlingwale's real property, and another entity, which held a security interest in Sterlingwale's machinery and equipment]. . . . Ansin also hired a professional liquidator to dispose of the company's remaining assets, mostly its inventory, at auction.

During this same period, Herbert Chace [a former Sterlingwale employee and officer] and Arthur Friedman [the president of one of Sterlingwale's major customers, Marcamy Sales Corporation] formed petitioner Fall River Dyeing & Finishing Corp. Chace, who had resigned from Sterlingwale in February 1982, had worked there for 27 years, had been vice president in charge of sales at the time of his departure, and had participated in collective bargaining with the Union during his tenure at Sterlingwale. . . . Chace and Friedman formed petitioner with the intention of engaging strictly in the commission-dyeing business and of taking advantage of the availability of Sterlingwale's assets and work force. . . . Accordingly, Friedman had [his company] acquire from [Sterlingwale's creditors] Sterlingwale's plant, real property, and equipment . . . and convey them to petitioner. . . . Petitioner also obtained some of Sterlingwale's remaining inventory at the liquidator's auction. . . . Chace became petitioner's vice president in charge of operations and Friedman became its president. . . .

In September 1982, petitioner began operating out of Sterlingwale's former facilities and began hiring employees. . . . It advertised for workers and supervisors in a local newspaper . . . and Chace personally got in touch with several prospective supervisors. . . . Petitioner hired 12 supervisors, of whom 8 had been supervisors with Sterlingwale and 3 had been production employees there. . . . In its hiring decisions for production employees, petitioner took into consideration recommendations from these supervisors and a prospective employee's former employment with Sterlingwale. . . . Petitioner's initial hiring goal was to attain one full shift of workers, which meant from 55 to 60 employees. . . . Petitioner planned to "see how business would be" after this initial goal had been met and, if business permitted, to expand to two shifts. . . . The employees who were hired first spent approximately four to six weeks in start-up operations and an additional month in experimental production.

By letter dated October 19, 1982, the Union requested petitioner to recognize it as the bargaining agent for petitioner's employees and to begin collective bargaining. . . . Petitioner refused the request, stating that, in its view, the request had "no legal basis." . . . At that time, 18 of petitioner's 21 employees were former employees of Sterlingwale. . . . By November of that year, petitioner had employees in a complete range of jobs, had its production process in operation, and was handling customer orders . . . ; by mid-January 1983, it had attained its initial goal of one shift of workers. . . . Of the 55 workers in this initial shift, a number that represented over half the workers petitioner would eventually hire, 36 were former Sterlingwale employees. . . . Petitioner continued to expand its work force, and by mid-April 1983, it had reached two full shifts. For the first time, ex-Sterlingwale employees were in the minority but just barely so (52 or 53 out of 107 employees).

Although petitioner engaged exclusively in commission dyeing, the employees experienced the same conditions they had when they were working for Sterlingwale. The production process was unchanged and the employees worked on the same machines, in the same building, with the same job classifications, under virtually the same supervisors. . . . Over half the volume of petitioner's business came from former Sterlingwale customers, and, in particular, [Friedman's company].

On November 1, 1982, the Union filed an unfair labor practice charge with the Board, alleging that in its refusal to bargain petitioner had violated §§ 8(a)(1) and (5) . . . . [The Board affirmed the decision of the ALJ that petitioner was a successor to Sterlingwale, and it would have an obligation to bargain with the Union if the majority its employees] were former employees of Sterlingwale . . . that the proper date for making this determination was not mid-April, when petitioner first had two shifts working, but mid-January, when petitioner had attained a "representative complement" of employees . . . that a demand for bargaining from the Union was necessary to trigger petitioner's obligation to bargain, but . . . that the Union's demand of October 1982, although premature, was "of a continuing nature." [Thus] petitioner's duty to bargain arose in mid-January because former Sterlingwale employees then were in the majority and because the Union's October demand was still in effect. Petitioner thus committed an unfair labor practice in refusing to bargain.

[The First Circuit enforced the Board's order]. . . .

Fifteen years ago in *NLRB v. Burns International Security Services, Inc.*, 406 U.S. 272 (1972), this Court first dealt with the issue of a successor employer's obligation to bargain with a union that had represented the employees of its predecessor. . . .

Although our reasoning in *Burns* was tied to the facts presented there . . . we suggested that our analysis would be equally applicable even if a union with which a successor had to bargain had not been certified just before the transition in employers. . . .

Moreover, in defining "the force of the Board's certification within the normal operative period," we referred in *Burns* to two presumptions regarding a union's majority status following certification. First, after a union has been certified by the Board as a bargaining-unit representative, it usually is entitled to a conclusive presumption of majority status for one year following the certification. . . . Second, after this period, the union is entitled to a rebuttable presumption of majority support. . . .

These presumptions are based not so much on an absolute certainty that the union's majority status will not erode following certification, as on a particular policy decision. The overriding policy of the NLRA is "industrial peace." *Brooks v. NLRB*, 348 U.S. at 103. The presumptions of majority support further this policy by "promot[ing] stability in collective-bargaining relationships, without impairing the free choice of employees." . . . In essence, they enable a union to concentrate on obtaining and fairly administering a collective-bargaining agreement without worrying that, unless it produces immediate results, it will lose majority support and will be decertified. [*See Brooks*, 348 U.S. at 100.] The presumptions also remove any temptation on the part of the employer to avoid good-faith bargaining in the hope that, by delaying, it will undermine the union's support among the employees. . . .

The rationale behind the presumptions is particularly pertinent in the successorship situation. . . . During a transition between employers, a union is in a peculiarly vulnerable position. It has no formal and established bargaining relationship with the new employer, is uncertain about the new employer's plans, and cannot be sure if or when the new employer must bargain with it. While being concerned with the future of its members with the new employer, the union also must protect whatever rights still exist for its members under the collective-bargaining agreement with the predecessor employer. Accordingly, during this unsettling transition period, the union needs the presumptions of majority status to which it is entitled to safeguard its members' rights and to develop a relationship with the successor.

The position of the employees also supports the application of the presumptions in the successorship situation. If the employees find themselves in a new enterprise that substantially resembles the old, but without their chosen bargaining representative, they may well feel that their choice of a union is subject to the vagaries of an enterprise's transformation. This feeling is not conducive to industrial peace. In addition, after being hired by a new company following a layoff from the old, employees initially will be concerned primarily with maintaining their new jobs. In fact, they might be inclined to shun support for their former union, especially if they believe that such support will jeopardize their jobs with the successor or if they are inclined to blame the union for their layoff and problems associated with it. Without the presumptions of majority support and with the wide variety of corporate transformations possible, an employer could use a successor enterprise as a way of getting rid of a labor contract and of exploiting the employees' hesitant attitude towards the union to eliminate its continuing presence.

In addition to recognizing the traditional presumptions of union majority status, however, the Court in *Burns* was careful to safeguard "'the rightful prerogative of owners independently to rearrange their businesses.'" . . . We observed in *Burns* that, although the successor has an obligation to bargain with the union, it "is ordinarily free to set initial terms on which it will hire the employees of a predecessor," and it is not bound by the substantive provisions of the predecessor's collective-bargaining agreement. We further explained that the successor is under no obligation to hire the employees of its predecessor, subject, of course, to the restriction that it not discriminate against union employees in its hiring. . . . Thus, to a substantial extent the applicability of *Burns* rests in the hands of the successor. If the new employer makes a conscious decision to maintain generally the same business and to hire a majority of its employees from the predecessor, then the bargaining obligation of §8(a)(5) is activated. This makes sense when one considers that the employer *intends* to take advantage of the trained work force of its predecessor.

Accordingly, in *Burns* we acknowledged the interest of the successor in its freedom to structure its business and the interest of the employees in continued representation by the union. We now hold that a successor's obligation to bargain is not limited to a situation where the union in question has been recently certified. Where, as here, the union has a rebuttable presumption of majority status, this status continues despite the change in employers. And the new employer has an obligation to bargain with that union so long as the new employer is in fact a successor of the old employer and the majority of its employees were employed by its predecessor.

We turn now to the three rules, as well as to their application to the facts of this case, that the Board has adopted for the successorship situation. The Board, of course, is given considerable authority to interpret the provisions of the NLRA. . . .

In *Burns* we approved the approach taken by the Board and accepted by courts with respect to determining whether a new company was indeed the successor to the old. This approach, which is primarily factual in nature and is based upon the totality of the circumstances of a given situation, requires that the Board focus on whether the new company has "acquired substantial assets of its predecessor and continued, without interruption or substantial change, the predecessor's business operations." *Golden State Bottling Co. v. NLRB*, 414 U.S. at 184. Hence, the focus is on whether there is "substantial continuity" between the enterprises. Under this approach, the Board examines a number of factors: whether the business of both employers is essentially the same; whether the employees of the new company are doing the same jobs in the same working conditions under the same supervisors; and whether the new entity has the same production process, produces the same products, and basically has the same body of customers.

In conducting the analysis, the Board keeps in mind the question whether "those employees who have been retained will understandably view their job situations as essentially unaltered." *See Golden State Bottling Co.*, 414 U.S. at 184. . . . This emphasis on the employees' perspective furthers the Act's policy of industrial peace. If the employees find themselves in essentially the same jobs after the employer transition and if their legitimate expectations in continued representation by their union are thwarted, their dissatisfaction may lead to labor unrest. . . .

Although petitioner does not challenge the Board's "substantial continuity" approach, it does contest the application of the rule to the facts of this case. . . . [W]e find that the Board's determination that there was "substantial continuity" between Sterlingwale and petitioner and that petitioner was Sterlingwale's successor is supported by substantial evidence in the record. Petitioner acquired most of Sterlingwale's real property, its machinery and equipment, and much of its inventory and materials. It introduced no new product line. Of particular significance is the fact that, from the perspective of the employees, their jobs did not change. Although petitioner abandoned converting dyeing in exclusive favor of commission dyeing, this change did not alter the essential nature of the employees' jobs, because both types of dyeing involved the same production process. The job classifications of petitioner were the same as those of Sterlingwale; petitioners' employees worked on the same machines under the direction of supervisors most of whom were former supervisors of Sterlingwale. The record, in fact, is clear that petitioner acquired Sterlingwale's assets with the express purpose of taking advantage of its predecessor's work force.

We do not find determinative of the successorship question the fact that there was a 7-month hiatus between Sterlingwale's demise and petitioner's start-up. Petitioner argues that this hiatus, coupled with the fact that its employees were hired through newspaper advertisements-not through Sterlingwale employment records, which were not transferred to it-resolves in its favor the "substantial continuity" question. . . . Yet such a hiatus is only one factor in the "substantial continuity" calculus and thus is relevant only when there are other indicia of discontinuity. . . . Conversely, if other factors indicate a continuity between the enterprises, and the hiatus is a normal start-up period, the "totality of the circumstances" will suggest that these circumstances present a successorship situation.

For the reasons given above, this is a case where the other factors suggest "substantial continuity" between the companies despite the 7-month hiatus. Here, moreover, the extent of the hiatus between the demise of Sterlingwale and the start-up of petitioner is somewhat less than certain. After the February layoff, Sterlingwale retained a skeleton crew of supervisors and employees that continued to ship goods to customers and to maintain the plant. In addition, until the assignment for the benefit of the creditors late in the summer, Ansin was seeking to resurrect the business or to find a buyer for Sterlingwale. The Union was aware of these efforts. Viewed from the employees' perspective, therefore, the hiatus may have been much less than seven months. Although petitioner hired the employees through advertisements, it often relied on recommendations from supervisors, themselves formerly employed by Sterlingwale, and intended the advertisements to reach the former Sterlingwale work force.

Accordingly, we hold that, under settled law, petitioner was a successor to Sterlingwale. We thus must consider if and when petitioner's duty to bargain arose.

In *Burns*, the Court determined that the successor had an obligation to bargain with the union because a majority of its employees had been employed by Wackenhut.... The "triggering" fact for the bargaining obligation was this composition of the successor's work force. The Court, however, did not have to consider the question *when* the successor's obligation to bargain arose: Wackenhut's contract expired on June 30 and Burns began its services with a majority of former Wackenhut guards on July 1.... In other situations, as in the present case, there is a start-up period by the new employer while it gradually builds its operations and hires employees. In these situations, the Board, with the approval of the Courts of Appeals, has adopted the "substantial and representative complement" rule for fixing the moment when the determination as to the composition of the successor's work force is to be made. If, at this particular moment, a majority of the successor's employees had been employed by its predecessor, then the successor has an obligation to bargain with the union that represented these employees.

This rule represents an effort to balance "'the objective of insuring maximum employee participation in the selection of a bargaining agent against the goal of permitting employees to be represented as quickly as possible.'"... In deciding when a "substantial and representative complement" exists in a particular employer transition, the Board examines a number of factors. It studies "whether the job classifications designated for the operation were filled or substantially filled and whether the operation was in normal or substantially normal production." *See Premium Foods, Inc. v. NLRB*, 709 F.2d 623, 628 (9th Cir. 1983). In addition, it takes into consideration "the size of the complement on that date and the time expected to elapse before a substantially larger complement would be at work ... as well as the relative certainty of the employer's expected expansion." *Id.*

Petitioner contends that the Board's "representative complement" rule is unreasonable, given that it injures the representation rights of many of the successor's employees and that it places significant burdens upon the successor, which is unsure whether and when the bargaining obligation will arise.... According to petitioner, if majority status is determined at the "full complement" stage, all the employees will have a voice in the selection of their bargaining representative, and this will reveal if the union truly has the support of most of the successor's employees. This approach, however, focuses only on the interest in having a bargaining representative selected by the majority of the employees. It fails to take into account the significant interest of employees in being represented as soon as possible. The latter interest is especially heightened in a situation where many of the successor's employees, who were formerly represented by a union, find themselves after the employer transition in essentially the same enterprise, but without their bargaining representative. Having the new employer refuse to bargain with the chosen representative of these employees "disrupts the employees' morale, deters their organizational activities, and discourages their membership in unions." *Franks Bros. Co. v. NLRB*, 321 U.S. 702, 704 (1944). Accordingly, petitioner's "full complement" proposal must fail.

Nor do we believe that this "substantial and representative complement" rule places an unreasonable burden on the employer. It is true that, if an employer refuses to bargain with the employees once the representative complement has been attained, it risks violating §8(a)(5). Furthermore, if an employer recognizes the union before this complement has been reached, this recognition could constitute a violation of §8(a)(2), which makes it an unfair labor practice for an employer to support a labor organization....

We conclude, however, that in this situation the successor is in the best position to follow a rule the criteria of which are straightforward. The employer generally will know with tolerable certainty when all its job classifications have been filled or substantially filled, when it has hired a majority of the employees it intends to hire, and when it has begun normal production. Moreover, the "full complement" standard advocated by petitioner is not *necessarily* easier for a successor to apply than is the "substantial and representative complement." In fact, given the expansionist dreams of many new entrepreneurs, it might well be more difficult for a successor to identify the moment when the "full complement" has been attained, which is when the business will reach the limits of the new employer's initial hopes, than it would be for this same employer to acknowledge the time when its business has begun normal production-the moment identified by the "substantial and representative complement" rule.

We therefore hold that the Board's "substantial and representative complement" rule is reasonable in the successorship context. Moreover, its application to the facts of this case is supported by substantial record evidence.... Although petitioner intended to expand to two shifts, and, in fact, reached this goal by mid-April, that expansion was contingent expressly upon the growth of the business. Accordingly... mid-January was the period when petitioner reached its "substantial and representative complement." Because at that time the majority of petitioner's employees were former Sterlingwale employees, petitioner had an obligation to bargain with the Union then.

We also hold that the Board's "continuing demand" rule is reasonable in the successorship situation. The successor's duty to bargain at the "substantial and representative complement" date is triggered only when the union has made a bargaining demand. Under the "continuing demand" rule, when a union has made a premature demand that has been rejected by the employer, this demand remains in force until the moment when the employer attains the "substantial and representative complement."

Such a rule, particularly when considered along with the "substantial and representative complement" rule, places a minimal burden on the successor and makes sense in light of the union's position. Once the employer has concluded that it has reached the appropriate complement, then, in order to determine whether its duty to bargain will be triggered, it has only to see whether the union already has made a demand for bargaining. Because the union has no established relationship with the successor and because it is unaware of the successor's plans for its operations and hiring, it is likely that, in many cases, a union's bargaining demand will be premature. It makes no sense to require the union repeatedly to renew its bargaining demand in the hope of having it correspond with the "substantial and representative complement" date, when, with little trouble, the employer can regard a previous demand as a continuing one. . . .

The judgment of the Court of Appeals is affirmed.

[POWELL, J., joined by THE CHIEF JUSTICE and O'CONNOR, J., dissenting, disagreed with much of what the Court held and was particularly concerned with the Board's substantial and representative complement rule. The dissent argued that it would better to wait for a full complement to be hired unless hiring is sporadic.]

Notes

1. How does the Court apply the substantial continuity test in this case? Does the *Fall River* substantial continuity test differ from *Burns'* requirement that the bargaining unit remain essentially unchanged? How did the seven-month hiatus affect the Court's analysis, and should it have made more of a difference?

2. What are the values involved here? Footnote 6 of the Court's opinion states: "The difficulty a union faces during an employer-transition period is graphically exhibited by the facts of this case. The Union was confronted with the layoff. . . . Although officials at Sterlingwale were willing to meet with it, the Union unsuccessfully attempted to have Sterlingwale honor its commitments under the collective-bargaining agreement, particularly those dealing with health benefits. . . . Moreover, despite the Union's desire to participate in the transition between employers, it was left entirely in the dark about petitioner's acquisition." 482 U.S. 27, 39 n.6.

3. A majority of whom? Footnote 12 of the Court's opinion states: "After *Burns*, there was some initial confusion concerning this Court's holding. It was unclear if work force continuity would turn on whether a majority of the successor's employees were those of the predecessor or on whether the successor had hired a majority of the predecessor's employees. . . . The Board, with the approval of the Courts of Appeals, has adopted the former interpretation. . . . *See Spruce Up Corp.*, 209 N.L.R.B. 194, 196 (1974), *enforced*, 529 F.2d 516 (4th Cir. 1975). . . . This issue is not presented by the instant case." 482 U.S. at 46 n.12.

Which test is preferable, and why? Consider this again after reading the *Howard Johnson* case, *infra*.

4. Under the substantial and representative complement test, how would you determine precisely when the successor's bargaining obligation is triggered?

5. *Fall River* relied in part on presumptions of majority status in various contexts. Along those lines, what sort of bar, if any, should there be to representation elections at successor employers? The NLRB has gone back and forth on the issue. In *UGL-UNICCO Serv. Co.*, 357 N.L.R.B. 801 (2011), the NLRB decided to restore the "successor bar" doctrine, which requires employers to recognize incumbent unions without challenge to their majority status after a business transition for a reasonable period. In 2002, the Board had held in *MV Transportation*, 337 N.L.R.B. 770 (2002), that an incumbent union in a successorship context had only a rebuttable presumption of majority status (and thus, that status could be challenged by, *e.g.*, decertification petitions). The *UGL* majority rejected *MV Transportation*, explaining that the successor bar "better achieves the overall policies of the Act, in the context of today's economy." *UGL,* at 801. In so doing, the Board returned to the rule in *St. Elizabeth Manor, Inc.*, 329 N.L.R.B. 341 (1999), but *UGL* also gave further guidance on the length of the successor bar: no less than six months after the parties' first bargaining session and no more than one year after the start of bargaining. *UGL,* at 809. Which approach is best?

In *NLRB v. Lily Transportation Corp.*, 853 F.3d 31 (1st Cir. 2017), the First Circuit, in an opinion by retired Associate Supreme Court Justice David Souter, sitting by designation and writing for the court, upheld the Board's rule in *UGL*.

6. In *Golden State Bottling Co. v. NLRB*, 414 U.S. 168 (1973), the Supreme Court held that a successor company is liable for the ULPs of the predecessor company if the successor had adequate notice of them at the time of acquisition. The Court thus held it was within the Board's power under § 10(c) to pursue reinstatement and backpay orders against a successor owing to the predecessor's ULPs. What type of knowledge of unremedied ULPs is sufficient to trigger liability for a successor? *See NLRB v. General Wood Preserving Co.*, 905 F.2d 803 (4th Cir. 1990) (successor employer knew or should have known that the predecessor employer had committed numerous ULPs during the union's campaign).

B. The Successor's Obligation to Arbitrate Under the Predecessor's CBA

In *John Wiley & Sons v. Livingston*, 376 U.S. 543 (1964), the Court held that a new employer is required to arbitrate cases that arose under a predecessor's CBA in the context of a merger. The Court held that the disappearance of the predecessor by merger did not necessarily end the union rights of employees under the CBA, so long as there was a "substantial continuity of identity in the business enterprise." In *Wiley,* substantial continuity was evidenced by the wholesale transfer of the predecessor's employees to the successor.

Ten years later, the court took up this issue in the context of a successor where there was plainly no substantial continuity of identity in the work force with the predecessor, and no express or implied assumption of the agreement to arbitrate.

Howard Johnson Co. v. Detroit Local Joint Executive Bd.

Supreme Court of the United States
417 U.S. 249 (1974)

MARSHALL, J.

Once again we are faced with the problem of defining the labor law obligations of a "successor" employer to the employees of its predecessors. In this case, petitioner Howard Johnson Co. is the bona fide purchaser of the assets of a restaurant and motor lodge. Respondent Union was the bargaining representative of the employees of the previous operators, and had successfully concluded collective-bargaining agreements with them. In commencing its operation of the restaurant, Howard Johnson hired only a small fraction of the predecessors' employees. The question presented in this case is whether the Union may compel Howard Johnson to arbitrate, under the arbitration provisions of the collective-bargaining agreements signed by its predecessors, the extent of its obligations under those agreements to the predecessors' employees.

[The Grissom family operated a Howard Johnson Motor Lodge and an adjacent restaurant under a franchise agreement. Employees at both locations were represented by unions, and their CBAs provided that the CBAs would be binding on successors and purchasers. Howard Johnson then bought the personal property used in the lodge and restaurant and leased the real property. It hired nine of its predecessor's fifty-three employees, and began operating with a total of forty-five employees. It refused to recognize the union or assume any obligations under the CBA. The lower courts held that Howard Johnson had to arbitrate with the union the extent of Howard Johnson's obligations to the former Grissom employees.]

We granted certiorari . . . to consider the important labor law question presented. We reverse.

Both courts below relied heavily on this Court's decision in *John Wiley & Sons v. Livingston*, 376 U.S. 543 (1964). In *Wiley*, the union representing the employees of a corporation which had disappeared through a merger sought to compel the surviving corporation, which had hired all of the merged corporation's employees and continued to operate the enterprise in a substantially identical form after the merger, to arbitrate under the merged corporation's collective-bargaining agreement. As *Wiley* was this Court's first experience with the difficult "successorship" question, its holding was properly cautious and narrow:

> "We hold that the disappearance by merger of a corporate employer which has entered into a collective bargaining agreement with a union does not automatically terminate all rights of the employees covered by the

agreement, and that, in appropriate circumstances, present here, the successor employer may be required to arbitrate with the union under the agreement."

Mr. Justice Harlan, writing for the Court, emphasized "the central role of arbitration in effectuating national labor policy" and preventing industrial strife, and the need to afford some protection to the interests of the employees during a change of corporate ownership.

The courts below recognized that the reasoning of *Wiley* was to some extent inconsistent with our more recent decision in *NLRB v. Burns International Security Services*, 406 U.S. 272 (1972). . . .

The courts below held that *Wiley* rather than *Burns* was controlling here on the ground that *Burns* involved an NLRB order holding the employer bound by the substantive terms of the collective-bargaining agreement, whereas this case, like *Wiley*, involved a § 301 suit to compel arbitration. Although this distinction was in fact suggested by the Court's opinion in *Burns, see id.* at 285–86, we do not believe that the fundamental policies outlined in *Burns* can be so lightly disregarded. In *Textile Workers Union v. Lincoln Mills*, 353 U.S. 448 (1957), this Court held that § 301 of the Labor Management Relations Act authorized the federal courts to develop a federal common law regarding enforcement of collective-bargaining agreements. But *Lincoln Mills* did not envision any freewheeling inquiry into what the federal courts might find to be the most desirable rule, irrespective of congressional pronouncements. Rather, *Lincoln Mills* makes clear that this federal common law must be "fashion(ed) from the policy of our national labor laws." . . .

It would be plainly inconsistent with this view to say that the basic policies found controlling in an unfair labor practice context may be disregarded by the courts in a suit under § 301, and thus to permit the rights enjoyed by the new employer in a successorship context to depend upon the forum in which the union presses its claims. Clearly the reasoning of *Burns* must be taken into account here.

We find it unnecessary, however, to decide in the circumstances of this case whether there is any irreconcilable conflict between *Wiley* and *Burns.* We believe that even on its own terms, *Wiley* does not support the decision of the courts below. The Court in *Burns* recognized that its decision "turn(ed) to a great extent on the precise facts involved here." . . .

When the focus is placed on the facts of these cases, it becomes apparent that the decision below is an unwarranted extension of *Wiley* beyond any factual context it may have contemplated. Although it is true that both *Wiley* and this case involve § 301 suits to compel arbitration, the similarity ends there. *Wiley* involved a merger, as a result of which the initial employing entity completely disappeared. In contrast, this case involves only a sale of some assets, and the initial employers remain in existence as viable corporate entities, with substantial revenues from the lease of the motor lodge and restaurant to Howard Johnson. Although we have recognized that ordinarily there is no basis for distinguishing among mergers, consolidations, or purchases of assets in the analysis of successorship problems, *see Golden State Bottling Co. v. NLRB*, 414 U.S. 168, 182–83, n. 5 (1973), we think these distinctions are relevant here for two reasons. First, the merger in *Wiley* was conducted "against a background of state law that embodied the general rule that in merger situations the surviving corporation is liable for the obligations of the disappearing corporation," *Burns*, 406 U.S. at 286, which suggests that holding Wiley bound to arbitrate under its predecessor's collective-bargaining agreement may have been fairly within the reasonable expectations of the parties. Second, the disappearance of the original employing entity in the Wiley merger meant that unless the union were afforded some remedy against Wiley, it would have no means to enforce the obligations voluntarily undertaken by the merged corporation, to the extent that those obligations vested prior to the merger or to the extent that its promises were intended to service a change of ownership. Here, in contrast, because the Grissom corporations continue as viable entities with substantial retained assets, the Union does have a realistic remedy to enforce their contractual obligations. Indeed, the Grissoms have agreed to arbitrate the extent of their liability to the Union and their former employees; presumably this arbitration will explore the question whether the Grissoms breached the successorship provisions of their collective-bargaining agreements, and what the remedy for this breach might be.

Even more important, in *Wiley* the surviving corporation hired all of the employees of the disappearing corporation. Although, under *Burns*, the surviving corporation may have been entitled to make substantial changes in its operation of the enterprise, the plain fact is that it did not. . . .

The claims which the union sought to compel Wiley to arbitrate were thus the claims of Wiley's employees as to the benefits they were entitled to receive in connection with their employment. It was on this basis that the Court in *Wiley* found that there was the "substantial continuity of identity in the business enterprise," 376 U.S. at 551, which it held necessary before the successor employer could be compelled to arbitrate.

Here, however, Howard Johnson decided to select and hire its own independent work force to commence its operation of the restaurant and motor lodge. It therefore hired only nine of the 53 former Grissom employees and none of the Grissom supervisors. The primary purpose of the Union in seeking arbitration here with Howard Johnson is not to protect the rights of Howard Johnson's employees; rather, the Union primarily seeks arbitration on behalf of the former Grissom employees who were not hired by Howard Johnson. It is the Union's position that Howard Johnson was bound by the pre-existing collective-bargaining agreement to employ all of these former Grissom employees, except those who could be dismissed in accordance with the "just cause" provision or laid off in accordance with the seniority provision. . . .

What the Union seeks here is completely at odds with the basic principles this Court elaborated in *Burns*. We found there that nothing in the federal labor laws "requires that an employer . . . who purchases the assets of a business be obligated to hire all of the employees of the predecessor though it is possible that such an obligation might be assumed by the employer." . . . *Burns* emphasized that "(a) potential employer may be willing to take over a moribund business only if he can make changes in corporate structure, composition of the labor force . . . and nature of supervision." . . . We rejected the Board's position in part because "(i)t would seemingly follow that employees of the predecessor would be deemed employees of the successor, dischargeable only in accordance with provisions of the contract and subject to the grievance and arbitration provisions thereof. Burns would not have been free to replace Wackenhut's guards with its own except as the contract permitted." . . . Clearly, *Burns* establishes that Howard Johnson had the right not to hire any of the former Grissom employees, if it so desired. The Union's effort to circumvent this holding by asserting its claims in a § 301 suit to compel arbitration rather than in an unfair labor practice context cannot be permitted.

We do not believe that *Wiley* requires a successor employer to arbitrate in the circumstances of this case.[9] The Court there held that arbitration could not be compelled unless there was "substantial continuity of identity in the business enterprise" before and after a change of ownership, for otherwise the duty to arbitrate would be "something imposed from without, not reasonably to be found in the particular bargaining agreement and the acts of the parties involved." . . . This continuity of identity in the business enterprise necessarily includes, we think, a substantial continuity in the identity of the work force across the change in ownership. The *Wiley* Court seemingly recognized this, as it found the requisite continuity present there in reliance on the "wholesale transfer" of Interscience employees to Wiley. This view is reflected in the emphasis most of the lower courts have placed on whether the successor employer hires a majority of the predecessor's employees in determining the legal obligations of the successor in § 301 suits under *Wiley*. This interpretation of *Wiley* is consistent also with the Court's concern with affording protection to those employees who are in fact retained in "(t)he transition from one corporate organization to another" from sudden changes in the terms and conditions of their employment, and with its belief that industrial strife would be avoided if these employees' claims were resolved by arbitration rather than by "the relative strength . . . of the contending forces." *Wiley*, at 549. . . . At the same time, it recognizes that the employees of the terminating employer have no legal right to continued employment with the new

---

9. The Court of Appeals stated that "[t]he first question we must face is whether Howard Johnson is a successor employer," and, finding that it was, that the next question was whether a successor is required to arbitrate under the collective bargaining agreement of its predecessor, which the court found was resolved by *Wiley*. We do not believe that this artificial division between these questions is a helpful or appropriate way to approach these problems. The question whether Howard Johnson is a "successor" is simply not meaningful in the abstract. . . . [T]he real question in each of these "successorship" cases is, on the particular facts, what are the legal obligations of the new employer to the employees of the former owner or their representative? The answer to this inquiry requires analysis of the interests of the new employer and the employees and of the policies of the labor laws in light of the facts of each case and the particular legal obligation which is at issue. . . .

employer, and avoids the difficulties inherent in the Union's position in this case. This holding is compelled, in our view, if the protection afforded employee interests in a change of ownership by *Wiley* is to be reconciled with the new employer's right to operate the enterprise with his own independent labor force.

Since there was plainly no substantial continuity of identity in the work force hired by Howard Johnson with that of the Grissoms, and no express or implied assumption of the agreement to arbitrate, the courts below erred in compelling the Company to arbitrate the extent of its obligations to the former Grissom employees. Accordingly, the judgment of the Court of Appeals must be reversed.

[Douglas, J., dissenting, would have found a duty to arbitrate under *Wiley*.]

Notes

1. How does the Court distinguish this case from *Wiley*? Is that distinction persuasive? For example, was the *Wiley* holding really as narrow as *Howard Johnson* suggests? How does the Court attempt to avoid "any irreconcilable conflict" between *Wiley* and *Burns*? Is there in fact a conflict—in legal rules or in policies? If so, what is the nature of that conflict, and what approach best expresses the policies undergirding the NLRA?

2. In *Howard Johnson*, the Court found no substantial continuity between the predecessor and the new enterprises. Does that factual finding limit the holding of this case? What precedential value does *Howard Johnson* have? Does this case help guide the Board and lower courts as to when they should find substantial continuity between a predecessor and successor employer, or is the approach always fact-based? Does footnote 9 in this case make these issues clearer, or less clear?

3. In analyzing whether substantial continuity existed, *Burns* and *Fall River* stressed the proportion of the successor's workforce that had previously been employed by the predecessor. In contrast, *Howard Johnson* stressed the proportion of the predecessor's workforce that the successor retains. Can you imagine factual situations in which the first approach would give a substantially different result than the second approach? Which is the better approach?

4. Did the Union in this case have any other options? If so, what were they?

III. Special Rules for Employers in Bankruptcy

A. Overlapping Rules in the NLRA and the Bankruptcy Code

Courts have long held that a bankruptcy petition does not relieve an employer from liability under the NLRA. *See Nathanson v. NLRB*, 344 U.S. 25, 30 (1952). Normally, a debtor in bankruptcy enjoys many protections, including the "automatic stay," which enjoins civil litigation against that debtor. 11 U.S.C. § 362(b)(4). Although the Board is exempt from the "automatic stay," *NLRB v. P*I*E Nationwide*,

Inc., 923 F.2d 506, 512 (7th Cir. 1991), the Board's recovery may be limited by the bankruptcy rules.

Specifically, the NLRB maintains authority over determining whether a debtor has engaged in a ULP and what backpay is owed, while bankruptcy courts have jurisdiction over the debtor's estate and therefore over the priority and distribution of backpay claims. The "fixing of the back pay is one of the functions confided solely to the Board." *Nathanson*, 344 U.S. at 29–30. With respect to employers in bankruptcy, the Board can (1) prosecute a ULP case, (2) proceed to a final decision, and (3) liquidate the backpay amount, as long as it does not seek collection outside the bankruptcy court.

In bankruptcy proceedings involving ULP remedies, the Board is the creditor. This is because the Board's backpay remedy not only makes individual discriminatees whole for the wrongs suffered, but also serves the public purpose of deterring future ULPs. *NLRB v. Mastro Plastics Corp.*, 354 F.2d 170, 175 (2d Cir. 1965). This public purpose means the Board—not any individual employee—is the creditor under the Bankruptcy Code for backpay owed due to employer ULPs. *See Nathanson, supra.* Thus, the Board must file a timely proof of claims and otherwise comply with bankruptcy rules for creditors.

Under the Bankruptcy Code, a hierarchy of creditor classes controls how much each creditor is paid, including the NLRB. *See* 11 U.S.C. § 507. Often, only higher classes share in the distribution; lower "priority" claims are not paid until those with higher priority are satisfied. Administrative priority claims (defined in 11 U.S.C. § 503(b)), arising after the commencement of the bankruptcy, have a higher priority than most other unsecured claims.

This leaves us with the following question: What type of claim does the Board hold? The answer depends upon when the backpay accrued: before or after the bankruptcy petition. For years, courts differed over whether post-petition backpay deserved administrative priority, regardless of when the NLRA violation was committed or whether the employees were actually working post-petition. This issue was clarified by a 2005 amendment to the Bankruptcy Code. Now, under § 503(b)(1)(A)(ii), post-petition wages and benefits awarded in a judicial or NLRB proceeding resulting from the debtor-employer's violation of federal law are administrative expenses under the Bankruptcy Code—regardless of the time of the unlawful conduct or whether services have been rendered—if the court determines that payment of such wages and benefits will not substantially increase the probability of layoff or termination of current employees, or of nonpayment of domestic support obligations, during the bankruptcy case.

B. The Bankrupt Employer's Collective Bargaining Agreements

Employers can violate § 8(a)(5) by refusing to honor the terms of a CBA or by unilaterally terminating such an agreement. *See* Chapter 9. Bankruptcy Code § 365 permits a debtor to "assume or reject any executor contract," subject to bank-ruptcy court approval. May a bankruptcy debtor unilaterally reject a CBA under Code § 365, notwithstanding the NLRA's prohibition of such conduct? In *NLRB v. Bildisco & Bildisco*, 465 U.S. 513 (1984), the Supreme Court held that Congress intended § 365 to apply to CBAs, and that debtors-in-possession may lawfully ter-minate or modify the CBA after filing a bankruptcy petition, even before court approval.

That same year, in response, Congress enacted Bankruptcy Code § 1113. Under § 1113, a debtor may *not* "unilaterally terminate or alter any provisions of a collec-tive bargaining agreement" until it has complied with the provisions of that section and secured court authorization. Accordingly, absent bankruptcy court approval of a request to reject a CBA, the NLRB may find that an employer's post-petition, unilateral contract modification or termination violates § 8(a)(5). Section 1113 was designed to foster negotiations between the debtor and union and to discourage a debtor's unilateral repudiation of the agreement. Accordingly, similar to private suits which may be brought in court by a union or employer under 29 U.S.C. § 185 to resolve an alleged breach of a CBA, Congress provided a special mechanism for bankruptcy courts to determine the enforceability of such agreements against employers in bankruptcy. In both circumstances, it is unusual for the NLRB to become directly involved in the court dispute.

In *In re Trump Entertainment Resorts*, 810 F.3d 161, 164 (3d Cir. 2016) — a case of first impression among the courts of appeal — the Third Circuit held that a bank-ruptcy court, under § 1113(c) of the Bankruptcy Code, can authorize trustees or debtors in possession to reject terms and conditions of employment maintained post-contract expiration. The court explained that in resolving the question pre-sented, it was required to resolve a potential conflict between the NLRA, which does not permit employers to unilaterally change terms and conditions of employment without first bargaining with the union, and Bankruptcy Code § 1113(c), which allows Chapter 11 debtors to reject collective-bargaining agreements in certain circumstances. Under the court's decision, those circumstances include situations where the collective-bargaining agreement has expired. The court based its con-clusion on its finding that "§ 1113 does not distinguish between the terms of an unexpired CBA and the terms and conditions that continue to govern after the CBA expires." *Id.*

IV. Public-Sector Successorship: Contracting Out Public-Sector Work to the Private Sector

The most important "successorship" issue in the public sector arises when a pub-lic employer "contracts out" work formerly done by its unionized workforce to a private-sector employer. Should the same rules apply as when a private-sector suc-cessor takes over from a private-sector predecessor?

Dean Transportation v. NLRB

D.C. Circuit Court of Appeals
551 F.3d 1055 (2009)

GARLAND, J.

When petitioner Dean Transportation, Inc. took over operations at a facility that provided bus transportation for the Grand Rapids Public Schools (GRPS), it refused to recognize and bargain with the Grand Rapids Educational Support Personnel Association (GRESPA), the union that had been representing employees at the facility. Instead, Dean recognized the union that represented bus drivers at Dean's seven other facilities, the Dean Transportation Employees Union (DTEU). The [NLRB] determined that, in so doing, Dean and DTEU violated the [NLRA]. The Board's determination was based on the following findings: Dean was a successor to GRPS as the employer of bus drivers, mechanics, and route planners at the facility it acquired by lease from GRPS; a unit consisting of those employees was an appropriate bargaining unit; . . . and GRESPA had made a proper demand for recognition and bargaining. We deny the company's petition for review and grant in full the Board's applications for enforcement of its order. . . .

A "new employer has an obligation to bargain with" the union representing its predecessor's employees if, inter alia, "the new employer is in fact a successor of the old employer and the majority of its employees were employed by its predecessor." *Fall River Dyeing & Finishing Corp. v. NLRB*. . . . It is undisputed that a majority of Dean's employees at Union Street were formerly employed by GRPS in the same capacity, including 100 of 137 drivers, 4 of 5 mechanics, and 2 of 3 route planners. All of these former employees were represented by GRESPA when GRPS operated the Union Street facility. Dean contends, however, that it is not in fact a successor employer.

A new employer qualifies as a successor to its predecessor if there is "substantial continuity" between the enterprises. *Fall River*, 482 U.S. at 43. The determination of substantial continuity "is based upon the totality of the circumstances of a given situation, [and] requires that the Board focus on whether the new company has 'acquired substantial assets of its predecessor and continued, without interruption or substantial change, the predecessor's business operations.'" *Id.* In *Fall River*, the Supreme Court identified the following factors as relevant to the determination of substantial continuity:

> [W]hether the business of both employers is essentially the same; whether the employees of the new company are doing the same jobs in the same working conditions under the same supervisors; and whether the new entity has the same production process, produces the same products, and basically has the same body of customers. *Fall River*, at 43.

These factors are assessed from "the employees' perspective," and the court asks "whether 'those employees who have been retained will understandably view their job situations as essentially unaltered.'" *Id.*

There is no dispute that Dean acquired substantial transportation assets from GRPS—namely, all of GRPS' buses and the Union Street physical facilities—and that it continued, without interruption, GRPS' transportation operations. The ALJ found that, "when viewed from the perspective of the employees, there has been very little change in their working conditions." As the ALJ explained:

> The bus drivers continue to report to the same location, drive the same buses, transport the same group of students to essentially the same schools. They report to the same supervisors . . . that they did when they worked for GRPS and KISD. . . . The route planners . . . continue to work in the same office, doing the same jobs, using the same computer software, and reporting to the same supervisor. . . . The mechanics, likewise, work in the same garage, with the same equipment and tools, repairing and maintaining the same buses.

Substantial evidence supports all of these findings, and Dean does not seriously contest them. Instead, the company focuses on several factors that it contends should count against a finding of substantial continuity.

First, Dean argues that it "implemented a number of significant changes" when it took over operations at Union Street, "including changes with respect to wages and benefits, supervision, work rules, policies, training programs," paperwork, and the method for assigning routes. . . . But as we have noted before, "[p]ointing to differences in size, wages, benefits, training, customer base, [and] managerial philosophy . . . is unresponsive to the question we face. We ask not whether [the petitioner's] view of the facts supports its version of what happened, but rather whether the Board's interpretation of the facts is reasonably defensible." . . .

Moreover, the Board's finding of substantial continuity here is directly in line with its decision in *Van Lear Equipment, Inc.*, 336 N.L.R.B. 1059 (2001). That case involved strikingly similar facts: a private employer engaged in school bus transportation took over the provision of services to a public school district but refused to recognize the union that had previously represented the district's bus drivers. The company maintained that substantial continuity was absent because it had implemented many operational changes. Although the Board recognized those changes, it rejected the company's argument because, "viewed from the drivers' perspective, the drivers are performing the same work that they performed as [school district] employees—transporting school children to and from [district] schools by school bus and van."

Second, the company argues against a finding of substantial continuity on the ground that it only took over GRPS' Union Street facility and not the entire 536-employee GRESPA unit. But as the NLRB recognized, "[i]t is well established that the Board may find substantial continuity even where, as here, a successor employer has taken over only a discrete portion of the predecessor's bargaining unit." . . . Once again, *Van Lear* is directly on point. Although the bus drivers in that case had previously been represented in a larger unit that also included custodians, maintenance workers, and secretaries, the Board found substantial continuity "even though [the new employer] did not take over all the operations and functions of the prior [school district] bargaining unit." *Van Lear*, 336 N.L.R.B. at 1064. . . .

Finally, before the agency Dean argued against a finding of substantial continuity on the ground that the Union Street workers, who at GRPS had been public-sector employees governed by Michigan law, were now private-sector employees subject to a different statutory scheme. In response, the ALJ correctly noted that "[t]he Board has applied [the usual successorship test] even where, as here, the predecessor is a public entity." *Dean*, 350 N.L.R.B. No. 4, at 11 (ALJ Op.) [collecting cases]. Indeed, in *Van Lear*, the Board held that "the successorship doctrine continue[d] to apply even though the predecessor [school district] . . . [wa]s a public employer" and the successor bus transportation company was not. . . . And in *Community Hospitals*, this court likewise ruled that "[t]he change from public to private ownership of the hospital does not undermine the Board's finding that Community was a successor." *Community Hosps.*, 335 F.3d at 1084.

On appeal, Dean focuses not simply on the general differences between public and private employment, but on the fact that the employees "will now have the right to 'strike'" under the NLRA, a right that was unavailable to them as public employees under Michigan law. Dean suggests that employees who acquire the right to strike under the NLRA may not want to be represented by the same union that represented them under a state statute that barred strikes. In response, NLRB counsel argues the opposite, contending that "the acquisition of the right to strike is more likely than not to support former public employees' desire" for continued representation.

We do not resolve this dispute. Dean did not mention this right-to-strike argument in any of its filings before the Board and offers no excuse for not doing so. Section 10(e) of the NLRA therefore prevents us from considering it. . . .

For the foregoing reasons, we deny Dean's petition for review and grant the Board's applications for enforcement of its order. *So ordered.*

Notes

1. Are there any valid reasons to treat a successorship differently in this "public to private" sector context? Or should courts simply apply private-sector precedent?

2. The employer in *Dean Transportation* tried to argue that the lack of a right to strike made an important difference, but the court held the employer had waived this argument. Should this factual difference (where it exists) change the legal analysis for successorship? If so, how? Note that the NLRB in this case argued that this difference supported the NLRB's position, not the position of the employer. How would you make that argument?

3. *Burns* explained that it would have been a very different case if the Board had determined that the Lockheed bargaining unit was no longer an appropriate one because of differences in Burns's operational structure and practices. In part of

Dean Transportation not excerpted above, the Court rejected the employer's argument that the new bargaining unit was inappropriate. Consider, however, when this would be a valid objection in the "public to private" context. For example, recall (from Chapter 7) the presumption in the private sector that single-facility units are appropriate and, in contrast, the common preference in the public sector for larger, "unfragmented" units.

4. *Grane Health Care v. NLRB*, 712 F.3d 145 (3d Cir. 2013) came to the same conclusion as *Dean Transportation*. In *Grane*, a private company had purchased a nursing home formerly run by a Pennsylvania county. The Third Circuit enforced the NLRB's order that the company had an obligation, as a successor, to recognize and bargain with the union that had represented the nursing home's employees when it had been a public entity. The court found that the majority support the union had established under the Pennsylvania public-sector statute was sufficient to establish a presumption of support among the same group of employees under the NLRA. 712 F.3d 145, 152. The court cited *Fall River* for the proposition that the "purpose of the successorship doctrine is to encourage stability at a time of transition." 712 F.3d at 153. "We see no reason why the Board's determination that this policy applies equally to a public-to-private transition is inconsistent with the Act." *Id.*

Chapter 16

Modern Authority Over Labor Relations: Federalism, Delegation, and Preemption

I. Introduction

This chapter addresses labor law's preemptive effect. Because the NLRA is a broadly applicable federal law, the Supreme Court has held that it preempts certain state laws under the Supremacy Clause of the U.S. Constitution: "[T]he law of the United States . . . shall be the supreme law of the land; and the judges in every state shall be bound thereby, anything in the Constitution or law of any State to the contrary notwithstanding." U.S. Const. Art. VI. Courts have held that the NLRA has a broad preemptive sweep — that is, in most circumstances, states may not regulate labor relations for employers and employees covered by the NLRA.

This prohibition takes several forms examined in this chapter. The chapter begins with a discussion of the Board's primary jurisdiction over substantive labor law claims. Following the leading case on this subject, this is called "*Garmon* preemption." The chapter continues by describing the preemption of laws regulating economic weapons left unregulated by the NLRA, or "*Machinists* preemption." The chapter proceeds to a discussion of preemption under § 301, which is the provision authorizing suits in federal courts by and against labor unions, including those relating to collective bargaining agreements.

There is no analogous issue of federal preemption in the public sector. This is because public-sector labor law is generally a matter of state or local law, and because the federal statutes that govern labor relations in federal government agencies do not cover state or local governments. Note that this is not true of many federal employment laws. Title VII, the Fair Labor Standards Act, the Americans with Disabilities Act, and various other federal employment laws cover state and local government employers as well as private employers (although a few such laws, *e.g.*, the Employee Retirement Income Security Act and the Occupational Health and Safety Act, do not cover the public sector). A short section at the end of this chapter considers a proposed federal law that would have governed certain aspects of labor relations between state and local government employers and unions of state and local government employees.

II. NLRA Preemption of State Action

A. The Board's Primary Jurisdiction over Employees' Substantive Labor Rights

As Chapter 1 explained, before the NLRA was enacted, state courts routinely issued injunctions against strikes, pickets, and other activities by labor unions. *Garner v. Teamsters*, 346 U.S. 485 (1953) presented the issue whether a state court interfered with the NLRB's primary jurisdiction when it found a violation of state law and enjoined labor picketing. The Supreme Court held that the NLRA preempts state law when the state law interferes with the NLRB's primary jurisdiction as the agency to which Congress delegated its authority to apply and elaborate upon national private-sector labor policy. The Court provided two reasons for its conclusion. First, it explained that Congress, in enacting the NLRA, did not merely lay down a substantive rule of law to be enforced by any tribunal competent to apply law generally to the parties. Rather, Congress bestowed on the Board primary jurisdiction over most private-sector labor law matters. Primary jurisdiction is necessary to ensure centralized administration of specially designed procedures necessary to obtain uniform application of substantive rules and to avoid undue diversity and conflicts likely to result from a variety of local procedures and attitudes toward labor disputes. Second, the state's application of its own law could upset the substantive balance of the rights of employees, unions and the general public that Congress struck in the NLRA.

Over time, the Court's preemption doctrine, introduced to the private-sector labor law context in *Garner*, evolved into two preemption doctrines: *Garmon* preemption and *Machinists* preemption. The dispute in *Garmon* reached the U.S. Supreme Court twice. At first, the Court held that the state court was without jurisdiction to enjoin peaceful union picketing. The second decision, excerpted below, addressed whether the state court had jurisdiction to award damages arising out of the peaceful union activity that it could not enjoin.

San Diego Bldg. Trades Council v. Garmon

Supreme Court of the United States
359 U.S. 236 (1959)

FRANKFURTER, J.

This case is before us for the second time. The present litigation began with a dispute between the petitioning unions and respondents, co-partners in the business of selling lumber and other materials in California. Respondents began an action in the Superior Court ... asking for an injunction and damages. Upon hearing, the trial court found the following facts. In March of 1953 the unions sought from respondents an agreement to retain in their employ only those workers who were already members of the unions, or who applied for membership within thirty days. Respondents refused. . . . The unions began at once peacefully to picket the respondents' place of business, and to exert pressure on customers and suppliers in order to persuade them to stop dealing with respondents. The sole purpose of these pressures was to compel execution of the proposed contract. The unions contested this finding, claiming that the only purpose of their activities was to educate the workers and persuade them to become members. On the basis of its findings, the court enjoined the unions from picketing and from the use of other pressures to force an agreement, until one of them had been properly designated as a collective bargaining agent. The court also awarded $1,000 damages for losses found to have been sustained.

At the time the suit in the state court was started, respondents had begun a representation proceeding before the NLRB. The Regional Director declined jurisdiction, presumably because the amount of interstate commerce involved did not meet the Board's monetary standards in taking jurisdiction.

On appeal, the California Supreme Court sustained the judgment of the Superior Court . . . holding that, since the NLRB had declined to exercise its jurisdiction, the California courts had power over the dispute. They further decided that the conduct of the union constituted an unfair labor practice under §8(b)(2) of the NLRA and hence was not privileged under California law. As the California court itself later pointed out this decision did not specify what law, state or federal, was the basis of the relief granted. Both state and federal law played a part but, "(a)ny distinction as between those laws was not thoroughly explored."

We granted certiorari . . . and decided the case together with *Guss v. Utah Labor Relations Board*, 353 U.S. 1, and *Amalgamated Meat Cutters v. Fairlawn Meats, Inc.*, 353 U.S. 20. In those cases, we held that the refusal of the NLRB to assert jurisdiction did not leave with the states power over activities they otherwise would be pre-empted from regulating. Both *Guss* and *Fairlawn* involved relief of an equitable nature. In vacating and remanding the judgment of the California court in this case, we pointed out that those cases controlled this one, "in its major aspects." 353 U.S. at 28. However, since it was not clear whether the judgment for damages would be sustained under California law, we remanded to the state court for consideration of that local law issue. The federal question, namely, whether the NLRA precluded California from granting an award for damages arising out of the conduct in question, could not be appropriately decided until the antecedent state law question was decided by the state court.

On remand, the California court, in accordance with our decision in *Guss*, set aside the injunction, but sustained the award of damages. . . . After deciding that California had jurisdiction to award damages for injuries caused by the union's activities, the California court held that those activities constituted a tort based on an unfair labor practice under state law. In so holding the court relied on general tort provisions of the [California Civil Code] as well as state enactments dealing specifically with labor relations [under the California Labor Code].

We again granted certiorari . . . to determine whether the California court had jurisdiction to award damages arising out of peaceful union activity which it could not enjoin.

The issue is a variant of a familiar theme. It began with *Allen-Bradley Local No. 1111 v. Wisconsin Employment Relations Board*, 315 U.S. 740, was greatly intensified by litigation flowing from the Taft-Hartley Act, and has recurred here in almost a score of cases during the last decade. The comprehensive regulation of industrial relations by Congress, novel federal legislation twenty-five years ago but now an integral part of our economic life, inevitably gave rise to difficult problems of federal-state relations. To be sure, in the abstract these problems came to us as ordinary questions of statutory construction. But they involved a more complicated and perceptive process than . . . "ascertaining the intent of the legislature." Many of these problems probably could not have been . . . foreseen by the Congress. Others were only dimly perceived and their precise scope only vaguely defined. This Court was called upon to apply a new and complicated legislative scheme, the aims and social policy of which were drawn with broad strokes while the details had to be filled in, to no small extent, by the judicial process. Recently we indicated the task that was thus cast upon this Court in carrying out with fidelity the purposes of Congress, but doing so by giving application to congressional incompletion. What we said in *Weber v. Anheuser-Busch, Inc.*, 348 U.S. 468, deserves repetition, because the considerations there outlined guide this day's decision:

> "By the Taft-Hartley Act, Congress did not exhaust the full sweep of legislative power over industrial relations given by the Commerce Clause. Congress formulated a code whereby it outlawed some aspects of labor activities and left others free for the operation of economic forces. As to both categories, the areas that have been pre-empted by federal authority and thereby withdrawn from state power are not susceptible of delimitation by fixed metes and bounds. Obvious conflict, actual or potential, leads to easy judicial exclusion of state action. . . . But . . . the Labor Management Relations Act 'leaves much to the states, though Congress has refrained from telling us how much.' . . . This penumbral area can be rendered progressively clear only by the course of litigation." . . .

The case before us concerns one of the most teasing and frequently litigated areas of industrial relations, the multitude of activities regulated by §§ 7 and 8 of the NLRA. These broad provisions govern both protected "concerted activities" and unfair labor practices. They regulate the vital, economic instruments of the strike and the picket line, and impinge on the clash of the still unsettled claims between employers and labor unions. The extent to which the variegated laws of the several States are displaced by a single, uniform, national rule has been a matter of frequent and recurring concern. As we pointed out the other day, "the statutory implications concerning what has been taken from the states and what has been left to them are of a Delphic nature, to be translated into concreteness by the process of litigating elucidation." *International Ass'n of Machinists v. Gonzales*, 356 U.S. 617, 619. . . .

In determining the extent to which state regulation must yield to subordinating federal authority, we have been concerned with delimiting areas of potential conflict; potential conflict of rules of law, of remedy, and of administration. The nature of the judicial process precludes an ad hoc inquiry into the special problems of labor-management relations involved in a particular set of occurrences in order to ascertain the precise nature and degree of federal-state conflict there involved, and more particularly what exact mischief such a conflict would cause. Nor is it our business to attempt this. Such determinations inevitably depend upon judgments on the impact of these particular conflicts on the entire scheme of federal labor policy and administration. Our task is confined to dealing with classes of situations. To the NLRB and to Congress must be left those precise and closely limited demarcations that can be adequately fashioned only by legislation and administration. We have necessarily been concerned with the potential conflict of two law-enforcing authorities, with the disharmonies inherent in two systems, one federal the other state, of inconsistent standards of substantive law and differing remedial schemes. But the unifying consideration of our decisions has been regard to the fact that Congress has entrusted administration of the labor policy for the Nation to a centralized administrative agency, armed with its own procedures, and equipped with its specialized knowledge and cumulative experience:

> "Congress did not merely lay down a substantive rule of law to be enforced by any tribunal competent to apply law generally to the parties. It went on to confide primary interpretation and application of its rules to a specific and specially constituted tribunal and prescribed a particular procedure for investigation, complaint and notice, and hearing and decision, including judicial relief pending a final administrative order. Congress evidently considered that centralized administration of specially designed procedures was necessary to obtain uniform application of its substantive rules and to avoid these diversities and conflicts likely to result from a variety of local procedures and attitudes towards labor controversies. . . . A multiplicity of tribunals and a diversity of procedures are quite as apt to produce incompatible or conflicting adjudications as are different rules of substantive law. . . ." *Garner v. Teamsters*, 346 U.S. 485, 490–91.

Administration is more than a means of regulation; administration is regulation. We have been concerned with conflict in its broadest sense; conflict with a complex and interrelated federal scheme of law, remedy, and administration. Thus, judicial concern has necessarily focused on the nature of the activities which the states have sought to regulate, rather than on the method of regulation adopted. When the exercise of state power over a particular area of activity threatened interference with the clearly indicated policy of industrial relations, it has been judicially necessary to preclude the states from acting. However, due regard for the presuppositions of our embracing federal system, including the principle of diffusion of power not as a matter of doctrinaire localism but as a promoter of democracy, has required us not to find withdrawal from the states of power to regulate where the activity regulated was a merely peripheral concern of the Labor Management Relations Act. *See International Ass'n of Machinists v. Gonzales*, 356 U.S. 617. Or where the regulated conduct touched interests so deeply rooted in local feeling and responsibility that, in the absence of compelling congressional direction, we could not infer that Congress had deprived the states of the power to act.

When it is clear or may fairly be assumed that the activities which a State purports to regulate are protected by § 7 of the NLRA, or constitute an unfair labor practice under § 8, due regard for the federal enactment requires that state jurisdiction must yield. To leave the states free to regulate conduct so plainly within the central aim of federal regulation involves too great a danger of conflict between power asserted by Congress and requirements imposed by state law. Nor has it mattered whether the states have acted through laws of broad general application rather than laws specifically directed towards the governance of industrial relations. Regardless of the mode adopted, to allow the states to control conduct which is the subject of national regulation would create potential frustration of national purposes.

At times it has not been clear whether the particular activity regulated by the states was governed by § 7 or § 8 or was, perhaps, outside both these sections. But courts are not primary tribunals to adjudicate such issues. It is essential to the administration of the Act that these determinations be left in the first instance to the NLRB. What is outside the scope of this Court's authority cannot remain within a State's power and state jurisdiction too must yield to the exclusive primary competence of the Board. . . .

The case before us is such a case. The adjudication in California has throughout been based on the assumption that the behavior of the petitioning unions constituted an unfair labor practice. This conclusion was derived by the California courts from the facts as well as from their view of the Act. It is not for us to decide whether the NLRB would have, or should have, decided these questions in the same manner. When an activity is arguably subject to § 7 or § 8 of the Act, the states as well as the federal courts must defer to the exclusive competence of the NLRB if the danger of state interference with national policy is to be averted.

To require the states to yield to the primary jurisdiction of the National Board does not ensure Board adjudication of the status of a disputed activity. If the Board decides, subject to appropriate federal judicial review, that conduct is protected by § 7, or prohibited by § 8, then the matter is at an end, and the states are ousted of all jurisdiction. Or, the Board may decide that an activity is neither protected nor prohibited, and thereby raise the question whether such activity may be regulated by the states. However, the Board may also fail to determine the status of the disputed conduct by declining to assert jurisdiction, or by refusal of the General Counsel to file a charge, or by adopting some other disposition which does not define the nature of the activity with unclouded legal significance. This was the basic problem underlying our decision in *Guss v. Utah Labor Relations Board*, 353 U.S. 1. In that case we held that the failure of the NLRB to assume jurisdiction did not leave the states free to regulate activities they would otherwise be precluded from regulating. It follows that the failure of the Board to define the legal significance under the Act of a particular activity does not give the states the power to act. In the absence of the Board's clear determination that an activity is neither protected nor prohibited or of compelling precedent applied to essentially undisputed facts, it is not for this Court to decide whether such activities are subject to state jurisdiction. The withdrawal of this narrow area from possible state activity follows from our decisions in Weber and Guss. The governing consideration is that to allow the states to control activities that are potentially subject to federal regulation involves too great a danger of conflict with national labor policy.

In the light of these principles the case before us is clear. Since the NLRB has not adjudicated the status of the conduct for which the State of California seeks to give a remedy in damages, and since such activity is arguably within the compass of §7 or §8 of the Act, the State's jurisdiction is displaced. . . . Reversed.

Notes

1. *Garmon* addressed ULP cases and the substantive law of §8. What about more process-focused concerns, such as election procedures, that fall under §9? Courts have explained that the NLRB has exclusive jurisdiction over these processes as well, and that state action is also preempted in this area. *See Minn-Dak Farmers Co-op. Emps. Org. v. Minn-Dak Farmers Co-op.*, 3 F.3d 1199, 1200–01 (8th Cir. 1993). Accordingly, consider whether the NLRA would preempt the following state laws:

> "The right to vote by secret ballot for employee representation is fundamental and shall be guaranteed where local, state or federal law permits or requires elections, designations or authorizations for employee representation." ARIZ. CONST. art. II, §37; *see also, e.g.,* S.C. CONST. art. II, §12 ("The fundamental right of an individual to vote by secret ballot is guaranteed for a designation, a selection, or an authorization for employee representation by a labor organization"); S.D. CONST. art. VI, §28 ("The rights of individuals to vote by secret ballot is fundamental. If any state or federal law requires or permits an election for public office, for any initiative or referendum, or for any designation or authorization of employee representation, the right of any individual to vote by secret ballot shall be guaranteed"); UTAH CONST. art. IV, §8 ("All elections, including elections . . . to designate or authorize employee representation or individual representation, shall be by secret ballot").

2. Federal courts must also respect the primary jurisdiction of the Board to determine whether conduct is (arguably) protected or (arguably) prohibited, although not for reasons of preemption. The courts are limited by the principle of separation of powers which requires that they respect Congress' decision to delegate administration of most aspects of private-sector labor relations to the Board with judicial review only in those circumstances Congress has specified in the Act. Accordingly, parties may not turn to a federal district court to determine whether a union's picketing is protected by §7. But what if Congress passes a law that arguably conflicts with the NLRA? Courts do not conduct a preemption analysis. Instead, courts would conduct a conflict analysis or interpret the conflicting statutes in light of one another. *See, e.g., Epic Systems v. Lewis*, 138 S. Ct. 1612 (2018) (reconciling the

NLRA with the Federal Arbitration Act); *Hoffman Plastic Compounds, Inc. v. NLRB*, 535 U.S. 137 (2002) (reconciling the NLRA with federal immigration law); *NLRB v. Bildisco and Bildisco*, 465 U.S. 513 (1984) (reconciling the NLRA with federal bankruptcy law).

3. As with questions of judicial review, presidential executive orders in the labor relations realm raise a slightly different legal question than those raised by state or local laws. A president's intervention in private-sector labor relations implicates the separation of powers granted by the Constitution to the executive and legislative branches of the federal government. Nonetheless, courts of appeals have borrowed the regulatory/proprietary dichotomy from *Boston Harbor, Gould*, and *Golden State Transit*, discussed below, to analyze certain presidential actions. For example, in *Chamber of Commerce v. Reich*, 74 F.3d 1322 (D.C. Cir. 1996), the D.C. Circuit held that President Clinton improperly acted to regulate private-sector labor relations when he issued an Executive Order essentially prohibiting federal contractors from permanently replacing striking workers. By contrast, in *Bldg. & Constr. Trades Dep't v. Allbaugh*, 295 F.3d 28 (D.C. Cir. 2002), the same court held that President George W. Bush properly acted in a non-regulatory proprietary role when he issued an Executive Order barring federal agencies from requiring or prohibiting project labor agreements when they funded construction projects. The court conditioned its conclusion on the fact that the president limited the scope of his order to projects where the federal government had a proprietary interest. *Id.* at 36. *See generally Nat'l Ass'n of Mfrs. v. Perez*, 2015 U.S. Dist. LEXIS 60467 (D.D.C. May 7, 2015) (Memorandum Opinion) (upholding President Obama's executive order requiring federal contractors to post notices of employees' rights under the NLRA, including the right to join a union, and citing *UAW-Labor Emp't & Training Corp. v. Chao*, 325 F.3d 360 (D.C. Cir. 2003) which upheld President Bush's executive order requiring the posting of a notice informing employees of their right *not* to join a union).

4. *Garmon* preemption is grounded in a policy of averting the danger of states' interference with national labor policy. *See Garmon*, 359 U.S. at 244; *Amalgamated Ass'n of Street, Electric Ry. & Motor Coach Emps. v. Lockridge*, 403 U.S. 274, 286–90 (1971). This policy of federal supremacy has a number of implications that courts have addressed over the years:

a. The Supremacy Clause and preemption are issues only when there is a conflict between state or local law and federal law. Congress delegated jurisdiction to the Board only over statutory "employers" and "employees." *See* 29 U.S.C. §§ 152(2), (3). Accordingly, the states are generally free to regulate the labor relations between employers and other workers who do not meet the statutory definition of "employee." Perhaps the most obvious example of this principle is state regulation of public-sector labor relations. In short, the NLRA does not preempt public-sector labor laws because state and local government employees are not covered by the Act and subject to the Board's jurisdiction. See discussion in Chapter 2. What about the other exemptions? Several states have enacted laws providing agricultural workers with collective bargaining rights. See discussion in Chapter 2. Further, the Ninth Circuit held that the NLRA did not preempt a local law allowing ride-hail drivers who were classified as independent contractors to unionize. (However, the statute ran into problems under antitrust law, and the case was settled before those problems were conclusively resolved.) *Chamber of Commerce v. Seattle*, 890 F.3d 769 (9th Cir. 2018). What about supervisors? *See Int'l Longshoremen's Ass'n v. Davis*, 476 U.S. 380, 399 (1986) (holding, in the context of determining whether the NLRA preempted a putative supervisor's state fraud claim, that "the party asserting preemption [the union] must make an affirmative showing that the activity is arguably subject to the Act").

One important recent case concerns a New York City law requiring fast food restaurants to allow workers to pay money to "alt-labor" and other qualifying non-profit groups via payroll deduction. The statute specifically bars "labor organizations" as defined in the NLRA from qualifying to receive contributions under this system. The National Restaurant Association sued, arguing in part that the law was preempted under *Garmon*. The NRA's argument turned on the fact that the ordinance put a New York agency in charge of deciding what groups were "labor organizations." Specifically, the NRA argued that the NLRB was the only body permitted to decide what groups were labor organizations, and relatedly, that the statute inevitably placed the New York agency in the position of having to make close calls involving groups that were "arguably" labor organizations. However, a district court rejected these arguments, at least insofar as the NRA argued that they provided a basis to strike down the statue on its face. The district court held that many situations covered by the statute would not present close calls; where that was not the case, the court signaled that an as-applied preemption challenge might succeed. *Restaurant Law Center v. City of New York*, 360 F. Supp. 3d 192 (S.D.N.Y. 2019). (This case was on appeal as of the date this book went to print.)

b. The NLRA preempts state prohibition of (arguably) protected activity. For example, in *UAW v. O'Brien*, 339 U.S. 454 (1950), the Court held that the states were without jurisdiction to regulate peaceful strikes. There, the Court struck down a state law imposing a notice period and requiring unions to call a membership vote before striking. *See Amalgamated Ass'n of Street, Elec., Ry. & Motor Coach Emps. v. Employment Rel. Bd.*, 340 U.S. 383 (1951) (states lack jurisdiction to regulate peaceful strikes of public utilities).

c. The NLRA also preempts state prohibition of acts that the NLRA (at least arguably) prohibits. For example, a state may not provide relief to an employee discharged for engaging in an NLRA-protected activity such as union organizing. Instead the employee must file a charge with the NLRB, alleging that the employer violated the NLRA. *See, e.g., Gouveia v. Napili-Kai*, 649 P.2d 1119, 1125 (Haw. 1982) (NLRA preempts mental distress state claim of employee—discharged for attempting to negotiating union wage scale—absent a showing that alleged outrageous conduct which caused mental distress was "unrelated to practice prohibited by [NLRA] or did not form basis of prohibited practice").

5. There are several exceptions to the *Garmon* preemption doctrine even when states seek to regulate conduct by covered employers and employees that is (arguably) protected by § 7 or (arguably) prohibited by § 8. As *Garmon* states, the Court has refused to apply the pre-emption doctrine to activity that "was a merely peripheral concern of the Labor Management Relations Act . . . (or) touched interests so deeply rooted in local feeling and responsibility that, in the absence of compelling congressional direction, we could not infer that Congress had deprived the states of the power to act." With these two tests in mind, consider whether the states may regulate the following conduct:

a. Mass picketing and threats of violence? In *United Constr. Workers v. Laburnum Corp.*, 347 U.S. 656, 657 (1954), the union, using intimidation and threats of violence in concert with its demands for recognition, forced an employer to abandon a construction contract resulting in lost profits. In *Auto. Workers v. Russell*, 356 U.S. 634 (1958), the Court held that the state court had jurisdiction to entertain an employee's common-law tort claim against a union that utilized mass picketing and threats of violence to prevent that employee from crossing a picket line so that he could go to work. In both cases, absent these coercive elements, the causes of action would have been preempted.

Recall *NLRB v. Washington Aluminum Co.*, 370 U.S. 9 (1962), discussed in Chapter 4, in which the Court observed in dicta that activity loses its protected character if, among other things, it is violent or otherwise unlawful. In *Riesbeck v. UFCW, Local 23*, 404 S.E.2d 404 (W. Va. 1991), the West Virginia Supreme Court of Appeals observed that state courts may enjoin concerted activity that is violent or destructive because such conduct is unprotected and the state has a strong interest in protecting its people and their property. The court further observed that, absent such violence and destruction, a state court is without jurisdiction to enjoin peaceful trespassory picketing upon the filing of the ULP charge. *Accord UMW v. Waters*, 489 S.E.2d 266 (W. Va. 1997). In *Loehmann's Plaza*, 305 N.L.R.B. 663 (1991), *enforced sub nom. Davis Supermkts. v. NLRB*, 2 F.3d 1162 (D.C. Cir. 1993), the Board considered this question, holding that a state law action is preempted upon issuance of the General Counsel's complaint.

b. Malicious libel? In *Linn v. Plant Guard Workers*, 383 U.S. 53 (1966), the Court held that a malicious libel suit was not preempted, even though the subject matter of the dispute constituted a ULP, where statements made during the course of a labor dispute were maliciously false and injurious. The Court explained that allowing states to remedy reputational injury was of peripheral concern to national labor policy because such conduct was unprotected by § 7.

c. Wrongful expulsion from union membership? *See Machinists v. Gonzales*, 356 U.S. 617 (1958) (action for breach of contract not preempted because it was a matter of peripheral concern to the NLRA).

d. Tort suits? In *Farmer v. United Bhd. of Carpenters and Joiners of Am., Local 25*, 430 U.S. 290 (1977), the Court held that the NLRA did not preempt an intentional infliction of emotional distress lawsuit, where the conduct alleged was outrageous. The Court suggested, however, that a state law tort suit resting on claims of breach of contract and discriminatory hiring hall referrals would be preempted.

e. Trespass? In *Sears, Roebuck & Co. v. San Diego Cnty. Dist. Council of Carpenters*, 436 U.S. 180 (1978), the employer obtained a state court injunction (which the California Supreme Court reversed) enjoining nonviolent union picketing (protesting a work assignment and requesting recognition with regard to that work assignment) on the employer's property. The United States Supreme Court reversed, holding that the NLRA did not preempt the state injunction on several grounds. First, the Court observed that the picketing was arguably prohibited under §§ 8(b)(4)(D) or 8(b)(7)(C). (See Chapter 12.) The Court concluded, however, there was little chance that a state injunction would interfere with the Board's primary jurisdiction because the state court's concern in issuing the injunction would be to protect the employer's private property, whereas the NLRB's concern would be determining whether the union was coercing a work assignment or recognition. Second, the picketing was arguably protected as area standards picketing. The Court concluded, however, that the NLRA did not preempt the state regulation where the union refused to invoke the Board's jurisdiction to determine whether the employer's eviction of the picketers violated the NLRA. Does this mean that the Court would have found that the NLRA would have preempted a state court's order enjoining protected picketing?

Recently, the UFCW-linked group OURWalmart engaged in a series of protests inside and around Wal-Mart stores, and Wal-Mart responded by filing trespass lawsuits in a number of state courts. With one exception, these state courts have concluded that Wal-Mart's claims are not preempted. *See UFCW v. Wal-Mart Stores, Inc.*, No. 02-C-13-181974, 2017 WL 2691235 (Md. 2017) (holding trespass and nuisance suit fell under *Garmon*'s "local feeling" exception and therefore was not preempted by NLRA); *UFCW v. Wal-Mart Stores, Inc.*, No. 02-15-00374-cv, 2016 WL 6277370 (Tex. App. Oct. 27, 2016) (holding trespass and nuisance actions not preempted, and discussing similar conclusions by state courts in California, Colorado, Florida, and Maryland); *but see Wal-Mart Stores, Inc. v. UFCW*, 354 P.3d 31 (Wash. Ct. App. 2015) (Wal-Mart's trespass action did not implicate "'deeply rooted' local interest because the UFCW's activities were not violent, intentional torts, or threat[s of] violence").

f. Wrongful discharge? In *Belknap, Inc. v. Hale*, 463 U.S. 491 (1983), permanent striker replacement workers sued an employer for wrongful discharge and deceit when the employer displaced those workers with the strikers shortly after settling the strike with the union. The Court held that the NLRA did not preempt this state cause of action and that the employer could have protected itself simply by hiring temporary replacement workers. In other words, employers may not avoid the striking employees' statutory rights (recall that such workers have a right to displace replacement workers where the concerted action is a ULP strike) by telling replacement workers that they are permanent.

By contrast, the Sixth Circuit held in *Lewis v. Whirlpool Corp.*, 630 F.3d 484 (6th Cir. 2011) that the NLRA preempted a wrongful discharge claim brought under Ohio's public policy exception to the at-will doctrine, where the question presented was identical to the question that could have been presented to the NLRB. In that case, Whirlpool had discharged Lewis, a former supervisor, for refusing to discharge employees for their union activity. The court observed that Lewis was not an employee protected under the NLRA, but noted that supervisors do have claims under the NLRA when disciplined for refusing to commit an ULP. *See id.* (citing, among others, *Auto. Salesmen's Union Local 1095, United Food & Commercial Workers Union, AFL-CIO v. NLRB*, 711 F.2d 383, 386 (D.C. Cir. 1983)).

6. The *Garmon* Court also suggested that preemption does not apply "where the particular rule of law sought to be invoked before another tribunal is so structured and administered that, in virtually all instances, it is safe to presume that judicial supervision will not disserve the interests promoted by the federal labor statutes." In *Vaca v. Sipes*, 386 U.S. 171 (1967), discussed in Chapter 14, an employee filed a lawsuit alleging that his union breached its duty of fair representation (DFR) when it refused to take the employees' grievance to arbitration on grounds that the grievance was weak. Although the DFR allegations also constituted a ULP and, therefore, conduct arguably prohibited by the NLRA, the Supreme Court held that the NLRA does not preempt § 301 lawsuits against unions for violating the DFR where the union has refused to take a grievance to arbitration, so long as the parties have fully exhausted internal remedies. 386 U.S. at 184–85; *see also Figueroa v. Foster*, 864 F.3d 222 (2d Cir. 2017) (holding that NLRA duty of fair representation did not preempt discrimination claims filed by union members against their union representative under the New York State Human Rights Law).

7. One criticism of labor law preemption doctrine is that it has contributed to the "ossification" of American labor law by foreclosing opportunities for innovation. *See, e.g.,* Cynthia Estlund, *The Ossification of American Labor Law*, 102 Colum. L. Rev. 1527 (2002) With limited exceptions, the text of the NLRA has not changed in seven decades, and many legal issues originally left open by Congress have been finally decided by the Supreme Court and rendered essentially unchangeable without further congressional action, even where workers' lives, the nature of work, and the state of the American economy have undeniably changed. As the principal interpreter of a static statute, the Board is limited in its ability to innovate. Because of preemption, states and local governments do not have an opportunity to innovate. As a result, this criticism suggests, labor law has been rendered obsolete or, at least, less effective than it might be were greater innovation permitted. What is your reaction to this argument? Does it have merit?

More generally, should advocates for unions or employers call for more relaxed pre-emption rules? Union advocates could push for more union-friendly state laws — for example, laws that barred employers from requiring employees to attend meetings for certain specified purposes, including (but not limited to) anti-union "captive audience" meetings. *See* Paul Secunda, *Toward the Viability of State-Based*

Legislation to Address Workplace Captive Audience Meetings in the United States, 29 Comp. Lab. L. & Pol'y J. 209 (2008). Employer advocates could push for rules that, for example, would bar voluntary recognition based on cards and require elections in all cases for union recognition. Note that the NLRB has sued or threatened to sue four states (Arizona, South Carolina, South Dakota, and Utah) over state laws with such provisions. *See* Steven Greenhouse, *U.S. Plans to Sue 4 States over Laws Requiring Secret Ballots for Unionizing*, N.Y. Times, Jan. 14, 2011, *available at* http://www .nytimes.com/2011/01/15/business/economy/15labor.html?_r=1. If NLRA preemption rules were relaxed, what do you think would happen? Would private-sector labor law become somewhat more like public-sector law, with significant variations among states? If so, would that be a good or bad thing?

B. The NLRA Preempts State Regulation of Conduct that Congress Intended to Leave Unregulated

Lodge 76, International Ass'n of Machinists v. Employment Rel. Bd.

Supreme Court of the United States
427 U.S. 132 (1976)

Brennan, J.

The question to be decided in this case is whether federal labor policy pre-empts the authority of a state labor relations board to grant an employer covered by the NLRA an order enjoining a union and its members from continuing to refuse to work overtime pursuant to a union policy to put economic pressure on the employer in negotiations for renewal of an expired collective-bargaining agreement.

A collective-bargaining agreement between petitioner Lodge 76 (Union) and respondent Kearney & Trecker Corp. (employer) was terminated by the employer pursuant to the terms of the agreement on June 19, 1971. Good-faith bargaining over the terms of a renewal agreement continued for over a year thereafter, finally resulting in the signing of a new agreement effective July 23, 1972. A particularly controverted issue during negotiations was the employer's demand that the provision of the expired agreement under which, as for the prior 17 years, the basic workday was seven and one-half hours, Monday through Friday, and the basic workweek was 37 ½ hours, be replaced with a new provision providing a basic workday of eight hours and a basic workweek of 40 hours, and that the terms on which overtime rates of pay were payable be changed accordingly.

A few days after the old agreement was terminated the employer unilaterally began to make changes in some conditions of employment provided in the expired contract, *e.g.*, eliminating the checkoff of Union dues, eliminating the Union's office in the plant, and eliminating Union lost time. No immediate change was made in the basic workweek or workday, but in March 1972, the employer announced that it would unilaterally implement, as of March 13, 1972, its proposal for a 40-hour week and eight-hour day. The Union response was a membership meeting on March 7 at which strike action was authorized and a resolution was adopted binding Union members to refuse to work any overtime, defined as work in excess of seven and one-half hours in any day or 37 1/2 hours in any week. Following the strike vote, the employer offered to "defer the implementation" of its workweek proposal if the Union would agree to call off the concerted refusal to work overtime. The Union, however, refused the offer and indicated its intent to continue the concerted ban on overtime. Thereafter, the employer did not make effective the proposed changes in the workday and workweek before the new agreement became effective on July 23, 1972. Although all but a very few employees complied with the Union's resolution against acceptance of overtime work during the negotiations, the employer did not discipline, or attempt to discipline, any employee for refusing to work overtime.

Instead, while negotiations continued, the employer filed a charge with the NLRB that the Union's resolution violated § 8(b)(3). The Regional Director dismissed the charge on the ground that the "policy prohibiting overtime work by its member employees . . . does not appear to be in violation of the Act" and therefore was not conduct cognizable by the Board under *NLRB v. Insurance Agents*, 361 U.S. 477 (1960). However, the employer also filed a complaint before the Wisconsin Employment Relations Commission charging that the refusal to work overtime constituted an unfair labor practice under state law. The Union filed a motion before the Commission to dismiss the complaint for want of "jurisdiction over the subject matter" in that jurisdiction over "the activity of the [Union] complained of [is] pre-empted by" the NLRA. The motion was denied and the Commission adopted the Conclusion of Law of its Examiner that "the concerted refusal to work overtime, is not an activity which is arguably protected under § 7 or arguably prohibited under § 8 of the NLRA, as amended, and . . . , therefore, the . . . Commission is not pre-empted from asserting its jurisdiction to regulate said conduct." The Commission also adopted the further Conclusion of Law that the Union "by authorizing . . . the concerted refusal to work overtime . . . engaged in a concerted effort to interfere with production and . . . committed an unfair labor practice within the meaning of § 111.06(2)(h) [making it an "unfair labor practice for an employee individually or in concert with others to take unauthorized possession of property of the employer or to engage in any concerted effort to interfere with production except by leaving the premises in an orderly manner for the purpose of going on strike"]." The Commission thereupon entered an order that the Union, Inter alia, "[i]mmediately cease and desist from authorizing, encouraging or condoning any concerted refusal to accept overtime assignments. . . . " The Wisconsin Circuit Court affirmed and entered judgment enforcing the Commission's order. The Wisconsin Supreme Court affirmed the Circuit Court. . . . We reverse.

I

"The national . . . Act . . . leaves much to the states, though Congress has refrained from telling us how much. We must spell out from conflicting indications of congressional will the area in which state action is still permissible." *Garner v.*

Teamsters, 346 U.S. 485, 488 (1953). Federal labor policy as reflected in the NLRA . . . has been construed not to preclude the states from regulating aspects of labor relations that involve "conduct touch[ing] interests so deeply rooted in local feeling and responsibility that . . . we could not infer that Congress had deprived the states of the power to act." *Garmon*, 359 U.S. at 244. Policing of actual or threatened violence to persons or destruction of property has been held most clearly a matter for the states. Similarly, the federal law governing labor relations does not withdraw "from the States . . . power to regulate where the activity regulated [is] a merely peripheral concern of the Labor Management Relations Act." *Id.* at 243.

Cases that have held state authority to be pre-empted by federal law tend to fall into one of two categories: (1) those that reflect the concern that "one forum would enjoin, as illegal, conduct which the other forum would find legal" and (2) those that reflect the concern "that the [application of state law by] state courts would restrict the exercise of rights guaranteed by the Federal Acts." . . . "[I]n referring to decisions holding state laws pre-empted by the NLRA, care must be taken to distinguish pre-emption based on federal protection of the conduct in question . . . from that based predominantly on the primary jurisdiction of the NLRB . . . , although the two are often not easily separable." . . . Each of these distinct aspects of labor law pre-emption has had its own history in our decisions, to which we now turn.

We consider first pre-emption based predominantly on the primary jurisdiction of the Board. This line of pre-emption analysis was developed in [*Garmon*]. . . .

However, a second line of pre-emption analysis has been developed in cases focusing upon the crucial inquiry whether Congress intended that the conduct involved be unregulated because left "to be controlled by the free play of economic forces." *NLRB v. Nash-Finch Co.*, 404 U.S. 138, 144, (1971). Concededly this inquiry was not made in 1949 in [*Briggs-Stratton*]. . . . [There], the union, in order to bring pressure on the employer during negotiations, adopted a plan whereby union meetings were called at irregular times during working hours without advance notice to the employer or any notice as to whether or when the workers would return. In a proceeding under the Wisconsin Employment Peace Act, the Wisconsin Employment Relations Board issued an order forbidding the union and its members to engage in concerted efforts to interfere with production by those methods. This Court did not inquire whether Congress meant that such methods should be reserved to the union "to be controlled by the free play of economic forces." Rather, because these methods were "neither made a right under federal law nor a violation if it" the Court held that there "was no basis for denying to Wisconsin the power, in governing her internal affairs, to regulate" such conduct.

However, the *Briggs-Stratton* holding that state power is not pre-empted as to peaceful conduct neither protected by § 7 nor prohibited by § 8 of the federal Act, a holding premised on the statement that "[t]his conduct is governable by the State or it is entirely ungoverned," . . . was undercut by subsequent decisions of this Court. For the Court soon recognized that a particular activity might be "protected" by federal law not only when it fell within § 7, but also when it was an activity that

Congress intended to be "unrestricted by any governmental power to regulate" because it was among the permissible "economic weapons in reserve, ... actual exercise [of which] on occasion by the parties, is part and parcel of the system that the Wagner and Taft-Hartley Acts have recognized." *NLRB v. Insurance Agents*, 361 U.S., at 488–89. "[T]he legislative purpose may ... dictate that certain activity 'neither protected nor prohibited' be deemed privileged against state regulation." ...

II

[*Insurance Agents*] involved a charge of a refusal by the union to bargain in good faith in violation of § 8(b)(3). ... The charge was based on union activities that occurred during good-faith bargaining over the terms of a collective-bargaining agreement. During the negotiations, the union directed concerted on-the-job activities by its members of a harassing nature designed to interfere with the conduct of the employer's business, for the avowed purpose of putting economic pressure on the employer to accede to the union's bargaining demands. The harassing activities, all peaceful, by the member insurance agents included refusal for a time to solicit new business, and refusal (after the writing of new business was resumed) to comply with the employer insurance company's reporting procedures; refusal to participate in a company campaign to solicit new business; reporting late at district offices the days the agents were scheduled to attend them; refusing to perform customary duties at the office, instead engaging there in "sit-in-mornings," "doing what comes naturally," and leaving at noon as a group; absenting themselves from special business conferences arranged by the company; picketing and distributing leaflets outside the various offices of the company on specified days and hours as directed by the union; distributing leaflets each day to policyholders and others and soliciting policyholders' signatures on petitions directed to the company; and presenting the signed policyholders' petitions to the company at its home office while simultaneously engaging in mass demonstrations there. ... We held that such tactics would not support a finding by the NLRB that the union had failed to bargain in good faith as required by § 8(b)(3) and rejected the per se rule applied by the Board that use of "economically harassing activities" alone sufficed to prove a violation of that section. The Court assumed "that the activities in question here were not 'protected' under § 7 of the Act," ... but held that the per se rule was beyond the authority of the NLRB to apply. ...

The Court had earlier recognized in pre-emption cases that Congress meant to leave some activities unregulated and to be controlled by the free play of economic forces. *Garner*, in finding pre-empted state power to restrict peaceful recognitional picketing, said:

> "The detailed prescription of a procedure for restraint of specified types of picketing would seem to imply that other picketing is to be free of other methods and sources of restraint. For the policy of the National Labor Management Relations Act is not to condemn all picketing but only that ascertained by its prescribed processes to fall within its prohibitions. Otherwise, it is implicit in the Act that the public interest is served by freedom of labor

to use the weapon of picketing. For a state to impinge on the area of labor combat designed to be free is quite as much an obstruction of federal policy as if the state were to declare picketing free for purposes or by methods which the federal Act prohibits." 346 U.S. at 499–500.

Moreover, *Garmon* expressly recognized that "the Board may decide that an activity is neither protected nor prohibited, and thereby raise the question whether such activity may be regulated by the states." . . .

III

There is simply no question that the Act's processes would be frustrated in [this] case were the State's ruling permitted to stand. The employer in this case invoked the Wisconsin law because it was unable to overcome the Union tactic with its own economic self-help means. Although it did employ economic weapons putting pressure on the Union when it terminated the previous agreement . . . , it apparently lacked sufficient economic strength to secure bargaining demands under "the balance of power between labor and management expressed in our national labor policy." But the economic weakness of the affected party cannot justify state aid contrary to federal law for, as we have developed, "the use of economic pressure by the parties to a labor dispute is not a grudging exception [under] . . . the [federal] Act; it is part and parcel of the process of collective bargaining." *Insurance Agents*, 361 U.S. at 495. The state action in this case is not filling "a regulatory void which Congress plainly assumed would not exist," . . . Rather, it is clearly beyond question that Wisconsin "[entered] into the substantive aspects of the bargaining process to an extent Congress has not countenanced." *Id.* at 498.

Our decisions hold that Congress meant that these activities, whether of employer or employees, were not to be regulable by States any more than by the NLRB, for neither States nor the Board is "afforded flexibility in picking and choosing which economic devices of labor and management shall be branded as unlawful." Ibid. Rather, both are without authority to attempt to "introduce some standard of properly 'balanced' bargaining power" *Id.* at 497 (footnote omitted), or to define "what economic sanctions might be permitted negotiating parties in an 'ideal' or 'balanced' state of collective bargaining." *Id.* at 500. To sanction state regulation of such economic pressure deemed by the federal Act "desirabl[y] . . . left for the free play of contending economic forces, . . . is not merely [to fill] a gap [by] outlaw[ing] what federal law fails to outlaw; it is denying one party to an economic contest a weapon that Congress meant him to have available." Lesnick, *Preemption Reconsidered: The Apparent Reaffirmation of Garmon*, 72 COLUM. L. REV. 469, 478 (1972). Accordingly, such regulation by the State is impermissible because it "'stands as an obstacle to the accomplishment and execution of the full purposes and objectives of Congress.'" *Hill v. Florida*, 325 U.S. 538, 542 (1945).

IV

There remains the question of the continuing vitality of *Briggs-Stratton*. . . . We hold today that the ruling of *Briggs-Stratton*, permitting state regulation of partial strike activities such as are involved in this case is likewise "no longer of general application."

Briggs-Stratton assumed "management . . . would be disabled from any kind of self-help to cope with these coercive tactics of the union" and could not "take any steps to resist or combat them without incurring the sanctions of the Act." 336 U.S. at 264. But as *Insurance Agents* held, where the union activity complained of is "protected," not because it is within § 7, but only because it is an activity Congress meant to leave unregulated, "the employer could have discharged or taken other appropriate disciplinary action against the employees participating." *Id.* at 493. Moreover, even were the activity presented in the instant case "protected" activity within the meaning of § 7, economic weapons were available to counter the Union's refusal to work overtime, *e.g.*, a lockout, *American Ship Bldg. Co. v. NLRB*, 380 U.S. 300 (1965), and the hiring of permanent replacements under *NLRB v. Mackay Radio & Tel. Co.*, 304 U.S. 333 (1938). . . .

Our decisions since *Briggs-Stratton* have made it abundantly clear that state attempts to influence the substantive terms of collective-bargaining agreements are as inconsistent with the federal regulatory scheme as are such attempts by the NLRB: "Since the federal law operates here, in an area where its authority is paramount, to leave the parties free, the inconsistent application of state law is necessarily outside the power of the State." *Local 24 Teamsters v. Oliver*, 358 U.S. 283, 296 (1959). And indubitably regulation, whether federal or State, of "the choice of economic weapons that may be used as part of collective bargaining [exerts] considerable influence upon the substantive terms on which the parties contract." *NLRB v. Insurance Agents*, 361 U.S. at 490. The availability or not of economic weapons that federal law leaves the parties free to use cannot "depend upon the forum in which the [opponent] presses its claims." *Howard Johnson Co. v. Hotel Employees*, 417 U.S. 249, 256 (1974).

Briggs-Stratton "stands as a significant departure from our . . . emphasis upon the congressional policy" central to the statutory scheme it has enacted[.] . . . [S]ince our later decisions make plain that *Briggs-Stratton* "does not further but rather frustrates realization of an important goal of our national labor policy," . . . *Briggs-Stratton* is expressly overruled. Its authority "has been 'so restricted by our later decisions' . . . that [it] must be regarded as having 'been worn away by the erosion of time' . . . and of contrary authority." . . .

V

This survey of the extent to which federal labor policy and the federal Act have pre-empted state regulatory authority to police the use by employees and employers of peaceful methods of putting economic pressure upon one another compels the conclusion that the judgment of the Wisconsin Supreme Court must be reversed. . . . [T]he Union policy against overtime work was [not] enforced by violence or threats of intimidation or injury to property. Workers simply left the plant at the end of their work shift and refused to volunteer for or accept overtime or Saturday work. In sustaining the order of the Wisconsin Commission, the Wisconsin Supreme Court relied on *Briggs-Stratton* as dispositive against the Union's claim of pre-emption. . . .

Since *Briggs-Stratton* is today overruled, and as we hold further that the Union's refusal to work overtime is peaceful conduct constituting activity which must be free of regulation by the states if the congressional intent in enacting the comprehensive federal law of labor relations is not to be frustrated, the judgment of the Wisconsin Supreme Court is [reversed].

Notes

1. As with *Garmon* preemption, there are exceptions to *Machinists* preemption. Generally applicable labor standards legislation that raises the floor of workers' wages, hours, and other terms and conditions of employment generally are not preempted by the NLRA, even though the existence and level of the floor might interfere with a freely bargained for exchange. As the Supreme Court explained:

> [T]he [state] statute gives employees something for which they otherwise might have to bargain. That is true, however, with regard to any state law that substantively regulates employment conditions. Both employers and employees come to the bargaining table with rights under state law that form a "backdrop" for their negotiations. . . . *Fort Halifax Packing Co. v. Coyne*, 482 U.S. 1, 21 (1987).

Here are a few examples of statutes that the NLRA does not preempt, even though they might have some effect on market forces at play.

a. Statutory benefits: In *New York Tel. Co. v. New York State Dept. of Labor*, 440 U.S. 519 (1979), the Court held that a state law authorizing unemployment benefits to strikers was not preempted by *Machinists*. The Court rejected the employer's argument that the law upset the free play of market forces in resolving labor disputes by forcing employers, who pay an unemployment tax, to essentially subsidize their workers' strikes. The Court also found no evidence in the legislative history of the Social Security Act of Congress's intent to preclude States from extending benefits to strikers. The Court grounded its holding on its observation that the state law was concerned primarily with creating an unemployment scheme and not with labor-management relations. Similarly, in *Metro. Life Ins. Co. v. Mass.*, 471 U.S. 724 (1985), the Court held not preempted a state law requiring employers who provide medical-insurance coverage for hospital expenses to include mental healthcare coverage. The Court rejected the union's argument that the law unfairly limited its bargaining leverage by preventing it from opting out of the mental healthcare coverage in exchange for another benefit that its members might prefer. Once again, the Court rejected these arguments in part on grounds that the state law was not concerned with primarily with creating a benefits mandate and not with labor-management relations.

A related issue involves minimum standards laws that contain an exemption for employees who are covered by a collective bargaining agreement. For example, in 2014, Los Angeles adopted a minimum wage ordinance for hotel workers that contained an exemption for hotels covered by a CBA. Non-union hotels sued to invalidate the law, arguing that either the law in general or the waiver for union hotels was preempted under *Machinists*. However, the Ninth Circuit disagreed, because the law did not interfere with labor dispute resolution. *Am. Hotel & Lodging Ass'n v. Los Angeles*, 834 F.3d 958 (9th Cir. 2016) (citing *Livadas v. Bradshaw*). In contrast, a federal district court in New York held that the NLRA preempted a city ordinance that required non-union car wash companies to post a $150,000 surety bond, but required only a $30,000 bond from car washes that entered into a CBA or an "active monitoring" agreement that would ensure timely and accurate wage payments. *Ass'n of Car Wash Owners, Inc. v. City of NY*, 15-cv-08157 (S.D.N.Y. May 26, 2017).

b. Severance Pay: In *Fort Halifax Packing Co. v. Coyne*, 482 U.S. 1 (1987), the Court held a state law mandating severance pay in cases of a plant closing was not preempted.

c. Wage Payment Acts: A wage payment act requires employers to pay discharged employees all wages due at the time of discharge or shortly thereafter. In cases where an employer refused to pay those wages, a state official can pursue the unpaid wages in court and obtain payment and damages on behalf of the discharged worker. In *Livadas v. Bradshaw*, 512 U.S. 107 (1994), the Court held preempted a state policy of pursuing the statutory rights only of non-union employees. The Court rejected the state's rationale for distinguishing unionized and non-union employees; the state had argued that it felt its resources were better spent on focusing its efforts on workers who did not have the luxury of a grievance-arbitration mechanism.

2. *Machinists* noted the following additional exception to its preemption rule: "To the extent . . . that the holding in *Briggs-Stratton* was premised on the Court's concern in that case with 'evidence of considerable injury to property and intimidation of other employees by threats,' that decision remains vital as an unexceptional instance of our consistent recognition of the power of the states to regulate conduct physically injuring or threatening injury to persons or property." This is consistent with the *Garmon* line of cases that States are free to regulate violence and threats to property.

The following case is the Court's most recent pronouncement on *Machinists* preemption and offers a worthwhile illustration of many of the arguments discussed above. Although the Court does a good job of explaining why the NLRA preempts the California statute, it does not reach the *Garmon* preemption question. While reading the case, consider why this statute might or might not be preempted under *Garmon*. Can a state action be preempted by both *Machinists* and *Garmon*?

Chamber of Commerce v. Brown

Supreme Court of the United States
554 U.S. 60 (2008)

STEVENS, J.

A California statute known as "Assembly Bill 1889" (AB 1889) prohibits several classes of employers that receive state funds from using the funds "to assist, promote, or deter union organizing." . . . The question presented to us is whether two of its provisions — § 16645.2, applicable to grant recipients, and § 16645.7, applicable to private employers receiving more than $10,000 in program funds in any year — are pre-empted by federal law mandating that certain zones of labor activity be unregulated. . . .

AB 1889 prohibits certain employers that receive state funds . . . from using such funds to "assist, promote, or deter union organizing." *See* CAL. GOVT. CODE ANN. §§ 16645.1 to 16645.7. This prohibition encompasses "any attempt by an employer to influence the decision of its employees" regarding "[w]hether to support or oppose a labor organization" and "[w]hether to become a member of any labor organization." § 16645(a). The statute specifies that the spending restriction applies to "any expense, including legal and consulting fees and salaries of supervisors and employees, incurred for . . . an activity to assist, promote, or deter union organizing." § 16646(a).

Despite the neutral statement of policy quoted above, AB 1889 expressly exempts "activit[ies] performed" or "expense[s] incurred" in connection with certain undertakings that promote unionization, including "[a]llowing a labor organization or its representatives access to the employer's facilities or property," and "[n]egotiating, entering into, or carrying out a voluntary recognition agreement with a labor organization." §§ 16647(b), (d).

To ensure compliance with the grant and program restrictions at issue in this case, AB 1889 establishes a formidable enforcement scheme. . . .

In April 2002, several organizations whose members do business with the State of California (collectively, Chamber of Commerce), brought this action against the California Department of Health Services and appropriate state officials (collectively, the State) to enjoin enforcement of AB 1889. Two labor unions (collectively, AFL-CIO) intervened to defend the statute's validity.

The District Court granted partial summary judgment in favor of the Chamber of Commerce . . . The [Ninth Circuit] . . . granted rehearing en banc and reversed. . . . We granted certiorari . . . and now reverse.

Although the NLRA itself contains no express pre-emption provision, we have held that Congress implicitly mandated two types of pre-emption as necessary to implement federal labor policy. The first, known as *Garmon* pre-emption . . . forbids States to "regulate activity that the NLRA protects, prohibits, or arguably protects or prohibits."... The second, known as *Machinists* pre-emption, forbids both the NLRB and States to regulate conduct that Congress intended "be unregulated because left 'to be controlled by the free play of economic forces.'" *Machinists v. Wisconsin Employment Relations Comm'n*, 427 U.S. 132, 140 (1976) ([citation omitted]). *Machinists* pre-emption is based on the premise that "'Congress struck a balance of protection, prohibition, and laissez-faire in respect to union organization, collective bargaining, and labor disputes.'" 427 U.S., at 140, n.4 ([citation omitted]).

Today we hold that §§ 16645.2 and 16645.7 are pre-empted under *Machinists* because they regulate within "a zone protected and reserved for market freedom." *Building & Constr. Trades Council v. Associated Builders & Contractors of Mass./R. I., Inc.*, 507 U.S. 218, 227 (1993) (*Boston Harbor*). We do not reach the question whether the provisions would also be pre-empted under *Garmon*. ...

As enacted in 1935, the NLRA ... did not include any provision that specifically addressed the intersection between employee organizational rights and employer speech rights. ... Rather, it was left to the NLRB, subject to review in federal court, to reconcile these interests in its construction of §§ 7 and 8. ...

Among the frequently litigated issues under the Wagner Act were charges that an employer's attempts to persuade employees not to join a union—or to join one favored by the employer rather than a rival—amounted to a form of coercion prohibited by § 8. The NLRB took the position that § 8 demanded complete employer neutrality during organizing campaigns, reasoning that any partisan employer speech about unions would interfere with the § 7 rights of employees. *See* 1 J. Higgins, THE DEVELOPING LABOR LAW 94 (5th ed. 2006). In 1941, this Court curtailed the NLRB's aggressive interpretation, clarifying that nothing in the NLRA prohibits an employer "from expressing its view on labor policies or problems" unless the employer's speech "in connection with other circumstances [amounts] to coercion within the meaning of the Act." *NLRB v. Virginia Elec. & Power Co.*, 314 U.S. 469, 477. We subsequently characterized *Virginia Electric* as recognizing the First Amendment right of employers to engage in noncoercive speech about unionization. *Thomas v. Collins*, 323 U.S. 516, 537–538, (1945). Notwithstanding these decisions, the NLRB continued to regulate employer speech too restrictively in the eyes of Congress.

Concerned that the Wagner Act had pushed the labor relations balance too far in favor of unions, Congress passed the Labor Management Relations Act, 1947 (Taft-Hartley Act). ... The Taft-Hartley Act ... added § 8(c), which protects speech by both unions and employers from regulation by the NLRB. 29 U.S.C. § 158(c). ...

From one vantage, § 8(c) "merely implements the First Amendment," *NLRB v. Gissel Packing Co.*, 395 U.S. 575, 617 (1969), in that it responded to particular constitutional rulings of the NLRB. ... But its enactment also manifested a "congressional intent to encourage free debate on issues dividing labor and management." *Linn v. Plant Guard Workers*, 383 U.S. 53, 62 (1966). It is indicative of how important Congress deemed such "free debate" that Congress amended the NLRA rather than leaving to the courts the task of correcting the NLRB's decisions on a case-by-case basis. We have characterized this policy judgment, which suffuses the NLRA as a whole, as "favoring uninhibited, robust, and wide-open debate in labor disputes," stressing that "freewheeling use of the written and spoken word . . . has been expressly fostered by Congress and approved by the NLRB." *Letter Carriers v. Austin*, 418 U.S. 264, 272–73 (1974).

Congress's express protection of free debate forcefully buttresses the pre-emption analysis in this case. Under *Machinists*, congressional intent to shield a zone of activity from regulation is usually found only "implicit[ly] in the structure of the Act," *Livadas v. Bradshaw*, 512 U.S. 107, 117, n. 11 (1994), drawing on the notion that "'[w]hat Congress left unregulated is as important as the regulations that it imposed'" . . . . In the case of noncoercive speech, however, the protection is both implicit and explicit. Sections 8(a) and 8(b) demonstrate that when Congress has sought to put limits on advocacy for or against union organization, it has expressly set forth the mechanisms for doing so. Moreover, the amendment to § 7 calls attention to the right of employees to refuse to join unions, which implies an underlying right to receive information opposing unionization. Finally, the addition of § 8(c) expressly precludes regulation of speech about unionization "so long as the communications do not contain a 'threat of reprisal or force or promise of benefit.'" *Gissel Packing*, 395 U.S. at 618.

The explicit direction from Congress to leave noncoercive speech unregulated makes this case easier, in at least one respect, than previous NLRA cases because it does not require us "to decipher the presumed intent of Congress in the face of that body's steadfast silence." *Sears, Roebuck & Co. v. Carpenters*, 436 U.S. 180, 188, n. 12 (1978). California's policy judgment that partisan employer speech necessarily "interfere[s] with an employee's choice about whether to join or to be represented by a labor union," 2000 Cal. Stats. ch. 872, § 1, is the same policy judgment that the NLRB advanced under the Wagner Act, and that Congress renounced in the Taft-Hartley Act. To the extent §§ 16645.2 and 16645.7 actually further the express goal of AB 1889, the provisions are unequivocally pre-empted. . . .

The Court of Appeals concluded that *Machinists* did not pre-empt §§ 16645.2 and 16645.7 for three reasons: (1) The spending restrictions apply only to the *use* of state funds, (2) Congress did not leave the zone of activity free from *all* regulation, and (3) California modeled AB 1889 on federal statutes. We find none of these arguments persuasive.

Use of State Funds

In NLRA pre-emption cases, "'judicial concern has necessarily focused on the nature of the activities which the States have sought to regulate, rather than on the method of regulation adopted.'" . . . [S]*ee also Livadas*, 512 U.S. at 119 ("Pre-emption analysis . . . turns on the actual content of [the State's] policy and its real effect on federal rights"). California plainly could not directly regulate noncoercive speech about unionization by means of an express prohibition. It is equally clear that California may not indirectly regulate such conduct by imposing spending restrictions on the use of state funds. . . .

It is beyond dispute that California enacted AB 1889 in its capacity as a regulator rather than a market participant. AB 1889 is neither "specifically tailored to one particular job" nor a "legitimate response to state procurement constraints or to local economic needs." *Gould*, 475 U.S. at 291. As the statute's preamble candidly acknowledges, the legislative purpose is not the efficient procurement of goods and services, but the furtherance of a labor policy. *See* 2000 CAL. STATS. ch. 872, § 1. Although a State has a legitimate proprietary interest in ensuring that state funds are spent in accordance with the purposes for which they are appropriated, this is not the objective of AB 1889. In contrast to a neutral affirmative requirement that funds be spent solely for the purposes of the relevant grant or program, AB 1889 imposes a targeted negative restriction on employer speech about unionization. Furthermore, the statute does not even apply this constraint uniformly. Instead of forbidding the use of state funds for *all* employer advocacy regarding unionization, AB 1889 permits use of state funds for *select* employer advocacy activities that promote unions. . . .

NLRB Regulation

We have characterized *Machinists* pre-emption as "creat[ing] a zone free from all regulations, whether state or federal." *Boston Harbor*, 507 U.S. at 226. Stressing that the NLRB has regulated employer speech that takes place on the eve of union elections, the Court of Appeals deemed *Machinists* inapplicable because "employer speech in the context of organizing" is not a zone of activity that Congress left free from "*all* regulation." *See* 463 F.3d at 1089 ([citation omitted]).

The NLRB has policed a narrow zone of speech to ensure free and fair elections under the aegis of § 9 of the NLRA, 29 U.S.C. § 159. Whatever the NLRB's regulatory authority within special settings such as imminent elections, however, Congress has clearly denied it the authority to regulate the broader category of noncoercive speech encompassed by AB 1889. It is equally obvious that the NLRA deprives California of this authority, since "'[t]he States have no more authority than the Board to upset the balance that Congress has struck between labor and management.'" *Metropolitan Life Ins. Co. v. Massachusetts*, 471 U.S. 724, 751 (1985).

Federal Statutes

Finally, the Court of Appeals reasoned that Congress could not have intended to pre-empt AB 1889 because Congress itself has imposed similar restrictions. . . . Specifically, three federal statutes include provisions that forbid the use of particular grant and program funds "to assist, promote, or deter union organizing." We are not persuaded that these few isolated restrictions, plucked from the multitude of federal spending programs, were either intended to alter or did in fact alter the "'wider contours of federal labor policy.'" *Metropolitan Life*, 471 U.S. at 753.

A federal statute will contract the pre-emptive scope of the NLRA if it demonstrates that "Congress has decided to tolerate a substantial measure of diversity" in the particular regulatory sphere. *New York Telephone*, 440 U.S. at 546 (plurality opinion). . . .

The three federal statutes relied on by the Court of Appeals neither conflict with the NLRA nor otherwise establish that Congress "decided to tolerate a substantial measure of diversity" in the regulation of employer speech. Unlike the States, Congress has the authority to create tailored exceptions to otherwise applicable federal policies, and (also unlike the States) it can do so in a manner that preserves national uniformity without opening the door to a 50-state patchwork of inconsistent labor policies. Consequently, the mere fact that Congress has imposed targeted federal restrictions on union-related advocacy in certain limited contexts does not invite the States to override federal labor policy in other settings.

Had Congress enacted a federal version of AB 1889 that applied analogous spending restrictions to *all* federal grants or expenditures, the pre-emption question would be closer. Cf. *Metropolitan Life*, 471 U.S. at 755 (citing federal minimum labor standards as evidence that Congress did not intend to pre-empt state minimum labor standards). But none of the cited statutes is Government-wide in scope, none contains comparable remedial provisions, and none contains express pro-union exemptions. . . . The Court of Appeals' judgment reversing the summary judgment entered for the Chamber of Commerce is reversed, and the case is remanded for further proceedings consistent with this opinion.

III. Section 301 Preemption of State Law Claims

As Chapter 13 describes, § 301 granted federal courts jurisdiction over suits alleging violations of collective-bargaining agreements. Courts reviewing such claims apply federal common law developed under § 301. *See, e.g., Teamsters Local 174 v. Lucas Flour*, 369 U.S. 95 (1962).

Congress did not state whether and to what extent § 301 would preempt state law claims. This is a problem because, just as contractual grievances can raise ULP issues, contractual disputes under collective-bargaining agreements can give rise to state law causes of action. Accordingly, courts have developed a body of law to determine whether such state law causes of action should be adjudicated under state law or whether they would be more properly adjudicated under § 301. Courts generally apply the principle that "when resolution of a state-law claim is substantially dependent upon analysis of the terms of an agreement made between the parties in a labor contract, that claim must either be treated as a § 301 claim . . . or dismissed as pre-empted by federal labor-contract law." *Allis-Chalmers Corp. v. Lueck*, 471 U.S. 202, 220 (1985) (citing *Avco Corp. v. Aero Lodge 735*, 390 U.S. 557 (1968)). This jurisprudential doctrine is known as Section 301 preemption.

Note

In *Bldg. & Constr. Trades Council of the Metro. Dist. v. Associated Builders & Contractors of Mass. (Boston Harbor)*, 507 U.S. 218 (1993), the Supreme Court distinguished between state action that is regulatory and state action that is proprietary, such as when the state purchases construction services or otherwise procures goods and services from the private sector. Applying that distinction, the Court concluded that the NLRA did not preempt the state from being party to a project labor agreement requiring, among other things, that building contractors bidding on a construction project recognize the union, secure workers through a union hiring hall, and abide by the union contract, including the union security clause. The Court found that the state acted as a market player and that Congress did not intend to preempt states from behaving in the manner of other market players, like private businesses.

Drawing a clear line between regulation and proprietary activities has proven more difficult than might be expected, although there are some obvious distinctions. The Court stated that "[w]hen the State acts as regulator, it performs a role that is characteristically a governmental rather than a private role." 507 U.S. at 229. For example, state common law, state legislation, and state executive or administration action would all be considered regulatory. But what about a statute that prohibited the state from purchasing goods from companies that were labor law recidivists? While states' own decisions to purchase goods and services would seem to be quintessentially proprietary, the Supreme Court reached a different result. In *Wisc. Dep't of Indus. v. Gould*, 475 U.S. 282 (1986), a precursor to *Boston Harbor*, the Court found that the state was, in fact, acting in a regulatory role. *Accord Golden State Transit Corp. v. Los Angeles*, 475 U.S. 608 (1986) (NLRA preempts a state from withholding renewal of a franchise license pending settlement of a taxi strike). In essence, *Gould* and *Golden State Transit* found that state and local entities had imposed additional penalties on employers that had violated the NLRA and been subject to its remedies. This was a regulatory act, essentially modifying the framework for punishing labor law violators that Congress had created and the Board had elaborated upon.

In *Airline Service Providers Ass'n v. Los Angeles World Airports*, 873 F.3d 1074 (9th Cir. 2017), the Ninth Circuit upheld a city law requiring companies engaged in refueling planes, handling baggage, taking tickets, and similar services at LAX airport to enter a "labor peace agreement" with "any employee organization that requests one." (The law also required companies to enter mediation and then arbitration to settle the terms of the agreement in the event that bargaining with the employee organization failed.) The court held that the city, which operates LAX, was acting as a market participant because "the challenged governmental action [was] undertaken in pursuit of the 'efficient procurement of needed goods and services,' as one might expect of a private business in the same situation," and "the narrow scope of the challenged action defeat[ed] an inference that its primary goal was to encourage a general policy rather than [to] address a specific proprietary problem." *See also Southeast La. Bldg. & Constr. Trades Council v. Jindal*, 107 F. Supp. 3d 584 (E.D. La. 2015) (state law prohibiting public entities from entering into project labor agreements or funding projects that include project labor agreements fell under the market participant exception).

Lingle v. Norge Div. of Magic Chef, Inc.

Supreme Court of the United States
486 U.S. 399 (1988)

STEVENS, J.

In Illinois an employee who is discharged for filing a worker's compensation claim may recover compensatory and punitive damages from her employer. The question presented in this case is whether an employee covered by a collective-bargaining agreement that provides her with a contractual remedy for discharge without just cause may enforce her state-law remedy for retaliatory discharge. The Court of Appeals [in an en banc decision] held that the application of the state tort remedy was pre-empted by §301 of the Labor Management Relations Act [LMRA]. . . . We disagree.

I

Petitioner was employed in respondent's manufacturing plant in Herrin, Illinois. On December 5, 1984, she notified respondent that she had been injured in the course of her employment and requested compensation for her medical expenses pursuant to the Illinois Workers' Compensation Act. On December 11, 1984, respondent discharged her for filing a "false worker's compensation claim." . . .

The union representing petitioner promptly filed a grievance pursuant to the collective-bargaining agreement that covered all production and maintenance employees in the Herrin plant. The agreement protected those employees, including petitioner, from discharge except for "proper" or "just" cause . . . and established a procedure for the arbitration of grievances. . . . The term grievance was broadly defined to encompass "any dispute between . . . the Employer and any employee, concerning the effect, interpretation, application, claim of breach or violation of this Agreement." . . . Ultimately, an arbitrator ruled in petitioner's favor and ordered respondent to reinstate her with full backpay. . . .

Meanwhile, on July 9, 1985, petitioner commenced this action against respondent by filing a complaint in the Illinois Circuit Court . . . alleging that she had been discharged for exercising her rights under the Illinois workers' compensation laws. . . . Respondent removed the case to the Federal District Court on the basis of diversity of citizenship, and then filed a motion praying that the court either dismiss the case on pre-emption grounds or stay further proceedings pending the completion of the arbitration. . . . Relying on our decision in *Allis-Chalmers Corp. v. Lueck*, 471 U.S. 202 (1985), the District Court dismissed the complaint. It concluded that the "claim for retaliatory discharge is 'inextricably intertwined' with the collective bargaining provision prohibiting wrongful discharge or discharge without just cause" and that allowing the state-law action to proceed would undermine the arbitration procedures set forth in the parties' contract. . . .

The Court of Appeals agreed that the state-law claim was pre-empted by §301. In an en banc opinion, over the dissent of two judges, it rejected petitioner's argument that the tort action was not "inextricably intertwined" with the collective-bargaining agreement because the disposition of a retaliatory discharge claim in Illinois does not depend upon an interpretation of the agreement; on the contrary, the court concluded that "the same analysis of the facts" was implicated under both procedures. . . . We granted certiorari to resolve the conflict in the Circuits.

II

. . . In *Textile Workers v. Lincoln Mills*, 353 U.S. 448 (1957), we held that § 301 not only provides federal-court jurisdiction over controversies involving collective-bargaining agreements, but also "authorizes federal courts to fashion a body of federal law for the enforcement of these collective bargaining agreements." *Id.* at 451.

In *Teamsters v. Lucas Flour Co.*, 369 U.S. 95 (1962), we . . . held that § 301 mandated resort to federal rules of law in order to ensure uniform interpretation of collective-bargaining agreements, and thus to promote the peaceable, consistent resolution of labor-management disputes.

In *Allis-Chalmers Corp. v. Lueck*, 471 U.S. 202 (1985), we considered whether the Wisconsin tort remedy for bad-faith handling of an insurance claim could be applied to the handling of a claim for disability benefits that were authorized by a collective-bargaining agreement. We began by examining the collective-bargaining agreement, and determined that it provided the basis not only for the benefits, but also for the right to have payments made in a timely manner. . . . We then analyzed the Wisconsin tort remedy, explaining that it "exists for breach of a 'duty devolv[ed] upon the insurer by reasonable implication from the express terms of the contract,' the scope of which, crucially, is 'ascertained from a consideration of the contract itself.'" . . . Since the "parties' agreement as to the manner in which a benefit claim would be handled [would] necessarily [have been] relevant to any allegation that the claim was handled in a dilatory manner," . . . we concluded that § 301 pre-empted the application of the Wisconsin tort remedy in this setting.

Thus, *Lueck* faithfully applied the principle of § 301 preemption developed in *Lucas Flour*: if the resolution of a state-law claim depends upon the meaning of a collective-bargaining agreement, the application of state law (which might lead to inconsistent results since there could be as many state-law principles as there are States) is pre-empted and federal labor-law principles—necessarily uniform throughout the Nation—must be employed to resolve the dispute.

III

Illinois courts have recognized the tort of retaliatory discharge for filing a worker's compensation claim . . . and have held that it is applicable to employees covered by union contracts. . . . "[T]o show retaliatory discharge, the plaintiff must set forth sufficient facts from which it can be inferred that (1) he was discharged or threatened with discharge and (2) the employer's motive in discharging or threatening to discharge him was to deter him from exercising his rights under the Act or to interfere with his exercise of those rights." *Horton v. Miller Chemical Co.*, 776 F.2d 1351, 1356 (7th Cir. 1985) (summarizing Illinois state-court decisions). . . . Each of these purely factual questions pertains to the conduct of the employee and the conduct and motivation of the employer. Neither of the elements requires a court to interpret any term of a collective-bargaining agreement. To defend against a retaliatory discharge claim, an employer must show that it had a nonretaliatory reason for the discharge . . . ; this purely factual inquiry likewise does not turn on the meaning of any provision of a collective-bargaining agreement. Thus, the state-law remedy in this case is "independent" of the collective-bargaining agreement in the sense of "independent" that matters for § 301 pre-emption purposes: resolution of the state-law claim does not require construing the collective-bargaining agreement.

The Court of Appeals seems to have relied upon a different way in which a state-law claim may be considered "independent" of a collective-bargaining agreement. The court wrote that "the just cause provision in the collective-bargaining agreement may well prohibit such retaliatory discharge," and went on to say that if the state-law cause of action could go forward, "a state court would be deciding precisely the *same issue* as would an arbitrator: whether there was 'just cause' to discharge the worker." . . . The court concluded, "the state tort of retaliatory discharge is inextricably intertwined with the collective-bargaining agreements here, because it implicates the *same analysis of the facts* as would an inquiry under the just cause provisions of the agreements." . . . We agree with the court's explanation that the state-law analysis might well involve attention to the same factual considerations as the contractual determination of whether Lingle was fired for just cause. But we disagree with the court's conclusion that such parallelism renders the state-law analysis dependent upon the contractual analysis. For while there may be instances in which the NLRA pre-empts state law on the basis of the subject matter of the law in question, § 301 pre-emption merely ensures that federal law will be the basis for interpreting collective-bargaining agreements, and says nothing about the substantive rights a State may provide to workers when adjudication of those rights does not depend upon the interpretation of such agreements. In other words, even if dispute resolution pursuant to a collective-bargaining agreement, on the one hand, and state law, on the other, would require addressing precisely the same set of facts, as long as the state-law claim can be resolved without interpreting the agreement itself, the claim is "independent" of the agreement for § 301 pre-emption purposes.

IV

The result we reach today is consistent both with the policy of fostering uniform, certain adjudication of disputes over the meaning of collective-bargaining agreements and with cases that have permitted separate fonts of substantive rights to remain unpre-empted by other federal labor-law statutes.

First, as we explained in *Lueck*, "[t]he need to preserve the effectiveness of arbitration was one of the central reasons that underlay the Court's holding in *Lucas Flour*." 471 U.S. at 219. "A rule that permitted an individual to sidestep available grievance procedures would cause arbitration to lose most of its effectiveness, . . . as well as eviscerate a central tenet of federal labor contract law under § 301 that it is the arbitrator, not the court, who has the responsibility to interpret the labor contract in the first instance." *Id.* at 220. . . . Today's decision should make clear that interpretation of collective-bargaining agreements remains firmly in the arbitral realm; judges can determine questions of state law involving labor-management relations only if such questions do not require construing collective-bargaining agreements.

Second, there is nothing novel about recognizing that substantive rights in the labor relations context can exist without interpreting collective-bargaining agreements.

> "This Court has, on numerous occasions, declined to hold that individual employees are, because of the availability of arbitration, barred from bringing claims under federal statutes. *See, e.g., McDonald v. West Branch*, 466 U.S. 284 (1984); *Barrentine v. Arkansas-Best Freight System, Inc.*, 450 U.S. 728 (1981); *Alexander v. Gardner-Denver Co.*, 415 U.S. 36 (1974). Although the analysis of the question under each statute is quite distinct, the theory running through these cases is that notwithstanding the strong policies encouraging arbitration, 'different considerations apply *where the employee's claim is based on rights arising out of a statute designed to provide minimum substantive guarantees to individual workers.'* *Barrentine*, 450 U.S. at 737." *Atchison, T. & S. F. R. Co. v. Buell*, 480 U.S. 557, 564–65 (1987) (emphasis added).

Although our comments in *Buell*, construing the scope of Railway Labor Act pre-emption, referred to independent *federal* statutory rights, we subsequently rejected a claim that federal labor law pre-empted a *state* statute providing a one-time severance benefit to employees in the event of a plant closing. In *Fort Halifax Packing Co. v. Coyne*, 482 U.S. 1, 21 (1987), we emphasized that "pre-emption should not be lightly inferred in this area, since the establishment of labor standards falls within the traditional police power of the State." We specifically held that the Maine law in question was not pre-empted by the NLRA, "since its establishment of a minimum labor standard does not impermissibly intrude upon the collective-bargaining process." . . .

The Court of Appeals "recognize[d] that § 301 does not pre-empt state anti-discrimination laws, even though a suit under these laws, like a suit alleging retaliatory discharge, requires a state court to determine whether just cause existed to justify the discharge." . . . The court distinguished those laws because Congress has affirmatively endorsed state antidiscrimination remedies in Title VII of the Civil Rights Act of 1964 . . . , whereas there is no such explicit endorsement of state workers' compensation laws. . . . [T]his distinction is unnecessary for determining whether § 301 pre-empts the state law in question. . . . [T]he mere fact that a broad contractual protection against discriminatory-or retaliatory discharge may provide a remedy for conduct that coincidentally violates state-law does not make the existence or the contours of the state law violation dependent upon the terms of the private contract. For even if an arbitrator should conclude that the contract does not prohibit a particular discriminatory or retaliatory discharge, that conclusion might or might not be consistent with a proper interpretation of state law. In the typical case a state tribunal could resolve either a discriminatory or retaliatory discharge claim without interpreting the "just cause" language of a collective-bargaining agreement. . . .

In sum, we hold that an application of state law is pre-empted by [LMRA] § 301 only if such application requires the interpretation of a collective-bargaining agreement.

The judgment of the Court of Appeals is reversed.

Notes

1. *Lingle* is part of a long line of cases that developed § 301 preemption law, some of which are recounted in the excerpt from the Court's decision. In *Avco Corp. v. Machinists*, the employer filed a state court law suit to enjoin the union from striking at its plant. The Sixth Circuit held that "[s]tate law does not exist as an independent source of private rights to enforce collective bargaining contracts." 376 F.2d 337, 340 (6th Cir. 1967), *aff'd*, 390 U.S. 557 (1968). In affirming, the Supreme Court explained that the "heart of the complaint was a 'no-strike' clause in the collective bargaining agreement by which 'grievances' were to be settled amicably or by binding arbitration." *Avco Corp. v. Aero Lodge No. 735*, 390 U.S. 557, 558 (1968). In *Franchise Tax Board of the State of Cal. v. Constr. Laborers Vacation Trust for Southern Cal.*, 463 U.S. 1, 23 (1983), the Court added that "the pre-emptive force of § 301 is so powerful as to displace entirely any state cause of action 'for violation of contracts between an employer and a labor organization.' Any such suit is purely a creature of federal law, notwithstanding the fact that state law would provide a cause of action in the absence of § 301."

Allis-Chalmers Corp. v. Lueck, 471 U.S. 202 (1985), the immediate precursor to *Lingle*, held that "when resolution of a state-law claim is substantially dependent upon analysis of the terms of an agreement made between the parties in a labor contract, that claim must either be treated as a § 301 claim . . . or dismissed as preempted by federal labor-contract law." In *Lueck*, a worker, covered by a collective-bargaining agreement that incorporated by reference separately negotiated group health and disability plans funded by Allis-Chalmers and administered by Aetna, chose to sue those companies in state court as a tort claim (rather than grieve) when he met with repeated resistance from the companies to pay his disability claims. The Supreme Court concluded that Lueck should have made use of the grievance arbitration procedures of the collective-bargaining agreement before suing in court. Having failed to exhaust his administrative remedies, the Court dismissed the complaint as preempted by § 301.

2. After *Lueck* and *Lingle*, § 301 preemption can be thought of as a two-pronged analysis:

a. Is the state-law right, which the employee claims that the employer violated, waivable by the union?

b. If waivable, is the state-law right either (a) independent of the contractual right established by the collective bargaining agreement or (b) "inextricably intertwined" with the collective bargaining provision?

Whereas the *Lueck* Court concluded that the worker's state law tort claim, based on the employer's allegedly harrying conduct, was preempted, the *Lingle* Court concluded that a worker's state law retaliation claim was not preempted.

For a recent example of a claim that is preempted under Section 301, consider *Curtis v. Irwin Indus., Inc.*, 913 F.3d 1146 (9th Cir. 2019). Curtis was employed on an oil platform off the coast of California. His typical schedule called for him to stay on the platform for seven days at a time, during which he would work for 12 hours, then rest for 12 hours. Curtis filed a lawsuit, alleging that under California law, he was entitled to compensation for all hours that he was required to be on the platform.

The court held that Curtis' claim was preempted because California's wage and hour law contains a carve-out for employees "working pursuant to . . . [a]n alternative workweek schedule adopted pursuant to a [qualifying] collective bargaining agreement." Curtis argued that he should not fall under the carve-out, because his CBA defined overtime differently than California law. But the court rejected that argument, because it would make the carve-out nearly meaningless. Accordingly, the court held that, "[b]ecause Curtis's right to overtime 'exists solely as a result of the CBA,' . . . his claim that Irwin violated overtime requirements . . . is preempted under § 301. Thus, his claim fails at step one of the preemption analysis."

3. Recall that § 301 grants jurisdiction to courts to enforce contractual promises to arbitrate under collective-bargaining agreements. When thinking of § 301 in this way, § 301 preemption becomes more intuitive.

a. Imagine a case where a supervisor accepts a demotion to a bargaining-unit position in exchange for job security. The parties memorialize that promise in an individual contract. Shortly thereafter, the employer shuts down the plant and dismisses the employee. Does § 301 preempt a state law breach-of-contract claim grounded in the individual contract? *See Caterpillar, Inc. v. Williams*, 482 U.S. 386 (1987) (no § 301 preemption). Would such a claim implicate *Garmon* preemption? Does *J.I. Case Co. v. NLRB*, 321 U.S. 332 (1944), discussed in Chapter 5, help to answer this question?

b. In general, an employer commits an ULP if it enters into individual side agreements with bargaining-unit employees. *J.I. Case Co. v. NLRB, supra.* The parties to a collective-bargaining agreement can, however, bargain around this by negotiating a clause expressly permitting individual bargaining. For example, the parties might negotiate a wage floor below which no employee may be paid, but allow individual employees to bargain above that floor. This model is used in many professional sports leagues. Given this background, can a professional athlete who is a member of a players' union with this type of contract sue his or her employer in state court for breach of the individual wage contract? The answer most likely depends on what the collective-bargaining agreement states about how wage disputes are handled—under the grievance-arbitration mechanism of the collective-bargaining agreement or in some other manner.

c. *14 Penn Plaza LLC v. Pyett*, 556 U.S. 247 (2009), discussed in Chapter 13, held that unions can waive their members' right to file in court where the "collective-bargaining agreement . . . clearly and unmistakably requires union members to arbitrate ADEA [Age Discrimination in Employment Act] claims" against the employer. What contractual language would you look for to determine whether a discrimination law suit arising under a state's human rights statute is preempted by § 301?

4. The Court distinguishes § 301 preemption from (and leaves unresolved) the question "[w]hether a union may *waive* its members' individual, [non-preempted] state-law rights. . . . Before deciding whether such a state-law bar to waiver could be pre-empted under federal law by the parties to a collective-bargaining agreement, we would require 'clear and unmistakable' evidence, *see Metro. Edison Co. v. NLRB*, 460 U.S. 693, 708 (1983), in order to conclude that such a waiver had been intended. No such evidence is available in this case." *Lingle*, 486 U.S. at 409 n.9.

5. Does § 301 preempt lawsuits to invalidate contracts? In *Textron Lycoming Reciprocating Engine Div. v. UAW*, 523 U.S. 653 (1998), in the context of a union suit against an employer for fraudulently inducing the union to sign a collective-bargaining agreement, the Supreme Court held that § 301 jurisdiction is conferred over suits alleging *contract breach*, not suits alleging *contract invalidity*. The Court explained that § 301(a) confers jurisdiction over "'suits for violation of contracts.'" *Id.* at 656. Applying these principles, § 301 jurisdiction did not lie over a suit for fraud in the execution and/or mistake because the purpose of such a suit is not to show contract violation, but rather contract invalidity. *Id.* at 657–58.

6. The courts have repeatedly warned parties against "attempting an end run around [the NLRB] under the guise of contract interpretation." *Int'l Woodworkers of Am., Local 3-193 v. Ketchikan Pulp Co.*, 611 F.2d 1295, 1299 (9th Cir. 1980) (district court properly dismissed § 301 action concerning union's attempt to represent employees at later-acquired facilities). *See also Amalgamated Clothing & Textile Workers Union v. Facetglas, Inc.*, 845 F.2d 1250, 1252 (4th Cir. 1988) (cautioning against allowing parties to use § 301 to "circumvent an existing Board disposition of the merits of their representational claims"); *Local Union 204, Int'l B'hood of Elec. Workers v. Iowa Elec. Light & Power Co.*, 668 F.2d 413, 419 (8th Cir. 1982) ("To fail to apply this policy to § 301 actions would allow an 'end run' around provisions of the NLRA under the guise of contract interpretation." Thus, because plaintiff's complaint sought to avoid the appropriate forum for adjudication, the Court dismissed the complaint.).

7. What are the drawbacks of § 301 preemption? Can it discourage union organization of a workplace, if employees know that certain state law claims are preempted by § 301?

III. Note on the Public Sector: Should the Federal Government Guarantee Basic Collective Bargaining Rights for (Some) Employees of State and Local Governments?

Again, the federal government has not attempted to regulate the labor relations of state and local governments, so there are no preemption issues analogous to those described above. However, such a federal law has been proposed. Consider the following.

The Public Service Freedom to Negotiate Act, H.R. 6238, introduced in 2018, would have required the Federal Labor Relations Authority (FLRA) to determine whether a state substantially provides for certain collective bargaining rights. If the state does not substantially provide for such rights, the state would be subject to nationwide standards the FLRA would create and enforce to guarantee collective bargaining rights, including the duty to bargain in good faith. The bill contained few details as to some of the key issues discussed in this casebook: *e.g.,* the scope of bargaining. It expressly allowed for binding interest arbitration. It did not bar all strikes, but it did provide that "no employer, emergency services employee, or law enforcement officer may engage in a lockout, strike, or any other organized job action of which a reasonably probable result is a measurable disruption of the delivery of emergency or public safety services."

In a number of previous years, bills were introduced in Congress along similar lines, except that they only covered public-safety employees. *See, e.g.,* the proposed Public Safety Employer-Employee Cooperation Act of 2009, House Bill 413.

None of these bills have become law, but proponents of such bills have not given up. For the many states that grant collective bargaining rights to public employees generally, the bill would not change anything. In states that grant few or no public employees collective bargaining rights, however, this bill would preempt often longstanding practices.

In some ways, this bill would be a major departure from traditional public-sector labor law in the U.S. The only time the federal government has granted bargaining rights to any state or local government employees involved the Urban Mass Transit Act of 1964. That law provided funds for local governments to take over previously private mass transit systems and required that collective bargaining rights of their employees be preserved.

Yet in other ways, this law would not be a significant departure. Most federal employment laws cover both private- and public-sector employees. In some cases, there are a few special rules, but in many cases the coverage is mostly identical. For example, the Fair Labor Standards Act [FLSA] covers state and local government employees, although it contains some overtime rules that apply only to the public sector. Title VII generally applies to the public sector in the same ways as it does to the private sector.

Were such a bill to become law, one would expect constitutional challenges. As late as 1976, the Supreme Court held that applying the FLSA to state and local government employers violated the Tenth Amendment. *Nat'l League of Cities v. Usery*, 426 U.S. 833 (1976). That case was overruled in 1985. *Garcia v. San Antonio Metro. Transp. Auth.*, 469 U.S. 528, 531 (1985). But a federal law granting collective bargaining rights to employees in states that have not authorized such rights could give the Court a chance to revisit this issue. Notably, in recent decades, the Court has arguably become more conservative and sensitive to issues of state sovereignty in public employment. *See, e.g.*, its Eleventh Amendment jurisprudence in cases such as *Alden v. Maine*, 527 U.S. 706 (1999) (holding, at least in part because of the Eleventh Amendment, that states are immune from monetary damages in private suits brought by state employees under the FLSA). On the other hand, this Eleventh Amendment limited immunity only applies to *state* employers and their employees; it does not protect local government employers. Further, it does not grant even state employers immunity from money damages when federal agencies sue. *See Alden*, *supra*. Under these bills, the primary enforcer of labor law rights would be a federal agency: the FLRA.

Notes

1. These bills would have created a "floor" but not a ceiling, guaranteeing certain minimum collective bargaining rights to state and local government employees in jurisdictions where they currently do not have them. Would this be good policy? Does your answer depend on precisely what sort of rules the FLRA would craft as basic minimums?

2. Again, many federal *employment* laws (Title VII, the FLSA, the Americans with Disabilities Act, etc.) apply to state and local government employers and employees. Is it more intrusive for the federal government to apply anti-discrimination laws and wage-and-hour rules to state and local governments than to mandate minimal collective bargaining rights? Or is it just an historical accident that it has evolved that way in the U.S.?

3. The Public Service Freedom to Negotiate Act went beyond previous attempts in this area by covering public employees generally, rather than just public safety employees. Are there principled (or other) reasons to preempt some state laws to provide minimum collective bargaining rights only for public safety employees? Recall from Chapter 1 that Wisconsin Act 10, the 2011 law which removed almost all collective bargaining rights from most Wisconsin employees, specifically excluded certain public safety officers (thus leaving such employees with their pre-existing, fairly robust, collective bargaining rights). Finally, to bring the history full circle,

one might find it ironic here that, as Chapter 1 explains, the fear of giving collective bargaining rights to police officers (in light of the Boston police strike) was one of the main obstacles to the development of public-sector labor laws in the U.S.

4. For an argument in favor of the Public Service Freedom to Negotiate Act, see Joseph Slater, *House Committee on Education and Labor Hearing, "Standing with Public Servants: Protecting the Right to Organize,"* https://papers.ssrn.com/sol3/papers.cfm?abstract_id=3439645 (2019).

Index

[References are to sections.]